Presenting

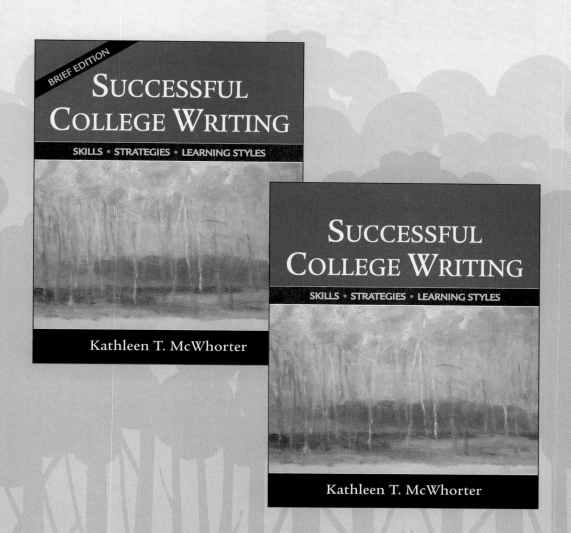

Covers what other texts assume students know

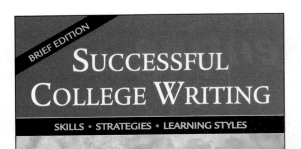

The book that gives students the extra help they need

Successful College Writing is a first-year composition text that covers the skills other college-level texts assume students already possess. For a variety of reasons, many students today need a review of basic reading skills and writing conventions before they are ready for college-level writing. In addition, many students have not examined *how* they learn, nor have they identified the approaches that work best for them. *Successful College Writing* addresses these realities.

An all-in-one text for first-year composition

Successful College Writing provides everything students need for a first-year writing course, with comprehensive coverage of writing and research, more help with reading and study skills than any other rhetoric on the market, and a thorough, easy-to-use handbook in the complete edition. This text truly gives students the support they need to become successful college writers.

"I am so impressed with this text. I can't state that enough. . . . The entire book covers everything a first-year student needs for writing for the rest of his or her academic career."
–Sue Serrano, *Sierra College*

Gives students an academic "Quick Start"

The text opens with three chapters that prepare students for the work required in first-year composition. These chapters help students learn about themselves as writers and strengthen their reading skills in preparation for the demands of college work.

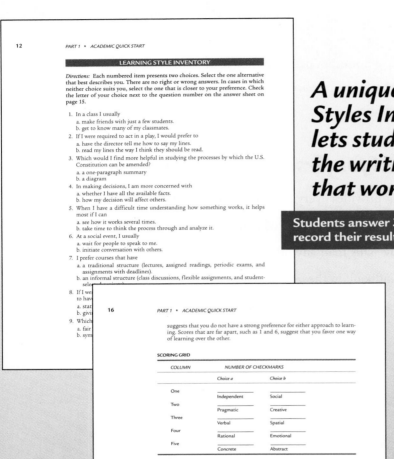

A unique Learning Styles Inventory that lets students discover the writing strategies that work best for them

Students answer 35 questions and record their results in a scoring grid.

Successful College Writing is the first rhetoric to respond to the fact that each student learns —and writes—differently. The **Learning Styles Inventory** in Chapter 1 helps students discover more about the ways they naturally prefer to approach writing tasks. By increasing their awareness of their own learning styles, *Successful College Writing* will benefit students in their writing class as well as throughout their academic career.

The scoring grid indicates the student's particular learning-style profile. Each aspect of a student's learning style is then explained to give students a better understanding of how to interpret the results.

Two chapters that help students make the reading-writing connection

Chapters 2 and 3 demonstrate strategies that will help students become more active, critical readers and provide complete guidelines for questioning a text and writing a response paper.

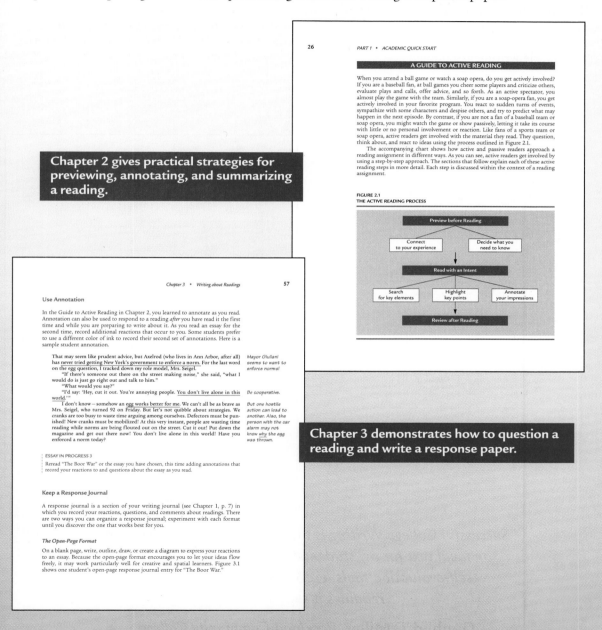

Chapter 2 gives practical strategies for previewing, annotating, and summarizing a reading.

A GUIDE TO ACTIVE READING

When you attend a ball game or watch a soap opera, do you get actively involved? If you are a baseball fan, at ball games you cheer some players and criticize others, evaluate plays and calls, offer advice, and so forth. As an active spectator, you almost play the game with the team. Similarly, if you are a soap-opera fan, you get actively involved in your favorite program. You react to sudden turns of events, sympathize with some characters and despise others, and try to predict what may happen in the next episode. By contrast, if you are not a fan of a baseball team or soap opera, you might watch the game or show passively, letting it take its course with little or no personal involvement or reaction. Like fans of a sports team or soap opera, active readers get involved with the material they read. They question, think about, and react to ideas using the process outlined in Figure 2.1.

The accompanying chart shows how active and passive readers approach a reading assignment in different ways. As you can see, active readers get involved by using a step-by-step approach. The sections that follow explain each of these active reading steps in more detail. Each step is discussed within the context of a reading assignment.

FIGURE 2.1
THE ACTIVE READING PROCESS

Preview before Reading

Connect to your experience   Decide what you need to know

Read with an Intent

Search for key elements   Highlight key points   Annotate your impressions

Review after Reading

Chapter 3 • Writing about Readings   57

Use Annotation

In the Guide to Active Reading in Chapter 2, you learned to annotate as you read. Annotation can also be used to respond to a reading *after* you have read it the first time and while you are preparing to write about it. As you read an essay for the second time, record additional reactions that occur to you. Some students prefer to use a different color of ink to record their second set of annotations. Here is a sample student annotation.

That may seem like prudent advice, but Axelrod (who lives in Ann Arbor, after all) has never tried getting New York's government to enforce a norm. For the last word on the egg question, I tracked down my role model, Mrs. Seigel.

Mayor Giuliani seems to want to enforce norms!

"If there's someone out there on the street making noise," she said, "what I would do is just go right out and talk to him."

"What would you say?"

"I'd say: 'Hey, cut it out. You're annoying people. You don't live alone in this world.'"

Be cooperative.

I don't know — somehow an egg works better for me. We can't all be as brave as Mrs. Seigel, who turned 92 on Friday. But let's not quibble about strategies. We cranks are too busy to waste time arguing among ourselves. Defectors must be punished! New cranks must be mobilized! At this very instant, people are wasting time reading while norms are being flouted out on the street. Cut it out! Put down the magazine and get out there now! You don't live alone in this world! Have you enforced a norm today?

But one hostile action can lead to another. Also, the person with the car alarm may not know why the egg was thrown.

ESSAY IN PROGRESS 3

Reread "The Boor War" or the essay you have chosen, this time adding annotations that record your reactions to and questions about the essay as you read.

Keep a Response Journal

A response journal is a section of your writing journal (see Chapter 1, p. 7) in which you record your reactions, questions, and comments about readings. There are two ways you can organize a response journal; experiment with each format until you discover the one that works best for you.

The Open-Page Format

On a blank page, write, outline, draw, or create a diagram to express your reactions to an essay. Because the open-page format encourages you to let your ideas flow freely, it may work particularly well for creative and spatial learners. Figure 3.1 shows one student's open-page response journal entry for "The Boor War."

Chapter 3 demonstrates how to question a reading and write a response paper.

Gives students the extra help they need with their writing

Writing activities for any learning style

Throughout the text, students are presented with **learning style options**—writing activities that are designed for different learning styles. Students can choose the activities that are the most helpful for them. The attention to learning styles will make *all* students feel more confident as they tackle writing assignments.

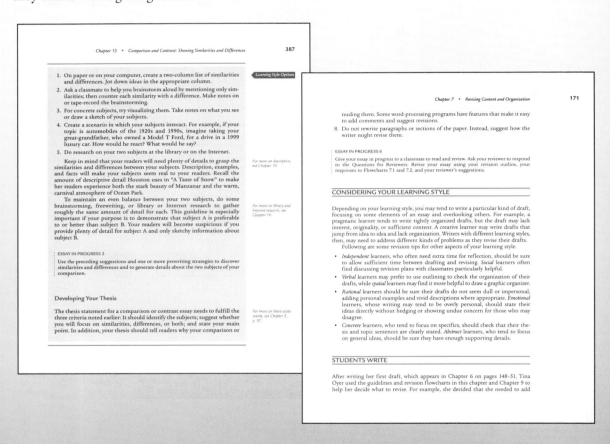

"Successful College Writing is the closest thing I have seen to an ideal text for my students, who really need the . . . self-evaluation tools, exercises, and stimulating readings it supplies."

–Gunhild T. Miller, *Rockland Community College*

Practical, step-by-step writing assignments

Guided Writing Assignments lead students step by step through the process of writing an essay. The assignments cover the methods of development that students will need to master for academic success as well as success on the job.

A GUIDED WRITING ASSIGNMENT

The following guide will help you write a process analysis essay. It may be a how-to or a how-it-works essay. Although you will focus on process analysis, you may need to integrate one or more other patterns of development in your essay. Depending on your learning style, you may choose different ways of gathering ideas or evaluating your first draft. This Guided Writing Assignment will provide you with alternatives.

The Assignment

Write a process analysis essay on one of the following topics or one that you choose on your own. Be sure the process you choose is one you know enough about to explain to others, or can learn about through observation or research. Your audience consists of readers who are unfamiliar with the process, including your classmates.

How-to Essay Topics

1. How to improve _____ (your study habits, your wardrobe, your batting average)
2. How to be a successful _____ (diver, parent, gardener)
3. How to make or buy _____ (an object for personal use or enjoyment)
4. How to prepare for _____ (a test, a job interview, an oral presentation)

How-It-Works Essay Topics

1. How your college _____ (spends tuition revenues, hires professors, raises money)
2. How _____ works (an answering machine, a generator, email, or a search engine)
3. How a decision is made to _____ (accept a student at a college, add or eliminate a local or state agency)
4. How _____ is put together (a quilt, a news broadcast, a football team, a Web site)

As you develop your process analysis essay, you will probably use narrative strategies, description (for example, to describe equipment or objects), or illustration (such as to show an example of part of the process).

For more on narration, description, and illustration, see Chapters 9–11.

Thorough coverage of combining patterns of development

Every chapter on a pattern of development includes a section on integrating that pattern in an essay. An accompanying reading demonstrates the pattern used in combination with other methods. This approach encourages students to view the patterns of development realistically while they learn how to combine the patterns in their own essays for more effective writing.

Tools to help students identify their writing problems

Successful College Writing is the first writing text to make two diagnostic tests available to students and instructors within the book itself. A **Writing Test**—a brief essay exam—is provided so instructors can help students discover and start to solve basic problems with organization and paragraph development. A **Grammar Assessment Test** helps students determine their own sentence-level problems. Drawing on resources in the text and in the ancillary package, students can develop an **Action Plan** for solving their writing problems.

More visual aids than any other first-year rhetoric

Successful College Writing makes the writing process visual by using photographs, cartoons, and other images to begin each chapter as well as graphic organizers and flowcharts to help students analyze and revise their essays.

Every chapter begins with a *Quick Start activity* that gets students immediately involved with the chapter's topic by asking them to write about a lively and engaging visual such as a photograph, a cartoon, or a Web site.

"The Quick Starts...are a fantastic way to begin each chapter. Students and professors will equally enjoy them."

–Bill Stiffler, *Harford Community College*

organizer can help you structure your writing, analyze a reading, and recall key events as you generate ideas for an essay.

Use Figure 9.1 as a basic model. However, keep in mind that narrative essays vary in organization and may lack one or more of the elements included in the model. When you incorporate narration into an essay in which you also use other patterns of development, you will probably need to condense or eliminate some of the elements shown in Figure 9.1. Whether you write a narrative essay or incorporate narration in a different kind of essay, use a graphic organizer to help you visualize the structure of your essay.

The following selection, "A Primitive Ritual," is an example of a narrative. Read it first, and then study the graphic organizer for it (Figure 9.2).

FIGURE 9.1
GRAPHIC ORGANIZER FOR A NARRATIVE ESSAY

Unique *Graphic Organizers* for each type of writing give students an appealing visual tool that makes it easier to analyze readings and plan their own essays.

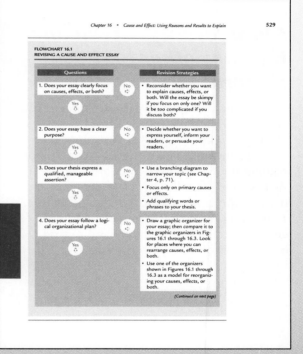

Revision Flowcharts help students read their own essays as well as those of other students with a critical eye and provide practical suggestions for revision.

"The book is great! The author's thorough explanations and examples make it easy for the students to understand and follow the writing process...The graphic organizers and flowcharts are a great idea, especially for those students who are visual learners!"

–Barbara J. Robedeau, *San Antonio College*

Gives students the extra help they need with their reading and study skills

The author of a number of best-selling college textbooks, Kathleen McWhorter is a learning specialist with over 30 years' experience in teaching reading and study skills. Her knowledge of what works best for students and her determination to help them succeed are apparent throughout *Successful College Writing*.

More coverage of reading than any other first-year rhetoric

In addition to the coverage in Chapters 2 and 3, reading skills are reinforced in every writing assignment chapter. In a unique section, students learn practical strategies for reading the type of essay they are writing. By becoming familiar with the elements a reader expects in a particular type of writing, students are more likely to include those elements in their own writing and to read other essays of that type critically.

"I greatly appreciate the way reading and writing skills have been integrated into the text. The lack of reading skills seems to be a major weakness with my students....I do like the way McWhorter integrates these skills."

–Michael Mackey, *Community College of Denver*

High-interest readings—reviewed by a student panel

The 64 readings were selected using the results of a national survey of students on topics they want to read about. Evaluated by a group of student reviewers, the readings are drawn from a variety of sources, including popular magazines, scholarly journals, newspapers, and textbooks. Along with 14 student essays, the professional readings are a mix of new voices and familiar authors such as Maxine Hong Kingston, Daniel Goleman, Terry Tempest Williams, Brent Staples, Charles Krauthammer, George Will, and Barbara Ehrenreich. The combination of student-selected topics and the variety of sources and authors will motivate students and excite them about reading.

"In general the readings were very interesting....The readings were short, so it was easy to read the essay twice if I needed to because it only took a few minutes....I think these essays will help me in writing and reading next semester."

–Donald G. Harris, *Student Reviewer*

"Great variety! Reading these essays has been a true pleasure."

–Murcia Moressa Hunte, *Student Reviewer*

Useful chapter on reading arguments

A unique chapter on reading arguments reinforces the text's strong emphasis on developing critical reading skills by giving students informative, practical guidelines for analyzing and evaluating arguments.

Serious attention to study skills

The only first-year rhetoric with coverage of study skills, *Successful College Writing* gives students practical survival strategies for all of their college work, including guidelines for reading different types of texts, valuable advice on taking essay examinations (Chapter 22), and a unique appendix that offers helpful tips on basic study strategies such as organizing a study area and managing time.

Gives instructors the extra help they need too!

Bedford/St. Martin's is pleased to provide an extensive ancillary package to support the needs of all instructors.

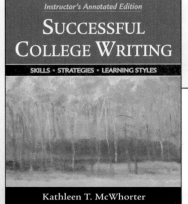

Instructor's Annotated Edition

This helpful volume contains useful teaching tips, suggestions for using computers, notes on additional resources, and answers to the exercises and the questions following the readings.

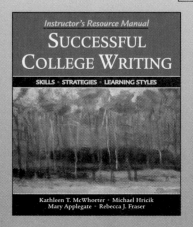

Instructor's Resource Manual

This extensive collection of materials provides extra support for adjuncts and new instructors. It includes a chapter on teaching with *Successful College Writing*, sample syllabi, and chapters on helping underprepared students in the first-year writing classroom, evaluating student writing, and using the writing center. It also includes a bibliography for rhetoric and composition, with a list of books and articles on learning styles.

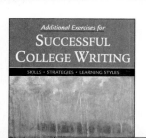

Exercise Booklet

Available free with the text, these additional exercises are keyed specifically to the *Writing Assessment Test* and the *Handbook*.

Transparency Masters

These reproducible masters include *Graphic Organizers*, *Revision Flowcharts*, and other helpful charts and images from the text.

Writing Guide Software

Developed specifically for *Successful College Writing*, this software leads students through the process of writing essays in response to the assignments in the text. At each step, a variety of resources—detailed instructions, models, examples, etc.—are available but not intrusive. At the end, students will have a completed paper that they can print, save, or send to their instructors. The software also includes reading workshops, online versions of the Learning Style Inventory and grammar assessment test, and grammar tutorials.

Exercise Central

This extensive collection of additional grammar exercises is easy to use and convenient for students and instructors alike. Multiple exercise sets on every grammar topic, at a variety of levels, ensure that students get as much practice as they need. Customized instant feedback turns skills practice into a learning experience, and the reporting feature allows both students and instructors to monitor and assess student progress. Accessed through the *Successful College Writing* Web site.

Web site

Designed specifically for *Successful College Writing*, this Web site includes information on conducting online research and useful links for students and instructors.

www.bedfordstmartins.com/composition /successfulwriting

About the Author

KATHLEEN T. McWHORTER is the author of a number of widely adopted books on reading and writing skills for developmental students, including *The Writer's Express*, 2/e (1997), *The Writer's Guide: A Basic Handbook* (1997), and *The Writer's Compass*, 2/e (1999), as well as *College Reading and Study Skills*, 7/e (1998). She is Professor of Humanities and Director of the Learning Skills Center at Niagara County Community College. She has also been on the faculty of the State University College at Buffalo.

"I heartily endorse the notion of promoting success in college writing...by having students understand the effects of variations in learning styles. This approach is long overdue in composition studies and in composition textbooks. The method for discovering and using various learning styles presented here seems natural and easy to use, and it should be effective in supporting the teaching and learning of writing."

–Ronald A. Sudol, *Oakland University*

Successful
College
Writing

Instructor's Annotated Edition

Successful College Writing

SKILLS
STRATEGIES
LEARNING STYLES

Kathleen T. McWhorter
NIAGARA COUNTY COMMUNITY COLLEGE

BEDFORD/ST. MARTIN'S
Boston ◆ New York

For Bedford/St. Martin's

Executive Editor: Carla Kay Samodulski
Development Editor for the Handbook: Kristin Bowen
Production Editor: Harold Chester
Production Supervisor: Dennis J. Conroy
Marketing Manager: Brian Wheel
Art Director: Lucy Krikorian
Text Design: Anna George
Cover Design: Donna Lee Dennison
Cover Art: Wolf Kahn, *Sunset Orange.* Pastel on paper, 1997. 22"×30". Courtesy Diane
    Nelson Fine Art, Long Beach, CA. Photo, Peter Muscato.
Copy Editor: Wendy Polhemus-Annibell
Composition: Monotype Composition Company, Inc.
Printing and Binding: RR Donnelley & Sons Company

President: Charles H. Christensen
Editorial Director: Joan E. Feinberg
Editor in Chief: Nancy Perry
Marketing Director: Karen Melton
Director of Editing, Design, and Production: Marcia Cohen
Managing Editor: Erica T. Appel

Library of Congress Catalogue Numbers: 99-62110 (with Handbook)
                                         99-66670 (without Handbook)

Manufactured in the United States of America

5   4   3   2   1
f   e   d   c   b   a

For information, write: Bedford/St. Martin's, 75 Arlington Street, Boston, MA 02116
(617-426-7440)

ISBN: 0-312-15276-0 (Student Edition with Handbook)
      0-312-24534-3 (Student Edition without Handbook)
      0-312-24367-7 (Instructor's Annotated Edition)

Credits

Successful College Writing is a first-year composition text that covers the skills other college-level texts assume students already possess. During over thirty years of teaching at both two-year and four-year colleges, I have found that the number of underprepared students increases every year. For a variety of reasons, many students today need a review of basic writing conventions before they can be equipped with college-level skills in writing, reading, or critical thinking. Many students, although serious and hard working, also have not examined *how* they learn, nor have they identified the approaches that work best for them. *Successful College Writing* addresses these realities.

I have designed this text to be flexible. Instruction in reading and in basic writing conventions is presented in self-contained segments within the chapters or in print and electronic ancillaries. Instructors can devote class time to this instruction, or they can encourage students to complete these sections and activities on their own. Through its unique, highly visual, student-centered approach, *Successful College Writing* teaches basic skills and, at the same time, engages students immediately in the thinking-writing process, guiding them through the writing strategies and activities that form the core of composition instruction.

"ACADEMIC QUICK START" CHAPTERS

From the very first chapter, *Successful College Writing* provides students with the kind of extra help they will need to meet the demands of their first-year writing course as well as their other courses. Chapter 1 includes a unique *Learning Style Inventory* that helps students discover how they naturally prefer to approach writing assignments, and Chapters 2 and 3 provide practical guidelines that will help students handle college-level reading.

Learning Style Assessment. Research conducted by George Jensen, John DiTiberio, Robert Sternberg, and others has demonstrated that students differ in how they learn, depending upon their individual cognitive style or orientation. In particular, research by Jensen and DiTiberio, based on the *Myers-Briggs Type Indicator,* has applied learning-style theory to the composition classroom. They demonstrate that the writing strategies students find effective depend, in part, on dimensions of their learning styles. In this text, I have focused on five aspects of learning style that are relevant for writing and have used commonly accepted terms to describe them. Some students learn best using verbal modes—for example, by listing or freewriting—while others do better with spatial modes—for example, by drawing diagrams or maps. Some students are creative learners who prefer to experiment, while others are more pragmatic and approach tasks systematically. Some are concrete learners who tend to concentrate on details, while others are more abstract, preferring to focus on broader issues. Socially oriented students enjoy working with others, while independently focused students like to work alone. Since students learn in different ways, they learn to write in different ways as well, yet most writing texts do not take this variety into account. This text uses learning style as a springboard, a way to encourage students to explore alternative writing strategies.

A brief questionnaire in Chapter 1, field-tested using a national sample of first-year students, enables students to assess their learning style. Throughout the text, students are encouraged to take these results into account as they choose writing and revision strategies. This learning style approach will be particularly refreshing to students who incorrectly perceive writing to be a rigid, lock-step process. I have found that emphasizing learning style demonstrates to students that writing is a flexible, multifaceted process and alleviates some of the frustration they often associate with writing.

Guidelines for Active, Critical Reading.   Many students entering college today also need help with basic reading skills. To provide students with solid, proven strategies for working with text, Chapter 2 presents a _Guide for Active Reading_, which helps students improve their comprehension and build skills that they can apply to the readings within this text as well as to all of their other college reading assignments. In addition, Chapter 3, "Writing about Readings," includes guidelines for questioning a text, relating it to a student's own experience, and writing a response paper.

EXTENSIVE SUPPORT FOR INEXPERIENCED COLLEGE WRITERS THROUGHOUT

In addition to these "Quick Start" chapters, _Successful College Writing_ provides guidance and support for inexperienced writers in every chapter of the text. Each chapter includes practical, student-oriented instruction in the writing process, along with extra help for those students who need it.

Learning Style Options.   To help students apply what they discover about their learning style in Chapter 1, the text offers them an abundance of alternatives as they write and revise their essays. Recognizing that students need choices—that no one strategy works for every student — the text includes a variety of strategies for generating ideas and revising an essay. Alternative strategies are identified by the heading "Learning Style Options" throughout the text.

Detailed Coverage of Each Stage of the Writing Process.   Part 2 of the text, "Strategies for Writing Essays," consists of five chapters that cover each stage of the writing process in detail, with plenty of skill-building exercises, many of them collaborative; a running student example; and "Essay in Progress" activities that lead students through each step in writing an essay.

Appealing, Helpful Visuals.   Because inexperienced writers often are more comfortable with images than with text, *Successful College Writing* employs a highly visual approach to writing instruction. The *Chapter Quick Start* at the beginning of each chapter provides an engaging image for students to respond to. This opener gets students immediately involved with the chapter's topic by asking them to write about a photograph, a cartoon, a page from the World Wide Web, or another kind of visual. In addition, the text presents students with an alternative to traditional outlines: *Graphic Organizers*. These are maps that display relationships among ideas. Students are encouraged to use them as tools both for analyzing readings and for planning and revising their own essays. I have found that structuring information with graphic organizers is particularly helpful for those students who find outlining cumbersome but respond positively to a more visual method. Finally, *Revision Flowcharts* help students read their own essays as well as those of others with a critical eye, and other figures and boxes reinforce points made in the text and summarize information for students.

Practical, Step-by-Step Writing Assignments.   In Part 3, each chapter covers one of the patterns of development that students will frequently encounter in college and on the job. (The box on page vi describes the elements of these chapters.) The chapters in Part 3, as well as the chapter on writing arguments in Part 4 and on writing a literary analysis in Part 5, include *Guided Writing Assignments* that lead students step by step through the process of writing an essay. These guided assignments give student writers the support they need whether they are working in class or on their own. The guided assignments will also appeal to faculty members who often have limited time to become familiar with a complex text.

Writing Skills Assessment and Action Plan.   Time constraints and the amount of material that needs to be covered in a typical first-year composition course often do not permit the instruction in basic writing conventions that many students need. To enable students to identify their own writing problems and develop an action plan for improving their own skills, I have included two writing assessment tests in Appendix A. The first is a writing assignment to be evaluated by the instructor. Guidelines for evaluating and scoring this assignment are provided in the Instructor's Resource Manual. The second, an error recognition test, will

CHAPTERS THAT TEACH WRITING SKILLS AND STRATEGIES

Every chapter in Part 3 follows a consistent organization and includes the following elements:

Scenes from College and the Workplace.   The opening section of each chapter presents several typical writing situations that call for the type of writing taught in the chapter.

Essays by Professional Writers.   One reading in each chapter appears near the beginning and serves as a model of the type of essay covered in the chapter. In the section on visualizing the pattern, a second reading, along with a graphic organizer, demonstrates the structure of a typical essay of that type. Two more professional readings appear at the end of the chapter along with questions that ask students to analyze and react to the reading.

Exercises.   In the first part of the chapter, exercises, many of them collaborative, reinforce the writing strategies that students are learning.

Integration of Rhetorical Patterns.   Since patterns are seldom used in isolation, each chapter in Part 3 contains a section on how the pattern covered in that chapter can be combined with other patterns. The chapter also includes a reading that shows the pattern combined with other patterns of development.

A Guided Writing Assignment.   Demonstrating step-by-step how to generate ideas, formulate a thesis, draft an essay, revise it, and polish it through editing and proofreading, each Guided Writing Assignment includes Learning Style Options, a Revision Flowchart, and help with two grammar problems.

Students Write.   Students learn from reading, and evaluating, good student writing. Therefore, a sample student essay is provided in each chapter. Questions following the essay encourage students to consider the strategies the student writer has used and to react to the content.

Reading the Type of Essay.   This section presents reading strategies that will enable students to read more efficiently and critically the two final professional essays and other essays of the type covered in the chapter.

Applying Your Skills: Additional Essay Assignments.   This final section offers a variety of alternative writing assignments, including cases that provide students with a real-world context for writing.

identify the particular conventions of sentence structure, punctuation, and grammar that students need to work on. With the results of these two forms of assessment in hand, students can develop an action plan and use sections of the handbook, the book of additional exercises, and the computer software that accompanies *Successful College Writing* to improve their skills.

Thorough Reference Handbook. Designed to work with an individual student's action plan, the handbook in Part 6 covers basic grammar, sentence problems, punctuation, mechanics, spelling, and ESL troublespots. It also reinforces students' learning with plenty of opportunities for practice. The handbook includes hand-corrected examples, key grammatical terms defined in the margin, helpful charts and boxes, and sentence and paragraph exercises.

An Accent on Technology. Increasingly, the ability to use computers is crucial to college writing and research and to success in the working world. Therefore, I have provided practical advice on writing with computers throughout the text. This advice is marked with an icon. In addition, new research techniques that take advantage of computerized library resources, the Internet, and email are covered in Chapter 19, "Planning a Paper with Sources," and the sections on the MLA and APA documentation styles in Chapter 20, "Writing a Research Paper," incorporate the latest guidelines for citing Internet sources.

AN EMPHASIS ON READING AND STUDY SKILLS

Over the years, my work with students has convinced me that skills taught in isolation are seldom learned well or applied. Because reading and study skills are essential to successful writing, instruction in these skills is integrated throughout *Successful College Writing*. By becoming proficient, enthusiastic readers, students learn to be better writers and improve their chances for success in the writing classroom and in their other courses.

Thorough Coverage of Reading Skills. The reading skills that are taught in Chapters 2 and 3 are reinforced in each of the chapters on the patterns of development. As students develop their writing skills by writing a particular type of essay, they learn practical strategies for reading that type of essay at the same time. In addition, Chapter 17, "Reading Arguments," gives students guidelines for analyzing and evaluating arguments. By becoming familiar with the elements a reader expects in a particular type of writing, students are more likely to include those elements in their own writing. Furthermore, as their reading skills improve, students are better able to approach readings critically, freeing them to express their own ideas on important issues.

High-Interest Readings — Reviewed by a Student Panel. Students who enjoy what they are reading become more proficient readers. Therefore, the 64 readings in this text have been carefully chosen to interest students as well as to function as strong rhetorical models. To help guide the choice of readings, Bedford/St. Martin's conducted a survey of students to determine those topics that they find most interesting. Then all of the readings, including the fourteen student essays, were read and evaluated by a student review panel. The professional readings come from a wide range of sources, including newspapers, popular magazines, special-interest magazines, textbooks, and scholarly journals, representing the diverse texts students encounter in both their personal and their academic life.

Attention to Study Skills. *Successful College Writing* gives students practical survival strategies for all of their college work, not only in their writing course but in all of their courses. In addition to guidelines for reading different types of texts, the text includes excerpts from college textbooks in marketing, biology, communication, and anthropology; practical advice on study strategies in Chapter 22 on essay examinations; and advice on organizing a study area, managing time, setting goals, and building a positive academic image in Appendix B, "Five Steps to Academic Success."

USEFUL ANCILLARIES FOR INSTRUCTORS AND STUDENTS

The print and electronic ancillaries that accompany *Successful College Writing* offer plenty of support for both students and instructors. The exercise book and software are designed so that students can use them along with the text to improve the problem areas they identify when they develop their action plan. The Instructor's Annotated Edition and the Instructor's Resource Manual are valuable resources for all instructors but are especially helpful for adjunct instructors, who often don't receive their teaching assignments until the last minute.

Print Ancillaries

- **Instructor's Annotated Edition,** with annotations prepared by Kathleen McCoy, Adirondack Community College. This useful volume provides abundant teaching tips, including suggestions for collaborative activities and applying learning styles to the writing classroom, along with computer hints, notes on additional resources, and answers to exercises and questions following readings.
- **Instructor's Resource Manual,** by Kathleen T. McWhorter; Michael Hricik, Westmoreland County Community College; Mary Applegate, D'Youville Col-

lege; and Rebecca J. Fraser, Nassau Community College. This extensive collection of materials provides extra support for adjuncts and new instructors. It includes sample syllabi along with chapters on teaching with *Successful College Writing,* helping underprepared students in the first-year writing classroom, evaluating student writing, and using the writing center. It also provides a bibliography of books and articles in rhetoric and composition.

- **Transparency Masters.** These reproducible masters include Graphic Organizers, Revision Flowcharts, and other helpful charts and images from the text.
- **Additional Exercises for *Successful College Writing,*** by Carolyn Lengel, Hunter College. Available free with the text, these additional exercises are keyed specifically to Appendix A, "Writing Assessment," and the Handbook.

Electronic Ancillaries

- *Writing Guide Software for Successful College Writing.* Developed specifically for *Successful College Writing,* the software leads students through the process of writing essays in response to the assignments in the text. At each step, a variety of resources—detailed instructions, models, examples, and so on—are available but not intrusive. At the end, students will have a completed paper that they can print, save, or send to their instructors. The software also includes reading workshops, online versions of the Learning Style Inventory and the grammar assessment test from Appendix A, "Writing Assessment," and grammar tutorials.
- **Exercise Central.** This extensive collection of additional grammar exercises is easy to use and convenient for students and instructors alike. Multiple exercise sets on every grammar topic, at two levels, ensure that students get as much practice as they need. Customized feedback turns skills practice into a learning experience, and the reporting feature allows both students and instructors to monitor and assess student progress. Exercise Central can be accessed through the *Successful College Writing* Web site.
- **Web site** (www.bedfordstmartins.com/composition/successfulwriting). The Web site includes information on conducting online research and useful links for students and instructors.

ACKNOWLEDGMENTS

A number of instructors and students from across the country have helped me to develop *Successful College Writing.* I would like to express my gratitude to the following instructors, who served as members of the advisory board for the text. They provided detailed, valuable comments and suggestions about the manuscript as well as student essays and additional help and advice during its development: Marvin Austin, Columbia State Community College; Sarah H. Harrison, Tyler Junior College; Dan Holt, Lansing Community College; Michael Mackey, Community College of Denver; Lucille M. Schultz, University of Cincinnati; Sue Serrano, Sierra College; Linda R. Spain, Linn-Benton Community College; and Jacqueline Zimmerman, Lewis and Clark Community College.

I would also like to thank the following instructors and their students, who class tested chapters from *Successful College Writing* and provided valuable feedback about how its features and organization worked in the classroom: Mary Applegate, D'Youville College; Michael Hricik, Westmoreland County Community College; Lee Brewer Jones, DeKalb College; Edwina Jordan, Illinois Central College; Susan H. Lassiter, Mississippi College; Mildred C. Melendez, Sinclair Community College; Steve Rayshich, Westmoreland County Community College; Barbara J. Robedeau, San Antonio College; and Deanna White, University of Texas at San Antonio.

The following instructors have given me the benefit of their experience and expertise by reviewing drafts of *Successful College Writing;* I am very grateful to them for all of their comments and advice: Andrea Berta, University of Texas at El Paso; Larry T. Blades, Highline Community College; Laurie Warshal Cohen, Seattle Central Community College; Mark Coley, Tarrant County College; Patricia Delamer, University of Dayton; Marla Dinchak, Glendale Community College; Elizabeth Griffey, Florida Community College at Jacksonville; Avon Bisson Hadoulis, Long Island University, C. W. Post Campus; Michael Hricik, Westmoreland County Community College; Becky Johnen, West Virginia Northern Community College; Lee Brewer Jones, DeKalb College; Edwina Jordan, Illinois Central College; Peter Jordan, Tennessee State University; Earnest Lee, Carson-Newman College; Jane Maher, Nassau Community College; Mildred C. Melendez, Sinclair Community College; Dianne S. Metzar, Broome Community College; Gunhild T. Miller, Rockland Community College (SUNY); Patrice A. Quarg, Community College of Baltimore County—Catonsville Campus; Barbara J. Robedeau, San Antonio College; Eileen B. Seifert, DePaul University; Lauren Sewell, University of Tennessee at Chattanooga; Bill M. Stiffler, Harford Community College; William Tucker, Eastern Michigan University; Susan A. VanSchuyver, Oklahoma City Community College; Deanna M. White, University of Texas at San Antonio; and Ruth Windhover, Highline Community College.

For their comments on the coverage of learning styles in this text, I would like to thank John K. DiTiberio, Saint Louis University; Ronald A. Sudol, Oakland University; and Thomas C. Thompson, The Citadel. For useful comments on the chapters on argument, I would like to thank Heather Graves, DePaul University, and Gary Mitchner, Sinclair Community College. For her advice on the chapter on library research, I am grateful to Barbara Fister, and for useful comments on the ESL chapters in the handbook, I would like to thank Craig Kleinman, City College of San Francisco, and Bob Hemmer.

My thanks go to Mary Jane Feldman, Niagara County Community College, for designing the field test of the Learning Styles Inventory and conducting the statistical analysis of the results. I would also like to thank the instructors and students who participated in a field test of the Learning Styles Inventory: Laurie Warshal Cohen, Seattle Central Community College; Lee Brewer Jones, DeKalb College; Edwina Jordan, Illinois Central College; Jennifer Manning, John Jay College; Mildred Melendez, Sinclair Community College; Paul Resnick, Illinois Central College; and Deanna M. White, University of Texas at San Antonio. Four instructors at Adirondack Community College field tested the grammar assessment test and provided me with useful feedback. I would like to thank Elizabeth Cassidy, Patricia J. Duncan, Kathleen McCoy, and Nancy Seid.

I am grateful to the following students whose essays appear in this text: Andrew Decker, Nicholas Destino, Robin Ferguson, Heather Gianakos, Melinda Hunter, Michael Jacobsohn, Sarah McCreight, Sharon McLaughlin, Tina Oyer, Ryan Porter, Maria Rodriguez, Harley Tong, Jennifer Tumiel, and Aphonetip Vasavong.

Finally, I would like to thank the instructors and students at the following colleges who participated in our survey on student interests: Amarillo College; Bunker Hill Community College; Broome Community College; Illinois Central College; Portland Community College, Sylvania; and the University of South Alabama.

Judy Voss deserves much credit and recognition for her thoughtful editing of the manuscript, as does Wendy Polhemus-Annibell for her careful and judicious copyediting of my final draft. I offer special thanks to Carolyn Lengel, who wrote the exercises and examples for the Handbook. Marica Muth, too, deserves recognition and thanks for coordinating the development of the Instructor's Resource Manual. I also want to thank Beverly Ponzi for her clerical work in preparing the manuscript and Linda Herman for her research assistance.

Many people at Bedford/St Martin's have contributed to the creation and development of *Successful College Writing*. Each person with whom I have worked is a true professional; each demonstrates high standards and expertise; each is committed to producing a book focused on student needs. First of all, I would like to thank Barbara Heinssen for her many contributions to the planning of the book. To Kristin Bowen, development editor, I give special thanks for coordinating the development of the handbook and for her skillful editing and thoughtful advice. To Harold Chester, project editor, I extend my thanks for thoroughly and carefully checking and cross-checking every detail and for helping me adhere to a demanding production schedule. Gregory Johnson, editorial assistant, and Leah Edmunds, associate editor, have helped in a number of ways, and I thank them.

To Chuck Christensen, president and publisher of Bedford/St. Martin's, I attribute much of my success in writing college textbooks. Twenty-one years ago, I signed a contract for my first textbook with Chuck. Under his guidance, it became a best-seller. From Chuck I learned how to translate what I teach to the printed page. I respect Chuck's knowledge of publishing and value his expertise in the field of college English, his judgment, and his friendship. Joan Feinberg, editorial director, has become another trusted advisor. I value her editorial experience and appreciate the creative energy she brings to each issue and to each conversation. I also must thank Nancy Perry, editor in chief, for her forthright advice and for valuable assistance in making some of the more difficult decisions about the book.

I also appreciate the advice and guidance that Karen Melton, marketing director, and Brian Wheel, marketing manager, have provided at various junctures in the writing of this text. Thanks also to Denise Wydra, director of new media, for coordinating the development of the software that accompanies this text.

I owe the largest debt of gratitude to Carla Samodulski, executive editor, for guiding this book from its inception to its publication. To the day-to-day writing of this book, Carla has contributed energy, creativity, enthusiasm, and scholarship, as well as practicality. Her knowledge of and experience with our student audience kept the book focused; her perceptive advice and skillful editing were invaluable. She insists on excellence and inspired me to do the same. Carla and I have worked on the book for three years; she has become much more than an editor. She has become a collaborator, a colleague, and a friend.

Finally, I must thank the many students who inspired me to write this book. From them I have learned how to teach, and they have shown me how they think and learn. My students, then, have made the largest contribution to this book, for without them I would have little to say and no reason to write.

Kathleen T. McWhorter

Contents

PART ONE   ACADEMIC QUICK START   *1*

1 STARTING WITH AN ADVANTAGE   *3*

14 CLASSIFICATION AND DIVISION: EXPLAINING CATEGORIES AND PARTS   *413*

PART FOUR   READING AND WRITING ARGUMENTS   *547*

17 READING ARGUMENTS   *549*

22 ESSAY EXAMINATIONS AND TIMED WRITINGS   *753*

PART SIX   HANDBOOK: Writing Problems and How to Correct Them   **767**

Thematic Contents

EVERYDAY LIFE

CURRENT ISSUES

NATURE AND THE ENVIRONMENT

Our goal has been to make the readings in *Successful College Writing* as interesting and accessible to students as possible. The student reviewers listed below each reviewed and rated readings from the text and provided insightful comments and suggestions as well as information about how they use writing in their courses and careers. The text has benefited from their contributions, and we thank them.

Sherry P. Bosley *University of Baltimore*

An English major and psychology minor, Sherry uses writing in her courses and as a peer writing tutor at her college.

Crystal Arrie Brown *University of Baltimore*

Crystal uses her writing and critical thinking skills every day as a writing and math tutor and as a jurisprudence major.

Kirsten S. Giddings *Linn-Benton Community College*

An elementary education major, Kirsten uses writing to demonstrate her mastery of course material. She also notes that her writing abilities will be a crucial part of her teaching career.

Dan Graybill *Linn-Benton Community College*

As a chemical engineering major, Dan writes technical reports: "You have to be able to document everything."

Donald G. Harris *St. John Fisher College*

A business management major, Don writes papers and also uses writing when applying for internships.

Murcia Moressa Hunte *Seattle Central Community College*

Murcia, a school counseling major, writes fliers about campus news, articles in the school newspaper, and submissions to the *Caribbean Compass*.

Khililah Jackson *Niagara County Community College*

Khililah, an education major, writes essays and reports for school.

Virginia Jimenez *Community College of Denver*

A general studies major, Virginia writes term papers for her courses and uses writing as part of her job as a tutor.

Joanne R. Nelson *Seattle Central Community College*

Joanne, a psychology major, enjoys reading. She also loves to write and is currently writing a book.

James M. Otis *Niagara County Community College*

James majors in psychology, with a minor in social work. He uses writing mostly in school for assignments, papers, and research.

Lucius Perdue Jr. *Niagara County Community College*

Lucius, a first-year student, is a business management major. He writes essays for his writing classes and when taking exams in his business courses.

Karen M. Arnett Rodriguez *University of Baltimore*

According to Karen, "My life is writing!" As an English major and as a writing tutor, she uses writing in "every conceivable manner."

Elisha Scheiblauer *Seattle Central Community College*

Elisha, a journalism major, writes research papers, reading responses, book analyses, and essays for many of her classes.

To the Student

As a college student, you probably have many responsibilities. You may need to balance the demands of college with the needs of your family and the requirements of your job. In addition, you are probably attending college to make a change in your life — to better your prospects. You may not have chosen a specific career path as yet, but you eventually want a rewarding, secure future. Consequently, you are ready to pursue a course of study that will lead you there.

I have been teaching students like you for over thirty years in both two and four year colleges. I have written this book to help you achieve your goals by becoming a successful college writer. In writing the book, I have taken into account your busy lifestyle. It is practical and easy to read. As simply and directly as possible, the text explains what you need to know to sharpen your writing skills. You will also find it easy to locate the information you need within the text. You can use the brief contents on the inside front cover, the detailed contents, or the comprehensive index to locate information. In addition, numerous flowcharts, boxes, and other visual aids appear throughout to help you find the information or writing assistance you need quickly. (You will find a list of helpful flowcharts, figures, and boxes near the back of the text.) I also show how the writing strategies you are learning apply to other college courses and to the workplace. Throughout the book you will find tips for completing reading and writing assignments in your other college courses; Appendix B, "Five Steps to Academic Success," contains useful study skills advice, as well.

How This Book Can Help You Succeed

There are no secrets to success in writing — no tricks or miracle short-cuts. Rather, becoming a successful student writer requires hard work, guidance and feedback, and the application of skills and strategies. You must provide the hard work; your instructor and classmates will provide the guidance and feedback. This book introduces you to the skills and strategies that successful writers need to know. Specifically, this book will help you succeed in your writing course in the following ways.

- **By emphasizing the connection between reading and writing.** You have been reading nearly your entire life. You could probably read sentences and paragraphs before you could write them. This book shows you how reading and writing are connected so that you can use your reading skills to improve your writing.

- **By helping you become and stay involved with the course by including readings on topics and issues of interest and concern to college students.** The readings in this text were chosen with the help of students across the country and reviewed by a Student Review Panel. They have been selected from a wide range of sources, including newspapers, popular magazines, special-interest magazines, textbooks, and scholarly journals, representing the diverse texts you will encounter in both your personal and academic life.

- **By offering you both professional and student models of good writing.** As you work with the essays in this book, you will discover that both professional writers and student writers follow the same principles in organizing and presenting their ideas. You will also have opportunities to examine, react to, and discuss the ideas presented in these essays and relate them to your own life.

- **By helping you discover the writing strategies that work best for you.** You may have noticed that you don't learn in the same way as your best friend or the person who sits next to you in class. For example, some students learn better by listening, while others learn better by reading. Because not all students learn in the same way, Chapter 1 includes a *Learning Style Inventory* that will help you discover how you learn. As you work through the writing assignments throughout the book, you will find lists of different ways to approach a given writing task; these alternatives are designated "Learning Style Options." Feel free to experiment with these options; try one, then another. You will probably discover some techniques that work better or take less time than those you are currently using.

- **By helping you identify and eliminate basic problems with writing paragraphs and in sentence structure, grammar, punctuation, and mechanics.** In Appendix A, "Writing Assessment," you will find two ways to assess your mastery of writing basics. Your instructor may assign either or both. These assessments will help you pinpoint the types of errors you commonly make and to develop an action plan for correcting the areas in which you have problems. For each error you identify, the Action Plan Checklist on page A–9 refers to the specific section in Chapter 6, "Drafting an Essay," Chapter 8, "Editing Sentences and Words," or Part Six, "Handbook: Writing Problems and How to Correct Them," where you can review rules and practice their application. The Action Plan Checklist also refers to a student workbook, *Additional Exercises for Successful College Writing,* and to the software that accompanies this text, which offers tutorials for skills taught in the book.

How to Use This Book

In writing this book, I have included many features that I use when I am actually teaching a class. Each is described below along with suggestions for how the feature can help you become a skilled, successful writer.

A Guide to Active Reading

Chapter 2, "Working with Text: Active Reading Strategies," includes specific, practical strategies that will help you get the most out of the selections in this book as well as the reading assignments in your other courses. The *Guide to Active Reading* on page 26 explains, step by step, how to improve your comprehension and build your critical reading skills.

Detailed Coverage of Each Stage of the Writing Process

Part 2 of the text, "Strategies for Writing Essays," includes five chapters that cover each stage of the writing process in detail. Each step in the process is illustrated by the example of a student, Tina Oyer, who generates ideas for, drafts, and revises an essay. Chapter 7, "Revising Content and Organization," includes an important section on working with classmates to revise an essay (p. 166), with plenty of practical suggestions for you to use as both a writer seeking advice and as a peer reviewer.

Student Essays

Throughout the text, student essays illustrate different types of writing or different writing strategies. These student examples are usually found in sections entitled "Students Write." Use the questions following these student essays to help you discover how other students apply the techniques you are learning in their writing.

Computer Tips

Today more than ever before, computers affect every aspect of the writing process. Using a computer at a computer lab on campus or at home can help you to write and revise your papers more efficiently, and using the Internet for research opens up an almost unlimited number of sources for you to consider. Throughout the text, I suggest particular ways computers, and specifically word processing programs, can be especially helpful as you write and revise an essay; this advice is designated by the icon .

Graphic Organizers

Throughout the text you will find diagrams, called *Graphic Organizers,* that offer a visual approach to organizing and revising essays. These organizers present a picture or map of an essay. A sample Graphic Organizer appears on the next page. As you draft and revise, you can refer frequently to the graphic organizer for the particular type of essay you are writing. The text also demonstrates how to draw your own organizers to help you analyze a reading, structure your ideas, and write and revise drafts.

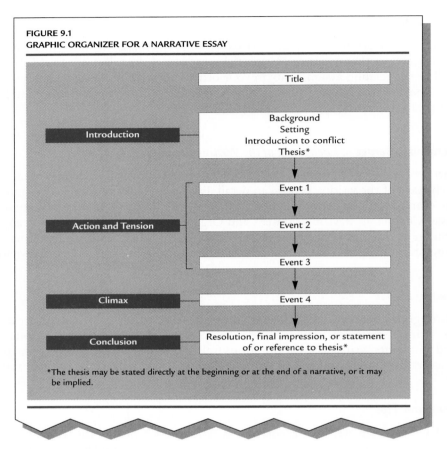

FIGURE 9.1
GRAPHIC ORGANIZER FOR A NARRATIVE ESSAY

Title

Introduction → Background
Setting
Introduction to conflict
Thesis*

Action and Tension → Event 1

Event 2

Event 3

Climax → Event 4

Conclusion → Resolution, final impression, or statement
of or reference to thesis*

*The thesis may be stated directly at the beginning or at the end of a narrative, or it may
be implied.

GRAPHIC ORGANIZER

Guided Writing Assignments

Chapters 9–16, 18, and 21 contain writing guides that "walk you through" a writing assignment step by step. The Guided Writing Assignments are shaded, as in the sample on page xxxvii. You can refer to this guide as often as you need to while you complete the assignment in the chapter or other similar assignments. Think of it as a tutorial to which you can always turn for tips, examples, and advice.

Revision Flowcharts

Many chapters include flowcharts that will help you identify what you need to revise in a first draft. Each flowchart lists key questions to ask about a draft and offers suggestions for how to revise to correct any weaknesses you uncover. (See the sample on page xxxvii.) You can also use the questions in the appropriate revision flowchart to guide classmates who are reviewing your essay.

A GUIDED WRITING ASSIGNMENT

The following guide will help you write a process analysis essay. It may be a how-to or a how-it-works essay. Although you will focus on process analysis, you may need to integrate one or more other patterns of development in your essay. Depending on your learning style, you may choose different ways of gathering ideas or evaluating your first draft. This Guided Writing Assignment will provide you with alternatives.

The Assignment

Write a process analysis essay on one of the following topics or one that you choose on your own. Be sure the process you choose is one you know enough about to explain to others, or can learn about through observation or research. Your audience consists of readers who are unfamiliar with the process, including your classmates.

How-to Essay Topics

1. How to improve _____ (your study habits, your wardrobe, your batting average)

PART OF A GUIDED WRITING ASSIGNMENT

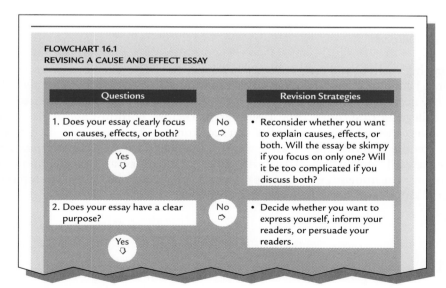

FLOWCHART 16.1
REVISING A CAUSE AND EFFECT ESSAY

Questions		Revision Strategies
1. Does your essay clearly focus on causes, effects, or both?	No ⇨	• Reconsider whether you want to explain causes, effects, or both. Will the essay be skimpy if you focus on only one? Will it be too complicated if you discuss both?
Yes ⇩		
2. Does your essay have a clear purpose?	No ⇨	• Decide whether you want to express yourself, inform your readers, or persuade your readers.
Yes ⇩		

A PORTION OF A REVISION FLOWCHART

Writing Using Sources

Often, as you write and revise an essay you will find that you need facts, statistics, or the viewpoint of an expert to strengthen your own ideas. Chapter 19, "Planning a Paper with Sources," will acquaint you with basic information on how to locate information in the library and on the Internet. Chapter 20, "Writing a Research Paper," demonstrates how to use, and document, information from sources within an essay. For your convenience, this book includes guidelines for using two widely recommended styles for documenting sources: MLA and APA. You can find guidelines for using MLA style on pages with a green bar at the edge and guidelines for using APA style on pages with a gray bar at the edge.

Handbook

Part Six, "Handbook: Writing Problems and How to Correct Them," is a user-friendly reference that you can consult to review problem areas or to check rules about grammar, punctuation, or mechanics that you are uncertain about. Refer to this section often to make sure your papers are error-free. Your instructor may also refer you to this part of the book by writing either revision symbols (such as *cs* for "comma splice") or the numbers and letters of specific sections (such as "7a" for a pronoun reference problem) on your papers. You can refer to the list of revision symbols at the back of the book or to the complete contents for the Handbook on the last page of the text and the inside back cover to find the information you need. You can also look up grammar concepts, punctuation marks, or problem areas in the index.

A Final Word

In my high school and early college years, I was an "OK" writer, but never a skilled writer. I could not have imagined myself writing a textbook. Now, *Successful College Writing* is my tenth college textbook. How did I learn to write well? I learned from my college writing courses and from my instructors, both in English classes and those in other disciplines as well. I learned from my husband, who used to read and comment on my papers while we were in college. I learned from friends and classmates; I continue to learn from colleagues, editors, and most importantly from my own students, who deserve clear and concise expression. Never stop learning — I know I will not. I wish you success.

Kathleen T. McWhorter

Academic
Quick Start

Chapter *1*

The three photographs on the opposite page illustrate three important parts of most students' lives — classes, jobs, and friends and family.

Writing Quick Start

Open a new computer file or take out a blank sheet of paper and write at the top, "I am a (an) _____." Under this statement, write a vertical list of the numbers *1* through *10*. Working rapidly, complete the statement by writing down next to the numbers whatever words or phrases come to mind that describe you. Try to be as honest as possible. Remember, there are no right or wrong answers. Responses such as "great math student," "procrastinator," "good outfielder," or "slow reader" are all acceptable. Once your list is complete, take a few minutes to reread it. Then renumber the items in order of importance.

Starting with an Advantage

TEACHING TIP

To initiate class discussion, ask the class how the subject of each photograph — a college classroom, a job situation, and a family scene — relates to writing. For instance, college classes may require writing, inspire writing, and teach writing. Ask students to talk about examples of writing they do for their classes, jobs, and friends and family, and spend five minutes discussing their responses.

What did your list tell you about yourself? Did this exercise help you see what is important in your life? Many kinds of writing help you explore and learn about yourself and your values, especially journal writing and personal essays. You will learn more about these and other kinds of writing as you take various college courses.

College is a challenging, often competitive environment. Hard work and a strong commitment to learning are essential to success: You must be willing to devote time and effort to reading, writing, and learning. If you are like most students, however, you have other commitments—to a job or a family, for example, or perhaps to both. Although your goal is certainly to succeed, you need to manage your studies so that you don't have to shut down the rest of your life for the next few years. The main purpose of this chapter, as well as the other chapters in the book, is to help you succeed in your writing course. However, you'll find that many of the suggestions offered here will help you with your other courses as well.

One key to academic success is to give yourself an advantage—a competitive edge that will help you learn efficiently and get the most out of the time you spend studying and writing. The process of *assessment,* discussed later in this chapter, will help you gain such an advantage. You will discover not only *how* you learn but *what* your strengths and weaknesses are as well. You will also discover effective approaches to your own learning and writing—ones that work for *you.* First, though, let's consider why writing skills are so very important and look at some general writing strategies.

WHY STRIVE TO IMPROVE YOUR WRITING SKILLS?

Most college students ask themselves the following two questions:

- How can I improve my grades?
- How can I improve my chances of getting a good job?

The answer to both questions is the same: Improve your writing, reading, and thinking skills. The following sections explain how these skills, especially writing, are essential to your success in college and on the job and discuss other benefits of improving your writing skills.

Writing Skills Help You Succeed in College and in Your Career

College courses such as psychology, biology, and political science demand that you read, write, and think about concepts and issues in particular fields of study. You will be expected to read articles, essays, reports, and textbooks and then to react to and write about what you have read. In many courses, your grade depends on your written work—you demonstrate what you have learned by writing exams, reports, and papers.

Writing is important on the job as well. In most jobs, workers need to communicate effectively with others, such as supervisors, co-workers, patients, clients, and customers. You can expect to write plenty of letters, email messages, memos, and reports. In fact, social scientist Patrick Scheetz, reporting the results of a 1995 national survey of employers of recent college graduates, notes that strong oral and written communication skills are rated as the two most highly desired skills by employers.*

Because your writing course offers both immediate and long-range benefits, it is one of the most important college courses you will ever take. Your writing course will teach you how to write more effectively. You will learn how to express your ideas clearly, structure convincing arguments, prepare research papers, and write essay exams. Your writing course will also help you improve your reading and thinking skills. As you read the variety of selections offered in this book, you will develop more efficient ways of approaching reading assignments. As you read, respond to, and write about the readings, you will learn how to analyze, synthesize, and evaluate ideas. Approach your writing course as a valuable experience that can make a difference in the next few years of your life. In addition to improving your chances for academic and career success, your writing course offers you the following other advantages.

TEACHING TIP

If pressed, some students may admit that they believe writing will not help them in their chosen profession. You can demonstrate Patrick Scheetz's point by bringing to class the employment section of the latest Sunday edition of the *New York Times* or another large city newspaper. The employment ads will demonstrate the importance of strong oral and written communication skills.

Writing Facilitates Learning and Recall

Writing is a way to learn. For example, you can often remember something more easily if you write it down. Whether you are taking notes, outlining, summarizing, or annotating, the act of writing focuses your attention on and gets you thinking about the material to be learned. In addition, writing facilitates learning by engaging two senses at once. Whereas you take in information visually by reading or aurally by listening, writing engages your sense of touch, as you put your pen to paper or your fingers on a keyboard, as well as your sense of sight. In general, researchers have found that the more senses you use in a learning task, the more easily learning occurs and the more you remember about the task later on. Writing also forces you to think about the subject matter at hand as you sort, connect, and define ideas. Each of these mental activities facilitates learning. In fact, numerous research studies demonstrate that students who read an assignment and then write about it retain more information than students who only read the assignment.

TEACHING TIP

Point out that while writing facilitates both learning and recall, not all learning is limited to recall. Analysis, interpretation, and other critical thinking skills begin with recall but go beyond it, requiring a high degree of independent thought. Writing facilitates these levels of thinking as well.

Writing Clarifies Thinking

Let's suppose you are given the task of awarding ten $10,000 grants to needy students on your campus. How would you determine who would receive the awards? Take three to four minutes to write a list of possible criteria that you could use to

TEACHING TIP

For an example of how writing clarifies organization, point out that students may already have experience with organizing lists. For instance, to save time a busy shopper might reorganize a list to correspond to the layout of the store — produce first, and so on.

Scheetz, L. Patrick. *Recruiting Trends 1995–96. A Study of 527 Businesses, Industries and Governmental Agencies Employing New College Graduates.* ERIC. Database. Dec. 1995.

judge each candidate. Next, reread your list; circle the criteria that would be useful, cross out any that do not seem workable, and add any new criteria that occur to you. By writing and revising this list, you are on your way to building a useful set of criteria.

As this activity demonstrates, writing forces you to think through a task. Getting your ideas down on paper or on a computer screen helps you to evaluate them. Writing, then, is a means of sorting ideas, exploring relationships, weighing alternatives, and clarifying values.

Writing Helps You Solve Problems

TEACHING TIP:
COLLABORATIVE
WRITING

(10–15 minutes) Divide
the class into small
groups. Have each
group

• assign one person the
  role of recorder.
• brainstorm a short list
  of personal problems
  (real or imagined) and
  possible solutions.
• discuss what discoveries they might make
  about how to define
  or solve each problem
  through writing.

When you solve problems, you identify possible actions that may change undesirable situations (your car won't start) to desirable ones (your car starts). Writing makes problem solving easier by helping you define the problem. That is, by describing the problem in writing, you can often see new aspects of it.

One student, for example, had a problem with her father-in-law. He seemed hostile and uncooperative when she tried to be open and friendly with him. The student described her problem in a letter to a friend: "He looks at me as if I'm going to take his son to the end of the earth and never bring him back." When she reread this statement, the student realized that her father-in-law may have resented her because he was afraid of losing contact with his son. Recognizing that this fear might be the root of the problem, the student began to think of ways to reassure her father-in-law and strengthen their relationship. In this example, writing about the problem helped the student to define it and discover ways to solve it. Similarly, writing can help you to think through confusing situations, make difficult decisions, and clarify your position on important issues.

DEVELOPING STRATEGIES FOR WRITING

*For more help with study
strategies, see Appendix B.*

Establishing a study area, planning your time, using academic services such as the writing center, and consulting your instructor are all strategies that will help you succeed in your writing course as well as in your other courses. Using the following tips will also make a big difference in how much and how quickly you are able to improve your writing skills in your writing course.

Start with a Positive Attitude

As a college student, you have the potential and ability to be a successful writer. All you need is a process to follow, opportunities to practice, and feedback from your classmates and instructor to bring out your writing potential. Your writing course will provide this process, practice, and feedback. To approach your writing course positively and to get the most out of it, use the following suggestions.

1. **Think of writing as a process.** Writing is not, as some students think, a single act of getting words down on paper. Instead, it is a series of steps that you work through—a process of planning, organizing, drafting, revising, and editing and proofreading. In addition, most writers go back and forth among these steps. Chapters 4–8 cover these steps of the writing process in detail.

2. **Be patient.** Writing is a skill that improves gradually. Don't expect to see dramatic differences in your writing immediately. As you draft and revise your essays, your writing will improve in small ways that build on one another.

3. **Expect writing to take time, often more time than you planned.** Realize, too, that on some days writing will be easier than on other days. As with many skills, there will be days when ideas flow easily and days when you'll say, "I just can't think of anything to write."

4. **Focus on learning.** When you are given a writing assignment, don't ask, "Why do I have to do this?" Ask instead, "What can I learn from this?" As you learn more about your own writing process, write your observations in one place for easy review (such as in a journal; see the section on journal writing on page 7).

5. **Use the support and guidance available to you.** Your instructor, your classmates, and this book can all help you become a better writer. In Parts 3 and 4 of the text , Guided Writing Assignments will lead you, step-by-step, through each chapter assignment. You will find tips, advice, and alternative ways of approaching the assignment.

6. **Look for ideas in the readings.** The essays in this book have been chosen to spark your interest, to open windows to ideas, and to touch on current issues. Think of every assigned reading as an opportunity to learn about a topic that you might not otherwise have the time to read or think about. Chapter 2 provides a Guide to Active Reading and helpful strategies for getting the most out of the reading assignments in this book. As you will see, the readings themselves will serve as sources of ideas for writing essays of your own.

7. **Attend all classes.** Writing is a skill, not a set of facts you can read about in a book; it is best learned through interaction with your instructor and classmates.

Keep a Writing Journal

Whether you keep your writing journal in a notebook or a computer file, use it to record your ideas for later use. You should write in your journal frequently; every day, if possible. Use it to record daily impressions, reflect on events or on reading assignments, comment on experiences and observations, explore relationships among people or ideas, ask questions, and test ideas. You will soon discover the many benefits of journal writing.

TEACHING TIP

• Either provide or have students purchase write-on tabs to paste into their journals to mark freewriting space, the error log, and the misspelled word log.

• Remind students to write the date at the top of each journal entry. This practice makes it easy to distinguish one entry from another; more importantly, it allows students to chronicle their progress in writing and thinking.

COMPUTER HINT

Have students create separate files for freewriting, the error log, and the misspelled word log. Remind them to save each file on disk as they work.

Benefits of Journal Writing

• **A journal is a place to practice writing.** Like most skills, writing can best be improved through practice. Record conversations, summarize or react to meaningful experiences, or release pent-up frustrations. Remember, regardless of what you write about, you are writing and thereby improving your skills.

• **A journal is a place to experiment.** Try out new ideas and express things that you are learning about yourself—your beliefs and values. Experiment with different voices, different topics, and different approaches to a topic.

• **A journal is a place to warm up.** Like an athlete, a writer benefits from warming up. Use a journal to activate your thought processes, loosen up, and stretch your mind before you tackle your writing assignments.

• **A journal is a place to reflect on your writing.** Record problems, strategies you have learned, and ways to get started on assignments. You might also find it helpful to keep an error log and a misspelled word log.

• **A journal is a source of ideas for papers.** If you are asked to choose your own topic for an essay, leaf through your journal. You'll find plenty of possibilities.

• **A journal is a place to respond to readings.** Use it to collect your thoughts about and respond to a reading before writing an assigned essay. (You will learn more about response journals in Chapter 3.)

• **A journal can help you work through problems.** Use it to define a problem, brainstorm options, weigh alternatives, and arrive at possible solutions. You may discover that writing helps you think more clearly.

• **A journal can be therapeutic.** Writing in a journal can make you feel better about yourself. Explore your feelings and emotions, consider solutions to personal problems, or just react to the events of the day.

How to Get Started

Your first journal entry is often the most difficult one to write. Once you've written a few entries, you'll begin to feel more comfortable. Here's how to get started.

TEACHING TIP

Distinguish journal writing from essay writing to illustrate why the emphasis in journals is not on correctness but on ideas.

• Journal writing is primarily *personal,* whereas essay writing is *social,* shared writing.

• Journal writing is largely *prewriting,* whereas essay writing is *polished* writing.

1. Write in an 8-½-by-11-inch spiral-bound notebook, or type your entries on a computer, print them out, and compile them in a loose-leaf notebook.

2. Set aside five to ten minutes each day for journal writing. "Waiting times" at the bus stop, the laundromat, or a drive-through window provide opportunities for journal writing, as do "down times" such as the ten minutes before a class begins or the few minutes before you leave for work.

3. Concentrate on capturing your ideas—not on being grammatically correct. Try to write correct sentences, but do not focus on grammar and punctuation.

4. If you are not sure what to write about, consult Figure 1.1, Starting Points for Journal Writing. You may want to code your journal entries by using the symbols shown in the figure. Coding your entries will make you more aware of your thought processes and help you to distinguish different types of entries.

FIGURE 1.1
STARTING POINTS FOR JOURNAL WRITING

Get started by . . .

< >	Describing	a daily event a sporting event an object a cartoon or photograph an overheard conversation
!!	Reacting to	a person a world, national, local, or campus event a passage from a book a magazine or newspaper article a film, song, or concert a television program a radio personality a fashion or fad
←	Recollecting	an important event a childhood experience an impression or dream a favorite relative or friend
?	Questioning	a policy a trend a position on an issue
↔	Comparing or contrasting	two people two events or actions two issues
ex	Thinking of examples of	a personality type a type of teacher, supervisor, or doctor
+ **−**	Judging (evaluating)	a rule or law a decision a musician or other performer an assignment a radio or television personality a political candidate

5. Reread your journal entries on a regular basis. By doing so you will discover that rereading entries is similar to looking at old photographs: They will bring back vivid snippets of the past for reflection and appreciation.

TEACHING TIP

Give students at least 20 minutes to write this first journal entry. They may feel most comfortable working independently for now; later in the chapter and throughout this course, however, they will benefit from working in cooperative groups.

WRITING ACTIVITY 1

Write a journal entry describing your reaction to one or more of your classes this semester. For example, you might write about which classes you expect to be most or least difficult, most or least enjoyable, and most or least time consuming.

Get the Most out of Writing Conferences

Many writing instructors schedule periodic writing conferences with individual students. These conferences are designed to give you and your instructor an opportunity to discuss your work and your progress in the course. Such conferences are not interviews, oral tests, or evaluation sessions. Rather, they are opportunities for you to get individualized help with improving your writing skills. If the conferences are optional, be sure to schedule one.

The following tips will help you get the most out of a writing conference.

TEACHING TIP

To promote critical thinking and self-assessment, suggest that students summarize conferences throughout the year and review their notes to analyze their writing progress

• before submitting final drafts.
• before midterm grades are assigned.
• before final grades are assigned (to predict the grade they feel they deserve).

1. Arrive on time or a few minutes early.

2. Bring copies of the draft essay you are currently working on as well as previously returned papers. Have them in hand when your conference begins, not buried in your book bag, since you may want to refer to them.

3. Reread recently returned papers ahead of time, so that your instructor's comments are fresh in your mind. If the purpose of the conference is to discuss one recently returned paper, reread it and your instructor's comments closely on the day of the conference. Also review your notes from any previous conferences.

4. Allow your instructor to set the agenda, but come prepared with questions you need answered. Write the questions down so you won't forget to ask them.

5. Take notes, either during or immediately after the conference. Include the comments and suggestions offered by your instructor. You might also consider writing a journal entry that summarizes the conference.

6. Revise the draft essay you and your instructor discussed as soon as possible after the conference, while the suggestions for revision you received are still fresh in your mind.

ASSESSING YOUR LEARNING STYLE

The writing strategies discussed thus far in this chapter are appropriate for just about every student writer. But you also need to know how *you* learn. How do you discover this information? The key is assessment.

What Is Assessment?

Assessment is an essential part of many daily tasks. When shopping for a birthday gift for a close friend, you might assess what she needs, what she already has, and what she might like to have. Before starting to search for an apartment, you might assess what you can afford, what locations are desirable, and what your minimum space requirements are. Assessment is essential to academic learning as well. Before you plan a speech for a communication class, you assess your audience and decide which approaches, examples, and visual aids might appeal to its particular members. Before you solve a math problem, you determine what information is given and what is asked for. *Assessment,* then, means evaluating or appraising.

Assessment is also an important part of learning to write more effectively. Not everyone learns in the same way, and not everyone needs to learn the same set of skills and approaches. Depending in part on a person's past experiences, personality, and prior learning, each person learns and writes in a unique way. Discovering your learning style will give you an important advantage in your writing course and in your other courses.

Therefore, in this section and the following one, you will (1) assess how you learn by using a learning style inventory and (2) identify your strengths and weaknesses as a writer by using the assessment tests in Appendix A. If you discover areas in which you need improvement, you can use the exercise workbook or computer software that accompanies this text to strengthen your skills. These assessment activities will help you devise specific strategies to learn more effectively, capitalizing on your strengths and overcoming your weaknesses.

What Is Your Learning Style?

Have you noticed that you differ from some of your friends in the types of tasks you can perform easily and how you perform them? Do you have a friend who is mechanically inclined and can assemble toys or repair appliances with ease? Have you noticed differences in how you and your friends solve problems and take in information? You may be methodical and analytical, whereas a friend may get flashes of insight. You may be able to read printed information and recall it easily, but a friend finds it easier to learn from class lectures or a videotape. Have you noticed that some students prefer to work alone on a project, while others enjoy working as part of a group?

These differences can be explained by what is known as learning style. **Learning style** refers to the set of preferences that describes how you learn. The following Learning Style Inventory is intended to help you assess your learning style. Complete the questionnaire now, before continuing with the chapter. After you have completed the Learning Style Inventory, you'll find directions for scoring on page 16.

LEARNING STYLE INVENTORY

Directions: **Each numbered item presents two choices. Select the one alternative that best describes you. There are no right or wrong answers. In cases in which neither choice suits you, select the one that is closer to your preference. Check the letter of your choice next to the question number on the answer sheet on page 15.**

1. In a class I usually
   a. make friends with just a few students.
   b. get to know many of my classmates.

2. If I were required to act in a play, I would prefer to
   a. have the director tell me how to say my lines.
   b. read my lines the way I think they should be read.

3. Which would I find more helpful in studying the processes by which the U.S. Constitution can be amended?
   a. a one-paragraph summary
   b. a diagram

4. In making decisions, I am more concerned with
   a. whether I have all the available facts.
   b. how my decision will affect others.

5. When I have a difficult time understanding how something works, it helps most if I can
   a. see how it works several times.
   b. take time to think the process through and analyze it.

6. At a social event, I usually
   a. wait for people to speak to me.
   b. initiate conversation with others.

7. I prefer courses that have
   a. a traditional structure (lectures, assigned readings, periodic exams, and assignments with deadlines).
   b. an informal structure (class discussions, flexible assignments, and student-selected projects).

8. If I were studying one of the laws of motion in a physics course, I would prefer to have my instructor begin the class by
   a. stating the law and discussing examples.
   b. giving a demonstration of how the law works.

9. Which set of terms best describes me?
   a. fair and objective
   b. sympathetic and understanding

10. When I learn something new, I am more interested in
    a. the facts about it.
    b. the principles behind it.

11. As a volunteer for a community organization that is raising funds for a hospice, which of the following tasks would I prefer?
    a. stuffing envelopes for a mail campaign
    b. making phone calls asking for contributions

12. I would begin an ideal day by
    a. planning what I want to do during each hour of the day.
    b. doing whatever comes to mind.

13. If I wanted to learn the proper way to prune a rosebush, I would prefer to
    a. have someone explain it to me.
    b. watch someone do it.

14. It is more important for me to be
    a. consistent in thought and action.
    b. responsive to the feelings of others.

15. If I kept a journal or diary, it would most likely contain entries about
    a. what happens to me each day.
    b. the insights and ideas that occur to me each day.

16. If I decided to learn a musical instrument, I would prefer to take
    a. one-on-one lessons.
    b. group lessons.

17. If I worked in a factory, I would prefer to be a
    a. machine operator.
    b. troubleshooter.

18. I learn best when I
    a. write down the information.
    b. form a mental picture of the information.

19. If I gave a wrong answer in class, my main concern would be
    a. finding out the correct answer.
    b. what others in class thought of me.

20. I prefer television news programs that
    a. summarize events through film footage and factual description.
    b. deal with the issues behind the events.

21. Whenever possible, I choose to
    a. study alone.
    b. study with a study group.

22. In selecting a topic for a research paper, my more important concern is

    a. choosing a topic for which there is adequate information.
    b. choosing a topic I find interesting.

23. If I took apart a complicated toy or machine to repair it, to help me reassemble it I would

    a. write a list of the steps I followed when taking it apart.
    b. draw a diagram of the toy or machine.

24. As a member of a jury for a criminal trial, I would be primarily concerned with

    a. determining how witness testimony fits with the other evidence.
    b. judging the believability of witnesses.

25. If I were an author, I would most likely write

    a. biographies or how-to books.
    b. novels or poetry.

26. A career in which my work depends on that of others is

    a. less appealing than working alone.
    b. more appealing than working alone.

27. When I am able to solve a problem, it is usually because I

    a. worked through the solution step by step.
    b. brainstormed until I arrived at a solution.

28. I prefer to keep up with the news by

    a. reading a newspaper.
    b. watching television news programs.

29. If I came upon a serious auto accident, my first impulse would be to

    a. assess the situation.
    b. comfort any injured people.

30. I pride myself on my ability to

    a. remember numbers and facts.
    b. see how ideas are related.

31. To solve a personal problem, I prefer to

    a. think about it myself.
    b. talk it through with friends.

32. If I had one last elective course to take before graduation, I would choose one that presents

    a. practical information that I can use immediately.
    b. ideas that make me think and stimulate my imagination.

33. For recreation I would rather do a

    a. crossword puzzle.
    b. jig-saw puzzle.

34. I can best be described as
    a. reasonable and levelheaded.
    b. sensitive and caring.
35. When I read a story or watch a film, I prefer one with a plot that is
    a. clear and direct.
    b. intricate and complex.

Answer Sheet

Directions: Check either *a* or *b* in the boxes next to each question number.

Column One			Column Two			Column Three			Column Four			Column Five		
	a	*b*		*a*	*b*		*a*	*b*		*a*	*b*		*a*	*b*
1			2			3			4			5		
6			7			8			9			10		
11			12			13			14			15		
16			17			18			19			20		
21			22			23			24			25		
26			27			28			29			30		
31			32			33			34			35		
Total														

Directions for Scoring

1. On your answer sheet, add the checkmarks in each *a* and *b* column, counting first the number of *a*s checked, then the number of *b*s.
2. Enter the number of *a*s and *b*s you checked in the boxes at the bottom of each column.
3. Transfer these numbers to the Scoring Grid on p. 16. Enter the number of *a* choices in column one in the blank labeled "Independent," the number of *b* choices in column one in the blank labeled "Social," and so on.
4. Circle your higher score in each row. For example, If you scored 2 for Independent and 5 for Social, circle "5" and "Social."
5. Your higher score in each row indicates a characteristic of your learning style. If the scores in a particular row are close to one another, such as 3 and 4, this

suggests that you do not have a strong preference for either approach to learning. Scores that are far apart, such as 1 and 6, suggest that you favor one way of learning over the other.

SCORING GRID

COLUMN	NUMBER OF CHECKMARKS	
	Choice a	*Choice b*
One	_____	_____
	Independent	Social
Two	_____	_____
	Pragmatic	Creative
Three	_____	_____
	Verbal	Spatial
Four	_____	_____
	Rational	Emotional
Five	_____	_____
	Concrete	Abstract

Interpreting Your Scores

The Learning Style Inventory is divided into five parts; each question in the inventory assesses one of five aspects of your learning style. Here is how to interpret the five aspects of your learning style.

1. Independent or Social

These scores indicate the level of interaction with others that you prefer, both in general and when you have a specific task to perform. *Independent* learners prefer to work and study alone. They focus on the task at hand rather than on the people around them. Independent learners are often goal-oriented and self-motivated. *Social* learners are more people-oriented. Because interaction with others is important to them, social learners often prefer to learn and study with classmates. They often focus their attention on those around them and see a task as an opportunity for social interaction.

2. Pragmatic or Creative

These scores suggest how you prefer to approach learning tasks. *Pragmatic* learners are practical and systematic. They approach tasks in an orderly, sequential manner.

They like rules and learn step by step. *Creative* learners, in contrast, approach tasks imaginatively. They prefer to learn through discovery or experiment. They enjoy flexible, open-ended tasks and tend to dislike following rules.

3. Verbal or Spatial

These scores indicate the way you prefer to take in and process information. *Verbal* learners rely on language, usually written text, to acquire information. They are skilled in the use of language and can work with other symbol systems as well. *Spatial* learners prefer to take in information by studying graphics such as drawings, diagrams, films, or videos. They can visualize in their minds how things work or how things are positioned in space.

4. Rational or Emotional

These scores suggest your preferred approach to decision making and problem solving. *Rational* learners are objective and impersonal; they rely on facts and information when making decisions or solving problems. Rational learners are logical, often challenging or questioning a task. They enjoy prioritizing, analyzing, and arguing. In contrast, *emotional* learners are subjective; they focus on feelings and values. Emotional decision makers are socially conscious and often concerned with what others think. In making a decision, they seek harmony and may base a decision in part on the effect it may have on others. Emotional decision makers are often skilled at persuasion.

5. Concrete or Abstract

These scores indicate how you prefer to perceive information. *Concrete* learners pay attention to what is concrete and observable. They focus on details and tend to perceive tasks in parts or steps. Concrete learners prefer actual, tangible tasks and usually take a no-nonsense approach to learning. *Abstract* learners look at a task from a broader perspective. They tend to focus on the "big picture" or an overview of a task. Abstract learners focus on large ideas, meanings, and relationships.

A Word about Your Findings

The results of the learning style inventory probably confirmed some things you already knew about yourself as a learner and provided you with some new insights as well. Keep in mind, though, that there are other ways to measure learning style.

- The inventory you completed is an informal measure of your learning style. Other, more formal measures of learning style are available, including Kolb's *Learning Style Inventory,* the *Canfield Instructional Styles Inventory,* and the *Myers-Briggs Type Indicator.* These tests may be available at your college through the counseling or academic skills centers.

TEACHING TIP: LEARNING STYLES

To reinforce the concept of learning styles with a little humor, take a poll: How do students approach the task of assembling furniture or toys from do-it-yourself kits? Do they

- read all of the directions first? (probably verbal learners)
- follow the instructions step by step? (pragmatic learners)
- prefer to follow the diagram? (spatial learners)
- prefer to figure it out without instructions or diagrams? (independent, creative, or concrete learners)
- call a friend or family member for help? (social learners)
- assume each part has a purpose, because there must be some logic behind this product? (rational learners)
- become either upset or ecstatic during the assembly process? (emotional learners)
- set the item aside and sit down to read a book instead? (abstract learners)

Briefly discuss how students' responses to the poll relate to their inventory results.

- The inventory you completed measures the five aspects of learning style that are most relevant to the writing process. However, many other aspects of learning style exist.
- You are the best judge of the accuracy of the results of this inventory and how they apply to you. If you think that one or more of the aspects of your learning style indicated by the inventory do not describe you, trust your instincts.

TEACHING TIP:
LEARNING STYLES

Discuss the benefits of working with other students who share the same learning preferences versus the benefits of working with students who have different learning styles.

How to Use Your Findings

Now that you have identified important characteristics of your learning style, you are ready to use the findings to your advantage—to make learning easier and improve your writing skills. As you do so, keep the following suggestions in mind.

1. **Understand that if you have a strength in one area, you can still function in the opposite way.** For example, if you scored highly on the pragmatic scale, you are still capable of creative thinking as well.

2. **Recognize that learning style tendencies are not fixed, unchangeable characteristics.** Although you may have a higher score on the independent scale, for example, you *can* learn to function effectively in groups.

3. **Experiment with approaches that are not necessarily suited to your learning style.** Some students find that when they try an approach that never seemed to work before, they sometimes discover situations in which the approach is helpful. A verbal learner, for example, may discover that drawing a diagram of how a process works is an effective learning strategy.

4. **Do not use your learning style as an excuse to avoid learning.** Don't make the mistake of saying, "I can't write poetry because I'm not a creative learner." Instead, use what you know about your learning style to guide your approach to each task. If you are a pragmatic learner, try writing a poem about a tangible object or place or a real event: a favorite keepsake, a place where you go to sort out problems, or an event that made a lasting impression on you.

APPLYING YOUR LEARNING STYLE TO YOUR WRITING

Writing is a process that involves planning, organizing, drafting, revising, and editing and proofreading. You'll learn more about each of these steps in Chapters 4–8. At this point, however, it is important to realize that you can approach each step in the writing process in more than one way. For example, one of the first steps in that process is to select a topic to write about. Depending on your learning style, there are a number of ways to go about this task. A social learner may prefer to brainstorm about possible topics with a friend. A verbal learner may find that flipping through a newsmagazine brings topics to mind. A spatial learner may see a photograph that generates ideas for topics. Someone who is a social as well as a spatial learner may prefer to select a topic by discussing photographs with a classmate.

Let's consider an example involving two hypothetical students with different learning styles. Yolanda and Andrea, classmates in a first-year writing course, are assigned to write an essay describing an event that has influenced their lives, either positively or negatively. Yolanda writes a list of possible events and arranges them in order of importance in her life. After selecting one of these events to explore further, she draws a diagram showing the circumstances that led up to the event and those that followed it. Next, she highlights those circumstances that show how the event has affected her. Before she begins writing, Yolanda decides on the best way to organize her ideas and creates an outline.

Andrea chooses to let her mind roam freely over various events in her life while she is out jogging. All of a sudden an idea comes to mind and she knows what she wants to write about. To get started, Andrea jots down everything she can recall about the event, in the haphazard order that each remembered detail, incident, or bit of dialogue comes to her. From these notes, she selects ideas and writes her first draft. Eventually, Andrea writes numerous drafts, experimenting with different organizations. Finally, she produces an essay with which she is satisfied.

Although Yolanda and Andrea approach the same assignment in different ways, they both write effective essays. Yolanda prefers a deliberate and systematic approach because she is a pragmatic learner. Andrea, a creative learner, prefers a less structured approach, one that allows ideas to come to her in any form. Yolanda spends a great deal of time planning before writing, while Andrea prefers to experiment with various versions of her paper.

Because students' learning styles differ, this book presents alternative strategies for generating ideas and for revising your writing. These choices are indicated by the heading "Learning Style Options" (see p. 46 for an example). The following advice will help you take advantage of these learning style alternatives.

1. **Select an alternative that fits with how you learn.** For instance, if you are writing an essay on insurance fraud and are given the choice of interviewing an expert on insurance fraud or finding several articles in the library on the topic, choose the option that best suits the way you prefer to acquire information.

2. **Experiment with options.** To sustain your interest and broaden your skills, you should sometimes choose an option that does not match your preferred style of learning. For example, if you are an independent learner, conducting an interview with the insurance fraud expert may provide a refreshing change and help you strengthen your interpersonal skills.

3. **Don't expect the option that is consistent with your learning style to require less attention or effort.** Even if you are a social learner, an interview must still be carefully planned and well executed.

4. **Keep logs of the skills and approaches that work for you and the ones you need to work on.** The logs may be part of your writing journal (see p. 7). Be specific; record the assignment, the topic you chose, and the skills you applied.

TEACHING TIP: COMPUTER HINT

- Concrete or spatial learners may appreciate creating graphs, charts, and diagrams to help organize or illustrate ideas, using the draw function of a word-processing or spreadsheet program.
- Creative and verbal learners may prefer to compose and then cut and paste text using a standard word-processing program.

TEACHING TIP: LEARNING STYLES

(10–15 minutes) As a class, discuss how students approached this activity. Did they use approaches that reflect their learning styles? Did concrete learners outline or list? Did creative learners discover their reactions as they wrote? If you find consistency between learning styles and students' approaches, encourage students to try a different approach in Writing Activity 3. If you find little correlation, however, encourage students to try approaches that are compatible with their learning styles in Writing Activity 3.

TEACHING TIPS

Students may not realize that assessment is advantageous. A useful analogy might include an Olympic athlete or professional musician whose coach or tutor assesses strengths and weaknesses in order to discover how to approach a particular task. You may wish to monitor students' work on their action plans incrementally throughout this course and evaluate their success at the end of the term.

ADDITIONAL RESOURCES

For extra help with writing problems, refer students to the computer software that accompanies this text.

Analyze your log, looking for patterns. Over time, you will discover more about the writing strategies and approaches that work best for you.

Your learning style profile also indicates your strengths as a writer. As with any skill, you should try to build on your strengths, using them as a foundation. Work with Figure 1.2 to identify your strengths. First, circle or highlight the characteristics that you scored higher on in the five areas of learning style. Then refer to the right-hand column to see your strengths as a writer in each area.

WRITING ACTIVITY 2

Write a two-page essay describing your reactions to the results of the Learning Style Inventory. Explain how you expect to use the results in your writing course or other courses.

ASSESSING AND CORRECTING YOUR WRITING PROBLEMS

Even writers who are able to select pertinent and vivid details to explain an idea may have difficulty with punctuation or sentence style. Left uncorrected, errors in grammar, punctuation, and mechanics can interfere with your progress in your courses. Consequently, you may not earn the grades you think you deserve, and your writing will not be considered of college-level quality.

Many first-year college students find that they lack some of the fundamental skills that are important to good writing. Other students discover that their skills are rusty from disuse. If you have not done any formal writing for a while, you may be out of touch with some of the standards, conventions, and rules of academic writing. Usually, a quick review or refresher course will bring these fundamentals to mind, and you will be well on your way to clear, effective writing. Other students have a few trouble spots they have never been able to overcome. For instance, you may have trouble with spelling.

To eliminate these weaknesses and trouble spots, you first need to identify them, and then you need to commit yourself to overcoming them. Appendix A includes two forms of writing assessment. The first is an essay assignment that will be evaluated by your instructor. The second is a multiple-choice test in grammar and mechanics that you can grade yourself. Your instructor may assign one or the other or both. After you have completed your assigned assessment(s), take some time to develop an action plan for correcting any problems you and your instructor have identified.

By identifying and working to overcome any writing problems you may have, you can take control of your own learning and take positive steps toward writing error-free papers.

WRITING ACTIVITY 3

Using your responses to the Writing Quick Start on page 3 and the results of the Learning Style Inventory, write a two-page profile of yourself as a student or as a writer.

FIGURE 1.2
YOUR STRENGTHS AS A WRITER

Learning Style Characteristic	Strengths as a Writer
Independent	You are willing to spend time thinking about a topic and are able to pull ideas together easily.
Social	You usually find it easy to write from experience. Writing realistic dialogue may be one of your strengths. You tend to have a good sense of who you are writing for (your audience) and what you hope to accomplish (your purpose).
Pragmatic	You can meet deadlines easily. You recognize the need for organization in an essay. You tend to approach writing systematically and work through the steps in the writing process.
Creative	You tend to enjoy exploring a topic and often do so thoroughly and completely. Your writing is not usually hindered or restricted by rules or requirements.
Verbal	You may have a talent for generating ideas to write about and expressing them clearly.
Spatial	You can visualize or draw a map of the organization of your paper. Descriptions of physical objects, places, and people come easily.
Rational	You tend to write logically developed, well-organized essays. You usually analyze ideas objectively.
Emotional	Expressive and descriptive writing usually go well for you. You have a strong awareness of your audience.
Concrete	You find it easy to supply details to support an idea. You are able to write accurate, detailed descriptions and observations. You can organize facts effectively and present them clearly.
Abstract	You can develop unique approaches to a topic; you can grasp the point to which supporting ideas lead.

TEACHING TIP

Ask students to include in their profile what they would like to change about themselves as students or as writers.

TEACHING TIP: COLLABORATIVE WRITING

(10–15 minutes) Create groups of four or five students that mix pragmatic, creative, verbal, and spatial learners (if possible). Ask group members to share their responses to Writing Activity 1 (p. 10), discussing how they could apply what they now know about their learning styles to further writing on the topic (for example, they might consider which aspects of their learning style help them in each of their classes).

Chapter 2

The photograph on the opposite page is taken from a mass communication textbook. Your mass communications instructor has asked your class to study the photograph and discuss its significance.

Write a paragraph explaining what you think the photograph means and why it might have been included in the communication textbook.

Working with Text: Active Reading Strategies

o

TEACHING TIP

To initiate discussion, ask the class to brainstorm about the photograph and how it is related to the topic of communication.

• What key elements of the photo are ironic or surprising?
• What is the photographer's intent? Why does the photographer include both the satellite dish and the camel in the desert scene rather than one or the other?

TEACHING TIP:
CHAPTER OVERVIEW

• Pragmatic learners
  may be predisposed to
  active reading strate-
  gies, but other learners
  often need encourage-
  ment to mark their
  texts and may even
  seek reassurance that
  it is "okay" to do so.
• It is helpful to point
  out that writers as
  different as the poet
  Samuel Taylor
  Coleridge and the
  science writer Isaac
  Asimov have found it
  valuable to annotate
  their favorite books.
• Mention that while it
  may be easier at first
  to write annotations
  directly on the text, it
  is also possible to
  make annotations in a
  notebook, journal, or
  computer file.

To explain the meaning of the photograph, you had to think beyond the obvious action it portrays: A camel in the desert is standing near a satellite dish. You had to interpret and evaluate the photograph to arrive at its possible meaning. To complete this evaluation, you did two things. First, you grasped what the photograph *showed;* then you analyzed what it *meant*.

Reading involves a similar process of evaluation. First, you must know what the author *says;* then you must interpret what the author *means*. Both parts of the process are essential. If you learn only what the author says, you may be able to answer factual questions about the reading, but you will not be able to write papers or take tests that require interpretation of the author's meaning. This chapter will help you succeed with both parts of the reading process.

In this chapter you will learn to be a more active reader, a reader who becomes engaged and involved with a reading assignment by thinking about, challenging, and evaluating ideas. The chapter contains a Guide to Active Reading in which you will learn what to do before, during, and after reading to strengthen your comprehension and increase your recall. You will also learn how to approach difficult assignments and how to draw a diagram, called a graphic organizer, that will help you grasp both the content and organization of an assignment.

The skills you learn in this chapter will help you not only in your writing course but in your other college courses as well. As you improve your ability to read thoroughly and carefully, you'll begin to learn more about what you read. You'll also do better on exams and quizzes that ask you to apply, connect, and evaluate ideas—skills that you will learn in this chapter.

The examples in the accompanying box demonstrate why active, critical reading is essential to your success in college and on the job.

SCENES FROM COLLEGE AND THE WORKPLACE

• Each week a *political science* instructor requires students to locate and read a current newspaper article that illustrates a political principle they are studying in class.

• A *biology* professor distributes an article on cloning from *Science* magazine and asks students to agree or disagree with the position the writer takes.

• You are working as an *inspector* for the Occupational Safety and Health Administration (OSHA). Part of your job is to evaluate and critique corporate plans to comply with OSHA safety standards.

CHANGING SOME MISCONCEPTIONS ABOUT READING

Much misinformation exists about how to read effectively and efficiently. This section dispels some popular misconceptions about reading.

- **You do not always have to read everything.** Although your instructors generally expect you to read textbook assignments completely and carefully, you can sometimes read selectively, depending on your purpose, the nature of the material, and your familiarity with it. A newspaper, for example, is almost always read selectively. You choose only those articles and news reports that interest you. On occasion, you might read selectively in academic situations as well. For example, if you have recently studied chemistry in high school and your college chemistry text begins with basic definitions, you should be able to skim through the introductory explanations.

- **Not everything on a page is equally important.** Whether you are reading an article in a sports magazine, a biography of a president, or an essay in this book, each text contains a mixture of important and not-so-important ideas and information. Your task as a reader is to sort through the material and evaluate what you need to know.

- **You should not read everything the same way.** What you read, how rapidly and how carefully you read, what you pay attention to, and what, if anything, you skip are all affected by your purpose. For instance, if your psychology instructor assigns an article from *Psychology Today* as a basis for class discussion, you would read it differently than if you were preparing for a quiz based on the article. For a class discussion, you would have the article in front of you; you could refer to it to check facts and details. For a quiz, however, you would need to study the material carefully and remember it. Your familiarity with a topic also affects how you read. If you are not familiar with the topic of in-vitro fertilization, for example, you would read an essay about it much more slowly than would a doctor with considerable knowledge of the subject. Effective readers, then, vary their reading techniques to suit what they are reading and why they are reading it.

- **Not everything in print is true.** Just as you don't believe everything you hear, neither should you believe everything you read. Be sure to read with a critical, questioning eye and, at times, with a raised eyebrow. To evaluate a text, consider the authority of the author and the author's purpose for writing. As you read, try to distinguish facts from opinions, value judgments, and generalizations. (You will learn more about these topics in later chapters.) If you were to read an article titled "Woman Loses 30 Pounds in One Week," for example, your critical, questioning eye would probably be wide open. Be sure to keep that eye open when you read scholarly essays as well.

For more on how to read selectively by scanning and skimming, see Working with Text: Reading Sources in Chapter 19, p. 648.

TEACHING TIP

- Point out that because good readers read critically, it is important for writers to establish their credibility through writing that is accurate, precise, well supported, and logical as well as engaging.
- Emphasize that such standards are easier to meet when student writers are supported by their peers, their instructor, and tutors in the writing center.

A GUIDE TO ACTIVE READING

When you attend a ball game or watch a soap opera, do you get actively involved? If you are a baseball fan, at ball games you cheer some players and criticize others, evaluate plays and calls, offer advice, and so forth. As an active spectator, you almost play the game with the team. Similarly, if you are a soap-opera fan, you get actively involved in your favorite program. You react to sudden turns of events, sympathize with some characters and despise others, and try to predict what may happen in the next episode. By contrast, if you are not a fan of a baseball team or soap opera, you might watch the game or show passively, letting it take its course with little or no personal involvement or reaction. Like fans of a sports team or soap opera, active readers get involved with the material they read. They question, think about, and react to ideas using the process outlined in Figure 2.1.

The accompanying chart shows how active and passive readers approach a reading assignment in different ways. As you can see, active readers get involved by using a step-by-step approach. The sections that follow explain each of these active reading steps in more detail. Each step is discussed within the context of a reading assignment.

FIGURE 2.1
THE ACTIVE READING PROCESS

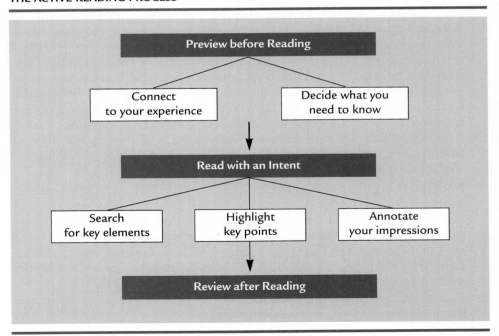

APPROACHES TO READING: ACTIVE VERSUS PASSIVE

Passive Reading	*Active Reading*
Passive readers begin reading.	Active readers begin by reading the title, evaluating the author, and thinking about what they already know about the subject. Then they decide what they need to know before they begin reading.
Passive readers read the essay only because it is assigned.	Active readers read the essay while looking for answers to questions and key elements.
Passive readers read but do not write.	Active readers read with a pen in hand. They highlight or underline, annotate, and write notes as they read.
Passive readers close the book when finished.	Active readers review, analyze, and evaluate the essay.

TEACHING TIP: LEARNING STYLES

Emphasize that students can be active readers regardless of their learning style. However, the nature of their comments, questions, and notes may differ depending on their particular learning style.

- Pragmatic learners may prefer to list main points or details.
- Creative learners may focus on the "big picture."
- Emotional learners may fill the margins with personal reactions.

What matters most is that students feel both the need and the freedom to engage with the text meaningfully.

Preview before Reading

You probably wouldn't pay to see a movie unless you knew something about it. You wouldn't dive into a pool unless it had water in it, cross a street without checking for traffic, or prepare a recipe unless you had some idea of how the dish might turn out. Similarly, you should not start reading an essay without checking its content to get a sense of what it is about. **Previewing**, then, is a quick way to familiarize yourself with an essay's content and organization. Previewing also enables you to connect the essay to your own experience and to decide what you need to know from the material. Previewing has a number of other benefits as well.

- It helps you get interested in the material.
- It provides you with a mental outline of the material before you read it.
- It enables you to concentrate more easily on the material because you know what to expect.
- It helps you remember more of what you read.

To preview a reading assignment, use the guidelines in the following list. Remember to read *only* the parts of an essay that are listed.

1. **Read the title, subtitle, and the author.** The title and subtitle may tell you what the reading is about. Check the author's name to see if it is one you recognize.
2. **Read the introduction and the first paragraph.** These sections often provide an overview of the essay.

TEACHING TIP

Remind students (who may feel pressed for time) that previewing *saves* time by providing a sort of map of the text.

TEACHING TIP:
LEARNING STYLES

Emphasize that all students need to use various strategies when previewing an assignment. At first, however, students might be inclined to use familiar strategies in previewing, such as the following:

• Emotional learners might ask, "How do I feel about this subject?" or "How does the author feel?"
• Rational learners might ask, "Where does the writer support ideas with logic or facts?"
• Pragmatic learners might prefer to list main ideas or steps.
• Spatial learners might compose a flowchart or an outline of ideas.
• Independent, creative, verbal, or abstract learners may prefer to freewrite reponses to prereading questions.

PREREADING
QUESTION

• Why don't heroics in sports necessarily produce real-life heroes?

3. **Read any headings and the first sentence following each one.** Headings, taken together, often form a mini-outline of the essay. The first sentence following a heading often explains the heading further.

4. **For an essay without headings, read the first sentence in a few of the paragraphs on each page.**

5. **Look at any photographs, tables, charts, and drawings.**

6. **Read the conclusion or summary.** A conclusion will draw the reading to a close. If the reading concludes with a summary, it will give you a condensed view of the reading.

7. **Read any end-of-assignment questions.** These questions will help focus your attention on what is important in the reading and on what you might be expected to know after you have read it.

The following essay, "Where Have You Gone, Joe DiMaggio?" has been highlighted to illustrate the parts you should read while previewing. Preview it now.

 Where Have You Gone, Joe DiMaggio*?
Heroics in the sports arena don't necessarily produce real-life heroes
Matthew Goodman

1   These days, it seems, the sports pages have come to resemble a police blotter. The fan seeking box scores and game recaps must first wade through news stories about drug abuse among athletes, arrests for drunk driving, betting and recruiting scandals, and, most disturbingly, reports of rape and other sex-related crimes. What's going on here? American sports fans ask over their morning toast and coffee. *What's happening to our heroes?*

2   It's not difficult to understand our desire for athletes to be heroes. On the surface, at least, athletes display many of the classical heroic attributes. They possess a vital and indomitable spirit; they are gloriously alive inside their bodies. And sports does allow us to witness acts that can legitimately be described as courageous, thrilling, beautiful, even noble. In an increasingly complicated and disorderly world, sports is still an arena in which we can regularly witness a certain kind of greatness.

3   Yet there's something of a paradox here, for the very qualities a society tends to seek in its heroes — selflessness, social consciousness, and the like — are precisely the *opposite* of those needed to transform a talented but otherwise unremarkable neighborhood kid into a

Joe DiMaggio (1914–1999): A legendary baseball player, he was a member of the New York Yankees from 1936 to 1951. The title refers to a line from the song "Mrs. Robinson" by Paul Simon and Art Garfunkel.

Michael Jordan or a Joe Montana. Becoming a star athlete requires a profound and long-term kind of self-absorption, a single-minded attention to the development of a few rather odd physical skills, and an overarching competitive outlook. These qualities may well make a great athlete, but they don't necessarily make a great person. On top of this, our society reinforces these traits by the system it has created to produce athletes—a system characterized by limited responsibility and enormous privilege.

The athletes themselves suffer the costs of this system. Trained to   4
measure themselves perpetually against the achievements of those around them, many young athletes develop a sense of what sociologist Walter Schafer has termed "conditional self-worth": They learn very quickly that they will be accepted by the important figures in their lives—parents, coaches, peers—to the extent they are perceived as "winners." Their egos come to rest, all too precariously, upon the narrow plank of athletic success.

Young athletes learn that success, rather than hard and honest   5
play, is what brings rewards. And for those successful enough to rise to the level of big-time college sports, the "reward" is often an artificially controlled social environment, one that shields them from many of the responsibilities other students face. Coaches—whose own jobs, of course, depend on maintaining winning programs—hover over their athletes to ensure that nothing threatens their eligibility to compete. If an athlete gets into trouble with the law, for instance, a coach will very likely intervene—hiring an attorney, perhaps even managing to have the case quietly dismissed. In some schools, athletes don't even choose their own classes or buy their own books; the athletic department does all this for them. It's not unheard of for athletic department staff to wake up athletes in the morning and to take them to class.

Given this situation, it's not too surprising that many young Amer-   6
ican athletes seem to have been left with a stunted ethical sense. Professor Sharon Stoll of the University of Idaho has tested more than 10,000 student athletes from all over the country, ranging from junior high to college age; she reports that in the area of moral reasoning, athletes invariably score lower than non-athletes—and that they grow worse the longer they participate in athletics.

Coddled by universities, lionized by local communities, accorded   7
star status by the public, endowed with six- and seven-figure salaries,
successful athletes inevitably develop a sense of themselves as privi-
leged beings—as indeed they are. The danger arises when the realistic (and thus probably healthy) understanding of personal privilege mutates into a sense of personal entitlement.

Mike Tyson, of course, is the most blatant example of this phe-   8
nomenon. Having been taught as a young man that he was special—his mentor, Cus D'Amato, reportedly had one set of rules for Tyson and

another, more stringent, set for all his other boxing protégés—and having lived his entire adult life surrounded by a cortege of fawning attendants, Tyson eventually came to believe, like a medieval king, that all he saw rightfully belonged to him. Blessed with money and fame enough to last a lifetime, he spent his time outside the ring acquiring and discarding the objects of his desire: houses, automobiles, jewelry, clothes, and women. In the wake of the publicity surrounding his rape trial, countless women have come forward to relate stories of Tyson propositioning them and then, upon being rebuffed, exclaiming in what was apparently genuine surprise, "Don't you know who I am? *I'm the heavyweight champion of the world."* Needless to say, not all athletes are Mike Tyson; there are plenty of athletes who recognize that they have been granted some extraordinary gifts in this life and want to give something back to the community.

9   Some remarkable individuals will always rise above the deforming athletic system we've created. After retiring from football, defensive tackle Alan Page of the Minnesota Vikings became a successful lawyer and established the Page Education Foundation, which helps minority and disadvantaged kids around the country pay for college. Frustrated by the old-boy network by which Minnesota judges had traditionally been appointed, Page challenged the system in court and finally won election to the state Supreme Court, becoming the first black ever elected to statewide office in Minnesota. Tennis star Martina Navratilova recently joined six other lesbians and gay men as a plaintiff in a lawsuit filed by the cities of Denver, Boulder, and Aspen challenging Colorado's recent anti-gay law as unconstitutional. Thankfully, there will always be some legitimate heroes (or, to use the more contemporary term, role models) to be found among professional athletes.

10   Still, it's probably misguided for society to look to athletes for its heroes—anymore than we look among the ranks of, say, actors or lawyers or pipefitters. The social role played by athletes is indeed important (imagine a society without sports; I wouldn't want to live in it), but it's fundamentally different from that of heroes.

11   **Thanks to the years of hard and uncompromising work that athletes have invested in themselves, sports is often able to provide us a glimpse of that "supreme beauty" that Bertrand Russell wrote of as characteristic of mathematics: "sublimely pure, and capable of a stern perfection such as only the greatest art can show."**

12   **Can't we just leave it at that?**   ■

EXERCISE 2.1

Based only on your preview of the essay "Where Have You Gone, Joe DiMaggio?" answer the following true-false questions to determine whether you have gained a sense of the essay's content and organization. If most of your answers are correct, you will know that previewing worked. (For the answers to this exercise, see p. 47).

_____ 1. The reading is primarily about heroes in sports.

_____ 2. The author thinks athletics is an acceptable source of real-life heroes.

_____ 3. The author thinks athletes are catered to by our society.

_____ 4. The qualities that make a hero will also produce a star athlete.

_____ 5. Athletes quickly learn that success is more important than honest, hard work.

_____ 6. Star athletes often consider themselves privileged.

Connect the Essay to Your Own Experience

Once you have previewed an essay, take a few moments to discover what you already know about its subject matter. At first, you may assume that you know very little about the subject, but with a little effort, you may discover you know quite a bit. To connect the subject of any essay to your experience, try the following suggestions.

1. **Think of familiar situations or examples that illustrate the subject.** For example, if you are going to read an essay about fads and fashions, you might try thinking of fads you have followed and popular fashions you have worn. You could then write an entry in your journal describing those examples.

2. **Ask questions and then answer them.** Suppose you are assigned to read an essay about mercy killing. You might ask yourself, "Under what circumstances is it done? Who is involved? Who should make the decision?" In answering these questions, you'll probably recall having read or heard about cases of medically assisted suicide or about legislation governing it. Such questions and answers can also be entered in your journal.

3. **Let your mind jump from idea to idea.** In your journal, or working with a classmate, jot down facts about, questions about, and examples of the subject. If you work quickly and write whatever comes to mind, this process will create a flow of thoughts and ideas related to the subject.

The preceding techniques can be adapted to any learning style. Use them whether you work alone or in a group, whether you write in a journal or tape-record a group discussion. Make your questions abstract or concrete, or emotional or rational, depending on your learning style. Once you discover what you already know about the subject of an essay, you will feel "tuned in" to it. You will be able to sustain your interest in the essay and grasp its content more easily.

EXERCISE 2.2

Review the three preceding techniques for connecting the subject of an essay to your own experience. Choose *one* of those techniques and try it out on the topic *sports heroes*.

TEACHING TIP: COLLABORATIVE WRITING

(5–10 minutes) In pairs, students can "grade" each other's responses and discuss their success with previewing. This activity promotes honesty and helps students open up for class discussion.

For more about journal writing, see Chapter 1, p. 7.

TEACHING TIP

Point out that in this activity, students create their own prereading questions, which can help them remember and understand what they read.

For more on flow of thought, see Brainstorming in Chapter 4, p. 82.

TEACHING TIP: LEARNING STYLES

Allow students to choose to work on this exercise independently or in pairs and to record their responses on paper or, if possible, using a tape recorder.

POSSIBLE ANSWERS

Approaches will vary. Students may choose to create lists, compose questions and answers, or relate anecdotes.

TEACHING TIP:
COLLABORATIVE
WRITING

(10–15 minutes) Initiate
a brief discussion of the
value of intent in recall:

• Ask students to sketch
the face side of a
one-dollar bill from
memory.
• Students should then
examine the face side
of a one-dollar bill
carefully, put the bill
away, and sketch it
again.
• In pairs, ask students
to discuss briefly the
differences between
the two sketches.

TEACHING TIP:
LEARNING STYLES

All learners should prac-
tice devising questions,
though this technique
may be most appealing
to pragmatic and verbal
learners. Spatial or emo-
tional learners may need
to be encouraged to use
this method.

Decide What You Need to Know and Remember

If you tried to draw the face side of a one-dollar bill from memory, you would prob-ably remember little about its appearance, despite the hundreds of bills that have passed through your hands. In much the same way, if you read an essay with the attitude, "Well, it was assigned, so I had better read it," you probably won't remem-ber much of what you read. Why does this happen? According to a psychological principle known as *intent to remember,* you remember what you decide to remem-ber. So, if you begin reading an essay without first deciding what you need to know and remember, you won't be able to recall any more about the essay than you could about the dollar bill.

Before you begin reading, then, you will want to improve your intent to remember. Look again at the items in the preview list—title, subtitle, headings, and so forth—on page 27. You can use these parts of an essay to form questions. Then, as you read, you can answer those questions and thereby strengthen your comprehension and memory of the material. The following suggestions will help you get started with devising your questions.

• **Use the title of an essay to devise questions.** Then read to find the answers. Here are a few examples of titles and relevant questions.

Essay Title	Question
"Part-time Employment Undermines Students' Commitment to School "	Why does part-time employment undermine commitment to school?
"Where *Marriage* Is a Scary Word"	Why and for whom is *marriage* a scary word?

• **Use headings to devise questions.** For example, in the essay "How to Say Nothing in 500 Words," Professor Paul Roberts offers advice on writing worth-while essays. His headings include "Avoid the Obvious Content," "Take the Less Usual Side," and "Get Rid of Obvious Padding." Each of these headings can easily be turned into a question that becomes a guide as you read: "What is too obvious? Why take the less usual side? How can I get rid of obvious padding?"

Not all essays, of course, lend themselves to these particular techniques. For some essays, you may need to dig deeper into the introductory and final para-graphs to form questions. Or, you may discover that the subtitle is more use-ful than the title. Look again at your preview of "Where Have You Gone, Joe DiMaggio?" Using the subtitle and the introductory paragraph of that essay, you might decide to look for answers to these questions: Why are sports heroes not real-life heroes? How are sports heroes different from real-life heroes? Is the author suggesting that sports heroes are negative role models?

Read with an Intent

As you already know, active reading involves much more than moving your eyes across lines of print. It is a process of actively searching for ideas and sorting important ideas from less important ones. You may need to read an essay more than once. Comprehension is often gradual. On the first reading, you may grasp some ideas but not others. On the second reading, other ideas may become clear. Do not hesitate to reread.

You know from the preceding section that you need to seek answers to your questions as you read. You should also be on the lookout for several key elements.

Search for Key Elements

If you know what to look for as you read, you will find that reading is easier and goes faster and that less rereading is necessary. When you read assigned articles, essays, or chapters, search for the following key elements:

1. **The meaning of the title and subtitle.** In some essays, the title announces the topic and reveals the author's point of view. In others, though, the meaning or the significance of the title becomes clear only after you have read the entire essay.

2. **The introduction.** The opening paragraph of an essay should provide background information, announce the subject of the essay, and get the reader's attention.

3. **The author's main point.** The author's main point is often stated directly in the **thesis statement.** That is, the thesis states the one big idea that the whole piece of writing explains, explores, or supports. For example, in an essay about who should receive organ transplants, the thesis may state the writer's position on the issue: "Whether a person smokes or drinks alcohol should be a factor in determining whether he or she is eligible for an organ transplant." The thesis is often placed in the first or second paragraph of an essay to let the reader know what lies ahead. But it may at times appear at the end of an essay instead. Occasionally, an essay's thesis will be implied or suggested rather than stated directly.

   For more about thesis statements see Chapter 5, p. 97 on Developing Your Thesis Statement.

4. **The support and explanation.** The body of the piece of writing should support or give reasons for the author's main point. For example, if an essay's thesis is that gay marriages should be legalized, then the body of the essay should offer reasons to support that position. Each paragraph in the body has a **topic sentence,** which states what the paragraph is about. Each topic sentence should in some way explain or support the essay's thesis statement.

5. **The conclusion.** The concluding paragraph or paragraphs of an essay bring the piece of writing to a close. A conclusion may restate the author's main point, offer ideas for further thought, or suggest new directions.

TEACHING TIP: LEARNING STYLES

Pragmatic or spatial learners appreciate a mathematical presentation of the relation between the thesis statement and topic sentences: *the thesis statement: [is to] the essay :: [as] the topic sentence: [is to] the paragraph.*

You'll learn much more about each part of an essay in Chapters 4–8.

Now read the entire essay, "Where Have You Gone, Joe DiMaggio?" with an intent. Remember to look out for key elements as you read.

Where Have You Gone, Joe DiMaggio?

*Heroics in the sports arena don't
necessarily produce real-life heroes*

Matthew Goodman

Matthew Goodman is a sportswriter whose essays have appeared in numerous publications, including the Village Voice *and* Washington Monthly. *This essay was first published in* Utne Reader *in 1993. As you read, pay attention to the marginal notes that identify and explain various parts of the essay.*

Introductory headline: summarizes main point of essay

Introductory paragraph: builds interest and provides background

1   These days, it seems, the sports pages have come to resemble a police blotter. The fan seeking box scores and game recaps must first wade through news stories about drug abuse among athletes, arrests for drunk driving, betting and recruiting scandals, and, most disturbingly, reports of rape and other sex-related crimes. What's going on here? American sports fans ask over their morning toast and coffee.

Support: explains concept of heroes in athletics

2   It's not difficult to understand our desire for athletes to be heroes. On the surface, at least, athletes display many of the classical heroic attributes. They possess a vital and indomitable spirit; they are gloriously alive inside their bodies. And sports does allow us to witness acts that can legitimately be described as courageous, thrilling, beautiful, even noble. In an increasingly complicated and disorderly world, sports is still an arena in which we can regularly witness a certain kind of greatness.

Thesis statement

3   Yet there's something of a paradox here, for the very qualities a society tends to seek in its heroes — selflessness, social consciousness, and the like — are precisely the *opposite* of those needed to transform a talented but otherwise unremarkable neighborhood kid into a Michael Jordan or a Joe Montana. Becoming a star athlete requires a profound and long-term kind of self-absorption, a single-minded attention to the develop-

Support: explains paradox

ment of a few rather odd physical skills, and an overarching competitive outlook. These qualities may well
make a great athlete, but they don't necessarily make a
great person. On top of this, our society reinforces these
traits by the system it has created to produce athletes—
a system characterized by limited responsibility and
enormous privilege.

The athletes themselves suffer the costs of this system. Trained to measure themselves perpetually against
the achievements of those around them, many young
athletes develop a sense of what sociologist Walter
Schafer has termed "conditional self-worth": They learn
very quickly that they will be accepted by the important
figures in their lives—parents, coaches, peers—to the
extent they are perceived as "winners." Their egos come
to rest, all too precariously, upon the narrow plank of
athletic success.

4   Support: effects of system on athletes

Young athletes learn that success, rather than hard
and honest play, is what brings rewards. And for those
successful enough to rise to the level of big-time college
sports, the "reward" is often an artificially controlled
social environment, one that shields them from many
of the responsibilities other students face. Coaches—
whose own jobs, of course, depend on maintaining winning programs—hover over their athletes to ensure that
nothing threatens their eligibility to compete. If an athlete gets into trouble with the law, for instance, a coach
will very likely intervene—hiring an attorney, perhaps
even managing to have the case quietly dismissed. In
some schools, athletes don't even choose their own
classes or buy their own books; the athletic department
does all this for them. It's not unheard of for athletic
department staff to wake up athletes in the morning
and to take them to class.

5   Support: rewards athletes seek

Given this situation, it's not too surprising that
many young American athletes seem to have been left
with a stunted ethical sense. Professor Sharon Stoll of
the University of Idaho has tested more than 10,000 student athletes from all over the country, ranging from
junior high to college age; she reports that in the area of
moral reasoning, athletes invariably score lower than
non-athletes—and that they grow worse the longer they
participate in athletics.

6   Support: lack of ethical
sense

Support: athletes
become privileged

7   Coddled by universities, lionized by local communities, accorded star status by the public, endowed with six- and seven-figure salaries, successful athletes inevitably develop a sense of themselves as privileged beings—as indeed they are. The danger arises when the realistic (and thus probably healthy) understanding of personal privilege mutates into a sense of personal entitlement.

Support: Mike Tyson
example

8   Mike Tyson, of course, is the most blatant example of this phenomenon. Having been taught as a young man that he was special—his mentor, Cus D'Amato, reportedly had one set of rules for Tyson and another, more stringent, set for all his other boxing protégés—and having lived his entire adult life surrounded by a cortege of fawning attendants, Tyson eventually came to believe, like a medieval king, that all he saw rightfully belonged to him. Blessed with money and fame enough to last a lifetime, he spent his time outside the ring acquiring and discarding the objects of his desire: houses, automobiles, jewelry, clothes, and women. In the wake of the publicity surrounding his rape trial, countless women have come forward to relate stories of Tyson propositioning them and then, upon being rebuffed, exclaiming in what was apparently genuine surprise, "Don't you know who I am? *I'm the heavyweight champion of the world.*" Needless to say, not all athletes are Mike Tyson; there are plenty of athletes who recognize that they have been granted some extraordinary gifts in this life and want to give something back to the community.

Support: there are
exceptions

9   Some remarkable individuals will always rise above the deforming athletic system we've created. After retiring from football, defensive tackle Alan Page of the Minnesota Vikings became a successful lawyer and established the Page Education Foundation, which helps minority and disadvantaged kids around the country pay for college. Frustrated by the old-boy network by which Minnesota judges had traditionally been appointed, Page challenged the system in court and finally won election to the state Supreme Court, becoming the first black ever elected to statewide office in Minnesota. Tennis star Martina Navratilova recently joined six other lesbians and gay men as a plaintiff in a lawsuit filed by the cities of Denver, Boulder, and

Aspen challenging Colorado's recent anti-gay law as unconstitutional. Thankfully, there will always be some legitimate heroes (or, to use the more contemporary term, role models) to be found among professional athletes.

    Still, it's probably misguided for society to look to athletes for its heroes — anymore than we look among the ranks of, say, actors or lawyers or pipefitters. The social role played by athletes is indeed important (imagine a society without sports; I wouldn't want to live in it), but it's fundamentally different from that of heroes.

    Thanks to the years of hard and uncompromising work that athletes have invested in themselves, sports is often able to provide us a glimpse of that "supreme beauty" that Bertrand Russell wrote of as characteristic of mathematics: "sublimely pure, and capable of a stern perfection such as only the greatest art can show."

    Can't we just leave it at that? ■

10 — Support: compares with other occupations

11 — New direction: value of sports

12 — Final word

Highlight or Underline Key Points

As you read, you will encounter many new ideas. You will find some ideas more important than others. You will agree with some and disagree with others. Later, as you write about what you have read, you will want to return to the main points to refresh your memory. To locate and remember these points easily, it is a good idea to read with a highlighter or pen in hand. Develop a system of highlighting or underlining that you can use as you read to identify ideas you plan to reread or review later on. Use the following guidelines to make your highlighting or underlining as useful as possible.

1. **Decide what kinds of information to highlight or underline before you begin.** What types of tasks will you be doing as a result of your reading? Will you write a paper, participate in a class discussion, or take an exam? Think about what you need to know, and tailor your highlighting to the particular needs of the task.

2. **Read first; then highlight.** First read a paragraph or section; then go back and mark what is important within it. This approach will help you control the tendency to highlight or underline too much.

3. **Be selective.** If you highlight or underline every idea, none will stand out.

4. **Highlight or underline key elements, words, and phrases.** Mark the thesis statement, the topic sentence in each paragraph, important terms and definitions, and key words and phrases that relate to the thesis.

TEACHING TIP

If students complain that they are "lost" in a reading assignment and are unable to pick out important points, ask to see what they have highlighted. Often, students highlight so much of the reading that they have to reread the entire piece to make sense of it. Working with a clean copy, the students should try again, using the guidelines provided here.

Annotate Your Impressions

Annotating is a way to keep track of your impressions, reactions, and questions as you read. When you annotate, you jot down your ideas about what you are reading. Think of your annotations as a personal response to the author's ideas: You might question, agree with, or express surprise at those ideas. Write your annotations in the margins of the essay. Your annotations can take several forms, including questions that come to mind, personal reactions (such as disagreement or anger), or brief phrases that summarize important points. Later on, when you are ready to write about or discuss the reading, your annotations will help you focus on major issues and questions. Following is a partial list of what you might annotate.

- Important points (such as the thesis) that initiate personal responses
- Sections about which you need further information
- Sections in which the author reveals his or her reasons for writing
- Ideas you disagree or agree with
- Inconsistencies

Sample annotations for a portion of "Where Have You Gone, Joe DiMaggio?" are shown in Figure 2.2.

EXERCISE 2.3

Reread "Where Have You Gone, Joe DiMaggio?" on page 34. Highlight and annotate the essay as you read.

Review after Reading

Do you simply close a book or put away an article after you have read it? If so, you are missing an opportunity to reinforce your learning. If you are willing to spend a few minutes reviewing and evaluating what you read, you can increase dramatically the amount of information you remember.

To review material after reading, you use the same steps used to preview a reading (see p. 27). You should do your review immediately after you have finished reading. Reviewing does not take much time. Your goal is to touch on each main point one more time, not to embark on a long and thorough study. Pay particular attention to the following elements.

- The headings
- Your highlighting or underlining
- Your annotations
- The conclusion

FIGURE 2.2
SAMPLE ANNOTATIONS

Young athletes learn that success, rather than hard and honest play, is what brings rewards. And for those successful enough to rise to the level of big-time college sports, the "reward" is often an artificially controlled social environment, one that shields them from many of the responsibilities other students face. Coaches — whose own jobs, of course, depend on maintaining winning programs — hover over their athletes to ensure that nothing threatens their eligibility to compete. If an athlete gets into trouble with the law, for instance, a coach will very likely intervene — hiring an attorney, perhaps even managing to have the case quietly dismissed. In some schools, athletes don't even choose their own classes or buy their own books; the athletic department does all this for them. It's not unheard of for athletic department staff to wake up athletes in the morning and to take them to class.

*How wide-
spread is this?*

*Not on my
campus!*

Given this situation, it's not too surprising that many young American athletes seem to have been left with a stunted ethical sense. Professor Sharon Stoll of the University of Idaho has tested more than 10,000 student athletes from all over the country, ranging from junior high to college age; she reports that in the area of moral reasoning, athletes invariably score lower than non-athletes — and that they grow worse the longer they participate in athletics.

*Is it true
in other
countries?*

*How was this
measured?*

Coddled by universities, lionized by local communities, accorded star status by the public, endowed with six- and seven-figure salaries, successful athletes inevitably develop a sense of themselves as privileged beings — as indeed they are. The danger arises when the realistic (and thus probably healthy) understanding of personal privilege mutates into a sense of personal entitlement.

*Many certainly
behave as
such.*

TEACHING TIP

To emphasize the importance of reviewing, ask students if they think they could earn an *A* in a science class in which they took copious notes but never studied outside of class. Odds are most students would not do well in the course.

As part of your review, it is also helpful to write a brief summary of the essay, using your highlighting and annotations. If you need to write an essay about a reading, your summary will help you get started. Here is a sample summary for "Where Have You Gone, Joe DiMaggio?"

SUMMARY

Since sports is an integral part of our lives, society tends to regard all athletes as heroes. We tend to credit them with certain personal characteristics that they may not have, such as selflessness. We should keep in mind that in order to become a devoted athlete, it is necessary to be the opposite—that is, selfish.

Athletes learn at an early age that they need to win in order to gain approval. Since winning is so important, especially to a coach whose job depends on a winning team, coaches and other authority figures tend to cater to college athletes. Such catering prevents athletes from learning to accept responsibility for their actions. This lack of responsibility leads the athletes to expect that they should be treated in a privileged manner and to assume that they are above the law. Society should simply appreciate the extraordinary gifts of its athletes instead of making athletes seem like heroes endowed with personal characteristics that they may not even possess.

For more on journal writing, see Chapter 1, p. 7.

TEACHING TIP

You may choose to require students to summarize readings and/or research in their journals throughout the course.

Many students keep a journal in which they write summaries of essays as well as personal reactions to what they read. Journal writing is a good way to generate and record ideas about an essay, and your journal entries can serve as useful sources of ideas for writing papers.

UNDERSTANDING DIFFICULT TEXT

For more help with understanding difficult text, see Appendix B.

All students experience difficulty with a reading assignment at one time or another. Perhaps this will happen because you just can't "connect" with the author, or because you find the topic uninteresting or the writing style confusing. Regardless of the problem, however, you know you must complete the assignment. Table 2.1 lists some typical problems that students experience with difficult reading material and identifies strategies for solving them.

TEACHING TIP:
LEARNING STYLES

Whatever their learning style, all students can write outlines or draw graphic organizers and should be encouraged to do so when they have difficulty discerning or creating an effective organization. Keep in mind that this technique may be more comfortable for spatial and pragmatic learners than for verbal and creative learners.

Draw a Graphic Organizer

If you are having difficulty following a long or complicated essay, try drawing a **graphic organizer**—a diagram of the structure of an essay's main points. Even if you are not a spatial learner, you will probably find a graphic organizer helpful. Many people, for example, draw maps to show friends where their home is located. Just as a map shows the relationship of streets and highways to one another, a graphic organizer—a diagram or map of ideas—shows you how an essay's main points are related.

Drawing a graphic organizer is an active way to review and connect major ideas. Some students find that once they have drawn the organizer, they understand the essay and no longer need the organizer. The sample graphic organizers

TABLE 2.1
DIFFICULT READINGS: SPECIFIC PROBLEMS AND STRATEGIES FOR SOLVING THEM

TEACHING TIP:
LEARNING STYLES

Help students become
interested in the mater-
ial by encouraging them
to develop creative and
social learning styles.

Problems	*Strategies*
You cannot concentrate.	1. Take limited breaks. 2. Tackle the assignment at peak periods of attention. 3. Divide the material into sections. Make it your goal to complete one section at a time. 4. Give yourself a reasonable deadline for completing the assignment.
The sentences are long and confusing.	1. Read aloud. 2. Divide each sentence into parts and analyze the function of each part. 3. Express each sentence in your own words.
The ideas are complicated and hard to understand.	1. Reread the material several times. 2. Rephrase or explain each idea in your own words. 3. Make outline notes. 4. Study with a classmate; discuss difficult ideas. 5. Look up the meanings of unfamiliar words in a dictionary.
The material seems disorganized or poorly organized.	1. Study the introduction for clues to organization. 2. Pay more attention to headings. 3. Read the summary or conclusion. 4. Try to discover the organization by writing an outline or drawing a graphic organizer (see pp. 42 and 43).
You cannot get interested in the material.	1. Think about something you've experienced that is related to the topic. 2. Work with a classmate, discussing each section as you go.
You cannot relate to the writer's ideas or experiences.	1. Find out some background information about the author. 2. Put yourself in the writer's position. How would you react?
The subject is unfamiliar; you lack background information on the subject.	1. Obtain a more basic text or other source that moves slower, offers more explanation, and reviews fundamental principles and concepts. 2. For unfamiliar terminology, consult a specialized dictionary within the field of study. 3. Ask your instructor to recommend useful references.

**TEACHING TIP:
LEARNING STYLES**

The structured format
may appeal to prag-
matic, spatial, rational,
and concrete learners,
whereas the free-form
format may appeal to
creative, verbal, emo-
tional, and abstract
learners.

shown in Figures 2.3 and 2.4 indicate the type and placement of information in two possible formats: a structured format (Figure 2.3) and a free-form format (Figure 2.4). Use the format that appeals to you, or develop your own format to record the main points in an essay. The particular format you use is not important — just be sure it includes all the key elements of an essay listed on page 33. An example of a graphic organizer for "Where Have You Gone, Joe DiMaggio?" appears in Figure 2.5. Work through the organizer and reread the essay (pp. 34–37), paragraph by paragraph, at the same time.

**FIGURE 2.3
GRAPHIC ORGANIZER: STRUCTURED FORMAT**

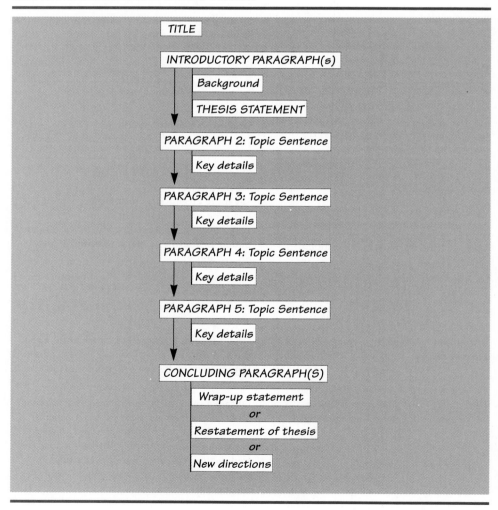

FIGURE 2.4
GRAPHIC ORGANIZER: FREE-FORM FORMAT

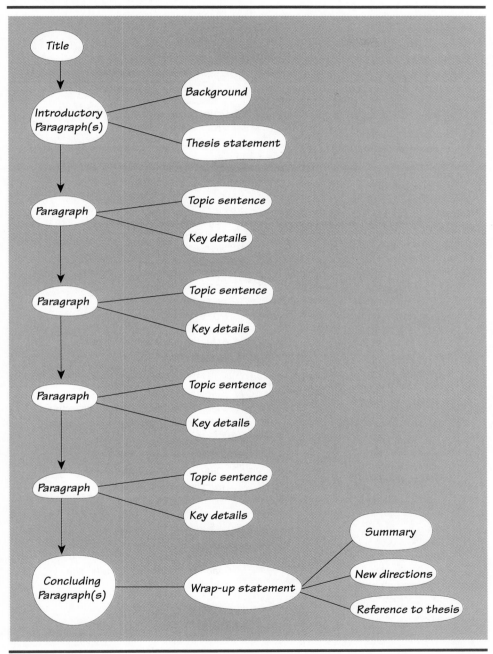

FIGURE 2.5
GRAPHIC ORGANIZER FOR "WHERE HAVE YOU GONE, JOE DIMAGGIO?"

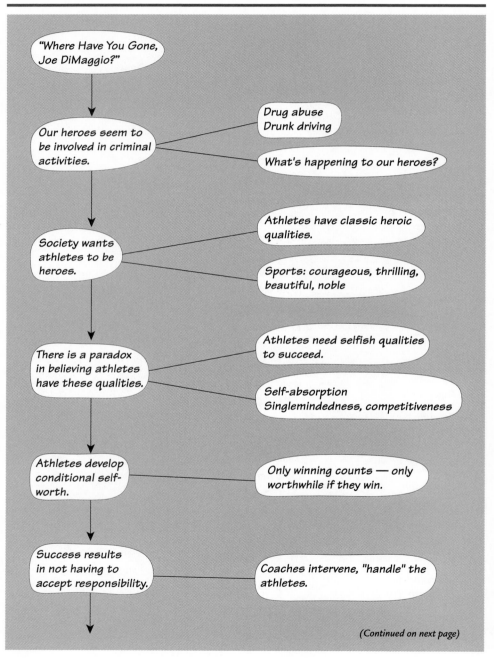

(Continued on next page)

FIGURE 2.5 *(continued)*

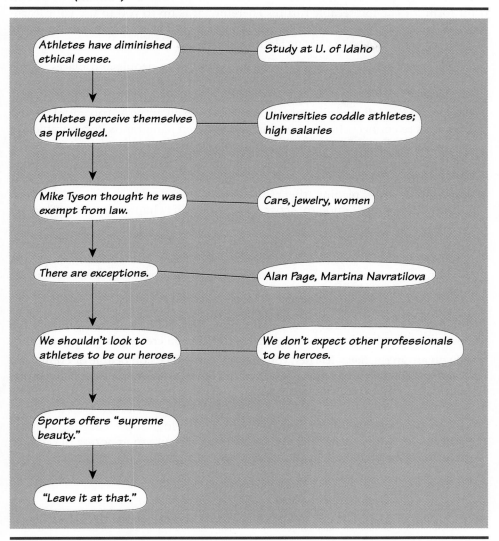

USING YOUR LEARNING STYLE TO IMPROVE YOUR READING

If you are a *verbal* learner, a *social* learner, or both, you probably find reading a comfortable and convenient way to obtain information. If you are a *spatial* learner, though, you may prefer the graphic images of video and film to those of printed material. Regardless of your learning style, most of your assignments will be in print form for the foreseeable future. Therefore, it is up to you to use your learning style in a way that enhances your reading. The following guidelines for active reading are tailored to the various learning styles.

Learning Style Options

TEACHING TIP: LEARNING STYLES

Remind students that collaborative writing groups provide them with feedback from peers whose learning approaches may be different from their own.

- If you are a *spatial* learner, create mental pictures of people and places. While reading the essay "Where Have You Gone, Joe DiMaggio?" for example, you might create a mental image of a spoiled athlete. In addition, use graphic organizers and diagrams to organize the ideas in an essay. As you annotate, use symbols to connect the ideas within and between paragraphs (for example, see the symbols listed for the reading response journal on p. 9).

- If you are a *social* learner, discuss a reading assignment with a classmate both before and after reading. Preview the essay together, sharing ideas about the topic. After reading the essay, discuss your reactions to it. In both instances, use the Guide to Active Reading in this chapter (pp. 26–40) to get started.

- If you are an *abstract* learner, a *creative* learner, or both, you may tend to overlook details while focusing instead on the "big ideas" and overall message of a reading. Be sure to highlight or underline important points and to concentrate on facts and supporting details.

- If you are a *concrete* learner, a *pragmatic* learner, or both, you may like to focus on details instead of seeing how ideas fit together and contribute to an author's overall message. Use graphic organizers to help you create a larger picture.

- If you are an *emotional* learner, you may generally focus on people or events and overlook the way an author uses them to convey an overall message. Keep this question in mind: How does the author use these people or events to get his or her message across?

- If you are a *rational* learner, you may zero in on a logical presentation of ideas and overlook more subtle shades of meaning. Be sure to annotate in order to draw out your personal reactions to a piece of writing.

COMPUTER HINT

By this time students should be comfortable with one another and with the act of sharing their writing.

- If possible, have students use networked computers to share essays and responses to each other's writing.
- If a network is not available, encourage students to share writing and comments by attaching essay files to email messages.

APPLYING YOUR SKILLS: WRITING ABOUT THE READING

Use your highlighting, annotating, and graphic organizers as sources of ideas for the following writing assignments based on "Where Have You Gone, Joe DiMaggio?"

1. Write an essay describing someone you consider to be a hero. Describe the traits and qualities that make the person heroic.

2. Write an essay describing a famous athlete. Explain why you think the athlete does or does not qualify as a hero.

3. Many current American heroes tend to be sports stars or entertainment celebrities. Write an essay discussing what the lack of heroes in other areas of public life suggests about American values.

ANSWERS TO EXERCISE 2.1

1. True   2. False   3. True   4. False   5. True   6. True

Back   Forward   Reload   Home   Search   Guide   Images   Print   Security   Stop

Location: http://www.altculture.com/aentries/e/extremexsp.html

alt.culture

home   new   subscribe   vote   email   boards   random   autopilot   a-z   categories   help

extreme sports

Catch-all term, coined circa 1990, for a variety of athletic challenges that have virtually nothing in common except high risk and an appeal to men ages 18-34--the dream demographic for a lot of advertisers. Many extreme sports developed as variations on previously existing non-extreme sports: snowboarding, sky-surfing, free climbing, barefoot waterskiing, street luge, etc. After gaining popularity in fitness-obsessed locales like Colorado, extreme sports caught on with the media: magazines like *Details* lavished space on these hyperkinetic, photogenic activities, and *MTV Sports* and ESPN's *Extreme Sports* (both started in 1991) brought them to television, with a rock-video style and soundtrack. Advertisers, including Nike ("Just Do It") and Mountain Dew ("Been There, Done That"), also found the "extreme" credo to their liking. In 1993, ESPN2--the younger, wilder brother of ESPN"--was born; in 1995, ESPN developed the $10 million first annual Olympics-style Extreme Games, which featured competitions in dozens of events from skateboarding to bungee jumping.

Charged!
Everything Extreme
AdventureTime Magazine

The X-Games on ESPN2 (ESPN).

submit search

Eno, Brian
ephemeral films
Estep, Maggie
Eurotrash
▲
extreme sports
▼
Extropians
Faludi, Susan
family values
Fantagraphics Books

Chapter 3

CHAPTER QUICK START

You have decided to write a paper on sports and are browsing on the Internet to discover a specific topic. As you browse, you come upon the Web page reprinted on the opposite page.

Writing Quick Start

Read the text and study the photograph on the Web page, highlighting or underlining key words and phrases and writing notes about how the content relates to your own experience with or knowledge about this topic. Then write a few sentences that summarize the content of the page and your reaction to it.

Writing about Readings

TEACHING TIP

Take an informal poll to determine students' experience with the Internet: How many have just "surfed" and how many have done online research? Briefly discuss how to analyze the relative usefulness of an online source: Is the information clear and relevant? Is the date of publication provided? Is credible supporting evidence given?

TEACHING TIP:
CHAPTER OVERVIEW

• Students often feel
empowered and vali-
dated in their writing
when their responses
to reading are encour-
aged, as they are in
this chapter.

• Responsive writing
involves using critical
thinking skills, which
this chapter fosters.

In many college classes and work situations, you will be asked to read something and then respond to it in writing, as you have just done with the Web page. Some other assignments you might encounter are listed in the box below.

If you were asked to complete one of these assignments, how would you start? What would you write about?

When you finish your first reading of an article or essay, you may think you have nothing to say or write about. Such thoughts are normal and to be expected. This chapter will help you think constructively about what you read, so that you can respond to readings in writing.

WHAT IS A RESPONSE PAPER?

Usually, your instructor will expect you to read an essay and then to analyze and write about some aspect of it. This kind of writing is often called a **response paper.** In some assignments, your instructor may suggest a particular direction for the paper. At other times, your instructor may not suggest where to start. It will be up to you to decide how you are going to respond to what you have read.

In a response paper, your instructor does not want you to simply summarize an essay. Although you may include a brief summary as part of your introduction, you should concentrate on analyzing the reading and linking it to your own experience. Try to explain how *you* react to or interpret what you have read. Keep in mind, however, that you should not attempt to discuss all of your reactions. Instead, choose one key idea, one question the essay raises, or one issue it explores.

SCENES FROM COLLEGE AND THE WORKPLACE

- In an *art history* class, your instructor distributes a critical review of an exhibit your class recently visited. She asks you to write an essay agreeing or disagreeing with the critic's viewpoint and expressing your own views.

- For a *zoology* course, your instructor distributes an excerpt from the book *When Elephants Weep: The Emotional Lives of Animals* and asks you to write a paper on your own observations about whether animals experience emotions.

- For your job as an *accountant,* your supervisor refers you to an article from the *Online Journal of Accounting Studies* and asks you to evaluate whether the procedures described in the article could be implemented within the company.

Before beginning any response paper, make sure you understand the assignment. If you are uncertain of what your instructor expects, be sure to ask. You may also want to check with other students to find out how they are approaching the assignment. If your instructor does not mention length requirements, be sure to ask how long the paper should be.

For example, suppose your instructor asks you to read an article titled "Advertising—A Form of Institutional Lying," which tries to show that advertisements deceive consumers by presenting half-truths, distortions, and misinformation. Your instructor asks you to write a two-page paper about the essay but gives you no other directions. In writing this response paper, you might take one of the following approaches:

- Discuss how you were once deceived by an advertisement.
- Evaluate the evidence and examples the author provides to support his claim; determine whether the evidence is relevant and sufficient.
- Discuss the causes or effects of deception in advertising that the author overlooks (you might need to consult other sources to take this approach).
- Evaluate the assumptions the author makes about advertising or about consumers.

For an assignment like this one, or for any response paper, how do you decide on an issue to write about? How do you come up with ideas about a reading? The following section will help you.

DISCOVERING IDEAS FOR A RESPONSE PAPER

This chapter presents a number of ways to discover ideas for response papers. After you become familiar with each approach, experiment with it to see if it suits your learning style. Be sure to try out several approaches. The subject matter of an essay may also help you to determine which method is most effective.

Before reading about these approaches, take a few minutes to read the following essay: "The Boor War" by John Tierney. As you read the essay, follow the steps in the Guide to Active Reading in Chapter 2 (pp. 26–40). After you have read the essay, create a brief summary, outline, or graphic organizer to make sure you have grasped the essay's thesis and key supporting details. In the sections that follow the reading, "The Boor War" will be used to demonstrate various ways to discover ideas for response papers. You will then have the opportunity to practice each approach using either "The Boor War" or another brief essay of your choice.

For more on summaries and graphic organizers, see Chapter 2, pp. 39–45.

TEACHING TIP

Point out the title's pun:
A *boor* is an ill-mannered
person; the *Boër War*
(1899–1902), also called
the South African War,
was fought between the
English and the Orange
Free State and Transvaal
Republic. The English
were known for treating
their colonial subjects
with condescension.

PREREADING
QUESTIONS

• What kinds of people
does Tierney call
"urban cranks"?

• What important role
do they play in city
life?

The Boor War

John Tierney

John Tierney is a business writer for the New York Times *and has written numerous articles for the* New York Times Magazine, *where this essay originally appeared in 1997. The essay explores a type of city dweller known as the "urban crank."*

1   I never appreciated the importance of urban cranks until I met a woman named Miriam Seigel one afternoon on West 23d Street. She was struggling with a heavy grocery cart, and when I gave her a hand she introduced herself. It turned out she was the grandmother of David Remnick of *The New Yorker.* As she began extolling his writing talents, she was distracted by a couple of teen-age girls who were loudly exchanging obscenities. One of them threw an empty bottle on the ground. She seemed to be in a dangerously unhappy state of mind, but Mrs. Seigel promptly intervened.

2   "You pick that up," Mrs. Seigel said sternly to the girl, who was twice her size. "The sidewalk is not a trash can."

3   It was a wonderful moment. The girl was so stunned that she stopped swearing and stared open-mouthed at Mrs. Seigel. She didn't obey, but she didn't try to argue either. She seemed to be experiencing a novel sensation — shame — and it occurred to me that New York might be a better place if more of us emulated Mrs. Seigel.

4   I soon found myself asking carriers of boom boxes to turn down the volume. When a man started urinating one morning from the top of the bleachers in Riverside Park, I yelled at him to stop. I discovered that someone who discards a piece of paper on the sidewalk gets flustered if you pretend to be helpful by returning it and saying, "You dropped this." My friends began to worry about me.

5   Eventually, after a particularly unpleasant confrontation with a young man scratching his initials into the window of a subway car, *I* began to worry about me. Was there a rational case to be made for crankdom? I sought guidance from Robert Axelrod, a professor of political science and public policy at the University of Michigan who uses game theory to devise strategies for dealing with boors. . . .

6   "A cooperative norm* can collapse completely in a big anonymous city," Axelrod said, "because the cost imposed by a defector is diffused over so many people that no one bothers to punish him. We

---

cooperative norm: a shared rule that specifies how people should behave.

need to find new ways to encourage the enforcement of useful cooperative norms."

Which is to say, we need more cranks. We need cab passengers to 7
punish noise pollution by refusing to tip drivers who honk. Guests at
dinner parties should refuse to sit next to anyone who owns a car
alarm. Apartment dwellers who live above wailing cars should contemplate today's most hotly debated moral question among urban
cranks: to egg or not to egg?

"Throwing an egg at a car is a low-cost way to impose a relatively 8
high-cost penalty on the violator of a norm," Axelrod said, "so it
could well work as an enforcement strategy. But it makes me uncomfortable. You're violating the law. In this case, citizens are probably
better off pressuring the government to enforce the norm."

That may seem like prudent advice, but Axelrod (who lives in 9
Ann Arbor, after all) has never tried getting New York's government
to enforce a norm. For the last word on the egg question, I tracked
down my role model, Mrs. Seigel.

"If there's someone out there on the street making noise," she 10
said, "what I would do is just go right out and talk to him."

"What would you say?" 11

"I'd say: 'Hey, cut it out. You're annoying people. You don't live 12
alone in this world.'"

I don't know—somehow an egg works better for me. We can't all 13
be as brave as Mrs. Seigel, who turned 92 on Friday. But let's not
quibble about strategies. We cranks are too busy to waste time arguing among ourselves. Defectors must be punished! New cranks must
be mobilized! At this very instant, people are wasting time reading
while norms are being flouted out on the street. Cut it out! Put down
the magazine and get out there now! You don't live alone in this
world! Have you enforced a norm today? ■

Link the Reading to Your Own Experience

One way to come up with ideas for a response paper is to think about how the
reading relates to your own experience. You might begin by looking for useful
information in the essay and considering how you could apply that information
to other real-life situations. Your reading of "The Boor War," for example, might
lead you to think about a time when you observed boorish behavior and either
were tempted to correct or actually did correct the offender. Or, you might consider writing about a "Mrs. Seigel" you know, perhaps someone who lives in your
neighborhood.

Try to think beyond the reading itself. Recall other material you have read and events you have experienced that are related to the reading. In thinking about "The Boor War," for example, you might recall an article about a noise ordinance that prohibits playing car radios or stereo systems above a specific decibel level, or you might recall a visit to a park in which picnickers had left garbage strewn about. The following paragraph shows how one student connected "The Boor War" to her own experience.

> Last Halloween, a neighborhood kid who is around eleven or twelve years old threw a frozen egg through my brother's screen door. The egg splattered all over the living room floor. Furious, my brother went outside and walked down the street, looking for the culprit. He thought he knew who the kid was, and when the boy ran out from behind another house, my brother grabbed him and threatened to tell his mother if he didn't come back to the house and clean up the mess. The boy did as my brother asked. I guess that night my brother was a suburban crank.

This writer discovered two possible topics to write about: suburban cranks and taking action against irresponsible behavior.

Devise Critical Questions

Another useful method of discovering ideas for a response paper involves asking critical questions. Ask *why* things are the way they are, *how* they happened, and *what* makes them work — that is, look at causes, effects, and consequences. Here are some critical questions you might ask about "The Boor War":

- What makes people behave boorishly?
- How did Mrs. Seigel become an urban crank?
- Are there other types of cranks, such as rural cranks? What types of behavior might annoy them?
- Why do some people fail to see the effects of their actions on others?
- Why can it be dangerous to correct boorish behavior?

The answers to any of the preceding questions might serve as the basis for a paper responding to "The Boor War." Here are three sample questions and the answers that one student wrote in response to them after reading the essay.

TEACHING TIP

Ask the class to explain how critical questions differ from comprehension questions. (Critical questions cannot be answered simply by reading the essay, but require further independent thought, extending the reasoning from the world of the essay to the wider world of readers.)

POSSIBLE ANSWERS

Example: **What makes people behave boorishly?**

- Selfishness; an inability to get along with others
- Insensitivity; single-mindedness
- Lack of morals or ethics

What makes people brave enough to correct boorish behavior?

I think my brother responded as he did because he knew the boy and his mother and because he grew up in our neighborhood and cares about it. He was also really angry. The egg tore a hole in our screen door.

Why do people tend to ignore boorish behavior instead of correcting it?

I think people are afraid of getting hurt themselves. It's similar to road rage. People are afraid hostilities will increase--that angry words will lead to angry actions.

Why aren't there more Mrs. Seigels?

Mrs. Seigel and my brother have one thing in common: They've lived in their neighborhood a long time and it matters to them. (If Mrs. Seigel isn't a longtime New Yorker, she sure seems like one!) I think people who ignore boorish behavior are either afraid or they don't feel any particular connection to the area and don't worry about keeping it nice.

Her questions and answers enabled this student to discover several more possible writing topics: motivations for correcting boorish behavior and motivations for ignoring boorish behavior.

COMPUTER HINT

(20–30 minutes) Encouraging students to do short writing activities like this one on a computer helps them feel comfortable at the keyboard. Have students trade disks or email messages to comment on each other's lists and critical questions.

ESSAY IN PROGRESS 1

Connect "The Boor War" or another essay you have chosen to your own experience by writing a list of your experiences with or ideas about the subject of the essay. Then write a list of critical questions about the reading. Use *why, how,* and *what* to generate ideas about causes and effects.

Use Key-Word Response

When you use the key-word response method for generating ideas, you record your initial response to a reading and then let associations and reactions flow from that response. Begin by choosing one or more key words that describe your initial response, such as *angered, amused, surprised, confused, annoyed, curious,* or *shocked.* For example, fill in one of the following blanks with key words describing your response to "The Boor War."

1. "After reading the essay I was _____."
2. "After reading the essay I felt _____."

The key-word response you just wrote will serve as a point of departure for further thinking. Start by explaining your response; then write down ideas as they come to you, trying to approach the reading from many different perspectives.

For more on freewriting, see Chapter 4, p. 78.

Here is the result of one student's key-word response to "The Boor War."

> After reading "The Boor War," I felt <u>encouraged,</u> <u>but worried and concerned.</u> I felt encouraged after reading "The Boor War" because I was glad that someone, particularly an older person, had both the gall and the common sense to tell someone to stop doing something, but I wonder what would happen if Mrs. Seigel were confronted or even attacked by a person she corrected. Once I was tempted to shout at a person in the car next to me to turn down his blaring radio, but he looked like a person I would not want to meet alone on the street, so I decided to do nothing. But I am concerned about what a person can do safely to control unacceptable behavior.

As you can see, this student uncovered two possible topics — the potential repercussions of urban crankiness and safe actions to take — from her key-word response.

TEACHING TIP:
COLLABORATIVE
WRITING

(10–15 minutes) Students can complete this activity independently or in pairs. If students are paired, have one student provide the prompt and the other fill in the blanks; then ask the students to reverse roles. Have students discuss their key-word choices and write down ideas that they generate.

ESSAY IN PROGRESS 2

For "The Boor War" or another essay, use the key-word response method to generate ideas.

Use Annotation

In the Guide to Active Reading in Chapter 2, you learned to annotate as you read. Annotation can also be used to respond to a reading *after* you have read it the first time and while you are preparing to write about it. As you read an essay for the second time, record additional reactions that occur to you. Some students prefer to use a different color of ink to record their second set of annotations. Here is a sample student annotation.

> That may seem like prudent advice, but Axelrod (who lives in Ann Arbor, after all) has never tried getting New York's government to enforce a norm. For the last word on the egg question, I tracked down my role model, Mrs. Seigel.
>
> *Mayor Giuliani seems to want to enforce norms!*
>
> "If there's someone out there on the street making noise," she said, "what I would do is just go right out and talk to him."
>
> "What would you say?"
>
> "I'd say: 'Hey, cut it out. You're annoying people. You don't live alone in this world.'"
>
> *Be cooperative.*
>
> I don't know—somehow an egg works better for me. We can't all be as brave as Mrs. Seigel, who turned 92 on Friday. But let's not quibble about strategies. We cranks are too busy to waste time arguing among ourselves. Defectors must be punished! New cranks must be mobilized! At this very instant, people are wasting time reading while norms are being flouted out on the street. Cut it out! Put down the magazine and get out there now! You don't live alone in this world! Have you enforced a norm today?
>
> *But one hostile action can lead to another. Also, the person with the car alarm may not know why the egg was thrown.*

ESSAY IN PROGRESS 3

Reread "The Boor War" or the essay you have chosen, this time adding annotations that record your reactions to and questions about the essay as you read.

Keep a Response Journal

A response journal is a section of your writing journal (see Chapter 1, p. 7) in which you record your reactions, questions, and comments about readings. There are two ways you can organize a response journal; experiment with each format until you discover the one that works best for you.

The Open-Page Format

On a blank page, write, outline, draw, or create a diagram to express your reactions to an essay. Because the open-page format encourages you to let your ideas flow freely, it may work particularly well for creative and spatial learners. Figure 3.1 shows one student's open-page response journal entry for "The Boor War."

TEACHING TIP: LEARNING STYLES

• Give students the opportunity to experiment with both journal formats in class. Students will choose one format for Essay in Progress 4 (p. 60); allot 20 minutes at an appropriate time to allow students to try the format they did *not* use in Essay in Progress 4.

• Sometimes only creative and spatial learners will be willing to try the open-page format. Emphasize

(Continued on next page)

that both formats are options for all learners —opportunities to expand their approaches to learning beyond their preferred learning styles. This increased flexibility is why students should be encouraged to try both methods.

FIGURE 3.1
SAMPLE OPEN-PAGE JOURNAL FORMAT

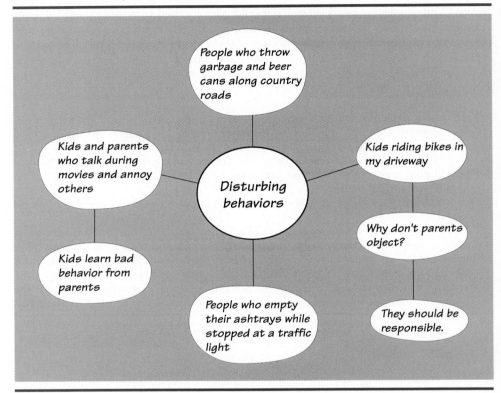

This entry suggests several possible topics to write about: parental responsibility for boorish behavior and how boorish behavior is learned from adult models.

The Two-Column Format

Divide several pages of your journal or computer file into two vertical columns. Label the left side "Quotations" and the right side "Reactions." Under "Quotations" jot down five to ten quotations from the text. Choose remarks that seem important: that state an opinion, summarize a viewpoint, and so forth. In the right column, directly opposite each quotation, write your reaction to the quotation. You might explain it, disagree with or question it, relate it to other information in the reading or in another reading, or tie it to your own experience. The two-column format forces you to think actively about an essay while you question what you have read and draw connections. Figure 3.2 follows the two-column format.

FIGURE 3.2
SAMPLE TWO-COLUMN JOURNAL FORMAT

TEACHING TIP:
LEARNING STYLES

Quotations	Reactions
"She seemed to be experiencing a novel sensation--shame--and it occurred to me that New York might be a better place if more of us emulated Mrs. Seigel."	Someone once wrote about New Yorkers' "glassy-eyed stare"--the way they learn to ignore unusual behavior so that the person exhibiting the behavior won't notice them. Also, city dwellers are often too busy or distracted to notice bad behavior.
"Was there a rational case to be made for crankdom?"	Yes, there's a rational case, if you can be sure the person you are confronting is sane and doesn't carry a concealed weapon. But you can't always be sure. It's not worth losing your life over an empty bottle.
"'We need to find new ways to encourage the enforcement of useful cooperative norms.'"	By "new ways" does he mean that "old ways" no longer work? Was Mrs. Seigel practicing one of these old ways? What could these "new ways" be?

All students can use the two-column format, but it may be most appealing to learners with pragmatic, rational, and verbal styles. This format offers students practice in personal response and analysis.

In this entry, the writer has uncovered several possible topics—risks of crankdom, new means of enforcing norms, and problems of enforcement. Because the two-column format provides more structure, students who tend to be pragmatic or concrete learners may find it effective.

You may find it useful to paraphrase the quotation before writing your reaction. Paraphrasing forces you to think about the meaning of the quotation, and

For more on paraphrasing, see Chapter 19, p. 656.

ideas for writing may come to mind as a result. To use paraphrasing, add a "Paraphrase" column to your journal between the "Quotation" column and the "Reaction" column.

ESSAY IN PROGRESS 4

For "The Boor War" or another essay, write a response in your journal using the open-page format or the two-column format.

Use Your Learning Style

Depending on your learning style, you may find that some of the methods we have discussed for discovering ideas about a reading work better for you than others. Your learning style may suggest new approaches as well.

If you tend to be a *social* learner, you may find that discussing a reading with classmates can be a helpful way to discover ideas to write about. Be sure to make brief notes as you discuss so you don't lose track of worthwhile ideas. Consider using one or more of the strategies suggested earlier in this chapter to guide your discussion, adapting them to group response. For instance, you could work on devising critical questions, or share how the reading ties to your experiences. Each student could first select meaningful quotations, and then read them aloud and respond to them. If you tend to be an *independent* learner, however, you may prefer working alone through the strategies suggested in this chapter.

If you tend to be a *pragmatic* or *verbal* learner, a structured, systematic approach that involves writing—such as the two-column response journal—may work well. When devising questions, create a structure by listing the headings "What?" "How?" and "Why?" on your paper or computer screen and creating questions for each category. For *creative* or *spatial* learners, an open-page journal or a diagram may be appealing because it offers flexibility and may foster creativity.

If you tend to be a *rational* learner, try to analyze and evaluate each piece of supporting evidence the writer provides by asking questions or writing annotations. *Emotional* learners may find it helpful to work with a classmate, examining ideas together, possibly arriving at a consensus on important questions or key quotations to paraphrase and react to. If you tend to be a *concrete* learner, try to make the essay as "real" as possible; visualize events occurring, or the author writing. You might visualize yourself interviewing the author, alone or with a panel of classmates. You may also focus on the details the writer provides, analyzing how they work together. *Abstract* learners may find it helpful to focus on the larger issues raised by the essay, considering the overall message and its implications.

TEACHING TIP: COLLABORATIVE WRITING

(30 minutes) Have students work independently at first, spending 15–20 minutes writing responses to the essay. Then, to gain the benefits of social learning, have them

• share their responses with one another in pairs.
• discuss their responses as a class.

TEACHING TIP: LEARNING STYLES

Social learners may have difficulty taking adequate notes, focusing instead on the pace of their conversation, and may benefit from using a tape recorder during conversations with peers or tutors, independent brainstorming, and personal interviews. Encourage students to borrow or purchase a standard tape recorder, which uses cassette tapes that can be played back on a car stereo, or a minitranscriber, which is compact and easy to slip into a pocket or backpack. Students should always obtain a fellow student's, tutor's, or interviewee's consent before recording a conversation.

ESSAY IN PROGRESS 5

Discuss "The Boor War" with a classmate. Make notes as you discuss. If you chose another essay, pair up with a classmate who also chose that essay or else ask your classmate to read the essay you have chosen.

ESSAY IN PROGRESS 6

Write a two- to four-page paper in response to "The Boor War" or the essay you have chosen. Use the following steps to shape the ideas you generated in Essay in Progress 1–5.

1. **Reread the writing you did in response to the reading.** Look for ideas, comments, statements, or annotations that seem worthwhile and that are important enough to become the basis of your essay.
2. **Look for related ideas.** Try to find ideas that fit together to produce a viewpoint or position toward the reading.
3. **Do not attempt to cover all your ideas.** Your essay should not analyze every aspect of the essay. Instead, you should choose some feature or aspect on which to focus.
4. **Write a sentence that states your central point.** This sentence will become your thesis statement. It should state what your essay will assert or explain.
5. **Collect ideas and evidence from the reading to support your ideas.** Your ideas should be backed up by specifics in the reading.
6. **Organize your ideas into essay form.** Your paper should have a title, introduction, body, and conclusion.
7. **Revise your essay.** Evaluate and revise your essay to be sure that you have explained your ideas fully and that you have provided clear support for each of your ideas by referring to the reading.
8. **Proofread for accuracy and correctness.** Use the Proofreading Checklist.

STUDENTS WRITE

Sharon McLaughlin was a student returning to college after several years in the work force when she wrote the following essay. Her essay, written in response to "The Boor War," was assigned by her writing instructor. As you read, notice how McLaughlin describes her reactions to Tierney's methods of dealing with urban cranks.

```
Confronting Boors Can Be Hazardous to Your Health
                 Sharon McLaughlin
```

In John Tierney's essay "The Boor War," the author suggests that if more New Yorkers became "cranks" and confronted litterers, noisemakers, and other rude,

1

Introduction

TEACHING TIP

In order to allow students to work at their own pace, assign this Essay in Progress to be completed outside of class. Encourage students to use the writing center for support during any phase of the writing process.

For more on thesis statements, see Chapter 5. For more on organizing your ideas, see Chapter 6. To help you revise your essay, see Chapter 7. For more on editing and proofreading, see Chapter 8.

PREREADING QUESTIONS

• To what extent does McLaughlin agree that it is important to confront boors?
• What historical example does McLaughlin use to support the idea that someone who confronts a rude person cannot depend on strangers for assistance should the rude person become aggressive?

thoughtless people, the quality of life in New York would improve. I've lived in New York and in a suburban town, and I agree that unless rude people are con-fronted--unless their selfish behavior has consequences--they will continue to be rude. I don't think the author's, or Mrs. Seigel's, methods always work, however, and they can be very dangerous.

Thesis statement

Supporting paragraph

2   When people have lived in a neighborhood for a long time, I think they are probably more likely to respond to rude, obnoxious behavior than a newcomer or a person who is just passing through. From Tierney's description of her, Mrs. Seigel seems very much like a life-long New Yorker. Because she is struggling with a grocery cart when Tierney meets her, she is undoubtedly in her own neighborhood (and New York is really a big collection of neighborhoods). When I first lived in New York and had friends over for a visit one day, a rock flew through my window, thrown by a group of boys in the street below. My friends, who had lived in that neighborhood for many years, immediately called 911. The police came right away. If I had been alone I'm not sure that I would have called them. Last Halloween, my brother, who has lived in his suburban neighborhood all his life, chased an eleven-year-old boy who threw a frozen egg through his screen door, caught up with the boy, and made him clean up the mess he had caused.

McLaughlin is connecting the reading to her own experience.

Supporting paragraph

3   By contrast, many New Yorkers ignore rude or unusual behavior. They are often too busy and distracted by other things to notice, and correct, every instance of rudeness. Robert Axelrod, the professor of political science and public policy who is quoted in Tierney's article, observes that people will get away with rudeness most of the time in a big city; therefore, being embar-rassed a few times by someone like Mrs. Seigel will not stop them. In addition, since any large city is filled with all sorts of people, including people who might be carrying concealed weapons, ignoring bad behavior can be

McLaughlin is questioning whether it is safe to become an urban crank.

a wise course of action. Especially if you are in an unfamiliar part of town, you can't always be sure that someone will come to your aid if the person you are confronting attacks you. Many people are familiar with the story of Kitty Genovese, who was murdered on a street in New York while neighbors ignored her screams for help. People who live in a big city have to learn to be "street smart"--to avoid danger and not to take unnecessary risks.

McLaughlin is relating the reading to another event.

If Tierney hopes to recruit more cranks, then he needs to find ways to make people feel at home--to feel that they are part of a neighborhood. He also needs to think about more creative, less aggressive ways to deal with rudeness than throwing an egg at a noisy car.

4

Conclusion

Analyzing the Reading

1. What is McLaughlin's thesis (central point)?
2. What kind of information does McLaughlin include to support her thesis?
3. What additional information, if any, would you suggest McLaughlin include in her essay?

Reacting to the Reading: Discussion and Journal Writing

1. How do you think you or your neighbors would react to one of the situations described in McLaughlin's essay?
2. What creative approaches might be effective in dealing with boorish behavior?
3. Write a journal entry describing a situation in which you confronted (or thought about confronting) boorish behavior.

POSSIBLE ANSWERS: ANALYZING THE READING

1. While confronting rude people would improve the quality of urban life, it can be dangerous.
2. McLaughlin uses several types of support in her brief essay, including personal experience (her own experiences and her brother's), expert testimony (the opinion of the professor of political science and public policy cited in "The Boor War"), common knowledge and reason (city dwellers' "street smarts" prompt them to avoid confrontation), and example (Kitty Genovese).
3. She spends as much time relating her personal experiences of confrontation as she does in using less personal types of support. Her essay might benefit if she developed the ideas in paragraphs 3 and 4.

POSSIBLE ANSWERS: REACTING TO THE READING

Responses will vary.

PART 2

Strategies for
Writing Essays

Chapter *4*

Study the photo on the opposite page. What is happening in the photo? What do you think the man could be reacting to?

Writing Quick Start

Take out a sheet of paper or open a new computer file and write whatever comes to mind about the photo and what you think might be happening in it. You might write about times when you've felt the same emotions you think the man is expressing, or you might write about times when you've seen people express strong emotions in a public place. Try to write nonstop for at least five minutes, jotting down or typing whatever ideas cross your mind. Don't stop to evaluate your writing or to phrase your ideas in complete sentences or correct grammatical form. Don't worry about correctness; just record your thinking.

Prewriting: How to Find and Focus Ideas

TEACHING TIP: COLLABORATIVE WRITING

(20–30 minutes) In order to give students practice with choosing a topic, using a journal, and brainstorming, divide students into small groups to share and discuss the results of their freewriting. Have each group choose a sentence from one student's freewriting; then each person should add one sentence to further the story, with one student in each group recording the story in a journal. *Optional:* Groups can then share their collaborative stories with the class.

You have just used *freewriting*, a method of discovering ideas about a topic. Read over what you wrote. Suppose you were asked to write an essay about joy or exuberance. Do you see some starting points and usable ideas in your freewriting? In this chapter you will learn more about freewriting as well as a number of other methods, in addition to those described in Chapter 3, that will help you find ideas to write about. You will also learn how to focus an essay by considering why you are writing (your purpose), who you are writing for (your audience), and the perspective from which you are approaching your topic (point of view). These steps are all part of the beginning of the process of writing an essay, as illustrated in Figure 4.1. First, you will learn how to choose and narrow a topic.

CHOOSING AND NARROWING A TOPIC

When you begin an essay assignment, it's a good idea to take some time choosing your broad topic and then narrowing it so that it is manageable within the assigned length of your paper. Skipping this step is one of the biggest mistakes you can make in beginning a writing assignment. You can waste a great deal of time working part way through an essay only to discover that the topic is too large or that you don't have enough to say about it.

Choosing a Topic

In some writing situations, your instructor will assign the topic. In others, your instructor will allow you to write on a topic of your choice. Or you may be given a number of possible topics to choose from, as in the Guided Writing Assignments in Chapters 9–16, 18 and 21 of this text. In the latter cases, use the following guidelines to choose a successful topic.

1. **Invest time in making your choice.** It may be tempting to grab the first topic that comes to mind and get on with the assignment. Often, however, deciding too quickly is a mistake. You will produce a better, more successful essay if you work with a topic that interests you and that you know something about.

2. **Choose a topic that is substantive, meaningful, and worthwhile.** Even the most mundane subjects can lead you in surprising directions. If you are interested in soap operas, for example, you might write about why people watch them or do some research to discover who writes them or how they are made.

3. **Focus on questions and ideas, rather than topics.** You may find it easier to think of questions or ideas, rather than topics. For example, the question "Do television commercials really sell products?" may come to mind more easily than the broad topic of advertising or television commercials.

FIGURE 4.1
AN OVERVIEW OF THE WRITING PROCESS

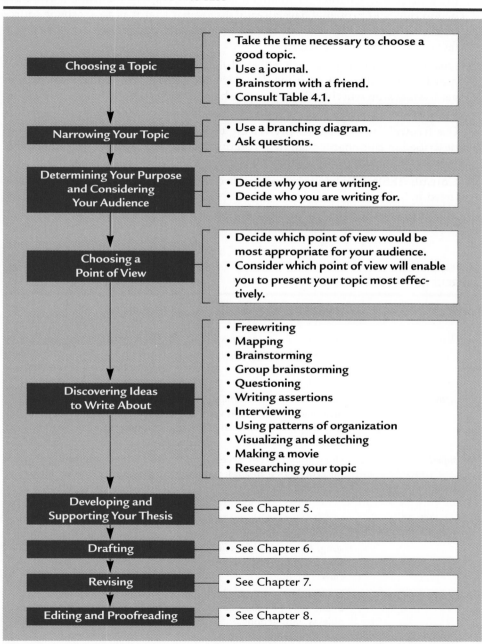

Choosing a Topic
- Take the time necessary to choose a good topic.
- Use a journal.
- Brainstorm with a friend.
- Consult Table 4.1.

Narrowing Your Topic
- Use a branching diagram.
- Ask questions.

Determining Your Purpose and Considering Your Audience
- Decide why you are writing.
- Decide who you are writing for.

Choosing a Point of View
- Decide which point of view would be most appropriate for your audience.
- Consider which point of view will enable you to present your topic most effectively.

Discovering Ideas to Write About
- Freewriting
- Mapping
- Brainstorming
- Group brainstorming
- Questioning
- Writing assertions
- Interviewing
- Using patterns of organization
- Visualizing and sketching
- Making a movie
- Researching your topic

Developing and Supporting Your Thesis
- See Chapter 5.

Drafting
- See Chapter 6.

Revising
- See Chapter 7.

Editing and Proofreading
- See Chapter 8.

TEACHING TIP

Encourage students to purchase pocket-size notebooks to serve as out-of-class idea journals. Point out that professional writers often use such notebooks to record ideas wherever they are—on the bus, in line, in waiting rooms, at restaurants, and so on.

COMPUTER HINT

Some students will enjoy keeping a journal on computer. Again, remind them to save their work on a floppy disk.

4. **Use your journal as a source of ideas.** Chapter 1 describes how to keep a writing journal and Chapter 3 explains how to use a response journal. If you have begun one, you probably have already discovered that it is an excellent source of ideas for essays. If you have not, start a journal now; try writing in it for a few weeks to see if it is helpful.

5. **Discuss possible topics with a friend.** Discussing possibilities with a friend may help you discover worthwhile topics and, at the same time, allow you to get feedback on whether the topics you have already thought of are interesting to others.

6. **Use freewriting or another prewriting technique.** The prewriting techniques described in this chapter can help you discover an interesting topic and decide whether you have enough to say about it (see pp. 78–91).

7. **Consult Table 4.1.** A number of specific sources of ideas for essay topics are listed in Table 4.

TABLE 4.1
SOURCES OF IDEAS FOR ESSAY TOPICS

SOURCE	*WHAT TO LOOK FOR*	*EXAMPLE*
Your classes	Listen for issues, controversies, and new ideas that might be worth exploring.	A discussion in your education class on education reform leads you to the topic of teacher evaluation.
Daily activities	Take note of memorable or meaningful incidents at work and at sporting or social events.	A health inspector's visit at work suggests an essay on restaurant food safety.
Newspapers and magazines	Flip through recent issues; look for articles that might lead to promising topics.	You find an interesting article on rap music and decide to write about a popular rap musician.
Radio and television	Listen to your favorite radio station for a thought-provoking song, or look for ideas in television programs and commercials.	Commercials for diet soda suggest an essay on the diet food industry.
The world around you	Look within your household or outside of it. Notice people, objects, interactions.	You notice family members reading books or newspapers and decide to write about the value of leisure time.

ESSAY IN PROGRESS 1

Using the suggestions on pages 68 and 70 and in Table 4.1 to stimulate your thinking, list at least three broad topics.

TEACHING TIP: COLLABORATIVE WRITING

(10 minutes) In small groups, have students share their lists of possible topics and provide feedback to one another: Which topics are most interesting? Which might require research? Which are specific enough for a two- to four-page essay?

Narrowing a Topic

Once you have chosen a topic, the next step is to narrow or limit it so that it is manageable within the length of the essay your instructor has assigned. If you are assigned to write a two- to four-page essay, for example, a broad topic such as gun control is too large. Entire books have been written on this issue; you could not possibly cover all of the aspects of gun control in two to four pages. If you did try to write on this broad subject, your essay would probably ramble from issue to issue without a focus. Fortunately, most broad subjects contain manageable topics within them. For gun control, you might write about a plan to raise the minimum age for owning a handgun or argue for a complete ban of a particular type of weapon.

To narrow a topic, then, you limit it to a specific part or aspect. The following techniques—branching and questioning—will help you do so. Later in the chapter you will learn other techniques for narrowing a broad topic (see pp. 78–91).

Using a Branching Diagram

Start by writing your broad topic at the far left side of your paper or computer screen. Then subdivide the topic into three or more subcategories or aspects. Here is an example for the broad topic of wild game hunting.

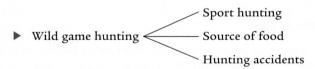

Then choose one subcategory and subdivide it further, as shown here.

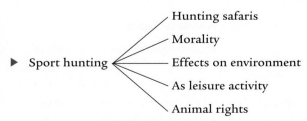

Continue narrowing the topic in this way until you feel you have found one that is both interesting and manageable.

Keep in mind that once you begin planning, researching, and drafting the essay, you may need to narrow your topic even further. The following example shows additional narrowing of the topic *effects on environment*.

▶ Effects on environment $\Big\langle$
— Hunted species may become endangered.
— Hunters may spoil pristine wilderness areas.
— Hunting helps control some animal populations.

Any one of these narrowed topics would be workable for a two- to four-page essay. Did you notice that as the narrowing progressed, the topics changed from words and phrases to statements of ideas?

<table>
<tr><td>

POSSIBLE ANSWERS

Example: **3. Population explosion**

• "Population explosion" could be narrowed to effects on environment, birth control methods, and declining quality of life in the Third World.

• Subsequently, effects on environment could be narrowed to global food shortages, increasing air pollution, excess solid waste, and increased damage to the ozone layer.

</td><td>

EXERCISE 4.1

Use branching diagrams to narrow three of the following broad topics to more manageable topics for a two- to four-page essay.

1. Divorce
2. Safe transportation
3. Population explosion
4. Military spending
5. Birth control
6. Early childhood education

ESSAY IN PROGRESS 2

Narrow one of the broad topics you chose in Essay in Progress 1 to a topic manageable for a two- to four-page essay.

</td></tr>
</table>

Asking Questions to Narrow a Broad Topic

Use questions that begin with *who, what, when, where, why,* and *how* to narrow your topic. Questioning will lead you to consider and focus your attention on specific aspects of the topic. Here is an example of questioning for the broad topic of divorce.

Questions	*Narrowed Topics*
Why does divorce occur?	• Lifestyle differences as a cause of divorce
	• Infidelity as a cause of divorce
How do couples divide their property?	• Division of assets during a divorce
Who can help couples work through a divorce?	• Role of divorce mediators
	• Marital counselor's or attorney's role in divorce

What are the effects of divorce on children?

- Emotional effects of divorce on children
- Financial effects of divorce on children

When might it be advisable for a couple considering divorce to remain married?

- Couples who stay together for the sake of their children
- Financial benefit of remaining married

As you can see, the questions about divorce produced several workable topics. At times, however, you may need to ask additional questions to get to a topic that is sufficiently limited. The topic *emotional effects of divorce on children,* for example, is still too broad for an essay. "What are the most typical emotional effects?" and "How do divorcing parents prevent emotional problems?"—would lead to more specific topics.

EXERCISE 4.2

Use questioning to narrow three of the following subjects to topics that would be manageable within a two- to four-page essay.

1. Senior citizens
2. Mental illness
3. Environmental protection
4. Affirmative action
5. Radio programming

THINKING ABOUT YOUR PURPOSE, AUDIENCE, AND POINT OF VIEW

Once you have decided on a manageable topic, you are ready to determine your purpose, consider your audience, and choose a point of view.

Determining Your Purpose

While the general goal of most writing is to communicate, a well-written essay should have a specific **purpose**—a goal the essay intends to accomplish. There are three main purposes for writing: to *express* yourself, to *inform* your reader, and to *persuade* your reader. For example, an essay might express the writer's feelings about an incident of "road rage" that he or she observed. Another essay may inform readers about the dangers of lead poisoning. Still another essay might attempt to persuade readers to vote for congressional representatives who support health care reform.

Before you begin developing ideas for writing your draft essay, ask yourself two critical questions.

- Why am I writing this essay?
- What do I want to accomplish?

Often, thinking about your topic will help you determine your purpose. If your topic is snowboarding, for instance, think about why you are writing about that subject: Do you want to re-create its thrills for readers (express yourself), explain to readers how to do it (inform), or urge readers to try it (persuade)? Some essays can have more than one purpose. An essay on snowboarding could be both informative and persuasive. The essay could explain the benefits of snowboarding and then urge readers to take up the sport because it is good aerobic exercise.

Considering Your Audience

TEACHING TIP

(15–20 minutes) For a role-playing exercise, have students work in pairs. One student plays the other's parent; the second student "confesses" to the student playing parent that he or she has just wrecked the family car. Then have the parent figure play the role of the son or daughter, telling the same story to his or her best friend. As a whole class, discuss the differences between the two conversations.

If you were getting ready to go to a rock concert, you probably would not choose the same outfit you would wear to a job interview. In other words, you would select your clothing to suit the event and situation. Likewise, if you were describing a student orientation session to a friend, you would use a different tone and select different details than you would if you were describing the orientation in an article for the student newspaper. Consider the following examples.

TELLING A FRIEND

Remember I told you how I'll be attending college in the fall? Well, guess what? I went to my student orientation over the weekend, and it was much better than I had expected! I even met one of my psych teachers — they call them "instructors" here — and he was so nice and down-to-earth that now I'm starting to get excited about going to college. Some of the welcoming speeches were really boring, but after that things got better. At first, I was worried that I wouldn't know anyone (I didn't), but all the students were so friendly that before long I was talking to them as if we had known each other for a long time. I almost didn't go to the orientation — it started on a Friday night and I thought I'd be going to Peter's party. But I'm really glad I got to go. Now I'm sure I made the right decision about starting college.

WRITING FOR THE STUDENT NEWSAPER

College student orientations are often thought to be stuffy, high-brow affairs where high-achieving students mix with aloof professors. For this reason, I am pleased to report that the college orientation held on campus last weekend was a major success. Along with my fellow incoming first-year students, I was impressed with the friendly atmosphere and camaraderie that developed. I would have preferred fewer "welcome-to-the-college" speeches, but once they were over, more practical information on registration, grading policies, and college services followed. Like most new students, I admit to deep feelings of apprehension mixed with a tinge of excitement as I thought about professors, grades, expectations, time limitations, and the dreaded fear of failure. However, my anxieties were quickly alleviated by the orientation. I met my future classmates who, as it turned out, harbored many of the same doubts. The college arranged for us to meet our advisers — not to chart our academic futures but to lay the groundwork for a solid working relationship. With most self-doubt erased, I can begin my college career with newly found confidence.

Notice how the two examples differ in terms of word choice, sentence structure, and the type of information that is provided. The tone varies as well: the paragraph spoken to a friend has a casual tone, whereas the article written for the student newspaper is more formal.

Considering your audience is an important part of writing an essay. How you express yourself (the type of sentence structure you use, for example); the words you choose; your **tone** — how you sound to your reader — and what you say, the details and examples you include; and the attitude you take toward your topic all depend on the **audience,** the people who will read your essay.

How to Consider Your Audience

As you consider your audience, keep the following points in mind.

- **Your readers are not present and cannot observe or participate in what you are writing about.** If you are writing about your apartment, for example, they cannot visualize it unless you describe it in sufficient detail.

- **Your readers do not know everything you do.** They may not have the same knowledge about and experience with the topic that you do. If you are writing about basketball, for instance, they may not know what a slam-dunk or a rebound is.

- **Your readers may not necessarily share your opinions and values.** If you are writing about raising children and assume that strict discipline and authoritative parenting are undesirable, for example, some readers may not agree with you.

- **Your readers may not respond in the same way you do to situations or issues.** Some readers may not see any humor in a situation that you find funny. An issue that you consider only mildly disturbing may make some readers angry.

Ask the following questions to analyze your audience.

- **What does your audience know or not know about your topic?** If you are proposing a community garden project to an audience of city residents who know little about gardening, you would need to describe the pleasures and benefits of gardening in order to capture their interest.

- **What is the education, background, and experience of your audience?** If you are writing your garden-project proposal for an audience of low-income residents, you might emphasize the money they could save by growing vegetables, but if you are proposing the project to middle-income residents, you might stress instead how relaxing gardening can be and how a garden can beautify a neighborhood.

- **What attitudes, beliefs, opinions, or biases is your audience likely to hold?** If, for example, your audience believes that most development is harmful to the environment, and you are writing an essay urging your audience to agree to a new housing development, consider emphasizing the increased tax revenues, which could be used to improve local parks and recreational facilities.

As you can see, an awareness of your audience should influence the kinds of information you include in your essay. If you have difficulty analyzing your audience, try writing directly to one member of that audience or imagining a profile of a typical audience member. If your audience consists of teachers in your local school district, for example, pick one teacher and write directly to him or her. If you are writing a letter of application to the personnel director of a company, try to visualize or imagine that person, his or her workload, the challenges he or she faces, and so forth.

When Your Audience Is Your Instructor

Some students find it difficult to develop a sense of audience for an essay they are writing for their instructor. You might be tempted to assume that your instructor understands why you are writing and what you are writing about, since he or she made the assignment. For example, many students mistakenly think that they do not need to supply introductory or background information in an essay written in response to an assignment.

Instructors occasionally direct students to write for a particular audience, such as readers of a certain magazine or newspaper. Usually, however, you can assume that your audience is your instructor. You should not, however, automatically assume that he or she is an expert on your topic. In most cases, it is best to write as if your instructor were unfamiliar with your topic. Suppose, for example, that you are writing a paper on personality disorders for your psychology class and your audience is your instructor who is obviously knowledgeable about your topic. He or she wants to see if *you* understand the topic, however, and can write and think clearly about it. For academic papers, then, you should provide enough information to demonstrate your knowledge of the subject. Include background information, definitions of technical terms, and relevant details to make your essay clear and understandable.

EXERCISE 4.3

1. Write a one-paragraph description of a current television commercial for a particular product. Your audience is another college student.
2. Write a description of the same commercial for one of the following writing situations.
   a. An assignment in a business marketing class: Analyze the factors that make the advertisement interesting and appealing. Your audience is a marketing instructor.
   b. A letter to the company that produces the product: Describe your response to the advertisement. Your audience is the consumer relations director of the company.
   c. A letter to your local television station: Comment favorably on or complain about the advertisement. Your audience is the station director.

Choosing a Point of View

Point of view is the perspective from which you write an essay. There are three types: *first, second,* and *third person.* In choosing a point of view, consider your topic, your purpose, and your audience.

Think of point of view as the "person" you become as you write. For some essays you may find first-person pronouns (*I, me, mine, we, ours*) effective and appropriate, such as in an essay narrating an event in which you participated. For other types of essays, second-person pronouns (*you, your, yours*) are appropriate. If you are explaining how to build a fence, for instance, it would sound awkward or overly formal to write in the third person: "First the *fence builder* should measure. . . ." For this kind of explanation, you need to address readers directly, telling them what to do: "First *you* should measure. . . ." At times, the word *you* may be understood but not directly stated, as in "First measure. . . ." Many textbooks, including this one, use the second person to address student readers.

The third-person point of view is less personal, more formal, and more detached than both the first person and the second person. People's names and third-person pronouns (*he, she, they*) are used. In academic writing, the third-person point of view is prevalent. Think of the third person as public rather than private or personal. The writer is looking in on and reporting what he or she sees.

EXERCISE 4.4

Working with a classmate, discuss which point of view (first, second, or third person) would be most appropriate in each of the following writing situations.

1. An essay urging students on your campus to participate in a march against hunger to support a local food drive
2. A description of a car accident on a form that your insurance company requires you to submit in order to collect benefits
3. A paper for an ecology course on the effects of air pollution caused by a local industry

TEACHING TIP: COLLABORATIVE WRITING

(15–25 minutes) Divide the class into three groups. Assign each group one of the assignments in Exercise 4.3. Ask students to choose a commercial they have all seen and to determine what main points to include in their writing while one student takes notes. Each student should then write a version of the assignment and read it aloud to the group. *Optional:* Have each group choose one version to present to the class.

POSSIBLE ANSWERS

Answers will vary.

TEACHING TIP

Some students respond better to the term *voice.* Explain that the warmth or distance of the voice corresponds to the level of formality and the point of view. That is, the first and second person address the reader more directly and informally than does the third person.

POSSIBLE ANSWERS

1. Second person; first person would work if the student incorporates personal observations or experience.
2. First person would allow the student to convey his or her view of the accident.
3. Third person is the most appropriate choice for an academic paper.

DISCOVERING IDEAS TO WRITE ABOUT

Many students report that one of the most difficult parts of writing an essay is finding enough to say about a narrowed topic. Most of these students simply pick up a pen or turn on a computer and try to start writing. They soon run out of ideas. For many students, writing is easier when they make the effort to do some thinking and planning first. You wouldn't leave for a vacation without choosing a route and a destination beforehand. Similarly, you should not start writing a paper until you have a route and destination for it in mind. Before writing actual sentences and paragraphs, you should have some sense of what your paper will accomplish — your purpose — and how you will accomplish it — what you will say and how you will organize your ideas. In the following sections you will learn a number of useful strategies for discovering ideas to write about. Chapters 5 and 6 will show you how to focus your ideas and organize them into an effective essay. In addition, in the Guided Writing Assignments in Chapters 9–16 and 18 you will use various strategies for choosing and narrowing a topic and generating ideas about it.

Writers use many techniques for generating ideas. The most common methods are described here. Experiment with each before deciding which will work for you. Depending on your learning style, you will probably discover that some strategies work better than others. You may also find that the technique you choose for a given essay may depend in part on your topic.

Freewriting

When you use **freewriting,** you write nonstop for a specific, limited period of time, usually five to ten minutes. As you learned in the activity that opens this chapter, freewriting involves writing whatever comes to mind, regardless of its relevance to your topic. If nothing comes to mind, just write the topic, your name, or "I can't think of anything to write." Then let your mind run free: explore ideas, make associations, jump from one idea to another. The following tips will help you make freewriting work for you.

- Be sure to write nonstop. Writing often forces thought.
- Don't be concerned with grammar, punctuation, or spelling.
- Write fast! Try to keep up with your thinking. (Most people can think faster than they can write.)
- Record ideas as they come to you and in whatever form they appear — words, phrases, questions, or sentences.
- If you are freewriting on a computer, darken the screen so you are not distracted by errors, formatting issues, and what you have already written.

Next, reread your freewriting and highlight or underline ideas that seem useful. Look for patterns and connections. Do several ideas together make a point, reflect a sequence, or suggest a larger, unifying idea? Here is an annotated excerpt from one student's freewriting on the broad topic of violence in the media.

> There seems to be a lot of <u>violence</u> in the media these days particularly on TV. For example, last night when I watched the news, the camera man showed people <u>getting shot in the street</u>. What kind of people watch this stuff? I'd rather watch a movie. It really bothered me because people get so turned off by such an ugly, <u>gruesome scene</u> that they won't want to watch the news anymore. Then we'll have a lot of <u>uninformed citizens</u>. There are too many already. Some people do not even know who the vice president of the U.S. is. A negative thing-- that is the media <u>has a negative impact</u> on anyone or group who want to do something about violence in the inner city. And they create <u>negative impressions of minority and ethnic groups</u>, too. If the media shows one Latino man committing a crime, viewers falsely assume <u>all Latinos</u> are criminals. It's difficult to think of something positive that can be done when you're surrounded by so much violence. It's all so overwhelming. What we need in the inner city is not more coverage of violence but viable solutions to the violence we have. The media coverage of violent acts only serves to make people think that this violence is a normal state of affairs and nothing can be done about it.

Portrayal of violence

Negative impact on viewers

Portrayal of minority & ethnic groups

A number of different subtopics surfaced from this student's freewriting:

The media's graphic portrayal of violence
The media's negative impact on viewers
The media's portrayal of minority and ethnic groups

Any one of these broad topics could be narrowed into a manageable topic for an essay. The student chose the subtopic *the media's portrayal of minority and ethnic groups* and used freewriting to narrow it further. Finally, she chose to write an essay on the media's portrayal of African American teenagers.

TEACHING TIP:
COLLABORATIVE
WRITING

(15–20 minutes) Group
students together who
are interested in the
same topic, and then
ask them to share their
freewritings with one
another the first time
around. Their peers can
help them identify
phrases and concepts
worth highlighting and
developing further.

POSSIBLE ANSWERS

Answers will vary.

If you are a creative learner or feel restricted by organization and structure, freewriting may appeal to you because it allows you to give your imagination free rein.

EXERCISE 4.5

Set a clock or timer for five minutes and freewrite on one of the following broad topics. Then review and highlight your freewriting, identifying usable ideas with a common theme that might serve as a topic for an essay. Starting with this potential topic, freewrite for another five minutes to narrow your topic further and develop your ideas.

1. Rock 'n' roll
2. World Wide Web sites
3. How to be self-sufficient
4. Urban problems
5. Job interviews

Mapping

Mapping, or **clustering,** is a visual way of discovering ideas and relationships. It is also a powerful tool for some writers. Here is how it works.

1. Write your topic in the middle of a blank sheet of paper and draw a box or circle around it.
2. Think of ideas that are related to or suggested by your topic. As you think of them, write them down in clusters around the topic, connecting them to the topic with lines (see Figure 4.2). Think of your topic as a tree trunk and the related ideas as branches.
3. Draw arrows and lines or use highlighting to show relationships and connect groups of related ideas.
4. Think of still more ideas, clustering them around the ideas already on your map.
5. If possible, experiment with mapping on a computer, using a graphics program such as the draw function available in Microsoft Word™. You can then cut and paste items from your map into an outline or draft of your essay.

The sample map in Figure 4.2 was done by a student working on the topic of the costs of higher education. In this map, the student compared attending a local community college and attending an out-of-town four-year college. A number of different subtopics evolved, including the following.

• Tuition costs
• Social life
• Availability of degree programs
• Room and board costs

FIGURE 4.2
SAMPLE MAP

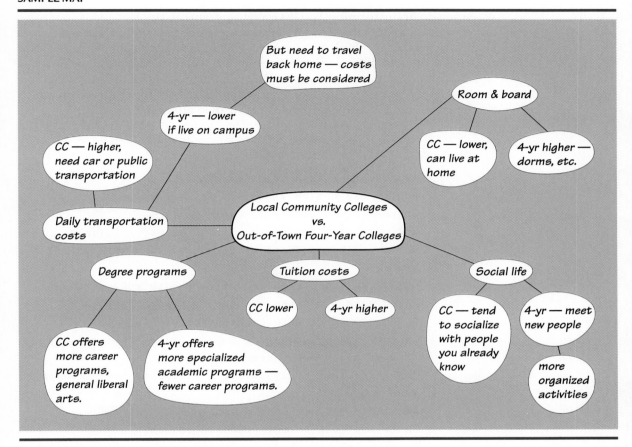

Mapping may appeal to you if you prefer a spatial method of dealing with information and ideas. It also appeals to creative learners who like to devise their own structure or framework within which to work.

EXERCISE 4.6

Narrow one of the following topics. Then select one of your narrowed topics and draw a map of related ideas as they come to mind.

1. Presidential politics
2. Daydreaming
3. Library facilities
4. The function of jewelry
5. Radio stations

POSSIBLE ANSWERS

Example: **1. Presidential politics**

• Possible ideas for *presidential politics:* fundraising, running mates, caucuses, endorsements, scandals, pundits, primaries, loss of privacy, diplomacy.

• Possible ideas for *diplomacy:* Middle East peace talks, UN arms inspections, terrorism, economic sanctions

Brainstorming

When you do **brainstorming,** you list everything you can think of about your topic on paper or on a computer. Record impressions, emotions, and reactions as well as facts. List them as you think of them, recording brief words or phrases rather than complete sentences. Give yourself a time limit; it will force ideas to come faster.

The following example shows a student's brainstorming on the narrowed topic *disadvantages of home schooling.* Home schooling is a form of education in which children are taught at home by parents rather than attending school.

TOPIC: DISADVANTAGES OF HOME SCHOOLING

- Child not exposed to other children
- Parent may not be an expert in each subject
- Libraries not easily accessible
- Wide range of equipment, resources not available
- Child may be confused by parent playing the role of teacher
- Child does not learn to interact with other children
- Child does not learn to compete against others
- Parents may not enforce standards
- Parents may be unable to be objective about child's strengths and weaknesses
- Child may learn only parent's viewpoint--not exposed to wide range of opinions
- Special programs (art, music) may be omitted
- Child may feel strong pressure to achieve
- Services of school nurse, counselors, reading specialists not available

Two clusters of topics are evident: unavailable services and resources and problems of social development. In the sample, ideas that belong in the first cluster are highlighted in green, ideas that belong in the second cluster are highlighted in gray. Once the student selected a cluster of topics, he did further brainstorming to generate ideas about his narrowed topic.

Brainstorming is somewhat more structured than freewriting because the writer focuses only on the topic at hand instead of writing whatever comes to mind. If you are a pragmatic learner, brainstorming may help you release your creative potential.

Group Brainstorming

Brainstorming can also work well when it is done in groups of two or three class-mates. Use a chalkboard in an empty classroom, share a large sheet of paper, sit together in front of a computer screen, or use networked computers. Say your ideas aloud as you write. You'll find that your classmates' ideas will trigger more of your own. *Group brainstorming* often appeals to students who are social learners and who find it stimulating and enjoyable to exchange ideas with other students.

EXERCISE 4.7

Choose one of the following subjects and narrow it to a manageable topic for a two- to four-page paper. Then brainstorm, either alone or with one or two classmates, to generate ideas to write about.

1. Value of music
2. National parks
3. Misuse of credit cards
4. Teenage fashions
5. Telemarketing

Questioning

Questioning is another way to discover ideas about a narrowed topic. Working either alone or with a classmate, write down every question you can think of about your topic. As with other prewriting strategies, focus on ideas, not correctness. Don't judge or evaluate ideas as you write. It may help to imagine that you have an expert on your topic present in the room and you are free to ask him or her any-thing that comes to mind.

Here is a partial list of questions one student generated on the narrow topic of the financial problems faced by single parents.

```
Why do many female single parents earn less than male single
   parents?
How can single parents afford to pay for day care?
Is there a support group for single parents that offers financial
   advice and planning?
How do single parents find time to attend college to improve
   their employability?
How can women force their ex-husbands to keep up with child sup-
   port payments?
```

TEACHING TIP

If you had students do the collaborative activity for Exercise 4.3 (p. 77), point out that they have already engaged in group brainstorming.

COMPUTER HINT

Email is particularly use-ful if networked comput-ers are not available and students have access to computers outside of class. Encourage stu-dents to send ideas for group brainstorming to each other via email. Compile a directory of class email addresses and distribute it to students for pasting into their notebooks or journals.

POSSIBLE ANSWERS

Example: **1. Value of music**

- Music serves as a mood-setter for social activities (it is essential to dancing and sets the mood of parties and celebrations).
- Music is therapeutic (it can help "bring out" autistic children, can calm colicky new-borns, and is used in hospitals and nursing homes to create a calm atmosphere for healing, resting, and childbirth).
- Music stimulates intel-ligence (it involves both sides of the brain, intelligence and creativity; enhances children's abilities in math and science; and, in the case of Mozart's music, has been used to improve students' ability to remember facts before tests).

TEACHING TIP

Warn students to
beware of questions that
can be answered with a
simple *yes* or *no*.
Although some *yes/no*
questions can lead to a
paper that explains the
reasons for that simple
answer, most *yes/no*
questions cut the writer
off at the start.

TEACHING TIP:
COLLABORATIVE
WRITING

(15 minutes) Pair up
students and have them
share their ideas for the
exercise. After one stu-
dent reads a topic he or
she has brainstormed,
have the other student
ask questions about it.
Then the first student
can follow up with other
questions. Students
should then reverse
roles. Have students
record their questions.

POSSIBLE ANSWERS

Example: The campus
newspaper

• How is it funded?
• Where is it printed?
• Who chooses the arti-
  cles for it?

CONNECTIONS

Ask students to tell you
what steps are involved
in Exercise 4.8: probably
clustering or branching,
then selecting a nar-
rowed topic, then brain-
storming questions.
Point out that students
must apply reading skills
covered in Chapter 2
(such as asking ques-
tions, underlining key
words) to each writing
exercise in this chapter.

How can single female parents who don't work outside the home
   still establish credit?

Are employers reluctant to hire women who are single parents?

Is it more difficult for a working single parent to get a mortgage than for a couple in which only one spouse works?

These questions yielded several possible ideas for further development: income
disparity, financial planning, establishment of credit, and child support.

You may find questioning effective if you are an analytical, inquisitive person,
and social learners will enjoy using this technique with classmates. Since questions
often tend to focus on specifics and details, questioning is also an appealing strategy for concrete learners.

EXERCISE 4.8

Working either alone or with a classmate, choose one of the following topics, narrow it,
and write a series of questions to discover ideas about it.

1. The campus newspaper
2. Learning a foreign language
3. Financial aid regulations
4. Late-night talk radio shows
5. Government aid to developing countries

Writing Assertions

The technique of **writing assertions** forces you to look at your topic from a number of different perspectives. Begin by writing five to ten statements that take a
position on or make an assertion about your topic. Here are a few possible assertions for the topic *the growing popularity of health food.*

Supermarkets have increased their marketing of health foods.

Health food is popular because buying it makes people think they
   are hip and current.

Health food is popular because it is chemical-free.

Health food tricks people into thinking they have a healthy
   lifestyle.

Review your list of assertions, choose one statement, and try brainstorming,
freewriting, or mapping to generate more ideas about it.

Abstract learners who prefer to deal with wholes rather than parts or who tend
to focus on larger ideas rather than details often find this technique appealing.

EXERCISE 4.9

Working either alone or with one or two classmates, write assertions about one of the following topics.

1. Advertising directed toward young adults
2. Buying a used car from a private individual
3. Needed improvements in public education
4. Characteristics of a good teacher
5. Attempts to regulate speech on campus

Interviewing

Interview a classmate about your topic; then ask your classmate to interview you about your topic. As you ask each other questions, make notes on interesting issues and subtopics that arise. Use questions that begin with *Who, What, When, Where, Why,* and *How* to get your interview started.

Here is a transcription of a conversation between two students on the topic of *how holidays are celebrated.*

MARY: How did you celebrate holidays at your house when you were a child? Let's start by talking about a particularly memorable holiday.

CHRISTINA: Well, on Christmas Eve — coming from a traditional Italian American family — my mother always prepared a meatless dinner.

MARY: Such as?

CHRISTINA: Eel and codfish. We also had squid and pasta with a fish sauce.

MARY: Was it good? Did you eat it?

CHRISTINA: No, it was like doing penance. We tried. But mostly we waited for the dessert — which was Italian cookies like cuccidati and ciccalane. But as we got older, we appreciated the tradition more and ate the fish — but no fish sauce.

MARY: What other traditions did you have?

CHRISTINA: For one, we sang Christmas songs. That is, everyone but my mother. She whistled. My father's favorite song was "Oh, Holy Night" and sometimes he held our dog, Mickey, on his arm while he sang, and Mickey's eyes got big and his ears perked up — like he was enjoying it, too.

MARY: What else did you do on Christmas Eve?

CHRISTINA: We went to midnight mass. We always walked to church as a family. It took about an hour.

From this interview, narrowed topics emerged: special holiday foods and the importance of family and tradition. In addition, Christina recalled a number of details about Christmas Eve celebrations that she might use in an essay.

TEACHING TIP

If students used group brainstorming in Exercise 4.7, point out the difference between this exercise and the group brainstorming of main points in the earlier one. This exercise requires students to look at the topic from various angles and points of view.

TEACHING TIP: COLLABORATIVE WRITING

(10–15 minutes) Working in pairs or small groups, have students comment on each other's assertions. Ask them to evaluate each assertion according to the following criteria.

- Is it merely an opinion argued from a personal standpoint, or can it be substantiated with reasons and evidence?
- Is it a surprising or an unfamiliar assertion or one that might interest a particular audience?

POSSIBLE ANSWERS

Example: 1. Advertising directed toward children

- Advertising is most often directed toward children during children's television shows.
- Television advertising for children is rarely good for them since it encourages them to buy sugary foods or toys they do not need.
- Advertising directed toward children is harmless in a free market economy because parents need to spend money on their children anyway.

(Continued on next page)

• Advertising directed toward children unfairly manipulates them by using cartoon characters, celebrities, and appealing jingles .

TEACHING TIP

Ask each student to write *P* (planned) beside those questions in the interview on p. 85 that seem prepared and *S* (spontaneous) beside those questions that seem to arise naturally from what the intervie-wee has to say.

TEACHING TIP: COLLABORATIVE WRITING

(10–15 minutes) Have interviewers use tape recorders, if possible, or to take careful notes of main ideas and quota-tions. Ask them to type up transcripts of their interviews to refer to while looking for possi-ble topics and subtopics.

POSSIBLE ANSWERS

Answers will vary.

Interviewing provides both social interaction and an opportunity to focus on details and specifics. Also, since it involves questioning, interviewing appeals to students who enjoy analyzing ideas and issues.

EXERCISE 4.10

Interview a classmate on one of the following topics.

1. Nicknames, uses and abuses
2. A favorite sports team
3. A part-time job as a learning experience
4. His or her long-term goals after college
5. The effects of peer pressure

Using the Patterns of Development

In Parts 3 and 4 of this book you will learn nine different ways to develop an essay: narration, description, illustration, process, comparison and contrast, classifica-tion and division, definition, cause and effect, and argument. These methods are often called **patterns of development**. In addition to providing ways to develop an essay, the patterns of development may be used to generate ideas about a topic. Think of the patterns as doors through which you can gain access to your topic. Just as a building or room looks different depending on which door you enter, so you will see your topic in various ways by approaching it through different pat-terns of development.

Once you work through the chapters in Parts 3 and 4, you will become more familiar with the patterns of development; for now, the list of questions in Fig-ure 4.3 will help you approach your topic through these different "doors." For any given topic, some questions will work better than others. If your topic is voter reg-istration, for example, the questions listed for definition and process would be more helpful than those listed for description.

As you write your answers to the questions, also record any related ideas that come to mind. Think of this technique as a way of finding new perspectives from which to approach your topic. If you are working on a computer, use a tabular format to brainstorm ideas about various rhetorical approaches. Pragmatic and creative learners will find this technique helpful.

Here are the answers that one student wrote in response to questions relevant to the topic *extra sensory perception (ESP)*.

```
Narration (What stories does my topic remind me of?)
• Stories about ghosts, haunted houses--particularly the famous
  one in Amityville on Long Island.
• Stories of cats with ESP--they find their way to the new house
  when their owners move away and leave them behind (sometimes
  traveling across states).
```

FIGURE 4.3
USING THE PATTERNS OF DEVELOPMENT TO EXPLORE A TOPIC

Pattern of Development	Questions to Ask
Narration (Chapter 9)	• What stories or events does this topic remind you of?
Description (Chapter 10)	• What does the topic look, smell, taste, feel, or sound like?
Illustration (Chapter 11)	• What examples of this topic are particularly helpful in explaining it?
Process (Chapter 12)	• How does this topic work? • How do you do this topic?
Comparison and Contrast (Chapter 13)	• To what is the topic similar? In what ways? • Is the topic more or less desirable than those things to which it is similar?
Classification and Division (Chapter 14)	• Of what larger group of things is this topic a member? What are its parts? • How can the topic be subdivided? • Are there certain types or kinds of the topic?
Definition (Chapter 15)	• How do you define the topic? • How does the dictionary define it? • What is the history of the term? • Does everyone agree on its definition? Why or why not? If not, what points are in dispute?
Cause and Effect (Chapter 16)	• What causes the topic? • How often does it happen? • What might prevent it from happening? • What are its effects? • What may happen because of it in the short term? • What may happen as a result of it over time?
Argument (Chapters 17 and 18)	• What issues surround this topic?

Description (What does my topic look, feel, smell, taste, or
sound like?)
• Some people report experiencing dizziness, eery feelings, foggy
  vision, unnatural sounds, cold winds.

POSSIBLE ANSWERS
(p. 89)

Example: 1. Buying only
American-made prod-
ucts

• *Narration:* Write about
a relative who insists
on buying only
American-made prod-
ucts.
• *Description:* Describe
the characteristics of
an American-made
product.
• *Illustration:* List all the
big-ticket items you
can think of that are
made in America.
• *Process analysis:* Write
about the process of
marketing American-
made products.
• *Comparison and contrast:*
Compare a particular
"American" car with a
particular "foreign"
car.
• *Classification and division:* Categorize goods
that are made in
America, such as
foods, clothing, cars,
and so on.
• *Definition:* What makes
a product "American"
— the materials, the
labor, or both?
• *Cause and effect:* People
may buy American
goods because of their
quality or because
doing so helps keep
jobs in America and

Illustration (What examples of my topic come to mind?)
• Feelings of déjà vu--that you have experienced something before.
• When a husband and wife or two friends have the same thought simultaneously.

Process (How does my topic work?)
• The theory is that ESP works by way of one person transmitting a thought telepathically (not through the usual senses) to another person. This is said to happen particularly in times of distress (for example, a wife "has a feeling" that her husband's plane will crash and sends a telepathic message to him not to board the plane).

Comparison and Contrast (What is similar to my topic?)
• Some people might say ESP is similar to guessing.
• Strange coincidences--two movies with similar plots released at the same time.

Classification and Division (How can my topic be classified or divided?)
• ESP may be subdivided by time: those who experience events in advance, those who experience events as they are happening, and those who experience events after they have happened.

Definition (How can my topic be defined?)
• ESP, or extra sensory perception, is the ability to perceive information not through the ordinary senses but as a result of a "sixth sense" (as yet undeveloped in most people).
• Scientists disagree on whether ESP exists and how it should be tested.

Cause and Effect (Why does my topic happen? What are its effects?)
• Scientists do not know the cause of ESP nor have they confirmed its existence, just the possibility of its existence.
• The effects of ESP are that some people know information that they would (seemingly) have no other way of knowing.
• Some people with ESP claim to have avoided disasters such as airplane crashes.

Argument (What issues surround my topic?)
• Is ESP always a desirable trait?
• Can ESP be learned or developed?

A number of interesting topics and ideas emerged from this student's answers, including types of ESP, ESP research, precognition, and mental telepathy.

Using the patterns of development helps to direct or focus your mind on specific issues related to a topic. The strategy may appeal to you if you are a pragmatic learner who enjoys structured tasks or a creative learner who likes to analyze ideas from different viewpoints.

EXERCISE 4.11

Use the patterns of development to generate ideas on one of the following topics. Refer to Figure 4.3 to form questions based on the patterns.

1. Buying only American-made products
2. The increase in incidents of carjacking
3. Community policing in urban areas
4. Effects of labor union strikes on workers
5. Internet chat sessions

Visualizing or Sketching

Especially if you enjoy working with graphics, **visualizing** or actually **sketching** your topic may be an effective way to discover ideas. If you are writing a description of a person, for example, close your eyes and visualize or draw that person in your mind. "See" what he or she is wearing; study facial expressions and gestures. If you are writing about shopping malls as a social scene, visualize the mall, the people in the mall, their actions and interactions. Or you may prefer to draw an actual sketch of some of the people or of the mall itself, labeling areas where socializing occurs. In each case, make notes on what you "see" or draw.

Here is what one student "saw" when visualizing a shopping mall.

As I walked through the local mall, I crossed the walkway to get to Sears and noticed a large group of excited women all dressed in jogging suits; they were part of a shopping tour, I think. I saw a tour bus parked outside. Across the walkway was a bunch of teenagers, shouting and laughing and commenting on each other's hairstyles. They all wore T-shirts and jeans; some had body adornments--pierced noses and lips. They seemed to have no interest in shopping. Their focus was on one another. Along the walkway came an obvious mother-daughter pair. They seemed to be on an outing, escaping from their day-to-day routine for some shopping, joking, and laughing. Then I noticed a tired-looking

stimulates the economy.
- *Argument:* Is buying only American-made goods patriotic, or is it an outdated nationalistic approach to consumerism?

TEACHING TIPS:
LEARNING STYLES

- Ask students who may think they can't draw or verbally describe an object or a person in detail to try a looser form of this technique —doodling—which can include realistic images, abstract forms, and words. While observing or envisioning a certain scene, students can doodle glimpses of what they see and use their doodles as a source of writing ideas. This approach may work well with creative and abstract learners.
- Point out that a good verbal sketch both shows and tells: Some passages are descriptive or graphic while others convey abstract ideas.

TEACHING TIP:
COLLABORATIVE
WRITING

(20 minutes) Ask stu-
dents to pair up and to
note in each other's
writing which phrases
are descriptive or
graphic and which
phrases convey abstract
ideas, using underlining
or highlighting and
notes in the margins.
They can also discuss
ideas in sketches and
doodles.

POSSIBLE ANSWERS

Notes or sketches will
vary.

elderly couple sitting on one of the benches. They
seemed to enjoy just sitting there and watching the people walk by, every now and then commenting on the fashions they observed people wearing.

After visualizing the mall, this student came up with several possible topics related
to malls as social gathering places as well as a number of subtopics: body piercing,
tour-group shopping, and teenage behavior. Visualization is a technique particularly well-suited to spatial and creative learners.

EXERCISE 4.12

Visualize one of the following situations. Make notes on or sketch what you "see."

1. A traffic jam
2. A couple obviously "in love"
3. A class you recently attended
4. The campus snack bar
5. A sporting event

Making a Mental Movie

If you are a spatial learner or a creative learner, you may find it helpful to explore
a topic by making a **mental movie**. Begin by imagining an event or situation that
illustrates or exemplifies your topic. Create scenes, characters, and action. Imagine
the scenes taking place in a particular setting. Devise a conflict or controversy that
builds interest and that ultimately is resolved.

TEACHING TIP

Relate approaches to
mental movie-making to
the rhetorical patterns
of development. In this
example, the movie
might lead to a *narrative*
approach (narrating the
story of the pregnant
teen) or a *process*
approach (how to
decide what to do).
Using another approach,
a student might describe
how the pregnant girl's
appearance reveals her
emotions, leading to a
paper whose purpose is
to create empathy rather
than to devise solutions.

As an example, suppose your topic is *counseling support for pregnant teenagers.*
You might begin your mental movie by imagining as the main character a sixteen-
year-old girl who has just discovered she is pregnant. She is crying and wondering
how she will ever arrive at the difficult decision of whether to raise the baby herself or give it up for adoption. You can then play out the possible scenarios of your
mental movie. For instance, you might have the teenager tell her parents about the
pregnancy. Their reaction is not what she had expected. Instead of criticizing her,
they tell her that they had suspected her condition, and while they're not happy
about it, they love her and want to support her in making the best possible decisions. They suggest that she see a counselor to sort out her confusion and consider
her options. At first she is hostile and reluctant. Then she agrees to see a counselor,
and her parents help her find one and go with her to the counselor's office. The
counselor discusses adoption as one possible option. By the end of your movie, the
teenager still feels awful but no longer views her problem as hopeless. She now
trusts her counselor and is ready to focus on solutions.

You, in turn, have identified several possible ideas to write about and explore
further: parental support, attitudes about counseling, adoption, and decision
making.

Researching Your Topic

Do some preliminary research on your topic in the library or on the Internet. Find three or four related books or articles in the library or online sources of information. Reading what others have written about your topic may suggest new approaches, reveal issues or controversies, and help you determine what you do and do not already know about the topic. This method is especially useful when you are working on an assigned essay with an unfamiliar topic or when you have chosen a topic you want to learn more about.

Take notes while reading sources. In addition, be sure to record the publication data you will need to cite each source (author, title, publisher, page numbers, and so on). If you use ideas or information from sources in your essay, you must give credit to the sources of the borrowed material. While research may be particularly appealing to concrete or rational learners, all students may need to use it at one time or another depending on their topic.

EXERCISE 4.13

Make a mental movie or do library or Internet research to generate ideas on one of the narrowed topics listed here.

1. A recent local disaster (hurricane, flood)
2. Shopping for clothes on the Internet or on television
3. Preventing terrorism in public buildings
4. Controlling children's access to television programs
5. Advantages or disadvantages of belonging to a health maintenance organization (HMO)

EXERCISE 4.14

Choose two prewriting techniques discussed in this chapter that appeal to you. Experiment with each method by generating ideas about one of the topics in the following list. Use a different topic for each prewriting technique you choose.

1. Nuisance phone calls
2. Budgeting money
3. Dorm life
4. Pop music icons
5. Couch potatoes
6. Recycling
7. Time management
8. Internet Web sites
9. Slang expressions

ESSAY IN PROGRESS 3

Keeping your audience and purpose in mind, use one of the prewriting strategies discussed in this chapter to generate details about the topic you narrowed in Essay in Progress 2 on page 72.

For more information on locating, using, and crediting sources, refer to Chapter 19, "Planning a Paper with Sources" and Chapter 20, "Writing a Research Paper."

COMPUTER HINT

Using databases provides good practice in refining a search, which is related to narrowing a topic. For instance, point out that a search on "guns" could turn up over a thousand hits, while one on "handgun control" that requests journal articles published after 1997 could limit hits to fifty or fewer.

POSSIBLE ANSWERS

Answers will vary.

CONNECTIONS

Remind students conducting Internet searches to note URL addresses for documentation purposes and to evaluate the credibility of online sources. Refer them to Chapters 19 and 20.

POSSIBLE ANSWERS

Answers will vary.

TEACHING TIP

In order for the class to view a range of prewriting approaches, consider distributing blank transparencies instead of asking students to do this exercise on paper or on computer. After using two prewriting techniques, students can take turns displaying their transparencies on an overhead projector to demonstrate their preferred methods of prewriting to the class.

TEACHING TIP

Emphasize that prewriting strategies can help students discover more about themselves as people and as writers as well as help them present information they learn or know about a topic.

STUDENTS WRITE

In this and the remaining four chapters of Part 2, we will follow the work of Tina Oyer, a student in a first-year writing course at Niagara Community College who was assigned to write a narrative essay by her instructor. She chose to write about an event that caused her to learn something about herself (which she selected from the list of possible topics in Chapter 9, p. 218).

Oyer decided to use questioning to narrow her topic and freewriting to generate ideas about the topic. Here is an example of her questioning.

Sample Questioning

```
What were some learning experiences for me?

having my first child
my first semester in college
getting married
working in the pharmacy
becoming a Christian
my mom's death
```

Oyer decided to explore two of these experiences further: *having my first child* and *working in the pharmacy*. She did so by asking another question.

```
What did I learn about myself in these situations?

Having my first child:
    I learned that a child can be very demanding.
    I learned how to manage my time.
    I learned to put my child's needs before my own.

Working in the pharmacy:
    I learned that people can be hypocrites.
    I learned to look out for myself.
    I learned how to spot a shoplifter.
```

After looking over the answers to her questions, Oyer chose *working in the pharmacy* as her topic, and she decided to focus on an event that had taught her something about herself as a worker. The following excerpt from her freewriting shows how she started to develop her topic.

Sample Freewriting

I remember that night when a woman had left her keys in the store and the store was closed. I was the manager that night on an alternate weekend shift, so I could go back in the store and look for the keys. But the owner of the store said he'd already looked and told the woman the keys weren't in the store. If I went back in, I would have to shut the alarm off, using my security code. The owner left knowing he had put his personal code into the alarm. So the owner would want to know why I went back into the store. It could have definitely cost me my job. But I also knew that the woman needed help. What to do?

As you work through the remaining chapters of Part 2, you will see how Oyer develops her tentative thesis statement in Chapter 5, her first draft in Chapter 6, and her final draft in Chapter 7. In addition, in Chapter 8, you will also see a portion of her final draft, edited and proofread to correct sentence-level errors.

Study the cartoon on the opposite page; it humorously depicts a serious situation.

Writing Quick Start

Working alone or with one or two class-mates, write a statement that expresses the main point of the cartoon. Your statement should not just describe what is happening in the cartoon. It should also state the idea that the cartoonist is trying to communicate to his audience.

Developing and Supporting a Thesis

TEACHING TIP

To help students distinguish between descriptions (facts) and ideas (assertions of facts), and to help them realize that not all facts are equally important, you might have students list all of the details in the cartoon, then compare this list to their statement of the main point. Ask which details were included in their statement and which were not. Relate the results of the Chapter Quick Start activity to Figure 5.1.

The statement you have just written is an assertion around which you could build an essay. Such an assertion is called a *thesis statement*. In this chapter, you will learn how to write effective thesis statements and how to support them with evidence. Developing a thesis is an important part of the writing process shown in Figure 5.1, which lists the skills presented in this chapter while placing them within the context of the writing process.

FIGURE 5.1
AN OVERVIEW OF THE WRITING PROCESS

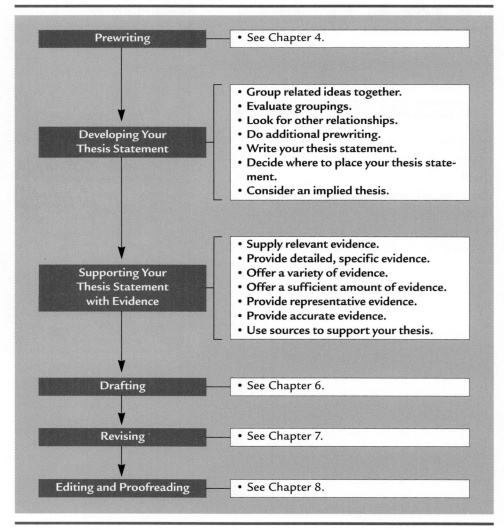

WHAT IS A THESIS STATEMENT?

A **thesis statement** is the main point of an essay; it identifies and explains what the essay will be about and often gives clues about how the essay will develop. Usually it is expressed in a single sentence. Think of a thesis statement as a promise to your reader. The rest of your essay delivers on your promise.

Here is a sample thesis statement.

Playing team sports, especially football and baseball, develops skills and qualities that can make you successful in life because these sports demand communication, teamwork, and responsibility.

In this thesis, the writer promises to show how team sports, especially football and baseball, equip players with important skills and qualities. The reader, then, expects to discover what skills and qualities football and baseball players learn and how these contribute to success in life.

DEVELOPING YOUR THESIS STATEMENT

Once in a while, for a topic that you are interested in and familiar with, a thesis may come to mind immediately. Most of the time, however, you will not be able simply to sit down and write a thesis statement. Usually, a thesis statement needs to evolve or develop as you explore your topic during prewriting. In addition to prewriting, for some topics you'll need to do research to develop a thesis. You may need to consult library sources, interview an expert, search the World Wide Web, or check statistics in an almanac, for example. Your thesis may change, too, as you work through the process of organizing supporting evidence, drafting, and revising.

For more on prewriting, see Chapter 4.

For more on library and Internet research, see Chapter 19, p.635.

TEACHING TIP: LEARNING STYLES

Remind students to tailor their thesis to the scope of the assignment. This advice is important for creative or abstract learners, who may initially choose a thesis too broad for an essay.

Your learning style can influence how you approach developing a thesis statement. If you tend to be a pragmatic or concrete learner, you may find it helpful to concentrate first on generating facts and details about your narrowed topic. Then you can develop a thesis statement that reveals what the details, taken together, demonstrate. However, if you tend to be a creative or abstract learner, you may find it easier to begin with a large idea, focus it into a thesis statement, and then generate details to support the thesis.

Coming Up with a Working Thesis Statement

To come up with a preliminary or working thesis for your paper, use the following suggestions.

CONNECTIONS

Refer students back to the Writing Quick Start on p. 95. Ask students to note which details in the cartoon are *not* relevant to the thesis they wrote.

Highlight Details that Seem to Fit Together

As you reread your prewriting, look for and highlight details that seem to fit together or those that all have to do with the same subtopic. Some students find that recopying their highlighted details on a separate sheet of paper or index cards or cutting and pasting them in a separate computer file makes it easier to rearrange the details into meaningful groups.

Here is the brainstorming that one student did on the broad topic of *animal intelligence.* As she reread her brainstorming, she noticed that most of her details dealt with the intelligence of dogs, so she highlighted those details as well as others she thought might help her come up with a working thesis.

Sample Brainstorming

Topic: Animal Intelligence

dogs seem smarter than cats

hard to know about wild animals

female dogs instinctively know how to deliver and care for their
    puppies

how to separate intelligence from instinct?

how can we measure intelligence?

there are different types

understanding commands is intelligence

choosing the best food source is intelligence

some dogs smarter than others

may vary by canine breed

dolphins have click-whistle communication system

dogs avoid danger

dogs may have learned some behaviors from ancestry as wolves

finding shelter

avoiding predators--is this instinct?

how dogs avoid predators may require intelligence

dogs can learn new behaviors--tricks

elephants recognize family members

cats know how to mark their scent on humans

my dog knows when I'm angry or depressed

ex-neighbor's dog used to pick up and bring empty water dish
    to her

retrievers can solve problems

most dogs adapt to new situations, new owners

not sure if dogs respond more to human language or nonverbal
  messages
birds can learn to imitate human speech
dogs learn to become housebroken
cats know to use litter boxes
retrievers have memory--remember where a decoy dropped
rescue dogs solve problems--missing persons
retriever rolls up clothing in order to carry it more easily

Look for Groups of Related Details

Look at the details you have highlighted, and try to find groups or sets of details
that all have to do with the same subtopic. Group these similar details together
and write a word or phrase that describes each group of related ideas.

For example, the student working on animal intelligence noticed in her brainstormed list that the details she highlighted could be grouped into three general
categories: details about learning, details about problem solving, and details about
instinct. Here is how the student rearranged her list of ideas into these three categories, rephrasing some items and adding new details as she worked.

Learning

learn to take commands
learn new tricks
learn to read master's emotions
learn to adapt to new owners
learn housebreaking
retrievers have memory--decoy; serve as guide dogs for blind
  people

Problem Solving

roll up clothing to carry it more easily
rescue dogs find victims
can warn owners about upcoming epileptic seizures
can carry empty water dish to owner

Instinct

females deliver and care for puppies
avoid danger

```
avoid predators
seek shelter
automatically raise hair on back in response to aggression
```

Evaluate Your Groupings

Once you've grouped similar details together, the next step is to decide which group or groups of ideas best represent the focus your paper should take. In some instances, one group of details will be enough to develop a working thesis for your paper. At other times, you need to use the details in two or three groups.

The student working on a thesis for the topic of animal intelligence evaluated her three groups of details on learning, problem solving, and instinct. She decided that instinct was unrelated to her topic. Consequently, she decided to write about learning and problem solving.

Do Additional Prewriting

For more on prewriting, see Chapter 4.

If you are not satisfied with how you have grouped or arranged your details or if you were not able to do so, you probably don't have enough details to come up with a good working thesis. In this case, you will need to generate more ideas through prewriting. Be sure to try a different prewriting strategy than the one you used previously. A new strategy may help you see your narrowed topic from a different perspective. If your second prewriting does not produce better results, consider refocusing or changing your topic. (It is better to realize now that a narrowed topic is not workable than after you have spent time and effort drafting your essay.)

ESSAY IN PROGRESS 1

1. If you used a prewriting strategy to generate details about your topic in response to Essay in Progress 3 in Chapter 4 (p. 91), review your prewriting, highlight useful ideas, and identify several sets of related details among those you have highlighted.
2. If you have not yet done any prewriting, choose and narrow a topic, using the guidelines provided in Chapter 4, and use one of the prewriting strategies discussed in that chapter to generate details about your narrowed topic. Then review your prewriting, highlight useful ideas, and identify several sets of related details among those you have highlighted.

Writing an Effective Thesis Statement

A thesis statement should introduce your narrowed topic, revealing what your essay is about, and state the point you will make about that topic. Your thesis statement, or a sentence following it, may also preview the organization of your essay. Use the following guidelines to write an effective thesis statement or to evaluate and revise your working thesis.

1. **Make an assertion about your narrowed topic.** An *assertion* states an idea that the remainder of the essay explains or supports. Unlike a fact, which is a statement of information, an assertion takes a position, expresses a viewpoint, or suggests your slant or angle on the narrowed topic (the approach you will take toward the topic).

TEACHING TIP

Explain that a thesis cannot be answered "yes" or "no," "true" or false"; it contains an element of explanation.

LACKS AN ASSERTION:	My Uncle George was falsely arrested for shoplifting.
REVISED:	My Uncle George's false arrest for shoplifting taught me a valuable lesson about selecting friends.

   The first thesis states a fact; the revised thesis develops an idea about the fact.

2. **Be specific and provide enough detail.** Try to provide as much information as possible about your main point.

TOO GENERAL:	I learned a great deal from my experiences as a teenage parent.
REVISED:	From my experiences as a teenage parent, I learned to accept responsibility for my own life and for that of my son.

   The first thesis is too general because it does not suggest what the student learned.

3. **Focus on *one* central point.** Limit your essay to stating and explaining one major idea.

FOCUSES ON SEVERAL POINTS:	This college should improve its tutoring services, sponsor more activities of interest to Latino students, and speed up the registration process for students.
REVISED:	To better represent the student population it serves, this college should sponsor more activities of interest to Latino students.

   The first thesis makes three separate points (the need for tutoring, activities for Latino students, and faster registration), each of which by itself could become the main point of an essay.

4. **Offer an original perspective on your narrowed topic.** If your thesis seems dull or ordinary, it probably needs more work. Search your prewriting for an interesting angle on or fresh insight about your narrowed topic.

TOO ORDINARY:	Many traffic accidents are a result of carelessness.
REVISED:	When a driver has an accident, it can change his or her entire approach to driving.

TEACHING TIP

Ask if all students agree with this thesis. Point out that a thesis is an assertion of the writer's point of view or opinion — and this is why a writer needs to provide sufficient evidence to support a thesis.

   The first thesis makes an assertion that few would dispute.

5. **Avoid announcing your main point.** Don't use phrases such as "This essay will discuss" or "The subject of my paper is." Instead, state your main point directly.

Announces the Main Point
The point I am trying to make is that people should not be allowed to smoke on campus.

This essay will discuss whether the campus newspaper represents the interests of older adult students.

Revised
The college should prohibit smoking on campus.

Our campus newspaper does not represent the needs and interests of older students.

6. **Do not hesitate to revise or change your thesis.** As you work on your essay, you may realize that your thesis is still too broad, or you may discover a more interesting approach to your narrowed topic.

7. **Use your thesis to preview the organization of the essay.** Consider using your thesis to mention the two or three key concepts on which your essay will focus, in the order in which you will discuss them.

ORIGINAL: Access to the Internet will have positive effects on high school students.

REVISED: Access to the Internet will improve the research abilities and communication skills of high school students.

POSSIBLE ANSWERS

1. It has no one central point. *Revised:* The most common cause of asthma is an allergic reaction.
2. It is neither specific nor original. *Revised:* Because it requires only a good pair of shoes and a place to run, jogging is one of the easiest aerobic sports to pursue.
3. This is a fact, not an assertion. *Revised:* The crime rate is decreasing in American cities because of more effective policing.
4. It is too broad and does not tell what the essay is about. *Revised:* Apartment dwellers have the advantages of fewer responsibilities for maintenance than home owners and more opportunities to interact with neighbors.
5. It does not tell how the points are related. *Revised:* Parents should buy toys for their children that encourage creativity.

EXERCISE 5.1

Working in a group of two or three students, discuss what is wrong with each of the following thesis statements. Then revise each thesis to make it more effective.

1. In this paper, I will discuss the causes of asthma, which include exposure to smoke, chemicals, and allergic reactions.
2. Jogging is an enjoyable aerobic sport.
3. The crime rate is decreasing in American cities.
4. Living in an apartment has many advantages.
5. Children's toys can be dangerous, instructional, or creative.

If you find it difficult to come up with a working thesis statement, one or more of the following strategies may help you.

• Arrange your details chronologically, according to their occurrence in time. You may discover a trend or sequence.

WORKING THESIS: A speaker can use numerous strategies to prepare for a speech, including planning, researching, rehearsing, and thinking positively.

• Divide your details into similarities and differences.

WORKING THESIS: The famous Kentucky Derby is similar to most other horse races, yet the consequences of winning are more far-reaching than those of any other race.

- Divide your details into causes and effects.

  WORKING THESIS:　　Because the justices who sit on the Supreme Court are appointed by the president, their attitudes and viewpoints always become a political issue during confirmation hearings.

- Divide your details into advantages and disadvantages.

  WORKING THESIS:　　Before electing to take a course on a pass-fail basis, students should weigh both the advantages and disadvantages of forgoing a letter grade.

- Divide your details into pros and cons.

  WORKING THESIS:　　A divorce may provide immediate benefits but also cause unexpected long-range problems for both the couple and their children.

ESSAY IN PROGRESS 2

Keeping your audience in mind, select one or more of the groups of ideas you identified in Essay in Progress 1 (page 100), and write a working thesis statement based on these ideas.

Placing the Thesis Statement

Your thesis statement can appear anywhere in your essay, but it is usually best to place it in the first or second paragraph as part of your introduction. When your thesis appears at the beginning of the essay, your readers will know what to pay attention to and what to expect in the rest of the essay. When your thesis is placed later in the essay, you can build up to the thesis gradually in order to prepare readers for it.

Using an Implied Thesis

In some professional writing, especially in narrative or descriptive essays, the writer may choose not to state the thesis directly. Instead, the thesis may be strongly implied by the details the writer chooses and the way those details are organized. The reader can still grasp the writer's main point even though it is not stated directly anywhere in the essay. A professional writer may use an **implied thesis** to achieve a particular dramatic or creative effect or because the thesis is so obvious it does not need to be stated directly. Until you become more practiced with essay writing, however, it is best to state your thesis directly. By doing so, you will make certain that readers will grasp the main point of your essay.

TEACHING TIP

Students who have learned the standard five-paragraph essay (introduction, three body paragraphs, conclusion), may also have learned that the thesis *must* be the last sentence of the first paragraph. Point out that while this placement has the advantage of preparing the reader, there are also advantages in using the first paragraph for an interesting anecdote or description (such as in "Pet Therapy for Heart and Soul," p. 111) before presenting the thesis of an essay in a subsequent paragraph.

TEACHING TIP

Ask students what they normally think of when they hear the word *evidence*. If they associate evidence with a legal case, they can think of the thesis as the verdict. The rest of the essay shows how the case was decided by presenting the evidence.

CONNECTIONS

Relate the concept of evidence to "Placing the Thesis Statement" on p. 103. Suggest that an important piece of evidence can serve as an effective introduction. For example, an essay on why motorists should be required to wear seat belts might begin with a story of how a life was saved by a seat belt or statistics on the number of lives seat belts save each year. The thesis statement might then be placed in the second paragraph, which would clarify or explain the introduction.

SUPPORTING YOUR THESIS STATEMENT WITH EVIDENCE

Once you have written a working thesis statement, the next step is to develop evidence that supports your thesis. **Evidence** is any type of information that clarifies, explains, or justifies your thesis. Think of evidence as reasons and other information (such as examples, statistics, or expert opinion) that will convince your reader that your thesis is reasonable or correct. This evidence, organized into well-developed paragraphs, makes up the body of your essay. To visualize the basic structure of an essay, look ahead to Figure 6.2 (p. 119).

Choosing Types of Evidence

There are many types of evidence; you need not use them all. In fact, it is usually best not to try. Instead, analyze your purpose, audience, and thesis to determine which types of evidence will be most effective. Figure 5.2 lists various types of evidence and gives examples of how each type could be used to support a working thesis on acupuncture. Note that many of the types of evidence correspond to the patterns of development discussed in Parts 3 and 4 of this text.

FIGURE 5.2
TYPES OF EVIDENCE USED TO SUPPORT A THESIS

WORKING THESIS: Acupuncture, a form of alternative medicine, is becoming more widely accepted in the United States.

Types of Evidence	*Example*
Definition	Explain that in acupuncture, needles are inserted into specific points of the body to control pain or relieve symptoms.
Historical background	Explain that acupuncture is a medical treatment that originated in ancient China.
Explanation of a process	Explain the principles on which acupuncture is based and how scientists think it works.
Factual details	Explain who uses acupuncture, on what parts of the body it is used, and under what circumstances it is applied.

(Continued on next page)

FIGURE 5.2 (continued)

Descriptive details	Explain what acupuncture needles look and feel like.
Narrative story	Relate a personal experience that illustrates the use of acupuncture.
Causes or effects	Discuss one or two theories that explain why acupuncture works. Offer reasons for its increasing popularity.
Classification	Explain types of acupuncture treatments.
Comparison and contrast	Compare acupuncture to other forms of alternative medicine, such as massage and herbal medicines. Explain how acupuncture differs from these other treatments.
Advantages and disadvantages	Describe the pros (nonsurgical, relatively painless) and cons (fear of needles) of acupuncture.
Examples	Describe situations in which acupuncture has been used successfully: by dentists, in treating alcoholism, for pain control.
Problems	Explain that acupuncture is not always practiced by medical doctors; licensing and oversight of acupuncturists may thus be lax.
Statistics	Indicate how many acupuncturists practice in the United States.
Quotations	Quote medical experts who attest to the effectiveness of acupuncture as well as those who question its value.

TEACHING TIP

Many students assume that they cannot use the first person in their essays and thus rule out certain kinds of evidence such as personal experience and anecdotal evidence. Discuss your position on this issue with your students.

EXERCISE 5.2

1. Working in a group of two to three students, discuss and list the types of evidence that could be used to support the following thesis statement for an informative essay.

   The pressure to become financially independent is a challenge for many young adults and often causes them to develop social and emotional problems.

2. For each audience here, discuss and list the types of evidence that would offer the best support for the preceding thesis.

POSSIBLE ANSWERS

1. *Types of evidence:* Personal experience; anecdotes about friends or relatives; the causes of such pressure (demands of peers or parents); comparison with other types of pressure; examples of social or emotional problems; statistics on the cost of living, average salaries and levels of debt for young adults; quotations from experts on financial planning or mental health.

2. (a) *Young adults:* Personal experience or anecdotes; examples of social or emotional problems; comparison with other types

(Continued on next page)

of pressure; statistics.
(b) *Parents of young adults:* Anecdotes about friends or relatives; causes of such pressure, comparison with other types of pressure; statistics; quotations from experts. (c) *Counselors of young adults:* causes of such pressure; statistics; quotations from experts.

a. Young adults
b. Parents of young adults
c. Counselors of young adults

Collecting Evidence to Support Your Thesis

Prewriting may help you collect evidence for your thesis. Try a different prewriting strategy than the one you used previously to arrive at a working thesis statement. Depending on your learning style, select one or more of the following suggestions to generate evidence that supports your thesis.

Learning Style Options

1. Complete the worksheet shown in Figure 5.3. For one or more types of evidence listed in the left column of the worksheet, give examples that support your thesis in the right column. It is *not* necessary to collect evidence for all of the listed types. Choose only those types that are appropriate for your thesis.

FIGURE 5.3
A WORKSHEET FOR COLLECTING EVIDENCE

TEACHING TIP: COLLABORATIVE WRITING

(30 minutes) Emphasize the difference between a thesis and the evidence provided to support it by involving students in a class debate. Choose a thesis with two clearly defined opposing positions (such as the right of states to require motorists to wear seat belts). Divide the class into two groups—one for each position. The groups should brainstorm a list of supporting evidence for their positions before carrying out the debate.

Purpose: _____

Audience: _____

Point of View: _____

Thesis Statement: _____

_____

Type of Evidence	Actual Evidence
Definition	
Historical background	
Explanation of a process	
Factual details	

(Continued on next page)

FIGURE 5.3 (*continued*)

Type of Evidence	Actual Evidence
Descriptive details	
Narrative story	
Causes or effects	
Classification	
Comparison and contrast	
Advantages and disadvantages	
Examples	
Problems	
Statistics	
Quotations	

2. Visualize yourself speaking to your audience. What would you say to convince your audience of your thesis? Jot down ideas as they come to you.

3. On a sheet of paper or in a computer file, develop a skeletal outline of major headings. Leave plenty of blank space under each heading. Fill in ideas about each heading as they come to you.

4. Draw a graphic organizer of your essay, filling in supporting evidence as you think of it.

5. Discuss your thesis statement with a classmate; try to explain why he or she should accept your thesis as valid.

For more on outlining, see Chapter 6, p. 125.

See p. 40 in Chapter 2 for instructions on drawing a graphic organizer. For samples of graphic organizers for each pattern of development, see Parts 3 and 4.

ESSAY IN PROGRESS 3

Using the preceding list of suggestions for collecting evidence to support a thesis, generate at least three different types of evidence to support the working thesis statement you wrote in Essay in Progress 2 (p. 103).

Choosing the Best Evidence

In collecting evidence in support of a thesis, you will probably generate more than you need. Consequently, you will need to identify the evidence that best supports your thesis and that suits your purpose and audience. Your learning style can also influence the way you select evidence and the kinds of evidence you favor. If you are a creative or an abstract learner, for example, you may tend to focus on large ideas and overlook the need for supporting detail. However, if you are a pragmatic or concrete learner, you may tend to generate too many facts and details, in which case you would need to select the most essential information and then concentrate on organizing your evidence logically.

The following guidelines will also help you select the types of evidence that will best support your thesis.

1. **Make sure the evidence is relevant.** All of your evidence must clearly and directly support your thesis. Irrelevant evidence will only distract your readers and cause them to question the validity of your thesis. Suppose your thesis is that acupuncture, as a form of alternative medicine, is useful for controlling pain. You would not need to describe other, less popular alternative therapies because that information would not establish acupuncture as a means of controlling pain.

TEACHING TIP
Demonstrate the effectiveness of specific rather than general evidence by offering examples of both to students and asking them which is most convincing and memorable. For example, compare "In the nineteenth century, immigrants had inadequate housing" with "Two or more immigrant families were often forced to share an apartment and sleep three to a bed."

2. **Provide specific evidence.** Avoid general statements that will neither engage your readers nor help you make a convincing case for your thesis. Instead, be as specific as possible. For instance, to support the thesis that acupuncture is becoming more widely accepted by patients in the United States, the statements "It is becoming more widely accepted because it is relatively painless" and "A growing number of acupuncturists practice in the United States" are too broad to be effective. Readers are more likely to be convinced that acupuncture is painless by precise details about how acupuncture feels: "Most patients report feeling only a mild pin prick or a slight tingling sensation." Similarly, statistics that demonstrate an increase in the number of practicing acupuncturists in the United States over the past five years would help to demonstrate that the demand for acupuncture is growing.

For more on conducting research, see Chapter 19.

To locate detailed, specific evidence, return to your prewriting or use a different prewriting strategy to generate concrete evidence. If, for example, you already used mapping, try visualizing or questioning to help you concentrate on details. You may also need to conduct research to find evidence for your thesis.

3. **Offer a variety of evidence.** Try to offer your readers several different types of evidence. Using diverse kinds of evidence increases the likelihood that your evidence will convince your readers. That is, some readers may not be convinced by one type of evidence, but they may be convinced by another. If you provide only four examples of people who have found acupuncture helpful, for example, many of your readers may conclude that these few isolated examples are not convincing. If you provide statistics and quotations from experts along with an example or two, however, more readers are likely to accept your thesis because you have quoted experts and cited statistics that they find credible and convincing. Using different types of evidence also shows readers that you are knowledgeable and informed about your topic, thus enhancing your credibility.

4. **Provide a sufficient amount of evidence.** In order for readers to accept your thesis, you must provide enough evidence, but the amount you need will vary according to your audience and your topic. To discover whether you have provided a sufficient amount of evidence, ask a classmate to read your essay and tell you whether he or she is convinced. If your reader is not convinced, ask him or her what additional evidence is needed.

5. **Provide representative evidence.** Be sure the evidence you supply is typical and usual. Do not choose unusual, rare, or exceptional situations as evidence. Suppose your thesis is that acupuncture is widely used for various types of surgery. An example of a person who underwent painless heart surgery using only acupuncture without anesthesia will not support your thesis unless the use of acupuncture in heart surgery is routine. Including such an example would mislead your reader and, should your reader realize that the example is not typical, would bring your credibility into question.

6. **Provide accurate evidence from reliable sources.** Gather your information from reliable sources. Do not guess at statistics or make estimates. If you are not certain of the accuracy of a fact or statistic, verify it through research. For example, do not estimate that "hundreds of acupuncturists who are also medical doctors are now licensed to practice in the United States." Instead, find out and state exactly how many U.S. physicians are licensed to practice acupuncture.

ESSAY IN PROGRESS 4

Evaluate the evidence you generated in Essay in Progress 3 (p. 108). Select from it the evidence that you could use to support your thesis in a two- to four-page essay.

Using Sources to Support Your Thesis

For many topics you will need to research library or Internet sources or interview an expert on your topic in order to collect enough supporting evidence for your thesis. Chapter 19 provides a thorough guide to locating sources in the library and

TEACHING TIP

Point out that some forms of evidence appeal to a reader's emotions (narrative and descriptive details) while other forms appeal more to the intellect (factual details, statistics, definitions). (Refer to Figure 5.2.) Also point out that, depending on the writer's purpose and audience, one or both kinds of evidence may be appropriate.

For more on choosing reliable sources, see Chapter 19, p. 645.

on the Internet, and it also includes tips for conducting interviews (p. 662). See especially the section on "Using Sources to Add Detail to an Essay" on page 629. Chapter 20 provides guidelines for incorporating and documenting sources.

ESSAY IN PROGRESS 5

For the thesis statement you wrote in Essay in Progress 2 (p. 103), locate and consult at least two sources to find evidence that supports your thesis.

STUDENTS WRITE

In the Students Write section of Chapter 4, you saw how student writer Tina Oyer narrowed her topic and generated ideas for her narrative essay about an event that caused her to learn something about herself. You also saw how she decided to focus on an incident at work when a customer had left her keys in the store.

CONNECTIONS

Refer students to Chapter 6, p. 148, to see where Tina Oyer places her thesis in the first draft of her essay.

After reviewing her responses to questions about her topic and her freewriting, Oyer decided that the event taught her that she could rely on her own instincts. She then wrote the following working thesis statement.

```
When faced with a difficult situation, I can trust my
instincts and rely on my ability to make good decisions.
```

To generate more details that would support her thesis, Oyer did more freewriting and brainstorming to help her recall the events of that evening at work. She also used visualization to recreate the main events of the evening. Here's an excerpt from what she wrote:

```
    --Stormy, cold wintry night
    --Everybody was busy all evening; some clerks bagging
customer's purchases, others pricing stock.
    --Owner was wearing his usual "white, 'I am in charge'
uniform."
    --It is the end of the evening and I am putting cash in the
iron safe, getting ready to close.
    --A woman dressed in leggings and a ski parka rushes up to
the store.
    --Looking for keys to her car--asks owner to check for them.
    --She seems distraught and nervous.
    --Owner never said a word to her--just went back in.
    --He wasn't gone but 20 or 30 seconds--or at least it seemed
only that long.
```

WORKING WITH TEXT

Pet Therapy for Heart and Soul
Kerry Pechter

The following essay by Kerry Pechter was first published in 1985 in Preven-tion *magazine, a periodical that focuses on promoting a healthy lifestyle. Later the article appeared in a collection of essays,* Your Emotional Health and Well-Being (1989). *Pechter supports the essay's thesis with a variety of evidence. As you read, underline the thesis statement and highlight the types of evidence that are offered to support it.*

PREREADING
QUESTIONS
• Who would be a typi-
cal reader of *Prevention*
magazine?
• What are the benefits
of pet therapy?

1   It's exercise hour at the Tacoma Lutheran Home in the state of Washington, and P.T., an exotic yellow-crested bird called a cockatiel, is having the time of his life. He's sitting on the foot of 81-year-old Ben Ereth, riding in circles while Ben pedals vigorously on an exercise bicycle. The bird likes it so much that if Mr. Ereth stops too soon, he'll squawk at him.

2   A bizarre sort of activity to find in a nursing home? Not at Tacoma Lutheran. Three years ago, the nursing home adopted an angora rabbit. Then a puppy. Then tropical birds. The home's elderly residents have taken to these animals with a passion. And, says Virginia Davis, director of resident services, the animals have breathed enthusiasm into what otherwise might have been a listless nursing home atmosphere.

3   "The animals help in several ways," says Davis. "One of the cockatiels gives a wolf whistle whenever anyone passes its cage. That gives them an unexpected boost in morale. And the birds seem to alleviate the tension associated with exercise. They make exercise more acceptable and relaxing."

4   What's happening at Tacoma Lutheran is just one example of an increasingly popular phenomenon called pet therapy. Although humans have adopted pets for thousands of years, only recently have social scientists taken a close look at the nature of the relationship that people form with dogs, cats and other "companion animals."

5   At places like the Center for the Interaction of Animals and Society in Philadelphia and the Center for the Study of Human Animal Relationships and Environments (CENSHARE) in Minneapolis, they've discovered that there is something mutually therapeutic about these relationships. They say that pets relax us, help us communicate with each other, build our self-esteem and comfort us when we're feeling down.

TEACHING TIP

Paragraphs 1–6 Ask students: What kind of evidence begins this essay? Why does the evidence precede the thesis? Does the evidence appeal more to the intellect or the emotions?

TEACHING TIP

Paragraph 2 Identify the intentional sentence fragments here and explain why they are used in this context.

6   In fact, many now believe that pets play a small but very significant role in determining how well, for example, a heart attack survivor recuperates, how a family handles domestic strife, whether a disturbed teenager grows up straight or even whether a nursing home resident like Mr. Ereth enjoys and sticks to his daily exercycle program.

7   Pet animals, in short, may affect our health.

ANIMAL MAGNETISM AT WORK

8   Pet therapists have put these capacities to work in a variety of ways. Pet therapy is very often used, for example, to combat the isolation and loneliness so common in nursing homes. At the Tacoma Lutheran Home, Davis has found that the pets help many residents break their customary silence.

9   "Animals are a catalyst for conversation," she says. "Most people can remember a story from their past about a pet animal. And people are more comfortable talking to animals than they are to people. Sometimes a person who hasn't spoken for a long time, or one who has had a stroke and doesn't talk, will talk to an animal."

10   Animals also seem to draw everyone into the conversation. "Even in a nursing home, there are some people who are more attractive or responsive than others," says Phil Arkow, of the Humane Society of the Pike's Peak Region in Colorado, who drives a "Petmobile" to local nursing homes. "Human visitors try not to do it, but they inevitably focus on those who are most attractive. But animals don't make those distinctions. They focus on everyone equally."

11   A person doesn't have to live in a nursing home, however, in order to reap the benefits of a pet. Pets typically influence the communication that goes on between family members in a normal household. During a research project a few years ago, University of Maryland professor Ann Cain, Ph.D., discovered that pets help spouses and siblings express highly charged feelings.

12   "When family members want to say something to each other that they can't say directly," Dr. Cain says, "they might say it to the pet and let the other person overhear it. That also lets the listener off the hook, because he doesn't have to respond directly."

13   Though it's still in the experimental stage, researchers are discovering that watching or petting friendly animals—not only dogs and cats but almost any pet—can produce the kind of deep relaxation usually associated with meditation, biofeedback and hypnosis. This kind of relaxing effect is so good that it can actually lower blood pressure.

14   At the University of Pennsylvania's Center for the Interaction of Animals and Society, for instance, Dr. Katcher and Dr. Friedmann monitored the blood pressure of healthy children while the children

were sitting quietly or reading aloud, either with or without a dog in the room. Their blood pressure was always lower when the dog was in the room.

The researchers went on to discover, remarkably, that looking at fish could temporarily reduce the blood pressure of patients with hypertension. In one widely reported study, they found that the systolic and diastolic pressure of people with high blood pressure dipped into the normal range when they gazed at an aquarium full of colorful tropical fish, green plants and rocks for 20 minutes. 15

This calming power of pets has found at least a few noteworthy applications. In Chicago, one volunteer from the Anti-Cruelty Society took an animal to a hospital and arranged for a surgical patient to be greeted by it when he awoke from anesthesia. "It's a comforting way to come back to reality," says one volunteer. "For children, pets can make a hospital seem safer. It's a reminder of home." 16

TEACHING TIP

Ask students to identify successful transitions that allow the reader to move smoothly from one idea to another (such as in the first sentence of paragraph 16).

Animals may also have the power to soften the aggressive tendencies of disturbed adolescents. At Winslow Therapeutic Riding Unlimited, Inc., in Warwick, New York, where horseback riding is used to help handicapped children of all kinds, problem teenagers seem to behave differently when they're put on a horse. 17

"These are kids who fight in school. Some of their fathers are alcoholics," says Mickey Pulis of the nonprofit facility. "But when they come here, they're different. When they groom and tack the horses, they learn about the gentle and caring side of life." 18

"The horse seems to act like an equalizer," she says. "It doesn't care what reading levels these kids are at. It accepts them as they are." 19

Ultimately, researchers like Dr. Friedmann believe that the companionship of pets can reduce a person's risk of dying from stress-related illnesses, such as heart disease. 20

"The leading causes of mortality and morbidity in the United States are stress-related or life-style related," she says. "Pets, by decreasing the level of arousal and moderating the stress response, can help slow the progression of those diseases or even prevent them." 21

PETS ARE COMFORTING

But what is it about pets that make them capable of all this? And why do millions of people go to the trouble and expense of keeping them? Pet therapists offer several answers. 22

For one thing, animals don't talk back to us. Researchers have discovered that a person's blood pressure goes up whenever he talks to another person. But we talk to animals in a different way, often touching them at the same time, which minimizes stress. 23

24   Another theory holds that pets remind us of our ancestral link with other animals. "By domesticating an animal, man demonstrates his kinship to nature," Dr. Levinson once wrote. "A human being has to remain in contact with all of nature throughout his lifetime if he is to maintain good mental health."

25   Dr. Corson, on the other hand, says that we love pets because they are perpetual infants. Human infants charm us, but they eventually grow up. Pets never do. They never stop being cuddly and dependent. Likewise, pets are faithful. "Pets can offer a relationship that is more constant than relationships with people," says Dr. Cain. "You can count on them."

26   Some argue that the most important ingredient in our relationships with animals is that we can touch them whenever we want to. "Having access to affectionate touch that is not related to sex is important," says Dr. Katcher. "If you want to touch another person, you can't always do it immediately. But with pets you can."   ■

Examining the Reading

1. Describe the effects of placing animals in nursing homes.
2. In what situations, other than nursing homes, are pets beneficial?
3. What reasons does Pechter offer to explain the positive effects of pets on humans?
4. Define each of the following words as it is used in the essay: *bizarre* (paragraph 2), *alleviate* (paragraph 3), *therapeutic* (paragraph 5), *catalyst* (paragraph 9), and *morbidity* (paragraph 21).

Analyzing the Reading

1. State the author's thesis in your own words. Then, using the guidelines on pages 101–102, evaluate the effectiveness of the thesis.
2. To what audience does Pechter address this essay? What purpose does the essay fulfill? How do you think the audience and purpose affect the author's choice of evidence?
3. What types of evidence does the author use to support the thesis? Which type does the author rely on most? What other types of evidence could the author have used? (Refer to Figure 5.2 for a summary of the various types of evidence.)
4. Do you think the author provides sufficient evidence for you to accept the thesis? Why or why not?

5. Cite one paragraph from the essay in which you think the author provides detailed, specific information. Explain why you chose it.

Reacting to the Reading: Discussion and Journal Writing

1. How do you think this essay would change if the writer wrote it for readers of *Dog Fancy*, a magazine for dog owners?
2. Most pet owners talk to their pets even though the pets probably do not understand most of what is said. In what sense is this "talk" therapeutic?
3. In your journal, write about other activities or types of recreation that you find relaxing or comforting because they remind you of your kinship to nature.

tion that will help them improve their health. The essay's purpose is to inform readers about the benefits of having a pet. Because *Prevention* is a general-interest magazine, not a journal for health care professionals, Pechter chooses evidence that is interesting and amusing, but not overly technical.

3. Pechter cites examples (paragraph 1), expert opinion (11 and 12), the results of research studies (14), and causes (23–25), but relies most heavily on examples. Pechter could also possibly have used personal experience, comparisons with other types of therapy, and statistics.
4. Answers will vary.
5. Answers will vary.

POSSIBLE ANSWERS: REACTING TO THE READING

1. The thesis would be narrowed further to cover only the therapeutic effects of dogs; the author would probably include examples of how dogs and humans interact. (As a follow-up to this question, ask students to rewrite the introduction to the essay for the readers of *Dog Fancy.*)
2. Responses will vary. One possibility: Pet owners probably feel safe in letting out their feelings, knowing that the animal will provide affection but will not judge them.
3. Responses will vary.

Phyllis Itoka, from Liberia, is 21 years old. The clothes she is wearing are the kind she wears in Liberia, where, she says, "anything Western is popular."

Adolfo Sarni, from Italy, is 23 years old. He bought his sweater in Rome, his pants in Milan, and his shoes in the United States. He notes that his look is "very trendy."

Rona Aharonson, from Israel, is 19 years old. Her jeans are from a Levi's store in Israel. According to Aharonson, jeans and T-shirts are popular in Israel.

Chapter 6

Suppose an anthropology instructor begins a lecture by asking the question, "What is 'typical' casual dress in today's world?" Then she projects the three photographs shown on the opposite page on a screen and asks the same question again. She notes that each photograph portrays a young person from a different country dressed in casual attire.

Drafting an Essay

Writing Quick Start

Assume you are in this instructor's anthropology class. Working alone or in a group of two or three classmates, write a topic sentence that asserts a point the three photographs illustrate about casual dress in today's global society. Then, list details (evidence) from the three photo-graphs and their captions that support the topic sentence. Number the details in your list so that the strongest evidence for your topic sentence is labeled *1*, the next strongest is *2*, and so on. Finally, write a paragraph that begins with the topic sentence and includes the evidence you have listed, arranged in the order you have determined.

TEACHING TIP:
COLLABORATIVE
WRITING

(15 minutes) Discuss
the importance of
understanding a reader's
assumptions.

• Have students work
together to brainstorm
contrasts between the
casual dress depicted
in the photos on page
116 and other types of
dress they might wear
in other situations,
such as a job inter-
view.

• Have students discuss
what people in these
other situations might
expect them to wear.

• As a class, briefly discuss the importance of
understanding what
the reader expects in a
piece of writing.

The paragraph you have just written could be part of an essay on the topic of how "casual dress" is similar, or different, in different countries. To write an essay of two to four pages, you would need to do additional prewriting and research to learn more about this narrowed topic and to obtain more supporting information. Then you would write a thesis statement, draft your essay by developing supporting paragraphs, write an effective introduction and conclusion, and choose a good title. This chapter will guide you through the process of developing an essay in support of a thesis statement, as part of the writing process shown in Figure 6.1.

THE STRUCTURE OF AN ESSAY

Think of an essay as a complete piece of writing, much as a textbook chapter is. A textbook chapter has a title that suggests the main topic. For example, *human rights* might be the main topic of a chapter in a textbook on international relations. The first few paragraphs of the chapter would probably introduce the concept of human rights by defining it and describing several situations in which

TEACHING TIP:
CHAPTER OVERVIEW

• Point out that all peo-
ple have the instinct to
prioritize and orga-
nize, even though
some seem to do so
more naturally than
others. Ask students to
give examples of how
they set priorities and
organize in their every-
day lives.

• For this chapter, con-
sider grouping spatial
learners and others
with strong organiza-
tional skills with cre-
ative learners and
others with weak orga-
nizational skills.

**FIGURE 6.1
AN OVERVIEW OF THE WRITING PROCESS**

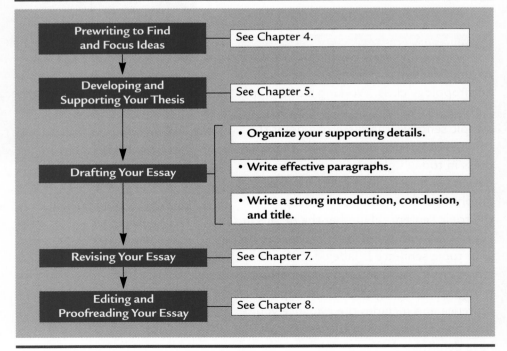

Prewriting to Find and Focus Ideas — See Chapter 4.

Developing and Supporting Your Thesis — See Chapter 5.

Drafting Your Essay
• Organize your supporting details.
• Write effective paragraphs.
• Write a strong introduction, conclusion, and title.

Revising Your Essay — See Chapter 7.

Editing and Proofreading Your Essay — See Chapter 8.

human rights is an issue. The chapter might then assert that human rights is a controversial global issue of growing importance. The rest of the chapter would explain the issue by tracing its history, examining why it is a world issue, and discussing its current status. The chapter would conclude with a summary.

Similarly, as you can see in Figure 6.2, an essay has a title and an introduction. It also makes an assertion, called the **thesis statement**, and that assertion is

FIGURE 6.2
THE STRUCTURE OF AN ESSAY: PARTS AND FUNCTIONS

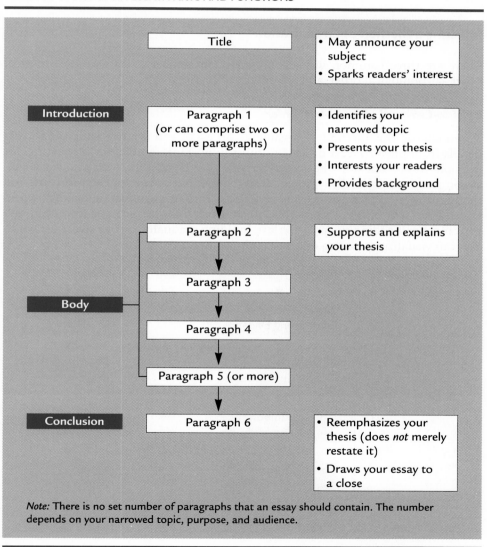

| Title | • May announce your subject |
| | • Sparks readers' interest |

Introduction
Paragraph 1 (or can comprise two or more paragraphs)
• Identifies your narrowed topic
• Presents your thesis
• Interests your readers
• Provides background

Paragraph 2
• Supports and explains your thesis

Paragraph 3

Body

Paragraph 4

Paragraph 5 (or more)

Conclusion
Paragraph 6
• Reemphasizes your thesis (does *not* merely restate it)
• Draws your essay to a close

Note: There is no set number of paragraphs that an essay should contain. The number depends on your narrowed topic, purpose, and audience.

explained and supported throughout the body of the essay. The essay ends with a final statement, its conclusion.

ORGANIZING YOUR SUPPORTING DETAILS

For more on developing a thesis and selecting evidence to support it, see Chapter 5.

CONNECTIONS
Explain that these sequencing strategies also work with the patterns of development discussed in Chapters 9–16 and 18. Most Guided Writing Assignments in these chapters discuss how to use one or more methods of organization.

The body of your essay contains the paragraphs that support your thesis. Before you begin writing these body paragraphs, decide on the supporting evidence you will use and the order in which you will present your evidence.

Selecting a Method of Organization

There are three common ways to organize ideas: most-to-least or least-to-most order, chronological order, and spatial order

Most-to-Least or Least-to-Most Order

If you choose this method of organizing an essay, you arrange your supporting details from most to least or least to most important, familiar, or interesting, for example, or by some other key characteristic. You might begin with your most convincing evidence and then present less compelling evidence to reinforce it. You might arrange facts, statistics, and examples from most to least shocking, expensive, difficult, or serious. Alternately, if you work from least to most, you can save your most compelling evidence for last, building gradually to your strongest point. You can visualize these two options as shown here.

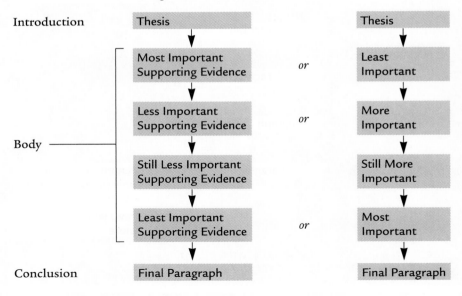

A student, Robin Ferguson, working on the thesis statement "Work as a literacy volunteer taught me more about learning and friendship than I ever expected," identified four primary benefits related to her thesis.

BENEFITS

- I learned about the learning process.
- I developed a permanent friendship with my student, Marie.
- Marie built self-confidence.
- I discovered the importance of reading.

Ferguson then chose to arrange these benefits from least to most important and decided that the friendship was the most important benefit. Here is how she organized her supporting evidence.

WORKING THESIS

Working as a literacy volunteer taught me more about learning and friendship than I ever expected.

LEAST	Supporting paragraph 1:	Learned about the learning process
TO	Supporting paragraph 2:	Discovered the importance of reading for Marie
MOST	Supporting paragraph 3:	Marie increased her self-confidence
IMPORTANT	Supporting paragraph 4:	Developed a permanent friendship

EXERCISE 6.1

For each of the following narrowed topics, identify several qualities or characteristics that you could use to organize details in most-to-least or least-to-most order.

1. Three stores in which you shop
2. Three friends
3. Three members of a sports team
4. Three fast-food restaurants
5. Three television shows you watched this week

TEACHING TIP:
LEARNING STYLES

(15–20 minutes) Give students the option of working independently or in small groups.

POSSIBLE ANSWERS

1. Clothing stores: expense of merchan-
(Continued on next page)

Chronological Order

When you arrange your supporting details in **chronological order,** you put them in the order in which they happened, according to a clock or calendar. When using this method of organization, begin the body of your essay with the first example or event and progress through the others as they occurred, ending with the one that happened last. Chronological order is commonly used in narrative essays and process analyses. You can visualize this order as follows.

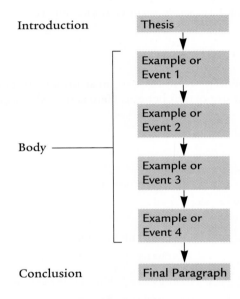

As an example, let's suppose Robin Ferguson, writing about her experiences as a literacy volunteer, decides to demonstrate her thesis by relating the events of a typical tutoring session. In this case, she might organize her essay by narrating the events in the order in which they usually occur. She might begin by describing her client's friendly but anxious greeting: "Wonderful! You're here. Every week, I worry that you won't be able to come." She might then move through other events and conversations in the order in which they typically happened, using each detail about the session to demonstrate what tutoring taught her about learning and friendship.

EXERCISE 6.2

Working alone or with a classmate, identify at least one thesis statement from those listed below that could be supported by chronological paragraphs. Write a few sentences explaining how you would use chronological order to support this thesis.

1. European mealtimes differ from those of many American visitors, much to the visitors' surprise and discomfort.

2. Despite the many pitfalls that await those who shop at auctions, people can find bargains if they prepare in advance.
3. My first day of kindergarten was the most traumatic experience of my childhood, one that permanently shaped my view of education.

Spatial Order

When you use **spatial order,** you organize details about your subject according to their location or position in space. Consider, for example, how you might use spatial order to support the thesis that modern movie theaters are designed to shut out the outside world and create a separate reality within. You could begin by describing the ticket booth, then the lobby, and finally the individual theaters, mentioning details that support your thesis. Similarly, to support the thesis that the layout of a football stadium is carefully planned to handle large crowds, you might start by describing the size and organization of the parking lot, then discuss how the ticket booths and entrance gates are structured, and finally explain the arrangement of the stands. You might describe a basketball court from right to left or a person from head to toe. The student writing about her experience as a literacy volunteer could describe her classroom or meeting area from front to back or left to right. Spatial organization is commonly used in descriptive essays as well as in classification and division essays.

You can best visualize spatial organization by picturing your subject in your mind or by sketching it on paper. "Look" at your subject systematically—from top to bottom, inside to outside, front to back. Cut it into imaginary sections or pieces and describe each piece.

You can visualize an essay that uses spatial order as follows.

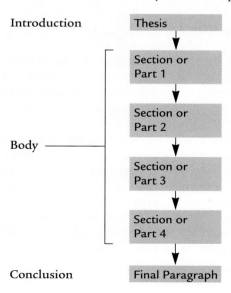

POSSIBLE ANSWERS

1. A writer could narrate the events of a day spent as a tourist in another country, describing when he or she was hungry and when meals were available.
2. A writer could narrate the events of a typical auction, first describing the process of preparing to attend the auction.
3. A writer could describe the events of that day in chronological order, building up to the most traumatic event.

EXERCISE 6.3

Working alone or with a classmate, identify one thesis statement listed below that could be supported by means of spatial organization. Write a few sentences explaining how you would use spatial order to support this thesis.

1. Our family's yearly vacation at a cabin in Maine provides us with a much needed opportunity to renew family ties.
2. The Allentown Theatre's set for Tennessee Williams's play *A Streetcar Named Desire* was simple, yet striking and effective.
3. Although a pond in winter may seem frozen and lifeless, this appearance is deceptive.

ESSAY IN PROGRESS 1

Choose one of the follow activities.

1. Using the thesis statement and evidence you gathered for the Essay in Progress activities in Chapter 5, choose a method for organizing your essay. Then explain briefly how you will use that method of organization.
2. Choose one of the following narrowed topics. Then, using the steps in the Overview of the Writing Process, (see Figure 6.1 on p. 118), prewrite to produce ideas, develop a thesis, and generate evidence to support the thesis. Next, choose a method for organizing your essay. Explain briefly how you will use that method of organization.
   a. Positive or negative experiences with computers
   b. Stricter (or more lenient) regulations for teenage drivers
   c. Factors that account for the popularity of Disney films (or children's films in general)
   d. Discipline in public elementary schools
   e. Advantages or disadvantages of health maintenance organizations (HMOs)

Writing or Drawing an Organizational Plan

Once you have written a thesis statement and chosen a method of organization for your essay, take a few minutes to write an outline or draw a graphic organizer of the essay's main points, in the order you plan to discuss them. Making an organizational plan is an especially important step when your essay is long or deals with a complex topic.

Outlining, or drawing a graphic organizer, can help you plan your essay as well as discover new ideas to include. Either method will help you see how ideas fit together and may reveal places where you need to add supporting information.

There are three types of outlines—informal, topic, and sentence outlines. An *informal* outline, also called a scratch outline, is a list of main points and subpoints, written in key words and phrases. An informal outline does not necessarily follow the standard outline format of numbered and lettered headings (described below). The outline of Robin Ferguson's essay on p. 126 is an example of an informal outline.

Two other types of outlines are topic and sentence outlines. A *topic* outline uses only key words and phrases, while a *sentence* outline uses complete sentences. Both follow the standard outline format, with Roman numerals (I, II), capital letters (A, B), Arabic numbers (1, 2), and lowercase letters (a, b) designating levels of importance. In a topic or sentence outline, less important entries are indented, as the example below shows.

Standard Outline Format

I.   First main topic

   A.   First subtopic of I

   B.   Second subtopic of I

      1.   First detail about I.B

      2.   Second detail about I.B

   C.   Third subtopic of I

      1.   First detail about I.C

         (a)   First detail or example about I.C.1

         (b)   Second detail or example about I.C.1

      2.   Second detail about I.C.

II.   Second main topic

Remember that all items labeled with the same designation (capital letters, for example) should be of parallel importance, and each must explain or support the topic or subtopic under which it is placed. Also, all items at the same level should be grammatically parallel.

NOT PARALLEL:	I.	Dietary Problems
	A.	Consuming too much fat
	B.	High refined-sugar consumption
PARALLEL:	I.	Dietary Problems
	A.	Consuming too much fat
	B.	Consuming too much refined sugar

Be sure to indent your outline as shown in the standard outline format above and begin each topic or sentence with a capital letter.

If your instructor allows, you can use both phrases and sentences within an outline, as long as you do so consistently. You might write all subtopics (designated by capital letters A, B, and so on) as sentences and supporting details (designated by 1, 2, and so on) as phrases, for instance.

2. Have students work solo for 15–20 minutes, brainstorming, developing a thesis, and generating supporting evidence. Then pair up students who have chosen option 2 to share and respond to one other's writing. Students should determine whether their partner's thesis is clear, specific, and supportable and evaluate the writer's method of organization.

TEACHING TIP: LEARNING STYLES

• Rational or concrete learners may benefit from rearranging their informal outlines, marking their changes with arrows or numbers as they experiment to discover an effective organization.

For more on parallel structure, see Chapter 8, p. 195.

• Creative, verbal, pragmatic, and spatial learners may benefit from using 4- by 6-inch index cards. Have them write one main point on each card (corresponding to one roman numeral section in a formal outline), arrange the cards on a flat surface, and move the cards around to discover the most effective organization.

If you have a pragmatic learning style, a verbal learning style, or both, preparing an outline will probably appeal to you. If you are a creative or spatial learner, however, you may prefer to draw a graphic organizer. Whichever method you find most appealing, begin by putting your working thesis statement at the top of a piece of paper or word-processing document. Then list your main points below your thesis. Be sure to leave plenty of space between main points. While you are filling in the details that support one main point, you will often think of details or examples to use in support of a different main point. As these details or examples occur to you, jot them down under, or next to, the appropriate main point of your outline or graphic organizer.

The following sample outline and the graphic organizer shown in Figure 6.3 were done for Ferguson's essay. Recall that Ferguson had decided to use a least-to-most important method of organization. As you read her outline, notice that she follows the organization shown in the graphic organizer on p. 127.

For more about graphic organizers, see Chapter 2, p. 40.

COMPUTER HINT

Students who prefer to work on a computer may experiment with an informal outline or graphic organizer (see Figure 6.3).

- Most word-processing programs have tabs and bullets that make it easy to construct informal outlines.
- Some computer programs — e.g., spreadsheet programs — construct flowcharts with a few mouse clicks.

INFORMAL OUTLINE

<u>Thesis</u>   Working as a literacy volunteer taught me more about learning and friendship than I ever expected.

<u>Paragraph 1</u>   Learned about the learning process
- Went through staff training program
- Learned about words "in context"

<u>Paragraph 2</u>   Discovered the importance of reading for Marie
- Couldn't take bus, walked to grocery store
- Couldn't buy certain products
- Couldn't write out grocery list

<u>Paragraph 3</u>   Marie increased her self-confidence
- Made rapid progress
- Began taking bus
- Helped son with reading

<u>Paragraph 4</u>   Developed a permanent friendship
- Saw each other often
- Both single parents
- Helped each other baby-sit

<u>Conclusion</u>   I benefited more than Marie did.

FIGURE 6.3
SAMPLE GRAPHIC ORGANIZER

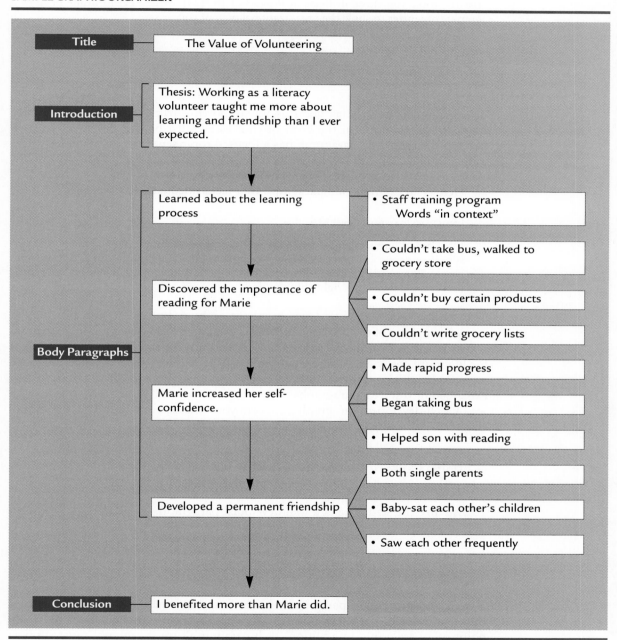

ESSAY IN PROGRESS 2

For the topic you chose in Essay in Progress 1 (p. 124), write a brief outline or draw a graphic organizer to show the organizational plan of your essay.

WRITING EFFECTIVE PARAGRAPHS

Your essay can only be as good as its supporting paragraphs. Therefore, each supporting paragraph in the body of your essay must be well developed. A well-developed supporting paragraph has a focused topic sentence and includes definitions, explanations, examples, or other evidence that supports the thesis of the essay. It must also use transitions and repetition to show how ideas are related.

Here is an example of a paragraph that lacks adequate development.

UNDERDEVELOPED PARAGRAPH

Capital punishment is wrong for several reasons. It's not right to kill another person. If someone kills another person, he or she should be given life in prison without parole. This sentence is probably worse than capital punishment. It may be more costly for society, but it's the right thing to do.

This paragraph offers several statements of opinion, but it does not provide evidence in support of those opinions. Why should a murderer be given life imprisonment? Why is a life sentence worse than capital punishment? Why is imprisonment for life more costly and the right thing to do? As is often true of underdeveloped paragraphs, this paragraph contains several broad topics, each of which should be expanded into several paragraphs.

A well-developed paragraph supports your thesis, contributes to the overall effectiveness of your essay, and contains three parts:

- A well-focused topic sentence
- Unified, specific supporting details
- Transitions and repetition to show how the ideas are related

To visualize the structure of a well-developed paragraph, see Figure 6.4.

Writing Well-Focused Topic Sentences

A topic sentence is to a paragraph what a thesis statement is to an essay. Just as a thesis announces the main point of an essay, a **topic sentence** states the main point of a paragraph. In addition, each paragraph's topic sentence must support

FIGURE 6.4
THE STRUCTURE OF A PARAGRAPH

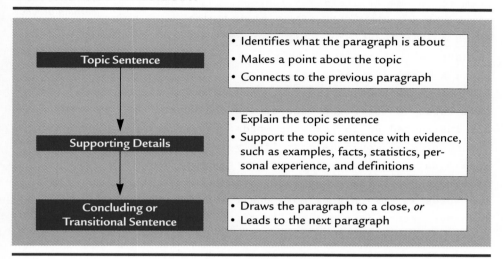

the thesis of the essay. In the following student essay by Robin Ferguson on volunteering in a literacy program, which you have been learning about in earlier sections of this chapter, the thesis statement and topic sentences are underlined.

Robin Ferguson was a first-year college student studying to become a physical therapy assistant when she wrote this essay. She wrote it in response to an assignment in a community studies course. As you read the essay and the annotations, note how each topic sentence states the main point of the paragraph and supports the essay's thesis.

The Value of Volunteering

Robin Ferguson

I began working as a literacy volunteer as part of a community service course I was taking last semester. The course required a community service project, and I chose literacy volunteers simply as a means of fulfilling a course requirement. <u>Now I realize that working as a literacy volunteer taught me more about learning and friendship than I ever expected.</u>

1   Background

Thesis statement

*Topic
sentence*

2   When I first went through the training program to become a literacy volunteer, I learned
about the process of learning--that is, the way in
which people learn new words most effectively. To
illustrate this concept, the person who trained me
wrote a brief list of simple words on the left
side of a chalkboard and wrote phrases using the
same words on the right side of the chalkboard.
She instructed us to read the words, then asked
which words we would be most likely to remember.
We all said the words on the right because they
made more sense. In other words, we could remember
the words in the phrases more easily because they
made more sense in context. The trainer showed us
several more examples of words in context so we
could get a grasp of how people learn new information by connecting it to what they already know.

*Benefit 1:
learned about
learning process*

— *Example*

3   The training I received, though excellent,
was no substitute for working with a real student,
however. When I began to discover what other people's lives are like because they cannot read, I
realized the true importance of reading. For example, when I had my first tutoring session with my
client, Marie, a 44-year-old single mother of
three, I found out she walked two miles to the
nearest grocery store twice a week because she
didn't know which bus to take. When I told her I
would get her a bus schedule, she confided to me
that it would not help because she could not read
it, and therefore, she wouldn't know which bus to
take. She also said she had difficulty once she
got to the grocery store because she couldn't
always remember what she needed. Since she did
not know words, she could not write out a grocery
list. Also, she could only identify items by
sight, so if the manufacturer changed a label,

*Topic
sentence*

*Benefit 2:
importance of
reading*

— *Example*

she would not recognize it as the product she
wanted.

*Topic
sentence*

   As we worked together, learning how to read   4   *Benefit 3:*
built Marie's self-confidence, which gave her an   *self-confidence*
incentive to continue in her studies. She began to
make rapid progress and was even able to take the
bus to the grocery store. After this successful
trip, she reported how self-assured she felt.
Eventually, she began helping her youngest son,
Mark, a shy first grader, with his reading. She   *Example*
sat with him before he went to sleep and together
they would read bedtime stories. When his eyes
became wide with excitement as she read, her
pride swelled, and she began to see how her own
hard work in learning to read paid off. As she
described this experience, I swelled with pride
as well. I found that helping Marie to build her
self-confidence was more rewarding than anything I
had ever done before.

*Topic
sentence*

   As time went by, Marie and I developed a   5   *Benefit 4:*
friendship that became permanent. Because we saw   *friendship*
each other several times a week, we spent a lot of
time getting to know each other, and we discovered
we had certain things in common. For instance, I'm
also a single parent. So we began to share our   *Example*
similar experiences with each other. In fact, we   5
have even baby-sat for each other's children. I
would drop my children off at her house while I
taught an evening adult class, and in return, I
watched her children while she worked on Saturday
mornings.

   As a literacy volunteer, I learned a great   6   *Conclusion*
deal about learning, teaching, and helping others.
I also established what I hope will be a lifelong
friendship. In fact, I may have benefited more
from the experience than Marie did.

The following guidelines will help you write effective topic sentences.

A Topic Sentence Supports Your Thesis

Each topic sentence must in some way explain the thesis or show why the thesis is believable or correct. The following sample thesis, for example, could be supported by the topic sentences shown here.

THESIS: Adoption files should not be made available to adult children seeking their biological parents.

TOPIC SENTENCES

- Research has shown that not all biological parents want to meet with the sons or daughters they gave up many years before.
- If a woman gives up a child for adoption, it is probable that she does not ever intend to have a relationship with that child.
- Adult children who try to contact their biological parents often meet resistance and even hostility, which can cause them to feel hurt and rejected.
- A woman who gave up her biological child because she became pregnant as a result of rape or incest should not have to live in fear that her child will one day confront her.

All of these topic sentences support the thesis because they offer valid reasons for keeping adoption files closed.

POSSIBLE ANSWERS

1. *b* (*a* addresses understanding; *c*, communication; *d*, trust)
2. *c* (it does not support the thesis about mail-order sales capturing a large market share)

EXERCISE 6.4

For each of the following thesis statements, identify the one topic sentence in the list that does *not* support the thesis.

1. To make a marriage work, a couple must build trust, communication, and understanding.
   a. Knowing why a spouse behaves as he or she does can improve a relationship.
   b. People get married for reasons other than love.
   c. The ability to talk about feelings, problems, likes, and dislikes should grow as a marriage develops.
   d. Marital partners must rely on each other to make sensible decisions that benefit both of them.
2. For numerous products, mail-order sales are capturing a larger market share.
   a. Mail-order firms that target a specific audience tend to be most successful.
   b. The increasing number of women in the work force accounts, in part, for increased mail-order sales.
   c. Mail-order customers may order merchandise in a variety of ways: by phone, fax, mail, or computer.
   d. Products most commonly purchased through mail order are clothing and home furnishings.

A Topic Sentence States What the Paragraph Is About

A topic sentence should be focused, stating exactly what the paragraph will explain. Avoid vague or general statements. Instead, tell the reader precisely what to expect in the paragraph. Often, a topic sentence also previews the organization of the paragraph. Compare these examples of unfocused and focused topic sentences.

UNFOCUSED: Some members of minority groups do not approve of affirmative action.

FOCUSED: Some members of minority groups disapprove of affirmative action because it implies that they are not capable of obtaining employment based on their own accomplishments.

UNFOCUSED: Many students believe that hate groups shouldn't be allowed on campus.

FOCUSED: The Neo-Nazis, a group that promotes hate crimes, should not be permitted to speak in our local community college because most students find its members' views objectionable.

If you have trouble focusing your topic sentences, review the guidelines for writing an effective thesis statement in Chapter 5 (pp. 101–102), many of which also apply to writing effective topic sentences.

EXERCISE 6.5

Revise each topic sentence to make it focused and specific. At least two of your revised topic sentences should also preview the organization of the paragraph.

1. In society today, there is always a new fad or fashion in clothing.
2. People watch television talk shows because they find them irresistible.
3. Body piercing is a popular trend.
4. Procrastinating can have a negative effect on your success in college.
5. In our state, the lottery is a big issue.

A Topic Sentence Can Appear in Any Position within a Paragraph

Where you place the topic sentence will determine the order and structure of the rest of the paragraph.

Topic Sentence First. The most common position for a topic sentence is at the beginning of the paragraph. Unless you have a good reason for placing a topic sentence elsewhere in a paragraph, it is usually best to place it first. A paragraph that opens with the topic sentence should follow a logical sequence: You state your main point and then you explain it. In other words, the topic sentence tells readers what to expect in the rest of the paragraph, making it clear and easy for them to follow. This paragraph about advertising begins by telling readers what it is about.

TEACHING TIP

Emphasize that in both examples the focused topic sentence includes a *because* clause that introduces *reasons* for the reader to believe the assertion. While this structure is not the only possible one, it does assure the reader that the writer is focused on proving the assertion.

TEACHING TIP

Point out that phrases such as *In society today* are so broad and vague that they should be edited out.

POSSIBLE ANSWERS

1. New clothing fashions are churned out every season in the Western world, largely because of the influence of Parisian and New York designers, who flood the market with new or recycled designs to attract buyers.
2. People watch television talk shows like Jerry Springer's because they enjoy lurid stories, conflict, and audience participation.
3. Body piercing is popular among men and women aged eighteen to twenty-four.

(Continued on next page)

4. Procrastinating can have a negative effect on college success because most courses require sustained effort.

5. In our state, the lottery is a big issue because of concerns about gambling addiction and organized crime.

Advertising is first and foremost based on the principle of visibility—the customer must notice the product. Manufacturers often package products in glitzy, even garish, containers to grab the consumer's attention. For example, one candy company always packages its candy in neon wrappers. When the hurried and hungry consumer glances at the candy counter, the neon wrappers are easy to spot. It is only natural for the impatient customer to grab the candy and go.

Topic Sentence Early in the Paragraph.   When one or two sentences at the beginning of a paragraph are needed to smooth the transition from one paragraph to the next, the topic sentence may follow these transitional sentences. In the following example, the topic sentence comes after two transitional sentences. Note also that the paragraph explains the main point stated in the topic sentence.

However, visibility is not the only principle in advertising. It is simply the first. A second and perhaps more subtle principle is identity. The manufacturer attempts to lure the consumer into buying a product by linking it to a concept with which the consumer can identify. For instance, Boundaries perfume is advertised on television as the choice of "independent" women. Since independent women are admired in our culture, women identify with the concept and therefore are attracted to the perfume. Once the consumer identifies with the product, a sale is more likely to occur.

Topic Sentence Last.   The topic sentence can also appear last in a paragraph. You first present the supporting details and then end the paragraph with the topic sentence, which usually states the conclusion that can be drawn from the details. Common in argumentative writing, this arrangement allows you to present convincing evidence before stating your point about the issue, as the following paragraph from a student essay on gun control shows.

The saying "guns don't kill people; people kill people" always makes me even more certain of my own position on gun control. That statement is deceptive in the same way that the statement "Heroin doesn't kill people; people kill themselves" is deceptive. Naturally, people need to pull the trigger of a gun in order to make the gun kill other people, just as it is necessary for a person to ingest heroin in order to for it to kill him or her. However, these facts do not excuse us from the responsibility of keeping guns (or heroin) out of people's hands as much as possible. People cannot shoot people unless they have a gun. This fact alone should persuade the government to institute stiff gun control laws.

Including Unified, Specific Supporting Details

In addition to including well-focused topic sentences, effective paragraphs are unified and provide concrete details that work together to support the main point.

Effective Paragraphs Have Unity

In a unified paragraph, all of the sentences in the paragraph directly support the topic sentence. Together they provide adequate and convincing evidence for the assertion in the topic sentence. The following sample paragraph lacks unity. As you read it, try to pick out the sentences that do not support the topic sentence.

PARAGRAPH LACKING UNITY

(*1*) Much of the violence we see in the world today may be caused by the emphasis on violence in the media. (*2*) More often than not, the front page of the local newspaper contains stories involving violence. (*3*) In fact, one recent issue of my local newspaper contained seven references to violent acts. (*4*) There is also violence in public school systems. (*5*) Television reporters frequently hasten to crime and accident scenes and film every grim, violent detail. (*6*) The other day, there was a drive-by shooting downtown. (*7*) If the media were a little more careful about the ways in which they glamorize violence, there might be less violence in the world today and children would be less influenced by it.

Although sentences 4 and 6 deal with the broad topic of violence, neither is directly related to the main point about the media promoting violence that is stated in the topic sentence. Both should be deleted.

EXERCISE 6.6

Working alone or in a group of two or three students, read each paragraph and identify the sentences that do *not* support the topic sentence. In each paragraph, the topic sentence is underlined.

1. (*a*) Today many options and services for the elderly are available that did not exist years ago. (*b*) My grandmother is eighty-five years old now. (*c*) Adult care for the elderly is now provided in many parts of the country. (*d*) Similar to day care, adult care provides places where the elderly can go for meals and social activities. (*e*) Retirement homes for the elderly, where they can live fairly independently with minimal supervision, are another option. (*f*) My grandfather is also among the elderly at eighty-two. (*g*) Even many nursing homes have changed so that residents are afforded some level of privacy and independence while their needs are being met.

2. (*a*) Just as history repeats itself, fashions have a tendency to do the same. (*b*) In the late 1960s, for example, women wore long peasant dresses with beads; some thirty years later, the fashion magazines are featuring this same type of dress. (*c*) This peasant style has always seemed feminine and flattering. (*d*) I wonder if the fashion industry deliberately recycles fashions. (*e*) Men wore their hair long in the 1960s. (*f*) Today, some men are again letting their hair grow. (*g*) Goatees, considered "in" during the beatnik period of the 1950s, have once again made an appearance in the 1990s.

POSSIBLE ANSWERS

1. b, f
2. c, d (Though these sentences speculate about reasons, they do not directly support the topic sentence.)

Effective Paragraphs Provide Specific Supporting Details

The evidence you provide to support your topic sentences should be *concrete* and *specific*. Specific details interest your readers and make your meaning clear and forceful. Look at the following two examples. The first paragraph contains vague, general statements about psychologists and psychiatrists, while the revised paragraph provides concrete details that make the distinction between psychologists and psychiatrists clear.

VAGUE

Many people are confused about the difference between a psychologist and a psychiatrist. Both have a license, but a psychiatrist has more education than a psychologist. Also, a psychiatrist can prescribe medication.

CONCRETE AND SPECIFIC

Many people are confused about the difference between psychiatrists and psychologists. Both are licensed by the state to practice psychotherapy. However, a psychiatrist has earned a degree from medical school and can also practice medicine. Additionally, a psychiatrist can prescribe psychotropic medications. A psychologist, on the other hand, usually has earned a Ph.D. but has not attended medical school and, therefore, cannot prescribe medication of any type.

To make your paragraphs concrete and specific, use the following guidelines.

1. **Provide exact details.** If, for example, you use a magazine advertisement as an example of a marketing strategy, name the product and describe the advertisement: its features, type, use of color, and copy. Notice how the following vague sentences become clearer and livelier with the addition of exact details in the revised version.

   VAGUE: Peter has been driving around in his new car. It's yellow and low to the ground. It looks like the kind of car you see on racetracks.

   SPECIFIC: Peter's new canary yellow Stingray has a black pinstripe down each side. Its mag wheels are shiny with new chrome, and the headlights pop up at the push of a button.

CONNECTIONS

Link this strategy with writing prereading questions (Chapter 3) and prewriting questions (Chapter 4).

2. **Focus on: Who, What, When, Where, How and Why? questions.** Ask yourself these questions about your supporting details, and use the answers to expand and revise your paragraph. For instance, if you are writing about why violent crime has declined, you could ask at least two questions about the following sentence: "Recently some cities have increased the number of police patrols on the streets." *Where* were police patrols increased? (Name the cities.) *When* did this increase occur? (Give a specific year.) Notice how adding the answers to questions makes the following sentence more concrete.

VAGUE: Some animals hibernate for part of the year.

What animals? *When* do they hibernate?

SPECIFIC: Some bears hibernate for three to four months each winter.

3. **Name names.** Include the names of people, places, brands, and objects.

VAGUE: When my sixty-three-year-old aunt was refused a job, she became an angry victim of age discrimination.

SPECIFIC: When my sixty-three-year-old aunt *Angela* was refused a job at *Vicki's Nail Salon,* she became an angry victim of age discrimination.

4. **Use action verbs.** Select strong verbs that will help your readers visualize the action.

VAGUE: When Silina came on stage, the audience became excited.

SPECIFIC: When Silina *burst* onto the stage, the audience *screamed, cheered,* and *chanted* "Silina, Silina!"

5. **Use descriptive language that appeals to the senses (smell, touch, taste, sound, sight).** Words that appeal to the senses enable your readers to feel as if they are observing or participating in the experience you are describing.

For more about descriptive language, see Chapter 10, p. 248.

VAGUE: It's relaxing to walk on the beach.

SPECIFIC: I walked in the sand next to the ocean, breathing in the smell of the salt water and listening to the rhythmic sound of the waves.

6. **Use adjectives and adverbs.** Including carefully chosen adjectives and adverbs in your description of a person, a place, or an experience can make your writing more concrete.

VAGUE: Working in the garden can be enjoyable.

SPECIFIC: As I slowly weeded my perennial garden, I let my eyes wander over the pink meadow sweets and blue hydrangeas, all the while listening to the chirping of a bright red cardinal.

EXERCISE 6.7

Working alone or in a group of two or three students, revise and expand each sentence in the following paragraph to make it specific and concrete. Feel free to add new information and new sentences.

> I saw a great concert the other night in Dallas. Two groups were performing. The music was great, and there was a large crowd. In fact, the crowd was so enthusiastic that the second group performed one hour longer than scheduled.

TEACHING TIP: COLLABORATIVE WRITING

If students work independently, have them take a few minutes to share their revised paragraphs with peer reviewers to get feedback on needed revisions.

Connecting Your Supporting Details with Transitions and Repetition

All of the details in a paragraph must fit together and function as a connected unit of information. When a paragraph has **coherence**, its ideas flow smoothly, allowing readers to follow their progression with ease. Using one of the methods of organization discussed earlier in this chapter can help you show the connections among details and ideas. Transitions, used both within and between paragraphs, and repeated words are also useful devices for linking details. Look back, for example, at the student essay, "The Value of Volunteering," you read earlier (see p. 129); notice that each paragraph is organized chronologically and that transitions such as *after, eventually,* and *for example* are used to link ideas.

Coherent Paragraphs Include Transitional Words and Phrases

Transitions are words or phrases that lead your reader from one idea to another. Think of transitional expressions as guideposts or signals of what is coming next in a paragraph. Some commonly used transitions are shown in the accompanying box, grouped according to the type of connections they show.

In the two examples that follow, notice that the first paragraph is disjointed and choppy because it lacks transitions, whereas the revised version with transitions is easier to follow.

WITHOUT TRANSITIONS

Most films are structured much like a short story. The film begins with an opening scene that captures the audience's attention. The writers build up tension, preparing for the climax of the story. They complicate the situation by revealing other elements of the plot, perhaps by introducing a surprise or additional characters. They introduce a problem. It will be solved either for the betterment or to the detriment of the characters and the situation. A resolution brings the film to a close.

WITH TRANSITIONS

Most films are structured much like a short story. The film begins with an opening scene that captures the audience's attention. Gradually, the writers build up tension, preparing for the climax of the story. Soon after the first scene, they complicate the situation by revealing other elements of the plot, perhaps by introducing a surprise or additional characters. Next, they introduce a problem. Eventually, the problem will be solved either for the betterment or to the detriment of the characters and the situation. Finally, a resolution brings the film to a close.

Coherent Essays Include Transitional Phrases and Sentences

Transitional phrases and sentences show connections between sentences and paragraphs. A transitional phrase or sentence signals the reader about what is to follow or shows the reader how a new sentence or paragraph is connected to the one that precedes it. It may also remind the reader of an idea discussed earlier in the essay.

COMMONLY USED TRANSITIONAL EXPRESSIONS

Type of Connection	*Transitions*
Logical Connections	
Items in a series	then, first, second, next, another, furthermore, finally, as well as
Illustration	for instance, for example, namely, that is
Result or cause	consequently, therefore, so, hence, thus, because, then, as a result
Restatement	in other words, that is, in simpler terms
Summary or conclusion	finally, in conclusion, to sum up, all in all, evidently, actually
Opposing viewpoint	but, however, on the contrary, nevertheless, neither, nor, on the one/other hand, still, yet
Spatial Connections	
Direction	inside/outside, along, above/below, up/down, across, to the right/left, in front of/behind
Nearness	next to, near, nearby, facing, adjacent to
Distance	beyond, in the distance, away, over there
Time Connections	
Frequency	often, frequently, now and then, gradually, week by week, occasionally, daily, rarely
Duration	during, briefly, hour by hour
Reference to a particular time	at two o'clock, on April 27, in 1998, last Thanksgiving, three days ago
Beginning	before then, at the beginning, at first
Middle	meanwhile, simultaneously, next, then, at that time
End	finally, at last, eventually, later, at the end, subsequently, afterward

In the example that follows, the underlined transitional phrase connects the two paragraphs by reminding the reader of the main point of the first.

> A compliment is a brief and pleasant way of opening lines of communication and demonstrating goodwill. _____
> _____ [remainder of paragraph] _____ .
> <u>Although compliments do demonstrate goodwill</u>, they should be used sparingly; otherwise they may seem contrived. _____ .
> _____ .

Especially in lengthy essays (five pages or longer), you may find it helpful to include one or more transitional phrases or sentences that recap what you have said so far and suggest the direction of the essay from that point forward.

> Thus, the invasion of privacy is not limited to financial and consumer information; invasion of medical and workplace privacy is increasingly common. What can individuals do to protect their privacy in each of these areas?

The first sentence summarizes the four types of invasion of privacy already discussed in the essay. The second sentence signals that the discussion will shift to the preventive measures that individuals can take.

Coherent Essays Use Repeated Words to Connect Ideas

Repeating key words or their *synonyms* (words that have similar meanings) or using pronouns that refer to key words in the essay also helps readers follow your ideas. Such repetition can reinforce a main point in your essay. In the following paragraph, notice how the underlined words help to keep the reader's attention on the issue — the legal drinking age.

> Many years ago the <u>drinking age</u> in New York State was 18; now <u>it</u> is 21. Some young adults continue to argue that <u>it</u> should be 18 again. Whether a <u>young adult</u> is 20 or 21 does not make a big difference when he or she is <u>consuming alcoholic beverages</u>, <u>young people</u> say. However, statistics indicate that 20-year-olds who <u>drink alcohol</u> are at a greater risk for having an automobile accident than 21-year-olds. That difference is the reason the <u>drinking age</u> was changed.

WRITING YOUR INTRODUCTION, CONCLUSION, AND TITLE

It is not necessary to start writing an essay at the beginning and write straight through to the end. In fact, some students prefer to write the body of the essay first and then the introduction and conclusion. Others prefer to write a tentative introduction as a way of getting started. Some students think of a title before they start writing; others find it easier to add a title when the essay is nearly finished. Regardless of when you write them, the introduction, conclusion, and title are important components of a well-written essay. Following are some suggestions for writing strong introductions, conclusions, and titles.

Writing a Strong Introduction

Your introduction creates a first, and often lasting, impression. It also focuses your readers on your narrowed topic and establishes the tone of your essay. Based on your introduction, your readers will form an expectation of what the essay will be about and the approach it will take. In addition, they will become aware of your **tone**—how you "sound" about your topic and your attitude toward your readers. Because the introduction is crucial, take the time to get it right.

Two sample introductions to student essays follow. Although they are written on the same topic, notice how each creates an entirely different impression and set of expectations.

INTRODUCTION 1

The issue of sexual harassment has received a great deal of attention in recent years. From the highest office in the country—the presidency—to factories in small towns, sexual harassment cases have been tried in court and publicized on national television for all Americans to witness. This focus on sexual harassment has been, in and of itself, a good and necessary thing. However, when a little boy in first grade makes national headlines for having kissed a little girl of the same age, and the incident is labeled "sexual harassment," the American public needs to take a serious look at the definition of sexual harassment.

INTRODUCTION 2

Sexual harassment in the workplace seems to be happening with alarming frequency. As a woman who works part time in a male-dominated office, I have witnessed at least six incidents of sexual harassment aimed at me and my female colleagues on various occasions during the past three months alone. For example, in one incident, a male co-worker repeatedly made kissing sounds whenever I passed his desk, even after I explained that his actions made me uncomfortable. A female co-worker was invited to dinner several times by her male supervisor; each time she refused. The last time she refused, he made a veiled threat, "You obviously aren't happy working with me. Perhaps a transfer is in order." These incidents were not isolated, did not happen to only one woman, and were initiated by more than one man. My colleagues and I are not the only victims. Sexual harassment is on the rise and will continue to increase unless women speak out against it loudly and to a receptive audience.

CONNECTIONS

The revision flowcharts in Chapters 9–16 and 18 ask students to evaluate their introductions.

TEACHING TIP

(5 minutes) To review elements of development covered so far while also analyzing effective introductions, ask the whole class to:

- identify and highlight the thesis in each introduction.
- locate transitional words and phrases.
- orally describe the type of organization they would expect from each paper.

Introduction 1: Final sentence is thesis; transitional word: *however;* type of development: chronological (probably the story of the boy) or least-to-most order (outrageous examples of oversensitivity)

Introduction 2: Final sentence is thesis; transitional words and phrases: *for example, even after, the last time;* type of development: least-to-most or most-to-least order (outrageous examples and alarming statistics)

In introduction 1, the writer focuses on the definition of sexual harassment. Introduction 2 has an entirely different emphasis — the frequency of incidents of sexual harassment. Each introductory paragraph reveals a different tone as well. Introduction 1 suggests a sense of mild disbelief, whereas introduction 2 suggests anger and outrage. From introduction 1, you expect the writer to examine seriously definitions of sexual harassment and, perhaps, suggest his or her own definition. From introduction 2, you expect the writer to present additional cases of sexual harassment and suggest ways women can speak out against it.

In addition to establishing a focus and tone, your introduction should accomplish four other objectives:

- Announce the narrowed topic of your essay (see Chapter 4)
- Present your thesis statement
- Interest your reader
- Provide any background information your readers may need.

Introductions are often difficult to write. If you have trouble, write a tentative introductory paragraph and return to it later. Once you have written the body of your essay, you may find it easier to complete the introduction. In fact, as you work out your ideas in the body of the essay, you may think of a better way to introduce them in the opening.

Tips for Writing a Strong Introduction

The following suggestions for writing a strong introduction will help you capture your readers' interest.

1. **Ask a provocative or disturbing question.** Pose a question that will interest or intrigue your readers. Or, consider posing a series of short, related questions that will direct your readers' attention to the key points in your essay.

    Should health insurance companies pay for more than one stay in a drug rehabilitation center? Should health insurance companies continue to pay for rehab services when patients consciously and consistently put themselves back into danger by using drugs again?

2. **Begin with a story or anecdote.** Choose a story or anecdote that will appeal to your audience and is relevant to or illustrates your thesis.

    I used to believe that it was possible to stop smoking by simply quitting cold turkey. When I tried this approach, I soon realized that quitting was not so simple. When I did not smoke for even a short period of time, I became so uncomfortable that I started again just to alleviate the discomfort. I realized then that in order to quit smoking, I would need a practical solution that would overcome my cravings.

3. **Offer a quotation.** The quotation should illustrate or emphasize your thesis.

> As Indira Gandhi once said, "You cannot shake hands with a clenched fist." This truism is important to remember whenever people communicate with one another, but particularly when they are attempting to resolve a conflict. Both parties need to agree that there is a problem and then agree to listen to each other with an open mind. Shaking hands is a productive way to begin working toward a resolution.

4. **Cite a little-known or shocking fact or statistic.** An unfamiliar or unusual fact or statistic can interest your readers and focus their attention on the topic of your essay.

> Between 1963 and 1993, there was a 26 percent increase in the number of college students who admitted copying academic work from another student. This increase suggests that students' attitude toward cheating changed dramatically during that thirty-year period.

5. **Move from general to specific.** Begin with the category or general subject area to which your topic belongs and narrow it to arrive at your thesis.

> The First Amendment is the basis for several cherished rights in the United States, and free speech is among them. Therefore, it would seem unlawful—even anti-American—for a disc jockey to be fired for expressing his or her views on the radio, regardless of whether those views are unpopular or offensive.

6. **State a commonly held misconception or a position that you oppose.** Your thesis would then correct the misconception or state your position on the issue.

> Many people have the mistaken notion that only homosexuals and drug users are in danger of contracting AIDS. In fact, many heterosexuals also suffer from this debilitating disease. Furthermore, the number of heterosexuals who test HIV-positive has increased substantially over the past decade. It is time the American public became better informed about the prevention and treatment of AIDS.

7. **Describe a hypothetical situation.** A situation that illustrates your thesis provides a realistic opening to your essay.

> Suppose you were in a serious car accident and became unconscious. Suppose further that you slipped into a coma, with little hope for recovery. Unless you had a prewritten health care proxy that designated someone familiar with your wishes to act on your behalf, your fate would be left in the hands of medical doctors who knew nothing about you or your preferences for treatment.

8. **Begin with an intriguing statement.** A provocative or intriguing statement may encourage your readers to continue reading.

> Recent research has shown that the color pink has a calming effect on people. In fact, a prison detention center in western New York was recently painted pink to make prisoners more controllable in the days following their arrest.

9. **Begin with a striking example.** A compelling example makes your topic immediate and relevant to your readers.

> The penal system is sometimes too concerned with protecting the rights of the criminal instead of the victim. For example, during a rape trial, the victim is often questioned about his or her sexual history by the defense attorney. However, the prosecuting attorney is forbidden by law to raise the question of whether the defendant has been charged with rape in a previous trial. In fact, if the prosecution even hints at the defendant's sexual history, the defense can request a mistrial.

10. **Make a comparison.** Compare your topic to one that is familiar or of special interest to your readers.

> The process a researcher uses to locate a specific piece of information in the library is similar to the process an investigator follows in tracking a criminal; both use a series of questions and follow clues to accomplish their task.

Mistakes to Avoid

The following advice will help you avoid the most common mistakes students make in writing introductions.

1. **Do not make an announcement.** Avoid opening comments such as "I am writing to explain . . ." or "This essay will discuss. . . ." They are unnecessary.

2. **Keep your introduction short.** Often one or two paragraphs is sufficient. In some cases, more than two paragraphs may be appropriate, but be careful not to lose your readers' attention. But an introduction that goes beyond two paragraphs will probably sound long-winded and make your readers impatient.

3. **Avoid statements that may create negative attitudes.** Statements such as "This process may seem complicated, but . . ." may make your readers apprehensive.

4. **Avoid a casual, overly familiar, or chatty tone.** Opening comments such as "Man, did it surprise me when . . ." or "You'll never in a million years believe what happened. . . ." are not effective.

5. **Be sure your topic is clear or explained adequately for your readers.** Do not begin an essay by stating, for example, "I oppose Proposition 413 and urge you to vote against it." Before stating your position on your topic, you need to explain the topic adequately. Readers of an essay on Proposition 413 would need to understand what that legislation is and what it proposes before they could consider your position against it.

CONNECTIONS

The revision flowcharts in Chapters 9–16 and 18 ask students to evaluate their conclusions.

Writing an Effective Conclusion

Your essay should not end abruptly with your last supporting paragraph. Instead, it should end with a conclusion, a separate paragraph that reiterates the importance of your thesis—without directly restating it—and that brings your essay to a satisfying close.

Tips for Writing a Solid Conclusion

For an especially lengthy or complicated essay, it may be appropriate to summarize your main points and restate your thesis. For most other essays, however, it is best to avoid ending with a summary and a restatement of the thesis. Instead, use one of the following suggestions to conclude your essay effectively.

1. **Look ahead.** Take your readers beyond the scope and time frame of your essay.

   > For now, then, the present system for policing the Internet appears to be working. In the future, though, it may be necessary to put a more formal, structured procedure in place.

2. **Remind readers of the relevance of the issue.** Suggest why your thesis is important.

   > As stated earlier, research has shown that implementing the seat-belt law has saved thousands of lives. These lives would almost certainly have been lost had this law not been enacted.

3. **Offer a recommendation or make a call to action.** Urge your readers to take specific steps that follow logically from your thesis.

   > To convince MTV to eliminate R-rated material, concerned citizens should contact their local cable station and threaten to cancel their MTV coverage.

4. **Discuss broader implications.** Point to larger issues not fully addressed in the essay.

   > When fair-minded people consider whether the FBI should be allowed to tap private phone lines, the issue inevitably leads them to the larger issue of First Amendment rights.

5. **Conclude with a fact, a quotation, an anecdote, or an example that emphasizes your thesis.** These endings will bring a sense of closure and realism to your essay.

   > The next time you are tempted to send a strongly worded message to an Internet newsgroup, consider this fact: At the Internet address <www.dejanews.com> your friends and your enemies can recover messages you have posted on Usenet newsgroups since 1995.

Mistakes to Avoid

The following advice will help you avoid the types of mistakes students tend to make when writing conclusions.

1. **Avoid a direct restatement of your thesis.** An exact repetition of your thesis will make your essay seem dull and mechanical.

2. **Avoid standard phrases.** Don't use phrases such as "To sum up," "In conclusion," or "It can be seen, then." They are routine and tiresome.

3. **Avoid introducing new points in your conclusion.** Major points belong in the body of your essay.

4. **Avoid apologizing for yourself, your work, or your ideas.** Do not say, for example, "Although I am only twenty-one, it seems to me. . . ."

5. **Avoid softening or reversing your stance in the conclusion.** If, for instance, your essay criticizes the behavior of a particular political candidate, do not back down by saying "After all, she's only human. . . ." Backing down will weaken the impact of your thesis or argument.

Writing a Good Title

The title of your essay should suggest your topic and spark your readers' interest. Depending on the purpose, intended audience, and tone of your essay, your title may be direct and informative, witty, or intriguing. The following suggestions will help you write effective titles.

1. **Write straightforward, descriptive titles for most academic essays.**

   The Economic Disadvantages of Single Parenthood

   Hunger in Cleveland: A Practical Solution

2. **Ask a question that your essay answers.**

   What Are Your Rights as a Tenant?

3. **Use alliteration.** Repeating initial sounds (called *alliteration*) often produces a catchy title.

   Lotteries: Dreaming about Dollars

4. **Consider using a play on words or a humorous expression.** Though not appropriate for most academic essays, this technique may work well for less formal essays.

   The Rub against Ribs

   (*Rub* is both a seasoning for barbecue ribs and a word that suggests problems or disadvantages.)

5. **Avoid broad, vague titles that sound like labels.** Titles such as "Baseball Fans" or "Gun Control" provide your reader with too little information.

ESSAY IN PROGRESS 3

Using the outline or graphic organizer you created in Essay in Progress 2 (p. 128), write a first draft of your essay. Be sure to write clear and effective topic sentences that support your thesis and unified paragraphs that support each topic sentence.

DRAFTING WITH A COMPUTER

The word processing programs that are available on most computers are ideally suited to drafting essays. Drafting on a computer has a number of advantages for writers. First of all, because a word processor takes care of many of the mechanics of drafting (setting margins, for example) you are free to concentrate on the most important part of drafting—developing and expressing your ideas clearly. Second, often when you are drafting a paragraph within your essay, you will think of ideas for a previous or later paragraph. On a computer, you can move back and forth within your draft, adding these ideas in the appropriate places whenever they occur to you. Finally, word processing programs allow you to make insertions and revisions easily within the paragraph you are working on.

When drafting an essay on computer, use the flexibility it affords you to your advantage. Experiment with different ways to express an idea, different ways to organize the essay, different positions for a topic sentence, or different word choices. For example, on a computer you can rewrite a paragraph that you are uncertain about in two or three different ways by copying it and making changes in each copy. You can then make comparisons. When comparing several drafts, you may find it helpful to print each draft so that you can place them side by side and study each.

Be sure to save your work frequently as you draft, make back-up copies for security, and note file names so that you can find your essay again easily.

STUDENTS WRITE

The first draft of a narrative essay by Tina Oyer follows. Oyer used her freewriting (see Chapter 4) and her working thesis (see Chapter 5) as the basis for her draft, adding events and details that she came up with by doing additional brainstorming (see Chapter 5). Because she was writing a first draft, Oyer did not worry about correcting errors in grammar, punctuation, and mechanics. (You will see her revised draft in Chapter 7 and an excerpt that shows Oyer's final editing and proofreading in Chapter 8.)

First Draft

• To whom or what does
  the title refer?
• Can you predict some
  of the changes Oyer
  will make in her draft?

Hypocritically Warm

1   It was a cold snowy night, when I learned something
unexpected about myself. I can trust my instincts. The
temperature was about ten degrees, something we are especially mindful of in Buffalo. We are used to it; we
expect it. You never can tell by the blinding glare when
you look out the window. The sun appears to be beaming a
tale of the hottest summer day, but when you step outside the cold has the upper hand. That night, the wind
that stung my face wasn't the only thing that was
frigid.

2   Walking into a small store, I could feel the
refreshing heat dominate the cold on my skin. The
clerks, all dressed in identical attire, were busy: waiting on customers, bagging and pricing stock. The owner,
also the pharmacist, waited on customers. The customers
are his priority. They get first-class service. They are
always catered to, and pleased when they leave the
store. If we don't have it, we will order it. He goes to
any lengths to please them. He even goes to the extreme
of being sickeningly sweet at times. If they ask him a
question, he stops what he is doing and speaks to them
in a very kind and friendly manner. If they don't feel
like waiting around for their prescription to be ready,
he tells them he'll have it delivered. So unlike the
personality he displays to us, his workers!

3   We are his on-the-clock toilers! If we have a question, we are lucky to get an answer. When we do, his
eyes never leave the task at hand, and it's most often a
quick short answer. Unless of course we are fulfilling a
customer's request. His hypocritical personality is so
familiar to us. It makes you wonder how anyone could put
on such a phony front, and have a heart of stone. He
missed his calling, he should be in Hollywood. Sometimes
you don't know whether to chuckle or disgorge. At times

it keeps me entertained. If the customers only knew they were buying more than just his merchandise.

Quitting time arrived none too soon for me. As the last customer leaves the store, I locked the doors. As I am collecting the cash register drawers to put in the safe, I feel a sense of relief. I'll soon be on my way home, something I looked forward to, as the clock was ticking away the last hour. 4

As we started through the parking lot, enroute to our cars, a customer stopped us. We recognized her as a customer who had been in the store earlier. She looked at the owner and told him she left her keys in the store. Without saying a word he ran back into the store and took a quick look. As he locked the doors again, he told her he didn't find them. Then he left. I was left standing there with the woman and a couple of co-workers. His quick answer and departure didn't surprise us, but the customer was in what appeared to be total confusion. If I could read her mind, I would guess she caught a glimpse of the side of him we know so well. She probably wondered what happened to the royal service she had received earlier. I'm sure she felt another sense of cold, besides the chill from the blowing, drifting snow we were experiencing at that moment. 5

As the shock wore off, the woman confronted her next hurdle: She was stranded. She made a couple of phone calls to get in touch with someone to help her, but to no avail. My two colleagues looked at me. I worked with them long enough to know what they were thinking. Just as they look to me to take care of problems in the store, they felt this situation was no different. 6

As the manager of the night, alternate weekend shift, I could go back in the store and look for the keys. If I did, I would have an important decision to make. I would need enough time to walk around the store and look for the keys. The owner would want to know why I went back into the store. It could definitely cost me my job. 7

8   As I stood there in the blowing snow, it seemed to
melt as soon as it hit my face. I no longer felt the
cold as I had known it earlier. The decision I was facing filled my thoughts. The woman once again walked next
door to make another phone call. As I saw her punch the
first numbers into the phone in desperation, I turned
back to my own thoughts.

9   I took the store keys out of my pocket, feeling as
if I still didn't make a final decision and my body was
going through the motions. I unlocked the doors, locked
them behind me and ran and put my security code into the
alarm. I looked around the store, feeling like a criminal. I made my way over to the video counter. Laying
right there in plain sight were the keys. Made me wonder
if the owner's glasses were fogged up from the change in
temperature. At that point, I was glad I had gone back
into the store. I picked up the keys, set the alarm and
locked the doors.

10   As I joined my co-workers and the woman in the
parking lot. I held up the keys and placed them in the
woman's hand. She hugged me and told me if I needed her
to confirm my story to the owner, she would be glad to
speak with him. That was probably the first time in the
past hour that I had to deal with only one emotion at a
time. I was happy; I could help her, and now she could
go home.

11   As I watched her brush off her car, I'm sure she
was still in a state of confusion. She probably was
wondering, as we once did, how someone could be so
friendly and caring one time and so cold the next. She
perhaps could have felt that when she was a paying customer in the store, she was worth his time and effort,
but outside the store he could care less. I'm sure
these thoughts or similar ones were with her all the
way home.

12   As for me, I said goodnight to my co-workers, and
they headed for their cars. As I headed for my car, my
sense of happiness wore off. As my thoughts left the

POSSIBLE ANSWERS: ANALYZING THE FIRST DRAFT

1. *Title:* contrasts the warmth of the owner to customers with his coldness to his employees, as the indoor warmth contrasts with the weather.
Introduction: first two sentences = thesis; support: describes weather; last sentence creates suspense. The paragraph is a bit disjointed; the author might consider adding transitions and combining sentences.

2. "It was a cold . . . instincts." Prepares for narrative development; suggests what the author learned about herself; con-

events of the past hour, I was relieved to be going home.

As I drove, I thought again of the woman and how she must be feeling. I know I had feelings that were all mixed up. I was elated that I could help the woman. On the other hand, I had a huge knot in my stomach. I could soon be among the unemployed. The longer I drove, the more content I felt with my decision. By the time I reached my house, I realized that when faced with a difficult situation, I can trust my instincts and rely on my ability to make wise decisions.

As I pulled into my driveway, I pushed the button to the garage door opener, and was not surprised that in the middle of the garage was a little pink bike, with tiny training wheels. Ah, the realities of home. I got out of the car to move the bike and once again the cold wind stung my face, and it felt good!

13

14

trasts inclement weather with positive experience of self-confidence.
3. Background seems adequate; students may offer suggestions.
4. Primarily chronological.
5. Answers will vary. Paragraphs 5 and 10, e.g., could use more narrative detail or dialogue to enliven the scene.
6. The pink bike suggests innocence, contrasts with the hypocritical officiousness of the pharmacist. Repetition of the image of cold resonates with the introduction, suggesting a contrast with the title: warmth is hypocritical; coldness, in this context, is genuine and uplifting.

Analyzing the First Draft

1. Evaluate Oyer's title and introduction.
2. Evaluate Oyer's thesis statement.
3. Does Oyer provide adequate background for her essay? If not, what additional information might she include?
4. How does Oyer organize her ideas?
5. Evaluate her supporting paragraphs. Which paragraphs need more detail?
6. Evaluate the conclusion.

WORKING WITH TEXT

Black Men and Public Space
Brent Staples

Brent Staples is a journalist who has written numerous articles and editorials as well as a memoir, Parallel Time: Growing Up in Black and White *(1994). Staples holds a Ph.D. in psychology and is currently an editor at the*

PREREADING QUESTION

What is the relation between "black men and public space," according to the author?

New York Times. *This essay, first published in* Harper's *magazine in 1986, is a good model of a well-structured essay. As you read the selection, highlight or underline the author's thesis and topic sentences.*

CONNECTIONS

Staples's essay can also serve as a strong model of an illustration essay—see Chapter 11.

1   My first victim was a woman—white, well dressed, probably in her early twenties. I came upon her late one evening on a deserted street in Hyde Park, a relatively affluent neighborhood in an otherwise mean, impoverished section of Chicago. As I swung onto the avenue behind her, there seemed to be a discreet, uninflammatory distance between us. Not so. She cast back a worried glance. To her, the youngish black man—a broad six feet two inches with a beard and billowing hair, both hands shoved into the pockets of a bulky military jacket—seemed menacingly close. After a few more quick glimpses, she picked up her pace and was soon running in earnest. Within seconds she disappeared into a cross street.

2   That was more than a decade ago. I was twenty-two years old, a graduate student newly arrived at the University of Chicago. It was in the echo of that terrified woman's footfalls that I first began to know the unwieldy inheritance I'd come into—the ability to alter public space in ugly ways. It was clear that she thought herself the quarry of a mugger, a rapist, or worse. Suffering a bout of insomnia, however, I was stalking sleep, not defenseless wayfarers. As a softy who is scarcely able to take a knife to a raw chicken—let alone hold one to a person's throat—I was surprised, embarrassed, and dismayed all at once. Her flight made me feel like an accomplice in tyranny. It also made it clear that I was indistinguishable from the muggers who occasionally seeped into the area from the surrounding ghetto. That first encounter, and those that followed, signified that a vast, unnerving gulf lay between nighttime pedestrians—particularly women—and me. And I soon gathered that being perceived as dangerous is a hazard in itself. I only needed to turn a corner into a dicey situation, or crowd some frightened, armed person in a foyer somewhere, or make an errant move after being pulled over by a policeman. Where fear and weapons meet—and they often do in urban America—there is always the possibility of death.

3   In that first year, my first away from my hometown, I was to become thoroughly familiar with the language of fear. At dark, shadowy intersections, I could cross in front of a car stopped at a traffic light and elicit the *thunk, thunk, thunk, thunk* of the driver—black, white, male, or female—hammering down the door locks. On less traveled streets after dark, I grew accustomed to but never comfortable with people crossing to the other side of the street rather than pass me. Then there were the standard unpleasantries with police-

men, doormen, bouncers, cabdrivers, and others whose business it is to screen out troublesome individuals *before* there is any nastiness.

I moved to New York nearly two years ago and I have remained an avid night walker. In central Manhattan, the near-constant crowd cover minimizes tense one-on-one street encounters. Elsewhere—in SoHo, for example, where sidewalks are narrow and tightly spaced buildings shut out the sky—things can get very taut indeed.

4

After dark, on the warrenlike streets of Brooklyn where I live, I often see women who fear the worst from me. They seem to have set their faces on neutral, and with their purse straps strung across their chests bandolier-style, they forge ahead as though bracing themselves against being tackled. I understand, of course, that the danger they perceive is not a hallucination. Women are particularly vulnerable to street violence, and young black males are drastically overrepresented among the perpetrators of that violence. Yet these truths are no solace against the kind of alienation that comes of being ever the suspect, a fearsome entity with whom pedestrians avoid making eye contact.

5

It is not altogether clear to me how I reached the ripe old age of twenty-two without being conscious of the lethality nighttime pedestrians attributed to me. Perhaps it was because in Chester, Pennsylvania, the small, angry industrial town where I came of age in the 1960s, I was scarcely noticeable against a backdrop of gang warfare, street knifings, and murders. I grew up one of the good boys, had perhaps a half-dozen fistfights. In retrospect, my shyness of combat has clear sources.

6

As a boy, I saw countless tough guys locked away; I have since buried several, too. They were babies, really—a teenage cousin, a brother of twenty-two, a childhood friend in his mid-twenties—all gone down in episodes of bravado played out in the streets. I came to doubt the virtues of intimidation early on. I chose, perhaps unconsciously, to remain a shadow—timid, but a survivor.

7

The fearsomeness mistakenly attributed to me in public places often has a perilous flavor. The most frightening of these confusions occurred in the late 1970s and early 1980s, when I worked as a journalist in Chicago. One day, rushing into the office of a magazine I was writing for with a deadline story in hand, I was mistaken for a burglar. The office manager called security and, with an ad hoc posse, pursued me through the labyrinthine halls, nearly to my editor's door. I had no way of proving who I was. I could only move briskly toward the company of someone who knew me.

8

Another time I was on assignment for a local paper and killing time before an interview. I entered a jewelry store on the city's affluent Near North Side. The proprietor excused herself and returned

9

POSSIBLE ANSWERS: EXAMINING THE READING (p. 154)

1. Strangers insist he keep his distance; a shopkeeper brings out a guard dog; pedestrians and women avoid him; drivers lock their doors at intersections.
2. His attitude of nonaggression
3. He gives strangers "wide berth," remains "calm and extremely congenial" when confronted by police, and hums classical music while strolling at night.
4. *uninflammatory:* incapable of irritating or inciting anger; *unwieldy:* awkward, difficult to handle; *vulnerable:* likely to be victimized; *retrospect:* a later view, upon reflection; *constitutionals:* walks

with an enormous red Doberman pinscher straining at the end of a leash. She stood, the dog extended toward me, silent to my questions, her eyes bulging nearly out of her head. I took a cursory look around, nodded, and bade her good night.

10   Relatively speaking, however, I never fared as badly as another black male journalist. He went to nearby Waukegan, Illinois, a couple of summers ago to work on a story about a murderer who was born there. Mistaking the reporter for the killer, police officers hauled him from his car at gunpoint and but for his press credentials would probably have tried to book him. Such episodes are not uncommon. Black men trade tales like this all the time.

11   Over the years, I learned to smother the rage I felt at so often being taken for a criminal. Not to do so would surely have led to madness. I now take precautions to make myself less threatening. I move about with care, particularly late in the evening. I give a wide berth to nervous people on subway platforms during the wee hours, particularly when I have exchanged business clothes for jeans. If I happen to be entering a building behind some people who appear skittish, I may walk by, letting them clear the lobby before I return, so as not to seem to be following them. I have been calm and extremely congenial on those rare occasions when I've been pulled over by the police.

12   And on late-evening constitutionals I employ what has proved to be an excellent tension-reducing measure: I whistle melodies from Beethoven and Vivaldi and the more popular classical composers. Even steely New Yorkers hunching toward nighttime destinations seem to relax, and occasionally they even join in the tune. Virtually everybody seems to sense that a mugger wouldn't be warbling bright sunny selections from Vivaldi's *Four Seasons*. It is my equivalent of the cowbell that hikers wear when they know they are in bear country. ∎

Examining the Reading

1. Explain what Staples means by "the ability to alter public space" (paragraph 2).
2. Staples considers himself a survivor (paragraph 7). To what does he attribute his survival?
3. What does Staples do to make himself seem less threatening to others?
4. Explain the meaning of each of the following words as it is used in the reading: *uninflammatory* (paragraph 1), *unwieldy* (2), *vulnerable* (5), *retrospect* (6), and *constitutionals* (12).

Analyzing the Reading

1. Evaluate Staples's opening paragraph. Does it spark your interest? Why or why not?

2. Identify Staples's thesis statement. How does the author support his thesis? What types of information does he include?

3. Cite several examples of places in the essay where Staples uses specific supporting details and transitions effectively. Explain your choices.

4. Evaluate Staples's conclusion. Does it leave you satisfied? Why or why not?

5. What is Staples's method of organization in this essay? What other method of organization could he have used?

6. Many of the paragraphs in this essay begin with clearly stated topic sentences. Identify at least one topic sentence. What kind of support does Staples offer for this topic sentence?

Reacting to the Reading: Discussion and Journal Writing

1. Why is Staples's whistling of classical music similar to hikers wearing cowbells in bear country?

2. In what other ways can an individual "alter public space"?

3. Do you think Staples *should* alter his behavior in public to accommodate the reactions of others? Write a journal entry explaining whether you agree or disagree with Staples's actions.

6. For instance, "In that first year . . . language of fear" (paragraph 3). Support: recurring incidents such as the image of drivers locking their doors; sight of pedestrians crossing the street to avoid him.

POSSIBLE ANSWERS: REACTING TO THE READING

1. The similarity is ironic: The music warns other urbanites of his presence yet puts them at ease, unlike the bear bell, which is designed to frighten bears away.

2. Have students brainstorm answers (e.g. people with disabilities "alter public space," as do those with body odor and those who are famous). Then note the sociopolitical implications: People who do not fit the status quo "alter public space."

3. Responses will vary.

TEACHING TIP

To foster critical thinking about the subject of racial discrimination, initiate a class discussion on the assumptions people make about others at first sight.

• Discuss situations in which students' intentions were misunderstood or in which someone made false assumptions about them.

• Discuss times when students had to alter their behavior to accommodate others' needs or expectations.

Chapter 7

Revising Content and Organization

A drawing of The Orange Bowl Stadium appears on the opposite page. With a pencil, make a drawing similar to this one of a sports stadium, an arena, a convention center, a theater, or of another building, such as the one in which your class meets. Your sketch of the building's floor plan doesn't have to be exact, but it should be good enough to allow someone to use it to find his or her way from one place to another within the building.

Writing Quick Start

Reexamine your floor plan, looking for ways to make it clearer and easier for someone to use. Write a few sentences describing the changes you would make. After you make these changes, will it be easier for someone to find his or her way around the building? Exchange sketches with a classmate, and examine your classmate's sketch. Look for parts of it that you find confusing and that need more detail. Write down your comments for your classmate. Finally, using your own comments and those of your classmate, make changes to improve your drawing.

When you changed your sketch, did you mark gates, entrances and exits, or eleva-
tors; label nearby streets or important rooms; add parking ramps or lots; or indicate the location of snack bars and restroom facilities? The changes you made
improved the content of the drawing. In other words, you have *revised* the drawing.

Revising an essay works in much the same way. **Revision** is a process of making changes to improve both what your essay says and how it is said. This chapter
offers several different approaches to revising an essay. It lists some general suggestions, describes how to use a graphic organizer for revision, offers specific questions to guide your revision, and discusses the implications of learning style for the
revision process. You will notice in Figure 7.1 that revision is an essential part of
the writing process.

WHY REVISE?

A thorough, thoughtful revision can change a *C* paper to an *A* paper! Revising is
one of the most important steps in the writing process and can make a significant
difference in how well your paper achieves your purpose and how effectively it

FIGURE 7.1
AN OVERVIEW OF THE WRITING PROCESS

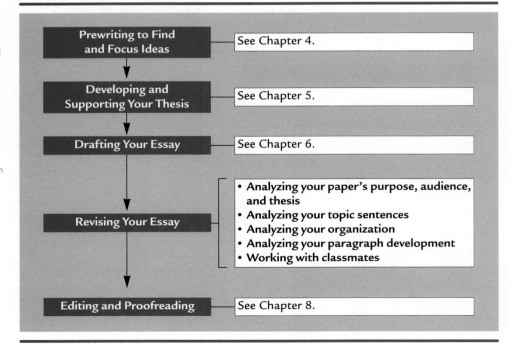

expresses your ideas to your intended audience. Although revision takes time and hard work, it pays off and produces results.

Most professional writers revise frequently and thoroughly, as do successful student writers. For example, this writer revised this chapter five times before it was published. Each time, I added *ideas,* deleted *ideas,* changed the order of *ideas,* or reworded *ideas.* Notice the emphasis on *ideas.* Revision is a process of looking again at your *ideas* in order to make them clearer and easier to understand. Sometimes, it even involves rethinking your ideas. It is not merely a process of cleaning up sentences, correcting surface errors, and changing a word or two here and there. It may mean adding, eliminating, or reorganizing key elements within the essay. It may even mean revising your thesis statement and refocusing the entire essay. Even though a thorough revision may be time-consuming, it is better to discover the problems in an essay while you still have time to correct them rather than discovering later that your audience misunderstood your message or that your supporting evidence was not convincing.

The amount of revision you will need to do will depend, in part, on how you approach the task of writing. Good writing requires an investment of time; it is simply a matter of how you prefer to spend it. Some writers spend more time planning; others spend more time in revision. For example, students who tend to be pragmatic learners take a highly structured approach to writing. They plan in detail what they will say before they draft. More creative learners, however, may dash off a draft as ideas come to mind. A well-planned draft usually requires less revision than one that was spontaneously written. Regardless of how carefully planned an essay may be, however, any first draft will require at least some revision.

Revision is frequently an ongoing process. While you are writing a draft, you will often pause to reread parts of what you have written. While doing so, you may think of new points to add or realize that a main point needs more support. Add new ideas as they come to mind; don't wait until you've finished your paper.

USEFUL TECHNIQUES FOR REVISION

The following techniques will help you to get the most benefit from the time you spend revising your essays.

- **Allow time between drafting and revision.** Once you have finished writing, set your draft aside for a while, overnight if possible. When you return to your draft, you will be able to approach it from a fresh perspective. Right after finishing a draft, you are usually too involved with it to look at it impartially. A day later, however, you will begin to see what does and does not work.

- **Read your draft aloud.** Hearing what you have written will help you discover main points that are unclear or that lack adequate support. You will notice paragraphs that sound confusing. You will also "hear" awkward wording and vague or overused expressions.

**TEACHING TIP:
LEARNING STYLES**

Most students, especially creative learners, seem inspired to hear that people often get ideas for revising papers while they are in the shower, taking a walk, or doing some other mundane task. In "The Eureka Phenomenon," e.g., Isaac Asimov describes the doubleness of the mind—the way the conscious and unconscious minds work together to come up with ideas.

- **Ask a friend to read your draft aloud to you.** Listen for clues that tell you whether your draft flows logically and whether it makes sense to the reader. When your reader hesitates, slows down, misreads, or sounds confused, it could be a signal that your message is not as clear as it should be. Keep a copy of your draft in front of you as you listen, and mark places where your reader falters or seems baffled.

- **Seek the opinions of classmates.** Ask a classmate to read and comment on your paper. This process, called peer review, is discussed in more detail later in this chapter (see p. 166).

- **Look for consistent problem areas.** Over the course of writing and revising several essays, many students discover consistent problem areas. One student might discover, for example, that she often has problems with organization. Another might notice that his writing often lacks concrete details to support his main points and that he usually needs to state and focus his thesis more clearly.

- **Work with typed or printed copy.** Even if you prefer to handwrite your draft, be sure to type, keyboard, or print it before you revise. Because computer-generated, typed, or printed copy will seem less personal, you will be able to analyze and evaluate it more impartially. You will also be able to see a full page at a time on a printed copy, instead of only a paragraph at a time on a computer screen. Finally, on a printed copy you can write marginal annotations, circle troublesome words or sentences, and draw arrows to connect details.

- **Prepare readable copy.** If you cannot type or keyboard your paper, write on one side of the page, in case you want to cut your paper into pieces and rearrange them. Leave wide margins so you have plenty of room to jot down new main points or supporting details as they occur to you.

USING A GRAPHIC ORGANIZER FOR REVISION

One of the best ways to reexamine your essay is to draw a graphic organizer—a visual display of your thesis statement and supporting paragraphs. A graphic organizer allows you to see how your thesis and topic sentences relate and connect to one another. It will also help you evaluate both the content and organization of your essay.

For instructions on creating a graphic organizer, see Chapter 2, page 40. If you are working on an assignment in Chapters 9–16 or Chapter 18, each of those chapters includes a model graphic organizer for the type of writing covered in the chapter. As you are drawing your graphic organizer, if you spot a detail or an example that does not support a topic sentence, as well as any other problems, write notes to the right of your organizer, as shown in Figure 7.2.

Another option, instead of drawing a graphic organizer, is to write an outline of your draft. For more information on outlining, see p. 124.

COMPUTER HINT

Encourage students to try making a graphic organizer using a word-processing or graphics program. Using a computer will allow them to try out different ways of revising an essay.

ESSAY IN PROGRESS 1

Make a graphic organizer or an outline for the draft essay you wrote in Essay in Progress 3 in Chapter 6 (p. 147), or for any essay that you are working on.

FIGURE 7.2
SAMPLE GRAPHIC ORGANIZER FOR REVISION

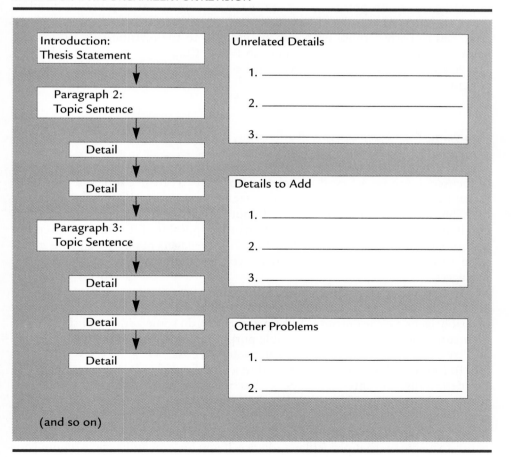

KEY QUESTIONS FOR REVISION

The four key questions listed below will help you know what to look for when you revise. Use the questions to identify broad areas of weakness in your essay.

- Are you unsure of your essay's purpose, audience, and thesis?
- Do you have enough reasons and evidence to support your thesis?
- Does your essay seem to drift or lack structure? Does it have a strong introduction and conclusion?
- Is each paragraph well developed?

After reading your draft or after discussing it with a classmate, try to pinpoint areas that need improvement by answering each of these four questions. Then refer to the self-help flowcharts in the following section. Once you become more familiar with the revision process, you can use the four questions to pinpoint problem areas, and then you can go directly to the appropriate section to discover revision strategies to correct those problems. In addition to the revision suggestions and flowcharts in this chapter, the chapters in Part 3, Chapter 18 in Part 4, and Chapters 20 and 21 in Part 5 provide revision flowcharts that are tailored to the specific assignments in those chapters.

Analyzing Your Purpose and Audience

For more information about purpose and audience, see Chapter 4, p. 73. For more on developing a thesis, see Chapter 5, pp. 97–103.

A good essay reflects your sense of purpose and audience. First drafts are often unfocused, however. A first draft might go off in two or three different directions rather than having a clear purpose. For instance, one section of an essay on divorce may inform readers of its causes, and another section may argue that it harms children. A first draft may contain sections that appeal to different audiences. For instance, one section of an essay on counseling teenagers about drug abuse might seem to be written for parents; other sections might be more appropriate for teenagers.

To find out if your paper has a clear focus, write a sentence stating what your paper is supposed to accomplish. If you cannot write such a sentence, your essay probably lacks a clear purpose. To find a purpose, do some additional thinking or brainstorming, listing as many possible purposes as you can think of. Choose one and try again to write a sentence stating your purpose.

To find out if your essay is directed to a specific audience, write a sentence or two describing your intended readers. Describe their knowledge, beliefs, and experience with your topic. If you are unable to do so, and you are allowed to choose your own audience, reread your essay, considering to whom various portions of the essay may appeal; decide which of these portions is most effective. Revise your paper, focusing on that particular audience. If you have an audience to whom your essay must be directed, brainstorm a list of its characteristics, and add details to your essay that will appeal to people with those characteristics.

ESSAY IN PROGRESS 2

Evaluate the purpose and audience of the draft essay you wrote in Essay in Progress 3 in Chapter 6 (p. 147) or of any essay that you have written. Make notes on your graphic organizer or annotate your outline.

Analyzing Your Thesis, Topic Sentences, and Evidence

Once your paper is focused on a specific purpose and audience, your next step is to evaluate your thesis statement and how well you have supported that thesis. Use Flowchart 7.1 to examine your thesis statement, topic sentences, and evidence.

ESSAY IN PROGRESS 3

Using Flowchart 7.1, evaluate the thesis statement, topic sentences, and evidence of your essay in progress. Make notes on your graphic organizer or annotate your outline.

FLOWCHART 7.1
EVALUATING YOUR THESIS STATEMENT, TOPIC SENTENCES, AND EVIDENCE

Question	Revision Strategies
1. Does your essay have a thesis statement that (a) identifies your topic and (b) states your position or suggests your slant or angle on the topic? (To find out, state your thesis aloud without looking at your essay; then find the sentence in your draft essay that matches or is close to what you have just said. If you cannot find such a sentence, you have probably not written a well-focused thesis statement.)	• Reread your essay and answer this question: What one main point is most of this essay concerned with? • Write a thesis statement that expresses that main point. • Revise your paper to focus on that main point. • Delete parts of the essay that do not support your thesis statement.

No ⇨

Yes ⇩

(Continued on next page)

TEACHING TIP: COLLABORATIVE WRITING AND COMPUTER HINT

(15–20 minutes) Have students draft responses to the flowchart questions on a computer and share their drafts and responses to the flowchart in small groups, online if possible. They should comment on each other's responses, agreeing or disagreeing and offering reasons for their own view of their thesis, topic sentences, and evidence. (This Teaching Tip also applies to Essay in Progress 5. Students should remain in the same groups for both activities.)

FLOWCHART 7.1 (*continued*)

Question	Revision Strategies
2. Have you supplied your readers with all of the background information they need to understand your thesis? (To find out, ask someone unfamiliar with your topic to read your essay, encouraging your reader to ask questions as he or she reads.)	• Answer *Who, What, When, Where, Why,* and *How* questions to discover more background information.

 No

Yes

| 3. Have you presented enough convincing evidence to support your thesis? (To find out, study your graphic organizer or outline. Ask yourself this question: Would I accept the thesis, or does it need more evidence to be convincing?) | • Use prewriting strategies or do additional research to discover more supporting evidence.
• Evaluate this new evidence and add the most convincing evidence to your essay. |

 No

Yes

| 4. Does each topic sentence logically connect to and support the thesis? (To find out, read the thesis and then read each topic sentence. For example, read the thesis and the topic sentence of paragraph 2, then the thesis and the topic sentence of paragraph 3, and so on. When the connection is not obvious, revision is needed.) | • Rewrite the topic sentence so that it clearly supports the thesis.
• If necessary, broaden your thesis so that it encompasses all your supporting points. |

No

Yes

(Continued on next page)

FLOWCHART 7.1 (*continued*)

Question		Revision Strategies
5. Is your evidence specific and detailed? (To find out, go through your draft and underline each piece of information that answers one of these questions: *Who? What? When? Where? Why? How?* If you have not underlined anything in a particular paragraph or have underlined only one sentence or part of a sentence, you need to add more detailed evidence to that paragraph.)	No ⇨	• Name names, give dates, specify places. • Use action verbs and descriptive language, including carefully chosen adjectives and adverbs. • Answer *Who, What, When, Where, Why* and *How* questions to discover more detailed evidence.

Yes

Analyzing Your Organization

Your readers will not be able to follow your ideas if your essay does not hold together as a unified piece of writing. To be sure that it does, examine your essay's organization. The graphic organizer or outline of your draft (see p. 160) that you completed in order to analyze your ideas and evidence will also help you analyze the draft's organization and discover any flaws.

To determine if the organization of your draft is clear and effective, you can also ask a friend to read your draft and then explain how your essay is organized. If your friend cannot describe its organization, it probably needs further work. Use one of the methods in Chapter 6 (pp. 120–24) or one of the patterns of development described in Parts 3 and 4 to organize your ideas.

Once you are satisfied with the draft's organization, evaluate your introduction, conclusion, and title. Use the following questions as guidelines:

1. **Does your introduction interest your reader and provide needed background information?** If your essay jumps into the topic without preparing readers for it, your introduction needs to be revised. Use the suggestions on page 142 to create interest. Ask the "W" questions—*Who, What, When, Where, Why,* and *How*—to determine what background information you need.

2. **Does your conclusion draw your essay to a satisfactory close and reinforce your thesis statement?** To find out, read your introduction and then your

conclusion. Does the conclusion follow logically from the introduction? If it does not, use the suggestions for writing conclusions in Chapter 6 on page 145. Also try imagining yourself explaining the significance or importance of your essay to a friend. Use this explanation to rewrite your conclusion.

3. **Does your title accurately reflect the content of your essay?** To improve your title, think of it as a label. Write a few words that "label" your essay. Also, reread your thesis statement, looking for a few key words that can serve as part of your title. Finally, use the suggestions in Chapter 6 (p. 146) to help you choose a title.

ESSAY IN PROGRESS 4

Evaluate the organization of your essay in progress. Make notes on your graphic organizer or annotate your outline.

Analyzing Your Paragraph Development

See Chapter 6 for more on paragraph development.

Each paragraph within your essay must fully develop a single idea that supports your thesis. (Narrative essays are an exception to this rule. As you will see in Chapter 9, in a narrative essay, each paragraph needs to focus on a separate part of the action.)

In a typical first draft, paragraphs are often weak or loosely structured. They may contain irrelevant information or lack a clearly focused topic sentence. To evaluate your paragraph development, study each paragraph separately in conjunction with your thesis statement. You may need to delete some paragraphs, rework or reorganize other paragraphs, or move selected paragraphs to a more appropriate part of the essay. If you need to supply additional information to support your thesis, you may need to add paragraphs to the draft. Use Flowchart 7.2 to help you analyze and revise your paragraphs.

ESSAY IN PROGRESS 5

Using Flowchart 7.2, examine each paragraph of your essay in progress. Make notes on your graphic organizer or annotate your outline.

WORKING WITH CLASSMATES TO REVISE YOUR ESSAY

TEACHING TIP

If students have done any of the Essay in Progress activities in this chapter collaboratively, point out that they have already engaged in a highly structured version of peer review.

Increasingly, writing instructors, as well as instructors in other academic disciplines, use **peer review** to help students know what to revise. Peer review is a process in which two or more students read and comment on each other's papers. Students might work together in class or outside of class, or communicate via email or a computer network that links class members to one another. Working

FLOWCHART 7.2
EVALUATING YOUR PARAGRAPHS

Question	Revision Strategies
1. Does each paragraph have a clearly focused topic sentence that expresses the main point of the paragraph? (To find out, underline the topic sentence in each paragraph of your draft. Then evaluate whether the topic sentence makes a statement that the rest of the paragraph supports.)	• Revise a sentence that is currently within the paragraph so that it clearly states the main point. • Write a new sentence that states the one main point of the paragraph.

 No

 Yes

2. Do all sentences in each paragraph support the topic sentence? (To find out, read the topic sentence and then read each supporting sentence in turn. The topic sentence and each supporting sentence should fit together.)	• Revise supporting sentences to make their connection to the topic sentence clear. • Delete any sentences that do not support the topic sentence.

 No

 Yes

3. Does the paragraph need further explanation or more supporting details? (To find out, ask yourself this question: Is there other information readers will want or need to know?)	• Add additional details if your paragraph seems skimpy. • Use the *Who, What, When, Where, Why,* and *How* questions to generate the details you need. • Use the prewriting strategies in Chapter 4 to generate additional details.

 No

 Yes

(Continued on next page)

FLOWCHART 7.2 (*continued*)

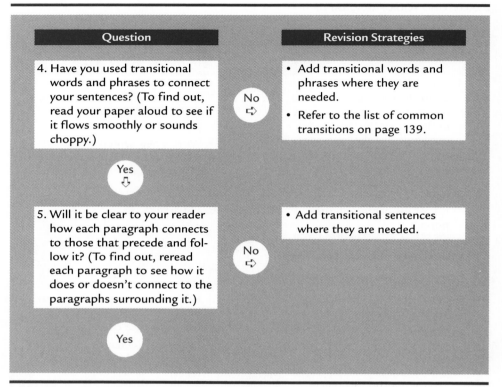

Question	Revision Strategies
4. Have you used transitional words and phrases to connect your sentences? (To find out, read your paper aloud to see if it flows smoothly or sounds choppy.)	• Add transitional words and phrases where they are needed. • Refer to the list of common transitions on page 139.
5. Will it be clear to your reader how each paragraph connects to those that precede and follow it? (To find out, reread each paragraph to see how it does or doesn't connect to the paragraphs surrounding it.)	• Add transitional sentences where they are needed.

with classmates is an excellent way to get ideas for improving your essays. As you read and discuss other students' work, you'll also have the opportunity to discover how they view and approach the writing process. The following suggestions will help both the writer and the reviewer get the most out of the peer review process.

How to Find a Good Reviewer

Your instructor may pair you with another class member or leave it to you to find your own reviewer, either a classmate or someone outside of class. Class members make good reviewers since they are familiar with the assignment and with what you have learned so far in the course. If you need to find someone outside your class, try to choose a person who has already taken the writing course you are taking, preferably someone who has done well. Best friends are not necessarily the best reviewers; they may be reluctant to offer criticism, or they may be too critical. Instead, choose someone who is serious, skillful, and willing to spend the time needed to provide useful comments. If your college has a writing center, you might ask a tutor in the center to read and comment on your draft. Consider using more than one reviewer so you can get several different perspectives on your draft.

COMPUTER HINT

(50 minutes) In order to help students become comfortable at the keyboard, allow one class period for students to evaluate each other's draft essays online or on disk.

• If a network is available, have students engage in real-time virtual conversations, referring to specific passages and topic sentences.

• If a network is not available, encourage students to comment on each other's drafts on disk, adding their comments at the end of the essay or writing them in a separate file.

QUESTIONS FOR REVIEWERS

1. What is the purpose of the paper?
2. Who is the intended audience?
3. Is the introduction fully developed?
4. What is the main point or thesis statement of the draft? Is it easy to identify?
5. Does the essay offer evidence to support each important point? Where is more evidence needed (indicate specific paragraphs)?
6. Is each paragraph clear and well organized?
7. Are transitions used to connect ideas within and between paragraphs?
8. Is the organization easy to follow? Point out places where the organization needs to be improved and suggest ways to do so.
9. Does the conclusion draw the essay to a satisfying close?
10. What do you like about the draft?
11. What are its weaknesses and how could they be eliminated? Underline or highlight sentences that are unclear or confusing.

Suggestions for the Writer

To get the greatest benefit from having another student review your paper, use the following suggestions.

1. Be sure to provide readable copy; a typed, double-spaced draft is preferred.

2. Don't submit a very rough or preliminary draft. If your essay is not very far along, think it through a little more and make additions and revisions. The more developed your draft is, the more helpful the reviewer's comments will be.

3. Define the reviewer's task. Offer specific questions or guidelines so that he or she will know what to do. A sample set of Questions for Reviewers is provided above. Some of these questions will become more meaningful as you work through subsequent chapters of this book. Give your reviewer a copy of these questions, adding others that you need answered. You might also give your reviewer questions from one of the revision flowcharts in this chapter. For example, using questions from Flowchart 7.1, you might ask a reviewer to evaluate your background information or evidence. If you have written an essay in response to an assignment in Chapters 9–16, 18, 20, or 21, consider giving your reviewer the revision flowchart for that assignment.

4. Be open to criticism and new ideas. As much as possible, try not to be defensive; instead, look at your essay objectively, seeing it as your reviewer sees it.

TEACHING TIP

- Emphasize the importance of ownership: Students must *own* responsibility for strengthening their own papers, even when seeking help from peers or writing center tutors.
- Explain that in the writing center, e.g., students may receive more useful guidance if they ask the tutor for help with specific areas (such as the thesis and transitions) than if they have no idea of the strengths and weaknesses of their draft.

5. Don't feel obligated to accept all of the advice you are given. In fact, a reviewer might suggest a change that will not work well in your paper or identify as an error something that is correct. If you are uncertain about a suggestion, discuss it with your instructor.

Suggestions for the Reviewer

Be honest, but tactful. Criticism is never easy to accept, so keep your reader's feelings in mind. The following tips will help you provide useful comments and suggestions to the writer.

1. Read the draft through completely before making any judgments or comments. You will need to read it at least one more time to evaluate it.

2. Concentrate on content; pay attention to what the paper says. Evaluate the writer's train of thought; focus on the main points and how clearly they are expressed. If you notice a misspelling or a grammatical error you can circle it, but spotting errors is not your primary task. Do not correct errors that you discover.

3. Offer some positive comments. It will help the writer to know what is good as well as what needs improvement.

4. Be specific. For instance, instead of saying that more examples are needed, tell the writer which ideas in which paragraphs are unclear without examples.

5. Use the Questions for Reviewers in the accompanying box to guide your review as well as any additional questions that the writer provides. If the essay was written in response to an assignment in one of the chapters in Parts 3, 4, and 5, you might use the revision flowchart in that chapter as an alternative. Keep these questions in mind as you read, and try to answer each one in your response. You might make a copy of the questions and jot your responses next to each question.

6. Write notes and comments directly on the draft. Then, at the end, write a final note summarizing your overall reaction, pointing out both strengths and weaknesses. Here is a sample final note written by a reviewer.

    Overall, I think your paper has great ideas, and I found that it held my interest. The example about the judge did prove your point. I think you should organize it better. The last three paragraphs do not seem connected to the rest of the essay. Maybe better transitions would help, too. Also work on the conclusion. It just says the same thing as your thesis statement.

 7. If you are reviewing a draft on a computer, consider typing your comments in brackets following the appropriate sentence or paragraph or highlighting them in some other way. The writer can easily delete your comments after

reading them. Some word-processing programs have features that make it easy to add comments and suggest revisions.

8. Do not rewrite paragraphs or sections of the paper. Instead, suggest how the writer might revise them.

ESSAY IN PROGRESS 6

Give your essay in progress to a classmate to read and review. Ask your reviewer to respond to the Questions for Reviewers. Revise your essay using your revision outline, your responses to Flowcharts 7.1 and 7.2, and your reviewer's suggestions.

TEACHING TIP

• If students worked in groups for the preceding Essay in Progress activities, have them choose a reviewer who has not yet seen their work.

• Alternatively, ask students to take their drafts to the campus writing center for review by a tutor.

CONSIDERING YOUR LEARNING STYLE

Depending on your learning style, you may tend to write a particular kind of draft, focusing on some elements of an essay and overlooking others. For example, a pragmatic learner tends to write tightly organized drafts, but the draft may lack interest, originality, or sufficient content. A creative learner may write drafts that jump from idea to idea and lack organization. Writers with different learning styles, then, may need to address different kinds of problems as they revise their drafts.

Following are some revision tips for other aspects of your learning style.

• *Independent* learners, who often need extra time for reflection, should be sure to allow sufficient time between drafting and revising. *Social* learners often find discussing revision plans with classmates particularly helpful.

• *Verbal* learners may prefer to use outlining to check the organization of their drafts, while *spatial* learners may find it more helpful to draw a graphic organizer.

• *Rational* learners should be sure their drafts do not seem dull or impersonal, adding personal examples and vivid descriptions where appropriate. *Emotional* learners, whose writing may tend to be overly personal, should state their ideas directly without hedging or showing undue concern for those who may disagree.

• *Concrete* learners, who tend to focus on specifics, should check that their thesis and topic sentences are clearly stated. *Abstract* learners, who tend to focus on general ideas, should be sure they have enough supporting details.

STUDENTS WRITE

After writing her first draft, which appears in Chapter 6 on pages 148–51, Tina Oyer used the guidelines and revision flowcharts in this chapter and Chapter 9 to help her decide what to revise. For example, she decided that she needed to add more details about the store in which she worked and to describe her position as head clerk of the night shift earlier in the essay. She also decided to add more detail about her evening routine in the store and about the customer's reasons for being in the store earlier in the evening.

Oyer asked a classmate named Meg to review her essay. A portion of Meg's comments is shown here.

REVIEWER'S COMMENTS

This is a really interesting incident. It takes several paragraphs before the story picks up, though. Consider adding a scene that shows the store owner interacting with the customer who will later lose her keys, and with his employees. This would make the later scene when he is rude to the customer more striking than it is now.

Also, there is very little dialogue in the essay. You might consider adding some in the paragraph where you give the keys to the customer. You might also add some dialogue that shows how the clerks feel about the store manager.

I like the ending where you return home and find the tricycle. It shows what is really important to you. But I'm still not sure what the incident means to you. You risked your job, but you seem more worried about the woman and what she thinks of the manager.

Using her own analysis and her classmate's suggestions, Oyer created a graphic organizer to help her decide how to revise her draft, using the format for a narrative essay provided in Chapter 9 (p. 214). Oyer's graphic organizer, which includes her notes for revision, is shown in Figure 7.3.

After using Meg's comments, the graphic organizer, and her notes to help her think through her revision, Oyer revised her first draft. A portion of her revised draft, with her revisions marked, follows.

FIGURE 7.3
GRAPHIC ORGANIZER FOR TINA OYER'S FIRST DRAFT

Title	Hypocritically Warm

Introduction Thesis
I learned something unexpected about myself: I can trust my instincts.

Background
The scene in the store

Details about the manager's hypocrisy. The way he treats customers vs. the way he treats workers.

Unnecessary details
- Need less about the manager's behavior toward customers in general.
- How the woman might be feeling about the owner—how would I know?

Event 1
Quitting time. I help close the store.

Event 2
Customer stops us. Tells us about leaving her keys. The owner looks for but doesn't find them. He leaves.

Event 3
The woman makes phone calls. My colleagues look to me to help.

Event 4
The woman walks back to the phone. I think some more.

Event 5
I go back and find the keys.

More details needed
- Need more specific details about the owner: how he looks, what he says.
- Need to add that the owner sets the alarm before leaving—how would he know I went back?
- Need more about the woman's situation: how she left her keys, how the owner treats her—details about how nice he is in the store.
- Need more at the conclusion: What does this incident mean?

Event 6
I return and give the woman her keys. She hugs me—offers to back me up.

Event 7
Woman brushes off her car. I think about how confused she must be.

Other problems
- Need to rethink my thesis—the essay is also about my reaction to the owner's hypocrisy.
- Need to make it more interesting at the beginning (Meg's comment)

Event 8
I say good night and drive home with conflicting feelings, afraid for my job.

Conclusion
I find the pink bike in the garage. The cold wind feels good.

One cold evening in Buffalo I stood in an almost empty parking lot with snow blowing around me, my colleagues and a customer facing me, and a tough choice to make. The snow seemed to melt as soon as it hit my face but I didn't feel the cold. All I could think of was the decision I was facing, a decision that filled me with fear.

~~It was a cold night, when I learned something~~

new ¶

~~unexpected about myself; I can trust my instincts~~. The

temperature was about ten degrees, something we are

used to

especially ~~mindful of~~ in Buffalo /; ~~We are used to it;~~ we

^ During the day, we

expect it. ~~You~~ never can tell by the blinding glare when

we   *can*   *as if*

~~you~~ look out the window. The sun appears to be beaming ~~a~~

it were the   *we*

~~tale of the~~ hottest summer day, but when ~~you~~ step out-

side the cold has the upper hand. That night, the wind

that stung my face wasn't the only thing that was

and I was about to learn just how much chilliness I could tolerate

freezing /, *before I decided to do things my own way.*

Earlier I walked   Hilltop Pharmacy.

~~Walking~~ into ~~a small store,~~ It was time for my

regular shift as evening supervisor. I could feel the

refreshing heat dominate the cold on my skin. The

clerks, all dressed in identical attire, were busy/ wait-

in his immaculate

ing on customers, bagging, and pricing stock. The owner, ^

white coat and aviator glasses, stood at the pharmacy counter, talking to the

~~also the pharmacist, waited on~~ customers. The customers

He always caters to them, and goes to any lengths

are his priority. ~~They get first-class service. They are~~

to please them. "What a nice man"! I've heard more than one customer say on

~~always catered to, and pleased when they leave the~~

the way out of the store.

~~store. If we don't have it, we will order it. He goes to~~

~~any lengths to please them. He even goes to the extreme~~

~~of being sickening sweet at times. If they ask him a~~

~~question, he stops what he is doing and speaks to them~~

~~in a very kind and friendly manner. If they don't feel~~

~~like waiting around for their prescription to be ready,~~

~~he tells them he'll have it delivered. So unlike the~~

~~personality he displays to us, his workers!~~
We employees, however, are not worth this royal treatment.
~~We are his on-the-clock toilers!~~ If we have a

question, we are lucky to get an answer. ~~When we do,~~ his
When he does answer,
eyes never leave the ~~task at hand, and it's most often a~~
pills he is counting or the label he is typing. "Yes,"
~~quick short answer. Unless of course we are fulfilling a~~
"No," or "I don't know" is the most he'll usually say, unless of course we are
standing next to a customer.
~~customer's request. His hypocritical personality is so~~

~~familiar to us. It makes you wonder how anyone could put~~

~~on such a phony front, and have a heart of stone. He~~

~~missed his calling, he should be in Hollywood. Sometimes~~

~~you don't know whether to chuckle or disgorge. At times~~

~~it keeps me entertained. If the customers only knew they~~

~~were buying more than just his merchandise.~~

Before Oyer submitted her final draft, she read her essay several more times, editing it for sentence structure and word choice. She also proofread it once to catch errors in grammar and punctuation as well as typographical errors. (A portion of Oyer's revised essay, with editing and proofreading changes marked, appears in Chapter 8, page 202.) The final version of Oyer's essay follows.

Revised Student Essay

Hypocritically Warm

One cold evening in Buffalo, I stood in an almost 1
empty parking lot with snow blowing around me, my colleagues and a customer facing me, and a tough choice to
make. The snow seemed to melt as soon as it hit my face,

CONNECTIONS

Oyer's essay can serve as a model of a narrative essay—see Chapter 9.

but I didn't feel the cold. All I could think of was the decision I was facing, a decision that filled me with fear.

2   The temperature was about ten degrees, something we are used to in Buffalo; we expect it. During the day, we can never tell the temperature by the blinding glare when we look out the window. The sun can appear to be beaming as if it were the hottest summer day, but when we step outside the cold assaults our senses. That night, the wind that stung my face wasn't the only thing that was freezing, and I was about to learn just how much chilliness I could tolerate before I decided to do things my own way.

3   Earlier, when I had walked into Hilltop Pharmacy to start my regular shift as the evening supervisor, the refreshing heat of the store had made my cold skin tingle. The clerks, all dressed in identical uniforms, were busy waiting on customers, bagging, and pricing stock. The owner, in his immaculate white coat and aviator glasses, stood at the pharmacy counter, talking to the customers, his priority. He always caters to them, and goes to any lengths to please them. "What a nice man!" I've heard more than one customer say on the way out of the store.

4   We employees, however, are not worth this royal treatment. If we have a question, we are lucky to get an answer. When he does answer, his eyes never leave the pills he is counting or the label he is typing. "Yes," "No," or "I don't know" is the most he'll usually say, unless of course we are standing next to a customer.

5   Nothing unusual had happened that evening. I signed time cards for employees who "forgot to punch in," assigned jobs, answered the phone, and helped at the pharmacy counter when the line started to build up. With twenty minutes to go before we could lock up, as I was putting a prescription into a bag for a customer, I heard a familiar voice. It was a woman who always comes into the store right before closing time.

"Any chance I could run next door to the supermarket   6
and pick up a few things while my prescription is being
filled?" she asked the owner breathlessly.

"No problem," he said, his phony smile plastered on   7
his face. "We'll hold the store open a few minutes if we
have to so you don't have to come back tomorrow." She
hurried out.

About fifteen minutes later, she rushed back into   8
the store like a whirlwind and practically ran to the
pharmacy counter. The owner told her that her prescription had expired but said, "I'll give you a couple of
pills to hold you over until you can file your new prescription, then we'll be glad to deliver it." He smiled
his phony smile again, and she thanked him profusely. As
I left the pharmacy counter to start collecting the cash
register drawers to put in the safe, I rolled my eyes. A
nearby clerk rolled her eyes too.

After the safe was locked, the other employees and   9
I retrieved our coats and waited at the door while the
owner set the alarm by punching in his code. Then he
shut the lights off. As we started through the parking
lot on our way to our cars, though, a customer stopped
us. She was the customer who had come in right before
closing. Obviously flustered, she looked at the owner and
said, "I think I left my keys in the store." Without
saying a word, he turned around and ran back into the
store. In what seemed like less than a minute, he came
outside and locked the doors again.

"They're not there," he said. "Sorry." Then he got   10
into his car and drove away, leaving me standing there
with the woman and a couple of co-workers. His curt
answer and quick departure didn't seem out of character
to me, but I was surprised to see him treat a customer
in that way. The customer looked confused. We were all
silent and motionless for a moment, and then the
stranded woman walked over to the pay phone in front of
the pharmacy and picked up the receiver. She punched the
buttons, waited, then hung up and tried again.

11   My two colleagues looked at me. They knew that, as the manager of the night shift on alternate weekends, I could go back in the store and look for the woman's keys. In order to do so, though, I would have to shut the alarm off, using my security code. The owner left knowing that he put his code into the alarm and would want to know why I went back into the store. Helping the woman could cost me my job.

12   Finally, the woman hung up the phone with a bang and walked toward us. "Do you have any change you could lend me?" she asked. Instead of change, I took the keys to the store out of my pocket, feeling as if I still hadn't made a final decision and was just going through the motions. As if I were a robot, I walked back to the pharmacy, unlocked the doors, locked them behind me, and ran and put my security code into the alarm. Then I hurried through the store, feeling like a criminal. Finally, I spotted the keys on the video counter and laughed. I wondered if the owner's glasses had been fogged up from the change in temperature. I picked up the keys, reset the alarm, and locked the doors again.

13   When I returned to the parking lot, I held up the keys, jingled them, and placed them in the woman's hand. "Oh, thank you so much. You saved my life!" she exclaimed, hugging me. "I'll call the owner tomorrow, if you want me to, and tell him exactly what happened." I smiled weakly, but inside I was panicking. Even if the woman did call him, I didn't know what his reaction would be.

14   I said good night to my co-workers, and we all headed for our cars. As I started my car and brushed off the snow, any lingering sense of happiness wore off. I was just relieved to be going home.

15   My feelings were still all mixed up as I drove through the icy streets toward home. I was elated that I had helped the woman, but I had a huge knot in my stomach as I realized that I might soon be unemployed. The longer I drove, though, the more I began to feel content

TEACHING TIP: COLLABORATIVE WRITING AND LEARNING STYLES

Try pairing independent learners with social learners, verbal learners with spatial learners, rational learners with emotional learners, and concrete learners with abstract learners to analyze Oyer's revision.

POSSIBLE ANSWERS: ANALYZING THE REVISION

1. Oyer added a new opening paragraph, added more specific details about the incident involving the woman who lost her keys, cut back on her description of the owner's treatment of customers and employees, cut out speculation about how the woman felt about the owner's behavior, and added dialogue. Her revisions make the introduction more interesting and the event more vivid for readers; they also focus the essay on what the incident meant to the writer.

with my decision. By the time I reached my house, I had
realized that it was more important to me not to leave
the woman stranded than to protect my job. Unlike the
owner, I couldn't stop being considerate to my customers
just because I had punched out on the time clock.

    As I pulled into my driveway, I pushed the button   16
to open the garage door. In the middle of the garage was
a little pink bike with tiny training wheels. I got out
of the car to move the bike, and once again the cold
wind stung my face. It felt good.

Analyzing the Revision

1. Identify the major revisions that Oyer made. How did she carry out the plan indicated in her graphic organizer?

2. Choose one major revision that Oyer made and explain why you think it improved her essay.

3. Evaluate Oyer's introduction and conclusion. In what ways are they more effective than the introduction and conclusion in her first draft? What additional improvements could she make?

4. Choose one paragraph and compare the details provided in it with those in the corresponding paragraph of the first draft. Which added details are particularly effective, and why?

2. Two possibilities: (a) Oyer moved her thesis to the end and sharpened it: "... I couldn't stop being considerate to my customers just because I had punched out on the time clock." The events naturally led her to this conclusion. (b) Her description of the owner ("his immaculate white coat and aviator glasses"), his dialogue with the customer, and his behavior in the parking lot show readers what he was like much more effectively than the general description given in the first draft.

3. Oyer's revised introduction gets readers right into the action and her crisis from the start of the essay. The revised conclusion includes her thesis and a final reference to the imagery of cold versus heat. Some readers may be left wondering how the owner reacted, although others may consider the ambiguity more effective than a resolution.

4. *Possible paragraph:* The first draft of paragraph 6 includes only the information that the woman made a few phone calls. In contrast, paragraph 10 of the final draft increases the tension by describing the action: the woman walking over to the pay phone and making several calls without success.

"GOT IDEA. TALK BETTER. COMBINE WORDS. MAKE SENTENCES."

"LET ME GET THIS STRAIGHT NOW. IS WHAT YOU WANT TO BUILD A JEAN FACTORY OR A GENE FACTORY?"

Chapter **8**

CHAPTER QUICK START

The cartoons on the facing page take a humorous view of language; however, each makes a point about writing as well.

Writing Quick Start

Write a few sentences describing what you think the cartoons suggest about writing and about the focus of this chapter — editing sentences and words.

Editing Sentences and Words

TEACHING TIP
- Discuss what each cartoon reveals about the topic of this chapter.
- Encourage students to bring in other cartoons and humorous articles about words and sentences to make the chapter topic less forbidding and more approachable.

Once you have revised an essay for content and organization as discussed in Chapter 7, you are ready to edit and proofread the essay. Your task is to examine individual sentences and words with care, to be sure that each conveys your meaning accurately, concisely, and in an interesting way. This chapter will help you sharpen your sentences and refine your word choice.

Like most student writers, and especially if you are an abstract or a creative learner, you may tend to concentrate on developing your ideas in an essay and may overlook the more concrete or pragmatic aspects of the writing process. But even an essay with good ideas will be ineffective if its sentences are vague and imprecise or if its words convey an inappropriate tone and level of diction. Therefore, your goal at this point is to improve your revised draft through the use of clear, correct sentences and effective word choice. This chapter offers specific guidelines for editing sentences and words.

As shown in Figure 8.1, editing and proofreading are the final steps in the writing process. Because you are almost finished, you may be tempted to hurry through these steps, or skip them altogether. Careful editing and proofreading will always pay off in the end, however, because an error-free essay makes a good impression on the reader.

**FIGURE 8.1
AN OVERVIEW OF THE WRITING PROCESS**

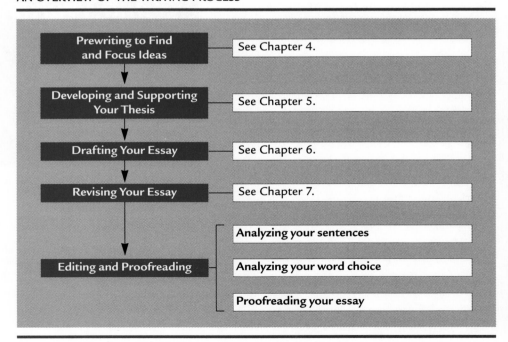

ANALYZING YOUR SENTENCES

Each sentence in your essay should be concise and clear. Overall, you should use a variety of sentence types to add interest, and your sentence elements should be parallel in structure, and you should use strong, active verbs. For each section that follows, consider the question in the heading, and then use the suggestions given after the heading for improving your sentences.

Are Your Sentences Concise?

Sentences that are concise convey their meaning in as few words as possible. Use the following suggestions to make your sentences concise.

1. **Avoid wordy expressions.** Search your essay for sentences with empty phrases that contribute little or no meaning to the sentence. Use this rule: If the sentence is clear without a particular phrase, or if the phrase can be replaced by a more direct word or phrase, take it out or replace it. Here are a few examples.

▶ ~~In the near future,~~ *A*nother revolution in computer technology is bound to occur/ *soon.*

▶ ~~In light of the fact that~~ *Since* computer technology changes ~~every month or so~~ *monthly,* software upgrades are ~~what everybody has to do.~~ *necessary.*

2. **Eliminate redundancy.** A common problem, **redundancy** is the unnecessary repetition of words or ideas. Redundant sentences say the same thing twice by using the same words or different words that have the same meaning. Here are some examples.

▶ ~~My decision to choose the field of~~ *Choosing* accounting as my major will lead to steady, rewarding employment.

▶ ~~The type of slang I notice~~ *T*eenagers ~~using is part of the way they~~ *use slang to* establish ~~who they are and what~~ their identity.~~is.~~

3. **Eliminate unnecessary sentence openings.** When you first write down an idea, you may express it indirectly or awkwardly. As you revise, look for and edit sentence openings that sound indirect or tentative. Consider these examples.

▶ ~~It is my opinion that~~ *F*ast-food restaurants should post nutritional information for each menu item.

▶ ~~Many people would agree that~~ nutritious food and snacks ~~are~~ a priority for health-conscious people.

Selecting ... *is* ... *many*

An **adverb** modifies a verb, an adjective, or another adverb.

4. Eliminate unnecessary adverbs. Using too many **adverbs** can weaken your writing. Adverbs such as *extremely, really,* and *very,* known as intensifiers, add nothing and can actually weaken the word they modify. Notice that the following sentence is stronger without the adverb.

▶ The journalist was ~~very~~ elated when he learned that he had won a Pulitzer Prize.

Other adverbs, such as *somewhat, rather,* and *quite,* also add little or no meaning and are often unnecessary.

▶ The college president was ~~quite~~ disturbed by the findings of the Presidential Panel on Sex Equity.

5. Eliminate unnecessary phrases and clauses. Wordy phrases and clauses can make it difficult for readers to find and understand the main point of your sentence. This problem often occurs when you use too many **prepositional phrases** and clauses that begin with *who, which,* or *that.*

A **prepositional phrase** is a group of words that begins with a preposition and includes the object or objects of the preposition and all their modifiers: *above the low wooden table.*

▶ The complaints ~~of students in the college~~ encouraged the dean to create additional parking ~~spaces for cars~~.

students' ... *areas.*

▶ The ~~teenagers who were~~ mall walkers disagreed with the editorial ~~in the newspaper~~ ~~that supported the~~ shopping mall regulations.

teenage ... *newspaper* ... *supporting*

POSSIBLE REVISIONS

1. Because Professor Wu assigned twenty-five math problems for tomorrow, I must miss the U.S. vice president's lecture this evening.
2. Workers are often forced to use old equipment because of a policy that forbids replacement.
3. Bill Cosby is a prime example of an over-publicized entertainment celebrity.
4. The president of Warehouse Industries has the ability and power to hire and fire.
5. The soccer league's sponsor purchased league jerseys as advertisements.

EXERCISE 8.1

Edit the following sentences to make them concise.

1. Due to the fact that Professor Wu assigned twenty-five math problems for tomorrow, I am forced to make the decision to miss this evening's lecture to be given by the vice president of the United States.
2. In many cases, workers are forced to use old equipment that needs replacing due to the fact that there is a policy that does not permit replacement.
3. Bill Cosby is one of the best examples of an entertainment celebrity being given too much publicity.
4. The president of Warehouse Industries has the ability and power to decide who should and who should not be hired and who should and who should not be fired.
5. The soccer league's sponsor, as a matter of fact, purchased league jerseys for the purpose of advertisement and publicity.

Are Your Sentences Varied?

Sentences that are varied will help to hold your reader's interest and make your writing flow more smoothly. Vary the type, length, and pattern of your sentences.

How to Vary Sentence Type

There are four basic types of sentences: *simple, compound, complex,* and *compound-complex.* Each type consists of one or more clauses. A **clause** is a group of words with both a subject and a verb. There are two types of clauses. An **independent clause** can stand alone as a complete sentence. A **dependent clause** cannot stand alone as a complete sentence. It begins with a subordinating conjunction (for example, *because* or *although*) or a relative pronoun (for example, *when, which,* or *that*).

Here is a brief summary of each sentence type and its clauses.

Sentence Type	Clauses That Comprise It	Example
Simple	One independent clause	Credit card fraud is increasing in the United States.
Compound	Two or more independent clauses	Credit card fraud is increasing in the United States; it is a violation of financial privacy.
Complex	One or more dependent clauses joined to one independent clause	Because credit card fraud is increasing in America, consumers must become more cautious.
Compound-Complex	One or more dependent clauses and two or more independent clauses	Because credit card fraud is increasing in America, consumers must be cautious, and retailers must take steps to protect consumers.

Use the following suggestions to vary your sentence types.

1. Use simple sentences for emphasis and clarity. A **simple sentence** contains only one independent clause, but it is not necessarily short. It can have more than one subject, more than one verb, and several modifiers.

▶ Both <u>retailers</u> and <u>consumers</u> <u>have</u> and <u>must exercise</u> the responsibility <u>to curtail</u>
     subject   subject   verb   verb   modifier

<u>fraud</u> by reporting suspicious use of credit cards.
          modifier

TEACHING TIP

Some students may mistake long sentences for run-ons, while other students may mistake long dependent clauses for complete sentences. Be certain students *see* the difference. Write a long sentence on the board (e.g., "You must prepare and revise several essays to become comfortable with the writing process") and label the parts of the sentence to demonstrate that there is only one independent clause. Then add *Although* at the beginning of the sentence to demonstrate how a long sentence can become a fragment.

A short, simple sentence can be used to emphasize an important point or to make a dramatic statement.

▶   Credit card fraud is rampant.

If you use too many simple sentences, however, your writing will sound choppy and disjointed.

▶   It was a cold, drizzly spring morning. I was driving to school. A teenage hitchhiker stood alongside the road. He seemed distraught.

2. Use compound sentences to clarify relationships. A compound sentence consists of two or more independent clauses joined in one of the following ways.

Coordinating conjunctions *(and, but, or, nor, for, so, yet)* connect sentence elements that are of equal importance.

- With a comma and **coordinating conjunction** *(and, but, or, nor, so, for, yet)*:

  ▶   Leon asked a question, *and* the whole class was surprised.

- With a semicolon:

  ▶   Graffiti had been scrawled on the subway walls; passersby ignored it.

A conjunctive adverb is a word (such as *also, however,* or *still*) that links two independent clauses.

- With a semicolon and a **conjunctive adverb**:

  ▶   Each year thousands of children are adopted; *consequently,* adoption service agencies have increased in number.

A correlative conjunction is a word pair (such as *not only . . . but also*) that works together to join elements within a sentence.

- With a correlative conjunction:

  ▶   *Either* the jury will reach a verdict tonight, *or* they will recess until Monday morning.

Use compound sentences to join ideas of equal importance. For instance, in the following sentence, both ideas are equally important and receive equal emphasis.

▶   Several air disasters have involved small commuter planes; consequently, some air travelers try to avoid flying in them.

You can also use compound sentences to explain *how* ideas are related. You can, for example, suggest each of the following relationships, depending on the coordinating conjunction you choose.

Coordinating Conjunction	Relationship	Example
and	Additional information	The three teenage vandals were apprehended, *and* their parents were required to pay damages.
but, yet	Contrasts or opposites	Fares on major airlines are increasing, *yet* discount airlines are struggling to survive.

| *for, so* | Causes or effects | Telephone calls can interrupt a busy worker constantly, *so* answering machines are a necessity. |
| *or, nor* | Choices or options | Quebec may become a separate country, *or* it may settle its differences with the Canadian government. |

3. Use complex sentences to show subordinate relationships. A **complex sentence** consists of one independent clause and at least one dependent clause; either type of clause may come first. When the dependent clause appears first, it is followed by a comma. When the independent clause comes first, a comma is not used.

▶ **Because the dam broke, the village flooded.**

▶ **The village flooded because the dam broke.**

Use complex sentences to show that one or more ideas are less important than (or subordinate to) another idea. In the preceding sentence, the main point is that the village flooded. The dependent clause explains *why* the flood happened. A dependent clause often begins with a *subordinating conjunction* that indicates how the less important (dependent) idea is related to the more important (independent) idea.

Here is a list of some subordinating conjunctions and the relationships they suggest.

Subordinating Conjunction	*Relationship*	*Example*
as, as far as, as soon as, as if, as though, although, even though, even if, in order to	Circumstance	*Even though* cable television has expanded, it is still unavailable in some rural areas.
because, since, so that	Causes or effects	*Because* the movie industry has changed, the way theaters are built has changed.
before, after, while, until, when	Time	*When* prices rise, demand falls.
whether, if, unless, even if	Condition	More people will purchase satellite dishes *if* they become less expensive.

Dependent clauses can also begin with a relative pronoun (*that, who, which*).

▶ **Many medical doctors *who are affiliated with a teaching hospital* use interns in their practice.**

TEACHING TIP

Some students think it is incorrect to begin a sentence with a subordinating conjunction. Write a sample sentence on the board; then demonstrate that the entire subordinate clause can appear at the beginning or end of the sentence.

To see how complex sentences can improve your writing, study the following two paragraphs. The first paragraph consists primarily of simple and compound sentences. The revised paragraph uses complex sentences that show relationships.

ORIGINAL

Are you one of the many people who has tried to quit smoking? Well, don't give up trying. Help is here in the form of a nonprescription drug. A new nicotine patch has been developed. This patch will help you to quit gradually. That way, you will experience less severe withdrawal symptoms. Quitting will be easier than ever before. You need to be psychologically ready to quit smoking. Otherwise, you may not be successful.

REVISED

If you are one of the many people who has tried to quit smoking, don't give up trying. Help is now here in the form of a nonprescription nicotine patch, which has been developed to help you quit gradually. Because you experience less severe withdrawal symptoms, quitting is easier than ever before. However, for this patch to be successful, you need to be psychologically ready to quit.

4. Use compound-complex sentences occasionally to express complicated relationships. A **compound-complex sentence** contains one or more dependent clauses and two or more independent clauses.

▶   If you expect to study medicine, you must take courses in biology and chemistry, and you must prepare for three more years of study after college.

Use compound-complex sentences sparingly; when overused, they tend to make your writing sound wordy and labored.

POSSIBLE REVISIONS

1. When a day-care center looks respectable, parents assume it is safe and well run.
2. In some . . . minimal, and on-the-job . . . is infrequent.
3. Although restaurants . . . violations, day-care centers rarely are.
4. Because more and more . . . work force, the need . . . dramatically.
5. Day-care workers naturally . . . children, yet few . . . stimulation.

EXERCISE 8.2

Combine each of the following sentence pairs into a single compound or complex sentence.

1. A day-care center may look respectable.
    Parents assume a day-care center is safe and run well.

2. In some states, the training required to become a day-care worker is minimal.
    On-the-job supervision and evaluation of day-care workers are infrequent.

3. Restaurants are often fined or shut down for minor hygiene violations.
    Day-care centers are rarely fined or closed down for hygiene violations.

4. More and more mothers have entered the work force.
    The need for quality day care has increased dramatically.

5. Naturally, day-care workers provide emotional support for children.
    Few day-care workers are trained to provide intellectual stimulation.

How to Vary Sentence Length

Usually, if you vary sentence type, you will automatically vary sentence length as well. Simple sentences tend to be short, whereas compound and complex sentences tend to be longer. Compound-complex sentences tend to be the longest. You can, however, use sentence length for specific effects. Short sentences tend to be sharp and emphatic; they move ideas forward quickly, creating a fast-paced essay. In the following example, a series of short sentences creates a dramatic pace.

▶ The jury had little to debate. The incriminating evidence was clear and incontrovertible. The jury announced its verdict with astonishing speed.

Longer sentences, in contrast, move the reader more slowly through the essay. Notice that the lengthy sentence in this example suggests a leisurely, unhurried pace.

▶ While standing in line, impatient to ride the antique steam-powered train, a child begins to imagine how the train will crawl deliberately, endlessly along the tracks, slowly gathering speed as it spews grayish steam and emits hissing noises.

How to Vary Sentence Patterns

A sentence is usually made up of subject(s), verb(s), and modifiers. **Modifiers** are words (adjectives or adverbs), phrases, or clauses that describe, qualify, or limit another part of the sentence (a noun, pronoun, verb, phrase, or clause). Think of a modifier as a word or group of words that provides additional information about a part of the sentence. Here are some examples of modifiers in sentences.

WORDS AS MODIFIERS:	The *empty* classroom was unlocked. [adjective] The office runs *smoothly.* [adverb]
PHRASES AS MODIFIERS:	The student *in the back* raised his hand. Schools should not have the right *to mandate community service.*
CLAUSES AS MODIFIERS:	The baseball *that flew into the stands* was caught by a fan. *When the exam was over,* I knew I had earned an *A.*

As you can see, the placement of modifiers may vary, depending on the pattern of the sentence. The most common sentence patterns (or sentence structures) are described here.

1. **Modifier last: subject-verb-modifier.** In this sentence pattern, the main message (expressed in the subject and verb) comes first, followed by information that clarifies or explains the message.

subject   verb   modifier

▶ The instructor announced that class was canceled. [clause as modifier]

LEARNING STYLES

• Spatial learners may find sentence diagramming an effective strategy for understanding sentence structure. To

(Continued on next page)

save time, you can offer an informal diagram of the first sample sentence ("The instructor announced . . ."): Draw a vertical line between *instructor* and *announced;* draw a vertical line below *announced* and write the modifier next to the line to indicate its connection to the verb.
• Other learners may find it helpful to underline subjects, double-underline main verbs, place brackets around modifiers, and draw an arrow from each modifier to the word or phrase it modifies.

TEACHING TIPS
• Explain that a periodic sentence creates suspense because the main action is withheld until the end of the sentence.
• (5 minutes) Have students compose a long periodic sentence leading up to a surprising situation at the end.

In some cases, a string of modifiers follows the subject and verb.

               subject   verb   modifiers

▶ The salesperson demonstrated the word-processing software, creating and deleting files, moving text, creating directories, and formatting tables.

2. Modifier first: modifier-subject-verb. Sentences that follow this pattern are called **periodic sentences.** Notice that most explanatory information precedes the main point, shifting the emphasis to the end of the sentence and slowing the overall pace.

                     modifier   subject verb

▶ Tired and depressed from hours of work, divers left the scene of the accident.

Use this sentence pattern sparingly. Too many periodic sentences will make your writing sound stiff and unnatural.

3. Modifier in the middle: subject-modifier-verb. In sentences that follow this pattern, the modifier or modifiers appear between the subject and the verb. The modifier thus interrupts the main point and tends to slow the pace of the sentence. The emphasis is on the subject because it comes first in the sentence.

             subject   modifier   verb

▶ The paramedic, trained and experienced in water rescue, was first on the scene of the boating accident.

Avoid placing too many modifiers between the subject and verb in a sentence. Doing so may cause your reader to miss the sentence's key idea.

4. Modifiers used throughout. In this pattern, modifiers are used throughout a sentence.

                 modifier   subject

▶ Because human organs are in short supply, awarding an organ transplant, especially

       modifier   verb   modifier

hearts and kidneys, to patients has become a controversial issue, requiring difficult medical and ethical decisions.

By varying the order of subjects, verbs, and modifiers, you can give emphasis where it is needed as well as vary sentence patterns. In the first paragraph that follows, notice the monotonous effect of using the same subject-verb-modifier pattern in all of the sentences. In the revised paragraph, the ideas are better developed and the main point comes alive as a result of the varied sentence patterns.

ORIGINAL

Theme parks are growing in number and popularity. Theme parks have a single purpose — to provide family entertainment centered around high-action activities. The most famous theme parks are Disney World and Disneyland. They serve as models for other, smaller parks. Theme parks always have amusement rides. Theme parks can offer other activities such as swimming. Theme parks will probably continue to be popular.

TEACHING TIP

Ask the class to analyze why this paragraph sounds monotonous. In addition to the repetition of a single sentence pattern, the sentence beginnings are repetitive and boring ("Theme parks . . .").

REVISED

Theme parks are growing in number and popularity. Offering high-action activities, theme parks fulfill a single purpose — to provide family entertainment. The most famous parks, Disney World and Disneyland, serve as models for other, smaller parks. Parks always offer amusement rides, which appeal to both children and adults. Added attractions such as swimming, water slides, and boat rides provide thrills and recreation. Because of their family focus, theme parks are likely to grow in popularity.

EXERCISE 8.3

Add modifiers to the following sentences to create varied sentence patterns.

1. The divers jumped into the chilly waters.
2. The beach was closed because of pollution.
3. Coffee-flavored drinks are becoming popular.
4. The dorm was crowded and noisy.
5. The exam was more challenging than we expected.

POSSIBLE REVISIONS

1. *Working quickly to find the missing child,* the divers jumped into the chilly waters; The divers, *some in wetsuits and others in their bathing suits,* jumped . . . ; *In spite of their hunger and fatigue,* the divers . . . waters, *which were thick with algae.*
2. *To the disappointment of sweltering city dwellers,* the beach was closed because of pollution; The beach, *empty and desolate,* was closed . . . ; The beach . . . pollution, *a slick black ooze that covered the rocks and sand.*
3. *With coffee bars opening all over the country,* coffee-flavored drinks are becoming popular; Coffee-flavored drinks, *with exotic names and sometimes outrageous ingredients,* are . . . ; Coffee-flavored drinks . . . popular *despite worries about the effects of caffeine.*

Are Your Sentences Parallel in Structure?

Parallelism means that similar ideas in a sentence are expressed in similar grammatical form. It means balancing words with words, phrases with phrases, and clauses with clauses. Use parallelism to make your sentences flow smoothly and your thoughts easy to follow. Study the following pairs of sentences. Which sentence in each pair is easier to read?

▸ The horse was large, had a bony frame, and it was friendly.
▸ The horse was large, bony, and friendly.

▸ Maria enjoys swimming and drag races cars.
▸ Maria enjoys swimming and drag racing.

In each pair, the second sentence sounds better because it is balanced grammatically. *Large, bony,* and *friendly* are all adjectives. *Swimming* and *drag racing* are nouns ending in *-ing.*

The following sentence elements should be parallel in structure.

4. *An old brick building with faded carpeting,* the dorm was crowded and noisy; *The dorm, my least favorite place to be on a Saturday night,* was . . . ; *The dorm was . . . because of a huge party on the third floor.*

5. *Taking more than an hour to complete,* the exam was more challenging than we expected; *The exam was more challenging, but less comprehensive,* than . . . ; *The exam . . . expected, lulled into a false sense of security as we were.*

1. **Nouns in a series should be parallel.**

   ▶ A thesis statement, ~~that is clear~~ *clear*, strong supporting paragraphs, and ~~a~~ *an interesting* conclusion ~~that should be interesting~~ are all elements of a well-written essay.

2. **Adjectives in a series should be parallel.**

   ▶ The concertgoers were rowdy and ~~making a great deal of noise.~~ *noisy.*

3. **Verbs in a series should be parallel.**

   ▶ The sports fans jumped and ~~were applauding.~~ *applauded.*

4. **Phrases and clauses within a sentence should be parallel.**

   ▶ The parents who supervised the new playground were pleased ~~about~~ *that* the preschoolers ~~playing~~ *played* congenially and that everyone enjoyed the sandbox.

5. **Items being compared should be parallel.** When items within a sentence are compared or contrasted, use the same grammatical form for each item.

   ▶ It is usually better to study for an exam over a period of time than ~~cramming~~ *to cram* the night before.

POSSIBLE REVISIONS

1. The biology . . . reviewing his weekly textbook assignments, writing a research report, and going over lab reports.
2. The career counselor . . . courses and to register. . . .
3. Three reasons . . . prices, and serve food that most people like.
4. Driving to Boston is as expensive as taking the train.
5. While . . . first to look both ways and then to proceed with caution.

EXERCISE 8.4

Edit the following sentences to eliminate problems with parallelism.

1. The biology student spent Saturday morning reviewing his weekly textbook assignments, writing a research report, and with lab reports.
2. The career counselor advised Althea to take several math courses and that she should also register for at least one computer course.
3. Three reasons for the popularity of fast-food restaurants are that they are efficient, offer reasonable prices, and most people like the food they serve.
4. Driving to Boston is as expensive as it is to take the train.
5. While at a stop sign, it is important first to look both ways and then proceeding with caution is wise.

Do Your Sentences Have Strong, Active Verbs?

Strong, active verbs make your writing lively and vivid. By contrast, *to be* verbs (*is, was, were, has been,* and so on) and other **linking verbs** (*feels, became, seems, appears*), which connect a noun or pronoun to words that describe it, can make your writing sound dull. Often, these verbs contribute little meaning to a sentence. Whenever possible use stronger, more active verbs.

TO BE VERB:	The puppy *was* afraid of thunder.
ACTION VERBS:	The puppy *whimpered* and *quivered* during the thunderstorm.
LINKING VERB:	The child *looked* frightened as she boarded the bus for her first day of kindergarten.
ACTION VERBS:	The child *trembled* and *clung* to her sister as she boarded the bus for her first day of kindergarten.

In order to strengthen your writing, try to use active verbs rather than passive verbs as much as possible. A **passive verb** is a form of the verb *to be* combined with a past participle (*walked, drank, shouted*). In a sentence with a passive verb, the subject is acted upon rather than performing the action. By contrast, in a sentence with an **active verb,** the subject performs the action.

PASSIVE:	It *was claimed* by the cyclist that the motorist failed to yield the right of way.
ACTIVE:	The cyclist *claimed* that the motorist failed to yield the right of way.

Notice that the first sentence emphasizes the claim, not the person who made the claim. In the second sentence, the person who made the claim is the subject and the verb is active.

Unless you decide deliberately to de-emphasize the subject, try to avoid using passive verbs. On occasion, you may need to use passive verbs, however, to emphasize the object or person receiving the action.

▶ The irreplaceable Steinway grand piano *was destroyed* by the flood.

Passive verbs may also be appropriate if you do not know or choose not to reveal who performed an action. Journalists often use passive verbs for this reason.

▶ It *was confirmed* late Tuesday that Senator Kraemer *is resigning.*

EXERCISE 8.5

Edit the following sentences by changing passive verbs to active ones, adding a subject when necessary.

1. Songs about peace were composed by folk singers in the 1960s.
2. The exam was thought to be difficult because it covered thirteen chapters.
3. For water conservation, it is recommended that low-water consumption dishwashers be purchased.

POSSIBLE REVISIONS

1. In the 1960s, folk singers composed songs about peace.
2. Some students thought the exam was difficult . . . chapters.
3. To conserve water, consumers should purchase low-water consumption dishwashers.

(Continued on next page)

4. The university opened the new satellite center so that . . . homes.
5. In aggressive telemarketing sales calls, the caller urges the consumer to make . . . change.

4. The new satellite center was opened by the university so that students could attend classes nearer their homes.
5. In aggressive telemarketing sales calls, the consumer is urged by the caller to make an immediate decision before prices change.

Evaluating Your Sentences

Always read through your essay once to check for wordy, unclear, or monotonous sentences. If you have trouble identifying sentences that need revision, ask a classmate or friend to read and evaluate your essay by marking any problematic sentences.

ESSAY IN PROGRESS 1

For your essay in progress (the one you worked on in Chapters 6 and 7) or any essay you are working on, evaluate and edit your sentences.

ANALYZING YOUR WORD CHOICE

Each word you select contributes to the meaning of your essay. Consequently, when you are revising be sure to analyze your word choice, or **diction.** The words you choose should suit your purpose, audience, and tone. Suppose, for instance, that you are writing an editorial for your local newspaper in which you are protesting an incident of vandalism in your neighborhood. You would not write "those jerks should be penalized" because the word *jerks* is not appropriate for your audience or your purpose. Instead, you might say "the *vandals* should be penalized." This section describes five aspects of word choice to consider as you evaluate and revise your essay.

- Tone and level of diction
- Word connotations
- Concrete and specific language
- Figures of speech
- Verb-noun combinations

Are Your Tone and Level of Diction Appropriate?

Imagine that as a technician at a computer software company you discover a time-saving shortcut for installing the company's best-selling software program. Your supervisor asks you to write two memos describing your discovery and how it works: one for your fellow technicians at the company, and the other for customers who might purchase the program. Would both memos say the same thing in the same way? Definitely not. The two memos would differ not only in content but also in tone and level of diction. The memo addressed to the other technicians would be technical and concise, explaining how to use the shortcut and why it works. The memo directed to customers would praise the discovery, mention the time customers will save, and explain in nontechnical terms how to use the shortcut.

Tone refers to how you sound to your readers and how you feel about your topic. Your word choice should be consistent with your tone. Your memo to the technicians would have a direct, no-nonsense tone. Your memo to the customers would be enthusiastic.

There are three common *levels of diction:* formal, popular, and informal. The **formal** level of diction is serious and dignified. Think of it as the kind of language that judges use in interpreting laws, presidents employ when greeting foreign dignitaries, or speakers choose for commencement addresses. Formal diction is often written in the third person, tends to include long sentences and multisyllabic words, and contains no slang or contractions. It has a slow, rhythmic flow and an authoritative, distant, and impersonal tone. Here is an example taken from *The Federalist, No. 51,* a political tract written by James Madison in 1788 to explain constitutional theory.

> It is of great importance in a republic, not only to guard the society against the oppression of its rulers, but to guard one part of the society against the injustice of the other part. Different interests necessarily exist in different classes of citizens. If a majority be united by a common interest, the rights of the minority will be insecure.

Formal diction is also used in scholarly publications, in operation manuals, and in most academic fields. Notice in the following excerpt from a chemistry textbook that the language is concise, exact, and marked by specialized terms, called *jargon,* used within the particular field of study. The examples of jargon are in italics.

> A *catalyst* is classified as *homogeneous* if it is present in the same *phase* as that of the *reactants.* For *reactants* that are *gases,* a *homogeneous catalyst* is also a *gas.*
> ATKINS AND PERKINS, *Chemistry: Molecules, Matter, and Change*

Popular or casual diction is common in magazines and newspapers. It sounds more conversational and personal than formal diction. Contractions may be used, and sentences tend to be shorter and less varied than in formal diction. The first person (*I, me, mine, we*) or second person (*you, your*) may be used. Consider this example taken from a popular newsmagazine, *US News & World Report.*

> Add Joe Camel to the list of extinct species. After a 10-year run in which he has been everything from marketing tool extraordinaire to anti-smoking-lobby lighting rod, tobacco giant R. J. Reynolds has already decided to end the ad campaign featuring the cartoon dromedary.
> JASON VEST, "Joe Camel Walks His Last Mile"

In this excerpt, the writer conveys a light, casual tone.

Informal diction, also known as **colloquial language,** is the language of every-day speech and conversation. It is friendly and casual. Contractions (*wasn't, I'll*), slang expressions (*cops, chill out, "What's happening?"*), sentence fragments, and first-person and second-person pronouns are all common in informal diction. This level of diction should not be used in essays and academic writing, except when it is part of a quotation or a block of dialogue. Here is an example of informal diction.

> This guy in my history class is a candidate for the Hall of Fame of Annoying People. He drives us crazy. He's nuts! He doesn't allow anybody to have a real conversation. I mean, this guy interrupts constantly. He's brutal — get a life, Jeffrey.

Notice the use of the first person, slang expressions, and a loose sentence structure.

TEACHING TIP

Note that to formalize this passage, students should change the first person to the third person and replace slang with more formal diction. This process is called *upwriting*. (Conversely, lowering the level of formality is called *downwriting*.)

EXERCISE 8.6

Revise the following informal statement by giving it a more formal level of diction.

> It hadn't occurred to me that I might be exercising wrong, though I suppose the signs were there. I would drag myself to the gym semi-regularly and go through the motions of walking (sometimes jogging) on the treadmill and doing light weight training. But I rarely broke a sweat. I just didn't have the energy. "Just doing it" wasn't cutting it. My body wasn't improving. In fact, certain areas were getting bigger, overly muscular. I needed someone to kick my butt — and reduce it too.
>
> WENDY SCHMID, "Roped In," *Vogue*

POSSIBLE REVISION

The average person can exercise incorrectly without realizing it. Going to the gym semi-regularly, walking or occasionally jogging on the treadmill, and doing light weight training do not assure a healthful workout. The casual exerciser who rarely elevates his or her heart rate to the level recommended for cardiovascular exercise will not experience physical improvement. In fact, certain areas of the body may become enlarged and overly muscular.

Do You Use Words with Appropriate Connotations?

Many words have two levels of meaning — a denotative meaning and a connotative meaning. A word's **denotation** is its precise dictionary definition. For example, the denotative meaning of the word *mother* is "female parent." A word's **connotation** is the collection of feelings and attitudes the word evokes, its emotional colorings or shades of meaning. A word's connotation may vary, of course, from one person to another. One common connotation of *mother* is a warm, caring person. Some people, however, may think of a mother as someone with strong authoritarian control. Similarly, the phrase *horror films* may conjure up memories of scary but fun-filled evenings for some people and terrifying experiences for others.

Since the connotations of words can elicit a wide range of responses, be sure the words you choose convey only the meanings you intend. In each pair of words that follows, notice that the two words have a similar denotation but different connotations.

artificial/ fake
firm/stubborn
lasting/endless

EXERCISE 8.7

Describe the different connotations of the three words in each group of words.

1. crowd/mob/gathering
2. proverb/motto/saying
3. prudent/penny-pinching/frugal
4. token/gift/keepsake
5. display/show/expose

Do You Use Concrete Language?

Specific words convey much more information than do general words. The following examples show how you might move from general to specific word choices.

General	Less General	Specific	More Specific
store	department store	Sear's	Sear's at the Galleria Mall
music	popular music	country and western music	Garth Brooks's "Friends in Low Places"

Concrete words add life and meaning to your writing. In each of the following sentence pairs, notice how the underlined words in the first sentence provide little information, whereas the underlined words in the second sentence provide interesting details and add meaning.

▶ Our <u>vacation</u> was <u>great fun</u>.
▶ Our <u>rafting trip</u> was filled with <u>adventure</u>.

▶ The <u>red flowers</u> were blooming in our yard.
▶ <u>Crimson and white petunias</u> were blooming in our yard.

Suppose you are writing about a shopping mall that has outlived its usefulness. Instead of saying "a number of stores were unoccupied, and those that were still in business were shabby," you could describe the mall in concrete, specific terms that would enable your readers to visualize it.

The vacant storefronts with "For Rent" signs slathered across the glass, the half-empty racks in the stores that were still open, and the empty corridors suggested that the mall was soon to close.

EXERCISE 8.8

Revise the following sentences by adding concrete, specific details.

1. The book I took on vacation was exciting reading.
2. The students watched as the instructor entered the lecture hall.

3. The antique blue and white vase featured a relief of a young woman with ringlet curls extending her hand toward a suitor under a blossoming tree.

4. Standing beside the outline of a woman's body on the floor, the reporter questioned the middle-aged couple from across the hall, who shook as they grasped their coffee cups.

5. Although the gift shop was closed, we noticed that the lights were on and that a sign in the window said "Back in half an hour."

TEACHING TIP

• To help students think of figures of speech, have them list the topics in Exercise 8.9 in the left column and all the abstract nouns they can think of for each topic in the right column (e.g., item 1 might evoke the words *anxiety, exhaustion, pride*).

• Next, have students select one abstract noun and write down all the concrete nouns they associate with it (e.g., *anxiety* might lead to *spiders, snakes, heights, exams*).

• Finally, have students compare their lists of concrete nouns and topics, looking for possible figures of speech.

For more on figures of speech, see Chapter 10, p. 267.

3. The vase in the museum was an antique.
4. At the crime scene, the reporter questioned the witnesses.
5. Although the shop was closed, we expected someone to return at any moment.

Do You Use Fresh, Appropriate Figures of Speech?

A **figure of speech** is a comparison that makes sense imaginatively or creatively, but not literally. For example, if you say "the movie was *a ride on a roller coaster,*" you do not mean the movie was an actual ride. Rather, you mean the movie was thrilling, just like a ride on a roller coaster. This figure of speech, like all others, compares two seemingly unlike objects or situations by finding one point of similarity.

Fresh and imaginative figures of speech can help you create vivid images for your readers. However, overused figures of speech can detract from your essay. Be sure to avoid common **clichés** (trite or overused expressions) such as *blind as a bat, green with envy,* or *sick as a dog.*

Although there are many kinds of figures of speech, the most useful types are simile, metaphor, and personification. In a **simile**, the word *like* or *as* is used to make a direct comparison of two unlike things.

The child acts *like a tiger.*

The noise in a crowded high school cafeteria is as deafening *as a caucus of crows.*

A **metaphor** also makes a comparison of unlike things, but a metaphor does not use the word *like* or *as.* Instead, the comparison is implied.

That child is a tiger.

If you're born in America with black skin, you're born in prison.

MALCOLM X, "Interview"

In the second example, Malcolm X compares having black skin to being born in prison.

Personification describes an idea or object by giving it human qualities or characteristics.

A sailboat, or any other pleasure vehicle, devours money.

In this example, the ability to eat is ascribed to an inanimate object, the sailboat.

When you edit an essay, look for and eliminate overused figures of speech, replacing them with creative, fresh images. If you have not used any figures of speech, look for descriptions that could be improved by using a simile, a metaphor, or personification.

EXERCISE 8.9

Invent fresh figures of speech for two items in the following list.

1. Parents of a newborn baby
2. A lengthy supermarket line or a traffic jam
3. A relative's old refrigerator
4. A man and woman obviously in love
5. Your team's star quarterback or important player

Do You Avoid Weak Verb-Noun Combinations?

Weak verb-noun combinations such as *wrote a draft* instead of *drafted* or *made a change* instead of *changed* tend to make sentences wordy.

▶ The attorney ~~made an assessment of~~ *assessed* the company's liability in the accident.

▶ The professor ~~gave a lecture~~ *lectured* on Asian-American relations in the 1990s.

Evaluating Your Word Choice

Use Flowchart 8.1 on page 200 to help you evaluate your word choice. If you have difficulty identifying which words to revise, ask a classmate or friend to read and evaluate your essay by using the flowchart as a guide and marking any words that may need revision.

A word-processing program is a useful editing tool. For example, you might experiment with several different word choices in a paragraph, print out all versions, and make comparisons. Because it is difficult to spot ineffective word choices on a computer screen, print a copy of your essay and work with the print copy, circling words or phrases that may need revision.

ESSAY IN PROGRESS 2

For the essay you worked on in Essay in Progress 1 (p. 194), use Flowchart 8.1 to evaluate and edit your word choice.

SUGGESTIONS FOR PROOFREADING

Once you are satisfied with your sentences and words and your edited essay as a whole, you are ready for the final step of the writing process—*proofreading*. When you proofread, you make sure your essay is error-free and is presented in acceptable manuscript format. Your goals are to catch and correct surface errors—such as

For information on manuscript format, see Chapter 20, p. 703.

FLOWCHART 8.1
EVALUATING YOUR WORD CHOICE

Question	Revision Strategies
1. Have you used an appropriate tone and level of diction?	• Imagine you are talking to a member of your audience. Circle any words or phrases that seem inappropriate. • Skim your draft and circle any words that are too formal or too informal, especially any instances of slang or jargon. Replace these words with words appropriate for your audience.
No →	
Yes ⬇	
2. Have you chosen words with appropriate connotations?	• Circle all words that might convey a negative connotation. • Circle all words whose connotations you are not sure of. • Check the meanings of the circled words in a dictionary.
No →	
Yes ⬇	
3. Is your language concrete and specific?	• Skim your draft for general, vague words that contribute little or no meaning. • Replace general words with concrete, specific words.
No →	
Yes ⬇	
4. Have you used fresh, appropriate figures of speech?	• Underline all figures of speech. If any are commonly used, create new ones or delete them.
No →	
Yes ⬇	
5. Have you avoided weak noun-verb combinations?	• Skim your draft looking for places where you can strengthen the verb.
No →	
Yes	

errors in grammar, punctuation, spelling, and mechanics — as well as keyboarding or typographical errors. Making sure your essay is free of surface errors will help create a favorable impression in readers — of both the essay and of you as its writer. An essay that is riddled with errors in grammar, punctuation, spelling, and so on is not only difficult to read, it is also likely to reflect negatively on you. Your readers may assume that careless proofreading is a sign of a careless writer. The guidelines in this section will help you become a careful proofreader.

If you are using a word processor or computer, print out a clean copy of your essay specifically for proofreading. Do not attempt to work with a previously marked-up, edited copy or on a computer screen. Spotting errors in grammar, spelling, punctuation, and mechanics is easier when you work with a clean printed copy. Be sure to double-space the copy to allow room for you to mark corrections between lines.

Use the following suggestions to produce an error-free essay.

1. **Review your paper once for each type of error.** Because it is difficult to spot all types of surface errors simultaneously during a single proofreading, you should read your essay several times, each time focusing on *one* error type: errors in spelling, punctuation, grammar, mechanics, and so on.

2. **Read your essay backward, from the last sentence to the first.** Reading in this way will help you concentrate on spotting errors without being distracted by the flow of ideas.

3. **Use the spell-check and grammar-check functions cautiously.** If you are working with a word processor or computer, the spell-check function can help you spot some spelling and keyboarding errors, but you cannot rely on it to catch all spelling errors. A spell-check program can detect misspelled words but it cannot detect the difference in meaning between *there* and *their* or *to* and *too,* for example. Similarly, the grammar-check function can identify only certain kinds of errors and is not a reliable substitute for a careful proofreading.

4. **Read your essay aloud.** By reading aloud slowly and deliberately, you can catch certain errors that sound awkward, such as missing words, errors in verb tense, and errors in the singular or plural forms of nouns.

5. **Ask a classmate to proofread your paper.** Another reader may spot errors you have overlooked.

TEACHING TIP

Advise students to use the spell- and grammar-check functions as *one* of several necessary steps. They should also use a print dictionary and a current handbook (print or online), which are more useful resources.

Keeping an Error Log

You may find it helpful to keep an error log as part of your writing journal. Start by recording errors from several graded or peer-reviewed papers in the log. Then look for patterns in the types of errors you tend to make. Once you identify these types of errors, you can proofread your essays specifically for them.

In the accompanying Sample Error Log, notice that the student kept track of five types of errors in three writing assignments. By doing so, she discovered that most of her errors fell into the categories of subject-verb agreement, spelling, and verb tense. She was then able to proofread for those errors specifically. The error log also allowed the student to keep track of her progress in avoiding these types of errors over time.

SAMPLE ERROR LOG

Type of Error	Assignment 1	Assignment 2	Assignment 3
Subject-verb agreement	X	XX	XX
Spelling	XXXX	XXX	XXX
Verb tense	XX	XX	XXX
Word choice	X		X
Parallelism			X

The Proofreading Checklist on the inside cover will help you systematically review your essays for surface errors.

ESSAY IN PROGRESS 3

For the essay you edited in Essay in Progress 2 (p. 199), use the Proofreading Checklist to catch and correct errors in spelling, punctuation, grammar, and mechanics.

STUDENTS WRITE

Recall that Tina Oyer's essay, "Hypocritically Warm," was developed, drafted, and revised in the Students Write sections of Chapters 4–7. Printed here are the first three paragraphs of Oyer's essay with Oyer's final editing and proofreading changes. Each revision has been numbered. The list following the excerpt explains the reason for each change. The final draft of Oyer's essay, with these changes incorporated into it, appears in Chapter 7, on pages 175–79.

1

One cold evening in Buffalo, I stood in an almost

empty parking lot with snow blowing around me, my col-

TEACHING TIP: LEARNING STYLES

Most students (with the possible exception of pragmatic or concrete learners) find it difficult to pay close attention to detail, particularly in papers longer than a page or two.

- Encourage all students to read their papers aloud (to themselves or another student) to help them locate errors.
- To facilitate independent learning, remind students to record proofreading errors in their error logs.

leagues and a customer facing me, and a tough choice to

make. The snow seemed to melt as soon as it hit my face, **②**

but I didn't feel the cold. All I could think of was the

decision I was facing, a decision that filled me with

fear.

The temperature was about ten degrees, something we

are ~~especially~~ **③** used to in Buffalo; we expect it. During

the day, we can never tell the temperature by the blind-

ing glare when we look out the window. The sun can

appear to be beaming as if it were the hottest summer

assaults our senses. **④**
day, but when we step outside the cold ~~has the upper~~

~~hand,~~ That night, the wind that stung my face wasn't the

only thing that was freezing, and I was about to learn

just how much chilliness I could tolerate before I

decided to do things my own way.

when I had   *to start* **⑤**
Earlier, ~~I~~ walked into Hilltop Pharmacy, ~~It was~~

~~time for~~ my regular shift as evening supervisor, ~~I~~

of the store
~~could feel~~ the refreshing heat ~~dominate the cold on my~~

had made my cold skin tingle. **⑥**   *uniforms,* **⑦**
~~skin,~~ The clerks, all dressed in identical ~~attire,~~ were

busy waiting on customers, bagging, and pricing stock.

The owner, in his immaculate white coat and aviator

glasses, stood at the pharmacy counter, talking to the

customers, **⑧** ~~The customers are~~ his priority. He always

TEACHING TIP

To demonstrate the importance of word choice, ask students to analyze Oyer's changes in word choice and how they affect her essay.

• Replacing *attire* with *uniforms*, e.g., makes the tone less formal and more engaging for the reader.
• Word-choice changes and use of the first person create an informal tone, which is appropriate for a personal experience essay.

```
caters to them, and goes to any lengths to please them.
```

```
                      9
"What a nice man"    I've heard more than one customer say
```

```
on the way out of the store.
```

Notice that in editing and proofreading these paragraphs, Oyer improved the clarity and variety of her sentences, chose clearer, more specific words, and corrected errors in punctuation.

1. A comma was needed to separate the opening phrase from the rest of the sentence.

2. A comma was needed between two independent clauses joined by *but.*

3. Oyer decided that the sentence would be stronger without the intensifier *especially.* (see p. 184 for more on unnecessary adverbs.)

4. Oyer changed a cliché, *has the upper hand,* to a fresher figure of speech. (See p. 198 for more on figures of speech.)

5. Oyer decided to combine three simple sentences into one complex sentence in order to show the chronological sequence and emphasize the warmth she felt on entering the store. (See p. 185 for more on varying sentence types.)

6. Oyer decided that the word *dominate,* which suggests controlling or ruling, had the wrong connotation, so she changed *dominate the cold on my skin* to a more concrete description of how the warm air made her feel. (See p. 196 for more on the connotations of words.)

7. Oyer substituted *uniforms,* a more specific noun, for *attire.* (See p. 197 for more on using concrete language.)

8. Oyer combined two sentences to eliminate redundancy and emphasize the owner's priority: his customers. (See p. 183 for more on eliminating redundancies and p. 185 for more on varying sentence patterns.)

9. The exclamation point is part of the quoted sentence and needs to come before the quotation mark.

Patterns of
Development

Chapter 9

CHAPTER QUICK START

Homelessness is a serious national problem with many possible causes. The photograph on the opposite page shows a homeless family. Imagine the series of events that might have caused this particular family to become homeless. Did the parents lose their jobs? If so, how? Did they spend their entire savings on life-saving surgery for one of the children? Did a fire destroy their home?

Writing Quick Start

Working by yourself or with a classmate, construct a series of events that may have caused the family in the photograph to become homeless. Write a brief summary of the events you imagined.

Narration: Recounting Events

TEACHING TIP

List one student's series of events on the blackboard; then point out the features of a narrative (conflict, tension, climax, and so on).

COMPUTER HINT

Have students brainstorm on computer, sharing their ideas by posting them on a network or attaching files to email messages.

WRITING A NARRATIVE

As you imagined this family's path to homelessness, you constructed the beginnings of a narrative. You began to describe a series of events or turning points, and you probably wrote them in the order in which they occurred. In this chapter you will learn how to write narrative essays as well as how to use narratives in essays that rely on one or more other patterns of development.

WHAT IS NARRATION?

A **narrative** relates a series of events, real or imaginary, in an organized sequence. It is a story, but it is *a story that makes a point.* You began listening to, telling, and watching narratives when you were a small child and have continued to do so nearly every day since. Today, you probably exchange family stories, tell jokes, read biographies or novels, and watch television situation comedies or dramas—all of which are examples of the narrative form. In addition, narratives are an important part of the writing you will do in college and in your career, as the examples in the accompanying box illustrate.

Narratives provide human interest, spark our curiosity, and draw us close to the storyteller. In addition, narratives can do the following.

• *Create a sense of shared history,* linking people together. The members of a culture share certain stories and events, true or untrue, that unite them. Examples of American stories include the Boston Tea Party and the first Thanksgiving.

• *Provide entertainment.* Most people enjoy a thrilling movie or an intriguing book.

SCENES FROM COLLEGE AND THE WORKPLACE

• Each student in a *business law* course must attend a court trial and complete the following written assignment: Describe what happened and what the proceedings illustrated about the judicial process.

• In a *sociology* course, the class is scheduled to discuss the nature and types of authority figures in U.S. society. Your instructor begins by asking class members to describe situations in which they found themselves in conflict with an authority figure.

• Your job in *sales* involves frequent business travel, and your company requires you to submit a report for each trip. You are expected to recount the meetings you attended, your contacts with current clients, and new sales leads.

- *Offer instruction.* Children learn about good and bad behavior and moral and immoral actions through stories. "Pinocchio" teaches children not to tell lies, and "The Boy Who Cried Wolf" admonishes them not to raise false alarms.

- *Provide psychological healing.* Reading or listening to the story of someone who faced a life crisis similar to one you are experiencing can help you through the crisis.

- *Provide insight.* Stories can help you discover values, explore options, and examine motives. By reading a story, you can think through a dilemma without actually experiencing it.

The following narrative is a Native American legend about the origin of a bothersome insect. As you read, notice how the narrative makes a point by relating a series of events that build to a climax.

How Mosquitoes Came to Be

This legend appears in the anthology American Indian Myths and Legends *(1984), edited by Richard Erdoes and Alfonso Ortiz. Erdoes, active in Native American civil rights movements, is a freelance writer and a lecturer at Yale and Princeton. Ortiz was a professor of anthropology at the University of New Mexico and is a past president of the Association on American Indian Affairs.*

Long ago there was a giant who loved to kill humans, eat their flesh, and drink their blood. He was especially fond of human hearts. "Unless we can get rid of this giant," people said, "none of us will be left," and they called a council to discuss ways and means.

One man said, "I think I know how to kill the monster," and he went to the place where the giant had last been seen. There he lay down and pretended to be dead.

Soon the giant came along. Seeing the man lying there, he said: "These humans are making it easy for me. Now I don't even have to catch and kill them; they die right on my trail, probably from fear of me!"

The giant touched the body. "Ah, good," he said, "this one is still warm and fresh. What a tasty meal he'll make; I can't wait to roast his heart."

The giant flung the man over his shoulder, and the man let his head hang down as if he were dead. Carrying the man home, the giant dropped him in the middle of the floor right near the fireplace. Then he saw that there was no firewood and went to get some.

TEACHING TIP

Introduce this piece as *folklore*—an oral narrative intended to explain a natural phenomenon or human situation and one of the oldest forms of literature. As part of the *oral tradition* of a culture, folklore is comprised of stories that predate written literature and that often aim to instruct, entertain, or preserve values within a culture.

PREREADING QUESTION

What lesson does this folktale teach, if any?

6   As soon as the monster had left, the man got up and grabbed the giant's huge skinning knife. Just then the giant's son came in, bending low to enter. He was still small as giants go, and the man held the big knife to his throat. "Quick, tell me, where's your father's heart? Tell me or I'll slit your throat!"

7   The giant's son was scared. He said: "My father's heart is in his left heel."

8   Just then the giant's left foot appeared in the entrance, and the man swiftly plunged the knife into the heel. The monster screamed and fell down dead.

9   Yet the giant still spoke. "Though I'm dead, though you killed me, I'm going to keep on eating you and all the other humans in the world forever!"

10   "That's what you think!" said the man. "I'm about to make sure that you never eat anyone again." He cut the giant's body into pieces and burned each one in the fire. Then he took the ashes and threw them into the air for the wind to scatter.

11   Instantly each of the particles turned into a mosquito. The cloud of ashes became a cloud of mosquitoes, and from their midst the man heard the giant's voice laughing, saying: "Yes, I'll eat you people until the end of time."

12   And as the monster spoke, the man felt a sting, and a mosquito started sucking blood, and then many mosquitoes stung him, and he began to scratch himself.   ■

Characteristics of a Narrative

As you can see from "How Mosquitoes Came to Be," a narrative does not merely report events; a narrative is *not* a transcript of a conversation or a news report. Although it does include events, conversations, and vivid descriptions, a narrative is more than a list; it is a story that conveys a particular meaning. It presents actions and details that build toward a climax, the point at which the conflict of the narrative is resolved. Most narratives use dialogue to present selected portions of conversations that move the story along.

Narratives Make a Point

A narrative makes a point or supports a thesis by telling readers about an event or a series of events. The point may be to describe the significance of the event or events, make an observation, or present information. Often a writer will state the point directly, using an explicit thesis statement. Other times a writer may leave the main point unstated, using an implied thesis. Either way, the point must always be clear to your readers. The point also determines the details the writer selects and the way they are presented.

The following excerpt is from a brief narrative, written by a student, that is based on the photo at the start of this chapter. After imagining the series of events that might have brought the family to homelessness, the student wrote this final paragraph.

> Jack and Melissa are kind, patient people who want nothing more than to live in a house or an apartment instead of camping out on a street curb. Unfortunately, their unhappy story and circumstances are not uncommon. Thousands of Americans, through no fault of their own, share their hopeless plight. The homeless can be found on street corners, in parks, and under bridges in the coldest months of winter. Too often, passersby shun them and their need for a helping hand. They either look away, repulsed by the conditions in which the homeless live, and assume they live this way out of choice rather than necessity, or they gaze at them with disapproving looks, walk away, and wonder why such people do not want to work.

Notice that the writer makes a point about the homeless and about people's attitudes toward them directly. Note, too, how the details support the writer's point.

Narratives Convey Action and Detail

A narrative presents a detailed account of an event or a series of events. In other words, a narrative is like a camera lens that zooms in on an event and makes readers feel like they can see the details and experience the action.

Writers of narratives can involve readers in several ways: through *dialogue,* with *physical description,* and by *recounting action.* In "How Mosquitoes Came to Be," both dialogue and the recounting of events help to build suspense and make the story come alive. To a lesser degree, this narrative includes description as well. (For more about dialogue, see page 212.)

For more on descriptive writing, see Chapter 10.

Narratives Present a Conflict and Create Tension

An effective narrative presents a **conflict**—such as a struggle, question, or problem—and works toward its resolution. The conflict can be between participants or between a participant and some external force, such as a law, value, moral, or act of nature. **Tension** is the suspense created as the story unfolds and as the reader wonders how the conflict will be resolved. In "How Mosquitoes Came to Be," for example, tension is created in the first paragraph: "Long ago there was a giant who loved to kill humans. . . ." The tension is sustained in paragraphs 2–7 through dialogue and the events. The conflict is resolved in paragraph 8, when the giant is killed. The point at which the conflict is resolved is called the **climax.** The main point of the story—how mosquitoes were created—concludes the narrative.

POSSIBLE ANSWERS

Answers will vary. Possible completed first sentences:

1. . . . you remember you have a project due today that you haven't started.
2. . . . you forgot to answer the questions on the last page.
3. . . . just as guests begin arriving for a party.
4. . . . his friends are pressuring him to try an alcoholic beverage.
5. . . . he or she is at the local police station.

EXERCISE 9.1

Working alone or with a classmate, complete each of the following statements by setting up a conflict. Then for one of the completed statements, write three to four sentences that build tension through action or dialogue (or both).

1. You are about ready to leave the house when . . .
2. You have just turned in your first math exam when you realize that . . .
3. You just moved to a new town when your spouse suddenly becomes seriously ill . . .
4. Your child just told you that . . .
5. Your best friend phones you in the middle of the night to tell you . . .

Narratives Sequence Events

The events in a narrative must be arranged in an order that is easy for readers to follow. Often, but not always, a narrative presents events in chronological order—the order in which they happened. "How Mosquitoes Came to Be," for example, uses this straightforward sequence. At other times, writers may use the techniques of flashback and foreshadowing to make their point more effectively. A **flashback** returns the reader to events that took place in the past, while **foreshadowing** jumps ahead in time to the future. Both of these techniques are used frequently in drama, fiction, and film. A soap opera, for instance, might open with a scene showing a woman lying in a hospital bed, flash back to a scene showing the accident that put her there, then return to the scene in the hospital. A television show might foreshadow what is to come by beginning with a wedding that is the result of preceding events and conflicts the program then dramatizes. When used sparingly, these techniques can build interest and add variety to a narrative, especially a lengthy chronological account.

Narratives Use Dialogue

TEACHING TIP

Briefly review the conventions for written dialogue.

• Phrases such as *he said* are preceded and/or followed by a comma.
• Periods and commas go inside closing quotation marks.
• A new paragraph signals a change in speakers.

CONNECTIONS

Have students briefly turn to "The Discus Thrower" in Chapter 10 (p. 255) to see an example of dialogue.

Just as people reveal much about themselves by what they say and how they say it, dialogue can reveal much about the characters in a narrative. **Dialogue** is often used to dramatize the action, emphasize the conflict, and reveal the personalities or motives of the key participants in a narrative. Notice how the dialogue in "How Mosquitoes Came to Be" makes the narrative lively and reveals the characteristics of both the hunter and the giant. For example, in paragraph 3, the giant reveals his arrogance through what he says about humans and their fear of him. Keep in mind that dialogue should resemble everyday speech; it should sound natural, not forced or formal. Consider these examples.

FORCED DIALOGUE: Maria confided to her grandfather, "I enjoy talking with you. I especially like hearing you tell of your life in Mexico long ago. I wish I could visit there with you. . . ."

NATURAL: Maria confided to her grandfather, "Your stories about Mexico when you were a kid are great. I'd like to go there with you. . . ."

EXERCISE 9.2

For one of the following situations, imagine what the person might say and how he or she would say it. Then write five or six sentences of natural-sounding dialogue. If your dialogue sounds forced or too formal, try saying it out loud into a tape recorder.

1. An assistant manager trying to explain to a supervisor that an employee offends customers
2. A man or a woman who just discovered that he or she and a best friend are dating the same person
3. A babysitter disciplining an eight-year-old girl for pouring chocolate syrup on her brother's head

Narratives Are Told from a Particular Point of View

Many narratives use the first-person point of view, in which the key participant speaks directly to the reader ("*I* first realized the problem when . . ."). Other narratives use the third-person point of view, in which an unknown storyteller describes what happens to the key participants ("The problem began when Saul Overtone . . ."). The third person is used in "How Mosquitoes Came to Be."

The first and third person each offer a distinct set of advantages. The first person allows you to assume a personal tone and to speak directly to your audience. You can easily express your attitudes and feelings and offer your interpretation and commentary. When you narrate an event that occurred in your own life, for example, the first person is probably your best choice. One drawback to using the first person, however, is that you cannot easily convey the inner thoughts of other participants unless they are shared with you. Both the first and third person are used to narrate actions performed by people other than the narrator, but the third person point of view gives the narrator more distance from the action. In "How Mosquitoes Came to Be," the narrator was not a participant in the events. The third-person point of view often provides a broader, more objective perspective.

EXERCISE 9.3

For each of the following situations, discuss with your classmates the advantages and disadvantages of using the first- and third-person points of view to develop a narrative essay.

1. The day you and several friends played a practical joke on another friend
2. An incident of sexual or racial discrimination that happened to you or someone you know
3. An incident at work that a co-worker told you about

Visualizing a Narrative: A Graphic Organizer

Whether or not you are a spatial learner, it is often helpful to see the content and organization of an essay in simplified, visual form. The graphic organizer shown in Figure 9.1 is a visual diagram of the basic structure of a narrative. A graphic

TEACHING TIP: COLLABORATIVE WRITING

(30 minutes)
- Have students work in pairs or small groups on this exercise (15 minutes).
- Ask one student from each group to read the dialogue aloud to the class (10 minutes).
- Discuss which groups' dialogues sound most realistic and why. Have students suggest ways to make their dialogues sound more realistic (5 minutes).

POSSIBLE ANSWERS

Answers will vary.

TEACHING TIP

- First-person narratives students might be familiar with: *Catcher in the Rye, The Adventures of Huckleberry Finn,* and *Jane Eyre.*
- Third-person narratives students might be familiar with: *The Red Badge of Courage* and *The Scarlet Letter.*

POSSIBLE ANSWERS

Example: **The day you and several friends played a practical joke . . .**

- *First person:* would convey the narrator's feelings and experiences directly and show action through the point of view of one of the jokers; but readers would have to decide whether to believe the narrator's account.
- *Third person:* would provide distance and allow the reader to learn about the characters through their actions; but it lacks the immediacy of the first person.

For more on graphic organizers, see Chapter 2, p. 40.

organizer can help you structure your writing, analyze a reading, and recall key events as you generate ideas for an essay.

Use Figure 9.1 as a basic model. However, keep in mind that narrative essays vary in organization and may lack one or more of the elements included in the model. When you incorporate narration into an essay in which you also use other patterns of development, you will probably need to condense or eliminate some of the elements shown in Figure 9.1. Whether you write a narrative essay or incorporate narration in a different kind of essay, use a graphic organizer to help you visualize the structure of your essay.

The following selection, "A Primitive Ritual," is an example of a narrative. Read it first, and then study the graphic organizer for it (Figure 9.2).

FIGURE 9.1
GRAPHIC ORGANIZER FOR A NARRATIVE ESSAY

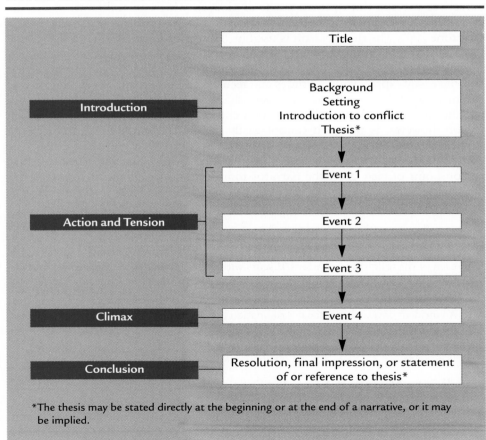

A Primitive Ritual

David Hicks and Margaret A. Gwynne

The following brief narrative first appeared as an introduction to the chapter "Culture and the Human Body" in Cultural Anthropology (1996), *a textbook written by David Hicks and Margaret A. Gwynne, both professors at the State University of New York at Stony Brook. Hicks is the recipient of numerous research awards, including one from the National Science Foundation. Gwynne serves as a consultant in eastern Caribbean countries for the World Health Organization. As you read the selection, look for the elements of a narrative essay. Compare your findings with the graphic organizer shown in Figure 9.1. Then study the graphic organizer for this reading in Figure 9.2.*

The professor in a big introductory course in anthropology at a state university often illustrated his lectures with ethnographic films. Most films portrayed events in the lives of people living in small-scale societies in faraway parts of the world. Over the course of the semester, students in the class saw Inuit hunters celebrating a successful seal hunt with drumming, dancing, and singing; a group of Middle Eastern nomads walking hundreds of miles to take their sheep to new pastures; Balinese dancers performing a religious drama to the eerie accompaniment of strange-looking stringed instruments; and opposing groups of Pacific islanders, wearing elaborate feather headdresses, fighting each other with homemade spears. The reaction of the students to these films was mixed. Some viewers were intrigued, others were bored, and still others admitted that at times they were shocked or even repelled. In general, however, the students were more struck by the strangeness of what they saw on the screen than by similarities between the filmed scenes and events in their own lives.

One day, toward the end of the semester, the professor dimmed the lecture hall lights for yet another film. This one, like several of the others, began with a darkened screen and the heavy thump of distant drumming, and some students groaned inwardly at the thought of having to sit through what they anticipated would be another strange, incomprehensible, or even repellent dance, drama, sacrifice, or other ritual. As the screen slowly brightened, shadowy human figures became visible—moving shapes with flapping clothing and grotesque, voluminous hairdos. Smoke swirled around the silhouetted figures who bounced up and down rhythmically to the faint but steady beat of the drums.

PREREADING QUESTION

What is an example of a "primitive ritual"?

TEACHING TIP: POSTREADING DISCUSSION

Ask students to discuss:

• how scientists from another culture might interpret social rituals in the United States, such as dancing.
• how Hicks and Gwynne build readers' curiosity about the film.
• how the authors imply their thesis through the account of the students and their reaction to the film. How is this strategy more or less effective than stating the thesis directly?

3   As the sound track gradually grew louder and musical tones surfaced above the percussive thumping, the students began to listen
more intently, for they thought they recognized something familiar.
Soon the screen brightened, and they began to laugh, for this
footage, far from showing a primitive rite filmed in some remote
land, had been filmed at a popular nightclub near the campus, and
the mysterious figures gyrating rhythmically to the music were none
other than the students themselves.   ■

POSSIBLE ANSWER

Answers will vary. See
the *Instructor's Resource
Manual* for a possible
graphic organizer.

EXERCISE 9.4

Using the graphic organizers in Figures 9.1 and 9.2 as models, draw a graphic organizer
for "How Mosquitoes Came to Be" (pp. 209–210).

FIGURE 9.2
GRAPHIC ORGANIZER FOR "A PRIMITIVE RITUAL"

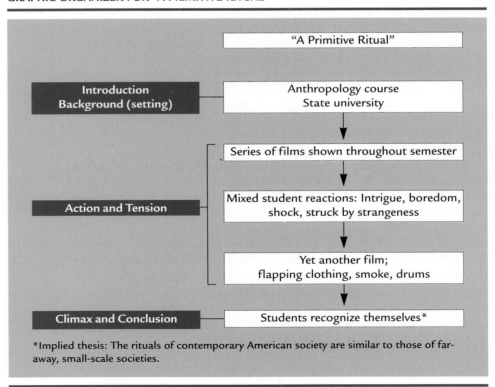

INTEGRATING A NARRATIVE INTO AN ESSAY

In many of your essays, you will want to use a narrative along with one or more other patterns of development in order to support your thesis effectively. In much of the writing you encounter in newspapers, magazines, and textbooks, the patterns of development often mix and overlap. Similarly, although "How Mosquitoes Came to Be" is primarily a narrative, it also uses cause and effect to explain why mosquitoes exist today. "A Primitive Ritual" is a narrative that contains descriptions of the films the students watched in class.

For more on description and cause and effect, see Chapters 10 and 16.

Although most of your college essays will *not* be primarily narrative, you can often use stories to illustrate a point, clarify an idea, support an argument, or capture readers' interest in essays that rely on another pattern of development or on several patterns. Here are a few suggestions for using narration effectively in the essays you write.

1. **Be sure that your story illustrates your point accurately and well.** Don't include a story just because it's funny or interesting.

2. **Keep the narrative short.** An extended narrative within, for example, a process analysis essay may divert your reader's attention from your main point.

3. **Introduce the story with a transitional sentence or clause that indicates you are about to shift to a narrative.** Otherwise, your readers may wonder, "What's this story doing here?" Your transition should also make clear the connection between the story and the point it illustrates. For example, in introducing a story that illustrates how Internet chatrooms can lead to new friendships and even marriages, you might write: "Chatroom friendships can lead to lifelong relationships, as Fred Garcia, who 'dated' his wife on the Internet for two years, discovered."

4. **Use descriptive language, dialogue, and action.** These elements make narratives vivid, lively, and interesting in any essay.

In "Another Mother's Child" on p. 240, Norma Molen incorporates narration into a persuasive essay.

ADDITIONAL RESOURCES

The writing process soft-ware that accompanies this text includes an electronic Guided Writing Assignment for a narrative essay.

A GUIDED WRITING ASSIGNMENT

The following guide will lead you through the process of writing a narrative essay. Although your essay will be primarily a narrative, you may choose to use one or more other patterns of development as well. Depending on your learning style, you might decide to start at various points and move back and forth within the process. If you are a spatial learner, for example, you might begin by visualizing and sketching the details of your narrative. If you are a social learner, you might prefer to start out by evaluating your audience.

The Assignment

Write a narrative essay about an incident or experience in your life that had a significant effect on you or that changed your views in some important way. Choose one of the following topics or one that you think of on your own. The readers of your campus newspaper are your audience.

1. An experience that caused you to learn something about yourself.
2. An incident that revealed the true character of someone you knew.
3. An experience that helped you discover a principle to live by.
4. An experience that explains how a particular object became a valued personal possession.
5. An incident that has become a family legend, perhaps one that reveals the character of a family member or illustrates a clash of generations or cultures.
6. An incident that has allowed you to develop an appreciation or aware-ness of your ethnic identity.

As you develop your narrative essay, be sure to consider using one or more of the other patterns of development. You might use description to present details about a family member's appearance, for example, or com-parison and contrast to compare your attitudes or ideas to those of a par-ent or child.

For more on description and comparison and contrast, see Chapters 10 and 13.

Generating Ideas

Use the following steps to help you choose a topic and generate ideas about the experience or incident you decide to write about.

Choosing an Experience or Incident That Leads to a Working Thesis

Take your time in choosing the experience or incident to write about. Be sure that the experience or incident is memorable and vivid and that you are comfortable writing about it. No student wants to discover, when a draft is nearly completed, that he or she cannot remember important details about an experience or that it does not fulfill the requirements of the assignment.

The following suggestions will help you choose an experience or incident. Some will be more appealing to you than others. Experiment and use whatever suggestions prove helpful. After you have chosen one, make sure that you can develop it by formulating a working thesis.

1. Brainstorm with another student, discussing and describing experiences or incidents that fit one or more of the suggested topics.

2. You can probably eliminate one or more topic choices right away. List those that remain across the top of a piece of paper or on your computer screen, for example, *Learn about Self, Principle to Live By,* and *Family Legend.* Then brainstorm about significant experiences or incidents in your life and write each one you think of beneath the appropriate heading.

3. Flip through a family photo album or page through a scrapbook, diary, or yearbook. Your search will remind you of people and events from the past.

4. Work backward. Think of a principle you live by, an object you value, or a family legend. How did it become so?

5. Using freewriting or another prewriting technique, write down any experiences or incidents that come to mind. The memory of one incident will trigger memories of other incidents. Then sort your list to see if any of these experiences or incidents fulfill the assignment.

ESSAY IN PROGRESS 1

For the assignment on page 218, use one or more of the preceding suggestions to choose an experience or incident to write about and formulate a working thesis for your choice.

For more on formulating a working thesis, see Chapter 5, p. 97

Learning Style Options

For more on prewriting strategies, see Chapter 4.

**TEACHING TIP:
LEARNING STYLES**

1. For social learners
2. For rational or pragmatic learners
3. For spatial or emotional learners
4. For abstract or independent learners
5. For all learners

TEACHING TIP

(30 minutes)

- Have students work alone at first, using at least two prewriting strategies from Chapter 4 — freewriting, mapping, brainstorming, questioning, writing assertions — to generate ideas (20 minutes).
- Then ask students to work in pairs to evaluate their prewriting (10 minutes).

For more on purpose,
audience, and point of
view, see Chapter 4,
pp. 73–77.

TEACHING TIP:
COLLABORATIVE
WRITING

(15 minutes)

• Pair students and have
them role-play this
scenario: A college
basketball player had
been penalized for
committing a foul. He
claims the "fouled"
player faked; the other
team then wins the
game when the
"fouled" player makes
the extra baskets. Have
one student role-play
the penalized player,
telling the story to the
other student. Have
the other student play
a television sports-
caster, reporting the
incident (10 minutes).

• Ask one pair of stu-
dents to "replay" their
version of the incident
for the class. Then dis-
cuss the different pur-
pose and point of view
of the basketball
player and the sports-
caster (5 minutes).

Learning Style Options

TEACHING TIP:
LEARNING STYLES

1. For a broad range of
learners: spatial, con-
crete, creative, and
emotional

2. For pragmatic and
rational learners

3. For social and verbal
learners

Considering Your Purpose, Audience, and Point of View

Once you have chosen an experience or incident to write about, the next step is to consider your purpose, audience, and point of view. Recall from Chapter 4 that most essays have one of three possible purposes: to inform, to express thoughts or feelings to, or to persuade readers.

Thinking about your audience may help you clarify your purpose and decide what to include in your essay. For this Guided Writing Assignment, your audience is readers of your campus newspaper. In an essay about a dispute at a basketball game, for example, you would need to explain the relevant plays, rules, and penalties because not all readers of the campus newspaper could be expected to know the sport. However, if your audience consisted solely of basketball players, you could assume that they were already familiar with the rules, and you could omit the explanations.

At this stage of planning your narrative essay, you should also decide on a point of view. If the basketball narrative was written to express your feelings about the incident, it would probably be most effective in the first person. But if the narrative's purpose was instead to inform readers about what happened at the game, the third person would be appropriate. Consider the pros and cons of using each point of view for your narrative. In most cases, you will use the first person to relate an experience or incident in your own life.

Gathering Details about the Experience or Incident

This step involves recollecting as many details about the experience or incident as possible and recording them on paper or in a computer file. Reenact the story, sketching the scene or scenes in your mind. Identify key actions, describe key participants, and describe your feelings. Here are a few ways to generate ideas.

1. Replay the experience or incident in your mind. If you have a strong visual memory, you can sit back, close your eyes, and imagine the incident or experience taking place. Jot down what you see, hear, smell, and feel—colors, dialogue, sounds, odors, and sensations. Also note how these details make you feel.

2. Write the following headings on a piece of paper, or type them on your computer screen: *Key Actions, Key Details, Sounds and Smells, Key Participants, Key Lines of Dialogue,* and *Feelings.* Then list ideas under each heading systematically.

3. Describe the incident or experience to a friend. Have your friend ask you questions as you retell the story. Jot down the details that the retelling and questioning help you recall.

4. Describe the incident or experience aloud while you tape-record it. Then listen to the tape and make notes.

5. Consider different aspects of the incident or experience by asking *Who, What, When, Where, How,* and *Why* questions. Record your answers.

4. For a range of learners
5. For pragmatic or rational learners

In addition, as you gather details for your narrative, be sure to include the types of details that are essential to an effective narrative.

- **Scene: Choose relevant sensory details.** Include enough detail about the scene or place where the experience or incident occurred to allow your readers to feel as if they are there, especially details that appeal to the senses of touch, taste, smell, hearing, and sight. Try also to recall memorable or important details that direct your readers' attention to the main points of the narrative and to avoid irrelevant details that distract readers and cause them to lose interest.

For more on sensory details, see Chapter 10.

- **Key actions: Choose actions that create tension, build it to a climax, and resolve it.** Be sure to gather details about the conflict of your narrative. Answer the following questions:

  Why did the experience or incident occur?
  What events led up to it?
  How was it resolved?
  What were its short- and long-term outcomes?
  What is its significance now?

- **Key participants: Concentrate only on the appearance and action of those people who were directly involved.** People who were present but not part of the incident or experience need not be described in detail or perhaps even included.

- **Dialogue: Include dialogue that is interesting, revealing, and related to the main point of the story.** To make sure the dialogue sounds natural, read the lines aloud, or ask a friend to do so.

- **Your feelings: Record your feelings before, during, and after the experience or incident.** Did you reveal your feelings then? If so, how? How did others react to you? How do you feel about the experience or incident now? What have you learned from it? Write a few sentences that summarize your feelings.

ESSAY IN PROGRESS 2

For the experience or incident you chose in Essay in Progress 1, use one or more of the preceding suggestions to generate details.

Evaluating Your Ideas

CONNECTIONS
Point out that the active reading strategies learned in Chapter 2 (such as highlighting and annotating) are also useful for evaluating prewriting.

Evaluate the ideas you have gathered about your topic now, before you begin drafting your narrative. You want to make sure you have enough details to describe the experience or incident vividly and meaningfully.

Begin by rereading everything you have written thus far with a critical eye. As you do so, add dialogue, descriptions of actions, or striking details as they come to mind. Then highlight the most usable material and cross out any that does not directly support your main point. You might use a two-color highlighting system—one color for key actions and dialogue, another for key details about the experience or incident. Some students find it helpful to read their notes aloud. If you are working on a computer, highlight usable ideas by making them bold or moving them to a separate page or document for easy access when drafting.

TEACHING TIP:
COLLABORATIVE
WRITING

(15 minutes) After students discuss the questions in groups (10 minutes), ask them to write a brief response to each group member's narrative and to give the feedback sheets to the student writer (5 minutes).

TRYING OUT YOUR IDEAS ON OTHERS

Once you are satisfied with the details you have generated about your incident or experience, you are ready to discuss your ideas with others. Working in a group of two or three students, each student should narrate his or her experience or incident and state the main point of the narrative. Then work together to answer the following questions about the narrative.

1. What more do you need to know about the experience or incident?
2. What is your reaction to the story?
3. How do the events of the narrative support or not support the main point?

ESSAY IN PROGRESS 3

Gather your prewriting and any comments you have received from your classmates or instructor, and evaluate the details you have developed so far. Based on your findings, generate additional details. Highlight the most useful details and omit those that do not support the main point.

Developing Your Thesis

For more on thesis statements, see Chapter 5, p. 97.

As noted earlier, not all narratives have a clearly stated thesis; the thesis may be implied rather than directly stated. However, if you have not written many narratives, it may be best to state your thesis directly. In either case, your thesis should make clear the main point of your narrative. You should already have a working thesis in mind. Now is the time to focus it. For example, a student who decided to write about her family's antique silver plate after brainstorming a list of ideas wrote the following focused thesis statement for her narrative. Notice that the thesis identifies the object, introduces the experience that made the object a valuable family possession, and expresses the main point of the narrative.

> The silver serving platter, originally owned by my great-grandmother, became our most prized family heirloom after a robbery terrorized our family.

A thesis statement may be placed at the beginning of a narrative essay. In "The Village Watchman" (p. 234), for example, the thesis appears near the beginning of the essay. A thesis may also be placed at the end of a narrative. "A Primitive Ritual" ends with the main point, but it uses an implied thesis rather than one that is stated directly.

ESSAY IN PROGRESS 4

Develop a thesis statement for the narrative you worked on in Essay in Progress 1–3. Make sure the thesis expresses the main point of the incident or experience you have chosen to write about.

Once you have a thesis, you need to do some additional prewriting to develop support and collect evidence for the thesis. In a narrative essay, the "evidence" includes dialogue, action, and details. Your prewriting at this stage may involve elaborating on some of the details you've already collected or typed into a computer file. Be sure your events and details will create or contribute to the tension or suspense of the narrative. Eliminate details that will sidetrack your reader instead of helping to establish or maintain the tension.

Organizing and Drafting

Once you are satisfied with your thesis and your support for it, you are ready to organize your ideas and write your first draft. Use the following suggestions for organizing and drafting your narrative.

Choosing a Narrative Sequence

As noted earlier in the chapter, the events of a narrative may follow a chronological order from beginning to end, or some events may be presented as flashbacks or foreshadowing for dramatic effect. Consider, for

TEACHING TIP
• Have students write their thesis statement in their journal and bring a copy to class.
• Collect students' theses and select several to write on the blackboard. Without mentioning the students' names, have the class analyze the thesis statements for clarity, specificity, and interest.

See Chapter 5, p. 104, for more on supporting a thesis with evidence.

For more on drafting an essay, see Chapter 6.

example, the options available to the student writing about her family's antique plate. Chronological order could be used to describe the events of the robbery in the order they happened. Or, the writer could start with her sister's discovery of the platter in the bushes, and then flash back to tell how it got there. Another option would be to foreshadow the robbery by describing a relevant scene from the past, such as when she polished the platter and wondered why her family valued the antique.

The following strategies will help you determine the best sequence for your narrative.

1. Write a brief description of each event on a 4- by 6-inch index card. Be sure to highlight the card that contains the climax. Experiment with various ways of arranging your details by rearranging the cards. When you have chosen a narrative sequence, prepare an outline of your narrative.

2. Dictate the narrative into a tape recorder. Then listen to the tape, taking note of the story's sequence of events. Evaluate the order of events.

3. Draw a graphic organizer of the experience or incident (see p. 214).

4. Use a word-processing program to create a list of the events. Rearrange the events using the cut-and-paste function, experimenting with different sequences.

ESSAY IN PROGRESS 5

Using one or more of the preceding suggestions, plan the order of the events for your narrative essay.

Drafting the Narrative Essay

Now that you've determined your narrative sequence, you are ready to begin drafting your essay. As you write, use the following guidelines to help keep your narrative on track.

The Introduction.   Your essay's introduction should catch your reader's attention, provide useful background information, and set up the sequence of events. Your introduction should also contain your thesis, if you have decided to place it at the beginning of the essay.

The Story.   The story should build tension as it leads up to the final outcome, resolution, or climax. The student writing about the antique platter,

Learning Style Options

TEACHING TIP:
LEARNING STYLES

1. For pragmatic learners
2. For a range of learners
3. For spatial learners
4. For verbal learners (and others comfortable with working on a computer)

For more on writing effective paragraphs, including introductions and conclusions, see Chapter 6.

for example, would need to set the scene of the robbery, describe the events that occurred when the thief entered the house, and explain what happened to the platter during the robbery.

As you draft your narrative, be conscious of your paragraphing, devoting a separate paragraph to each major action or distinct part of the story. Use transitional words and phrases such as *during, after,* and *finally* to connect events and guide readers along.

For more on transitions, see Chapter 6, p. 138.

In addition, be consistent in your use of verb tense. Most narratives are told in the past tense ("Yolanda *discovered* the platter . . ."). Fast-paced, short narratives, however, are sometimes related in the present tense ("Yolanda *discovers* the platter . . ."). Whichever tense you choose, be sure to use it consistently. Avoid switching between the past and present tenses unless the context of the narrative clearly requires it.

The Ending.   Your final paragraph should conclude the essay in a satisfying manner. A summary is usually unnecessary and may detract from the impact of the narrative. Instead, try ending in one of the following ways.

- Make a final observation about the experience or incident.
- Ask a probing question.
- Suggest a new but related direction of thought.
- Reveal a surprising piece of information.
- Refer back to the beginning.
- Restate the thesis in different words.

ESSAY IN PROGRESS 6

Using the narrative sequence you developed in Essay in Progress 5 and the preceding guidelines for drafting, write a first draft of your narrative essay.

Analyzing and Revising

If possible, set your draft aside for a day or two before rereading and revising it. As you reread your draft, don't worry about misspellings or errors in grammar and mechanics; focus instead on improving the overall effectiveness of your narrative. Will it interest readers and make them want to know what happens next? Does it make your point clear? To discover weaknesses in your draft, try the following strategies.

TEACHING TIP

Students who have followed the steps in the Guided Writing Assignment should be ready to compose a first draft independently. However, check to see if any students need to rethink their thesis, conflict, organization, or dialogue before drafting. Encourage them to seek further assistance from a peer reviewer or writing center tutor.

Learning Style Options

TEACHING TIP:
LEARNING STYLES

1. Encourage all stu-
   dents to try this
   approach.
2. For verbal or spatial
   learners.

1. Reread your paper aloud or ask a friend to do so as you listen. Hearing your essay read out loud may help you identify parts in need of revision.

2. Write an outline or draw a graphic organizer, or review the one you created earlier. Does your narrative follow the intended sequence?

As you analyze your narrative, be on the lookout for dialogue that doesn't support your thesis, events that need further explanation or description, and details that contribute nothing to the overall impression you want to convey. Use Flowchart 9.1 to help you discover the strengths and weaknesses of your narrative. You might also ask a classmate to review your essay using the questions in the flowchart. For each answer that refers you to the right column of the chart, ask your reviewer to explain why he or she answered in that way. Your reviewer's comments and impressions may reveal strengths and weaknesses in the narrative that you overlooked.

For more on the benefits of peer review, see Chapter 7, p. 166.

ESSAY IN PROGRESS 7

Revise your narrative essay, using Flowchart 9.1 and the suggestions of your classmates to guide you.

Editing and Proofreading

For more on keeping an error log, see Chapter 8, p. 201.

The last step is to check your revised narrative essay for errors in grammar, spelling, punctuation, and mechanics. In addition, be sure to look for the types of errors that you tend to make. (Refer to your error log. See also the Writing Self-Assessment in Appendix A.)

For narrative essays, pay particular attention to the following kinds of sentence problems.

For more on varying sentence structure, see Chapter 8, p. 185.

1. **Make certain that your sentences vary in structure.** A string of sentences that are similar in length and structure is tedious.

   ▶ The Ding Darling National Wildlife Preserve is located on Sanibel Island,

   Florida. ~~It was established~~ ^{Established} in 1945 as the Sanibel Refuge_∧, ^{, its} ~~Its~~ name was

   changed in 1967 to honor the man who helped found it.

FLOWCHART 9.1
REVISING A NARRATIVE ESSAY

Questions		Revision Strategies
1. Is the point of the story clear and do all details support it?	No ⇨	• Rework your thesis to make it more detailed and specific. • Locate and delete irrelevant details.
Yes ⇩		
2. Is each important scene, person, or action vividly described?	No ⇨	• Brainstorm to discover more vivid details. • Consider adding dialogue to bring people and events to life.
Yes ⇩		
3. Does the narrative present a conflict, create and sustain tension, and move at a pace that maintains interest?	No ⇨	• Add events or dialogue to draw more attention to the conflict. • Look for and delete distracting or extraneous material. • Speed up the pace of the narrative by condensing the introduction or eliminating nonessential descriptions.
Yes ⇩		
4. Is the sequence of and relationship among events clear?	No ⇨	• Look for gaps in the narrative and add any missing events. • Consider rearranging the events. • Use transitions to clarify the sequence of events.
Yes ⇩		

(Continued on next page)

FLOWCHART 9.1 *(continued)*

Questions		Revision Strategies

5. Is the dialogue realistic and effective?

Yes ⇩   No ⇨

- Revise by talking aloud for your participants. Record what you say.
- Eliminate dialogue that does not add anything to the story.

6. Do you use point of view and verb tense consistently?

Yes ⇩   No ⇨

- Reconsider your point of view and verb tense.
- Check for places where the tense changes for no reason and revise to make it consistent.

7. Is each paragraph well developed and focused on a separate part of the action? Have you written an effective introduction and conclusion?

Yes   No ⇨

- Be sure each paragraph has a topic sentence and supporting details (see Chapter 6).
- Consider combining closely related paragraphs.
- Split paragraphs that cover more than one event.
- Revise your introduction and conclusion so that they meet the guidelines given on pp. 140–46.

2. **Be sure to punctuate dialogue correctly.** Use commas to separate the quotation from the phrase that introduces it, unless the quotation is integrated into your sentence.

▶ The wildlife refuge guide noted, "American crocodiles are an endangered species and must be protected."

▶ The wildlife refuge guide noted that "American crocodiles are an endangered species and must be protected."

¦ **ESSAY IN PROGRESS 8**
¦ Edit and proofread your narrative essay, paying particular attention to varying
¦ sentence patterns and punctuating dialogue correctly. Don't forget to look for
¦ the types of errors you tend to make.

**TEACHING TIP:
COLLABORATIVE
WRITING**

After students revise
their drafts, have them
work in pairs to edit
each other's narratives
for varied sentence
structure and correct
punctuation of dialogue.

STUDENTS WRITE

Aphonetip Vasavong is a native of Laos who was a nursing student at Niagara University when she wrote this essay. She wrote it in response to an assignment given by her first-year writing instructor to describe an event that changed her life. As you read the essay, notice how Vasavong's narrative creates conflict and tension and builds to a climax and resolution. Highlight the sections where you think the tension is particularly intense.

CONNECTIONS

The student essay "Hypocritically Warm" by Tina Oyer, in Chapter 7 (p. 175), also narrates an event.

**PREREADING
QUESTION**

What kind of miracle does Vasavong write about?

You Can Count on Miracles

Aphonetip Vasavong

Most of us have experienced synchronicity at least   1
once in our lives. According to an article entitled "Do
Miracles Happen?" by Sherry Suib Cohen, synchronistic
experiences are "coincidences that are so unusual and
meaningful that they can't be attributed to chance alone"
(Cohen M6). Many events that seem coincidental often have
simple explanations; however, synchronistic incidents
have no simple explanations. I have had such an experience. My synchronistic experience happened when I was
eight years old and lost in the woods. Strange as it may
seem, a rabbit led me to safety. I would not be here
today if it were not for that rabbit.

Until I was eight, my family lived in Laos. In   2
1986, however, my family and I left Laos to prevent the
Communists from capturing my father. He is an educated
man, and at that time the Communist government wanted to
imprison educated people. The government would place such
people in concentration camps, similar to those used in

Germany and Eastern Europe during World War II, to prevent them from forming a party that might overthrow the
Communists. To protect my father from being captured and
imprisoned in Laos, my family decided to immigrate to
America.

3   We had to leave Laos quickly and secretively. In
order to prevent suspicion, we told our neighbors that
we were taking a two-week family vacation to see our
grandfather. Instead, we stayed with our grandmother for
two days, until we were able to find someone willing to
escort us across the river to Thailand. On the second
night, we planned to board a boat that would take us to
a small town where we could spend the night. I remember
it was around 2 a.m. when my father woke us up. He
divided the ten of us into two groups of five because it
was too risky to walk to the river as a large group.
People would be more likely to notice us and report us
to the Communist soldiers. We were not allowed to speak
or make any noise at all because we might have awakened
people or disturbed their dogs. My father instructed us
carefully: "Hold on to each other's jackets and stay in
line. Move carefully and quietly and we'll all be safe
soon."

4   In a group with my brothers, my sister, and an
escort lady, I was the last person in line. On the way
to the river, everyone else was walking fast through a
dark, wooded area, and I could not keep up with them.
Somehow I accidentally let go of my sister's jacket and
got left behind in the woods. I was alone in the middle
of what seemed like nowhere. It was so dark I could not
see anything or anyone. As I waited in terror for the
escort lady to come back to look for me, I started to
cry. I waited a while longer, and still no one came back
for me.

5   Suddenly, something ran out of the bushes onto a
nearby path. I could see that it was a rabbit. It was
beautiful and bright, like a light. It came back toward
me and stood in front of me. I reached out to pet it,

but it ran toward the same path that it had come from a moment ago. I decided to follow the rabbit along the path. As I did, I was able to see my way through the woods because the rabbit and the path were bright, while the trees and the dense groundcover remained dark. I continued to follow the rabbit along the path until it disappeared into the darkness and I no longer saw the light. I looked around for the rabbit, and what I saw instead was my family getting into the canoes. I turned back once more to look for the rabbit, but it was gone. When I got on the canoe, I was relieved and overjoyed to see my family again. My father pulled me close to him and whispered, "We thought you were lost forever. How did you find us?"

Synchronistic experiences such as mine occur to people everywhere, but most people do not take the time to think about their meaning. Some critics argue that these occurrences are merely coincidental. My experience leads me to believe otherwise. Being lost in the woods and having a brightly lit rabbit lead me safely to my family cannot be attributed to chance alone.

6

Work Cited

Cohen, Sherry Suib. "Do Miracles Happen? What Seems to Be Coincidence Could Really Be the Universe Talking to You, So Pay Attention." <u>Buffalo News</u> 23 June 1996: M6.

Analyzing the Essay

1. Evaluate the effectiveness of Vasavong's thesis.
2. What ideas do you think should be expanded? That is, where did you find yourself wanting or needing more detail?
3. How effectively does Vasavong establish conflict and create tension?
4. Where does Vasavong use foreshadowing? Explain its effectiveness.
5. Evaluate the title, introduction, and conclusion of the essay.

POSSIBLE ANSWERS:
ANALYZING THE ESSAY

1. The thesis—"My synchronistic experience . . . the woods" (paragraph 1)—is clear and specific.
2. It's not clear how many of the ten people were immediate family members (3). More detail is needed about Vasavong's situation (4).
3. *Conflict:* political situation. *Tension:* separation at night. *Effectiveness:* the essay conveys political oppression in explaining the need for silence (3) and builds tension in the account of the walk in the woods and her separation (4).
4. In the introduction, where she mentions the rabbit. *Effectiveness:* Vasavong creates suspense and heightens the readers' awareness of the importance of the rabbit to the story.
5. *Title:* makes an assertion some would say is not provable. *Introduction:* provides background, foreshadowing. *Conclusion:* attempts to universalize her experience by presenting it as an example of synchronicity.

Reacting to the Essay: Discussion and Journal Writing

1. Vasavong's family held a "trust no one" attitude. Why was that necessary? In what situation today, if any, would such an attitude be necessary?
2. Vasavong's father escaped Laos to avoid persecution because of his education. Where does persecution still exist today? Why does it occur?
3. Vasavong believes that the appearance of the rabbit was a synchronistic event, not one that happened by chance. Do you agree? Why or why not?
4. Write a journal entry describing your interpretation of an unusual coincidence or a memorable event from your childhood.

READING A NARRATIVE

The following section provides advice for reading narratives and models of narrative essays. Each essay illustrates the characteristics of narrative writing covered in this chapter and provides opportunities to examine, analyze, and react to the writer's ideas. The second essay uses a narrative to support an argument.

WORKING WITH TEXT: READING NARRATIVES

For more on previewing an
essay and other reading
strategies, see Chapter 2.

It is usually a good idea to read a narrative essay several times before you attempt to discuss or write about it. Preview the essay first, to get an overview of its content and organization. Then read it through to familiarize yourself with the events and action, noting also who did what, when, where, and how. Finally, reread the narrative, this time concentrating on its meaning (more than one reading for meaning may be necessary).

What to Look for, Highlight, and Annotate

1. Narrative elements. When reading a narrative, it is easy to become immersed in the story and to overlook its importance or significance. Therefore, as you read, look for the answers to the following questions. Highlight those sections of the essay that reveal or suggest the answers.

- What main point does the writer make in the narrative?
- What is the writer's thesis? Is it stated directly or implied?
- What is the role of each participant in the story?

- What does the dialogue reveal about or contribute to the main point?
- What is the conflict?
- How does the writer create tension?
- What is the climax?
- How is the conflict resolved?

2. **Sequence of events.** Especially for lengthy or complex narratives and for those that flash back and forward among events, it is helpful to draw a graphic organizer. Doing so will help you establish the sequence of key events.

3. **Keys to meaning.** The following questions will help you evaluate the reading and discover its main point.

CONNECTIONS

Another useful strategy is to prepare a timeline. See Chapter 21, p. 738, for more on creating a timeline for a narrative.

- What is the author's purpose in writing this narrative?
- For what audience is it intended?
- What is the lasting value or merit of this essay? What does it tell me about life, people, jobs, or friendships, for example?
- What techniques does the writer use to try to achieve his or her purpose? Is the writer successful?

4. **Reactions.** As you read, write down your reactions to and feelings about the events, participants, and outcome of the narrative. Include both positive and negative reactions; do not hesitate to challenge participants, their actions, and their motives.

How to Find Ideas to Write About

Since you may be asked to write a response to a narrative, keep an eye out for ideas to write about *as you read*. Pay particular attention to the issue, struggle, or dilemma at hand. Try to discover what broader issue the essay is concerned with. For example, a narrative about a worker's conflict with a supervisor is also concerned with the larger issue of authority. In a story about children who dislike eating vegetables, the larger issue might be food preferences, nutrition, or parental control. Once you've identified the larger issue, you can begin to develop your own ideas about it by relating it to your own experience.

For more about discovering ideas for a response paper, see Chapter 3.

THINKING CRITICALLY ABOUT NARRATION

A nonfiction narrative is often a highly personal, subjective account of an event or a series of events. It is one writer's perception of the event or series of events. Unless you have reason to believe otherwise, assume that the writer is honest—that he or she does not lie or purposely distort the version of the experiences or incidents presented in the essay. You should also assume, however, that the writer chooses details selectively—in order to advance his or her narrative point. Use the following questions to think critically about the narratives you read.

Is the Writer Subjective?

TEACHING TIP

(5 minutes) Ask for a volunteer to tell the class about an incident in which the student knew two sides of a story. Based on this example, what conclusions can the class draw about the subjectivity of experience?

Because a narrative is often highly personal, a critical reader must recognize that the information it contains is probably influenced by the author's values, beliefs, and attitudes. In "How Mosquitoes Came to Be," for example, the giant is presented as a blood-thirsty monster, but imagine if the giant were to tell the same story. Two writers, then, may present two very different versions of a single incident. For example, suppose two observers—one with pro-life views, the other pro-choice—watched a protest in front of an abortion clinic. The pro-life observer would tell a quite different story about the protesters than would the pro-choice observer. Each would make a different narrative point.

What Details Does the Writer Omit?

All of the events and details in a narrative are affected by the writer's perceptions. In a story about the abortion clinic protest, for example, the pro-life observer might include flattering details about the participants and comment on their constitutional right of free speech. The pro-choice writer, however, might focus on the disruption of the clinic and include dialogue from doctors and nurses employed there. Imagine again how the mosquito legend might be told if the narrator were the giant: Descriptions and dialogue would change, and the reader would end up with a very different impression of both the hunter and the giant. As you read a narrative, then, keep in mind that it is one person's version of an experience or incident and that the action, dialogue, and details all support the writer's perception.

NARRATIVE ESSAY

As you read the following essay by Terry Tempest Williams, consider how the writer uses the elements of narrative discussed in this chapter.

The Village Watchman
Terry Tempest Williams

Terry Tempest Williams is a naturalist-in-residence at the Utah Museum of Natural History. She has published several books, including An Unspoken

Hunger: Stories from the Field (1995), a collection of essays, and Refuge:
An Unnatural History of Family and Place *(1992). This essay is from*
Between Friends *(1994). As you read it, highlight or annotate each narrative
element in the essay.*

Stories carved in cedar rise from the deep woods of Sitka. These   1
totem poles are foreign to me, this vertical lineage of clans: Eagle,
Raven, Wolf, and Salmon. The Tlingit* craftsmen create a genealogy
of the earth, a reminder of mentors, a reminder that we come into
this world in need of proper instruction. I sit on the soft floor of this
Alaskan forest and feel the presence of Other. The totem before me is
called "Wolf Pole" by locals. The Village Watchman sits on top of
Wolf's head with his knees drawn to his chest, his hands holding
them tight against his body. He wears a red and black striped hat. His
eyes are direct, deep set, painted blue.

The expression on his face reminds me of a man I loved, a man   2
who was born into this world feet first. "Breech," my mother told me
of her brother's birth. "Alan was born feet first. As a result, his brain
was denied oxygen. He is special." As a child, I was impressed by this
information. I remember thinking that fish live underwater. Maybe
Alan had gills, maybe he didn't need a face-first gulp of air like the
rest of us. The amniotic sea he had floated in for nine months delivered him with a fluid memory. He knew something. Other.

There is a story of a boy who was kidnapped from his village by   3
the Salmon People. He was taken from his family to learn the ways of
water. When he returned many years later to his home, he was recognized by his own as a holy man privy to the mysteries of the unseen
world. Twenty years after my uncle's death, I wonder if Alan could
have been that boy.

But our culture tells a different story, more alien. My culture calls   4
people of sole births retarded, handicapped, mentally disabled or
challenged. We see them for who they are not, rather than for who
they are.

My grandmother, Lettie Romney Dixon, wrote in her journal, "It   5
wasn't until Alan was 16 months old that a busy doctor cruelly broke
the news to us. Others may have suspected our son's limitations but
to those of us who loved him so unquestionably, lightning struck
without warning. I hugged my sorrow to myself. I felt abandoned and
lost. I wouldn't accept the verdict. Then we started the trips to a mul-
titude of doctors. Most of them were kind and explained that our

PREREADING
QUESTION

Who is the "village
watchman," and what is
his function?

Tlingit: A group of Native American tribes living on reservations in British
Columbia and Alaska.

child was like a car without brakes, like an electric wire without insulation. They gave us no hope for a normal life."

6   Normal. Latin: *normalis; norma,* a rule; conforming with or constituting an accepted standard, model, or pattern, especially corresponding to the median or average of a large group in type, appearance, achievement, function, or development.

7   Alan was not normal. He was unique; one and only; single; sole; unusual; extraordinary; rare. His emotions were not measured, his curiosity not bridled. In a sense, he was wild like a mustang in the desert, and like most wild horses, he was eventually rounded up.

8   He was unpredictable. He created his own rules, and they changed from moment to moment. Alan was 12 years old, hyperactive, mischievous, easily frustrated, and unable to learn in traditional ways. The situation was intensified by his seizures. Suddenly, without warning, he would stiffen like a rake, fall forward, and crash to the ground, hitting his head. My grandparents could not keep him home any longer. They needed professional guidance and help. In 1957, they reluctantly placed their youngest child in an institution for handicapped children called the American Fork Training School. My grandmother's heart broke for the second time.

9   Once again, from her journal: "Many a night my pillow is wet from tears of sorrow and senseless dreamings of 'if things had only been different,' or wondering if he is tucked in snug and warm, if he is well and happy, if the wind still bothers him. . . ."

10   The wind may have continued to bother Alan; certainly the conditions he was living under were less than ideal, but there was much about his private life his family never knew. What we did know was that Alan had an enormous capacity for adaptation. We had no choice but to follow him.

11   I followed him for years.

12   Alan was ten years my senior. In my mind, he was mythic. Everything I was taught not to do, Alan did. We were taught to be polite, to not express displeasure or anger in public. Alan was sheer, physical expression. Whatever was on his mind he vocalized and usually punctuated with colorful speech. We would go bowling as a family on Sundays. Each of us would take our turn, hold the black ball to our chest, take a few steps, swing our arm back, forward, glide, and release. The ball would roll down the alley, hit a few pins; we would wait for the ball to return, and then take our second run. Little emotion was shown. When it was Alan's turn, it was an event. Nothing subtle. His style was Herculean. Big man. Big ball. Big roll. Big bang. Whether it was a strike or a gutter ball, he clapped his hands, spun around on the floor, slapped his thighs, and cried, "Goddamn! Did you see that one? Send me another ball, sweet Jesus!" And the ball was always returned.

I could count on my uncle for a straight answer. He taught me   13
that one of the remarkable aspects of being human was to hold
opposing views in our mind at once.

"How are you doing?" I would ask.   14

"Ask me how I am feeling?" he answered.   15

"Okay, how are you feeling?"   16

"Today? Right now?"   17

"Yes."   18

"I am very happy and very sad."   19

"How can you be both at the same time?" I asked in all serious-   20
ness, a girl of nine or ten.

"Because both require each other's company. They live in the   21
same house. Didn't you know?"

We would laugh and then go on to another topic. Talking to my   22
uncle was always like entering a maze of riddles. Ask a question.
Answer with a question and see where it leads you.

My younger brother Steve and I spent a lot of time with Alan. He   23
offered us shelter from the conventionality of a Mormon family. At
our home during Christmas, he would direct us in his own nativity
plays. "More—" he would say to us, making wide gestures with his
hands. "Give me more of yourself." He was not like anyone we knew.
In a culture where we were taught to be seen and not heard, Alan was
our mirror.

We could be different, too. His unquestioning belief in us as chil-   24
dren, as human beings, was in startling contrast to the way we saw
the public react to him. It hurt us. We could never tell if it hurt him.

Each week, Steve and I would accompany our grandparents south   25
to visit Alan. It was an hour's drive to the school from Salt Lake City,
mostly through farmlands. We would enter the grounds, pull into
the parking lot to a playground filled with huge papier-mâché story-
book figures (a 20-foot pied piper, a pumpkin carriage with Cin-
derella inside, the old woman who lived in a shoe), and nine times
out of ten, Alan would be standing outside his dormitory waiting for
us. We would get out of the car and he would run toward us and
throw his powerful arms around us. His hugs cracked my back and at
times I had to fight for my breath. My grandfather would calm him
down by simply saying, "We're here, son. You can relax now."

Alan was a formidable man, now in his early twenties, stocky and   26
strong. His head was large, with a protruding forehead that bore
many scars, a line-by-line history of seizures. He always had on someone else's clothes—a tweed jacket too small, brown pants too big, a
striped golf shirt that didn't match. He showed us that appearances
didn't matter, personality did. If you didn't know him, he could look
frightening. It was an unspoken rule in our family that the character
of others was gauged by how they treated Alan. The only consistent

thing about his attire was that he always wore a silver football helmet from Olympus High School, where my grandfather was coach. It was a loving, practical solution to protect Alan when he fell.

27   "Part of the team," my grandfather would say as he slapped Alan affectionately on the back. "You're a Titan, son, and I love you."

28   The windows to the dormitory were dark, reflecting Mount Timpanogos to the east. It was hard to see inside, but I knew what the interior held. It looked like an abandoned gymnasium without bleachers, filled with hospital beds. The stained white walls and yellow-waxed floors offered no warmth. The stench was nauseating: sweat and urine trapped in the oppression of stale air. I recall the dirty sheets, the lack of privacy, and the almond-eyed children who never rose from their beds. And then I would turn around and face Alan's cheerfulness, the open and loving manner in which he would introduce me to his friends, the pride he exhibited as he showed me around his home. I kept thinking, "Doesn't he see how bad this is, how poorly they are being treated?" His words would return to me: "I am very happy and very sad."

29   For my brother and me, Alan was guide, elder. He was fearless. But neither one of us will ever be able to escape the image of Alan kissing his parents good-bye after an afternoon with family and slowly walking back to his dormitory. Before we drove away, he would turn toward us, take off his silver helmet, and wave. The look on his face haunts me still.

30   Six years later, I found myself sitting with my uncle at a hospital where he was being treated for a severe ear infection. I was 18. He was 28.

31   "Alan," I asked, "what is it really like to live inside your body?"

32   He crossed his legs and placed both hands on the arms of the chair. His brown eyes were piercing.

33   "I can't tell you what it's like except to say I feel pain for not being seen as the person I am."

34   A few days later, Alan died—alone, unique, one and only, single —in American Fork, Utah.

35   The Village Watchman sits on top of his totem with Wolf and Salmon. It is beginning to rain in the forest. I find it curious that this spot in southeast Alaska has brought me back into relation with my uncle, this man who came into the world feet first. He reminds me of what it means to live and love with a broken heart; how nothing is sacred, how everything is sacred. He was a weather vane, at once a storm and a clearing.

36   Shortly after his death, Alan appeared to me in a dream. We were standing in my grandmother's kitchen. He was leaning against the white stove with his arms folded.

POSSIBLE ANSWERS:
EXAMINING THE
READING

1. He is mentally handi-
   capped; he is also
   unusual—more sensi-
   tive, honest, and
   unconventional than
   most other people.
2. This metaphor and
   others suggest Alan's
   unpredictability.
3. His honesty, kindness,
   originality, depth of
   feeling, fearlessness.
4. He is distinctive; he is
   the watchman of the
   institution, waiting for
   his family; he is a wise
   man, set apart from
   others.
5. *Genealogy:* a map or
   narrative chronicling
   lines of descent within
   a family; *privy:* let in
   on a secret; *Herculean:*
   as strong as Hercules;
   formidable: large, overpowering; *Titan:* a
   giant, after the Greek
   god Titan.

"Look at me now, Terry," he said, smiling. "I'm normal — per- 37
fectly normal." And then he laughed. We both laughed.

He handed me his silver football helmet, which was resting on 38
the counter, kissed me, and opened the back door.

"Do you recognize who I am?" 39

On this day in Sitka, I remember. ■ 40

Examining the Reading

1. Why is Alan considered "special"?
2. Explain Williams's comparison of Alan to a wild mustang.
3. What is it about Alan's personality that Williams admires most?
4. In what sense is Alan the Village Watchman?
5. Explain the meaning of each of the following words as it is used in the read-ing: *genealogy* (paragraph 1), *privy* (3), *Herculean* (12), *formidable* (26), and *Titan* (27). Refer to your dictionary as needed.

Analyzing the Reading

1. Reread the description of the totem poles in paragraph 1. What is the writer's purpose here? What do the details about the totem poles contribute to the essay?
2. What is the writer's thesis? Is it stated directly or implied?
3. Evaluate Williams's use of dialogue. What does the dialogue contribute to the essay?
4. Although the essay is primarily a narrative, Williams uses description and comparison as well. Locate examples of those patterns of development and explain what they contribute to the essay as a whole.
5. Does Williams present an objective or subjective view of Alan's institutional-ization? Mention several types of details that Williams does not discuss.

Reacting to the Reading: Discussion and Journal Writing

1. Do you agree with Williams's family that a good way to evaluate people is to observe their response to a mentally challenged person? Explain your reasons, giving examples from your experience.
2. Williams says her uncle taught her "that one of the remarkable aspects of being human [is] to hold opposing views in our mind at once" (paragraph 13). Alan also tells her that opposing feelings "require each other's company" (paragraph 21). Explain what it means to you to have ambivalent feelings.

POSSIBLE ANSWERS: ANALYZING THE READING

1. They are a multicul-tural metaphor for respect and reverence due to mentors or wisdom figures that implies a comparison between the strange and wise watchman and Alan.
2. Students might argue for a direct or an implied thesis. *Direct:* "We see them for who they are not, rather than for who they are" (paragraph 4). *Implied:* Alan repre-sents the value and wisdom of people who are different.
3. Dialogue conveys a sense of immediacy: Shows the relation-ship between the writer and Alan, the grandmother's sor-row, and Alan's per-sonality.
4. *Description:* totem poles (1) provide a metaphor for Alan; description of the institution (28) pro-vides the setting. *Com-parisons:* the village watchman (1); boy kidnapped by Salmon People (3); contrast between Alan and "normal" people (6–7) — all serve to enhance readers un-derstanding of Alan.
5. Subjective. Williams does not discuss the pain Alan experiences when he falls or his feelings as his family leaves him after a visit.

POSSIBLE ANSWERS: REACTING TO THE READING

1. Responses will vary.
2. Responses will vary.

(Continued on next page)

Alan probably means
that people must
know sadness to rec-
ognize its opposite:
happiness.
3. Responses will vary.

3. Williams laments that people with mental disabilities are seen "for who they are, rather than for who they are" (paragraph 4). Write a journal entry in response to her statement, giving examples from your experience.

NARRATION COMBINED WITH OTHER PATTERNS

*For more on reading and
writing arguments, see
Chapters 17 and 18.*

In the following selection, Norma Molen uses a narrative within an essay that presents an argument.

Another Mother's Child
A Letter to a Murdered Son
Norma Molen

Norma Molen read this letter on the steps of the Lincoln Memorial in Washington, D.C., during a Mother's Day rally against gun violence in 1992. This letter was later published in Catalyst, *a Salt Lake City–based alternative magazine, in 1993. Molen begins with the narrative, using it to grab her readers' attention and prepare them for her argument in favor of handgun restriction. As you read, notice how Molen integrates the narrative within her essay and makes it clear how the story illustrates her message.*

PREREADING
QUESTION

What is Molen's posi-
tion on the issue of gun
control?

Dear Steven,

1   We find it difficult to speak of your terrible tragedy, yet we feel we must. You told us at Christmas break you were dating a beautiful graduate student, Susan Clements, who lived in the women's wing of your dormitory. And just before you returned to school you casually mentioned that Susan had received threatening phone calls from an ex-boyfriend, a graduate student at Stanford. You said there was nothing to worry about, that he was all bluff, but that he was causing Susan a great deal of distress. We were not too concerned because he was 3,000 miles away, yet we warned you not to get involved. You insisted you could handle it.

2   On April 23, Andreas Drexler, the ex-boyfriend, appeared in the dormitory hall, just as Susan was unlocking the door to her room. Drexler shot once and missed. You ran to Susan's defense and he shot you in the stomach, then ran down the hall and shot Susan three times in the face. Susan died immediately, you lived five days on machines before you were pronounced dead, and Drexler, despairing over his unspeakable crime, shot himself with the same gun. An unimaginable nightmare.

Three talented students dead. And for what purpose? A moment 3
of passion from which there was no return.

We are sorry we brought you up in this violent land. Other 4
advanced nations are ten to fifty times safer from gun violence than
the United States. You would still be alive if you had been born in
England, France, Germany, or Japan. We are a free people, but with
this freedom we kill a staggering number with handguns. We have
learned to accept the intolerable.

There is no legitimate need for a handgun in a civilized society, a 5
technology designed specifically for killing, a weapon for the coward.
And we, like most Americans, were lethargic about this grotesque
carnage until you became a victim, not in a drug war, but on the 14th
floor of the graduate dormitory at Indiana University. The killing is
everywhere: 25,000 last year. And more people arm themselves each
day because we have allowed the gun industry to promote a solution
of complete madness.

Drexler, ironically a German, could never have committed this 6
crime in his own country because he couldn't have purchased a gun.
In civilized countries people don't buy handguns. The only exception
in European countries is for members of target shooting societies,
but the gun is never taken from the target range.

The immense tragedy that can never change is that we lost you, 7
our poet and writer, our scholar. You disdained material things,
always wore shorts and rode a bicycle, even in winter. You even
refused to have a driver's license. And every time we go to an outdoor
restaurant, for a bike ride, or a walk up the canyon, there will be an
empty place. You were cheated of a career already begun. You were a
published writer at age 22 with a short story in a collection called
Flash Fiction. Who knows what you might have contributed? Several
literature professors said you were the brightest student they ever
had. They also spoke of Susan in superlatives.

We think a wall like the Vietnam Memorial should be built in 8
front of the Capitol building, except this time it should record the
names of the victims killed in their own land because their senators
and representatives did not have the integrity and common sense to
establish laws that would protect the public. It would be a daily
reminder that your blood, Susan's blood, and the blood of thousands
of other victims stains the flag.

After you died, artist Randall Lake called to remind us of the por- 9
trait of you he'd begun to paint. We were thrilled to see it. He caught
your intelligent eyes, firm chin, and high cheekbones, your full, thick
hair, and he captured your stance. Yet it was not finished. An unfinished portrait is a perfect metaphor for your life. And Susan's. And
all the others. ∎

POSSIBLE ANSWERS:
EXAMINING THE
READING

1. Gun control
2. Molen favors gun
control because she
believes it prevents
crimes of passion and
deliberate murder.
She gives examples of
other countries whose
citizens are safer than
U.S. citizens because
of gun-control laws
(paragraph 4); argues
that "There is no
legitimate need for a
handgun in a civilized
society" and cites the
statistic of 25,000
killed in one year (5);
points out that hand-
gun violence kills peo-
ple who are valuable
to society (7).
3. *Grotesque:* abhorrent,
disgusting, absurd;
carnage: bloody killing;
ironically: in contrast
to what is expected;
disdained: did not
value; *superlatives:*
words of praise

POSSIBLE ANSWERS:
ANALYZING THE
READING

1. "There is no legiti-
mate need for a hand-
gun . . . coward." The
placement in para-
graph 5 emphasizes
the point that the nar-
rative illustrates.
2. It adds emotional
power by encouraging
the reader to
empathize with vic-
tims of gun violence.

*For more on locating and
documenting sources, see
Chapters 19 and 20.*

Examining the Reading

1. What main issue does Molen's essay address?

2. What is Molen's position on the issue? What reasons does she offer in support of her position?

3. Explain the meaning of each of the following words as it is used in the reading: *grotesque* (paragraph 5), *carnage* (5), *ironically* (6), *disdained* (7), and *superlatives* (7). Refer to your dictionary as needed.

Analyzing the Reading

1. What is Molen's thesis? (It is presented after the narrative.) Is its placement effective? Why or why not?

2. How does the opening narrative of her son's death contribute to the effectiveness of Molen's essay?

3. Explain how the narrative creates tension and builds to a climax.

4. Highlight several words or phrases that reveal Molen's subjective viewpoint.

Reacting to the Reading: Discussion and Journal Writing

1. Do you think the letter format is effective? Why or why not?

2. Does Molen seriously advocate a wall similar to the Vietnam Memorial? What, if anything, do you think should be done to commemorate handgun victims?

3. Write a journal entry exploring or explaining your position on handgun ownership.

APPLYING YOUR SKILLS: ADDITIONAL ESSAY ASSIGNMENTS

Write a narrative on one of the following topics, using the elements and techniques of narration you learned in this chapter. Depending on the topic you choose, you may need to do library or Internet research to gather enough support for your ideas.

To Express Your Ideas

1. Write a narrative about an incident or experience from the past that you see differently now than you did then.

2. In "A Primitive Ritual" students observe behavior that at first seems strange and bizarre, only to learn later that the behavior is similar to their own. Write a narrative describing an incident or experience that caused you to change your mind about a person or activity.

To Inform Your Reader

3. Write an essay informing your reader about the characteristics of a strong (or weak) relationship, the habits of successful (or unsuccessful) students, or the ways of keeping (or losing) a job. Use a narrative to support one or more of your main points.

To Persuade Your Reader

4. In "The Village Watchman," Williams observes that people with mental disabilities are not seen "for who they are." Write an essay persuading your reader to support a particular action or policy that would improve the way individuals with physical or mental disabilities are regarded on your campus. Include a narrative within your essay that supports your position.

5. "Another Mother's Child" is a persuasive essay that uses narration to support the writer's position on gun control. Write an essay persuading your reader to take a particular stand on an issue of your choosing. Use a narrative to support your position on the issue or tell how you arrived at it.

Cases Using Narration

6. Write a paper on the advantages of an urban or suburban lifestyle for a sociology course. Support some of your main points with events and examples from your own experience.

7. Write a draft of the presentation you will give as the new personnel director of a nursing care facility in charge of training new employees. You plan to hold your first orientation session next week, and you want to emphasize the importance of teamwork and communication by telling related stories from your previous job experiences.

3. Tension builds as Molen describes the ex-boyfriend's threats and reaches a climax in the sudden appearance of Drexler and the shootings.

4. Molen reveals her viewpoint through the following words and phrases: "beautiful graduate student" (paragraph 1), "violent land" (4), "lethargic about this grotesque carnage" (5), "our poet and writer, our scholar" (7).

POSSIBLE ANSWERS: REACTING TO THE READING

1. The letter format is poignant and ironic (in that Molen will never be able to communicate with her son again).

2. Responses will vary.

3. Responses will vary.

TEACHING TIP: REACTING TO THE READING

Choose one question. After students respond to it individually in their journals, discuss the question as a whole class.

TEACHING TIP: APPLYING YOUR SKILLS

Suggest that students use at least one prewriting strategy—drawing a graphic organizer, freewriting, brainstorming, questioning, writing assertions—to get started. Remind students to consult the learning style options (p. 219) and the revision flowchart (p. 227).

CHAPTER QUICK START

Suppose you have to find a home for your puppy because your new landlord does not allow pets. You decide to place the following advertisement in the campus newspaper:

Four-month-old, male puppy needs new home. Free to caring individual. Call 555-2298.

Although you run the ad for two weeks, you don't get a single call. Then a friend advises you to write a more appealing description of your puppy, one that will make people *want* to adopt him.

Writing Quick Start

Rewrite the advertisement, describing the puppy in a way that will help convince readers to adopt him.

Description: Portraying People, Places, and Things

TEACHING TIP

To introduce elements of description, ask students to brainstorm as a class a list of the additional information they would need about the puppy before responding to the ad (e.g., whether the puppy is healthy, housebroken, friendly with children, and well behaved).

TEACHING TIP:
CHAPTER OVERVIEW

• Explain that students
will use what they have
learned about *audience*
in writing descriptions.
Readers are drawn to
the immediacy and
vividness of good
descriptive writing, but
different details appeal
to different audiences.

• Remind students that
showing is more effec-
tive than *telling* in
descriptive writing.
Readers should be
able to see the people
or places being
described. Have stu-
dents brainstorm
details about a cam-
pus building or area
that would allow a
reader unfamiliar with
it to form a mental
image.

WRITING A DESCRIPTION

In rewriting the advertisement, did you describe how the puppy looks, feels, responds, or behaves? Did you choose details that emphasize one or more of the puppy's features—his soft, cuddly appearance, his desire to please, or his training? If so, you just wrote a successful description. In this chapter, you will learn how to write descriptions and how to use description to support and develop your ideas.

WHAT IS DESCRIPTION?

Description presents information in a way that appeals to one or more of the five senses, usually with the purpose of creating an overall impression or feeling. Descriptive writing makes your ideas vivid for your audience—so they can almost see, hear, smell, taste, or touch what you are writing about. We use description every day. In a conversation with a friend, you might describe a pair of shoes you bought, a flavor of ice cream you tasted, or a wedding you recently attended.

Description is an important and useful communication skill. If you were an eyewitness to a car theft, for example, the detective investigating the crime would no doubt ask you to describe what you saw. You would need to describe clearly and accurately what the thief looked like and what he or she did. Or suppose you work at an aquarium and part of your job is to explain to visiting groups of school-children how the resident dolphins are trained. You would probably describe the sign language trainers use, the tasks dolphins perform, and the rewards they receive. When you write vivid descriptions, you not only make your writing more lively and interesting, but you also indicate your attitude toward the subject through your choice of words and details.

You will use description in many situations in college and on the job, as the examples in the accompanying box show.

In the following lively description of a sensory experience of taste, you will feel as if you, too, are eating chilli peppers.

SCENES FROM COLLEGE AND THE WORKPLACE

- For a *chemistry* lab report, you are asked to describe the odor and appearance of a substance made by combining two chemicals.

- In an *art history* class, your instructor asks you to visit a local gallery, choose a particular painting, and describe in a two-page paper the artist's use of line or color.

- As a *nurse* at a local burn treatment center, one of your responsibilities is to record on each patient's chart the overall appearance of and change in second- and third-degree burns.

Eating Chilli Peppers
Jeremy MacClancy

Jeremy MacClancy is an anthropologist and tutor at Oxford University in England who has written several scholarly works in the field of anthropology. This essay is taken from his book Consuming Culture: Why You Eat What You Eat *(1993). As you read the selection, underline or highlight the descriptive words and phrases that convey what it's like to eat chilli peppers.*

PREREADING QUESTION

If you have eaten chilli peppers, what was the experience like?

TEACHING TIP

• MacClancy uses *modifiers, active verbs, figurative language,* and *abstractions* to describe the taste of chilli peppers. Have students identify descriptions with these elements; e.g., "powerful chemical irritant" (paragraph 1); "chilli mush" (2); "The sweat glands open, your eyes stream" (2); "go for the burn" (3); "belching flames" (6).

• To prepare students to identify figurative language, point out a few examples: "like aiming a flame-thrower at your parted lips" (2); "your mouth belches fire like a dragon" (2); "like going to a horror movie" (4); "like experienced surfers" (4); "hot sauce for their lives" (5).

• Mention that occasionally description can also be abstract; e.g., "the thrill of anticipation . . . normality" (4); "non-sexist form of acquired love" (5).

1   How come over half of the world's population have made a powerful chemical irritant the center of their gastronomic lives? How can so many millions stomach chillies?

2   Biting into a tabasco pepper is like aiming a flame-thrower at your parted lips. There might be little reaction at first, but then the burn starts to grow. A few seconds later the chilli mush in your mouth reaches critical mass and your palate prepares for liftoff. The message spreads. The sweat glands open, your eyes stream, your nose runs, your stomach warms up, your heart accelerates, and your lungs breathe faster. All this is normal. But bite off more than your body can take, and you will be left coughing, sneezing, and spitting. Tears stripe your cheeks, and your mouth belches fire like a dragon celebrating its return to life. Eater beware!

3   As a general stimulant, chilli is similar to amphetamines — only quicker, cheaper, non-addictive, and beneficial to boot. Employees at the tabasco plant in Louisiana rarely complain of coughs, hay fever, or sinusitis. (Recent evidence, however, suggests that too many chillies can bring on stomach cancer.) Over the centuries, people have used hot peppers as a folk medicine to treat sore throats or inflamed gums, to relieve respiratory distress, and to ease gastritis induced by alcoholism. For aching muscles and tendons, a chilli plaster is more effective than one of mustard, with the added advantage that it does not blister the skin. But people do not eat tabasco, jalapeno, or cayenne peppers because of their pharmacological side-effects. They eat them for the taste — different varieties have different flavors — and for the fire they give off. In other words, they go for the burn.

4   Eating chillies makes for exciting times: the thrill of anticipation, the extremity of the flames, and then the slow descent back to normality. This is a benign form of masochism, like going to a horror movie, riding a roller coaster, or stepping into a cold bath after a sauna. The body flashes danger signals, but the brain knows the threat is not too great. *Aficionados,* self-absorbed in their burning passion, know exactly how to pace their whole-chilli eating so that the flames are maintained at a steady maximum. Wrenched out of

normal routines by the continuing assault on their mouths, they concentrate on the sensation and ignore almost everything else. They play with fire and just ride the burn, like experienced surfers cresting along a wave. For them, without hot peppers, food would lose its zest and their days would seem too dull. A cheap, legal thrill, chilli is the spice of their life.

5   In the rural areas of Mexico, men can turn their chilli habit into a contest of strength by seeing who can stomach the most hot peppers in a set time. This gastronomic test, however, is not used as a way to prove one's machismo, for women can play the game as well. In this context, chillies are a non-sexist form of acquired love for those with strong hearts and fiery passions — a steady source of hot sauce for their lives.

6   The enjoyable sensations of a running nose, crying eyes, and dragon-like mouth belching flames are clearly not for the timorous.

7   More tabasco, anyone?   ■

Characteristics of Descriptive Writing

Successful descriptions offer readers more than just a list of sensory details or a catalog of characteristics. In a good description, the details work together to create a single effect or impression. Descriptive writing uses sensory detail selectively to create a dominant impression. Writers often use comparison to help readers experience what they are writing about.

Description Uses Sensory Details

Sensory details appeal to one or more of the five senses — sight, sound, smell, taste, and touch. For example, in the second paragraph of "Eating Chilli Peppers," MacClancy describes the physical sensations that chilli peppers create. The third paragraph focuses on their drug-like effects, while the fourth and fifth paragraphs emphasize their psychological effects. Throughout the essay the writer uses vivid language. Can you almost feel a chilli pepper burning in your mouth? MacClancy achieves this effect by using words that appeal to the senses of sight and taste. By appealing to the senses in your writing, you too can help your readers experience the object, sensation, event, or person you aim to describe.

Sight.   When you describe what something looks like, you help your reader create a mental picture of the subject. In the following excerpt, notice how Loren Eiseley uses visual detail to describe what he comes across in a field.

One day as I cut across the field which at that time extended on one side of our suburban shopping center, I found a giant slug feeding from a funnel of pink ice cream in an abandoned Dixie cup. I could see his eyes telescope and protrude in a kind of dim, uncertain ecstasy as his dark body bunched and elongated in the curve of the cup.

LOREN EISELEY, "The Brown Wasps"

The description allows the reader to imagine the slug eating the ice cream in a way that a bare statement of the facts—"On my way to the mall, I saw a slug in a paper cup"—would not do. Eiseley describes shape ("funnel of pink ice cream"), action ("bunched and elongated"), color ("pink funnel," "dark body"), and size ("giant"). Notice also how Eiseley includes specific details ("suburban shopping center," "Dixie cup") to help readers visualize the scene.

Sound.   Sound can also be a powerful descriptive tool. Can you "hear" the engines in the following description?

> They were one-cylinder and two-cylinder engines, and some were make-and-break and some were jump-spark, but they all made a sleepy sound across the lake. The one-lungers throbbed and fluttered, and the twin-cylinder ones purred and purred, and that was a quiet sound too. But now the campers all had outboards. In the daytime, in the hot mornings, these motors made a petulant, irritable sound; at night, in the still evening when the afterglow lit the water, they whined about one's ears like mosquitoes.
>
> E. B. WHITE, "Once More to the Lake"

White conveys the sounds of the engines by using active verbs ("throbbed and fluttered," "purred and purred," "whined"), descriptive adjectives ("sleepy," "petulant," "irritable") and a comparison ("whined about one's ears like mosquitoes").

Writers of description also use *onomatopoeia,* words that approximate the sounds they describe. The words *hiss, whine, spurt,* and *sizzle* are common examples.

Smell.   Smells are sometimes difficult to describe, partly because we do not have as many adjectives for smells as we do for sights and sounds. Smell can be an effective descriptive device, however, as shown here.

> Driving through farm country at summer sunset provides a cavalcade of smells: manure, cut grass, honeysuckle, spearmint, wheat chaff, scallions, chicory, tar from the macadam road.   DIANE ACKERMAN, *A Natural History of the Senses*

Notice how Ackerman lists nouns that evoke distinct odors and leaves it to the reader to imagine how they smell.

Taste.   Words that evoke the sense of taste can make descriptions lively, as you saw in "Eating Chilli Peppers." Consider also this restaurant critic's description of Vietnamese cuisine.

> In addition to balancing the primary flavors—the sweet, sour, bitter, salty and peppery tastes whose sensations are, in the ancient Chinese system, directly related to physical and spiritual health—medicinal herbs were used in most dishes. . . . For

instance, the orange-red annatto seed is used for its "cooling" effect as well as for the mildly tangy flavor it lends and the orange color it imparts.

MOLLY O'NEILL, "Vietnam's Cuisine: Echoes of Empires"

Notice that O'Neill describes the variety of flavors ("sweet, sour, bitter, salty and peppery") in Vietnamese cuisine.

Touch.   Descriptions of texture, temperature, and weight allow a reader not only to visualize but almost to experience an object or scene. In the excerpt that follows, Annie Dillard describes the experience of holding a Polyphemus moth cocoon.

> We passed the cocoon around; it was heavy. As we held it in our hands, the creature within warmed and squirmed. We were delighted, and wrapped it tighter in our fists. The pupa began to jerk violently, in heart-stopping knocks. Who's there? I can still feel those thumps, urgent through a muffling of spun silk and leaf, urgent through the swaddling of many years, against the curve of my palm. We kept passing it around. When it came to me again it was hot as a bun; it jumped half out of my hand. The teacher intervened. She put it, still heaving and banging, in the ubiquitous Mason Jar.
>
> ANNIE DILLARD, *Pilgrim at Tinker Creek*

Dillard describes the texture of the cocoon ("a muffling of spun silk and leaf"), its temperature ("hot as a bun"), and its weight ("heavy") to give readers an accurate sense of what it felt like to hold it.

Description Uses Active Verbs and Varied Sentences

Sensory details are often best presented by using active, vivid verbs and by varying your sentences. Look, for instance, at the active verbs in this sentence from paragraph 2 of MacClancy's essay.

> The sweat glands *open,* your eyes *stream,* your nose *runs,* your stomach *warms up,* your heart *accelerates,* and your lungs *breathe* faster.

In fact, active verbs are often more effective than adverbs in creating striking and lasting impressions, as the following example demonstrates.

ORIGINAL: **The team captain *proudly* accepted the award.**

REVISED: **The team captain *marched* to the podium, *grasped* the trophy, and *gestured* toward his teammates.**

For more on varying sentence patterns and using active verbs, see Chapter 8, pp. 189 and 192.

Using varied sentences also contributes to the effective expression of sensory details. Be sure to use different types and patterns of sentences and to vary their lengths. Look again at the second paragraph in MacClancy's essay. Note how he varies his sentences to make the description interesting. Avoid wordy or repetitive sentences, especially those with strings of mediocre adjectives or adverbs *(pretty, really),* which tend to detract from the impression you are trying to create.

EXERCISE 10.1

Using sensory details, active verbs, and varied sentences, describe one of the common objects in the following list or one of your own choosing. Do not name the object in your description. Exchange papers with a classmate. Your reader should be able to guess the item you are describing from the details you provide.

1. A piece of clothing
2. A food item
3. An appliance
4. A machine
5. A computer keyboard

POSSIBLE ANSWERS

Answers will vary

Description Creates a Dominant Impression

An effective description leaves the reader with a **dominant impression** — an overall attitude, mood, or feeling about the subject. The impression may be awe, inspiration, anger, or distaste, for example.

Let's suppose you are writing about an old storage box you found in your parents' attic and that the aspect of the box you want to emphasize (your slant) is *memories of childhood.* Given this slant or angle, you might describe the box in several different ways, each of which would convey a different dominant impression.

For more on thesis statements, see Chapter 5, p. 97.

- "A box filled with treasures from my childhood brought back memories of long, sunny afternoons playing in our backyard."
- "Opening the box was like lifting the lid of a time machine, revealing toys and games from another era."
- "When I opened the box, I was eight years old again, fighting over my favorite doll with my twin sister, Erica."

Notice that each example provides a different impression of the contents of the storage box and would require a different type of support. That is, only selected objects from within the box would be relevant to each impression. Note, too, that in all of these examples, the dominant impression is stated directly rather than implied. Many times writers rely on descriptive language to imply a dominant impression.

In "Eating Chilli Peppers," notice how all the details evoke the thrill of eating the peppers for those who love them; as MacClancy says, "they go for the burn." The first two sentences of the essay pose the questions that the remaining paragraphs answer. The answer is the dominant impression — eating chilli peppers is thrilling. To write an effective description, you need to select details carefully, including only those that contribute to the dominant impression you are trying to create. Details that do not support your dominant impression can clutter a description and distract your reader. Notice that MacClancy does not clutter his description by describing the size, shape, texture, or color of chilli peppers. Instead, he focuses on their thrilling, fiery hotness and the side effects they cause.

EXERCISE 10.2

Read the following paragraph and cross out details that do not contribute to the dominant impression.

> All morning I had had some vague sense that something untoward was about to happen. I suspected bad news was on its way. As I stepped outside, the heat of the summer sun, unusually oppressive for ten o'clock, seemed to sear right through me. In fact, now that I think about it, everything seemed slightly out of kilter that morning. The car, which had been newly painted the week before, had stalled several times. The flowers in the garden, planted for me by my husband, purchased from a nursery down the road, were drooping. It was as though they were wilting before they even had a chance to grow. Even my two cats, who look like furry puffballs, moved listlessly across the room, ignoring my invitation to play. It was then that I received the phone call from the emergency room telling me about my son's accident.

Description Uses Connotative Language Effectively

As noted in Chapter 8, most words have two levels of meaning—*denotative* and *connotative*. The denotation of a word is its precise dictionary meaning. For instance, the denotation of the word *flag* is "a piece of cloth used as a national emblem." Usually, however, feelings and attitudes are also associated with a word—emotional colorings or shades of meaning. These are the word's connotations. A common connotation of *flag* is patriotism—love and respect for one's country. Because connotations vary, for some people the connotation of *flag* may be an interesting decoration for a jacket or other article of clothing. As you write, be careful about the connotations of the words you choose. Select words that help to strengthen the dominant impression you are creating.

Description Uses Comparisons

When describing a person or an object, you can help your readers by comparing it to something with which they are familiar. Several types of comparison are used in descriptive writing: similes, metaphors, personification, and analogies. In a **simile** the comparison is direct and is introduced by the word *like* or *as*. MacClancy uses a number of telling similes in "Eating Chilli Peppers."

- "Biting into a tabasco pepper is like aiming a flame-thrower at your parted lips."
- Eating chillies is "like going to a horror movie, riding a roller coaster, or stepping into a cold bath after a sauna."

A **metaphor** is indirect, implying the comparison by describing one thing as if it is another. Instead of the similes listed above, MacClancy could have used metaphors to describe the experience of eating chillies.

- Eating chilli peppers is a descent into a fiery hell.
- To eat chilli peppers is to ride the crest of a wave, waiting for the thrill.

Personification is a figure of speech in which an object is given human qualities or characteristics. "The television screen stared back at me" is an example. An **analogy** is an extended comparison in which one subject is used to explain the other. Often, a more familiar subject is used to explain one that is less familiar. For example, you might explain the elements of an essay—introduction, thesis, body, and conclusion—by comparing them to a documentary film containing those elements. Like similes and metaphors, analogies add interest to your writing while making your ideas more real and accessible.

For more on similes, metaphors, and personification, see Chapter 8, p. 198.

EXERCISE 10.3

Write a paragraph describing a food you enjoy eating. Focus on one sense, as MacClancy does, or appeal to several senses. If possible, try to draw a comparison using a simile or metaphor.

TEACHING TIP
• Ask for a student volunteer to read his or her paragraph aloud to the class. Discuss the vividness of the description and the senses to which it appeals.
• The concept *vicarious experience* is useful here: good descriptive writing appeals to readers' senses and emotions so that they remember the writing almost as vividly as if it were a personal experience.

Description Assumes a Vantage Point

A **vantage point** is the point or position from which you write a description. You can use either a fixed or a moving vantage point. With a *fixed vantage point,* you describe what you see from a particular position. With a *moving vantage point,* you describe your subject from a number of different positions. In this way, your vantage point is similar to a movie camera. A fixed vantage point is like a stationary camera trained on a subject from one direction. A moving vantage point is like a handheld camera that moves around the subject, capturing it from many directions.

In "Eating Chilli Peppers," MacClancy uses a moving vantage point; he first reports sensations within the mouth and then moves on to other body parts. When you use a moving vantage point, be sure to signal your readers when you change positions. MacClancy gives his readers clues that his vantage point is changing. For example, in paragraph 2 he states, "the message spreads" to indicate that he is moving from the palate to sweat glands, eyes, and so forth.

POSSIBLE ANSWERS
Answers will vary.

Description Follows a Method of Organization

Effective descriptions, like other kinds of writing, must follow a clear method of organization in order to be easy to read. Three common methods of organization used in descriptive writing are spatial order, chronological order, and most-to-least or least-to-most order.

For more on these methods of organization, see Chapter 6, p. 120.

• When you use spatial order, you systematically describe a subject from top to bottom, from inside to outside, or from near to far away. Or you may start from a central focal point and then describe the objects that surround it. For example, if you are describing a college campus, you might start by describing a building at the center of the campus—the library, perhaps. You would then describe the buildings, parking lots, and so forth that are near the library, and you would conclude by describing anything on the outskirts of the campus.

- Chronological order works well when you need to describe events or changes that occur in objects or places over a period of time. You might use chronological order to describe the changes in a puppy's behavior as it grows or to relate changing patterns of light and shadow as the sun sets.
- You might use least-to-most or most-to-least order to describe the different smells in a flower garden or the sounds of an orchestra tuning up for a concert.

Visualizing a Description: A Graphic Organizer

For more on graphic organizers, see Chapter 2, p. 40.

The graphic organizer shown in Figure 10.1 will help you visualize the elements of a description. When you write an essay in which your primary purpose is to describe something, you'll need to follow the standard essay format—title, introduction, body, and conclusion—with slight adaptations and adjustments. In a descriptive essay, the introduction provides a context for the description and presents the thesis statement, which states or suggests the dominant impression.

FIGURE 10.1
GRAPHIC ORGANIZER FOR A DESCRIPTIVE ESSAY

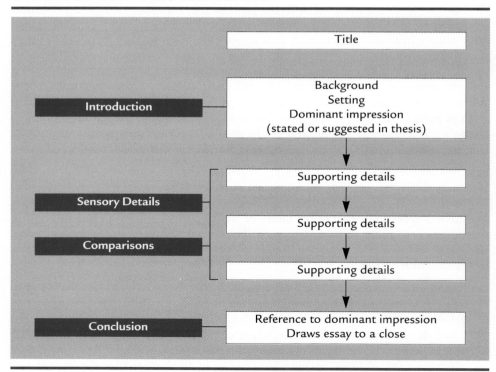

The body of the essay presents sensory details that support the dominant impression. The conclusion draws the description to a close and makes a final reference to the dominant impression. It may offer a final detail or pull various details together into a closing statement.

When you incorporate a description into an essay in which you also use other patterns of development, you will probably need to condense or eliminate one or more of these elements of a description essay.

The following essay, "The Discus Thrower," is a good example of descriptive writing. Read the essay and then study the graphic organizer for it in Figure 10.2.

The Discus Thrower
Richard Selzer

Richard Selzer is a medical doctor who has written several books and articles. His books include Mortal Lessons *(1977),* Confessions of a Knife *(1979),* Raising the Dead *(1994), and* The Doctor Stories *(1998). This essay first appeared in* Harper's *magazine in 1977. As you read the selection, notice how Selzer uses sensory details to create an impression of his patient. Highlight the sensory details and other details that contribute to the writer's dominant impression.*

I spy on my patients. Ought not a doctor to observe his patients by any means and from any stance, that he might the more fully assemble evidence? So I stand in the doorways of hospital rooms and gaze. Oh, it is not all that furtive an act. Those in bed need only look up to discover me. But they never do.

From the doorway of Room 542 the man in the bed seems deeply tanned. Blue eyes and close-cropped white hair give him the appearance of vigor and good health. But I know that his skin is not brown from the sun. It is rusted, rather, in the last stage of containing the vile repose within. And the blue eyes are frosted, looking inward like the windows of a snowbound cottage. This man is blind. This man is also legless — the right leg missing from midthigh down, the left from just below the knee. It gives him the look of a bonsai, roots and branches pruned into the dwarfed facsimile of a great tree.

Propped on pillows, he cups his right thigh in both hands. Now and then he shakes his head as though acknowledging the intensity of his suffering. In all of this he makes no sound. Is he mute as well as blind?

The room in which he dwells is empty of all possessions — no get-well cards, small, private caches of food, day-old flowers, slippers, all the usual kickshaws of the sickroom. There is only the bed, a chair, a

PREREADING QUESTIONS
• What is a "discus thrower"?
• What kinds of experiences have you had with hospitals and doctors?

TEACHING TIP: POSTREADING DISCUSSION
• Ask students to identify examples of *irony* in the essay. E.g., "'Get me my shoes'" (paragraph 42); "Room 542 is deceased" (49); "His face is relaxed, grave . . ." (50); "the wall looks very clean and very white" (50).
• Ask students: What *dominant impression* does Selzer convey about the man? What does he imply about the nurse? About death?
• The dialogue in the essay is more notable for what is *not* said than for what *is* said. Ask students to express the attitudes behind the words: the
(Continued on next page)

1

2

3

4

pain behind the
patient's stoic exterior;
the concern behind
the doctor's busi-
nesslike demeanor; the
hollow disapproval of
the nurse.

nightstand, and a tray on wheels that can be swung across his lap for meals.

5   "What time is it?" he asks.

6   "Three o'clock."

7   "Morning or afternoon?"

8   "Afternoon."

9   He is silent. There is nothing else he wants to know.

10   "How are you?" I say.

11   "Who is it?" he asks.

12   "It's the doctor. How do you feel?"

13   He does not answer right away.

14   "Feel?" he says.

15   "I hope you feel better," I say.

16   I press the button at the side of the bed.

17   "Down you go," I say.

18   "Yes, down," he says.

19   He falls back upon the bed awkwardly. His stumps, unweighted by legs and feet, rise in the air, presenting themselves. I unwrap the bandages from the stumps, and begin to cut away the black scabs and the dead, glazed fat with scissors and forceps. A shard of white bone comes loose. I pick it away. I wash the wounds with disinfectant and redress the stumps. All this while, he does not speak. What is he thinking behind those lids that do not blink? Is he remembering a time when he was whole? Does he dream of feet? Of when his body was not a rotting log?

20   He lies solid and inert. In spite of everything, he remains impressive, as though he were a sailor standing athwart a slanting deck.

21   "Anything more I can do for you?" I ask.

22   For a long moment he is silent.

23   "Yes," he says at last and without the least irony. "You can bring me a pair of shoes."

24   In the corridor, the head nurse is waiting for me.

25   "We have to do something about him," she says. "Every morning he orders scrambled eggs for breakfast, and, instead of eating them, he picks up the plate and throws it against the wall."

26   "Throws his plate?"

27   "Nasty. That's what he is. No wonder his family doesn't come to visit. They probably can't stand him any more than we can."

28   She is waiting for me to do something.

29   "Well?"

30   "We'll see," I say.

31   The next morning I am waiting in the corridor when the kitchen delivers his breakfast. I watch the aide place the tray on the stand and

swing it across his lap. She presses the button to raise the head of the bed. Then she leaves.

In time the man reaches to find the rim of the tray, then on to find the dome of the covered dish. He lifts off the cover and places it on the stand. He fingers across the plate until he probes the eggs. He lifts the plate in both hands, sets it on the palm of his right hand, centers it, balances it. He hefts it up and down slightly, getting the feel of it. Abruptly, he draws back his right arm as far as he can. 32

There is the crack of the plate breaking against the wall at the foot of his bed and the small wet sound of the scrambled eggs dropping to the floor. 33

And then he laughs. It is a sound you have never heard. It is something new under the sun. It could cure cancer. 34

Out in the corridor, the eyes of the head nurse narrow. 35

"Laughed, did he?" 36

She writes something down on her clipboard. 37

A second aide arrives, brings a second breakfast tray, puts it on the nightstand, out of his reach. She looks over at me shaking her head and making her mouth go. I see that we are to be accomplices. 38

"I've got to feed you," she says to the man. 39

"Oh, no you don't," the man says. 40

"Oh, yes I do," the aide says, "after the way you just did. Nurse says so." 41

"Get me my shoes," the man says. 42

"Here's oatmeal," the aide says. "Open." And she touches the spoon to his lower lip. 43

"I ordered scrambled eggs," says the man. 44

"That's right," the aide says. 45

I step forward. 46

"Is there anything I can do?" I say. 47

"Who are you?" the man asks. 48

In the evening I go once more to that ward to make my rounds. The head nurse reports to me that Room 542 is deceased. She has discovered this quite by accident, she says. No, there had been no sound. Nothing. It's a blessing, she says. 49

I go into his room, a spy looking for secrets. He is still there in his bed. His face is relaxed, grave, dignified. After a while, I turn to leave. My gaze sweeps the wall at the foot of the bed, and I see the place where it has been repeatedly washed, where the wall looks very clean and very white. 50 ■

FIGURE 10.2
GRAPHIC ORGANIZER FOR "THE DISCUS THROWER"

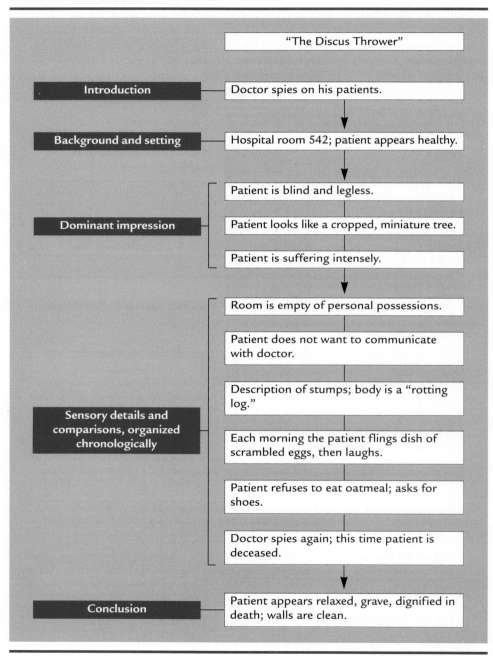

EXERCISE 10.4

Draw a graphic organizer of MacClancy's "Eating Chilli Peppers" (pp. 247–48).

INTEGRATING DESCRIPTION INTO AN ESSAY

There are times when description alone fulfills the purpose of an essay. In most cases, however, you will use descriptions in other types of essays. For instance, in a narrative essay, description plays an important role in helping readers experience events, reconstruct scenes, and visualize action. Similarly, you would use descriptions to explain the causes or effects of a phenomenon, to compare or contrast animal species, and to provide examples of defensive behavior in children (illustration). Description, then, is essential to many types of academic and business writing.

Use the following guidelines to build effective descriptions into the essays you write.

1. **Include only relevant details.** Whether you describe an event, a person, or a scene, the sensory details you choose should enhance the reader's understanding of your subject.

2. **Keep the description focused.** Select enough details to make your essential points and dominant impression clear. Readers may become impatient if you include too many details.

3. **Make sure the description fits the essay's tone and point of view.** A personal description, for example, is not appropriate in an essay explaining a technical process.

In "The Lion of Kabul" on page 281, Christine Aziz incorporates description into an essay that is primarily a narrative.

A GUIDED WRITING ASSIGNMENT

TEACHING TIP:
LEARNING STYLES

Suggest that some stu-
dents, especially creative
learners, begin by creat-
ing metaphors or similes
to describe their topic.

ADDITIONAL
RESOURCES

The writing process soft-
ware that accompanies
this text includes an
electronic Guided Writ-
ing Assignment for a
descriptive essay.

The following guide will lead you through the process of writing an essay that uses description. You may choose to write a descriptive essay or to employ description within an essay that relies on another pattern of development. Depending on your learning style, you may choose to work through this Guided Writing Assignment in various ways. If you are an abstract learner, for example, you might begin by brainstorming about the general subject. If you are a concrete learner, you might prefer to begin by freewriting specific details. If you are a pragmatic learner, you might start by thinking about how to organize your description.

The Assignment

Write a descriptive essay or an essay that uses description and one or more other patterns of development. Choose one of the following topics or one that you think of on your own. Your classmates are your audience.

1. An adult toy, such as a camera, CD player, computer, golf clubs, cooking gadget, and so on
2. A hobby, sport, or activity, either one that you enjoy or one that you do not engage in but can observe others doing on campus, in your neighborhood, or on television
3. An annoying or obnoxious person or a pleasant, courteous one

As you develop your description, consider using other patterns of development. For example, you might compare and contrast an unfamiliar activity to one you engage in regularly, or you might narrate an incident that reveals a person's positive or negative qualities.

*For more on comparison
and contrast, see Chapter
13. For more on narra-
tion, see Chapter 9.*

Generating Ideas and Details

Use the following steps to help you choose a topic and generate ideas to write about.

Choosing a Topic

In order to write an effective description, you must be familiar with the subject or have the opportunity to observe the subject directly. Never try to describe the campus computer lab without visiting it or the pizza served in the snack bar without tasting it. You will quickly discover you have little or nothing to say.

Use the following suggestions to choose an appropriate topic.

For more on conducting observations, see Chapter 19, p. 664.

1. Once you have selected one of the assignments or a topic you have thought of yourself, take time to do some prewriting about possible subjects. Use freewriting, mapping, group brainstorming, or another prewriting technique to generate a list of specific objects, activities, or people that fit the assignment.

For more on prewriting strategies, see Chapter 4.

2. Look over your list of possible topics. Narrow your list down to the one or two subjects that you find most interesting and that you can describe in detail.

3. Make sure your subject is one you are familiar with or one you can readily observe. Also take into account that you may need to observe the object, activity, or person several times as you work through your essay.

ESSAY IN PROGRESS 1

Using the preceding suggestions, choose a topic to write about for the assignment option you selected on page 260.

TEACHING TIP

Have students do their prewriting at home (in a journal or on a computer) and bring it to class to share and refer to as they continue working on this assignment.

Considering Your Purpose, Audience, and Point of View

A descriptive essay may be objective, subjective, or both, depending on the writer's purpose. In an *objective* essay, the writer's purpose is to inform—to present information or communicate ideas without obvious bias or emotion. All writers convey their feelings to some extent, but in an objective essay the writer strives to focus on giving information. For example, a geologist's description of a rock formation written for a scientific journal would be largely objective; its purpose would be to inform readers of the height of the formation, the type of rock it contains, and other characteristics of the subject. Objective essays are generally written in the third person.

For more on purpose, audience, and point of view, see Chapter 4.

In a *subjective* essay, which is often written in the first person, the writer's purpose is to create an emotional response. Whereas an objective essay describes only what the writer observes or experiences, a subjective essay describes both the observation or experience *and* how the writer feels about it. Therefore, a rock climber's description of a rock formation would focus on the writer's impressions of and reactions to the experience of climbing it, such as the feeling of the smooth rock on a hot day and the exhilaration of reaching the top. But the rock climber's description might also include objective details about the height and composition of the rock formation to help readers see and feel what it's like to climb one.

Once you've chosen a subject and considered your purpose and point of view, think about your audience. For this assignment your audience is your classmates. How familiar are your classmates with your subject? If they are unfamiliar with the subject, you will need to provide a more thorough introduction and a greater amount of detail than if your audience has some knowledge of it. For example, if the rock climber is describing the difficulty of a climb to an audience of other climbers, the writer could omit explanations of technique and other details that a more general audience would require.

Choosing an Aspect of Your Subject to Emphasize

Most any subject you choose will be made up of many more details than you could possibly include in an essay. Start by selecting several possible slants or angles on your subject—that is, aspects of the subject that you would like to emphasize. In "Eating Chilli Peppers," MacClancy emphasizes the *taste* of chilli peppers. If your subject is a person, you might focus on a particular character trait, such as compulsiveness or sense of humor, and then generate a list of descriptive terms that illustrate the trait. To describe an object, you might emphasize its usefulness, value, or beauty.

In descriptive writing, choosing which aspect of your subject to emphasize is similar to narrowing a topic—a process you use in writing other kinds of essays. To come up with an appropriate slant or angle on your subject, first list several possible slants and then record details about each one as they come to mind. Choose the one slant that seems most promising and for which you generated plenty of sensory details.

> ESSAY IN PROGRESS 2
>
> Using one or more prewriting techniques, come up with several possible slants on your subject and details to support them. Then choose the slant about which you can write the most effective description.

Collecting Details That Describe Your Subject

Once you've decided on a slant or angle to emphasize, you're ready for the next step—collecting and recording additional sensory details. The following suggestions will help you generate details. Use those that suit your learning style. Also refer to Table 10.1 to stimulate your thinking.

TEACHING TIP:
LEARNING STYLES

Rational, pragmatic, and concrete learners may prefer to use listing or branching, whereas creative, emotional, and abstract learners may prefer mapping or clustering to generate and sort their ideas. Spatial learners may be equally drawn to branching and mapping.

For more on narrowing a topic, see Chapter 4, p. 71.

TEACHING TIP:
COLLABORATIVE WRITING

(30 minutes)

• Have students work alone at first, using at least two prewriting strategies from Chapter 4—freewriting, mapping, brainstorming, questioning, writing assertions—to generate details (20 minutes).
• Then ask students to work in pairs to evaluate their prewriting (10 minutes).

For more on generating details, see Chapter 4, p. 78.

1. Brainstorm about your subject. Record any sensory details that support the slant or angle you have chosen.

2. Try describing your subject to a friend, concentrating on the slant you have chosen. You may discover that details come quickly during conversation. Make notes on what you said and on your friend's response.

3. Draw a quick sketch of your subject and label the parts. You may find yourself recalling additional details as you draw.

4. Divide a piece of paper or a computer file into five horizontal sections. Label the sections *sight, sound, taste, touch,* and *smell.* Work through each section in turn, systematically recording what the subject looks like, sounds like, and so forth.

▸ Learning Style Options

For more on prewriting strategies, see Chapter 4.

TEACHING TIP:
LEARNING STYLES

1. For all learners
2. For all learners, especially social or verbal learners
3. For creative, spatial, and concrete learners
4. For rational or pragmatic learners

TABLE 10.1
CHARACTERISTICS TO CONSIDER IN DEVELOPING SENSORY DETAILS

Sight	Color
	Pattern
	Shape
	Size
Sound	Volume (loud or soft)
	Pitch
	Quality
Taste	Pleasant or unpleasant
	Salty, sweet, sour, or bitter
Touch	Texture
	Weight
	Temperature
Smell	Agreeable or disagreeable
	Strength

Finding Comparisons and Choosing a Vantage Point

Look over your list of details. Try to think of appropriate comparisons — similes, metaphors, or analogies — for as many details as possible. Jot down your comparisons in the margin next to the relevant details in your list. Don't expect to find a comparison for each detail. Instead, your goal is to discover one or two strong comparisons that you can use in your essay.

Next, consider whether to use a fixed or moving vantage point. Think about the aspect of your subject you have chosen to emphasize and how it can best be communicated, from one or several locations. Ask yourself the following questions.

1. What vantage point(s) will give the reader the most useful information?
2. From which vantage point(s) can I provide the most revealing or striking details?

TEACHING TIP:
COLLABORATIVE
WRITING

(10 minutes) Have students work in pairs to evaluate the comparisons they came up with. (Students will evaluate their slants in Trying Out Your Ideas on Others in the following section).

CONNECTIONS

Point out that the active reading strategies learned in Chapter 2 (such as highlighting and annotating) are also useful for evaluating prewriting.

ESSAY IN PROGRESS 3

Use one or more of the preceding suggestions to develop details that support the aspect or slant of your subject that you are emphasizing. Then find comparisons and decide on a vantage point.

Evaluating Your Details

Evaluate the details you have collected to determine which ones you can use in your essay. Begin by rereading all of your notes with a critical eye. Highlight vivid, concrete details that will create pictures in your reader's mind. Eliminate vague details as well as those that do not support your slant on the subject. For example, for the subject *fast food* and the slant *fast food is not nutritional,* you would eliminate any details about convenience, cost, taste, and others not directly related to nutrition. If you are working on a computer, highlight usable ideas by making them bold or moving them to a separate page or document for easy access when drafting.

TRYING OUT YOUR IDEAS ON OTHERS

Working in a group of two or three students, discuss your ideas and details for this chapter's assignment. Each writer should explain his or her slant or angle on the subject and provide a list of the details collected for the subject. Then as a group, evaluate the writer's details and suggest improvements.

ESSAY IN PROGRESS 4

Use your notes and the comments of your classmates to evaluate the details you have collected so far. Omit irrelevant and vague details and add more vivid and concrete details if they are needed.

Creating a Dominant Impression

As noted earlier, think of the dominant impression as your thesis in that it conveys your main point and holds the rest of your essay together. The dominant impression also creates a mood or feeling about the subject, which all other details in your essay explain or support.

The dominant impression you decide on should be the one about which you feel most knowledgeable and confident. It should also appeal to your audience, offer an unusual perspective, and provide new insights on your subject. Finally, keep in mind that you may need to do additional prewriting to gather support for your dominant impression. This step is similar to collecting evidence for a thesis (see Chapter 5), except the "evidence" for a descriptive essay consists of sensory details. Therefore, before you begin drafting your essay, check to see if you have enough sensory details to support your dominant impression.

ESSAY IN PROGRESS 5

Using the preceding guidelines, select the dominant impression you want to convey about your subject and do additional prewriting, if necessary, to gather enough details to support it.

Organizing and Drafting

Once you are satisfied with your dominant impression and your support for it, you are ready to organize your ideas and draft your essay.

Choosing a Method of Organization

Select the method of organization that will best support your dominant impression. For example, if you have chosen to focus on a person's slovenly appearance, then a spatial (top to bottom, left to right) organization may be effective. If you are describing a scary visit to a wildlife preserve, then chronological order would be a useful method of organization. A most-to-least or least-to-most arrangement might work best for a description of the symptoms of pneumonia. Also consider organizing your details by the five senses. For instance, to describe a chocolate-chip cookie, you could give details about how it looks, then how it smells, and then how it tastes and feels (chocolaty, with a crunchy texture).

If you are working on a computer, use your word-processing program's cut-and-paste function to try different methods of organization.

TEACHING TIP

Emphasize that the *purpose* of description often includes an element of surprise. Whereas a dry description is a chore to read, a description with an unexpected slant is more likely to engage the reader's imagination.

TEACHING TIP: COLLABORATIVE WRITING

(15 minutes) After students complete this activity, have them work in pairs to evaluate each other's dominant impression. Each student reviewer should underline or highlight any problematic wording in the other's work and give feedback for revising it.

For more on drafting an essay, see Chapter 6.

TEACHING TIP

• Have students write the dominant impression in their journal or on a computer and bring a copy to class.
• Collect students' work and select several examples to write on the blackboard. Without mentioning the students' names, have the class analyze the dominant impressions for clarity, specificity, and interest.

For a list of transitions, see Chapter 6, p. 139.

Regardless of which method you choose for organizing your details, be sure to connect your ideas and guide your reader with transitional words and phrases.

Drafting the Description

For more on writing effective paragraphs, including introductions and conclusions, see Chapter 6.

As you draft your essay, remember that all of your details must support your dominant impression. Other details, no matter how interesting or important they may seem, should not be included. For example, if you are describing the way apes in a zoo imitate one another and humans, only details about how the apes mimic people and other apes should be included. Other details, such as the condition of the apes' environment and types of animals nearby, do not belong in the essay. Be careful as well about the *number* of details you include. Too many details will tire your readers, but an insufficient number will leave your readers unconvinced of your main point. Select striking sensory details that make your point effectively; leave out details that tell the reader little or nothing. For example, instead of selecting five or six ordinary details to describe a concert, choose one revealing detail such as the following.

> As the band performed the final song, the lights dimmed and every single member of the audience of twelve hundred people silently held a lighted candle before his or her face.

Try also to include one or two telling metaphors or similes. If you cannot think of any, however, don't stretch to construct them. Most effective comparisons come to mind naturally from how you view the subject. Contrived comparisons will only lessen the impact of your essay.

As you write your description, remember that the sensory language you use should enable your readers to re-create the person, object, or scene in their minds. Keep the following three guidelines in mind as you write.

1. Create images that appeal to the five senses. As noted earlier, your descriptions should appeal to one or more of the senses. See pages 248–50 for examples of ways to engage each of the five senses.

2. Avoid vague, general descriptions. Use specific, not vague, language to describe your subject. Notice the difference between the following pair of descriptions.

CONNECTIONS

The reading "Be Specific," by Natalie Goldberg, in Chapter 11, p. 297, addresses this topic.

VAGUE: The pizza was cheaply prepared.

CONCRETE: The supposedly "large" pizza was miniature, with a nearly imperceptible layer of sauce, a light dusting of cheese, a few paper-thin slices of pepperoni, and one or two stray mushroom slices.

Vivid descriptions hold your readers' interest and give them a more complete picture of your subject. For example, notice how the list below becomes increasingly more concrete.

Animal $\longrightarrow$ dog $\longrightarrow$ golden retriever $\longrightarrow$ male golden retriever $\longrightarrow$ six-month-old male golden retriever puppy $\longrightarrow$ Ivan, my six-month-old male golden retriever puppy

You can create a similar progression of descriptive words for any person, object, or place that you want to describe.

3. Use figures of speech and analogies effectively. Figures of speech (similes, metaphors) and analogies create memorable images that enliven your writing and capture your readers' attention. Here are some tips for using figurative language in your writing.

- Choose fresh, surprising images. Avoid overused clichés such as *cool as a cucumber* and *it's a hop, skip, and a jump away.*

- Make sure the similarity between the two items being compared is apparent. If you write *"Peter* looked like an *unpeeled tangerine,"* your reader will not be able to guess what characteristics Peter shares with the tangerine. "Peter's *skin* was as *dimpled* as a *tangerine peel"* gives the reader a clearer idea of what Peter looks like.

- Don't mix or combine figures of speech. Such expressions, called **mixed metaphors**, are confusing and often unintentionally humorous. For example, the following sentence mixes images of a hawk and a wolf.

The fighter jet was a hawk soaring into the clouds, growling as it sought its prey.

ESSAY IN PROGRESS 6

Draft your essay. Use the preceding suggestions to organize your details and support your dominant impression. Even if your essay is primarily descriptive, consider incorporating a narrative, an illustration, or a comparison (or another pattern of development) to strengthen the dominant impression.

Analyzing and Revising

If possible, set your draft aside for a day or two before rereading and revising it. As you reread your draft, focus on its overall effectiveness, not on

TEACHING TIP

Students who have followed the steps in the Guided Writing Assignment should be ready to compose a first draft independently. However, check to see if any students need to rethink their dominant impression, comparisons, vantage point, or language before drafting. Encourage them to seek further assistance from a peer reviewer or writing center tutor.

grammar and mechanics. To analyze your draft, use one or more of the following strategies.

1. Reread your paper aloud or ask a friend to do so as you listen. You may "hear" parts that seem contrived or skimpy or notice descriptions that do not work.

2. Ask a classmate to read your draft and describe the dominant impression, comparing his or her version to the one you intended. Note ideas that your reader overlooked or misinterpreted.

3. Write an outline or draw a graphic organizer (using the format shown on p. 254) or update the outline or graphic organizer you prepared earlier. Look for ideas that do not seem to fit or that lack supporting details and for places where your organization needs tightening.

Use Flowchart 10.1 to help you discover the strengths and weaknesses of your descriptive essay. You might also ask a classmate to review your essay using the questions in the flowchart. For each answer that refers you to the right column of the chart, ask your reviewer to explain why he or she answered in that way.

FLOWCHART 10.1
REVISING A DESCRIPTIVE ESSAY

Questions		Revision Strategies
1. Does the essay contain enough sensory detail and vivid language?	No ⇨	• Brainstorm to discover additional sensory details (see Table 10.1). • Highlight sentences that contain little or no sensory description. Work paragraph by paragraph. • Replace passive verbs with active ones. Vary your sentences. • Tape-record the description of your subject. Play the tape and listen for where more detail is needed.
Yes ⬇		

(Continued on next page)

Learning Style Options

TEACHING TIP:
LEARNING STYLES

1. For all learners, especially social and verbal learners
2. For social and verbal learners
3. For all learners (spatial learners may prefer the graphic organizer; others may prefer the outline).

For more on the benefits of peer review, see Chapter 7, p. 166.

FLOWCHART 10.1 *(continued)*

Questions	Revision Strategies

2. Does the essay establish a single dominant impression?

 No

 Yes

- Reread your essay. Make a list of the different impressions it conveys.
- Choose one impression about which you have the most to say and brainstorm to develop additional details that support it.
- If none of the impressions seems promising, try to find a new aspect of your subject to emphasize or change subjects and start over.

3. Does each detail support the dominant impression? Are your connotations appropriate?

 No

Yes

- Read through each paragraph, highlighting and eliminating irrelevant details.
- Analyze the connotations of the descriptive words you use. For any with inappropriate connotations, substitute words that better support your dominant impression.

4. Are the comparisons (similes, metaphors, and analogies) fresh and effective?

 No

 Yes

- Look for and eliminate clichés.
- Brainstorm to find fresh comparisons.
- Instead of writing, try speaking to a friend or into a tape recorder to free up ideas.

(Continued on next page)

TEACHING TIP

If the dominant impression is too obvious, encourage students to make their thesis statement more subtle. If the dominant impression is too subtle, encourage them to make the thesis statement explicit and to add concrete details.

FLOWCHART 10.1 *(continued)*

Questions		Revision Strategies
5. Does the vantage point(s) give the clearest possible view of your subject?	No ⇨	• If your essay seems dull or limited, consider adding more vantage points. • If your essay seems too busy or unfocused, consider switching to a single or different vantage point.
Yes ⇩		
6. Are the details effectively organized?	No ⇨	• Arrange your details using a different order: spatial, chronological, or most-to-least or least-to-most order. • Experiment with several different arrangements to see which one works best. • Add transitions where necessary to connect your ideas.
Yes ⇩		
7. Is each paragraph well developed and focused on a separate part of the description? Are your introduction and conclusion effective?	No ⇨	• Be sure each paragraph has a topic sentence and supporting details (see Chapter 6). • Consider combining closely related paragraphs. • Split paragraphs that cover more than one part of the description. • Revise your introduction and conclusion so that they meet the guidelines in Chapter 6 (pp. 140-46).
Yes		

ESSAY IN PROGRESS 7

Using Flowchart 10.1 as a guide, as well as suggestions made by your classmates, revise your essay.

Editing and Proofreading

The last step is to check your revised essay for errors in grammar, spelling, punctuation, and mechanics. In addition, be sure to look for the types of errors you tend to make. (Refer to your error log. See also the Writing Assessment in Appendix A.)

For descriptive writing, pay particular attention to the punctuation of adjectives. Keep the following rules in mind.

For more on keeping an error log, see Chapter 8, p. 201.

1. Use a comma between coordinate adjectives not joined by *and*.

▶ Singh was a *confident, skilled* pianist.

The order of coordinate adjectives can be scrambled (*skilled, confident pianist* or *confident, skilled pianist*).

2. Do not use commas between cumulative adjectives.

▶ *Two frightened brown* eyes peered at us from under the sofa.

You would not write *frightened two brown eyes*.

3. Use a hyphen to connect two words that work together as an adjective before a noun. Here are a few examples.

▶ *well-used* book
▶ *perfect-fitting* shoes
▶ *foil-wrapped* pizza

ESSAY IN PROGRESS 8

Edit and proofread your essay, paying particular attention to the use and punctuation of adjectives, as well as errors listed in your error log.

STUDENTS WRITE

Maria Rodriguez, a 25-year-old returning student, wrote the following essay in response to an assignment for a writing class. She was asked to describe a rewarding or frustrating experience. As you read, highlight words, phrases, and sentences that have sensory appeal and that help you see and hear what the writer experienced.

PREREADING
QUESTIONS

• What clues does the
  title give to the
  author's slant?
• What experiences have
  you had with health
  clubs?

CONNECTIONS

The opening sentence
of the essay is a good
example of a periodic
sentence (see Chapter 8,
p. 190).

Health Clubs--Only for the Beautiful and the Fit
Maria Rodriguez

1   If you are like the average sedentary adult who
enjoys a fair amount of junk food, is slightly but not
noticeably overweight, and whose exercise threshold is
such that 15 minutes on the stationary bicycle at level
zero leaves you wondering whether you should dial 911,
do not join a health club to get physically fit. You
will feel like a failure before you have begun.

2   Going to the gym where my first aerobics class was
held was like being thrown into a glitzy, overdecorated,
migraine-inducing discotheque with a bunch of adult-sized
cheerleaders, each of whom had a cute name like "Mimi"
or "Didi" or "Gigi." Little did I know when I put on my
tattered gray sweats and my discount sneakers that I
would be expected to conform to a rigid dress code: a
spandex outfit with a matching headband. The "beautiful
people," who arrived for class already physically fit,
with hair sprayed and makeup intact, looked at me as
though I had just landed from Jupiter. Pretending not to
notice their haughty stares, I decided to participate
actively in the class. "Why yes, this could be fun," I
thought, and it might have been, too, except that everyone was doing some sort of complicated dance that
involved simultaneously jumping, turning, counting, and
applauding--all to extremely loud-pitched, fast-paced,
ear-aching music. Most disturbingly, they were doing this
dance gleefully, as if they enjoyed it. And while I know
that it shouldn't have, all this cheerful jumping and
happy clapping really got on my normally inactive nerves.

3   Feeling defeated both in appearance and performance,
I decided to leave the aerobics class and head for the
weight room. Now, if you have never been to a weight
room, the one piece of information you need to know
before you go is that these people, mostly men with
huge, hard muscles, take weight lifting very seriously.
They grunt and groan and gyrate while lifting metal bars
weighing several hundred pounds above their heads. Then
they bring this heavy metal object down to their slim,

oil-slicked waists and then down to their feet. Finally, they drop the metal on the ground with a thunderous thud and a gut-wrenching moan. They look up at themselves in a mirror and stare purposefully at their overdeveloped bodies with a sober "I look very healthy" look. It's not clear to me why the mirror is there in the first place, nor why they would want to look at themselves with pained facial expressions, oozing oil all over a shiny metal dumbbell and contemplating how many more times they should repeat this bizarre ritual. However, unlike the aerobics enthusiasts, who at least give the impression of being jolly, these weight-lifting zealots are evidently an unhappy lot--so much so that when I attempted to have a conversation with one of them, he growled.

Having lost all hope of ever fitting in with the somber weight-lifting crowd, I chose to walk on the track. While I walked, I overheard parts of other walkers' conversations. These were not particularly interesting conversations, but I hoped they might be at least somewhat instructive on the subject of fitness. Although I listened intently, I had difficulty following the conversations because they were peppered with health-club jargon completely foreign to the unfit and not-so-beautiful. Words like "abs" and "pecs" kept creeping into the conversation. I kept hearing the terms "carbs" and "crunches," the latter term evidently denoting some sort of exercise as well.

Later, in the dressing room, it occurred to me that walking in the mall is cheaper than a fitness center, and it doesn't require wearing spandex, being maniacally cheerful, acting morosely serious, or learning a new language. In fact, mall walking is the perfect solution to my fitting-in-while-getting-fit problem. Also, there is an additional advantage to walking the mall. I will be forced to pass a candy shop while walking. I can get good nutrition and exercise at the same time. After all, I don't want to get totally fit; then I would have to join a health club.

4

5

POSSIBLE ANSWERS:
ANALYZING THE ESSAY
(p. 274)

1. The dominant impression is that health clubs are discouraging. It is explicit and appears in the first two sentences of paragraph 1.
2. *Visual:* "glitzy, overdecorated" (paragraph 2); "tattered gray sweats and my discount sneakers" (2); *Auditory:* "cute name like 'Mimi' or 'Didi' or 'Gigi' " (2); "extremely loud-pitched . . . music" (2); "grunt and groan" (3); "words like 'abs' and 'pecs' " (4).
3. Responses will vary. The description of an aerobics class in paragraph 2 includes concrete, specific details that support the dominant impression. The description of walking on the track in paragraph 10 could use more specific details.

(Continued on next page)

4. Narration, comparison and contrast, illustration, cause and effect, and argument support the dominant impression (that health clubs make normal people feel like failures); e.g., the writer compares herself with the other members of the aerobics class (2).

Analyzing the Essay

1. Describe the writer's dominant impression about health clubs. Is it stated explicitly or implied?
2. To which senses does the writer appeal? Cite several examples from the essay.
3. Which descriptions do you find particularly strong? What makes them effective? Which, if any, are weak, and how can they be improved?
4. In addition to description, what other patterns of development does the writer use? How do these patterns work to make the description more effective?

POSSIBLE ANSWERS: REACTING TO THE ESSAY

1. Responses will vary.
2. Body image is important enough to Rodriguez to get her to go to the gym, but not important enough to keep her going there.
3. Responses will vary. Factors include media images, exercise videos, and medical studies.

Reacting to the Essay: Discussion and Journal Writing

1. Explain why you agree or disagree with the writer's attitude toward aerobics and weight lifting.
2. Body image is important to many people who belong to health clubs. How important is body image to Rodriguez? How important is it to your friends and family?
3. Exercise has grown in popularity in recent years. To what factors do you attribute its increased popularity? Write an entry about these factors in your journal.

READING A DESCRIPTION

The following section provides advice for reading description and models of descriptive essays. Each essay illustrates the characteristics of description covered in this chapter and provides opportunities to examine, analyze, and react to the writer's ideas. The second essay uses a description as part of a narrative.

WORKING WITH TEXT: READING DESCRIPTIVE ESSAYS

For more on reading strategies, see Chapter 2.

When you read descriptive essays, you are more concerned with impressions and images than you are with the logical progression of ideas. To get the full benefit of descriptive writing, you need to connect what you are reading to your own senses of sight, sound, smell, touch, and taste. Here are some guidelines for reading descriptive essays.

What to Look for, Highlight, and Annotate

1. Plan on reading the essay more than once. Read it a first time to get a general sense of what's going on in the essay. Then reread it, this time paying attention to sensory details.

2. Be alert for the dominant impression as you read. If it is not directly stated, ask yourself this question: "How does the author want me to feel about the subject?" Your answer will be the dominant impression the writer wants to convey.

3. Highlight particularly striking details and images that you may want to refer to again or that may help you analyze the essay's effectiveness.

4. Identify the author's vantage point and method of organization.

5. Analyze each paragraph and decide how it contributes to the dominant impression. In a marginal annotation, summarize your analysis.

6. Observe how the author uses language to achieve his or her effect; notice types of images, sentence structure, use of and placement of adjectives and adverbs.

7. Study the introduction and conclusion. What is the purpose of each?

8. Evaluate the title. What meaning does it contribute to the essay?

9. Use marginal annotations or your journal to record the thoughts and feelings the essay evokes in you. Try to answer these questions: "What did I feel as I read? How did I respond? What feelings was I left with after reading the essay?"

How to Find Ideas to Write About

Since you may be asked to write a response to a descriptive essay, keep an eye out for ideas to write about *as you read*. Try to think of parallel situations that evoked similar images and feelings in you. For example, for an essay describing the peace and serenity the author experienced while sitting beside a remote lake in a forest, try to think of situations in which you felt peace and serenity or how you felt when you visited a national park or wilderness area. Perhaps you had contradictory feelings, such as a sense of insecurity in the remote spot. Such contradictory feelings may be worth exploring as well.

For more on discovering ideas for a response paper, see Chapter 3.

THINKING CRITICALLY ABOUT DESCRIPTION

Words are powerful. They can create lasting impressions, shape attitudes, and evoke responses. The words a writer chooses to describe a subject, then, can largely determine how readers view and respond to that subject. For example, suppose you want to describe a person's physical appearance. You can make the person seem attractive and appealing or ugly and repellent, depending on the details you choose and the meanings of the words you select.

APPEALING: The stranger had an impish, childlike grin, a smooth complexion with high cheekbones, and strong yet gentle hands.

REPELLENT: The stranger had limp, blond hair, cold, vacant eyes, and teeth stained by tobacco.

Writers use details and word connotations to shape their essays and affect their readers' response. Use the following questions to think critically about the descriptions you read.

What Details Does the Writer Omit?

As you read an essay, ask yourself: "What hasn't the writer told me?" or "What else would I like to know about the subject?" As you have seen, writers often omit details because they are not relevant; they may also omit them because they contradict the dominant impression they intend to convey.

To be sure you are getting a complete and fairly objective picture of a subject, consult more than one source of information. You have probably noticed that each news program you watch usually has a slightly different slant on a news event; each offers different details or film footage. Once you view several versions of the same event, you eventually form your own impression of it by combining and synthesizing the various reports. Often, you must do the same thing when reading descriptions. Pull together information from several sources and form your own impression.

How Does the Writer Use Connotative Language?

The sensory details writers choose often reveal their feelings and attitudes toward the subject and help to convey the dominant impression. If a writer describes a car as "fast and sleek," the wording suggests approval, whereas if the writer describes it as "bold and glitzy," the wording suggests a less favorable attitude.

As you read, pay particular attention to connotations; they are often used intentionally to create a particular emotional response. Get in the habit of highlighting words with strong connotations or annotating them in the margin. As you write, you can and should use connotative language. Be certain to recognize, however, that you are nudging your reader in a particular direction by doing so.

DESCRIPTIVE ESSAY

As you read the following essay by Maxine Hong Kingston consider how she uses the characteristics of description discussed in this chapter.

A Sea Worry

Maxine Hong Kingston

Maxine Hong Kingston, whose first language is a dialect of Cantonese, grew up in a village where the stories she heard influenced her later writings. King-ston is well known for her books The Woman Warrior *(1976),* China Men *(1980), and* Tripmaster Monkey *(1989). While living and teaching creative writing in Hawaii, Kingston published her first book,* The Woman Warrior. *This essay was originally published in 1978 in the* New York Times *and was later published as part of an anthology titled* Hawai'i One Summer *(1987). As you read the selection, highlight the descriptions you find most effective.*

This summer my son body-surfs. He says it's his "job" and rises each morning at 5:30 to catch the bus to Sandy Beach. I hope that by September he will have had enough of the ocean. Tall waves throw surfers against the shallow bottom. Undertows have snatched them away. Sharks prowl Sandy's. Joseph told me that once he got out of the water because he saw an enormous shark. "Did you tell the life-guard?" I asked. "No." "Why not?" "I didn't want to spoil the surf-ing." The ocean pulls at the boys, who turn into surfing addicts. At sunset you can see the surfers waiting for the last golden wave. 1

"Why do you go surfing so often?" I ask my students. 2

"It feels so good," they say. "Inside the tube, I can't describe it. There are no words for it." 3

"You can describe it," I scold, and I am very angry. "Everything can be described. Find the words for it, you lazy boy. Why don't you go home and read?" I am afraid that the boys give themselves up to the ocean's mindlessness. 4

When the waves are up, surfers all over Hawaii don't do their homework. They cut school. They know how the surf is breaking at any moment because every fifteen minutes the reports come over the radio; in fact, one of my former students is the surf reporter. 5

Some boys leave for mainland colleges, and write their parents heartrending letters. They beg to come home for Thanksgiving. "If I can just touch the ocean," they write from Missouri and Kansas, "I'll last for the rest of the semester." Some come home for Christmas and don't go back. 6

Even when the assignment is about something else, the students write about surfing. They try to describe what it is to be inside the wave as it curls over them, making a tube or "chamber" or "green room" or "pipeline" or "time warp." They write about the silence, the peace, "no hassles," the feeling of being reborn as they shoot out the end. They've written about the perfect wave. Their writing is full of clichés. "The endless summer," they say. "Unreal." 7

PREREADING QUESTION

What is the author worried about?

8   Surfing is like a religion. Among the martyrs are George Helm, Kimo Mitchell, and Eddie Aikau. Helm and Mitchell were lost at sea riding their surfboards from Kaho'olawe, where they had gone to protest the Navy's bombing of that island. Eddie Aikau was a champion surfer and lifeguard. A storm had capsized the *Holule'a,* the ship that traced the route that the Polynesian ancestors sailed from Tahiti, and Eddie Aikau set out on his board to get help.

9   Since the ocean captivates our son, we decided to go with him to Sandy's.

10   We got up before dawn, picked up his friend, Marty, and drove out to Honolulu. Almost all the traffic was going in the opposite direction, the freeway coned to make more lanes into the city. We came to a place where raw mountains rose on our left and the sea fell on our right, smashing against the cliffs. The strip of cliff pulverized into sand is Sandy's. "Dangerous Current Exist," said the ungrammatical sign.

11   Earll and I sat on the shore with our blankets and thermos of coffee. Joseph and Marty put on their fins and stood at the edge of the sea for a moment, touching the water with their fingers and crossing their hearts before going in. There were fifteen boys out there, all about the same age, fourteen to twenty, all with the same kind of lean v-shaped build, most of them with black hair that made their wet heads look like sea lions. It was hard to tell whether our kid was one of those who popped up after a big wave. A few had surfboards, which are against the rules at a body-surfing beach, but the lifeguard wasn't on duty that day.

12   As they watched the next wave, the boys turned toward the ocean. They gazed slightly upward; I thought of altar boys before a great god. When a good wave arrived, they turned, faced shore, and came shooting in, some taking the wave to the right and some to the left, their bodies fish-like, one arm out in front, the hand and fingers pointed before them, like a swordfish's beak. A few held credit card trays, and some slid in on trays from McDonald's.

13   "That is no country for middle-aged women," I said. We had on bathing suits underneath our clothes in case we felt moved to participate. There were no older men either.

14   Even from the shore, we could see inside the tubes. Sometimes, when they came at an angle, we saw into them a long way. When the wave dug into the sand, it formed a brown tube or a golden one. The magic ones, though, were made out of just water, green and turquoise rooms, translucent walls and ceilings. I saw one that was powder-blue, perfect, then; the sun filled it with sky blue and white light. The best thing, the kids say, is when you are in the middle of the tube, and there is water all around you but you're dry.

The waves came in sets; the boys passed up the smaller ones. 15
Inside a big one, you could see their bodies hanging upright, knees
bent, duckfeet fins paddling, bodies dangling there in the wave.

Once in a while, we heard a boy yell, "Aa-whoo!" "Poon-tah!" 16
"Aaroo!" And then we noticed how rare a human voice was here; the
surfers did not talk, but silently, silently rode the waves.

Since Joseph and Marty were considerate of us, they stopped after 17
two hours, and we took them out for breakfast. We kept asking them
how it felt, so they would not lose language.

"Like a stairwell in an apartment building," said Joseph, which I 18
liked immensely. He hasn't been in very many apartment buildings,
so had to reach a bit to get the simile. "I saw somebody I knew coming toward me in the tube, and I shouted, 'Jeff. Hey, Jeff,' and my
voice echoed like a stairwell in an apartment building. Jeff and I came
straight at each other — mirror tube."

"Are there ever girls out there?" Earll asked. 19

"There's a few who come out at about eleven," said Marty. 20

"How old are they?" 21

"About twenty." 22

"Why do you cross your heart with water?" 23

"So the ocean doesn't kill us." 24

I describe the powder-blue tube I had seen. "That part of Sandy's 25
is called Chambers," they said.

I have gotten some surfing magazines, the ones kids steal from 26
the school library, to see if the professionals try to describe the tube.
Bradford Baker writes: 27

> . . . Round and pregnant in Emptiness
>   I slide,
>   Laughing,
>   into the sun,
>   into the night.

Frank Miller calls the surfer 28
    . . . mother's fumbling
        curly-haired
        tubey-laired
        son.

"Ooh, offshores —" writes Reno Abbellira, "where wind and wave 29
most often form that terminal rendezvous of love — when the wave
can reveal her deepest longings, her crest caressed, cannily covered to
form those peeling concavities we know, perhaps a bit irreverently, as
tubes. Here we strive to spend every second — enclosed, encased,
sometimes fatefully entombed, and hopefully, gleefully ejected —
Whoosh!"

POSSIBLE ANSWERS:
EXAMINING THE
READING (p. 280)

1. To gain an under-
standing of the
appeal the ocean has
for her son

2. She states her con-
cerns directly: "I hope
that by September he
will have had enough
. . ." (paragraph 1);
"The ocean pulls . . .
surfing addicts" (1);
"I am afraid . . .
mindlessness" (4);
"Among the martyrs
. . . lifeguard" (8).

3. She is relieved to be
traveling with older
people on dry land
rather than taking the
risks of body-surfing
the waves with young
people.

4. Perhaps she means to
refer to the addiction
she alludes to — the
thrill-chasing that
encourages surfers to
embrace the emo-
tional experience and
forgo the verbal
expression of the
experience of body-
surfing.

5. *Martyrs:* those who die
for a cause; *captivates:*
enthralls, captures the
attention of; *entombed:*
as a corpse is placed
in a tomb; *encased:*
surrounded.

POSSIBLE ANSWERS:
ANALYZING THE
READING

1. Despite the thrilling
experience it provides,
body-surfing is an
addictive, life-threat-
ening sport that
appeals to young peo-
ple. Dominant
impression is implied
in paragraphs 1, 4, 8.
2. Figures of speech:
" 'Chamber' or 'green
room' or 'pipeline' or
'time warp' " (7);
"black hair . . . sea
lions" (11); "altar
boys before a great
god" (12); " 'Like a
stairwell' " (18).
3. Especially in para-
graphs 11–12 and
14–16, Kingston's sen-
sory details are vivid
and strong: "lean
v-shaped build" (11);
"bodies fish-like"
(12).
4. The quotations sug-
gest the poetic, tran-
scendent nature of
the body-surfing
experience, one that is
effectively communi-
cated through figura-
tive language. The
quotations also rein-
force her earlier con-
cern about finding a
way to describe the
experience.
5. Examples of connota-
tive language include
"surfing addicts"
(paragraph 1); "lazy
boy" (4); "power-
blue" (14); the first
two convey disap-
proval; the last, a
sense of enchantment.

30   "An iridescent ride through the entrails of God," says Gary L. Crandall.

31   I am relieved that the surfers keep asking one another for descriptions. I also find some comfort in the stream of commuter traffic, cars filled with men over twenty, passing Sandy Beach on their way to work. ■

Examining the Reading

1. Why does Kingston accompany her son to Sandy Beach?
2. Describe how Kingston's concerns about her son are revealed in the essay.
3. Why do you think the writer finds "some comfort in the stream of commuter traffic, cars filled with men over twenty, passing Sandy Beach on their way to work" (paragraph 31)?
4. What does Kingston mean by the "ocean's mindlessness" (paragraph 4)?
5. Explain the meaning of each of the following words as it is used in the reading: *martyrs* (paragraph 8), *captivates* (9), *entombed* (29), and *encased* (29). Refer to your dictionary as needed.

Analyzing the Reading

1. What dominant impression does Kingston convey about surfing? Is the dominant impression stated or implied? Support your answers with examples from the reading.
2. Kingston uses comparisons to describe the experience of surfing. Find several figures of speech in the essay and explain why they are effective.
3. Using examples from the essay, evaluate Kingston's use of sensory detail.
4. Near the end of the essay, Kingston quotes others who have attempted to describe the tube. What do these quotations add to her essay? Why do you think she includes them?
5. Highlight several examples of connotative language that convey Kingston's attitude toward her subject.

Reacting to the Reading: Discussion and Journal Writing

1. In what way does the author believe surfing is like religion? Do you agree? Why or why not?

2. Why is the author "relieved that the surfers keep asking one another for descriptions" of the tube (paragraph 31)?

3. In your journal, describe an activity you engage in that produces feelings similar to those the surfers experience.

POSSIBLE ANSWERS: REACTING TO THE READING

1. She believes surfing has martyrs and inspires devotion.
2. She wants to be able to describe the experience and thereby to understand it.
3. Responses will vary.

DESCRIPTION COMBINED WITH OTHER PATTERNS

As you read the following essay by Christine Aziz, notice how description is used within a narrative essay.

The Lion of Kabul
Christine Aziz

Christine Aziz is a freelance journalist based in Amsterdam in the Netherlands. The following essay was published in 1996 in the New Internationalist, *a periodical that focuses on current issues. As you read the selection, notice how the writer incorporates vivid descriptions into a narrative about her visit to Kabul, the capital of Afghanistan. Highlight the descriptions you consider most striking and note what they add to the narrative essay.*

PREREADING QUESTION

What qualities does a lion usually symbolize?

Somehow a sightseeing tour of Kabul, the despoiled capital of Afghanistan,* seems obscene. Amir Shah, our taxi driver, insists on taking us on what he calls the "scenic route." He refers to everything in the past tense: "This was our university. This was the palace. This was one of our finest hotels." There is a retrospective pride in his voice that I have to respond to. "It must have been lovely," I mumble.

"I'll take you to the zoo," he says in an attempt to cheer me and my companion up. We pull up outside what must have been a pleasant garden, but all that's left now is twisted stumps of trees, their branches torn off for firewood. Cages line the walkways, but the bars are twisted steel and the walls nothing more than rubble. "Most of the animals and birds have been stolen and cooked," Amir Shah explains. "But we do have a lion," he says in an effort to make the visit worthwhile. "I don't remember his name anymore. I just call him Lion."

Lion lies in the only cage that remains intact, his head resting sulkily on his huge front paws. His eyes are missing, and his face is

1

2

3

---

*Afghanistan: A country in south central Asia. Following a coup in 1979 the Soviet Union invaded Afghanistan, precipitating a war. The Soviet Union withdrew its troops in 1989, but civil war continues.

heavily scarred. His mane has been reduced to a few tufts. We stare at the sightless bald lion who is now making a halfhearted attempt to stand up, and as he shuffles forward Amir Shah tells us his story.

4   "Some mujahideen [guerrillas] came to visit the zoo and they saw Lion. They goaded one of their friends into climbing into the cage and dared him to touch Lion. Lion was sleeping, so the man got out unhurt. Then the mujahideen dared him to go in again, but this time he touched a female and Lion attacked him. The mujahideen's brother threw in a hand grenade that blew up Lion's face, but it was too late. Lion killed him."

5   It is hard to believe that the mangy specimen now growling weakly in front of us could have managed it. "Lion was taken to the Red Cross hospital," Amir Shah says. "He was in the best hospital in Kabul, and the doctors tried to save his sight. But he was too badly injured. They did the best they could."

6   The people of Kabul clearly wanted Lion to live. It's as if this proud animal has become a symbol for the city itself and the grisly drama a metaphor for the senseless battles that have been played out in the city's streets. Both Lion and Kabul are the victims of wanton destruction inspired by a warped belief in "honor" and an obstinate, macho pride. If Lion dies, then the foolishness of men has triumphed.

7   We settle silently into the back of Amir Shah's taxi. By now we are in respectful awe of this man who can laugh, smile, and joke as he guides us around such utter desolation. Like other Kabul residents, he displays courage and resilience that belie 16 years of a war that began when the Russians arrived to occupy the city in 1979 and then turned into a civil war the moment they left, 10 years later. Whatever destruction the Russians wreaked on Afghanistan, the mujahideen of the various warring factions managed to continue: Schools and universities were looted. Books and equipment were sent to Pakistan to be sold. Water pipes were used as target practice — making the water rehabilitation programs of a number of aid agencies almost impossible. Homes were destroyed in the crossfire as rival groups fought each other from different ends of the city.

8   The sun begins to set, turning the snow on the mountains that surround Kabul a delicate rose pink. Amir Shah starts to sing a song about love and a beautiful woman and then turns off into a side street. He stops the car. "I want to show you where I used to live," he says and ushers us out, warning us not to step off the road because of the land mines that litter the residential areas. He points to a wall standing amid a pile of rubble. "That was my house," he says. We notice that part of the wall has been freshly bricked up. "That was the front door once," he explains, "but I bricked it up to stop people getting into the garden."

POSSIBLE ANSWERS: EXAMINING THE READING

1. The observation foreshadows her description of Kabul — the buildings have been destroyed; tourist sites are reduced to rubble and memories.

2. Both are crippled yet miraculously alive; proud yet weak: "Lion and Kabul are the victims of wanton destruction inspired by a warped belief in 'honor' " (paragraph 6).

3. Because Lion symbolizes the city's pride and refusal to be destroyed by war.

4. He is waiting for it to be restored to greatness: refers to tour of devastated sites as " 'scenic route' " (1); implies analogy between Lion and people of Afghanistan (5–6); reveals his optimism by singing a love song (8); wants to protect budding tree behind his wrecked house (9–10).

5. *Despoiled:* stripped down, plundered; *retrospective:* nostalgic, looking to the past; *wanton:* senseless; *resilience:* ability to adapt to adversity; *belie:* stand in contrast to or opposition.

We can see no sign of a garden until we notice tree branches ris- 9
ing out of the rubble. "I didn't want people coming into my home
and tearing down the tree for firewood," he says. "I wanted to protect
it for when my family and I return home."

In the fading light we notice that the tree is covered in sweet- 10
smelling white blossoms. ■

Examining the Reading

1. Why does the writer open her essay by telling us that the taxi driver, Amir
   Shah, "refers to everything in the past tense"?
2. In what ways does the writer use the lion as a symbol of the capital and people of Afghanistan?
3. Why do the people of Kabul want the injured lion to live?
4. Describe Amir Shah's attitude toward his homeland. Give examples from the
   reading to support your ideas.
5. Explain the meaning of each of the following words as it is used in the reading: *despoiled* (paragraph 1), *retrospective* (1), *wanton* (6), *resilience* (7), and *belie*
   (7). Refer to your dictionary as needed.

Analyzing the Reading

1. Citing examples from the essay, explain how the writer uses both narrative and
   descriptive elements.
2. What dominant impression does the writer establish?
3. Aziz's narrative tells a story within a story. What does this strategy accomplish? Is it effective? Why or why not?
4. How does the writer capture and hold your interest? Cite examples from the
   essay.
5. What type of details about Kabul would Aziz have included if her primary purpose had been to criticize the Russians and the mujahideen for the destruction
   of Kabul?

Reacting to the Reading: Discussion and Journal Writing

1. Why do you think Amir Shah begins singing "a song about love and a beautiful woman" (paragraph 8)?

POSSIBLE ANSWERS:
ANALYZING THE
READING

1. *Narrative elements:*
   Aziz presents action
   throughout and
   quotes Amir Shah,
   who relates the story
   of the lion (4). *De-
   scriptive elements:* the
   descriptions of the
   lion (3, 5), Amir Shah
   (7), the sunset (8),
   the symbolic bloom-
   ing tree (9–10). De-
   scriptions are carefully
   selected to convey the
   dominant impressions
   of Amir Shah, Lion,
   and the people of
   Kabul.
2. Amir Shah, Lion, and
   the people of Kabul
   are at once humbled
   victims and deter-
   mined optimists.
3. The story of Lion is
   told by Amir Shah;
   in a literary sense, it
   symbolizes Shah, his
   people, and their
   country.
4. Responses will vary.
   Students might notice
   Aziz's use of irony:
   Shah's use of the
   terms "scenic route"
   (paragraph 1) and
   "garden" (8).
5. Details about loss
   of life, more details
   about destruction of
   property, and mone-
   tary losses.

POSSIBLE ANSWERS:
REACTING TO THE
READING

1. Seems to have faith
   that Kabul will be
   rebuilt; still sees the
   beauty and nobility
   the city represents

(Continued on next page)

2. Irony: beauty amidst rubble; symbol of spring, possibility, continuance of life, and resilience of the Afghan people
3. Responses will vary.

2. What is the significance of the tree in bloom in Amir Shah's garden (paragraphs 9–10)? Why does the writer save the description of the tree and its "sweet-smelling white blossoms" for the end of the essay?

3. Write a journal entry describing a place (or a person) you know that changed in some significant way. Describe the place (or person) as it was in the past and as it is now. Also try to explain why the change occurred.

APPLYING YOUR SKILLS: ADDITIONAL ESSAY ASSIGNMENTS

For more on locating and documenting sources, see Chapters 19 and 20.

Write a descriptive essay on one of the following topics, using what you learned about description in this chapter. Depending on the topic you choose, you may need to conduct library or Internet research.

TEACHING TIP
Suggest that students use at least one prewriting strategy — drawing a graphic organizer, freewriting, brainstorming, questioning, writing assertions — to get started. Remind students to consult the learning style options (p. 263) and the revision flowchart (p. 268).

To Express Your Ideas

1. Suppose you had a famous person, living or dead, over for dinner. Write an essay describing the person and the evening, and expressing your feelings about the occasion.

2. In "A Sea Worry," parents observe a sport that their son enjoys but for which they do not share his enthusiasm. Write an essay for your classmates describing a sport, an activity, or a fashion that a family member or close friend enjoys but that you disapprove of or dislike.

To Inform Your Reader

3. "The Lion of Kabul" describes the devastation of a city as a result of war. Write an essay describing destruction or devastation you have observed as result of a natural disaster (hurricane, flood), accident, or a form of violence.

4. Write a report for your local newspaper on a local sporting event you recently observed or participated in.

To Persuade Your Reader

5. Suppose you want to persuade your parents to loan you money. The loan may be to purchase a used car or to rent a more expensive apartment, for example. Write a letter to them persuading them to make the loan. Include a description of your current car or apartment.

6. "The Discus Thrower" describes a patient's response to hospitalization, serious illness, and physical debilitation. Write a letter to a hospital administrator describing a seriously ill patient you know or have known and suggesting alternative methods of dealing with a patient's anger and frustration.

Cases Using Description

7. Write a letter for a business marketing course about a new product or invention (such as an electronic gadget, an advice book on parenting, or a new cosmetic) that you have developed and designed. Direct the letter to the director of the new products division of a company you hope will distribute your product, and describe the product in a way that will help convince the company to market it.

8. Write an essay to accompany your application for a summer internship. The sponsoring agency requires all applicants to describe in essay format the knowledge and experience they can bring to the internship and how the position would benefit them personally and professionally. Write a brief description of your ideal internship and an essay that fulfills the preceding requirements.

Chapter *11*

In an American government class, the instructor projects the photograph shown on the opposite page on a screen. The photo shows a group of physically challenged Americans demonstrating in front of the U.S. Capitol for improved access to public buildings. The instructor makes the following statement: "Protest has become an integral part of the American political process." She asks the class to think of several examples of situations similar to the one shown in the photograph that support this statement.

Writing Quick Start

Using the instructor's statement as your topic sentence, write a paragraph that supports the topic sentence with several examples of political protests from recent news reports, your own experience, or both.

Illustration: Explaining with Examples

TEACHING TIP: LEARNING STYLES

To facilitate brainstorming about similar situations, have students work in groups. Each student in the group should think of one example of a protest demonstration or movement.

TEACHING TIP:
CHAPTER OVERVIEW

• In this chapter students will see that examples lend support and authority to narratives, comparisons, arguments, and so on.

• Have students consider the forms that examples can take (i.e., as narratives, supporting details, definitions, statistics, points of comparison or contrast, causes or effects).

• Ask students to recall a time when they engaged in a conversation with a friend who had an opposing view on an issue. Did the friend make assertions or generalizations but fail to provide support for them? How did the student feel about the friend's avoidance of examples? Point out that it is easy to refute arguments that offer insufficient supporting examples.

WRITING AN ILLUSTRATION ESSAY

The sentences you have just written could be part of an illustration essay. Your essay might explain specific situations that illustrate your thesis about the neighborhood in question. When writers use illustration, they support their points with clear, specific examples. This chapter will show you how to write an essay that uses illustration as the primary method of development, as well as how to use illustration in other types of essays.

WHAT IS ILLUSTRATION?

Illustration is a means of explaining a topic or supporting a thesis by describing specific situations that reveal the essential characteristics of the topic or that reinforce the thesis. In arguing that horror films are harmful, for instance, you might mention several films that demonstrate the qualities you object to. Or if you are making a point about the high cost of attending a movie, you could quote prices at several movie theaters in your neighborhood. Examples make ideas concrete, often connecting them to situations within the reader's experience. Examples are especially appealing to readers with a concrete learning style. An unfamiliar term or an abstract idea often becomes clear once an example is provided. Most textbooks are filled with examples for this reason. Writers in academic and work situations commonly use illustration as well (see the accompanying box for several examples).

In the following illustration essay, "Rambos of the Road," Martin Gottfried uses examples to support a thesis.

SCENES FROM COLLEGE AND THE WORKPLACE

• For a *literature* class, you are assigned to write an analysis of the poet Emily Dickinson's use of metaphor and simile. To explain your point about her use of animals in metaphors, you provide specific examples from several of her poems.

• You are studying sexual dimorphism — differences in appearance between the sexes — for a *biology* course. The following question appears on an exam: Define sexual dimorphism and illustrate its occurrence in several different species. In your answer you give examples of peacocks, geese, and chickens, explaining how the males and females in each species differ in physical appearance.

• You are an *elementary school reading teacher* and have been asked by your principal to write a justification to the school board for the new computer software you have requested. You decide to give several examples of how the software will benefit particular types of students.

Rambos of the Road

Martin Gottfried

Martin Gottfried has been a drama critic for such publications as the New York Post, *the* Saturday Review, *and* New York. *He has also written several books, including* In Person: The Great Entertainers *(1985),* All His Jazz: The Life and Death of Bob Fosse *(1990),* George Burns and the Hundred-Year Dash *(1996), and* Balancing Act: The Authorized Biography of Angela Lansbury *(1998). This essay was first published in* Newsweek, *a popular weekly newsmagazine, in 1986. As you read the selection, notice where Gottfried employs compelling examples to support his thesis, and highlight those you find particularly striking.*

PREREADING QUESTION

What experiences have you had with overly aggressive drivers?

The car pulled up and its driver glared at us with such sullen intensity, such hatred, that I was truly afraid for our lives. Except for the Mohawk haircut he didn't have, he looked like Robert De Niro in "Taxi Driver," the sort of young man who, delirious for notoriety, might kill a president.

He was glaring because we had passed him and for that affront he pursued us to the next stoplight so as to express his indignation and affirm his masculinity. I was with two women and, believe it, was afraid for all three of us. It was nearly midnight and we were in a small, sleeping town with no other cars on the road.

When the light turned green, I raced ahead, knowing it was foolish and that I was not in a movie. He didn't merely follow, he chased, and with his headlights turned off. No matter what sudden turn I took, he followed. My passengers were silent. I knew they were alarmed, and I prayed that I wouldn't be called upon to protect them. In that cheerful frame of mind, I turned off my own lights so I couldn't be followed. It was lunacy. I was responding to a crazy *as* a crazy.

"I'll just drive to the police station," I finally said, and as if those were the magic words, he disappeared.

It seems to me that there has recently been an epidemic of auto macho—a competition perceived and expressed in driving. People fight it out over parking spaces. They bully into line at the gas pump. A toll booth becomes a signal for elbowing fenders. And beetle-eyed drivers hunch over their steering wheels, squeezing the rims, glowering, preparing the excuse of not having seen you as they muscle you off the road. Approaching a highway on an entrance ramp recently, I was strong-armed by a trailer truck, so immense that its driver all but blew me away by blasting his horn. The behemoth was just inches from my hopelessly mismatched coupe when I fled for the safety of the shoulder.

TEACHING TIP

The writer supports his thesis (stated in the opening sentence of paragraph 5) with such vivid examples as the description of the car driver's expression (1), the New York taxi driver quote (6), and the extended narrative of the incident involving the enraged car driver and belligerent bus driver (8–10). The conclusion reinforces the thesis, extending it to include the concept that passive drivers who accept others' road rage play a role in its continuance.

1

2

3

4

5

6   And this is happening on city streets, too. A New York taxi driver told me that "intimidation is the name of the game. Drive as if you're deaf and blind. You don't hear the other guy's horn and you sure as hell don't see him."

7   The odd thing is that long before I was even able to drive, it seemed to me that people were at their finest and most civilized when in their cars. They seemed so orderly and considerate, so reasonable, staying in the right-hand lane unless passing, signaling all intentions. In those days you really eased into highway traffic, and the long, neat rows of cars seemed mobile testimony to the sanity of most people. Perhaps memory fails, perhaps there were always testy drivers, perhaps — but everyone didn't give you the finger.

8   A most amazing example of driver rage occurred recently at the Manhattan end of the Lincoln Tunnel. We were four cars abreast, stopped at a traffic light. And there was no moving even when the light had changed. A bus had stopped in the cross traffic, blocking our paths: it was a normal-for-New-York-City gridlock. Perhaps impatient, perhaps late for important appointments, three of us nonetheless accepted what, after all, we could not alter. One, however, would not. He would not be helpless. He would go where he was going even if he couldn't get there. A Wall Street type in suit and tie, he got out of his car and strode toward the bus, rapping smartly on its doors. When they opened, he exchanged words with the driver. The doors folded shut. He then stepped in front of the bus, took hold of one of its large windshield wipers and broke it.

9   The bus doors reopened and the driver appeared, apparently giving the fellow a good piece of his mind. If so, the lecture was wasted, for the man started his car and proceeded to drive directly *into the bus*. He rammed it. Even though the point at which he struck the bus, the folding doors, was its most vulnerable point, ramming the side of a bus with your car has to rank very high on a futility index. My first thought was that it had to be a rental car.

10   To tell the truth, I could not believe my eyes. The bus driver opened his doors as much as they could be opened and he stepped directly onto the hood of the attacking car, jumping up and down with both his feet. He then retreated into the bus, closing the doors behind him. Obviously a man of action, the car driver backed up and rammed the bus again. How this exercise in absurdity would have been resolved none of us will ever know for at that point the traffic unclogged and the bus moved on. And the rest of us, we passives of the world, proceeded, our cars crossing a field of battle as if nothing untoward had happened.

11   It is tempting to blame such belligerent, uncivil and even neurotic behavior on the nuts of the world, but in our cars we all become

a little crazy. How many of us speed up when a driver signals his intention of pulling in front of us? Are we resentful and anxious to pass him? How many of us try to squeeze in, or race along the shoulder of a lane merger? We may not jump on hoods, but driving the gantlet, we seethe, cursing not so silently in the safety of our steel bodies on wheels — fortresses for cowards.

What is it within us that gives birth to such antisocial behavior   12
and why, all of a sudden, have so many drivers gone around the bend? My friend Joel Katz, a Manhattan psychiatrist, calls it, "a Rambo pattern. People are running around thinking the American way is to take the law into your own hands when anyone does anything wrong. And what constitutes 'wrong'? Anything that cramps your style."

It seems to me that it is a new America we see on the road now. It   13
has the mentality of a hoodlum and the backbone of a coward. The car is its weapon and hiding place, and it is still a symbol even in this. Road Rambos no longer bespeak a self-reliant, civil people tooling around in family cruisers. In fact, there aren't families in these machines that charge headlong with their brights on in broad daylight, demanding we get out of their way. Bullies are loners, and they have perverted our liberty of the open road into drivers' license. They represent an America that derides the values of decency and good manners, then roam the highways riding shotgun and shrieking freedom. By allowing this to happen, the rest of us approve.   ■

Characteristics of Illustration Essays

Effective illustration essays support a generalization with specific, pertinent examples that maintain readers' interest and help to fulfill the author's purpose. Because an illustration essay needs to be more than a list of examples, a well-thought-out organization is essential.

Illustration Uses Examples to Support Generalizations

Examples are an effective way to support generalizations. A **generalization** is a broad statement about a topic. Often, the thesis of an essay contains a generalization. In "Rambos of the Road," Gottfried's thesis contains a generalization about "an epidemic of auto macho" behavior.

The following statements are generalizations because they make assertions about an entire group or category.

- Most college students are energetic, ambitious, and eager to get ahead in life.
- Gestures play an important role in nonverbal communications.
- Boys are more willing to participate in class discussions than are girls.

To explain and support any one of these generalizations, you would need to provide specific examples to show how or why the statement is accurate. For instance, you could support the first generalization about college students by describing several students who demonstrate energy and ambition: one student works two part-time jobs to cover tuition costs; another is the mother of two young children as well as a full-time student; a third never misses a class despite having suffered a severe back injury in a recent auto accident. However, because this general statement says "*Most* college students are energetic . . ." other types of support would need to accompany the examples of individual college students. Relevant facts, statistics, expert opinions, anecdotes, personal observations, or descriptions could be used to show that the generalization does indeed apply to the majority of college students.

TEACHING TIP:
COLLABORATIVE
WRITING

Students can complete
this exercise indepen-
dently and share their
examples in small
groups.

POSSIBLE ANSWERS

1. *Sesame Street,* news
   programs
2. Children who wander
   around in restaurants
3. Ratings and demo-
   graphics for profes-
   sional basketball or
   football

EXERCISE 11.1

Using one or more prewriting strategies for generating ideas, think of at least one example that supports each general statement.

1. Television offers some programs with educational or social value.
2. Today's parents are not strict enough with their children.
3. The favorite pastime of most men is watching sports on television.

Illustration Uses Examples to Explain or Clarify

Examples are also useful when you need to explain an unfamiliar topic, a difficult concept, or an abstract term for your readers.

Unfamiliar Topics.   When your audience has little or no knowledge of your topic, consider using examples to help your readers understand it. In "Rambos of the Road," Gottfried uses an extended example of real-life road rage to help his readers understand that topic. Similarly, note how examples are used in the following excerpt from a book about the English language.

> The complexities of the English language are such that even native speakers cannot always communicate effectively, as almost every American learns on his first day in Britain. . . . That may be. But if the Briton and American of the twenty-second century baffle each other, it seems altogether likely that they won't confuse many others—not, at least, if the rest of the world continues expropriating words and phrases at its present rate. Already Germans talk about *ein Image Problem* and *das Cash-Flow,* Italians program their computers with *il software,* French motorists going away for a *weekend break* pause for *les refueling stops,* Poles watch *telewizja,* Spaniards have a *flirt,* Austrians eat *Big Macs,* and the Japanese go on a *pikunikku.* For better or worse, English has become the most global of languages, the lingua franca of business, science, education, politics, and pop music.
>   BILL BRYSON, *The Mother Tongue*

Difficult Concepts.   Many concepts are difficult for readers to grasp by definition alone. For instance, a reader might guess that the term *urbanization,* a key concept in sociology, has something to do with cities. Defining the concept as, say, "the process by which an area becomes part of a city" would give the reader more to go on. But examples of formerly suburban areas that have become urban would make the concept immediately understandable. Notice how the following passage uses examples to explain the limitations of the human senses.

> The human senses detect only a fraction of reality: We can't see the ultraviolet markers that guide a honeybee to nectar; we can't hear most of the noises emitted by a dolphin. In this way, the senses define the boundaries of mental awareness. But the brain also defines the limits of what we perceive. Human beings see, feel, taste, touch and smell not the world around them but a version of the world, one their brains have concocted. "People imagine that they're seeing what's really there, but they're not," says neuroscientist John Maunsell of Baylor College of Medicine in Houston. The eyes take in the light reflecting off objects around us, but the brain only pays attention to part of the scene. Looking for a pen on a messy desk, for example, you can scan the surface without noticing the papers scattered across it.
>
> SHANON BROWNLEE and TRACI WATSON, "The Senses,"
> *US News & World Report,* January 13, 1997

Abstract Terms. Abstract terms refer to ideas, rather than to people or to concrete things you can see and touch. Terms such as *truth* and *justice* are abstract. Because abstractions are difficult to understand and often mean different things to different people, examples help to clarify them. If your psychology instructor explains the term *rationalization* by both defining it ("making excuses for one's failures") and giving examples of it (such as a gambler who justifies a loss by blaming the casino or a student who rationalizes a failing grade by claiming grades are unimportant), you can understand the abstract term by relating it to what you already know about gamblers and students who rationalize failures. In this case, then, familiar examples are used to clarify unfamiliar or hard-to-grasp ideas.

In other cases, however, abstract terms mean different things to different people. Here you give examples to clarify what *you* mean by an abstract term. Suppose you use the term *unfair* to describe your employer's treatment of employees. Some readers might assume she applies company rules unfairly; other readers may think she is unfair in scheduling employees for weekend hours. Examples of the employer's unfair treatment would make your meaning clear.

EXERCISE 11.2

The following list contains a mix of unfamiliar topics, difficult concepts, and abstract terms. Choose three items from the list and think of examples that illustrate their meanings.

1. Phobia
2. Conformity
3. Gender roles
4. The self-fulfilling prophecy
5. Sexual harassment

Illustration Maintains Readers' Interest

Examples that give readers a glimpse of an event or a circumstance and that allow them to imagine themselves there also help to maintain readers' interest. In "Rambos of the Road," we can visualize Gottfried's example of a bus driver leaping out of the bus and stamping on the hood of the car. Similarly, Gottfried's opening example of being followed by an angry driver creates tension; we want to keep reading to learn the outcome.

Illustration Takes Purpose and Audience into Account

A successful illustration essay uses either a series of related examples or one extended example to support its thesis. The number and type of examples to include will depend on your purpose and audience. In an essay arguing that a Toyota Tercel is a better buy than a Ford Taurus, you would need to give a series of examples to show the various models, years, and options available to potential car buyers. But a single poignant example would be appropriate in an essay written for an audience of high school students about the consequences of dropping out of school.

Your audience also plays a role in deciding what type of examples to include in an essay. At times, technical examples may be appropriate; at other times, more personal or nontechnical ones are effective. For instance, suppose you want to persuade readers that the Food and Drug Administration should approve a new cancer drug. If your audience is composed of doctors, your examples would include statistical studies and technical explanations of the drug's effectiveness. But if your audience is the general public, you would include personal anecdotes about lives being saved and nontechnical examples of the drug's safety. In addition, try to choose examples that represent different aspects of or viewpoints on your topic. In writing about the new drug, for instance, you might include expert opinion from researchers as well as the views of doctors, patients, and a representative of the company that manufactures the drug.

POSSIBLE ANSWERS

1. (a) A hypothetical example of a situation that would lead to dismissal; (b) an example of an offense similar to the student's; (c) an example of the consequences of not enforcing the policy.
2. (a) An example of an accident caused by an elderly driver who didn't react quickly enough; (b) statistics comparing the accident rate for elderly drivers versus those for the general population; (c) anecdotes from adult children of elderly drivers

EXERCISE 11.3

For one of the following topics, suggest examples that would suit the different audiences listed.

1. Your college's policy on academic dismissal
   a. First-year students attending a college orientation session
   b. Students facing academic dismissal
   c. Parents or spouses of students who have been dismissed for academic reasons
2. A proposal recommending that drivers over the age of sixty-five undergo periodic assessment of their ability to operate a motor vehicle safely
   a. Senior citizens
   b. State senators
   c. Adult children of elderly drivers

Illustration Uses Carefully Selected Examples

The examples you use to explain your thesis should be carefully chosen. Select examples that are relevant, representative, accurate and striking. *Relevant* examples have a direct and clear relationship to your thesis. If your essay advocates publicly funded and operated preschool programs, support your case with examples of successful publicly funded programs, not privately operated ones.

An example is *representative* when it shows a typical or real-life situation, not a rare or unusual one. In many cases, you will need to give several representative examples. For instance, in an essay arguing that preschool programs advance children's reading skills, one example of a preschool whose students later achieved high-level reading skills would not be representative of all or most children who attend these programs.

Be sure the examples you include are *accurate*. Report statistics objectively, and provide readers with enough information so that they can evaluate the reliability of the data. Do not, for instance, simply report that "Most students in preschool programs have better language skills than children who don't attend such programs." Instead, report details about the research. Explain how it was done, how many children participated, which language skills (such as speaking or listening) improved, and to whom the children were compared.

Finally, choose examples that are *striking and dramatic* and that will make a strong, lasting impression on your readers. A poignant example of an extremely shy child who learned to participate in small groups would dramatically illustrate the point that preschool programs can help children develop social skills.

At times, it may be necessary to conduct research to find examples outside of your knowledge and experience. For the essay on preschool programs, you would need to do library or Internet research to obtain the statistical information mentioned earlier. You might also interview a preschool administrator or teacher to gather firsthand anecdotes and opinions or visit a preschool classroom to observe the program in action.

Illustration Organizes Details Effectively

When you use examples to support a thesis, you need to decide how to organize both the examples and the details that accompany them. Often, one of the methods of organization discussed in Chapter 6 will be useful: most-to-least, least-to-most, chronological, or spatial order. For example, in an essay explaining why people wear unconventional dress, the examples might be arranged spatially, from outlandish footwear to headgear. In some instances, you may want to organize your examples according to another pattern of development, such as comparison and contrast or cause and effect. To support the thesis that a local department store needs to improve its customer services, you might begin by contrasting the department store with several computer stores that do have have better customer services, and offering examples of the services provided by each. Regardless of the method of organization you choose, use transitions to link your examples.

Visualizing an Illustration Essay: A Graphic Organizer

For more on graphic organizers, see Chapter 2, p. 40.

The graphic organizer shown in Figure 11.1 will help you visualize the components of an illustration essay. As you can see, the structure is straightforward: The introduction contains background information and usually includes the thesis, the body paragraphs give one or more related examples, and the conclusion presents a final statement. For an essay using one extended example — such as a highly descriptive account of an auto accident intended to persuade readers to wear seat belts — the body of the essay would focus on the details of that one example.

When you incorporate examples into an essay that uses other patterns of development, you might develop an example over several paragraphs or include a brief, one-paragraph example to illustrate a point.

The following essay, "Be Specific," is an example of an illustration essay. Read the selection, and then study the graphic organizer for it (see Figure 11.2).

FIGURE 11.1
GRAPHIC ORGANIZER FOR AN ILLUSTRATION ESSAY

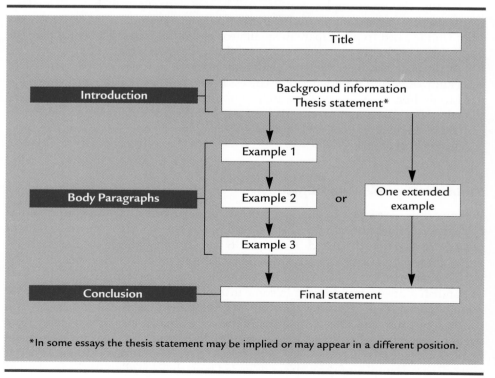

*In some essays the thesis statement may be implied or may appear in a different position.

Be Specific

Natalie Goldberg

Natalie Goldberg often writes about writing and has written several books on the subject, including Writing Down the Bones: Freeing the Writer Within *(1986), from which this excerpt was taken;* Wild Mind: Living the Writer's Life *(1990); and* Living Color: A Writer Paints Her World *(1996). Her books offer practical advice on both writing well and living well. She has also written several fictional works, including a novel,* Banana Rose *(1994). As you read this selection, highlight the examples Goldberg uses to support her thesis.*

PREREADING QUESTION

What does the author want readers to "be specific" about?

Be specific. Don't say "fruit." Tell what kind of fruit—"It is a pomegranate." Give things the dignity of their names. Just as with human beings, it is rude to say, "Hey, girl, get in line." That "girl" has a name. (As a matter of fact, if she's at least twenty years old, she's a woman, not a "girl" at all.) Things, too, have names. It is much better to say "the geranium in the window" than "the flower in the window." "Geranium"—that one word gives us a much more specific picture. It penetrates more deeply into the beingness of that flower. It immediately gives us the scene by the window—red petals, green circular leaves, all straining toward sunlight. [1]

About ten years ago I decided I had to learn the names of plants and flowers in my environment. I bought a book on them and walked down the tree-lined streets of Boulder, examining leaf, bark, and seed, trying to match them up with their descriptions and names in the book. Maple, elm, oak, locust. I usually tried to cheat by asking people working in their yards the names of the flowers and trees growing there. I was amazed how few people had any idea of the names of the live beings inhabiting their little plot of land. [2]

When we know the name of something, it brings us closer to the ground. It takes the blur out of our mind; it connects us to the earth. If I walk down the street and see "dogwood," "forsythia," I feel more friendly toward the environment. I am noticing what is around me and can name it. It makes me more awake. [3]

If you read the poems of William Carlos Williams, you will see how specific he is about plants, trees, flowers—chicory, daisy, locust, poplar, quince, primrose, black-eyed Susan, lilacs—each has its own integrity. Williams says, "Write what's in front of your nose." It's good for us to know what is in front of our noses. Not just "daisy," but how the flower is in the season we are looking at it—"The days-eye hugging the earth/in August . . . brownedged,/green and pointed scales/armor his yellow." Continue to hone your awareness: to the name, to the month, to the day, and finally to the moment. [4]

TEACHING TIP: POSTREADING DISCUSSION

Ask students to discuss:

- the examples the author uses and their effectiveness.
- the short, staccato sentences in paragraph 1 and what they contribute to the essay.
- the writing class example (6). Does knowing other group members' names help the group work more effectively? In what other situations might this apply?

5   Williams also says: "No idea, but in things." Study what is "in front of your nose." By saying "geranium" instead of "flower," you are penetrating more deeply into the present and being there. The closer we can get to what's in front of our nose, the more it can teach us everything. "To see the World in a Grain of Sand, and a heaven in a Wild Flower . . ."

6   In writing groups and classes too, it is good to quickly learn the names of all the other group members. It helps to ground you in the group and make you more attentive to each other's work.

7   Learn the names of everything: birds, cheese, tractors, cars, buildings. A writer is all at once everything—an architect, French cook, farmer—and at the same time, a writer is none of these things.   ■

FIGURE 11.2
GRAPHIC ORGANIZER FOR "BE SPECIFIC"

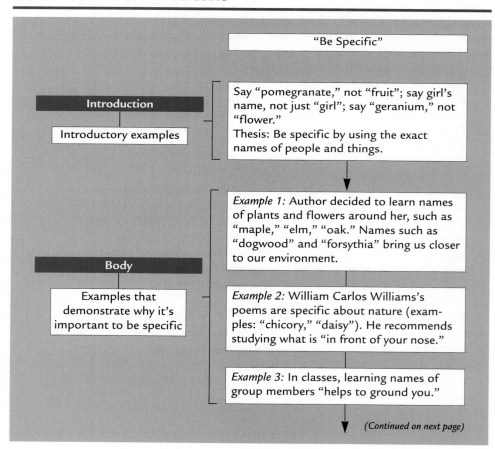

"Be Specific"

Introduction

Introductory examples

Say "pomegranate," not "fruit"; say girl's name, not just "girl"; say "geranium," not "flower."
Thesis: Be specific by using the exact names of people and things.

Body

Examples that demonstrate why it's important to be specific

Example 1: Author decided to learn names of plants and flowers around her, such as "maple," "elm," "oak." Names such as "dogwood" and "forsythia" bring us closer to our environment.

Example 2: William Carlos Williams's poems are specific about nature (examples: "chicory," "daisy"). He recommends studying what is "in front of your nose."

Example 3: In classes, learning names of group members "helps to ground you."

(Continued on next page)

FIGURE 11.2 *(continued)*

Conclusion — Learn names because a writer has many occupations, and none.

EXERCISE 11.4

Draw a graphic organizer for "Rambos of the Road" (pp. 289–91).

POSSIBLE ANSWERS

Answers will vary. See the *Instructor's Resource Manual* for a possible graphic organizer.

INTEGRATING ILLUSTRATION INTO AN ESSAY

Examples are an effective way to explain concepts or to support a thesis in an essay that relies on one or more other patterns of development. You might, for instance, use examples in the following ways.

- To *define* a particular advertising ploy.
- To *compare* two types of small businesses.
- To *classify* types of movies.
- To *show the effects* of aerobic exercise.
- To *argue* that junk food is unhealthy because of its high fat and salt content.

When using examples in an essay, keep the following tips in mind.

1. **Choose examples that are relevant, representative, accurate, and striking.** In most cases, you will include only one or two examples. Therefore, you need to choose them carefully.

2. **Use clear transitions.** Be sure to use a clear transition to introduce each new example. In essays organized by other methods, make it clear that an example is to follow.

3. **Limit descriptive detail.** Provide enough details so that your reader can understand how an example illustrates your generalization, but don't overwhelm your reader with too many details. Extended examples that are too detailed may distract your reader from the main point you are trying to make.

In "The Meanings of a Word" on page 319, Gloria Naylor uses illustration along with several other patterns of development to make a point about the various meanings of a word.

TEACHING TIP:
LEARNING STYLES AND
COMPUTER HINT

• Emphasize that stu-
dents should keep
their learning style
strengths in mind as
they work through this
assignment. While
some students may
prefer to work through
each Essay in Progress
step in sequence, oth-
ers may prefer to vary
the sequence (e.g., by
writing a rough first
draft before generating
ideas).
• Although students are
free to work through
this assignment in
their own ways,
encourage *all* students
to do some prewriting
on a computer and to
email each other with
questions and sugges-
tions as they work.

ADDITIONAL
RESOURCES

The writing process soft-
ware that accompanies
this text includes an
electronic Guided Writ-
ing Assignment for an
illustration essay.

*For more on narration,
description, and compari-
son and contrast, see
Chapters 9, 10, and 13.*

A GUIDED WRITING ASSIGNMENT

The following guide will lead you through the process of writing an illus-tration essay. You will use examples to support your thesis, but you may need to use one or more of the other patterns of development to organize your examples or relate them to one another. Depending on your learning style, you may choose to work through this Guided Writing Assignment in different ways. If you are a creative learner, you may prefer to begin by brainstorming a list of examples related to your topic. If you are a prag-matic learner, you may prefer to work through the assignment sequen-tially. If you are a social learner, you might discuss each part of the assignment with a classmate, or if you are an independent learner, you may prefer to work on your own.

The Assignment

Write an illustration essay. Select one of the following topics or one that you think of on your own. Your audience consists of readers of your cam-pus newspaper.

1. The connection between clothing and personality
2. The long-term benefits of a part-time job
3. The idea that you are what you eat
4. The problems of balancing school, job, and a family
5. Controlling or eliminating stress
6. Decision-making techniques
7. Effective (or ineffective) parenting
8. The popularity of a particular sport, television show, or hobby

As you develop your essay, consider using one or more of the other patterns of development. For example, you might use narration to present an extended example that illustrates the difficulties of balancing school-work with a job and family. You might compare decision-making tech-niques. Or you might describe your favorite television show.

Generating Ideas

Use the following guidelines to help you narrow a topic and generate ideas.

Narrowing Your Topic

Once you have chosen an assignment topic, your first step is to narrow it so that it becomes a manageable topic for your essay. Use brainstorming, freewriting, questioning, branching, or another prewriting technique to discover possible narrowed topics. Each of these might then lead to a thesis for your essay.

For more on prewriting strategies, see Chapter 4.

When you think you have done enough prewriting, review your work and select a narrowed topic that can be supported by one or more examples. For instance, suppose you have come up with two manageable topics about anxiety. One is to discuss methods for controlling test anxiety; another is to discuss its effects. If you decide to write about controlling test anxiety, you would need to explain a process. You might use an extended example to show how one person overcame test anxiety. The second narrowed topic, the effects of test anxiety, could be explained by using several examples of test situations in which individuals "freeze" or "go blank."

Considering Your Purpose, Audience, and Point of View

Your purpose and audience will affect the type and number of examples you include. If you are writing a persuasive essay, examples may be part of your essay but seldom are they sufficient evidence. However, if you are writing an informative essay in which you explain how to select educational toys, one extended example may be sufficient.

For more on purpose, audience, and point of view, see Chapter 4, p. 73.

Consider your audience in deciding what kinds of examples to include. For this assignment, your audience is made up of the readers of your campus newspaper. Think about whether this audience is interested in and familiar with your topic. If your audience is familiar with your topic, you may want to use complex examples. However, simpler, more straightforward examples would be appropriate for an audience unfamiliar with your topic. For instance, in an essay urging closer regulation of airline safety, readers knowledgeable about aircraft construction would appreciate technical examples of safety violations, but a general audience would require nontechnical examples.

You also need to consider which point of view to use to present your examples. In most illustration essays, the emphasis is on the subject at hand—the examples. For this reason, illustration is often written in the third person, as in "Goin' Gangsta, Choosin' Cholita!: Claiming Identity" later in this chapter (page 314). When personal examples are used, however, writers may decide to use the first person, as in "Rambos of the Road," (page 289) and "The Meanings of a Word" (page 319).

Developing Your Thesis

For more on thesis statements, see Chapter 5, p. 97.

Your next step is to develop a working thesis about your narrowed topic. The thesis in an illustration essay is the idea that all of the examples help to support. To write an effective thesis statement, use the following guidelines.

- Identify the narrowed topic of your essay.
- Make a generalization about your narrowed topic that you will support through the use of examples.

TEACHING TIP: LEARNING STYLES

Creative and abstract learners may have difficulty composing an illustration essay because they tend to focus on big ideas and gloss over details. Try grouping creative or abstract learners with pragmatic or concrete learners, who can assist each other with the steps of the writing process.

You can develop a thesis statement in several different ways, depending on your learning style. For instance, a concrete learner writing about the effects of absent fathers on families may begin by listing the problems and behaviors that children in such single-parent families exhibit. The list might suggest a thesis such as the following.

> Children in families in which the father is absent often lack a male role model, which can result in behavioral problems.

An abstract learner, on the other hand, might write the thesis first and then go on to generate examples that support the generalization.

Once you are satisfied with your thesis statement, use the following suggestions to help you think of examples that illustrate it. As you brainstorm examples, you may think of situations that illustrate a different or more interesting thesis. Don't hesitate to revise or change your thesis as you discover more about your topic.

For more on prewriting strategies, see Chapter 4.

1. Jot down all of the instances or situations you can think of that illustrate your thesis.
2. Close your eyes and visualize situations that relate to your thesis.
3. Systematically review your life—year-by-year, place-by-place, or job-by-job—to recall situations that illustrate your thesis.
4. Discuss your thesis with a classmate. Try to match or better each other's examples.
5. Create two columns on a piece of paper or in a computer file. In the first column, type a list of words describing how you feel about your

▶ *Learning Style Options*

TEACHING TIP: LEARNING STYLES

1. For all learners, particularly verbal, concrete, or pragmatic
2. For creative learners
3. For pragmatic or concrete learners
4. For all learners, particularly social

narrowed topic. (For example, the topic *cheating on college exams* might generate such feelings as anger, surprise, and confusion.) In the second column, elaborate on these words by adding details about specific situations. (For example, you might write about how surprised you were to discover your best friend had cheated on an exam.)

6. Research your topic in the library or on the Internet to uncover examples outside of your own experience.

5. An excellent strategy for all learners (the first column requires emotional thinking; the second, pragmatic and concrete thinking)
6. For all learners

For more on library and Internet research, see Chapter 19.

ESSAY IN PROGRESS 1

Using the preceding guidelines, choose and narrow your topic. Then develop a working thesis statement and brainstorm possible examples that illustrate the thesis.

Choosing and Evaluating Your Examples

Brainstorming will lead you to discover a wealth of examples — many more than you could possibly use in your essay. Your task, then, is to select the examples that will best support your thesis. Use the following criteria in choosing examples.

1. **Choose relevant examples.** The examples you choose must clearly demonstrate the point or idea you want to illustrate. To support the thesis that high schools do not provide students with the instruction and training in physical education necessary to maintain a healthy lifestyle, you would not use as an example a student who is underweight because of a recent illness. Since lack of preparation in high school is not responsible for this student's problem, the case would be irrelevant to your thesis.

2. **Choose a variety of useful examples.** If you are using more than one example, choose examples that reveal different aspects of your topic or that contribute new information. In writing about students who lack physical education skills, for instance, you would need to provide examples of students who lack different kinds of skills: one student who lacks strength, one who lacks agility, and so forth. You can also add variety by using expert opinion, quotations, observations, or statistics to illustrate your thesis.

3. **Choose representative examples.** Choose typical cases, not rare or unusual ones, to illustrate your point. To continue with the thesis about physical education, a high school all-star football player who

lacks adequate strength or muscular control would be an exceptional case and a nonrepresentative example. A recent high school graduate who did not learn to play a single sport and failed to develop a habit of regular exercise would be a more representative example.

4. **Choose striking examples.** Include examples that capture your readers' attention and make a vivid impression. In "Rambos of the Road," Gottfried's example of the car-bus confrontation is a striking illustration of road rage. It is much more memorable than, say, an ordinary example of drivers gesturing toward or cutting in front of one another.

5. **Choose accurate examples.** Be sure the examples you include are accurate. They should be neither exaggerated nor understated; your examples should present the situation realistically. For the thesis about high school students, for example, you would lose credibility if you exaggerated the students' physical condition.

6. **Choose examples that appeal to your audience.** Some examples will appeal to one type of audience more than to another type. If you want to illustrate high school graduates' lack of training in physical education for an audience of high school seniors, examples involving actual students may be most appealing, whereas for an audience of parents, expert opinion and statistics would be appropriate.

If you are working on a computer, highlight strong examples by making them bold or moving them to a separate page or document for easy access when drafting.

TRYING OUT YOUR IDEAS ON OTHERS

Working in a group of two or three students, discuss your thesis and supporting examples for this chapter's assignment. Use the list of criteria on pages 303–304 to guide the discussion and to make suggestions for improving each student's thesis and examples.

ESSAY IN PROGRESS 2

Using the preceding suggestions, and the feedback you have received from classmates, evaluate your examples and decide which ones you will include.

Organizing and Drafting

Once you are satisfied with your thesis and the examples you have chosen to illustrate it, you are ready to organize your ideas and write your draft essay.

TEACHING TIP: COLLABORATIVE WRITING

(10 minutes) Encourage students to evaluate each other's thesis statements. For multiple peer reviews, have students pass their draft thesis statements to the student on the right for comments, and then to the student on the left for comments.

COMPUTER HINT

Encourage students to email their working theses and examples to each other, if networked computers are not available. Suggest that they review the characteristics of illustration essays before preparing their responses.

For more on drafting an essay, see Chapter 6.

Choosing a Method of Organization

Use the following guidelines to organize your essay.

1. **If you are using a single, extended example, relate events in the order in which they happened or choose another method of organization.** If the example is not made up of events, you might use a most-to-least, a least-to-most, or a spatial organization. For instance, if you want to use in-line skating as an example of why protective gear should be worn during athletic activities, you might arrange the details spatially, describing the skater's head gear first, then the elbow and wrist pads, and then the knee protection.

2. **If you are using several examples, decide how you will order them.** Many illustration essays order examples in terms of their importance, such as from most to least important or from least to most important. However, other arrangements are possible. Examples of childhood memories, for instance, could follow chronological order, beginning with your earliest memory and moving forward in time.

3. **If you have many examples, consider grouping them in categories.** For instance, in an essay about the use of informal language, you might classify examples of slang words according to how they are used by teenagers, by adults, and by other groups. Draw a graphic organizer or write an outline to plan your categories.

For more on chronological organization, see Chapter 9.

For more on classification and division, see Chapter 14.

ESSAY IN PROGRESS 3

Using the preceding suggestions, choose a method for organizing your examples. Then draw a graphic organizer or write an outline of your essay.

Drafting the Illustration Essay

Once you have decided on a method of organization, your next step is to write a first draft. Here are some tips for drafting an illustration essay.

1. **Each paragraph should express one key idea; the example or examples in that paragraph should illustrate that key idea.** Develop your body paragraphs so that each one presents a single example or group of closely related examples.

2. **Use the topic sentence in each paragraph to make clear the particular idea each example or set of examples illustrates.** In an essay that informs readers about the kinds of students who drop out of high school, you might focus on students who drop out for social reasons, for economic reasons, and for academic reasons and discuss each type

TEACHING TIP: LEARNING STYLES

Spatial learners may prefer to draw a graphic organizer, whereas others may prefer to write an outline.

CONNECTIONS

Emphasize the importance of topic sentences by referring to what students learned in Chapter 9 about narration: Just as a narrative must make a point to be interesting and relevant to readers, so must examples exemplify *something*, a main point presented in a thesis or topic sentence.

of student in a separate paragraph. Each topic sentence would focus on one type.

For more on description, see Chapter 10. For more on using sufficient detail, see Chapter 6, p. 136.

3. **Provide sufficient detail about each example.** Explain each example using vivid descriptive language. Your goal is to make your readers feel as if they are experiencing or observing the situation.

For more on transitions, see Chapter 6, p. 138.

4. **Use transitions to move your readers from one example to another.** Without transitions, your essay will seem choppy and disconnected. Use transitions such as *for example* and *in particular* to keep your readers on track.

For more on writing effective paragraphs, including introductions and conclusions, see Chapter 6.

5. **Begin with a clear introduction.** In most illustration essays, the thesis is stated at the outset. Your introduction should also spark readers' interest and include background information about the topic.

6. **End with an effective conclusion.** Your essay should not end with your last example. Instead, it should conclude with a final statement that pulls your ideas together and reminds readers of your thesis. In an essay about why students decide to drop out of high school, you might conclude with a memorable quotation from a student who regrets the decision or with a statistic indicating a recent increase in the dropout rate.

TEACHING TIP

Students who have followed the Guided Writing Assignment should be ready to compose a first draft independently. However, check to see if any students need to rethink their thesis and examples before drafting. Encourage them to seek further assistance from a peer reviewer or writing center tutor.

ESSAY IN PROGRESS 4

Using the preceding guidelines, write a first draft of your illustration essay.

Analyzing and Revising

If possible, set your draft aside for a day or two before rereading and revising it. As you reread and review your draft, concentrate on its organization, level of detail, and overall effectiveness, not on grammar or mechanics. To evaluate and revise your draft, use the following strategies.

Learning Style Options

For more on the benefits of peer review, see Chapter 7, p. 166.

1. Reread your paper aloud or ask a friend to do so as you listen.

2. Write an outline or draw a graphic organizer, or update the one you created earlier. Look for weaknesses in how examples are organized.

TEACHING TIP: LEARNING STYLES

1. For all learners, particularly social learners
2. For all learners (spatial learners may prefer the graphic organizer; others may prefer the outline)

Use Flowchart 11.1 to help you discover the strengths and weaknesses of your illustration essay. You might also ask a classmate to review your essay using the questions in the flowchart. For each answer that refers you to the right column of the chart, ask your reviewer to explain why he or she answered in that way.

FLOWCHART 11.1
REVISING AN ILLUSTRATION ESSAY

Questions	Revision Strategies

1. Is your thesis statement focused? Does it clearly indicate the generalization that your examples will support?

No ⇨

- Revise your thesis, focusing only on the ideas that your examples illustrate.
- Reconsider your thesis, changing your generalization so that it fits your examples.

Yes ⇩

2. Have you used examples that explain and clarify unfamiliar topics, difficult concepts, or abstract terms?

No ⇨

- Highlight terms that might be problematic in your essay, and see if a classmate or friend can define them.
- List terms or concepts in one column. For each item, think of at least two examples.

Yes ⇩

3. Will your examples appeal to your audience?

No ⇨

- Replace obvious, predictable examples with more striking or interesting ones.
- Add examples that represent different aspects of or viewpoints on your topic.

Yes ⇩

4. Are your examples appropriate for your audience and purpose?

No ⇨

- Replace examples that are too technical with more familiar examples.
- Consider using more than one example or cutting back and using one extended example, depending on your subject.

Yes ⇩

(Continued on next page)

FLOWCHART 11.1 *(continued)*

Questions	Revision Strategies
5. Are your examples relevant, varied, striking, representative, accurate, and appealing?	• Eliminate examples that do not illustrate your thesis. • Brainstorm or conduct research to discover relevant or more striking examples. • Expand your examples to include more details. • Consider adding other kinds of examples (such as expert opinion and statistics).

Yes ⇩   No ⇨

| 6. Do you use an effective method of organization to arrange your examples? Do you use transitions to move from one example to the next? | • Review the methods of organization in Chapter 6.
• Consider using a different organizing strategy: most-to-least, least-to-most, chronological, or spatial order.
• Add transitions if your essay sounds choppy. |

No ⇨   Yes ⇩

| 7. Does the topic sentence of each paragraph clearly make a point that the example(s) in that paragraph illustrate? | • Reorganize your essay, grouping examples according to the point or idea they illustrate.
• Add topic sentences that clearly indicate the point each example or group of examples illustrates. |

No ⇨   Yes ⇩

| 8. Have you written an effective introduction and conclusion? | • Revise your introduction and conclusion so that they meet the guidelines in Chapter 6 (pp. 140–46). |

No ⇨   Yes

ESSAY IN PROGRESS 5

Revise your draft using Flowchart 11.1 and any comments you have received from peer reviewers.

TEACHING TIP

Encourage students to get feedback on the revised essay from a peer reviewer or writing center tutor.

Editing and Proofreading

The last step is to check your revised essay for errors in grammar, spelling, punctuation, and mechanics. In addition, look for the types of errors you commonly make. (Refer to your error log. See also the Writing Assessment in Appendix A.)

For more on keeping an error log, See Chapter 8, p. 201.

For illustration essays, pay particular attention to the following common errors.

1. **Inconsistent verb tense.** Be consistent in your use of verb tense in extended examples. If you are using the present tense but citing an event from the past as an example, however, use the past tense to describe it.

   ▶ Special events *are* an important part of children's lives. Parent visitation day at school *was* an event my daughter *talked* about for an entire week. . . . Children *are* also excited by . . .

2. **Inconsistent use of first, second, or third person.** Be sure to use the first person (*I*, *me*), the second person (*you*), or the third person (*he*, *she*, *it*, *him*, *her*) consistently throughout your essay.

   ▶ I visited my daughter's first-grade classroom during parents' week last month. Each parent was invited to read a story to the class and ~~you~~ *we* were encouraged to ask the children questions afterward.

ESSAY IN PROGRESS 6

Edit and proofread your illustration essay, paying particular attention to consistent use of verb tense and point of view. Don't forget to look for the types of errors you tend to make.

STUDENTS WRITE

Michael Jacobsohn originally wrote the following essay as part of his application to Harvard University. It was later published as "The Harmony of Life" in *Harvard Magazine,* in 1996. As you read the illustration essay, highlight the examples that best convey the writer's love of musicals.

CONNECTIONS

"The Value of Volunteering" by Robin Ferguson is another student essay that uses illustration (see Chapter 6, p. 129).

PREREADING QUESTION

What does the word *harmony* connote?

The Harmony of Life

Michael Jacobsohn

1   I am first in my class, an all-state football player, weigh 220 pounds, and can lift up small cars, yet I have a secret which I have kept hidden for years. It rages within me, yearning to break free and reveal itself in both shame and splendor. I can contain it no longer. I must shed my inhibitions and proclaim aloud, "So help me, God, I love musicals!"

2   Until now, only my family and those who have had the experience of calling my house in the midst of one of my renditions of the confrontation scene between Javert and Valjean from Les Misérables knew about my passion for musical theater. For years I have endured ridicule from my sisters and their friends who have overheard me belting out the lyrics to "Sunrise, Sunset" from Fiddler on the Roof while in the shower. Ever since my first musical, Jesus Christ Superstar, seven years ago, I have been obsessed with the telling of stories through melody and verse. My heart leaps when I see that Phantom of the Opera is coming to the local theater, or when Guys and Dolls is appearing on television at one in the morning.

3   Music is the most beautiful and powerful way to relate emotion. Thus, the entire structure of a story is enhanced by presenting action and dialogue through song. The topic of a story can deal with anything from religion, such as Godspell, to a ravenous man-eating plant (Audrey II in Little Shop of Horrors), but no matter which, music brings to life a story line and places a

production forever in one's head by providing a harmony
to be continually associated with it.

Musicals also provide me with an emotional outlet.   4
When enthralled by a member of the opposite sex, I am
wont to burst into a performance of "Maria" from West
Side Story. After an exhaustive football practice, my
lips chant "I'm Free" from the rock opera Tommy; and at
my desk, feeling haughty after getting the highest grade
on a calculus test, I sing quietly, "I am the very model
of a modern Major-General," from The Pirates of Penzance.
I can delve into the recesses of my mind and produce a
piece fitting for any occasion, and I take pride in this
ability.

While preparing this confession, a less musically   5
inclined friend of mine happened upon a rough draft of
the revelation. As he heartily laughed at me, he asked,
"Can this be? Can the fact that Michael Jacobsohn is
both an academic and football colossus and a lover of
musicals be reconciled?" I replied, "The bald, fat Marlon
Brando of Apocalypse Now is the same Marlon Brando in
Guys and Dolls. Just as Kurtz and Sky Masterson* are one
and the same, so does my love for musicals reconcile
itself with the other facets of my personality. It is
unwise to stereotype, just as it is unwise to typecast."
Inside, I shall sing forever.

Kurtz and Sky Masterson: Kurtz is a character played by Marlon Brando in the film *Apocalypse Now* (1979). Sky Masterson is the male lead in the musical *Guys and Dolls* and was played by Brando in the 1955 movie version.

Analyzing the Essay

1. What is Jacobsohn's thesis, and what does it tell us about him?
2. How does Jacobsohn's introduction capture your interest?
3. Evaluate the quantity and types of examples the writer provides.
4. How are the details in the essay organized? Is the organization effective?
5. Evaluate paragraph 3. What suggested revisions would you offer the writer?

POSSIBLE ANSWERS:
ANALYZING THE ESSAY

1. Although it is unexpected and possibly unpopular for him to admit it, Jacobsohn loves musicals.
2. The periodic sentence that opens the essay sets up expectation, suspense, and irony, which build to the thesis.
3. There is an ample supply of examples of classic musicals and of situations in which he recites songs from musicals, but more quotes of lyrics (e.g., in paragraph 4) would add variety to the example types.
4. One could say they are ordered from most important to least important or that they are listed point by point, without ranking of points.
5. Although it names musicals and their subjects, the discussion is too abstract and could be improved by quoting lyrics and analyzing their relation to the story structure.

POSSIBLE ANSWERS:
REACTING TO THE
ESSAY

1. Responses will vary;
possibilities include
dance, writing, and
painting.
2. The title has double
meanings: *Harmony*
suggests music as well
as the way aspects of
something work
together.
3. Responses will vary.

TEACHING TIP

Question 3 indirectly
asks students to evalu-
ate an *irony* in their personal experience—the
discrepancy between a
special interest and their
other interests and tal-
ents. Point out that
irony is used in various
types of writing, includ-
ing literary works.

Reacting to the Essay: Discussion and Journal Writing

1. Jacobsohn says that musicals provide an emotional outlet for him. Discuss whether other art forms can serve the same function.
2. Discuss the meaning and effectiveness of the essay's title.
3. Jacobsohn claims that his love of musicals is his hidden secret, a passion that no one who knows him would have expected. What interests or hobbies do you have that do not seem to fit the image others hold of you? Write a journal entry describing such an interest and the discrepancy between it and your other interests and talents.

READING AN ILLUSTRATION ESSAY

The following section provides advice for reading illustration essays as well as two model essays. Each essay exemplifies the characteristics of illustration covered in this chapter and provides opportunities to examine, analyze, and react to the writer's ideas. The second essay uses illustration along with other methods of development.

WORKING WITH TEXT: READING ILLUSTRATION ESSAYS

*For more on reading
strategies, see Chapter 2.*

When reading essays that use examples to explain or persuade, you may find yourself paying too much attention to the examples and losing sight of the key points the examples are meant to illustrate. Moreover, when the examples are especially exciting and dramatic, or when one extended example is used, it is easy to become distracted from the main point of the reading. Here are some suggestions for reading illustration essays with a focused eye.

What to Look for, Highlight, and Annotate

1. Read the essay more than once. As with other types of essays, several readings may be necessary. Read the essay once to grasp its basic ideas; reread it to analyze its structure and content.
2. Begin by identifying and highlighting the thesis statement. If the thesis is not directly stated, ask yourself this question: "What one major point do all of the examples illustrate?"
3. Study and highlight the examples. What characteristics or aspects of the thesis do they illustrate? Note in the margin the characteristics or aspects of the thesis each example illustrates.

4. Record your response to each example, either by using annotations or by writing in a journal. Try to answer these questions: "How well do the examples explain or clarify the thesis? Do I feel convinced of the writer's thesis after reading the essay? Would more or different examples have been more effective?"

5. Notice how the examples are organized. Are they organized in order of importance, in chronological order, in spatial order, or by some other method?

6. Note how the examples fit with any other patterns of development used in the essay.

How to Find Ideas to Write About

When you are asked to write a response to an illustration essay, keep an eye out for ideas to write about *as you read*. Try to think of similar or related examples from your personal experience. While reading "Rambos of the Road," for instance, you might have thought of driving behaviors you have observed. You might have recalled other examples of road rage, of drivers oblivious to those around them, of drivers who are reckless or careful and considerate. Each of these examples could lead you to a thesis and ideas for writing.

For more on discovering ideas for a response paper, see Chapter 3.

THINKING CRITICALLY ABOUT ILLUSTRATION

When you read text that uses illustration to support generalizations, read with a critical eye. Study the examples and how they are used in the essay. Use the following questions to think critically about the examples you read.

What Is the Emotional Impact of the Examples?

Examples are primarily a means of explaining or persuading, but they can also be used to evoke emotional responses. A vivid description of a forlorn tiger in a zoo pacing and rubbing its body against a fence while deepening an open sore would provide a clear example of the behavior exhibited by wild animals in captivity. At the same time, such an example evokes feelings of pity, sympathy, even outrage.

For more on emotional appeals, see Chapter 17, p. 555.

Writers often choose examples with emotional appeal in order to manipulate their readers' feelings. This strategy is especially common in persuasive writing. Although it is not necessarily wrong for a writer to use examples that evoke emotional responses, as a critical reader you should be aware of their use so that you can avoid being manipulated. When you encounter an example that evokes an emotional response, try to set your emotions aside and look at the example objectively. In the case of the tiger, for instance, consider such questions as: Why are animals held in captivity? What are the benefits of zoos?

Are the Examples Representative?

Not all writers choose examples that convey a full picture of the subject. In the example about zoos, you might ask if the animals in all zoos are treated as badly as the tiger is treated. Especially when you read persuasive writing, attempt to confirm through alternate sources or research that the writer's examples are fair and representative and try to think of examples that might contradict the writer's point.

Is the Generalization Supported?

Evaluate whether the writer provides enough relevant examples to support the generalization and lead you to accept the thesis. Study each example closely: Is it clear and fully explained? Does it illustrate the thesis? What other types of examples, such as statistics or expert opinion, might strengthen the essay? In the hypothetical essay about zoos, for instance, the expert opinion of zoologists would support the generalization that the primary function of a zoo should be to preserve animal species. Similarly, statistics on the number of species preserved in zoos would be relevant.

ILLUSTRATION ESSAY

As you read the following essay by Nell Bernstein, consider how the author uses the elements of illustration discussed in this chapter.

Goin' Gangsta, Choosin' Cholita: Claiming Identity
Nell Bernstein

PREREADING
QUESTION

What is your cultural
identity?

CONNECTIONS

"The Bilingual Ed Trap"
and "Melting Pot or
Tossed Salad" in Chap-
ter 17 also consider the
implications of a multi-
cultural society.

Nell Bernstein is a San Francisco journalist who writes about current issues and is the editor of YO! (Youth Outlook). *The following excerpt from an essay that originally appeared in 1994 in* West *magazine, the Sunday supplement to the* San Jose Mercury News, *describes several California teenagers and their viewpoints on ethnic and racial identity. As you read the selection, highlight the statements and examples that reveal the teenagers' views.*

1   Her lipstick is dark, the lip liner even darker, nearly black. In baggy pants, a blue plaid Pendleton, her bangs pulled back tight off her forehead, 15-year-old April is a perfect cholita, a Mexican gangsta girl.

2   But April Miller is Anglo. "And I don't like it!" she complains. "I'd rather be Mexican."

April's father wanders into the family room of their home in San 3
Leandro, California, a suburb near Oakland. "Hey, cholita," he teases.
"Go get a suntan. We'll put you in a barrio and see how much you like
it."

A large, sandy-haired man with "April" tattooed on one arm and 4
"Kelly" — the name of his older daughter — on the other, Miller spent
21 years working in a San Leandro glass factory that shut down and
moved to Mexico a couple of years ago. He recently got a job in
another factory, but he expects NAFTA* to swallow that one, too.

"Sooner or later we'll all get nailed," he says. "Just another stab in 5
the back of the American middle class."

Later, April gets her revenge: "Hey, Mr. White Man's Last Stand," 6
she teases. "Wait till you see how well I manage my welfare check.
You'll be asking me for money."

A once almost exclusively white, now increasingly Latin and black 7
working-class suburb, San Leandro borders on predominantly black
East Oakland. For decades, the boundary was strictly policed and
practically impermeable. In 1970 April Miller's hometown was 97
percent white. By 1990 San Leandro was 65 percent white, 6 percent
black, 15 percent Hispanic, and 13 percent Asian or Pacific Islander.
With minorities moving into suburbs in growing numbers and cities
becoming ever more diverse, the boundary between city and suburb
is dissolving, and suburban teenagers are changing with the times.

In April's bedroom, her past and present selves lie in layers, the 8
pink walls of girlhood almost obscured, Guns N' Roses and Pearl Jam
posters overlaid by rappers Paris and Ice Cube. "I don't have a big
enough attitude to be a black girl," says April, explaining her current
choice of ethnic identification.

What matters is that she thinks the choice is hers. For April and 9
her friends, identity is not a matter of where you come from, what
you were born into, what color your skin is. It's what you wear, the
music you listen to, the words you use — everything to which you
pledge allegiance, no matter how fleetingly.

The hybridization of American teens has become talk show fod- 10
der, with "wiggers" — white kids who dress and talk "black" — appearing on TV in full gangsta regalia. In Indiana a group of white high
school girls raised a national stir when they triggered an imitation
race war at their virtually all white high school last fall simply by
dressing "black."

In many parts of the country, it's television and radio, not neigh- 11
bors, that introduce teens to the allure of ethnic difference. But in
California, which demographers predict will be the first state with no

---

NAFTA (North American Free Trade Agreement): An agreement among North American countries to ease restrictions on the exchange of goods and services.

racial majority by the year 2000, the influences are more immediate. The California public schools are the most diverse in the country: 42 percent white, 36 percent Hispanic, 9 percent black, 8 percent Asian.

12   Sometimes young people fight over their differences. Students at virtually any school in the Bay Area can recount the details of at least one "race riot" in which a conflict between individuals escalated into a battle between their clans. More often, though, teens would rather join than fight. Adolescence, after all, is the period when you're most inclined to mimic the power closest at hand, from stealing your older sister's clothes to copying the ruling clique at school.

13   White skaters and Mexican would-be gangbangers listen to gangsta rap and call each other "nigga" as a term of endearment; white girls sometimes affect Spanish accents; blond cheerleaders claim Cherokee ancestors.

14   "Claiming" is the central concept here. A Vietnamese teen in Hayward, another Oakland suburb, "claims" Oakland—and by implication blackness—because he lived there as a child. A law-abiding white kid "claims" a Mexican gang he says he hangs with. A brown-skinned girl with a Mexican father and a white mother "claims" her Mexican side, while her fair-skinned sister "claims" white. The word comes up over and over, as if identity were territory, the self a kind of turf.

15   Will Mosley says he and his friends listen to rap groups like Compton's Most Wanted, NWA, and Above the Law because they "sing about life" . . . that is, what happens in Oakland, Los Angeles, anyplace but where Will is sitting today, an empty Round Table Pizza in a minimall.

16   "No matter what race you are," Will says, "if you live like we do, then that's the kind of music you like."

17   And how do they live?

18   "We don't live bad or anything," Will admits. "We live in a pretty good neighborhood, there's no violence or crime. I was just . . . we're just city people, I guess."

19   Will and his friend Adolfo Garcia, 16, say they've outgrown trying to be something they're not. "When I was 11 or 12," Will says, "I thought I was becoming a big gangsta and stuff. Because I liked that music, and thought it was the coolest, I wanted to become that. I wore big clothes, like you wear in jail. But then I kind of woke up. I looked at myself and thought, 'Who am I trying to be?'"

20   They may have outgrown blatant mimicry, but Will and his friends remain convinced that they can live in a suburban tract house with a well-kept lawn on a tree-lined street in "not a bad neighborhood" and still call themselves "city" people on the basis of musical tastes. "City" for these young people means crime, graffiti, drugs. The kids are law-abiding, but these activities connote what Will

admiringly calls "action." With pride in his voice, Will predicts that "in a couple of years, Hayward will be like Oakland. It's starting to get more known, because of crime and things. I think it'll be bigger, more things happening, more crime, more graffiti, stealing cars."

"That's good," chimes in 15-year-old Matt Jenkins, whose new beeper—an item that once connoted gangsta chic but now means little more than an active social life—goes off periodically. "More fun." 21

The three young men imagine with disdain life in a gangsta-free zone. "Too bland, too boring," Adolfo says. "You have to have something going on. You can't just have everyday life." 22

"Mowing your lawn," Matt sneers. 23

"Like Beaver Cleaver's house," Adolfo adds. "It's too clean out here." 24

Not only white kids believe that identity is a matter of choice or taste, or that the power of "claiming" can transcend ethnicity. The Manor Park Locos—a group of mostly Mexican-Americans who hang out in San Leandro's Manor Park—say they descend from the Manor Lords, tough white guys who ruled the neighborhood a generation ago. 25

Not every young Californian embraces the new racial hybridism. Andrea Jones, 20, an African-American who grew up in the Bay Area suburbs of Union City and Hayward, is unimpressed by what she sees mainly as shallow mimicry. "It's full of posers out here," she says. "When *Boyz N the Hood* came out on video, it was sold out for weeks. The boys all wanna be black, the girls all wanna be Mexican. It's the glamour." 26

Driving down the quiet, shaded streets of her old neighborhood in Union City, Andrea spots two white preteen boys in Raiders jackets and hugely baggy pants strutting erratically down the empty sidewalk. "Look at them," she says. "Dislocated." 27

She knows why. "In a lot of these schools out here, it's hard being white," she says. "I don't think these kids were prepared for the backlash that is going on, all the pride now in people of color's ethnicity, and our boldness with it. They have nothing like that, no identity, nothing they can say they're proud of. 28

"So they latch onto their great-grandmother who's a Cherokee, or they take on the most stereotypical aspects of being black or Mexican. It's beautiful to appreciate different aspects of other people's culture—that's like the dream of what the 21st century should be. But to garnish yourself with pop culture stereotypes just to blend—that's really sad." 29

Those who dismiss the gangsta and cholo styles as affectations can point to the fact that several companies market overpriced knockoffs of "ghetto wear" targeted at teens. 30

POSSIBLE ANSWERS:
EXAMINING THE
READING (p. 318).

1. To Miller it means cultural identification: "It's what you wear, the music you listen to, the words you use" (paragraph 9).
2. An increasingly multicultural society, in which races become mixed and cultural heritage becomes less important than cultural identification

(Continued on next page)

3. Choosing the culture with which one wishes to identify, one's own or another culture
4. As Hispanic, African, and Asian Americans have migrated to suburbs and cities, these areas have become more multicultural and the music and fashions of multicultural groups have become more popular, leading adolescents to want to identify with them.
5. *impermeable:* impossible to cross; *hybridization:* adopting cultural attributes of another race; *connoted:* suggested; *affectations:* put on for show, a pretense

POSSIBLE ANSWERS:
ANALYZING THE
READING

1. American adolescents' adoption of cultural attributes of other races is a trend symptomatic of the drift away from clear biological roots toward a more multicultural society.
2. It provides unity and closure.
3. Real "cases" — examples of actual teenagers going through "hybridization" — dramatize Bernstein's point. Most examples come from California, but other U.S. areas are also mentioned; although relevant, one might question whether they are geographically biased.
4. Through examples of how actual U.S. teens dress and talk.

31   But there's also something going on out here that transcends adolescent faddishness and pop culture exoticism. When white kids call their parents "racist" for nagging them about their baggy pants; when they learn Spanish to talk to their boyfriends; when Mexican-American boys feel themselves descended in spirit from white "uncles"; when children of mixed marriages insist that they are whatever race they say they are, all of them are more than just confused.

32   They're inching toward what Andrea Jones calls "the dream of what the 21st century should be." In the ever more diverse communities of Northern California, they're also facing the complicated reality of what their 21st century will be.

33   Meanwhile, in the living room of the Miller family's San Leandro home, the argument continues unabated. "You don't know what you are," April's father has told her more than once. But she just keeps on telling him he doesn't know what time it is. ■

Examining the Reading

1. What does racial or ethnic identity mean to April Miller? According to Bernstein, by what standards does she define herself?

2. What does Bernstein mean by "the complicated reality" of the twenty-first century (paragraph 32)?

3. Explain the meaning of "claiming" as it is used in this essay.

4. What possible causes does Bernstein offer to explain why the teenagers developed such attitudes about their racial and ethnic identity?

5. Explain the meaning of each of the following words as it is used in the reading: *impermeable* (paragraph 7), *hybridization* (10), *connoted* (21), and *affectations* (30). Refer to your dictionary as needed.

Analyzing the Reading

1. What generalization does Bernstein make and support in this essay?

2. The writer uses the example involving April Miller in the introduction and conclusion. Do you find this strategy effective? Why or why not?

3. Evaluate Bernstein's use of illustration: Are the examples relevant and representative? Striking and dramatic? Does Bernstein include enough examples? Explain your responses.

4. *Identity* is an abstract term. How does Bernstein make this term real and understandable?

Reacting to the Reading: Discussion and Journal Writing

1. Discuss why you agree or disagree with this statement: Teenagers who establish their identities by copying members of racial or ethnic groups only strengthen unwanted stereotypes.

2. Have you observed teenagers claiming an ethnic or a racial identity? How do they look and behave? What seems to motivate them?

3. What factors most contribute to your sense of identity? Write a journal entry describing who you are and how you define yourself. Include examples.

POSSIBLE ANSWERS:
REACTING TO THE
READING

1. Responses will vary.
2. Responses will vary.
3. Responses will vary;
possible examples
include interests and
hobbies, sports
teams, and heroes the
student may identify
with.

ILLUSTRATION COMBINED WITH OTHER PATTERNS

As you read the following essay by Gloria Naylor, notice how she uses examples along with other patterns of development to support her main point.

The Meanings of a Word
Gloria Naylor

Gloria Naylor is a writer of fiction and nonfiction. Her novels include The Women of Brewster Place *(1982),* Linden Hills *(1985), and* Bailey's Café *(1992). She has a master's degree from Yale in African American literature and has taught writing workshops at George Washington University, New York University, and Cornell University, among others. This essay was originally published in the* New York Times, *in 1986. As you read the selection, look for and highlight the examples Naylor uses to support her thesis.*

PREREADING
QUESTION

How are the meanings
of a word determined?

Language is the subject. It is the written form with which I've managed to keep the wolf away from the door and, in diaries, to keep my sanity. In spite of this, I consider the written word inferior to the spoken, and much of the frustration experienced by novelists is the awareness that whatever we manage to capture in even the most transcendent passages falls far short of the richness of life. Dialogue achieves its power in the dynamics of a fleeting moment of sight, sound, smell, and touch.

I'm not going to enter the debate here about whether it is language that shapes reality or vice versa. That battle is doomed to be waged whenever we seek intermittent reprieve from the chicken and egg dispute. I will simply take the position that the spoken word, like the written word, amounts to a nonsensical arrangement of sounds or letters without a consensus that assigns "meaning." And building from the meanings of what we hear, we order reality. Words themselves are innocuous; it is the consensus that gives them true power.

3   I remember the first time I heard the word *nigger*. In my third-grade class, our math tests were being passed down the rows, and as I handed the papers to a little boy in back of me, I remarked that once again he had received a much lower mark than I did. He snatched his test from me and spit out that word. Had he called me a nymphomaniac or a necrophiliac, I couldn't have been more puzzled. I didn't know what a nigger was, but I knew that whatever it meant, it was something he shouldn't have called me. This was verified when I raised my hand, and in a loud voice repeated what he had said and watched the teacher scold him for using a "bad" word. I was later to go home and ask the inevitable question that every black parent must face — "Mommy, what does *nigger* mean?"

4   And what exactly did it mean? Thinking back, I realize that this could not have been the first time the word was used in my presence. I was part of a large extended family that had migrated from the rural South after World War II and formed a close-knit network that gravitated around my maternal grandparents. Their ground-floor apartment in one of the buildings they owned in Harlem was a weekend mecca for my immediate family, along with countless aunts, uncles, and cousins who brought along assorted friends. It was a bustling and open house with assorted neighbors and tenants popping in and out to exchange bits of gossip, pick up an old quarrel, or referee the ongoing checkers game in which my grandmother cheated shamelessly. They were all there to let down their hair and put up their feet after a week of labor in the factories, laundries, and shipyards of New York.

5   Amid the clamor, which could reach deafening proportions — two or three conversations going on simultaneously, punctuated by the sound of a baby's crying somewhere in the back rooms or out on the street — there was still a rigid set of rules about what was said and how. Older children were sent out of the living room when it was time to get into the juicy details about "you-know-who" up on the third floor who had gone and gotten herself "p-r-e-g-n-a-n-t!" But my parents, knowing that I could spell well beyond my years, always demanded that I follow the others out to play. Beyond sexual misconduct and death, everything else was considered harmless for our young ears. And so among the anecdotes of the triumphs and disappointments in the various workings of their lives, the word *nigger* was used in my presence, but it was set within contexts and inflections that caused it to register in my mind as something else.

6   In the singular, the word was always applied to a man who had distinguished himself in some situation that brought their approval for his strength, intelligence, or drive.

"Did Johnny *really* do that?"   7

"I'm telling you, that nigger pulled in $6,000 of overtime last   8
year. Said he got enough for a down payment on a house."

When used with a possessive adjective by a woman — "my nigger"   9
— it became a term of endearment for her husband or boyfriend. But
it could be more than just a term applied to a man. In their mouths
it became the pure essence of manhood — a disembodied force that
channeled their past history of struggle and present survival against
the odds into a victorious statement of being: "Yeah, that old foreman found out quick enough — you don't mess with a nigger."

In the plural, it became a description of some group within the   10
community that had overstepped the bounds of decency as my family defined it. Parents who neglected their children, a drunken couple
who fought in public, people who simply refused to look for work,
those with excessively dirty mouths or unkempt households were all
"trifling niggers." This particular circle could forgive hard times,
unemployment, the occasional bout of depression — they had gone
through all of that themselves — but the unforgivable sin was a lack
of self-respect.

A woman could never be a "nigger" in the singular, with its con-   11
notation of confirming worth. The noun *girl* was its closest equivalent in that sense, but only when used in direct address and regardless
of the gender doing the addressing. *Girl* was a token of respect for a
woman. The one-syllable word was drawn out to sound like three in
recognition of the extra ounce of wit, nerve, or daring that the
woman had shown in the situation under discussion.

"G-i-r-l, stop. You mean you said that to his face?"   12

But if the word was used in a third-person reference or shortened   13
so that it almost snapped out of the mouth, it always involved some
element of communal disapproval. And age became an important
factor in these exchanges. It was only between individuals of the same
generation, or from any older person to a younger (but never the
other way around), that *girl* would be considered a compliment.

I don't agree with the argument that use of the word *nigger* at this   14
social stratum of the black community was an internalization of
racism. The dynamics were the exact opposite: the people in my
grandmother's living room took a word that whites used to signify
worthlessness or degradation and rendered it impotent. Gathering
there together, they transformed *nigger* to signify the varied and complex human beings they knew themselves to be. If the word was to
disappear totally from the mouths of even the most liberal of white
society, no one in that room was naive enough to believe it would disappear from white minds. Meeting the word head-on, they proved it
had absolutely nothing to do with the way they were determined to
live their lives.

POSSIBLE ANSWERS:
EXAMINING THE
READING (p. 322)

1. Words spoken within
the context of real life
"achieve . . . power in
the dynamics of a
fleeting moment of
sight, sound, smell,
and touch" (para-
graph 1).

2. A word can have radi-
cally different conno-
tations depending on
how and by whom it
is used.

3. She learns that a
word her family treats
as a compliment or a
pejorative (depending
on its context) is
always a pejorative
when spoken by a
white person.

4. Compliment: for
"strength, intelligence,
or drive" (6); "term of
endearment for her
husband or boyfriend"
(9); represents the
"essence of man-
hood" (9). Pejorative:
"a description of
some group . . . that
had overstepped the
bounds of decency
. . ." (10).

5. *Transcendent:* a pas-
sage so eloquent that
it rises above others;
intermittent: occa-
sional; *consensus:* a
general agreement
among most people;
communal: shared by
the community, col-
lective; *internalization:*
accepting a social
concept as one's own.

POSSIBLE ANSWERS:
ANALYZING THE
READING

1. Thesis: The word *nig-ger* is in itself harm-less; the context in which it is used gives it a positive or nega-tive meaning.
2. Comparison and con-trast (e.g., the word's use by her family ver-sus her classmate, the use of *girl* versus *nigger*) and narration (e.g., the story of the first time she hears the word used in a racist way).
3. It is effective because it illustrates Naylor's bewilderment and sets the stage for the other examples that follow. Readers sense and share her surprise and hurt feelings.
4. Responses will vary.
5. The definitions of *girl* reinforce and explain the positive meanings of *nigger* within the black community.

POSSIBLE ANSWERS:
REACTING TO THE
READING

1. Possible reason for agreeing: Spoken lan-guage is accompanied by facial expressions and gestures that add meaning. Possible rea-sons for disagreeing: Written language is more permanent; writers can think through and refine what they want to say.
2. Where do babies come from? What happens to people after death?
3. Responses will vary.

15   So there must have been dozens of times that *nigger* was spoken in front of me before I reached the third grade. But I didn't "hear" it until it was said by a small pair of lips that had already learned it could be a way to humiliate me. That was the word I went home and asked my mother about. And since she knew that I had to grow up in America, she took me in her lap and explained. ■

Examining the Reading

1. Why does Naylor think the spoken word is more powerful than the written word?
2. What does Naylor mean by "the spoken word, like the written word, amounts to a nonsensical arrangement of sounds or letters without a consensus that assigns 'meaning'" (paragraph 2)?
3. What does Naylor learn as a third grader from the incident in which a class-mate calls her "nigger"?
4. Explain the meanings of the word *nigger* to Naylor as a child.
5. Explain the meaning of each of the following words as it is used in the read-ing: *transcendent* (paragraph 1), *intermittent* (2), *consensus* (2), *communal* (13), and *internalization* (14).

Analyzing the Reading

1. Restate Naylor's thesis in your own words.
2. In addition to illustration, what other patterns of development does the writer use to support her thesis? Give examples from the reading.
3. Naylor builds her essay around an extended example: the time her third-grade classmate called her "nigger." Is this example effective? Why or why not? What is its emotional impact?
4. The essay begins with an abstract discussion of the functions of language and moves to a concrete example. Evaluate the effectiveness of Naylor's introduction.
5. Why does Naylor give definitions of the word *girl*? What function do they serve?

Reacting to the Reading: Discussion and Journal Writing

1. Is spoken language more powerful than written language? Explain why you agree or disagree with Naylor's views.
2. What other questions do parents inevitably face?
3. Write a journal entry identifying a word that has both positive and negative meanings, depending on how, by whom, or where it is used.

APPLYING YOUR SKILLS: ADDITIONAL ESSAY ASSIGNMENTS

Write an illustration essay on one of the following topics, using what you learned about illustration in this chapter. Depending on the topic you choose, you may need to conduct library or Internet research.

For more on locating and documenting sources, see Chapters 19 and 20.

To Express Your Ideas

1. Explain what you consider to be the three most important qualities of a college instructor, in an article for the campus newspaper. Support your opinion with vivid examples from your own experience.

2. Explain to a general audience the importance or role of grandparents within a family, citing examples from your family.

To Inform Your Reader

3. In "Rambos of the Road," Martin Gottfried explains the concept of "auto macho," also known as "road rage," using examples from his own experience. Explain the concept *peer pressure*, using examples from your experience.

4. Describe to an audience of college students the qualities or achievements you think should be emphasized during job interviews. Give examples that show why the qualities or achievements you choose are important to potential employers.

5. In "The Meanings of a Word," Gloria Naylor describes an incident of racial discrimination from her childhood. Explain to a general audience your views on whether progress has been made in curbing racial discrimination in the United States. Give examples from your own and others' experience.

To Persuade Your Reader

6. Argue for or against an increased emphasis on physical education within public schools. Your audience is members of your local school board.

7. Argue for or against the establishment of a neighborhood watch group in your hometown, in a letter to the editor for the local newspaper.

Cases Using Illustration

8. Prepare the oral presentation you will give to your local town board in order to convince the board to lower the speed limit on your street. Use examples as well as other types of evidence.

9. You are the director of a day-care center. Write a letter to parents whose three-year-old children will attend your day-care center this year, explaining how the parents can prepare their children for the day-care experience. Support your advice with brief but relevant examples.

TEACHING TIP

Suggest that students use at least one prewriting strategy—drawing a graphic organizer, freewriting, brainstorming, questioning, writing assertions—to get started. Remind students to consult the learning style options (p. 302 and the revision flowchart (p. 307).

Loading a Camera

Chapter 12

Process Analysis: Explaining How Something Works or Is Done

The diagram on the opposite page shows how to load film into a camera. Suppose you are a technical writer and have been asked to write the instructions to accompany the diagram.

Writing Quick Start

Write a brief paragraph describing how to load film into the camera as shown in the diagram. Your audience consists of people who have just purchased the camera.

TEACHING TIP

• Ask students to think about a time they followed instructions for assembling a new purchase and whether they found them confusing or inaccurate. How could the instructions have been improved?

• *Audience* is key here, since the subject and purpose are givens. Emphasize that the task is to make it clear to the average consumer how to load the film.

WRITING A PROCESS ANALYSIS

In order to describe the steps involved in loading a camera, you had to explain a process. You use process analysis whenever you explain how something is done or how it works—how to make lasagna, how to change a flat tire, or how a bill becomes law. This chapter will show you how to write a well-organized, easy-to-understand process analysis essay and how to incorporate process analysis into essays that use other patterns of development.

WHAT IS PROCESS ANALYSIS?

A **process analysis** explains in step-by-step fashion how something works or how something is done or made. Process analyses provide people with practical infor-mation: directions for assembling equipment, instructions for registering for classes, and directions for using a search engine on the World Wide Web. Some-times, process analyses inform people about things that affect their lives, such as an explanation of how a medication works or how a child learns to read. Whatever the purpose, the information in a process analysis must be accurate, clear, and easy to follow.

Process analysis is a common type of writing in college and on the job (see the accompanying box for a few examples).

Whether you are writing for a college course or for your colleagues at work, two types of writing situations call for the use of process analysis:

• To explain how something works or is done to readers *who want or need to per-form the process*

• To explain how something works or is done to readers *who want to understand the process but not actually perform it*

SCENES FROM COLLEGE AND THE WORKPLACE

• For a *child development* course, you are assigned to visit a day-care center, choose one child–teacher confrontation, and explain how the teacher resolved the conflict.

• As part of a *chemistry* lab report, you are asked to summarize the proce-dure you followed in preparing a solution or conducting an experiment.

• While working as an *engineer* at a water treatment plant, you are asked by your supervisor to write a description of how the city's drinking water is tested and treated for contamination.

The first type, a *how-to essay*, may explain how to teach a child the alphabet, for example. Your primary purpose is to present the steps in the process clearly and completely so that your readers can perform the task you describe. For the second type of process analysis, a *how-it-works essay*, you might explain how a popular radio talk show screens its callers. Your purpose is to present a clear, straightforward description of the steps in the process so that your readers can fully understand it. At times, you may read or write essays that contain elements of both types of process analysis. In writing about how a car alarm system works, for example, you might find it necessary to explain how to activate and deactivate the system.

The following essay exemplifies the first type of process analysis: a how-to essay.

Fender Benders: Legal Do's and Don'ts
Armond D. Budish

Armond D. Budish is an attorney and a consumer-law journalist. He is also the author of How to Beat Catastrophic Costs of Nursing Home Care *(1989) and writes columns for the* Cleveland Plain Dealer *and* Family Circle, *from which the following essay, published in 1994, is excerpted. The article is written in journalistic style, using headings and numbered lists, and it does not have a conclusion. As you read, highlight the thesis and notice the trouble spots in the process that Budish anticipates for his readers.*

The car ahead of you stops suddenly. You hit the brakes, but you just can't stop in time. Your front bumper meets the rear end of the other car. *Ouch!*   1

There doesn't seem to be any damage, and it must be your lucky day because the driver you hit agrees that it's not worth hassling with insurance claims and risking a premium increase. So after exchanging addresses, you go your separate ways.   2

Imagine your surprise when you open the mail a few weeks later only to discover a letter from your "victim's" lawyer demanding $10,000 to cover car repairs, pain and suffering. Apparently the agreeable gentleman decided to disagree, then went ahead and filed a police report blaming you for the incident and for his damages.   3

When automobiles meet by accident, do you know how to respond? Here are 10 practical tips that can help you avoid costly legal and insurance hassles.   4

1. STOP! IT'S THE LAW.

No matter how serious or minor the accident, stop immediately. If possible, don't move your car—especially if someone has been   5 injured. Leaving the cars as they were when the accident occurred helps the police determine what happened. Of course, if your car is blocking traffic or will cause another accident where it is, then move it to the nearest safe location.

6   For every rule there are exceptions, though. If, for example, you are rear-ended at night in an unsafe area, it's wisest to keep on going and notify the police later. There have been cases in which people were robbed or assaulted when they got out of their cars.

2. Zip Loose Lips.

7   Watch what you say after an accident. Although this may sound harsh, even an innocent "I'm sorry" could later be construed as an admission of fault. Also be sure not to accuse the other driver of causing the accident. Since you don't know how a stranger will react to your remarks, you run the risk of making a bad situation worse.

8   Remember, you are not the judge or jury; it's not up to you to decide who is or is not at fault. Even if you think you caused the accident, you might be wrong. For example: Assume you were driving 15 miles over the speed limit. What you probably were not aware of is that the other driver's blood-alcohol level exceeded the legal limits, so he was at least equally at fault.

3. Provide Required Information.

9   If you are involved in an accident, you are required in most states to give your name, address and car registration number to any person injured in the accident; the owner, driver or passenger in any car that was damaged in the accident; a police officer on the scene. If you don't own the car (say it belongs to a friend or your parents), you should provide the name and address of the owner.

10   You must produce this information even if there are no apparent injuries or damages and even if you didn't cause the accident. Most states don't require you to provide the name of your insurance company, although it's usually a good idea to do so. However, *don't* discuss the amount of your coverage—that might inspire the other person to "realize" his injuries are more serious than he originally thought.

11   What should you do if you hit a parked car and the owner is not around? The law requires you to leave a note with your name, and the other identifying information previously mentioned, in a secure place on the car (such as under the windshield wiper).

4. GET REQUIRED INFORMATION.

You should obtain from the others involved in the accident the   12
same information that you provide them with. However, if the other
driver refuses to cooperate, at least get the license number and the
make and model of the car to help police track down the owner.

5. CALL THE POLICE.

It's obvious that if it's a serious accident in which someone is   13
injured, the police should be called immediately. That's both the law
and common sense. But what if the accident seems minor? Say you're
stopped, [and] another car taps you in the rear. If it's absolutely clear
to both drivers that there is no damage or injury, you each can go
your merry way. But that's the exception.

Normally, you should call the police to substantiate what   14
occurred. In most cities police officers will come to the scene, even
for minor accidents, but if they won't, you and the other driver
should go to the station (of the city where the accident occurred) to
file a report. Ask to have an officer check out both cars.

If you are not at fault, be wary of accepting the other driver's sug-   15
gestion that you leave the police out of it and arrange a private settlement. When you submit your $500 car-repair estimate several
weeks later, you could discover that the other driver has developed
"amnesia" and denies being anywhere near the accident. If the police
weren't present on the scene, you may not have a legal leg to stand on.

Even if you *are* at fault, it's a good idea to involve the police. Why?   16
Because a police officer will note the extent of the other driver's damages in his or her report, limiting your liability. Without police presence the other driver can easily inflate the amount of the damages.

6. IDENTIFY WITNESSES.

Get the names and addresses of any witnesses, in case there's a   17
legal battle some time in the future. Ask bystanders or other
motorists who stop whether they saw the accident; if they answer
"yes," get their identifying information. It is also helpful to note the
names and badge numbers of all police officers on the scene.

7. GO TO THE HOSPITAL.

If there's a chance that you've been injured, go directly to a hos-   18
pital emergency room or to your doctor. The longer you wait, the

more you may jeopardize your health and the more difficult it may be to get reimbursed for your injuries if they turn out to be serious.

8. FILE A REPORT.

19   Every driver who is involved in an automobile incident in which injuries occur must fill out an accident report. Even if the property damage is only in the range of $200 to $1,000, most states require that an accident report be filed. You must do this fairly quickly, usually in 1 to 30 days. Forms may be obtained and filed with the local motor vehicle department or police station in the city where the accident occurred.

9. CONSIDER FILING AN INSURANCE CLAIM.

20   Talk with your insurance agent as soon as possible after an accident. He or she can help you decide if you should file an insurance claim or pay out of your own pocket.

21   For example, let's say you caused an accident and the damages totaled $800. You carry a $250 deductible, leaving you with a possible $550 insurance claim. If you do submit a claim, your insurance rates are likely to go up, an increase that will probably continue for about three years. You should compare that figure to the $550 claim to determine whether to file a claim or to pay the cost yourself. (Also keep in mind that multiple claims sometimes make it harder to renew your coverage.)

10. DON'T BE TOO QUICK TO ACCEPT A SETTLEMENT.

22   If the other driver is at fault and there's any chance you've been injured, don't rush to accept a settlement from that person's insurance company. You may not know the extent of your injuries for some time, and once you accept a settlement, it's difficult to get an "upgrade." Before settling, consult with a lawyer who handles personal injury cases.

23   When you *haven't* been injured and you receive a fair offer to cover the damage to your car, you can go ahead and accept it.   ■

Characteristics of Process Analysis Essays

A process analysis essay should include everything your reader needs to know in order to understand or perform the process. In addition to presenting an explicit thesis, the essay should provide a clear, step-by-step description of the process, define key terms, give any necessary background information, describe any equipment needed to perform the process, supply an adequate amount of detail, and, for a how-to essay, anticipate and offer help with potential problems.

Process Analysis Usually Includes an Explicit Thesis Statement

A process analysis usually contains a clear thesis that identifies the process to be discussed and suggests the writer's attitude or approach toward it. The thesis statement tells why the process is important or useful to the reader. In "Fender Benders: Legal Do's and Don'ts," for instance, Budish offers a clear-cut reason for why the process following an automobile accident is important: The advice can help the driver avoid costly legal and insurance hassles.

Here are two examples of thesis statements for how-to process analyses that suggest the usefulness or importance of the process.

> Switching to a low-fat diet, a recent nutritional trend, can improve weight control dramatically.

> By carefully preparing for a vacation in a foreign country, you can save time and prevent hassles.

In a how-it-works essay, the writer either reveals why the information is worth knowing or makes an assertion about the nature of the process itself. Here are two examples of thesis statements for how-it-works essays.

> Although understanding the grieving process will not make the grief that you experience after the death of a loved one any easier, it is comforting to know that your experiences are normal.

> Advertisers often appeal to the emotions of the audience for whom a product is targeted; some of these appeals may be unethical.

Process Analysis Is Organized Chronologically

The steps or events in a process analysis are usually organized in chronological order; that is, the order in which the steps are normally completed. Think of process analysis as being organized by the clock or calendar. A process essay presents what happens first in time, then what happens next in time, and so forth. In "Fender Benders: Legal Do's and Don'ts," Budish uses a numbered list to show the chronological organization of his advice to drivers involved in an accident. For essays that explain lengthy processes, the steps may be grouped into categories to make the process easier to understand.

On occasion, the steps of a process may not have to occur in any particular order. For example, in an essay on how to resolve a dispute between two co-workers, the recommended actions may not have an exact order; instead, the order may depend on the nature of the dispute. In this situation, some logical progression of recommended actions should be used, such as starting with informal or simple steps and progressing to more formal or complex ones.

For more on defining terms, see Chapter 15, p. 464.

EXERCISE 12.1

Choose one of the following processes. It should be one you are familiar with and are able to explain to others. Draft a working thesis statement and a chronological list of the steps or stages of the process.

1. Learning how to use a computer program
2. Studying for an exam
3. Performing a task at work
4. How a machine operates
5. How an application process works (for example, applying for college, a job, or a credit card)

Process Analysis Defines Technical Terms

In most cases, you can assume your audience is not familiar with the technical terms associated with the process. Therefore, in a process essay, be sure to define specialized terms for your readers. In describing how cardiopulmonary resuscitation (CPR) works, for instance, you would need to explain the meanings of such terms as *airway*, *sternum*, and *cardiac compression*.

EXERCISE 12.2

Choose one of the following processes. It should be one you are familiar with and are able to explain to others. For the process you choose, list the technical terms and definitions you would need to include to explain the process.

1. How to perform a task at home or at work (such as changing the oil in a car or taking notes during a court hearing).
2. How a piece of equipment or a machine works (such as a treadmill or a lawn mower).
3. How to repair an object (such as re-stringing a tennis racket or a violin bow).

Process Analysis Provides Background Information

In some process analysis essays, readers may need background information to understand the process. For example, in an explanation of how CPR works, general readers might need background information on how the heart functions before they could understand how pressing down on a person's breastbone propels blood into the arteries. In "Fender Benders: Legal Do's and Don'ts," Budish opens with a scenario that illustrates why his essay is important to drivers involved in accidents.

Process Analysis Describes Necessary Equipment

When special equipment is needed to perform or understand the process, you should describe the equipment for readers. If necessary, you should also explain where to obtain it. For example, in an essay explaining how to use a computer system to readers unfamiliar with computers, you would need to describe the keyboard, monitor, printer, and so forth.

EXERCISE 12.3

For the process you selected in Exercise 12.2 (p. 332), consider what background information and equipment are needed to understand and perform the process.

Process Analysis Provides an Appropriate Level of Detail

In deciding the level of detail to include in a process analysis essay, you should be careful not to overwhelm your readers with too many technical details. An essay about how to perform CPR written by and for physicians would be highly technical, but it would be less technical if written for paramedics, and even less so if written for a friend who is considering whether to enroll in a CPR course. At the same time, you would need to include enough detail to show your readers how to perform the steps of the CPR process.

Budish, in "Fender Benders: Legal Do's and Don'ts," writing for a general audience, is careful to provide details about legal implications because he assumes his audience is unfamiliar with legal matters.

Keep in mind that when you write essays explaining technical or scientific processes, you can use sensory details and figures of speech to make your writing lively and interesting. Rather than giving dry technical details, try using descriptive language.

For a process involving many complex steps or an assortment of highly specialized equipment, consider using a drawing or schematic diagram to help your readers visualize the steps they need to follow or details you need to provide. For example, in an essay explaining how to detect a wiring problem in an electric stove, you might include a diagram of the stove's circuitry.

Process Analysis Anticipates Trouble Spots and Offers Solutions

Especially in a how-to essay, you need to anticipate potential trouble spots or areas of confusion and offer advice to the reader on how to avoid or resolve them. In an essay explaining how to apply for a mortgage, for instance, you would need to anticipate the difficulty of finding a co-signer and give advice on how to resolve that problem.

A how-to process analysis essay should also warn readers of any difficult, complicated, or critical steps, encouraging them to pay special attention to a difficult step or to take extra care in performing a critical one. In "Fender Benders: Legal Do's and Don'ts," Budish warns readers about the possible results of not calling the police to the scene of an accident. You should also warn readers of any steps in the process that they may have trouble completing. For instance, in a how-to essay on hanging wallpaper, you would warn readers about the difficulties of handling lengthy sheets of wallpaper and perhaps suggest folding the sheets to make them easier to work with.

TEACHING TIP: COLLABORATIVE WRITING

Pair students for this exercise. Try to include a concrete and an abstract thinker in each pair. Have students help one another determine what background information and equipment are needed to describe and perform the process.

POSSIBLE ANSWERS

Answers will vary.

TEACHING TIP: LEARNING STYLES

(10–15 minutes) For the process students chose in Exercise 12.2, have them work independently on generating details. Spatial and concrete learners can make a drawing or schematic diagram, while verbal and abstract learners can create relevant similes or metaphors.

EXERCISE 12.4

For one of the processes listed in Exercise 12.1 or Exercise 12.2 (p. 332), identify potential trouble spots in the process and describe how to avoid or resolve them.

Visualizing a Process Analysis Essay: A Graphic Organizer

The graphic organizer in Figure 12.1 shows the basic organization of a process analysis essay. When your primary purpose is to explain a process, you should follow this standard format, including a title, an introduction, body paragraphs, and a conclusion. Your introduction should include any necessary background information and present your thesis statement. Your body paragraphs should explain the steps of the process in chronological order. Your conclusion should draw the essay to a satisfying close and refer back to the thesis.

FIGURE 12.1
GRAPHIC ORGANIZER FOR A PROCESS ANALYSIS ESSAY

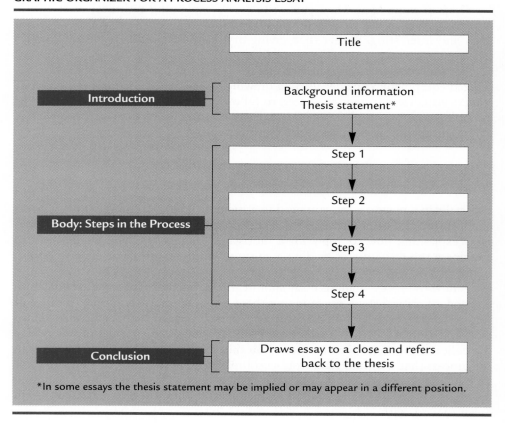

When you incorporate process analysis into an essay using one or more other patterns of development, briefly introduce the process and then move directly to the steps involved. If the process is complex, you may want to add a brief summary of it before the transition back to the main topic of the essay.

Read the following how-it-works essay, "Fertile Minds," and then study the graphic organizer for it (see Figure 12.2).

Fertile Minds
J. Madeline Nash

J. Madeline Nash, a researcher, a freelance writer, and a correspondent for Time, *a popular weekly newsmagazine, has written numerous articles and essays on science-related topics. "Fertile Minds" is excerpted from an article that first appeared in a 1997 issue of* Time. *In it, Nash explains how an infant's brain responds to environmental stimuli and how a child's future may be shaped by those stimuli. As you read the selection, highlight the thesis and the steps of the process. Notice, too, how Nash uses sensory details and figures of speech to capture her readers' interest and explain her subject.*

PREREADING QUESTION

Whose minds are "fertile," and in what way?

TEACHING TIP: POSTREADING DISCUSSION

After students read the essay, have them discuss

• other developmental processes (e.g., learning to walk).

• how Nash presents her technical topic to a general audience. Point out definitions of technical terms (e.g., "neurons" in paragraph 2) and analogies ("like teenagers with telephones" in paragraph 1).

• Nash's conclusion and how it is supported in the essay.

Rat-a-tat-tat. Rat-a-tat-tat. Rat-a-tat-tat. If scientists could eavesdrop on the brain of a human embryo 10, maybe 12 weeks after conception, they would hear an astonishing racket. Inside the womb, long before light first strikes the retina of the eye or the earliest dreamy images flicker through the cortex, nerve cells in the developing brain crackle with purposeful activity. Like teenagers with telephones, cells in one neighborhood of the brain are calling friends in another, and these cells are calling their friends, and they keep calling one another over and over again, "almost," says neurobiologist Carla Shatz of the University of California, Berkeley, "as if they were autodialing."

But these neurons—as the long, wiry cells that carry electrical messages through the nervous system and the brain are called—are not transmitting signals in scattershot fashion. That would produce a featureless static, the sort of noise picked up by a radio tuned between stations. On the contrary, evidence is growing that the staccato bursts of electricity that form those distinctive rat-a-tat-tats arise from coordinated waves of neural activity, and that those pulsing waves, like currents shifting sand on the ocean floor, actually change the shape of the brain, carving mental circuits into patterns that over time will enable the newborn infant to perceive a father's voice, a mother's touch, a shiny mobile twirling over the crib.

3   Of all the discoveries that have poured out of neuroscience labs in recent years, the finding that the electrical activity of brain cells changes the physical structure of the brain is perhaps the most breathtaking. For the rhythmic firing of neurons is no longer assumed to be a by-product of building the brain but essential to the process, and it begins, scientists have established, well before birth. A brain is not a computer. Nature does not cobble it together, then turn it on. No, the brain begins working long before it is finished. And the same processes that wire the brain before birth, neuroscientists are finding, also drive the explosion of learning that occurs immediately afterward.

4   During the first years of life, the brain undergoes a series of extraordinary changes. Starting shortly after birth, a baby's brain, in a display of biological exuberance, produces trillions more connections between neurons than it can possibly use. Then, through a process that resembles Darwinian competition, the brain eliminates connections, or synapses, that are seldom or never used. The excess synapses in a child's brain undergo a draconian pruning, starting around the age of 10 or earlier, leaving behind a mind whose patterns of emotion and thought are, for better or worse, unique.

5   "There is a time scale to brain development, and the most important year is the first," notes Frank Newman, president of the Education Commission of the States. By the age of three, a child who is neglected or abused bears marks that, if not indelible, are exceedingly difficult to erase.

6   But the new research offers hope as well. Scientists have found that the brain during the first years of life is so malleable that very young children who suffer strokes or injuries that wipe out an entire hemisphere can still mature into highly functional adults. Moreover, it is becoming increasingly clear that well-designed preschool programs can help many children overcome glaring deficits in their home environment. With appropriate therapy, say researchers, even serious disorders like dyslexia may be treatable. While inherited problems may place certain children at greater risk than others, says Dr. Harry Chugani, a pediatric neurologist at Wayne State University in Detroit, that is no excuse for ignoring the environment's power to remodel the brain. "We may not do much to change what happens before birth, but we can change what happens after a baby is born," he observes.

7   When a baby is born, it can see and hear and smell and respond to touch, but only dimly. The brain stem, a primitive region that con-

trols vital functions like heartbeat and breathing, has completed its wiring. Elsewhere the connections between neurons are wispy and weak. But over the first few months of life, the brain's higher centers explode with new synapses. And as dendrites and axons swell with buds and branches like trees in spring, metabolism soars. By the age of two, a child's brain contains twice as many synapses and consumes twice as much energy as the brain of a normal adult.

University of Chicago pediatric neurologist Dr. Peter Hutten-   8
locher has chronicled this extraordinary epoch in brain development by autopsying the brains of infants and young children who have died unexpectedly. The number of synapses in one layer of the visual cortex, Huttenlocher reports, rises from around 2,500 per neuron at birth to as many as 18,000 about six months later. Other regions of the cortex score similarly spectacular increases but on slightly different schedules. And while these microscopic connections between nerve fibers continue to form throughout life, they reach their highest average densities (15,000 synapses per neuron) at around the age of two and remain at that level until the age of 10 or 11.

This profusion of connections lends the growing brain excep-   9
tional flexibility and resilience. Consider the case of 13-year-old Brandi Binder, who developed such severe epilepsy that surgeons at UCLA had to remove the entire right side of her cortex when she was six. Binder lost virtually all the control she had established over muscles on the left side of her body, the side controlled by the right side of the brain. Yet today, after years of therapy ranging from leg lifts to math and music drills, Binder is an A student at the Holmes Middle School in Colorado Springs, Colorado. She loves music, math and art—skills usually associated with the right half of the brain. And while Binder's recuperation is not 100%—for example, she has never regained the use of her left arm—it comes close. Says UCLA pediatric neurologist Dr. Donald Shields: "If there's a way to compensate, the developing brain will find it."

What wires a child's brain, say neuroscientists—or rewires it after   10
physical trauma—is repeated experience. Each time a baby tries to touch a tantalizing object or gazes intently at a face or listens to a lullaby, tiny bursts of electricity shoot through the brain, knitting neurons into circuits as well defined as those etched onto silicon chips. The results are those behavioral mileposts that never cease to delight and awe parents. Around the age of two months, for example, the motor-control centers of the brain develop to the point that infants can suddenly reach out and grab a nearby object. Around the age of four months, the cortex begins to refine the connections needed for depth perception and binocular vision. And around the

age of 12 months, the speech centers of the brain are poised to produce what is perhaps the most magical moment of childhood: the first word that marks the flowering of language.

11   Indeed, parents are the brain's first and most important teachers. Among other things, they appear to help babies learn by adopting the rhythmic, high-pitched speaking style known as Parentese. When speaking to babies, Stanford University psychologist Anne Fernald has found, mothers and fathers from many cultures change their speech patterns in the same peculiar ways. "They put their faces very close to the child," she reports. "They use shorter utterances, and they speak in an unusually melodious fashion." The heart rate of infants increases while listening to Parentese, even Parentese delivered in a foreign language. Moreover, Fernald says, Parentese appears to hasten the process of connecting words to the objects they denote. Twelve-month-olds, directed to "look at the ball" in Parentese, direct their eyes to the correct picture more frequently than when the instruction is delivered in normal English.

12   In some ways the exaggerated, vowel-rich sounds of Parentese appear to resemble the choice morsels fed to hatchlings by adult birds. The University of Washington's Patricia Kuhl and her colleagues have conditioned dozens of newborns to turn their heads when they detect the *ee* sound emitted by American parents, vs. the *eu* favored by doting Swedes. Very young babies, says Kuhl, invariably perceive slight variations in pronunciation as totally different sounds. But by the age of six months, American babies no longer react when they hear variants of *ee,* and Swedish babies have become impervious to differences in *eu.* "It's as though their brains have formed little magnets," says Kuhl, "and all the sounds in the vicinity are swept in."

13   Rat-a-tat-tat. Rat-a-tat-tat. Rat-a-tat-tat. Just last week, in the U.S. alone, some 77,000 newborns began the miraculous process of wiring their brains for a lifetime of learning. If parents and policymakers don't pay attention to the conditions under which this delicate process takes place, we will all suffer the consequences — starting around the year 2010. ∎

FIGURE 12.2
GRAPHIC ORGANIZER FOR "FERTILE MINDS"

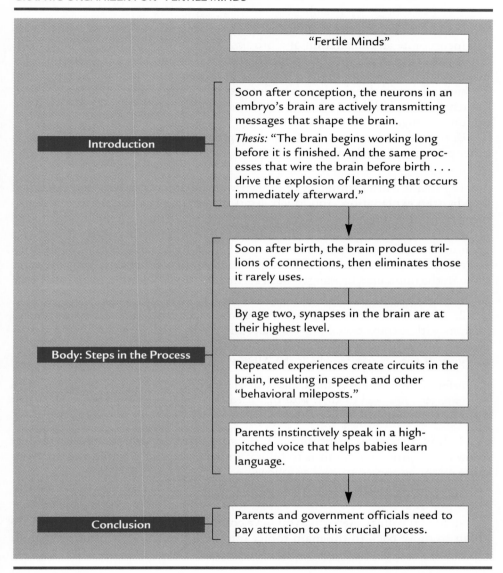

EXERCISE 12.5

Draw a graphic organizer for "Fender Benders: Legal Do's and Don'ts" (pp. 327–30).

INTEGRATING PROCESS ANALYSIS INTO AN ESSAY

While some essays you write will focus solely on explaining a process, other essays will incorporate an explanation of a process into a discussion that relies on a different pattern of development, such as description or narration. Let's suppose, for instance, that you are writing a descriptive essay about an alcohol abuse program for high school students. Although description is your primary pattern of development, you decide to include a brief process analysis of how alcohol impairs mental functioning.

Use the following tips to incorporate process analysis into essays based on other patterns of development.

1. **Provide a brief summary or overview of the process rather than a detailed step-by-step explanation.** Too much detail will divert your readers from the primary focus of your essay. Consider explaining only the major steps in the process rather than every step in detail. In "Fender Benders," for example, Budish gives a great deal of information about what to do following a traffic accident, but if his essay were intended to describe the responsibilities of owning a car, only the steps given in the numbered headings would suffice; he would not need to go into detail about each step.

2. **Make it clear** *why* **the process analysis is included.** Introduce your process analysis with a transitional sentence alerting readers that it will follow and suggesting why it is included. For example, here is how you might introduce an overview of the process by which the AIDS virus is spread.

> Before considering *how* the dangers of contracting AIDS should be explained to teenagers, you need to know *what* they need to be told. Teenagers need to know that AIDS is transmitted by. . . .

3. **It is sometimes helpful to use the word** *process* **or** *procedure* **to let readers know that a process analysis is to follow.** In the preceding example, the final sentence might be revised to read as follows.

> Teenagers need to know that AIDS is transmitted by the following process.

4. **Signal your readers that you have completed the process analysis and are about to move back to the main topic.** You might conclude the process analysis of the way AIDS is transmitted with a summary statement.

> Above all, teenagers need to know that AIDS is transmitted through an exchange of bodily fluids.

In "For Man and Beast, Language of Love Shares Many Traits" on page 363, Daniel Goleman uses process analysis along with other patterns of development to explain an aspect of human behavior.

ADDITIONAL
RESOURCES

The writing process soft-
ware that accompanies
this text includes an
electronic Guided Writ-
ing Assignment for a
process analysis.

A GUIDED WRITING ASSIGNMENT

The following guide will help you write a process analysis essay. It may be a how-to or a how-it-works essay. Although you will focus on process analysis, you may need to integrate one or more other patterns of development in your essay. Depending on your learning style, you may choose different ways of gathering ideas or evaluating your first draft. This Guided Writing Assignment will provide you with alternatives.

The Assignment

Write a process analysis essay on one of the following topics or one that you choose on your own. Be sure the process you choose is one you know enough about to explain to others, or can learn about through observation or research. Your audience consists of readers who are unfamiliar with the process, including your classmates.

How-to Essay Topics

1. How to improve _____ (your study habits, your wardrobe, your batting average)

2. How to be a successful _____ (diver, parent, gardener)

3. How to make or buy _____ (an object for personal use or enjoyment)

4. How to prepare for _____ (a test, a job interview, an oral presentation)

How-It-Works Essay Topics

1. How your college _____ (spends tuition revenues, hires professors, raises money)

2. How _____ works (an answering machine, a generator, email, or a search engine)

3. How a decision is made to _____ (accept a student at a college, add or eliminate a local or state agency)

4. How _____ is put together (a quilt, a news broadcast, a football team, a Web site)

As you develop your process analysis essay, you will probably use narrative strategies, description (for example, to describe equipment or objects), or illustration (such as to show an example of part of the process).

*For more on narration,
description, and illustration, see Chapters 9–11.*

TEACHING TIP:
LEARNING STYLES

The process analysis essay gives students an opportunity to challenge their natural learning styles and learn new ways to think and write.

• *Topic choices:* Encourage pragmatic and abstract learners to try the creative learning approach of visualizing steps in how-to essays, creative learners to exercise their self-discipline by slowing down to set out detailed steps, and concrete learners to convey the importance of the "big picture" of a social process in a how-it-works essay.
• *Techniques:* Try grouping social learners together for group brainstorming, while allowing independent learners to work on their own for now. For other learners, suggest the following: Rational learners/questioning, spatial learners/drawing a diagram, verbal learners/freewriting, pragmatic learners/branching, creative learners/mapping or clustering.

COMPUTER HINT

Several prewriting techniques can be done with a word-processing program or composition software. Remind students who freewrite on a computer to try dimming the screen to filter out distractions.

Selecting a Process

The following guidelines will help you to select a process to write about. You may want to use one of the prewriting techniques in Chapter 4 to help you select a process to write about. Consider your learning style when you select a prewriting technique. You might try group brainstorming, questioning, or sketching a diagram of a potential process. Be sure to keep the following tips in mind.

• For a how-to essay, choose a process that you can visualize or actually perform as you write. Keep the object or equipment nearby for easy reference. In explaining how to scuba dive, for example, it may be helpful to have your scuba equipment in front of you.

• For a how-it-works essay, choose a topic about which you have background knowledge or for which you can find information. Unless you are experienced in woodworking, for example, do not try to explain how certain stains produce different effects on different kinds of wood.

• Choose a topic that is useful and of interest to your readers. Unless you can find a way to make an essay about how to do the laundry interesting, do not write about it.

ESSAY IN PROGRESS 1

Using the preceding suggestions, choose a process to write about from the list of essay topics on page 341, or choose a topic of your own.

Considering Your Purpose, Audience, and Point of View

Once you choose a process to write about, consider your purpose and audience as well as what your readers need to know about the process. How-to and how-it-works essays can be informative, persuasive, or both. Your aim is always to inform readers about the process; in addition, you may want to persuade them to try it (how-to), or that it is beneficial or should be changed (how-it-works) as well.

For this Guided Writing Assignment, your audience consists of general readers who are unfamiliar with the process, including your classmates. As you develop your essay, then, think about what your audience wants and needs to know about the process. Keep the following questions about your audience in mind.

1. What background information does my audience need?

2. What terms should I define?
3. What equipment should I describe?
4. How much detail does my audience need?
5. What trouble spots require special attention and explanation?

When considering your audience, you also need to think about point of view—that is, how you will address your readers. Writers of how-to essays commonly use the second person, addressing the reader directly as *you*. The second person point of view is informal and draws the reader in, as can be seen in Budish's essay earlier in the chapter. For how-it-works essays, the third person (*he, she, it*) is commonly used, as in Nash's essay.

For more on purpose, audience, and point of view, see Chapter 4, p. 73.

ESSAY IN PROGRESS 2

For the process you selected in Essay in Progress 1, use the preceding guidelines to decide on your purpose, consider the needs of your audience, and choose your point of view.

TEACHING TIP

Encourage all students to work independently on this activity in their journals.

Developing Your Thesis

Once you have chosen a process to write about and carefully considered your purpose, audience, and point of view, your next step is to develop a working thesis. As noted earlier, the thesis of a process analysis essay tells readers *why* the process is important, beneficial, or relevant to them—why they would want to know how to do something or why they need to know how something works or is made (see p. 331). In a how-to essay on jogging, for instance, your thesis might reveal why readers would find the activity beneficial.

For more on thesis statements, see Chapter 5, p. 97.

> Jogging, an excellent aerobic activity, provides both exercise and a chance for solitary reflection.

Considering your audience is especially important in developing a thesis for a process analysis, since what may be of interest or importance to one audience may be of little interest to another audience.

ESSAY IN PROGRESS 3

Write a working thesis statement that tells readers why the process you have chosen for your essay is important, beneficial, or relevant to them.

TEACHING TIP: COLLABORATIVE WRITING

(10 minutes) Encourage students to evaluate each other's theses. For multiple peer reviews, have students pass their draft theses to the student on the right for comments, and then to the student on the left for comments.

COMPUTER HINT (p. 343)

Encourage students to email their working theses and examples to each other, if networked computers are not available. Suggest that they review the characteristics of process analysis essays before preparing their responses.

> **Learning Style Options**

For more on prewriting strategies, see Chapter 4.

TEACHING TIP: LEARNING STYLES

1. For all learners, especially pragmatic and concrete learners
2. For verbal learners
3. For all learners, especially social and emotional learners
4. For all learners

For more on library and Internet research, see Chapter 19.

Listing the Steps and Gathering Details

Once you are satisfied with your working thesis statement, your next task is to list the steps in the process and to gather appropriate and interesting details. You will probably need to do additional prewriting at this point as well in order to generate ideas and details that will help you explain the process. Use the following suggestions.

1. On paper or on your computer, list the steps in the process as they occur to you, keeping these questions in mind.
   - What separate actions are involved?
   - What steps are obvious to me but may not be obvious to someone unfamiliar with the process?
   - What steps, if omitted, will lead to problems or failure?

2. Describe the process aloud into a tape recorder and then take notes as you play the recording back.

3. Discuss your process with classmates to see what kinds of details they would need to know about your topic.

4. Once you have a list of steps, do additional prewriting or research in the library or on the Internet to generate details. If you are explaining how to go hiking in the Grand Canyon, for example, you might include sensory details about the narrow, winding trails or the vibrant colors of the canyon walls. Of course, you should also add whatever details readers need to understand the process itself. Check the five questions on pages 342–43 to make sure you have sufficient detail.

ESSAY IN PROGRESS 4

Using the preceding guidelines, brainstorm a list of the steps in the process. Then add details that will help you explain the steps. If necessary, interview someone knowledgeable about the process or do library or Internet research to gather more details.

Evaluating Your Ideas and Thesis

Take a few minutes to evaluate the process you have chosen and determine whether your analysis of it is meaningful, worthwhile, and relevant to your audience. Start by rereading everything you have written with a critical eye. Highlight usable details; cross out any that seem unnecessary or repetitious. As you review your work, do not hesitate to add a step, a detail, a definition, or background information where it is needed.

For more on drafting an
essay, see Chapter 6.

TRYING OUT YOUR IDEAS ON OTHERS

Working in a group of two or three students, discuss your ideas and thesis for this chapter's assignment. Each writer should state his or her topic and thesis and describe the steps in the process. Then, as a group, evaluate each writer's work. The group should provide each writer with responses to the following questions.

1. How familiar are you with the process the writer has chosen?
2. Is the writer's explanation of the process detailed and complete?
3. What additional information do you need to understand or perform the process?
4. What unanswered questions do you have about the process?

ESSAY IN PROGRESS 5

Using the preceding suggestions and the feedback you have received from classmates, evaluate your thesis and your steps and decide whether you need to add details.

Organizing and Drafting

Once you have gathered enough details to explain the steps in the process, developed your thesis statement, and considered the advice of peer reviewers, you are ready to organize your ideas and draft your essay.

Organizing the Steps in the Process

For a process that involves fewer than ten steps, you can usually arrange the steps in chronological order, devoting one paragraph to each step. However, for a more complex process with ten or more steps, group the steps into related categories to avoid overwhelming your reader with a long list that may seem unmanageable or monotonous. To avoid these problems, divide the steps of a complex process into three or four major groups, devoting one paragraph to each group of steps.

Try moving steps around and experimenting with different groupings. Working on a computer will make it easy to rearrange your groupings, using the computer's cut-and-paste function. For an essay on how to run a successful garage sale, the steps might be organized into these main groups.

Group 1: Locating and collecting merchandise
Group 2: Advertising
Group 3: Pricing and setting up
Group 4: Conducting the sale

Then, below each main group you would list the steps related to it.

Group 1: Steps for Locating and Collecting Merchandise

1. Clean out closets, basement, and attic.
2. Offer to clear out the closets, attics, and basements of friends and relatives.
3. Pick up merchandise discarded at the town dump.

Usually you can devote one paragraph to each group of steps. A topic sentence introduces the group, and the rest of the paragraph explains the individual steps involved. For example, the body of the essay about the garage sale would devote a paragraph to group 1. That paragraph would include a topic sentence about locating and collecting merchandise and a discussion of the three steps related to this task. The next paragraph would address group 2 on advertising, giving a topic sentence and discussing the steps specific to it (such as running ads in local newspapers, preparing signs, and so forth).

> **ESSAY IN PROGRESS 6**
>
> Review the list of steps you generated in Essay in Progress 5. If your process involves ten or more steps, use the preceding guidelines to group the steps into related categories. Write an outline or draw a graphic organizer to ensure that your steps are in chronological sequence.

Drafting the Process Analysis Essay

Once you have organized the steps of the process, your next task is to write a first draft. Use the following guidelines to draft your essay.

1. **Include reasons for the steps.** Unless the reason is obvious, explain why each step or group of steps is important and necessary. For example, locating merchandise is obviously an important step in running a successful garage sale and does not need justification, but the importance of other details about conducting the sale may not be as apparent. For instance, your readers may not realize that robberies often occur during garage sales. Once they know this fact, they will be more likely to take the precautions you suggest, such as locking the house and wearing a waist-wallet. In explaining why a step is important, consider including a brief anecdote as an example.

2. **Consider using graphics and headings.** For some processes, a drawing or diagram is helpful and, at times, necessary to provide readers

with an accurate and complete process analysis. Use the drawing or diagram to make your steps easier to understand. Suppose you are explaining how seat belts protect passengers from injury. A diagram that illustrates how, upon sudden deceleration, a pendulum activates a locking device that prevent passengers from pitching forward would be useful. Remember, however, that a diagram or drawing is no substitute for a clearly written explanation.

When using a graphic, be sure to introduce it in your essay and refer to it by its title. If you are including more than one graphic, assign a number to each one (*Figure 1, Figure 2*) and include the number in your text reference.

When writing about a lengthy or complicated process, consider adding headings to your essay. Headings divide the body of an essay into manageable segments. They also call attention to your main topics and signal your reader that a change in topic is about to occur. Notice that Budish uses headings in "Fender Benders" to identify steps in the process he describes.

3. Use transitions. To avoid writing a process analysis that sounds monotonous, use transitions such as *before, next,* and *finally.*

For more on transitions, see Chapter 6, p. 138.

4. Write an effective introduction. The introduction usually presents your thesis statement and includes necessary background information. It should also capture your readers' interest and focus their attention on the process. Notice how Budish starts "Fender Benders" with an anecdote about a traffic accident and its unexpected consequences — an outcome that readers can avoid by following the process he presents. For some essays, you may want to explain that related processes and ideas depend on the process you are describing, as Nash does in "Fertile Minds." For a lengthy or complex process, consider including an overview of the steps or providing an introductory list.

For more on writing effective paragraphs, including introductions and conclusions, see Chapter 6.

5. Use an appropriate tone. By the time your readers move from your introduction to the first body paragraph, they should have a good idea of the tone of your essay. Recall from "Fender Benders" how Budish establishes a direct yet friendly tone in his introductory paragraphs by choosing words and phrases that convey that tone (such as *"Ouch!"* and "Imagine your surprise"). The tone you choose should be appropriate for your audience and purpose. In some situations, a direct, matter-of-fact tone is appropriate; other times, an emotional or humorous tone may be suitable.

For more on tone, see Chapter 8, p. 194.

6. Write a satisfying conclusion. An essay that ends with the final step in the process may sound incomplete to your readers. Especially in a how-it-works essay, readers appreciate a satisfying conclusion. In your conclusion, you might emphasize the value or importance of the process, describe particular situations in which it is useful, or offer a final amusing or emphatic comment or anecdote. In "Fertile Minds," for example, Nash ends with a warning about the need for parents and educators to "pay attention" to the process she describes and the conditions under which it occurs.

TEACHING TIP

Students who have followed the Guided Writing Assignment should be ready to compose a first draft independently. However, check to see if any students need to rethink their thesis, steps, and descriptions before drafting. Encourage them to seek further assistance from a peer reviewer or writing center tutor.

ESSAY IN PROGRESS 7

Draft your process essay, using the organization you developed in Essay in Progress 6 and the preceding guidelines for drafting.

Analyzing and Revising

If possible, wait at least a day before rereading and revising your draft. As you reread your draft, concentrate on the organization and your ideas, not on grammar or mechanics. Use one or more of the following suggestions to analyze your draft.

Learning Style Options

TEACHING TIP: LEARNING STYLES

1. For all learners, especially social learners; independent learners will learn the benefits of peer response
2. Encourage students working on a how-to essay to do this visualization exercise prior to seeking peer or tutor review. The discipline and practice are important independent learning skills.
3. For all learners (spatial learners may prefer the graphic organizer, whereas verbal learners may prefer the outline)

For more on the benefits of peer review, see Chapter 7, p. 166.

1. Read your essay aloud to one or two friends or classmates. Ask them to interrupt you if they have questions or if a step is unclear.
2. For a how-to essay, evaluate by visualizing the steps or following them exactly. Be careful to complete only the steps included in your essay. Following your directions to the letter will help you discover gaps and identify sections that are unclear or wordy.
3. Update the graphic organizer or outline you prepared earlier. Look to see if the steps are sequenced correctly and if each step is covered in enough detail.

Use Flowchart 12.1 to guide your analysis. You might also ask a classmate to review your draft essay using the questions in the flowchart. For each answer that refers you to the right column of the chart, ask your reviewer to explain why he or she answered in that way. For a how-to essay, ask your reviewer to try out the process, if possible, or to imagine himself or herself doing so. Encourage your reader to ask questions wherever necessary. These questions will help you discover where and what to add or revise. For a how-it-works essay, ask your reviewer to describe the process to you. As you listen to the explanation, you may discover sections in which your information is sketchy or incomplete as well as sections that are unclear.

FLOWCHART 12.1
REVISING A PROCESS ANALYSIS ESSAY

Questions		Revision Strategies

1. Is the importance of the process made clear to readers in your thesis statement?

No ⇨

- Ask yourself: "Why do I need to know this process? Why is it important?" Incorporate the answers into your thesis statement.

Yes ⇩

2. Is the process organized in easy-to-follow steps or groups and presented in chronological order (or some other logical progression)?

No ⇨

- Visualize or actually complete the process to discover the best order in which to do it.
- Study your graphic organizer or outline to determine if any steps are out of order.

Yes ⇩

3. Do you define technical terms for readers unfamiliar with them?

No ⇨

- Skim your essay, highlighting any specialized terms. Consider whether readers are likely to know each term that you have highlighted.
- Ask a classmate to point out any unfamiliar terms.

Yes ⇩

4. Does your introduction provide sufficient background information and an overview, if needed?

No ⇨

- Give an example of a situation in which the process might be used.
- Explain that related processes and ideas depend on the process you are describing.

Yes ⇩

(Continued on next page)

FLOWCHART 12.1 *(continued)*

Questions		Revision Strategies
5. Do you describe all of the necessary equipment?	No ⇨	• Describe equipment you have overlooked. • Describe equipment that might be unfamiliar to readers.
Yes ⇩		
6. Do you include an appropriate level of detail for your readers?	No ⇨	• Add or delete background information in your introduction. • Add or delete definitions of technical terms. • Add or delete detail.
Yes ⇩		
7. For a how-to essay, do you anticipate problems and difficulties for your readers?	No ⇨	• Add more detail about critical steps. • Warn your readers about confusing or difficult steps. • Offer advice on what to do if things go wrong.
Yes ⇩		
8. Is each paragraph well developed and focused on a separate step or group of steps? Is the conclusion satisfying?	No ⇨	• Be sure each paragraph has a topic sentence and supporting details (see Chapter 6). • Ask a classmate whether more or less detail is needed for each step. • Revise your conclusion so that it meets the guidelines in Chapter 6 (pp. 144–46).
Yes		

TEACHING TIP:
COLLABORATIVE
WRITING

Encourage students to
get feedback on the
revised draft from a peer
reviewer or writing center tutor.

ESSAY IN PROGRESS 8

Revise your draft using Flowchart 12.1 and any comments you received from peer reviewers.

Editing and Proofreading

The last step is to check your revised essay for errors in grammar, spelling, punctuation, and mechanics. In addition, be sure to look for errors that you tend to make. (Refer to your error log. See also the Writing Assessment in Appendix A.)

For more on keeping an error log, see Chapter 8, p. 201.

As you edit and proofread your process analysis essay watch out for two grammatical errors in particular: comma splices and shifts in verb tense and mood.

   1. **Avoid comma splices.** A **comma splice** occurs when two independent clauses are joined only by a comma.

COMMA SPLICE   The first step in creating a flower arrangement is to choose an attractive container, the container should not be the focal point of the arrangement.

To correct a comma splice, add a coordinating conjunction (*and, but, for, nor, or, so,* or *yet*), change the comma to a semicolon, or divide the sentence into two sentences. You can also subordinate one clause to the other.

   ▶ The first step in creating a flower arrangement is to choose an attractive
       but
       container, the container should not be the focal point of the arrangement.

   ▶ Following signs is one way to navigate a busy airport, looking for a map is
       another.

   ▶ To place a long-distance call using a credit card, first dial 0 and the 10 digit
       Next
       number, next punch in your credit card number and PIN.

       After you have placed
   ▶ Place the pill on the cat's tongue, hold its mouth closed, rubbing its chin
       until it swallows the pill.

   2. **Avoid shifts in verb mood.** There are three *moods* of a verb: indicative, imperative, and subjunctive. The **indicative mood** is used to express ordinary statements and to ask questions.

TEACHING TIP

• Point out that the subjunctive mood requires the base form of the verb when the sentence makes a recommendation: *I suggest that a new phone line be installed.*

• Mention that when a sentence presents a hypothetical circumstance (useful in process essays) and the verb follows the word *if,* it takes a plural form, even with a singular subject: *If I were a rich man.* . . .

▶ The modem is built into the computer.

The **imperative mood** is used for giving orders, advice, and directions. The subject of a verb in the imperative mood is understood to be *you*, but it is not expressed.

▶ (You) Plant your feet firmly before swinging the club.

The **subjunctive mood** is used for making statements contrary to fact or for wishes and recommendations.

▶ I suggest that a new phone line be installed.

When writing a process analysis, be sure to use a consistent mood throughout your essay.

▶ The firefighters instructed the third-grade class about procedures to follow in the event of a fire in the school. They emphasized that children should leave
they should
the building quickly. Also, ^move at least 100 feet away from the building.

TEACHING TIP:
COLLABORATIVE
WRITING

(50 minutes) After stu-
dents edit and proofread
their essays indepen-
dently, set aside a class
period (if possible) for
peer review. Have them
work in small groups or
on a computer to look
for and correct errors
involving comma splices
and shifts in tense and
mood.

ESSAY IN PROGRESS 9

Edit and proofread your essay, paying particular attention to avoiding comma splices and shifts in verb mood.

STUDENTS WRITE

Melinda Hunter was a first-year student at Daemen College when she wrote the following essay for her writing class. She was asked to write an essay explaining a worthwhile skill or craft that she had mastered. Hunter is a member of the Mohawks of the Bay of Quinte, a Native American tribe located in Ontario, Canada. Her family resides on the Tyenginaga Reservation. As you read the essay, highlight the main categories of steps as well as the writer's thesis.

How to Make a Dream Catcher
Melinda Hunter

PREREADING
QUESTION
• What is a dream
catcher?
• Why would someone
want to make a dream
catcher?

Dream catchers are a type of Native American craft.   1
The dream catcher is a circle with leather on the outside. The inside of the leather is webbed with a bead in
the middle. The dream catcher is hung in a window above
a bed. The webbing catches bad dreams and puts them in
the bead. In the morning, when the sunlight shines
through the webbing, the bad dreams are gone. Native
American people believe that a dream catcher will only
work if it is made by a Native American. They often give
dream catchers as gifts to newborn babies. In addition
to chasing away bad dreams, dream catchers are useful as
decorations and are sometimes worn as earrings or hung
on the rearview mirror of a car. The construction of a
dream catcher includes many different steps, and may take
a long time for beginners.

Before you begin to make a dream catcher, get   2
together all the necessary supplies. You will need a
spool of leather in a color of your choice. Also, you
need tacky glue and a brass ring the size you want the
dream catcher to be in diameter. You will also need
beads and feathers in two different colors that coordinate with the color of the leather. Finally, you will
need thin waxed string. Now you are ready to begin making a dream catcher.

First, estimate how much leather you will need to   3
wrap around the brass ring. Keep in mind that you must
leave a long piece of leather at the top of the ring.
You should also leave a long piece at the bottom when
you finish wrapping the leather around the ring. You are
leaving these strips so you can hang the dream catcher
when it is finished. Cut the leather to the proper size.
Put a small drop of glue on the brass ring and rub the
glue around the ring. Then begin wrapping the leather
around the ring. Because it is very easy to twist the
leather, wrapping must be done very carefully. You must

remember to angle the leather strips in the same direction and make sure they don't overlap. If the leather is
twisted or overlapping, it will make the dream catcher
look sloppy. The leather is crucial to the look of the
dream catcher because it accents the inner webbing.

4   The second step in making a dream catcher is to
make the waxed string webbing. This step is very complicated and takes much practice and skill. Cut a length of
waxed string about 2 feet long and pick a starting point
on the leather-covered ring. Begin by tying a knot
around the ring with the string, then wrap the string
around the ring at 1-1/2- to 2-inch intervals. For each
stitch, place the string over the ring and behind it,
creating a space between the ring and the string. Bring
the end of the string through this space, pulling the
stitch taut, until you get to an inch from the original
knot, as shown in Figure 1. Then create the webbed look
by taking the end of the string and inserting it through
the middle of the first stitch. Pull the string down
through the middle of the first stitch and bring it back

Fig. 1 A single stitch, adapted from
Tara Prindle, "Instructions for Making Dream Catchers."

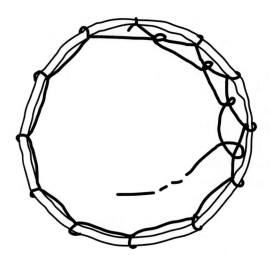

Fig. 2 Creating the web, adapted
from Tara Prindle, "Instructions
for Making Dream Catchers."

up and across and make it tight. (See Figure 2.) Go
around the circle many times, each time making sure you
pull the string tight. Make sure that you never flip the
dream catcher over because flipping it will cause the
waxed string to knot up, thus ruining the whole webbing.
When you are finished weaving the strings, you should
arrive at the middle of the dream catcher. Put a bead on
the string and tie a knot. If there is any excess string
after you have made a knot, you can wrap it around the
other string or you can cut it off. Now the waxed string
webbing step is complete.

The third step in making a dream catcher is to add   5
the feather and beads. Cut a piece of leather as long as
the one you left for hanging the dream catcher. Cut the
leather in half and tie the two pieces onto the bottom
of the dream catcher on either side of the strip you
will hang the dream catcher from. Now you have two short
strips of leather. Take the three beads (each has a hole
through the middle) and insert them over the leather for

each of the two strips. Next get two different colored feathers and glue them onto the bottom of the two leather pieces. After you do this, pull the beads down over the feathers and your dream catcher is done. (See Figure 3.)

6   If you follow these instructions, you should be able to make a basic dream catcher. Changing the pattern in the center to make it more complex is a craft that takes Native Americans many years to master. So, if you find making the middle webbing difficult when you start, do not worry; it takes experience to do this step well. Making a dream catcher is a beautiful craft to master. You may not do it well the first time, but after you have made a few dream catchers, you will feel as if you have been making them for a long time. Making a dream catcher is an art form, one that you can be proud to learn. Hang your dream catcher up and see if you have good dreams.

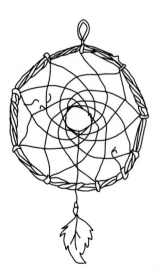

Fig. 3 A finished dream catcher, adapted from Tara Prindle, "Instructions for Making Dream Catchers."

Work Cited

Prindle, Tara. "Instructions for Making Dream Catchers."
Native Web: Resources for Indigenous Cultures
around the World. 1996. 2 Feb. 1999 <http://
www.nativeweb.org/NativeTech/dreamcat/dreminst.html>

Analyzing the Essay

1. Evaluate the writer's thesis statement. Does it suggest why making a dream catcher is useful and important to readers? Explain.
2. Where does Hunter alert readers to potential trouble spots in the process?
3. Does the introduction provide enough background information, or do you wish the writer had included more information? Explain.
4. Evaluate the essay's level of detail. Do you think you could make a dream catcher using Hunter's instructions? If not, where is additional detail needed? How helpful are the diagrams Hunter provides?
5. Does Hunter's conclusion bring her essay to a satisfying close? Why or why not?

Reacting to the Essay: Discussion and Journal Writing

1. What crafts or hobbies do you enjoy making or doing? Discuss why you find them enjoyable.
2. Hunter says it takes a great deal of time to master making a dream catcher. Write a journal entry explaining why such an investment of time might be worthwhile for this craft, or for another craft with which you are familiar.

READING A PROCESS ANALYSIS

The following section provides advice for reading a process analysis as well as model essays. Each essay illustrates the characteristics of process analysis covered in this chapter and provides opportunities to examine, analyze, and react to the writer's ideas. The second essay uses process analysis along with other methods of development.

WORKING WITH TEXT: READING PROCESS ANALYSIS ESSAYS

For more on reading strategies, see Chapter 2.

Process analysis is a common method of explaining; it is often used in textbooks, including this one, and in other forms of academic writing. To read a process analysis effectively, use the following suggestions.

What to Look for, Highlight, and Annotate

1. Look for and highlight the thesis statement. Try to discover why the writer believes the process is important or useful.
2. For a how-to essay, look for difficulties you might experience in the process or questions you may need to ask about it.
3. Highlight or underline each step or grouping of steps. Using a different colored highlighter or an asterisk (*), mark steps that the author warns are difficult or troublesome.
4. For a complex or especially important process (such as one you will need to apply on an exam), outline or draw a graphic organizer of the steps. Try explaining each step in your own words without referring to the text.
5. For a how-to essay, imagine yourself carrying out the process as you read.
6. Highlight or use a symbol to mark new terms as they are introduced.
7. Annotate the sections that summarize complex steps.

How to Find Ideas to Write About

For more on discovering ideas for a response paper, see Chapter 3.

Look for ideas to write about *as you read*. Record your ideas and impressions as marginal annotations. Think about why *you* want or need to understand the process. Think of situations in which you can use or apply the information. Also try to think of processes similar to the one described in the essay. If you think of metaphors or analogies, such as the similarity of a dream catcher to a spider's web, make a note of them. Consider how other processes are the same and how they are different from the one in the essay. Finally, evaluate the usefulness and completeness of the information provided.

THINKING CRITICALLY ABOUT PROCESS ANALYSIS

Although most process analyses are straightforward and informative, you should still consider the author's motives for writing and knowledge of the topic. Use the following questions to think critically about the process analyses you read.

What Are the Writer's Motives?

As you read, ask yourself: "Why does the writer want me to understand or carry out this process? What is his or her motive?" At times, an author may have a hidden motive for explaining a process. For example, a writer opposed to the death penalty may describe the process of carrying out executions in graphic detail, with the purpose of shocking readers and persuading them to oppose the death penalty. Since the writer may seek this outcome without stating so, it is your job as a critical reader to detect the hidden motives. Even a how-to article on a noncontroversial topic can have a hidden agenda, such as one entitled "How to Lose Ten Pounds" and written by the owner of a weight-loss clinic.

Is the Writer Knowledgeable and Experienced?

When you read process analyses, always consider whether the writer is sufficiently knowledgeable about or has experience with the process. This step is especially important if you intend to perform the task. Following the advice of someone who is not qualified to give it can be a waste of time or even dangerous. For scholarly, academic, popular, and most other types of writers, it is possible to check credentials and determine whether the writer is considered an expert in the field. An article about a new treatment for asthma by an author who has no credentials in medicine would not be a reliable source of information on that topic. In addition to checking the writer's credentials, consider whether sources, expert opinion, and quotes from authorities are used in the process analysis to support the writer's assertions.

PROCESS ANALYSIS ESSAY

As you read the following essay, notice how the author uses the elements of process analysis discussed in this chapter.

Remote Control: How to Raise a Media Skeptic
Susan Douglas

Susan Douglas is a media critic for The Progressive *and a lecturer on media literacy. She has written the book* Where the Girls Are: Growing Up Female with the Mass Media *(1994) and contributed articles to such periodicals as the* Village Voice, Nation, *and* Journal of American History. *The following selection—a how-to essay—is from a 1997 issue of* Utne Reader, *a periodical that publishes selected articles from specialized magazines known as alternative media. As you read the selection, highlight the steps that Douglas outlines and consider the order in which she presents them.*

PREREADING
QUESTION

What do you think the author means by "media skeptic"?

1   "Mommy, Mommy, come here now! Hurry, you're gonna miss it. It's Barbie's High-Steppin' Pony, and its legs really move! Hurreeeeey!"

2   "No!" I bark, as I'm wiping the dog barf up from the carpet, stirring the onions again so they don't burn, and slamming the phone down on a caller from Citibank who wants to know how I'm doin' today. It is 5:56 p.m., and I'm in no mood. "I don't come for commercials, and besides, the horse doesn't really move — they just make it look that way."

3   "Oh yeah?" demands my daughter, sounding like a federal prosecutor. "It can too. It's not like those old ones where you told me they faked it — this one really does move."

4   So now I have to go see and, indeed, the sucker takes batteries, and the stupid horse moves — sort of. "See, Mommy, the commercials don't always lie."

5   Moments like this prompt me to wonder whether I'm a weak-kneed, lazy slug or, dare I say it, a hypocrite. See, I teach media studies, and, even worse, I go around the country lecturing about the importance of media literacy. One of my talking points is how network children's programming is, ideologically, a toxic waste dump. Yet here I am, just like millions of parents during that portion of the day rightly known as hell hour — dinnertime — shoving my kid in front of Nickelodeon so my husband and I can get dinner on the table while we whisper sweet nothings like "It's your turn to take her to Brownies tomorrow" and "Oh, I forgot to tell you that your mother called three days ago with an urgent message."

6   We let her watch Nickelodeon, but I still pop in to ridicule Kool-Aid commercials or to ask her why Clarissa's parents (on *Clarissa Explains It All*) are so dopey. I am trying to have it both ways: to let television distract her, which I desperately need, and to help her see through its lies and banalities. I am very good at rationalizing this approach, but I also think it isn't a bad compromise for overworked parents who believe Barbie is the anti-Christ* yet still need to wash out grotty lunch boxes and zap leftovers at the end of the day.

7   It's best to be honest up front: My house is not media proofed. I am not one of those virtuous, haloed parents who has banished the box from the home. I actually believe that there are interesting, fun shows for my daughter to watch on TV. (And I'm not about to give up *ER*.)

8   But I'm also convinced that knowing about television, and growing up with it, provides my daughter with a form of cultural literacy

---

anti-Christ: In the Christian religion, the figure who will be opposed to Christ in the days before Christ returns.

that she will need, that will tie her to her friends and her generation and help her understand her place in the world. So instead of killing my TV, I've tried to show my daughter basic nonsense-detecting techniques. Don't think your choices are either no TV or a zombified kid. Studies show that the simple act of intervening — of talking to your child about what's on television and why it's on there — is one of the most important factors in helping children understand and distance themselves from some of the box's more repugnant imagery.

I recommend the quick surgical strike, between throwing the 9 laundry in and picking up the Legos. Watch a few commercials with them and point out that commercials lie about the toys they show, making them look much better than they are in real life. Count how many male and female characters there are in a particular show or commercial and talk about what we see boys doing and what we see girls doing. Why, you might ask, do we always see girls playing with makeup kits and boys playing with little Johnny Exocet missiles? Real life dads change diapers, push strollers, and feed kids, but you never see boys doing this with dolls on commercials. Ask where the Asian and African-American kids are. Point out how most of the parents in shows geared to kids are much more stupid than real-life parents. (By the way, children report that TV shows encourage them to talk back to their folks.) Tell them that all those cereals advertised with cartoon characters and rap music (like Cocoa Puffs and Trix) will put giant black holes in their teeth that only a dentist with a drill the size of the space shuttle can fix.

One of the best words to use when you're watching TV with your 10 kids is *stupid*, as in "Aren't Barbie's feet — the way she's always forced to walk on her tiptoes — really stupid?" or "Isn't it stupid that Lassie is smarter than the mom on this show?" (My favorite Barbie exercise: Put your kitchen timer on for a minute and make your daughter walk around on her tiptoes just like Barbie; she'll get the point real fast.) *Cool* — a word that never seems to go out of style — is also helpful, as in "Isn't it cool that on *Legends of the Hidden Temple* (a game show on Nickelodeon) the girls are as strong and as fast as the boys?" Pointing out what's good on TV is important too.

See, I think complete media-proofing is impossible, because the 11 shallow, consumerist, anti-intellectual values of the mass media permeate our culture. And we parents shouldn't beat ourselves up for failing to quarantine our kids. But we can inoculate them — which means exposing them to the virus and showing them how to build up a few antibodies. So don't feel so guilty about letting them watch TV. Instead, have fun teaching them how to talk back to it rather than to you. ∎

Examining the Reading

1. What is the author's view of children's television programming and of commercial advertisements? What, in particular, does she dislike?
2. What techniques does Douglas suggest to teach children to be critical of what
   they view on television?
3. What benefits of television does Douglas recognize?
4. Explain the meaning of each of the following words as it is used in the reading: *hypocrite* (paragraph 5), *ideologically* (5), *banalities* (6), *rationalizing* (6), and
   permeate (11). Refer to your dictionary as needed.

Analyzing the Reading

1. Identify Douglas's thesis statement. What background information does she
   provide to support the thesis?
2. Do you think the narrative in the introduction is effective? Why or why not?
3. Where does Douglas anticipate trouble spots in the process and offer solutions? In what places, if any, would more advice have been helpful to you?
4. Where does Douglas provide adequate detail? Identify those sections as well as
   any places where you think more detail is needed.
5. Does Douglas appear to be knowledgeable about her subject? Support your
   answer with evidence.

Reacting to the Reading: Discussion and Journal Writing

1. Discuss what Douglas's use of exaggeration contributes to the essay.
2. Explain why you agree or disagree with the writer's critical views of the "shallow, consumerist, anti-intellectual values of the mass media" (paragraph 11).
3. Look for misleading images or stereotypes in the television programs you
   watch. Then write a journal entry describing one such image or stereotype.

PROCESS ANALYSIS COMBINED WITH OTHER PATTERNS

As you read the following essay by Daniel Goleman, notice how he combines
process analysis with other patterns of development.

For Man and Beast, Language of Love Shares Many Traits

Daniel Goleman

Daniel Goleman holds a Ph.D. in behavioral and brain sciences and has published several books on psychology, including Emotional Intelligence *(1995) and* Working with Emotional Intelligence *(1998). He has taught at Harvard University and has been a senior editor at* Psychology Today. *This essay appeared in the* New York Times *in February 1995. As you read the selection, highlight the thesis and the steps in the process.*

1   With the same ethological methods they have long used in studies of animals, scientists are turning their attention to the nuances of human courtship rituals — otherwise known as flirting.

2   By turning the ethologist's lens on human courtship, scientists are finding striking similarities with other species, suggesting that the nonverbal template used by *Homo sapiens* for attracting and approaching a prospective mate is to some extent part of a larger, shared animal heritage.

3   A woman parades past a crowded bar to the women's room, hips swaying, eyes resting momentarily on a likely man and then coyly looking away just as she notices his look. This scenario exemplifies a standard opening move in courtship, getting attention, said Dr. David Givens, an anthropologist in Washington who is writing a book about evolution and behavior. "In the first phase of courting, humans broadcast widely a nonverbal message that amounts to 'notice me,'" said Dr. Givens. "They do it through movement, through their dress, through gesture."

4   From hundreds of hours of observations in bars and at parties, Dr. Givens discovered that women, more than men, tend to promenade, making numerous trips to the women's room, for instance, both to scout and to be seen.

5   A second nonverbal message in this earliest stage is "I am harmless," Dr. Givens has found. The gestures and postures humans use to send this message are shared with other mammals, particularly primates. Charles Darwin, who noted the same gestures in his 1859 book, *The Expressions of the Emotions in Man and Animals,* called them "submissive displays."

6   Perhaps the first serious study of flirting was done in the 1960's by Dr. Irenaus Eibl-Eibesfeldt, an eminent ethologist at the Max Planck Institute in Germany. Dr. Eibl-Eibesfeldt traveled to cultures

children to talk back to their parents (9). More advice: Possibly more on pointing out what's good on TV. (Have students debate this point.)

4. Plenty of detail in personal background narrative; good detail in the process section (9–10); could possibly use more detail in making the point about cultural literacy (8).

5. Yes, Douglas is a media critic and has written a book on girls and the media. Because she is also a parent, she has first-hand experience to share.

POSSIBLE ANSWERS: REACTING TO THE READING (p. 362)

1. Her exaggerations add humor and, therefore, interest.
2. Responses will vary.
3. Responses will vary; one possibility is beer-guzzling sports fans.

PREREADING QUESTION

What steps do you follow when flirting?

TEACHING TIP

Thesis: "By turning the ethologist's lens on human courtship, scientists are finding striking similarities with other species . . ." (paragraph 2). Steps of process (nonverbal messages): Gestures conveying "notice me" (3); "I am harmless" (5–7); coy, flirtatious looks (16); conversation (21).

around the world with a camera that took pictures from the side so he could stand near couples and take their pictures without their realizing they were being observed. In research in Samoa, Brazil, Paris, Sydney and New York, Dr. Eibl-Eibesfeldt discovered an apparently universal nonverbal human vocabulary for flirting and courtship.

7   In humans, one such gesture is a palm-up placement of the hand, whether on a table or a knee, a reassuring sign of harmlessness. Another submissive display is the shoulder shrug, which, ethologists suggest, derives from an ancient vertebrate reflex, a posture signifying helplessness. A posture combining the partly shrugged shoulder and a tilted head — which displays the vulnerability of the neck — is commonly seen when two people who are sexually drawn to each other are having their first conversation, Dr. Givens said.

8   Being playful and childish is another way potential lovers often communicate harmlessness. "You see the same thing in the gray wolf," said Dr. Givens.

9   When wolves encounter each other, they usually give a show of dominance, keeping their distance. But in a sexual encounter, they become playful and frisky, "like puppies," said Dr. Givens, "so they can accept closeness." The next step is a mutual show of submission, all of which paves the way for physical intimacy.

10   "We still go through the ritual of courtship much like our mammalian ancestors," said Dr. Givens. "These gestures are subcortical, regulated by the more primitive part of our brain. They have nothing to do with the intellect, with our great neocortex."

11   The nonverbal repertoire for flirting is "part of a natural sequence for courtship worldwide," said Dr. Helen Fisher, an anthropologist at Rutgers University in New Brunswick, N.J., and author of *The Anatomy of Love* (Fawcett, 1993). "Mothers don't teach this to their daughters."

12   "In evolutionary terms, the payoff for each sex in parental investment differs: to produce a child a woman has an obligatory nine-month commitment, while for a man it's just one sexual act," said Dr. David Buss, a psychologist at the University of Michigan in Ann Arbor and author of *The Evolution of Desire* (Basic Books, 1994). "For men in evolutionary terms what pays is sexual access to a wide variety of women, while for women it's having a man who will commit time and resources to helping raise children."

13   From this view, the coyness of courtship is a way to "test a prospective partner for commitment," said Dr. Jane Lancaster, an anthropologist at the University of New Mexico in Albuqerque. "Women, in particular, need to be sure they're not going to be deserted."

14   Coyness is not seen in species where the female does not need the sustained help or resources of a male to raise her young, said Dr. Lancaster. In species where a single act of copulation is the only

contact a female requires with the father of her young, "there's a direct assertion of sexual interest by the female," said Dr. Lancaster.

But in species where two parents appreciably enhance the sur- 15 vival of offspring, "females don't want to mate with a male who will abandon them," said Dr. Lancaster. In such species, "the courtship dances are coy, a test to see if the male is willing to persist and pursue or simply wants a momentary dalliance," he said. "Instead of the female simply getting in a posture for mating, she repeats a promise-withdraw sequence, getting in the mating posture and then moving away."

In humans, flirtatious looks imitate this sequence. The coy look 16 a woman gives a man is the beginning of a continuing series of approach-withdraw strategies that will unfold over the course of their courtship. These feminine stratagems signal the man, "I'm so hard to win that if you do win me you won't have to worry about me getting pregnant by another male," said Dr. Lancaster.

A taxonomy of 52 "nonverbal solicitation behaviors" observed in 17 flirting women has been garnered by Dr. Monica Moore, a psychologist at Webster University in St. Louis. In her research, conducted in singles bars, shopping malls and other places young people go to meet those of the opposite sex, Dr. Moore has found that the women who send flirtatious signals most frequently are most likely to be approached by men — even more so than are women who are rated as more attractive.

"It's not who's most physically appealing," said Dr. Moore, "but 18 the woman who's signaling availability that men approach."

Flirting is the opening gambit in a continuing series of negotia- 19 tions at every step of the way in courtship. Indeed, the first major negotiation point is signaled by the flirtatious look itself.

"When a man is looking at a woman and she senses it, her first 20 decision is, 'Do I have further interest in him?'" said Dr. Beverly Palmer, a psychologist at California State University in Dominguez Hills who has studied flirting. "If so, by flirting she sends the next signal: 'I'm interested in you, and yes, you can approach me.'"

Once the first conversation begins, there is "a major escalation 21 point," said Dr. Fisher.

"The woman has a whole new basis for judging the man," she 22 said. "A large number of prospective pickups end here."

Though men may say they are well aware of the tentativeness of 23 flirting, Dr. Buss's findings suggest a male tendency — at least among college-age men — toward wishful thinking in interpreting flirtatious looks. In settings where men and women go to meet someone of the opposite sex, Dr. Buss said, "we find that when you ask men what it means for a woman to smile at them, they interpret it as a sexual invitation."

24   "But when you ask women what it means," he continued, "they'll say it just indicates she wants to get to know him better."

25   In interviews with 208 college-age men and women published this month in the *Journal of Sex Research*, Dr. Buss and colleagues found that when it comes to seduction, "the sexual signals that work for a woman backfire for men."

26   "There's a huge sex difference in how effective different tactics are," he added.

27   Perhaps not surprisingly, the research showed that for women, direct sexual approaches—dressing seductively, dancing close, staring into a man's eyes—worked well in leading to sexual contact. But for men similar direct strategies were failures.

28   Instead, for men the less overtly seductive tried-and-true romantic strategems fared best. "For men the most effective approaches are displays of love and commitment," said Dr. Buss. "Telling her he really loves her, that he cares and is committed." ∎

Examining the Reading

1. What is Goleman's purpose?
2. In what courtship behaviors are humans and animals similar?
3. According to Goleman, how do male and female flirting behaviors differ?
4. Explain the meaning of each of the following words as it is used in the reading: *ethological* (paragraph 1), *template* (2), *mammalian* (10), *repertoire* (11), *evolutionary* (12), and *escalation* (21). Refer to your dictionary as needed.

Analyzing the Reading

1. Goleman uses process analysis to explain how human courtship works. What other patterns of development does the writer use in the essay? Choose one pattern and explain how Goleman uses it to develop his thesis.
2. What technical terms does Goleman explain? What other terms, if any, do you think he should have explained?
3. What method of organization does this essay follow? Give examples from the reading to support your answer.
4. Evaluate Goleman's use of detail. Why does he explain some steps in the courtship process in greater detail than other steps?
5. Explain why Goleman is qualified to write this essay.

Reacting to the Reading: Discussion and Journal Writing

1. Discuss why you agree or disagree with Goleman's description of flirtatious behavior in humans.

2. Observe couples in a public place, such as in restaurants or on campus. What flirtatious behaviors do you notice? Are the behaviors consistent with Goleman's description? Why or why not?

3. In a journal entry, discuss why you agree or disagree with Goleman that women and men flirt for different reasons.

APPLYING YOUR SKILLS: ADDITIONAL ESSAY ASSIGNMENTS

Write a process analysis essay on one of the following topics. Depending on the topic you choose, you may need to conduct library or Internet research.

To Express Your Ideas

1. How children manage their parents
2. How to relax and do nothing
3. How to find enough time for your children

To Inform Your Reader

4. How to avoid or speed up red-tape procedures
5. How a particular type of sports equipment protects an athlete
6. How to remain calm while giving a speech

To Persuade Your Reader

7. How important it is to vote in a presidential election
8. How important it is to select the right courses in order to graduate on time
9. How important it is to exercise every day

Cases Using Process Analysis

10. You are taking a communication course, and you are studying friendship development and the strategies people use to meet others. Your instructor has asked you to write an essay describing the strategies people use to meet new people and develop friendships.

11. You are employed by a toy manufacturer and you have been asked to write a brochure for elementary school children. The brochure is intended to encourage children to use toys safely. As you prepare the brochure, describe at least three steps children can follow to avoid injury.

the opening gambit in a continuing series of negotiations at every step of the way in courtship" (19); "direct sexual approaches — dressing seductively, dancing close, staring into a man's eyes" (27).

3. The sequence of steps in human courtship is

For more on locating and documenting sources, see Chapters 19 and 20.

presented in chronological order, though definitions and comparisons are woven into the body paragraphs.

4. He uses more details to explain behaviors that resemble those of animals, such as gestures that convey harmlessness (similarity with wolves) and coyness (similarity and difference with animals). These details support his thesis.

POSSIBLE ANSWERS: REACTING TO THE READING (p. 366)

Responses will vary.

TEACHING TIP

Suggest that students use at least one prewriting strategy — drawing a graphic organizer, freewriting, brainstorming, questioning, writing assertions — to get started. Remind students to consult the learning style options (p. 344) and the revision flowchart (p. 349).

Chapter **13**

CHAPTER QUICK START

The two photographs on the opposite page were taken at wedding ceremonies. Study the photographs and make two lists — one of the ways the two wedding scenes are similar and another of the ways the wedding scenes are different. Include in your lists any details that you notice about the people and setting, such as clothing, facial expressions, and background details.

Writing Quick Start

Write a paragraph about the photos that answers these questions: How are these two wedding scenes the same and how are they different?

Comparison and Contrast: Showing Similarities and Differences

TEACHING TIP: COLLABORATIVE WRITING

(15 minutes) As a class, brainstorm lists of similarities and differences on the blackboard. Then examine the lists for points of comparison (clothing, setting, and so on).

TEACHING TIP:
CHAPTER OVERVIEW

• This chapter chal-
lenges creative learners
to adopt pragmatic
organizational tech-
niques and pragmatic
learners to develop
creative analogies and
comparisons.

• This chapter empha-
sizes the importance
of *analysis* in identifying
key comparisons and
contrasts and of
description in conveying
them.

• All learners will need
to use outlines or
graphic organizers to
plan a *point-by-point* or
subject-by-subject
method of organiza-
tion. Both methods
rely on *transitions* to
maintain clear organi-
zation.

• The chapter fosters the
critical thinking skill of
synthesis: Students are
required to *break down*
a subject into compo-
nents or essential traits
and *put together* the
essential similarities
between subjects.

• Students may need to
conduct research to
develop and substanti-
ate their ideas.

WRITING A COMPARISON OR CONTRAST ESSAY

Your paragraph about the wedding ceremonies is an example of comparison and contrast writing. In it you probably wrote about similarities and differences in dress, location of the ceremony, and so forth. In addition, you probably organized your paragraph in one of two ways: (1) by writing about one wedding and then the other or (2) by alternating back and forth between the two weddings as you discussed each point of similarity or difference. This chapter will show you how to write effective comparison or contrast essays as well as how to incorporate comparison and contrast into essays using other patterns of development.

WHAT ARE COMPARISON AND CONTRAST?

As you saw in your paragraph about the two weddings, using **comparison and contrast** involves looking at both similarities and differences. For example, when you compare and contrast two used cars, you consider how they are similar (in terms of size, body type, gas mileage) and how they are different (in terms of price, color, engine size). Analyzing similarities and differences is a common and useful decision-making skill that you use daily. You make comparisons when you shop for a pair of jeans, select a sandwich in the cafeteria, or decide which television program to watch. You also make important decisions about which college to attend, which field to major in, and which person to date by weighing (or comparing) options and alternatives.

You will find many occasions to use comparison and contrast in the writing you do in college and on the job (see the accompanying box for a few examples).

SCENES FROM COLLEGE AND THE WORKPLACE

- For a course in *deviant behavior,* your instructor asks you to participate in a panel discussion comparing organized crime in three societies: Italy, Japan, and Russia.

- For a *journalism* course, you are assigned to interview two local television news reporters and write a paper contrasting their views on journalistic responsibility.

- As a *computer technician* for a pharmaceutical firm, you are asked to compare and contrast several models of notebook computers and recommend the one the company should purchase for its salespeople.

In addition, in most essays of this type you will use one of two primary methods of organization. As the following two readings illustrate, comparison or contrast essays are usually organized *point by point* or *subject by subject*. The first essay, "Lincoln and Roosevelt: Two Master Politicians" by Geoffrey Ward, uses a **point-by-point organization**. The writer moves back and forth between his two subjects (Lincoln and Roosevelt), comparing them on the basis of several key points or characteristics. The second essay, Jeanne Wakatsuki Houston's "A Taste of Snow," uses a **subject-by-subject organization**. Here the author describes the key points or characteristics of one subject (Christmas in the California Desert) before moving on to those of her other subject (Christmas at Ocean Park).

POINT BY POINT ORGANIZATION

Lincoln and Roosevelt: Two Master Politicians
Geoffrey Ward

Geoffrey Ward is the author of three books about Franklin Roosevelt, Before the Trumpet *(1985),* A First-Class Temperament *(1989), and* Closest Companion *(1995). In the following essay, originally published in the* New York Times *in 1997, Ward makes a point-by-point comparison of two U.S. presidents, Abraham Lincoln and Franklin Roosevelt. As you read the selection, highlight each point of comparison.*

PREREADING QUESTION

How might the political careers of Lincoln and Roosevelt counter the notion that "career politician" is a "dirty word"?

As of today, each of the three Presidents whom American historians routinely rate most highly has his own oversized memorial in the nation's capital. It took George Washington 86 years to reach the Mall. Abraham Lincoln had to wait 57 years. F.D.R. made it to the Tidal Basin in just 52.

Washington was sui generis, of course; he invented the job. And at first glance, his two ablest successors seem wholly dissimilar. The Roosevelt estate, high above the Hudson River at Hyde Park, was very far in every sense from the log cabin on Nolin Creek in Kentucky where Lincoln was born.

Lincoln had never managed anything larger than a two-man law office when he became President; F.D.R. had helped run the Navy Department in wartime and was twice Governor of New York. Lincoln was plagued by melancholy; Roosevelt remained so relentlessly sunny, despite paraplegia and the pressures of 12 years in the

White House, that one dazzled aide said he seemed to have been "psychoanalyzed by God."

4   Yet the two had much in common. Each was hugely ambitious. Lincoln declared himself a candidate for state office at 23, before he owned so much as a suit of clothes. F.D.R. was just 25 when he began outlining for friends the path he planned to follow to the Presidency.

5   Both believed that the United States had a unique part to play in the world and that the Presidency was, as Roosevelt said, "preeminently a place of moral leadership." Each found solace in the conviction that he was merely the instrument of a higher power whose purposes were unknowable but who was nonetheless active in the affairs of men.

6   Both were denounced as unprincipled for failing to move as fast or as consistently as their more ideologically inclined contemporaries would have liked. "Lincoln was a sad man because he couldn't get it all at once," Roosevelt told a friend. "Nobody can." In the interest of getting all they could, both Roosevelt and Lincoln were often accused of being too clever by half.

7   Above all, they were masterful politicians who managed to overcome seemingly insurmountable obstacles to win power—polio in Roosevelt's case, abject poverty in Lincoln's.

8   Along the way, each learned hard lessons about the value of keeping one's own counsel, the pace at which public opinion can be shaped, the strategic uses of delay and flattery and the miraculous power of patronage to change men's minds.

9   We've heard a great deal about the sins of "career politicians." Everything would run more smoothly, we are told, if government were just placed in the hands of gifted amateurs, distinguished men and women who would contribute a limited amount of their valuable time to bringing efficiency and objectivity to government, then return to their real jobs to give someone else a chance.

10   But the achievements of Franklin Roosevelt and Abraham Lincoln are the most vivid possible refutation of that notion. When the survival of this country was most seriously threatened—by domestic enemies during Lincoln's watch, and, when Roosevelt was at the helm, by economic disaster and the crippling self-doubt it fostered, and then by foreign enemies—the American people wisely turned to men who had devoted their whole lives to politics.

11   In that sweaty, sometimes squalid world, they had mastered the essential skills of Presidential leadership. Had we turned to amateurs, no matter how well-intentioned, in those anxious times, government of the people, by the people, and for the people might long since have perished from the earth. ∎

SUBJECT BY SUBJECT ORGANIZATION

A Taste of Snow
Jeanne Wakatsuki Houston

Jeanne Wakatsuki Houston has written a number of books, including Farewell to Manzanar *(1973),* Don't Cry, It's Only Thunder *(1984), and* Beyond Manzanar *(1985), from which this essay is taken. It opens with a description of her first snowy Christmas in northern California during World War II, when Houston and many other Japanese Americans were detained in internment camps. Then the writer goes on to describe a Christmas at Ocean Park, near the beach. As you read the selection, highlight the key points Houston makes about each place and note how her two concluding paragraphs pull the comparison together. You will notice that Houston's essay does not include an introduction but begins with a description of her first subject.*

TEACHING TIP

"A Taste of Snow" exemplifies the use of description in comparison and contrast.

PREREADING QUESTIONS

• Why does Houston choose to contrast two Christmas memories?
• What does Houston mean when she says that in her mind they coexist, "a memory within a memory"?

I first saw snow one Christmas when I lived in the high desert of Owens Valley, California. I was nine years old. It was during the Second World War, the first winter my family and I spent at Manzanar. When the crystal flakes floated down, like translucent coconut chips dancing in the breeze, I ran out into the clear area between the barracks, twirling and dancing and opening my mouth to catch the powdery ice. The snow reminded me of cotton candy, wispy and delicate, and gone with one whisk of the tongue.   1

I was surprised by the sharp coldness of the air and somehow disappointed that such beauty had its price to be paid—icy feet and hands, and uncomfortable wetness when the snow melted upon contact with my clothes and face. Still, the utter loveliness of this new phenomenon was so overpowering I soon forgot my discomfort.   2

Other people began coming out of the barracks into a transformed world. Some carried brightly colored Japanese parasols and wore high wooden *getas* to raise their stockinged feet above the snow. It was odd not to hear the "kata-kata" clatter of wooden clogs scraping across sand and gravel. The blanket of snow muffled sound and thickened the thin planed roofs of the barracks, softening the stark landscape of white on white. It was strangely soothing to me, silent and tranquil. I found myself moved to tears.   3

This particular imprint in my memory is easily explained. Before being sent to Manzanar we lived in Ocean Park, on Dudley Avenue, a block from the beach. Ocean Park Pier was my playground. All the kids in the neighborhood played ball and skated along the wide   4 cement promenade that bordered the beach from Ocean Park to Venice.

5   Memories of Ocean Park are warm ones of sunshine, hot days on the beach, building sand castles, playing *Tarzan* and *Jungle Girl,* jumping off lifeguard stands and spraining ankles. Fourth of July was a balmy evening of crowds milling around the pier waiting for fireworks to spray the sky with luminous explosives. Easter was as colorful as the many-hued eggs the local service club buried in the sand for the kids to uncover. And Christmas was just another version of this type of buoyant, high-spirited celebration my family enjoyed before the war. In my memory Christmas morning seemed always sunny and clear. Strolling along the promenade in my orange-flowered dress and white high-topped shoes, pushing the doll carriage Santa left under the big tree in our living room, I proudly displayed myself and my gifts as did the other children of the neighborhood. My oldest brother Bill, who was then in his twenties, walked with me and helped me feed popcorn to the pigeons warbling and pecking around our feet. Then he rushed me off in his old blue roadster to visit his girlfriend Molly who played the violin while he sang, and I slept.

6   Like a story within a story, or a memory within a memory, I cannot think of one memorable Christmas, but of these two. They are yin and yang, each necessary to appreciate the other. I don't remember Christmas trees in Manzanar. But we gathered driftwood from the creeks that poured down from the nearby Sierras and across the high desert. With these we improvised. In my mind's eye they co-exist: a lush, brilliantly lit fir tree; and a bare manzanita limb embellished with origami cranes.

7   To this day, when I travel in the high country, I can cry seeing nature's exquisite winter garb and remembering my first taste of snow.   ■

Characteristics of Comparison or Contrast Essays

When writers use comparison and contrast, they consider subjects with characteristics in common, examining similarities, differences, or both. Whether used as the primary pattern of development or alongside another pattern, comparison and contrast can help writers achieve their purpose and make a point about their subjects.

Comparison or Contrast Has a Clear Purpose

A comparison or contrast essay usually has one of three purposes: *to express ideas,* *to inform,* or *to persuade.* In an essay about the two weddings shown in the chapter-opening photographs, the purpose could be to evaluate the ceremonies, persuading readers that one is more formal or more bound in tradition. Or the purpose could be to inform readers about variations in wedding ceremonies. Finally, the purpose might be to express the bride's ideas about her unconventional wedding by showing how it is similar to and different from more traditional American weddings. Whatever the purpose of a comparison or contrast, it should be made clear to readers. In "Lincoln and Roosevelt: Two Master Politicians," for example, it's clear that Ward wants to persuade readers to accept his evaluation of the two presidents.

Comparison or Contrast Considers Shared Characteristics

You have probably heard the familiar expression, "you can't compare apples and oranges." Although overused, the cliché makes a useful point about comparisons: You cannot compare two unlike things unless they have something in common. Apples and oranges *can* be compared if they share at least one characteristic — nutritional value, for instance.

When making a comparison, then, a writer needs to choose a **basis of comparison** — a common characteristic on which to base the essay. Baseball and football might be compared on the basis of their entertainment value or the types of athletic skill they require. The basis of comparison determines the type of details the essay should include. In an essay about the value of baseball and football as forms of entertainment, for example, the number of people who watch the Superbowl versus the World Series on television would be relevant, whereas the types of equipment used by the players of each sport would not be relevant to the basis of comparison.

EXERCISE 13.1

For three items in the following list, identify two possible bases of comparison you could use to compare each pair of topics.

1. Two means of travel or transportation
2. Two means of communication (email, telephone, postal letters)
3. Two pieces of equipment
4. Two magazines or books
5. Two types of television programming

POSSIBLE ANSWERS

1. Cruise ship, airplane: fares; passenger amenities
2. Email, letters: speed; cost
3. CD player, tape player: quality of sound; expense
4. *Forbes, Business Week:* quality of writing; amount of advertising
5. Situation comedies, dramas: complexity of plots; timeliness

Comparison or Contrast Fairly Examines Similarities, Differences, or Both

Depending on their purpose, writers using comparison and contrast in essays may focus on similarities, differences, or both. In an essay intended to *persuade* readers that baseball players Mark McGwire and Sammy Sosa have much in common both on and off the field, the writer would focus on similarities — home-run records, camaraderie with teammates, and attitudes toward family, for example. However, an essay intended to *inform* readers about the two home-run hitters would probably cover both similarities and differences, discussing the players' different childhoods or major league experiences in addition to covering similarities.

An essay that focuses on differences often mentions a few key similarities, usually in the introduction, to let readers know the writer is aware of the similarities. Conversely, an essay focusing on similarities might mention a few differences. Ward takes this approach in "Lincoln and Roosevelt: Two Master Politicians," mentioning a few differences between the presidents in paragraph 3 before discussing the more important similarities.

Whether you cover similarities, differences, or both in an essay, you should strive to treat your subjects fairly. Relevant information should not be purposely omitted in order to show one subject in a more favorable light. In an essay about McGwire and Sosa, for instance, you would not leave out information about McGwire's friendliness in an effort to make Sosa appear to be a nicer person. Notice that in "A Taste of Snow" Houston is open-minded about Manzanar, even though she was interned there; she recognizes the beauty of the snowfall and the silent landscape on Christmas Day.

Comparison or Contrast Makes a Point

Whatever the purpose of a comparison or contrast, the essay should make a main point about its subjects in a way that sparks readers' interest, rather than boring them with a mechanical listing of similarities or differences. This main point can serve as the thesis for the essay, or the thesis can be implied in the writer's choice of details. In "Lincoln and Roosevelt," for example, Ward states his main point and thesis explicitly in the last sentence of paragraph 10 when he notes that Lincoln and Roosevelt were successful presidents because they were career politicians. In "A Taste of Snow," Houston implies her main point by her choice of details: the sunshine and doll carriage during Christmas at Ocean Park; the snowy landscape and silence of the high desert during Christmas in Manzanar.

An explicit thesis has three functions:

1. It identifies the *subjects* being compared or contrasted.
2. It suggests whether the focus is on *similarities*, *differences*, or *both*.
3. It states the *main point* of the comparison or contrast.

Notice how the following three sample theses meet the above criteria. Note, too, that each thesis suggests why the comparison or contrast is meaningful and worth reading about.

┌──────── similarities ────────┐   ┌──────── subjects ────────┐
Similar appeals in commercials for three popular breakfast cereals reveal

┌──────── main point ────────┐
America's obsession with fitness and health.

┌──── difference ────┐ ┌──── subjects ────┐ ┌── similarities ──┐
Although different in purpose, weddings and funerals each draw families

┌────────── main point ──────────┐
together and confirm family values.

┌──────────────── subjects ────────────────┐
The cities Niagara Falls, Ontario, and Niagara Falls, New York, demonstrate

┌──── differences ────┐ ┌──────────────── main point ────────────────┐
two different approaches to appreciating nature and preserving the environment.

EXERCISE 13.2

For one of the topic pairs you worked on in Exercise 13.1, select the basis of comparison that seems most promising. Then write a thesis statement that identifies the subjects, the focus (similarities, differences, or both), and the main point.

Comparison or Contrast Considers a Sufficient Number of Significant Characteristics and Details

A comparison or contrast essay considers characteristics that are significant as well as relevant to the essay's purpose and thesis. In "Lincoln and Roosevelt," for example, Ward considers several significant characteristics of the two presidents, including their ambition, their view of the presidency, and their denouncement by contemporaries.

Although the number of details can vary by topic, usually at least three or four significant characteristics are needed to support a thesis. Each characteristic should be fully described or explained so readers can grasp the main point of the comparison or contrast. A writer may use sensory details, dialogue, examples, expert testimony, and other kinds of detail in a comparison or contrast essay. Houston offers numerous details in "A Taste of Snow," describing, for example, the cold air, crystal snowflakes, muffled sounds, and silence at Manzanar.

Visualizing a Comparison or Contrast Essay: Two Graphic Organizers

Suppose you want to compare two houses (house A and house B) built by the same architect for the purpose of evaluating how the architect's style has changed over time. After brainstorming ideas, you decide to base your essay on these points of comparison: layout, size, building materials, and landscaping. You could organize your essay in one of two ways: point by point or subject by subject.

Point-by-Point Organization

In a *point-by-point organization,* you would first discuss the layout of each house, then their size, then building materials, and finally landscaping. You would go

TEACHING TIP: COLLABORATIVE WRITING

(15 minutes) Have students draft their theses independently and then work in groups to review each other's statements for focus and clarity.

POSSIBLE ANSWERS

Answers will vary.

For more on graphic organizers, see Chapter 2, p. 40.

back and forth between the two houses, noting similarities and differences between them on each of the four points of comparison. You can visualize this pattern as shown in the graphic organizer in Figure 13.1.

FIGURE 13.1
GRAPHIC ORGANIZER FOR A POINT-BY-POINT COMPARISON AND CONTRAST

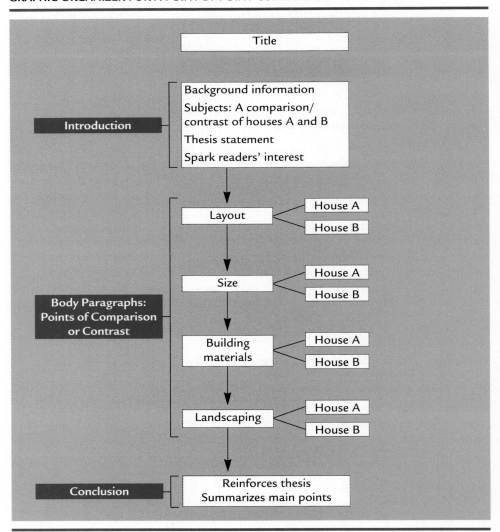

Subject-by-Subject Organization

In the *subject-by-subject organization,* you would first discuss all points about house A: its layout, size, building materials, and landscaping. Then you would do the same for house B. This pattern is shown in the graphic organizer in Figure 13.2.

FIGURE 13.2
GRAPHIC ORGANIZER FOR A SUBJECT-BY-SUBJECT COMPARISON AND CONTRAST

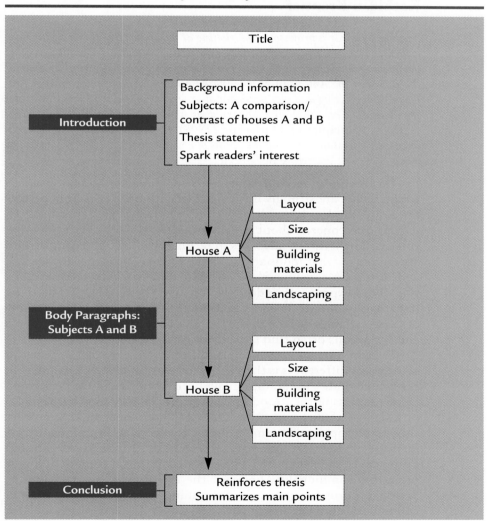

TEACHING TIP

Note that if points of comparison cannot be presented in a parallel fashion throughout an essay, the subject-by-subject organization may be the better choice.

The following essay uses a point-by-point organization. Read the essay, and then study the graphic organizer for it in Figure 13.3.

Who's Eating What, and Why in the United States and Europe?

Thomas Kinnear
Kenneth Bernhardt
Kathleen Krentler

Thomas Kinnear is professor of marketing at the University of Michigan. He is a former editor of the Journal of Marketing. *Kenneth Bernhardt is regents professor of marketing at Georgia State University and has served as chair of the Board of the American Marketing Association. Kathleen Krentler is professor of marketing and vice president of programs at the Academy of Marketing Science. This essay first appeared as a marketing profile in a college textbook,* Principles of Marketing *(1995). As you read the selection, highlight the thesis statement and the points of comparison.*

**PREREADING
QUESTIONS**

• How do you think
European and Ameri-
can consumers com-
pare in terms of the
fat content of their
food? The vitamin
content? The cost?
The variety?
• How might other
factors affect food
choices?

**TEACHING TIP:
POSTREADING
DISCUSSION**

Ask students to discuss

• differences between
the eating habits of
two groups or cultures
they know of (e.g.,
their families versus
their friends' families).
• why this information is
presented in a market-
ing textbook (to
inform students and
help them learn how
to analyze a market).
• the authors' points
of comparison as well
as others they might
have presented (e.g.,
cultural traditions or
foods grown in partic-
ular areas).

1   Do European and U.S. consumers eat alike? Yes and no. People's eating habits are strongly influenced by a number of factors besides taste. Cultural values, demographic characteristics, personal finances, and concern about the environment all help determine what you eat. Furthermore, advances in technology, laws, and competition are factors in what foods are available to you. To the extent that U.S. and European consumers are influenced similarly by these factors, you would expect and, indeed, would find their eating habits to be remarkably similar. However, because the relative influence of many of these variables differs on the two sides of the Atlantic, U.S. diners and Europeans often find themselves eating different things.

2   Perhaps one of the most significant factors that appears to account for differences is the variation in social values. Consumers in the United States, for example, have been interested in the health and fitness aspects of their food for some time. This interest has resulted in a deluge of diet and other types of "lite" food on U.S. grocery shelves. European consumers, however, are just beginning to get interested in diet and "lite" foods. A recent study found both U.S. and European consumers primarily interested in the fat content of foods. After this commonality, however, the concerns of the two groups diverged. Europeans want (in descending order) freshness, vitamin and mineral content, and nutritional value while Americans look for foods low in salt, cholesterol, and sugar.

3   Ironically, as European interest in diet and "lite" goods is increasing, many U.S. consumers appear to be switching back to what has

been called real food. Increasingly, healthy eating in the U.S. alternates with the consumption of heartier fare. Like other food producers, McDonald's appears to be responding to this move by downplaying its reduced-fat McLean Deluxe Burger (dubbed the McFlopper by some cynics) and introducing the Mega Mac, a half-pound hamburger patty.

Recent statistics reveal a demographic difference that may also account for variation in eating habits. A study found that 44 percent of Western European women reported being homemakers and only 33 percent said they worked outside the home. This is approximately the reverse of U.S. statistics on these same factors. Marketers realize that the presence of a full-time homemaker in a home is likely to account for different shopping, cooking, and eating habits for the entire family. 4

Economic and ecological factors can also help shape our eating habits. Consumers in the United States have traditionally been concerned with price. In the last few years, European consumers have become increasingly cost-conscious as well, due in large part to a recessionary economy throughout the early 1990s. Consumers with less money to spend and less optimism about the economy are likely to eat differently. Consumers on both sides of the Atlantic are also increasingly concerned about the environment. Marketers have found themselves having to respond to demands for reductions in excessive packaging, for example. 5

Advances in technology mean changes in what consumers eat. The introduction of the microwave oven, for example, has affected what's for dinner in U.S. households for the last twenty years. Microwavable food is a relatively new phenomenon in Europe, however. 6

Traditionally, European consumers have claimed that having a wide variety is much less important to them than it is to residents of the United States. However, increased competition from popular private-label products is pushing producers in industries like breakfast cereals to introduce more products into the European market. Time will tell whether European consumers will become more like U.S. consumers and respond to broader product offerings or whether they reject the strategy. 7

The changes in the European market brought on by economic, competitive, and social upheaval [are] providing opportunities for marketers who respond appropriately. Pepsico Corporation, for example, entered the Polish market in 1993 with "3-in-1" outlets combining Pizza Hut, Taco Bell, and KFC. The outlets have been very successful. 8

Smart marketers should be less concerned with whether U.S. and European consumers are alike and more concerned with monitoring the variety of factors that account for potential similarities and differences. Attention to the dynamic nature of those factors will produce opportunities for the alert marketer. ∎ 9

FIGURE 13.3
GRAPHIC ORGANIZER FOR "WHO'S EATING WHAT, AND WHY IN THE UNITED STATES AND EUROPE?"

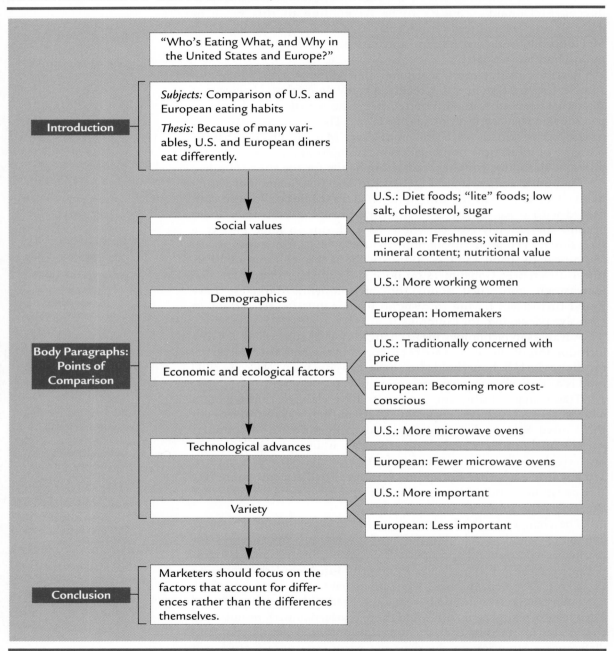

EXERCISE 13.3

Draw a graphic organizer for "Lincoln and Roosevelt: Two Master Politicians" (p. 371) or "A Taste of Snow" (p. 373).

POSSIBLE ANSWERS

Answers will vary. See the *Instructor's Resource Manual* for a possible graphic organizer.

INTEGRATING COMPARISON AND CONTRAST INTO AN ESSAY

While some essays you write will use comparison and contrast as the primary pattern of development, in most cases you will integrate comparisons or contrasts into essays that rely on other patterns, such as description, process analysis, or argument. Comparisons or contrasts can be particularly effective in essays intended to be persuasive.

Use the following tips to incorporate a comparison or contrast into essays based on other patterns of development.

1. **Determine the purpose of the comparison or contrast.** What will it contribute to your essay?

2. **Introduce the comparison or contrast clearly.** Tell your readers how it supports the main point of the essay. Do not leave it to them to figure out why the comparison is included.

3. **Keep the comparison or contrast short and to the point.** An extended comparison will distract readers from the overall point of your essay.

4. **Organize the points of the comparison or contrast.** Even though it is part of a larger essay, the comparison or contrast should follow a point-by-point or subject-by-subject organization.

5. **Use transitions.** Transitional words and expressions are especially important in easing the flow into the comparison or contrast and then back to the essay's primary pattern of development.

In "By Being Honest about Violence, Spielberg Wins" on page 407, Janet Maslin uses comparison and contrast along with other patterns of development to support her evaluation of Steven Spielberg's film, *Saving Private Ryan.*

ADDITIONAL
RESOURCES

The writing process soft-
ware that accompanies
this text includes an
electronic Guided Writ-
ing Assignment for a
comparison or contrast
essay.

A GUIDED WRITING ASSIGNMENT

The following guide will lead you through the process of writing a comparison or contrast essay. Although you will focus on comparing or contrasting your subjects, you may need to integrate one or more other patterns of development in your essay. Depending on your learning style, you may use different approaches to choosing subjects or generating ideas. This Guided Writing Assignment will provide you with alternatives.

The Assignment

Write a comparison or contrast essay on one of the following topic pairs or one of your own choice. Depending on the topic pair you choose, you may need to use Internet or library sources to develop and support your ideas about the subjects. Your audience is your classmates.

1. Two public figures
2. Two forms of entertainment (such as movies, concerts, radio, music videos) or one form of entertainment as it is used today versus ten or more years ago
3. Two styles of communication, dress, or teaching
4. The right and wrong ways of doing something
5. Your views versus your parents' or grandparents' views on an issue
6. Two different cultures' approaches to a rite of passage, such as weddings or funerals
7. Two different cultures' views on the roles of men and women in society
8. Two products from two different eras

As you develop your comparison or contrast essay, consider using one or more other patterns of development. For example, you might use process analysis to explain the right and wrong ways of doing something or cause and effect to show the results of two teaching styles on learners.

For more on process analysis, see Chapter 12. For more on cause and effect, see Chapter 16.

Generating Ideas

Generating ideas involves choosing subjects to compare and prewriting to discover similarities, differences, and other details about the subjects.

Choosing Subjects to Compare

Take your time in selecting the assignment option you want to write about and in identifying specific subjects for the option you choose. A hasty decision at the beginning of the writing process can cost time later if you have to refocus or change your topic. Use the following guidelines to get started.

For more on prewriting strategies, see Chapter 4.

1. Some of the options listed on page 384 are concrete (comparing two public figures); others are more abstract (comparing teaching styles or views on an issue). Consider your learning style and choose the option with which you are most comfortable.

2. If you are a social learner, choose subjects that your classmates are familiar with so you can discuss your subjects with them. Try group brainstorming about various possible subjects.

3. Choose subjects with which you have some firsthand experience or that you are willing to learn about through research. You might try the techniques of questioning or writing assertions to help you generate ideas.

4. Choose subjects that interest you. You will have more fun writing about them, and your enthusiasm will enliven your essay. Try mapping or sketching to come up with interesting subjects.

Learning Style Options

TEACHING TIP: LEARNING STYLES

Encourage students to brainstorm (alone or in groups) a list of subjects they feel comfortable working with. Point out that comparison and contrast can work with any two comparable subjects, so that pragmatic and creative learners, for example, should both be able to find engaging subjects.

ESSAY IN PROGRESS 1

Using the preceding suggestions, choose an assignment option from the list on page 384 or an option you think of on your own. Then do some prewriting to help you select two specific subjects for your comparison or contrast essay.

Choosing a Basis of Comparison and a Purpose

Suppose you want to compare or contrast two well-known football players, a quarterback, and a linebacker. If you merely present various similarities and differences about the two players—their awards, unusual plays, and so forth—your essay will lack direction. To avoid this problem, you need to choose a basis of comparison and a purpose for writing. To compare or contrast the two football players, you could compare the players on the basis of the positions they play, describing the skills and training needed for each position. Your purpose in this instance would be to *inform* readers about the two positions. Alternately, you could base your comparison on their performance on the field; in this case, your purpose might be to *persuade* readers to accept your evaluation of both players and

TEACHING TIP: LEARNING STYLES

Encourage students to use at least one prewriting strategy.

• Creative learners may pair up with social learners to brainstorm about human or animal subjects.
• Verbal learners may freewrite in their journals or on a computer about possible subjects and then highlight essential points of comparison and contrast. The subjects about which they have the most to say will probably be their most promising choice.
• Spatial learners may prefer to draw a map or cluster diagram of promising subjects.

your opinion on who is the better athlete. Other bases of comparison might be the players' media images, contributions to their respective teams, or service to the community.

Once you have a basis of comparison and a purpose in mind, try to state them clearly in a few sentences that you can refer to as you work through the rest of the process of writing your essay. Doing so will help you keep your essay on track.

ESSAY IN PROGRESS 2

For the assignment option and subjects you selected in Essay in Progress 1, decide on a tentative basis of comparison and purpose for your essay. Describe both clearly in a few sentences. Keep in mind that you may revise your basis of comparison and purpose as your essay develops.

Considering Your Audience and Point of View

As you develop your comparison or contrast and gather details, keep your audience in mind. Choose points of comparison that will interest your readers and that support your purpose for writing. For example, if you were evaluating two local summer recreation programs for children and your audience was other parents, they would be interested in the details of the programs' operations, such as costs, hours, activities, and supervision. However, if your audience was a group of elementary school principals, they might be more interested in the programs' goals and objectives and how the programs are administered and funded. For this assignment, your audience is made up of your classmates. Keep them in mind as you develop your essay.

When considering your audience, you also need to think about point of view, or how you should address your readers. Most comparison or contrast essays are written in the third person (see Ward's essay on p. 371 for an example). However, the first person may be appropriate when you use comparison or contrast to express personal thoughts or feelings (see Houston's essay on p. 373 for an example).

Discovering Similarities and Differences and Generating Details

Your next step is to discover how your two subjects are similar, how they are different, or both. Depending on your learning style, you can approach this task in a number of different ways.

TEACHING TIP

Ask students to write their tentative bases of comparison and purpose in their journals or on a computer. Remind them to refer to and revise these elements throughout this assignment.

For more on purpose, audience, and point of view, see Chapter 4, p. 73.

1. On paper or on your computer, create a two-column list of similarities and differences. Jot down ideas in the appropriate column.

2. Ask a classmate to help you brainstorm aloud by mentioning only similarities; then counter each similarity with a difference. Make notes on or tape-record the brainstorming.

3. For concrete subjects, try visualizing them. Take notes on what you see or draw a sketch of your subjects.

4. Create a scenario in which your subjects interact. For example, if your topic is automobiles of the 1920s and 1990s, imagine taking your great-grandfather, who owned a Model T Ford, for a drive in a 1999 luxury car. How would he react? What would he say?

5. Do research on your two subjects at the library or on the Internet.

Keep in mind that your readers will need plenty of details to grasp the similarities and differences between your subjects. Description, examples, and facts will make your subjects seem real to your readers. Recall the amount of descriptive detail Houston uses in "A Taste of Snow" to make her readers experience both the stark beauty of Manzanar and the warm, carnival atmosphere of Ocean Park.

To maintain an even balance between your two subjects, do some brainstorming, freewriting, or library or Internet research to gather roughly the same amount of detail for each. This guideline is especially important if your purpose is to demonstrate that subject A is preferable to or better than subject B. Your readers will become suspicious if you provide plenty of detail for subject A and only sketchy information about subject B.

ESSAY IN PROGRESS 3

Use the preceding suggestions and one or more prewriting strategies to discover similarities and differences and to generate details about the two subjects of your comparison.

Developing Your Thesis

The thesis statement for a comparison or contrast essay needs to fulfill the three criteria noted earlier: It should identify the subjects; suggest whether you will focus on similarities, differences, or both; and state your main point. In addition, your thesis should tell readers why your comparison or

Learning Style Options

TEACHING TIP:
LEARNING STYLES

1. For all learners, especially rational or pragmatic learners
2. For social learners
3. For concrete, spatial, and creative learners
4. For emotional learners
5. For all learners

For more on description, see Chapter 10.

For more on library and Internet research, see Chapter 19.

For more on thesis statements, see Chapter 5, p. 97.

contrast of the two subjects is important or useful to them. Look at the following sample thesis statements.

WEAK: The books by Robert Parker and Sue Grafton are similar.

REVISED: The novels of Robert Parker and Sue Grafton are popular because readers are fascinated by the intrigues of sassy, independent private detectives.

The first thesis is weak because it presents the two subjects in isolation, without placing the comparison within a context or giving the reader a reason to care about it. The second thesis is more detailed and specific. It indicates why the similarity is worth reading about. As you develop your thesis, think about what your comparison says about people, life, or behavior. In "Lincoln and Roosevelt: Two Master Politicians," for example, Ward's thesis makes a point about political leadership skills that is relevant to current issues in politics and government.

ESSAY IN PROGRESS 4

Using the preceding suggestions, write a thesis statement for this chapter's essay assignment. The thesis should identify the two subjects of your comparison; tell whether you will focus on similarities, differences, or both; and convey your main point to readers.

Evaluating Your Ideas and Thesis

Your prewriting no doubt yielded numerous ideas and details about the subjects of your comparison. Your next steps are to evaluate your ideas and thesis and to choose the points and details of comparison to include in your essay.

Selecting Points of Comparison

With your thesis in mind, review your prewriting by underlining or highlighting ideas that pertain to your thesis and eliminating those that do not. If you are working on a computer, highlight these key ideas in bold type or move them to a separate file, using the cut-and-paste function of your word-processing program. Try to identify the points or characteristics by which you can best compare your subjects. For example, if your thesis is about evaluating the performance of the two football players, you would probably select various facts and details about their training, the plays they make, and their records.

TEACHING TIP: COLLABORATIVE WRITING

(10 minutes) Encourage students to evaluate each other's draft theses. To ensure multiple peer reviews, have students pass their draft thesis to the student on the right for comments; then to the student on the left for comments. Ask peer reviewers to evaluate whether the thesis identifies the subjects, the focus, and the main point.

COMPUTER HINT

Ask each student to email his or her tentative thesis statement to two other students for review, if networked computers are not available.

Think of points of comparison as the main similarities or differences that support your thesis. As noted earlier, in "Lincoln and Roosevelt: Two Master Politicians," Ward discusses several important similarities between the two presidents — their ambition, their attitude toward the presidency, and their political savvy — but avoids including minor points that could sidetrack readers and weaken the effect of his essay.

Take a few minutes to evaluate your ideas and thesis. Make sure you have enough points of comparison to support your thesis and enough details to develop those points. If necessary, do additional brainstorming (or use another prewriting technique) to generate sufficient support for your thesis.

TRYING OUT YOUR IDEAS ON OTHERS

Working in a group of two or three students, discuss your ideas and thesis for this chapter's assignment. Each writer should state his or her topic, thesis, and points of comparison. Then, as a group, evaluate each writer's work.

ESSAY IN PROGRESS 5

Using the preceding suggestions and comments from your classmates, list the points of comparison you plan to use in your essay and evaluate your ideas and thesis. Refer to the list of characteristics on pages 374–77 to help you with your evaluation.

Organizing and Drafting

Once you have evaluated your thesis, points of comparison, and details, you are ready to organize your ideas and draft your essay.

For more on drafting an essay, see Chapter 6.

Choosing a Method of Organization

Before you begin writing, decide whether you will use a point-by-point or a subject-by-subject organization. Recall that a point-by-point organization compares two subjects on each point of comparison, whereas a subject-by-subject organization discusses all points of comparison about one subject before moving on to the second subject (review Figures 13.1 and 13.2). To select a method of organization, consider the complexity of your subjects and the length of your essay. You may also need to experiment with the two approaches to see which works better. It is a good idea to make an outline or draw a graphic organizer at this stage. To experiment with different methods of organization, create a new computer file for each possibility and try each one out.

Here are a few other guidelines to consider.

1. The subject-by-subject method tends to emphasize the larger picture, whereas the point-by-point method emphasizes details and specifics.

2. The point-by-point method often works better for lengthy essays because it keeps both subjects current in your reader's mind. For example, if five pages of a ten-page essay are devoted to each subject, by the time a reader finishes the five pages on subject B, he or she may have forgotten the main points about subject A.

3. The point-by-point method is often preferable for complicated or technical subjects. For example, if you compare two computer systems, it would be easier to explain the function of a memory card once and then describe the memory cards in each of the two systems than it would be to mention memory cards at two different points in the essay.

ESSAY IN PROGRESS 6

Choose a method of organization—point by point or subject by subject—and organize the points of comparison you generated in Essay in Progress 5.

Drafting the Comparison or Contrast Essay

Now that you know how to organize your essay, your next step is to write a first draft. Use the following guidelines.

1. If you are drafting a point-by-point essay, keep the following suggestions in mind.

- Work back and forth between your two subjects, generally mentioning the subjects in the same order. If both subjects share a particular characteristic (as they do in paragraph 4 of Ward's essay on p. 371), then you may want to mention the two subjects together.

- Arrange your points of comparison carefully; start with the clearest, simplest points and then move on to more complex ones.

2. If you are drafting a subject-by-subject essay, keep the following suggestions in mind.

TEACHING TIP

Students who experience difficulty in organizing their writing, especially creative learners, may seek your help during the drafting stage. Check whether these students are using a consistent method of organization in their graphic organizer or outline (whether point by point or subject by subject). Encourage them to work with a peer reviewer or writing center tutor.

- Be sure to cover the same points for both subjects.

- Cover the points of comparison in the same order in both halves of your essay.

- Write a clear statement of transition wherever you switch from one subject to the other. (For an example, see paragraph 4 in Houston's essay on p. 373, where she makes the transition from Manzanar to Ocean Park.)

3. Use analogies. An **analogy** is a special type of comparison in which one subject is used to explain the other. Sometimes called an *extended metaphor,* an analogy uses a familiar subject to explain a less familiar one. You can use an analogy as part of a comparison or contrast essay or as a way to make comparisons within an essay that relies on some other pattern of development.

For example, a writer could compare the sounds of early spring in a marsh to those made by an orchestra or explain the evolution of the universe by comparing it to the stages of a human's life. In this sense, analogies differ from similes and metaphors (see p. 198), which make comparisons based on a single shared point.

4. Use transitions. Transitions are especially important in helping readers to follow the points you make in a comparison or contrast essay. Transitions alert readers to the organization of the essay as well as to shifts between subjects or to new points of comparison. An essay that lacks transitions sounds choppy and unconnected. Transitional words and phrases that are useful in moving among ideas in essays using comparison and contrast include *similarly, in contrast, on the one hand, on the other hand,* and *not only . . . but also.*

For more on transitions, see Chapter 6, p. 138.

5. Write an effective introduction. Although Houston's "A Taste of Snow" is effective without an introduction, most of the comparison or contrast essays you write should have a clear introduction. In it you want to spark your readers' interest, introduce your subjects, state your thesis, and include any background information your readers may need. If your focus is on similarities, you may want to mention some differences between your subjects at the outset, as Ward does in "Lincoln and Roosevelt."

For more on writing effective paragraphs, including introductions and conclusions, see Chapter 6.

6. Write a satisfying conclusion. Your conclusion should offer a final comment on your comparison or contrast, reminding readers of your

TEACHING TIP

Students who have fol-
lowed the steps in the
Guided Writing Assign-
ment should be ready to
compose a first draft
independently. However,
check to see if any stu-
dents need to rethink
their thesis, points of
comparison, or method
of organization before
drafting. Encourage
them to seek the assis-
tance of a peer reviewer
or writing center tutor.

thesis. For a lengthy or complex essay, you might want to summarize
your main points as well. Reread the two concluding paragraphs of
Houston's essay, "A Taste of Snow" (p. 373), to see how the writer ties her
two subjects together.

ESSAY IN PROGRESS 7

Using the organization you developed in Essay in Progress 6 and the preceding guidelines for drafting, write a first draft of your comparison or contrast
essay.

Analyzing and Revising

If possible, set your draft aside for a day or two before rereading and revising it. As you reread your draft, concentrate on your ideas, not on grammar or mechanics. Use one or more of the following suggestions to analyze
your draft.

Learning Style Options

LEARNING STYLES

1. For social learners;
   encourage other stu-
   dents to try this
   technique.
2. Spatial learners
   should have already
   drawn a graphic orga-
   nizer; encourage other
   students to do so.
3. For all learners;
   encourage students
   to seek out a writing
   center tutor to discuss
   weak paragraphs.

*For more on the benefits
of peer review, see Chap-
ter 7, p. 166.*

1. Reread your essay aloud or ask a friend or classmate to do so as you listen. Use a tape recorder. Play the tape back, listening for parts that
   sound choppy or monotonous.

2. Draw a graphic organizer or make an outline, or update the one you
   prepared earlier to reflect the organization of your essay. A graphic
   organizer or outline will indicate whether your method of organization is clear or if your essay contains inconsistencies or gaps.

3. Read each paragraph with this question in mind: "So what?" If any
   paragraph does not answer that question, it may not contribute to
   your comparison. Revise the paragraph or delete it.

Use Flowchart 13.1 to guide your analysis of the strengths and weaknesses in your draft essay. You might also ask a classmate to review your
draft essay using the questions in the flowchart. Encourage your reader to
ask questions wherever necessary about the purpose of the essay and the
major points of comparison or contrast and to give you feedback on any
parts that are unclear. Your reviewer should consider each question listed
in the flowchart, explaining each "No" answer.

FLOWCHART 13.1
REVISING A COMPARISON OR CONTRAST ESSAY

Questions		Revision Strategies

1. Does your essay have a clear purpose? Does it express ideas, inform, or persuade?

 No

- Brainstorm a list of reasons the comparison is worth making. Make the most promising reason your purpose.
- If you cannot discover why the comparison is worth making, broaden or narrow your topic or choose a new one.

Yes ⇩

2. Do you compare subjects with shared characteristics? Do you use a workable basis of comparison?

 No

- Use *Who, What, Where, When,* and *How* questions to generate characteristics about your subjects or to find those common to both.
- Ask a friend or classmate to help you think of a basis of comparison.

Yes ⇩

3. Do you fairly examine similarities, differences, or both?

 No

- Add details to provide a more balanced examination.
- If you have trouble thinking of similar or opposing points, conduct research or ask a classmate to suggest ideas.

Yes

(Continued on next page)

FLOWCHART 13.1 *(continued)*

Questions	Revision Strategies

4. Do you use your comparison or contrast to make an interesting point about your subjects? Does your thesis identify the subjects being compared; indicate whether you focus on similarities, differences, or both; and state your main point?

 No

- Make sure your essay includes a thesis statement.
- Revise your thesis to include the three required elements (p. 376).
- Research your subjects to come up with a more interesting main point.

 Yes

5. Do you include only significant similarities and differences that support your thesis? Do you include enough details to make your comparisons vivid and interesting to your readers? (Do you tell enough for readers to understand each subject?)

 No

- Reread each key point; then reread your thesis. Delete any points that do not directly support the thesis.
- Review your prewriting to see if you overlooked any significant points or details about your subjects.
- Research your subjects to come up with more interesting examples and details.

 Yes

6. Do you use either a point-by-point or subject-by-subject organization throughout the entire essay? Do you discuss the same features in the same order consistently throughout?

 No

- Outline your existing organization to find inconsistencies or gaps.
- Reorganize your essay using only one method of organization consistently.

 Yes

(Continued on next page)

FLOWCHART 13.1 *(continued)*

Questions		Revision Strategies
7. Is each body paragraph well developed and focused on a separate point? Is your introduction effective?	No ⇨	• Check to see if each paragraph has a topic sentence and supporting details (see Chapter 6). • Add transitions and vary the length and pattern of sentences. • Revise your introduction so that it meets the guidelines in Chapter 6 (pp 141–44).
Yes ⇩		
8. Is the conclusion satisfying and relevant to the comparison?	No ⇨	• Review what the comparison suggests; then revise your conclusion. • Propose an action or way of thinking that is appropriate in light of the comparison. • Revise your conclusion so that it meets the guidelines in Chapter 6 (pp. 144–46).
Yes		

ESSAY IN PROGRESS 8

Revise your draft using Flowchart 13.1 and any comments you received from peer reviewers.

TEACHING TIP

Encourage students to seek a writing center tutor for further review of the revision.

Editing and Proofreading

The last step is to check your revised essay for errors in grammar, spelling, punctuation, and mechanics. In addition, be sure to check your error log for the types of errors you tend to make.

As you edit and proofread your comparison or contrast essay, watch out for the following types of errors.

For more on keeping an error log, see Chapter 8, p. 201.

1. Look at adjectives and adverbs and their degrees of comparison—*positive, comparative,* and *superlative.* Make sure you change the form of adjectives and adverbs when you compare two items (comparative) and when you compare three or more items (superlative). The following examples show how adjectives and adverbs change forms:

	Adjectives	Adverbs
Positive	sharp	early
Comparative	sharper	earlier
Superlative	sharpest	earliest

▶ Both *L.A. Confidential* and *Devil in a Blue Dress* were suspenseful movies, but I liked *Devil in a Blue Dress* ~~best.~~ *better.*

▶ George, Casey, and Bob all play basketball badly, but Bob's game is ~~worse.~~ *the worst.*

2. Make sure that items in a pair linked by correlative conjunctions (*either . . . or, neither . . . nor, not only . . . but also*) are in the same grammatical form.

▶ The Grand Canyon is not only a spectacular tourist attraction, but also scientists *a useful geological record for* ~~consider it a useful geological record.~~

ESSAY IN PROGRESS 9

Edit and proofread your essay, paying particular attention to adjectives and adverbs used to compare and to items linked by correlative conjunctions.

STUDENTS WRITE

Heather Gianakos was a first-year student when she wrote the following comparison and contrast essay for her composition course. Although she has always enjoyed both styles of cooking she discusses, she needed to do some research in the library and on the Internet to learn more about their history. As you read the essay, highlight the writer's thesis and points of comparison.

Border Bites

Heather Gianakos

Chili peppers, tortillas, tacos: All these foods belong to the styles of cooking known as Mexican, Tex-Mex, and Southwestern. These internationally popular styles often overlap; sometimes it can be hard to tell which style a particular dish belongs to. Two particular traditions of cooking, however, play an especially important role in the kitchens of Mexico and the American Southwest: native-derived Mexican cooking ("Mexican"), and Anglo-influenced Southwestern cooking, particularly from Texas ("Southwestern"). The different traditions and geographic locations of the inhabitants of Mexico and of the Anglo-American settlers in the Southwest have resulted in subtle, flavorful differences between the foods featured in Mexican and Southwestern cuisine.

Many of the traditions of Southwestern cooking grew out of difficult situations--cowboys and ranchers cooking over open fires, for example. Chili, which can contain beans, beef, tomatoes, corn, and many other ingredients, was a good dish to cook over a campfire because everything could be combined in one pot. Dry foods, such as beef jerky, were a convenient way to solve food storage problems and could be easily tucked into saddlebags. In Mexico, by contrast, fresh fruits and vegetables such as avocados and tomatoes were widely available and did not need to be dried or stored. They could be made into spicy salsa and guacamole. Mexicans living in coastal areas could also enjoy fish and lobster dishes (Jamison and Jamison 5).

Corn has been a staple in the American Southwest and Mexico since the time of the Aztecs, who made tortillas (flat, unleavened bread, originally made from stone-ground corn and water) similar to the ones served in Mexico today (Jamison and Jamison 5). Southwesterners, often of European descent, adopted the tortilla but often prepared it with wheat flour, which was easily available

1

2

3

PREREADING
QUESTION

What difficult circumstances might have contributed to the development of a Southwestern cuisine?

TEACHING TIP

Thesis: "The different traditions and geographic locations . . . cuisine" (paragraph 1).

to them. Wheat-flour tortillas can now be found in both Mexican and Southwestern cooking, but corn is usually the primary grain in dishes with precolonial origins. Tamales (whose name derives from a word in Nahuatl, the Aztec group of languages) are a delicious example: A hunk of cornmeal dough, sometimes combined with ground meat, is wrapped in corn husks and steamed. In Southwestern cooking, corn is often used for leavened corn bread, which is made with corn flour rather than cornmeal and can be flavored with jalapeños or back bacon.

4   Meat of various kinds is often the centerpiece of both Mexican and Southwestern tables. However, although beef, pork, and chicken are staples in both traditions, they are often prepared quite differently. Fried chicken rolled in flour and dunked into sizzling oil or fat is a popular dish throughout the American Southwest. In traditional Mexican cooking, however, chicken is often cooked more slowly, in stews or baked dishes, with a variety of seasonings, including ancho chiles, garlic, and onions.

5   Ever since Southwestern cattle farming began with the early Spanish missions in Texas, beef has been eaten both north and south of the border. In Southwestern cooking, steak--flank, rib eye, or sirloin--grilled quickly and served rare is often a chef's crowning glory. In Mexican cooking, beef may be combined with vegetables and spices and rolled into a fajita or served ground in a taco. For a Mexican food purist, in fact, the only true fajita is made from skirt steak, although Mexican food as it is served in the United States often features chicken fajitas.

6   In Texas and the Southwest United States, barbecued pork ribs are often prepared in barbecue cookoffs, similar to chili-cooking competitions (Raven 1). However, while the BBQ is seen as a Southwestern specialty, barbecue ribs as they are served in Southwestern-themed restaurants today actually come from a Hispanic and Southwest Mexican tradition dating from the days before refrigeration: since pork fat, unlike beef fat, has a

tendency to become rancid, pork ribs were often marinated in vinegar and spices and then hung to dry. Later the ribs were basted with the same sauce and grilled (Campa 278). The resulting dish has become a favorite both north and south of the border, although in Mexican cooking, where beef is somewhat less important than in Southwestern cooking, pork is equally popular in many other forms, such as chorizo sausage.

    Cooks in San Antonio or Albuquerque would probably   7 tell you that the food they cook is as much Mexican as it is Southwestern. Regional cuisines in such areas of the Southwest as New Mexico, southern California, and Arizona feature elements of both traditions; Chimichangas, deep-fried burritos, actually originated in Arizona (Jamison and Jamison 11). Food lovers who sample regional specialties, however, will note, and savor, the contrast between the spicy, fried or grilled, beef-heavy style of Southwestern food and the richly seasoned, corn- and tomato-heavy style of Mexican food.

Works Cited

Campa, Arthur L. Hispanic Culture in the Southwest.
    Norman: U of Oklahoma P, 1979.
Jamison, Cheryl Alters, and Bill Jamison. The Border
    Cookbook. Boston: Harvard Common, 1995.
Raven, John. "Competition Barbecuing." Texas Cooking
    Magazine Apr. 1998. 9 June 1998 <http://
    www.texascooking.com/features/
    apr98ravencompetition.htm>.

Analyzing the Essay

1. Evaluate Gianakos's title and introduction. Do they provide the reader with enough background on her topic?

2. What method of organization does Gianakos use in her essay?

POSSIBLE ANSWERS: ANALYZING THE ESSAY

1. The title sounds clever but does not reveal much about the topic. The introduction provides adequate background, though the body of the essay develops the interrelations between Southwestern and Mexican cuisine, which are only hinted at in the introduction.

2. Point-by-point organization.

(Continued on next page)

3. Points of comparison: convenience versus fresh foods; use of corn, chicken, beef, pork.
4. The sources enhance her credibility (on origins of particular foods and other historical notes) and give readers sources of further information.

POSSIBLE ANSWERS: REACTING TO THE ESSAY

1. Responses will vary; possibilities include customs, industries, and popular culture.
2. Responses will vary; possibilities include California, New Orleans, and the Southeast.
3. Responses will vary.

3. Identify Gianakos's points of comparison.

4. How does Gianakos's use of sources contribute to her essay?

Reacting to the Essay: Discussion and Journal Writing

1. Gianakos compares the cuisines of the American Southwest and Mexico. Suggest several other possible bases of comparison that could be used to compare these geographic regions.

2. What other regional cuisines might make effective topics for a comparison and contrast essay?

3. Write a journal entry describing your reaction to Southwestern and Mexican foods or two other regional cuisines.

READING COMPARISON AND CONTRAST

The following section provides advice for reading comparison and contrast as well as two model essays. Each essay illustrates the characteristics of comparison and contrast covered in this chapter and provides opportunities to examine, analyze, and react to the writer's ideas. The second essay uses comparison and contrast along with other methods of development.

WORKING WITH TEXT: READING COMPARISON OR CONTRAST ESSAYS

For more on reading strategies, see Chapter 2.

Reading a comparison or contrast essay is somewhat different from reading other kinds of essays. First, the essay contains two or more subjects, instead of one. Second, the subjects are being compared, contrasted, or both, so you must follow the author's points of comparison between or among them. Use the following guidelines to read comparison or contrast essays effectively.

What to Look for, Highlight, and Annotate

For more on previewing, see Chapter 2, p. 27.

1. As you preview the essay, determine whether it uses the point-by-point or subject-by-subject organization. Knowing the method of organization will help you move through the essay more easily.

2. Identify and highlight the thesis statement, if it is stated explicitly. Use it to guide your reading: What does it tell you about the essay's purpose, direction, and organization?

3. Read the essay once to get an overall sense of how it develops. As you read, watch for the points of comparison that the writer makes. Highlight each point of comparison as you discover it.

4. Review the essay by drawing a graphic organizer (see Figures 13.1 and 13.2). Doing so will help you learn and recall the key points of the essay.

How to Find Ideas to Write About

To respond to or write about a comparison or contrast essay, consider the following strategies.

For more on discovering ideas for a response paper, see Chapter 3.

- Compare the subjects using a different basis of comparison. If, for example, an essay compares or contrasts athletes in various sports on the basis of salary, you could compare them according to the training required for each sport.

- For an essay that emphasizes differences, consider writing about similarities, and vice versa. For example, in response to an essay on the differences between two late-night television hosts, you might write about their similarities.

- To write an essay that looks at one point of comparison in more depth, you might do research to discover further information or interview an expert on the topic.

THINKING CRITICALLY ABOUT COMPARISON AND CONTRAST

In many academic situations, you will be called upon to read and compare two or more sources on a given topic. This skill, called *synthesis*, involves drawing together two or more sets of ideas and discovering similarities and differences. You will need to synthesize sources for research papers, articles and essays for class discussion, and even lecture notes and textbook readings on the same topic as you study for tests. For example, you might be asked to read a number of articles on movie rating systems and then recommend a system that you think might work. You might be asked to read three excerpts from different biographies of Martin Luther King Jr., and then write a summary of his religious views. Notice that in each situation, you are asked to discover a new idea or viewpoint, one that did not appear in any of the sources. Synthesis is a process of putting ideas together to create new ideas

CONNECTIONS

Chapter 20 also provides advice for synthesizing sources.

or to discover new insights about them. Here are some questions to ask when synthesizing sources.

- On what points do the sources agree?
- On what points do the sources disagree?
- How do the sources differ in viewpoint, approach, purpose, and type of support?

After you have read and analyzed your sources, develop your own ideas about the topic. Start by brainstorming about the topic without referring to the sources. Try to answer the following questions.

- What did I learn about this topic from the sources?
- What can I conclude about this topic based on what I read?
- With which sources do I agree?
- How can I support my views on this topic?

COMPARISON AND CONTRAST ESSAY

As you read the following essay by psychologist Daniel Goleman, notice how the writer uses the elements of comparison and contrast discussed in this chapter.

 His Marriage and Hers: Childhood Roots
Daniel Goleman

PREREADING
QUESTION

In what ways do you
think men and women
differ in communication
style?

Daniel Goleman holds a Ph.D. in behavioral and brain sciences and has published a number of books on psychology, including Vital Lies, Simple Truths *(1985),* The Meditative Mind *(1988),* Working with Emotional Intelligence *(1998), and, as coauthor,* The Creative Spirit *(1992). In his book* Emotional Intelligence *(1995), from which the following selection was taken, Goleman asserts that daily living requires skill in handling emotions. He describes the skill and explains how to develop it. As you read the selection, notice how the writer uses comparison and contrast to explore his subject—differences between the sexes—and highlight his key points of comparison.*

1   As I was entering a restaurant on a recent evening, a young man stalked out the door, his face set in an expression both stony and sullen. Close on his heels a young woman came running, her fists desperately pummeling his back while she yelled, "Goddamn you! Come back here and be nice to me!" That poignant, impossibly self-

contradictory plea aimed at a retreating back epitomizes the pattern most commonly seen in couples whose relationship is distressed: She seeks to engage, he withdraws. Marital therapists have long noted that by the time a couple finds their way to the therapy office they are in this pattern of engage-withdraw, with his complaint about her "unreasonable" demands and outbursts, and her lamenting his indifference to what she is saying.

This marital endgame reflects the fact that there are, in effect, two emotional realities in a couple, his and hers. The roots of these emotional differences, while they may be partly biological, also can be traced back to childhood, and to the separate emotional worlds boys and girls inhabit while growing up. There is a vast amount of research on these separate worlds, their barriers reinforced not just by the different games boys and girls prefer, but by young children's fear of being teased for having a "girlfriend" or "boyfriend."[1] One study of children's friendships found that three-year-olds say about half their friends are of the opposite sex; for five-year-olds it's about 20 percent, and by age seven almost no boys or girls say they have a best friend of the opposite sex.[2] These separate social universes intersect little until teenagers start dating.

Meanwhile, boys and girls are taught very different lessons about handling emotions. Parents, in general, discuss emotions—with the exception of anger—more with their daughters than their sons.[3] Girls are exposed to more information about emotions than are boys: when parents make up stories to tell their preschool children, they use more emotion words when talking to daughters than to sons; when mothers play with their infants, they display a wider range of emotions to daughters than to sons; when mothers talk to daughters about feelings, they discuss in more detail the emotional state itself than they do with their sons—though with the sons they go into more detail about the causes and consequences of emotions like anger (probably as a cautionary tale).

Leslie Brody and Judith Hall, who have summarized the research on differences in emotions between the sexes, propose that because girls develop facility with language more quickly than do boys, this leads them to be more experienced at articulating their feelings and more skilled than boys at using words to explore and substitute for emotional reactions such as physical fights; in contrast, they note, "boys, for whom the verbalization of affects is de-emphasized, may become largely unconscious of their emotional states, both in themselves and others."[4]

At age ten, roughly the same percent of girls as boys are overtly aggressive, given to open confrontation when angered. But by age thirteen, a telling difference between the sexes emerges: Girls become more adept than boys at artful aggressive tactics like ostracism, vicious gossip, and indirect vendettas. Boys, by and large, simply continue being confrontational when angered, oblivious to these more covert strategies.[5] This is just one of many ways that boys — and later, men — are less sophisticated than the opposite sex in the byways of emotional life.

6   When girls play together, they do so in small, intimate groups, with an emphasis on minimizing hostility and maximizing cooperation, while boys' games are in larger groups, with an emphasis on competition. One key difference can be seen in what happens when games boys or girls are playing get disrupted by someone getting hurt. If a boy who has gotten hurt gets upset, he is expected to get out of the way and stop crying so the game can go on. If the same happens among a group of girls who are playing, the *game stops* while everyone gathers around to help the girl who is crying. This difference between boys and girls at play epitomizes what Harvard's Carol Gilligan points to as a key disparity between the sexes: boys take pride in a lone, tough-minded independence and autonomy, while girls see themselves as part of a web of connectedness. Thus boys are threatened by anything that might challenge their independence, while girls are more threatened by a rupture in their relationships. And, as Deborah Tannen has pointed out in her book *You Just Don't Understand,* these differing perspectives mean that men and women want and expect very different things out of a conversation, with men content to talk about "things," while women seek emotional connection.

7   In short, these contrasts in schooling in the emotions foster very different skills, with girls becoming "adept at reading both verbal and nonverbal emotional signals, at expressing and communicating their feelings," and boys becoming adept at "minimizing emotions having to do with vulnerability, guilt, fear and hurt."[6] Evidence for these different stances is very strong in the scientific literature. Hundreds of studies have found, for example, that on average women are more empathic than men, at least as measured by the ability to read someone else's unstated feelings from facial expression, tone of voice, and other nonverbal cues. Likewise, it is generally easier to read feelings from a woman's face than a man's; while there is no difference in facial expressiveness among very young boys and girls, as they go through the elementary-school grades boys become less expressive, girls more so. This may partly reflect another key difference: women, on average, experience the entire range of emotions with greater intensity and more volatility than men — in this sense, women *are* more "emotional" than men.[7]

8   All of this means that, in general, women come into a marriage groomed for the role of emotional manager, while men arrive with

much less appreciation of the importance of this task for helping a relationship survive. Indeed, the most important element for women —but not for men—in satisfaction with their relationship reported in a study of 264 couples was the sense that the couple has "good communication."[8] Ted Huston, a psychologist at the University of Texas who has studied couples in depth, observes, "For the wives, intimacy means talking things over, especially talking about the relationship itself. The men, by and large, don't understand what the wives want from them. They say, 'I want to do things with her, and all she wants to do is talk.'" During courtship, Huston found, men were much more willing to spend time talking in ways that suited the wish for intimacy of their wives-to-be. But once married, as time went on the men—especially in more traditional couples—spent less and less time talking in this way with their wives, finding a sense of closeness simply in doing things like gardening together rather than talking things over.

This growing silence on the part of husbands may be partly due   9
to the fact that, if anything, men are a bit Pollyannaish about the state of their marriage, while their wives are attuned to the trouble spots: in one study of marriages, men had a rosier view than their wives of just about everything in their relationship—lovemaking, finances, ties with in-laws, how well they listened to each other, how much their flaws mattered.[9] Wives, in general, are more vocal about their complaints than are their husbands, particularly among unhappy couples. Combine men's rosy view of marriage with their aversion to emotional confrontations, and it is clear why wives so often complain that their husbands try to wiggle out of discussing the troubling things about their relationship. (Of course this gender difference is a generalization, and is not true in every case; a psychiatrist friend complained that in his marriage his wife is reluctant to discuss emotional matters between them, and he is the one who is left to bring them up.)

The slowness of men to bring up problems in a relationship is no   10
doubt compounded by their relative lack of skill when it comes to reading facial expressions of emotions. Women, for example, are more sensitive to a sad expression on a man's face than are men in detecting sadness from a woman's expression.[10] Thus a woman has to be all the sadder for a man to notice her feelings in the first place, let alone for him to raise the question of what is making her so sad.

Consider the implications of this emotional gender gap for how   11
couples handle the grievances and disagreements that any intimate relationship inevitably spawns. In fact, specific issues such as how often a couple has sex, how to discipline the children, or how much debt and savings a couple feels comfortable with are not what make

or break a marriage. Rather, it is *how* a couple discusses such sore points that matters more for the fate of their marriage. Simply having reached an agreement about *how* to disagree is key to marital survival; men and women have to overcome the innate gender differences in approaching rocky emotions. Failing this, couples are vulnerable to emotional rifts that eventually can tear their relationship apart. . . . [T]hese rifts are far more likely to develop if one or both partners have certain deficits in emotional intelligence.   ■

NOTES:

1. The separate worlds of boys and girls: Eleanor Maccoby and C. N. Jacklin, "Gender Segregation in Childhood," in H. Reese, ed., *Advances in Child Development and Behavior* (New York: Academic Press, 1987).
2. Same-sex playmates: John Gottman, "Same and Cross Sex Friendship in Young Children," in J. Gottman and J. Parker, eds., *Conversation of Friends* (New York: Cambridge University Press, 1986).
3. This and the following summary of sex differences in socialization of emotions are based on the excellent review in Leslie R. Brody and Judith A. Hall, "Gender and Emotion," in Michael Lewis and Jeannette Haviland, eds., *Handbook of Emotions* (New York: Guilford Press, 1993).
4. Brody and Hall, "Gender and Emotion," p. 456.
5. Girls and the arts of aggression: Robert B. Cairns and Beverley D. Cairns, *Lifelines and Risks* (New York: Cambridge University Press, 1994).
6. Brody and Hall, "Gender and Emotion," p. 454.
7. The findings about gender differences in emotion are reviewed in Brody and Hall, "Gender and Emotion."
8. The importance of good communication for women was reported in Mark H. Davis and H. Alan Oathout, "Maintenance of Satisfaction in Romantic Relationships: Empathy and Relational Competence," *Journal of Personality and Social Psychology* 53, 2 (1987), pp. 397–410.
9. The study of husbands' and wives' complaints: Robert J. Sternberg, "Triangulating Love," in Robert Sternberg and Michael Barnes, eds., *The Psychology of Love* (New Haven: Yale University Press, 1988).
10. Reading sad faces: The research is by Dr. Ruben C. Gur at the University of Pennsylvania School of Medicine.

Examining the Reading

1. Summarize the differences Goleman claims exist between men's and women's ways of expressing emotion.
2. According to Goleman, what are the roots or causes of the differences between men's and women's expression of emotion?
3. How can the emotional differences between spouses cause marital difficulties, according to the writer?

4. Explain how boys and girls play differently, according to Goleman.

5. Explain the meaning of each of the following words as it is used in the reading: *epitomizes* (paragraph 1), *articulating* (4), *ostracism* (5), *vendetta* (5), *disparity* (6), and *empathic* (7). Refer to your dictionary as needed.

Analyzing the Reading

1. What is Goleman's thesis?

2. Identify the purpose of the essay and list the points of comparison.

3. For each point of comparison, evaluate the evidence Goleman offers to substantiate his findings. Do you find the evidence sufficient and convincing? Why or why not? What other information might the writer have included?

4. What types of details does Goleman provide to explain each point of comparison?

5. Evaluate the effectiveness of the introduction and conclusion.

Reacting to the Reading: Discussion and Journal Writing

1. Do you think any of Goleman's generalizations about men and women are inaccurate? Discuss the evidence, if any, that would prove Goleman wrong.

2. Discuss a situation from your experience that either confirms or contradicts one of Goleman's generalizations.

3. Make a list of the emotional differences and resulting behavioral conflicts between men and women that you have observed. Decide which differences are explained by Goleman. Write a journal entry describing your findings.

COMPARISON AND CONTRAST COMBINED WITH OTHER PATTERNS

In the following reading, notice how Janet Maslin uses comparison and contrast to support her evaluation of a recent film, *Saving Private Ryan*.

By Being Honest about Violence, Spielberg Wins
Janet Maslin

Janet Maslin is a film and music critic. Her reviews have appeared in the **Boston Phoenix,** **Newsweek,** *and the* **New York Times,** *where she is currently chief film critic. This essay was originally published in the* **New York Times** *in August 1998. As you read the selection, highlight where the writer draws comparisons or makes analogies.*

---

differently about emotions; (b) different rates of acquiring verbal skills; (c) different ways of handling emotional life; (d) cooperation versus competition in childhood play; (e) different values; (f) different emotional skills; (g) talking versus doing; (h) different sensitivities to the conditions of marriage; (i) differences in the ability to read facial expressions

3. (a) Bald assertions; section would be stronger if Goleman had cited research; (b) common knowledge; (c) common knowledge; (d) presents empirical evidence; cites Harvard expert Carol Gilligan; (e) cites Deborah Tannen, expert on gender differences in communication; (f) refers to "hundreds of studies"; (g) cites University of Texas research; (h) a self-admitted generalization with exceptions; (i) generalization

4. Narrative with quote (introduction); references to scholarly research; supporting generalizations; quotations from experts.

5. Both are effective: The introduction sets up the issue; the conclusion considers "implications of this emotional gender gap."

POSSIBLE ANSWERS: REACTING TO THE READING

1. Responses will vary. Goleman notes that

(Continued on next page)

the generalizations do not apply to all men and women (9), thereby strengthening his credibility. More such examples would weaken his case, however.

2. Responses will vary.
3. Responses will vary.

PREREADING
QUESTION

How might the "honesty" alluded to in the title help distinguish the type of violence in *Saving Private Ryan* versus the violence in other movies?

1   Though the landmark film event that is Steven Spielberg's *Saving Private Ryan* opened last weekend to strong attendance and critical cartwheels, it also set off a flurry of talk-show trepidations. Worries spread about the violence level in this already famously harrowing World War II epic. Was it too much to bear? A decent date movie? Upsetting to veterans? In no time this tour de force had taken on the medicinal whiff of something punishing, instead of the aura of so-called entertainment value that we associate with *Armageddon, Deep Impact, The Negotiator* or *Lethal Weapon 4.**

2   Meanwhile, at the United States Capitol, our notion of acceptable violence raged out of control. In what sounded exactly like a pistol-packing summer-movie scene, a man found his way to the Rotunda, pulled out a concealed weapon and opened fire, mowing down two guards as screaming tourists fled.

3   This horrific event conformed so well to movie-style terrorism that it became all the more shocking for its sense of déjà vu. Real life has hard acts to follow these days: what's one more shaky skyscraper in midtown Manhattan after *Godzilla*? What's a gunfight at the Capitol when the White House has been incinerated by spaceships and the Chrysler Building is Hollywood's favorite punching bag?

4   In a week that brought *The Negotiator,* another hostage-crisis drama in which the apparent terrorist becomes an instant celebrity and finds himself suddenly able to wield enormous power, why should it be *Saving Private Ryan* that gives anyone pause? Because Mr. Spielberg's war games are not played by the usual rules, which means they don't offer the reassurance of playing games at all. Ordinarily, the movie that thrills audiences with over-the-top violence also creates its own buffer zone, protecting us from uncertainty as it indicates when to be frightened, when to breathe easy, where to find an above-the-title hero who can save the day.

5   Many of these films can match *Saving Private Ryan* for graphic bloodshed, but it's more pernicious in a context of pure fantasy. They kill off armies without eliciting a twitch.

6   For instance, *Starship Troopers,* last year's super-violent film in which cute earthling military units fought huge extraterrestrial bugs, was a much more gruesome battle film than Mr. Spielberg's. But it passed for light entertainment thanks to its slavish pandering to teen-age boys. Like *Saving Private Ryan, Starship Troopers* included early in its story the casual sight of a military officer who is missing a limb. In each case this served as a harbinger of the toll taken by warfare, but for *Starship Troopers* that just meant a hint at ugly, formulaic com-

---

Armageddon, Deep Impact, The Negotiator, and *Lethal Weapon 4:* action films that were released in the summer of 1998.

bat sequences featuring abundant mutilation. Without itself exploiting such misery, *Saving Private Ryan* is frank about what war does to the body and even more so about what it does to the soul.

Mr. Spielberg's film has been widely admired for its breathtaking D-Day sequence, which surpasses any known special effects in immersing audiences into the fierce chaos of the battlefield. No less astounding is its final showdown in a bombed-out French town, as all of the film's dramatic and historic events fuse into a crescendo of visceral terror.

But within that second long section of the film, one episode stands out as unforgettably as the shower scene from *Psycho*,* a brilliantly edited model of furious clarity and shattered audience expectations. The incident has to do with a failure of nerve at a crucial dramatic juncture, and it defines this film's way of breaking through conventional storytelling into terra incognita. It goes beyond the spectacle of killing, and even the immediate experience of violence, to contemplate a fate worse than death.

There's more to be gained from the core of bitter honesty in this one episode than there is in watching the whole planet get rescued to a rock-video beat, *Armageddon*-style.

And between those two films, incidentally, it's *Saving Private Ryan* that has by far the greater entertainment value. While everything about *Armageddon*, including its prettified violence, hurtles forward on automatic pilot, and while its characters' asteroid-sized triumphs are so inflated that they bear no relationship to life on earth, *Saving Private Ryan* opens a window onto real men in real turmoil and leaves us sharing every nuance of their experience.

Anyone can bombard viewers with gaudy, unrelated images and a lot of noise, but it takes a storyteller of Mr. Spielberg's stature to draw an audience so deeply, and so movingly, into the unknown.

It's that quality of the unfamiliar, and not the actual ravages of war, that makes *Saving Private Ryan* so disturbing—and also so vital. Here's a film with no interest in reinforcing what we already know. Nor does it care to keep us within the collective *Truman Show** of toothless violence that constitutes most Hollywood action fare. When real life imitates, or is shaped by, such Hollywood ideas of bloodshed, the trigger-happy action genre leaves us all the more stymied and bereft. The same films that feed fantasies of vicious omnipotence—of the gun in the Rotunda—haven't a clue about the nature of real strength.

7

8

9

10

11

12

Psycho: a 1960 horror film directed by Alfred Hitchcock (1899–1980).

The Truman Show: a 1998 film about a man who has unknowingly been the main character of a television show all of his life.

POSSIBLE ANSWERS: EXAMINING THE READING (p. 410)

1. Spielberg "goes beyond the spectacle of killing . . . to contemplate a fate worse than death" (paragraph 8) and "the core of bitter honesty" (9) is unconventional; the violence is realistic, not fantastic, though not what audiences might expect.

(Continued on next page)

2. *Armageddon* bombards
   viewers with familiar,
   "prettified violence"
   (10), "gaudy, unre-
   lated images and a lot
   of noise" (11).
3. Most such films pre-
   sent gratuitous vio-
   lence and special
   effects not to move
   viewers but merely to
   create memorable
   images.
4. *Trepidations:* expressions of fear; *tour de
   force:* an ingenious
   work; *pernicious:* injuri-
   ous, malicious; *vis-
   ceral:* gut-wrenching;
   omnipotence: quality of
   being all-powerful.

POSSIBLE ANSWERS:
ANALYZING THE
READING

1. *Saving Private Ryan*
   has been criticized
   because it depicts violence realistically and
   is more honest and
   original than most
   Hollywood war films.
   "In a week . . . why
   should it be *Saving
   Private Ryan* that gives
   anyone pause? Be-
   cause Mr. Spielberg's
   war games are not
   played by the usual
   rules" (paragraph 4).
2. Narrative, cause-
   effect, illustration,
   description, argument
3. Violence at the Capi-
   tol versus in a Holly-
   wood movie; *Saving
   Private Ryan* versus
   Armageddon. The com-
   parisons support the
   thesis that the vio-
   lence simulated by
   Ryan is ultimately
   more humane and
   true to actual human
   experience.
4. It shows that we are
   too willing to accept
   violence in real life

13   *Saving Private Ryan* does. That's why, for all its terrifying candor, it is an inspiration and not an ordeal. It is Mr. Spielberg's triumph this time to restore a sense of courage and sacrifice to a medium in which boisterous, empty victories are all the rage, and in which another kind of rage grows out of feeling cheated and impoverished by such deceptions. This surfeit of cartoon blowhards and fake conquests is junk food of the spirit. No wonder we yearn for something better. No wonder the two most lingering words in *Saving Private Ryan* are "Earn this." ■

Examining the Reading

1. According to Maslin, in what ways does Spielberg stray from the usual rules for portraying violence in movies and incorporate unconventional approaches?
2. Explain how *Saving Private Ryan* is different from other films, such as *Armageddon*.
3. Describe Maslin's attitude toward most films that portray violence.
4. Define each of the following terms as it is used in the reading: *trepidations* (paragraph 1), *tour de force* (1), *pernicious* (5), *visceral* (7), and *omnipotence* (12). Refer to your dictionary as needed.

Analyzing the Reading

1. What is Maslin's thesis?
2. What patterns of development, other than comparison and contrast, does Maslin use?
3. Identify several comparisons that you think make the essay particularly effective. Explain your choices.
4. How does Maslin use a current example of violence at the U.S. Capitol to support her thesis about *Saving Private Ryan*?
5. In paragraph 8, why doesn't Maslin give complete information about the event she refers to?

Reacting to the Reading: Discussion and Journal Writing

1. Discuss whether you think films that portray violence should be realistic or offer a buffer zone to protect viewers from the horror they show.
2. Discuss why you think *Saving Private Ryan* was a 1998 box-office success.

3. Write a journal entry describing your reaction to the violence depicted in *Saving Private Ryan* or another film of your choice.

APPLYING YOUR SKILLS: ADDITIONAL ESSAY ASSIGNMENTS

Write a comparison or contrast essay on one of the following topics, using what you have learned in this chapter. Depending on the topic you choose, you may need to conduct library or Internet research.

To Express Your Ideas

1. Compare two families that you know or are part of. Include points of comparison that reveal what is valuable and important in family life.

2. Compare your values and priorities today to those you held when you were in high school.

3. Compare your lifestyle today to the way you intend it to be after you graduate from college.

To Inform Your Reader

4. Compare library resources to those available on the World Wide Web.

5. Compare two places (neighborhoods in your area; cities, vacation spots), as Houston does in "A Taste of Snow."

6. Compare two advances in technology on the basis of their effects on people.

To Persuade Your Reader

7. Compare two views on a controversial issue, arguing in favor of one of them.

8. Compare two recent films of a certain type (for example, two action films), evaluating them as Maslin does in "By Being Honest About Violence, Spielberg Wins."

9. Compare two methods of doing something (such as disciplining a child or training a pet), arguing that one method is more effective than the other.

Cases Using Comparison and Contrast

10. You are taking a course in photography and have been asked to write a paper comparing and contrasting the advantages and uses of black-and-white versus color film. Your instructor is your audience.

11. You are working in the advertising department of a company that manufactures in-line skates. Your manager has asked you to evaluate two periodicals and recommend which one the company should use to run its advertisements.

and that we need a realistic look at violence to restore the humanity within us.
5. To do so would reveal one of the film's secrets to her audience, which professional film reviewers usually try to avoid doing.

For more on locating and documenting sources, see Chapters 19 and 20.

POSSIBLE ANSWERS: REACTING TO THE READING

1. Responses will vary.
2. Responses will vary; some possibilities include current interest in the World War II generation, and Spielberg's reputation as a filmmaker.
3. Responses will vary.

TEACHING TIP

Suggest that students use at least one prewriting strategy—drawing a graphic organizer, freewriting, brainstorming, questioning, writing assertions—to get started. Remind students to consult the learning style options (p. 387) and revision flowchart (p. 393).

The four basic personality types

Chapter 14

The cartoon on the opposite page shows four different personality types. Take a few minutes to think about the categories and people you know who seem to fit each type.

Writing Quick Start

Come up with a name for each type of person shown in the cartoon, then make a list of people you know that fit each category. To test whether this system works, consider whether you know people who would fit into more than one category.

Classification and Division: Explaining Categories and Parts

TEACHING TIP: COLLABORATIVE WRITING

(15 minutes) Have students work in groups of two or three to name categories. Possible labels or names of groups include *optimist, pessimist, indecisive,* and *impatient.*

TEACHING TIP:
CHAPTER OVERVIEW

• Reinforce the point
  that classification and
  division are skills
  students use and
  encounter in everyday
  situations, from gro-
  cery shopping (where
  items are classified
  and shelved by type),
  to sorting laundry, to
  preparing a recipe that
  is divided into groups
  of ingredients.
• Point out that *transi-
  tions* help clarify classifications and divisions
  for the reader.
• Encourage rational
  learners to assist their
  peers in selecting an
  appropriate method of
  organization. *Organization* is an important
  choice for writers,
  both in helping them
  determine the most
  appropriate sequence
  or emphasis and in
  helping readers follow
  the text.

WRITING A CLASSIFICATION OR DIVISION ESSAY

By categorizing the types of personalities, you used a process called classification. You grouped people you know into categories based on specific characteristics, and by doing so you made a successful start with classification and division writing. This chapter will show you how to write effective classification and division essays as well as how to incorporate classification or division into essays using other patterns of development.

WHAT ARE CLASSIFICATION AND DIVISION?

You use classification to organize things and ideas daily. Your dresser drawers and kitchen cupboards are probably organized by categories; you might put socks in one drawer, sweatshirts in another; pots and pans in one cupboard, dishes in another. Grocery stores, phone directories, libraries, even restaurant menus arrange items in groups according to similar characteristics.

Classification, then, is a process of sorting people, things, or ideas into groups or categories to help make them more understandable. For example, your college classifies its course offerings by schools, divisions, and departments. The college catalog and the courses offered each semester are arranged using that classification system. Think of how difficult it would be to find courses in a catalog or schedule if it were arranged alphabetically instead of by categories.

Division is similar to classification in that it groups or divides something into components. Whereas classification groups numerous items into categories, division begins with *one* item and breaks it down into parts. Thus, for example, the humanities department at your college may be divided into English, modern language, literature, and philosophy, and the modern language courses might be

---

SCENES FROM COLLEGE AND THE WORKPLACE

• For a course in *anatomy and physiology,* you are asked to study the structure and parts of the human ear by identifying the function of each part.

• As part of a *business management* report, you need to consider how debt liability differs for three types of businesses — a single proprietorship, a partnership, and a corporation.

• While working as a *facilities planner,* you are asked to conduct a feasibility study of several new sites. You begin by sorting the sites into three categories: "within-state," "out-of-state," and "out-of-country."

further divided into Spanish, French, Chinese, and Russian. Division is often closely related to process analysis, which is covered in Chapter 12.

A classification or division essay explains a topic by describing types or parts. For example, a classification essay might explore types of advertising: direct mail, radio, television, newspaper, and so forth. A division essay might describe the parts of an art museum: exhibit areas, museum store, visitor services desk, and the like.

Classification and division are effective ways to explain a topic. You will find many occasions to use these patterns of development in the writing you do in college and the workplace (see the accompanying box for a few examples). In the following essay, Paula M. White classifies the kinds of intelligence found in children. An example of a division essay, "A Brush with Reality: Surprises in the Tube" by David Bodanis, appears on page 423.

Bringing out Your Child's Gifts
Paula M. White

Paula M. White is an editor and the author of numerous articles published in Essence *and* Black Enterprise *magazines. This essay is from the September 1997 issue of* Essence, *a periodical for African American women. White describes seven types of intelligence a child may demonstrate. As you read the selection, highlight the types of intelligence and their key characteristics.*

As a child, I loved books so much that I would get a flashlight and try to read under the covers after my parents had put me to bed at night. I also kept a journal, wrote and produced plays for family and friends, and composed stories using my friends as the characters. Because of my natural verbal skills, I did well on standardized tests and was always near the top of my class.   1

My brother, Keith, on the other hand, was good at making friends. He never met a stranger, and whenever someone needed a helping hand, he was there. He was always lending his video games and designer clothes, and when he began driving, he frequently volunteered to shuttle his friends around. Keith was also an active member of numerous community-service clubs. But rarely did his good deeds and unselfish works translate into a stellar report card.   2

Keith and I were very different kids who learned in very different ways. And like most folks, we grew up in a household where a premium was placed on education. Good grades were rewarded and bad grades meant grief. Yet, despite our mother's high expectations, she always gave us the freedom to learn in our own way. When we weren't   3

PREREADING QUESTION

Is it wise to single out a child's greatest natural ability and encourage development in that area alone? Why or why not?

TEACHING TIP: LEARNING STYLES

(10–15 minutes) To reinforce the concept of learning styles, ask students to write in their journals or on a computer about one of the following topics, comparing the multiple intelligences that White describes with the learning styles presented in this book.

• Linguistic intelligence correlates with a verbal learning style
• Logical-mathematical: rational and abstract
• Visual-spatial: concrete and spatial
• Musical: creative

(Continued on next page)

• Bodily-kinesthetic:
  possibly concrete
• Interpersonal: social
  and emotional
• Intrapersonal: inde-
  pendent

doing homework, Mom was shuttling us to street festivals and puppet shows, animal farms and children's museums. Keith played soccer and the clarinet; I took tap and ballet classes (to tame my wayward feet). We explored worlds that we were good—and not so good—at. And we grew.

4   Although she didn't know it then, my mother was a proponent of the theory of multiple intelligences. According to this theory, everyone has talents or gifts in many areas, and when we play to our strongest suits, the most effective learning usually occurs. Sometimes, however, these strong suits aren't where parents want them to be.

5   "If we look at children only in traditional ways, and the child doesn't have 'schoolhouse' intelligence [is strong in linguistics or math], parents will figure they don't have a promising child," says psychologist Thomas Armstrong of Sonoma County, California. "However, by considering multiple intelligences, parents can look deeper and see talents they may have neglected."

6   Ellen Winner, a professor of psychology at Boston College and the author of *Gifted Children: Myths and Realities,* explains that if you want to identify where your child's potential lies, simply take note of the activities she naturally gravitates toward. Winner says she believes that if parents recognize and nurture a child's inborn abilities, the child will be able to build her confidence and self-esteem much more than any IQ or other standardized-test result ever could.

7   "IQ tests are very limited," says Winner. "They're pretty good for predicting how well your child will do in school because they test subject matter that schools value. But they don't predict how well your child is going to do in life."

MULTIPLE INTELLIGENCES MADE SIMPLE

8   Uncovering your child's strengths and providing opportunities for him to develop do not have to be complicated or costly. In his books *Awakening Your Child's Natural Genius* and *In Their Own Way: Discovering and Encouraging Your Child's Personal Learning Style,* Armstrong offers these guidelines for recognizing and cultivating the seven intelligences in your child.

9   **A verbal-linguistic child** speaks and/or reads at an early age; enjoys writing; spins tall tales or tells jokes and stories; has a good memory for names, places, dates or trivia; enjoys reading in her spare time; spells words easily; appreciates nonsense rhymes and tongue twisters; likes doing crossword puzzles.

How they learn: These kids learn best by saying, hearing and see- 10
ing words.

How to nurture them: Provide them with books, records and tapes 11
of the spoken word; create opportunities for writing; engage them in
discussions; give them access to such tools as a tape recorder, a typewriter and a computer for word making; read books together; have
evenings of storytelling; take them places where words are important,
including bookstores and libraries; play games such as *Black Heritage
Brain Quest, Scrabble, Trivial Pursuit, Boggle, Jeopardy* or *Wheel of Fortune.*

A logical-mathematical child computes arithmetic problems 12
quickly in his head; enjoys using computers; asks questions like
"Where does the universe end?" "What happens after we die?" and
"When did time begin?"; plays chess, checkers or other strategy
games and wins; enjoys brainteasers, logical puzzles; devises experiments to test things he doesn't understand; likes patterns.

How they learn: These children think in terms of concepts and 13
look for abstract patterns and relationships.

How to nurture them: Provide them with materials they can experi- 14
ment with, such as science resources. Visit science museums, computer
fairs and electronics exhibitions. They enjoy logical puzzles and games
like backgammon, *Clue,* dominoes, *Mastermind, Monopoly* and *Othello.*

A visual-spatial child spends free time drawing, designing things 15
or building articles with Lego blocks; reports clear visual images
when thinking; easily reads maps, charts and diagrams; likes it when
you show movies, slides or photographs; enjoys doing jigsaw puzzles
or mazes; daydreams a lot; is fascinated with machines and contrap-
tions and sometimes comes up with her own inventions.

How they learn: These youngsters usually learn visually and need 16
to be taught through images, pictures, metaphor and color.

How to nurture them: Use films, slides, diagrams, maps, charts, art 17
activities, construction kits, visualization exercises and vivid stories.
Visit architectural landmarks, planetariums and art museums. Play
games such as checkers, chess, *Classic Concentration, Connect Four,
Pictionary* and ticktacktoe.

A musical child frequently sings, hums or whistles quietly to 18
himself; has strong opinions about the music you play on the radio
or stereo; is sensitive to nonverbal sounds in the environment, such
as crickets chirping, distant bells ringing; remembers melodies of
songs; tells you when a musical note is off-key; needs music to study;
collects records or tapes.

How they learn: These children learn best through rhythm and 19
melody. They can learn almost anything more easily if it's sung,
tapped or whistled.

20   *How to nurture them:* Provide music lessons (if the child wants them), play different types of music around the house, involve them in rhythmic activities and sing-along time. Use percussion instruments or metronomes to help them learn rote material. Good games include *Encore, NoteAbility, Hot Potato, Simon* and *Song Burst.*

21   **A bodily-kinesthetic child** does well in competitive sports; moves, twitches, taps or fidgets while sitting in a chair; enjoys physical activities like swimming, biking, hiking or skateboarding; needs to touch people when talking to them; enjoys scary amusement rides; demonstrates skill in a craft like woodworking, sewing or carving; cleverly mimics other people's gestures, mannerisms or behaviors; communicates well through body language.

22   *How they learn:* These kids learn best by moving their bodies and working with their hands.

23   *How to nurture them:* Provide them with access to playgrounds, swimming pools and gyms. Let them fix machines, build models and care for small animals. Play games like *Twister,* jacks, *Jenga, Pick-Up Sticks, Operation* and charades.

24   **An interpersonal child** enjoys socializing; knows everybody's business, such as who has a crush on whom, who's mad at whom and where the fight is going to be after school; serves as mediator when disputes arise; seems particularly streetsmart; gets involved in after-school group activities; has empathy for others' feelings.

25   *How they learn:* These children learn best by relating to and cooperating with people.

26   *How to nurture them:* Let them teach other kids; get them involved in community projects, school clubs and volunteer organizations where they can learn by interacting with others; have family discussions and problem-solving sessions. Play games like *LifeStories* and *Therapy: The Game.*

27   **An intrapersonal child** shies away from group activities; keeps a diary or has ongoing projects and hobbies that are semisecretive in nature; displays a sense of independence or strong will; seems to live in her own private, inner world; likes to play alone; seems to have a deep sense of self-confidence; often is labeled eccentric; is self-motivated.

28   *How they learn:* These kids frequently learn best when they're left to themselves.

29   *How to nurture them:* Give them a chance to pursue independent study and individualized projects or games. Respect their privacy; let them know it's okay to be independent. Play games like *Scruples* and *The Ungame.*

Caveat Emptor

"It's wisest to look at all your child's abilities and foster each of   30
them," Armstrong says. He warns against simply finding the greatest
strength and teaching everything through that one entry point; you
run the risk of pigeonholing your youngster, and your child also
misses out on the chance to develop in other areas.

"The most important thing is for parents to be balanced and take   31
it a step at a time," Armstrong concludes. "Parents shouldn't make it
a job to develop their child's intelligences."

My brother Keith is now a teacher. I'm a writer and editor. We   32
ultimately ended up in professions that matched our natural-born
gifts. I suppose my mom knew without knowing that nurturing
our strengths and working with us on our weaknesses was the way
to get us to the other side of childhood, well-adjusted, productive
and confident. I pray that I can follow her lead and do the same for
my kids.   ■

Characteristics of Classification or Division Essays

A successful classification or division essay is meaningful to its audience. The
writer uses one principle of classification or division, with exclusive categories or
parts that are broad enough to include all of the members of the group.

Classification or Division Groups or Divides Ideas According to One Principle

To sort items into groups, a writer needs to decide how to categorize them. For
example, types of birds could be classified in terms of their size, habitat, or diet,
while microwave ovens could be classified by price, size, and wattage. For a division
essay, the writer must decide into what parts to divide the topic. A journalist writing about a new aquarium could divide the topic according to type of fish displayed, suitability for children of different ages, or the quality of the exhibits.

To develop an effective set of categories or parts, a writer needs to choose one
principle of classification or division and use it consistently throughout the essay
or within a particular section of the essay. For instance, a college president might
classify professors by age or teaching style, but he or she would not mix categories
by classifying some professors by age and others by teaching style. The president
could, however, classify all professors by age in the first part of a report and then
classify all professors by teaching style in another part of the report. In "Bringing
out Your Child's Gifts," White uses the principle of types of intelligence to categorize children's gifts throughout her essay.

Once a writer chooses an appropriate principle of classification or division, the next step is to identify a manageable number of categories or parts. An essay classifying birds according to diet, for example, might use five or six types of diet, not twenty. Likewise, an essay that divides the aquarium according to its suitability for children might use four or five divisions by age.

Classification or Division Is Meaningful to Its Audience

Because there are usually several different bases—or principles—a writer can use to categorize any particular group, the principle of classification chosen depends on the writer's purpose. The personnel director of a college might classify professors by age in preparing a financial report that projects upcoming retirements, whereas a student writing a paper about effective teaching methods might choose to categorize professors by teaching style.

To develop a meaningful classification, therefore, focus on your readers as well as on what you intend to accomplish. When your purpose is to inform, choose a principle of classification that will be of value and interest to your readers. If, for instance, you want to inform parents about the types of day-care facilities in your town, you could classify the day-care centers according to the services they offer because that principle would be a primary concern of your readers.

Division essays, too, are guided by purpose and audience. For example, the journalist who divides the aquarium exhibits according to their suitability for children of different ages might be writing to persuade readers that the aquarium is designed for children. His audience would be readers of the entertainment section of the newspaper he writes for.

POSSIBLE ANSWERS

1. Strong offensive/ defensive teams; overall win/loss records; personnel
2. Types; ethnic fast-food restaurants; parts of a typical restaurant (grill, counter, condiment stand, and so on)
3. Those that are open all night versus those with daytime hours; kinds of products or services offered; locations
4. Type of instruction (lecture versus lab); level of difficulty; amount of writing and type of thinking required
5. Length; complexity of plot; parts of a typical novel (opening, introduction of conflict, climax, and so on); intended audience

EXERCISE 14.1

Brainstorm three different principles of classification or division you might use for each of the following topics.

1. Sports teams
2. Fast-food restaurants
3. Convenience stores
4. Academic subjects
5. Novels

Classification or Division Uses Categories or Parts That Are Exclusive and Comprehensive

The categories or parts you choose should not overlap. In other words, a particular item or person should fit in no more than one category. A familiar example is age: the categories *25 to 30* and *30 to 35* are not mutually exclusive since someone who is thirty would fit in both. The second category should be changed to *31 to 35*.

In an essay about the nutritional value of pizza, you could divide your topic into carbohydrates, proteins, and fats, but you would not add a separate category for saturated fat, since saturated fat is already contained in the fats category.

The categories or parts you choose should also be comprehensive. In a division essay, all the major parts of an item should be included. In a classification essay, the categories need to include all of the items in the group or all of the major items. Each member of the group should fit into one category or another. For example, an essay categorizing fast-food restaurants according to the type of food they serve would have to include a category for take-out pizza because a fair number of fast-food establishments in most areas would fit into that category.

EXERCISE 14.2

Choose a principle of classification or division for two of the topics listed in Exercise 14.1. Then make a list of the categories or parts into which each item could be sorted or divided.

Classification or Division Fully Explains Each Category or Part

A classification or division essay contains adequate detail so that each category or part can be well understood by readers. In "Bringing out Your Child's Gifts," White clearly describes each of the seven types of intelligence, using expert testimony, personal observation, and other kinds of details to make her classification interesting and understandable. Consider how she elaborates on her description of the interpersonal child as someone who "knows everybody's business" by detailing what the child knows: "who has a crush on whom, who's mad at whom, and where the fight is going to be after school" (paragraph 24). Details such as these enable readers to "see" the writer's categories or parts in a classification or division essay.

Classification or Division Develops a Thesis

The thesis statement in a classification or division essay identifies the topic and may reveal the principle used to classify or divide the topic. In most cases, it also suggests why the classification or division is relevant or important. In "Bringing out Your Child's Gifts," for example, the thesis is that "everyone has talents or gifts in many areas, and when we play to our strongest suits, the most effective learning usually occurs" (paragraph 4).

Here are a few other examples of thesis statements.

Most people consider videos a form of entertainment; however, videos can also serve educational, commercial, and political functions.

The Grand Canyon is divided into two distinct geographical areas, the North Rim and the South Rim; each offers different views, facilities, and climatic conditions.

TEACHING TIP:
LEARNING STYLES

Pragmatic and rational learners may have the easiest time with this exercise. Try pairing them with creative and emotional learners.

POSSIBLE ANSWERS

Example: **Sports teams**

Personnel: managers, owners, players

Example: **Fast-food restaurants**

Types of ethnic fast-food restaurants: Chinese, Italian, Mexican

Visualizing a Classification or Division Essay: A Graphic Organizer

For more on graphic organizers, see Chapter 2, p. 40.

The graphic organizer shown in Figure 14.1 outlines the basic organization of a classification or division essay. The introduction announces the topic, gives back-

FIGURE 14.1
GRAPHIC ORGANIZER FOR A CLASSIFICATION OR DIVISION ESSAY

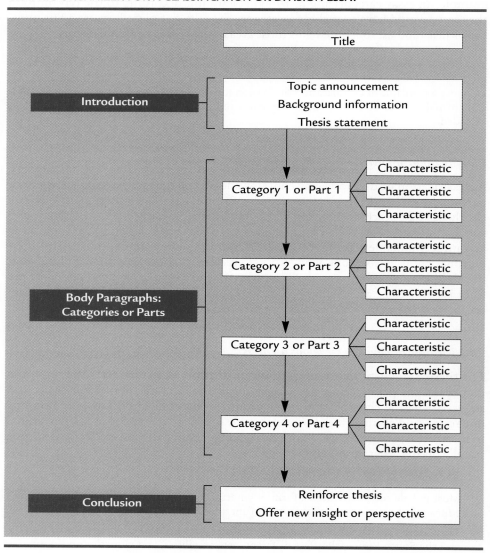

ground information, and states the thesis. The body paragraphs explain the categories or parts and their characteristics. The conclusion brings the essay to a satisfying close by reinforcing the thesis and offering a new insight on the topic.

When you incorporate classification or division into an essay using one or more other patterns of development, you may need to condense the introduction to your system of classification.

Read the following division essay and then study the graphic organizer for it in Figure 14.2.

A Brush with Reality: Surprises in the Tube
David Bodanis

David Bodanis is a journalist and the author of several books, including **The Body Book** *(1984),* **The Secret Garden** *(1992), and* **The Secret Family** *(1997). The following essay is from* **The Secret House** *(1986), a book that traces a family of five through a day, analyzing foods they eat and products they use. As you read the selection, highlight the writer's thesis and the sections where he divides his topic into parts.*

Into the bathroom goes our male resident, and after the most pressing need is satisfied it's time to brush the teeth. The tube of toothpaste is squeezed, its pinched metal seams are splayed, pressure waves are generated inside, and the paste begins to flow. But what's in this toothpaste, so carefully being extruded out?

Water mostly, 30 to 45 percent in most brands: ordinary, everyday simple tap water. It's there because people like to have a big gob of toothpaste to spread on the brush, and water is the cheapest stuff there is when it comes to making big gobs. Dripping a bit from the tap onto your brush would cost virtually nothing; whipped in with the rest of the toothpaste the manufacturers can sell it at a neat and accountant-pleasing $2 per pound equivalent. Toothpaste manufacture is a very lucrative occupation.

Second to water in quantity is chalk: exactly the same material that schoolteachers use to write on blackboards. It is collected from the crushed remains of long-dead ocean creatures. In the Cretaceous seas chalk particles served as part of the wickedly sharp outer skeleton that these creatures had to wrap around themselves to keep from getting chomped by all the slightly larger other ocean creatures they met. Their massed graves are our present chalk deposits.

PREREADING QUESTION

Do you think using commercial toothpaste is necessary to maintaining good dental hygiene? Why or why not?

TEACHING TIP: POSTREADING DISCUSSION

Ask students to discuss

• the author's thesis, which is implied rather than stated (the ingredients in toothpaste are surprising, and a bit disturbing).

• major divisions (such as chalk, water, paint, seaweed, antifreeze, paraffin oil, detergent, peppermint, formaldehyde, and fluoride).

• the author's purpose in describing the ingredients of toothpaste in detail (such as to surprise or amuse readers or to make them think about the ingredients in other household products).

4   The individual chalk particles — the size of the smallest mud particles in your garden — have kept their toughness over the aeons, and now on the toothbrush they'll need it. The enamel outer coating of the tooth they'll have to face is the hardest substance in the body — tougher than skull, or bone, or nail. Only the chalk particles in toothpaste can successfully grind into the teeth during brushing, ripping off the surface layers like an abrading wheel grinding down a boulder in a quarry.

5   The craters, slashes, and channels that the chalk tears into the teeth will also remove a certain amount of build-up yellow in the carnage, and it is for that polishing function that it's there. A certain amount of unduly enlarged extra-abrasive chalk fragments tear such cavernous pits into the teeth that future decay bacteria will be able to bunker down there and thrive; the quality control people find it almost impossible to screen out these errant super-chalk pieces, and government regulations allow them to stay in.

6   In case even the gouging doesn't get all the yellow off, another substance is worked into the toothpaste cream. This is titanium dioxide. It comes in tiny spheres, and it's the stuff bobbing around in white wall paint to make it come out white. Splashed around onto your teeth during the brushing it coats much of the yellow that remains. Being water soluble it leaks off in the next few hours and is swallowed, but at least for the quick glance up in the mirror after finishing it will make the user think his teeth are truly white. Some manufacturers add optical whitening dyes — the stuff more commonly found in washing machine bleach — to make extra sure that that glance in the mirror shows reassuring white.

7   These ingredients alone would not make a very attractive concoction. They would stick in the tube like a sloppy white plastic lump, hard to squeeze out as well as revolting to the touch. Few consumers would savor rubbing in a mixture of water, ground-up blackboard chalk, and the whitener from latex paint first thing in the morning. To get around that finicky distaste the manufacturers have mixed in a host of other goodies.

8   To keep the glop from drying out, a mixture including glycerine glycol — related to the most common car antifreeze ingredient — is whipped in with the chalk and water, and to give *that* concoction a bit of substance (all we really have so far is wet colored chalk) a large helping is added of gummy molecules from the seaweed *Chondrus Crispus*. This seaweed ooze spreads in among the chalk, paint, and antifreeze, then stretches itself in all directions to hold the whole mass together. A bit of paraffin oil (the fuel that flickers in camping

lamps) is pumped in with it to help the moss ooze keep the whole substance smooth.

With the glycol, ooze, and paraffin we're almost there. Only two major chemicals are left to make the refreshing, cleansing substance we know as toothpaste. The ingredients so far are fine for cleaning, but they wouldn't make much of the satisfying foam we have come to expect in the morning brushing.

To remedy that, every toothpaste on the market has a big dollop of detergent added too. You've seen the suds detergent will make in a washing machine. The same substance added here will duplicate that inside the mouth. It's not particularly necessary, but it sells.

The only problem is that by itself this ingredient tastes, well, too like detergent. It's horribly bitter and harsh. The chalk put in toothpaste is pretty foul-tasting too for that matter. It's to get around that gustatory discomfort that the manufacturers put in the ingredient they tout perhaps the most of all. This is the flavoring, and it has to be strong. Double rectified peppermint oil is used—a flavorer so powerful that chemists know better than to sniff it in the raw state in the laboratory. Menthol crystals and saccharin or other sugar simulators are added to complete the camouflage operation.

Is that it? Chalk, water, paint, seaweed, antifreeze, paraffin oil, detergent, and peppermint? Not quite. A mix like that would be irresistible to the hundreds of thousands of individual bacteria lying on the surface of even an immaculately cleaned bathroom sink. They would get in, float in the water bubbles, ingest the ooze and paraffin, maybe even spray out enzymes to break down the chalk. The result would be an uninviting mess. The way manufacturers avoid that final obstacle is by putting something in to kill the bacteria. Something good and strong is needed, something that will zap any accidentally intrudant bacteria into oblivion. And that something is formaldehyde—the disinfectant used in anatomy labs.

So it's chalk, water, paint, seaweed, antifreeze, paraffin oil, detergent, peppermint, formaldehyde, and fluoride (which can go some way towards preserving children's teeth)—that's the usual mixture raised to the mouth on the toothbrush for a fresh morning's clean. If it sounds too unfortunate, take heart. Studies show that thorough brushing with just plain water will often do as good a job. ∎

9

10

11

12

13

EXERCISE 14.3

Draw a graphic organizer for "Bringing out Your Child's Gifts" (p. 415).

POSSIBLE ANSWERS

Answers will vary. See the *Instructor's Resource Manual* for a possible graphic organizer.

FIGURE 14.2
A GRAPHIC ORGANIZER FOR "A BRUSH WITH REALITY"

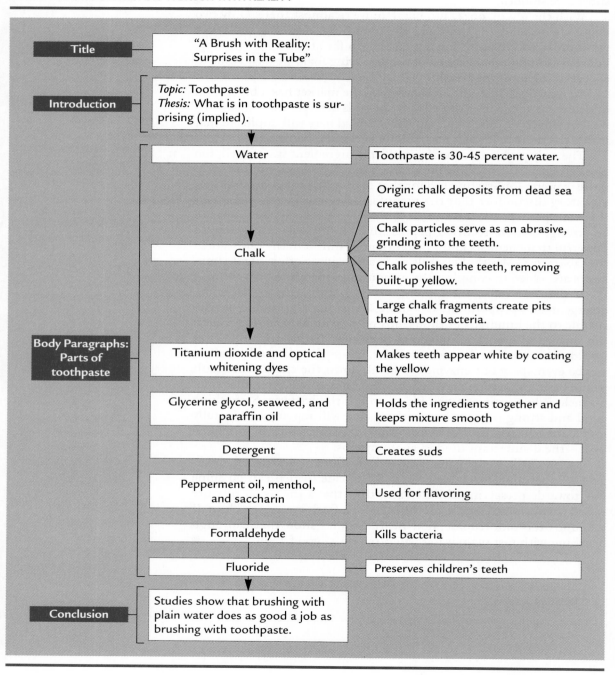

INTEGRATING CLASSIFICATION OR DIVISION INTO AN ESSAY

Classification or division is often used along with one or more other patterns of development. For example, an essay that describes the origins of sports teams' names may also classify them as geographic names, animal names, and ethnic names. Similarly, an essay that argues for gun control may categorize guns in terms of their firepower, use, or availability. A narrative about a writer's frustrating experience in a crowded international airport terminal may describe the different parts or areas of the airport.

Use the following tips to incorporate classification or division into an essay based on another pattern of development.

1. **Avoid focusing on why the classification or division is meaningful.** When used as a secondary pattern, its significance should be clear from the context in which the classification or division is presented.

2. **State the principle of classification.** Do so briefly, but make sure it is clear to your readers.

3. **Name the categories or parts.** In the sentence that introduces the classification or division, name the categories or parts to focus your readers' attention on the explanation that follows.

4. **Make the classification or division comprehensive and exclusive.** The categories or parts should be complete and should not overlap.

5. **Include both classification and division or more than one system of classification, if necessary.** In a persuasive essay on gun control, for instance, you might classify types of guns early in the essay. Then, later in the essay, you might divide the process of buying a gun into a series of steps. Keep in mind that when you use two or more systems of classification or division, it must be clear that each system is separate.

In "The Men We Carry in Our Minds" on page 452, Scott Russell Sanders uses classification along with other patterns of development to develop his thesis about the lives of men.

ADDITIONAL RESOURCES

The writing process software that accompanies this text includes an Electronic Guided Writing Assignment for a classification and division essay.

TEACHING TIP: LEARNING STYLES

(25 minutes total) Try this role-playing exercise to encourage students to use different learning styles for generating ideas. Students should work in groups of two; if possible, each group should include one pragmatic learner and one creative learner.

- (5 minutes) Have students choose one topic from the "Classification" or "Division" list.
- (10 minutes) Pragmatic learners should share their topic with their partner, who can use creative techniques such as brainstorming and freewriting to generate ideas and details about the topic before experimenting with classifications or divisions.
- (10 minutes) Creative learners should then share their topic with their partner, who can use pragmatic techniques to generate ideas and details about the topic and to list categories or parts.

A GUIDED WRITING ASSIGNMENT

The following guide will lead you through the process of writing a classification or division essay. Although you will focus primarily on classifying or dividing your subject, you may need to integrate one or more other patterns of development in your essay to develop your thesis or make a point. Depending on your learning style, you may choose various ways of generating and organizing ideas. A pragmatic learner, for instance, might get started by listing categories or parts, whereas a creative learner might feel more comfortable with brainstorming a list of details before trying out different ways of classifying or dividing them. This Guided Writing Assignment will provide you with alternatives.

The Assignment

Write a classification or division essay on a topic in one of the following lists or on a topic you choose on your own. Depending on the topic you select, you may need to use Internet or library sources to develop and support your ideas about it. You may also need to narrow the topic. Your audience consists of readers of your local newspapers.

Classification

Mark Twain once said that the world is made up of two groups of people — those who sort the world into groups of people and those who do not. Become a member of Twain's first group by devising a classification system for one of the topics suggested below or a topic of your choice. Write an essay that explains your categories.

1. Types of pets
2. Types of sports fans
3. Types of movies
4. Types of classmates
5. Types of shoppers
6. Types of television dramas

Division

Choose one of the following topics, or devise your own topic, and write an essay using division as the main pattern of development.

1. Your family
2. A machine or piece of equipment

3. An organization
4. A sports team or club
5. A public place (a building, stadium, department store, or theme park)
6. Your college campus

As you develop your classification or division essay, consider using one or more other patterns of development. For example, in a classification essay, you might compare and contrast types of sports fans or give examples of types of movies. In a division essay, you might describe the parts of a theme park or other public place.

For more on description, illustration, and comparison and contrast, see Chapters 10, 11, and 13.

Generating Ideas

There are two primary methods for generating ideas and developing a system for classifying or dividing them.

Classification
1. Think of details that describe the group and then use the details to categorize group members.
2. Identify categories and then think of details that fit each category.

Division
1. Brainstorm details about your topic and then group the details into parts or sections.
2. Think about how your topic can be divided into easy-to-understand parts.

Depending on your learning style and topic, one method may be more appealing or easier to work with than the other. Before you try either method, however, it is important to consider your purpose, audience, and point of view.

Considering Your Purpose, Audience, and Point of View

Your principle of classification or division, your categories or parts, and your details must all fit your purpose, audience, and point of view. If your purpose is to inform your audience about the components of a personal computer (PC), and your audience is made up of novice computer users, then your parts and details must be straightforward and nontechnical. However, if your purpose is to persuade an audience of computer

For more on purpose, audience, and point of view, see Chapter 4, p. 73.

technicians to purchase a particular kind of PC, then your parts and details would be necessarily more technical. Keep in mind that for this Guided Writing Assignment, your audience consists of the readers of your local newspaper.

As you work on your classification or division essay, ask yourself the following questions.

- Do my details and categories advance the purpose of the essay?
- Will my readers understand the categories or parts?
- Is my principle of classification or division appropriate for my purpose and audience?
- What point of view will best suit my purpose and audience—first, second, or third person?

You are now ready to try method 1 or method 2 for generating ideas.

Method 1: Generating Details and Grouping Them into Categories or Parts

To use method 1, try the following techniques for generating details, deciding on a principle of classification or division, and choosing categories or parts.

Generating Details.   Begin with one or more of the following strategies for generating details about your topic.

1. Visit a place where you can observe your topic or the people associated with it. For example, to generate details about pets, visit a pet store or an animal shelter; to generate details about sports fans, attend a sporting event or watch one on television. Make notes on or tape-record what you see and hear. Be specific; record conversations, physical characteristics, behaviors, and so forth.
2. Discuss your topic with a classmate or friend. Focus your talk on the qualities and characteristics of your topic.
3. Brainstorm a list of all the features or characteristics of your topic that come to mind. Work on a computer, on a piece of paper, or with a tape recorder.
4. Draw a map or diagram that illustrates your topic's features and characteristics.
5. Conduct library or Internet research to discover facts, examples, and other details about your topic.

For more on prewriting strategies, see Chapter 4.

Learning Style Options

For more on observation, see Chapter 19, p. 664.

TEACHING TIP: LEARNING STYLES

1. For concrete learners, but creative learners will also enjoy this method
2. For social learners
3. For all learners, especially pragmatic and independent learners
4. For all learners, especially spatial learners
5. For all learners

For more on library and Internet research, see Chapter 19.

Choosing a Principle of Classification or Division.   Your next task is to decide which principle or basis you will use to classify or divide your subject. Read through your details, looking for shared features or characteristics. If your topic is highway drivers, for instance, you could classify them by gender, age, type of car driven, or driving habits. Your principle of classification or division should be interesting and meaningful to your audience. It should also enable you to make a worthwhile point about your classification or division. For the essay on highway drivers, you might decide to classify drivers according to their driving habits, focusing on annoying or unsafe habits that you have observed. Experiment with several principles of classification or division until you find one that fits your purpose and audience.

Choosing Categories or Parts.   With your principle of classification or division in mind, use the following suggestions to determine your categories or parts.

1. *In a classification essay,* make sure most or all members of the group fit into one of your categories; few, if any, members should be left out. For example, in choosing categories of local businesses, one student writer chose privately owned small businesses, franchises, and corporation branches. *In a division essay,* no essential parts should be left out. You probably would not exclude the infield or bleachers in a division essay about the parts of a baseball stadium, for example.

2. *In a classification essay,* be sure the categories are exclusive; each group member should fit into one category only. For example, the categories of family-owned businesses and franchises would overlap, so exclusive categories should be used instead. *In a division essay,* make sure the parts do not overlap. For example, the parts "playing field" and "infield" would overlap, so it would be better to use the three distinct parts of the field: infield, outfield, and foul-ball area.

3. Create specific categories or parts that will engage your readers. *In a classification essay,* categorizing drivers by their annoying driving habits would be more interesting than simply distinguishing between "good" and "bad" drivers. In classifying drivers with annoying habits, you might choose the following categories: aggressive drivers, slow drivers, and inattentive drivers. *A division essay* on players' facilities in a baseball stadium — dugout, locker room, and bullpen — would be more interesting to sports fans than an essay describing different seating sections of the stadium.

4. Once you establish your categories or parts, you may need to do additional brainstorming or observing (or use some other type of prewriting) to come up with enough details (examples, facts, anecdotes, and observations) to explain each category or part adequately.

5. Choose descriptive names for your categories or parts. Each name should emphasize the distinguishing feature of the category or part. *In a classification essay* categorizing highway drivers with annoying habits, you might assign the names "I-own-the-road" drivers, "I'm-in-no-hurry" drivers, and "I'm-daydreaming" drivers. *In a division essay* about the parts of a baseball stadium, you might use "homerun heaven" to name one part of the stadium.

Method 1 is effective when you approach the classification or division from part to whole — identifying characteristics and then grouping the characteristics. Depending on your learning style and your topic, it may be easier to start by creating categories or parts and then filling in details about each one. In this case, use method 2.

Method 2: Generating Categories or Parts and Supplying Details

Especially when you are familiar with your topic, you may begin by exploring categories into which items may be sorted (or parts into which something can be divided). Once you have a tentative list of categories or parts, you can work on generating details and examples relevant to each one. To use method 2, try the following techniques.

Choosing Categories or Parts.   To explore and choose categories or parts, try one or more of the following strategies.

Learning Style Options ▶

LEARNING STYLES

1. For social learners
2. For concrete and creative learners
3. For all learners, especially pragmatic learners
4. For all learners, especially spatial learners
5. For verbal and social learners
6. For all learners

1. Discuss your topic with a classmate or friend. Question each other about how the topic can be categorized or divided.

2. Visit a place where you can observe your topic or the people associated with it. Make notes on what you see and hear.

3. Brainstorm principles of classification or division. List as many different ways to classify or divide the topic as you can think of. Then test the effectiveness of each principle by quickly listing the categories or parts into which the topic may be divided.

4. Draw graphic organizers, experimenting with several different categories or parts into which your topic may be classified or divided (see Figures 14.1 and 14.2 for examples of graphic organizers).

5. Use a tape recorder while you describe your topic aloud. Mention as many categories or parts as you can think of. Then listen to the tape.

6. Conduct library or Internet research. Try to discover information that will help you classify or divide your topic.

Before moving on to the next step, make sure your categories or parts meet the criteria discussed earlier in the chapter (see pp. 419–21).

Identifying the Key Features of Each Category or Part.   Once you have a workable list of categories or parts, the next step is to identify key features. These are the features that you will use to explain and differentiate each category or part for your readers. Recall how White, in "Bringing out Your Child's Gifts," clearly describes the major characteristics of each type of intelligence that children exhibit.

Consider again the three categories of annoying highway drivers. You might distinguish each type of driver by the key characteristics listed here.

1. "I-Own-the-Road" Drivers
   - Inconsiderate of other drivers
   - Weave in and out of traffic
   - Honk horns or flash lights to intimidate others into letting them pass

2. "I'm-in-No-Hurry" Drivers
   - Drive below the speed limit
   - Cause other drivers to become impatient
   - Drive in the left lane

3. "I'm-Daydreaming" Drivers
   - Fail to observe other drivers
   - Fail to signal when changing lanes
   - Wander over the dividing line or onto the shoulder of the road

As you identify characteristics for each category, you may find that two categories overlap or that a category is too broad. You may discover similar problems with the parts of a division essay. Do not hesitate to create, combine, or eliminate categories or parts as you work.

Generating Details.   For each category or part, you need to supply specific details that will make it clear and understandable to your readers. It is not enough to simply state major features. As you work on your essay, then, write down examples, situations, or sensory details that illustrate each category or part. In "Bringing out Your Child's Gifts," for example, White explains each category of intelligence and then describes how each type of child can learn and be nurtured.

For more on thesis statements, see Chapter 5, p. 97.

ESSAY IN PROGRESS 1

Choose a topic for your classification or division essay from the list of assignment options on pages 428–29, or choose one on your own. Then use the preceding guidelines for method 1 *or* method 2 to generate details about your topic, choose a principle of classification or division, and devise a set of categories or parts. Whatever method you use, list the examples, situations, or other details that you will use to describe each category or part. You might try drawing a graphic organizer.

Developing Your Thesis

Once you choose categories or parts and are satisfied with your details, you are ready to develop a thesis for your essay. Remember that your thesis statement should identify your topic and reveal your principle of division or classification. In most cases, it should also suggest why your classification or division is useful or important. Avoid writing a thesis statement that merely announces your categories, as in "There are four kinds of. . . ." Notice how the following weak theses have been strengthened.

WEAK: There are four types of insurance that most people can purchase.

REVISED: If you are familiar with the four types of insurance that are available, you will be able to make sure that you, your family members, and your property are protected.

WEAK: Conventional stores are only one type of retailing; other types are becoming more popular.

REVISED: Although shopping in conventional stores is still the most common way to purchase products, three new types of shopping are becoming increasingly popular: face-to-face sales conducted in the home, sales via telephone or computer, and sales from automatic vending machines.

Draft your thesis; then check your prewriting to make sure you have enough details to support the thesis. If necessary, do some additional prewriting to gather the supporting details you need. In addition, keep in mind that a lengthy or complex topic may require a more elaborate thesis

TEACHING TIP: LEARNING STYLES
Remind students that method 1 is a creative approach (details first, then categories or parts) and method 2 is a pragmatic approach (categories or parts first, then details).

and introduction. You may need to provide more detailed information about your principle of classification or division or its importance.

ESSAY IN PROGRESS 2

Using the preceding guidelines, develop a thesis for your classification or division essay.

Evaluating Your Ideas and Thesis

Take a few minutes to evaluate your ideas and thesis. Start by rereading everything you have written with a critical eye. Highlight the most useful details and delete those that are repetitious or irrelevant. If you are working on a computer, highlight useful details in bold type or move them to a separate file. As you review your work, do not hesitate to add useful ideas that come to mind.

TRYING OUT YOUR IDEAS ON OTHERS

Working in a group of two or three students, discuss your ideas and thesis for this chapter's assignment. Each writer should describe his or her topic, principle of classification or division, and categories or parts to the group. Then, as a group, evaluate each writer's work and suggest recommendations for improvement.

ESSAY IN PROGRESS 3

Using the preceding suggestions and comments from your classmates, evaluate your thesis, your categories or parts, and the details you plan to use in your essay. Refer to the list of characteristics on pages 419–21 to help you with your evaluation.

Organizing and Drafting

Once you have evaluated your categories or parts, reviewed your thesis, and considered the advice of your classmates, you are ready to organize your ideas and draft your essay.

Choosing a Method of Organization

Choose the method of organization that best suits your purpose. One method that works well in classification essays is the least-to-most

TEACHING TIP: LEARNING STYLES

Challenge creative learners to examine their categories or parts closely, and encourage pragmatic learners to strengthen their details.

TEACHING TIP: COLLABORATIVE WRITING

(10 minutes) Encourage students to evaluate each other's theses. To ensure multiple peer reviews, have students pass their draft theses to the student on the right for comments; then to the student on the left for comments. Ask peer reviewers to evaluate whether the thesis identifies the topic and principle of classification or division and suggests why the classification or division is important.

COMPUTER HINT

Ask each student to email his or her tentative thesis statement to two other students for review, if networked computers are not available.

For more on drafting an essay, see Chapter 6.

CONNECTIONS

Here students will be called on to apply their understanding of the methods of organization covered in Chapter 6.

For more on methods of organization, see Chapter 6, p. 120.

arrangement. You might arrange your categories in increasing order of importance or from least to most common, difficult, or frequent. Other possible sequences include chronological order (when one category occurs or is observable before another) or spatial order (when you classify physical objects).

Spatial order often works well in division essays, as does order of importance. In describing the parts of a baseball stadium you might move from stands to playing field (spatial order). In writing about the parts of a hospital, you might describe the most important areas first (operating rooms and emergency room) and then move to less important facilities (waiting rooms and visitor cafeteria).

To experiment with different methods of organization, create a new computer file for each possible method and try out each one.

Drafting the Classification or Division Essay

Once you decide how to organize your categories or parts, your next step is to write a first draft. Use the following guidelines to draft your essay.

1. Explain each category or part. Begin by defining each category or part, taking into account the complexity of your topic and the background knowledge of your audience. For example, if you classify types of behavioral disorders in an essay written for a general audience, you would need to define such terms as *schizophrenic* and *delusional*. In a division essay about a baseball stadium, you might need to define *infield* and *outfield* if your audience includes a large number of people who are not sports fans.

2. Provide details that describe each category or part. Be sure to show how each category or part is distinct from the others. Include a wide range of details: sensory details, personal experiences, examples, and comparisons and contrasts. In the following excerpt from a student essay on types of sales, the writer describes one type of consumer purchase — vending machines. The annotations indicate how the writer explains her category.

Operation

Advantages

Types of products

Automatic vending machines are an increasingly popular option for consumers. They operate simply: The consumer inserts cash and the machine dispenses the product. Vending machines are cost effective because they do not require sales staff or a high-maintenance selling floor. They are accessible twenty-four hours a day and can be placed in convenient locations, such as hotels, malls, and office buildings. A wide assortment of goods can be purchased through vending machines: snacks, common grocery items (milk), stamps, cosmetics, and even travel insurance at airports.

3. Generally, allow one or more paragraphs for each category or part.

4. Use transitions. Your reader needs transitions to keep on track as you move from one category or part to another. In addition, notice how the transitions in the following examples help to distinguish key features between and within categories or parts.

For more on transitions, see Chapter 6, p. 138.

TRANSITIONS BETWEEN CATEGORIES OR PARTS

The *third* class of mental disorder is . . .
A *final* category of mental disorder is . . .
The *fourth* area of the campground is . . .

TRANSITIONS WITHIN CATEGORIES OR PARTS

Another feature that characterizes a neurosis is . . .
The observation tower *also* contains . . .
An *additional* characteristic of neurosis is . . .

5. Provide roughly the same amount and kind of detail and description for each of your categories or parts. For instance, if you give an example of one type of mental disorder, you should then give an example for every other type discussed in the essay.

6. Consider adding headings or lists. Presenting the parts or categories within a numbered list or in sections with headings can help make them clear and distinct. Headings or lists can be especially useful when you have a large number of categories or parts.

7. Consider adding a visual such as a diagram or flowchart. Diagrams, flowcharts, or other visuals can make your system of classification or division clearer for your readers. Graphics software, available with some word-processing programs, can help you produce professional looking charts and diagrams.

8. Write an effective introduction. Your introduction, which usually includes your thesis statement, should provide background information, and explain further, if needed, your principle of classification or division. It may also suggest why the classification or division is worth reading about.

9. Write a satisfying conclusion. Your conclusion should do more than just repeat your categories or parts. It should bring your essay to a

For more on writing effective paragraphs, including introductions and conclusions, see Chapter 6.

TEACHING TIP
Caution students that while explicit transitions ("The first type . . . is") enhance clarity, when overused they make prose sound labored. Remind students to use active verbs wherever possible to help counteract this potential problem, and to look for creative ways to make a transition from one category or part to another.

satisfying close, reemphasizing your thesis or offering a new insight or perspective on the topic. A division essay about the parts of a baseball stadium might conclude with a comment on the value of baseball as the all-American sport. A classification essay on types of mental disorders might urge tolerance in interpersonal relationships or emphasize the need for improved treatment programs.

If you have trouble finding an appropriate way to conclude your essay, return to your statement about why the classification or division is useful and important and try to extend or elaborate on that statement.

ESSAY IN PROGRESS 4

Draft your classification or division essay, using an appropriate method of organization and the preceding guidelines for drafting.

Analyzing and Revising

If possible, set your draft aside for a day or two before rereading and revising it. As you review your draft, remember your goal is to revise your classification or division essay to make it clearer and more effective. Focus on content and ideas, then, not on grammar, punctuation, or mechanics. Use one or more of the following strategies to analyze your draft.

1. Reread your essay aloud, using a tape recorder if possible. You may "hear" parts that need revision.

2. Ask a friend or classmate to read your draft and to give you his or her impression of the principle of classification or division and its significance. Compare your reader's impressions with what you intend to convey and revise your draft accordingly.

3. Draw a graphic organizer or make an outline, or update the one you drew or made earlier. In particular, look for any categories or parts that lack sufficient details and revise to include them.

Use Flowchart 14.1 to guide your analysis of the strengths and weaknesses in your draft essay. You might also ask a classmate to review your draft using the questions in the flowchart. For each "No" response, ask your reviewer to explain his or her answer.

TEACHING TIP

Students who have followed the steps in the Guided Writing Assignment should be ready to compose a first draft independently. However, check to see if any students need to rethink their principle of classification or division and their categories or parts before drafting. Encourage them to seek the assistance of a peer reviewer or writing center tutor. Remind all students to keep their prewriting handy.

Learning Style Options

TEACHING TIP: LEARNING STYLES

1. For verbal and some social learners
2. For social learners and others
3. Spatial learners may have already drawn a graphic organizer; encourage all other students to draw one, or prepare an outline.

For more on the benefits of peer review, see Chapter 7, p. 166.

FLOWCHART 14.1
REVISING A CLASSIFICATION AND DIVISION ESSAY

Questions		Revision Strategies
1. Do you have a manageable number of categories or parts?	No ⇨	• For a classification essay, narrow your topic to a smaller, more manageable group (for example, narrow types of shoppers to types of shoppers for women's clothing). For a division essay, divide your topic into fewer parts.
Yes ⇩		
2. Do you use one principle of classification or division consistently throughout the essay or throughout a particular section?	No ⇨	• Review your categories or parts to be sure that they all are related to the same principle. • If they are not, choose the principle that best fits your purpose and rethink your categories or parts.
Yes ⇩		
3. Is your principle of classification or division meaningful to your audience?	No ⇨	• Brainstorm to find other bases of classification or division. • Ask friends or classmates what they would want to know about your topic.
Yes ⇩		
4. For a classification essay, do your categories cover all or most members of the group? For a division essay, do you cover all major parts of the topic?	No ⇨	• Revise your categories or parts so that each item fits into one group only. • Brainstorm or do research to add categories or parts.
Yes ⇩		

(Continued on next page)

FLOWCHART 14.1 *(continued)*

Questions		Revision Strategies

5. Does your essay fully explain each category or part. (If it reads like a list, answer "No.")

No ⇨

- Brainstorm or do research to discover more details.
- Add examples, definitions, facts, and expert testimony to improve your explanations.

Yes ⇩

6. Do your thesis and introduction explain your principle of classification or division and tell why it is important?

No ⇨

- Revise your thesis to make your justification stronger or more apparent.
- Add explanatory information to the introduction.

Yes ⇩

7. Are the categories or parts organized in a way that suits your purpose? (If you are unsure, answer "No.")

No ⇨

- Draw a graphic organizer to evaluate your present organization.
- Refer to Chapter 6 to discover an organizing plan.

Yes ⇩

8. Is each paragraph well developed and focused on a separate category or part? Does the conclusion offer a new insight or perspective on the topic?

No ⇨

- Be sure each paragraph has a topic sentence and supporting details (see Chapter 6).
- Consider combining closely related paragraphs.
- Split paragraphs that cover more than one category or part.
- Ask yourself: "So what? What does this mean?" Build your answers into the conclusion.

Yes

TEACHING TIP

Remind students to allow ample time for revising the draft and to preview their error logs for potential problems with mechanics and grammar.

TEACHING TIP

Encourage students to seek a writing center tutor for further review of the revision.

ESSAY IN PROGRESS 5

Revise your draft using Flowchart 14.1 and any comments you received from peer reviewers.

Editing and Proofreading

The last step is to check your revised essay for errors in grammar, spelling, punctuation, and mechanics. In addition, watch out for the types of errors you tend to make (refer to your error log).

For more on keeping an error log, see Chapter 8, p. 201.

When editing a classification or division essay, pay particular attention to two particular kinds of grammatical error: omitted commas following introductory elements and choppy sentences.

1. Add a comma after opening phrases or clauses that are longer than four words.

▶ When describing types of college students, be sure to consider variations in age.
          ^

▶ Although there are many types of cameras, most are easy to operate.
          ^

2. Avoid short, choppy sentences, which can make a classification or division sound dull and mechanical. Try combining a series of short sentences and varying sentence patterns and lengths.

For more on combining sentences and varying sentence patterns, see Chapter 8.

          such as German shepherds and sheep herding dogs
▶ Working dogs are another one of the American Kennel Club's breed cate-
          ^
gories. ~~These include German shepherds and sheep herding dogs.~~

          The fountain pen, one
▶ ~~One~~ standard type of writing instrument, ~~is the fountain pen. It~~ is some-
  ^   ^
times messy and inconvenient to use. It often leaks.

TEACHING TIP: COLLABORATIVE WRITING

• Have students work in pairs to look for missing commas after introductory phrases.
• (30 minutes) If possible, have students read their drafts aloud in groups of two or three, listening for choppy passages and suggesting needed revisions (combining short, related sentences and eliminating redundancies).

ESSAY IN PROGRESS 6

Edit and proofread your essay, paying particular attention to comma usage and sentence variety and length.

STUDENTS WRITE

PREREADING
QUESTION

As you read about
Porter's classification
of "car nuts," consider
whether the various
types are similar or very
different.

Ryan Porter was a first-year student when he wrote the following essay in response to an assignment for his writing course. He is an avid reader of car magazines and enjoys antique cars, especially cars of the 1950s. As you read the essay, identify the basis of classification and the categories he uses, and annotate your reactions to Porter's details.

Motor Heads
Ryan Porter

1   As you probably realize, we live in an automobile-oriented society; car culture is everywhere. Can you really say that you don't care about cars, or that you are not a car lover on some level? Although your interest may be merely practical, there are multitudes of people who are car nuts to some degree.

2   You see them on Sundays in spring, gathered around the glittering external exhaust pipes of a classic Duesenberg dual-cowl phaeton parked on the fairway at an antique auto show, or on Saturday nights in summer in a fast-food parking lot, jostling each other to peek at the chromed engine bay of a chopped and channeled '56 Chevy Bel Air. You see them bunched up at the parts counter at Pep Boys or poring over the car magazines at Borders Books. These are the motor heads or the car nuts. Like all nuts, they come in many varieties. You can tell the type of car nut by the kind of car the nut worships.

3   The first variety, the afficionado, is usually wealthy or has pretensions of wealth. Afficionados own classic cars from the 1920s and 1930s, such as the fabled Duesenberg, Hispano-Suiza, Packard, or Bentley. If they own more than one, you might hear them talk of the cars in their "stable," as if these machines were thoroughbred horses. These autos are extremely valuable--

often selling at auction for hundreds of thousands of dollars--and can be considered part of their investment portfolios. Because of this, afficionados rarely, if ever, drive their cars, preferring instead to have the vehicles trailered to shows. Afficionados never actually put a wrench to any lug nut on one of their classic cars; instead they hire a mechanic who specializes in maintaining antiques and classics. Afficionados treat their classic cars like fine crystal. Maybe they should collect crystal instead; it takes up less room and is a lot easier to maintain.

The second type of car nut, the gear head, can be seen sporting grease-smeared T-shirts with faded Camaro, Mustang, or Corvette logos. Unlike the afficionados, the gear heads are ready, willing, and able to thrust a wrench-wielding hand into the engines of their Camaros, Mustangs, or Corvettes. They can disassemble a turbo hydramatic transmission, and then reassemble it, at a moment's notice. They have wrenches in their jeans pocket. Gear heads seem to have ESP when it comes to automobile engines. A gear head can pop open the hood of your car, listen with head cocked and eyes closed for a second or two, and tell you that you have nine hundred miles left on your timing belt. You say, "Sure I do, buddy." Five weeks later you're stranded on the side of the road as a friendly police officer observes "Sounds like the timing belt is gone." When most people think of a car nut, it is the gear head who comes to mind. Hollywood has been using the gear head in movies and television shows for decades: James Dean in the 1950s, the Fonz in the 1970s, and Tim Allen in Home Improvement in the 1990s. On a practical level, you may not ever want to be a gear head, but you'd want your brother-in-law to be one.

On a more specialized level, there is the make-specific car nut. This is not your uncle Walter, who always drove Fords and swore by them. The make-specific car nuts go far beyond that, knowing every detail about every model of one specific brand of automobile. They might love Porsches, for instance, rattling off observations like, "The '96 Turbo's machined rather than cast cylinder fins dissipate hot air better than those of the Carrera 2." Make-specific car nuts bore their friends to tears with descriptions of the differences between the drip-rail moldings on the 1959 versus 1960 Oldsmobile Super 88 Vista Cruiser sedans. Upon spotting two old Woodstock-era Volkswagen (VW) Beetles putt-putting down the road, the make-specific car nut will handily determine the year they were made. It's eerie; everyone knows you can't tell one year's vintage VW from another. Make-specific car nuts dress like you and me, except they wear accessories--tie clips, cuff links, pens, and dress shirts--adorned with their favorite car's logo. Will coffee served in a Firebird mug stay warm longer?

6   <u>Orphan-make hoarders</u> are the twin of make-specific car nuts, except orphan-make hoarders love only the cars manufactured by companies no longer in business. They are determined to collect every model of every Packard or Kaiser-Frazer ever produced. Usually residing in rural areas, the hoarder often owns a thirty-acre parcel of land upon which are parked a hundred or more examples of the make in various stages of decomposition, not one of which is drivable. Do you need the horn-ring for a 1951 Studebaker President Land Cruiser? The orphan-make hoarder has fourteen of them.

7   Finally, closer in orbit to our own planet, we have the <u>wishful thinkers</u>. They read <u>Road & Track</u>, <u>Car and Driver</u>, and <u>Automobile</u> every month and dream of someday owning a Ferrari Testarossa or Porsche 911 Turbo. Wishful thinkers drag their families or friends to car shows, auto races, and antique auto events. You find them in auto showrooms whenever a new model is introduced, demanding to road-test the new BMW roadster or Mustang GT that they have no intention of buying. The sales-

POSSIBLE ANSWERS:
ANALYZING THE ESSAY

1. Thesis: "You can tell the type of car nut by the kind of car the nut worships" (paragraph 2)

2. By giving examples in paragraph 2 (introduction), and for each category

3. *Principle:* Types of car nuts. *Categories:* aficionado, gear head, make-specific car nut, orphan-make hoarder, and wishful thinker.

people call them "tire-kickers." The wishful thinker owns a five-year-old Honda Civic sedan.

As you can see, car nuts cross all social and eco- 8 nomic levels, reflecting the diversity of our society. You probably know a car nut or may be one yourself. America is a nation in love with the automobile. Whatever their variety, car nuts take that love to the next level: obsession.

Analyzing the Essay

1. Identify Porter's thesis.
2. How does the writer establish the importance or meaningfulness of his classification?
3. Identify Porter's principle of classification and the categories he establishes.
4. What other patterns of development does Porter use to develop each category?
5. Evaluate the title, introduction, and conclusion.
6. Consider Porter's tone. What kind of audience does he address?

Reacting to the Essay: Discussion and Journal Writing

1. Evaluate the categories Porter establishes. Are they realistic? Describe someone you know who fits into one of the categories.
2. Discuss other principles that might be used in a classification essay about automobiles.
3. Write a journal entry describing what you sense is Porter's attitude toward three or more of his categories of "car nuts."

READING A CLASSIFICATION OR DIVISION ESSAY

The following section provides advice for reading classification or division as well as two model essays. The first essay illustrates the characteristics of classification covered in this chapter. The second essay uses classification along with other methods of development. Both essays provide opportunities to examine, analyze, and react to the writers' ideas.

WORKING WITH TEXT: READING CLASSIFICATION OR DIVISION

For more on reading strategies, see Chapter 2.

A classification or division essay is usually tightly organized and relatively easy to follow. Use the following suggestions to read classification or division essays, or any writing that uses classification or division, effectively.

What to Look for, Highlight, and Annotate

1. Highlight the thesis statement, principle of classification, and the name or title of each category or part. Also look for visual clues provided by the writer.
2. Use a different color highlighter (or another marking method, such as asterisks or numbers) to identify the key features of each category. In a textbook reading, for example, the characteristics of each category are what you are expected to learn.
3. Mark important definitions and vivid examples for later reference.
4. Add annotations indicating where you find a category or part confusing or where you think more detail is needed.

How to Find Ideas to Write About

For more on discovering ideas for a response paper, see Chapter 3.

To gain a different perspective on the reading, think of other ways of classifying or dividing the topic. For example, consider an essay that classifies types of exercise programs at health clubs according to the benefits they offer for cardiovascular health. Such exercise programs could also be classified according their cost, degree of strenuousness, type of exercise, and so forth.

A classification or division, then, provides the reader with one particular viewpoint on the subject. Be sure to keep in mind that it is *only* one viewpoint. Once you identify alternative viewpoints, choose one to write about.

TEACHING TIP

Classifications and divisions are good examples of the subjective nature of analysis. Students need to recognize that what they read and write necessarily reflects the biases, experiences, and purposes of the writer to some degree.

THINKING CRITICALLY ABOUT CLASSIFICATION AND DIVISION

The writer's purpose often shapes the nature of a classification or division essay. It is your job as a critical reader to determine how the writer's purpose affects the principle of classification or division used in an essay as well as the overall impression conveyed about the topic. For example, a writer might intend to give adult readers an unfavorable impression of high school students by classifying—and thereby emphasizing—their leisure-time activities. By contrast, high school students could be presented more favorably to the same group of readers if the writer instead categorizes the types of part-time jobs students hold or students' contributions to family life.

As a critical reader, then, keep the following questions in mind.

- How does the writer's principle of classification or division serve his or her purpose?

- What effect does the classification or division have on the reader's attitude toward and impression of the topic being classified or divided?

- What alternative classifications or divisions would give the reader a different viewpoint?

CLASSIFICATION ESSAY

As you read the following selection by Joseph A. DeVito, consider how the writer employs the elements of classification or division discussed in this chapter.

Territoriality
Joseph A. DeVito

Joseph A. DeVito holds a Ph.D. from the University of Illinois and is a professor of communication at Hunter College. He is also the author of numerous college textbooks, including Messages: Building Interpersonal Communication, *Third Edition (1996);* Essentials of Human Communication, *Second Edition (1996); and* Human Communication, *Seventh Edition (1997), from which this excerpt is taken. As you read the selection, highlight the categories the writer uses to explain the territoriality of human behavior.*

PREREADING QUESTIONS

- How does power or status in a group affect a person's or an animal's territoriality?
- What are three types of territories?

One of the most interesting concepts in ethology (the study of animals in their natural surroundings) is *territoriality*. For example, male animals will stake out a particular territory and consider it their own. They will allow prospective mates to enter but will defend it against entrance by others, especially other males of the same species. Among deer, the size of the territory signifies the power of the buck, which in turn determines how many females he will mate with. Less powerful bucks will be able to control only small parcels of land and so will mate with only one or two females. This is a particularly adaptive measure, since it ensures that the stronger members will produce most of the offspring. When the "landowner" takes possession of an area — either because it is vacant or because he gains it through

1

battle—he marks it, for example, by urinating around the boundaries. The size of the animal's territory indicates the status of the animal within the herd.

2   The size and location of human territory also say something
about status (Mehrabian, 1976; Sommer, 1969). An apartment or
office in midtown Manhattan or downtown Tokyo, for example, indicates extremely high status. The cost of the territory restricts it to
those who have lots of money.

3   Status is also signaled by the unwritten law granting the right of
invasion. Higher-status individuals have more of a right to invade the
territory of others than vice versa. The boss of a large company, for
example, can invade the territory of a junior executive by barging into
her or his office, but the reverse would be unthinkable.

4   Some researchers claim that territoriality is innate and demonstrates the innate aggressiveness of humans. Others claim that territoriality is learned behavior and is culturally based. Most, however,
agree that a great deal of human behavior can be understood and
described as territorial, regardless of its origin.

TYPES OF TERRITORIES

5   ***Primary Territory.***   Primary territories are your exclusive preserve;
your desk, room, house, or backyard, for example. In these areas you
are in control. It's similar to the home field advantage that a sports
team has when playing in its own ballpark. When you are in these primary areas, you generally have greater influence over others than you
would in someone else's territory. For example, when in their own
home or office people take on a kind of leadership role; they initiate
conversations, fill in silences, assume relaxed and comfortable postures, and maintain their positions with greater conviction. Because
the territorial owner is dominant, you stand a better chance of getting your raise, your point accepted, and the contract resolved in your
favor if you are in your own primary territory (Marsh, 1988).

6   ***Secondary Territory.***   Secondary territories, although they do not
belong to you, are associated with you perhaps because you have
occupied them for a long period of time or they have been assigned
to you. For example, your desk in a classroom may be a secondary territory if it was assigned to you or if you have regularly occupied it and
others treat it as yours. Your neighborhood turf, a cafeteria table that
you regularly occupy, or a favorite corner of a local coffee shop may
be secondary territories. You feel a certain "ownership-like" attach-
ment to the place although it is really not yours in any legal sense.

Public Territory.   Public territories are those areas that are open to   7
all people: a park, movie house, restaurant, or beach, for example.
The European café, the food court in a suburban mall, and the public spaces in large city office buildings are public spaces that,
although established for eating, also serve to bring people together
and to stimulate communication. The electronic revolution, however,
may well change the role of public space in stimulating communication (Drucker & Gumpert, 1991; Gumpert & Drucker, 1995). For
example, home shopping clubs make it less necessary for people to
go shopping "downtown" or to the mall, and consequently they have
less opportunity to run into other people and to talk and to exchange
news. Similarly, electronic mail permits communication without
talking and without even going out of one's home to mail a letter.
Perhaps the greatest change is telecommuting (Giordano 1989)
which allows people to work without even leaving their homes. The
face-to-face communication that normally takes place in an office is
replaced by communication via computer.

TERRITORIAL ENCROACHMENT

Look around your home. You probably see certain territories that   8
different people have staked out and where invasions are cause for at
least mildly defensive action. This is perhaps seen most clearly with
siblings who each have (or "own") a specific chair, room, radio, and
so on. Father has his chair and Mother has her chair.

In classrooms where seats are not assigned, territoriality can also   9
be observed. When a student sits in a seat that has normally been
occupied by another student, the regular occupant will often become
disturbed and resentful.

Following Lyman and Scott (1967; DeVito & Hecht, 1990), Table   10
[1] identifies the three major types of territorial encroachment: violation, invasion, and contamination.

You can react to encroachment in several ways (Lyman & Scott,   11
1967; DeVito & Hecht, 1990). The most extreme form is *turf defense.*
When you cannot tolerate the intruders, you may choose to defend
the territory against them and try to expel them. This is the method
of gangs that defend "their" streets and neighborhoods by fighting
off members of rival gangs (intruders) who enter the territory.

A less extreme defense is *insulation,* a tactic in which you erect   12
some sort of barrier between yourself and the invaders. Some people
do this by wearing sunglasses to avoid eye contact. Others erect
fences to let others know that they do not welcome interpersonal
interaction.

TABLE 1
THREE TYPES OF TERRITORIAL ENCROACHMENT

Name	Definition	Example
Violation	Unwarranted use of another's territory and thereby changing the meaning of that territory	Entering another's office or home without permission
Invasion	Entering the territory of another and thereby changing the meaning of that territory	Parents entering a teen's social group
Contamination	Rendering a territory impure	Smoking a cigar in a kitchen

13   *Linguistic collusion,* another method of separating yourself from unwanted invaders, involves speaking in a language unknown to these outsiders. Or you might use professional jargon to which they are not privy. Linguistic collusion groups together those who speak that language and excludes those who do not know the linguistic code. Still another type of response is withdrawal; you leave the territory altogether.

MARKERS

14   Much as animals mark their territory, humans mark theirs with three types of markers: central, boundary, and earmarkers (Hickson & Stacks 1993). *Central markers* are items you place in a territory to reserve it. For example, you place a drink at the bar, books on your desk, and a sweater over the chair to let others know that this territory belongs to you.

15   *Boundary markers* set boundaries that divide your territory from "theirs." In the supermarket checkout line, the bar placed between your groceries and those of the person behind you is a boundary marker. Similarly, the armrests separating seats in movie theaters and the rises on each side of the molded plastic seats on a bus or train are boundary markers.

16   *Earmarkers*—a term taken from the practice of branding animals on their ears—are those identifying marks that indicate your possession of a territory or object. Trademarks, nameplates, and initials on a shirt or attaché case are all examples of earmarkers. ∎

REFERENCES

DeVito, J. A., & Hecht, M. L., (Eds.) (1990). *The nonverbal communication reader.* Prospect Heights, IL: Waveland.

Drucker, S. J., & Gumpert, G. (1991). Public space and communication: The zoning of public interaction. *Communication Theory, 1* (November), 294–310.

Giordano, J. (1989). *Telecommuting and organizational culture: A study of corporate consciousness and identification.* Unpublished doctoral dissertation, University of Massachusetts, Amherst, MA.

Gumpert, G., & Drucker, S. J. (1995). Place as medium: Exegesis of the café drinking coffee, the art of watching others, civil conversation — with excursions into the effects of architecture and interior design. *The Speech Communication Annual, 9* (Spring), 7–32.

Hickson, M. L., & Stacks, D. W. (1993). *NVC: Nonverbal communication: Studies and applications,* 3rd ed. Dubuque, IA: Wm. C. Brown.

Lyman, S. M., & Scott, M. B. (1967). Territoriality: A neglected sociological dimension. *Social problems, 15,* 236–249.

Marsh, P. (1988). *Eye to eye: How people interact.* Topfield, MA: Salem House.

Mehrabian, A. (1976). *Public places and private spaces.* New York: Basic Books.

Sommer, R. (1969). *Personal space: The behavioral basis of design.* Upper Saddle River, NJ: Prentice-Hall/Spectrum.

Examining the Reading

1. Describe the three types of territories that DeVito identifies in his classification.

2. According to the writer, in what ways do humans react to territorial encroachment?

3. Describe the three types of territorial markers that DeVito discusses and classifies.

4. Define each of the following words as it is used in the reading: *innate* (paragraph 4), *dominant* (5), *encroachment* (10), *expel* (11), and *collusion* (13). Refer to your dictionary as needed.

Analyzing the Reading

1. What is DeVito's thesis?

2. What principle of classification does the writer use to establish the three types of territories? Does he employ the same principle or a different one in his classifications of encroachment and markers?

3. What other patterns of development does DeVito use to explain his classification of territoriality, encroachment, and markers?

4. Evaluate the introduction. What methods are employed to spark readers' interest in the topic of territoriality?

POSSIBLE ANSWERS: EXAMINING THE READING

1. Primary territory, "your exclusive preserve" (paragraph 5); secondary territory, a place "associated with you" (6); public territory, a space open to all (7).

2. Turf defense, expelling intruders; insulation, erecting a barrier between self and intruders; linguistic collusion, speaking a language unknown to intruders; withdrawal, leaving the territory

3. Central markers, "items you place in a territory to mark it" such as a sweater on a chair (14); boundary markers, which "set boundaries that divide your territory from 'theirs,'" such as supermarket dividers (15); earmarkers, emblems that identify personal property, such as trademarks and monograms (16)

4. *Innate:* natural, inborn; *dominant:* having the greatest social power in a group; *encroachment:* intrusion upon another's territory; *expel:* to send away; *collusion:* conspiracy, secret agreement to band together against a common enemy

POSSIBLE ANSWERS: ANALYZING THE READING

1. Thesis: Territoriality underlies "a great deal of human behavior" (paragraph 4)

2. Classifies territories in terms of the relation

(Continued on next page)

of the person to the place, encroachment by the type of disturbance, markers by the position of the marker.

3. Definition, comparison, illustration, cause-effect

4. The introduction uses a variety of methods of development (see item 3 above); the analogy of the territoriality of animals and discussion of research lead up to the thesis. Perhaps the most interesting example is the deer.

POSSIBLE ANSWERS: REACTING TO THE READING

1. Responses will vary; possibilities include a place at the dinner table and a seat on a bus or train.

2. Other possible principles: by purpose or function (social, private); by type of activity (study, worship)

3. Responses will vary.

PREREADING QUESTION

As you read, consider Sanders's attitude toward the kinds of men he knew in childhood.

Reacting to the Reading: Discussion and Journal Writing

1. Discuss examples of secondary territoriality that you have observed or experienced.

2. Discuss other possible principles of classification that might be used to classify human territories.

3. Write a journal entry describing how you dealt with a situation involving territorial encroachment.

CLASSIFICATION COMBINED WITH OTHER PATTERNS

In the following essay, Scott Russell Sanders combines classification with other patterns of development to support a thesis about types of men.

The Men We Carry in Our Minds
Scott Russell Sanders

Scott Russell Sanders is a professor of English at Indiana University. He is also the author of numerous works of fiction, including two novels, Terrarium *(1985) and* The Invisible Company *(1989); several short story collections; and two children's books,* Aurora Means Dawn *(1989) and* Here Comes the Mystery Man *(1993). His other works include* Staying Put: Making a Home in a Restless World *(1993),* Writing from the Center *(1995), and articles published in* Harper's, *the* New York Times, *and the* Georgia Review. *This essay was originally published in 1984 in the* Milkweed Chronicle, *a journal of literature and the arts. As you read the selection, notice that Sanders uses classification as well as description and illustration to develop his ideas. Highlight the categories that the writer establishes.*

1   The first men, besides my father, I remember seeing were black convicts and white guards, in the cottonfield across the road from our farm on the outskirts of Memphis. I must have been three or four. The prisoners wore dingy gray-and-black zebra suits, heavy as canvas, sodden with sweat. Hatless, stooped, they chopped weeds in the fierce heat, row after row, breathing the acrid dust of boll-weevil poison. The overseers wore dazzling white shirts and broad shadowy hats. The oiled barrels of their shotguns flashed in the sunlight. Their faces in memory are utterly blank. Of course those men, white and black, have become for me an emblem of racial hatred. But they have also come to stand for the twin poles of my early vision of manhood — the brute toiling animal and the boss.

When I was a boy, the men I knew labored with their bodies. They 2
were marginal farmers, just scraping by, or welders, steel workers, car-
penters; they swept floors, dug ditches, mined coal, or drove trucks,
their forearms ropy with muscle; they trained horses, stoked fur-
naces, built tires, stood on assembly lines wrestling parts onto cars
and refrigerators. They got up before light, worked all day long whatever the weather, and when they came home at night they looked as
though somebody had been whipping them. In the evenings and on
weekends they worked on their own places, tilling gardens that were
lumpy with clay, fixing broken-down cars, hammering on houses
that were always too drafty, too leaky, too small.

The bodies of the men I knew were twisted and maimed in ways 3
visible and invisible. The nails of their hands were black and split, the
hands tattooed with scars. Some had lost fingers. Heavy lifting had
given many of them finicky backs and guts weak from hernias. Racing against conveyor belts had given them ulcers. Their ankles and
knees ached from years of standing on concrete. Anyone who had
worked for long around machines was hard of hearing. They
squinted, and the skin of their faces was creased like the leather of
old work gloves. There were times, studying them, when I dreaded
growing up. Most of them coughed, from dust or cigarettes, and
most of them drank cheap wine or whiskey, so their eyes looked
bloodshot and bruised. The fathers of my friends always seemed
older than the mothers. Men wore out sooner. Only women lived into
old age.

As a boy I also knew another sort of men, who did not sweat and 4
break down like mules. They were soldiers, and so far as I could tell
they scarcely worked at all. During my early school years we lived on
a military base, an arsenal in Ohio, and every day I saw GIs in the
guardshacks, on the stoops of barracks, at the wheels of olive drab
Chevrolets. The chief fact of their lives was boredom. Long after I left
the Arsenal I came to recognize the sour smell the soldiers gave off as
that of souls in limbo. They were all waiting — for wars, for transfers,
for leaves, for promotions, for the end of their hitch — like so many
braves waiting for the hunt to begin. Unlike the warriors of older
tribes, however, they would have no say about when the battle would
start or how it would be waged. Their waiting was broken only when
they practiced for war. They fired guns at targets, drove tanks across
the churned-up fields of the military reservation, set off bombs in
the wrecks of old fighter planes. I knew this was all play. But I also
felt certain that when the hour for killing arrived, they would kill.
When the real shooting started, many of them would die. This was
what soldiers were *for*, just as a hammer was for driving nails.

Warriors and toilers: those seemed, in my boyhood vision, to be 5
the chief destinies for men. They weren't the only destinies, as I

learned from having a few male teachers, from reading books, and from watching television. But the men on television — the politicians, the astronauts, the generals, the savvy lawyers, the philosophical doctors, the bosses who gave orders to both soldiers and laborers — seemed as remote and unreal to me as the figures in tapestries. I could no more imagine growing up to become one of these cool, potent creatures than I could imagine becoming a prince.

6   A nearer and more hopeful example was that of my father, who had escaped from a red-dirt farm to a tire factory, and from the assembly line to the front office. Eventually he dressed in a white shirt and tie. He carried himself as if he had been born to work with his mind. But his body, remembering the earlier years of slogging work, began to give out on him in his fifties, and it quit on him entirely before he turned sixty-five. Even such a partial escape from man's fate as he had accomplished did not seem possible for most of the boys I knew. They joined the Army, stood in line for jobs in the smoky plants, helped build highways. They were bound to work as their fathers had worked, killing themselves or preparing to kill others.

7   A scholarship enabled me not only to attend college, a rare enough feat in my circle, but even to study in a university meant for the children of the rich. Here I met for the first time young men who had assumed from birth that they would lead lives of comfort and power. And for the first time I met women who told me that men were guilty of having kept all the joys and privileges of the earth for themselves. I was baffled. What privileges? What joys? I thought about the maimed, dismal lives of most of the men back home. What had they stolen from their wives and daughters? The right to go five days a week, twelve months a year, for thirty or forty years to a steel mill or a coal mine? The right to drop bombs and die in war? The right to feel every leak in the roof, every gap in the fence, every cough in the engine, as a wound they must mend? The right to feel, when the layoff comes or the plant shuts down, not only afraid but ashamed?

8   I was slow to understand the deep grievances of women. This was because, as a boy, I had envied them. Before college, the only people I had ever known who were interested in art or music or literature, the only ones who read books, the only ones who ever seemed to enjoy a sense of ease and grace were the mothers and daughters. Like the menfolk, they fretted about money, they scrimped and made-do. But, when the pay stopped coming in, they were not the ones who had failed. Nor did they have to go to war, and that seemed to me a blessed fact. By comparison with the narrow, ironclad days of fathers, there was an expansiveness, I thought, in the days of mothers. They went to see neighbors, to shop in town, to run errands at school, at

the library, at church. No doubt, had I looked harder at their lives, I would have envied them less. It was not my fate to become a woman, so it was easier for me to see the graces. Few of them held jobs outside the home, and those who did filled thankless roles as clerks and waitresses. I didn't see, then, what a prison a house could be, since houses seemed to me brighter, handsomer places than any factory. I did not realize—because such things were never spoken of—how often women suffered from men's bullying. I did learn about the wretchedness of abandoned wives, single mothers, widows; but I also learned about the wretchedness of lone men. Even then I could see how exhausting it was for a mother to cater all day to the needs of young children. But if I had been asked, as a boy, to choose between tending a baby and tending a machine, I think I would have chosen the baby. (Having now tended both, I know I would choose the baby.)

So I was baffled when the women at college accused me and my sex of having cornered the world's pleasures. I think something like my bafflement has been felt by other boys (and by girls as well) who grew up in dirt-poor farm country, in mining country, in black ghettos, in Hispanic barrios, in the shadows of factories, in Third World nations—any place where the fate of men is as grim and bleak as the fate of women. Toilers and warriors. I realize now how ancient these identities are, how deep the tug they exert on men, the undertow of a thousand generations. The miseries I saw, as a boy, in the lives of nearly all men I continue to see in the lives of many—the body-breaking toil, the tedium, the call to be tough, the humiliating powerlessness, the battle for a living and for territory.

When the women I met at college thought about the joys and privileges of men, they did not carry in their minds the sort of men I had known in my childhood. They thought of their fathers, who were bankers, physicians, architects, stockbrokers, the big wheels of the big cities. These fathers rode the train to work or drove cars that cost more than any of my childhood houses. They were attended from morning to night by female helpers, wives and nurses and secretaries. They were never laid off, never short of cash at month's end, never lined up for welfare. These fathers made decisions that mattered. They ran the world.

The daughters of such men wanted to share in this power, this glory. So did I. They yearned for a say over their future, for jobs worthy of their abilities, for the right to live at peace, unmolested, whole. Yes, I thought, yes yes. The difference between me and these daughters was that they saw me, because of my sex, as destined from birth to become like their fathers, and therefore as an enemy to their desires. But I knew better. I wasn't an enemy, in fact or in feeling. I was an ally. If I had known, then, how to tell them so, would they have believed me? Would they now? ∎

9

10

11

POSSIBLE ANSWERS: EXAMINING THE READING (p. 456)

1. Toilers (blue-collar workers); warriors (soldiers); the boss
2. Because women tended to the house and the children and lived to an old age
3. He encountered young feminists who rejected the patriarchy of their white-collar fathers.
4. *Emblem:* symbol; *limbo:* spiritual homelessness, state of being lost; *expansiveness:* vastness, considerable size; *undertow:* an ocean current that pulls one toward or under the water; *tedium:* exhausting boredom

POSSIBLE ANSWERS: ANALYZING THE READING (p. 456)

1. Thesis: "Warriors and toilers . . . men" (paragraph 5)
2. The kinds of work the men did
3. Comparisons include "like so many braves waiting for the hunt . . ." (4); "But the men on television . . .

(Continued on next page)

Examining the Reading

1. Identify the categories of men that Sanders establishes.
2. Why, as a boy, did Sanders envy women?
3. How did Sanders's view of women change while he was in college?
4. Explain the meaning of each of the following words as it is used in the read-ing: *emblem* (paragraph 1), *limbo* (4), *expansiveness* (8), *undertow* (9), and *tedium* (9). Refer to your dictionary as needed.

Analyzing the Reading

1. Identify Sanders's thesis statement.
2. What principle does the writer use to establish his categories of men?
3. Sanders makes numerous comparisons in the essay. Identify two comparisons that you think are particularly effective. Give reasons to support your choices.
4. Identify several descriptions and examples that Sanders uses to explain his views of men and women.
5. What is the meaning of the essay's title?

Reacting to the Reading: Discussion and Journal Writing

1. Discuss alternative principles that could be used to classify men.
2. Discuss whether Sanders's views of men and women are applicable today.
3. Write a journal entry explaining how you think Sanders would answer the two questions he poses in the conclusion.

APPLYING YOUR SKILLS: ADDITIONAL ESSAY ASSIGNMENTS

*For more on locating and
documenting sources, see
Chapters 19 and 20.*

Write a classification or division essay on one of the following topics, using what you learned about classification and division in this chapter. Depending on the topic you choose, you may need to conduct library or Internet research.

To Express Your Ideas

1. Explain whether you are proud of or frustrated with your ability to budget money. For example, you might classify budget categories that are easy to mas-ter versus those that cause problems.

2. Explain why you chose your career or major. Categorize the types of job opportunities or benefits of your chosen field and indicate why they are important to you.

3. Divide a store, such as a media shop, department store, or grocery store, into departments. Describe where you are most and least tempted to overspend.

started. Remind students to consult the learning style options (pp. 430 and 432) and the revision flowchart (p. 439).

To Inform Your Reader

4. Write an essay classifying college instructors' teaching styles for the readers of your college newspaper.

5. Explain the parts of a ceremony or event you have attended or participated in.

6. Divide a familiar substance into its components, as Bodanis does in "A Brush with Reality: Surprises in the Tube."

To Persuade Your Reader

7. Categorize types of television violence to develop the argument that violence on television is harmful to children.

8. Categorize types of parenting skills and demonstrate how they are learned to develop the argument that effective parenting skills can be acquired through practice, training, or observation.

9. Classify the men and women you have known. Use your classification to support a thesis about men and women in general, as Sanders does in "The Men We Carry in Our Minds."

Cases Using Classification or Division

10. Write an essay for an introductory education class, identifying a problem you have experienced or observed in the public education system. Divide public education into parts in order to better explain your problem.

11. You oversee the development of the annual catalog for a large community college, including the section describing the services offered to students. Decide how that section of the catalog should be organized; then list the categories it should include. Finally, write a description of the services in *one* category.

Chapter 15

Study the photograph on the opposite page. How might you explain what the people in the photograph are doing to someone who is unfamiliar with the activity?

Writing Quick Start

Write a paragraph explaining what the people in the photograph are doing. Include the name of the activity, and the type of activity it is (for example, physical versus mental).

Definition: Explaining What You Mean

TEACHING TIP

Advise students to *describe* the people and their actions in the photograph. They may also distinguish the activity pictured in the photo from other, similar ones.

TEACHING TIP:
CHAPTER OVERVIEW

• In all oral and written communication, students should be encouraged to use clear, precise language.

• In this chapter, students consider complex ideas in extended definition essays.

• Students should recognize the relevance of definition in essays using other patterns of development, such as narration, description, illustration, comparison and contrast, classification and division, cause and effect, and argument.

• Thinking Critically about Definition (p. 490) emphasizes the subjectivity of some definitions and the importance of considering the writer's bias, particularly when *euphemisms* may be used to influence readers' thinking.

WRITING A DEFINITION

In your paragraph, you named and described the activity in the photo, perhaps including one or more characteristics that distinguish it from other similar activities. In other words, you have just written a brief definition. This chapter will show you how to write effective definitions, how to explore and explain a topic using an extended definition, and how to incorporate definition into essays using other patterns of development.

WHAT IS DEFINITION?

A **definition** is a way of explaining what a term means or which meaning is intended when a word has a number of different meanings. Often, but not always, a definition is intended for someone who is unfamiliar with the thing or idea being defined. You might define *slicing* to someone unfamiliar with golf or explain the term *koi* to a person unfamiliar with tropical fish.

You use definitions every day in a variety of situations. You might explain the term *disk drive* to someone unfamiliar with personal computers or be asked to explain what you mean by the term *vintage clothing*. If you call a friend a *nonconformist*, she might ask you exactly what you mean, or you and a friend might disagree over what constitutes *feminism*. Definitions, then, are an important part of daily communication.

When a group shares a set of terms with commonly understood meanings, communication is simplified. For example, many sports and hobbies have their own language. Hockey fans know terms such as *high-sticking, icing, puck,* and *blueline;* when a sports announcer uses one of these terms, fans know what is meant. Photographers speak of *f-stop, ASA,* and *sky filters;* cooking enthusiasts know such terms as *sauté, parboil,* and *fillet.* Professions and academic fields of study also have

---

SCENES FROM COLLEGE AND THE WORKPLACE

• On an exam for a *health and fitness* course, the following short answer question appears: "Define the term *wellness.*"

• Your *philosophy* instructor asks you to write a paper exploring the ethics of mercy killing; as part of the essay, you need to define the concepts *terminal illness* and *chronic condition.*

• As a *chemical engineer* responsible for your department's compliance with the company's standards for *safety* and *work efficiency,* you write a brief memo to your staff defining each term.

their own specialized terminology. A surgeon, for example, does not need to ask the surgical nurse for the small, straight knife with the thin, sharp blade; he or she asks for a *scalpel*. Terms and meanings, then, make communication precise, helping to avoid misunderstandings and confusion.

Many academic and work situations require that you write or learn definitions, as the examples in the accompanying box indicate.

The essay that follows is an example of a definition of a Hispanic tradition, cracking *cascarones*.

Cracking Cascarones
Yleana Martinez

Yleana Martinez's essay first appeared in 1996 in Hispanic, *a magazine that covers social and cultural issues but also includes current information on a wide range of subjects. Martinez has written numerous other articles for* Hispanic *magazine on such topics as AIDS, education, and Hispanic traditions. As you read the selection, pay particular attention to how Martinez defines* cascarones. *Highlight the characteristics of the tradition of cracking* cascarones *that the writer identifies.*

PREREADING
QUESTIONS

• In your opinion, are *cascarones* works of art? Why or why not?
• Why do you think the writer cites Dr. Jim Griffith's claim that there has been a "'*cascarón* revolution' in the past two decades" (paragraph 9)?

This April 7, on Easter Sunday morning, many Hispanic families will celebrate the religious holiday by attending Mass. And for some, the solemnity of observing Christ's resurrection will give way to the mischievous fun of cracking confetti-filled *cascarones*, or eggshells, on unsuspecting heads.   1

Eggs have had symbolic meaning for centuries. They were used in ancient fertility rites to ensure a bountiful harvest or that a marriage produced a child. These rituals were held at the start of the spring season. Easter, with its message of renewal and hope, is celebrated on the first Sunday after the full moon of the vernal equinox. The Easter of modern times shares with its pre-Christian counterparts the fertility symbols of rabbits and eggs. My own memories of this holiday, however, barely contain a religious aspect and instead, concentrate on the fun and excitement of *cascarones*.   2

CONNECTIONS

Ask the class to identify the other patterns of development used in this essay (e.g., description, narration, process analysis) and to discuss how Martinez weaves them into her definition essay.

Growing up in South Texas, my siblings and I awakened on warm spring mornings for the egg hunt. Barefooted and in pajamas, we'd race outside, first to search for the basket left by *La Coneja*,* then to collect the *cascarones* we decorated in the days leading up to Easter. The basket always had foil-wrapped chocolate eggs and rabbits as well as hideously sweet neon-pink and yellow marshmallow chicks.   3

La Coneja: the Easter bunny.

4   We'd hold up the hems of our pajama tops to carry the *cascarones* —a delicate task since we also lugged our basket of candy treasures with the same hand. We'd use our free hand to scoop the eggs from their hiding places. Woe to the child who carelessly smashed some of his or her precious arsenal, for that was how we regarded our *cascarones*.

5   After Mass, the family would drive to a ranch for a reunion and the traditional *carne asada*.* Just before sundown, we'd get the signal from a grownup that the moment had arrived. All manners and civility were lost as everyone chased each other around, smashing dozens of painted eggshells on delicate craniums.

6   The *cascarón* activity may seem irreverent, but it has a respectable tradition. Along the Mexico border, *cascarones* have long been a part of the Easter tradition. References to the craft have been documented as early as 1897, when the Folklore Society of London published a catalogue with illustrations of elaborate eggshell figures and decorated eggs from all over Mexico. The Mexican tradition of painting eggs and filling them with colored bits of paper is practiced in the U.S. Southwest from California to Texas. The popularity of this tradition may stem from the view that *cascarones* are more fun to decorate than hard-boiled eggs because you're not stuck with having to eat them all.

7   *Cascarones* are found in some Hispanic communities throughout the year. In cities from Tucson to San Antonio, they can be purchased in folk art shops and at fiestas and church festivals. They're cheap and easy to make and can bring a nice profit to those who make them. Some people along the border have even turned *cascarones* into beautiful art.

8   Consider Doña Gloria Moroyoqui, a half-Mayo, half-Yaquí Indian who lives in Nogales, Sonora, Mexico. Her creations go beyond the typical painted egg with a tissue paper "hat." Moroyoqui, who is recognized mainly for her skill at making paper flowers and *pinatas*,* constructs elaborate human figures with painted eggshell heads. She often demonstrates her craft at the Tumacacori National Historical Park in Arizona. Her *cascarones* are often described as "phenomenal."

9   Dr. Jim Griffith, coordinator at the University of Arizona Libraries Southwest Folklore Center, says he has seen a "*cascarón* revolution" in the past two decades. Because the eggshells are used for any festive occasion, many women who decorate them professionally are able to support their families, he says. According to Griffith, the *cascarón*-makers of southern Arizona's Santa Clara Valley favor

---

carne asada: grilled meat, barbecue.

piñatas: containers, usually made of papier-mâché, that are filled with treats and hung from the ceiling.

putting cone-shaped "hats," sometimes almost a foot tall, over the egg's opening. They then add strips of fringed *papel de china** in alternating layers, like streamers. The eggs are adorned with glitter, feathers, and other material. He's seen the eggs painted with human faces, as well as animals like cows and penguins. "They've gone visually wild," Griffith says. *Cascarones* are no longer just eggshells with different colors painted on them and paper glued on them to keep the confetti in. They're very, very elaborate. Until you've seen them, it's hard to know what they look like."

In Laredo, Texas, Maria Villarreal uses felt-tip markers to paint 10 more than 3,000 eggs a year. Villarreal, a homemaker, was never enamored of the single-colored, water-dipped eggs, so she started painting the eggs with markers during her free time. She lets her imagination take over as she holds the eggshell over her finger, rotating it to paint clowns, cartoon characters, flowerbeds, and other fanciful images. Some of her Easter eggs have complex scenes that need to be viewed from all sides to fully appreciate them. One features a desert scene with cactus, jackrabbits, and snakes; another depicts an underwater scene with brilliant tropical fish skirting among the kelp.

Villarreal, who has seven grandchildren, sells her eggs to friends 11 and co-workers referred by her family. She charges $1.25 a dozen. Her children collect the eggs year-round for her, and weeks before Easter, she begins to get orders from people who want to buy them. "I've been doing this twenty years. It's my hobby," Villarreal says. "But now I do it all year long. It's become a habit for my children to bring me the empty eggshells."

Like so many other customs, *cascarones* involve days, sometimes 12 weeks, of preparation and constitute a fun family project. *Cascarón*-making starts in the kitchen. The family's chief cook takes special care to crack open the eggs at one end. The eggs are drained into a bowl; then the shells are carefully rinsed out and left to dry. When a sufficient number have been collected, all the artist needs is egg dye, glue, tissue paper, and confetti. After the eggs are dry, they are filled with confetti. The artist cuts circles from tissue paper (or forms cones), then pastes them over the opening.

Cascarones are usually stored in egg cartons and left within easy 13 reach of the Easter Bunny, who magically hides them outside before the kids wake up on Easter Sunday (remember, *cascarones* are for cracking on the hardest part of the body—the crown of the head— and not for throwing). Huge quantities of confetti and eggshells will fly all over the place, so it's best to perform the ceremony outdoors. *Cascarones* do make a mess, but considering the fun and laughter they produce, you'll find they are worth it. ■

---

papel de china: crepe paper; crinkled tissue paper.

Characteristics of Extended Definitions

You will have many occasions to use definition in your writing. When you suspect your reader may not understand a key term, offer a brief definition. Often, however, a standard definition will not be sufficient to explain the meaning of a complex idea or concept. At times, you may need a paragraph or an entire essay to define a term. For example, if you were asked to define the term *happiness,* you would probably have trouble coming up with a brief definition because the emotion is experienced in a variety of different situations. In an essay-length piece of writing, however, you could explore the term and explain all that it means to you. Such a lengthy, detailed definition is called an **extended definition.**

Extended definitions are particularly useful in exploring a topic — in examining its various meanings and applications. In some instances, an extended definition may begin with a standard definition that anchors the essay's thesis statement. At other times, an extended definition may begin by introducing a new way of thinking about the term. Whatever approach is used, the remainder of the definition then clarifies the term by using one or more other patterns of development.

An Extended Definition Often Includes a Brief Explanation of the Term

In almost any kind of essay, it is often necessary to include a brief definition of an important term. Even in an essay that provides an extended definition, it is useful to include a brief definition to help readers begin to grasp the concept. A brief or standard definition is the kind found in a dictionary. It consists of three parts:

- The *term* itself
- The *class* to which the term belongs
- The *characteristics* that distinguish the term from all others in its class

For example, to define a wedding band, you would first say it is a piece of jewelry. "Jewelry" is the **class** or group of objects to which a wedding band belongs. To show how a wedding band differs from other members of that class, you would need to define its **distinguishing characteristics** — how it is different from other types of jewelry. You could say that it is a ring, often made of gold, given by the groom to the bride or the bride to the groom during a marriage ceremony.

Here are a few more examples of this three-part structure.

Term	Class	Distinguishing Characteristics
fork	utensil	—Two or more prongs
		—Used for eating or serving food
Dalmatian	breed of dog	—Originated in Dalmatia
		—Has short, smooth coat with black or dark brown spots

To write a standard definition, use the following guidelines.

1. **Describe the class as specifically as possible.** In the preceding example, notice that for *Dalmatian* the class is not *animal* or *mammal,* but a *breed of dog.* Narrowing the class as much as possible will make it easier for your reader to understand the term you define.

2. **Do not use the term (or forms of the term) as part of your definition.** Do not write, "*Mastery* means that one has *mastered* a skill" or "A *firefighter* is a person who *fights fires.*" Synonyms may be helpful as substitutes for a term. In place of *mastered,* you could use *learned,* for example.

3. **Include enough distinguishing characteristics so that your readers will not mistake the term for something similar within the class.** If you define *answering machine* as "a machine that records messages," your definition would be incomplete because tape recorders and computers also record messages.

4. **Do not limit the definition so much that it becomes inaccurate.** Defining *bacon* as "a smoked, salted meat from a pig that is served at breakfast" would be too limited because bacon is also served at other mealtimes (at lunch, for instance, as part of a bacon, lettuce, and tomato sandwich).

Look at the following definition of the term *bully,* taken from a magazine article on the topic. As you read it, study the highlighting and marginal notes.

Term

Three characteristics —

Distinguishes this term from similar — terms

The term *bully* does not have a standard definition, but Dan Olweus, professor of psychology at the University of Bergen, has honed the definition to three core elements—bullying involves a pattern of *repeated aggressive behavior* with *negative intent* directed from one child to another where there is a *power difference.* Either a larger child or several children pick on one child, or one child is clearly more dominant than the others. Bullying is not the same as garden-variety aggression; although aggression may involve similar acts, it happens between two people of equal status. By definition, the bully's target has difficulty defending him- or herself, and the bully's aggressive behavior is intended to cause distress.

— Example of power difference

HARA ESTROFF MARANO, "Big. Bad. Bully."

EXERCISE 15.1

Write a standard definition for two of the following terms.

1. hero
2. giraffe
3. science fiction

POSSIBLE ANSWERS

1. *hero:* a person who possesses outstanding qualities and/or who may engage in acts of selflessness.
2. *giraffe:* a jungle mammal with spots and an extremely long neck, which allows the animal to graze from treetops.
3. *science fiction:* a type of imaginative literature set in the future, usually including high technology and such themes as good versus evil.

(Continued on next page)

4. *ATM machine:* an "automatic teller machine" that is connected to a bank's main computer and is designed to perform simple banking functions such as deposits and withdrawals.
5. *friendship:* a relationship between two or more people or animals based on mutual respect and some common bond, such as compatible personalities, similar ages, or similar interests.

4. ATM machine
5. friendship

An Extended Definition Is Specific and Focused

An extended definition focuses on a specific term and discusses it in detail. In "Cracking *Cascarones*," Martinez concentrates on a specific Hispanic tradition. She recalls childhood memories of cracking *cascarones*, relates the history of the tradition, describes their preparation, and introduces some people who make them. Although *cascarones* are only one part of her family's traditional Easter celebration, Martinez focuses solely on that part. She does not sidetrack readers by discussing other parts of the celebration.

An Extended Definition Makes a Point

The thesis of an extended definition essay often includes a brief standard definition of the term and tells why it is worth reading about. In "Cracking *Cascarones*," Martinez includes a brief definition of the term in her thesis and tells readers that cracking *cascarones* is "mischievous fun" (paragraph 1). She wants her readers to join in the fun of her family's tradition.

The following thesis statements include a brief definition and make a point about the term.

> Produced by the body, hormones are chemicals that are important to physical as well as emotional development.

> Euthanasia, the act of ending the life of someone suffering from a terminal illness, is an issue that should not be legislated; rather, it should be a matter of personal choice.

An Extended Definition Uses Other Patterns of Development

To explain the meaning of a term, writers usually integrate one or more other patterns of development. Here are some examples of how other patterns might be used in an extended definition.

- *Narrate* a term's history (or etymology) or a story that demonstrates its use (Chapter 9).
- *Describe* the item a term stands for (Chapter 10).
- Offer *examples* of how a term is used (Chapter 11).
- Explain how something works, its *process* (Chapter 12).
- *Compare* or *contrast* a term to similar terms (Chapter 13).
- *Classify* a term or *divide* it into its parts (Chapter 14).
- Examine the *causes* or *effects* of a term (Chapter 16).
- *Argue* in favor of a particular definition of a term (Chapter 18).

In "Cracking *Cascarones,*" for example, Martinez relies on several patterns of development. She uses narration to present the history of *cascarones,* includes examples of *cascarones* as artwork, describes the *cascarones* made by several artists, and presents the process by which *cascarones* are made.

EXERCISE 15.2

For one of the terms listed in Exercise 15.1, describe how you might use two or three patterns of development in an extended definition of the term.

An Extended Definition Includes Sufficient Distinguishing Characteristics and Details

An extended definition includes enough distinguishing characteristics and details so that readers can fully understand the term. In "Cracking *Cascarones,*" Martinez gives vivid descriptions of numerous characteristics of *cascarones,* allowing her readers to visualize both the *cascarones* and the celebration in which they are used. Consider this description of the elaborate artwork on some of them: "One features a desert scene with cactus, jackrabbits, and snakes; another depicts an underwater scene with brilliant tropical fish skirting among the kelp" (paragraph 10).

EXERCISE 15.3

For one of the terms listed in Exercise 15.1, list the distinguishing characteristics that you might use in building an extended definition.

An Extended Definition May Use Negation and Address Misconceptions

When the term being defined is very similar to other terms in the same class and may be confused with them, a writer may use negation to explain how the term is different from the other terms. For example, in an essay defining *Szechuan* food, you might clarify how it is unlike *Hunan,* which is a different type of spicy Chinese cuisine but one that readers may confuse with Szechuan. This strategy is known as **negation** because you explain what a term *is not* as well as what it *is.* You can also use negation to clarify personal meanings. In defining what you mean by *relaxing vacation,* you might include examples of what is *not* relaxing: the pressure to see something new every day, crowded scenic areas, and driving too many miles a day.

In addition, an extended definition may need to address popular misconceptions about the term being defined. In an essay defining *potatoes,* for instance, you might correct the mistaken idea that potatoes are high in calories, explaining that it is the butter or sour cream that is put on potatoes that greatly increases the number of calories consumed.

EXERCISE 15.4

For two of the following broad topics, select a narrowed term and develop a standard definition of it. Then, for each term, consider how you could address misconceptions and use
negation in an extended definition of the term.

1. A type of dance
2. A play, call, or player position in a sport
3. A piece of clothing (hat, jacket, or jeans)
4. A term related to a course you are taking
5. A type of business

Visualizing an Extended Definition Essay: A Graphic Organizer

The graphic organizer in Figure 15.1 shows the basic organization of an extended
definition essay. The introduction announces the term, provides background

FIGURE 15.1
GRAPHIC ORGANIZER FOR AN EXTENDED DEFINITION ESSAY

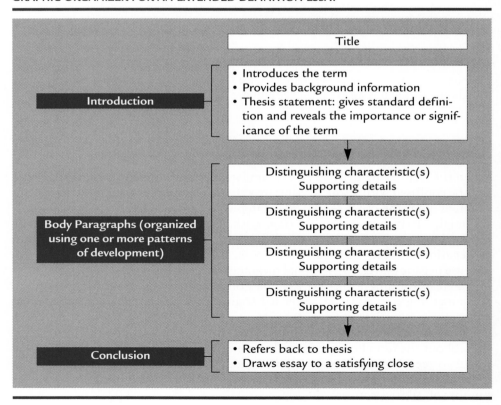

information, and usually includes the thesis statement (which briefly defines the term and indicates its significance to readers). The body paragraphs, which are organized using one or more patterns of development, present the term's distinguishing characteristics along with supporting details. The conclusion refers back to the thesis and brings the essay to a satisfying close, perhaps by citing a memorable quotation, making a final observation, or indicating a new direction of thought.

For more on graphic organizers, see Chapter 2, p. 40.

As you read the following essay, "The Case for Frivolity," look for the elements illustrated in the basic graphic organizer for an extended definition. Then study the graphic organizer for the essay in Figure 15.2.

The Case for Frivolity
Shannon Brownlee

Shannon Brownlee has written articles for Sports Illustrated *and has worked as a science reporter for* Discover *magazine. This essay was first published in* US News & World Report *in February 1997. In it Brownlee uses a variety of strategies to explore the meaning of play. As you read the selection, highlight the thesis, the standard definition, and the distinguishing characteristics of play.*

PREREADING QUESTION

Is play important in animal and human development? Why or why not?

TEACHING TIP: POSTREADING DISCUSSION

Ask students to discuss

• how their preconceived notion of play differed from Brownlee's definition.

• the techniques Brownlee uses to interest readers and establish the importance of play (humorous examples of play, quotations from experts).

• the writer's method of citing experts (introduces them within the text but without using a conventional system of documentation; although not appropriate in academic writing, this method is commonly used in articles written for popular magazines).

1 If the nature of life on Earth were judged by the space textbooks devote to the subject of play, the planet would seem joyless indeed. It's not that biologists have failed to notice animals playing. They have watched the frolicsome tussles of bighorn sheep over which will be king of the mountain, have seen dolphins push each other through the water, have observed ravens sliding down snowy slopes with all the abandon of human 6-year-olds. But until relatively recently, scientists could not make sense of what appeared to be a behavior with no purpose. Courtship has an obvious point. Fighting usually provides the winner with wider access to food or to sex. But play seemed entirely frivolous—and, by extension, so did anybody who studied it.

2 No longer. In the past decade, the study of play has gained a badge of respect as biologists have found increasing evidence that to a variety of species it is nearly as important as food and sleep. "We are finally beginning to understand that play is serious business," says Marc Bekoff, an ethologist at the University of Colorado–Boulder. In several papers and new books to be published this year, Bekoff and other scientists explore why play evolved and what young animals gain from it. They have found, for example, that all young mammals

play, as do some birds and even the odd reptile. Highly intelligent social species, such as wolves and some primates, continue playing as adults as a way of cementing social bonds.

3   **Something Freud forgot.** These new findings have important implications for the most playful species of all — our own. Without play, particularly imaginative games, children fail to gain a sense of mastery and are less adept at social interactions than their more playful counterparts. "Freud said human beings need love, sex, and work, but he forgot play," says California psychiatrist Stuart Brown. "I think we get in trouble socially, physically, and culturally if we neglect it." Play is so vital, say Brown and others, in part because it lays the groundwork for creative thinking in adulthood.

4   Early in animal evolution, play probably did not have so lofty a purpose. Rather, some researchers believe, it served as practice for adulthood. "If you are a prey species, you practice running away," says University of Idaho evolutionary biologist John Byers. "If you are a predator, you practice pouncing and chomping."

5   Byers has observed young pronghorn antelopes, native to the American West, executing leaps and twirls that would put Mikhail Baryshnikov* to shame. "After nursing, a young fawn will stand there looking dazed," says Byers. "Then it will start to jerk around, as if it has a fly in its brain." The fawn typically executes a series of wild vertical leaps, then takes off, running away from the herd as fast as 40 miles an hour, then back again. Finally, says Byers, it "comes to rest next to its mother, sides heaving and little black tongue hanging out." Such "locomotor play," Byers believes, helps forge connections between neurons in a young animal's brain, especially in the cerebellum, the region that controls and coordinates movement.

6   **Can't we all just get along?** Over the eons, play has acquired other, more subtle roles as well, especially in highly social, intelligent species. In the adults of some species, playing helps patch up disagreements. And for young animals, social play — tickling, wrestling, and chasing — also provides lessons in getting along with others: Young, captive rhesus monkeys, which spend about half their waking hours in play, learn to restrain aggressive impulses, safeguarding alliances they will need in adulthood.

7   "Social play helps animals learn to interpret signals and actions of others and then respond appropriately," says Robert Fagen of the University of Alaska–Juneau. A leading play biologist, Fagen draws his conclusions from a 10-year study of grizzly bears that congregate

---

Mikhail Baryshnikov (b. 1948): famous ballet dancer, born in Riga, Latvia.

during salmon season at Pack Creek on Admiralty Island. In early July, the salmon swim upstream to spawn in the creek's shallow waters. Like families out camping, the bears spend the summer gorging on fish and having fun. Fagen and his wife and son have observed adult female bears tossing a salmon in the air, then snatching it out of the water again, and cubs prancing across the meadow with a flower in their teeth. Teenage bears chase each other and wrestle, displaying the open-mouthed "play face" that indicates they are just fooling around.

These exuberant outbursts serve a serious purpose, allowing young bears to learn how to gauge the intentions of other bears and to find out which bear is easygoing and which is not. "To correctly judge what is a threat and what isn't is a big deal for a bear," says Fagen.   8

Making such judgments, it turns out, is easier for the animals than for the researchers watching them. The University of Colorado's Bekoff and others have just begun to decode the signals their subjects use to keep mock battles from turning ugly. "Play involves negotiation," says Bekoff. "When my dog, Jethro, wants to play, he needs to be able to say, 'Look, I'm going to bite you, but don't take it seriously.'" A dog makes its desires known with the familiar "play bow," putting its head down between its front paws and waving its hind end in the air. Other species have different signals: The short-tailed vole exudes a special scent; chimpanzees smile and laugh; young calves approach playmates at a galumph or a gambol.   9

A number of species employ these signals with surprising sophistication. For example, some animals may indicate they want to play simply by stringing together an absurd series of unrelated acts: a nip to the ears followed by a leap in the air followed by a sloppy attempt at sexual mounting. Young dogs, wolves, and coyotes are most likely to perform a play bow when an action that was meant in fun is apt to be misinterpreted, says Bekoff. Of the three species, coyotes are usually the most aggressive and least cooperative, and consequently must bow far more often to avoid giving the wrong impression.   10

Just kidding! In another example, primatologist Frans de Waal of Yerkes Regional Primate Research Center at Atlanta's Emory University found that Socko, an adolescent chimpanzee, was a master at using play signals to mollify his younger playmates' worried mothers. Mother chimps will break up a game that threatens to hurt their offspring. But Socko stressed his benign intentions by laughing loudly and displaying his play face when his playmate's mother was in view.   11

Play may be instructive, but for animals — as for people — it's of course fun. Early evidence suggests that play taps into the brain   12 chemicals involved in pleasure. When rats play, says Stephen Siviy, a psychobiologist at Gettysburg College in Pennsylvania, their brains release dopamine, a chemical that in people induces elation and excitement. In one experiment, Siviy taught rats that they would be allowed to play with another rat after being placed in a plexiglass chamber. After eight days of training, he says, "a rat will go back and forth, looking about as happy as a rat can look, in anticipation of a play partner." But when Siviy administered a drug that blocks dopamine, the rats no longer got excited. Researchers suspect that play also increases brain levels of pleasure-inducing endorphins and norepinephrine, which heightens attention.

13   Though research into the meaning of play is still nascent, many scientists have come to believe it is critical not only to a young animal's development but to a human child's as well. Children gain physical skills through exuberant motion, just like any young animal. They also gain emotional and mental mastery through play, particularly through imaginative games, according to Jerome and Dorothy Singer, child psychologists at Yale University and authors of *The House of Make-Believe* (Harvard University Press). When a child plays pretend, says Jerome Singer, "he is taking a complicated world and cutting it down to size. [When] you are the doctor and the teddy bear is the patient, you have reduced a frightening situation to one you can control." Kids who initiate imaginative play, the Singers have found, show leadership skills in school. They cooperate more with other children than kids who don't make believe, and they are less likely to antagonize and intimidate others.

14   The capacity for play may, in fact, be the hallmark of *Homo sapiens*'s unparalleled flexibility. More than any other species, human beings can adapt to change—in their diets, in their mates, in political systems, in social conventions, even in climate. What makes that possible, argues Brian Sutton-Smith, a psychologist who pioneered studies of human play 30 years ago, is that evolution gave people an appetite for fun throughout their lives. "Whether we are talking about children or adults, a sense of play makes people optimistic, and it rewards variability," he says. Tennis, anyone?   ■

EXERCISE 15.5

Draw a graphic organizer for "Cracking *Cascarones*" on page 461.

FIGURE 15.2
GRAPHIC ORGANIZER FOR "THE CASE FOR FRIVOLITY"

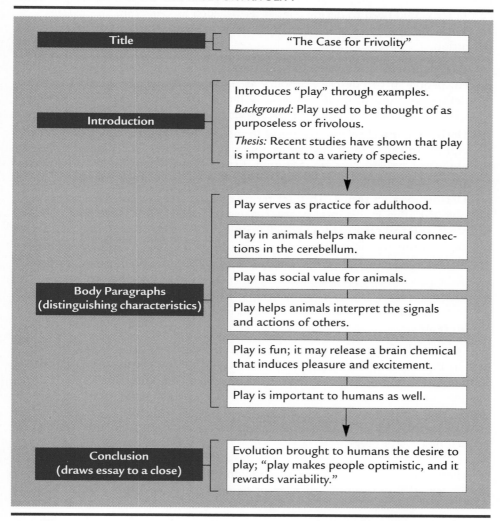

Title — "The Case for Frivolity"

Introduction —
Introduces "play" through examples.
Background: Play used to be thought of as purposeless or frivolous.
Thesis: Recent studies have shown that play is important to a variety of species.

Body Paragraphs (distinguishing characteristics) —
Play serves as practice for adulthood.

Play in animals helps make neural connections in the cerebellum.

Play has social value for animals.

Play helps animals interpret the signals and actions of others.

Play is fun; it may release a brain chemical that induces pleasure and excitement.

Play is important to humans as well.

Conclusion (draws essay to a close) —
Evolution brought to humans the desire to play; "play makes people optimistic, and it rewards variability."

INTEGRATING DEFINITIONS INTO AN ESSAY

On many occasions, you will need to include either standard or extended definitions in your writing. College exams may ask you to write a standard definition in response to a short-answer question or an extended definition in response to an essay question. Definitions are also useful for defining unfamiliar terms in any type of essay. For example, an essay explaining the process of installing a home computer would need to define related terms, such as *sound card* and *modem.*

Whatever the type of essay, the following kinds of terms usually require definition.

- **Define judgmental terms.** Judgmental terms mean different things to different people. If you describe a policy as "fiscally unsound," you would need to define your use of *fiscally unsound.* What you think is fiscally unsound and what another person thinks is fiscally unsound may be very different.

- **Define technical terms.** Technical terms are used in a particular field or discipline. In the field of law, for example, such terms as *writ, deposition, hearing,* and *plea* have very specific meanings. Especially when writing for an audience that is unfamiliar with your topic, be sure to define technical terms.

- **Define abstract terms.** Abstract terms refer to ideas or concepts rather than physical objects. Examples are *happiness, heroism,* and *conformity.* Because abstract terms refer to ideas, which people cannot see or touch, they often need explanation and definition.

- **Define controversial terms.** Because they evoke strong emotions, controversial terms — such as *politically correct, affirmative action,* and *chemical warfare* — are often subject to several interpretations. When writing about controversial subjects, be sure to define exactly how you interpret and use each related term in an essay.

In general, if you are not sure whether a term needs a definition, it is usually best to include a brief definition in order to avoid any confusion or misunderstanding. Definitions can be added to an essay in several different ways. At times, you may want to offer a standard definition in a separate sentence.

> An intermezzo is a piece of music that connects sections of a larger work, such as the acts of a play or opera.

At other times, a brief definition or synonym can be incorporated into a sentence. In this case, you use commas, dashes, or parentheses to set off the definition.

> Implicit memory, the nonconscious retention of information about prior experiences, is important in eyewitness accounts of crimes.

> Empathy — a shared feeling of joy for people who are happy or distress for people who are in pain — explains the success of many popular films.

> The Celsius (Centigrade) scale, used throughout Canada, is still not widely used in the United States.

In "High-Tech Piracy" (p. 496), Andrew Kimbrell uses definition within an essay that mixes several other methods of development.

A GUIDED WRITING ASSIGNMENT

ADDITIONAL RESOURCES

The writing process software that accompanies this text includes an Electronic Guided Writing Assignment for an extended definition essay.

The following guide will lead you through the process of writing an extended definition essay. Although you will focus on definition, you will need to integrate one or more other patterns of development to develop your essay. Depending on your learning style, you may choose different strategies as you work through the guide. This Guided Writing Assignment will provide you with alternatives.

The Assignment

Write an extended definition essay on one of the following topics or one that you choose on your own. You will need to narrow the general topic to a more specific term for your definition essay. Your audience is made up of your classmates.

1. A type of music (rock, jazz, classical)
2. Charisma
3. A form of entertainment
4. A social problem
5. Leisure time
6. Rudeness or politeness

As you develop your extended definition essay, consider using one or more other patterns of development. For example, you might include several examples to illustrate charisma, or you might explain rap music by comparing it to and contrasting it with rock music. For more on patterns of development, see p. 466.

For more on using examples or comparison and contrast, see Chapters 11 and 13.

Generating Ideas

The following guidelines will help you narrow your general topic and identify distinguishing characteristics.

Narrowing the General Topic to a Specific Term

Your first step is to narrow the broad topic you have selected to a more specific term. For example, the term *celebrity* is probably too broad a topic

For more on narrowing a topic, see Chapter 4, p. 71.

for a brief essay, but the topic can be narrowed to a particular type of celebrity, such as a *sports celebrity, Hollywood celebrity, local celebrity,* or *political celebrity.* You might then focus your definition on sports celebrities, using Michael Jordan and Monica Seles as examples to illustrate the characteristics of sports celebrities.

Use the following suggestions for finding a suitable narrowed term for your definition essay.

For more on prewriting strategies, see Chapter 4.

Learning Style Options

For more on classification and division, see Chapter 14.

TEACHING TIP:
LEARNING STYLES

1. For pragmatic and rational learners
2. For concrete learners
3. For social and verbal learners

1. Use a branching diagram or clustering to classify the general topic into specific categories. Choose the category that you are especially interested in or familiar with.

2. Think of someone who might serve as an example of the general topic, and consider focusing your definition essay on that person.

3. Discuss your general topic with a classmate to come up with specific terms related to it.

ESSAY IN PROGRESS 1

For the assignment option you chose on p. 475 or on your own, narrow your general term into several specific categories of terms. Then choose one narrowed term for your extended definition essay.

Considering Your Purpose, Audience, and Point of View

For more on purpose, audience, and point of view, see Chapter 4, p. 73.

Carefully consider your purpose and audience before you develop details for your essay. The purpose of a definition essay can be expressive, informative, or persuasive. You might, for example, write an essay defining search engines for researching on the Internet that expresses your frustration or success with using them to locate information. Or you might write an informative essay on search engines in which you relate their origins and uses and discuss the most commonly used ones. Finally, you might write a persuasive essay in which you argue that one search engine is superior to all others or that they all have many faults or quirks. To determine a purpose, ask yourself this question: "Do I want to inform, persuade, or express myself, or do I have more than one purpose?"

When your audience is unfamiliar with the term, you will need to explain the term in greater detail than when your audience is familiar with the term. For a novice audience, then, you will need to present detailed background information and define all specialized terms that you use.

Your audience for this Guided Writing Assignment is your classmates. As you develop your essay, keep the following questions in mind.

1. What, if anything, can I assume my audience already knows?
2. What does my audience need to know to understand or accept my definition?

In addition, consider which point of view will be most effective for your essay. Most definition essays are written in the third person, while the first person is used occasionally, as in "Cracking *Cascarones*."

Identifying Distinguishing Characteristics and Supporting Details

The following suggestions will help you identify distinguishing characteristics and supporting details for the specific term you intend to define in your essay.

1. Define the term for a classmate; tape-record what you say. Then, discuss the term with him or her, making notes as you talk.
2. Brainstorm a list of (a) words that describe your term, (b) people and actions that might serve as examples of the term, and (c) everything a person would need to know to understand the term.
3. Observe a person who is associated with the term or who performs some aspect of it. Take notes on your observations, including the qualities and characteristics of what you see.
4. Look up the term's *etymology*, or origin, in the *Oxford English Dictionary, A Dictionary of American English*, or *A Dictionary of Americanisms*, all of which are available in the reference section of your library. Take notes; the word's etymology may give you some characteristics and details as well as ideas on how to organize your essay.
5. Think of incidents or situations that reveal the meaning of the term.
6. Think of similar and different terms with which your reader is likely to be more familiar.
7. Do a search on the Internet for the term. Visit three or four Web sites and take notes on or print out what you discover at each site.

ESSAY IN PROGRESS 2

For the narrowed term you selected in Essay in Progress 1, use the preceding suggestions to generate a list of distinguishing characteristics and supporting details.

> **Learning Style Options**

TEACHING TIP: LEARNING STYLES

1. For all learners, especially social learners
2. For verbal, pragmatic, and rational learners

For more on observation, see Chapter 19, p. 664.

3. For emotional and spatial learners
4. For abstract and independent learners
5. For concrete learners
6. For abstract learners
7. For all learners, including creative learners

For more on Internet research, see Chapter 19, p. 635.

Developing Your Thesis

*For more on thesis state-
ments, see Chapter 5,
p. 97.*

Once you have gathered the distinguishing characteristics and supporting details for your term, you are ready to develop your thesis. It is a good idea to include a brief standard definition within your thesis, in addition to suggesting why your extended definition of the term is useful, interesting, or important to readers.

Notice how the following weak thesis statement can be revised to the reveal writer's main point.

WEAK: Wireless cable is a means of transmitting television signals through the air by microwave.

REVISED: The future of wireless cable, a method of transmitting television signals through the air using microwaves, is uncertain.

Also avoid statements that begin *Friendship is when . . .* or *Laziness is when. . . .* Instead, name the class to which the term belongs. (See page 485.)

WEAK: Discrimination is when a person is treated unfairly because of the group or class to which that person belongs.

REVISED: More prevalent today than many people realize, discrimination is an unfair attitude toward or action taken against a person because of the group or class to which that person belongs.

Notice that both of the preceding revised theses include a standard definition as well as an assertion about the term, which the essay will support with details and other evidence.

ESSAY IN PROGRESS 3

Write a working thesis statement that briefly defines your term and tells readers why your extended definition of it is useful or important to them.

Evaluating Your Ideas and Thesis

Take a few minutes to evaluate your notes, ideas, and thesis. Highlight characteristics and details that best support your thesis—those that will help your readers to distinguish your term from other similar terms. If you are writing on a computer, highlight key information in bold type or move

TEACHING TIP:
COLLABORATIVE
WRITING

(10 minutes) Peer
review: after students
have drafted tentative
thesis statements, have
them review each other's
thesis statements in
groups of two or three
classmates. Students
should make sure that
each thesis statement
indicates the writer's
main point about the
term.

COMPUTER HINT

Ask each student to
email his or her tentative
thesis statements to two
other students, if net-
worked computers are
not available. Suggest
that peer reviewers refer
to the character-
istics of extended
definitions be-
fore preparing their
responses.

it to a separate file. Also check your prewriting to see if you have enough details — examples, facts, descriptions, expert testimony, and so forth. If you find that your characteristics or details are skimpy, choose a different method from the list on page 477 to generate additional material. Think about how you can use one or more other patterns of development (such as narration or classification) to support your thesis. If you find you still need more details, research the term in the library or on the Internet.

TRYING OUT YOUR IDEAS ON OTHERS

Working in a group of two or three students, discuss your ideas and thesis for this chapter's assignment. Each writer should state his or her term, thesis, distinguishing characteristics, and supporting details. Then, as a group, evaluate each writer's work and offer suggestions for improvement.

ESSAY IN PROGRESS 4

Using the preceding suggestions and comments from your classmates, evaluate your thesis, distinguishing characteristics and details. Refer to the list of characteristics on pages 464–67 to help you with your evaluation.

Organizing and Drafting

Once you have evaluated your distinguishing characteristics, supporting details, and thesis and considered the advice of your classmates, you are ready to organize your ideas and draft your essay.

For more on drafting an essay, see Chapter 6.

Choosing Other Patterns of Development

To a considerable extent, the organization of an extended definition essay depends on the patterns of development you decide to use. Try to choose the patterns before you begin drafting your essay.

Suppose you want to define the term *lurking* as it is used in the context of the Internet, where it usually means reading newsgroup or listserv messages without directly participating in the ongoing discussion among others in the group. Once you give a brief standard definition of *lurking*, you could develop and expand it by using one or more other patterns of development as noted in the following list.

CONNECTIONS

(25 minutes total) To give students practice in using multiple patterns of development, try this exercise, using the term *cramming* (last-minute studying).

• (10 minutes) Have students work independently. Assign each student one pattern of development. Students should use their pattern to develop a definition of *cramming*.

• (15 minutes) Have one volunteer for each pattern of development read his or her definition to the class. Discuss the major strengths and weaknesses of each draft read aloud.

Pattern of Development	*Defining the Term* Lurking
Narration (Chapter 9)	Relate a story about someone who learned something unusual or important by lurking.
Description (Chapter 10)	Describe the experience of lurking.
Illustration (Chapter 11)	Give examples of typical situations involving the act of lurking.
Process analysis (Chapter 12)	Explain how to lurk in an Internet chatroom.
Comparison and contrast (Chapter 13)	Compare or contrast lurking to other forms of observation.
Classification and division (Chapter 14)	Classify the reasons people lurk — for information, entertainment, and so on.
Cause and effect (Chapter 16)	Explain the benefits or outcomes of lurking.
Argument (Chapters 17 and 18)	Argue that lurking is an ethical *or* unethical practice.

You could use one or more of the patterns in the list to create an interesting extended definition of "lurking," choosing the pattern or patterns that suit your audience and purpose as well as the term. For instance, narrating a story about lurking might capture the interest of an audience unfamiliar with the Internet, whereas classifying different types of people who lurk might be of interest to an audience familiar with online environments.

For more on organizing an essay, see Chapter 6.

With your pattern(s) firmly in mind, think about how to organize your characteristics and details. An essay classifying different types of people who lurk would probably follow a least-to-most or most-to-least arrangement. An essay narrating a story about lurking might be most effectively related in chronological order. An essay incorporating several patterns of development might use a number of arrangements. At this stage, it is a good idea to make an outline or draw a graphic organizer. To experiment with different organizational plans, create a computer file for each possibility and try each one out.

ESSAY IN PROGRESS 5

For the thesis you wrote in Essay in Progress 3, decide which pattern(s) of development you will use to develop your characteristics and details. Draw a graphic organizer or write an outline to help you see how each pattern will work.

Drafting an Extended Definition Essay

Use the following guidelines to draft your essay.

1. Include enough details. Be sure you include sufficient information to enable your reader to understand each characteristic.

2. Consider including the history or etymology of the term. As noted earlier, the etymology, or origin, of a term may be of interest to readers. You might include a brief history of your term in the introduction or in some other part of your essay. Consider, for example, how the following brief history of the term *peeping Tom* both entertains and clarifies meaning.

> In an age when we can speak of *peeping Tom cameras* or *electronic peeping Toms* we have indeed come far from the time of the legendary peeping Tom. Godgifu . . . , Lady Godiva to us, pledged her legendary ride as a means of persuading her husband, Leofric, Earl of Mercia, to lower taxes. In the original version of the story she was observed by all the townspeople as she disrobed, but in a much later version of the story a tailor or butcher named Tom was the only person to observe her as she rode by, everyone else having shuttered their windows as they had been asked. *Peeping Tom,* first recorded around 1796, has become a term for a voyeur, not at all a pleasant fate for this legendary fellow.
>
> *American Heritage Dictionary*

3. Use transitions. As you move from characteristic to characteristic, be sure to use a transitional word or phrase to signal each change and guide your readers along. The transitions *another, also,* and *in addition* are especially useful in extended definitions.

For more on transitions, see Chapter 6, p. 138.

4. Write an effective introduction and a satisfying conclusion. As noted earlier, your introduction should introduce the term, provide any needed background information, and state your thesis (which includes a standard definition as well as your main point). Also, when introducing your term, it may be helpful to use negation, explaining what the term *is* and what it *is not.* Recall that negation is useful when a term is likely to be confused with other terms in the same class. Alternatively, you might use your introduction to justify the importance of your topic, as Brownlee does in "The Case for Frivolity."

Your conclusion should reinforce your thesis and draw the essay to a satisfying close, as Martinez's conclusion does in "Cracking *Cascarones.*"

For more on writing effective paragraphs, including introductions and conclusions, see Chapter 6.

TEACHING TIP

Students who have followed the steps in the Guided Writing Assignment should be ready to compose a first draft independently. However, check to see if any students need to rethink their thesis or characteristics before drafting. Encourage them to seek the assistance of a peer reviewer or writing center tutor.

ESSAY IN PROGRESS 6

Draft your extended definition essay, using the pattern(s) of development you selected in Essay in Progress 5 and the preceding guidelines for drafting.

Analyzing and Revising

If possible, set your draft aside for a day or two before rereading and revising it. As you review your draft, concentrate on your ideas and organization, not on grammar or mechanics. Use one or more of the following suggestions to analyze your draft.

Learning Style Options ▶

TEACHING TIP:
LEARNING STYLES

1. For all students; if possible, allow 30–50 minutes (depending on the length of students' essays) for students to work in pairs or small groups
2. For all learners
3. For all learners; especially spatial learners (graphic organizer)

1. Delete or make unreadable the title and all mentions of the term, then ask a classmate to read your essay. Alternately, you could read your essay aloud, substituting "Term X" each time the term occurs. Then ask your classmate to identify the term you are defining. If your reader or listener cannot come up with the term or a synonym for it, most likely your distinguishing characteristics are not specific enough or you need to add additional details.

2. Test your definition by trying to think of exceptions to it as well as other terms that might be defined in the same way.

- *Exceptions.* Try to identify exceptions to your distinguishing characteristics. Suppose, for example, you define *sports stars* as people who exemplify sportsmanlike behavior. Since most people can name current sports stars who indulge in unsportsmanlike behavior, this distinguishing characteristic needs to be modified. You might say "people who *are expected to* exemplify" or "who *should* exemplify." Alternately, you could delete this characteristic and substitute a different one.

- *Other terms that fit all of your characteristics.* For example, in defining the term *bulletproof vest,* you explain that it is a piece of clothing worn by law-enforcement officers, among others, to protect them from bullets and other life-threatening blows. You also provide details about its effectiveness, when it is worn, and so forth. According to this definition, however, another kind of protective clothing—a helmet—would also fit your description. You would need to add information about *where* a bulletproof vest is worn.

3. Draw a graphic organizer or make an outline (or update the one you made earlier) to see if your essay follows the organization you intend.

For more on the benefits of peer review, see Chapter 7, p. 166.

Use Flowchart 15.1 to guide your analysis. You might also ask a classmate to review your draft using the questions in the flowchart. For each "No" answer, ask your reviewer to explain his or her answer. In addition, ask your reviewer to describe his or her impressions of your main point and distinguishing characteristics. Your reviewer's comments will help you identify the parts of your essay in need of revision.

FLOWCHART 15.1
REVISING AN EXTENDED DEFINITION ESSAY

Questions		Revision Strategies

1. Does your thesis include a brief definition of the term?

No ⇨

- Use the guidelines on pp. 464–65 to identify the class and distinguishing characteristics of your term.
- Write a standard definition and incorporate it into your thesis.

Yes ⇩

2. Is your extended definition specific and focused?

No ⇨

- Delete any details that do not help to define your term.
- Narrow your term further (for example, the broad term *leisure time activities* could be narrowed to *television addiction*).

Yes ⇩

3. Does your thesis statement indicate why extended definition is useful, interesting or important?

No ⇨

- Ask yourself: "Why is this definition worth reading about?" Add your answer to your thesis.

Yes ⇩

4. Do you use one or more other patterns of development to explain the distinguishing characteristics of your term?

No ⇨

- Review the list of patterns on p. 466.
- Think of details, examples, and comparisons you might use.
- Consider adding a narrative.
- Explain a process related to the term.
- Classify the term, or explain its causes or effects.

Yes ⇩

(Continued on next page)

FLOWCHART 15.1 *(continued)*

Questions		Revision Strategies

5. Do you include enough distinguishing characteristics and details to explain the term adequately?

 No

- Do additional research or prewriting to discover more characteristics and details.

 Yes

6. Do you use negation appropriately and address misconceptions about the term?

 No

- If appropriate for your purpose, explain what your term is not.
- Add facts or expert opinion to correct readers' mistaken notions about the term.

 Yes

7. Is each body paragraph well developed and focused on a particular characteristic? Are the introduction and conclusion effective?

 No

- Be sure each body paragraph has a topic sentence and supporting details (see Chapter 6).
- Consider combining closely related paragraphs.
- Split paragraphs that cover more than one characteristic.
- Revise your introduction and conclusion so that they meet the guidelines in Chapter 6 (pp. 141–146).

Yes

TEACHING TIP

Encourage students to seek a writing center tutor for further review of the revision.

ESSAY IN PROGRESS 7

Revise your draft using Flowchart 15.1 and any comments you received from peer reviewers.

Editing and Proofreading

The final step is to check your revised essay for errors in grammar, spelling, punctuation, and mechanics. In addition, be sure to check your error log for the types of errors you commonly make.

As you edit and proofread your extended definition essay, watch out for the following types of errors commonly found in this type of writing.

For more on keeping an error log, see Chapter 8, p. 201.

1. Make sure you avoid the awkward expressions *is when* or *is where* in defining your term. Name the class to which the term belongs.

▶ Early bird specials ~~is when~~ restaurants ~~offer reduced-price dinners~~ *are reduced-price dinners served in* late in the afternoon and early in the evening.

▶ A rollover is ~~where~~ *a transaction in which* an employee transfers money from one retirement account to another.

2. Make sure subjects and verbs agree in number. When two subjects are joined by *and*, the verb should be plural.

▶ Taken together, the military and Medicare ~~costs~~ *cost* U.S. taxpayers an enormous amount of money.

When two nouns are joined by *or*, the verb should agree with the noun closest to it.

▶ For most birds, the markings or wing span ~~are~~ *is* easily observed with a pair of good binoculars.

When the subject and verb are separated by a prepositional phrase, the verb should agree with the subject, not with the noun in the phrase.

▶ The features of a hot-air balloon ~~is~~ *are* best learned by studying the attached diagram.

ESSAY IN PROGRESS 8

Edit and proofread your essay, paying particular attention to avoiding *is when* or *is where* expressions and correcting errors in subject-verb agreement.

TEACHING TIP: COLLABORATIVE WRITING

After students revise their drafts, have them work in pairs to look for the expressions *is when* and *is where* and problems with subject-verb agreement.

CONNECTIONS

(10 minutes) To ensure that students understand subject-verb agreement, analyze subject-verb agreement in one or two paragraphs from any essay in this book as a whole class. Address questions and help students focus on simple subject and main verbs in order to determine agreement.

STUDENTS WRITE

Jennifer Tumiel was a first-year nursing student at Niagara County Community College when she wrote the following essay in response to an assignment for her writing class. As you read the essay, highlight the characteristics of hip hop music that Tumiel identifies.

PREREADING
QUESTIONS
• How did hip hop
  music get its name?
• What experiences have
  you had with hip hop
  music?

Hip Hop Music

Jennifer Tumiel

1   In the 1980s, a new sound emerged from the ghettos of New York City. This new music was known as hip hop. Since that time, hip hop has moved up through the ranks of the pop charts. Today it's in a class of its own.

2   Hip hop music is one of the most, if not <u>the</u> most, popular types of music among high school and college students. It mixes an upbeat rhythm with lyrics that make its fans want to move. This combination is how hip hop got its name. <u>Hip</u> means "cool" and <u>hop</u> means movement or dance. Without a doubt, it is the sound that is usually pumping through the large speakers at any dance club. The music of artists such as Adena Howard has a beat that would make anybody want to get up and dance.

3   A hip hop song usually has the same smooth and continuous beat throughout, but at the climax, the beat gets faster or slower and the lyrics get more intense. This is the point where dancers usually get excited and begin to move faster or slower. These songs are often sung by African American musical artists who are known for their ability to sing and dance to this kind of beat.

4   On the serious side, however, this type of music can have a positive impact on society. Such songs as "Gangsta's Paradise," by the artist Coolio, have lyrics that discourage young teenagers from choosing gangs as their way of life. Another well-known artist, MC Hammer, performs a song entitled "Pray" to help people escape

the ghetto through gospel music and positive thinking. The members of Salt-N-Pepa, a female hip hop group, have produced a song that combines their background music with lyrics written by a high school drama team. The tune, played on radio stations across the country, promotes safe sex in an attempt to stop the spread of AIDS.

Despite all the positive messages in this music, however, hip hop has also been heavily criticized. The negative feedback is usually aimed at a specific category of hip hop known as rap music. There are two categories of rap music: one is soft rap and the other is hard-core or gangsta rap (derived from the slang word for gang- ster), and they are very different.   5

The first category, soft rap, is the type of hip hop music most often heard on the radio. Soft rap lyrics are clean or at least tolerable. Most of the messages these artists convey are positive. The music of Queen Latifah, for example, influences young, single parents to make responsible decisions.   6

Although there are some sexual and violent messages in soft rap, it receives less criticism than hard-core rap for two reasons: (1) much of soft rap is set to dance music, so the emphasis is less on the lyrics and more on the beat, and (2) the critics pay more attention to gangsta rap.   7

Gangsta rap is performed by such hard-core groups as 2 Live Crew, Geto Boys, and Notorious B.I.G. These groups get their message across with very explicit lyrics. They are political rappers, but instead of using positive or appropriate messages, they choose to rap about "fighting the system" through violent opposition. For example, the Geto Boys claim that "a knife is real- ity" to them. Geffen Records, their recording company, refused to release one of the band's albums because it was considered to be too sick-minded. The Geto Boys use sexual and violent themes to sell their music. Another controversial aspect of gangsta rap is the pathetic degradation of women. In these songs, women are raped   8 because they are "asking for it," and they are frequently killed. Because of such violent, degrading lyrics, much of the negative criticism of gangsta rap is justified.

9   The dangers of this category are obvious. Gangsta rap influences young adult listeners who look to the artists as role models. The government can put all the warning labels it wants to on these albums, but once a few teenagers get hold of them, their popularity spreads like wildfire among the teens' peers. Many young people can listen to a gangsta rap number and realize that it is just a song, but others may take the song's message seriously and be influenced by it.

10   Hip hop is not just a passing fad; it has been around for about twenty years and shows no sign of disappearing. However, some hip hop groups have been censored, and this may be the only solution to the problem. Although many people oppose censorship, in the case of gangsta rap it provides a needed safety net. It is a way to stop these artists' violent messages from reaching children and adolescents.

Analyzing the Essay

1. Identify Tumiel's thesis. Where does she suggest why her extended definition of hip hop is interesting or important?

2. What patterns of development does Tumiel use to define hip hop? What other patterns do you think she might have used?

3. What characteristics of hip hop does Tumiel discuss? How does she differentiate soft rap from gangsta rap?

4. Evaluate the effectiveness of the essay's title, introduction, and conclusion.

Reacting to the Essay: Discussion and Journal Writing

1. Discuss whether popular music groups and recording companies have a moral responsibility to promote or uphold the values held by the majority of the population.

2. Discuss whether particular songs that promote violence or racism should be banned or restricted.

3. Write a journal entry defining a type of music you enjoy and explaining its positive or negative impact on society.

READING DEFINITIONS

The following section provides advice for reading definitions as well as model essays. The first essay illustrates the characteristics of an extended definition covered in this chapter. The second essay uses definition along with other methods of development. Both essays provide opportunities to examine, analyze, and react to the writers' ideas.

WORKING WITH TEXT: READING DEFINITIONS

As you encounter new fields of study throughout college, you will be called upon to learn many new academic languages (sets of terms that are specific to an academic discipline). Articles in academic journals, as well as most textbooks, especially in their first few chapters, contain many new terms.

For more on reading strategies, see Chapter 2.

If you need to learn a large number of specialized terms presented in a textbook, try the index-card system. Using 3-by-5-inch cards, write a word on the front of each card and its meaning on the back. Also include its pronunciation and any details or examples that will help you remember it. Be sure to write the definition in your own words; don't copy the author's definition. To study, test yourself by reading the front of the cards and trying to recall the definition on the back of the cards. Then reverse the process. Shuffle the pack of cards to avoid learning terms in a particular order.

What to Look for, Highlight, and Annotate

1. As you read a definition, whether in a textbook or an essay, be sure to identify the class and highlight or underline the distinguishing characteristics. Mark any that are unclear or for which you need further information.

2. Make sure that you understand how the term differs from similar terms, especially those presented in the same article or chapter. If a textbook or article does not explain sufficiently how two or more terms differ, check a standard dictionary. If you are still unclear, check a subject dictionary. Each academic field of

study also has its own dictionaries that list terms specific to the discipline. Examples include *Music Index, Taber's Cyclopedic Medical Dictionary,* and *A Dictionary of Economics.*

3. Many students find it useful to highlight definitions using a special color of pen or highlighter, or to designate them using annotations. You might use *V* for vocabulary, *Def.* for definition, and so forth.

How to Find Ideas to Write About

For more on discovering ideas for a response paper, see Chapter 3.

As you read an extended definition or an article containing brief definitions, mark additional characteristics or examples that you think of as you read. Then, when you respond to the article, you might write about how the definition could be expanded to include these additional characteristics or examples. You might also try the following strategies.

- Think of other terms in the same class that you might write about.
- Try to relate the definitions to your own experience. Where or when have you observed the characteristics described? Your personal experiences might be used in an essay in which you agree with or challenge the writer's definitions.
- If the writer has not already done so, you might use negation to expand the meaning of the term or you might explore the word's etymology.

TEACHING TIP:
COLLABORATIVE
WRITING

(15 minutes total) Bring a recent issue of a tabloid newspaper to class.

- (10 minutes) Have students work in small groups with one section of the tabloid to identify biased definitions or euphemisms and other uses of slanted language. One student in each group should take notes.
- (5 minutes) Reconvene the class. Have the recorder from each group present one or two examples of slanted uses of language.

THINKING CRITICALLY ABOUT DEFINITION

Some definitions are more straightforward and factual than others. Standard definitions of terms such as *calendar, automobile,* or *taxes* are not apt to be disputed by most readers. At other times, however, definitions can reflect bias, hide unpleasantness, and evoke conflicting reactions and emotions in readers. Use the following questions to think critically about the definitions you read.

Are the Writer's Definitions Objective?

Especially in persuasive essays, definitions are sometimes expressed in subjective, emotional language that is intended to influence the reader. For example, a writer who defines a *liberal* as "someone who wants to allow criminals to run free on the streets while sacrificing the rights of innocent victims" reveals a negative bias toward liberals and obviously intends to make the reader dislike them. However, a writer who defines a *conservative* as "a person who is willing to watch children starve as long as his or her taxes won't be raised" is trying to turn the reader against conservatives. When reading definitions, think critically. Ask yourself the following questions.

1. Do I agree with the writer's definition of this term?
2. Do I think these characteristics apply to all members of this group?
3. Is the writer's language meant to inflame my emotions?

Are the Writer's Definitions Evasive?

A **euphemism** is a word or phrase that is used in place of an unpleasant or objectionable word. For example, the phrase *suffers occasional irregularity* is a euphemism for *constipation,* while *passed away* is often used instead of *died* and *men's room* or *women's room* substitutes for *toilet*. At times, a writer may offer a euphemism as a synonym. For example, in describing a terrorist incident in which innocent civilians were killed, a writer may characterize the killings as "civilian damage." When a writer offers a synonym, be alert to the use of euphemisms. Like persuasive definitions, they are intended to shape your thinking.

EXTENDED DEFINITION ESSAY

As you read the following selection by David Blankenhorn, consider how the writer uses the elements of extended definitions covered in this chapter.

Life without Father
David Blankenhorn

David Blankenhorn is the author of Fatherless America: Confronting Our Most Urgent Social Problem *(1995), from which this selection is taken. Blankenhorn is the editor of several other nonfiction works and has published articles in the* New Republic, Washington Post, *and* Journal of Marriage and Family. *As you read the selection, notice how Blankenhorn defines the concept of* fatherhood *and highlight the terms he introduces and defines.*

PREREADING QUESTIONS

• Why do you think cultures should work to encourage responsible fatherhood?
• What might be the key consequences of a "culture of fatherlessness"?

The United States is becoming an increasingly fatherless society.   1
A generation ago, a child could reasonably expect to grow up with his or her father. Today, a child can reasonably expect not to. Fatherlessness is approaching a rough parity with fatherhood as a defining feature of childhood.

2   This astonishing fact is reflected in many statistics, but here are the two most important: Tonight, about 40 percent of U.S. children will go to sleep in homes in which their fathers do not live [see the accompanying chart]. More than half of our children are likely to spend a significant portion of childhood living apart from their fathers. Never before in this country have so many children been voluntarily abandoned by their fathers. Never before have so many children grown up without knowing what it means to have a father.

3   Fatherlessness is the most harmful demographic trend of this generation. It is the leading cause of the decline in the well-being of children. It is also the engine driving our most urgent social problems, from crime to adolescent pregnancy to domestic violence. Yet, despite its scale and social consequences, fatherlessness is frequently ignored or denied. Especially within our elite discourse, it remains a problem with no name.

4   Surely a crisis of this scale merits a name — and a response. At a minimum, it requires a serious debate: Why is fatherhood declining? What can be done about it? Can our society find ways to invigorate effective fatherhood as a norm of male behavior? Yet, to date, our public discussion has been remarkably weak and defeatist. There is a prevailing belief that not much can or even should be done to reverse the trend.

5   As a society, we are changing our minds about men's role in family life. Our inherited understanding of fatherhood is under siege. Men are increasingly viewed as superfluous to family life: either expendable or part of the problem. Masculinity itself often is treated with suspicion, and even hostility, in our cultural discourse. Consequently, our society is unable to sustain fatherhood as a distinctive domain of male activity.

DISAPPEARING DADS

U.S. KIDS LIVING WITH . . .	1960	1980	1990
Father and mother	80.6%	62.3%	57.7%
Mother only	7.7	18	21.6
Father only	1	1.7	3.1
Father and stepmother	0.8	1.1	0.9
Mother and stepfather	5.9	8.4	10.4
Neither parent	3.9	5.8	4.3

Sources: *America's Children* by Donald Hernandez, U.S. Census Bureau. Because the statistics are from separate sources, they don't total 100%.

The core question is simple: Does every child need a father? 6
Increasingly, our society's answer is "no." Few idea shifts in this century are as consequential as this one. At stake is nothing less than
what it means to be a man, who our children will be and what kind
of society we will become.

My . . . criticism [is] not simply of fatherlessness but of a *culture* 7
of fatherlessness. For, in addition to fathers, we are losing something
larger: our idea of fatherhood. Unlike earlier periods of father
absence in our history, such as wartime, we now face more than a
physical loss affecting some homes. The 1940s child could say: My
father had to leave for a while to do something important. The '90s
child must say: My father left me permanently because he wanted to.

This is a cultural criticism because fatherhood, much more than 8
motherhood, is a cultural invention. Its meaning is shaped less by
biology than by a cultural script, a societal code that guides — and at
times pressures — a man into certain ways of acting and understanding himself.

Like motherhood, fatherhood is made up of both a biological 9
and a social dimension. Yet, across the world, mothers are far more
successful than fathers at fusing these dimensions into a coherent
identity. Is the nursing mother playing a biological or a social role?
Feeding or bonding? We can hardly separate the two, so seamlessly
are they woven together. But fatherhood is a different matter. A
father makes his sole biological contribution at the moment of conception, nine months before the infant enters the world. Because
social paternity is linked only indirectly to biological paternity, a connection cannot be assumed. The phrase "to father a child" usually
refers only to the act of insemination, not the responsibility for raising the child. What fathers contribute after conception is largely a
matter of cultural devising.

Moreover, despite their other virtues, men are not ideally suited 10
to responsible fatherhood. Men are inclined to sexual promiscuity
and paternal waywardness. Anthropologically, fatherhood constitutes what might be termed a necessary problem. It is necessary
because child well-being and societal success hinge largely on a high
level of paternal investment: men's willingness to devote energy and
resources to the care of their offspring. It is a problem because men
frequently are unwilling or unable to make that vital investment.

Because fatherhood is universally problematic, cultures must 11
mobilize to enforce the father role, guiding men with legal and
extralegal pressures that require them to maintain a close alliance
with their children's mother and invest in their children. Because
men don't volunteer for fatherhood as much as they are conscripted

into it by the surrounding culture, only an authoritative cultural commitment to fatherhood can fuse biological and social paternity into a coherent male identity. For exactly this reason, anthropologist Margaret Mead and others have observed that the supreme test of any civilization is whether it can socialize men by teaching them to nurture their offspring.

12   The stakes could hardly be higher. Our society's conspicuous failure to sustain norms of fatherhood reveals a failure of collective memory and a collapse of moral imagination. It undermines families, neglects children, causes or aggravates our worst social problems and makes individual adult happiness, both female and male, harder to achieve.

13   Ultimately, this failure reflects nothing less than a culture gone awry, unable to establish the boundaries and erect the signposts that can harmonize individual happiness with collective well-being. In short, it reflects a culture that fails to "enculture" individual men and women, mothers and fathers.

14   In personal terms, the main result of this failure is the spread of a me-first egotism hostile to all except the most puerile understandings of personal happiness. In social terms, the results are a decline in children's well-being and a rise in male violence, especially against women. The most significant result is our society's steady fragmentation into atomized individuals, isolated from one another and estranged from the aspirations and realities of common membership in a family, a community, a nation, bound by mutual commitment and shared memory.

15   Many voices today, including many expert voices, urge us to accept the decline of fatherhood with equanimity. Be realistic, they tell us. Divorce and out-of-wedlock childbearing are here to stay. Growing numbers of children will not have fathers. Nothing can be done to reverse the trend itself. The only solution is to remedy some of its consequences: More help for poor children. More sympathy for single mothers. Better divorce. More child-support payments. More prisons. More programs aimed at substituting for fathers.

16   Yet what Abraham Lincoln called the better angels of our nature always have guided us in the opposite direction. Passivity in the face of crisis is inconsistent with the American tradition. Managing decline never has been the hallmark of American expertise. In the inevitable and valuable tension between conditions and aspirations — between the social "is" and the moral "ought" — our birthright as Americans always has been our confidence that we can change for the better.

Does every child need a father? Our current answer hovers between "not necessarily" and "no." But we need not make permanent the lowering of our standards. We can change our minds. We can change our minds without passing new laws, spending more tax dollars or empaneling more expert commissions. Once we change our philosophy, we might well decide to pass laws, create programs or commission research. But the first and most important thing to change is not policies, but ideas.

17

Our essential goal must be the rediscovery of the fatherhood idea: For every child, a legally and morally responsible man.

18

If my goal could be distilled into one sentence, it would be this: A good society celebrates the ideal of the man who puts his family first. Because our society is lurching in the opposite direction, I see the Good Family Man as the principal casualty of today's weakening focus on fatherhood. Yet I cannot imagine a good society without him. ■

19

Examining the Reading

1. Why is fatherhood a "cultural invention," according to Blankenhorn?
2. According to the author, why are men not ideally suited to fatherhood?
3. What are the effects of fatherlessness?
4. What solutions to the problem of fatherless families does Blankenhorn offer?
5. Explain the meaning of each of the following words as it is used in the reading: *demographic* (paragraph 3), *conscripted* (11), *collective* (12, 13), *puerile* (14), and *equanimity* (15). Refer to your dictionary as needed.

Analyzing the Reading

1. Identify Blankenhorn's thesis statement.
2. What characteristics of fatherlessness does Blankenhorn include in his essay?
3. What patterns of development, in addition to definition, does Blankenhorn employ?
4. Evaluate the essay's introduction and conclusion.

Reacting to the Reading: Discussion and Journal Writing

1. What problems have you observed or experienced in fatherless families?
2. Discuss what actions can be taken to encourage responsible fatherhood.

3. Write a journal entry agreeing or disagreeing with Blankenhorn's statement: "Men are not ideally suited to responsible fatherhood" (paragraph 10).

DEFINITION COMBINED WITH OTHER PATTERNS

In the following essay, Andrew Kimbrell uses definitions as part of an argument.

 High-Tech Piracy
Andrew Kimbrell

PREREADING
QUESTION

Kimbrell's essay is about
what type of theft
(piracy)?

Andrew Kimbrell, an attorney and environmental activist, is founder of the International Center for Technology Assessment, an organization that studies the effects of technology on people, societies, economies, and politics. The following essay, adapted from his book The Case against the Global Economy *(1996), was published in* Utne Reader *in March/April 1996. In it Kimbrell describes the effects of biotechnology companies on the Third World. As you read the selection, notice how the writer builds definitions into his essay and highlight where he introduces new terms and definitions.*

1   [The] biotechnology boom in the industrialized world has massively increased corporate demand for an unconventional form of natural resources: not the minerals and fossil fuels of the industrial age, but rather living materials found primarily in the Southern Hemisphere. According to the World Resources Institute, more than half the world's plant and animal species live in the rainforests of the Third World* and nowhere else on earth. Ironically, as industrial expansion and pollution reduce the number of species, we are witnessing a "gene rush" as governments and multinational corporations aggressively scout the continents in search of genetic material.

2   "Bioprospecting" is a potential gold mine for both science and business, since genetic material found in the developing world may yield cures for diseases as well as cash. But what also looms on the horizon, and in fact is already occurring in many parts of the developing world, is "biopiracy," where corporations use the folk wisdom of indigenous peoples to locate and understand the use of medicinal plants and then exploit them commercially. U.S. and European scientists hoping to find cures worth billions of dollars have even taken samples of the blood, hair, and saliva of indigenous peoples. Indige-

---

Third World: underdeveloped or developing nations of the world.

nous peoples' knowledge, their resources, and even their bodies are being pirated, and they receive little or nothing in return.

THE PATENTING OF LIFE

Biotechnology and new patent law have allowed companies to capitalize on even the smallest of life forms. The Merck pharmaceutical company has patented microbial samples from nine countries. These include soil bacteria from a heather forest on Mount Kilimanjaro, a Mexican soil fungus useful in the manufacturing of male hormones, a fungus found in Namibian soil of potential use in treating manic depression, a soil bacteria in India that serves as an antifungal agent, and a Venezuelan soil bacteria patented for use in the production of antibiotics.

Merck is not alone in its corporate ownership of microorganisms. Pfizer and Bristol-Myers Squibb both have more bacteria and fungi holdings than Merck. Each year the drug industry spends billions searching the world's soils for valuable microorganisms.

The biopirates are also on the lookout for profitable, patentable plants. In one remarkable example, several Northern corporations, including W.R. Grace, have been granted more than 30 U.S. patents on the neem tree of India — and not only on the tree, but also on the indigenous knowledge about its many uses.

In another act of biopiracy, two drugs derived from the rosy periwinkle — vincristine and vinblastine — earn $100 million annually for Eli Lilly. The plant is indigenous to the rainforest of Madagascar, and the country has received nothing in return.

Pharmaceuticals are among the most lucrative areas for the international biopirates: Some 25 percent of U.S. prescriptions are filled with drugs whose active ingredients are derived from plants. Sales of these plant-based drugs amounted to some $4.5 billion in 1980 and $15.5 billion in 1990. In Europe, Australia, Canada, and the United States, the market value for both prescription and over-the-counter drugs based on plants is estimated to be in excess of $70 billion. Transnational companies know where to find the plants: Well over 50 percent of the world's estimated 250,000 plant species are in tropical rainforests. Only a small fraction of them have been investigated as a source of potential new drugs, and the rapid destruction of tropical forests has hastened corporations' screening, appropriation, and patenting processes.

The mounting intensity of the biopirates' assault on Third World genetic resources can also be seen in the enormous pressures placed on governments by agricultural and drug companies to pass the General Agreement on Tariffs and Trade (GATT) and other international trade structures, including the Convention on Biological Diversity, that cement the right of private actors to patent the resources and indigenous knowledge of the Third World. The result is an ever-increasing use of patenting and licensing agreements by transnational corporations to secure a monopoly over valuable genetic materials that can be developed into profitable drugs and energy sources.

THE NEW VAMPIRES

9   The biopirates are interested not only in microbes and plants, but also in the very bodies of indigenous peoples. For decades the United States and other industrialized countries have been buying the blood of the poor in the Third World and selling it on the open market. Now scientists and researchers are racing to locate, identify, and find commercial uses for human genes from various indigenous populations. The search for valuable human genetic material is fueled by the fact that human genes and cells are now patentable. Relying on the *Chakrabarty* decision, over the past decade the U.S. Patent Office has allowed patents on human genes, cells, and cell lines. The lure of patent profits is leading a growing army of international gene hunters hoping to find potentially profitable genetic material to collect and analyze blood and other materials from Third World peoples. For example, in May 1989 researchers took blood samples from 24 members of the Hagahai tribe of Papua New Guinea. The patent application describes the Hagahai as "a 260-member hunter-horticulturist group" that inhabits New Guinea's Madang Province. A cell line developed from the Hagahai might be valuable in diagnosing adult leukemia and chronic degenerative neurologic disease. Another patent claim filed on behalf of the U.S. government involves a human cell line derived from a 40-year-old woman and a 58-year-old man, both of the Solomon Islands; this cell line, too, may be useful in diagnosing disease. In neither case were the people asked for their consent, nor were their traditions and values considered.

10   Despite the growing number of patents, biopirating the genetic material of indigenous peoples is only in early stages, and scientists are making plans for expansion. Starting in 1991, an informal consortium of scientists in North America and Europe launched a campaign to take blood, tissue, and hair samples from hundreds of "endangered" and unique human communities throughout the world. The initiative is called the Human Genome Diversity Project (HGDP), and the samples it gathers will be used to create "transformed" cell lines of each community.

11   Many indigenous communities have condemned the HGDP. In February 1995, leaders representing indigenous nations throughout

Canada, the United States, Panama, Ecuador, Peru, Bolivia, and Argentina issued a statement opposing the HGDP and noting that it "opens the door for potential widespread abuse of human genetic materials for scientific, commercial, or military purposes. . . . The proposed research holds little or no benefit to the donor populations, but could be highly profitable to various researchers, patent holders, and corporations, which may find commercial application [from collected material] such as the production of pharmaceuticals."

"This project is another form of the extremely racist process by which indigenous lands and resources have been pirated for the benefit of almost everyone except indigenous peoples," says Jeanette Armstrong, an Okanagan from British Columbia.

12

BIODEMOCRACY

To reverse the rapidly increasing biopiracy that is sweeping the globe, it is imperative that the current regime of bioimperialism be replaced by international structures based on biodemocracy: recognition of the intrinsic value of all life forms and preservation of their genetic integrity. Biodemocracy recognizes the contributions and rights of source communities and requires that nation-states renounce the patenting of life and the international trade structures — such as GATT — that support patenting.

13

Biodemocracy also requires that there be an immediate moratorium on the genetic engineering of the permanent genetic code of plant and animal species. Until a sophisticated means of predicting the effects of gene alterations on the environment is established and adequate regulations are enacted, the genetic engineering must stop. Collection of cells and blood from indigenous peoples through projects that violate all legal principles of informed consent and represent a threat to their dignity and survival must end.

14

As people in the North struggle to halt biopiracy, the South must also stand behind the principles and policies of biodemocracy and refuse to allow its resources and its people to become commodities of the North. ■

15

Examining the Reading

1. Explain the term *biopiracy*. What is being pirated and why?
2. How are indigenous peoples being exploited, according to Kimbrell?

3. Why does Kimbrell consider the harvesting of drugs from the rosy periwinkle plant in Madagascar an example of piracy?
4. Why is biopiracy intensifying and what is being done to control it?
5. Explain the meanings of each of the following words as it is used in the reading: *indigenous* (paragraph 2), *transnational* (7), *intrinsic* (13), *moratorium* (14), and *commodities* (15). Refer to your dictionary as needed.

Analyzing the Reading

1. What main point does the writer make about biopiracy?
2. What terms related to biopiracy are defined in the essay?
3. What methods of development does the writer use to develop his definition?
4. Evaluate the essay's title, introduction, and conclusion.

Reacting to the Reading: Discussion and Journal Writing

1. Discuss what actions, if any, should be taken to control biopiracy.
2. Is the writer's definition of biopiracy objective or subjective? Explain your answer.
3. Write a journal entry describing how you think a spokesperson for a pharmaceutical company might defend what Kimbrell calls biopiracy.

APPLYING YOUR SKILLS: ADDITIONAL ESSAY ASSIGNMENTS

Write an extended definition essay on one of the following topics, using what you learned about definition in this chapter. Depending on the topic you choose, you may need to conduct library or Internet research.

To Express Your Ideas

Define your audience and write an essay defining and expressing your views on one of the following terms.

1. Parenting
2. Assertiveness
3. Sexual harassment

To Inform Your Reader

4. Write an essay defining a term from a sport, hobby, or form of entertainment. Your audience is a classmate who is unfamiliar with the sport, hobby, or pastime.

5. Write an essay defining the characteristics of the "perfect job" you hope to hold after graduation. Your audience is your instructor.

6. As Brownlee does, write an essay defining an important concept in a field of study, perhaps from one of your other courses. Your audience is other students not enrolled in the course.

To Persuade Your Reader

As Blankenhorn does, write an essay defining a term and demonstrating that it is either increasing or decreasing in your community. Your audience is readers of your local newspaper. Choose a term from the following list.

7. Racism or ethnic stereotyping
8. Sexual discrimination
9. Age discrimination

Cases Using Definition

10. You are a fifth-grade teacher and are working on a lesson plan entitled "What Is American Democracy?" How will you limit the term in order to define it for your audience? What characteristics and details will you include?

11. Write a press release for a new menu item as part of your job as public relations manager for a restaurant chain. First, decide what the new menu item is, and then define the item and describe its characteristics using sensory details.

TEACHING TIP

Suggest that students use at lease one prewriting strategy—drawing a graphic organizer, freewriting, brainstorming, questioning, writing assertions—to get started. Remind students to consult the learning style options (p. 477) and the revision flowchart (p. 483).

TEACHING TIP: LEARNING STYLES

Give students the option of working in small groups on these assignments. Encourage pragmatic and rational learners to help with organization; creative, emotional, and social learners to consider the audience; and verbal learners to suggest appropriate word choices.

Chapter **16**

Assume you are a journalist for your local newspaper reporting on a natural disaster that has occurred in a nearby town. Your immediate task is to write a story to accompany the photograph shown on the opposite page.

Writing Quick Start

Write a paragraph telling your readers why the disaster occurred and what happened as a result of it. For the purpose of this activity, you should make up a plausible account of the event you see in the photograph.

Cause and Effect: Using Reasons and Results to Explain

TEACHING TIP: LEARNING STYLES

Have students work independently to generate a list of possible causes and effects of the fire, using techniques suited to their learning styles. For instance, creative learners might envision the devastation or other effects of the fire before considering its causes, while pragmatic learners might use listing or branching to come up with causes first, then effects.

TEACHING TIP:
CHAPTER OVERVIEW

• To demonstrate the
relevance of causal
analysis in everyday
life, ask students to list
the *What if . . .?* questions they routinely ask
themselves ("What if I
fail history, forget to
set my alarm, or
change my major?").
• This chapter empha-
sizes that unsupported
assertions and faulty
reasoning can weaken
a causal analysis, (e.g.,
post hoc, ergo propter hoc,
or "after this, there-
fore because of this,"
confuses chronology
with causation).
• Emphasize that *organi-
zation* is essential in a
cause or effect essay,
which must follow a
clear sequence
(whether chronologi-
cal or some other
method). Encourage
pragmatic and ratio-
nal learners to share
their graphic organiz-
ers with peers.
• Point out that *supporting evidence,* especially
evidence generated by
research, is particu-
larly important in
causal analysis
because unsupported
assertions mislead
readers and misrepre-
sent the issue.

WRITING A CAUSE AND EFFECT ESSAY

Your paragraph is an example of cause and effect. By describing why the disaster happened, you explained *causes*. By explaining what happened as a result of the disaster, you explained *effects*. This chapter will show you how to write effective causal analyses as well as how to incorporate cause and effect into essays using other patterns of development.

WHAT ARE CAUSE AND EFFECT?

A **cause and effect** essay, also called a **causal analysis**, analyzes (1) why an event or phenomenon happens (its *causes*), (2) what happens because of the event or phenomenon (its *effects*), or (3) both causes and effects. The essay generally shows how one event or phenomenon brings about another: Losing your car keys (the *cause*) is why you are late for class (the *effect*).

Almost everything you do has a cause and produces an effect. If you skip lunch because you need to study for a test, you feel hungry. If you drop a glass because it is slippery, it breaks. Young children attempting to discover and make sense of the complex world around them continually ask "Why?" Adults also think about and govern their lives in terms of causes and effects: "What would happen if I dropped a class or turned a paper in late?" or "Why did that happen?" (for example, "Why wouldn't my car start this morning?" or "Why do I get dizzy on roller coasters?" or "Why does the wind pick up before a storm?"). Many academic disciplines also focus on why questions: Psychologists are concerned with *why* people behave as they do; biologists study *why* the human body functions and reacts as it does; historians consider *why* historical events occurred.

Many everyday occasions require you to use causal analyses. If your child is hurt in an accident, the doctor may ask you to describe the accident and its effects on your child. In a note to a manufacturer, you may need to explain that a prod-

---

SCENES FROM COLLEGE AND THE WORKPLACE

• For an essay exam in your *twentieth-century history* course, you are required to discuss the causes of U.S. involvement in the 1991 Persian Gulf War.

• For a *health and nutrition* course, you decide to write a paper on the relationship between diet and heart disease.

• For your job as an *elementary school teacher,* you need to explain to a student's parents why the student is failing mathematics.

uct is defective and, therefore, that you deserve a refund. Finally, you will find many occasions to use causal analysis in the writing you do in college and on the job (see the accompanying box for examples).

In the following essay, "Personality Is What Makes Woods Special," Charles Krauthammer analyzes the causes of professional golfer Tiger Woods's popularity.

Personality Is What Makes Woods Special
Charles Krauthammer

Charles Krauthammer, a syndicated columnist who writes on national affairs, was awarded a Pulitzer Prize for commentary in 1987 for his columns on politics and society. His essays have appeared in the New Republic, Time, Nation, *and* The New York Times Book Review. *This essay was originally published in April 1997 in the* Washington Post, *shortly after Tiger Woods became the youngest person in history to win the Masters golf tournament. As you read the selection, highlight and label the causes of Woods's popularity that the writer mentions.*

PREREADING QUESTION

What do you think makes Tiger Woods special?

Why is everybody in America pulling for Tiger Woods?   1

Yes, he's good, very good. Record-breaking, field-lapping good.   2
But there are dozens of other great sportsmen in the country, and golf is generally not a sport that quickens America's pulse.

Yes, he's young, 21. But in individual sports, young phenoms are   3
not that unusual. We've had 17-year-old tennis champions (Becker, Chang, Seles, Graf). We have gymnastics champions barely out of infancy.

Of course, there is race. An African- and Asian-American Masters   4
champion is as rare as April snow in Augusta. But almost as rare is a black hockey player and nothing remotely like the Woods phenomenon greeted the emergence of Grant Fuhr, an extremely talented black goalie who in the '80s won five Stanley Cups with the Edmonton Oilers. And Hideo Nomo—splendid pitcher, rookie of the year, Dodger, and Japanese—became a local hero but hardly a national obsession.

Yes, excellence, youth and ethnicity—combined—account for   5
much of Tiger Woods mania. But it is not quite enough to explain the most remarkable wave of adulation to sweep this continent since Trudeaumania* swept an obscure ex-professor to the premiership of Canada in 1968.

Pierre Trudeau (b. 1919): Prime minister of Canada, 1968–1970 and 1980–1984.

6   What then? Woods is more than just good, young, black and Asian. He is gracious. In an age of the commercially hyped, trash-talking, in-your-face sports star, here is someone who combines great athleticism with decency, poise and manners and simple soft-spoken politeness.

7   He has not just the old-fashioned virtues of respect for his parents, his elders, his competitors. He has a deep respect for the difficulty of his own craft. He knows its history. He speaks with genuine gratitude of his debt to the black golfers that preceded him. What so impresses about Woods is that, for all of his greatness and for all of his awareness of his greatness, he is so situated, so anchored in the history and mystery of his game.

8   Woods' pride in his game does not extend to the braggart denigration of the competition and the naked promotion of self over sport that you find in so many young stars today.

9   This, after all, is the age of the athlete with attitude. Total self-regard and self-promotion are hip. Andre Agassi* and Deion Sanders* have mastered this very lucrative pose of chest-beating, almost parodic individualism. Dennis Rodman has taken it to its logical grinning conclusion with his groin-kicking, body-piercing, barely literate anarchism.

10   The bad boys, by the way, did not start, as is often assumed, with young black basketballers. It began with young, white tennis players like Jimmy Connors and, especially, John McEnroe, who turned bad manners and quick tempers into a shtick and a ticket to celebrity that took them far beyond tennis.

11   Rodman's pose has taken him far beyond basketball. In fact, just two weeks before Woods' miraculous Masters, we reached a kind of apogee of Rodmanism: his elevation to movie star—the highest rung in our hierarchy of celebrity—with the release of *Double Team,* an action flick in which he co-stars with Jean-Claude Van Damme.

12   Mercifully, the film tanked. Meanwhile, Woods' final-round Masters performance, despite being devoid of any competition, earned the highest ratings in golf history. One caller to a local radio station noted with amazement that during the tournament he had been frantically checking his car radio for updates. For a golf match!

13   Why did this happen? Americans are simply overcome with relief to find, rising out of this swamp of bad-boy athletes, a mensch* like Woods.

Andre Agassi: a top-ranked professional tennis player.

Deion Sanders: a well-known professional football player.

mensch: a Yiddish term meaning "a decent, responsible person."

A paragon in sports is easy to define: Someone whom you would 14
be pleased to have your child emulate. One of the main reasons baseball is dying is that, with the exception of Cal Ripken and but a hand-
ful of others, the best players are repulsive louts. Who can possibly
care about the fortunes of a sport populated by growling freebooters
with contempt not just for their followers but for their game?

Enter Tiger. It is not that we tuned in to see possibly the best 15
golfer ever, though seeing any craft executed so brilliantly is beautiful and satisfying. More than anything, we tuned in to see a good
man excel. America is mesmerized not just because he is champion.
Not just because he is a young, gifted, African- and Asian-American
champion. But because he is a paragon and a rarity: a gentleman
athlete.   ■

Characteristics of Cause and Effect Essays

As you can see from Krauthammer's essay on Tiger Woods, a causal analysis has a
clear purpose: to explain causes or effects or both. In addition, a cause and effect
essay includes a thesis, follows a logical organizational plan, develops each cause or
effect fully, and may recognize or dispel readers' assumptions about the topic.

Causal Analysis Focuses on Causes, Effects, or Both

In deciding whether to consider causes, effects, or both, it is important to distinguish the causes from the effects. Some are relatively easy to identify.

Cause	*Effect*
You get a flat tire. ⟶	You are late for work.
You forget to mail a loan payment. ⟶	You receive a past-due notification.
There is a power failure. ⟶	You lose changes made to a computer file.

In more complex situations, however, the causes and effects are less clear. For
example, the issue of what causes a weight problem is complex, and causes may
not always be clearly separable from effects. Some people have an obsession with
dieting (*effect*) because they have a poor body image (*cause*). Yet an obsession
with dieting (*cause*) can lead to a poor body image (*effect*).

To identify causes and effects, think of causes as *why something happened* and
effects as the *results of the thing that happened*.

POSSIBLE ANSWERS

1. It escaped from a zoo; it escaped from a truck; it is wild.
2. Inclement weather; computer failure; too few passengers on the flight
3. Someone is harassing you; problem with phone; problem with line; wrong number
4. Surplus of local tax revenues; bequest to city; pressure from citizens; desire to attract tourists
5. Friend really is busy; friend is upset and avoiding you; friend is depressed

POSSIBLE ANSWERS

1. You have to get a ride to the bus company to retrieve it; you have to cancel your credit cards; you cannot buy your mother's birthday present.
2. You have to stay in school an extra semester to meet requirements; you become a professional in a different field than the one you had envisioned; your grades improve.
3. You decide to move; you decide to live separately during the week; you decide to divorce.
4. You convince a child to stay in school; you prevent a child from becoming a gang member; you teach a child to read.
5. The relative recovers and gains a new appreciation for life; you become your relative's caregiver; your family becomes closer.

Cause   *Effect*

Event *X* happened because . . . ◀——EVENT *X*——▶ The result of event *X* was . . .

EXERCISE 16.1

Working either alone or with a classmate, list one or more possible causes for each of the following events or phenomena.

1. You observe a peacock strutting down a city street.
2. You are notified by the airline that the flight you had planned to take tonight has been canceled.
3. Your phone frequently rings once and then stops ringing.
4. Your town decides to fund a new public park.
5. Your best friend keeps saying "I'm too busy to get together with you."

EXERCISE 16.2

Working either alone or with a classmate, list one or more possible effects for each of the following events.

1. You leave your bookbag containing your wallet on the bus.
2. You decide to change your major.
3. Your spouse is offered a job in a city five hundred miles away from where you live now.
4. You volunteer as a Big Brother or Big Sister.
5. A close relative becomes very ill.

Multiple Causes and Effects.   Causal analysis can be complex when it deals with an event or phenomenon that has multiple causes, effects, or both.

1. Several causes may produce a single effect. For example, you probably chose the college you attend now (*a single effect*) for a number of reasons, including the availability of courses in your major, the cost of tuition, the reputation of the school, and its distance from your home (*multiple causes*).

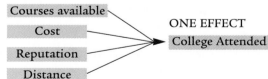

MULTIPLE CAUSES

Courses available
Cost
Reputation
Distance

ONE EFFECT
College Attended

2. One cause may have several effects. For instance, your decision to quit your part-time job (*one cause*) will result in more study time, less pressure, and less spending money (*multiple effects*).

3. Related events or phenomena may have both multiple causes and multiple effects. For instance, an increase in the number of police patrolling the street in urban areas along with the formation of citizen watch groups (*multiple causes*) will result in less street crime and the growth of small businesses (*multiple effects*).

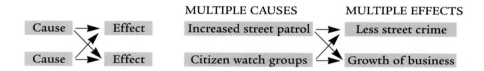

Chains of Events.   In some cases, a series of events forms a chain in which each event is both the effect of what happened before it and the cause of the next event. In other words, a simple event can produce a chain of consequences.

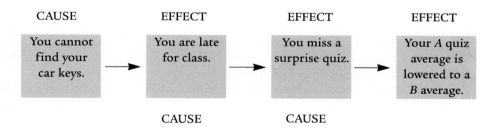

Once you clearly separate causes and effects, you can decide whether to focus on causes, effects, or both.

Causal Analysis Has a Clear Purpose

A cause and effect essay may be expressive, but more often it is informative, persuasive, or both. In an essay about the effects of the death of a close relative, for example, you would express your feelings about the person by showing how the loss affected you. An essay describing the sources (*causes*) of the pollution of a local river could be primarily informative, or it could be informative and persuasive if it also discussed the positive results (*effects*) of enforcing anti-pollution laws.

Some cause and effect essays have more than one purpose. For example, an essay may examine the causes of academic cheating (informative) and propose policies that could help alleviate the problem (persuasive). In "Personality Is What Makes Woods Special," Krauthammer aims to inform readers about Tiger Woods as well as persuade readers that Woods is "a gentleman athlete" (paragraph 15).

EXERCISE 16.3

In a small group or with a classmate as a partner, choose two topics from the following list. Then, for each topic, consider how you would write a causal analysis with (a) an informative purpose and (b) a persuasive purpose.

1. Changes in airline safety standards
2. Rapid changes in computer hardware
3. Sexual harassment in the workplace
4. The popularity of health clubs and fitness centers
5. The increasing amount of junk email on the Internet

Causal Analysis Includes a Clear Thesis Statement

Most cause and effect essays have a clear thesis statement that identifies the topic, makes an assertion about that topic, and suggests whether the essay focuses on causes, effects, or both. In "Personality Is What Makes Woods Special," Krauthammer makes it clear to readers that his focus is the causes of Tiger Woods's popularity. The writer also makes an assertion about his topic: Woods's popularity is due to his ability to combine "great athleticism with decency, poise and manners and simple soft-spoken politeness" (paragraph 6).

The following sample thesis statements show two other ways of approaching an essay about Tiger Woods, one emphasizing effects, the other emphasizing causes and effects, and both making assertions about the topic.

EFFECTS:	Tiger Woods has helped to create enthusiasm for golf, especially among African American and Asian American youngsters.
CAUSES AND EFFECTS:	Although the story of how Tiger Woods became a golf star is fascinating, the effects of his Masters victory will long outlive the tales of his childhood.

Causal Analysis Follows a Logical Organization

A cause and effect essay is organized logically and systematically. It may use chronological order to present causes or effects in the order in which they happened. An essay about the events that led to a decision to save a Civil War battle-field from development might be organized in this way. Or a most-to-least or least-to-most order may be used to sequence the causes or effects according to their importance. In "Personality Is What Makes Woods Special," Krauthammer uses the least-to-most important order, discussing the less important causes of Woods's popularity — athletic ability, age, and race — before moving on to the most important cause — Woods's graciousness.

Causal Analysis Explains Each Cause or Effect Fully

A causal analysis essay presents each cause or effect in a detailed and understandable way. Examples, facts, descriptions, comparisons, statistics, and anecdotes may be used to explain causes or effects. Krauthammer uses several of these elements to give readers a detailed description of Woods's graciousness. He uses such terms as "old-fashioned virtues," "deep respect," and "genuine gratitude" (paragraph 7). He also compares Woods to several less gracious athletes, such as Deion Sanders, Dennis Rodman, and John McEnroe (paragraphs 9–11), and includes a brief anecdote about a fan who frantically checked his car radio for news of Woods's score during the Masters tournament (paragraph 12).

For most cause and effect essays, you will need to research your topic to locate evidence that will support your thesis. In an essay about the effects on children of viewing violence on television, for instance, you might need to locate research or statistics that document changes in children's behavior after watching violent programs. In addition to statistical data, expert opinion is often used as evidence. For example, to support a thesis that reading aloud to preschool children helps them learn how to read, you might cite the opinions of reading specialists or psychologists who specialize in child development.

Causal Analysis May Recognize or Dispel Readers' Assumptions

Some cause and effect essays recognize or dispel popular ideas that readers may assume to be true. An essay on the effects of capital punishment might attempt to dispel the notion that it is a deterrent to crime. Similarly, in "Personality Is What Makes Woods Special," Krauthammer begins by recognizing three causes that many people think are responsible for Woods's popularity (athletic ability, age, and race) before moving on to his thesis about Woods's graciousness.

Dealing with the causes or effects that readers assume to be primary is an effective strategy, whether the purpose of the essay is informative or persuasive. In an informative essay, you create a sense of completeness or the impression that nothing has been overlooked. In a persuasive essay, you ensure readers that other viewpoints have been recognized.

Visualizing Cause and Effect Essays: Three Graphic Organizers

*For more on graphic orga-
nizers, see Chapter 2,
p. 40.*

The graphic organizers in Figures 16.1 through 16.3 show the basic organization of three types of causal analysis essays. Figure 16.1 shows the organization of an essay that examines *either* causes *or* effects. Figure 16.2 shows the organization of an essay that examines a chain of causes and effects, while Figure 16.3 shows two possible arrangements for an essay that focuses on multiple causes and effects. All three types of causal analyses include an introduction (which identifies the event, provides background information, and states a thesis) as well as a conclusion. Notice in Figures 16.2 and 16.3 that causes are presented before effects. Although this is the typical arrangement, writers sometimes reverse it, discussing effects first and then causes, to create a sense of drama or surprise.

When you incorporate causes, effects, or both into an essay that is not primarily a causal analysis, you can adapt one of these organizational plans to suit your purpose.

FIGURE 16.1
GRAPHIC ORGANIZER FOR AN ESSAY ON CAUSES *OR* EFFECTS

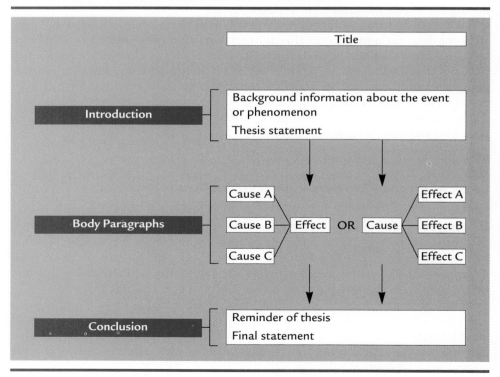

FIGURE 16.2
GRAPHIC ORGANIZER FOR AN ESSAY ON A CHAIN OF CAUSES AND EFFECTS

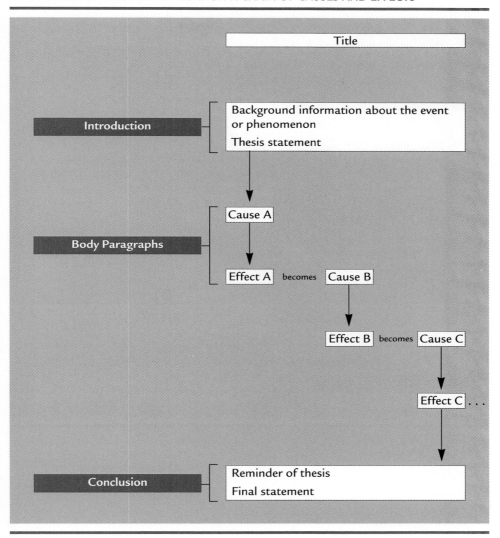

FIGURE 16.3
GRAPHIC ORGANIZER FOR AN ESSAY ON MULTIPLE CAUSES AND EFFECTS

The following essay, "Extinction and Us," is an example of a causal analysis. Read the essay and then study the graphic organizer for it in Figure 16.4.

Extinction and Us

Robert Wallace

Robert Wallace was a professor at the University of Florida, a contributing editor for Explorers Journal, *and a fellow of the Royal Geological Society of London. The following essay is taken from his* Biology: The World of Life

PREREADING
QUESTION

What is the primary
cause of present-day
extinction and how does
it differ from past causes
of extinction?

(1997), a college textbook used in introductory courses in biological science. As you read the selection, highlight the causes of extinction in one color and the effects of extinction in another color.

The very word extinction has a sad ring to it. It means that some-   1
thing, some fellow traveler on our small planet, is gone forever. Still, it has long been a natural part of things. There are two kinds of extinctions. One is the low level, background extinction that occurs constantly without dramatic effect. The other is the great mass extinctions that involve a large number and variety of species. These are important because such drastic losses have a major impact on the remaining life.

Scientists generally agree that there have been five great mass   2
extinctions, with the first occurring at the end of the Cambrian period (about 500 million years ago, or 500 mya). The next one was at the end of the Ordovician period (about 425 mya), followed by the one at the end of the Devonian period (about 345 mya). Then came the greatest mass extinction of all, at the close of the Permian period (some 225 mya). For some reason about 90 percent of marine life went extinct at that time. The most famous mass extinction occurred at the end of the Cretaceous period (65 mya) when the great dinosaurs died out along with many other species, including huge tracts of cycad forests. But it doesn't end there.

Now there is disconcerting evidence that we are apparently in the   3
midst of another, truly devastating mass extinction, and this time there is little question of the cause. As Pogo* once said, "We have met the enemy, and he is us." Indeed, the extinction rate is presently esti-mated by a number of experts to be between a thousand and several thousand species per year. If we continue on this course of environ-mental destruction, by the year 2000 the extinction rate could be about 100 species per day. Within the next several decades, we could lose one-quarter to one-third of all species now alive. This rate of loss is unprecedented on the planet. Furthermore, the problem is quali-tative, as well as quantitative. Not only are we losing *more* species, but we're also losing different *kinds* of species. The most recent mass extinction involved only certain groups of species, such as the cycads and the dinosaurs. The other groups of species were left more or less intact. At present, though, species are dying out across the board. That is, the current extinction affects all the major categories of species. Of particular note, this time the terrestrial plants are

------

Pogo: a cartoon character from a comic strip of the same name.

TEACHING TIP:
POSTREADING
DISCUSSION

Ask students to discuss

• the implications of Wallace's conclusion. (Is the process irre-versible? Why or why not?)
• the writer's purpose (primarily to inform, but also to persuade).
• the supporting evi-dence (historical events, facts about the loss of species and habitats).

involved. In the past, such plants provided resources that the surviving animals could use to launch their comeback. With the plants also devastated, any comeback (marked by a period of rapid expansion and speciation) by animals will be greatly slowed.

4   The present great extinction will also prove to deter a resurgence of species for another reason. This time we are killing the systems that are particularly rich in life, including tropical forests, coral reefs, saltwater marshes, river systems, and estuaries. In the past these systems have provided genetic reservoirs from which new species could spring and replenish the diversity of life on the planet. In effect, we are drying up the wellspring of future speciation.

5   In the past, extinctions have been due to two major processes, environmental forces (such as climatic change) and competition. For the first time, a single species (our own) has had the opportunity to cause mass extinctions at both levels. Much of the habitat destruction has been due to humans desiring the land where other species lived, forcing them into extinction as they failed in their competition with us. And now we find ourselves in the remarkable position of being able to alter environmental forces. As the Amazon basin is destroyed, the trees are no longer available to cycle water back to the atmosphere, causing many experts to predict sweeping changes in the weather.

6   We are continuing to interact in new ways with the environment. As we continue to release chlorofluorocarbons into the atmosphere, the ozone holes grow larger and the delicate veil of life on earth becomes increasingly bathed in destructive radiation. And we are learning that the oceans have become perilous places for many forms of life because we continue to use the great waters as dumps for dangerous or unknown chemicals.

7   There are those who say that our course, by now, is irreversible, that the damage is done and now we must sit back and prepare to reap what we have sown. Others, though, argue that there is still time to alter our course, to salvage much of what is left and to protect it from further damage. The danger is in accepting the first alternative if the second is really the case.   ■

POSSIBLE ANSWERS

Answers will vary. See the *Instructor's Resource Manual* for a possible graphic organizer.

EXERCISE 16.4

Draw a graphic organizer for "Personality Is What Makes Woods Special" on page 505.

FIGURE 16.4
GRAPHIC ORGANIZER FOR "EXTINCTION AND US"

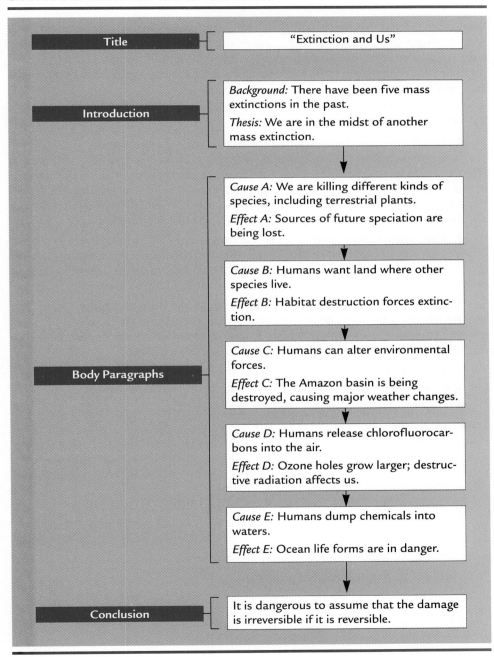

INTEGRATING CAUSE AND EFFECT INTO AN ESSAY

While some essays you write will focus solely on causal analysis, other essays will include cause and effect with other patterns, perhaps to explain *why* something happened or *what* happened as a result of something. In an essay comparing two popular newsmagazines with different journalistic styles, for example, you might explain the effects of each style on readers' attitudes.

Use the following tips to integrate causal analyses into essays that rely on other patterns of development.

1. **Use transitions to announce shifts to a causal explanation.** If your readers do not expect a causal explanation, launching into consideration of causes or effects without a transition may confuse them or cause them to misinterpret your message. In writing about your college president's decision to expand the Career Planning Center, for example, you might introduce your discussion of causes by writing "The three primary factors responsible for her decision are. . . ."

2. **Keep the causal explanation direct and simple.** Since your overall purpose is not to explore causal relationships, an in-depth analysis of causes and effects will distract your readers from your main point. Therefore, focus on the most important causes and effects.

3. **Emphasize why particular points or ideas are important.** For example, if you are writing a tip sheet on using a word-processing program for an audience of beginners, you need to explain why it is important to save material frequently by warning your readers of the effects of neglecting to save copy.

4. **Include only causal relationships you can support and justify.** If you do not have evidence to support a cause or effect, it is best to omit it.

To read an essay that integrates causal analysis with several other patterns of development, see "College President's Plan: Abolish High School" by George F. Will on page 542.

A GUIDED WRITING ASSIGNMENT

The following guide will lead you through the process of writing a cause and effect essay. Although you will focus primarily on causal analysis, you will probably need to integrate one or more other patterns of development in your essay. Depending on your learning style, you may work through this assignment in different ways. A creative learner may begin by brainstorming and recording causes and effects as they come to mind, whereas a pragmatic learner may begin by using questioning or writing assertions. A social learner might prefer to start by discussing the topic with friends or classmates. This Guided Writing Assignment will provide you with alternatives.

The Assignment

Write a cause and effect essay on one of the following topics or one that you choose on your own. Your essay may consider causes, effects, or both. Your audience consists of your classmates or members of the community in which you live.

1. The popularity (or lack of popularity) of a particular sport in the United States
2. The popularity (or lack of popularity) of a public figure
3. A miscommunication or misunderstanding between two people or two groups
4. Cheating on college exams
5. Rising college costs
6. A current trend or fad
7. A major change or decision in your life
8. A problem on campus or in the community

As you develop your causal analysis essay, consider how you can use one or more other patterns of development. For example, you might use narration to help explain the effects of a particular community problem. In an essay about the causes of a current fad, you might compare the fad to one that is obsolete. Or you might classify rising college costs in an essay covering the causes and effects of that phenomenon.

ADDITIONAL RESOURCES

The writing process software that accompanies this text includes an Electronic Guided Writing Assignment for a causal analysis essay.

For more on narration, see Chapter 9. For more on comparison and contrast, see Chapter 13. For more on classification, see Chapter 14.

Generating Ideas

When selecting an event or phenomenon to write about, be sure to choose one with which you are familiar or about which you can find information in the library or on the Internet.

Considering Your Purpose, Audience, and Point of View

For more on purpose, audience, and point of view, see Chapter 4, p. 73.

Once you choose a topic, your next step is to decide whether you want your essay to be informative, persuasive, or a mixture of both. Depending on your purpose, you may decide to explain why an event, problem, or phenomenon occurred (*causes*), or what happened as a result (*effects*), or both. Keep the length of your essay in mind as you think about these issues. It would be unrealistic, for example, to try to discuss both the causes and effects of child abuse in a five-page paper.

As you generate ideas, keep your audience in mind as well. For this Guided Writing Assignment, your audience consists of your classmates or members of your community. If they are unfamiliar with the event, problem, or phenomenon you are writing about, or if your topic is complex, consider limiting your essay to primary causes or effects (those that are obvious and easily understood). If your audience is generally familiar with your topic, then you can deal with secondary causes or effects.

The level of technical detail you include should also be determined by your audience. Suppose you are writing to explain the climatic conditions that cause hurricanes to an audience of your classmates. For this audience, far less technical detail would be needed than if your audience consisted of environmental science majors.

The point of view you choose should suit your audience and purpose. Although the third person is most often used in academic writing, the first person may be used to relate relevant personal experiences.

Discovering Causes and Effects

For more on prewriting strategies, see Chapter 4.

After considering your purpose, audience, and point of view, use one or more of the following suggestions to help you discover causes, effects, or both.

Learning Style Options

1. Write your topic in the middle of the page or at the top of your computer screen. Brainstorm all possible causes and effects, writing causes to the left and effects to the right.

2. Replay the event in your mind. Focus on one or both of these questions: "Why did the event happen?" and "What happened as a result of it?" Make notes on the answers.

3. Try asking questions and writing assertions about the problem or phenomenon. Did a chain of events cause the phenomenon? What effects are not so obvious?

4. Discuss your topic with a classmate or friend. Ask his or her opinion on the topic's causes, effects, or both.

5. Research your topic in the library or on the Internet. For example, you might begin by entering a keyword derived from the event, problem, or phenomenon into the search form of an Internet search engine. Then visit two or three promising Web sites turned up by your search. Make notes on possible causes and effects or print out copies of the relevant Web pages you discover.

6. Ask a friend or classmate to interview you about your topic. Assume you are an expert on the topic; try to explain causes, effects, or both as clearly as possible. Tape-record the interview and play it back to get ideas for your essay.

ESSAY IN PROGRESS 1

For the assignment option you chose on page 519 or on your own, use the preceding suggestions to generate a list of causes, effects, or both for your topic.

Identifying Primary Causes and Effects

Once you have a list of causes or effects (or both), your next task is to sort through them and decide which causes or effects are *primary,* or most important. For example, if your topic is the possible effects of television violence on young viewers, two primary effects might be an increase in aggressive behavior and a willingness to accept violence as normal. Less important or *secondary* effects might include learning inappropriate or offensive words and spending less time viewing family-oriented shows. In essays about controversial issues, primary causes or effects may differ depending on the writer.

Use the following questions to help you decide which causes and effects are most important.

TEACHING TIP:
LEARNING STYLES

1. For creative or abstract learners
2. For abstract learners
3. For rational and pragmatic learners
4. For social learners
5. For all learners, especially independent learners
6. For verbal and social learners

For more on library and Internet research, see Chapter 19.

TEACHING TIP:
LEARNING STYLES

Try sending independent learners to the computers to try assignment option 5, grouping social learners with verbal learners for option 4 or 6, grouping rational and pragmatic learners for option 3, and encouraging abstract learners to choose option 1 or 2.

Causes

What are the most obvious and immediate causes?
What cause(s), if eliminated, would drastically change the event, problem, or phenomenon?

Effects

What are the obvious effects of the event, problem, or phenomenon?
Which effects have the most serious consequences? For whom?

TEACHING TIP:
LEARNING STYLES
Encourage students to
work together in small
groups for a few min-
utes. Try to include an
abstract learner in each
group to keep the focus
on identifying primary
causes and effects.

ESSAY IN PROGRESS 2

Review the list you prepared in Essay in Progress 1. Separate primary causes and primary effects from secondary ones.

Checking for Hidden Causes and Effects and Errors in Reasoning

Once you identify primary and secondary causes and effects, examine them to be sure you have not overlooked any causes and effects and have avoided common reasoning errors.

Hidden Causes and Effects.   Be on the alert for the hidden causes or effects that may underlie a causal relationship. For example, if a child often reports to the nurse's office complaining of a stomachache, a parent may reason that the child has digestive problems. However, a closer study of the behavior may reveal that the child is worried about attending a physical education class and that the stomachaches are the result of stress and anxiety. The physical education class is the hidden cause. To avoid overlooking hidden causes or effects, be sure to examine a causal relationship closely. Do not assume the most obvious or simplest explanation is the only one.

Mistaking Chronology for Causation.   Avoid the *post hoc, ergo propter hoc* ("after this, therefore because of this") fallacy: the assumption that because event *B* followed event *A* in time, *A* caused *B* to occur. For example, suppose you decide against having a cup of coffee one morning, and later the same day you score higher than ever before on a political science exam. Although one event followed the other in time, the first event did not necessarily cause the second event to occur. That is, you cannot assume that reducing your coffee intake caused the high grade.

To avoid the *post hoc* fallacy, look for evidence that one event did indeed cause the other. Plausible evidence might include testimony from others who experienced the same sequence of events or documentation proving a causal relationship between the events. For instance, there are numerous examples of people who have contracted cancer after smoking cigarettes for a number of years as well as research documenting the link between cigarette smoking and cancer.

Mistaking Correlation for Causation.   Just because two events occur at about the same time does not mean they are causally related. For example, suppose sales of snow shovels in a city increased at the same time sales of gloves and mittens increased. The fact that the two events occurred simultaneously does not mean that snow shoveling causes people to buy more mittens and gloves. Most likely, a period of cold, snowy weather caused the increased sales of these items. Again, remember that evidence is needed to verify that the two events are related and that a causal relationship exists.

Unsupported Assumptions.   Assumptions are ideas or generalizations that you or your readers accept as truths without questioning their validity. For example, you may assume that someone you just met is honest or that your new math instructor treats all students fairly. Although assumptions can be true, in many cases people make sweeping generalizations that are untrue and unfair. For instance, it is unfair to say that senior citizens are nonproductive members of society because the evidence suggests that many seniors continue to work or contribute to their communities in other ways. Many assumptions are based on *stereotypes*—unfair generalizations about the characteristics or behaviors of an entire group or class of people or things. Because unsupported assumptions can interfere with your reasoning and lead to erroneous statements of cause and effect, examine your ideas carefully to be sure you avoid making this error in reasoning.

For more on errors in reasoning, see Chapter 17, p. 570.

Gathering Evidence

A convincing cause and effect essay does more than merely list causes, effects, or both and avoid errors in reasoning. Your readers expect a complete explanation of each primary cause or effect that you include. In order to explain your causes and effects, you'll probably use one or more other patterns of development. For example, you may need to narrate events;

present descriptive details about the event, problem, or phenomena; define important terms; explain processes unfamiliar to the reader; include examples that illustrate a cause or an effect; or make comparisons to explain unfamiliar concepts.

At this point, it is a good idea to do some additional prewriting or research to gather evidence to support your causes, effects, or both. You may want to do another search on the World Wide Web to obtain more specific information or details about your topic, or pay a visit to your college library. Whatever approach you take, try to discover several types of evidence, including facts, expert opinion, personal observation, quotations, and statistics.

CONNECTIONS

Refer students to Chapter 19 for more on Internet and library research.

Developing Your Thesis

Once you are satisfied with your causes and effects and the evidence you have generated to support them, your next step is to develop a working thesis. As noted earlier, the thesis for a causal analysis identifies the topic, makes an assertion about the topic, and tells whether the essay focuses on causes, effects, or both.

For more on thesis statements, see Chapter 5, p. 97.

Use the following tips to write a clear thesis statement.

1. State the cause and effect relationship. Do not leave it to your reader to figure out the causal relationship. In the following examples, note that the original thesis is weak and vague, whereas the revision clearly states the causal relationship.

TEACHING TIP

Students find it easy to recall the term *"because" clause*. It reminds them to include explicit reasons in the thesis and thereby to ensure the assertion is supported.

▶ Breathing paint fumes in a closed environment can be dangerous. ~~People~~ *for people*
~~suffering from asthma and emphysema~~ *because their lungs are especially sensitive to irritants.* ~~are particularly vulnerable.~~

The revised thesis makes the cause and effect connection explicit by using the word *because* and by including necessary information about the problem.

2. Avoid overly broad or absolute assertions. They are difficult or impossible to support.

▶ Drugs are ~~the root~~ *a major* cause of inner-city crime.

The revised thesis acknowledges drugs as one cause of crime but does not claim that drugs are the only cause.

3. Use qualifying words. Unless a cause and effect relationship is well established and accepted, qualify your thesis statement.

> ▶ Overemphasizing competitive sports ~~is~~ *may be* harmful to the psychological development of young children.

Changing the verb from *is* to *may be* qualifies the statement, allowing room for doubt.

4. Avoid an overly assertive or a dogmatic tone. The tone of your essay, including your thesis, should be confident but not overbearing. You want your readers to accept your ideas but not to be put off by an arrogant tone.

> ▶ *Substantial evidence suggests* ~~There is no question~~ that American youths have changed in response to the culture in which they live.

The phrase *Substantial evidence suggests* creates a less dogmatic tone than *There is no question*.

ESSAY IN PROGRESS 3

Using the preceding guidelines, study your list of causes, effects, or both, gather evidence, and develop a working thesis for your essay.

Evaluating Your Ideas and Thesis

Take a few minutes to evaluate the causal relationship you have chosen and determine whether your analysis of it is meaningful, worthwhile, and relevant to your audience. Start by rereading everything you have written with a critical eye. Highlight causes, effects, and evidence that seem usable; cross out items that are unnecessary or repetitious or that don't support your thesis. If you are working on a computer, highlight useful material in bold type, or move it to a separate file. If you find that your evidence is skimpy, do additional research or prewriting to generate

TEACHING TIP: COLLABORATIVE WRITING

(10 minutes) Encourage students to evaluate each other's draft theses in groups of two or three classmates. Remind the peer reviewers to refer to the tips for writing thesis statements above.

COMPUTER HINT

Ask each student to email his or her tentative thesis statement and primary and secondary causes, effects, or both to two other students, if networked computers are not available.

more information. Also think about how you can use other patterns of development (such as comparison or illustration) to further support your thesis.

TRYING OUT YOUR IDEAS ON OTHERS

Working in a group of two or three students, discuss your ideas and thesis for this chapter's assignment. Each writer should describe his or her topic (the event, problem, or phenomenon), thesis, causes or effects (or both), and supporting evidence. Then, as a group, evaluate each writer's work and causal analysis, pointing out any errors in reasoning and suggesting additional causes, effects, or evidence.

ESSAY IN PROGRESS 4

Using the preceding suggestions and your classmates' comments, evaluate your thesis and the evidence you have gathered to support it. Refer to the characteristics of cause and effect essays on pages 507–11 to help you with this step.

Organizing and Drafting

For more on drafting an essay, see Chapter 6.

Once you have evaluated your cause and effect relationship and thesis and considered the advice of your classmates, you are ready to organize your ideas and draft your essay.

Choosing a Method of Organization

Review Figures 16.1 through 16.3 to find the graphic organizer that is closest to your essay's basic structure. Then choose a method of organization that will help you present your ideas effectively. Chronological order works well when there is a clear sequence of events. In explaining why an entrepreneur was successful in opening a small business, for example, you might trace the causes in the order they occurred. However, if a key decision was crucial to the entrepreneur's success (such as the decision to advertise on a local television station), you might decide to focus on that

COMPUTER HINT

Try this exercise with a hypercard program or with the outline function of a standard word-processing program.

cause first. In this case, the causes would be arranged from most to least important. Use a word-processing program to experiment with different methods of organizing your ideas.

Drafting the Cause and Effect Essay

After deciding how to organize the essay, your next step is to write a first draft. Use the following guidelines to draft your essay.

1. **Provide well-developed explanations.** Be sure that you provide sufficient evidence that the causal relationship exists. Offer a number of reasons and choose a variety of types of evidence (examples, statistics, expert opinion, and so on) to demonstrate that you correctly perceived the relationship between causes and effects. Try to develop each cause or effect into a detailed paragraph with a clear topic sentence.

2. **Use strong transitions.** Use a transition each time you move from an explanation of one cause or effect to an explanation of another. When you move from discussing causes to discussing effects (or vice versa) or when you shift to a different pattern of development, use strong transitional sentences to alert your reader to the shift. Regardless of the organization you follow, you need to use clear transitions to guide your reader throughout the essay. Transitional words and phrases that are useful in cause and effect essays include *because, since, as a result,* and *therefore.*

For more on transitions, see Chapter 6, p. 138.

3. **Avoid overstating causal relationships.** When writing about causes and effects, avoid words and phrases that overstate the causal relationship, such as *it is obvious, without doubt, always,* and *never.* These words and phrases wrongly suggest that a causal relationship is absolute and without exception. Instead, use words and phrases that qualify, such as *it is possible, it is likely,* and *most likely.*

4. **Write an effective introduction.** Your introduction should identify the topic and causal relationship as well as draw your reader into the essay. For example, in "Personality Is What Makes Woods Special," Krauthammer opens with an intriguing question: "Why is everybody in America pulling for Tiger Woods?"

For more on writing effective paragraphs, including introductions and conclusions, see Chapter 6.

5. **Write a satisfying conclusion.** Your conclusion may remind readers of your thesis and should draw your essay to a satisfying close. In his conclusion, Krauthammer returns to the thesis, reiterating that it is not Woods's race that is the most important cause of his popularity but that he is "a gentleman athlete."

TEACHING TIP

Students who have fol-
lowed the steps in the
Guided Writing Assign-
ment should be ready to
compose a first draft
independently. However,
check to see if any stu-
dents need to rethink
their thesis, their pri-
mary and secondary
causes or effects, or
their organization before
drafting. Encourage
them to seek the assis-
tance of a peer reviewer
or writing center tutor.

Learning Style Options

TEACHING TIP:
LEARNING STYLES

1. For verbal and social
   learners
2. For all learners, especially spatial learners
3. For creative learners,
   who may combine
   this strategy with the
   use of a graphic orga-
   nizer; and for prag-
   matic and spatial
   learners, who will
   enjoy this creative
   technique.

*For more on the benefits
of peer review, see Chap-
ter 7, p. 166.*

ESSAY IN PROGRESS 5

Draft your cause and effect essay, using an appropriate method of organization
and the preceding guidelines for drafting.

Analyzing and Revising

If possible, set your draft aside for a day or two before rereading and
revising it. As you review your draft, concentrate on how you organize
and present your ideas, not on grammar, punctuation, or mechanics. Use
one or more of the following suggestions to analyze your draft.

1. Reread your essay aloud or ask a friend to do so as you listen. You may
   "hear" sections that are unclear or that require more evidence.

2. Draw a graphic organizer or update the one you drew earlier, using
   Figure 16.1, 16.2, or 16.3 as a model. Then study the visual organization of your ideas. Do they proceed logically? Do you see a way to organize your ideas more effectively for your readers? As an alternative,
   outline your essay, or update an outline you made earlier, in order to
   analyze your essay's structure.

3. Evaluate a chain of events essay by visualizing each step in the chain
   (review Figure 16.2). Does each effect become the next cause? Follow
   the chain exactly to identify any sections that are unclear.

Regardless of the technique you use, look for unsupported assumptions,
errors in reasoning, and primary or hidden causes or effects you may have
overlooked.

Use Flowchart 16.1 to guide your analysis of the strengths and weaknesses of your draft. You might also ask a classmate to read your paper and
then summarize the primary causes, effects, or both that your paper discusses. If he or she misses or misinterprets any causes or effects, focus
your revision on strengthening your explanation of the material that confused your reader. Also ask your classmate to use Flowchart 16.1 to react
to and critique your essay. Your reviewer should consider each question
listed in the flowchart and, for each "No" response, try to explain his or
her answer.

FLOWCHART 16.1
REVISING A CAUSE AND EFFECT ESSAY

Questions		Revision Strategies
1. Does your essay clearly focus on causes, effects, or both?	No ⇨	• Reconsider whether you want to explain causes, effects, or both. Will the essay be skimpy if you focus on only one? Will it be too complicated if you discuss both?
Yes ⇩		
2. Does your essay have a clear purpose?	No ⇨	• Decide whether you want to express yourself, inform your readers, or persuade your readers.
Yes ⇩		
3. Does your thesis express a qualified, manageable assertion?	No ⇨	• Use a branching diagram to narrow your topic (see Chapter 4, p. 71). • Focus only on primary causes or effects. • Add qualifying words or phrases to your thesis.
Yes ⇩		
4. Does your essay follow a logical organizational plan?	No ⇨	• Draw a graphic organizer for your essay; then compare it to the graphic organizers in Figures 16.1 through 16.3. Look for places where you can rearrange causes, effects, or both. • Use one of the organizers shown in Figures 16.1 through 16.3 as a model for reorganizing your causes, effects, or both.
Yes ⇩		

(Continued on next page)

FLOWCHART 16.1 *(continued)*

Questions		Revision Strategies

5. Is the order of presentation you use (chronological, least-to-most important, or most-to-least important) effective?

No ⇨
- Choose a different order and rearrange your draft.

Yes ⇩

6. Is each cause or effect explained fully?

No ⇨
- Add anecdotes or observations from personal experience.
- Add relevant details and examples.
- Research your topic to locate facts, research studies, statistics, and expert opinion.

Yes ⇩

7. Do you recognize or dispel readers' assumptions?

No ⇨
- Discuss or correct popular ideas readers might assume about your topic.

Yes ⇩

8. Is each paragraph well developed and focused on a separate cause or effect? Are your introduction and conclusion effective?

No ⇨
- Be sure each paragraph has a topic sentence and supporting details (see Chapter 6).
- Consider combining closely related paragraphs.
- Split paragraphs that cover more than one cause or effect.
- Revise your introduction and conclusion so that they meet the guidelines in Chapter 6 (pp. 141–46).

Yes

ESSAY IN PROGRESS 6
Revise your draft using Flowchart 16.1 and any comments you received from peer reviewers.

Editing and Proofreading

The final step is to check your revised essay for errors in grammar, spelling, punctuation, and mechanics. In addition, be sure to check your error log for the types of errors you commonly make.

As you edit and proofread your causal analysis essay, watch out for two types of errors commonly found in this type of writing: wordy sentences and mixed constructions.

1. Look for and revise wordy sentences. When explaining causal relationships, writers often use complex and compound-complex sentences. These sentences can sometimes become wordy and confusing. Look for ways to eliminate empty phrases and simplify your wording.

   ▸ As you are already well aware, viruses ~~of certain types in a computer file~~ *Certain types of computer* often create errors that you cannot explain ~~in documents~~ and may eventually result in lost data.

2. Revise to eliminate mixed constructions. A *mixed construction* happens when a writer connects phrases, clauses, or both that do not work together in a sentence.

   ▸ ~~Samantha, although~~ she was late for work, ~~but~~ was not reprimanded by her boss. *Although* *Samantha*

   Using both *although* and *but* makes this a mixed sentence. To avoid mixed constructions, check words that join your phrases and clauses. Pay attention to prepositions and conjunctions. Also, check to be sure that the subjects of your sentences can perform the actions described by the verbs. If not, revise the sentence to supply the appropriate verb.

   ▸ Higher academic standards ~~ignore~~ gifted but underprepared athletes who are motivated to improve their academic skills. *discourage*

TEACHING TIP
Encourage students to seek a writing center tutor for further review of the revision.

For more on keeping an error log, see Chapter 8, p. 201.

TEACHING TIP
• Students often find it useful to think of eliminating wordiness as "cutting the fat."
• Reading aloud to others makes it easier for students to identify wordy passages and mixed constructions.

TEACHING TIP: COLLABORATIVE WRITING
Have students work in pairs to identify wordiness and mixed constructions in each other's revised essays.

¦ **ESSAY IN PROGRESS 7**
¦ Edit and proofread your essay, paying particular attention to eliminating wordi-
¦ ness and mixed constructions.

STUDENTS WRITE

Harley Tong was a first-year liberal arts major at Niagara County Community
College when he wrote this essay in response to an assignment for his writing class.
He was asked to write a cause and effect essay explaining why and how he took
action to correct a frustrating or unpleasant situation or resolve a problem he
faced. As you read the essay, notice how Tong carefully presents the causes of his
leaving high school early. Highlight the causes he cites, and indicate which causes
are primary.

An Early Start

Harley Tong

PREREADING
QUESTION

What does Tong mean
by "an early start"?

1   For many students, high school is a place to enjoy
the company of friends while getting an education. For
some, it's a challenge to keep up with course work while
participating in clubs, organizations, and sports. For a
few others, though, it seems a waste of time and a
struggle to remain interested in schoolwork.

2   A year ago, I was a sophomore in high school and an
honor roll student with an average in the nineties, but
all of the courses I took seemed uninteresting. I felt
that high school was not the place for me. The combination of the unchallenging course work, hostile fellow
students, mediocre faculty, and unfair school policies
led me to make the decision to go directly to college
after my sophomore year.

3   First of all, the courses I was taking in high
school presented no challenge for me. Many of them were
at the Regents level rather than at the higher levels
like honors or advanced placement. Even though I had

been moved ahead in my science and language classes, I was never placed into honors level classes. I wanted to stay ahead and be challenged by my course work, but there wasn't much work to do. I became bored because the classes moved so slowly and became repetitive in certain areas.

The way I was treated by other students also played an important part in my decision. In high school, I never seemed to fit in with anyone. A lot of students belonged to their own groups of friends. These groups discriminated against anyone who didn't fit in. They often made me feel out of place. Many students verbally assaulted me in the halls and during homeroom. Some students also started fights with me, and as a result, I was suspended frequently.

In addition, I wanted to leave high school because I felt that many of my teachers and counselors were uninspiring and unsupportive. Many teachers were incapable of doing their jobs or just did them poorly. Most teachers taught by having us copy notes from the overhead projector or chalkboard, or they simply handed us our notes. Students were not introduced to computers unless they were taking computer classes and were not taught the use of calculators for complicated mathematics. I received little support from my counselor or any of the other faculty members in my attempt to leave high school early. My counselor thought that I wasn't mature enough to handle the college workload or the atmosphere. My global studies teacher, who had talked to my counselor and learned that I wanted to leave school early, told me how she felt about the idea in front of the entire class. She also told me that our principal would never approve of "such a stupid idea."

School policies were another major factor in my decision to leave high school. The administration's views on students' rights and how they should be interpreted were very unfair. Free speech was almost totally banned and other basic rights were denied to students. Students were not allowed to voice opinions about teachers and their teaching styles or actions in class. There were no teacher evaluation forms for students to fill out. Policies concerning fighting, harassment, and skipping class could be lightly or heavily enforced depending on whether or not you were a favorite of the teachers. My suspensions resulted from the school's policy regarding fighting: Even though I was attacked and did not do anything to defend myself, I was still punished for being involved. These suspension policies, which were allegedly designed by administrators to protect students, actually prevented students from keeping up with class work and maintaining good grades.

7   During my sophomore year, I came up with a plan that would allow me to attend the local community college instead of taking my junior and senior years at the high school. I would take equivalent course material at the college and transfer the grades and credits back to the high school. While I took the courses required for high school graduation, I would also be completing requirements for my graduation from college. As the year drew to a close, I arranged for a meeting between the principal and my father. My father gave his permission and the school finally agreed to my plan.

8   All of the things that made high school so miserable for me that year finally seemed unimportant because I was on my way to a better education. Over the summer, I held three jobs to earn money for tuition and then started to work for a local construction company, which I still work for. During my first semester, I took the maximum of eighteen credit hours and worked full time to raise money for the spring semester. I also worked at the college radio station and was given my own show for the spring semester. I worked hard over the semester and got good grades as a result.

9   My experiences since I left high school have been great. I have made many new friends, enjoyed all of my professors, and have joined a few clubs. Everyone at

POSSIBLE ANSWERS:
ANALYZING THE ESSAY

1. Thesis: "The combination . . . sophomore year" (paragraph 2)

college thinks my leaving high school early is an incredible opportunity and they are all very supportive. This was probably one of the best things I have ever done, and I hope I can keep on being successful not only in school but also in other aspects of life. I have no regrets about leaving high school and hope that what I did will make it easier for students in similar situations to realize that they can live up to their potential.

Analyzing the Essay

1. Identify Tong's thesis statement.
2. Describe Tong's audience and purpose.
3. Why did Tong leave high school early? Identify his primary and secondary causes.
4. What patterns of development does the writer use to support his thesis and maintain readers' interest?
5. Evaluate the introduction and conclusion.

Reacting to the Essay: Discussion and Journal Writing

1. How does your high school experience compare to Tong's? Did you experience or observe any similar problems?
2. Both George Will, in "College President's Plan: Abolish High School" (p. 542), and Tong point out problems with today's high schools. On what points do the two writers agree?
3. Tong devised an unconventional plan to solve a problem. Write a journal entry describing an unconventional step you either took or considered taking to solve a problem you faced.

READING CAUSE AND EFFECT ESSAYS

The following section provides advice for reading causal analyses and models of causal analysis essays. Each essay illustrates the characteristics of causal analysis covered in this chapter and provides opportunities to examine, analyze, and react to the writer's ideas. The second essay uses causal analysis with other patterns of development.

---

2. The audience could be other young adults, students in his class, or parents. The essay points out his need to attend college early because of the inadequacy of his high school in educating advanced or unpopular students.
3. Primary causes (set out in thesis) include "unchallenging course work, hostile fellow students, mediocre faculty, and unfair school policies" (2); no secondary causes.
4. Primarily causal analysis, supported by description, illustration, and narration (of personal experiences).
5. *Introduction:* Contrasts pleasant experience of some students in high school with the negative experience of others. *Conclusion:* Evaluates the effects of his decision to leave high school early; analyzes the outcome.

POSSIBLE ANSWERS: REACTING TO THE ESSAY

1. Responses will vary.
2. Responses will vary; both writers agree that high school can be a waste of time for students who are mature enough to handle the demands of college.
3. Responses will vary.

TEACHING TIP

Practice comparing essays on similar themes by discussing item 2 as a class.

WORKING WITH TEXT: READING CAUSAL ANALYSES

For more on reading strategies, see Chapter 2.

Reading cause and effect essays requires critical thinking and analysis as well as close attention to detail. The overall questions to keep in mind are these: What is the relationship between the events or phenomena the writer is describing and the proposed causes or effects? Has the writer perceived this relationship accurately and completely?

Use the following suggestions when reading text that deals with causes and effects.

What to Look for, Highlight, and Annotate

1. Identify the author's thesis. Look for evidence that suggests a causal relationship actually exists.

2. Make a specific effort to distinguish between causes and effects. Mark or highlight causes in one color, effects in another.

3. Annotate causes or effects that are unclear, or for which there is insufficient evidence.

4. Distinguish between primary and secondary causes or effects, especially in a lengthy or complex essay. Try marking primary causes *PC* and secondary causes *SC*.

5. Be alert for key words that signal a causal relationship. A writer may not always use obvious transitional words and phrases. Notice how each of the following examples suggests a cause or effect connection.

    CAUSES

    One *source* of confusion on the issue of gun control is . . .

    A court's decision *is motivated by* . . .

    EFFECTS

    One *impact* of the Supreme Court decision was . . .

    One *result* of a change in favored-nation status may be . . .

6. Use a graphic organizer to organize a complex causal relationship, sorting causes from effects (see Figures 16.1, 16.2, and 16.3). Fill in the organizer as you read.

7. Establish the sequence of events for an essay that is not organized chronologically. Some authors may discuss effects before presenting causes, as Wallace does in "Extinction and Us." An author who deals with a complex series of events may not mention key events in the order they occurred. To understand

and analyze a causal relationship, you may need to know the order in which the events occurred. Use your computer to draw a timeline or write a list of the events in chronological order.

How to Find Ideas to Write About

To respond to or write about a cause and effect essay, consider the following strategies.

For more on discovering ideas for a response paper, see Chapter 3.

- If the essay discusses the causes of an event, phenomenon, or problem, consider writing about the effects, or vice versa.
- Think of, and write about, other possible causes or effects.
- For a chain of events essay, write about what might have happened if the chain had been broken at some point.
- Write about the secondary causes or effects the writer does not mention.
- Write about a cause and effect relationship from your own life that is similar to one in the essay.

THINKING CRITICALLY ABOUT CAUSE AND EFFECT

Reading and evaluating causal relationships involves close analysis and may require that you do research to verify a writer's assertions. Use the following questions to think critically about the causal analyses you read.

What Is the Writer's Purpose?

Consider how the writer is describing certain effects and how this description advances his or her purpose, such as to persuade readers to accept a particular position on an issue. A wrenching description of the physical effects on animals used in experiments to test a new drug, for example, may strengthen a writer's argument against the use of animals in medical research.

CONNECTIONS

Since students are unlikely to be well prac-ticed at analyzing their own reasons at this point, encourage them to examine the underly-ing logic of each cause or effect. See page 536 for useful techniques.

Does the Writer Cover All Major Causes or Effects?

Consider whether the writer presents a fair and unbiased description of all major causes or effects. For example, a writer who favors using animals for medical research might fail to mention the harmful physical effects of testing on the animals. Conversely, a writer who opposes animal research might fail to mention that several human diseases are now controllable as a result of animal testing. In either case, the writer does not offer a complete, objective account.

Does the Writer Make Errors in Logical Reasoning?

For more on errors in reasoning, see Chapter 17, p. 570.

Consider whether the writer makes any errors in reasoning. Look for circular reasoning, the *post hoc* fallacy mistaking correlation for causation, and unsupported assumptions.

Does the Writer Provide Sufficient Evidence for the Causal Relationship?

Look to see whether the writer provides *sufficient* supporting evidence to prove the existence of a causal relationship between the events or phenomena. For example, suppose a writer makes this assertion: "Medical doctors waste the resources of health insurance companies by ordering unnecessary medical tests." For support, the writer relies on one example involving a grandparent who was required to undergo twenty-two tests and procedures before being approved for minor outpatient surgery. This one person's experience is relevant to the writer's assertion, but it is not enough to prove a causal relationship between unnecessary medical testing and wasted resources. In cases such as this one, consider whether the writer might have provided the additional support (such as statistics and expert opinion) or whether the assertion cannot be supported adequately.

CAUSAL ANALYSIS ESSAY

The following essay by Laurence Steinberg reports the results of his research into the causal relationship between students' part-time employment and diminished achievement in school.

Part-time Employment Undermines Students' Commitment to School
Laurence Steinberg

Laurence Steinberg holds a Ph.D. in psychology and is professor of psychology at Temple University. His books include Adolescence *(1985),* When Teenagers Work *(1986),* Childhood *(1995), and* Beyond the Classroom: Why School Reform Has Failed and What Parents Need to Do *(1996), from which this essay is taken. Steinberg reports the results of research he and his colleagues conducted on high school students. As you read the selection, highlight the causes and effects Steinberg discusses.*

PREREADING
QUESTIONS

• How might part-time employment undermine a student's commitment to school?
• What negative effects of working while a student might be reversible? How?

1   There are a variety of barometers by which one can measure the impact of employment on student achievement, and we used several in our research. We compared the grades of students who work a

great deal with those who work in limited amounts or not at all. We also contrasted workers with nonworkers, and those who work a lot with those who work a little, on different indicators of their commitment to education, such as how much time they spend on homework, how often they cut classes, or how far they want to go in school. And finally, we looked at the impact of employment on various measures of student engagement, such as how hard students try and how steadily they pay attention in class.

All in all, our research shows that heavy commitment to a part-time job during the school year — say, working 20 hours per week or more — significantly interferes with youngsters' school achievement and scholastic commitment. Students who work a lot perform worse in school, are less committed to their education, and are less engaged in class than their classmates who work less or not at all. For example, in our study, students who were working more than 20 hours weekly were earning lower grades, spending less time on homework, cutting class more often, and cheating more frequently, and they reported lower levels of commitment to school and more modest educational aspirations.

It has become clear from our research, as well as a host of other studies, that the key issue is not *whether* a student works, but *how much time* he or she devotes to a job. Working for more than 20 hours per week is likely to be harmful, but working for less than 10 hours per week does not seem to take a consistent toll on school performance. Most probably, the effects of working for between 10 and 20 hours weekly vary from student to student — some can handle it, while others can't. We should keep in mind, however, that half of all employed seniors, about one-third of all juniors, and about one-fifth of all sophomores work above the 20-hour threshold — indicating that large numbers of students are at risk of compromising their school careers by their part-time jobs. These findings suggest that one reason for widespread student disengagement is the fact that so many students are working at part-time jobs.

In our study, we were able to examine whether working long hours lessens youngsters' commitment to school or, alternatively, whether disengagement from school leads students to work. We did this by following students over time, as they increased or decreased their work hours, and studying how different patterns of employment affected school performance and engagement. When students increase their work hours, does their commitment to school decline as a result? When students cut back on their employment, does their school performance improve?

The answer to both of these questions is yes. While it is true that the more disengaged students are more likely to work long hours to begin with, it appears that working makes a bad situation worse. In other words, over time, the more students work, the less committed to school they become, even if they begin work with a more negative attitude toward school. (Working long hours also adversely affects students who enter the workplace with positive attitudes toward school.) When students withdraw from the labor force, however, or cut back on their work hours, their interest in school rises. The good news, then, is that the negative effects of working on schooling are reversible.

6   There are several explanations for the negative effects of working on students' engagement in school. First, when students work many hours each week, they have less time to devote to school assignments. According to our studies, one common response to this time pressure is for working students to cut corners by taking easier classes, copying assignments from other students, cutting class, or refusing to do work that is assigned by their teachers. Over time, as these become established practices, students' commitment to school is eroded bit by bit. About one-third of the students in our study said they take easier classes because of their jobs.

7   Second, in order to work 20 or more hours each week, many students must work on weekday evenings. Evening work may interfere not only with doing homework, but with both sleep and diet — studies show that working teenagers get less rest and eat less healthy meals than nonworking teenagers — and burning the midnight oil may make working teenagers more tired in school. Teachers frequently complain about working students falling asleep in class. Nearly a third of the students in our study said they were frequently too tired from work to do their homework.

8   Third, it appears that the excitement of earning large amounts of spending money may itself make school seem less rewarding and interesting. Although mind-wandering during school is considered a hallmark of adolescence, working students report significantly more of it than nonworkers. Indeed, the "rush" from earning and spending money may be so strong that students who have a history of prolonged intensive employment — those who, for example, have been working long hours since their sophomore year — are actually at greater risk than their classmates of dropping out before graduating.

9   Finally, working long hours is associated with increased alcohol and drug use. Students who work long hours use drugs and alcohol about 33 percent more often than students who do not work. Alcohol and drug use, in turn, are linked to disengagement from school, so any activity that leads adolescents to drink or experiment with drugs is likely to depress their school performance. Interestingly enough, our longitudinal studies show that working long hours *leads to* increased alcohol and marijuana use. Teenagers with between $200

POSSIBLE ANSWERS: EXAMINING THE READING

1. Research methods: "We compared the grades . . ."; "We also contrasted workers with nonworkers . . . on different indicators of their commitment to education . . ."; "And finally, we looked at the impact of employment on various measures of student engagement . . ." (paragraph 1)
2. Both: "While it is true that the more disengaged students are more likely to work long hours . . . working makes a bad situation worse" (5)
3. Working reduces students' commitment to study; causes students to fall asleep in class; and puts students at risk to drop out and become substance abusers.
4. "When students withdraw . . . or cut back on their work hours, their interest in school rises" (5).
5. *Barometers:* instruments for measuring weather conditions or (here) the effects of employment on student achievement; *engaged:* involved, participating; *toll:* negative effect, price; *eroded:* worn away; *longitudinal:* long term

and $300 of discretionary income per month have a lot more money to spend on drugs and alcohol than their peers, and this is one of the things they spend their earnings on.

Given the widespread belief that employment during adolescence   10
is supposed to be character-building, it no doubt will come as a surprise to many readers to hear that working at a part-time job *diminishes* students' engagement in school and increases their drug and alcohol use. But studies of how student workers actually spend their time on the job suggest that the real surprise is that we've held on to the myth of the benefits of adolescent work experience for as long as we have. ∎

Examining the Reading

1. What measures does Steinberg use to assess the effects of employment on students' academic performance?

2. Does Steinberg's study conclude that working long hours is a cause of students' disinterest in school, an effect of their disinterest, or both?

3. According to Steinberg, what negative effects does employment have on academic performance?

4. According to Steinberg's study, what happens when students stop working twenty or more hours per week?

5. Explain the meaning of each of the following words as it is used in the reading: *barometers* (paragraph 1), *engaged* (2), *toll* (3), *eroded* (6), and *longitudinal* (9). Refer to your dictionary as needed.

Analyzing the Reading

1. Identify Steinberg's thesis.

2. What is the writer's purpose?

3. Does the essay focus on causes, effects, or both? What type of evidence does Steinberg use?

4. Describe the overall organization of the essay. Can you identify a chain of events anywhere in the essay? If so, draw a graphic organizer of it.

5. Highlight the transitional words and phrases Steinberg uses to guide readers through the essay.

6. Evaluate the conclusion. How does Steinberg draw the essay to a close?

POSSIBLE ANSWERS: ANALYZING THE READING

1. Thesis: "Students who work a lot perform worse in school . . . at all" (paragraph 2)

2. To argue that high school students should not hold part-time jobs if possible, or should work as little as necessary, in order to maintain their commitment to school

3. Both: The causes of working students' poor commitment to school are followed in each paragraph by examples of effects. He presents the results of his study as evidence.

4. See Figure 16.3. *Example for body section:* Cause A: less time for school. Effects associated with A: taking easier classes, copying assignments, cutting class, refusing to do assigned work. Cause B: working weekday evenings. Effects associated with B: getting less rest, eating poorly, staying up late, falling asleep in class. Cause C: excitement of earning money. Effects associated with C: school seems less rewarding; students' minds wander in class; higher risk of dropping out. Cause D: increased alcohol and drug use. Effects associated with D: disengagement with school; substance abuse.

(Continued on next page)

Reacting to the Reading: Discussion and Journal Writing

1. Steinberg's research study involved high school students. Would you expect similar findings in a study of the effects of employment on the academic performance of college students? Explain your reasons.
2. Steinberg seems to overlook the fact that some students must work out of economic necessity. Do you think Steinberg is unfair to students who must work?
3. Steinberg claims there are four negative effects of employment on the academic performance of high school students. Write a journal entry explaining which effect you find most (or least) compelling. Can you think of additional effects? Use your experiences with work and school to support your answer.

PATTERNS COMBINED

In the following essay, George F. Will uses causal analysis, among other patterns, to support a provocative thesis about American high schools.

College President's Plan: Abolish High School
George F. Will

George F. Will is a well-known political commentator. He writes regular columns for the Washington Post *and* Newsweek *and has appeared on* World News Tonight *and* This Week with Sam Donaldson and Cokie Roberts. *His books include* Restoration: Congress, Term Limits, and the Recovery of Deliberative Democracy *(1992), a collection of essays, and* The Leveling Wind: Politics, the Culture and Other News, 1990–1994 *(1995), a collection of articles, columns, and speeches. The following essay was published in 1998 in his syndicated column. In it Will presents an argument for abolishing high schools. As you read the selection, highlight where the writer uses causal analysis, comparison, and examples of expert opinion to support his position.*

1   Three great creations of American civilization in the 19th century were judicial review, the curveball and high school. The first two are still robust. However, the time is ripe for rethinking the third.

2   For various reasons, some rooted in American history and others reflecting recent developments, education has become, for the moment, the most salient social concern and therefore the most potent political issue.

The world is less menacing than at any time since the 1920s. 3
Social learning about fiscal, monetary and regulatory management
has helped reduce the frequency and severity of business cycles.
Demography (fewer young males), better policing and more prison
cells have helped reduce crime.

As a result, public attention is concentrated, even more than 4
usual, on the Jeffersonian faith in education as the crucial ingredient
in personal independence and upward mobility. The focus of today's
anxiety is the highest institution from which a majority of Americans
— more than 75 percent—graduate. It is the sea of denim and hormones called high school.

America's education debates usually run in deep ruts. Liberals 5
want more money spent on schools, although there is scant evidence
of a positive correlation between increased financial inputs and
increased cognitive outputs from schools as currently constituted.
More constructively but still inadequately, conservatives call for
mechanisms to expand parental choice among schools as currently
constituted.

Now comes Leon Botstein with a radical argument for abolishing 6
the high school as we know it. He argues that puberty is not what it
once was, therefore high schools should not be what they have been
since taking their current form about 100 years ago.

Botstein, 51, has seen many products of America's high schools. 7
He has the longest tenure among current presidents of major colleges. He has been president of Bard College since 1975. At age 23 he
became the youngest college president in American history. He is
musical director of the American Symphony Orchestra in New York
and editor of the *Musical Quarterly*. In his spare time he has written a
book-length manifesto, *Jefferson's Children: Education and the Promise of
American Culture*, the third chapter of which argues that the American
high school is "obsolete."

The problem, Botstein says, is that the high school was created 8
for 15- to 18-year-olds who were still children, just approaching the
brink of adulthood. Today people that age are, physiologically and
psychologically, young adults who pose a teaching problem that the
traditional high school cannot solve.

Medical and nutritional advances have changed the relationship 9
between chronological age and physical development. Historians
estimate that during the last half of the 19th century, menstruation
began three to four months earlier each decade. The onset of puberty
is substantially earlier today than a century ago, when the high
school was invented. Then, says Botstein, the average age of the onset
of menstruation was between 15 and 16. Today it is 13.

10   As result, he says, educational practices no longer correspond to the freedoms and habits of young people's development. This is particularly so in today's adolescent culture, where money—meaning shopping—and ease of travel facilitate the young person's "self-declaration of independence."

11   Thus "today's first-year college students have lived the external appearances of an adult life for many more years than their counterparts 50 years ago did." Therefore, "what we have traditionally associated with the intellectual awakening during the college years must now occur in the high school."

12   Age 18 is too old for the intellectual regimentation and social confinements of today's high school. As a result, teachers are demoralized by the demands of keeping order. And age 18 is too old for starting serious education. It is too old to begin acquiring a love of reading, a level of comfort with mathematics and science, and good habits of concentration and memory.

13   Botstein believes that "linking learning to life in age-appropriate ways" requires "treating adolescents as young as 13 and 14 more the way we do college students and adults and less as children." Actually, he wants to abolish junior high and he wants students in high school—which he would end at 10th grade—treated better than college students often are, with classes, including many seminars, that are smaller than those in grade school.

14   Botstein is a Roman candle of ideas about curriculum reform and other matters, but every one of them likely would strain the sclerotic educational system's capacity for adaptation. Still, the fact that the changes he proposes are probably impossible does not mean that his thinking is wrong, or that lesser reforms will be satisfactory. ∎

Examining the Reading

1. According to Will, why has education become our most important national social concern?

2. How do liberals and conservatives differ in their positions on education?

3. Why does Botstein think American high schools are obsolete and should be abolished?

4. What additional reasons does Will offer for abolishing high schools?

5. Explain the meaning of each of the following words as it is used in the reading: *robust* (paragraph 1), *salient* (2), *manifesto* (7), *Roman candle* (14), *sclerotic* (14). Refer to your dictionary as needed.

Analyzing the Reading

1. Identify Will's thesis statement.
2. Will offers several types of evidence to support his thesis. Identify the types and evaluate their effectiveness.
3. Explain and evaluate the organization of the essay.
4. Do you find Will's introduction and conclusion effective? Why or why not?

Reacting to the Reading: Discussion and Journal Writing

1. Assume you are a member of your local school board. What further evidence would you need before deciding to modify the high school program in your district?
2. What short- and long-term effects can you anticipate if high schools were eliminated?
3. Write a journal entry agreeing or disagreeing with Botstein's argument that high schools are no longer appropriate for today's youth.

POSSIBLE ANSWERS: REACTING TO THE READING

1. Responses will vary; possibilities include test scores for local student population and more opinions from experts in child development.
2. Responses will vary; possibilities include huge influx of students in two-year and four-year colleges; large numbers of unemployed high school teachers; and people entering the work force at an earlier age.
3. Responses will vary.

APPLYING YOUR SKILLS: ADDITIONAL ESSAY ASSIGNMENTS

Write a cause and effect essay on one of the following topics, using what you learned about causal analysis in this chapter. Depending on the topic you choose, you may need to conduct library or Internet research.

For more on locating and documenting sources, see Chapters 19 and 20.

To Express Your Ideas

1. Write an essay reacting to George Will's essay "College President's Plan: Abolish High School." Give reasons why you think high schools have a positive effect on students and should not be abolished.
2. Write an essay explaining the causes of a "bad day" you recently experienced.
3. Suppose you or a friend or a relative won a large cash prize in a national contest. Write an essay about the effects of winning the prize.

TEACHING TIP

Suggest that students use at least one prewriting strategy—drawing a graphic organizer, freewriting, brainstorming, questioning, writing assertions—to get started. Remind students to consult the learning style options (p. 520) and the revision flowchart (p. 529).

To Inform Your Reader

4. Young children frequently ask the question "Why?" Choose a "Why" question you have been asked by a child, or think of a "Why" question you have always

wondered about (Examples: Why is the sky blue? Why are sunsets red? Why do parrots learn to talk?). Write an essay answering your question. Your audience is young children.

5. Write an essay explaining how you coped with a stressful situation.

6. Write a memo to your supervisor at work explaining the causes and effects of requiring employees to work overtime.

To Persuade Your Reader

7. Write a letter to the dean of academic affairs about a problem at your school. Discuss causes, effects, or both, and propose a solution to the problem.

8. Writer a letter to the editor of your local newspaper explaining the possible effects of a proposed change in your community and urging citizens to take action for or against it.

9. Write a letter to the sports editor of your city's newspaper. You are a fan of a professional sports team, and you just learned that the team was sold to new owners who may move the team to a different city. In your letter, explain the effects on the city and the fans if the team moves away.

Cases Using Cause and Effect

10. Write a paper for a psychology course, in preparation for a panel discussion on the psychology of humor. You are required to research this question: "What makes a joke funny?" Conduct research on the topic; then write a paper summarizing your findings for the panel discussion.

11. A scandal has arisen within the company. Employees have been sending email that contains ethnic and racial slurs to one another using company computers. In a letter to the head of personnel, either defend the employees' freedom of speech or call for their censure or dismissal. Also explain the immediate and long-term consequences of their actions and give reasons to support your position.

PART 4

Reading and
Writing Arguments

At least the fashion police won't give you a ticket. They may stop to admire the sophisticated lines of your 1998 Accord EX V-6 Coupe. Or take a moment to peruse the elegant interior, trimmed in leather. Or perhaps swoon at the performance of your 200-horsepower V-6 engine. But no tickets. Unless you're wearing fringe. Or rhinestones or something.

For more information, call 1-800-33-HONDA ext. 120 or visit us at www.honda.com. © 1997 American Honda Motor Co., Inc.

**An Accord
like no other.**

HONDA

Chapter 17

Suppose you work for an advertising agency and need to write ad copy for a new model of car. Study the ad on the opposite page as an example of how to appeal to car buyers. Note that the purpose of the advertisement is to convince readers to buy the car. The ad also makes a claim about the product: It claims that the Honda Accord is fashionable and stylish.

Writing Quick Start

Working alone or with one or two classmates, describe the appeal the advertisement makes and to whom the appeal is directed. Then describe how the ad might be revised to appeal to a different audience. Consider the visual as well as the written features of the advertisement.

Reading Arguments

TEACHING TIP: COLLABORATIVE WRITING

• Point out that the Honda ad presents a claim and implies (but does not prove) support for the claim. To generate class discussion about argument, ask students to compare and contrast a visual advertisement and a written argument. How does the *purpose* of each type of presentation differ? (E.g., a visual ad may try to sell a product, whereas an argument essay may try to convince readers to accept a view or proposal).

(Continued on next page)

The print advertisement you just evaluated is an example of a brief argument. An **argument** makes a claim and offers reasons and evidence in support of the claim. You evaluate arguments at home, work, and school every day. A friend may try to convince you to share an apartment, or your parents may urge you to postpone a wedding date. Many arguments, including print advertisements and television commercials, require you to analyze visual as well as verbal messages. A television commercial may try to persuade you to buy a running shoe or to vote for a political candidate by showing you appealing images. In your college courses and at work, you often need to judge the claims and weigh the evidence of arguments (see the accompanying box for a few examples).

In this chapter, you will learn how to read, analyze, and evaluate arguments. In Chapter 18, you will learn strategies for writing effective argument essays.

THE BASIC PARTS OF AN ARGUMENT

In everyday conversation, an argument can be a heated exchange of ideas between two people. College roommates might argue over who should clean the sink or who left the door unlocked last night. Colleagues in a company may argue over policies or procedures. An effective **argument** is a logical, well-thought-out presentation of ideas that makes a claim about an issue and supports that claim with evidence. An ineffective argument may be an irrational, emotional release of feelings and frustrations. Many sound arguments, however, combine emotion with logic. A casual conversation can also take the form of a reasoned argument, as in the following sample dialogue.

SCENES FROM COLLEGE AND THE WORKPLACE

• To prepare for a class discussion in a *sociology* course, you are asked to read and evaluate an essay proposing a solution to the decline of city centers in large urban areas.

• In a *mass communication* class, your instructor assigns three articles that take different positions on the issue of whether journalists should provide graphic coverage of accidents and other human tragedies. You are asked to articulate your own opinion on this issue.

• While working as a *purchasing agent* for a carpet manufacturer, you are listening to a sales pitch by a sales representative who is trying to convince you to purchase a new type of plastic wrapping that is used for shipping carpets.

DAMON: I'm upset that I've been called for jury duty! It's so unfair!

MARIA: Why? Everybody is supposed to do it.

DAMON: Well, first of all, we're forced to serve, whether we want to or not. And, as if being forced weren't enough, jurors are treated worse than the accused criminal. I had to sit all day in a hot, crowded room with other jurors while the TV was blaring. I couldn't read, study, or even think! How can that be fair?

• Students will work on identifying *faulty reasoning* and *emotional appeals.*

• Students will have the opportunity to *debate* an issue (bilingual education) after reading essays with differing views.

• Ask students to name the essays they have read in other chapters that present arguments (e.g., "Another Mother's Child" in Chapter 9, and "By Being Honest about Violence, Spielberg Wins" in Chapter 13). What other patterns of development do those essays use?

Damon argues that jurors are treated unfairly. He offers two reasons to support his claim and uses his personal experience to support the second reason — that "jurors are treated worse than the accused criminal" — which also serves as an emotional appeal.

    An argument has three basic parts: an *issue*, a *claim*, and *support*. In the preceding exchange between Damon and Maria, for instance, "fairness of jury duty" is the issue, "jury duty is unfair" is the claim, and Damon's two reasons are the support. In many cases an argument also recognizes or argues against opposing viewpoints, in which case it includes a fourth part — a *refutation*. Although this example does not include a refutation, consider how Damon might refute the opposing claim that jury duty gives citizens the privilege of participating in the justice system.

    As you read the following argument essay, note the issue, the writer's claim, and the support she offers. In addition, look for places where the writer recognizes or refutes opposing views.

When Volunteerism Isn't Noble
Lynn Steirer

Lynn Steirer was a student at Northampton County Area Community College when she wrote the following essay, which was published in the New York Times *in 1997. It appeared on the op-ed page of the* Times, *a forum for discussing current issues. The editor of the* New York Times's *editorial page selects articles for publication on the op-ed page.*

    Engraved in stone over the front entrance to my old high school is the statement, "No Man Is Free Who Is Not Master of Himself." No surprise for a school named Liberty.

    But in 1991, the Bethlehem school board turned its back on the principle for which my school was named when it began requiring students to perform community service or other volunteer work. Students would have to show that they had done 60 hours of such service, or they would not receive their high school diploma.

PREREADING QUESTION

How might making volunteerism a graduation requirement be contrary to the spirit of volunteerism?

1

2

3   That forced me to make a decision. Would I submit to the program even though I thought it was involuntary servitude, or would I stand against it on principle? I chose principle, and was denied a diploma.

4   Bethlehem is not alone in requiring students to do volunteer work to graduate. Other school districts around the country have adopted such policies, and in the state of Maryland, students must do volunteer work to graduate.

5   Volunteerism is a national preoccupation these days. Starting Sunday, retired Gen. Colin Powell, at President Clinton's request, will lead a three-day gathering in Philadelphia of political and business leaders and many others. General Powell is calling for more people to volunteer. That is a noble thought.

6   But what President Clinton has in mind goes far beyond volunteering. He has called for high schools across the country to make community service mandatory for graduation—in other words, he wants to *force* young people to do something that should be, by its very definition, voluntary.

7   That will destroy, not elevate, the American spirit of volunteerism. I saw firsthand how many of my classmates treated their required service as a joke, claiming credit for work they didn't do or exaggerating the time it actually took.

8   Volunteering has always been important to me. As a Meals on Wheels aide and a Girl Scout, I chose to give hundreds of hours to my community, at my own initiative.

9   While my family and I fought the school's mandatory service requirement, I continued my volunteering, but I would not submit my hours for credit. Two of my classmates joined me in this act of civil disobedience. At the same time, with the assistance of the Institute for Justice, a Washington legal-policy group, we sued the school board.

10   As graduation neared, a school official pulled me aside and said it was not too late to change my mind. That day, I really thought about giving in. Then he asked the question that settled it for me. "After all," he said, "what is more important, your values or your diploma?"

11   I chose to give up my diploma, eventually obtaining a graduate equivalency degree instead. The courts decided against us and, unfortunately, the Supreme Court declined to hear our case. The school has continued the program.

12   Volunteering is important. But in a country that values its liberty, we should make sure that student "service" is truly voluntary.   ■

The Issue

An argument is concerned with an **issue**—a controversy, a problem, or an idea about which people disagree and hold different points of view. In "When Volunteerism Isn't Noble," the issue is whether community service should be mandatory for high school graduation. Examples of other controversial issues are abortion, gun control, and the right of terminal patients to physician-assisted suicide.

The Claim

The **claim** is the point the writer tries to prove about the issue, usually the writer's view on the issue. Consider, for example, whether you think the death penalty is right or wrong. You could take three possible stands—or make three possible claims—on this issue.

The death penalty is never right.

The death penalty is always right.

The death penalty is the right choice under certain circumstances.

The claim often appears as part of the thesis statement in an argument essay. In Steirer's argument about volunteerism, the claim is that forcing students to volunteer "will destroy, not elevate, the American spirit of volunteerism" (paragraph 7). In some essays, however, the claim is implied rather than stated directly.

There are three types of claims: *claims of fact*, *claims of value*, and *claims of policy*. A **claim of fact** can be proven or verified. A writer employing a claim of fact bases the claim on verifiable facts or data, as in the following example.

The greenhouse effect is likely to take a serious toll on the environment within the next decade.

A **claim of value** focuses on showing how one thing or idea is better or more desirable than other things or ideas. Issues involving questions of right versus wrong or acceptable versus unacceptable often lead to claims of value. Such claims are subjective opinions or judgments that cannot be proven. In "When Volunteerism Isn't Noble," for instance, Steirer claims that community service should be "truly voluntary" (paragraph 12). Here is an example of a claim of value.

Doctor-assisted suicide is a violation of the Hippocratic oath and, therefore, should not be legalized.

A **claim of policy** offers one or more solutions to a problem. Often the verbs *should*, *must*, or *ought* appear in the statement of the claim.

The motion picture industry must accept greater responsibility for the consequences of violent films.

EXERCISE 17.1

Either on your own or with one or two classmates, choose two of the following issues and write two claims for each issue. Use different types of claims. For example, if one statement is a claim of value, the other should be a claim of policy or fact.

1. Legalization of drugs
2. Welfare reform
3. Television violence
4. Protection for endangered species
5. Mandatory public school uniforms

The Support

The **support** consists of the ideas and information intended to convince readers that the claim is sound or believable. Three common types of support are *reasons, evidence,* and *emotional appeals.*

Reasons

When writers make claims about issues, they have reasons for doing so. In "When Volunteerism Isn't Noble," for example, Steirer's claim—that community service should not be mandatory for high school graduation—is supported by several reasons, including her observation that students treat the mandatory community service "as a joke." A **reason**, then, is a general statement that backs up a claim. It explains why the writer's view on an issue is reasonable or correct. However, reasons alone are not sufficient support for an argument. Each reason must be supported by evidence and, often, by emotional appeals.

Evidence

In an argument, **evidence** usually consists of facts, statistics, and expert opinion. Examples and observations from personal experience can also serve as evidence. The following examples show how different types of evidence may be used to support a claim about the value of reading to children.

CLAIM:	Reading aloud to preschool and kindergarten children improves their chances of success in school.
FACTS:	First-grade children who were read to as preschoolers learn to read earlier than children who were not read to.

POSSIBLE ANSWERS

Sample claims of policy and of fact:

1. *Claim of policy:* In order to protect young people from further exposure and potential addiction, drugs such as marijuana should not be legalized. *Claim of fact:* The successful legalization of drugs like marijuana in certain European countries demonstrates that legalizing drugs can lower crime.
2. *Claim of policy:* Welfare benefits should be cut off after a specified period of time. *Claim of fact:* Private agencies do not have the resources to make up for cuts in welfare benefits.
3. *Claim of policy:* All television sets should be equipped with V-chips

For more on reasons as support in an argument, see Chapter 18, p. 588.

so that parents can block out access to violent programs. *Claim of value:* Attempts to regulate violent television programs violate the Constitution's protection of free speech.
4. *Claim of policy:* When the habitat of an endangered species is threatened, the government should protect the area from development. *Claim of fact:* Careful management can bring a species back from the brink of extinction.
5. *Claim of policy:* Children should not be

STATISTICS:
A 1998 study by Robbins and Ehri demonstrated that reading aloud to children produced a 16 percent improvement in the children's ability to recognize words used in a story.

EXPERT OPINION:
Dr. Maria Morealle, a child psychologist, urges parents to read two or three children's books to their children daily (Pearson 52).

EXAMPLES:
Stories about unfamiliar places or activities increase a child's vocabulary. For example, reading a story about a farm to a child who lives in a city apartment will acquaint the child with such new terms as *barn, silo,* and *tractor.*

PERSONAL EXPERIENCE:
When I read to my three-year-old son, I notice that he points to and tries to repeat words.

required to wear uniforms in school. *Claim of value:* Forcing children to wear uniforms suppresses their natural creativity.

In "When Volunteerism Isn't Noble," Steirer offers several examples of how high school students treat mandatory community service "as a joke": they claim credit unfairly and exaggerate their time spent doing volunteer work. The writer also uses her personal experience at Bethlehem High School to support her claim.

Emotional Appeals

Emotional appeals evoke the needs or values that readers care deeply about. For instance, a writer might appeal to readers' need for safety and security when urging them to install a deadbolt on their apartment door. You would appeal to the value a friend places on your friendship if, in urging him to visit a medical clinic when he has a bad case of the flu, you say, "If you won't go for your own good, then do it for me."

Appealing to Needs. People have various **needs**, including physiological needs (food and drink, health, shelter, safety, sex) and psychological needs (a sense of belonging or accomplishment, self-esteem, recognition by others, or self-realization). Advertisements often appeal directly or indirectly to one or more of these needs. An advertisement for an expensive necklace, for example, might appeal to a reader's need for self-esteem.

Appeals to needs are used not only by advertising copywriters. They are also used by your friends and family, by people who write letters to the editor, by personnel directors who write job listings, and so forth.

Appealing to Values. A **value** is a principle or quality that is judged to be important, worthwhile, or desirable. Some common examples of values include freedom, justice, loyalty, friendship, patriotism, duty, and equality. Values are difficult to define because not everyone considers the same principles or qualities important. Even when people agree on the importance of a value, they may not agree about what that value means. For example, although most people value honesty, some

For more on refutation, acknowledgment, and accommodation, see Chapter 18, pp. 591–92.

would say that white lies intended to protect a person's feelings are dishonest, while others would maintain that white lies are justified. Arguments often appeal to values that the writer assumes most readers will share. Steirer, in her essay on volunteerism, appeals to two widely held values: that it is worthy to stand up for one's own principles (paragraph 3) and that "No Man Is Free Who Is Not Master of Himself" (paragraph 1).

EXERCISE 17.2

As the director of a day-care center, you need to create a budget report for the following year. The report will itemize purchases and expenses as well as justify the need for each purchase or expenditure. Choose two of the following items and write a justification (reasons) for their purchase, explaining why each item would be beneficial to the children enrolled (evidence).

1. VCR
2. Tropical fish tank
3. Answering machine
4. Read-along books with tapes
5. Set of Dr. Suess books

The Refutation

The **refutation**, also called the *rebuttal*, recognizes and argues against opposing viewpoints. Suppose you want to argue that you deserve a raise at work (your claim). As support for your claim, you will remind your supervisor of the contributions and improvements you have made while you have been employed by the company, your length of employment, your conscientiousness, and your promptness. But you suspect that your supervisor may still turn you down, not because you don't deserve the raise but because other employees may expect the same raise and might quit if they don't get it. By anticipating this potential objection, you can build into your argument reasons for why the objection is not valid—that you have more time invested with the company and more responsibilities than the other employees, for example. In doing so, you would be offering a refutation.

Basically, refutation involves finding a weakness in the opponent's argument, either by casting doubt on the opponent's reasons or by questioning the accuracy, relevancy, and sufficiency of the opponent's evidence (facts, examples, statistics, and expert testimony).

Sometimes writers are unable to refute an opposing view or may choose not to, perhaps because the opposing view is weak. However, most writers of arguments recognize that the opposing viewpoint exists and, if they cannot refute it, acknowledge or accommodate it in some way. They **acknowledge** an opposing view by simply stating it. By **accommodating** an opposing view, they note that the view has merit and find a way of addressing it. In an argument opposing hunting, for example, a writer might simply *acknowledge* the view that hunting bans would cause a population explosion among wild animals. The writer might *accommodate* this opposing view by stating that if a population explosion were to occur, the problem could be solved by reintroducing natural predators into the area.

GENERAL STRATEGIES FOR READING ARGUMENTS

Arguments require a slow, careful reading in order to understand the complex relationships among ideas. Plan on reading an argument at least two times. Read it once to get an overview of the issue, claim, and support. Then reread it to identify the structure and evaluate the ideas and the relationships among them.

Because argument essays can be complex, you will find it helpful to annotate and summarize them. You may want to photocopy the essay before you begin reading, so that you can mark it up in the various ways suggested in this section. The following strategies, which you should use before and while reading, will help focus your attention on what is important and make the task of writing about what you have read easier.

Before You Read

Before you read an argument essay, look for information in the essay's main parts that will make your first reading more productive. Use the following strategies before reading.

1. **Think about the title.** The title may suggest the focus of the essay. The title of Steirer's essay, "When Volunteerism Isn't Noble," suggests her thesis. In some essays, the title may be a direct statement or synopsis of the claim. Here are a few more examples of titles.

   "In Defense of Voluntary Euthanasia"

   "The Case for Medicalizing Heroin"

   "Single-Sex Education Benefits Men, Too"

   You can tell from the title that the first essay argues for euthanasia, the second supports the use of heroin for medical purposes, and the third argues for single-sex schools.

EXERCISE 17.3

For each of the following essay titles, predict the issue and the claim you would expect the author to make.

---

machines are known to improve efficiency in all workplaces.

4. *Reasons:* Students need ample choices of reading material in order to learn to read; read-along books with tapes stimulate two senses at once and thereby facilitate learning. *Evidence:* Studies show that children who read along with tapes pick up new words faster

For more on reading strategies, see Chapter 2.

than children who read only print books.

5. *Reason:* Dr. Suess books help children learn to read. *Evidence:* The books have been used in preschools and elementary schools for many years; they provide an imaginative and phonics-based means of language acquisition for young children. Researchers advocate the type of rhyme and repetition found in Dr. Suess.

For more on evaluating sources, see Chapter 19, p. 645.

1. "What Drugs I Take Is None of Your Business"
2. "Watch That Leer, Stifle That Joke"
3. "Crazy in the Streets: A Call for Treatment"
4. "Penalize the Unwed Dad? Fat Chance"
5. "A Former Smoker Applauds New Laws"

2. **Check the author's name and credentials.** If you recognize the author's name, you may have some sense of what to expect, or what not to expect, in the essay. For example, an essay written by syndicated columnist Dave Barry, known for his humorous articles, would likely make a point through humor or sarcasm, whereas an essay by Martin Luther King Jr. would seriously address an issue current during his lifetime—most likely, civil rights. You also want to determine whether the author is qualified to write on the issue at hand. Essays in newspapers, magazines, and academic journals often include a brief review of the author's credentials and experiences related to the issue. Books include biographical notes about authors. When an article lacks an author's name, which often happens in newspapers, you need to evaluate the reliability of the publication in which the article appears.

3. **Check the original source of publication.** If the essay does not appear in its original source, use the headnote, footnotes, or citations provided to determine where the essay was originally published. Some publications have a particular viewpoint—liberal or conservative, for example. *Ms.* magazine, for instance, has a feminist slant. *Wired* is generally in favor of advances in technology. If you are aware of the viewpoint a particular publication advocates, you can sometimes predict the stand an essay will take on a particular issue. Knowing the publication's intended audience can also provide clues.

4. **Check the date of publication.** The date of publication provides a context for the essay and gives you a criterion for evaluating it. Generally, the more recent an article is, the more likely it is to reflect current research or debate on an issue. For instance, an essay on the existence of life on other planets written in the 1980s would lack recent scientific findings that might confirm or discredit the supporting evidence. When obtaining information from the World Wide Web, you should be especially careful to check the date the article was posted or last updated.

5. **Preview the essay.** Get a brief overview of the essay by reading the opening paragraph, any headings, the first sentence of one or two paragraphs per page, and the last paragraph. Previewing may also help you determine the author's claim.

6. **Think about the issue before you read.** It is often easier to read and evaluate an argument if you take a minute to explore the issue before you read. Write the issue at the top of a sheet of paper, in your journal, or in a computer file. Then create two columns for pros and cons, listing as many ideas as you can in each column.

When you think about an argument before reading, you may be less influenced by the writer's appeals and more likely to maintain an open mind and an objective, critical viewpoint. Use the preceding six suggestions to *get ready* to read the following argument essay, "Economic Affirmative Action." Do *not* read the essay until you have worked through the next section, While You Read.

Economic Affirmative Action
Ted Koerth

Ted Koerth was a first-year student at the University of Virginia when he wrote the following editorial in spring 1996 for the campus newspaper, the Cavalier Daily. *At the time he wrote the article, he was planning to major in government and Spanish.*

PREREADING
QUESTION

What type of policies might replace affirmative action?

1   Two words probably do not exist which can stir up more of a conversational frenzy than *affirmative action*. The debate surrounding such policies presents itself daily in the media, a seemingly never-ending saga destined to go back and forth forever.

2   Proponents of such policies argue that they not only give an advantage to underrepresented minority groups, but they help to settle some cosmic score that went askew during the first two hundred years of American history. People who oppose affirmative action measures argue that they encourage acceptance of underqualified applicants and that sufficient reparation time has elapsed. A growing majority of those opponents think that minorities do not deserve the push they get, hence the rise in complaints of reverse discrimination.

3   Despite the deeply felt emotions both sides of the debate harbor, a fair way to reform affirmative action's current state does exist. Many of the qualms some have with affirmative action have to do with the fact that it is based solely on race, for race is natural and unintentional. None of us chooses our race. So to treat someone differently because of his or her race demonstrates a glaring ignorance on the part of the prejudiced. We must consider, however, the opposite side of the coin which often does not receive as much thought. If we cannot judge people poorly because of their race, we cannot judge them superior for the same reason, nor should we use race to decide that a certain class of individuals needs a helping hand from any other.

4   Here the affirmative action argument comes into play. The problem starts when race becomes the basis for giving out advantages

such as college admissions. Choosing minority groups for special treatment in admissions implies that those groups lack the ability to achieve those things on their own, a bigoted assumption totally without founding. Granted, simple demographics demonstrate that certain ethnic groups are more highly represented in certain classes, but we cannot consider that an exclusive phenomenon, given that no group of people has all the same characteristics. Therefore, a generalization implying that any certain number of racial groups needs help lacks reason. For that reason, we need to fix affirmative action.

5   If two students have had the exact same opportunities during their lives but one is an American Indian and the other Caucasian, the American Indian will receive acceptance priority if her academic achievements are similar, simply because she belongs to an underrepresented group. That implies that an American Indian who achieves is out of the ordinary—a foolish assumption.

6   Take another example: Two students, one white and one Asian American, score the same on standardized tests and are equally qualified for a job. The white student, however, comes from a lower class, single-parent family, and the Asian student comes from the family of an affluent judge. If those two have equal academic achievements, affirmative action as it now exists would likely give a boost to the Asian student, though he has lived an easier life. The extra efforts the Caucasian student made go unnoticed, and he receives no boost.

7   For those reasons, America needs an affirmative action system that gives a boost not to members of groups that unfortunately suffered from past discrimination, because the days of rampant discrimination in the United States have passed for the most part. Continuing to pay back groups who previously had to deal with prejudice unfairly punishes other racial majorities for the sins of their ancestors. Instead, we need a system that gives a boost to those who have had to overcome considerable financial, physical, or other obstacles to achieve what they have achieved. Such a policy would not shut any ethnic group out of the process; it would only include anyone who has succeeded without financial assistance. If it occurs that a majority of those who benefit from that system still come from minority groups, that is fine. At least they have benefited from a system that recognizes their situation, not just their skin color.

8   The affirmative action debate roars on in the United States, with animosity on both sides building constantly. Our current system supposes a certain inherent inferiority of minority groups who in the past have experienced discrimination—an inferiority that simply does not exist. If the government were to institute an equal opportunity system that tries to help those who have had to deal with finan-

cial and physical obstacles, we could ease tensions and deal more fairly with admissions policies. Until we can respect the abilities of all ethnic groups, our country will divide its people along racial lines, as the tension rises to a fever pitch. ■

While You Read

The following tips will help you to read an argument essay carefully.

1. **Read first for an initial impression.** During your first reading, do not concentrate on specifics. Instead, read to get an overall impression of the argument and to identify the issue and the author's claim. Also try to get a general feel for the essay, the author, and the approach the author takes toward the topic. Do not judge or criticize; focus on what the author has to say.

2. **Read a second time with a pen in hand.** As you reread the essay, mark or highlight the claim, reasons, and key supporting evidence. Write annotations, noting appeals to needs and values. Jot down ideas, questions, or challenges to the writer's argument as they come to mind. Summarize reasons and key supporting evidence as you encounter them. Because an argument is built sequentially, one idea often hinges on the next. Consequently, readers often find it useful and necessary to refer to earlier statements or pieces of evidence, or to reread earlier sections before moving ahead.

3. **Underline key terms or unfamiliar words.** Because an argument can depend on defining terms in a specific way, it is especially important to make certain that you understand how the writer defines key terms and concepts. In arguments, precise definitions are crucial. For example, in an argument about options that should or shouldn't be available to infertile couples, you would need to understand what the author means by terms such as *in-vitro fertilization, surrogate parent,* and *artificial insemination.* If the author does not define terms precisely, look up their meanings in a dictionary. Jot down the definitions in the margins.

Using the preceding tips for reading arguments, turn back to page 559 and give "Economic Affirmative Action" a first and second reading. Then answer the questions that follow.

1. What is Koerth's claim?

2. Is Koerth's claim one of fact, value, or policy?

3. What reasons and types of evidence does Koerth provide to support his claim?

4. What types of emotional appeals does Koerth make, if any?

5. Does Koerth recognize or refute the opposing viewpoint? If so, how?

POSSIBLE ANSWERS

1. *Claim:* Instead of continuing with affirmative action policies, "we need a system that gives a boost to those who have had to overcome considerable financial, physical, or other obstacles . . ." (paragraph 7).
2. Policy
3. *Reasons:* No one chooses race, so a policy based on race is racist; affirmative action is unfair because it favors underrepresented groups rather than achievers of any group. *Evidence:* Hypothetical examples; essay would benefit from statistical evidence or expert opinion to back up the author's claim.
4. He appeals to readers' desire to succeed, sense of fairness, and anti-racist values.
5. He recognizes opposing views (2) and suggests that the system he proposes may benefit all people, including minority groups (7).

STRATEGIES FOR FOLLOWING THE STRUCTURE OF AN ARGUMENT

In some ways, an argument resembles a building. The writer lays a foundation and then builds on that foundation. Reasons and evidence presented early in the essay often support ideas introduced later on, as the lower floors in a building support the higher ones. Once you recognize an argument's plan or overall structure, you are in a better position to understand its content and evaluate its strengths and weaknesses. This section offers strategies for following the structure of an argument — including identifying key elements in a graphic organizer and writing a summary — that can help you analyze and evaluate an essay.

Using a Graphic Organizer

TEACHING TIP:
LEARNING STYLES

1. This option contrasts verbal learners with spatial learners.
2. For all learners, who will benefit from practice in summarizing main ideas
3. A basic study strategy for all learners
4. Encourage learners who are not primarily pragmatic or creative to collaborate with classmates who are.

Learning Style Options ▶

See Chapter 19 for suggestions on paraphrasing. For more on reading difficult material, see Chapter 2, p. 40.

The graphic organizer shown in Figure 17.1 outlines the basic relationships among ideas in an argument essay. However, unlike the graphic organizers in Part 3 of this text, this organizer does not necessarily reflect the order in which the ideas are presented in an argument essay. Instead, Figure 17.1 provides a way for you, as a reader, to organize those ideas. That is, an argument does not necessarily state (or imply) the issue in the first paragraph, but the issue is the first thing you need to identify in order to follow the structure of an argument. Similarly, the claim may not appear in the first paragraph (though it is often stated early in the essay) and the evidence may be presented at a number of different places within the essay. Regardless of the order a writer follows, his or her ideas can be shown in a graphic organizer like the one in Figure 17.1. To construct such an organizer, use the following suggestions.

1. You may find it helpful to read and highlight the essay before drawing a graphic organizer. If you are a visual learner, however, you may prefer to fill in the organizer as you read.
2. Record ideas in your own words, not in the author's words.
3. Reread difficult or confusing parts of the essay before filling in those sections of the organizer.
4. Try working through the graphic organizer with a classmate.

Study the graphic organizer for "Economic Affirmative Action" in Figure 17.2.

FIGURE 17.1
GRAPHIC ORGANIZER FOR AN ARGUMENT ESSAY

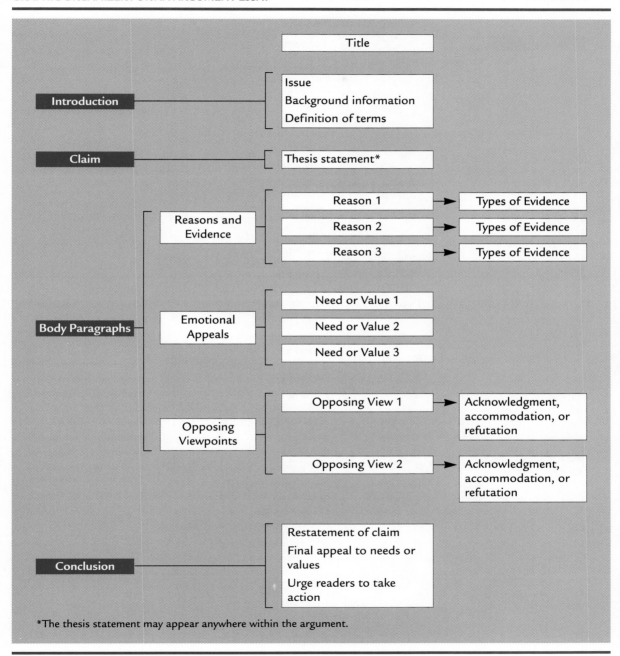

*The thesis statement may appear anywhere within the argument.

FIGURE 17.2
GRAPHIC ORGANIZER FOR "ECONOMIC AFFIRMATIVE ACTION"

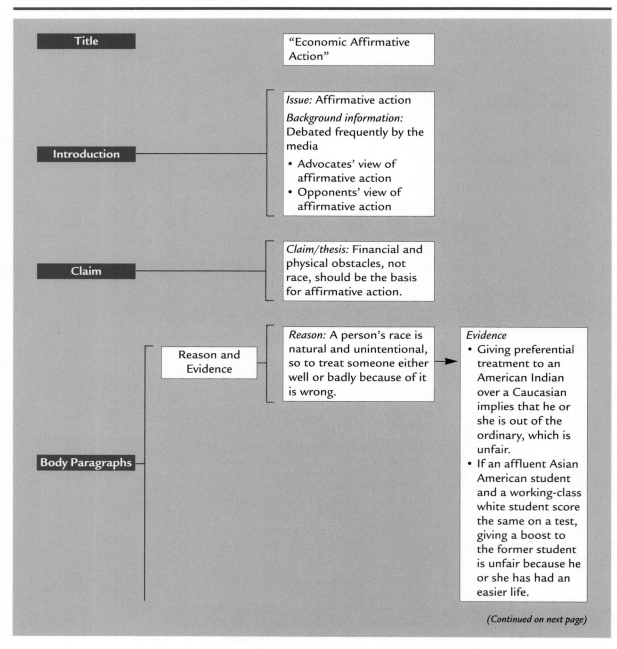

(Continued on next page)

FIGURE 17.2 *(continued)*

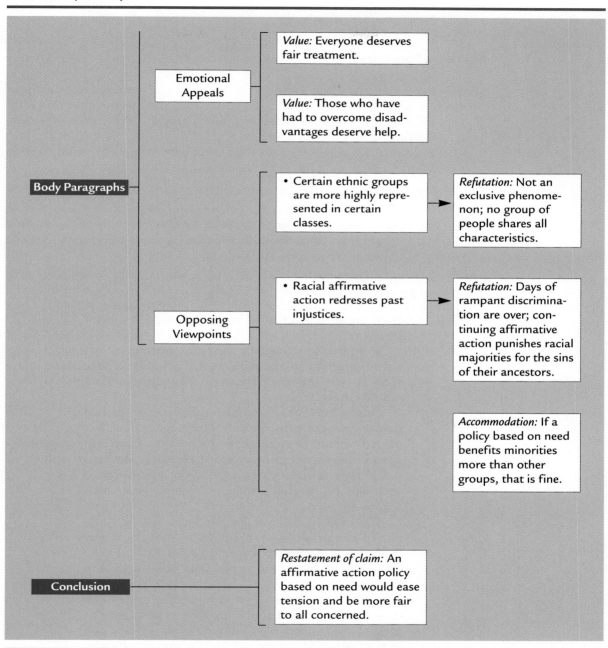

EXERCISE 17.4

Draw a graphic organizer for "When Volunteerism Isn't Noble" on page 551.

Writing a Summary

Writing a summary of an argument is another useful way to study the structure of
ideas in an essay. A summary eliminates detail; only the major supporting ideas
remain. You can write a summary after you draw a graphic organizer or use a summary to uncover an argument's structure.

The following guidelines will lead you through the process of writing a summary. (When you draw a graphic organizer first, start with summary step 4.)

1. Read the essay two or more times before you attempt to summarize it.

2. Divide the argument into sections or parts, noting the function of each section
   in the margin. You might write "offers examples" or "provides statistical
   backup," for instance. Label the issue, the claim, sections offering reasons and
   evidence, opposing viewpoints, and the conclusion.

3. Write brief marginal notes stating the main point of each paragraph or each
   related group of paragraphs. It may be helpful to use one margin for a content
   summary and the other to indicate function. Study the accompanying sample
   annotated portion of "When Volunteerism Isn't Noble."

Engraved in stone over the front entrance to my
old high school is the statement, "No Man Is Free
Who Is Not Master of Himself." No surprise for a
school named Liberty.

background

But in 1991, the Bethlehem school board turned
its back on the principle for which my school was
named when it began requiring students to perform
community service or other volunteer work. Students
would have to show that they had done 60 hours of
such service, or they would not receive their high
school diploma.

*mandatory
policy*

That forced me to make a decision. Would I submit to the program even though I thought it was
involuntary servitude, or would I stand against it on
principle? I chose principle, and was denied a
diploma.

*writer's
dilemma*

Bethlehem is not alone in requiring students to
do volunteer work to graduate. Other school districts
around the country have adopted such policies, and
in the state of Maryland, students must do volunteer
work to graduate.

*other
schools
have similar
policy*

Volunteerism is a national preoccupation these days. Starting Sunday, retired Gen. Colin Powell, at President Clinton's request, will lead a three-day gathering in Philadelphia of political and business leaders and many others. General Powell is calling for more people to volunteer. That is a noble thought.

opposing viewpoint

Powell & Clinton support

But what President Clinton has in mind goes far beyond volunteering. He has called for high schools across the country to make community service mandatory for graduation—in other words, he wants to *force* young people to do something that should be, by its very definition, voluntary.

forcing isn't voluntary

4. Once you identify the main sections of the argument and make notes about the content, you can develop a summary from your notes. Depending on your learning style, you may prefer to work from parts to whole or from whole to parts. Pragmatic learners often prefer to start by putting together the pieces of the argument (individual paragraphs) to see what they produce, whereas creative learners may prefer to begin with a one-sentence restatement of the argument and then expand it to a summary that includes the key points.

The following summary of "When Volunteerism Isn't Noble" shows an acceptable level of detail.

SAMPLE SUMMARY

The Bethlehem school board required 60 hours of community service for high school graduation, but the writer refused to submit her community service hours (as a volunteer for Meals on Wheels and as a Girl Scout) and was denied a diploma. Other school districts in other states have similar requirements. In addition, General Powell favors volunteerism, and President Clinton has called for a mandatory graduation requirement. Nevertheless, the writer maintains that making volunteerism mandatory destroys it. She cites the following personal observation as evidence: Her classmates treated the requirement as a joke and cheated in reporting their hours. The writer feels strongly that in a free society, community service should be voluntary. She gave up her diploma because of this conviction, though eventually she received a high school equivalency degree. She also sued the school board, but the Supreme Court refused to consider the case.

EXERCISE 17.5

Write a summary for "Economic Affirmative Action" on page 559.

TEACHING TIP: LEARNING STYLES

(20 minutes) Keeping their own learning styles in mind, students should try one of the strategies in step 4 for "Economic Affirmative Action:" working from parts to whole or from whole to parts. Have two students who used different methods share their summaries with the class.

POSSIBLE ANSWER

Sample summary: Affirmative action is frequently debated in the media. Proponents argue that affirmative action aids minorities who have been historically disadvantaged, while opponents argue that it encourages acceptance of under-qualified people and that reverse discrimination is now a problem. But widespread discrimination is now a thing of the past. Since race is not a choice, race should not be the basis of preference; rather, anyone experiencing financial and physical obstacles should receive the kinds of assistance that affirmative action now affords minorities. For instance, offering preferential treatment to an American Indian over a Caucasian implies the inferiority of the former, which is racist. Similarly,

(Continued on next page)

preferring an affluent
Asian student over a
blue-collar white student
with similar test scores is
unfair because the white
student has experienced
more obstacles to suc-
cess. If a needs-based
policy still benefits
minorities, that is fair,
but affirmative action as
it is now is not fair.

*For more on raising ques-
tions about an essay, see
Chapter 3.*

STRATEGIES FOR ANALYZING AND EVALUATING AN ARGUMENT

The graphic organizer shown in Figure 17.1 provides you with an easy way to lay out the ideas in an argument essay. Once you are familiar with an essay's content and organization, the next step is to analyze and evaluate the argument, including the writer's claim and support for the claim.

Review the pro-con list you wrote before reading (see p. 558), noting the points covered as well as those not covered. Think about the issue further by considering the ideas raised in the argument and writing about them in your journal. Explore your overall reaction and raise questions. Talk back to the author. Compare your ideas on the issue with those of the author. You will then be ready to analyze the argument more systematically. (For a checklist covering all of these elements, see Figure 17.3 on p. 572).

Analyzing the Elements of and Reasoning in an Argument

To analyze an argument, you need to study closely the writer's purpose, audience, definitions of key terms in the claim, and support (reasons and evidence). You also need to evaluate his or her emotional appeals, the way he or she deals with opposing viewpoints, whether the argument includes any faulty reasoning, and the conclusion.

The Basic Components

As you read an argument, consider the following aspects of any persuasive writing.

- **The writer's purpose.** Try to discover the writer's motive for writing. Ask yourself questions: "Why does the writer want to convince me of this? What does he or she stand to gain, if anything?" If a writer stands to profit personally from the acceptance of an argument, be especially careful to ask critical questions.
- **The intended audience.** Writers often reveal the intended audience by the language they use and the familiarity or formality of the tone. Also look at the reasons and types of evidence offered, the emotional appeals and examples, and the comparisons the writer makes.
- **Definitions of key terms.** Underline any terms in the statement of the claim that can have more than one meaning. Then read through the essay to see if these terms are clearly defined. The writer should offer definitions of ambiguous terms and use them consistently throughout the argument to avoid confusion.
- **The writer's credibility.** As you read an argument, judge the writer's *credibility* — his or her knowledge and trustworthiness. Ask yourself if the writer seems

to have a thorough understanding of the issue, acknowledges opposing views and addresses them respectfully, and establishes *common ground* with the reader by basing the argument in part on concerns shared by most audience members.

- **Support: reasons and evidence.** Does the writer supply sufficient reasons, as well as evidence that is relevant to the claim and accurate? Facts offered as evidence should be accurate, complete, and taken from reputable sources. In particular, statistical evidence should be current and from reliable sources. The evidence cited should be typical, and any authorities cited should be experts in their field.

For more on evaluating evidence, see Chapter 5, p. 108.

Emotional Appeals

As noted earlier in the chapter, writers of arguments appeal to or engage readers' emotions. Such appeals are a legitimate part of an argument. For example, in demonstrating the problems of a crime-ridden neighborhood, a writer may strengthen the argument by including two representative anecdotes that illustrate the despair and fear felt by its residents. However, it is unfair when a writer attempts to manipulate readers' emotions in order to distract them from the issue and the evidence. Table 17.1 presents some common unfair emotional appeals.

TABLE 17.1
COMMON UNFAIR EMOTIONAL APPEALS

Emotional Appeal	Example
Name-calling: using an emotionally loaded term to create a negative emotional response	"That reporter is an *egotistical bully*."
Ad hominem: attacking the opponent rather than his or her position on the issue	"How could anyone who didn't fight in a war criticize the president's foreign policy?"
False authority: quoting the opinions of well-known celebrities or public figures about topics on which they are not experts	"According to singer Jennifer Hope, welfare reform is America's most urgent social problem."
Appeal to pity: arousing sympathy by telling hard-luck stories or using excessive sentimentality	"Latchkey children come home to an empty house or apartment, a can of soup, and a note on the refrigerator."
Plain folks: urging readers to accept an idea or take an action because it is suggested by someone who is just like they are	"Vote for me, I'm just a regular guy."
Bandwagon: appealing to readers' desire to conform ("Everyone's doing it, so it must be right")	"It must be okay to exceed the speed limit, since so many people speed."

TEACHING TIP

Ask students to think of a time when they heard a campaign speech or political debate. Which types of emotional appeals do they recall being used by the speakers?

Opposing Viewpoints

If an argument essay takes into account opposing viewpoints, then you must evaluate these viewpoints and how the writer deals with them. Ask yourself the following questions.

- **Does the author state the opposing viewpoint clearly?** Can you tell from the essay what the opposition says?
- **Does the author present the opposing viewpoint fairly and completely?** That is, does the author recognize the opposing viewpoint and treat it with respect, or does he or she attempt to discredit or demean people holding an opposing view? Does the author present all the major parts of the opposing viewpoint or only those parts that he or she is able to refute?
- **Does the author clearly show why the opposing viewpoint is considered wrong or inappropriate?** Does the author apply sound logic? Are reasons and evidence provided?
- **Does the author acknowledge or accommodate points that cannot be refuted?**

As you read, jot down clues or answers to these questions in the margins of the essay.

Faulty Reasoning

For more on reasoning, see Chapter 18, p. 588.

In an argument essay, a writer may inadvertently introduce **fallacies**, or errors in reasoning or thinking. There are several types of fallacies that can weaken an argument, undermine a writer's claim, and call into question the relevancy, believability, or consistency of supporting evidence. Following is a brief review of the most common types of faulty reasoning.

Circular Reasoning.   Also called *begging the question,* this error in reasoning occurs when a writer uses the claim (or part of it) as evidence to support the claim. *Circular reasoning,* therefore, simply repeats the claim in different words. The statement "*Cruel* and unusual experimentation on helpless animals is *inhumane*" is an example.

Hasty Generalization.   A *hasty generalization* occurs when the writer draws a conclusion based on insufficient evidence or isolated examples. If you taste three pieces of chocolate cake and on the basis of that small sample conclude that all chocolate cakes are overly sweet, you would be making a hasty generalization.

Sweeping Generalization.   When a writer claims that something applies to *all* situations and instances without exception, the claim is called a *sweeping generalization.* To claim that all computers are easy to use is a sweeping generalization because the writer is probably referring only to the models with which he or she is familiar.

False Analogy.   When a writer compares two situations that are not sufficiently parallel or similar, the result is a *false analogy.* Just because two items or events are alike in *some* ways does not mean they are alike in *all* ways. If you wrote, "A human body needs rest after strenuous work, and a car needs rest after a long trip," you would falsely compare the human body with an automobile engine.

Non Sequitur. A *non sequitur*—which means "it does not follow"—occurs when no logical relationship exists between two or more connected ideas. For example, the comment, "Because my sister is financially independent, she will make a good parent," is a non sequitur because no logical relationship exists between financial independence and good parenting.

Red Herring. With a *red herring*, a writer attempts to distract readers from the main issue by raising an irrelevant point. For example, suppose you are arguing that television commercials for alcoholic beverages should be banned. To mention that some parents actually give sips of alcohol to their children is to create a red herring, distracting readers from the issue of television commercials.

Post hoc Fallacy. The *post hoc, ergo propter hoc* ("after this, therefore because of this") fallacy, or *post hoc* fallacy, occurs when a writer assumes that event *A* caused event *B* simply because *B* followed *A*. For example, the claim, "Student enrollment fell dramatically this semester because of the recent appointment of the new college president," is a *post hoc* fallacy because other factors may have contributed to the decline in enrollment (such as changes in the economy or in the availability of financial aid).

For more on the post hoc *fallacy, see Chapter 16, p. 522.*

Either-or Fallacy. An *either-or fallacy* argues that there are only two sides to an issue or two ways to solve a problem—and only one of them is correct. For instance, on the issue of legalizing drugs, a writer may argue that all drugs must be *either* legalized *or* banned, ignoring other positions or alternatives (such as legalizing marijuana use for cancer patients undergoing chemotherapy).

The Conclusion

The conclusion of an argument essay should leave you with a final impression of the argument. A conclusion may restate the thesis in a forceful way or make a final appeal to values. For example, in "When Volunteering Isn't Noble," Steirer makes a final appeal to values by referring to "a country that values its liberty." In "Economic Affirmative Action," Koerth makes a final appeal by reiterating a key reason for abandoning racial affirmative action—the presumed, but false, inferiority of minorities.

EXERCISE 17.6

Locate at least one brief argument essay or article and bring it to class. Working in a group of two or three students, analyze each argument using the preceding guidelines and the checklist in Figure 17.3.

FIGURE 17.3
CHECKLIST FOR ANALYZING AN ARGUMENT ESSAY

ELEMENT	QUESTIONS
1. The issue	• What is in dispute?
2. The claim	• Is the claim stated or implied?
	• Is it a claim of fact, value, or policy?
	• Does the author give reasons for making the claim?
3. The support	• What facts, statistics, expert opinions, examples, and personal experiences are presented?
	• Are appeals made to needs, values, or both?
4. The writer's purpose	• What is the author's purpose for writing the argument?
	• Why does the author want to convince readers to accept the claim?
	• What does the author stand to gain if the claim is accepted?
5. The intended audience	• Where is the argument essay published?
	• To whom do the reasons, evidence, and emotional appeals, examples, and comparisons seem targeted?
6. Definitions	• Are key terms in the author's claim clearly defined, especially terms that have ambiguous meanings?
7. The writer's credibility	• Is the author qualified, fair to the opposition, and knowledgeable?
	• Does the author establish a common ground with readers?
8. The strength of the argument: reasons and evidence	• Does the author supply several reasons to back up the claim?
	• Is the evidence relevant, accurate, current, and typical?
	• Are the authorities cited reliable experts?
	• Are fallacies or unfair emotional appeals used?
9. Opposing viewpoints	• Does the author address opposing viewpoints clearly, fairly, and completely?
	• Does the author acknowledge, accommodate, or refute opposing viewpoints with logic and relevant evidence?
	• Does the author use emotional appeals appropriately?
	• Has the author used any logical fallacies?
10. The conclusion	• Does the writer conclude the argument effectively?

APPLYING YOUR SKILLS: ADDITIONAL READINGS

The following essays take differing views on the issue of bilingual education. Use the Checklist in Figure 17.3 and the strategies for reading arguments presented in this chapter to analyze and evaluate each essay.

The Bilingual Ed Trap
Michael Gonzales

Michael Gonzales is a reporter for the Wall Street Journal, *a daily newspaper that reports on financial and world events. He has written numerous articles on economic and financial issues. This article first appeared in the* Wall Street Journal *in 1995. As you read the selection, highlight Gonzales's claim and the reasons he gives to support it.*

The push to make English the official language of the United States misses the point. If proponents of such a constitutional amendment aim to prevent Balkanization* and preserve the ideal of the melting pot, they would do far better to channel their efforts into radically changing bilingual education programs. Immigrants will learn English if the social engineers will only let them.   1

I know about bilingual education firsthand. When my family came to this country from Cuba via Spain more than twenty years ago, the New York City public school system, in its infinite wisdom, put me in a bilingual program, despite my family's doubts. The program delayed my immersion into English, created an added wedge between new immigrants and other students, and was sometimes used as a dumping ground for troubled Spanish-speakers more fluent in English.   2

When I tried to transfer to a regular class, the system threw roadblocks in my way. Administrators finally relented, though it took a lot to convince them. The process was an education in itself, but it wasn't one a fourteen-year-old should be asked to go through.   3

One year later, the students who had stayed in the bilingual class were still there, and their English-language skills were little improved. They were every bit as bright as I; it was the system that held them back. Sadly, this picture has not improved in the past two decades.   4

While a bilingual program of short duration that truly aims at quick immersion in the English-speaking culture would be of value,   5

Balkanization: when a region is divided into small, hostile countries.

PREREADING QUESTION

Is Gonzales's claim one of fact, value, or policy?

CONNECTIONS

Rachel Jones makes a similar point in "Not White, Just Right" (p. 592). Students might compare Jones's and Gonzales's use of personal experience as evidence in an argument essay.

POSSIBLE ANSWERS: EXAMINING THE READING (p. 575)

1. When Gonzales's family immigrated to the United States from Cuba via Spain in the 1970s, the New York City public school system placed Gonzales in a bilingual education program. The program delayed his language acquisition. He was blocked by administrators when he tried to transfer to regular classes, although he finally succeeded. He noticed that the other students who remained in the bilingual program experienced little improvement in English.

(Continued on next page)

2. He believes that they delay language acquisition, that they socially segregate new immigrants from the rest of the students, and that they are used as a "dumping ground" for troublesome students.

3. He is referring to the political movement to make English the official U.S. language. He sees it as politically extreme and counterproductive in that it would encourage isolationism; he suspects its proponents are motivated by "nativism, racism, and ignorance" (paragraph 10).

4. *Immersion:* complete involvement in and use of (the English language); *waif:* a stray or homeless child, an orphan; *agenda:* list of goals; *dissipated:* scattered, dispersed, lacking moral restraint; *nativism:* favoring interests of native citizens over those of immigrants

POSSIBLE ANSWERS: ANALYZING THE READING

1. *Claim:* Reforming bilingual education programs would preserve "the ideal of the melting pot" and, therefore, is preferable to making English the official U.S. language (paragraph 1). It is a claim of policy because it advocates a course of action.

2. *Reasons:* Both extremes—English-only and pro-bilingual

the lobbying groups that support bilingual education appear to have other aims in mind: chiefly, pushing the Spanish language as something in need of protection and creating a multicultural, multilingual nation.

6   Spanish is my native tongue, and it is the native tongue of every member of my family. I work hard at not losing it and speak it as often as I can, especially in the street. It is a beautiful, melodious tongue, especially suitable for poetry and other forms of literature. It is not a waif that needs the help of some concerned administrator. The language is alive and duly celebrated in Spain and eighteen countries in Latin America, as well as in any other country where individuals have chosen to add it to the particular inventory of the foreign languages they know.

7   Paul Hill, research professor at the University of Washington's graduate school of public policy, says one hidden agenda of bilingualism's proponents may be to create demand for teachers who speak a foreign language. He also suggests a more Machiavellian* agenda: Instilling in a child a self-consciousness as a member of a separate group virtually ensures that he or she will never fully feel a member of the larger society and will be more vulnerable to claims of ethnic pride, or resentment, by politicians and marketers alike. I fear Professor Hill may be right on target.

8   As a correspondent, I have witnessed countries such as South Korea and Japan use unity of purpose to compete globally. I have also witnessed strife in countries that are multilingual and multicultural, such as Afghanistan and Cyprus. We should think twice before we toss out the corny goal of having a melting pot.

9   Yes, Americans, an English-speaking people, had better start learning foreign languages, such as Spanish, in order to better compete in the world. Yes, our diversity is a real strength: Americans of Eastern European, Asian, and Latin American background are leading the charge in opening markets in those regions. But we cannot afford to become dissipated at the center—we have to understand one another, linguistically and culturally, back at the head office.

10   But if the liberals on one side confuse matters, the conservatives on the other side also send the wrong message with English-only drives. The first law that established English as the official language of a state, in Nebraska in the 1920s, restricted the learning of any other foreign language until secondary education. Any law that risks encouraging isolationism should be opposed. Globalism is real—anyone who doubts it should visit our business schools and see stu-

---

Machiavellian: Niccolò Machiavelli (1469–1527) was an Italian philosopher whose book *The Prince* asserts that a ruler's ends justify his or her means of obtaining them.

dents grappling with how to overcome America's natural seclusion. In addition, if it's fair to speculate about the motives of bilingual-ed supporters, it is also legitimate to hypothesize that supporters of English-only may be animated by nativism, racism, and ignorance.

Far from working toward union, making English an official lan- 11 guage risks creating further divisions. It goes against the grain of how things have traditionally been done in this country, where there is no official religion nor family that represents the state. Reforming bilingual ed and restricting government literature to English does not require an official language. We've done without one for 219 years. We don't need one now. ■

Examining the Reading

1. Summarize Gonzales's personal experiences with bilingual education.
2. Why does Gonzales oppose bilingual education programs?
3. What does the writer mean by "English-only drives" (paragraph 10)? Why does he oppose them?
4. Explain the meaning of each of the following words as it is used in the reading: *immersion* (paragraph 5), *waif* (6), *agenda* (7), *dissipated* (9), and *nativism* (10). Refer to your dictionary as needed.

Analyzing the Reading

1. What is Gonzales's claim? Is it a claim of fact, value, or policy? Explain how you know.
2. What reasons does Gonzales offer in support of his claim? What evidence does he use to support his reasons?
3. What emotional appeals does the writer make? Are his appeals fair or unfair?
4. Where does Gonzales recognize, accommodate, and/or refute opposing viewpoints?

Reacting to the Reading: Discussion and Journal Writing

1. Gonzales notes that students who remained in the bilingual program for the school year made little improvement. Discuss possible explanations for this lack of improvement.
2. Explain why you do or do not agree with Professor Hill that there may be a "hidden agenda" among proponents of bilingual education (paragraph 7).

education — are counterproductive because "[w]e should think twice before we toss out the corny goal of having a melting pot" (8). The English-only movement, backed by conservatives, is overly isolationist; bilingual education, backed by liberals, could lead to disunity. The most effective course is to abandon the English-only movement and overhaul bilingual education. *Evidence:* He offers personal experience, expert opinion, facts, and emotional appeals.

3. He appeals to the value of sustaining the melting pot, welcoming immigrants, embracing diversity, and fostering education for all. *Ad hominem* appeal: "supporters of English-only may be animated by nativism, racism, and ignorance" (10).

4. He concedes that short bilingual programs aimed at immersion would be valuable, but claims that proponents of bilingual education want to protect the Spanish language and create a multicultural nation (5). He concedes that Americans need to learn foreign languages and that diversity offers strength, but counters that the English-only and bilingual education movements weaken America (9).

3. Suppose you relocated to a country where the native language was different from your own. Write a journal entry describing the type of language instruction you would prefer and why you think it would help you learn the new language.

 ### Melting Pot or Tossed Salad?
Dudley Barlow

Dudley Barlow is an English teacher at Plymouth Rock High School in Canton, Michigan. He also writes two regular columns for Education Digest, *"Education Resources" and "The Teacher's Lounge." This essay is from the March 1996 issue of* Education Digest, *a journal that reports on education-related issues and research. As you read the selection, highlight Barlow's claim and the reasons he gives to support it.*

1   It was a student named Brian, during my first year of teaching, who introduced me to Hyman Kaplan, the main character in Leonard Q. Ross's wonderful little book, *The Education of H*y*m*a*n K*a*p*l*a*n.* The character is a German Jewish immigrant in his forties, and he is in Mr. Parkhill's class entitled "American Night Preparatory School for Adults." Kaplan first came to Parkhill's attention when the class turned in an assignment on common nouns and their plural forms. Kaplan's paper read: "house . . . makes . . . houses, dog . . . makes . . . doggies, library . . . makes Public library, cat . . . makes . . . Katz."

2   Throughout the book, we watch as Kaplan plunges enthusiastically into this puzzle of a new and difficult language. On the final exam, he writes Parkhill a note because, "In the recass was som students asking if is right to say Its Me or Its I . . . a planty hard question, no? Yes."

3   Kaplan has the whole puzzle neatly solved. "If I am in hall and knok, knok, knok; and I hear insite (insite the room) somebody hollers 'Whose there'—I anser strong *'Its Kaplan'*!!"

4   "Now is fine! Plain, clear like gold, no chance mixing up Me, I, Ect.

5   "By *Thinking* is Humans making big edvences on Enimals. This we call Progriss."

6   Kaplan came to my mind as I started writing this column. He was fortunate to be able to struggle with this new language in the company of the long-suffering Parkhill. A few weeks ago, I saw a news story on television about two non-English speakers who were not so fortunate.

The story concerned a bar owner somewhere in the state of Washington who refused to serve two Mexican patrons because they did not speak English. I believe she even went so far as to have the two men thrown out of the establishment. On the wall of the bar was a sign that said something like, "If you don't speak English, adios, amigo." When the TV reporter covering the story asked the woman about the incident, she said, "I thought this was America. In America, we speak English."

This woman reminded me of something my wife's uncle, Joe Zadzora, once told me. Joe was born in a coal town in Pennsylvania in the early 1920s, and he worked in the mines before joining the army during World War II. He told me about the ethnic groups — including Poles, Slavs, Russians, Irish, and Hungarians — who mined the coal and lived in the company town above the shafts. They had come to this country for the same reasons that immigrants have always come here: There was work to be had in America, and if they worked hard at difficult and sometimes dangerous jobs, maybe they could make it possible for their children to have better jobs and better lives.

Many, perhaps most, of them did not speak English. They did not need it. They could cut, blast, and shovel coal below ground with their compatriots, and above ground they lived in ethnic neighborhoods where the languages of their homelands worked just fine. But for their children, it was a different story. They went to school to learn, among other things, how to speak English to fit into this new land. English was the first key to assimilation into the broader culture beyond the company town.

The first generation born here would speak two languages with ease: the old world language used at home and English in the larger world. The next generation would have a new mother tongue, but would still be able to understand their grandparents. By the third generation, though, they would be monoglots again, and their ancestral languages would be lost.

This has been pretty much the normal course of events for immigrant families here. Big cities with their ethnic neighborhoods sometimes provided linguistic havens where the old languages could hang on for generations. Foreign-born folks less adventuresome than Hyman Kaplan could find everything they needed within the confines of a few blocks and within the familiar tongues of their former homes.

Ultimately, though, assimilation was what everyone wanted. Immigrants wanted to acquire our language to be able to partake of the American Dream, and we knew that they were right in wanting to be like us.

7

8

9

10

11

12

speak one language;
havens: safe places;
partake: participate in,
enjoy

POSSIBLE ANSWERS:
ANALYZING THE
READING (p. 579)

1. *Claim of policy:* Bilingual education that teaches English is the most auspicious method of dealing with the proliferation of non-native speakers (paragraph 19).
2. *Reasons:* The arguments for learning English have been weakened by demographics (13). "The melting pot is becoming a tossed salad" (14). *Evidence:* Barlow precedes these reasons with narrative examples and follows them with a classification of the responses of Americans to the abundance of non-native speakers.
3. His audience is mainstream American, native speakers of English. He addresses a range of responses to the problem of multilingualism; uses the first person (19), a narrative approach, and a straightforward tone.
4. He appeals to the need for education, the need to communicate, and the value of fairness in providing education to non-native speakers. He also uses a "plain folks" appeal to stress the idea that non-native speakers are like our ancestors.
5. Yes; he concisely but fairly addresses three

(Continued on next page)

viewpoints and deals
with the stories of
Hyman Kaplan and
the bar owner with
compassion. He
acknowledges in para-
graph 19 that stu-
dents must learn
English.

POSSIBLE ANSWERS:
REACTING TO THE
READING

Responses will vary.

POSSIBLE ANSWERS:
INTEGRATING THE
READINGS

1. Responses will vary.
2. Responses will vary.
Students may want to
know more about *how*
Gonzales thinks bilin-
gual education pro-
grams should be
changed and *why* Bar-
low thinks modern
Spanish-speaking
enclaves are different
from the older ethnic
neighborhoods he
describes in para-
graph 9.
3. Responses will vary.
4. Responses will vary.
Gonzales might iden-
tify with the anecdote
or find it irrelevant
since Kaplan is not a
child.

13   Now, though, things are changing. In some parts of our country, in the Southwest in particular, non-native English speakers are reaching a critical mass which has weakened the arguments for learning English.

14   The melting pot is becoming a tossed salad in which the various elements are mixed together but retain their individual identities. So, how do we respond to this new situation? What do government printing offices do? Does the Internal Revenue Service print forms in Spanish as well as English? What about road signs: Do cities in California, Arizona, and Texas print directions in both languages?

15   And how do those of us in the education business respond to this new situation? What are schools where Spanish-speaking students outnumber English-speaking students to do?

16   Some policymakers would respond the way the owner of that Washington pub did, and insist that "In America, we speak English." This "English only" approach would have all lessons taught only in English to force non-English speakers to learn our language.

17   Others would have us offer bilingual instruction designed to communicate with students in the language with which they are most familiar while trying to equip them with the language that would carry them beyond the confines of their own ethnic group.

18   There must also be a third group that would argue that, if a class is made up entirely or even predominantly of Spanish speakers, the lessons should be taught entirely in Spanish. To force these students to abandon Spanish for English, this group would argue, is a form of linguistic racism.

19   My sympathies are with the second group. If a school has a student population made up primarily of Spanish speakers, I think it would be foolhardy not to communicate with them in the language they understand best. At the same time, we need to recognize (and these students need to understand) that the language of commerce — the language of the widest range of opportunities in our country — is English. For this reason, these students also need to acquire English language skills.

20   And what about the road signs and IRS forms? We need to take a cue from business here. The instructions telling me how to set up my computer came in English and Spanish, and the instructions in a box of film or cough syrup come in several languages. As Kaplan would say, "This we call Progriss."

21   As a footnote, one final comment about the Washington bar owner who refused to serve the patrons who did not speak English. I believe her name was Orlander. Something tells me that her first ancestors to reach American soil didn't speak English, either. Someone must have served them. ∎

Examining the Reading

1. Why does Barlow open his essay with a story about a character in a book? What does Hyman Kaplan's story contribute to the essay as a whole?
2. Explain the meaning of the essay's title.
3. What three positions on bilingual education does Barlow identify?
4. What does the writer mean by "linguistic racism" (paragraph 18)?
5. Explain the meaning of each of the following words as it is used in the reading: *compatriots* (paragraph 9), *assimilation* (9), *monoglots* (10), *havens* (11), and *partake* (12). Refer to your dictionary as needed.

Analyzing the Reading

1. What is Barlow's claim?
2. What reasons does Barlow offer in support of his claim? What evidence does he use to support his reasons?
3. For whom is the essay written? How does Barlow establish a common ground with his audience?
4. To what needs and values does Barlow appeal?
5. Does the writer address opposing viewpoints clearly and fairly? Where does he accommodate and/or refute opposing views?

Reacting to the Reading: Discussion and Journal Writing

1. Describe a time when you or someone you know experienced unfair treatment as a result of speaking a non-native language or a dialect (or for using uncommon regional expressions and slang words).
2. Discuss why you agree or disagree that "English [is] the first key to assimilation into the broader [American] culture" (paragraph 9).
3. Write a journal entry in response to the bar owner's English-only policy.

Integrating the Readings

1. Gonzales and Barlow use different types of evidence to build their arguments. Which type of evidence do you think is more effective? Why?
2. If you could seek further information from each author, what questions would you ask?
3. Which writer's argument do you find most convincing? Explain your choice.
4. How might Gonzales respond to the anecdote about Hyman Kaplan at the start of Barlow's essay?

TEACHING TIP: COLLABORATIVE ACTIVITY

(50 minutes total) Conduct a class debate for question 3 under "Integrating the Readings." Divide the class into two groups, one for those who advocate reform of bilingual education (Gonzales's position) and the other for those who advocate current bilingual education programs (Barlow's position).

• (20 minutes) Have each group brainstorm a claim, reasons, and evidence. Remind students to anticipate the opposing argument and to consider possible refutations and concessions. One student in each group should take notes.

• (20 minutes) Have students rearrange their chairs so that opposing groups face each other. Allow 10 minutes for each side to present its case. You can require a spokesperson or panel from each group to do a formal presentation, or take a more informal approach, allowing anyone from each group to speak.

• (10 minutes) Open the issue for general class discussion, facing chairs toward the front of the room or in a circle. How did each group determine its main points and evidence? What "unfair" emotional appeals did students use? What did students learn about bilingual education? What did they learn about argument?

Location: http://www.safesci.com/chemsafe.htm

SafeScience®

| About SafeScience | Human Therapeutics | Distributor Information | Agriculture & Industrial | Consumer Products | Chemical Safety At Home | Shop SafeScience | SafeScience Community |

Chemical Safety At Home

Did you know?

- that the number one cause of fatal poisonings in the home is automatic dishwasher detergent?
- that the two most common household chemicals release a lethal gas when mixed together?
- that some name brand cleaning products contain a chemical proven to stimulate breast cancer cell growth?

Having a safe home is important to everyone. An increasing number of studies associate exposure to standard household chemicals with a wide range of serious health problems. As a consumer, you have the right to know which chemicals are hazardous and which are not in choosing the products you bring into your home.

SURPRISING FACTS ABOUT COMMON HOUSEHOLD CHEMICALS

HINTS ON READING LABELS

WHY NOT ANTIBACTERIAL?

THE PROS AND CONS OF SUDS

RELATED LINKS

DISPOSING OF OLD CHEMICALS AND PRODUCTS

Contact Us   Search SafeScience   Site Map

Chapter 18

Writing Arguments

Suppose you are doing research on the safety of household chemicals, and you locate the Web site shown on the opposite page. The Web site presents a brief argument: It identifies an issue (the safety of household chemicals), makes a claim (some household chemicals are hazardous), and offers evidence to support the claim (examples of unsafe products). It also establishes a rapport with readers who maintain households and use chemical products by appealing to their need for safety.

Working alone or with two or more classmates, rewrite the Web site as a brief argument of one to three paragraphs. The claim is your thesis. Add support of your own to strengthen the argument: evidence, emotional appeals, and so on. Also consider why some readers might disagree with the claim and offer reasons and evidence to refute this view. Finally, conclude your brief argument with a convincing statement.

TEACHING TIP

Brainstorm about evidence that might strengthen the argument (such as anecdotes about injuries caused by chemicals).

CONNECTIONS

Encourage students to do an Internet search for statistics and other information about the dangers of household chemicals. (See Chapter 19 for tips on Internet research.)

TEACHING TIP: CHAPTER OVERVIEW

• In this chapter, students practice writing clear, convincing claims, bolstering those claims with credible support, and choosing strategies for refuting opposing views.

• The chapter teaches the difference between *inductive* and *deductive reasoning* and continues to foster the effective use of logic, including *syllogisms,* and the avoidance of *fallacies.*

• Four methods of *organizing* an argument are covered, providing different ways of presenting the claim/thesis, opposing viewpoints, and support.

• Emphasize that in writing argument essays, students must choose an issue that is both *debatable* and *limited* in scope.

WRITING AN ARGUMENT

By following the steps in the Writing Quick Start, you made a successful start with building an argument. You made a claim, supported it with evidence, and refuted opposing views. This chapter will show you how to write clear, effective arguments.

WHAT IS AN ARGUMENT?

You encounter arguments daily in casual conversations, in newspapers, in classrooms, and on the job. A friend who asks to borrow your class notes, a writer who disagrees with a new drug-testing law, and a customer who requests a refund all argue their cases. Of the many arguments we hear and read, however, relatively few are convincing. A **sound argument** makes a claim and offers reasons and evidence in support of that claim. A sound argument also anticipates opposing viewpoints and acknowledges, accommodates, and/or refutes them.

The ability to construct and write sound arguments is an important skill in many aspects of life. In fact, much of what happens at all levels of society is a result of argument and debate. Many political, social, and economic issues, for instance, are resolved through public and private debate. Knowing how to construct a sound argument is also essential to success in college and on the job (see the accompanying box for a few examples).

The following essay presents an argument on the issue of human cloning.

SCENES FROM COLLEGE AND THE WORKPLACE

• For a *health science* course, you are part of a group working on an argument essay claiming that the results of genetic testing, which can predict a person's likelihood of contracting serious diseases, should be kept confidential.

• As a student member of the *Affirmative Action Committee* on campus, you are asked to write a letter to the editor of the campus newspaper, defending the committee's recently drafted affirmative action plan for minorities and women.

• As a *lawyer* representing a client whose hand was seriously injured on the job, you must argue to a jury that your client deserves compensation for the work-related injury.

Human Cloning? Don't Just Say No

Ruth Macklin

Ruth Macklin teaches courses in bioethics at Albert Einstein College of Medicine. This essay first appeared in U.S. News & World Report, *a weekly newsmagazine, in March 1997. As you read the selection, look for and highlight Macklin's claim and the evidence she offers to support it.*

Last week's news that scientists had cloned a sheep sent academics 1
and the public into a panic at the prospect that humans might be
next. That's an understandable reaction. Cloning is a radical challenge to the most fundamental laws of biology, so it's not unreasonable to be concerned that it might threaten human society and
dignity. Yet much of the ethical opposition seems also to grow out of
an unthinking disgust—a sort of "yuk factor." And that makes it hard
for even trained scientists and ethicists to see the matter clearly. While
human cloning might not offer great benefits to humanity, no one
has yet made a persuasive case that it would do any real harm, either.

Theologians contend that to clone a human would violate 2
human dignity. That would surely be true if a cloned individual were
treated as a lesser being, with fewer rights or lower stature. But why
suppose that cloned persons wouldn't share the same rights and
dignity as the rest of us? A leading lawyer-ethicist has suggested that
cloning would violate the "right to genetic identity." Where did he
come up with such a right? It makes perfect sense to say that adult
persons have a right not to be cloned without their voluntary,
informed consent. But if such consent is given, whose "right" to
genetic identity would be violated?

Many of the science-fiction scenarios prompted by the prospect of 3
human cloning turn out, upon reflection, to be absurdly improbable.
There's the fear, for instance, that parents might clone a child to have
"spare parts" in case the original child needs an organ transplant. But
parents of identical twins don't view one child as an organ farm for
the other. Why should cloned children's parents be any different?

Vast difference. Another disturbing thought is that cloning will 4
lead to efforts to breed individuals with genetic qualities perceived as
exceptional (math geniuses, basketball players). Such ideas are repulsive, not only because of the "yuk factor" but also because of the
horrors perpetrated by the Nazis in the name of eugenics.* But
there's a vast difference between "selective breeding" as practiced by
totalitarian regimes (where the urge to propagate certain types of

---

eugenics: a science that studies ways to improve a race or breed through selective
mating and other means.

TEACHING TIP

(10 minutes) Have students work independently to identify the
claim, background,
opposing views, refutations, and reasons for
cloning.

• Claim of value: "While
human cloning . . .
either" (paragraph 1)
• Background: Resistance to cloning (2–4)
• Opposing views/refutations: First half of
essay deals with several opposing views
followed by refutations
(theologians' view/
refutation [2]; science-
fiction scenarios/refutation [3]; fear of
eugenics/refutation
[4])
• Reasons: Second half
of essay includes hypothetical examples of
people who might use
cloning as a legitimate
means of reproduction
(5)
• Conclusion: Accommodations/proposals:
(a) moratorium on
further research into
human cloning; (b)
possible resumption of
research; (c) tight legal
oversight of cloning;
(d) human rights of
clones

people leads to efforts to eradicate other types) and the immeasurably more benign forms already practiced in democratic societies (where, say, lawyers freely choose to marry other lawyers). Banks stocked with the frozen sperm of geniuses already exist. They haven't created a master race because only a tiny number of women have wanted to impregnate themselves this way. Why think it will be different if human cloning becomes available?

5   So who will likely take advantage of cloning? Perhaps a grieving couple whose child is dying. This might seem psychologically twisted. But a cloned child born to such dubious parents stands no greater or lesser chance of being loved, or rejected, or warped than a child normally conceived. Infertile couples are also likely to seek out cloning. That such couples have other options (in vitro fertilization or adoption) is not an argument for denying them the right to clone. Or consider an example raised by Judge Richard Posner: a couple in which the husband has some tragic genetic defect. Currently, if this couple wants a genetically related child, they have four not altogether pleasant options. They can reproduce naturally and risk passing on the disease to the child. They can go to a sperm bank and take a chance on unknown genes. They can try in vitro fertilization and dispose of any afflicted embryo—though that might be objectionable, too. Or they can get a male relative of the father to donate sperm, if such a relative exists. This is one case where even people unnerved by cloning might see it as not the worst option.

6   Even if human cloning offers no obvious benefits to humanity, why ban it? In a democratic society we don't usually pass laws outlawing something before there is actual or probable evidence of harm. A moratorium on further research into human cloning might make sense, in order to consider calmly the grave questions it raises. If the moratorium is then lifted, human cloning should remain a research activity for an extended period. And if it is ever attempted, it should—and no doubt will—take place only with careful scrutiny and layers of legal oversight. Most important, human cloning should be governed by the same laws that now protect human rights. A world not safe for cloned humans would be a world not safe for the rest of us. ■

Characteristics of Argument Essays

All arguments are concerned with issues. In developing an argument essay, you need to narrow or limit the issue, make a clear and specific claim about the issue, analyze your audience, and give reasons and evidence to support the claim. In addition, you should follow a logical line of reasoning, use emotional appeals appropriately, and acknowledge, accommodate, and/or refute opposing views.

POSSIBLE ANSWERS: EXERCISE 18.1

1. *Limited topics:* The lottery in your home state; analysis of how the lottery is promoted in one state. *Background:* How many states have lotteries; how much money is raised; moral objections to state lotteries.

2. *Limited topics:* Privacy in the workplace or on the Internet; security of Internet transactions and accounts; corporate access to personal information without individual's knowledge. *Background:* Define the networks to be discussed; examples of privacy violations; relevant court cases.

An Argument Focuses on a Narrowed Issue

An **issue** is a controversy, problem, or idea about which people disagree. In choosing an issue, therefore, be sure it is arguable; that is, one that people have differing opinions on. For example, it is pointless to argue the position that education is important in today's job market because there is general agreement on that issue.

Depending on the issue you choose and the audience you write for, a clear definition of the issue may be required. Some well-known issues, such as gun control, capital punishment, and animal rights, need little definition. For less familiar issues, readers may need background information. In an argument about the awarding of organ transplants, for example, you would give readers information about the scarcity of organ donors versus the number of people who need transplants. Notice how Macklin, in "Human Cloning? Don't Just Say No," announces and defines the issue—the ethical implications of human cloning—in paragraph 1.

In addition, the issue you choose should be narrow enough to deal with adequately in an essay-length argument. For an essay on organ transplants, for instance, you could limit your argument to transplants of a particular organ or to one aspect of the issue, such as who does and does not receive them. When you narrow your issue, your thesis will be more precise and your evidence more specific. You can also provide more effective arguments against an opposing viewpoint. A detailed and specific argument is a strong argument, leaving no "holes" or gaps for opponents to uncover.

EXERCISE 18.1

Working alone or in a group of two or three students, choose two of the following issues. For each issue, consider ways to limit the topic and list the background information readers might need to understand the issue.

1. Moral implications of state-operated lotteries
2. Computer networks and the right to privacy
3. Speech codes on campus
4. Religious symbols on public property
5. Mandatory drug testing

An Argument States a Specific Claim in a Thesis

To build a convincing argument, you need to make a clear and specific **claim,** one that tells readers your position on the issue. If writing arguments is new to you, it is usually best to state your claim in a strong thesis early in the essay. Doing so will help you keep your argument on track. As you gain experience in writing arguments, you can experiment with placing your thesis later in the essay. In "Human Cloning? Don't Just Say No," Macklin makes a clear, specific claim in her opening paragraph: "While human cloning might not offer great benefits to humanity, no one has yet made a persuasive case that it would do any real harm, either."

3. Limited topics: A specific speech code on a specific campus; an incident or series of incidents that might justify speech codes. *Background:* Reasons for speech codes; purposes of typical speech codes; number of campuses that have enacted speech codes.

4. Limited topics: Controversy over displaying a crèche on public property at Christmas; attempts to display symbols meaningful to different religions. *Background:* Interpretations of what constitutes a religious symbol, relevant Supreme Court rulings.

5. Limited topics: Mandatory drug testing for members of particular professions (e.g., hospital workers, train engineers, police officers); mandatory testing of athletes for the use of steroids; mandatory testing for a specific drug. *Background:* Laws and company policies mandating drug testing; effects of drugs on job performance; relevant constitutional issues.

For more on types of claims, see Chapter 17, p. 553.

POSSIBLE ANSWERS:
EXERCISE 18.2

1. (a) While many parents approve of government control of pornography on the Internet, such controls *may* violate the First Amendment right to free speech. (b) Pornography is so readily available to children on the Internet that the government must pass legislation to control it.

For more on claims of policy, see Chapter 17, p. 553.

2. (a) Limiting immigration *may* open up more jobs for unemployed citizens. (b) While the government needs to control immigration, controls should be flexible so that people who can make valuable contributions to our society will be admitted.
3. (a) Strict controls on campaign spending would *very likely* decrease the number of political advertisements on television. (b) Laws limiting the amount of money a politician can raise and spend are a violation of First Amendment rights and should not be enacted.
4. (a) Computer literacy will *probably* be a mandatory requirement for *most* job applicants in the twenty-first century; every college graduate should be required to demonstrate profi-

Here are a few examples of how general claims can be narrowed into clear and specific thesis statements.

GENERAL: More standards are needed to protect children in day-care centers.

SPECIFIC: Statewide standards are needed to regulate the child–caregiver ratio and the qualifications of workers in day-care centers.

GENERAL: The use of animals in testing should be prohibited.

SPECIFIC: The testing of cosmetics and skin-care products on animals should be prohibited.

While all arguments make and support a claim, some also call for specific action to be taken. An essay opposing human cloning, for example, might argue for a ban on that practice as well as urge readers to take action against it, such as by voicing their opinions in letters to congressional representatives. Claims of policy often include a call for action.

Regardless of the argument, you need to be careful about the way you state your claim. Avoid a general or absolute statement; your claim will be more convincing if you qualify or limit it. For example, if a writer arguing in favor of single-sex education makes the claim "Single-sex educational institutions are *always* more beneficial to girls than are co-educational schools," opponents could easily cite exceptions to the claim and thereby show weaknesses in the argument. However, if the claim is qualified—as in "Single-sex educational institutions are *often* more beneficial to girls than are co-educational schools"—an exception would not necessarily weaken the argument. Similarly, the following example shows how a generalization might be revised by adding qualifying words.

▶ Unclear definitions and guidelines ~~are~~ *may be* responsible for the confusion between sexual harassment and mere insensitivity.

Notice that in "Human Cloning? Don't Just Say No," Macklin qualifies her claim by writing "While human cloning *might* not offer great benefits . . . (paragraph 1) and "Even if human cloning offers no *obvious* benefits . . ." (paragraph 6).

EXERCISE 18.2

Choose two of the following issues. Then, for each issue, write two thesis statements: one that makes a claim and contains a qualifying term, and another that makes a claim and calls for action.

1. Controlling pornography on the Internet
2. Limiting immigration
3. Limiting political campaign spending
4. Computer literacy as a graduation requirement
5. Competitive sports for young children

An Argument Depends on Careful Audience Analysis

To build a convincing argument, it is essential to know your audience. Because an argument is intended to influence readers' thinking, it is helpful to anticipate your readers' views. Begin by deciding whether your audience agrees or disagrees with your claim, or whether the audience is neutral about or wavering on the claim. You should also determine how familiar your audience is with the issue.

Agreeing Audiences.   When you write for an audience that agrees with your claim, the focus is usually on urging readers to take a specific action. Agreeing audiences are the easiest to write for because they are already likely to accept your claim. Instead of presenting large amounts of facts and statistics as evidence, you can concentrate on reinforcing your shared viewpoint and building emotional ties with your audience. By doing so, you encourage readers to act on their beliefs.

Neutral or Wavering Audiences.   Audiences are neutral or wavering when they have not made up their minds about or given much thought to an issue. Although they may be somewhat familiar with the issue, they usually do not have strong feelings about it. In fact, they may have questions about, misunderstandings about, or no interest in the issue.

In writing to a neutral or wavering audience, be straightforward. Emphasize the importance of the issue and offer explanations that clear up misunderstandings readers may have about it. Your goals are to establish yourself as a knowledgeable and credible writer, engender readers' trust, and present solid evidence in support of your claim.

Disagreeing Audiences.   The most challenging type of audience is the disagreeing audience—one that holds viewpoints in opposition to yours. Such an audience may also be hostile to your claim and have strong feelings about the issue. Disagreeing audiences may or may not make hasty judgments about an issue or rely on misinformation, but in either case they believe their position is correct and are not eager to accept your views. They may also tend to distrust you because you don't share their views on something they care deeply about.

In writing to a disagreeing audience, your goal is to persuade readers to consider your views on the issue. Be sure to follow a logical line of reasoning. Rather than stating your claim early in the essay, for a disagreeing audience it may be more effective to build slowly to your thesis. First establish a **common ground**—a basis of trust and goodwill—with your readers. Mentioning shared interests, concerns, or experiences as well as points in your argument about which you and your readers agree can help establish a common ground. Then, when you state your claim, the audience may be more open to considering your argument.

In "Human Cloning? Don't Just Say No," Macklin writes for a disagreeing audience. The title and opening sentences recognize that many people are opposed

ciency on the computer. (b) College students, who will need to use computers in all fields and professions, should be required to demonstrate computer literacy in order to graduate.

5. (a) Because they promote exercise and a competitive spirit, sports are *probably* among the best activities children can engage in. (b) Sports get inactive children away from the TV and into the fresh air; therefore, parents should encourage their children to engage in competitive sports.

For more on emotional appeals, see Chapter 17, p. 555.

to human cloning, even threatened or disgusted by it. Macklin openly acknowledges the opposing view and gives it a name—the "yuk factor" (paragraph 1). She then devotes several paragraphs to establishing a common ground with her readers. She mentions shared concerns (about human dignity and childless couples) and a key point of her argument (cloning would not necessarily violate human dignity and might help childless couples have children of their own).

EXERCISE 18.3

For one of the following claims, discuss how you would argue in support of it for an agreeing audience, a neutral or wavering audience, and a disagreeing audience.

1. Public school sex education classes should be mandatory because they help students make important decisions about their lives.
2. Portraying the effects of violent crime realistically on television may help to reduce the crime rate.
3. Children who spend too much time interacting with a computer may fail to learn how to interact with people.

An Argument Presents Reasons Supported by Convincing Evidence

In developing an argument, you need to have reasons for making a claim. A **reason** is a general statement that backs up a claim; it answers the question, "Why do I have this opinion about the issue?" You also need to support each reason with evidence. Suppose, for example, you argue that high school uniforms should be mandatory for three reasons: because the uniforms (1) reduce clothing costs for parents; (2) help to eliminate distractions in the classroom, thus improving academic performance; and (3) help to reduce peer pressure. Each of your reasons would need to be supported by evidence—facts, statistics, examples, personal experience, or expert testimony. Carefully linking your evidence to reasons helps readers to see how the evidence supports your claim.

Be sure to choose reasons and evidence that will appeal to your audience. In the argument about mandatory school uniforms, high school students would probably not be impressed by your first reason—reduced clothing costs for parents—but they might consider your second and third reasons if you cite evidence that appeals to them, such as personal anecdotes from students. For an audience of parents, facts and statistics about reduced clothing costs and improved academic performance would be appealing types of evidence. In "Human Cloning? Don't Just Say No," Macklin offers several reasons for her claim and supports them with examples (for instance, a couple grieving the loss of a child and a husband with a genetic defect might benefit from human cloning).

An Argument Follows a Logical Line of Reasoning

The reasons and evidence in an argument should follow a logical line of reasoning. The most common types of reasoning—induction and deduction—use evidence in different ways to arrive at a conclusion (see the accompanying diagrams). Whereas **inductive reasoning** begins with evidence and moves to a conclusion, **deductive reasoning** begins with a commonly accepted statement or premise and shows how a conclusion follows from it. You can use one or both types of reasoning in an argument essay to help keep your argument on a logical path.

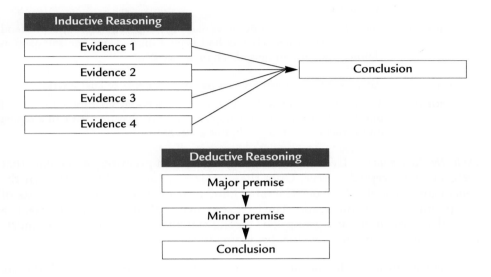

increased television viewing.
3. (a) Provide advice on ways to get computer-crazed children involved with social activities. (b) Provide examples of children who are too involved with computers along with expert testimony. (c) Concede that children will need to be comfortable using computers, but argue that other, more social skills are needed as well.

Inductive Reasoning.   Inductive reasoning starts with specific evidence and moves to a generalization or conclusion. For example, suppose you go shopping for a new pair of sneakers. You try on one style of Nikes. It doesn't fit, so you try a different style. It doesn't fit either. You try two more styles, neither of which fits. Finally, because of your experience, you draw the conclusion that Nike does not make a sneaker that fits your feet. Think of inductive reasoning as a process of coming to a conclusion about something after observing a number of cases or examples.

When you use inductive reasoning, you make an *inference* or guess about the cases that you have not experienced. In doing so, you run the risk of being wrong. Perhaps some other style of Nikes would have fit.

When building an inductive argument, be sure to consider all possible explanations for the cases you observe. In the shoe store, for example, perhaps the salesperson measured your foot incorrectly and brought you the wrong size sneakers. You also need to be sure that you have *sufficient* and *typical* evidence on which to base your conclusion. Suppose you observe one food stamp recipient selling food stamps for cash and another using them to buy candy bars. From these observations you conclude that the food stamp program should be abolished. Your reasoning is faulty, however, because these two cases are not typical of food stamp recipients and not sufficient for drawing a conclusion. When you use inductive reasoning in an argument, then, scrutinize your evidence. Make sure you have enough typical evidence to support the conclusion you draw or the claim you make.

TEACHING TIP

Point out that the Sherlock Holmes detective novels, by Arthur Conan Doyle, are classic examples of the use of inductive reasoning: Holmes starts with specific clues and eventually reaches a conclusion about the identity of the murderer, a conclusion that is "Elementary, my dear Watson."

When you use inductive reasoning in an argument essay, the conclusion becomes the claim and the specific pieces of evidence support your reasons for making the claim. For example, suppose you make a claim that Pat's Used Cars is unreliable. As support you might offer the following reasons and evidence.

REASON: Pat's Used Cars does not provide accurate information about its products.

EVIDENCE: My sister's car had its odometer reading tampered with. My best friend bought a car whose chassis had been damaged, yet the salesperson claimed the car had never been in an accident.

REASON: Pat's Used Cars doesn't honor its commitments to customers.

EVIDENCE: The dealership refused to honor the ninety-day guarantee for a car I purchased there. A local newspaper recently featured Pat's in a report on businesses that fail to honor guarantees.

Deductive Reasoning.   Deductive reasoning begins with **premises,** statements that are generally accepted as true. Once the premises are accepted as true, then the conclusion must also be true. The most familiar deductive argument consists of two premises and a conclusion. The first statement, called a **major premise,** is a general statement about a group. The second statement, called a **minor premise,** is a statement about an individual belonging to that group.

MAJOR PREMISE: All students who earn a 3.0 grade point average or better are eligible for the Dean's List.

MINOR PREMISE: Alphonso has earned a 3.2 grade point average.

CONCLUSION: Alphonso is eligible for the Dean's List.

Notice that this argument hinges on both of the premises being true. If the criterion for eligibility is incorrect or if Alphonso's average is less that 3.0, then the conclusion is not correct. You have probably used this three-step reasoning, called a **syllogism,** without realizing it. For example, suppose you know that any food containing dairy products makes you ill. Because frozen yogurt contains dairy products, you conclude that frozen yogurt will make you ill.

When you use deductive reasoning, it may be helpful to put your argument in the form of a syllogism. The syllogism will help you write your claim and organize and evaluate your reasons and evidence. Suppose you want to support the claim that state funding for Kids First, an early childhood program, should remain intact. You might use the following syllogism to build your argument.

MAJOR PREMISE: State-funded early childhood programs have increased at-risk children's readiness to attend school.

MINOR PREMISE: Kids First is a popular early childhood program in our state.

CONCLUSION: Kids First is likely to increase at-risk children's readiness to attend school.

Your thesis statement would be "Because early childhood programs are likely to increase at-risk children's readiness to attend school, state funding for Kids First should be continued." Your evidence would be the popularity and effectiveness of Kids First.

As you develop a logical argument, you also need to avoid introducing **fallacies,** or errors in reasoning.

For more on fallacies, see Chapter 17, pp. 570–71.

An Argument Appeals to Readers' Needs and Values

Although an effective argument relies mainly on credible evidence and logical reasoning, emotional appeals can help support and enhance a sound argument. **Emotional appeals** are directed toward readers' needs and values. **Needs** can be biological or psychological (food and drink, sex, a sense of belonging, and esteem, for example). **Values** are principles or qualities that readers consider important, worthwhile, or desirable. Examples include honesty, loyalty, privacy, and patriotism. In "Human Cloning? Don't Just Say No," Macklin appeals to the human need to reproduce and to the value of free choice, suggesting that childless couples should have the right to choose human cloning. Macklin also appeals to the value of democracy: "In a democratic society we don't usually pass laws outlawing something before there is actual or probable evidence of harm" (paragraph 6).

For more on emotional appeals, see Chapter 17, p. 555.

An Argument Recognizes Opposing Views

Recognizing or countering opposing arguments forces you to think hard about your own claims. When you pay attention to readers' objections, you may find reason to adjust your own reasoning and wind up with a stronger argument. In addition, readers who disagree with your claim may reconsider their position in light of your arguments. At the very least, readers will be more willing to consider your claim if you take their point of view into account.

There are three methods of recognizing opposing views in an argument essay: *acknowledgment, accommodation,* and *refutation.*

1. When you **acknowledge** an opposing viewpoint, you admit that it exists and that you have given it serious consideration. For example, in an essay arguing for mandatory high school uniforms, the opposition may argue that a uniform requirement will not eliminate peer pressure because students will find other objects with which to compete—backpacks, CDs, hairstyles, and cellular phones, for example. You could acknowledge this viewpoint by admitting there is no way to stop teenagers from finding ways to compete with one another.

2. When you **accommodate** an opposing viewpoint, you acknowledge readers' concerns, accept some of them, and incorporate them into your own argument. In arguing for mandatory high school uniforms, you might accommodate readers' view that uniforms will not eliminate peer pressure by arguing that the uniforms will eliminate one major and expensive means of competition.

POSSIBLE ANSWERS: EXERCISE 18.4 (p. 592)

1. Possible opposing arguments:
- Sex education exposes children to information that parents may want to withhold until the children are older. *Response:* Accommodate by proposing parental waivers, or refute by arguing students need to be informed about sex during adolescence, when many begin to experiment with it.
- Sex education sends the message that sex is acceptable behavior for teens. *Response:* Acknowledge the position, or accommodate it by noting that most teens experiment with sex, and therefore the program helps them protect themselves against disease and pregnancy.

2. Possible opposing arguments:
- Portraying violence more realistically on television will desensitize people to it, not deter them from it.

(Continued on next page)

Response: Refute by noting that portraying the effects of actual violence has deterred crime and changed people's minds, citing such examples as the televised images of the Vietnam War and the civil rights movement.

• Violent images have no effect on people who commit violent crimes. *Response:* Accommodate by noting that while realistic portrayals will have no effect on hardened criminals, they probably will keep some people from becoming criminals, or refute by citing studies that show a high crime rate among heavy television viewers.

3. Possible opposing arguments:

• There are many opportunities to interact with people on the Internet. *Response:* Accommodate by pointing out that interactions with strangers on the Internet can be valuable but limited, or refute by noting the uncertainty and possible dangers of interacting with strangers on the Internet.

• Children who take advantage of all the computer has to offer learn more than children with a more active social life. *Response:* Acknowledge; concede that there is much to learn from educational computer games and the Internet as well as from playing with other children.

3. When you **refute** an opposing viewpoint, you demonstrate the weakness of the opponent's argument. Macklin devotes several paragraphs (2–4) to refuting opposing views in her essay on human cloning. She considers several scary scenarios opponents of human cloning typically raise and counters each one with an example (for instance, that parents of identical twins "don't view one child as an organ farm for the other" in paragraph 3).

EXERCISE 18.4

For the three claims listed in Exercise 18.3, identify opposing viewpoints and consider how you could acknowledge, accommodate, or refute them.

Visualizing an Argument Essay: A Graphic Organizer

The graphic organizer shown in Figure 18.1 will help you analyze arguments as well as plan those that you write. Unlike the graphic organizers in Part 3, this organizer does not necessarily show the order in which an argument may be presented. Some arguments, for example, may begin with a claim, whereas others may start with evidence or opposing viewpoints. Whatever your argument's sequence, you can adapt this organizer to fit your essay. Note, however, that not every element will appear in every argument. Some arguments, such as those written for an agreeing audience, may not deal with opposing viewpoints.

Read the following essay by Rachel Jones; then study the graphic organizer for it in Figure 18.2.

Not White, Just Right
Rachel Jones

Rachel Jones is a national correspondent for Knight-Ridder newspapers and president of the Journalism and Women Symposium. Her column in the Chicago Reporter, *a monthly newsletter focusing on race and policy issues, won the 1995 Unity in Media Award for Editorial Writing. This essay first appeared in* Newsweek, *a weekly newsmagazine, in 1997. As you read the selection, highlight Jones's claim, supporting evidence, and counterarguments.*

1   In December of 1982, *Newsweek* published a My Turn column that launched my professional writing career and changed the course of my life. In that essay, entitled "What's Wrong with Black English," I argued that black youngsters need to become proficient in standard English. While the dialect known as black English is a valid part of our cultural history, I wrote, success in America requires a mastery of communications skills.

FIGURE 18.1
GRAPHIC ORGANIZER FOR AN ARGUMENT ESSAY

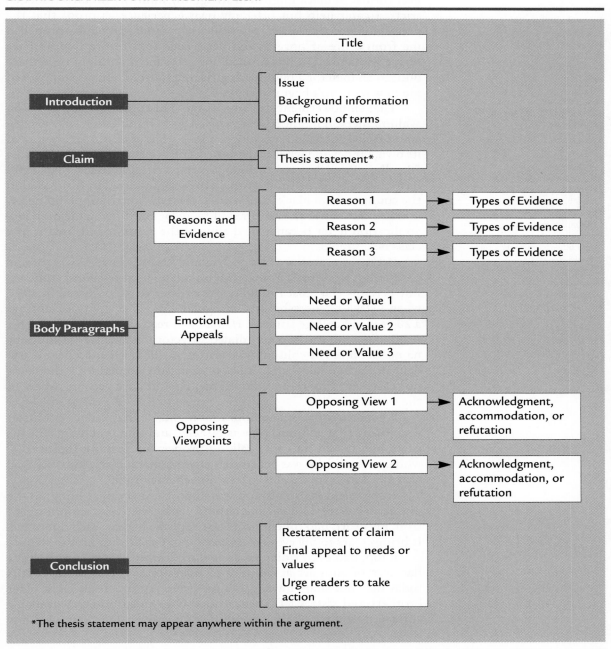

*The thesis statement may appear anywhere within the argument.

PREREADING
QUESTION

Do you think African
American students who
reject standard English
in favor of "black Eng-
lish" set themselves up
for failure? Why or why
not?

TEACHING TIP:
POSTREADING
DISCUSSION

Ask students to discuss

• Jones's use of personal
  experience as evidence
  (i.e., can her experi-
  ences be generalized?).
• other types of evidence
  Jones might have used
  to support her argu-
  ment (e.g., testimony
  from other prominent
  African Americans).
• other opposing argu-
  ments (e.g., that the
  support Jones received
  at home is not avail-
  able to all students, as
  noted in paragraph 7;
  that what constitutes
  "standard English"
  is open to interpreta-
  tion).

2   Fourteen years later, watching the increasingly heated debate over the use of black English in struggling minority urban school districts, I can't help but offer my own experience as proof that the premise is greatly flawed. My skill with standard English propelled me from a life of poverty and dead ends to a future I could have scarcely imagined. It has opened doors for me that might never have budged an inch for a poor black girl from Cairo, Ill. It has empowered me in ways I can't begin to explain.

3   That empowerment still amazes me. The column, one that Ralph Waldo Emerson might have described as "a frank and hearty expression of what force and meaning is in me," has assumed an identity of its own, far beyond what I envisioned. It has been reprinted in at least 50 college English texts, anthologies and writing course books. I still have a scrapbook of some of the letters that poured in from around the country, from blacks and whites, overwhelmingly applauding my opinion. An editor in Detroit said he recognized my name on a job-application letter because he'd clipped the column and used it in a class he'd taught.

4   Recently, a professor from Brigham Young University requested permission to record the material on a tape used for blind students. But perhaps the most humbling experience of all occurred in 1991, when I was on fellowship in Chicago and received a phone call from a 20-year-old college student. He had just read the essay in one of his textbooks and, on impulse, dialed directory assistance, seeking my name. Because the column was written in 1982, when I'd been a student in Carbondale—and Chicago wasn't my hometown—there was no reason for him to have found me; I could have been anywhere in the world.

5   We talked for about an hour that night. He thanked me profusely for writing that column. He was biracial, and said that all his life his peers had teased him for "talking proper, for wishing [he] was *all* white." He said he was frustrated that so many black kids believed that speaking articulately was a white characteristic.

6   He thanked me so often it was almost unnerving. I hung up the phone in a sort of daze. Something I had written, communicated from my heart, had touched him so deeply he had to reach out to me. It brings tears to my eyes remembering it; I related to him so well.

7   I, too, had been ridiculed as a youth for my proper speech. But I had lots of support at home, and many poor urban black youths today may not share my advantages. Every afternoon my eight older brothers and sisters left their schoolbooks piled on every available surface, so I was poking through *The Canterbury Tales** by age 8. My

---

The Canterbury Tales: a collection of poems written by English author Geoffrey Chaucer (1340?–1400).

sister Julie corrected me every time I used "ain't" or "nope." My brother Peter was a star on the high-school debate team. And my mother, Eloise, has one of the clearest, most resonant speaking voices I've ever known. Though she was a poor housekeeper when I was growing up, she was articulate and plain-spoken.

Knowing the price that was paid for me to develop my abilities, it's infuriating to hear that some young blacks still perceive clear speech as a Caucasian trait. Whether they know it or not, they're succumbing to a dangerous form of self-abnegation that rejects success as a "white thing." In an age of backlash against affirmative action, that's a truly frightening thought.

To me, this "whitewashing" is the crux of the problem. Don't tell me that calling Ebonics* a "bridge" or an "attempt to reach children where they are" will not deepen this perception in the minds of disadvantaged young blacks. And though Oakland, Calif., school administrators* have amended their original position on Ebonics, it still feels like a very pointed political statement to me, one rooted in the ongoing discussions about socioeconomic justice and educational equity for blacks. As much as I respect the cultural foundations of Ebonics, I think Oakland trivializes these discussions and stokes the fires of racial misunderstanding. Sen. Lauch Faircloth may have been too hasty in calling the Oakland school board's plan to introduce Ebonics "political correctness gone out of control," but he's hardly to be condemned for raising the flag of concern.

When immigrants worldwide fight to come to the United States, many seeking to gain even the most basic English skills, claiming a subset of language for black Americans is a damning commentary on our history of inequity and lack of access to equal educational opportunities in this country. Frankly, I'm still longing for a day when more young blacks born in poverty will subscribe to my personal philosophy. After a lifetime of hard work to achieve my goal of being a writer, of battling racism and forging my own path, I've decided that I really don't care if people like me or not. But I demand that they *understand* me, clearly, on my own terms. My mastery of standard English gave me a power that no one can take away from me, and it is important for any group of people hoping to succeed in America. As a great-granddaughter of slaves, I believe success is my birthright.

As I said back in December of 1982, I don't think I "talk white, I think I talk right." That's not quite grammatically correct, but it's a blessing to know the difference. ∎

Ebonics: the study of black English as a language.

Oakland School District: The school board originally voted to treat African American students as bilingual; the board later modified this plan to focus on teaching proficiency in standard English.

FIGURE 18.2
GRAPHIC ORGANIZER FOR "NOT WHITE, JUST RIGHT"

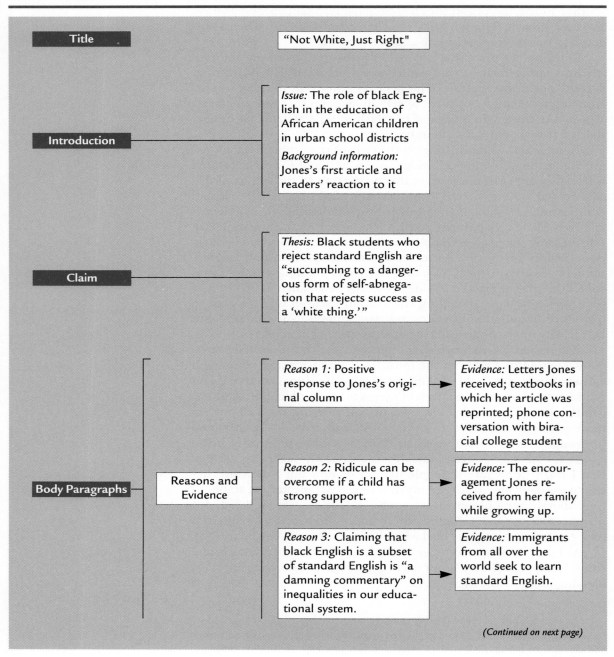

Title — "Not White, Just Right"

Introduction — *Issue:* The role of black English in the education of African American children in urban school districts
Background information: Jones's first article and readers' reaction to it

Claim — *Thesis:* Black students who reject standard English are "succumbing to a dangerous form of self-abnegation that rejects success as a 'white thing.'"

Body Paragraphs — Reasons and Evidence

Reason 1: Positive response to Jones's original column → *Evidence:* Letters Jones received; textbooks in which her article was reprinted; phone conversation with biracial college student

Reason 2: Ridicule can be overcome if a child has strong support. → *Evidence:* The encouragement Jones received from her family while growing up.

Reason 3: Claiming that black English is a subset of standard English is "a damning commentary" on inequalities in our educational system. → *Evidence:* Immigrants from all over the world seek to learn standard English.

(Continued on next page)

FIGURE 18.2 *(continued)*

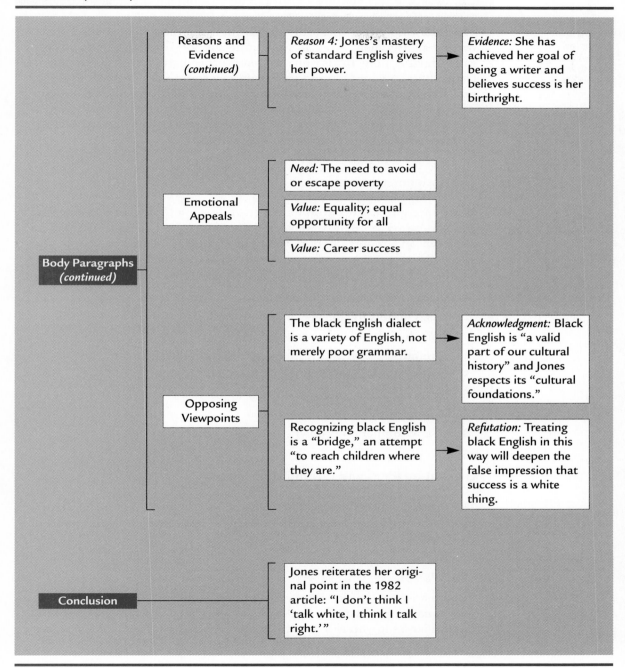

ADDITIONAL
RESOURCES

The writing process soft-
ware that accompanies
this text includes an
Electronic Guided Writ-
ing Assignment for an
argument essay.

A GUIDED WRITING ASSIGNMENT

The following guide will lead you through the process of planning and writing an argument essay. In presenting support for your argument, you will probably need to use one or more other patterns of development. Depending on your learning style, you may choose to approach the essay in different ways. A social learner may want to start by debating an issue with a classmate, whereas a pragmatic or concrete learner may want to research an issue in the library or on the Internet. This Guided Writing Assignment will provide you with alternatives.

The Assignment

For more on the patterns of development, see Chapters 9–16.

Write an argument essay on one of the following topic issues or one that you choose on your own. Make a claim about the issue and develop an argument in support of your claim. For this assignment, you should also select an audience. Analyze your readers' views on the issue and target your argument to the specific audience you choose to address.

1. Buying American-made products
2. Racial quotas in college admissions policies
3. Professional athletes as role models
4. Community service as a college graduation requirement
5. Competency exams for public educators
6. Providing a free college education to prisoners
7. Children's rights in a divorce
8. An environmental problem or issue in your community

Generating Ideas and Writing Your Thesis

The following guidelines will help you choose, explore, and make a tentative claim about an issue; consider your purpose, audience, and point of view; and research the issue.

Choosing and Exploring an Issue

Choose an issue that interests you and that you want to learn more about. Also consider how much you already know about a topic; if you choose an unfamiliar issue, you will need to conduct extensive research. For instance, to write an informed argument about children's rights in divorce cases, you would need to do research to learn about existing laws, the policies of social service agencies, and recent court decisions. Keep in mind that the issues listed in the assignment need to be narrowed. The issue about competency testing, for instance, might be limited to reading and writing competency tests for high school teachers in your state.

If you have trouble choosing an issue, move to the next step and explore several promising issues until you can make a decision. Experiment with the following strategies to discover those that work for you and fit your learning style.

For more on prewriting strategies, see Chapter 4.

1. Brainstorm about different sides of the issue. Try to point out why people disagree. Think of reasons and evidence that support various viewpoints.

2. Make a tentative claim, and then list reasons that support the claim. Then switch sides, state an opposing claim, and brainstorm to discover reasons and corresponding supporting evidence.

3. Draw a map of the issue, connecting ideas as they come to mind. Then narrow your issue: Start with one or two key ideas you generated and draw another map.

4. Conduct a mock argument with a classmate. Choose opposing views on the issue and defend your positions. Take notes on or tape-record the argument. Notice the reasons and evidence you and your opponent use to support your positions.

5. Make a two-column list of pros and cons about the issue. Write the issue at the top of a piece of paper or in a computer file. Then divide the list into two columns, listing pros in one column and cons in the other as you think of them.

6. Examine the issue by answering these key questions.
   - What is the issue? How can I best define it?
   - Is it an arguable issue?
   - What are some related issues?
   - How can I narrow the issue for an essay-length argument?
   - What are my views on the issue? How can I state my claim?
   - What evidence supports my claim?
   - Does my argument include a call for action? What do I want readers to do, if anything, about the issue?
   - Does the issue have a compromise position, or is there no middle ground?

Learning Style Options

TEACHING TIP: LEARNING STYLES

At this point, encourage students to use any methods they choose. However, hesitant students may want to start on comfortable ground, as follows:

1. For creative and emotional learners
2. For rational and creative learners
3. For spatial learners
4. For social learners
5. For pragmatic learners
6. For rational and abstract learners
7. For social and emotional learners
8. For all learners, especially concrete and pragmatic ones

*For more on conducting an
interview, see Chapter 19,
p. 662.*

*For more on Internet
research, see Chapter 19.*

7. Talk with others who have experience with the issue. Discuss the issue with an expert and ask questions. For example, if you argue for stricter laws to prevent child abuse and your sister is a case worker for a child welfare agency, she may be able to help you narrow the issue, gather evidence, and address opposing viewpoints. A friend who experienced abuse as a child could provide another perspective. Keep in mind that sensitive topics should be approached tactfully, and requests for confidentiality should be respected.

8. Use the Internet. Talk with others about the issue on the Internet — in a chatroom, newsgroup, or listserv. Use a search engine to locate discussion forums on your topic as well as Web sites that deal with the issue.

ESSAY IN PROGRESS 1

Use the preceding suggestions to choose an issue to write about (one from the list of assignments on page 598 or one you think of on your own) and to explore and narrow the issue.

**TEACHING TIP:
LEARNING STYLES**

Make sure students identify their purpose, their intended audience, their point of view, and the types of evidence and appeals on which they plan to base their arguments.

• Have students note their purpose, audience, evidence, and appeals in their journals or on a computer.

• Verbal learners may wish to freewrite about these aspects of their argument; pragmatic learners may wish to create lists or columns; social learners may wish to discuss them with classmates; and so on.

Considering Your Purpose, Audience, and Point of View

Once you choose an issue and begin to explore it, be sure to consider carefully your purpose, audience, and point of view. In an argument, your purpose is to persuade readers in some way. Think about what you want to happen as a result of your argument: Do you want your readers to change their minds? Do you want them to feel more certain of their existing beliefs? Or would you have them take some specific action?

An effective argument is tailored to its audience. The reasons and the types of evidence you offer, the needs and values to which you appeal, and the common ground you establish all depend on your audience. Remember that for this Guided Writing Assignment, you select the audience for your essay. Use the following questions to analyze your audience.

1. What do my readers already know about the issue? What do they need to know?

2. How familiar are my readers with the issue? Do they have firsthand experience with it or is their knowledge limited to what they've heard in the media and from other people?

3. Do my readers care about the issue? Why or why not?

4. Is my audience an agreeing or disagreeing audience, or one that is neutral or wavering? What opinions do my readers to have on the issue and how do their beliefs or values affect their views?

5. What do I have in common with my readers? What shared views or concerns can I use to establish a common ground?

In an argument essay, you can use the first-, second-, or third-person point of view, depending on the issue, your purpose for writing about it, and the reasons you offer in support of your claim. In "Not White, Just Right," Jones uses the first person because she is offering her personal experiences as evidence. In "Human Cloning? Don't Just Say No," Macklin uses the third person, which gives her essay a more impersonal tone. If it is important that your readers feel close to you and accept you or your experiences as part of your argument, the first person will help you achieve this closeness. If you want to establish a familiarity with your audience, the second person may be most effective. The third person creates the most distance between you and your readers and works well when you want to establish an objective, impersonal tone.

For more on purpose, audience, and point of view, see Chapter 4, p. 73.

Researching the Issue

Research is often an essential part of developing an argument. Reading what others have written on the issue helps you gather crucial components of your argument, such as background information, reliable evidence, and alternative viewpoints.

You might begin by looking for essays in this book that are relevant to your issue. For example, if your argument is about professional athletes as role models, Goodman's "Where Have You Gone Joe DiMaggio" (Chapter 2, p. 34) and Krauthammer's "Personality Is What Makes Woods Special" (Chapter 16, p. 505) would give you two writers' views on that issue. Similarly, if your issue is community service as a college graduation requirement, Steirer's "When Volunteerism Isn't Noble" (Chapter 17, p. 551) might be a good starting point.

You should also conduct library or Internet research to discover what others have written about the issue. Use the following guidelines to research and gather information on your topic.

For more on library and Internet research, see Chapter 19.

1. Consult library sources. Skim through many different sources, including books, magazine and newspaper articles, encyclopedia entries, and textbooks on your topic. Look for relevant background information, evidence (such as facts, statistics, and examples), and opposing views.

For more on reading sources, see Chapter 19, p. 648.

For more on note-taking and on avoiding plagiarism, see Chapter 19, pp. 654 and 659. For more on documenting sources, see Chapter 20.

TEACHING TIP

With the proliferation of information (and misinformation) in the mass media and on the Internet, students may not understand the meaning or appreciate the seriousness of plagiarism.

• Emphasize that students must cite the source of any *idea, phrase, sentence, statistic, table,* or *chart* that is not their own.

• Emphasize that they should take notes *as they read,* noting source information and page numbers so they can readily access this information later, if necessary.

• Discuss what is and is not considered "common knowledge."

For more on thesis statements, see Chapter 5, p. 97.

2. Watch television or videotape documentaries on your topic, or listen to debates on the radio. These sources can help you discover alternative viewpoints and expert testimony.

3. Research the issue on the World Wide Web. Use a search engine such as Yahoo! or AltaVista to help locate Web sites with information on your topic.

4. Select several key sources for careful reading. Key sources include a representative sample of the different points of view on your issue, essays by experts in the field, and reports that provide useful and current statistical data.

5. Take notes as you read your key sources. Also add ideas to your brainstormed lists, notes, or maps. As you jot down notes, take steps to avoid inadvertently plagiarizing the words and ideas of other writers. Enclose direct quotations from sources in quotation marks, summarize and paraphrase information from sources carefully, and record all of the publication details you will need to cite your sources (author, title, publisher and site, publication date, page numbers, and so on).

ESSAY IN PROGRESS 2

Using the preceding suggestions, consider your purpose, audience, and point of view. Be sure to answer the questions listed on pages 600–601; your responses will help you tailor your argument, including your evidence and emotional appeals, to suit your intended audience.

Developing Your Thesis and Making a Claim

After doing research and reading what others have to say about the issue, your views on it may have softened, hardened, or changed in some other way. For instance, research on the mandatory use of seat belts may turn up statistics, expert testimony, and firsthand accounts of lives saved by seat belts in automobile accidents, leading you to reconsider your earlier view opposing mandatory seat-belt use. Therefore, before you develop a thesis and make a claim about the issue, consider your views on it in light of your research.

As noted earlier in the chapter, the thesis for an argument essay makes a claim about the issue. As you draft your thesis, be careful to avoid general statements that are not arguable. Instead, clearly state your claim about the issue. Note the difference between a vague statement and a specific claim in the following examples.

> VAGUE: In recent years, U.S. citizens have experienced an increase in credit card fraud.
>
> SPECIFIC: Although the carelessness of merchants and electronic tampering contribute to the problem, U.S. consumers are largely to blame for the recent increase in credit card fraud.

The first example merely states a fact and is not a valid thesis for an argument. The second example makes a specific claim about an issue that is arguable.

ESSAY IN PROGRESS 3

Using the preceding suggestions, write a working thesis that clearly expresses your claim about the issue.

Evaluating Your Ideas, Evidence, and Claim

Once you are satisfied with your working thesis, take a few minutes to evaluate the reasons and evidence you will use to support your claim. Begin by rereading everything you have written with a critical eye. Look for ways to organize your reasons (such as in the order of their strength or importance) and group your evidence for each reason. Draw a graphic organizer of your reasons and evidence, using Figure 18.1 as a model.

TRYING OUT YOUR IDEAS ON OTHERS

Working in a group of two or three students, discuss your claim, reasons, and evidence. Each writer should state his or her issue, claim, reasons, and evidence for this chapter's assignment. Then, as a group, evaluate each writer's work.

ESSAY IN PROGRESS 4

Using the list of the characteristics of argument essays on pages 584–92 and comments from your classmates, evaluate your claim and the reasons and evidence you have gathered to support it. (You might also use the questions in Figure 17.3, page 572, to help you evaluate your claim, reasons, and evidence.)

Considering Opposing Viewpoints

Once you evaluate the key elements in your argument, you are ready to consider opposing viewpoints and plan how to acknowledge, accommodate,

COMPUTER HINT

Ask each student to email his or her tentative thesis statement to two other students, if networked computers are not available.

TEACHING TIP

Ask students to complete this essential step in their journals or on a computer. If possible, allow time in class for students to organize their reasons and evidence.

TEACHING TIP

Have students complete the step in Essay in Progress 4 independently.

TEACHING TIP

Inform students that recognizing, accommodating, and refuting opposing viewpoints can make a mark on the world. For instance, the 1960s civil rights movement was successful in part because Martin Luther King Jr. was careful to relate to educated whites, appeal to their love of the Bible, of Shakespeare, and of justice (appeals to values), and refute the position that African Americans would "eventually" gain civil rights if they would just wait patiently. King's "Letter from Birmingham Jail" and "I Have a Dream" demonstrate his ability to recognize, accommodate, and refute opposing arguments.

TEACHING TIP: LEARNING STYLES

Encourage creative, social, concrete, spatial, and emotional learners to develop their skill with pragmatic, verbal, rational, and abstract techniques. Independently listing opposing viewpoints and individually assigning strategies for dealing with the opposition are the most efficient ways to structure an argument at this stage.

For more on fallacies, see Chapter 17, p. 570.

and/or refute them. Your argument will be weak if you fail to at least acknowledge opposing viewpoints. Your readers may assume you did not think the issue through or that you dismissed alternative views without seriously considering them. In some situations, you may choose merely to acknowledge opposing ideas. At other times, you may need to accommodate opposing views, refute opposing views, or both.

Create a pro-con list or review the one you made earlier. Then make another list, one of all possible objections to your argument. Try to group the objections together to form two or more points of opposition.

To acknowledge an opposing viewpoint without refuting it, you can mention the opposition in your claim, as shown in this claim about enforcing speed limits.

▶ Although speed limit laws are intended to save lives, the conditions that apply to specific highways should be taken into account in enforcing them.

Notice that the opposing viewpoint appears in a dependent clause attached to an independent clause that states the claim. By including the opposing viewpoint as part of the claim, you show that you take it seriously.

To accommodate an opposing viewpoint, find a portion of the opposing argument that you can build into your argument. One common way to accommodate readers' objections is to suggest alternative causes for a particular situation. For example, suppose your argument defends the competency of most high school teachers. You suspect, however, that some readers think the quality of most high school instruction is poor and attribute it to teachers' laziness or lack of skill. You can accommodate this opposing view by recognizing that there are some high schools in which poor instruction exists. You could then suggest that the poor instruction is often due to a lack of instructional supplies and the disruptive behavior of class members rather than to teachers' incompetence.

If you choose to argue that an opposing view is not sound, you must refute it by pointing out problems or flaws in your opponent's reasoning or evidence. To refute an opponent's reasoning, check to see if your opponent uses faulty reasoning or fallacies. To refute an opponent's evidence, use one or more of the following guidelines.

1. **Give a counterexample** (one that is an exception to the opposing view). For instance, if the opponent argues that dogs are protective, give an example of a situation in which a dog did not protect its owner.

2. **Question the opponent's facts.** If an opponent claims that few professors give essay exams, present statistics demonstrating that a significant percentage of professors do give essay exams.

3. **Demonstrate that an example is not representative.** If an opponent argues that professional athletes are overpaid and cites the salaries of two famous quarterbacks, cite statistics that show that these salaries are not representative of all professional athletes.

4. **Demonstrate that the examples are insufficient.** If an opponent argues that horseback riding is a dangerous sport and offers two examples of riders who were seriously injured, point out that two examples are not sufficient proof.

5. **Question the credibility of an authority.** If an opponent quotes a television personality on welfare reform, point out that she is not a sociologist or public-policy expert and therefore is not an authority on welfare reform.

6. **Question outdated examples, facts, or statistics.** If your opponent presents evidence that is not recent on the need for more campus parking, you can argue that the situation has changed (enrollment has declined, bus service has increased).

7. **Present the full context of a quotation or group of statistical evidence.** If an opponent quotes an authority selectively or cites incomplete statistics from a research study on ozone depletion and its effects on skin cancer, the full context may show that your opponent has "edited" the evidence to suit his or her claim.

ESSAY IN PROGRESS 5

Write your claim on a piece of paper or in a computer file. Below it, list all possible opposing viewpoints. Then describe one or more strategies for acknowledging, accommodating, or refuting each opposing view.

TRYING OUT YOUR IDEAS ON OTHERS

Working in a group of two or three students, present your strategies for acknowledging, accommodating, or refuting opposing views. Critique each other's strategies and suggest others that each writer might use.

Organizing and Drafting

You are now ready to organize your ideas and draft your essay. Organizing and drafting an argument involves deciding on a line of reasoning, choosing a method of organization, and developing your essay accordingly.

Choosing a Line of Reasoning and a Method of Organization

To develop a method of organizing an argument, you need to decide on the line of reasoning you want to follow. As discussed earlier in this chapter, two common lines of reasoning are *induction* and *deduction*. Inductive reasoning begins with evidence and moves to a conclusion. Deductive reasoning starts with an observation that most people accept and shows how a certain conclusion follows from it. As you plan your argument, you may decide to use one or both lines of reasoning to arrive at your conclusion, and this decision will influence how you organize your essay.

Here are four common ways to organize an argument.

Method I	*Method II*	*Method III*	*Method IV*
Claim/thesis	Claim/thesis	Support	Opposing viewpoints
Support	Opposing viewpoints	Opposing viewpoints	Support
Opposing viewpoints	Support	Claim/thesis	Claim/thesis

The method you choose depends on your audience, your purpose, as well as the issue. Depending on your issue and audience, it may be best to state your claim at the outset. Other times, stating the claim at the end of your argument may be more effective. You also need to decide whether to present your reasons and supporting evidence before or after you discuss opposing viewpoints. Finally, decide the order in which you will discuss your reasons and supporting evidence. Will you arrange them from strongest to weakest? Most to least obvious? Familiar to unfamiliar? In planning your organization, try drawing a graphic organizer or making an outline. You might also try different ways of organizing your essay on the computer, creating a computer file for each alternative.

Drafting the Argument Essay

For more on drafting an essay, see Chapter 6.

Once you have chosen a method of organization for your argument, you are ready to write your first draft. Use the following guidelines to draft your essay.

For more on writing effective paragraphs, including introductions and conclusions, see Chapter 6.

1. **Write an effective introduction.** Your introduction should accomplish several things. It should *identify the issue* and *offer needed background information* based on your assessment of your audience's knowledge and experience. In addition, it should *define the terms* to be used in the

argument. For example, if you are writing about sexual harassment in the workplace, you would need to define that term. Most argument essays also include a thesis in the introduction, where you make your *claim*. The way you begin your essay will influence your readers' attitude toward you and your argument. Several strategies can help you to engage your readers right away.

- Open by relating a personal experience, ideally one with which your readers can identify. (See, for example, "When Volunteerism Isn't Noble" by Lynn Steirer, p. 551.)
- Open with an attention-getting remark. (See "Not White, Just Right" by Rachel Jones, p. 592.)
- Open by recognizing a counterargument. (See "Human Cloning? Don't Just Say No" by Ruth Macklin, p. 583.)

2. **Establish an appropriate tone.** The tone you adopt should depend on the issue and the type of claim you make as well as the audience to whom you write. For an argument on a serious issue such as the death penalty, you would probably use a serious, even somber tone. For a call-to-action argument, you might use an energetic, enthusiastic tone. For a disagreeing audience, you might use a friendly, nonthreatening tone. Be sure to avoid overly forceful or dogmatic language and statements that allow no room for opposing viewpoints (such as "It is obvious that . . . "). Also avoid language that may insult or alienate your reader ("Anybody who thinks . . . is . . .").

3. **State your reasons along with your evidence.** Be sure to state clearly the reasons for your claim. Each reason can be used to anchor the evidence that follows it. In an essay about mandatory high school uniforms, for example, you might use a reason (such as "Requiring high school uniforms will reduce clothing costs for parents") as a topic sentence for a paragraph. The rest of the paragraph and perhaps those that follow would then consist of evidence supporting that particular reason.

4. **Cite the sources of your research.** As you present your evidence, be sure to acknowledge and document the sources you use. You must include a citation for each quotation, summary, or paraphrase of ideas or information you borrow from sources. Even when you do not use an author's exact wording, you need to cite the original source.

5. **Use strong transitions.** Make sure you use transitions to move clearly from reason to reason in your argument, as in "*Also relevant* to the issue . . ." and "*Furthermore,* it is important to consider. . . ." Transitions help your reader follow your argument. Also be certain that you have distinguished your reasons and evidence from those of the opposition.

TEACHING TIP

Students who have followed the steps in the Guided Writing Assignment should be ready to compose a first draft independently. However, check to see if any students need to rethink their thesis, their reasons and evidence, or their responses to opposing arguments before drafting. Encourage them to seek the assistance of a peer reviewer or writing center tutor.

For more on documenting sources, see Chapters 19 and 20.

For more on transitions, see Chapter 6, p. 138.

Use a transitional sentence such as "Those opposed to the death penalty claim . . ." to indicate that you are about to introduce an opposing viewpoint. A transition such as "Contrary to what those in favor of the death penalty maintain . . ." can be used to signal a refutation.

6. **Write a satisfying conclusion.** You can end an argument essay in a number of different ways. You need to choose the strategy that will have the strongest impact on your audience.

   - Restate your thesis. (See, "Not White, Just Right" by Rachel Jones, p. 592.)
   - Make a final appeal to values. (See "When Volunteerism Isn't Noble" by Lynn Steirer, p. 551.)
   - Project into the future. (See "Economic Affirmative Action" by Ted Koerth, p. 559.)
   - Urge readers to take a specific action.
   - Call for further study and research. (See "Human Cloning? Don't Just Say No" by Ruth Macklin, p. 583.)

ESSAY IN PROGRESS 6

Using the preceding suggestions for organizing and drafting, choose the line of reasoning your argument will follow and a method of organization and write your first draft.

Analyzing and Revising

If possible, set your draft aside for a day or two before rereading and revising it. Then, as you review your draft, focus on discovering weak areas and on strengthening your overall argument, not on grammar or mechanics. Use one or more of the following suggestions to analyze your draft.

1. Read your draft essay; then put it aside and write one sentence that summarizes your argument. Compare your summary sentence and thesis (statement of claim) to see if they agree or disagree. If they do not agree, your argument needs a stronger focus.

2. Make an outline to help you see how your ideas fit together.

3. Read your essay aloud or ask a friend to do so as you listen. You may "hear" parts of your argument that do not seem to follow.

4. Draw a graphic organizer or update one you drew earlier, using Figure 18.1 as a model. Look to see if the graphic organizer reveals any weak-

Learning Style Options

TEACHING TIP:
LEARNING STYLES

1. For all learners
2. For verbal and ratio-nal learners, but encourage creative learners to work on a revision outline as well.
3. For social learners
4. For spatial learners, but encourage verbal learners to draw a graphic organizer as well.

nesses in your argument (for example, you don't have enough reasons to support your claim).

Use Flowchart 18.1 to guide your analysis. You might also ask a class-mate to review your draft essay using the questions in the flowchart. For each "No" response, ask your reviewer to explain why he or she responded in that way.

For more on the benefits of peer review, see Chapter 7, p. 166.

**FLOWCHART 18.1
REVISING AN ARGUMENT ESSAY**

Questions	Revision Strategies
1. Is the issue defined? Is enough background information provided? Is the issue sufficiently narrow? **No** ⇨	• Ask a friend who is unfamiliar with the issue to ask you questions about it or to tell you what else he or she needs to know. • Assume your reader has never heard of the issue. Write as if you are introducing the issue to the reader. • Use a branching diagram or questions to limit your issue (see Chapter 4, pp. 71–73).
Yes ⇩	
2. Is your claim stated clearly and specifically in your thesis? **No** ⇨	• Without looking at your essay, write a one-sentence summary of what your essay is intended to prove. • Try limiting the issue and claim to make it more specific. • Add a qualifying word or phrase (for example, *may, possibly*) to your thesis.
Yes ⇩	

(Continued on next page)

FLOWCHART 18.1 *(continued)*

Questions		Revision Strategies

3. Is your essay targeted to the intended audience? Do you appeal to your readers' needs and values?

No ⇨

- Examine each reason and piece of evidence. If it will not appeal to your audience, consider replacing it.
- Try to discover needs, values, and common experiences you share with your readers. Add appeals based on those needs, values, and experiences.
- If your audience is unfamiliar with the issue, add more background information.

Yes ⇩

4. Are your reasons and evidence convincing?

No ⇨

- State each reason clearly; then present evidence to support it.
- Brainstorm or conduct research to discover more reasons or stronger evidence.
- Consider using other types of evidence.

Yes ⇩

5. Are there any errors in your reasoning?

No ⇨

- Check for and omit faulty reasoning and fallacies (see Chapter 17, p. 570).
- Check the progression of your argument and your use of inductive and deductive reasoning by creating an outline or graphic organizer.

Yes ⇩

(Continued on next page)

FLOWCHART 18.1 *(continued)*

Questions		Revision Strategies

6. Do you acknowledge, accommodate, and/or refute opposing viewpoints?

 No

 Yes

- Try acknowledging an opposing view in your statement of claim.
- Ask a classmate to help you find a portion of an opposing argument that you can build into your argument.
- Look for ways to refute an opponent's evidence (see pp. 604–605) and for errors in your opponent's reasoning (see Chapter 17, pp. 570–71).

7. Is your method of organization effective for your argument?

 No

Yes

- Experiment with one or more other methods of organization (see p. 606).

8. Is each paragraph well developed and focused on a separate part of the argument? Are the introduction and conclusion effective?

 No

Yes

- Be sure each paragraph has a topic sentence and supporting evidence (see Chapter 6).
- Consider combining closely related paragraphs.
- Consider splitting a paragraph that covers more than one part of the argument.
- Revise your introduction and conclusion so that they meet the guidelines in Chapter 6 (pp. 140–46).

TEACHING TIP

Encourage students to consult a writing center tutor for further review of the revision.

For more on keeping an error log, see Chapter 8, p. 201.

TEACHING TIP: COLLABORATIVE WRITING

Have students work in pairs to edit their revised essays for errors in pronoun reference and in the use of *were* to indicate a hypothetical situation.

ESSAY IN PROGRESS 7

Revise your draft using Flowchart 18.1 and any comments you received from peer reviewers.

Editing and Proofreading

The last step is to check your revised essay for errors in grammar, spelling, punctuation, and mechanics. In addition, be sure to check your error log for the types of errors you tend to make.

As you edit and proofread your argument essay, watch out for the following two grammatical errors in particular.

1. Make sure that you use the subjunctive mood correctly. In an argument, you often write about what would or might happen in the future. When you use the verb *be* to speculate about conditions in the future, *were* is used in place of *was* to indicate a hypothetical situation.

   ▶ If all animal research ~~was~~ *were* outlawed, progress in the control of human diseases would be slowed dramatically.

2. Look for and correct pronouns that don't refer back to a clear antecedent. A pronoun must refer to another noun or pronoun, called its *antecedent*. The pronoun's antecedent should be clearly named—not just implied.

   ▶ Children of divorced parents often are shuttled between two homes, and ~~that~~ *this lack of stability* can be confusing and disturbing to them.

ESSAY IN PROGRESS 8

Edit and proofread your essay, paying particular attention to your use of the verb *be* in sentences that speculate about the future and to pronoun reference. Don't forget to look for errors you often make.

STUDENTS WRITE

Sarah McCreight was a student at Linn-Benton Community College when she wrote the following argument essay in response to an assignment. As you read the essay, notice that McCreight uses library and Internet sources to support her ideas and build her argument. Also highlight the writer's thesis, reasons, and evidence as you read.

PREREADING QUESTION

What do you think are McCreight's main reasons for riding the bus?

Spend a Little, Save a Lot

Sarah McCreight

If you're a driver, you can hop in your car at any   1
hour of the day or night and speed off to any destination you please. However, you may find that your lungs
hurt from the pollution on the roads, your wallet hurts
from the gas and repair bills, and your head hurts from
the stress of avoiding accidents and navigating through
heavy traffic. There is a very simple way to help reduce
pollution, save money, and be safer all at the same
time: ride the bus.

Cutting back on pollution is something that every-   2
body should consider doing. According to the American
Public Transit Association, "On average, riding mass
transit," more specifically the bus, "instead of driving
may cut hydrocarbon emissions that produce smog by 90%,
carbon monoxide by more than 75%, and nitrogen oxide by
a range of 15% to 75%" (Artunian 17). Even a single person can make a difference by riding the bus. By not driving a car for one year, that one person can save "9.1
pounds of hydrocarbons, 62.5 pounds of carbon monoxide,
and 4.9 pounds of nitrogen oxide" (Artunian 17). If more
people park their cars and ride the bus, there will be
fewer vehicles on the road to give off polluting fumes.

Along with helping the environment, riding the bus   3
will help you save money. The more you ride the bus, the
less money you will spend on gas and maintenance for
your car. Of course, you have to pay to ride the bus,

but you will spend far less on bus fares than you now
spend on gasoline and repairs for your vehicle. In Corvallis, Oregon, a one-year bus pass for an adult costs
$65, and a pass for a youth, a senior citizen, or a dis-
abled person costs $46 (<u>Transit</u> 1). Compare this to the
cost of driving a car for one year. The average annual
cost of driving a car is between $3,312 and $5,220
(Camph 3), and that does not include the cost of maintenance and insurance.

4   Another benefit of riding the bus is that it may
help save your life or someone else's life. Buses can be
hit just as cars can; however, the likelihood of injury
while riding a bus is not as great because buses are
nearly thirty-seven times less dangerous than automobiles
(Camph 3). Since buses are so large, they are able to
withstand the force of a collision, and you, as a passenger, are less at risk than you would be in a car. Of
course, there are fewer accidents in buses since the
drivers are trained professionals who know how to avoid
collisions. "Based on 1994 data, there are over 190,000
fewer annual deaths, injuries, and accidents than would
be the case if people who use transit made those same
trips via auto" (Camph 3).

5   Besides decreasing your chances of being injured in
a road accident, riding the bus can cut way back on your
stress level. While driving from point A to point B, you
may encounter careless drivers, traffic jams, and other
obstacles that may increase your level of anxiety. When
you ride the bus, you can let the driver worry about
problems on the road while you sit back and relax, read,
or even get some work done.

6   Of course, if you are on a tight schedule, riding
the bus can be somewhat inconvenient, since the bus may
not always reach its stop on time. However, because of
traffic jams and other unexpected delays, drivers often
do not arrive at their destination on time either. Driving offers its own set of inconveniences as well:
entering a cold car on a wintry morning or a hot car on

a ninety-degree day, having to stop to purchase gas when you're running late, and so forth. Besides, if you ride the bus you will never have to search for a parking space.

Without public transit, another five million cars 7 and 27,000 new lane miles would be added to our nation's highways, there would be 200,000 more fatalities, injuries, and accidents every year--costing billions of dollars--and there would be 367 million more hours spent sitting in traffic jams each year (Camph 1-2). Since we do have public transit, why not try riding the bus for a change? After all, riding the bus helps not only you but your fellow travelers as well.

Works Cited

Artunian, Judy. "Want to Clear the Air? Hop on the Bus!" Current Health 2 Jan. 1995: 16-17.

Transit Guide and Route Map. Map. Corvallis: Corvallis Transportation Services, 1996.

Camph, Donald H. "Dollars and Sense: The Economic Case for Public Transportation in America." CTTA Online. Community Transportation Association of America. 8 July 1997. 18 Nov. 1998 <http://www.ctaa.org/pubs/dollars>.

Analyzing the Essay

1. What types of evidence does McCreight offer to support her reasons?
2. Does McCreight acknowledge opposing viewpoints? If so, how? Does she attempt to accommodate them, or does she refute them?
3. McCreight mentions several disadvantages of driving a car. Do you feel this discussion belongs in the essay? Why or why not?
4. Evaluate McCreight's title, introduction, and conclusion.

Reacting to the Essay: Discussion and Journal Writing

1. Do you think McCreight's essay is convincing? Why or why not?

POSSIBLE ANSWERS: ANALYZING THE ESSAY

1. Statistics and common knowledge
2. Yes; she notes that buses may not always be on time, but refutes that objection by pointing out that drivers are often late as well.
3. Yes; the disadvantages of driving a car support the argument: Bus riding (a) causes less pollution than car driving; (b) saves the money that would otherwise be spent on gasoline, repairs, car payments, and insurance; (c) is safer than driving a car; (d) is less stressful than driving a car.
4. *Title:* Catchy, introduces idea of thriftiness of bus riding. *Introduction:* Concisely introduces main problems with driving a car. *Conclusion:* Extends argument to examine negative impact on society if public transit were eliminated.

POSSIBLE ANSWERS: REACTING TO THE ESSAY

1. Responses will vary.
2. Responses will vary; possible disadvantages include lack of seat belts on buses and lack of control over routes and schedules.

2. McCreight argues that riding the bus is beneficial to the environment. Write a journal entry discussing the disadvantages of bus riding that McCreight does not acknowledge.

READING AN ARGUMENT

The following section provides advice for reading an argument as well as two essays that take opposing views on a current issue: the effects of divorce on American children. Each essay illustrates the characteristics of argument covered in this chapter and provides opportunities to examine, analyze, and react to the writer's ideas. For additional information on reading arguments critically, see Chapter 17, "Reading Arguments."

WORKING WITH TEXT: RESPONDING TO ARGUMENTS

For more on reading arguments, see Chapter 17, especially the discussions of types of claims (p. 553) and types of evidence (p. 554).

Reading arguments requires careful attention and analysis; you not only must follow the writer's line of reasoning but also must analyze and evaluate it. Plan on reading an argument several times. Read it the first time to get an overview. Read it several times more to analyze and critique it. If you find an argument difficult to follow, fill in a graphic organizer (see p. 593) to help you as you read.

What to Look for, Highlight, and Annotate

1. **The issue.** Identify and highlight the issue and notice how the writer introduces it and the background information he or she provides. Highlight definitions of key terms.

2. **The claim.** Identify and highlight the writer's statement of claim about the issue. Notice any qualifying or limiting words.

3. **Evidence and reasons.** Study and highlight the types of evidence the writer uses to support the claim — facts, statistics, expert opinion, examples, and personal experience. Is the evidence relevant, accurate, current, and typical? Does the writer state reasons before introducing evidence? Write annotations indicating your initial reactions to or questions about the reasons or evidence.

For more on annotating, see Chapter 2, p. 38.

For more on needs and values, see Chapter 17, p. 555.

4. **Emotional appeals.** Analyze the needs and values to which the writer appeals.

5. **Organization and reasoning.** Is the argument organized effectively? Does the writer follow a deductive or an inductive line of reasoning? Evaluate the writer's premises and conclusions, and note whether any logical fallacies are made.

6. **Opposing viewpoints.** Does the writer acknowledge, accommodate, or refute opposing views? Highlight each instance.

How to Find Ideas to Write About

Since you may be asked to write a response to an argument, keep an eye out for ideas to write about as you read.

For more on discovering ideas for a response paper, see Chapter 3.

1. **Additional supporting evidence.** Use annotations to record additional examples, personal experiences, or other evidence that comes to mind in support of the claim. These ideas may be helpful in writing your own essay in support of this writer's claim. They might also provide a start for a paper on one aspect of the writer's argument.

2. **Opposing viewpoints and evidence.** Note any opposing views that come to mind as you read. Record events or phenomena that do not support the claim or that contradict one of the author's reasons. Keep the following question in mind: "When would this not be true?" The ideas you generate may be useful in writing an essay in which you support an opposing claim.

3. **Related issues.** Think of issues that are similar to the one under discussion in the essay. You may notice, for example, that the line of reasoning applied to the issue of "riding the bus rather than driving" may in part be applicable to the issue of "walking rather than riding."

Keep these guidelines in mind as you read the following pair of essays by Barbara Ehrenreich and John Leo on the issue of divorce reform.

In Defense of Splitting Up: The Growing Antidivorce Movement Is Blind to the Costs of Bad Marriages
Barbara Ehrenreich

Barbara Ehrenreich is a well-known social commentator and critic. She is the author or coauthor of a number of books, among them Fear of Falling: The Inner Life of the Middle Class *(1989),* The Worst Years of Our Life *(1990), and* The Snarling Citizen *(1995). The following essay appeared in* Time, *a weekly newsmagazine, in 1996. As you read the selection, highlight Ehrenreich's claim, reasons, and supporting evidence.*

PREREADING QUESTION

For what main reason does Ehrenreich defend divorce?

No one seems much concerned about children when the subject   1
is welfare or Medicaid cuts, but mention divorce, and tears flow for
their tender psyches. Legislators in half a dozen states are planning
to restrict divorce on the grounds that it may cause teen suicide, an

inability to "form lasting attachments" and possibly also the piercing of nipples and noses.

2   But if divorce itself hasn't reduced America's youth to emotional cripples, then the efforts to restrict it undoubtedly will. First, there's the effect all this antidivorce rhetoric is bound to have on the children of people already divorced—and we're not talking about some offbeat minority. At least 37% of American children live with divorced parents, and these children already face enough tricky interpersonal situations without having to cope with the public perception that they're damaged goods.

3   Fortunately for the future of the republic, the alleged psyche-scarring effects of divorce have been grossly exaggerated. The most frequently cited study, by California therapist Judith Wallerstein, found that 41% of the children of divorced couples are "doing poorly, worried, underachieving, deprecating and often angry" years after their parents' divorce. But this study has been faulted for including only 60 couples, two-thirds of whom were deemed to lack "adequate psychological functioning" even before they split, and all of whom were self-selected seekers of family therapy. Furthermore, there was no control group of, say, miserable couples who stayed together.

4   As for some of the wilder claims, such as "teen suicide has tripled as divorces have tripled": well, roller-blading has probably tripled in the same time period too, and that's hardly a reason to ban in-line skates.

5   In fact, the current antidivorce rhetoric slanders millions of perfectly wonderful, high-functioning young people, my own children and most of their friends included. Studies that attempt to distinguish between the effects of divorce and those of the income decline so often experienced by divorced mothers have found no lasting psychological damage attributable to divorce per se. Check out a typical college dorm, and you'll find people enthusiastically achieving and forming attachments until late into the night. Ask about family, and you'll hear about Mom and Dad . . . and Stepmom and Stepdad.

6   The real problems for kids will begin when the antidivorce movement starts getting its way. For one thing, the more militant among its members want to "re-stigmatize" divorce with the cultural equivalent of a scarlet D. Sadly though, divorce is already stigmatized in ways that are harmful to children. Studies show that teachers consistently interpret children's behavior more negatively when they are told that the children are from "broken" homes—and, as we know, teachers' expectations have an effect on children's performance. If the idea is to help the children of divorce, then the goal should be to de-stigmatize divorce among all who interact with them—teachers, neighbors, playmates.

Then there are the likely effects on children of the proposed
restrictions themselves. Antidivorce legislators want to repeal no-
fault divorce laws and return to the system in which one parent has
to prove the other guilty of adultery, addiction or worse. True, the
divorce rate rose after the introduction of no-fault divorce in the late
'60s and '70s. But the divorce rate was already rising at a healthy clip
before that, so there's no guarantee that the repeal of no-fault laws
will reduce the divorce rate now. In fact, one certain effect will be to
generate more divorces of the rancorous, potentially child-harming
variety. If you think, "Mommy and Daddy aren't getting along"
sounds a little too blithe, would you rather "Daddy (or Mommy) has
been sleeping around"?

Not that divorce is an enviable experience for any of the parties
involved. But just as there are bad marriages, there are, as sociologist
Constance Ahrons argues, "good divorces," in which both parents
maintain their financial and emotional responsibility for the kids.
Maybe the reformers should concentrate on improving the quality of
divorces—by, for example, requiring prenuptial agreements specify-
ing how the children will be cared for in the event of a split.

The antidivorce movement's interest in the emotional status of
children would be more convincing if it were linked to some concern
for their physical survival. The most destructive feature of divorce,
many experts argue, is the poverty that typically ensues when the children are left with a low-earning mother, and the way out of this
would be to toughen child-support collection and strengthen the
safety net of supportive services for low-income families—including
childcare, Medicaid and welfare.

Too difficult? Too costly? Too ideologically distasteful compared
with denouncing divorce and, by implication, the divorced and their
children? Perhaps. But sometimes grownups have to do difficult and
costly things, whether they feel like doing them or not. For the sake
of the children, that is. ∎

Examining the Reading

1. What is Ehrenreich's claim about the divorce issue?
2. What action does Ehrenreich call for?
3. Summarize the writer's argument.
4. Explain the meaning of each of the following words as it is used in the reading: *rhetoric* (paragraph 2), *deprecating* (3), *stigmatized* (6), *rancorous* (7), and *blithe*
   (7). Refer to your dictionary as needed.

POSSIBLE ANSWERS:
EXAMINING THE
READING

1. Claim: Efforts to
   restrict divorce will
   hurt America's youth:
   "But if divorce . . .
   will" (paragraph 2)
2. She calls for legisla-
   tors not to repeal no-
   fault divorce laws (7),
   for legislators to
   improve the quality of
   divorces (8), and for
   economic support for
   single-parent families
   (9).
3. The antidivorce move-
   ment is unfair to children of divorced
   couples because it
   stigmatizes them as
   damaged goods. The
   movement's rhetoric
   is based on a flawed
   study that claims children of divorce are
   lower functioning
   than children of intact
   families. The claim
   that suicide among
   teens has tripled
   along with divorce is
   based on a false
   cause-effect relation-
   ship. Repealing no-
   fault divorce laws will
   not eliminate divorces
   but will make them
   more painful. Just as
   there are good mar-
   riages, there are
   "good divorces."
   Reformers should
   improve the proce-
   dures for getting a
   divorce and ensure
   the economic well-
   being of children of
   divorce.
4. *Rhetoric:* slanted language used to per-
   suade; *deprecating:*
   protesting or belit-
   tling; *stigmatized:*
   branded as inferior;
   rancorous: full of ill
   will, malicious; *blithe:*
   casual, flippant

Analyzing the Reading

1. What reasons does Ehrenreich offer to support her claim? What types of evidence are used to support each reason? Evaluate the evidence: Choose several examples from the reading and explain how they are relevant, accurate, current, and typical.

2. Identify the opposing viewpoints that Ehrenreich addresses. How does she refute each one?

3. How does Ehrenreich establish her credibility on the issue? What, if anything, in the essay could possibly undermine her credibility?

4. What type of audience—agreeing, disagreeing, neutral or wavering—is Ehrenreich writing for? To what needs and values does the writer appeal? How do her emotional appeals suit her audience?

5. Describe the writer's tone. Does her use of such expressions as "grossly exaggerated" (paragraph 3) and "wilder claims" (4) strengthen or weaken her argument? Explain.

Reacting to the Reading: Discussion and Journal Writing

1. Do you agree that "No one seems much concerned about children when the subject is welfare or Medicaid cuts, but mention divorce, and tears flow for their tender psyches" (paragraph 1)? Why or why not?

2. Discuss why you agree or disagree with Ehrenreich's observation that "teachers' expectations have an effect on children's performance" (paragraph 6). Cite examples from your own or others' experience to support your view.

3. Write a journal entry in response to Ehrenreich's statement that "divorce is . . . stigmatized in ways that are harmful to children" (paragraph 6). Explain how your own observations of or experience with the effects of divorce on children do or do not support this view.

 ## *Where Marriage Is a Scary Word*
John Leo

John Leo is a contributing editor for U.S. News & World Report. *He previously held positions as an associate editor and senior writer at* Time *magazine and as a reporter for the* New York Times. *The following article originally appeared in* U.S. News & World Report, *a weekly newsmagazine, in February 1996. As you read the selection, highlight Leo's claim, reasons, and supporting evidence.*

If you go to a panel discussion in Washington, D.C., on "Reframing Family Values," do not expect much attention to either family or values. Instead you will be flooded with charts and graphs about heads of household and income distribution. The point of this exercise is to show that behavior and values have nothing to do with the crisis of the American family. Everything is economic. If the awkward term "family values" comes up, it will be discussed gingerly as some sort of mysterious and optional product that some households have while others do not. Then back to the charts.

This was true last week on a panel at the Woodrow Wilson Center. When my turn came, I attempted a few chart-free comments: To bolster the family, we certainly have to come to terms with '90s economics but also with '60s values, particularly the core value that self-fulfillment is a trump card over all obligations and expectations. By breaking the taboos against unwed motherhood and casual divorce, we have created the world's most dangerous environment for children—a new fatherless America filling up with kids who are so emotionally damaged by their parents' behavior that they may have a lot of trouble making commitments and forming families themselves.

The Murphy Brown* argument is now over, and Dan Quayle has won—an avalanche of evidence shows that single-parent kids are way more vulnerable than two-parent kids are to all sorts of damage, in all races and at all income levels, under all kinds of conditions. The mountain of evidence is just too high to keep arguing that different family forms are equally valuable or that "the quality of the home is the important thing, not the number of parents in it."

Children of divorce.   Barbara Dafoe Whitehead, who wrote the 1993 "Dan Quayle Was Right" article in the *Atlantic Monthly*, says that as she travels around the country to colleges, she is struck by the number of angry, emotionally scarred children of divorce she runs into. They can function and often get high marks, so researchers may not pick up the social cost, but it is being paid. And these are the privileged ones.

Since the obvious can come as a thunderbolt on Washington panels, much umbrage was taken at my comments. In closing the panel, the co-moderator, a well-known economist, said that a woman's right to have a baby without having the father around is what feminism is all about. In shaking her hand afterward, I remarked, perhaps a bit ungraciously, that intentionally planning to

---

Murphy Brown: a television series that ran from 1988 to 1998. Murphy, a television newswoman, had a child out of wedlock during the 1992 season; this plot development became an issue in the 1992 presidential campaign.

1

2

3

4

5

fair to children; amicability of divorce for children's sake.
5. Tone is somewhat sarcastic, as in "possibly also the piercing of nipples and noses" (1). The expressions denigrate the opposition; some readers might argue that she does not establish a common ground, whereas others may appreciate her pull-no-punches approach.

POSSIBLE ANSWERS: REACTING TO THE READING

Responses will vary.

PREREADING QUESTION

Do you think an "intellectual and cultural elite" has contributed to a decline in the nuclear family? Why or why not?

POSSIBLE ANSWERS: EXAMINING THE READING (p. 623)

1. Claim: "It's impossible to overestimate . . . nuclear family" (paragraph 6).
2. He calls for making divorce "rarer by trying to restore gravity to both marriage and separation" (10).
3. The author's experience on the panel suggests the current emphasis is on economics and on accepting a range of family styles, not on traditional marriage or family values. The 1960s values of self-fulfillment are catching up with kids of the 1990s; considerable evidence shows that

(Continued on next page)

have a fatherless family was like setting out intentionally to build a Yugo.*

6   It's impossible to overestimate how deeply our intellectual and cultural elite is implicated in the continuing decline of the American nuclear family. It's not just the constant jeering at the intact family as an Ozzie-and-Harriet* relic of the Eisenhower era. It's the constant broadening of the definition of what a family is (for example, a New Jersey judge said that six college kids on summer vacation constituted a family) and the equally constant attempt to undermine policies that might help the intact family survive.

7   Maggie Gallagher, in her . . . book, *The Abolition of Marriage,* says that marriage "has been ruthlessly dismantled, piece by piece, under the influence of those who . . . believed that the abolition of marriage was necessary to advance human freedom." Demoted to one lifestyle among many, marriage is no longer viewed by the elite as a crucial social institution but as a purely private act.

8   There are many ways to show this worldview in action. At its annual convention, the American Association for Marriage and Family Therapy conducts hundreds of workshops, but marriage is hardly ever listed as a topic. It showed up twice on the 1992 program, not at all in 1993. In 1994, the convention gave a major press award to a magazine article arguing that fathers weren't necessary in the home. At last November's convention, the status was still quo: Two mentions for marital on the entire program, none for marriage.

9   This is an odd business. The therapeutic custodians of marriage don't believe in it anymore and seem determined not to bolster, promote or even talk about it much. The "M" word seems to have disappeared from the association's basic vocabulary. Why? Probably because the group is committed to a nonjudgmental culture in which all relationships are equally valuable, endlessly negotiable and disposable. So talk about marriage as a long-term, serious commitment that must be shored up or preferred over other "lifestyles" becomes dicey and embarrassing.

10   The next skirmish in this continuing war between the elite and non-elite worldviews will be divorce reform. The elite will depict it as a punitive, backward, religious attempt to lock people into bad marriages. But that's not it. The point is that wide-open, anything-goes, no-fault divorce has unexpectedly created its own accelerating cul-

---

Yugo: a low-cost, no-frills automobile that was manufactured in Yugoslavia and sold in the United States from 1986 to 1991. It was unreliable and was often the subject of jokes.

The Adventures of Ozzie and Harriet: a television situation comedy that ran from 1952 to 1966. It portrayed a happy family with minor, easily resolved problems.

ture of noncommitment. Under no-fault divorce, marriage increasingly carries no more inherent social weight than a weekend fling in the Bahamas. The goal is not to halt divorce but to make it rarer by trying to restore gravity to both marriage and separation. But given the attitudes of our elite, the battle will be uphill all the way. ■

Examining the Reading

1. What is Leo's claim about the issue?
2. Does Leo make a call for action? If so, what action does he recommend?
3. Summarize the writer's argument.
4. Explain the meaning of each of the following words as it is used in the reading: *taboos* (paragraph 2), *umbrage* (5), *elite* (6), *dicey* (9), and *punitive* (10). Refer to your dictionary as needed.

Analyzing the Reading

1. What reasons does Leo offer to support his claim? What types of evidence are used to support each reason? Evaluate the evidence: Choose several examples from the reading and explain how they are relevant, accurate, current, and typical.
2. Identify the opposing viewpoints that Leo addresses. Does he refute opposing views? If so, how?
3. How does Leo establish his credibility on the issue? What, if anything, in the essay could possibly undermine his credibility?
4. What type of audience—agreeing, disagreeing, neutral, or wavering—is Leo writing for? To what needs and values does the writer appeal? How do his emotional appeals suit his audience?
5. Describe the writer's tone. How might Leo's tone appeal to his audience?

Reacting to the Reading: Discussion and Journal Writing

1. Do you agree that "unwed motherhood and casual divorce . . . have created the world's most dangerous environment for children" (paragraph 2)? Why or why not?
2. Discuss why you agree or disagree with the opponent's view that "'the quality of the home is the important thing, not the number of parents in it'" (paragraph 3). Cite examples from your own or others' experience to support your view.

of the AAMFT programs is relevant and current; it also seems accurate, but the concerns of convention speakers may not be typical of all marriage therapists.

2. *Opposing viewpoint:* The nuclear family is an outdated family model; we need to accept single-parent families. *Refutation:* Refers to the research as "a mountain of evidence" (3).

3. He establishes credibility by citing his invitation to speak at a conference on family values. He undermines his credibility by not citing more specific research studies in support of his claim.

4. *Audience:* Agreeing, neutral or wavering. *Needs and values:* Argues that strong families and marriages are social needs; appeals to traditional values of marriage and family by citing Quayle, Whitehead, Gallagher, and the AAMFT.

5. Tone is sarcastic; an agreeing audience might find his tone bracing, while a neutral or wavering audience might be put off by it.

POSSIBLE ANSWERS: REACTING TO THE READING

Responses will vary.

3. Write a journal entry in response to the economist's view "that a woman's right to have a baby without having the father around is what feminism is all about" (paragraph 5).

Integrating the Readings

1. Which author, Ehrenreich or Leo, deals with a broader issue concerning divorce? Explain your response.

2. Compare the reasons and types of evidence both writers offer in support of their claims. Which writer's argument do you find most convincing? Explain why you think so.

3. In your opinion, which writer refutes opposing views more effectively? Explain why you find the refutation convincing.

4. Compare how the two writers organize their argument essays. Then look for areas of strength and weakness in the organization.

APPLYING YOUR SKILLS: ADDITIONAL ESSAY ASSIGNMENTS

To Persuade Your Reader

Write an argument essay on one of the following topics. Narrow the topic to focus on an issue that can be debated, such as a problem that could be solved by reforms or legislation. Depending on the topic you choose, you may need to do library or Internet research. Your audience is made up of your classmates and instructor.

1. Professional sports

2. College policies

3. Traffic laws

4. Television or movie ratings

5. Term limits for members of Congress

Cases Using Argument

1. Write an essay for a sociology course, arguing your position on the following statement: The race of a child and that of the prospective parents should be taken into consideration in making adoption decisions.

2. Write a proposal, as part of your job as copy editor at a city newspaper, explaining and justifying your request to work at home one day per week. Incorporate into your argument the fact that you could use your home computer, which is connected to the newspaper's computer network.

Academic
Applications

Chapter 19

Suppose you are enrolled in a seminar on the environment. Your instructor gives the class a number of photographs and directs each student to choose one and write a paper about the environmental issue it reflects. You've chosen the picture shown on the opposite page.

Writing Quick Start

Write a brief statement describing the environmental issue the photograph represents. Consider where you might go to learn more about this issue, and make a list of the sources you would consult.

Planning a Paper with Sources

TEACHING TIP: COLLABORATIVE WRITING

In groups of two or three, students should think of one of each of the following types of sources: reference book, textbook, library book, periodical, government publication.

TEACHING TIP:
CHAPTER OVERVIEW

• In this chapter, stu-
dents learn about *pri-
mary* versus *secondary*
sources and how to
use them as support
in an essay (by citing
relevant examples, sta-
tistics, expert testi-
mony, background
information, and other
types of evidence).
• This chapter empha-
sizes that a paper with
sources does not just
string a series of
quotes or statistics
together but has a the-
sis, topic sentences,
analyses, and so forth.
Also, the writer's *voice*
guides readers through
a paper with sources.
Ask students to think
of voice as a master of
ceremonies and to
imagine a talk-show
host who merely
passes the microphone
around rather than
guiding the conversa-
tion.
• Students are intro-
duced to the interdis-
ciplinary technique
of *viewing a topic from
different perspectives*
(psychological, socio-
logical, scientific/
technical, historical,
political, economic) in
order to generate ideas
about it.
• Students learn three
systems of *note-taking*—
note cards, computer-
ized notes, and anno-
tated photocopies or
printouts—and other
strategies for avoiding
plagiarism.

What issue did you write about? What sources of information did you list? Now suppose you were to write a paper about the topic in your statement. What steps would you follow? What information would you need to support your ideas? How would you locate the sources you listed? What system would you use to extract information from the sources? This chapter will answer these and other questions about how to locate and use sources. It will also lead you through the process of planning a research paper.

Sources of information come in many forms. They include all print materials (books, newspapers, magazines, brochures, scholarly journals), media sources (television, radio, videotapes), and electronic sources (Internet, CD-ROM, email). Interviews, personal observations, and surveys are also sources of information. You can use sources in a variety of ways. Depending on the assignment, you may plan a paper that is based primarily on your own experience but discover aspects of the topic that need additional support. You would use sources to locate the needed information. At other times, you may start a paper by checking several sources to narrow your topic or to become more familiar with a topic before writing about it. Finally you may be asked to write a research paper, which requires the most extensive use of sources. Research papers are covered in detail in Chapter 20. Regardless of the kind of paper you write, always credit any source of information that is not your own.

You will have many opportunities to use sources in the writing you do in college and at work (see the accompanying box for a few examples).

WHEN SHOULD YOU USE SOURCES?

Sources are classified as *primary* or *secondary*. **Primary sources** include historical documents (letters, diaries, speeches), literary works, autobiographies, original research reports, eyewitness accounts, and your own interviews, observations, or correspondence. For example, a report on the results of a study on heart disease

---

SCENES FROM COLLEGE AND THE WORKPLACE

• For an *astronomy* course, you are asked to write a two-page report on black holes. Your textbook contains basic information on the subject, but you need to consult other sources to complete the assignment.

• For a *contemporary American history* assignment, you need to write a five-page paper on a current issue (such as national health insurance), explaining the issue and reporting on current developments.

• As *supervisor* of a health care facility, you decide to conduct a survey of the staff to determine employees' interest in flexible working hours.

written by the medical researcher who conducted the study is a primary source. A novel or short story by William Faulkner is also a primary source. In addition, what *you* say or write can be a primary source. If you conduct an interview with a heart-attack survivor for a paper on heart disease, your interview is a primary source.

Secondary sources report or comment on primary sources. A journal article that reviews several previously published research reports on heart disease is a secondary source. A book written about Faulkner by a literary critic or biographer is a secondary source.

TEACHING TIP

Schedule your class for a library tour with a reference librarian. Students will need to know how to use the library catalog; where to find reference books, microfilm, academic journals, and so on; as well as where and how to access the Internet.

Using Sources to Add Detail to an Essay

The following suggestions will help you use sources to add detail to a paper and thus provide stronger support for your thesis.

- **Make general comments more specific.** Instead of saying that "the crime rate in New York City has decreased over the past few years," offer statistics from a source that indicate by what percentage the rate has decreased.

- **Give specific examples that illustrate your main points.** If you are writing about why some companies refuse to accept orders over the Internet, locate a business that refuses to conduct business electronically and give details about its refusal.

- **Supply technical information.** If you are writing about a drug used to treat high blood pressure, gather information from sources about its manufacture, ingredients, effectiveness, cost, and side effects, so that you can make informed, accurate comments.

- **Support opinions with evidence.** If you state that more federal assistance is needed for public education, locate and provide statistics, facts, expert opinion, and other evidence that indicate why more funds are needed.

- **Provide historical information.** If you are writing about space stations, find out when the first one was established, what country launched it, and so forth to add background information to your paper.

- **Locate information about similar events.** If you are writing about an incident in which a president intervened in a labor strike, find out if presidents have intervened in similar strikes in the past. Use this information to make comparisons and point out unique actions.

Using Sources to Write a Research Paper

A research paper requires you to collect and analyze information on a topic from a variety of sources. Depending on your topic, you may use primary sources, secondary sources, or both. For a research paper comparing the speeches of Abraham

Lincoln to those of Franklin D. Roosevelt, you would probably read and analyze the speeches (primary sources). You might also create your own primary source by interviewing a local historian. But for a research paper comparing Lincoln's and Roosevelt's domestic policies, you would probably rely on several histories or biographies (secondary sources). Many research papers employ both primary and secondary sources. While researching Lincoln's and Roosevelt's domestic policies, for instance, you might consult some original documents (primary sources).

Regardless of the sources you use, your task is to organize and present your findings in a meaningful way. When you write a research paper, you don't simply "glue together" the facts, statistics, information, and quotations you find in the sources you consult. Like any other essay-length writing, a research paper has a thesis, and the thesis is supported throughout the paper. Although the information from outside sources is not your own, the interpretation you give it should be your own.

For more on systems for documenting sources, see Chapter 20, pp. 682 (MLA) and 693 (APA).

In a research paper, it is essential to acknowledge your sources fairly and correctly. To do so, you include parenthetical, or in-text, citations in the body of the paper and a corresponding list of works cited or references at the end of the paper.

Whether you use sources to add detail to an essay or to write a research paper, it is helpful to approach the process of locating, evaluating, and using sources in a systematic way. Figure 19.1 presents an overview of this process. The following sections of this chapter will guide you through the steps of the research process for planning a paper with sources.

FIGURE 19.1
LOCATING AND USING SOURCES: AN OVERVIEW

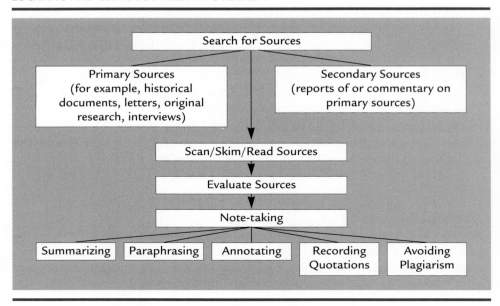

PLANNING YOUR PAPER

While it may seem like a good idea to start your research in the library or on the Internet, usually the best place to begin is at your desk. There you can think about and analyze the assignment and devise a plan for its completion. This section describes several tasks that you should accomplish before you begin your research.

Defining the Assignment

Not all assignments have the same purpose. Many are informative, asking you to *explain* (for example, "explain the treatment options for breast cancer") or to *explore* an issue (for example, "examine the pros and cons of legalizing casino gambling"). Still others are persuasive, asking you to take and support a particular position (for example, "defend or argue against your college's proposal to eliminate athletic scholarships"). Before you begin researching an assigned topic, be sure you understand what your instructor expects you to accomplish in the paper. If your instructor announces the assignment in class, write down what he or she says, including any examples that are given. Although this step may seem unnecessary at first, when you are ready to tackle the assignment days or weeks later, you may find it helpful to review exactly what the assignment requires. In addition, make sure you understand any limits on the topic, any minimum or maximum length requirements, the due date (and late penalties), and the minimum number of sources to be consulted. Finally, be sure you know which documentation style you are expected to use in the paper.

Choosing an Interesting and Workable Topic

Most assignments for essays as well as for research papers allow you to choose your topic. You will save time in the long run if you spend enough time at the outset choosing one that is interesting and workable. Too many students waste hours researching a topic that they finally realize is too difficult, broad, or ordinary. Here are some tips for choosing a topic.

1. **Choose an interesting topic.** You will find the assignment more enjoyable and you will be able to write more enthusiastically when you work with a topic that captures your interest. If you have trouble choosing a topic, brainstorm with a classmate or friend. A conversation will often help you discover new angles on ordinary topics.

2. **Choose a manageable topic.** Make sure you can adequately cover the topic within the required length of your paper. For example, don't try to write about all of the various family counseling programs in a five- to ten-page paper. Instead, limit your topic to one type of counseling program, such as programs for troubled adolescents.

3. **Avoid ordinary topics.** Familiar subjects that have been thoroughly explained in many sources seldom make good topics. For example, the topic of operant conditioning, which involves the use of rewards and punishments to change behavior, is explained in detail in most introductory psychology texts and may not leave much for you to research. However, the topic "Using operant conditioning to improve children's study habits" might be interesting and challenging.

4. **Avoid topics that are very current.** Topics that are currently in the news or for which a new breakthrough has just been reported often do not make good choices because in many cases sufficient, reliable information is not yet available. In February 1997, just after a sheep had been cloned by a Scottish researcher, sketchy reports appeared in newspapers and weekly newsmagazines, but it took some time for complete information about this breakthrough to be published. February 1997 would not have been a good time, then, to do a research paper on the cloning of animals.

5. **Choose a practical topic.** Unless you have unlimited time and energy, choose topics for which you can find sources on the Internet, in your college library, or through interlibrary loan. Avoid topics that require extensive technical knowledge that you lack. For example, a paper comparing the chemical makeup and effectiveness of two drugs might require the use of sources available only in medical libraries and background knowledge of pharmaceuticals that most of us do not have.

Narrowing and Discovering Ideas about Your Topic

The following techniques will help you narrow your topic and discover ideas about it.

1. **Do some preliminary reading.** It is often a good idea to do some preliminary reading to discover the scope, depth, and breadth of your topic. Although a **general encyclopedia,** such as *Encyclopaedia Britannica* or *World Book Encyclopedia,* contains limited information and may be somewhat out of date, it can give you a brief overview of your topic. For example, one student researching eating disorders quickly discovered through preliminary reading that the major types are obesity, anorexia nervosa, and bulimia. She then used this information to come up with a narrowed topic.

   In addition, you can check a **specialized encyclopedia** that focuses on a specific academic discipline related to your topic. Examples include the *Encyclopedia of Economics,* the *Harvard Guide to American History,* and the *McGraw-Hill Encyclopedia of Science and Technology.* A specialized encyclopedia can help you identify key terms pertinent to your topic, which you can use later on to locate material in library catalogs and indexes. To find a specialized encyclopedia on your topic, search the library catalog under the subject heading of the discipline (such as *psychology* or *philosophy*) and the keywords *dictionaries and encyclopedias*. A library's electronic catalog or card catalog can also help reveal the subtopics into which a topic can be broken.

The *CQ Researcher* is another useful reference to consult for background information on topics of current interest. Each report in the *CQ Researcher* focuses on a specific issue, such as health care reform or violence in the schools, and includes an analysis of the current situation, historical information, opposing viewpoints, and a bibliography. The *CQ Researcher* is also a good source of ideas for research paper topics. Also consider scanning a current magazine index for coverage of controversial issues. You may note different approaches or angles that will help you focus your topic. You can also ask a reference librarian for assistance.

2. **Try prewriting.** To uncover interesting topics or to narrow a broad topic to a more manageable one, use one or more prewriting techniques. Prewriting may also reveal an interesting approach to your topic that may eventually become your thesis. A branching diagram may be particularly helpful in narrowing a topic.

For more on branching and other prewriting strategies, see Chapter 4.

3. **View your topic from different perspectives.** To generate ideas about a topic, try asking questions about it from a variety of perspectives: psychological, sociological, scientific or technical, historical, political, and economic. Add other perspectives that apply to your topic. Here is how one student analyzed different perspectives on television advertising.

Topic: Television Advertising

Perspective	Questions
Psychological	• How does advertising affect people?
	• Does it affect everyone the same way?
	• What emotional appeals are used?
	• How do emotional appeals work?
Sociological	• How do different groups of people respond differently to ads?
	• Is advertising targeted toward specific racial and ethnic groups?
Scientific or technical	• How are ads produced?
	• Who writes them?
	• Are the ads tested before they are broadcast?
Historical	• What is the history of advertising?
	• When and where did it begin?
Political	• What is the history of political advertising?
	• Why are negative political advertisements effective?

Economic

- How much does a television ad cost?
- Is the cost of advertising added on to the price of the product?

This list of questions yielded a wide range of interesting subtopics about advertising, including emotional appeals, targeting ads to particular racial or ethnic groups, and negative political advertising, among others. You might try this technique with a friend or classmate, working together to devise questions.

EXERCISE 19.1

Working with one or two classmates, narrow each of the following topics until you reach a topic that would be manageable for a five- to ten-page research paper.

1. Job interviews
2. U.S. prison system
3. Mail-order companies
4. At-home schooling
5. Extinction of animal species

RESEARCH PAPER IN PROGRESS 1

Choose a broad topic for your research paper. In your paper you will state a thesis and provide evidence for your thesis. Your audience is your classmates. Begin by using one or more prewriting techniques to narrow and generate ideas about your topic. Then reread your work and highlight useful ideas. Choose one of the following broad topics or come up with one on your own.

1. Mandatory public works projects for the homeless
2. Cross-racial child adoptions
3. Sexual harassment: what it is and is not
4. How credit card use can lead to violations of privacy
5. Mandatory family planning

If you are uncertain about the topic you have chosen, be sure to check with your instructor. Most instructors don't mind if you clear your topic with them; in fact, some encourage or even require this step. Your instructor may also suggest a way to narrow your topic, recommend a useful source, or offer to review your outline at a later stage.

Writing a Working Thesis and Listing Research Questions

Once you choose and narrow a topic, try to determine, as specifically as possible, the kinds of information you need to know about it. Begin by writing a working thesis for your paper and listing the research questions you need to answer.

One student working on the general topic of child abuse, for example, used prewriting and preliminary reading to narrow his focus to physical abuse and its causes. Since he already had a few ideas about possible causes, he used those ideas to write a working thesis. He then used his thesis to generate a list of research questions. Notice how the student's questions follow from his working thesis.

WORKING THESIS: **The physical abuse of children often stems from parents' emotional instability and a family history of child abuse.**

RESEARCH QUESTIONS

If a person was physically abused as a child, how likely is that person to become an abusive parent?

What kinds of emotional problems seem to trigger the physical abuse of children?

Which cause is more significant — a family history of abuse or emotional problems?

Is there more physical abuse of children now than there was in the past, or is more abuse just being reported?

A working thesis and list of research questions will enable you to approach your research in a focused way. Instead of running helter-skelter from one aspect of your topic to another, you will be able to zero in on the specific information you need to obtain from sources.

EXERCISE 19.2

For one of the following topics, write a working thesis and four or more research questions.

1. Methods of controlling pornography on the Internet
2. The possibility that some form of life has existed on other planets
3. Reasons for the extinction of dinosaurs
4. Benefits of tracing your family's genealogy (family tree)
5. How elderly family members affect family life

RESEARCH PAPER IN PROGRESS 2

Review the list of ideas you generated in Research Paper in Progress 1. Underline ideas about which you need further information or supporting evidence and list the information you need. Then, using the preceding guidelines, write a working thesis and a list of research questions.

AN OVERVIEW OF LIBRARY AND INTERNET SOURCES

Your college library is your best and most immediate source of reference materials. It is an immense and amazing collection of print, media, and computerized sources on a wide variety of topics in all major academic disciplines. Within the

POSSIBLE ANSWERS

Example: **1. Methods of controlling pornography on the Internet**

Working thesis: The options available to lawmakers for controlling pornography include requiring pornographic Web site owners to install controls that effectively limit access to adults and requiring that personal computers used in homes, schools, and libraries be equipped with software that limits access to these sites. *Research questions:* Which options do lawmakers recommend? What technical glitches might hamper the controls? Might the controls be challenged in court on First Amendment grounds? How effective do experts predict the controls will be?

TEACHING TIP: COLLABORATIVE WRITING

After students complete this activity independently, have them work in small groups to review and comment on each other's working theses and research questions. Ask students to consider whether the topic is too broad for an essay-length writing assignment and whether the research questions are pertinent.

past ten years, however, the Internet has become another major resource for all types of research projects. To use the Internet, your computer must be equipped with either a modem, which is connected to a phone line, or a network card that hooks up to an Ethernet data line. Many colleges offer Internet access in dormitories, through campus computer centers, and in the library.

Learning Your Way around the Library

Over the course of your college career, you'll spend many hours in the library. Therefore, it is a good idea to become familiar with your college library *before* you need to use it. Following are a few ways to do so.

1. **Take a formal tour of the library.** Many colleges offer library tours during the first few weeks of a semester. On a tour, you'll learn where everything is located and discover how to use important services, such as interlibrary loans and computerized database searches.

2. **Take your own tour.** Visit the library for an hour, and just browse. Obtain a map or floor plan from the circulation desk and use it to guide your tour. Inspect the popular magazine collection; see what electronic resources are available. Check to see what sources the library has on your hobby or on a sport you enjoy. Your goal is to feel comfortable with the library so that the first time you need to use it, you can get to work easily. Keep the floor plan in your bag or notebook for future reference.

3. **Consult reference librarians.** In most libraries, one or more librarians are always available at the reference desk to assist you. They can advise you about what sources to use and where to locate them. Don't hesitate to ask reference librarians for help; they can save you time by offering shortcuts and directing you to appropriate sources.

Locating Useful Library and Online Sources

Technology is rapidly changing and, as a result, research procedures must change accordingly. Increasingly, the information you need is stored in electronic databases available through your college library or an online service.

Regardless of whether you use an online catalog, a database on CD-ROM (compact disk, read-only memory), or an online database to search for information on a topic, you will need to perform keyword searches to find relevant sources. Once you enter a keyword, the system searches its files and returns a list of pertinent sources. Many databases provide a dictionary of keywords as well as instructions for combining keywords and narrowing a search. For example, by connecting keywords with *and, or,* or *not,* or by enclosing a phrase within quotation marks, you can make your search more specific.

This section describes how to locate books and articles in the library, in electronic databases, and on the Internet.

Library of Congress Subject Headings (LCSH)

The *Library of Congress Subject Headings* (LCSH) is a major reference work that lists standard subject headings used by the Library of Congress. Consulting the LCSH can give you ideas for a topic or help you to narrow a broad topic. The LCSH can also provide headings to use when looking things up in your library's catalog. For example, if your broad subject is *animal communication* and you're interested in finding a narrowed topic for a ten-page research paper, the accompanying excerpt from the LCSH would give you several options to explore further, including *language learning by animals* and *human-animal communication*. You can also use subject headings from the LCSH to conduct library or Internet research. Although the LCSH is not the only source of subject headings, it is the most comprehensive reference work of its kind. It can be a useful starting point as well as a source of keywords for database and online searches.

SAMPLE ENTRY FROM THE LCSH

                        Animal communication
                              [QL776]
Used for ————————▶   UF   Animal language
                              Communication among animals
                              Language learning by animals
Broader term ————▶   BT   Animal behavior
Narrower term ————▶   NT   Animal sounds
                              Human-animal communication
                              Sound production by animals
                        Animal communication with humans
See or refer to ————▶ USE   Human-animal communication

Locating Books in the Library Catalog

A library's catalog lists books owned by the library. It may also list available magazines, newspapers, government documents, and electronic sources. It does not, however, list individual articles included in magazines and newspapers. Most libraries now have a computerized catalog, which allows you to search for sources electronically by title, author, or subject. You can access the computerized catalog at terminals in the library. Some libraries also allow access to their catalogs from a home computer or a computer lab on campus. Directions usually appear on or near the screen and are easy to follow.

When searching the library catalog for books on a specific topic, you may have to view two or three screens until you find information about a specific book. Figure 19.2 shows the results of a computerized search by subject for the topic *animal communication*. Computerized catalogs offer many conveniences. The screen often

FIGURE 19.2
SAMPLE ENTRY FROM A LIBRARY CATALOG

UB Libraries Catalog   Record Display

Search Request: S=ANIMAL COMMUNICATION   BOOK - Record 8 of 62 Entries Found

Please use these catalog buttons, not the browser back button:

| Previous Record | Next Record | Start Over | Index |

| Location: | Call Number: | Status: |
| UNDERGRADUATE Book Collection | QL776 .M66 1992 | Not checked out |

TITLE: Animal talk : science and the voices of nature / Eugene S. Morton, Jake Page.
AUTHOR: Morton, Eugene S.
CONTRIBUTORS: Page, Jake.
EDITION: 1st ed.
PUBLISHED: New York : Random House, c1992.
DESCRIPTION: 275 p. ; 22 cm.
SUBJECTS: Animal communication.
                  Sound production by animals.
                  Evolution (Biology)
NOTES: Includes bibliographical references and index.

COMPUTER HINT

Point out that often a *Boolean search* allows a specific search of the library's subject catalog. For example, the student can use *and* between two keywords to find sources that use both terms; use *or* to search for one of two key terms; or use *not* to exclude a term (as in *basketball not Knicks*). Advise students to check the help screen for detailed advice.

indicates whether the book is on the shelves or has been checked out and, if so, when it is due back. Some systems allow you to reserve the book by entering your request on the computer. Often, terminals are connected to printers that enable you to print the screen, providing you with an accurate record of each source and saving you the time it would take to write down information on each of your sources. Computerized catalogs have another important advantage: They allow you to enter more than one keyword at a time. For instance, if your topic is robbery but you want to limit your search to crimes committed in convenience stores, you could specify *robbery and convenience stores.*

A traditional card catalog consists of 3-by-5-inch cards that index all the books in the library's holdings. In libraries that are still in the process of switching to a computerized catalog, only older titles may be listed in the index-card version. The traditional catalog includes three types of cards: title, author, and subject. For works of fiction, only title and author cards are included. Arranged alphabetically, the three types of cards may be filed together, or there may be a separate catalog for the subject cards.

Both the computerized catalog and traditional card catalog provide *call numbers* that tell you where to locate books on the library's shelves. Use your library floor plan and the call-number guides posted on shelves to locate the particular section of the library indicated in the call number. Then scan the letters or numbers on the spines of books until you locate the book you need. Take a few minutes to scan the surrounding books, which are usually on similar or related topics. You may find other useful sources you overlooked in the card catalog.

Bibliographies

A **bibliography** lists sources on a particular subject, including books, articles, government publications, and other sources. Some bibliographies also provide brief summaries or descriptions of the sources they list.

To locate a bibliography on your subject, just combine the word *bibliography* with a relevant keyword for your topic. For example, you can search your library's online catalog for *animal communication and bibliography.* Another option is to check the *Bibliographic Index,* a reference work that lists available bibliographies. A new volume is published each year, so be sure to check several recent volumes of the index.

Locating Articles Using Periodical Indexes

Periodicals include newspapers, magazines, and scholarly journals. Because periodicals are published frequently (daily, weekly, or monthly), they often contain the most up-to-date information available on a subject. Although magazines the library subscribes to are listed in the catalog, specific articles are not. To find them, you must use periodical indexes and abstracts. **Indexes** list articles, usually by title, author, and subject. **Abstracts** list articles and provide a brief summary of each one. Library catalogs list the names of periodical indexes and abstracts held by the library.

Many indexes and abstracts are now available as computer databases as well as in print form. These online indexes and abstracts may be accessed through the Internet, or they may be available on a campus network. Keep in mind that the name of the electronic version of an index or abstract may be different from that of the print version. Check with your librarian to see what databases are available and whether the library charges a fee for online services. Because online indexes are updated frequently, sometimes every week, you can use them to locate very current information. Most computerized indexes and abstracts cover only the most recent years, however, so you may need to consult print indexes if you need older material. There are two types of periodical indexes—general and specialized.

General Periodical Indexes. General indexes list articles on a wide range of subjects that have been published in popular magazines. The following common general indexes are available in most college libraries.

- *Readers' Guide to Periodical Literature* (print, online, and CD-ROM). The print version indexes articles published in roughly two hundred popular periodicals beginning with the year 1900. It is useful for finding articles of general interest and on current topics. It is of limited use for academic topics because it does not index scholarly journals. It can be useful, however, for researching historical

COMPUTER HINT

Computer databases provide good practice in refining searches and narrowing topics, allowing users to search by *subject, type of material sought,* or *date of publication,* for instance. Point out that a search on a general term (e.g., *guns*) is likely to yield too many hits, whereas a narrowed term (*handgun control*) combined with specific requests (*journal articles,* published *after 1997*) will yield a more manageable number of relevant hits. A survey of titles in indexes and abstracts can then help students select appropriate sources.

events, social and political developments, and popular culture. It is also helpful for locating technical and literary articles written for a general audience. The accompanying example shows an excerpt from an entry for *animal communication.*

SAMPLE ENTRY FROM *READERS' GUIDE*

ANIMAL COMMUNICATION
> *See also*
> Bird communication
> Insect communication
> Bonobo dialogues [excerpt from Bonobo: the forgotten ape] F. de
>   Waal. il *Natural History* v106 p22-5 My '97
> Critter patter [C. N. Slobodchikoff studies prairie dog talk] il por
>   *People Weekly* v48 p111 N 24 '97
> How male animals gain an edge in the mating game [various
>   papers presented at the annual meeting of the Animal Behav-
>   ior Society] E. Pennisi. il *Science* v277 p317-18 Jl 18 '97
> Something smells: the language of animal scents [cover story] D.
>   G. Gordon. il *National Geographic World* v260 p2-6 Ap '97
> Using the power of dog-speak. L. Mueller. il *Outdoor Life* v199
>   p34+ Ap '97

• InfoTrac SearchBank (online and CD-ROM). This extensive computer database lists articles published in over 1,100 magazines, journals, and newspapers. Some entries include abstracts. InfoTrac SearchBank includes a wide range of databases, such as the following:

> *Magazine Index* (microfilm and online). It indexes articles published in over four hundred popular magazines by author, title, and subject, as well as numerous reference books and newspapers.
> *General Periodicals Index:* Indexes general interest articles for the most recent four-year period.
> *Academic Index:* Indexes over four hundred scholarly and general-interest articles for the most recent four-year period.
> *National Newspaper Index:* Indexes articles published in major newspapers during the most recent three-year period.

Since InfoTrac is organized by subject headings, it may list subdivisions of the topic being searched; a partial list of subdivisions for the topic "animal communication" is shown in the following example. Such listings can help you narrow a topic or discover facets of a topic you had not considered previously.

SAMPLE INFOTRAC ENTRY

InfoTrac: Subdivisions of Animal Communication
> analysis
>   View 15 articles

bibliography
    View 1 article
case studies
    View 2 articles
environmental aspects
    View 1 article
genetic aspects
    View 2 articles
illustrations, photographs, etc.
    View 1 article
models
    View 5 articles
moral and ethical aspects
    View 1 article

Specialized Periodical Indexes and Abstracts.   Specialized indexes and abstracts reference scholarly or technical articles within a specific academic field of study. The *Essay and General Literature Index* (1900–, online, CD-ROM) is useful for locating articles and essays published in books. Many academic disciplines have one or more specialized indexes or abstracts. Some are specialized by subject, others by the type of material they index. Here is a list of common specialized indexes. Each is available in a print version as well as on CD-ROM and on the Internet. CD-ROM and online versions, however, may contain only recent files, although many databases continue to add back files.

Applied Science and Technology Index (1958–).
Art Index (1929–).
Biological and Agricultural Index (1983–).
Book Review Digest (1905–).
Business Index (1958–).
Dissertation Abstracts (1933–).
Education Index (1929–).
Engineering Index (1920–).
Historical Abstracts (1955–).
Humanities Index (1974–).
MLA International Bibliography of Books and Articles in the Modern Languages and Literature (1921–).
Monthly Catalog of U.S. Government Publications (1895–).
Music Index (1949–).
Physics Abstracts (1898–).
Psychological Abstracts (1927–).
Science Index (1984–).
Sociological Abstracts (1952–).

Here is a sample entry on the topic of "animal communication, mammals," from the *Biological and Agricultural Index*.

SAMPLE ENTRY FROM *BIOLOGICAL AND AGRICULTURAL INDEX*

Mammals

Scent marking and responses to male castor fluid by beavers. B. A.
  Schulte. bibl il *J Mammal* v79 p191-203 F '98
Social calls coordinate foraging in greater spear-nosed bats. G. S.
  Wilkinson and J. W. Boughman. bibl il map *Anim Behav* v55
  p337-50 F '98

Locating Useful Internet Sources

The **Internet** is a system that connects computers worldwide and enables users to communicate with one another, share information, and exchange documents. Although the Internet offers vast amounts of information, it does have several drawbacks. Because anyone can post information and documents on the Internet, the information may be less reliable than that in print sources. Be sure to verify the accuracy of information you obtain from Internet sources. Another drawback of the Internet is that it lacks a central system for organizing or cataloging information. Despite these drawbacks, the Internet is a valuable resource, particularly for stimulating thought, exploring viewpoints, and discovering available print sources.

The World Wide Web.   The **World Wide Web** is made up of a vast collection of *Web sites* or linked electronic documents that can include video and audio as well as text and graphics. Web sites now exist on thousands of topics. Corporations, government agencies, nonprofit organizations, colleges and universities, and individuals create and publish Web sites for various purposes. Each Web site has a *home page,* which usually includes information about the site and a directory of links to other pages on the site. A Web site is accessed by way of a Web address, called a *uniform resource locator (URL),* and a Web browser, a computer program that enables you to view Web pages and navigate the Internet. Netscape Navigator and Microsoft Internet Explorer are two widely available Web browsers. Most Web pages also include underlined topics called *hyperlinks,* which you click on to access related pages or sites.

Search engines can help you find Web sites related to a topic. A **search engine** is a program designed to function with a Web browser that allows you to search by typing in keywords. Popular search engines include Lycos (http://www.lycos.com), Yahoo! (http://www.yahoo.com), and AltaVista (http://www.altavista.net). Keep in mind, when using a search engine, that a broad search term will yield a list of hundreds or even thousands of sites, most of them useless. Therefore, in formulating keywords, use a connecting word or symbol such as *and* or *or* or + or quotation marks around phrases to make your search as specific as possible (consult the help screen for each search engine you use for advice on how to limit your search). In addition, because different search engines yield different results, you should try searching your topic in two or more search engines. For a general search, it is probably best to start with a directory such as Yahoo!, which allows you to narrow your search by choosing categories. Figure 19.3 shows the results of an AltaVista search on *chimpanzee communication*. To make her search more specific, the researcher added "+language" to her search term.

Once you identify usable sources, be sure to keep track of their URLs so you can find the sites again easily and cite them in your paper. You can save Web

FIGURE 19.3
RESULTS OF A SEARCH ON ALTAVISTA

addresses on your own computer as *bookmarks* or *favorites* (depending on the Web browser you use) that allow you to return to a site by clicking on its name. Another option is to record Web addresses on index cards for easy reference.

Some Web sites function as guides to the World Wide Web, telling you what to look for and which sites are worthwhile. The World Wide Web Virtual Library at <http://vlib.org/overview.html> and the Argus Clearinghouse at <http://www.clearinghouse.net> are two examples.

Listservs and Newsgroups.   The Internet also offers listservs and newsgroups—discussion forums where people interested in a particular topic or field of research can communicate and share information about it. A **listserv** is an email discussion group; messages are sent automatically to subscribers' email accounts. To use a listserv, you must first request to be a member. Some listservs allow anyone to subscribe, whereas others require a moderator's permission. A **newsgroup,** in contrast, does not require membership, and messages are posted to a news server for anyone to read and respond to. A central network called *Usenet* provides access to thousands of newsgroups.

Consult the *frequently asked questions (FAQs)* for a listserv or newsgroup to determine if it suits your needs and, for a listserv, to see how to subscribe. Keep in mind that messages posted to listservs and newsgroups are not usually checked for accuracy and are not always reliable sources of information (though in general the discussion on listservs tends to be more serious and focused than newsgroup discussions). Electronic discussion forums are most useful for helping you become familiar with a topic; obtain background information; discover new issues, facets, or approaches; identify print sources of information; and build your interest in a topic. To locate discussion groups, search at <http://www.liszt.com>.

Email Addresses

Many authors, researchers, and corporations have email addresses that enable you to send correspondence directly to their computers. Many authorities are willing to respond to requests for specific information, but you should first make sure the information you need is not already available through more traditional sources. To locate email addresses, consult an email directory in your library's reference section or an online directory such as Bigfoot <http://bigfoot.com> or Internet Address Finder <http://www.iaf.net> (any directory may include obsolete entries). Email search directories are available through Yahoo! and elsewhere. While not complete, they do contain a great deal of information.

When you send an email message to someone you don't know, be sure to introduce yourself and briefly describe the purpose of your inquiry. Provide complete information about yourself, including the name of your school and how to contact you, and politely request the information you need.

RESEARCH PAPER IN PROGRESS 3

For the topic you worked on in Research Paper in Progress 1 and 2, locate a minimum of six sources that answer one or more of your research questions. Your sources must include at least one book, one magazine article, one scholarly article, one Internet source, and two other sources of any type. Experiment with the various ways of searching for sources. Finally, make a list of your sources, including the publication and online information you will need to find them again later.

CHOOSING RELEVANT AND RELIABLE SOURCES

Once you locate potential sources of information on your topic, you need to evaluate each one before you begin reading and taking notes. Many students make the mistake of photocopying many articles and lugging home numerous books only to find that the sources are not useful or that several contain identical information. Save yourself time by taking a few minutes to identify which sources will be most helpful and appropriate in fulfilling the purpose of your assignment. Once you've chosen these sources, the next step is to make sure they are relevant and reliable.

Choosing Relevant Sources

A *relevant* source contains information that helps you to answer one or more of your research questions. Answering the following questions will help you determine whether a source is relevant.

1. **Is the source too general or too specialized?** Some sources may be so basic that they don't contain the detailed information you need; others may be too technical and require background knowledge that you do not have. For example, suppose you are researching the environmental effects of recycling cans and bottles. An article in *Reader's Digest* may be too general, focusing on recycling efforts in the home but not discussing environmental effects in detail, whereas an article in *Environmental Science and Technology* may be too technical to be of use.

2. **Is the source recent enough for your purposes?** Especially in rapidly changing fields of study, outdated sources are not useful, except when you need to give a historical perspective. For example, a five-year-old article on the use of air bags to improve car safety may not include recent information on the dangers air bags pose to young children in the front passenger seat.

Choosing Reliable Sources

A *reliable* source is honest, accurate, and credible. Answering the following questions will help you determine whether a source is reliable.

1. **Is the source scholarly?** Although scholars often disagree with each other, they make a serious attempt to present accurate information. In addition, an article that appears in a scholarly journal or textbook has been reviewed by a panel of professionals in the field prior to publication. Therefore, scholarly sources tend to be trustworthy.

2. **Does the source have a solid reputation?** Some magazines, such as *Time* and *Newsweek,* are known for responsible reporting, whereas other periodicals have a reputation for sensationalism and should be avoided or approached skeptically.

3. **Is the author an expert in the field?** Check the author's credentials. Information about authors may be given in a headnote or at the end of an article, or on the title page or in the preface of a book. You might also check a reference book such as *Contemporary Authors* to verify an author's credentials.

4. **Does the author approach the topic fairly and objectively?** A writer who states a strong opinion or assertion is not necessarily biased. However, a writer who ignores opposing views, distorts facts, or ignores information that does not fit his or her opinion may present a biased and incomplete view of a topic. Although you can use a biased source to understand a particular viewpoint, you must also seek out other sources that present the alternative views.

POSSIBLE ANSWERS

1. (a) Textbook: preliminary reading, not a research source; (b) magazine article: possible source of anecdotes and general background information; (c) journal: credible scholarly source
2. (a) Newspaper article: useful source of examples of firsthand experiences but not for the broad picture; (b) journal article: excellent scholarly source, but may be too technical; (c) pamphlet: useful government source
3. (a) Article: credible newspaper but scan article to determine its relevance; (b) email: possible example but credibility may be questionable; (c) training manual: possible example of one company's policy

EXERCISE 19.3

Working in a small group, discuss why the sources listed for each topic would or would not be considered relevant and reliable.

1. Topic: Caring for family members with Alzheimer's disease
   a. Introductory health and nutrition textbook
   b. Article in *Women's Day,* titled "Mother, Where Are You?"
   c. Article from a gerontology journal on caring for aging family members
2. Topic: Analyzing the effects of heroin use on teenagers
   a. Article in a newspaper written by a former heroin user
   b. Article from the *Journal of Neurology* on the biochemical effects of heroin on the brain
   c. Pamphlet on teenage drug use published by the National Institutes of Health
3. Topic: Implementing training programs to reduce sexual harassment in the workplace
   a. Article from the *Christian Science Monitor* titled "Removing Barriers for Working Women"
   b. Email posting to a listserv relating an incident of harassment on the job
   c. Training manual for employees of General Motors

RESEARCH PAPER IN PROGRESS 4

Evaluate the sources you listed in Research Paper in Progress 3. On a scale from *1* to *5* (where *1* is low, *5* is high), rank each source in terms of its relevancy and reliability. Use the following chart to structure your responses.

Source	Relevancy Rating	Reliability Rating
1.		
2.		
3.		
4.		
5.		
6.		

Evaluating Internet Sources

Although many valuable and reliable Internet sources are available, keep in mind that rumors, misinformation, and exaggerations can spread easily through this medium. Use the following questions to evaluate the reliability of Internet sources.

1. **What are the author's credentials?** If information about an author is not available on the site or is sketchy, conduct a search for the author's name on the Web or Usenet. A home page for the author or biographical links may be available elsewhere.

2. **What is the date of posting?** Web sites often indicate the date on which they were posted or last updated. If no date is given, check some of the links. If links are outdated and nonfunctioning, the information at the site is probably outdated as well.

3. **Who is the site's sponsor?** The Web sites of government agencies and well-known organizations (such as universities and reputable newspapers like the *New York Times*) are generally reliable sources of information. If the last three letters in the URL are *gov* or *edu*, the site is published by the government or an educational institution.

4. **For an online publication, who sponsors and writes for it?** For example, *Slate* is published by Microsoft Corporation, and well-known journalists contribute to it.

5. **Why was the information posted?** Web sites are created for a variety of reasons—to promote products, advocate particular viewpoints, and so forth. Sometimes the purpose of the site is indicated on the home page. If not, look for clues to the site's purpose, such as the names of its sponsoring organization and advertisers.

6. **Can the information be verified elsewhere?** Confirm the accuracy of any questionable information you find on the Internet in another source, preferably a print source.

COMPUTER HINT

Point out that one simple way to judge the reliability of an Internet source is to note which three-letter extension appears in the site's URL or Internet address. In general, the sites of organizations (*.org*), government agencies (*.gov*), and educational institutions (*.edu*) are considered more reliable than commercial sites (*.com*) and sites hosted by Internet service providers (*.net*).

EXERCISE 19.4

Using the preceding guidelines for evaluating Internet sources, locate two of the following types of Web sites and determine whether each would be considered a reliable source.

1. The Web site of a textbook publisher
2. The Web site of a public service organization (Red Cross, American Cancer Society)
3. The Web site of your college or university
4. The Web site of an advocacy group (Planned Parenthood, the National Rifle Association)
5. The Web site of a federal or state government agency

WORKING WITH TEXT: READING SOURCES

Reading sources involves a special type of reading. Unlike textbook reading, where your purpose is to learn and recall the material, you read sources with a different purpose, usually to extract the information you need about a topic. Because your purpose differs, so should your reading strategy. Often you can read sources selectively, reading only the relevant parts and skipping over the rest. Use the following strategies for reading sources: 1) scan, 2) skim, and 3) read.

Scanning a Source

Scanning is a means of finding the information you seek within a source without reading it from beginning to end. Scanning involves more "looking" than actual reading. You look to see whether the source contains relevant information on your topic and, if so, where that information can be found. Just as you scan a phone directory to locate a phone number or an airport monitor to note a flight's departure time, you scan a print source to extract needed information. For electronic sources, often a search function will be available that can do the scanning for you and take you to the information you need.

Use the following guidelines to scan print sources effectively.

1. **Determine how the source is organized.** Is it organized by chapter? By subject? By author? Reference books, in particular, follow specific systems of organization.

2. **Check the abstract or summary for journal articles.** You can quickly determine whether articles contain the information you need and approximately where in the article to find it by reading abstracts and summaries.

3. **Scan the index and table of contents for books.** These are designed to help you locate the information you need.

4. **Keep key words or phrases in mind as you scan.** For example, if you are searching for information on welfare reform, key phrases might include *welfare system, entitlement programs, benefits,* and *welfare spending.*

5. **Scan systematically.** Don't scan a source randomly, hoping to see what you need. Instead, follow a pattern as you sweep your eyes across the material. For charts, tables, and indexes, use a downward sweep. For prose material, use a zigzag or Z-pattern, sweeping across several lines of print at a time.

EXERCISE 19.5

Scan "Virtual Reality" (on pp. 650–53) to locate the following information. Jot down notes on what you find. Then, working with another student, exchange and evaluate your notes.

1. A definition of *virtual reality*
2. The uses of virtual reality in law-enforcement training
3. The drawbacks of virtual reality

Skimming a Source

Skimming (also called *previewing*) is a quick way of finding out whether a source suits your purposes without taking the time to read it completely. Skimming also gives you an overview of the source and allows you to determine whether any sections deserve close reading. As you skim a source, mark or jot down sections to which you may want to return later.

Use the following guidelines to skim a source effectively. Keep in mind that you'll need to adapt these guidelines to fit the type of source with which you are working.

1. **Read the title.** It announces the subject and may provide clues about the author's approach to or attitude toward the subject.
2. **Read the introductory paragraph.** It may provide important background information, introduce the subject, and provide a brief overview.
3. **Read the headings.** A heading announces the topic to be discussed. When read successively, the headings may form a brief outline of the material.
4. **Read the first sentence of each paragraph.** Often it is the topic sentence of the paragraph and announces the main point. If it is transitional, then read the next sentence as well.
5. **Read key words and phrases.** Glance quickly through the remainder of each paragraph. Notice numbered lists, capitalized or italicized words, boldfaced terms, names, numbers, dates, and the like.
6. **Notice any graphics.** Read the legend or title given for any maps, charts, photographs, or diagrams.
7. **Read the last paragraph or summary.** It may review the key points in the article or essay.

For more on strategies for
close reading, see Chapter
2, p. 33.

EXERCISE 19.6

Skim "Virtual Reality" (below). Then write a few sentences that summarize the gist of the article.

Reading a Source Closely

Once you identify the sections within a source that contain the information you need — by scanning, skimming, or both — read those sections closely and carefully. To be sure you do not take information out of context, also read the paragraphs before and after the material you have chosen.

As you read the essay that follows, pay special attention to the parts you scanned or skimmed in the two preceding exercises.

 Virtual Reality
Jeffrey S. Hormann

Jeffrey S. Hormann is the special agent in charge of the Fort Belvoir Resident Agency, US Army Criminal Investigation Command. The article from which the following excerpt was taken was published in an FBI law-enforcement bulletin in July 1995.

1   A late night police pursuit of a suspected drunk driver winds through abandoned city streets. The short vehicle chase ends in a warehouse district where the suspect abandons his vehicle and continues his flight on foot. Before backup arrives, the rookie patrol officer exits his vehicle and gives chase. A quick run along a loading dock ends at the open door to an apparently unoccupied building. The suspect stops, brandishes a revolver, and fires in the direction of the pursuing officer before disappearing into the building. The officer, shaken but uninjured, radios in his location and follows the suspect into the building.

2   Did the officer make a good decision? Probably not by most departments' standards. Whether the officer's decision proves right or wrong, the training gained from this experience is immeasurable; that is, provided the officer lives through it. Fortunately for this officer, the scenario occurred in a realistic, high-tech world called virtual reality, where training can have a real-life impact without the accompanying risk.

WHAT IS VIRTUAL REALITY?

Simply stated, virtual reality is high-tech illusion. It is a computer-generated, three-dimensional environment that engulfs the senses of sight, sound, and touch. Once entered, it becomes reality to the user.

Within this virtual world, users travel among, and interact with, objects that are wholly the products of a computer or representations of other participants in the same environment. The limits of this virtual environment depend on the sophistication and capabilities of the computer and the software that drives the system.

HOW DOES VIRTUAL REALITY WORK?

Based on data entered by programmers, computers create virtual environments by generating three-dimensional images. Users usually view these images through a head-mounted device, which can be a helmet, goggles, or other apparatus that restricts their vision to two small video monitors, one in front of each eye. Each monitor displays a slightly different view of the environment, which gives users a sense of depth.

Another device, called a position tracker, monitors users' physical positions and provides input to the computer. This information instructs the computer to change the environment based upon users' actions. For example, when users look over their shoulders, they see what lies behind them.

Because virtual reality users remain stationary, they use a joy stick or track ball to move through the virtual environment. Users also may wear a special glove or use other devices to manipulate objects within the virtual environment. Similarly, they can employ virtual weapons to confront virtual aggressors.

To enhance the sense of reality, some researchers are experimenting with tactile feedback devices (TFDs). TFDs transmit pressure, force, or vibration, providing users with a simulated sense of touch. (1) For example, a user might want to open a door or move an object, which in reality would require the sense of touch. A TFD would simulate this sensation. At present, however, these devices are crude and somewhat cumbersome to use.

USES FOR VIRTUAL REALITY

In today's competitive business environment, organizations continuously strive to accomplish tasks faster, better, and inexpensively. This especially holds true in training.

10   Virtual reality is emerging rapidly as a potentially unlimited method for providing realistic, safe, and cost-effective training. For example, a firefighter can battle the flames of a virtual burning building. A police officer can struggle with virtual shoot/don't shoot dilemmas. (2)

11   Within a virtual environment, students can make decisions and act upon them without risk to themselves or others. Instructors can critique students' actions, enabling students to review and learn from their mistakes. This ability gives virtual reality a great advantage over most conventional training methods.

12   ***Military Training.***   The Department of Defense (DOD) leads public and private industry in developing virtual reality training. Since the early 1980s, DOD has actively researched, developed, and implemented virtual reality to train members of the armed forces to fight effectively in combat.

13   DOD's current approach to virtual reality training emphasizes team tactics. Groups of military personnel from around the world engage in combat safely on a virtual battlefield. Combatants never come together physically; rather, simulators located at various sites throughout the world transmit data to a central location, where the virtual battle is controlled. Because it costs less to move information than people, this form of training has proven quite cost-effective.

14   An additional benefit to this type of training is that battles can be fought under varying conditions. Virtual battlefields re-create real-world locations with interchangeable characteristics. To explore "what if" scenarios, participants can modify enemy capabilities, terrain, weather, and weapon systems.

15   ***Law Enforcement Training.***   While virtual reality has proven its value as a training and planning tool for the military, applications for this technology reach far beyond DOD. To varying degrees, many military uses can transfer to law enforcement, including training in firearms, stealth tactics, and assault skills.

16   Unfortunately, few organizations have dedicated resources to developing virtual reality for law enforcement. According to a recently published resource guide, more than 100 companies currently are developing and/or selling virtual reality hardware or software. However, none of these firms mentioned law enforcement uses. (3)

17   Further, a review of relevant literature revealed numerous articles on virtual reality technology, but only a few addressed law enforce-

ment applications. Yet, virtual reality clearly offers law enforcement benefits in a number of areas, including pursuit driving, firearms training, high-risk incident management, incident re-creation, and crime scene processing.

IS VIRTUAL REALITY VIRTUALLY PERFECT?

Though virtual reality may appear to be the ideal law enforcement tool, as with any new technology, some drawbacks exist. Currently, areas of concern range from cumbersome equipment to negative physical and psychological effects experienced by some users. Fortunately, however, the field is evolving and improving constantly, and as virtual reality gains widespread use, most major concerns should be dispelled. 18

CONCLUSION

At present, many individuals equate virtual reality with science fiction; yet, with numerous commercial firms and nonprofit organizations dedicated to its development, virtual reality soon will be an important part of life, especially for law enforcement personnel. By understanding how the technology works and what it can accomplish, law enforcement organizations can become active in research and development and request that applications be developed to meet their special needs. 19

In the case of the officer in the opening virtual reality scenario, he became caught up in the heat of the moment and entered a dangerous situation without backup. Fortunately, this officer could return to the real world, review his actions, and learn from his mistakes. Law enforcement officers who make errors in judgment sometimes pay for it with their lives. Virtual reality forgives mistakes and gives officers a second chance. ■ 20

NOTES

[1]Miller, Carmen, "Online Interviews Dr. Thomas A. Furness, III, Virtual Reality Pioneer," *Online*, Nov. 1992: 14.

[2]Emery, Glen, "The Radical Visions of Artificial Reality," *The Washington Times*, May 6, 1991.

[3]Berg, Tor, "Virtual Reality Resource Guide," *Virtual Reality Special Report*, Fall 1994, 39.

EXTRACTING INFORMATION FROM SOURCES

As you read sources, you will need to take notes to use later when you write your paper. The following section discusses systems for note-taking and types of notes, highlighting and annotating sources, and recording quotations. It also offers advice for avoiding plagiarism.

Systems of Note-Taking

When you take research notes, you'll probably need to copy quotes, write paraphrases, and make summary notes. There are three systems for recording research notes.

1. **Note cards.** Researchers who employ this system use 4-by-6-inch or 5-by-8-inch index cards for note-taking. If you use this system, put information from only one source or on only one subtopic on each card. At the top of the card, indicate the source from which the information came (by author's last name), along with the subtopic the note covers. Be sure to include page numbers in case you need to go back and reread the article or passage. If you copy an author's exact words, place the information in quotation marks and include the page number in parentheses. If you *paraphrase,* or record an author's complete idea in your own words (see p. 656), include a reminder for yourself on the card by writing "(paraphrase)" and the page number of the source. If you write a *summary* note, be sure to indicate the page and source; you may need to refer to it again. Write "(summary)" and the page number after the note. Figure 19.4 shows a sample note card. The advantage of using the note card system is that you can spread out your cards, rearrange them, and experiment with different ways of organizing as you plan your paper.

2. **Computerized note-taking.** If you have access to a computer, you can type your notes into computer files and organize your files by subtopic. You may use a computer notebook to create small "note cards," a hypertext card program, or an ordinary text file with page breaks between sources. As with note cards, be sure to keep track of sources by including the author's name and the page numbers for each source, and make a backup copy of your notes. If you have access to a laptop computer, you can type in summaries, paraphrases, and direct quotations while you are doing the research in the library, eliminating the need to type or recopy them later.

3. **Annotated photocopies or printouts from electronic sources.** This system is most appropriate for very short papers that do not involve numerous sources or extensive research. To use this system, photocopy or print the source material, underline or highlight useful information, and write your reactions and summary notes in the margins or attach them to the appropriate page. The

FIGURE 19.4
SAMPLE NOTE CARD

Schmoke & Roques, 17-25

Medicalization

    Medicalization is a system in which the government would control the release of narcotics to drug addicts.
    — would work like a prescription does now — only gov't official would write prescription
        — addicts would be required to get counseling and health services
        — would take drug control out of hands of drug traffickers   (paraphrase, 18)

advantage of this system is that it saves time by eliminating the need to write as much. The disadvantage is that in addition to the expense of photocopying, it does not allow you to sort and rearrange notes by subtopic. It also postpones thinking, since you do not have to express the ideas of others in your own words while you do your research.

Whichever system you use, be sure to record complete information for each source, including, for books, the author, title, edition, place of publication, name of publisher, date, and page numbers. For periodical articles, be sure to record the author, title, complete name of the journal, date, volume number, and page numbers. Record it in the correct form for use in your list of works cited or references (see Chapter 20), so that you do not need to rewrite it later. If you use the note card system, keep a separate bibliography card for each source you use. For annotated photocopies, be sure to copy or print full source information and attach it to your photocopies. For the computer system, create a separate bibliography file in which you enter complete information on each source.

It's also important to designate a place to record your own ideas, such as separate or different colored index cards, a notepad, or a computer file. Use this place to comment on what you've read or note topics related to your research.

When you use note cards or computerized note-taking, be careful not to simply record quotations. Writing summary notes or paraphrases is a thinking process. As you write, you think about the ideas in your source, how they fit with other ideas, and how they might work in your research paper.

Writing Summary Notes

Much of your note-taking will be in the form of **summary notes,** which condense or reduce information from sources. It is a good idea to take summary notes when you want to record the gist of an author's ideas but do not need the exact wording or a paraphrase. Use the following guidelines to write effective summary notes. Remember that everything you put in summary notes must be in your own words.

1. **Record only information that relates to your topic and purpose.** Do not include information that is irrelevant to your topic.

2. **Write notes that condense the author's ideas in your own words.** Include key terms and concepts, procedures, or principles. Do not include examples, descriptive details, quotations, or anything that is not essential to the main point. Do not include your opinion, even a positive one. (You can include any comments in a separate note. See p. 655.)

3. **Record the ideas in the order in which they appear in the original source.** Reordering ideas might affect the meaning.

4. **Reread your summary to determine whether it contains sufficient information.** Would it be understandable to someone who has not read the original source? If not, revise the summary to include additional information.

A sample summary note written for the section of "Virtual Reality" titled "Law Enforcement Training" (p. 652) is shown below. Read that section of the essay, and then study the summary note.

SUMMARY

Virtual reality could be used to train law enforcement personnel in the use of firearms, stealth techniques, and assault skills. Few companies, however, have developed hardware or software for such purposes. Not much has been published in professional literature on virtual reality applications for police work either, although the benefits of virtual reality are obvious.

POSSIBLE ANSWER
(Summary of pars. 9–11)

Because training is increasingly important in the corporate world, virtual reality is now recognized as an inexpensive, risk-free way to teach workers. Trainees can take action, and instructors can provide feedback, in a safe setting.

EXERCISE 19.7

Choose another section of "Virtual Reality" and write a summary note for it.

Writing Paraphrases

When you **paraphrase,** you restate the author's ideas in your own words. You do not condense ideas or eliminate details, as you do in a summary. You use different sentence patterns and vocabulary but keep the author's intended meaning. In most cases, a paraphrase is approximately the same length as the original material. Compose a paraphrase when you want to record the author's ideas and details but do not want to use a direct quotation. You should never paraphrase an entire article; instead, paraphrase only the ideas or details you intend to use.

Read this excerpt from a source; then compare it to the sample paraphrase that follows.

EXCERPT FROM ORIGINAL

Learning some items may interfere with retrieving others, especially when the items are similar. If someone gives you a phone number to remember, you may be able to recall it later. But if two more people give you their numbers, each successive number will be more difficult to recall. Such **proactive interference** occurs when something you learned earlier disrupts recall of something you experienced later. As you collect more and more information, your mental attic never fills, but it certainly gets cluttered.

DAVID G. MYERS, *Psychology*

PARAPHRASE

When proactive interference happens, things you have already learned prevent you from remembering things you learn later. In other words, details you learn first may make it harder to recall closely related details you learn subsequently. You can think of your memory as an attic. You can always add more junk to it. However, it will become messy and disorganized. For example, you can remember one new phone number, but if you have two or more new numbers to remember the task becomes harder.

Use the following guidelines to write effective paraphrases.

1. **Read first; then write.** You may find it wise to read material more than once before you try paraphrasing.

2. **If you must use any of the author's wording, enclose it in quotation marks.** If you do not use quotation marks, you may inadvertently use the same wording in your paper, which would result in plagiarism.

3. **Work sentence by sentence, restating each in your own words.** One easy way to avoid copying an author's words is to read a sentence, cover it up or look away, and then write. Check to be sure your version is accurate but not too similar to the original. As a rule of thumb, no more than two or three consecutive words should be the same as the original.

4. **Choose synonyms that do not change the author's meaning or intent.** Consult a dictionary, if necessary.

5. **Use your own sentence structure and sentence order.** Using an author's sentence structure can be considered plagiarism. Also rearrange the order of ideas within a sentence.

6. **Use two or more short sentences instead of a lengthy one.** If the original has a lengthy sentence, write your paraphrase of it in shorter sentences.

POSSIBLE ANSWER: EXERCISE 19.8 (p. 658)

Sample paraphrase: While we tend to think of language as a human capability, animals also communicate, some through body language, others through verbal language. Bees tell each other where to find food by performing an elaborate dance. Perhaps most impressive is the proven ability of several species of chimpanzees and other apes to master verbal language, both to express themselves and to communicate and follow requests. Primates who have learned to sign or push computer-connected buttons in order to communicate with human beings have amassed impressive vocabularies. While skeptics are quick to note that humans are superior to apes in their ability to sequence language correctly, studies indicate that primates are able to think and communicate.

Be sure to record the publication information (including page numbers) for the sources you paraphrase. You will need this information to document the sources in your paper.

EXERCISE 19.8

POSSIBLE ANSWER

Sample paraphrase of paragraph 5: Virtual reality illusions currently simulate sight. Computers use data inputted by programmers to generate three-dimensional images, which are viewed though small video monitors placed in front of the eyes by a head-mounted device (similar to a helmet with goggles). Users experience what photographers call "depth of field" because the two monitors provide slightly different views.

Write a paraphrase of the following excerpt from a source on animal communication.

> Another vigorously debated issue is whether language is uniquely human. Animals obviously communicate. Bees, for example, communicate the location of food through an intricate dance. And several teams of psychologists have taught various species of apes, including a number of chimpanzees, to communicate with humans by signing or by pushing buttons wired to a computer. Apes have developed considerable vocabularies. They string words together to express meaning and to make and follow requests. Skeptics point out important differences between apes' and humans' facilities with language, especially in their respective abilities to order words using proper syntax. Nevertheless, these studies reveal that apes have considerable cognitive ability.
>
> DAVID G. MYERS, *Psychology*

EXERCISE 19.9

Write a paraphrase of one paragraph from the section titled "How Does Virtual Reality Work?" in "Virtual Reality" on page 651.

Highlighting and Annotating Sources

For more on highlighting and annotating, including a sample, see Chapter 2, pp. 37–39.

If you have a printout or photocopy from a source, highlighting and writing annotations (marginal notes) are effective ways to identify what is important and record your own responses. You can *highlight* or *underline* key words and phrases and a writer's most important points, such as the thesis statement. You *annotate* by jotting down your ideas about what you are reading as you read. It is a way of "talking back" to the author—to question, challenge, agree, or disagree.

While highlighting or underlining helps you to find a writer's ideas, annotating helps you to respond to them. By annotating, you can discover new approaches to your topic, critically evaluate the source, and come up with new ideas to write about. Whether you use highlighting or annotating, be selective about what you mark or comment on, keeping the purpose of your research in mind.

The sample that follows shows an annotated excerpt from *When Elephants Weep: The Emotional Lives of Animals* by Jeffrey Masson and Susan McCarthy. Key points have been underlined. Notice how the annotations comment on, summarize key points of, and question the text.

SAMPLE ANNOTATIONS AND UNDERLINING

The greatest obstacle in science to investigating the emotions of other animals has been an inordinate desire to avoid anthropomorphism. <u>Anthropomorphism means</u>

the ascription of human characteristics — thought, feelings, consciousness, and motivation — to the nonhuman. When people claim that the elements are conspiring to ruin their picnic or that a tree is their friend, they are anthropomorphizing. Few believe that the weather is plotting against them, but anthropomorphic ideas about animals are held more widely. Outside scientific circles, it is common to speak of the thoughts and feelings of pets and wild and captive animals. Yet many scientists regard the notion that animals feel pain as the grossest sort of anthropomorphic error.

    Cats and dogs are prime targets of anthropomorphism, both wrongly and rightly. Ascribing unlikely thoughts and feelings to pets is common: "She understands every word you say." "He sings his little heart out to show how grateful he is." Some people deck reluctant pets in clothing, give them presents in which they have no interest, or assign their own opinions to the animals. Some dogs are even taught to attack people of races different from their owners'. Many dog lovers seem to enjoy believing that cats are selfish, unfeeling creatures who heartlessly use their deluded owners, compared with loving, loyal, and naive dogs. More often, however, people have quite realistic views about their pets' abilities and attributes. The experience of living with an animal often provides a strong sense of its abilities and limitations — although even here, as for people living intimately with people, preconceptions can be more persuasive than lived experience, and can create their own reality.

Jeffrey Masson and Susan McCarthy,
When Elephants Weep: The Emotional Lives of Animals

Margin notes:

*def

! Wrong! If so, then why do vets use anesthesia?

dog lovers vs. cat lovers

why?
People have preconceived notions of certain breeds of dogs as vicious.

Recording Quotations

Sometimes it is advisable, and even necessary, to use a **direct quotation** — which reproduces a writer's words exactly as they appear in the original source. You will probably need to use quotations often when referring to *primary sources,* especially when you analyze literature. Quote from *secondary sources* only when you want to reproduce the author's exact wording. Use quotations to record wording that is unusual or striking or when you want to report the exact words of an expert on your topic. Such quotations, when used sparingly, can be particularly effective in a paper. When using a direct quotation, be sure to record it *precisely* as it appears in the source. The author's spelling, punctuation, and capitalization must be recorded exactly. Also write down the page number on which the material being quoted appears in the original source. Be sure to indicate that you are copying a direct quotation by including the term "direct quotation" and the page number in parentheses.

    You may delete a phrase or sentence from a quotation as long as you do not change the meaning of the quotation. When you delete a phrase or sentence, use an ellipsis mark (. . .), three spaced periods, to indicate that you have made a deletion.

TEACHING TIP

Since students tend to rely too heavily on direct quotations in a research paper, consider limiting the number of quotes or quoted lines they can use in the paper. Explain that writers who rely too much on others' words shirk their responsibility to filter information through their own intelligence and thereby prevent their own voice from being heard.

For more on using ellipses, see Chapter 20, p. 676.

Avoiding Plagiarism

Plagiarism — using an author's ideas or words as if they were your own and neglecting to give the author credit — is a serious error. *All* quotations, summaries, and paraphrases *must* be documented. Most students do not plagiarize deliberately; they do not directly copy another writer's work and call it their own. Instead, plagiarism usually occurs unintentionally, as a result of careless note-taking or of the failure to acknowledge the ideas of others.

Especially when you paraphrase a source, check to be sure your wording is not too close to the original writer's. Compare the following plagiarized paraphrase to the original source quotation.

EXCERPT FROM ORIGINAL

Learning some items may interfere with retrieving others, especially when the items are similar. If someone gives you a phone number to remember, you may be able to recall it later. But if two more people give you their numbers, each successive number will be more difficult to recall. Such **proactive interference** occurs when something you learned earlier disrupts recall of something you experienced later. As you collect more and more information, your mental attic never fills, but it certainly gets cluttered.   DAVID G. MYERS, *Psychology*

EXAMPLE OF PLAGIARISM

When you learn some things, it may interfere with your ability to remember others. This happens when the things are similar. Suppose a person gives you a phone number to remember. You probably will be able to remember it later. Now, suppose two persons give you numbers. Each successive number will be harder to remember. Proactive interference happens when something you already learned prevents you from recalling something you experience later. As you learn more and more information your mental attic never gets full, but it will get cluttered.

For more on systems for documenting sources, see Chapter 20, pp. 682 (MLA) and 693 (APA).

TEACHING TIP

Point out to students that common knowledge is basic information about a *topic* or *field of study.* However, even basic terms and concepts that may be unfamiliar to readers require both definitions in the student's words, based on the information culled from sources, and corresponding citations for the multiple works the student used to define the terms.

Although this paraphrase does substitute some synonyms — *remembering* for *retrieving,* for example — it is still an example of plagiarism. The writer has changed neither the style nor the sentence order of the original.

Use the following tips to avoid plagiarizing sources in your writing.

1. Place in quotation marks *everything* you copy directly from a source.

2. Make sure that a paraphrase does not mix the author's wording and your own.

3. Always acknowledge the unique ideas or opinions of others, even if you do not quote them directly and regardless of whether they are in print or another medium. Movies, videos, documentaries, interviews, and computerized sources all require acknowledgment. Use an in-text citation to indicate that an idea or a point of view is not your own.

4. You do not need to acknowledge information that is *common knowledge,* such as well-known scientific facts and historical events. For instance, it would not be necessary to acknowledge Newton's Third Law of Motion, but it would be necessary to acknowledge a unique application or example of the law.

EXERCISE 19.10

The following piece of student writing is a paraphrase of a source on the history of advertising. Working with another student, evaluate the paraphrase and discuss whether it would be considered an example of plagiarism. If you decide the paraphrase is plagiarized, rewrite it so it is not.

ORIGINAL SOURCE

    Everyone knows that advertising lies. That has been an article of faith since the Middle Ages—and a legal doctrine, too. Sixteenth-century English courts began the Age of Caveat Emptor by ruling that commercial claims—fraudulent or not—should be sorted out by the buyer, not the legal system. ("If he be tame and have ben rydden upon, then caveat emptor.") In a 1615 case, a certain Baily agreed to transport Merrell's load of wood, which Merrell claimed weighed 800 pounds. When Baily's two horses collapsed and died, he discovered that Merrell's wood actually weighed 2,000 pounds. The court ruled the problem was Baily's for not checking the weight himself; Merrell bore no blame.
CYNTHIA CROSSEN, *Tainted Truth*

PARAPHRASE

    It is a well-known fact that advertising lies. This has been known ever since the Middle Ages. It is an article of faith as well as a legal doctrine. English courts in the sixteenth century started the Age of Caveat Emptor by finding that claims by businesses, whether legitimate or not, were the responsibility of the consumer, not the courts. For example, there was a case in which one person (Baily) used his horses to haul wood for a person named Merrell. Merrell told Baily that the wood weighed 800 pounds, but it actually weighed 2,000 pounds. Baily discovered this after his horses died. The court did not hold Merrell responsible; it stated that Baily should have weighed the wood himself instead of accepting Merrell's word.

RESEARCH PAPER IN PROGRESS 5

For the three most relevant and reliable sources you identified in Research Paper in Progress 4, use the preceding suggestions to take notes on your sources. Your goal is to provide information and support for the ideas you developed earlier. Choose a system of note-taking, write summary notes and paraphrases, and record quotations as needed. As you work, try to answer your research questions, and keep your preliminary thesis in mind.

    Note: You will continue working on this writing assignment in Chapter 20 (p. 672), where you will sort your research information, evaluate your working thesis, and develop an organizational plan for your research paper.

POSSIBLE ANSWER

The first half of the paraphrase is too close to the original. *Sample revised paraphrase:* Consumers have been legally responsible for checking out advertising claims since the sixteenth century, when the courts instituted the Age of Caveat Emptor in order to keep commercial claims out of the courts. In an example from the early seventeenth century, a man who suffered the loss of his workhorses in a business deal was denied compensation. Baily and Merrell entered into an agreement in which Baily consented to use his two horses to haul a load of wood that Merrell said weighed 800 pounds. After Baily's horses fell down exhausted and died during the job, Baily learned that the load actually weighed almost a ton. Though Baily sued Merrell, the court determined that Baily was responsible for weighing the wood himself.

CONDUCTING FIELD RESEARCH

Some instructors may encourage you to do field research to collect original information; others may prefer you to limit your research to the works of others. If you are unsure of whether to conduct field research, check with your instructor before doing so. This section discusses three common types of field research — *interviews, surveys,* and *observation* — all of which generate primary source material.

Interviewing

Suppose you choose the topic *treatment of teenage alcoholism* for a research paper. An interview with an experienced substance abuse counselor who works with teenagers may yield useful insights, opinions, and case examples. An **interview,** then, is a means of obtaining firsthand information from a person who is knowledgeable about or has experience with your topic.

Use the following suggestions to conduct effective interviews.

1. **Choose interview subjects carefully.** Be sure your subjects work in the field you are researching or are experts on your topic. Also try to choose subjects that may provide you with different points of view. If you are researching a corporation, for example, try to interview someone from upper management as well as white- and blue-collar workers.

2. **Arrange your interview by letter or phone well in advance.** Describe your project and state the purpose of your interview; be sure to explain that you are a student completing an assignment. Although some people may deny your request, others will welcome the opportunity to share their experiences. Request the amount of time you think you'll need, but don't be disappointed if the person needs to shorten the time allotted for the interview. In some instances, you may need to be somewhat flexible about whom you interview. A busy vice-president, for example, may refer you to his or her assistant or to another member of the management team.

3. **Plan the interview.** Write a list of questions you want to ask your subject and take them with you to the interview. Doing so will help the interview move along more efficiently, and your subject will appreciate the fact that you are prepared. Try to ask *open* rather than *closed* questions. Closed questions can be answered in a word or two. "Do you think your company has a promising future?" could be answered "yes" or "no," whereas "How do you account for your company's success in heavy manufacturing?" would encourage a detailed response. Open questions tend to encourage people to "open up" and reveal attitudes and feelings as well as factual information.

4. **Take notes during the interview.** Take a notebook to write in, since you probably will not be seated at a table or desk. Write the subject's responses in note form, and find out whether you may quote him or her directly. If you want to tape-record the interview, be sure to ask the subject's permission.

5. **Evaluate the interview.** As soon as possible after the interview, perhaps even before leaving the building, reread your notes. Fill in information you did not

have time to record. Also write down your reactions and impressions while they are still fresh in your mind. Record these in the margin or in a different color ink so they are distinguishable from the interview notes. Try to write down your overall impression and an answer to this question: "What did I learn from this interview?"

Using a Survey

A **survey** is a set of questions designed to get information quickly from a large number of people. Surveys can be conducted face-to-face, by phone, or by mail. Surveys are often used to assess people's attitudes, beliefs, or intended actions. For example, we frequently read or hear results of surveys that measure the popularity of political figures.

Use the following suggestions to prepare effective surveys.

1. **Clarify the purpose of the survey.** Write a detailed list of what you want to learn from the survey.

2. **Design your questions.** A survey can include either closed or open questions, or both, but most use closed questions in either a multiple-choice or ranking-scale format. Here is an example of each.

MULTIPLE CHOICE

How often do you purchase lunch in the campus cafeteria?

a. 1–2 days per week
b. 3–4 days per week
c. 5–6 days per week
d. Every day of the week

RANKING

On a scale of *1* to *5* (*1* = excellent and *5* = poor), rate the quality of food in the campus cafeteria.

Excellent				*Poor*
1	2	3	4	5

It is usually better to use closed questions in surveys because they are easy to tally and interpret. An open question such as "What do you think of the food served in the cafeteria?" would elicit a variety of responses that would be difficult to summarize in your paper.

3. **Test your survey questions.** Try out your questions on a few classmates, family members, or friends to be sure they are clear and that they will provide the information you need.

4. **Choose your respondents carefully.** Your *respondents,* the people who provide answers to your survey, should meet two requirements: They must be representative of the group you are studying, and they must be chosen at random. Suppose you want to conduct an opinion poll to learn what students on your campus think about mandatory drug testing for athletes. Since you cannot ask every enrolled student his or her opinion, you should choose a group of respondents—or a *sample*—that is similar to the entire population of students on your campus. For most campuses, then, your group of respondents would contain both men and women, be racially and ethnically diverse, and represent the various ages and socioeconomic groups of students. Your sample should also be random; respondents should be unknown to you and not chosen for a specific reason. One way to draw a random sample is to give the survey to every fifth or tenth name on a list or every fifteenth person who walks by.

5. **Summarize and report your results.** Tally the results of the survey and look for patterns in the data you have gathered. A computer spreadsheet can be useful in tabulating results from a large sample and in preparing tables that summarize data. In your paper, discuss your summary of your findings, not individual respondents' answers. Explain the purpose of the survey as well as how you designed it, selected a sample, and administered the survey to respondents. You may also want to include a copy of the survey and tabulations in an appendix at the end of your paper.

Conducting Observations

The results obtained from **observation**—the firsthand inspection of an event, scene, or activity—are also considered a primary source. For instance, depending on your research topic, you might observe and report on a demonstration at a government agency, a charity fund-raising event, or a field trial at a dog show. Observing your topic in action can give you valuable insight into it and enrich your research paper. Observation is also important on the job. You might, for example, need to observe and report on the condition of patients, the outcome of a negotiation, or the job performance of employees on your staff.

Use the following tips to conduct observations effectively.

1. **Arrange your visit in advance.** Unless you plan to visit a public place, you must obtain the advance permission of the company or organization to visit and observe. You should also make the purpose of your visit clear when arranging your appointment.

2. **Take detailed notes on what you observe.** Notice and write down the details you will need to describe the scene vividly in your paper. For instance, if you visit a mental health clinic, note details about patient care, security, hygiene, and the like. You might also try sketching the scene, especially if you are a spa-

tial learner, or using a tape recorder or video camera if you have obtained permission to do so. Your main goal is to gather enough information to reconstruct your visit in writing later, when you draft your research paper.

3. **Approach the visit with an open mind.** A close-minded approach defeats the purpose of conducting observations, whereas with an open mind you learn and discover more about what you observe. For example, if you observe a dog show with the preconceived notion that the dogs' owners are merely interested in winning prize ribbons, your close-minded view might prevent you from learning that dog shows serve many useful purposes (such as promoting responsible breeding of purebred dogs).

4. **Create a dominant impression.** As soon as possible after your visit, evaluate your observations. Ask yourself questions about what you saw and heard; then try to answer them. Also describe your dominant impression of what you observed and the details that contribute to your impression (such as facts and sensory details).

For more on formulating a dominant impression, see Chapter 10, p. 251.

Chapter 20

Suppose you have been assigned to write a research paper for a mass communication course on a topic related to one form of human communication involving more than two people. You struggle with choosing a topic for nearly a week, when suddenly, as you walk down a busy street, you notice several bumper stickers on a parked car. You decide to write about bumper stickers and begin to think about how to categorize them into types.

Writing a Research Paper

Writing Quick Start

Write a list of the bumper stickers in the photograph on the opposite page plus five or more bumper stickers you have seen. Then try to group the bumper stickers into categories.

TEACHING TIP

• Ask students to recall the categories of questions on p. 633 of Chapter 19 (psychological, sociological, economic, and so on). Suggest that they consider how those categories might apply to bumper stickers.

• Have students think of subcategories for bumper-sticker slogans within the same general category (e.g., bumper stickers about hobbies or interests). Write the subcategories on the board as students think of them; then discuss

(Continued on next page)

By creating categories of bumper stickers, you took the first steps in writing a research paper: synthesizing and condensing information from sources, in this case, a primary source. In Chapter 19, you learned how to locate and evaluate information from sources. Chapter 19 also showed how to formulate research questions and take notes. This chapter continues the research process by showing you how to plan, organize, draft, and revise a research paper, including how to document sources.

You will have numerous opportunities to write research papers in your college courses. Many jobs require research skills as well. You might, for instance, be asked to justify a proposed change in company policy by citing examples of other companies that have made a similar change, or you might need to research information about a company before going on a job interview. See the accompanying box for a few other examples of situations that would require research skills.

Think of a research paper as an opportunity to explore information about a topic, pull ideas from sources together, and present what you discover. This chapter will guide you through the process of writing a research paper. Figure 20.1 presents an overview of the process.

PLANNING AND WRITING YOUR FIRST DRAFT

After you conduct library and Internet research on your topic and take notes on your sources (as detailed in Chapter 19), you are ready to evaluate your work in preparation for writing a first draft. This stage of the research process involves evaluating your research and working thesis, developing an organizational plan, and drafting the research paper.

SCENES FROM COLLEGE AND THE WORKPLACE

• For a *business* course, you are required to research a Fortune 500 company and write a report on its history and current profitability. At least two of your sources must be from the Internet.

• For a *social problems* course, you are asked to conduct your own field research (interviews or surveys) on a local or campus issue and to report your findings in a research paper.

• As *plant manager,* you are asked by your supervisor to research a new type of machinery used in manufacturing your company's product and to submit a technical report that your company will use to decide whether it should invest in the new machinery.

FIGURE 20.1
WRITING A RESEARCH PAPER

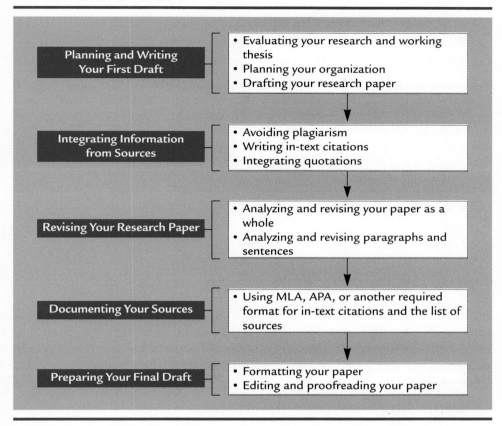

Evaluating Your Research and Working Thesis

Before you began researching your topic, you probably wrote a *working thesis*—a preliminary statement of your main point about the topic—and a list of research questions you hoped to answer. Then, as you researched your topic, you may have discovered new facts about your topic, statistics you were unaware of, or expert testimony that surprised you. In most cases, the discoveries you make during the research process influence your thinking on the topic, requiring you to modify your working thesis. In some cases, you may even need to rethink the direction of your paper.

For more on thesis statements, see Chapter 5.

As you evaluate your research notes and modify your thesis, keep the following questions in mind.

TEACHING TIP
Have students copy this list of questions in their journals for easy reference as they work through this chapter's research paper assignment. Later, they can freewrite responses to the questions and use their answers to help construct a rough draft.

1. What research questions did I begin with?
2. What answers did I find to those questions?
3. What other information did I discover about my topic?
4. What conclusions can I draw from what I've learned?
5. How does my research affect my working thesis?

To answer these questions, you'll need to **synthesize** the information you gathered from sources, pulling it together in a meaningful way. One way to arrive at a synthesis is to condense the information into categories. For example, one student found numerous sources on and answers to this research question: "What causes some parents to physically abuse their children?" He reread his research notes, looking for a way to pull the information together. The student realized he could synthesize the information by grouping aspects of it into categories: lack of parenting skills, emotional instability, and family history of child abuse. He then made this two-column list of the categories and his sources.

TEACHING TIP
Point out that the student had to consult seven sources to understand the range of views on his subject. Encourage students to consult a *variety of sources* and to avoid jumping to conclusions about issues that experts disagree on. Students need to recognize the importance of acknowledging any *ambiguities* and *dissent* they uncover in their research.

Category	*Sources*
Lack of parenting skills	Lopez, Wexler, Thomas
Emotional instability	Wexler, Harris, Thompson, Wong
Family history of child abuse	Thompson, Harris, Lopez, Strickler, Thomas

While evaluating his research in this way, the student also realized he needed to revise both his working thesis and the scope of his paper to include lack of parenting skills as a major cause of child abuse. Notice how he modified his working thesis accordingly.

WORKING THESIS

Some children are physically abused because of their parents' emotional instability and a family history of child abuse.

REVISED THESIS

Some children are physically abused because of their parents' emotional instability, a family history of child abuse, and a lack of parenting skills.

For more on categorizing information, see Chapter 14.

As you work on synthesizing information from sources, keep in mind that you can categorize many kinds of events or phenomena, such as types of life insurance, effects of education level on salary, views on environmental problems, and so forth.

POSSIBLE ANSWERS
1. *Information:* Statistics on types of toy-related injuries and

EXERCISE 20.1

Imagine that you have done research on one of the following topics; write a list of some of the information you have found. Then, working with one or two classmates, discuss how you might categorize the information. Write a thesis statement that reflects your research.

1. The health hazards of children's toys
2. The fairness of college entrance exams
3. The advantages of college athletic programs

Planning Your Organization

Your next step involves developing an organizational plan for your paper—deciding both what you'll say and the order in which you will say it. Think about whether you want to use chronological order, spatial order, or most-to-least or least-to-most important order, or whether one of the patterns of development discussed in Parts 3 and 4 of this text would be appropriate.

Following are some guidelines for organizing your research paper.

Arranging Your Information

If you used note cards, begin by sorting them into piles by subtopics or categories. (You may already have developed categories when you evaluated your research and thesis.) For example, note cards for the thesis "Prekindergarten programs provide children with long-lasting educational advantages" might be sorted by type of educational advantage, such as reading readiness, social skills, and positive self-image.

If you took notes on a computer, you may have arranged your research information by category as you went along. If not, this is the time to do so. As you move information within or among computer files, be careful to keep track of which material belongs to which source.

If you used photocopies of sources, attach Post-It notes to indicate the various subtopics each source covers.

Once your note cards, computer files, or photocopies are organized, you are ready to develop your outline or graphic organizer.

Developing an Outline or Graphic Organizer

Use an outline or a graphic organizer to show the planned divisions and subdivisions of your paper. There are several types of outlines: scratch outlines, informal outlines, and formal outlines.

1. Preparing an outline or graphic organizer is especially important for a research paper because you are working with a substantial amount of information. Without a plan to follow, it is easy to get lost and write an unfocused paper. If you are a creative learner, you may prefer to start writing and structure your paper as you work. Most students should not take this approach, however;

---

articles on how to protect children. *Categories:* Choking, cuts and puncture wounds, falls. *Thesis:* The major hazards of poorly designed toys include small parts that can choke a child, sharp edges that can cut, and equipment that can tip over or collapse onto a child.

2. *Information:* Demographics on students' scores and admission rates; information on how the exams are developed; expert opinion on their reliability. *Categories:* Types of students who do well (or poorly) on entrance exams. *Thesis:* Students from higher socioeconomic backgrounds tend to do better on college entrance exams than students from lower socioeconomic back-

grounds, although both student groups often have similar academic records.

3. *Information:* Data about the athletic program at your college; an interview with a college coach and/or athlete; the results of a survey on students' attitudes

For more on using outlines and graphic organizers, see Chapter 6, p. 124.

Learning Style Options

toward athletics. *Categories:* Help for under-privileged athletes;

(Continued on next page)

extra income for schools; increased visibility and prestige. *Thesis:* Athletic programs offer a college education to athletes who may not be able

to afford it, a source of income to schools whose teams are televised, and enhanced visibility that can help attract new students.

TEACHING TIP: LEARNING STYLES

Because creative learners may be tempted to jump into a first draft, encourage them to plan their organization, do note-taking, and possibly freewrite *before* they begin drafting. Most cre-

For more on the structure of an essay, see Chapter 6, p. 118.

ative learners will be more pleased with the final product if they devote time to prewriting, whereas others will need only some additional time for discovery through revision.

those who do should allow sufficient time for reorganizing and making extensive revisions.

2. Pragmatic learners tend to prefer organizing in detail before beginning to write. If this is your tendency, make sure that you are open to change and new ideas as you write your draft.

3. Whatever your learning style, consider writing your outline or graphic organizer on a computer. A word-processing program allows you to reorganize material easily and test out several different organizations. Be sure to save your original outline or graphic organizer and any revised versions as separate files, so that you can return to earlier versions if a new alternative doesn't work out.

RESEARCH PAPER IN PROGRESS 1

Using the research notes you developed in Chapter 19 for Research Paper in Progress 5 (p. 661) or for another assignment, sort your source notes and information into several categories and evaluate your working thesis. Then prepare an outline or a graphic organizer for your paper.

Drafting Your Research Paper

The following guidelines will help you write the first draft of a research paper.

1. **Follow the introduction, body, and conclusion format.** A straightforward organization is usually the best choice for a research paper.

2. **Employ a serious, academic tone and avoid using the first or second person.** Your credibility will be enhanced if you use the third person, which is more objective and gives you some distance from your topic.

3. **For most research papers, place your thesis in the introduction.** However, for papers analyzing a problem or proposing a solution, try placing your thesis near the end.

4. **Follow your outline or graphic organizer, but feel free to make changes as you work.** You may discover a better organization, think of new ideas about your topic, or realize that a subtopic belongs in a different section of your paper.

5. **Keep your audience in mind.** Although you now know a great deal about the topic you researched, your readers may have little knowledge of it. Be sure to provide background information, explain concepts and processes, and define terms for your readers.

For more on transitions, see Chapter 6, p. 138.

6. **Use strong transitions.** Because a research paper may be lengthy or complex, strong transitions are needed to hold the paper together as a whole. In addition, transitions help your readers understand how you have divided the topic and how one point relates to another.

7. **Support your key points with evidence.** Be sure to identify your major points *first;* then support each major point with evidence from several sources. Keep in mind that relying on one or two sources weakens your thesis, suggesting to readers that you did insufficient research. Bring together facts, statistics, details, expert testimony, and other types of evidence from a variety of sources to strengthen your thesis.

8. **Determine the purpose and main point of each paragraph.** State the main point of each body paragraph in a topic sentence. Then use your sources to substantiate, explain, or provide detail in support of that main point.

9. **Refer to your source notes frequently as you write.** If you do so, you will be less likely to overlook an important piece of evidence. If you suspect that a note is inaccurate in some way, check the original source.

10. **Use source information in a way that does not mislead your readers.** In other words, even though you are presenting only a portion of someone's ideas, make sure you are not using them in a way that is contrary to the writer's original intentions.

11. **Include source material only for a specific purpose.** Just because you discovered an interesting statistic or a fascinating quote, don't feel that you *must* use it. Information that doesn't support your thesis will only distract your reader and weaken your paper.

12. **Do not overuse sources.** Make sure your paper is not just a series of facts, quotations, and so forth taken from sources. The purpose of a research paper is not merely to summarize what others have written about the topic; be sure that *your* ideas and thesis are the basis of the paper.

INTEGRATING INFORMATION FROM SOURCES

The three methods for integrating information from sources into your paper—paraphrasing, summarizing, or quoting—have been discussed in the previous chapter. In general, try to paraphrase or summarize information rather than quote it directly. Quote a source directly only if the wording is unusual or unique or you want to provide the actual statement of an expert on the topic. For more information on each of these three options, refer to Chapter 19, pp. 656–61. Regardless of how you integrate sources, be sure to acknowledge and document all direct quotations as well as the paraphrased or summarized ideas of others. That is, you must make it clear to your readers when you borrow ideas or information from others by citing the source, whether it is a book, Web page, journal article, television show, or another type of source. The following section provides advice on what does and does not need to be documented as well as guidelines for using in-text citations and integrating quotations.

TEACHING TIP

Some teachers recommend limiting the number of direct quotations to no more than 10 percent of the paper. While this limitation is arbitrary, it helps beginning writers understand that the bulk of a research paper should contain original or paraphrased material, not a series of quotations strung together.

Deciding What to Document

You can use another person's material in your paper, as long as you give that person credit. **Plagiarism** occurs when you present the ideas of others as your own. Whether intentional or not, plagiarism is a serious error that must be avoided. The accompanying box identifies the types of material that *do* and *do not* require documentation.

WHAT DOES AND DOES NOT REQUIRE DOCUMENTATION

Documentation Required	*Documentation Not Required*
Summaries, paraphrases, and quotations	Common knowledge
Obscure or recently discovered facts	Everyday facts (presidential birth dates, names of Supreme Court Justices, and so forth)
Others' opinions	Standard definitions of academic terms
Others' field research (results of opinion polls, case studies, statistics)	Your own ideas or conclusions
Quotations or paraphrases from interviews you conduct	Your own field research (surveys or observations)

It is sometimes difficult to understand what constitutes plagiarism. Chapter 19 includes instructions for paraphrasing information from a source and examples of notes that are and are not plagiarized. See pages 656–61.

Writing In-text Citations

Many academic disciplines have their own preferred format or style for documenting sources within the text of a paper. For example, in English and the humanities, the preferred documentation format is that of the Modern Language Association and is known as the *MLA style*. In the social sciences, the guidelines of the American Psychological Association, commonly called the *APA style,* are often used. Many scientists follow a format developed by the Council of Biology Editors, known as the *CBE style*. The two most widely used formats—the MLA and the APA—are discussed in detail later in this chapter.

When you paraphrase, summarize, or quote from a source in the text of your paper, you must give credit to the source of the borrowed material. You give credit by way of providing an **in-text citation,** a brief reference that lets readers know there is a complete description of the source in a list of sources at the end of your paper. The list is headed *Works Cited* in the MLA style and *References* in the APA style. Because this list includes only those sources you cite in your paper, it is different from a bibliography, which includes all the sources you consulted in writing your paper, whether you used them or not.

Integrating Quotations

Quotations can lend interest to your paper as well as support for your ideas. They do, however, need to be used appropriately. The following section answers some common questions about the use of quotations. The in-text citations in this section follow the MLA format.

When and How Should I Use Quotations?

1. **Use quotations sparingly.** If a quote does not achieve one of the following purposes, use a paraphrase instead.
    - Quote when the author's wording is unusual, noteworthy, or striking. A quotation from Martin Luther King Jr.'s "Letter from Birmingham Jail" may have more impact than a paraphrase, for instance.
    - Quote when a paraphrase might alter or distort the statement's meaning.
    - Quote when the original words express the exact point you want to make.
    - Quote when the statement is a strong, opinionated, exaggerated, or disputed idea that you want to make clear is not your own.
2. **Use quotations to *support* your ideas.** Never use a quote as the topic sentence of a paragraph. The topic sentence should state in your own words the idea you are about to explain or prove.
3. **Use quotations that are self-explanatory.** If a quote needs to be restated or explained, paraphrase it instead.
4. **Copy quotations *exactly* as they appear in the original source.** Spelling, punctuation, and capitalization must be copied precisely, even if they are in error. If a source contains an error, copy it with the error and add the word *sic* (Latin for "thus") in brackets immediately following the error.

    ```
    According to Bernstein, "the family has undergone rapid decen-
    tralization since Word [sic] War II" (39).
    ```

How Can I Change Quotations?

1. You can emphasize words by underlining or italicizing them, but you must add the notation *emphasis added* in parentheses at the end of the sentence to indicate the change.

"In <u>unprecedented</u> and <u>increasing</u> numbers, patients are consulting practitioners of every type of complementary medicine"
(emphasis added) (Buckman and Sabbagh 73).

2. You can omit part of a quotation, but you must add an ellipsis mark, or three spaced periods (. . .), to indicate that material has been deleted. You may delete words, sentences, paragraphs, or entire pages, as long as you do not distort the author's meaning by doing so.

According to Buckman and Sabbagh, "Acupuncture . . . has been
rigorously tested and proven to be effective and valid" (188).

If you are following MLA style, the ellipsis mark should be enclosed in brackets to make it clear that the omission is yours.

According to Buckman and Sabbagh, "Acupuncture [. . .] has
been rigorously tested and proven to be effective and valid"
(188).

When an omission falls at the end of a quoted sentence, use the three spaced periods in addition to the sentence period.

Thompson maintains that "marketers need to establish ethical
standards for personal selling. . . . They must stress fairness and honesty in dealing with customers" (298).

If you are following MLA style, the ellipsis mark is enclosed in brackets, and the sentence period appears either before the first bracket or after the second, depending on what has been omitted.

According to Campbell, "We should, perhaps, strip adjectives
like <u>high</u>, <u>low</u>, <u>popular</u>, and <u>mass</u> from culture. [. . .] These
modifiers may artificially force media forms into predeter-
mined categories" (25).

Thompson maintains that "marketers need to establish ethical
standards for personal selling [. . .]. They must stress fairness and honesty in dealing with customers" (298).

3. You can add words or phrases in brackets to make a quotation clearer or to make it fit grammatically into your sentence.

Masson and McCarthy note that the well-known animal researcher
Jane Goodall finds that "the scientific reluctance to accept

```
anecdotal evidence [of emotional experience is] a serious
problem, one that colors all of science" (3).
```

4. You can change the first word of a quotation to a capital or lowercase letter to fit into your sentence. If you change it, enclose it in brackets.

```
As Aaron Smith said, "The . . ." (32).
Aaron Smith said that "[t]he . . ." (32).
```

How Do I Introduce Quotations?

Quotations should blend into your sentences and paragraphs; they should *not* pop up without a lead-in or introduction.

QUOTATION NOT INTEGRATED

```
Anecdotes that seem to indicate that animals experience emo-
tions are not considered scientifically valid. "Experimental
evidence is given almost exclusive credibility over personal
experience to a degree that seems almost religious" (Masson and
McCarthy 3).
```

QUOTATION INTEGRATED

```
Anecdotes that seem to indicate that animals experience emo-
tions are not considered scientifically valid. Masson and
McCarthy, who have done extensive field observation, comment,
"Experimental evidence is given almost exclusive credibility
over personal experience to a degree that seems almost reli-
gious" (3).
```

To introduce a quotation effectively, use an introductory phrase or clause: "As Markham points out" or "Bernstein observes that," for example. When you introduce several quotations in your paper, try to vary both the structure of the phrase as well as the verb used. The following verbs are useful for introducing quotations.

advocates	denies	proposes
argues	emphasizes	states
asserts	insists	suggests
believes	notes	
claims	points out	

TEACHING TIP

Some research manuals and handbooks refer to an attribution as a *tag phrase* or *signal phrase*. Be sure students understand that these terms are interchangeable.

What Format Do I Follow for Long Quotations?

In the MLA style, lengthy quotations (more than three lines of poetry or more than four typed lines of prose) are indented in *block form,* ten spaces from the left margin. In the APA style, the block format is used for quotations of more than forty words, and the block quotation is indented five spaces from the left margin. In both cases, omit the quotation marks from and double-space a block quotation. Introduce a block quotation in the sentence that precedes it; a colon is often used at the end of the introduction. Note that for a block quotation, the parenthetical citation appears *after* the final sentence period. This is different from the style for short quotations within the text, in which the parenthetical citation precedes the period.

BLOCK QUOTATION, MLA STYLE

Although a business is a profit-making organization, it is also a social organization. As Hicks and Gwynne note:

> In Western society, businesses are essentially economic organizations, with both the organizations themselves and the individuals in them dedicated to making as much money as possible in the most efficient way. But businesses are also <u>social</u> organizations, each of which has its unique culture. Like all social groups, businesses are made up of people of both sexes and a wide range of ages, who play different roles, occupy different positions in the group, and behave in different ways while at work. (174)

How Do I Punctuate Quotations?

There are specific rules and conventions for punctuating quotations. The most important rules follow.

1. **Use single quotation marks to enclose a quotation within a quotation.**

   Coleman and Cressey argue that "concern for the 'decaying family' is nothing new" (147).

2. **Use a comma after a verb that introduces a quotation.**

   As Thompson and Hickey report, "there are three major kinds of 'taste cultures' in complex industrial societies: high culture, folk culture, and popular culture" (76).

3. **Use a colon to introduce a quotation preceded by a complete sentence or independent clause.** Begin the first word of the quotation with a capital letter (enclosed in brackets if it is not capitalized in the source).

   The definition is clear: "Countercultures reject the conventional wisdom and standards of the dominant culture and provide alternatives to mainstream culture" (Thompson and Hickey 76).

4. **When a quotation is built into your own sentence, it is not necessary to use a comma or capitalize the first word.**

   Buck reports that "pets play a significant part in both physical and psychological therapy" (4).

5. **Place periods and commas inside quotation marks.**

   "The most valuable old cars," notes antique car collector Michael Patterson, "are the rarest ones."

   The Modern Language Association's style for in-text citations is an exception to this rule, however. In MLA style, when an in-text citation follows a short quotation that is integrated within the text, the period is placed *after* the quotation mark and the parentheses. (See the examples above.)

6. **Place colons and semicolons outside quotation marks.**

   "Petting a dog increases mobility of a limb or hand"; petting a dog, then, can be a form of physical therapy (Buck 4).

7. **Place question marks and exclamation points inside quotation marks when they are part of the original quotation.** No additional period is needed.

   The instructor asked, "Does the text's description of alternate lifestyles agree with your experience?"

8. **Place question marks and exclamation points that belong to your own sentence outside quotation marks.**

   Is the following definition accurate: "Sociolinguistics is the study of the relationship between language and society"?

RESEARCH PAPER IN PROGRESS 2

Using your research notes, revised thesis, and the organizational plan you developed for your research paper, write a first draft. Be sure to include in-text citations of sources. (See pp. 682–85 for MLA style guidelines for in-text citations; see pp. 693–96 for APA style.)

REVISING YOUR RESEARCH PAPER

Revise a research paper in two stages. First focus on the paper as a whole; then consider individual paragraphs and sentences for effectiveness and correctness. If time allows, wait at least a day before rereading your research paper.

Analyzing and Revising Your Paper as a Whole

Begin by evaluating your paper as a unified piece of writing; focus on general issues, overall organization, and the key points you provide in support of your thesis. Use Flowchart 20.1 to help you discover the strengths and weaknesses of your research paper as a whole. You might also ask a classmate to review your draft paper by using the questions in the flowchart.

FLOWCHART 20.1
REVISING A RESEARCH PAPER

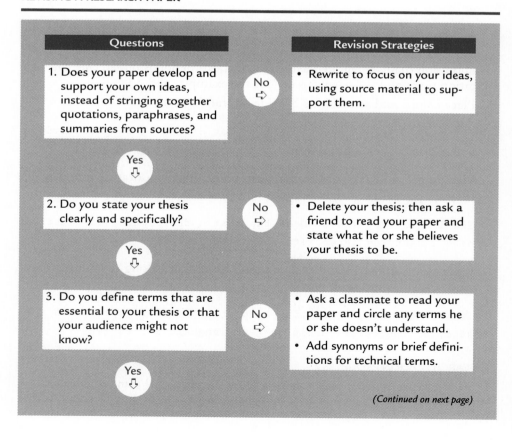

Questions		Revision Strategies
1. Does your paper develop and support your own ideas, instead of stringing together quotations, paraphrases, and summaries from sources?	No ⇨	• Rewrite to focus on your ideas, using source material to support them.
⇩ Yes		
2. Do you state your thesis clearly and specifically?	No ⇨	• Delete your thesis; then ask a friend to read your paper and state what he or she believes your thesis to be.
⇩ Yes		
3. Do you define terms that are essential to your thesis or that your audience might not know?	No ⇨	• Ask a classmate to read your paper and circle any terms he or she doesn't understand. • Add synonyms or brief definitions for technical terms.
⇩ Yes		

(Continued on next page)

FLOWCHART 20.1 *(continued)*

Questions		Revision Strategies
4. Do all of your key points support your thesis?	No ⇨	• Ask yourself, "Would my paper be stronger if this point were eliminated?" • Reread your research notes to see if you overlooked any major points.
Yes ⇩		
5. Does each paragraph have a clear topic sentence and evidence from your sources to support it?	No ⇨	• Revise topic sentences that don't adequately state what the paragraph is about. • Delete facts, statistics, and other evidence that does not support your topic sentence. • Reread your notes to find additional source information.
Yes ⇩		
6. Do you give credit to each source you cite in an in-text citation?	No ⇨	• Add in-text citations wherever you paraphrase, summarize, or quote from sources.
Yes ⇩		
7. Is it clear where information from each source begins and ends? Do you vary the way you introduce source material?	No ⇨	• Add phrases and clauses of attribution. • Change some of your introductory phrases so that you don't use the same phrase repeatedly.
Yes		

Analyzing and Revising Paragraphs and Sentences

After evaluating your paper as a whole, check each paragraph to be sure that it supports your thesis and integrates sources appropriately. Then check your sentences for correct structure, transitions, and in-text citation format. Use Flowchart 20.1 to guide your analysis.

RESEARCH PAPER IN PROGRESS 3

Using the questions in Flowchart 20.1, revise the first draft of your research paper.

DOCUMENTING SOURCES: MLA STYLE

The system described in this section is recommended by the Modern Language Association (MLA). If you are unsure of whether to use the MLA system, check with your instructor.

The MLA style uses in-text citations to identify sources within the text of a research paper. A corresponding list of works cited appears at the end of the paper.

MLA Style for In-Text Citations

The MLA style for citing sources is commonly used in English and the humanities. Both in-text citations and a list of works cited are used to document sources, as the models in this chapter show. For more information, consult the following sources.

> Gibaldi, Joseph. *MLA Handbook for Writers of Research Papers,* 5th ed. New York: MLA, 1999.
> Gilbadi, Joseph. *The MLA Style Manual and Guide to Scholarly Publishing,* 2nd ed. New York: MLA, 1998.

The student paper that appears later in this chapter uses MLA style (see pages 705–13).

Your paper must include in-text citations for all material you borrow or quote from sources. There are two basic ways to write an in-text citation.

1. **Use an attribution.** Mention the author's name early in the sentence or paragraph and include only the page number(s) in parentheses. Use the author's full name the first time you mention the author. After the first mention, give only the author's last name in subsequent citations to the same source.

2. **Use only a parenthetical citation.** Include both the author's last name and the page number(s) in parentheses at the end of the sentence. Do not separate the name and page number with a comma.

Many instructors prefer that you use attributions rather than parenthetical citations. For either type of citation, use the following rules.

- Do not use the word *page* or the abbreviation *p.* or *pp.*
- Place the sentence period after the closing parenthesis, unless the citation follows a block quotation. (See p. 678.)
- If a quotation ends the sentence, insert the closing quotation marks before the parentheses.

The following section provides guidelines for formatting in-text citations in the MLA style.

A single author

```
According to Vance Packard . . . (58).
. . . (Packard 58).
```

Two or three authors.   Include all authors' names, either in an attribution or a parenthetical citation.

```
Marquez and Allison assert . . . (74).
. . . (Marquez and Allison 74).
```

Four or more authors.   You may use either the first author's last name followed by *et al.* or all of the authors' last names. (The Latin *et al.* means "and others.") Whichever option you choose, apply it consistently within your paper.

```
Hong et al. maintain . . . (198).
. . . (Hong et al. 198).
```

Two or more works by the same author.   When you cite two or more sources by the same author or group of authors, include the full or abbreviated title in the citation.

```
In For God, Country, and Coca-Cola, Pendergrast describes . . .
(96).
Pendergrast describes . . . (Coca-Cola 96)
. . . (Pendergrast, Coca-Cola 96).
```

Unknown author.   If the author is unknown, use the full title in an attribution or a shortened form in parentheses.

```
According to the article "Medical Mysteries and Surprises,"
. . . (79).
. . . ("Medical Mysteries" 79).
```

Authors with the same last name.   Include the first initial of these authors in all parenthetical citations. Use the complete first name in an attribution or if both authors have the same first initial.

```
John Dillon proposes . . . (974).
. . . (J. Dillon 974).
```

Two or more sources in the same citation.   When citing two or more sources of one idea in parentheses, separate the citations with a semicolon.

```
. . . (Breakwater 33; Holden 198).
```

Entire work.   To refer to an entire work, use only the author's name, preferably within the text rather than in a parenthetical reference. The title is optional; do not include page numbers.

```
Pendergrast in For God, Country, and Coca-Cola presents an
unauthorized history of Coca-Cola, the soft drink, and of the
company that produces it.
```

Work within an anthology.   An *anthology* is a collection of writings (articles, stories, poems) by different authors. In the in-text citation, name the author who wrote the work (*not* the editor of the anthology) and include the page number(s) from the anthology. The corresponding works-cited entry begins with the author's last name; it also names the editor of the anthology.

IN-TEXT CITATION

```
According to Nora Crow . . . (226).
. . . (Crow 226).
```

WORKS-CITED ENTRY

```
Crow, Nora F. "Swift and the Woman Scholar." Pope, Swift and
     Women Writers. Ed. Donald C. Mell. Newark: U of Delaware
     P, 1996. 222-38.
```

Multivolume work.   When you cite two or more volumes of a multivolume work, indicate the volume number, followed by a colon and the page number.

```
Terman indicates . . . (2: 261).
. . . (Terman 2: 261).
```

Indirect sources.   When you quote an indirect source (someone whose ideas came to you through another source, such as a magazine article or book), make this clear by adding the last name and page number of the source in which the quote or information appeared in parentheses, preceded by the abbreviation *qtd. in.*

```
According to Ephron (qtd. in Thomas 33), . . .
```

Personal interviews, letters, email, conversations.   Give the name of the person in your text.

```
In an interview with Professor Lopez, . . .
```

Literature and poetry.   Include information that will help your readers locate the material in any edition of the literary work. Include page numbers from the edition you use.

- *For novels:* Cite page and chapter numbers.

```
(109; ch. 5)
```

- *For poems:* Cite line numbers instead of page numbers; use the word *line* or *lines* in the first reference only.

FIRST REFERENCE   `(lines 12-15)`

LATER REFERENCES `(16-18)`

- *For plays:* Give the act, scene, and line numbers in arabic numerals, separated by periods.

```
(Macbeth 2.1.32-37)
```

Include complete publication information for the edition you use in the list of works cited. (See pp. 686–88.)

Internet and nonprint sources.   Give enough information in the citation so that your readers can locate the source in your list of works cited. Include the author or title under which you list the source and paragraph numbers if they are included in the source. Use *par.* or *pars.* with paragraph numbers.

```
According to the Web site Buying Native American Arts and
Crafts, authentic arts and crafts are "handmade items produced
by a Native American craftsperson [. . .] using natural mate-
rials that are not machine stamped."
    . . . (Buying Native American).
```

MLA Style for the List of Works Cited

On a separate page at the end of your paper, you must include an alphabetical list of all the sources you cite. The list is headed *Works Cited*. Follow these general guidelines for preparing the list.

1. **List only the sources you cite in your paper.** If you consulted a source but did not cite it in your paper, do not include it in the list of works cited.
2. **Put the list on a separate page at the end of your paper.** The heading *Works Cited* should be centered about an inch below the top margin of the page. Do not use quotation marks, underlining, or bold type for the heading.
3. **Alphabetize the list by authors' last names.** For works with multiple authors, invert only the first author's name.

       Kaplan, Justine, and Anne Bernays. The Language of Names. New
            York: Simon, 1997.

4. **Capitalize the first word and all other words in a title except** *a, an, the, to,* **coordinating conjunctions, and prepositions.**
5. **Underline titles of books and names of journals.** If you are writing on a computer, you can use italics if your instructor approves.
6. **Give inclusive page numbers of articles in periodicals.** Do not use the word *page* or the abbreviation *p.* or *pp.*
7. **Indent the second and all subsequent lines five spaces.** This is known as the *hanging indent* style.
8. **Double-space the entire list.**

The following sections describe how to format works-cited entries for books, periodicals, Internet sources, and other sources.

Books

General guidelines and sample entries for books follow.

1. Begin with the author's last name, followed by the first name.
2. Provide the full title of the book, including the subtitle. It should be underlined and capitalized.
3. Give the place of publication. Do not abbreviate city names (use *Los Angeles,* not *LA*). It is not necessary to include an abbreviation for the state.
4. Use a shortened form of the publisher's name; usually one word is sufficient (*Houghton Mifflin* is listed as *Houghton*). For university presses, use the abbreviations *U* for *University* and *P* for *Press* with no periods.
5. Use the most recent publication date listed on the book's copyright page.

Book with one author

> Packard, Vance. <u>The Hidden Persuaders</u>. New York: McKay, 1957.

Book with two or more authors.

List the names in the order they appear on the title page of the book, and separate the names with commas. The second and subsequent authors' names are *not* reversed. For books with four or more authors, you can either list all names or list only the first author's name followed by *et al.*

TWO AUTHORS

> Wolpoff, Milford, and Rachael Caspari. <u>Race and Human Evolu-</u>
> <u>tion</u>. New York: Simon, 1997.

FOUR OR MORE AUTHORS

> Bullough, Bonnie, et al. <u>Gender Blending</u>. Amherst: Prometheus,
> 1997.

Book with no named author.

Put the title first and alphabetize the entry by title. (Do not consider the words *A, An,* and *The* when alphabetizing.)

> <u>The Ticker Symbol Book</u>. New York: McGraw, 1997.

Book by an agency or corporation.

List the agency as the author.

> Ford Foundation. <u>New Approaches to Conflict Resolution</u>. New
> York: Ford Foundation, 1978.

Edited book or anthology.

List the editor's name followed by a comma and the abbreviation *ed.* or *eds.*

> Wekesser, Carol, ed. <u>Pornography: Opposing Viewpoints</u>. San
> Diego: Greenhaven, 1997.

Work within an Anthology.

List the author and title of the work, followed by the title and editor of the anthology and the remainder of the citation.

> Tan, Amy. "Two Kinds." <u>The Story and Its Writer</u>. Ed. Ann Char-
> ters. Boston: Bedford, 1995. 62-67.

Translated book.

After the title include *Trans.* followed by the first and last names of the translator.

> Tolstoy, Leo. <u>War and Peace</u>. Trans. Constance Garnett. London:
> Pan, 1972.

Two or more works by the same author(s).   Use the author's name for only the first entry. For subsequent entries, use three hyphens followed by a period. List the entries in alphabetical order by title.

> Covey, Stephen R. <u>Principle-Centered Leadership</u>. New York:
>   Simon, 1991.
> ---. <u>The Seven Habits of Highly Effective People: Restoring
>   the Character Ethic</u>. New York: Simon, 1989.

Edition other than the first.   Indicate the number of the edition following the title.

> Myers, David G. <u>Psychology</u>. 5th ed. New York: Worth, 1998.

Multivolume work.   Give the number of volumes after the title.

> Ramachandran, V. S., ed. <u>Encyclopedia of Human Behavior</u>. 4
>   vols. San Diego: Academic, 1994.

One volume of a multivolume work.   Give the volume number after the title, and list the number of volumes in the complete work after the date, using the abbreviations *Vol.* and *vols.*

> Ramachandran, V. S., ed. <u>Encyclopedia of Human Behavior</u>. Vol.
>   1. San Diego: Academic, 1994. 4 vols.

Article or chapter in an anthology.   List the author and title of the article first and then the title of the anthology, the editor's name (introduced by the abbreviation *Ed.*), and the publication information.

> Spangler, L. C. "Buddies and Pals: A History of Male Friend-
>   ships on Prime-time Television." <u>Men, Masculinity and the
>   Media</u>. Ed. S. Craig. Newbury Park: Sage, 1992. 93-110.

Articles in Periodicals

General guidelines and sample entries for various types of periodical articles follow.

1. Use the basic format for listing authors' names (see p. 686). If no author is listed, begin the entry with the article title and alphabetize the entry by its title.

2. The title of the periodical should be underlined. Do *not* include the word *A, An,* or *The* at the beginning: *Journal of the American Medical Association, New York Times.*

3. Abbreviate the names of months except for *May, June,* and *July.*

4. List dates in the following order: day, month, year.

5. If an article begins in one place, such as pages 19 to 21, and is continued on pages 79 to 80, just write *19+* for the page numbers (do *not* write *19–80*).

Article in a scholarly journal when each issue begins with page 1.   After the journal title, include the volume number, a period, and the issue number, followed by the year in parentheses, a colon, and the inclusive page numbers.

> LaRosa, John. "Unemployment, Leisure and the Birth of
>   Creativity." Black Scholar 26.2 (1996): 29-31.

Article in a scholarly journal with issues paged continuously through each volume.   Only a volume number precedes the year.

> Ullman, Sarah E., and Judith M. Siegel. "Traumatic Events
>   and Physical Health in a Community Sample." Journal of
>   Traumatic Stress Disorder 9 (1996): 703-21.

Article in a newspaper

> Mathews, Jay. "Educators Differ on Whether Competitions Are in
>   the Best Interest of Students." Buffalo News 21 Aug.
>   1997: A3.

Article in a monthly magazine

> Dowd, Ann Reilly. "Protect Your Privacy." Money Aug. 1997:
>   104-16.

Article in a weekly magazine

> Shute, Nancy. "Why Do We Age?" U.S. News & World Report 18
>   Aug. 1997: 55-57.

Editorial or letter to the editor.   Cite the article or letter beginning with the author's name, and add the word *Editorial* or *Letter* followed by a period after the title. An author's name or a title may be missing.

> "Premature Praise for Welfare Reform." Editorial. New York
>   Times 20 Aug. 1997: A22.
> Seomin, Scott. Letter. Time 26 Jan. 1998: 9.

Book or film review.   List the reviewer's name and title of the review. After the title add the words *Rev. of* and give the title and author or director of the book or film reviewed. Include publication information for the review itself, *not* the material reviewed.

```
Stone, Andrea. "Muscular 'G.I. Jane' Pumps up Navy Dramatics."
     Rev. of G. I. Jane, dir. Ridley Scott. USA Today 22 Aug.
     1997: 7D.
```

Internet Sources

Citations for Internet sources should include enough information to allow readers to locate your sources. Because electronic sources change frequently, it is often necessary to provide more information than you do for print sources. To help your readers locate an online source easily, give its network address or URL (uniform resource locator) at the end of your citation, enclosed in angle brackets (< >). If a URL is too long to fit on one line, divide it only following a slash.

General guidelines and sample entries for Internet sources follow.

1. Include authors' names when they are available.
2. Include the full title of the work. Enclose titles of articles in quotation marks; underscore the titles of longer works.
3. Provide names of editors, compilers, or translators if appropriate.
4. Tell where and when the material was originally published, if it was originally published in print. Include volume and issue numbers, names of periodicals, and so forth.
5. Include the date the document was published electronically as well as the date you accessed the document.
6. Provide page, paragraph, or section numbers, if available.

For some Internet sources it may not be possible to locate all of the required information; provide the information that is available.

World Wide Web site.   Include the author's name (if it is not known, begin the entry with the title), title or site description (such as *Home page* if the site is untitled), date of publication, name of any sponsoring organization, date of access, and URL.

```
Rice, Scott. The Bulwer-Lytton Fiction Contest Home Page. 7
     Sept. 1997. San Jose State U. 29 Jan. 1999 <http://
     www.bulwer-lytton.com>.
Excerpts from Slave Narratives. Ed. Steven Mintz. 19 Nov.
     1997. U of Houston. 16 Dec. 1998 <http://vi.edu/
     pages/mintz/primary/htm>.
```

Electronic mail. Provide the author's name, the subject line (if available) in quotation marks, *E-mail to,* and the recipient's name. End with the date of the message.

> Johnson, Ann. "Antique American Blue Glass." E-mail to Ruth E.
> Thompson. 11 Aug. 1998.

Article from an online journal

> Herring, Susan C. "Gender and Democracy in Computer-mediated
> Communication." Electronic Journal of Communications 3.2
> (1993). 7 Sept. 1997 <http://www.cios.org/getfile/
> Herring_V3N293>.

Posting to a listserv or newsgroup. Include the author's name, the title or subject line enclosed in quotation marks, the phrase *Online posting,* the date of posting, the name of the list, the date of access, and the list's URL or the moderator's or supervisor's email address. If possible, cite an archival version.

> McCarty, Willard. "Disciplinarity, Mad Cows, and Smoke."
> Online posting. 8 May 1998. Humanist Discussion Group.
> 21 May 1999 <http://www.princeton.edu/~mccarty/humanist/>.

Online book. Include the author's name, title (underlined), the name of any editor, translator, or compiler, original publication information (if available), date of access, and URL.

> Twain, Mark. A Connecticut Yankee in King Arthur's Court.
> New York: Harper, 1889. 29 Jan. 1999 <http://
> etext.lib.virginia.edu/modeng/modengT.browse.html>.

Other Sources

Publication on diskette, CD-ROM, or another electronic medium. These sources are cited much like a book. Include the author's name and title. If the work is available in print, include publication information.

> The Time-Life Works of Shakespeare. Videodisc. Chicago:
> Clearvue, 1995.

Material from a CD-ROM database. Give the title of the material (in quotation marks), the title of the database (underlined), and all other publication details. Place the date at the end of the reference.

> Sternberg, Martin L. A. "History of ASL." The American Sign
>   Language Dictionary on CD-ROM. CD-ROM. New York: Harper-
>   Collins, 1995.

Personal interviews or personal communication.   Indicate the type of communication after the name of the person. For interviews you conducted, indicate the type of interview (telephone, personal, email, and so forth).

> Caulfield, Alan. Telephone interview. 18 Jan. 1998.
> Fields, Deborah. Letter to the author. 12 Aug. 1996.

See page 691 for help with citing an email message.

Published interviews.   List the person interviewed, and then list the title (if available) in quotation marks (underline the title if it is a complete work). If the interview has no title, label it *Interview* and give the source. Include the date of the interview.

> Gates, Bill. "A Kinder, Gentler Bill." Newsweek 14 Dec. 1998:
>   57.

Published letters.   If the letter was published, cite it as you would a selection in a book.

> Steinbeck, John. "Letter to His Son Thom." 10 Nov. 1958.
>   Letters of a Nation. Ed. Andrew Caroll. New York:
>   Kodansha, 1997. 313-14.

Film or video.   List the title, director, and key performer(s). Include the name of the distributor and the year of distribution.

> The Accidental Tourist. Dir. Lawrence Kasdan. Perf. William
>   Hurt, Kathleen Turner, and Geena Davis. Warner, 1989.

Television or radio program.   List the title of the program (underlined), then give key names (the narrator, producer, director, actors) as necessary and the title of the series (neither underlined nor in quotation marks). Identify the network, local station and city, and broadcast date. When you cite a particular episode or segment, include its title in quotation marks before the title of the program.

> High Stakes in Cyberspace. Prod. Frank and Martin Koughan.
>   Report. Robert Krulwich. Frontline. PBS. WGBH, Boston. 31
>   Oct. 1995.

Music recording.   List the composer or performer, the title of the recording or composition, the names of the artists, the medium if not a CD (audiocassette, LP, audiotape), the production company, and the date. Titles of recordings should be underlined, but titles of compositions identified by type (for example, Symphony no. 5) should not.

```
Lloyd-Webber, Andrew. Phantom of the Opera. Perf. Michael
     Crawford, Sarah Brightman, and Steve Barton. Polydor,
     1987.
```

DOCUMENTING YOUR SOURCES: APA STYLE

The APA style, recommended by the American Psychological Association, is commonly used in the social sciences. Both in-text citations and a list of references are used to document sources, as the following models show. For more information, consult the following reference work.

American Psychological Association. *Publication Manual of the American Psychological Association*. 4th ed. Washington, DC: APA, 1994.

APA Style for In-Text Citations

Your paper must include in-text citations for all material you borrow or quote from sources. There are two basic ways to write an in-text citation.

1. **Use an attribution.** Mention the author's name in a phrase or sentence introducing the material, and include the date in parentheses immediately following the author's name. For quotations, include a page number at the end of the cited material.
2. **Use only a parenthetical citation.** Include both the author's last name and the date of publication in parentheses at the end of the sentence. Separate the name, date, and page number with commas.

Many instructors prefer that you use attributions rather than parenthetical citations. For either type of citation, use the following rules.

- Place the sentence period after the closing parenthesis. When a quotation ends the sentence, insert the closing quotation mark before the parentheses. (Block quotations are an exception to these rules; see p. 678.)
- For direct quotations, include the page number after the date, separating it from the date with a comma. Use the abbreviation *p.* or *pp.* followed by a space and the page number.

```
The emotions of "captive wild animals are as real as those of
wild animals" (Masson & McCarthy, 1995, p. 7).
```

The following section provides guidelines for formatting in-text citations in the APA style.

A single author

```
According to Packard (1957), . . .
. . . (Packard, 1957).
```

Two authors.   Include both authors' last names and the date in an attribution or a parenthetical citation. In the latter case, use an ampersand (&) in place of the word *and*.

```
Masson and McCarthy (1995) assert. . . .
. . . (Masson & McCarthy, 1995).
```

Three to five authors.   Include all authors' last names the first time the source is mentioned. In subsequent references to the same source, use the first author's last name followed by *et al.* (Latin for "and others").

FIRST REFERENCE

```
Hong, Kingston, DeWitt, and Bell (1996) have found. . . .
. . . (Hong, Kingston, DeWitt, & Bell, 1996).
```

LATER REFERENCES

```
Hong et al. (1996) discovered. . . .
. . . (Hong et al., 1996).
```

Six or more authors.   Use the first author's last name followed by *et al.* in all in-text citations, but list all authors' names in the corresponding references entry.

Two or more works by the same author in the same year.   Add the lowercase letter *a* after the publication date for the first source as it appears alphabetically by title in your reference list. Add the letter *b* to the publication date for the source that appears next, and so forth. Include the dates with the corresponding lower-case letters in your in-text citations. (See p. 701 for the corresponding reference entries.)

```
Gardner (1995a) believes that. . . .
. . . (Gardner, 1995a).
```

Two or more works by the same author(s).   Cite the works chronologically, in order of publication.

> Gilbert (1988, 1993) believes that. . . .
> . . . (Gilbert, 1988, 1993).

Authors with the same last name.   Use the authors' initials with their last names.

> Research by F. P. Lopez (1997) demonstrated. . . .
> According to C. Lopez (1993), . . .

Unknown author.   Use the title and date in the attribution or parenthetical citation. Give only the first two or three important words of a long title. Underline a book title; put the title of a journal article in quotation marks. Unlike the entry in the list of references, use standard capitalization in the in-text citation. (See p. 697.)

> As noted in "Medical Mysteries" (1993), . . .
> . . . ("Medical Mysteries," 1993).

Two or more sources in the same citation.   When citing two or more sources in parentheses, put a semicolon between them and list them in alphabetical order.

> (Breakwater, 1986; Holden, 1996)

Entire work.   To refer to an entire work, give the author's name and the date. The title is optional; do not include page numbers.

> Pendergrast (1997) presents an unauthorized history of Coca-
> Cola, the soft drink, and of the company that produces it.

Work within an anthology.   An *anthology* is a collection of writings by different authors. In the in-text citation, name the author who wrote the work (*not* the editor of the anthology) and give the date. The corresponding entry in the list of references begins with the author's last name; it also names the editor of the anthology.

IN-TEXT CITATION

> As Kaul (1995) notes, . . .
> . . . (Kaul, 1995).

REFERENCES ENTRY

> Kaul, P. (1995). The unraveling of America. In L. Chiasson,
>   Jr. (Ed.), The press in times of crisis (pp. 169-187).
>   Westport, CT: Greenwood.

Multivolume work. When you cite one volume of a multivolume work, include the year of publication for that volume.

```
Terman (1990) indicates. . . .
. . . (Terman, 1990).
```

When you cite two or more volumes of a multivolume work, give inclusive dates for the volumes.

```
Terman (1990-1991) indicates. . . .
```

Indirect sources. When you quote a source indirectly (rather than from the original source), include the abbreviation *qtd. in* along with the information for the source in which you found the quote.

```
According to Ephron, . . . (qtd. in Thomas, 1994, p. 33).
```

Personal interviews, letters, email, and conversations. Give the last name and initial of the person, the source of the communication, and an exact date. Do not include these sources in the list of references.

```
Professor B. Lopez (personal communication, October 30, 1996)
asserts that. . . .
```

Internet sources. For direct quotations, give the author, year, and page number (if available) in the attribution or parenthetical citation. If the author is unknown, use the document title in place of the author.

```
Stevens (1997) maintains . . .
. . . (Stevens, 1997).
```

If you are citing a Web site in its entirety, include the address within the text. It is not necessary to provide an entry in the list of references.

```
Useful instructions for creating Native American crafts can be
found at Native Web: Resources for Indigenous Cultures around
the World (http://www.nativeweb.org).
```

APA Style for the List of References

On a separate page at the end of your paper, you must include an alphabetical list of all the sources you cite. The list is headed *References*. Follow these general guidelines for preparing the list.

1. **List only the sources you cite in your paper.** If you consulted a source but did not cite it in your paper, do not include it in the list of references.

CONNECTIONS

"Territoriality" by Joseph A. DeVito (p. 447) uses the APA style of documentation.

2. **Put the list on a separate page at the end of your paper.** The heading *References* should be centered about an inch below the top margin of the page. Do not use quotation marks, underlining, or bold type for the heading.

3. **Alphabetize the list by authors' last names.** Give the last name first followed by a comma and an initial or initials. Do not spell out authors' first names; use a space between initials: *Myers, D. G.* For works with multiple authors, list all authors' names in inverted order.

   Kaplan, J., & Bernays, A. (1997). <u>The language of names.</u> New
   York: Simon.

4. **Put the publication date in parentheses after the author's name.**

5. **Capitalize the first word of the titles of books and articles, the first word following a colon, and any proper nouns.** All other words are lowercase.

6. **Include the word *A, An,* or *The* at the beginning of titles.** The word *The* is dropped from the titles of journals, however.

7. **Underline titles of books and names of journals.** Do not underline or use quotation marks with article titles.

8. **For magazine and journal articles, underline the name of the publication and the volume number.** The punctuation and spaces between these elements are also underlined. Underline the names of newspapers. Capitalize all important words in the names of periodicals.

9. **Indent the second and all subsequent lines five spaces.** This is the *hanging indent* style, which the APA recommends for student papers.

10. **Double-space the entire list.**

The following sections describe how to format reference list entries for books, articles in periodicals, Internet sources, and other sources.

Books

The basic format for a book is as follows.

1. Give the author's last name and initial(s). Do not spell out authors' first names; include a space between initials: *Myers, D. G.*

2. Include the date in parentheses following the author's name. Use the most recent copyright date if more than one is given.

3. Underline the title of the book (including the period that follows the title).

4. Give the city of publication followed by a colon. If the city is not well known, add the postal abbreviation for the state *(Hillsdale, NJ:).*

5. Include the name of the publisher followed by a period. Use a shortened form of the publisher's name: *Houghton Mifflin* would be listed as *Houghton,* for example. Do not omit the word *Books* or *Press* if it is part of the publisher's name: *Academic Press, Basic Books.*

Book with one author

> Packard, V. (1957). The hidden persuaders. New York: McKay.

Book with two or more authors.   List all authors' names in the order they appear on the book's title page. Use inverted order (*last name, initial*) for all authors' names. Separate the names with commas and use an ampersand (*&*) in place of the word *and.* Do not use *et al.* in the reference list.

> Masson, J. M., & McCarthy, S. (1995). Why elephants weep: The
>   emotional lives of animals. New York: Delacorte Press.

Book with no named author.   Give the full title first, and alphabetize the entry by title. (Do not consider the word *A, An,* or *The* when alphabetizing.)

> The ticker symbol book. (1997). New York: McGraw.

Book by an agency or corporation.   List the agency as the author. If the publisher is the same as the author, write *Author* for the name of the publisher.

> Bureau of Justice Statistics. (1992). Drugs, crime, and the
>   justice system: A national report from the Bureau of Jus-
>   tice Statistics. Washington, DC: Author.

Edited book or anthology.   List the editor's or editors' names followed by the abbreviation *Ed.* or *Eds.* in parentheses followed by a period.

> Marcil, W. M., & Tigges, K. N. (Eds.). (1992). The person with
>   AIDS: A personal and professional perspective. Thorofare,
>   NJ: Slack.

Work within an anthology.   List the author of the work first, then the date the work was published in the anthology. The title of the work follows. Then name the editor of the anthology (not in inverted order), give the title of the anthology (under-lined), and include the inclusive page numbers in parentheses for the work (preceded by *pp.*). The publication information follows in normal order.

> Kaul, P. (1995). The unraveling of America. In L. Chiasson,
>   Jr. (Ed.), The press in times of crisis (pp. 169-187).
>   Westport, CT: Greenwood.

Translated book.   After the title, include the initial(s) and last name of the trans-lator followed by a comma and *Trans.*

> Tolstoy, L. (1972). War and peace. (C. Garnett, Trans.). Lon-
>   don: Pan. (Original work published 1869)

Two or more works by the same author(s).   Begin each entry with the author's name. Arrange the entries in chronological order of publication.

> Gilbert, L. A. (1988). <u>Sharing it all: The rewards and strug-</u>
> <u>gles of two-career families</u>. New York: Plenum.
> Gilbert, L. A. (1993). <u>Two careers, one family: The promise of</u>
> <u>gender equity</u>. Newbury Park, CA: Sage.

Edition other than the first

> Myers, D. G. (1998). <u>Psychology</u> (5th ed.). New York: Worth.

Multivolume work.   Give the inclusive volume numbers in parentheses after the title. If all volumes were not published in the same year, the publication date should include the range of years.

> Hawkins-Dady, M. (Ed.). (1992-1995). <u>International dictionary</u>
> <u>of theatre</u> (Vols. 1-3). New York: St. James Press.

Article in a multivolume work.   Include the author and title of the article, as well as the title, volume number, and publication information for the work.

> Norton, M. J. (1995). Sleep disorders. In <u>Encyclopedia of</u>
> <u>human behavior</u> (Vol. 4, pp. 738-741). San Diego: Academic
> Press.

Articles in Periodicals

General guidelines and sample entries for various types of periodical articles follow.

1. Follow the basic format for listing authors' names (see p. 697). If no author is listed, begin with the article title and alphabetize the entry by its title.
2. Do *not* enclose article titles in quotation marks and do *not* use standard capitalization. Only the first word of an article title is capitalized, along with any proper nouns and the first word following a colon.
3. The abbreviation *p.* or *pp.* is used only in entries for newspaper articles.
4. The year of publication appears in parentheses following the author's name.
5. Underline (or italicize) the name of the periodical and the volume number (including the comma appearing after the volume number).

Article in a scholarly journal when each issue begins with page 1

> Levy, S. J. (1998). The enjoyment of reading books. <u>Journal of</u>
> <u>Marketing, 62</u> (4), 99-101.

Article in a scholarly journal with issues paged continuously through each volume

> Triandis, H. C. (1989). The self and social behavior in differing cultural contexts. Psychological Review, 96, 506-520.

Article in a newspaper. Include the year, month, and day in parentheses following the author's name.

> Bennet, J. (1997, September 4). Clinton presses plan to test pupils on federal standards. The New York Times, p. A18.

Article in a monthly magazine. Include the month of publication after the year.

> Tobias, S. (1989, September). Tracked to fail. Psychology Today, 23, 54-60.

Article in a weekly magazine. Give year, month, and day of publication.

> Shute, N. (1997, August 18). Why do we age? U.S. News & World Report, 123, 55-57.

Editorial or letter to the editor. Cite the editorial or letter beginning with the author's name (if available); *Editorial* or *Letter to the editor* in brackets followed by a period after the title. If the author's name is not available, begin with the title.

> Change the term limits law [Editorial]. (1996, October 21). The New York Times, p. A16.
> Saginan, A. (1997, July/August). Facing up to feeling down [Letter to the editor]. Psychology Today, 30, 8.

Book or film review. List the reviewer's name, the date, and the title of the review. In brackets, give a description of the work reviewed, including the medium (book, video, or film) and the title.

> Quindlen, A. (1997, October 19). The past is another country. [Review of the book My brother]. The New York Times Book Review, p. 7.

Article with no author. Use the full title as the author.

> Fetal surgery. (1999, March). Discover, 20 (3), 28.

Two or more works by the same author in the same year.　Arrange the works alphabetically by title; then assign a lowercase letter (*a, b, c*) to the year of publication for each source. (See p. 694 for the corresponding in-text citation.)

```
Gardner, H. (1985a). Limited visions, limited means. Daedalus,
    124 (4), 101-105.
Gardner, H. (1985b). Reflections on multiple intelligences.
    Phi Delta Kappan, 77 (3), 200-208.
```

Two or more works by the same author published in different years.　See page 699.

Internet Sources

For Internet sources, include enough information to allow readers to locate the sources online. Guidelines for documenting Internet sources follow. For more help with formatting entries for Internet and other electronic sources in the APA style, consult *Electronic Reference Formats Recommended by The American Psychological Association,* available at < http://www.apa.org/journals/webref.html >.

1. Give the author's name, if available.
2. Include in parentheses the year of Internet publication or the year of the most recent update, if available.
3. Capitalize the first word of the title of the document or subject line of the message, the first word following a colon, and any proper nouns. The other words are lowercase.
4. Give the date you retrieved the document, preceded by "Retrieved" and followed by the words "from the World Wide Web," a colon, and the URL (the Internet address at which you accessed the source). The URL is not followed by a period.

```
Retrieved [date] from the World Wide Web: [URL]
```

A document posted on a World Wide Web site

```
Amnesty International. (1997). Amnesty International country
    report: United States of America: Death penalty develop-
    ments in 1996. London: Author. Retrieved January 31, 1999
    from the World Wide Web: http://www.amnesty.org/ailib
    /aipub/1997/AMR/25100197.htm
```

Article from an online journal   Provide page numbers if available.

> Steverson, B. K. (1997). Temporary employment and the social
>   contract. The Online Journal of Ethics, 1 (2). Retrieved
>   January 31, 1999 from the World Wide Web: http://www
>   .depaul.edu/ethics/tempemp.html

Posting to a listserv or newsgroup

> KEMP, F. (1999, March 20). Out on a limb. Alliance for
>   Computers and Writing Discussion List. Retrieved May 24,
>   1999 from the World Wide Web: ACWL@listserv.ttu.edu

Other Sources

Material from an information service or a database

> Anshel, M. (1996). Coping styles among adolescent competitive
>   athletes. Journal of Social Psychology, 136 (3), 311-323.
>   Retrieved January 31, 1999 from PsychINFO on-line data-
>   base (Record No: 84-28257)

Material from a CD-ROM database

> Gibbons, B. (1992) Alcohol: the legal drug. National Geo-
>   graphic, 181, 3-35. Retrieved from National Geographic
>   Interactive database (CD-ROM, 1997 release).

Film or video

> Jhally, S. (Producer and Director). (1995). Slim hopes:
>   Advertising and the obsession with thinness [Videotape].
>   Northampton, MA: Media Education Foundation.

Television program.   For a single episode of a series, the script writer's name
appears first and is used in the in-text citation.

> Carlin, J. (1999). The long walk of Nelson Mandela
>   (C. Bestall, Director). In M. Sullivan & D. Fanning
>   (Executive Producers), Frontline. Boston: WGBH.

Computer software.   If a person has proprietary rights to the software, list that
person's name. If not, use the format for a work with an unknown author.

> Mitterer, J. (1993). Dynamic concepts in psychology [Computer
>   software]. Orlando, FL: Harcourt.

RESEARCH PAPER IN PROGRESS 4

For the paper you revised in Research Paper in Progress 3, prepare a Works Cited or References list, following your instructor's preference.

PREPARING YOUR FINAL DRAFT

After you have revised your paper and compiled your list of references or works cited, you are ready to prepare your final draft. Following are some guidelines for formatting, editing, and proofreading your final draft.

Formatting Your Paper

Academic papers should follow a standard manuscript format whether or not they use sources. The following guidelines are recommended by the Modern Language Association (MLA). If your instructor suggests or requires a format that is different from that recommended by the MLA, be sure to follow it. If your instructor does not recommend a format, these guidelines would probably be acceptable.

1. **Paper.** Use 8½-by-11-inch white paper. Separate the sheets if you use continuous-feed printer paper. Use a paper clip; do not staple or use a binder.

2. **Your name and course information.** Do not use a title page unless your instructor requests one. Position your name at the left margin about one inch from the top of the page. Underneath it, list your instructor's name, your course name and number, and the date. Use separate lines for each and double-space between the lines.

3. **Title.** Place the title two lines below the date. Center the title on the page. Capitalize the first word and all other words except articles, coordinating conjunctions, and prepositions. Double space after the title and type your first paragraph. Do not underline your title or put quotation marks around it.

4. **Margins, spacing, and indentation.** Use 1-inch margins. Double-space between all lines of your paper. Indent each paragraph five spaces.

5. **Numbering of pages.** Number all pages in the upper-right corner. Place the numbers one-half inch below the top of the paper. (If your instructor requests a title page, do not number it and do not count it in your numbering.) Use arabic numerals (1, 2, 3), and include your last name, with a space between your name and the number.

6. **Headings.** The MLA does not provide any guidelines for using headings. However, the system recommended by the American Psychological Association (APA) should work for most papers. Main headings should be centered, and the first letter of key words capitalized. Subheadings, underlined, should begin at the left margin, with important words in the subheadings capitalized.

CONNECTIONS

"How to Make a Dream Catcher" by Melinda Hunter (p. 353) includes three figures and shows the MLA format for figure captions and in-text references to figures.

7. **Visuals.** You may include tables and figures (graphs, charts, maps, photographs, and drawings) in your paper. Label each table or figure with an arabic numeral (*Table 1, Table 2; Fig. 1, Fig. 2*) and give it a title. Place the title on a separate line above the table. Give each figure a number and title, and place the figure number and title on a separate line below the figure.

Editing and Proofreading Your Paper

TEACHING TIP:
COLLABORATIVE
WRITING

Have students work on editing each other's revised papers in small groups. Peer reviewers should circle problematic words and sentences and suggest corrections or improvements. Final decisions about editing should be left to the writers.

As a final step, edit and proofread your revised paper for errors in grammar, spelling, punctuation, mechanics, and documentation style. In addition, be sure to check your error log for the types of errors you commonly make.

As you edit and proofread, watch out for the following common problems.

1. Does your paper contain any long, cumbersome sentences? If so, try splitting them into two separate sentences.

2. Do you use a consistent verb tense throughout your paper? Don't shift from present to past to future tense, unless there is a good reason to do so.

3. Do you punctuate and style in-text citations correctly? Make sure that they conform to MLA style or that of another system of documentation.

TEACHING TIP

• *Thesis:* "As a result . . . conclusion that animals do exhibit a wide range of emotions . . . and joy" (paragraph 2)

• *Major supporting points:* Introduction includes example of grief among African elephants (1). "Grief has been observed in many different species" (4). Several species demonstrate sympathy (8); two types are "genetic altruism" and "mutual altruism" (9–10). Animals can express joy (11).

• Discuss as a class how Destino integrates quotations into the context of his argument. Also discuss how the writer introduces quotations — that is, with *active verbs* (*states*, not *stated*).

4. Do you reproduce direct quotations exactly as they appear in the original source? In addition to checking the accuracy of individual words, be sure to check your use of quotation marks, capital letters, commas, and ellipses within quotations.

5. Do you avoid plagiarism by carefully quoting, paraphrasing, and summarizing the ideas of others?

6. Is your paper typed and spaced according to the format you need to follow? Be sure that block quotations are also typed appropriately.

7. Is your list of works cited or references complete? Make sure all sources cited in your paper are included in the list and are formatted correctly.

RESEARCH PAPER IN PROGRESS 5

Edit and proofread your paper, paying particular attention to the questions in the preceding list.

STUDENTS WRITE

The following research paper was written by Nicholas Destino for his first-year writing course while he was a student at Niagara County Community College. Destino used the MLA style for formatting his paper and documenting sources. Notice his use of in-text citations and quotations to provide evidence in support of his thesis.

Destino 1

Nicholas Destino
Professor Thomas
English 101
10 November 1997

Double-spaced

Centered title

Do Animals Have Emotions?

Somewhere in the savannas of Africa a mother elephant is dying in the company of many other pachyderms.
Some of them are part of her family; some are fellow
members of her herd. The dying elephant tips from side
to side and seems to be balancing on a thin thread in
order to sustain her life. Many of the other elephants
surround her as she struggles to regain her balance.
They also try to help by feeding and caressing her.
After many attempts by the herd to save her life, they
seem to realize that there is simply nothing more that
can be done. She finally collapses to the ground in the
presence of her companions. Most of the other elephants
move away from the scene. There are, however, two
elephants who remain behind with the dead elephant--
another mother and her calf. The mother turns her back
to the body and taps it with one foot. Soon, the other
elephants call for them to follow and eventually they
do (Masson and McCarthy, Elephants 95). These movements, which are slow and ritualistic, suggest that
elephants may be capable of interpreting and responding
to the notion of death.

The topic of animal emotions is one that, until
recently, has rarely been discussed or studied by scientists. However, since the now famous comprehensive
field studies of chimpanzees by the internationally
renowned primatologist Jane Goodall, those who study
animal behavior have begun to look more closely at the

In-text citation of a
work with two
authors; short title
given because two
works by the authors
are cited

Destino 2

notion that animals feel emotions. As a result of their
observations of various species of animals, a number of
these researchers have come to the conclusion that animals do exhibit a wide range of emotions, such as
grief, sympathy, and joy.

One of the major reasons research into animal emotions has been avoided is that scientists fear being
accused of anthropomorphism--the act of attributing
human qualities to animals. To do so is perceived as
unscientific (Masson and McCarthy, "Hope and Joy"
xviii). Frans de Waal, of the Yerkes Regional Primate
Research Center in Atlanta, believes that if people are
not open to the possibility of animals having emotions,
they may be overlooking important information about
both animals and humans. He explains his position in
his article "Are We in Anthropodenial?" The term
anthropodenial, which he coined, refers to "a blindness
to the humanlike characteristics of other animals, or
the animal-like characteristics of ourselves" (52). He
proposes that because humans and animals are so closely
related, it would be impossible for one not to have
some characteristics of the other. He contends, "If two
closely related species act in the same manner, their
underlying mental processes are probably the same, too"
(53). If de Waal is correct, then humans can presume
that animals do have emotions because of the many similarities between human and animal behavior.

Grief has been observed in many different species.
In many instances, their behaviors (and presumably,
therefore, their emotions) are uncannily similar to the
behaviors of humans. Birds, which mate for life, have
been observed showing obvious signs of grief when their
mates die. In The Human Nature of Birds, Theodore

Thesis statement

Attribution of quota-
tion within text

Page number follows
quotation

First main point

Destino 3

Barber includes a report from one Dr. Franklin, who
witnessed a male parrot caring for his mate by feeding
her and trying to help her raise herself when she was
dying. Franklin observed the following scene:

> Her unhappy spouse moved around her inces-
> santly, his attention and tender cares redou-
> bled. He even tried to open her beak to give
> her some nourishment. [. . .] At intervals,
> he uttered the most plaintive cries, then
> with his eyes fixed on her, kept a mournful
> silence. At length his companion breathed her
> last; from that moment he pined away, and
> died in the course of a few weeks. (qtd. in
> Barber 116)

Veterinarian Susan Wynn, discussing the physiological symptoms brought on by emotional trauma in
animals, notes that "[a]nimals definitely exhibit
grief when they lose an owner or another companion animal. [. . .] Signs of grief vary widely, including
lethargy, loss of appetite, hiding [. . .]" (5). This
observation reinforces de Waal's position that animals
experience some of the same emotions as humans.

Perhaps the most extreme case of grief experienced
by an animal is exemplified by the true story of Flint,
a chimp, when Flo, his mother, died. In her book,
Through a Window, which elaborates on her thirty years
of experience studying and living among the chimps in
Gombe, Tanzania, Jane Goodall gives the following
account of Flint's experience with grief.

> Flint became increasingly lethargic, refused
> most food and, with his immune system thus
> weakened, fell sick. The last time I saw him
> alive, he was hollow-eyed, gaunt and utterly

Quotation longer than four lines indented ten spaces and not enclosed in quotation marks; period precedes citation

Citation for an indirect source

First letter of a quotation changed to lowercase to fit into sentence; ellipsis mark, enclosed in brackets, used to indicate omitted material

Source's credentials included within the text

Destino 4

> depressed, huddled in the vegetation close to
> where Flo had died. [. . .] The last short
> journey he made, pausing to rest every few
> feet, was to the very place where Flo's body
> had lain. There he stayed for several hours,
> sometimes staring and staring into the water.
> He struggled on a little further, then curled
> up--and never moved again. (196-97)

Of course, animal emotions are not limited to despair, sadness, and grief. Indeed, substantial evidence indicates that animals experience other, more uplifting emotions, such as sympathy, altruism, and joy.

Many scientists who study animal behavior have found that several species demonstrate sympathy to one another. In other words, they act as if they care about one another in much the same way as humans do. It is probably safe to assume that no animal is more sympathetic, or at least displays more behaviors associated with the emotion of sympathy, than chimpanzees. Those who have studied apes in the wild, including de Waal, have observed that animals who had been fighting making up with one another by kissing and hugging. Although other primates also engage in similar behaviors, chimps even go so far as to embrace, and attempt to console, the defeated animal ("Going Ape"). Another striking example of one animal showing sympathy for another is the account cited by Barber of a parrot comforting its sick mate. It is not, however, the only example of this type of behavior, especially among birds. Barber cites several other instances as well. According to Barber, documented records show that responsible observers have seen robins trying to keep each other alive. Also,

---

Transition to the second main point

Clear topic sentence

Information from a source paraphrased

Title used in citation since there is no author indicated

Page number not given since the article occupies only one page in the journal

Information from a source summarized

Destino 5

terns have been known to lift another handicapped tern
by its wing and transport it to safety. Likewise, a jay
has been known to successfully seek human help when a
newborn bird of a different species falls out of its
nest. What makes this latter example particularly noteworthy is that the newborn wasn't a jay but an altogether different type of bird.

Had the jay been helping another jay, it would be
easy to assume that the act of caring was the result of
what scientists call genetic altruism--the sociobiolog-
ical theory that animals help each other in order to
keep their own genes alive so they can reproduce and
not become extinct. Simply put, scientists who believe
in genetic altruism assume that when animals of the
same species help each other out, they do so because
there is something in it for them--namely the assurance
that their species will continue. This theory certainly
provides an adequate, unbiased scientific explanation
for why animals such as birds might behave in a caring
manner. However, if animals really help each other out
only when doing so will perpetuate their species, then
the jay would have had no genetic reason to help the
newborn bird.

There is another popular explanation for why a
bird of one species might help a bird of another
species, however. Scientists who favor a related scientific theory called mutual altruism believe that animals will help each other because some day they
themselves may need help, and then they will be able to
count on reciprocal help (Hemelrijk 479-81). This theory is a plausible, nonanthropomorphic explanation for
why animals show sympathy, regardless of whether they
actually feel sympathy. This point is crucial because

Transitional sentence refers to incident reported in preceding paragraph.

Common knowledge that does not need to be documented

after all, humans can't actually observe how an animal feels; we can only observe how it behaves. It is then up to the observer to draw some logical conclusion about why animals behave in the ways they do. The mutual altruism theory, however, also can be disputed. In many cases, animals have helped others even when the receiver of the help would probably never be in a position to return the favor. For example, there are many accounts of dolphins helping drowning or otherwise impaired humans to safety. Janine Benyus, in her book Beastly Behaviors, describes how dolphins find a struggling victim in a matter of seconds and lift him or her out of the water to breathe. According to swimmers whose lives have been saved by dolphins, their rescuers are "careful, efficient, and persistent" (235).

> Not only do animals show sympathy, but they are also clearly able to express joy. For example, on many occasions primate experts have heard apes laugh while in the presence of other apes. These experts are sure that the noise they heard was laughter because of the clarity and tone of the sound. In their book, Visions of Caliban, Dale Peterson and Jane Goodall describe this laughter in detail.

Transition to the final main point

> I'm not referring to a sort of pinched vocalization that might be roughly compared with human laughter, as in the "laughter" of a hyena. I'm referring to real laughter, fully recognizable laughter, the kind where you lie down on the ground and shake in a paroxysm of clear amusement and simple pleasure. According to Peterson and Goodall, only four species, in addition to humans, have the capacity to be amused and to show their

Destino 7

amusement by laughing: chimpanzees, gorillas, bonobos, and orangutans. (181)

Even the actions of animals who are not able to laugh uproariously indicate that they feel joy. Many animals engage in playful behavior that can only emanate from a sense of joy. In "Hope and Joy among the Animals," Masson and McCarthy tell an amusing, yet true, story about an elephant named Norma.

> A traveling circus once pitched its tents next to a schoolyard with a set of swings. The older elephants were chained, but Norma, a young elephant, was left loose. When Norma saw children swinging, she was greatly intrigued. Before long, she went over, waved the children away with her trunk, backed up to a swing, and attempted to sit on it. She was notably unsuccessful, even using her tail to hold the swing in place. (45)

Geese, according to experts, have an "emotional body language which can be read: goose posture, gestures, and sounds can indicate feelings such as uncertain, tense, glad, victorious, sad, alert, relaxed or threatening." Additionally, birds sometimes can be seen moving their wings back and forth while listening to sounds they find pleasant (McHugh).

In short, animals exhibit a large number of behaviors that indicate that they possess not only the capacity to feel but the capacity to express those feelings in some overt way, often through body language. If these are not proof enough that animals have emotions, people need look no further than their own beloved cat or dog. Pets are so frequently the cause of joy, humor, love, sympathy, empathy, and even grief

Entire title of article included in attribution because two works by Masson and McCarthy are cited

Citation of Internet source consists of author's name only; no page numbers available.

Transition to the conclusion of the essay

Destino presents his own conclusion about animal emotions.

that it is difficult to imagine animals could elicit such emotions in humans without actually having these emotions themselves. The question, then, is not "Do animals have emotions?" but rather, "Which emotions do animals have and to what degree do they feel them?"

Destino 9

Works Cited

Barber, Theodore Xenophone. The Human Nature of Birds.
    New York: St. Martin's, 1993.

Benyus, Janine M. Beastly Behaviors. New York: Addison,
    1992.

de Waal, Frans. "Are We in Anthropodenial?" Discover
    July 1997: 50-53.

"Going Ape." Economist 17 Feb. 1997: 78.

Goodall, Jane. The Chimpanzees of Gombe: Patterns of
    Behavior. Cambridge: Belknap Press, 1986.

---. Through a Window. Boston: Houghton, 1990.

Hemelrijk, Charlotte K. "Support for Being Groomed in
    Long-Tailed Macaques, Macaca Fascicularis." Animal
    Behaviour 48 (1994): 479-81.

Masson, Jeffrey Moussaleff, and Susan McCarthy. "Hope
    and Joy among the Animals." Utne Reader July-Aug.
    1995: 44-46.

---. When Elephants Weep: The Emotional Lives of
    Animals. New York: Delacorte, 1995.

McHugh, Mary. "The Emotional Lives of Animals." The
    Global Ideas Bank. Ed. Nicholas Albery and
    Stephanie Wienrich. 1998. Institute for Social
    Inventions, London. 19 Dec. 1998 <http://
    www.globalideasbank.org/BI/BI-170.html>.

Peterson, Dale, and Jane Goodall. Visions of Caliban.
    New York: Houghton, 1993.

Wynn, Susan G. "The Treatment of Trauma in Pet Animals:
    What Constitutes Trauma?" Homeopathy Online 5
    (1998): 7 pp. 15 Dec. 1998 <http://
    www.lyghtforce.com/HomeopathyOnline/issues/
    articles/wynn.html>.

Heading centered

Double-space
between heading
and first line, and
between all subse-
quent lines.

Entries are alphabet-
ized by authors' last
names.

First line of each
entry is flush with
the left margin; sub-
sequent lines indent
five spaces.

The Bean Eaters
Gwendolyn Brooks

They eat beans mostly, this old yellow pair.
Dinner is a casual affair.
Plain chipware on a plain and creaking wood,
Tin flatware.

Two who are Mostly Good.   5
Two who have lived their day,
But keep on putting on their clothes
And putting things away.

And remembering . . .
Remembering, with twinklings and twinges,   10
As they lean over the beans in their rented back room that
    is full of beads and receipts and dolls and cloths,
        tobacco crumbs, vases and fringes.

Chapter 21

Suppose your American literature instructor asks you to study the photograph on the facing page and to read carefully the accompanying poem by Gwendolyn Brooks (b. 1917), a major American writer of poetry as well as fiction and nonfiction prose. Brooks was the first African American woman to win a Pulitzer Prize for poetry (for *Annie Allen,* 1949). "The Bean Eaters" was originally published in a collection of poems, *The Bean Eaters,* in 1960.

Reading and Writing about Literature

Writing Quick Start

After reading Brooks's "The Bean Eaters," how can you describe the life of the elderly couple shown in the photo? Write a paragraph describing in your own words what you think the couple's relationship might be like.

TEACHING TIP: COLLABORATIVE WRITING

Have students work in groups of two or three on "The Bean Eaters." One student in each group should read the poem aloud slowly, paying attention to sound (e.g., "pair" / "affair"; "twinklings" / "twinges"), while the others read along silently. Then the group should brainstorm a list of modifiers and phrases that describe the couple in the poem.

TEACHING TIP:
CHAPTER OVERVIEW

• In this chapter, stu-
dents apply active
reading strategies to
works of literature in
order to identify
themes and analyze
subtle and complex
meanings.

• Students learn how
similes, metaphors,
personification, and
symbolism are used by
authors to express
ideas.

• Students learn general
guidelines for analyz-
ing short stories and
poetry and then work
through the process of
of writing a literary
analysis of their own.

Brooks's poem and the paragraph you just wrote both paint a picture of an elderly couple. Through carefully selected details, the poem tells about the couple's daily activities, memories of the past, and current economic situation (for example, "They eat beans mostly," "Plain chipware," and "rented back room" reveal that the couple is poor). Brooks also suggests that routine is important to the couple ("But keep on putting on their clothes / And putting things away") and that their memories of the past are both good ("twinklings") and bad ("twinges").

Now think of an elderly couple you know, such as your grandparents or neighbors. Do some of the characteristics of Brooks's couple apply to the couple you know? How does Brooks's picture of one elderly couple help you understand other elderly people?

"The Bean Eaters" suggests an answer to the question many students ask: "Why should I read or write about literature?" This poem, like all literature, is about the experiences people share. Literature often deals with large issues: "What is worthwhile in life?" "What is moral?" "What is beautiful?" When you read and write about literature, you gain new insights into many aspects of human experience, and thereby enrich your own life.

Understanding literature has practical purposes as well (see the accompanying box for a few examples). You may be asked to write about literature in many college courses—not only in English classes. Even in work situations, a knowledge of literature will make some tasks easier or more meaningful.

This chapter will help you read and respond to works of literature. The first half of the chapter offers a general approach to reading and understanding literature, including discussions of the language and other elements of short stories and poetry. The second half of the chapter focuses on the characteristics of literary analysis and helps you through the process of writing one in a Guided Writing Assignment. Although literature can take many forms, including poetry, short

---

SCENES FROM COLLEGE AND THE WORKPLACE

• Your *art history* professor asks you to read Ernest Hemingway's *For Whom the Bell Tolls* (a novel set in the time of the Spanish Civil War) and write a paper discussing its meaning in conjunction with Picasso's *Guernica,* a painting that vividly portrays a scene from that war.

• In a *film* class, you watch the film *Romeo and Juliet,* directed by Franco Zeffirelli. Your instructor then asks you to read excerpts from Shakespeare's *Romeo and Juliet* and write a paper evaluating how successfully Juliet is portrayed in the film.

• You work for a *children's book store.* Your supervisor has asked you to read several children's books that she is considering featuring during story hour and write an evaluation of each.

stories, biography, autobiography, drama, essays, and novels, this chapter concentrates on two literary genres: short stories and poetry.

A GENERAL APPROACH TO READING LITERATURE

Textbooks focus primarily on presenting factual information, but literature does not. Instead, *works of literature* are concerned with interpreting ideas, experiences, and events. They employ facts, description, and detail to convey larger meanings.

Use the following general guidelines to read a literary work effectively.

1. **Read with an open mind.** Be ready to respond to the work; don't make up your mind about it before you start reading.

2. **Preview the work before reading it.** Read background information about the author and the work and study the title. For a short story, read the first few and last few paragraphs and quickly skim through the pages in between, noticing the setting, the names of the characters, the amount of dialogue, and so forth. For a poem, read it through once to get an initial impression.

   For more on previewing, see Chapter 2, p. 27.

3. **Read slowly and carefully.** Works of literature use language in unique and creative ways, requiring you to read them slowly and carefully with a pen in hand. Mark interesting uses of language, such as striking phrases or descriptions, as well as sections that hint at the theme of the work.

4. **Note that literature often "bends the rules" of grammar and usage.** Writers of literature may use sentence fragments, ungrammatical dialogue, or unusual punctuation to create a particular *effect* in a short story or poem. When you see such instances in literature, remember that the writers bend the rules for a purpose.

5. **Establish the literal meaning first.** During the first reading of a work, try to establish its literal meaning. Who is doing what, when, and where? Identify the general subject, specific topic, and main character. What is happening? Describe the basic plot, action, or sequence of events. Establish where and during what time period the action occurs.

6. **Reread the work to focus on your interpretation.** To analyze a literary work, you will need to reread parts of the work or the entire work several times.

7. **Anticipate a gradual understanding.** Literary works are complex; you should not expect to understand a poem or short story immediately after reading it. As you reread and think about the work, its meanings will often come to mind gradually. Consider why the writer wrote the work and what message the writer is trying to communicate. Then ask "So what?" to discover deeper meanings. Try to determine the work's view of, comment on, or lesson about the human experience.

8. **Interact with the work.** Jot down your reactions to it in the margins as you read. Include hunches, insights, and feelings as well as questions about the work. Highlight or underline key words, phrases, or actions that seem important or that you want to reconsider later.

9. **Identify themes and patterns.** Study your annotations to discover how the ideas in the work link together to suggest a theme. **Themes** are large or universal topics that are important to nearly everyone. For example, the theme of a poem or short story might be that death is inescapable or that aging involves a loss of the innocence of youth. Think of the theme as the main point a poem or short story makes. (Themes are discussed in greater detail later in the chapter.)

THE LANGUAGE OF LITERATURE

Many writers, especially writers of literary works, use figures of speech to describe people, places, or objects and to communicate ideas. In general, **figures of speech** are comparisons that make sense imaginatively or creatively but not literally. Three common types of figurative language are *similes, metaphors,* and *personification.* Writers often use another literary device, *symbols,* to suggest larger themes. Finally, writers use *irony* to convey the incongruities of life.

Similes, Metaphors, and Personification

For more on figures of speech, see Chapter 8, p. 198, and Chapter 10, p. 252.

Similes and metaphors are comparisons between two unlike things that have one common trait. A **simile** uses the word *like* or *as* to make a comparison, whereas a **metaphor** states or implies that one thing *is* another thing. If you say, "My father's mustache is a housepainter's brush," your metaphor compares two dissimilar things — a mustache and paintbrush — that share one common trait — straight bristles. Such comparisons appeal to the reader's imagination. If you say, "Martha's hair looks like she just walked through a wind tunnel," your simile creates a more vivid image of Martha's hair than if you simply stated, "Martha's hair is messy." Here are examples from literary works.

SIMILE

My soul has grown deep like the rivers.

LANGSTON HUGHES, "The Negro Speaks of Rivers"

METAPHOR

Time is but the stream I go a-fishing in.

HENRY DAVID THOREAU, *Walden*

When writers use **personification,** they attribute human characteristics to objects or ideas. A well-known example of personification is found in Carl Sandburg's poem "Fog." Sandburg likens fog to a cat and says the fog "comes on little cat feet" and sits "on silent haunches" as it looks over the city. Like similes and metaphors, personification often creates a strong visual image.

Symbols

A **symbol** suggests more than its literal meaning. A flag, for instance, suggests patriotism; the color white often suggests innocence and purity. Because the abstract idea that a symbol represents is not stated but is left for the reader to infer, a symbol may suggest more than one meaning. A white handkerchief, for example, might symbolize retreat in one context but good manners in another. Some literary critics believe the white whale in Herman Melville's novel *Moby Dick* symbolizes evil, whereas others see the whale as representing the forces of nature.

To recognize symbols in a literary work, look for objects that are given a particular or unusual emphasis. The object may be mentioned often, suggested in the title, or appear at the beginning or end of the work. Also be on the lookout for familiar symbols, such as flowers, doves, and colors.

Irony

Irony is literary language or a literary style in which actions, events, or words are the opposite of what readers expect. For example, a prize fighter cowering at the sight of a spider is an ironic action, a fire station burning down is an ironic event, and a student saying that she is glad she failed an important exam is making an ironic statement.

EXERCISE 21.1

Working with another student, make a list of common metaphors and similes, examples of personification, and symbols you have heard or seen in everyday life, in films or television programs, or in works of literature.

TEACHING TIP

After students complete their lists, have them look for figures of speech that could be considered clichés.

POSSIBLE ANSWERS

Answers will vary.

ANALYZING SHORT STORIES

A **short story** is a brief fictional narrative. It contains five key elements: setting, characters, point of view, plot, and theme. Short stories are shorter than novels and their scope is much more limited. A short story, for example, may focus on one event in a person's life, whereas a novel may chronicle the events in the lives of an entire family. Like a novel, however, a short story makes a point about some aspect of the human experience.

Read the following short story, "The Secret Lion," before continuing with this section of the chapter. Then, as you continue with the chapter, you will discover how each of the key short-story elements works in "The Secret Lion."

 ## The Secret Lion
Alberto Ríos

Alberto Ríos (b. 1952), the son of a Guatemalan father and an English mother, was raised in Nogales, Arizona, near the Mexican border. His work has appeared in numerous national and international literature anthologies. In addition to fellowships from the Guggenheim Foundation and the National Endowment for the Arts, Ríos has won several awards: the Walt Whitman Award from the Academy of American Poets; the Arizona Governor's Arts Award; and the Western States Book Award for The Iguana Killer: Twelve Stories of the Heart *(1984), a collection of stories that includes the one reprinted here. Ríos is currently a Regents professor of English at Arizona State University.*

PREREADING QUESTIONS

• What is the "secret lion"?

• Is it a real thing or place?

• Why is it "secret"?

1   I was twelve and in junior high school and something happened that we didn't have a name for, but it was there nonetheless like a lion, and roaring, roaring that way the biggest things do. Everything changed. Just that. Like the rug, the one that gets pulled — or better, like the tablecloth those magicians pull where the stuff on the table stays the same but the gasp! from the audience makes the staying-the-same part not matter. Like that.

2   What happened was there were teachers now, not just one teacher, teach-erz, and we felt personally abandoned somehow. When a person had all these teachers now, he didn't get taken care of the same way, even though six was more than one. Arithmetic went out the door when we walked in. And we saw girls now, but they weren't the same girls we used to know because we couldn't talk to them anymore, not the same way we used to, certainly not to Sandy, even though she was my neighbor, too. Not even to her. She just played the piano all the time. And there were words, oh there were words in junior high school, and we wanted to know what they were, and how a person did them — that's what school was supposed to be for. Only, in junior high school, school wasn't school, everything was backward-like. If you went up to a teacher and said the word to try and find out what it meant you got in trouble for saying it. So we didn't. And we figured it must have been that way about other stuff, too, so we never said anything about anything — we weren't stupid.

But my friend Sergio and I, we solved junior high school. We would come home from school on the bus, put our books away, change shoes, and go across the highway to the arroyo.* It was the one place we were not supposed to go. So we did. This was, after all, what junior high had at least shown us. It was our river, though, our personal Mississippi, our friend from long back, and it was full of stories and all the branch forts we had built in it when we were still the Vikings of America, with our own symbol, which we had carved everywhere, even in the sand, which let the water take it. That was good, we had decided; whoever was at the end of this river would know about us.

At the very very top of our growing lungs, what we would do down there was shout every dirty word we could think of, in every combination we could come up with, and we would yell about girls, and all the things we wanted to do with them, as loud as we could—we didn't know what we wanted to do with them, just things—and we would yell about teachers, and how we loved some of them, like Miss Crevelone, and how we wanted to dissect some of them, making signs of the cross, like priests, and we would yell this stuff over and over because it felt good, we couldn't explain why, it just felt good and for the first time in our lives there was nobody to tell us we couldn't. So we did.

One Thursday we were walking along shouting this way, and the railroad, the Southern Pacific, which ran above and along the far side of the arroyo, had dropped a grinding ball down there, which was, we found out later, a cannonball thing used in mining. A bunch of them were put in a big vat which turned around and crushed the ore. One had been dropped, or thrown—what do caboose men do when they get bored—but it got down there regardless and as we were walking along yelling about one girl or another, a particular Claudia, we found it, one of these things, looked at it, picked it up, and got very very excited, and held it and passed it back and forth, and we were saying "Guythisis, this is, geeGuythis . . .": we had this perception about nature then, that nature is imperfect and that round things are perfect: we said "GuyGodthis is perfect, thisisthis is perfect, it's round, round and heavy, it'sit's the best thing we'veeverseen. Whatisit?" We didn't know. We just knew it was great. We just, whatever, we played with it, held it some more.

And then we had to decide what to do with it. We knew, because of a lot of things, that if we were going to take this and show it to anybody, this discovery, this best thing, was going to be taken away from us. That's the way it works with little kids, like all the polished quartz, the tons of it we had collected piece by piece over the years.

---

arroyo: a creek or stream in a dry part of the country.

Junior high kids too. If we took it home, my mother, we knew, was going to look at it and say "throw that dirty thing in the, get rid of it." Simple like, like that. "But ma it's the best thing I" "Getridofit." Simple.

7   So we didn't. Take it home. Instead, we came up with the answer. We dug a hole and buried it. And we marked it secretly. Lots of secret signs. And came back the next week to dig it up and, we didn't know, pass it around some more or something, but we didn't find it. We dug up that whole bank, and we never found it again. We tried.

8   Sergio and I talked about that ball or whatever it was when we couldn't find it. All we used were small words, neat, good. Kid words. What we were really saying, but didn't know the words, was how much that ball was like that place, that whole arroyo: couldn't tell anybody about it, didn't understand what it was, didn't have a name for it. It just felt good. It was just perfect in the way it was that place, that whole going to that place, that whole junior high school lion. It was just iron-heavy, it had no name, it felt good or not, we couldn't take it home to show our mothers, and once we buried it, it was gone forever.

9   The ball was gone, like the first reasons we had come to that arroyo years earlier, like the first time we had seen the arroyo, it was gone like everything else that had been taken away. This was not our first lesson. We stopped going to the arroyo after not finding the thing, the same way we had stopped going there years earlier and headed for the mountains. Nature seemed to keep pushing us around one way or another, teaching us the same thing every place we ended up. Nature's gang was tough that way, teaching us stuff.

10   When we were young we moved away from town, me and my family. Sergio's was already out there. Out in the wilds. Or at least the new place seemed like the wilds since everything looks bigger the smaller a man is. I was five, I guess, and we had moved three miles north of Nogales where we had lived, three miles north of the Mexican border. We looked across the highway in one direction and there was the arroyo; hills stood up in the other direction. Mountains, for a small man.

11   When the first summer came the very first place we went to was of course the one place we weren't supposed to go, the arroyo. We went down in there and found water running, summer rain water mostly, and we went swimming. But every third or fourth or fifth day, the sewage treatment plant that was, we found out, upstream, would release whatever it was that it released, and we would never know exactly what day that was, and a person really couldn't tell right off by looking at the water, not every time, not so a person could get out in time. So, we went swimming that summer and some days we had a

lot of fun. Some days we didn't. We found a thousand ways to explain what happened on those other days, constructing elaborate stories about the neighborhood dogs, and hadn't she, my mother, miscalculated her step before, too? But she knew something was up because we'd come running into the house those days, wanting to take a shower, even — if this can be imagined — in the middle of the day.

That was the first time we stopped going to the arroyo. It taught us to look the other way. We decided, as the second side of summer came, we wanted to go into the mountains. They were still mountains then. We went running in one summer Thursday morning, my friend Sergio and I, into my mother's kitchen, and said, well, what'zin, what'zin those hills over there — we used her word so she'd understand us — and she said nothingdon'tworryaboutit. So we went out, and we weren't dumb, we thought with our eyes to each other, ohhoshe'stryingtokeepsomethingfromus. We knew adults.   12

We had read the books, after all; we knew about bridges and castles and wildtreacherousraging alligatormouth rivers. We wanted them. So we were going to go out and get them. We went back that morning into that kitchen and we said, "We're going out there, we're going into the hills, we're going away for three days, don't worry." She said, "All right."   13

"You know," I said to Sergio, "if we're going to go away for three days, well, we ought to at least pack a lunch."   14

But we were two young boys with no patience for what we thought at the time was mom-stuff: making sa-and-wiches. My mother didn't offer. So we got out little kid knapsacks that my mother had sewn for us, and into them we put the jar of mustard. A loaf of bread. Knivesforksplates, bottles of Coke, a can opener. This was lunch for the two of us. And we were weighed down, humped over to be strong enough to carry this stuff. But we started walking anyway, into the hills. We were going to eat berries and stuff otherwise. "Goodbye." My mom said that.   15

After the first hill we were dead. But we walked. My mother could still see us. And we kept walking. We walked until we got to where the sun is straight overhead, noon. That place. Where that is doesn't matter; it's time to eat. The truth is we weren't anywhere close to that place. We just agreed that the sun was overhead and that it was time to eat, and by tilting our heads a little we could make that the truth.   16

"We really ought to start looking for a place to eat."   17

"Yeah. Let's look for a good place to eat." We went back and forth saying that for fifteen minutes, making it lunchtime because that's what we always said back and forth before lunchtimes at home. "Yeah, I'm hungry all right." I nodded my head. "Yeah, I'm hungry all right too. I'm hungry." He nodded his head. I nodded my head back.   18

After a good deal more nodding, we were ready, just as we came over a little hill. We hadn't found the mountains yet. This was a little hill.

19   And on the other side of this hill we found heaven.

20   It was just what we thought it would be.

21   Perfect. Heaven was green, like nothing else in Arizona. And it wasn't a cemetery or like that because we had seen cemeteries and they had gravestones and stuff and this didn't. This was perfect, had trees, lots of trees, had birds, like we had never seen before. It was like *The Wizard of Oz*, like when they got to Oz and everything was so green, so emerald, they had to wear those glasses, and we ran just like them, laughing, laughing that way we did that moment, and we went running down to this clearing in it all, hitting each other that good way we did.

22   We got down there, we kept laughing, we kept hitting each other, we unpacked our stuff, and we started acting "rich." We knew all about how to do that, like blowing on our nails, then rubbing them on our chests for the shine. We made our sandwiches, opened our Cokes, got out the rest of the stuff, the salt and pepper shakers. I found this particular hole and I put my Coke right into it, a perfect fit, and I called it my Coke-holder. I got down next to it on my back, because everyone knows that rich people eat lying down, and I got my sandwich in one hand and put my other arm around the Coke in its holder. When I wanted a drink, I lifted my neck a little, put out my lips, and tipped my Coke a little with the crook of my elbow. Ah.

23   We were there, lying down, eating our sandwiches, laughing, throwing bread at each other and out for the birds. This was heaven. We were laughing and we couldn't believe it. My mother was keeping something from us, ah ha, but we had found her out. We even found water over at the side of the clearing to wash our plates with — we had brought plates. Sergio started washing his plates when he was done, and I was being rich with my Coke, and this day in summer was right.

24   When suddenly these two men came, from around a corner of trees and the tallest grass we had ever seen. They had bags on their backs, leather bags, bags and sticks.

25   We didn't know what clubs were, but I learned later, like I learned about the grinding balls. The two men yelled at us. Most specifically, one wanted me to take my Coke out of my Coke-holder so he could sink his golf ball into it.

26   Something got taken away from us that moment. Heaven. We grew up a little bit, and couldn't go backward. We learned. No one had ever told us about golf. They had told us about heaven. And it went away. We got golf in exchange.

27   We went back to the arroyo for the rest of that summer, and tried to have fun the best we could. We learned to be ready for finding the

grinding ball. We loved it, and when we buried it we knew what would happen. The truth is, we didn't look so hard for it. We were two boys and twelve summers then, and not stupid. Things get taken away.

We buried it because it was perfect. We didn't tell my mother, but together it was all we talked about, till we forgot. It was the lion. ■   28

Setting

The **setting** of a short story is the time, place, and circumstance in which the story occurs. The setting provides the framework and atmosphere in which the plot develops and characters interact. For example, Charles Dickens's "A Christmas Carol" is set in nineteenth-century London. The setting of "The Secret Lion" is between the arroyo and the mountains just outside of Nogales, Arizona. The action occurs near the arroyo and on the golf course.

Characters

The **characters** are the actors in the story. They are revealed through their dialogue, actions, appearance, thoughts, and feelings. The **narrator,** the person who tells the story, may also comment on or reveal information about the characters. The narrator is not necessarily the author of the story. The narrator can be one of the characters in the story or an onlooker who observes but does not participate in the action. Therefore, you need to think critically about what the narrator reveals about the personalities, needs, and motives of the characters and whether the narrator's opinions may be colored by his or her perceptions and biases. "The Secret Lion" involves two principal characters: the narrator and his childhood friend, Sergio. Both twelve-year-old boys are playful, spirited, and inquisitive. They explore, disobey, and test ideas. The narrator's mother is a secondary character in the story.

Point of View

The **point of view** is the perspective from which a story is told. There are two common points of view: first person and third person. In the first-person (*I*) point of view, the narrator tells the story as he or she sees or experiences it ("*I* saw the crowd gather at the cemetery"). A first-person narrator may be one of the characters or someone observing but not participating in the story. In the third-person (*they*) point of view, the narrator tells the story as if someone else is experiencing it ("*Laura* saw the crowd gather at the cemetery"). A third-person narrator may be able to report only the actions that can be observed from the outside or may be able to enter the minds of one or more characters and tell about their thoughts and motives. An *omniscient* or all-knowing third-person narrator is aware of the thoughts and actions of all characters in the story.

To identify the point of view of a story, then, consider who is narrating and what the narrator knows about the characters' actions, thoughts, and motives. "The Secret Lion" is told by a first-person narrator who both participates in the action and looks back on the events to interpret them. For example, he says of their preparations for their trip to the mountains, "But we were two young boys with no patience for what we thought at the time was mom-stuff" (paragraph 15). He also uses a fast-talking narrative style characteristic of twelve-year-old boys, intentionally bending rules of spelling and grammar to achieve this effect. For example, he uses sentence fragments — "Lots of secret signs" (7), "Out in the wilds" (10) — and runs words together or emphasizes syllables to show how they are pronounced — "wildtreacherousraging alligatormouth rivers" (13), "sa-and-wiches" (15). He also uses slang words ("neat") and contractions to create an informal tone.

Plot

The **plot** is the basic story line — that is, the sequence of events and actions through which the story's meaning is expressed. The plot is often centered on a **conflict,** a problem or clash between opposing forces, and the resolution of the conflict. Once the scene is set and the characters are introduced, a problem or conflict arises. Suspense builds as the conflict unfolds and the characters wrestle with the problem. Near the end of the story, the events come to a **climax** — the point at which the conflict is resolved. The story ends with a conclusion.

In "The Secret Lion" two childhood friends, while playing near an arroyo, discover a grinding ball. They bury the ball but are unable to find it when they return. The narrator recollects an earlier time, when they had planned a trip to the mountains and stopped to have lunch on what they soon discovered was a golf course. The conflict, illustrated by several events, is between the boys' imaginations and adult realities.

Theme

The **theme** of a story is its central or dominant idea, the main point the author makes about the human experience. Readers do not always agree about a story's theme. Therefore, in a literary analysis of a short story, you must give evidence to support your interpretation of the theme. The following suggestions will help you uncover clues.

1. **Study the title.** What meanings does it suggest?
2. **Analyze the main characters.** Do the characters change? If so, how, and in response to what?
3. **Look for broad statements about the conflict.** What do the characters and narrator say about the conflict or their lives?
4. **Analyze important elements.** Look for symbols, figures of speech, and meaningful names (Young Goodman Brown, for example).

Once you uncover a theme, try expressing it in sentence form, rather than as a single word or brief phrase. For example, to say the theme is "dishonesty" or "parent-child relationships" does not reveal the meaning of a story. When expressed as a sentence, however, a story's theme becomes clear: "Dishonesty sometimes pays" or "Parent-child relationships are often struggles for power and control."

One possible theme of "The Secret Lion" is that change is inevitable, that nothing remains the same. After the boys discover that they can't find the buried grinding ball, the narrator hints at this theme: The ball was gone . . . like everything else that had been taken away" (9). Then, when the boys encounter the two men on the golf course, the narrator again comments on the theme of change: "Something got taken away from us that moment. Heaven. We grew up a little bit, and couldn't go backward" (26).

Another possible theme of Ríos's story is that perfection is unattainable. The boys are attracted to the ball because it is perfect: "GuyGodthis is perfect, thisisthis is perfect . . . it'sit's the best thing we'veeverseen" (5). But once the "perfect" ball is buried, it can never be found again. In much the same way, the boys cannot return to the "heaven" they once knew at the golf course.

EXERCISE 21.2

Working in groups of two or three, choose a television situation comedy and watch one episode, either together, if possible, or separately. After viewing the program, identify each of the following elements: setting, character, point of view, and plot. Then consider whether you think the episode has a theme.

TEACHING TIP

After students complete this group assignment, have them freewrite a journal entry for five minutes, exploring their findings.

POSSIBLE ANSWERS

Answers will vary.

Use the questions in the box on page 728 to guide your analysis of short stories. As you read the story that follows, "The Story of an Hour" by Kate Chopin, keep these questions in mind. You may choose to write an analysis of this story in response to the Guided Writing Assignment on page 737.

QUESTIONS FOR ANALYZING SHORT STORIES

Setting—Time

1. In what general time period (century or decade) does the story take place?
2. What major events (wars, revolutions, famines, political or cultural movements) occurred during that time and what bearing might they have on the story?

Setting—Place

1. In what geographic area does the story take place? (Try to identify the country and the city or town, as well as whether the area is an urban or rural one.)
2. Where does the action occur? (For example, on a battlefield, in a living room, or on a city street?)
3. Why is the place important? (Why couldn't the story occur elsewhere?)

Characters

1. Who are the main characters in the story?
2. What are the distinguishing qualities and characteristics of each character?
3. Why do you like or dislike each character?
4. How and why do characters change (or not change) as the story progresses?

Point of View

1. Is the narrator a character in the story or strictly an observer?
2. Is the narrator knowledgeable about the motives, feelings, and behavior of any or all of the characters?
3. Does the narrator affect what happens in the story? If so, how? What role does the narrator play?

Plot

1. What series of events occurs? Summarize the action.
2. What is the conflict? Why does it occur? How does it build to a climax?
3. How is the conflict resolved?
4. Is the outcome satisfying? Why or why not?

Theme

1. What is the theme? What broad statement about life or the human experience does the story suggest?
2. What evidence from the story supports your interpretation of the theme?

The Story of an Hour
Kate Chopin

Kate Chopin (1851–1904), a nineteenth-century American writer, is best known for her novel The Awakening *(1899), which portrays a woman in search of sexual and professional independence and outraged literary critics when it was first published. As you read the following short story, originally published in* Vogue *magazine in 1894, look for, highlight, and annotate the five primary elements of short stories discussed in this chapter.*

PREREADING QUESTIONS
• How would you describe the theme of this story?
• How does the climax of the story relate to the theme?

Knowing that Mrs. Mallard was afflicted with a heart trouble, great care was taken to break to her as gently as possible the news of her husband's death. 1

It was her sister Josephine who told her, in broken sentences, veiled hints that revealed in half concealing. Her husband's friend Richards was there, too, near her. It was he who had been in the newspaper office when intelligence of the railroad disaster was received, with Brently Mallard's name leading the list of "killed." He had only taken the time to assure himself of its truth by a second telegram, and had hastened to forestall any less careful, less tender friend in bearing the sad message. 2

She did not hear the story as many women have heard the same, with a paralyzed inability to accept its significance. She wept at once, with sudden, wild abandonment, in her sister's arms. When the storm of grief had spent itself she went away to her room alone. She would have no one follow her. 3

There stood, facing the open window, a comfortable, roomy armchair. Into this she sank, pressed down by a physical exhaustion that haunted her body and seemed to reach into her soul. 4

She could see in the open square before her house the tops of trees that were all aquiver with the new spring life. The delicious breath of rain was in the air. In the street below a peddler was crying his wares. The notes of a distant song which someone was singing reached her faintly, and countless sparrows were twittering in the eaves. 5

There were patches of blue sky showing here and there through the clouds that had met and piled one above the other in the west facing her window. 6

She sat with her head thrown back upon the cushion of the chair, quite motionless, except when a sob came up into her throat and shook her, as a child who has cried itself to sleep continues to sob in its dreams. 7

8   She was young, with a fair, calm face, whose lines bespoke repression and even a certain strength. But now there was a dull stare in her eyes, whose gaze was fixed away off yonder on one of those patches of blue sky. It was not a glance of reflection, but rather indicated a suspension of intelligent thought.

9   There was something coming to her and she was waiting for it, fearfully. What was it? She did not know, it was too subtle and elusive to name. But she felt it, creeping out of the sky, reaching toward her through the sounds, the scents, the color that filled the air.

10   Now her bosom rose and fell tumultuously. She was beginning to recognize this thing that was approaching to possess her, and she was striving to beat it back with her will—as powerless as her two white slender hands would have been.

11   When she abandoned herself a little whispered word escaped her slightly parted lips. She said it over and over under her breath: "Free, free, free!" The vacant stare and the look of terror that had followed it went from her eyes. They stayed keen and bright. Her pulses beat fast, and the coursing blood warmed and relaxed every inch of her body.

12   She did not stop to ask if it were not a monstrous joy that held her. A clear and exalted perception enabled her to dismiss the suggestion as trivial.

13   She knew that she would weep again when she saw the kind, tender hands folded in death; the face that had never looked save with love upon her, fixed and gray and dead. But she saw beyond that bitter moment a long procession of years to come that would belong to her absolutely. And she opened and spread her arms out to them in welcome.

14   There would be no one to live for during those coming years; she would live for herself. There would be no powerful will bending her in that blind persistence with which men and women believe they have a right to impose a private will upon a fellow creature. A kind intention or a cruel intention made the act seem no less a crime as she looked upon it in that brief moment of illumination.

15   And yet she had loved him—sometimes. Often she had not. What did it matter! What could love, the unsolved mystery, count for in face of this possession of self-assertion which she suddenly recognized as the strongest impulse of her being.

16   "Free! Body and soul free!" she kept whispering.

17   Josephine was kneeling before the closed door with her lips to the keyhole, imploring for admission. "Louise, open the door! I beg; open the door—you will make yourself ill. What are you doing, Louise? For heaven's sake open the door."

"Go away. I am not making myself ill." No; she was drinking in a   18
very elixir of life through that open window.

Her fancy was running riot along those days ahead of her. Spring   19
days, and summer days, and all sorts of days that would be her own.
She breathed a quick prayer that life might be long. It was only yesterday she had thought with a shudder that life might be long.

She arose at length and opened the door to her sister's importu-   20
nities. There was a feverish triumph in her eyes, and she carried herself unwittingly like a goddess of Victory. She clasped her sister's
waist, and together they descended the stairs. Richards stood waiting
for them at the bottom.

Some one was opening the front door with a latchkey. It was   21
Brently Mallard who entered, a little travel-stained, composedly carrying his gripsack and umbrella. He had been far from the scene of
accident, and did not even know there had been one. He stood
amazed at Josephine's piercing cry; at Richards' quick motion to
screen him from the view of his wife.

But Richards was too late.   22

When the doctors came they said she had died of heart disease—   23
of joy that kills. ■

ANALYZING POETRY

Poetry is written in lines and stanzas, instead of in paragraphs. Because of poetry's
unique format, ideas are often expressed in compact and concise language, requiring you to spend more time and effort reading and analyzing a poem than you do
for an essay or a short story. To grasp the meaning of a poem, it is important to
pay attention to the sound and meaning of individual words and to consider how
the words in the poem work together to convey meaning.

Use the following general guidelines to read and analyze poetry effectively.

1. **Read the poem through once, without any defined purpose.** Read with an
   open mind; try to get a general sense of what the poem is about. If you come
   across an unfamiliar word or a confusing reference, keep reading.

2. **Use punctuation to guide your comprehension.** Although poetry is written
   in lines, each line may not make sense by itself. Meaning often flows from line
   to line, and a single sentence can be comprised of several lines. Use the poem's
   punctuation to guide you. If there is no punctuation at the end of a line, read
   it with a slight pause at the end and with an emphasis on the last word. Think
   about how the poet breaks lines to achieve a certain effect.

**TEACHING TIP:
LEARNING STYLES**

(10 minutes) Encourage
social learners, some
verbal learners, and stu-
dents who feel uncom-
fortable or unfamiliar
with poetry to para-
phrase and respond to a
poem line by line or sen-
tence by sentence, in
order to gain a basic
understanding of its
meaning. Try this strat-
egy in class with the
poem "Mirror" (p. 735).
Read the first line or
sentence aloud. Ask the
class to paraphrase the
line or sentence and
then respond, either
orally or in their jour-
nals. This exercise also
works well when stu-
dents work in pairs or
with a tutor.

3. **Visualize as you read.** Especially if you tend to be a spatial or an abstract learner, try to visualize or see what the poem is about.

4. **Read the poem several more times.** The meaning of the poem will become clearer with each successive reading. At first, you may understand some parts but not others. If you tend to be a pragmatic or rational learner, you will probably want to work through the poem line by line, from beginning to end. With poetry, however, that approach does not always work. Instead, you may need to use later stanzas to help you understand earlier ones. If you find certain sections difficult or confusing, read these sections aloud several times. You might try copying them, word for word, on a piece of paper. Look up the meanings of any unfamiliar words in a dictionary.

5. **Check unfamiliar references.** A poet may make **allusions**—references to people, objects, or events outside of the poem. Understanding an allusion is often essential to understanding the overall meaning of a poem. If you see Oedipus mentioned in a poem, for example, you may need to use a dictionary or encyclopedia to learn that he was a figure in Greek mythology who unwittingly killed his father and unknowingly married his mother. Your knowledge of Oedipus would then help you interpret the poem.

6. **Identify the speaker and tone.** Poems often refer to an unidentified *I* or *we*. Try to describe the speaker's viewpoint or feelings to figure out who he or she is. Also consider the speaker's tone: Is it serious, challenging, sad, frustrated, or joyful? To help determine the tone, read the poem aloud. Your emphasis of certain words or the rise and fall of your voice may provide clues to the tone; that is, you may "hear" the poet's anger, despondency, or elation.

7. **Identify to whom the poem is addressed.** Is it written to a person, to the reader, to an object? Consider the possibility that the poet may be writing to work out a personal problem or to express strong emotions.

For more on connotations, see Chapter 8, p. 196; for more on descriptive language, see Chapter 10, p. 248.

8. **Analyze the language of the poem.** Consider the *connotations,* or shades of meaning of words in the poem. Study the poem's use of descriptive language, metaphors, similes, personification, and symbols (see p. 718).

9. **Analyze the poem's theme.** Does its overall meaning involve a feeling, a person, a memory, or an argument? Paraphrase the poem; express it in your own words and connect it to your own experience. Then link your ideas together to discover the poem's overall meaning. Ask yourself: "What is the poet trying to tell me?" and "What is the theme?"

Use questions in the accompanying box to guide your analysis of poetry. As you read the following poem by Robert Frost, "Two Look at Two," keep these questions in mind.

QUESTIONS FOR ANALYZING POETRY

1. How does the poem make you feel—shocked, saddened, angered, annoyed, happy? Write a sentence or two describing your reaction.

2. Who is the speaker? What do you know about him or her? What tone does the speaker use? To whom is he or she speaking?

3. What is the poem's setting? Or, if it is unclear, why does the poet not provide a setting?

4. What emotional atmosphere or mood does the poet create? Do you sense, for example, a mood of foreboding, excitement, or contentment?

5. How does the poet use language to create an effect? Does the poet use metaphors, similes, personification, or symbols?

6. Does the poem tell a story? If so, what is its point?

7. Does the poem express emotion? If so, for what purpose?

8. Does the poem rhyme? If so, does the rhyme affect the meaning? (For example, does the poet use rhyme to emphasize key words or phrases?)

9. What is the meaning of the poem's title?

10. What is the theme of the poem?

Two Look at Two
Robert Frost

Robert Frost (1874–1963) is a major American poet whose work often focuses on familiar objects, natural scenes, and the character of New England. In his early life, Frost was a farmer and teacher; later, he became a poet in residence at Amherst College and taught at Dartmouth, Yale, and Harvard. Frost was awarded Pulitzer Prizes for four collections of poems: New Hampshire *(1923), from which "Two Look at Two" is taken;* Collected Poems *(1930),* A Further Range *(1936), and* A Witness Tree *(1942). As you read the selection, use the questions in the accompanying box to think critically about the poem.*

Love and forgetting might have carried them
A little further up the mountain side
With night so near, but not much further up.
They must have halted soon in any case
With thoughts of the path back, how rough it was   5
With rock and washout, and unsafe in darkness;

PREREADING
QUESTION

How do the humans feel after their encounter with nature? Why?

When they were halted by a tumbled wall
With barbed-wire binding. They stood facing this,
Spending what onward impulse they still had
In one last look the way they must not go,   10
On up the failing path, where, if a stone
Or earthslide moved at night, it moved itself;
No footstep moved it. "This is all," they sighed,
"Good-night to woods." But not so; there was more.
A doe from round a spruce stood looking at them   15
Across the wall, as near the wall as they.
She saw them in their field, they her in hers.
The difficulty of seeing what stood still,
Like some up-ended boulder split in two,
Was in her clouded eyes: they saw no fear there.   20
She seemed to think that two thus they were safe.
Then, as if they were something that, though strange,
She could not trouble her mind with too long,
She sighed and passed unscared along the wall.
"*This,* then, is all. What more is there to ask?"   25
But no, not yet. A snort to bid them wait.
A buck from round the spruce stood looking at them
Across the wall, as near the wall as they.
This was an antlered buck of lusty nostril,
Not the same doe come back into her place.   30
He viewed them quizzically with jerks of head,
As if to ask, "Why don't you make some motion?
Or give some sign of life? Because you can't.
I doubt if you're as living as you look."
Thus till he had them almost feeling dared   35
To stretch a proffering hand — and a spell-breaking.
Then he too passed unscared along the wall.
Two had seen two, whichever side you spoke from.
"This *must* be all." It was all. Still they stood,
A great wave from it going over them,   40
As if the earth in one unlooked-for favor
Had made them certain earth returned their love.

The poem takes place on a mountainside path, near dusk. A couple walking the path comes upon a tumbled wall. Looking beyond the wall, the couple first encounters a doe and then a buck. The doe and buck stare at the human couple and vice versa; hence the title, "Two Look at Two." Neither the animals nor the humans are frightened; both couples observe each other and continue with their lives. The action is described by a third-person narrator who can read the thoughts of the humans. The speaker creates an objective tone by reporting events as they occur.

In "Two Look at Two," Frost considers the important relationship between humans and nature. The wall is symbolic of the separation between them. Beyond the wall the couple looks at "the way they must not go" (line 10). Although humans and nature are separate, they are also equal and in balance. These qualities are suggested by the title as well as by the actions of both couples as they observe each other in a nonthreatening way. The third-person point of view contributes to this balance in that the story is narrated by an outside observer rather than a participant. One possible theme of the poem, therefore, is the balance and equality between humans and nature.

As you read the following poem, "Mirror," by Sylvia Plath, use the guidelines on page 731 and the questions in the box on page 733 to help you analyze its elements and discover its meaning. You may choose to write an analysis of this poem in response to the Guided Writing Assignment on page 737.

Mirror
Sylvia Plath

Sylvia Plath (1932–1963), an American poet, published a collection of poems, The Colossus *(1960), and a novel,* The Bell Jar *(1962, under a pseudonym), before her suicide in 1963. Other works were published posthumously, including* Ariel *(1968) and* The Colossus and Other Poems *(1965), from which the following poem is taken. As you read it, add notes about your response as annotations.*

PREREADING
QUESTIONS
• What qualities does the mirror represent?
• How does the narrator respond to the reflection?

I am silver and exact. I have no preconceptions.
Whatever I see I swallow immediately
Just as it is, unmisted by love or dislike.
I am not cruel, only truthful —
The eye of a little god, four-cornered.   5
Most of the time I meditate on the opposite wall.
It is pink, with speckles. I have looked at it so long
I think it is a part of my heart. But it flickers.
Faces and darkness separate us over and over.

Now I am a lake. A woman bends over me,   10
Searching my reaches for what she really is.
Then she turns to those liars, the candles or the moon.
I see her back, and reflect it faithfully.

> She rewards me with tears and an agitation of hands.
> I am important to her. She comes and goes.   15
> Each morning it is her face that replaces the darkness.
> In me she has drowned a young girl, and in me an old woman
> Rises toward her day after day, like a terrible fish.

Now that you have a better understanding of the elements of poetry and short stories, you are ready to write about a literary work. In English and humanities courses, you will often be asked to read and analyze works of literature and then write literary analyses. The following sections will discuss this type of essay and take you step by step through a guided writing assignment.

WHAT IS LITERARY ANALYSIS?

A **literary analysis** essay, sometimes called *literary criticism* or a *critique,* analyzes and interprets one or more aspects of a literary work. As with other types of essays, writing a literary analysis involves generating ideas through prewriting, developing a thesis, collecting supporting evidence, organizing and drafting, analyzing and revising, and editing and proofreading.

Keep in mind that a literary analysis does *not* merely summarize the work; rather, it focuses on *analysis* and *interpretation* of the work. Therefore, in a literary analysis, you take a position on some aspect of the work and support your position with evidence. In other words, you assume the role of a critic, in much the same way that a film critic argues for his or her judgment of a film rather than simply reporting its plot. For this chapter's assignment, your literary analysis should focus on *one* element of the work, even though some literary analyses cover multiple elements or more than one work.

Characteristics of Literary Analysis

A literary analysis has the following characteristics.

- It makes a point about one or more elements of a literary work.
- It includes and accurately documents evidence from the work. (It may also include evidence from outside sources.)
- It assumes that the audience is somewhat familiar with the work, but not as familiar as the writer of the analysis.
- It has a serious tone and is written in the present tense.

A GUIDED WRITING ASSIGNMENT

The following guide will help you write a literary analysis of a poem or short story. Depending on your learning style, you may find some of the suggested strategies more suitable than others. Social or verbal learners, for instance, may prefer to generate ideas about the poem or short story through discussion with classmates. Spatial or creative learners may decide to draw a character map. Independent or concrete learners may choose to draw a time line or write a summary. This Guided Writing Assignment will provide you with alternatives.

The Assignment

Write a literary analysis of a poem or short story. Choose one of the following works reprinted in this chapter, a work you select on your own, or a work assigned by your instructor. Your classmates are your audience.

1. Gwendolyn Brooks, "The Bean Eaters" (p. 714)
2. Alberto Ríos, "The Secret Lion" (p. 720)
3. Kate Chopin, "The Story of an Hour" (p. 729)
4. Robert Frost, "Two Looked at Two" (p. 733)
5. Sylvia Plath, "Mirror" (p. 735)

As you develop your literary analysis essay, you will probably use one or more patterns of development. You will use illustration, for instance, to cite examples from the poem or short story that support your analysis of it. In addition, you might compare or contrast two main characters or analyze a plot by discussing causes and effects.

For more on illustration, comparison and contrast, and cause and effect, see Chapters 11, 13, and 16.

Generating Ideas

The following guidelines will help you explore the short story or poem you have selected and generate ideas for writing about it.

1. **Highlight and annotate as you read.** Record your initial impressions and responses to the work in marginal annotations as you read. For recording lengthy comments, use a separate sheet of paper. Look for and highlight figures of speech, symbols, revealing character descriptions, striking dialogue, and the like. Here is a sample annotated portion of Frost's "Two Look at Two."

Learning Style Options

For more on annotating, see Chapter 2, p. 38.

SAMPLE ANNOTATED PASSAGE

Love and forgetting might have carried them
A little further up the mountain side

limitations of humans →   With night so near, but not much further up.

They must have halted soon in any case

road of life? difficulty of life →   With thoughts of the path back, how rough it was

With rock and washout, and unsafe in darkness;

separates man and nature — Why is it tumbled? →   When they were halted by a tumbled wall

sharp, penetrating →   With barbed-wire binding. They stood facing this,

Spending what onward impulse they still had

prohibited from crossing →   In one last look the way they must not go,

ROBERT FROST, "Two Look at Two"

2. **Discuss the literary work with classmates.** Discussing the short story or poem with others will help you generate ideas about it. Plan your discussion, moving from the general meaning of the work to a more specific paragraph-by-paragraph or line-by-line examination. Then consider your interpretation of the work's theme.

For more on writing a summary, see Chapter 19, p. 656.

3. **Write a summary.** Especially when you draw a blank about a work, try writing a summary of it in your own words. You may find yourself raising and answering questions about the work as you summarize it. Jot down ideas as they occur to you, either on your summary page or a separate sheet of paper.

4. **Draw a time line.** For a short story, especially one with a complex plot that flashes back or forward in time, draw a time line of the action in chronological sequence on paper or a computer. Here is a sample time line for Ríos's "The Secret Lion."

Sample Time Line: "The Secret Lion"

Age 5 →   Main character moves three miles north of Nogales.

First half of summer →   He visits the arroyo with Sergio; goes swimming, mother suspects.

Second half of summer →   Boys visit mountains; think they have found heaven but learn it is a golf course.

→   They return to the arroyo; try to have fun.

Age 12 (Junior High School) →   They visit the arroyo.

→   They shout dirty words and yell about girls.

TEACHING TIP:
LEARNING STYLES

1. For all learners, especially verbal and independent learners
2. For social and emotional learners
3. For rational and pragmatic learners
4. For rational, pragmatic, and spatial learners
5. For spatial learners
6. For all learners
7. For all learners, especially verbal and pragmatic learners
8. For abstract learners
9. For all learners

One Thursday ⟶ They find grinding ball.

⟶ They bury grinding ball.

⟶ They can't find the buried ball; stop going to the arroyo.

5. **Draw a character map.** To explore the connections and interactions among the characters in a story, draw a character map. In the center of a blank piece of paper, put a main character's name inside a circle. Then add other characters' names, connecting them with lines to the main character. On the connecting lines, briefly describe the relationships between characters and the events or other factors (such as emotions) that affect their relationship. You might use a drawing or symbol to represent some aspect of a character or relationship (for instance, *$* for "wealthy" or a smiley face for "happy"). Here is a sample character map for Ríos's "The Secret Lion."

Sample Character Map: "The Secret Lion"

6. **Investigate the background of the work and author.** Research the historical context of the work and biographical information about the author. Look for connections among the work, the author's life, and the social, economic, and political events of the time. Investigating the background of a work and its author can give you valuable insights into the writer's meaning (or theme) and purpose. For example, an interpretation of Charles Dickens's "A Christmas Carol" might be

For more on conducting research, see Chapter 19.

more meaningful if you understood how the author's difficult child-hood and the conditions of the poor in nineteenth-century England contributed to his portrayal of the Cratchit family.

For more on journal writ-ing, see Chapter 1, p. 7, and Chapter 3, p. 57.

7. **Use a two-column response journal.** Divide several pages of your journal into two vertical columns. Label the left column *Text* and the right column *Response*. In the left column, record five to ten quotations from the poem or short story. Choose only quotations that convey a main point or opinion, reveal a character's motives, or say something important about the plot or theme. In the right column, describe your reaction to each quotation. You might interpret, disagree with, or question the quotation. Try to comment on the language of the quotation and to relate it to other quotations or elements in the work. Here is a sample two-column journal response to Frost's "Two Look at Two."

Sample Two-Column Response to "Two Look at Two"

Text	Response
"With thoughts of the path back, how rough it was" (line 5)	The couple's past has been difficult; returning to daily life may be difficult, too. Nature is rough and challenging.
"'This is all,' they sighed, / 'Good-night to woods.'" (lines 13–14)	The couple will soon come to the end—of their relationship or their lives.

8. **Discover parallel works or situations.** You can often evoke a response to a work by comparing it to other literary works, another narrative form (such as a film or television show), or a familiar situation. For example, after reading the poem "On His Blindness" by John Milton, one student connected it to the movie *Scent of a Woman*, in which one central character is blind. By comparing the literary work to the more familiar film, the student was better able to analyze the meaning of the poem.

9. **Use prewriting.** Prewriting helps you generate ideas for all types of essays, including a literary analysis. Try freewriting, brainstorming, sketching, questioning, or any of the other prewriting strategies discussed in Chapter 4.

TEACHING TIP

Before students pursue a more familiar prewriting method, ask them to write a few journal entries using the two-column response format to explore the meanings of particular passages or lines in the works they have chosen to analyze.

ESSAY IN PROGRESS 1

Use one or more of the preceding techniques to generate ideas about the short story or poem you've chosen for your analysis.

Evaluating Your Ideas

Once you generate sufficient ideas about the work, begin your evaluation by reviewing your notes and prewriting. Look for a perspective or position that reflects your understanding of some aspect of the work. Here are several possible approaches you might take in a literary analysis.

1. **Evaluate symbolism.** Discuss how the author's use of images and symbols creates a particular mood and contributes to the overall meaning of the work.

2. **Analyze conflicts.** Focus on their causes, effects, or both.

3. **Evaluate characterization.** Discuss the ways in which characters are presented, whether a particular character's actions are realistic or predictable, or what the author reveals or hides about a character.

4. **Interpret characters or relationships among them.** Analyze how the true nature of a character is revealed or how a character changes in response to circumstances.

5. **Explore themes.** Discover the important point or theme the work conveys, and back up your ideas with examples from the work.

Developing Your Thesis

After evaluating your ideas and choosing an aspect of the work to focus on, it is time to write a thesis statement. Your thesis should indicate the element of the work you will analyze (its theme, characters, or use of symbols, for example) and state the main point you will make about that element, as in the following sample thesis statements.

- In Flannery O'Connor's short story "A Good Man Is Hard to Find," color is used to depict various moods throughout the story.

- Susan Glaspell's play *Trifles* shows that the men's perception of women as only concerned with trivial matters is faulty when the women discover the major pieces of evidence that solve the murder mystery.

For more on thesis state-
ments, see Chapter 5,
p. 97.

Be sure your thesis statement focuses on your interpretation of *one* specific aspect of the work. As in other types of essays, the thesis for a literary analysis should identify your narrowed topic.

ESSAY IN PROGRESS 2

Using the preceding guidelines, write a working thesis for your literary analysis essay. Then review the poem or short story and your notes to make sure you have enough evidence to support your thesis. In the body paragraphs of your essay, you will need to cite examples from the work that show why your thesis is valid. You might, for example, include relevant descriptions of characters or events, snippets of dialogue, examples of imagery and figures of speech, or any other details from the work that confirm or explain your thesis.

As you review the work and your notes about it, try to meet with one or two classmates who are working on the same poem or short story, if possible. They may have noticed evidence that you have overlooked or offer insights into the work that enrich your own reading of it. No two readers will have the same interpretation of a literary work, however, so don't be alarmed if their ideas differ from yours.

TRYING OUT YOUR IDEAS ON OTHERS

Working in a group of two or three students, discuss each other's thesis and supporting evidence for this chapter's assignment. Encourage your peers to ask questions about your work and suggest improvements.

ESSAY IN PROGRESS 3

Use your own analysis and the feedback you received from peer reviewers to evaluate your thesis and supporting evidence. Gather additional examples from the work if necessary, and delete any examples that do not support your thesis.

Organizing and Drafting

Use the following guidelines to organize and draft your literary analysis.

1. **Choose a method of organization.** See Chapter 6 for more detailed suggestions about organizing an essay.

TEACHING TIP:
COLLABORATIVE
WRITING

Have students exchange their working thesis statements with at least two or three other students for comments via email, networked computers, or in small groups. Ask students to evaluate the specificity of each working thesis.

2. **Focus your essay on ideas, not events.** Remember that your literary analysis should not merely summarize the work or the plot. Instead, focus on your ideas and interpretations.

3. **Write in the present tense.** Treat the events in the work as if they are happening now rather than in the past. For example, write "Brooks describ*es* an elderly couple . . . ," *not* "Brooks describ*ed*. . . ."

4. **Include sufficient examples from the work and cite them correctly.** Use enough examples to support your thesis but not so many that your essay becomes one long string of examples with no clear main point. In addition, provide in-text citations (including page numbers for a short story or line numbers for a poem) in parentheses immediately after any quotations from the work. Include a works-cited entry at the end of your paper indicating the edition of the work you used.

For help with citing examples from a literary work, see Chapter 20, p. 685.

5. **Write an effective introduction.** The introduction for a literary analysis should engage readers, name the author and title of the work, present your thesis, and suggest why your analysis of the work is useful or important. For example, to engage your readers' interest, you might include a meaningful quotation from the work, comment on the universality of a character or theme, or briefly state your response to the work.

6. **Write a satisfying conclusion.** To conclude your essay, you can use techniques similar to those just described for introductions. Your purposes are to give the essay a sense of closure as well as to reaffirm your thesis. You may want to tie your conclusion directly to your introduction, offering a final word or comment on your main point.

For more on writing effective introductions and conclusions, see Chapter 6, p. 140.

TEACHING TIP

Students who have followed the steps in the Guided Writing Assignment should be ready to compose a first draft independently. However, check to see if any students need to rethink their thesis, organization, or examples from the work before drafting. Encourage them to seek further assistance from a peer reviewer or writing center tutor.

For more on the benefits of peer review, see Chapter 7, p. 166.

ESSAY IN PROGRESS 4

Using the preceding guidelines for organizing and drafting and the thesis you developed in Essay in Progress 2, draft your literary analysis essay.

Analyzing and Revising

If possible, set your draft aside for a day or two before rereading and revising it. Then, as you reread your draft, concentrate on your ideas and organization, not on grammar or mechanics. Use Flowchart 21.1 to guide your evaluation. You might also ask a classmate to review your draft by using the questions in the flowchart.

FLOWCHART 21.1
REVISING A LITERARY ANALYSIS ESSAY

Questions		Revision Strategies

1. Does your thesis identify the work, the one aspect of it you are analyzing, and the main point of your analysis?

 No

- Revise your thesis so that all of these items are included.
- Ask a classmate to read your thesis and convey his or her understanding of your main point.

 Yes

2. Do you support your thesis with sufficient evidence from the literary work? Is your evidence relevant to the one aspect of the work you identify in your thesis?

 No

- Delete examples that do not support your thesis or that might be confusing to readers.
- Include relevant quotations.

Yes

3. Do you include in-text citations with page or line numbers for all quotations from the work?

 No

- Add in-text citations where they are required.
- Give a works-cited entry for the edition of the work used at the end of the essay.

 Yes

4. Is your literary analysis written for the intended audience — one that is less familiar with the work than you are?

 No

- Assume your readers have only limited knowledge of the work and have read it only once or twice.
- Provide information (about the author, plot, characters, and so on) that your readers will need to understand your analysis of the work.

Yes

(Continued on next page)

FLOWCHART 21.1 *(continued)*

°Questions°	Revision Strategies

5. Does your tone suggest a serious, objective view of the work? Is your analysis written in the present tense?

No

Yes

- Eliminate any overly critical or enthusiastic statements.
- When writing about events in the work, maintain the present tense unless you are writing about an event that preceded another event in the story.

6. Does your introduction suggest the importance of your thesis and engage your readers' interest? Is your conclusion satisfying?

No

Yes

- Begin and end your essay with a meaningful quotation or brief statement about a character, a theme, or your response to the work.
- Ask yourself, "Why would my audience be interested in my thesis?" Incorporate the answer into your introduction.
- Revise your introduction and conclusion so that they meet the guidelines covered in Chapter 6 (pp. 140–46).

7. Is each body paragraph well developed and focused on one main point or idea?

No

Yes

- Be sure each body paragraph has a topic sentence (see Chapter 6) and supporting evidence from the work.
- Consider combining closely related paragraphs.
- Split paragraphs that cover two or more main points or ideas.

TEACHING TIP:
COLLABORATIVE
WRITING

Conduct a peer-review
session. Have students
work in small groups,
using Flowchart 21.1 as
a basis for their com-
ments and suggestions
for revision.

TEACHING TIP

Encourage students to
consult with a writing
center tutor for further
review of the revision.

*For more on keeping an
error log, see Chapter 8,
p. 201.*

ESSAY IN PROGRESS 5

Revise your draft essay using Flowchart 21.1 and the comments you received from peer reviewers.

Editing and Proofreading

The last step is to check your revised essay for errors in grammar, spelling, punctuation, and mechanics. In addition, be sure to check your error log for the types of errors you tend to make.

As you edit and proofread your literary analysis, watch out for the following errors that are often found in this type of writing.

1. **Use the literary present tense.** Even though the poem or short story was written in the past, as a general rule you should write about the events in it and the author's writing of it as if they were happening in the present. This is called the *literary present tense.* An exception to this rule occurs when you are referring to a time earlier than that in which the narrator speaks, in which case a switch to the past tense is appropriate.

   ▶ Keats in "Ode on a Grecian Urn" ~~referred~~ *refers* to the urn as a "silent form" (line 44).

   ▶ In "Two Look at Two," it is not clear why the couple *decided* to walk up the mountain side path.

   The couple made the decision before the action in the poem began.

2. **Punctuate quotations correctly.** Direct quotations from a literary work, whether spoken or written, must be placed in quotation marks. Omitted material is marked by an ellipsis mark, enclosed in brackets if you are following MLA style. The lines of a poem are separated by a slash (/).

   ▶ In "Two Look at Two," Frost concludes that "the earth in one unlooked-for favor / Had made them certain earth returned their love" (lines 41–42).

   Periods and commas appear within quotation marks. Question marks and exclamation points go within or outside of quotation marks, depending on the meaning of the sentence. Here the question mark goes inside the closing quotation marks because it is part of Frost's poem (line 32). Notice, too, that double and single quote marks are required for a quotation within a quotation.

▶ The buck seems "[...] to ask, 'Why don't you make some motion'"? (line 32).

TEACHING TIP

After students revise their drafts, have them work in pairs to look for shifts in tense and punctuation errors in quotations.

ESSAY IN PROGRESS 6

Edit and proofread your literary analysis essay, paying particular attention to verb tense and punctuation of quotations.

STUDENTS WRITE

Andrew Decker was a community college student at Niagara County Community College when he wrote the following literary analysis of Ríos's "The Secret Lion" in response to an assignment for his first-year writing class. As you read the essay, identify the one aspect of the literary work that Decker focuses on. Also underline or highlight his thesis and the evidence he uses to support it.

PREREADING QUESTION

What is the "secret" that Decker thinks is being kept?

The Keeping of "The Secret Lion"
Andrew Decker

Alberto Ríos's "The Secret Lion" charts the initia-   1
tion of a young boy into adolescence. During this climactic period of growth, the narrator experiences several
shifts in perception that change him from a child to an
adolescent by teaching him the value of secrets.

Within the first paragraph, the author introduces   2
the reader to the new and perplexing feelings of the
main character during his junior high years. His impression of what happened during those years remains name-
less, "but it was there nonetheless like a lion, and
roaring, roaring that way the biggest things do. Everything changed. Just that" (98). It is as if the boy is

being swept away by a great swell, the wave of anticipation traditionally associated with the child's entry into
adolescence.

3   He finds that these changes are confusing yet enticing. Evident within the context of the first page is the
boy's newfound curiosity about and fascination with the
opposite sex. He is also bewildered by the use of profanity, and delights in the opportunity to verbally (and
very loudly) explore his own feelings with respect to
the use of such words.

4   Although adults scold him when he questions them
about the meaning of these words, their dismay does not
discourage him from saying the words privately. He and
his friend Sergio like to hide away from such authoritarian voices, and so they cross the highway to the
arroyo where they are not supposed to play. In the
arroyo, they "shout every dirty word we could think of,
in every combination we could come up with, and we would
yell about girls, and all the things we wanted to do
with them, as loud as we could" (99). Of course, they
take great pleasure in this youthful audacity for "it
just felt good and for the first time in our lives there
was nobody to tell us we couldn't" (99). All is new. All
is fresh. Opportunity abounds, and possibilities remain
infinite, for time has not yet become an enemy.

5   One day when the two boys are playing and cussing
in the arroyo, they happen upon a perfectly round iron
ball. It is heavy and smooth and to them it is the perfect object. In the eyes of the two children, the world
is formless and pure, as is the ball. Similarly, they
consider the arroyo to be the perfect place--their perfect place. When faced with deciding what to do with the
ball, they choose to bury it so that nobody can take it
away--if only in a less literal sense.

6   Their minds are still free of the narrow vision of
an adult. They are free to roam and roar and echo the
spirit of the lion, which is for Sergio and the narrator

the spirit of that time. In their own words, when they
talk of that ball, they speak of

> how much that ball was like that place, that
> whole arroyo: couldn't tell anybody about it,
> didn't understand what it was, didn't have a
> name for it. It just felt good. It was just
> perfect in the way it was that place, that
> whole going to that place, that whole junior
> high school lion. (100)

They know that once they bury the grinding ball (they
only learn later what it is) it will be gone forever,
and yet thereby preserved.

The two boys are applying a lesson they have 7
already learned. They understand that an experience can
be stolen or changed by a shift in perception so that
the original feeling, the original reality, ceases to
exist in its more pure and innocent form. The boys had
experienced disillusion before; when they were very
young, they had also played in the arroyo and gone swimming in the stream. It was a time of naiveté, but their
naiveté had been challenged when they learned that the
water was at times filled with the waste flushed down-
stream by a local sewage plant.

Another shift in perception happened later that same 8
summer, when the boys thought they had found a new haven
across some mountains near their houses. Having come upon
a green clearing, they were swept away by the lush
beauty, and declared it their "heaven." They learned,
however, that this heaven was merely a product of their
unworldly imagination; the boys had youthfully glorified
a simple golf course, in which they were unwelcome
visitors.

These events and others teach the boys to protect 9
a new experience, to keep new feelings safe and virginal
so as not to lose them to the ravages of time and
change. When they return to the arroyo several years
later, when they are twelve and experiencing the exuber-

POSSIBLE ANSWERS:
ANALYZING THE ESSAY
(p. 750)

1. Decker analyzes the
theme of initiation
into adolescence.

2. *Thesis:* "During this
climactic period . . .
secrets" (paragraph
1). Yes, the thesis
yokes the theme of
initiation with "shifts
in perception" that
teach the narrator the
value of secrets,
thereby enabling his
maturation.

3. Examples of narra-
tor's shifts in percep-
tion: Fascination with
taboos of sex and
profanity (3–4); water
from the sewage plant
disrupts the boys'
swimming (7); realiza-
tion that "heaven" is
really a golf course
(8). All three are
effective examples.

(Continued on next page)

4. *Introduction:*
Announces theme,
specifies claim (that
shifts in perception
facilitated the narra-
tor's initiation into
adolescence by teach-
ing him the value of
secrets); could be
more developed. Sec-
ond paragraph pro-
vides background for
the essay, quoting the
"secret lion" passage
and associating it
with adolescence.
First two paragraphs
could possibly be
combined, with the
thesis moved to the
end of that section.
Conclusion: Analyzes
the boys' desire to
protect themselves
emotionally; relates
well to and reflects
the introduction.

5. Paragraphs 2, 4, 7,
and 8 are well devel-
oped. Paragraph 1
could use more back-
ground information
before the thesis is
introduced. Para-
graphs 3 and 5 need
specific details from
the work to support
such general state-
ments as "these
changes are confusing
yet enticing" (3) and
"In the eyes . . . as is
the ball" (5).

POSSIBLE ANSWERS:
REACTING TO THE
ESSAY
Responses will vary.

ance and excitement of adolescence, they know enough not to share or expose their experiences. The grinding ball is a symbol of that age, that sense of newness, and as they say, "when we buried it we knew what would happen" (102). Burying the ball is an attempt on their part to crystallize a certain time, a certain perception, "because it was perfect" (102). "It was the lion," and the lion was the "roaring" of both that time and that place, and they bury it so that it might never truly be lost.

Work Cited

Ríos, Alberto. <u>The Iguana Killer: Twelve Stories of the Heart</u>. 1984. Lewiston: Blue Moon, 1984.

Analyzing the Essay

1. What one element of "The Secret Lion" does Decker address?

2. Evaluate Decker's thesis statement. Does it indicate the element he analyzes and make a point about that element?

3. Does Decker provide sufficient evidence to support his thesis? Choose one example Decker offers and evaluate its effectiveness.

4. Evaluate Decker's introduction and conclusion. In what ways could they be improved?

5. Which paragraphs are particularly well developed? Which, if any, need further development?

Reacting to the Essay: Discussion and Journal Writing

1. How does Decker's interpretation of "The Secret Lion" compare with yours?

2. Evaluate Decker's perception of childhood and adolescence. Write a journal entry comparing his perception to your own.

"ALTHOUGH HUMANS MAKE SOUNDS WITH THEIR MOUTHS AND OCCASIONALLY LOOK AT EACH OTHER, THERE IS NO SOLID EVIDENCE THAT THEY ACTUALLY COMMUNICATE WITH EACH OTHER."

Chapter *22*

CHAPTER QUICK START

Suppose you have to take a short timed writing test. You have to write about one of the images on the opposite page. Assume that your grade on the test will influence your grade in the writing course.

Writing Quick Start

Write a paragraph explaining (1) your reaction to the activity in the photograph or (2) the meaning of the cartoon. You have fifteen minutes to complete the writing test.

Essay Examinations and Timed Writings

TEACHING TIP

Restrict students to the fifteen minutes indicated for completing the Writing Quick Start. Encourage them to prewrite on a separate sheet of paper or in their journals prior to drafting. Tell them when five minutes remain so they can read over what they have written and make final corrections.

In completing the timed writing test, did you feel pressured by the fifteen-minute limit? How did you decide which assignment to complete? Did you have as much time as you would have liked to organize, plan, develop, and revise your ideas? Probably not.

Many college instructors use timed writings and essay exams to assess students' knowledge and writing ability. As you progress through college, you will be required to take many essay exams, especially in advanced courses. In the workplace, too, you may be asked to produce a memo, report, or proposal and have it on your supervisor's desk "by five o'clock." See the accompanying box for a few examples of timed writing situations.

You may ask, "Why do instructors give essay exams and other kinds of timed writing assignments?" In many college courses, essay exams allow instructors to determine how well students have grasped important concepts and whether they can organize and integrate key concepts with other material. In addition, instructors realize that an essay exam requires students to use different and more advanced thinking skills than does a more objective type of exam, such as a multiple-choice test. For instance, an essay exam for a history course would require you to pull ideas together and focus on larger issues, perhaps analyzing historical trends or making comparisons between two political figures. Timed writing assignments serve a similar purpose in a composition course. When you are given forty-five minutes to write a brief process analysis of something you know how to do, a short comparison of two television shows, or a description of someone you admire, your instructor wants to make sure you are learning how to write various types of essays and can do so quickly and efficiently. Finally, some colleges require students to demonstrate their writing expertise in a mandatory competency test given upon admission to the college, at the end of a writing course, or at the completion of a program of study.

SCENES FROM COLLEGE AND THE WORKPLACE

• For an *introductory economics* course, you are given forty-five minutes to respond to the following essay question: "Unlike government agencies, private corporations must balance their budgets each year. What factors might force a financially healthy corporation to spend more than it earns in a given year?"

• For the midterm in a *philosophy of religion* course, you have one hour to complete the following essay: "Contrast the beliefs of Islam to those of Judaism or Christianity."

• As the *sales manager* of an auto parts store, you are required to write an evaluation of two sales trainees and to fax your report to national headquarters by noon today.

This chapter will help you prepare for the timed essay writings you will encounter in college and in your career. Developing good study skills is a key to success on such exams. You will learn how to anticipate the types of questions instructors ask, how to organize your ideas quickly and efficiently, and how to work within the time constraints of essay exams. Although the focus of the chapter is on essay exams, the skills you learn here also apply to other kinds of timed writing assignments.

PREPARING FOR ESSAY EXAMS

Because essay exams require you to produce a written response, the best way to prepare for them is by organizing and writing. The following guidelines will help you prepare for such exams.

Write Study Sheets That Synthesize Information

Most essay exams require you to *synthesize* or pull together information. To prepare for this task, try to identify the key topics in a course and write a study sheet for each main topic. Study sheets help you organize and consolidate complex or detailed information and give you brief topic outlines to study. To prepare a study sheet, draw on information from your textbook as well as from your class notes, in-class handouts, papers (note key topics), previous exams (look for emphasized topics), and assigned readings.

You can organize a study sheet in a variety of ways. For example, you might draw a graphic organizer to create a visual study sheet, create a time line to connect historical events, write an outline to organize information, or construct a comparison-contrast chart to see relationships between different topics. Whatever method of organization you use for your study sheet, be sure to include key information about topics: definitions, facts, principles, theories, events, research studies, and the like.

Here is part of one student's study sheet for a speech communication course on the topic *audience analysis*.

SAMPLE STUDY SHEET

Topic: Audience Analysis

1. Demographic characteristics
   — Age and gender
   — Educational background (type and level of education)
   — Group membership (people who share similar interests or goals)
   — Social activities

> —Religious activities
> —Hobbies and sports
> 2. Psychological characteristics
> —Beliefs (about what is true or false, right or wrong)
> —Attitudes (positive or negative)
> —Values (standards for judging worth of thoughts and actions)

TEACHING TIP:
COLLABORATIVE
WRITING

You may wish to allow
students who share
another class to work
together on a study
sheet for that class.

POSSIBLE ANSWERS

Responses will vary.

EXERCISE 22.1

For one of your courses, use the preceding guidelines to prepare a study sheet on a general topic that you expect will be covered on an upcoming exam.

Predict Essay Exam Questions

Once you prepare study sheets for a particular course, the next step is to predict questions that might be asked on an essay exam. Although essay exam questions usually focus on general topics, themes, or patterns, you will probably need to supply details in your response. For example, an essay question on an economics exam might ask you to compare and contrast the James-Lange and Cannon-Bard theories of motivation. Your answer would focus on the similarities and differences between these key theories, incorporating relevant details where necessary.

Use the following strategies to help you predict the types of questions you might be asked on an essay exam.

1. **Group topics into categories.** Review your textbook, class notes, and study sheets. Look to see how you can group topics into general subject areas or categories. For example, if you find several chapters that deal with kinship in your anthropology textbook, a question on kinship is likely to appear on one or more essay exams for the course.

2. **Study your course syllabus and objectives.** These documents contain important clues about what your instructor expects you to know at various points during the course.

3. **Study previous exams.** Notice which key ideas are emphasized in previous exams. If you had to explain the historical significance of the Boston Tea Party on your first American history exam, you can predict that you will be asked to explain the historical significance of other events on subsequent exams.

4. **Listen to your instructor's comments.** When your instructor announces or reviews material for an upcoming essay exam, pay close attention to what is said. He or she may reveal key topics or suggest areas that will be emphasized on the test.

5. **Draft some possible essay questions.** Use Table 22.1 (on p. 761) to help you draft possible essay questions using key verbs. The verb in a question affects

the way you answer it. It takes time to learn how to predict exam questions, so don't get discouraged if at first you predict only one question correctly. Even if you predict none of the questions, the attempt to do so will help you to learn the material.

EXERCISE 22.2

Suppose your business marketing textbook includes a chapter with the following headings. Using the preceding guidelines for predicting essay exam questions and the key verbs in Table 22.1 (p. 761), write three possible questions that the course instructor might ask about the chapter material.

Textbook: *Marketing,* by William G. Nickels and Marian Burk Wood
Chapter: "Consumer Buying Behavior"
Headings:
Marketing, Relationships, and Consumer Behavior
Real People, Real Individuals
Consumers as Moving Targets
How Consumers Buy
The Need-Recognition Stage
The Information-Seeking Stage
The Evaluation Stage
The Purchase Stage
The Postpurchase Evaluation Stage
Involvement and the Purchase-Decision Process
External Influences on Consumer Behavior
Family and Household Influences
Opinion Leaders and Word of Mouth
Reference Groups
Social Class
Culture, Subculture, and Core Values
Situational Influences
Internal Influences on Consumer Behavior
Perception
Motivation
Attitudes

POSSIBLE ANSWERS

1. Explain the five stages consumers go through when purchasing a product.
2. Contrast external influences on consumer behavior with internal influences.
3. Discuss what Nickels and Wood mean by calling consumers "moving targets."

ESSAY IN PROGRESS 1

For an upcoming essay exam in one of your courses, predict and write at least three possible questions your instructor might ask about the course material.

TEACHING TIP

Have students write their essay questions in their journals for future reference.

Draft Answers in Outline Form

Once you predict several possible essay exam questions, the next step is to write a brief, rough outline of the information that answers each question. Be sure each outline responds to the *wording* of the question; that is, it should *explain, compare, describe,* or do whatever else the question asks (see Table 22.1 on p. 761). Writing a rough outline will strengthen your recall of the material. It will also save you time during the actual exam because you will have already spent some time thinking about, organizing, and writing about the material.

Here is a sample essay question and an informal outline written in response to it.

ESSAY QUESTION

Explain the ways in which material passes in and out of cells by crossing plasma membranes.

INFORMAL OUTLINE

Types of Transport

1. Passive — no use of cellular energy; random movement of molecules
   a. Diffusion — movement of molecules from areas of high concentration to areas of low concentration. Example: open bottle of perfume; aroma spreads
   b. Facilitated diffusion — similar to simple diffusion; differs in that some kinds of molecules are moved more easily than others (helped by carrier proteins in cell membrane)
   c. Osmosis — diffusion of water across membranes, from area of lower to area of higher solute concentration
2. Active — requires cellular energy; usually movement against the concentration gradient
   a. Facilitated active transport — carrier molecules move ions across a membrane
   b. Endocytosis — material is surrounded by a plasma membrane and pinched off into a vacuole
   c. Exocytosis — cells expel materials

COMPUTER HINT

Have students share and review their informal outlines via networked computers or email, commenting on the usefulness and clarity of the outlines.

ESSAY IN PROGRESS 2

For one of the questions you predicted in Essay in Progress 1, prepare a brief informal outline in response to the question.

Reduce Informal Outlines to Key-word Outlines

To help you recall your outline answer at the time of the exam, reduce it to a brief key-word outline or list of key topics. Here is a sample key-word outline for the essay question about cells.

KEY-WORD OUTLINE

Types of Transport

1. Passive
   - Diffusion
   - Facilitated diffusion
   - Osmosis
2. Active
   - Facilitated active transport
   - Endocytosis
   - Exocytosis

ESSAY IN PROGRESS 3

Reduce the outline answer you wrote in Essay in Progress 2 to a key-word outline.

TEACHING TIP

Remind students that key-word outlines work well as a study tool for timed writings but are less effective in writing situations in which the outline will be evaluated by someone else.

TAKING ESSAY EXAMS

Once you have done some preparation, you should be more confident about taking an essay exam. Although the time limit for an essay exam may make you feel somewhat pressured, remember that your classmates are working under the same conditions.

Some General Guidelines

Keep the following general guidelines in mind when you take essay exams.

1. **Arrive at the room where the exam is to be given a few minutes early.** You can use this time to collect your thoughts and get organized.

2. **Sit in the front of the room.** You will be less distracted and better able to see and hear the instructor as last-minute directions or corrections are announced.

3. **Read the directions carefully.** For example, some exams may direct you to answer only one of three questions, whereas other exams may ask you to answer all questions.

4. **Preview the exam and plan your time carefully.** Get a complete picture of the task at hand, and then plan how you will complete the exam within the allotted time. For example, if you are given fifty minutes to complete an essay exam, spend roughly ten minutes planning, thirty minutes writing, and ten minutes editing, proofreading, and making last-minute changes. If an exam contains

both objective and essay questions, do the objective questions first so you have the remaining time to concentrate on the essay questions.

5. **Notice the point value of each question.** If your instructor assigns points to each question, use the point values to plan your time. For example, you would spend more time answering a thirty-point question than one worth ten points.

6. **Choose topics or questions carefully.** Often you will be given little or no choice of topic or question. If you do have a choice, choose the topics or answer the questions that you know the most about. If you are given a broad topic, such as a current social issue, narrow the topic to one you can write about in the specified amount of time.

7. **Answer the easiest question first.** Answering the easiest question first will boost your confidence and allow you to spend the remaining time working on the more difficult questions.

8. **Consider your audience and purpose.** For most essay exams, your instructor is your audience. Since your instructor is already knowledgeable about the topic, your purpose is to demonstrate what *you know* about the topic. Therefore, you should write thorough and complete answers, pretending that your instructor knows only what you tell him or her.

9. **Remember that your first draft is your final draft.** Plan on writing your first draft carefully and correctly so that it can serve as your final copy. You can always make minor changes and additions as you write or while you edit and proofread.

10. **Plan and organize your answer.** Because time is limited, your first response may be to start writing immediately. However, planning and organizing are especially important first steps because you will not have the opportunity to revise your essay. (If you usually write whatever comes to mind and then spend a great deal of time revising, you will need to modify your approach for essay exams.) Begin by writing a brief thesis statement. Then jot down the key supporting points and number them in the order you will present them. Leave space under each supporting point for your details. If the question is one you predicted earlier, write down your key-word outline. If an idea for an interesting introduction or an effective conclusion comes to mind, jot it down as well. As you write your answers, be sure to reserve enough time to reread your essay and correct surface errors.

TEACHING TIP: LEARNING STYLES

Creative learners may balk at the pressure of an essay exam. Remind them that timed-writing situations are opportunities to use what they have learned from the pragmatic and rational learners in class: how to generate a branching diagram or brainstorm a list before they write a working thesis and start drafting.

Analyzing Essay Exam Questions

Essay exam questions are often concise, and may at first seem to offer few clues about what to write. If you read them closely, you will find that they *do* tell you very specifically what to write about. Consider the following sample essay question from a sociology exam.

Choose a particular institution, define it, and identify its primary characteristics.

The question tells you exactly what to write about—*a particular institution*. In addition, the key verbs *define* and *identify* tell you how to approach the subject. For this essay question, then, you would give an accurate definition of an institution and discuss its primary characteristics.

Table 22.1 lists key verbs commonly used in essay exam questions along with sample questions and tips for answering them. As you study the list, notice that many of the verbs suggest a particular pattern of development. For example, *trace* suggests using a narrative sequence and *justify* suggests using argumentation. For a more vague key verb such as *explain* or *discuss,* you might use a combination of patterns.

TABLE 22.1
RESPONDING TO KEY VERBS IN ESSAY EXAM QUESTIONS

Key Verb	Sample Essay Question	Tips for Answering Questions
Compare	Compare the poetry of Judith Ortiz Cofer to that of a contemporary poet.	Show how poems are similar as well as different; use details and examples.
Contrast	Contrast classical and operant conditioning.	Show how they are different; use details and examples.
Define	Define *biofeedback* and describe its uses.	Give an accurate explanation of the term with enough detail to demonstrate that you understand it.
Discuss	Discuss the halo effect and give examples of its use.	Consider important characteristics and main points; include examples.
Evaluate	Evaluate the accomplishments of the feminist movement over the past fifty years.	Assess its merits, strengths, weaknesses, advantages, or limitations.
Explain	Explain the functions of amino acids.	Use facts and details to make the topic or concept clear and understandable.
Illustrate	Illustrate with examples from your experience how culture shapes human behavior.	Use examples that demonstrate a point or clarify an idea.
Justify	Justify laws outlawing smoking in federal buildings.	Give reasons and evidence that support an action, decision, or policy.
List	List the advantages and disadvantages of sales promotions.	List or discuss one by one; use most-to-least or least-to-most organization.
Summarize	Summarize Maslow's hierarchy of needs.	Briefly review all the major points.
Trace	Trace the life cycle of a typical household product.	Describe its development or progress in chronological order.

Writing Essay Answers

Since your final draft essay exam is also your final draft, be sure to write in complete and grammatically correct sentences, to supply sufficient detail, and to follow a logical organization. For essay exams, instructors do not expect your writing to be as polished as it might be for an essay or research paper assignment. It is acceptable to cross out words or sentences neatly and to indicate corrections in spelling or grammar. If you think of an idea to add, write the sentence at the top of your paper and draw an arrow to indicate where it should be inserted.

Essay exam answers tend to have brief introductions and conclusions. The introduction, for instance, may include only a thesis statement. If possible, include any necessary background information on the topic, and write a conclusion only if the question seems to require a final evaluative statement.

If you run out of time on an essay exam, jot the unfinished portion of your outline at the end of the essay. Your instructor may give you partial credit for your ideas.

Writing Your Thesis Statement

For more on thesis statements, see Chapter 5.

Your thesis statement should be clear and direct, identify your subject, and suggest your approach to the topic. Often the thesis rephrases or answers the essay exam question. Consider the following examples.

POSSIBLE ANSWERS

1. The term *freedom of the press* means that members of the press have the legal right to ask questions of any individual or corporate or government representative while investigating or reporting a story and to publish what they learn without fear of reprisal.
2. Private physicians tend to offer a higher level of care and a broader range of technologically sophisticated diagnostic tests than medical clinics, which often serve uninsured patients, do.
3. The talking Chihuahua featured in Taco Bell advertisements appeals to viewers' sense of humor and animal lovers' weakness for

Essay Exam Question	**Thesis Statement**
Explain how tides are produced in the earth's oceans. Account for seasonal variations.	The earth's gravitational forces are responsible for producing tides in the earth's oceans.
Distinguish between bureaucratic agencies and other government decision-making bodies.	Bureaucratic agencies are distinct from other government decision-making bodies because of their hierarchical organization, character and culture, and professionalism.

For some essay exam questions, your thesis should also suggest the organization of your essay. For example, if you are asked to explain the differences between primary and secondary groups, your thesis might be stated as follows: "Primary groups differ from secondary groups in their membership, purpose, level of interaction, and level of intimacy." Your essay, then, would be organized accordingly, discussing membership first, then purpose, and so forth.

EXERCISE 22.3

Write thesis statements for two of the following essay exam questions.

1. Define and illustrate the meaning of the term *freedom of the press*.

2. Distinguish between the medical care provided by private physicians and that provided by medical clinics.
3. Choose a recent television advertisement and describe its rational and emotional appeals.
4. Evaluate a current news program in terms of its breadth and depth of coverage, objectivity, and political and social viewpoints.

Developing Supporting Details

Write a separate paragraph for each of your key points. In an essay answer distinguishing primary from secondary groups, for example, you would devote one paragraph to each distinguishing feature: membership, purpose, level of interaction, and level of intimacy. The topic sentence for each paragraph should identify and briefly explain a key point. For example, a topic sentence for the first main point about groups might read like this: "Membership, or who belongs, is one factor that distinguishes primary from secondary groups." The rest of the paragraph would explain membership: what constitutes membership, what criteria are used to decide who belongs, and who decides. Whenever possible, supply examples to make it clear that you can apply the information you have learned. Keep in mind that on an essay exam your goal is to demonstrate *your* knowledge and understanding of the material.

Rereading and Proofreading Your Answer

Be sure to leave enough time to reread and proofread your essay answer. Begin by rereading the question to make sure you have answered all parts of it. Then reread your answer, checking it first for content. Add missing information, correct vague or unclear sentences, and add facts or details. Next, proofread for errors in spelling, punctuation, and grammar. Before taking an essay exam, check your error log and then evaluate your answer with those errors in mind. A neat, nearly error-free essay makes a positive impression on your instructor and identifies you as a serious, conscientious student. An error-free essay may also improve your grade.

ESSAY IN PROGRESS 4

For the essay question you worked on in Essay in Progress 1–3, use the preceding guidelines to write a complete essay answer.

STUDENTS WRITE

The following model essay exam response was written by Ronald Robinson for his sociology course. As you read the student's essay, note that it has been annotated to point out key elements of its organization and content.

cute little dogs; since dogs have no demonstrated preference for Mexican food, however, its rational appeal is nonexistent.
4. *"Viewpoints" covers issues in the local news fairly and objectively, but it fails to include enough coverage of issues that concern members of minority groups.*

For more on topic sentences, see Chapter 6, p. 128.

For more on proofreading and on keeping an error log, see Chapter 8, p. 199.

TEACHING TIP: COLLABORATIVE WRITING

After students complete the essay answers independently, have them work in small groups to evaluate each other's work. Remind them to assess the thesis, support, transitions, and clarity and correctness of the writing.

Essay Exam Response

ESSAY EXAM QUESTION

Distinguish between fads and fashions, explaining the characteristics of each type of group behavior and describing the phases each usually goes through.

Thesis statement

1   Fashions and fads, types of collective group behavior, are distinct from one another in terms of their duration, their predictability, and the number of people involved. Each type follows a five-stage process of development.

Definition and characteristics of *fashion*

2   A fashion is a temporary trend in behavior or appearance that is followed by a relatively large number of people. Although the word *fashion* often refers to a style of dress, there are fashions in music, art, and literature as well. Trends in clothing fashions are often engineered by clothing designers, advertisers, and the media to create a particular "look." The "grunge" look is an example of a heavily promoted fashion. Fashions are more universally subscribed to than fads. Wearing athletic shoes as casual attire is a good example of a universal fashion.

Definition and characteristics of *fads*

3   A fad is a more temporary adoption of a particular behavior or look. Fads are in-group behaviors that often serve as identity markers for a group. Fads also tend to be adopted by smaller groups, often made up of people who want to appear different or unconventional. Unlike fashions, fads tend to be shorter-lived, less predictable, and less influenced by people outside the group. Examples of recent fads are bungee jumping, wearing baggy pants and hooded sweatshirts, carrying a beeper, and buying a particular brand of toy doll. Fads are usually harmless and have no long-range effects.

Description of 5-step process

4   Fashions and fads each follow a five-phase process of development. In the first phase, latency, the trend exists in the minds of a few people but shows little evidence of spreading. In the second phase, the trend

```
spreads rapidly and reaches its peak. After that, the
trend begins a slow decline (phase three). In the fourth
phase, its newness is over and many users drop or aban-
don the trend. In its final phase, quiescence, nearly
everyone has dropped the trend, and it is followed by
only a few people.
```

THINKING CRITICALLY ABOUT ESSAY EXAMS

Read essay exam questions critically, approaching them from the viewpoint of the instructor. Try to discover the knowledge or skill that your instructor is attempting to assess by asking the question. Then, as you write your answer, make sure your response clearly demonstrates your knowledge or skill. For example, in posing the question "Discuss the issue of sexual behavior from the three major sociological perspectives," the instructor is assessing two things. First, the instructor wants to evaluate how well you *understand* the three sociological perspectives. Consequently, you would need to give a clear and complete, but brief, definition of each perspective (rather than focusing only on sexual behavior). Second, the instructor wants to assess how well you can *apply* the three sociological perspectives to a particular issue — sexual behavior. Therefore, you would need to explain each perspective's approach to the issue of sexual behavior.

Handbook
Writing Problems and How to Correct Them

HANDBOOK CONTENTS

REVIEW OF BASIC GRAMMAR

1   PARTS OF SPEECH

Each word in a sentence acts as one of eight parts of speech: *nouns, pronouns, verbs, adjectives, adverbs, conjunctions, prepositions,* and *interjections.* These are the building blocks of our language. Often, to revise your writing or to correct sentence errors, you will need to understand how a word or phrase functions in a particular sentence.

1a   Nouns

A **noun** names a person (*waiter, girlfriend*), a place (*classroom, beach*), a thing (*textbook, computer*), or an idea (*excitement, beauty*). **Proper nouns** name specific people (*Professor Wainwright*), places (*Texas*), things (*Game Boy*), or ideas (*Marxism*) and are always capitalized.

▶ *James drove to Williamsville in a Toyota in March.*

Common nouns name one or more of a general class or type of person, place, thing, or idea and are not capitalized.

▶ A *holiday* is a *celebration* of an *event.*

Collective nouns name groups: *class, jury, team.* **Concrete nouns** name tangible things that can be tasted, seen, touched, smelled, or heard: *instructor, exam, desk.* **Abstract nouns** name ideas, qualities, beliefs, and conditions: *love, faith, trust.*

Most nouns express **number** and can be singular or plural: *one test, two tests; one pen, five pens.* **Count nouns** name items that can be counted. Count nouns can be made plural, usually by adding *-s* or *-es: one telephone, three telephones; one speech, ten speeches.* Some count nouns form their plurals in an irregular way: *mouse, mice; goose, geese.* **Noncount nouns** such as *water, anger, courage,* and *knowledge* name ideas or entities that cannot be counted. Most noncount nouns do not have a plural form. (See Chapter 26 of the Handbook for more on count and noncount nouns.)

EXERCISE 1.1

Underline the nouns in the following sentences and identify each one as common or proper by writing *C* for common or *P* for proper above each.

          P
▶ Where did <u>English</u> come from?

1. The language we call Old English was spoken by tribes known as Angles and Saxons.
2. They invaded England from northern Europe.

TEACHING TIP:
HANDBOOK OVERVIEW

• The Handbook chapters review basic sentence grammar and provide help with the types of problems students have with grammar, punctuation, mechanics, and spelling.

• The final Handbook section consists of five chapters for ESL writers, covering nouns and articles, verbs, prepositions, adjectives, and common sentence problems.

• Part 6 is organized like a typical handbook; therefore, you should be able to refer your students to the appropriate section using either the section numbers and letters (e.g., 12a on using commas with coordinating conjunctions) or the correction symbols listed at the end of the book. You and your students can also refer to the complete contents for the Handbook on the inside back cover.

• Sentence and paragraph exercises are provided throughout the Handbook. Answers to all exercises are given in the margins of the *Instructor's Annotated Edition,* and answers to even-numbered sentence exercises are provided for students on pp. AK-1–AK-7.

EXERCISE 1.1: *Answers*

1. *language:* common;
   Old English: proper;
   tribes: common;
   Angles: proper; *Saxons:* proper

(Continued on next page)

2. *England:* proper;
   Europe: proper
3. *Old English:* proper;
   languages: common;
   time: common
4. *Normans:* proper;
   France: proper, *England:* proper
5. *language:* common;
   words: common; *characteristics:* common

   3. Old English was closely related to Germanic languages of that time.
   4. The Normans, who came from France, later conquered England.
   5. Our language then acquired many French words and characteristics.

1b Pronouns

Pronouns are words that take the place of nouns. The noun or pronoun to which a pronoun refers is called the pronoun's **antecedent**.

▶ Because the *researcher* developed a new drug, *she* became famous.

   The noun *researcher* is the antecedent of the pronoun *she.*

Personal pronouns name specific people, places, or things. Personal pronouns come in three cases that describe a pronoun's function in a sentence. The **subjective case** indicates that a pronoun is a subject, a doer of an action (*I, you, he, she, it, we, they*).

▶ *She* asked questions about the job.

The **objective case** indicates that a pronoun is an object, a receiver of an action (*me, you, him, her, it, us, them*).

▶ The career counselor has been advising *her.*

The **possessive case** indicates ownership or belonging (*my, mine, your, yours, his, her, hers, its, our, ours, your, yours, their, theirs*).

▶ *His* enthusiasm for the company does not match *theirs.*

Personal pronouns also indicate **person,** to distinguish among the speaker (first person: *I, we*), the person spoken to (second person: *you*), and the person or thing spoken about (third person: *he, she, it, they*). The **gender** of personal pronouns identifies them as masculine (*he, him*), feminine (*she, her*), or neuter (*it*). Personal pronouns also show **number**: singular (one person or thing: *I, you, he, she, it*) or plural (more than one person or thing: *we, you, they*).

Demonstrative pronouns point out a particular person or thing: *this, that, these,* and *those.* A demonstrative pronoun can be used as an adjective, to describe a noun.

▶ *These* research procedures are questionable.

Reflexive pronouns indicate that a subject performs actions to, for, or on itself. Reflexive pronouns end in *-self* or *-selves.*

	Singular	*Plural*
First person	myself	ourselves
Second person	yourself	yourselves
Third person	himself	themselves
	herself	
	itself	

▶ We allowed *ourselves* two hours to complete the experiment.

Intensive pronouns have the same forms as reflexive pronouns and are used to emphasize their antecedents.

▶ The computer programmer *herself* could not correct the error.

Reflexive and intensive pronouns cannot be used as the subject of a sentence, and their antecedents must appear in the same sentence as the pronoun.

INCORRECT	*Myself* disagreed with the speaker's proposal.
CORRECT	*I myself* disagreed with the speaker's proposal.

Interrogative pronouns introduce or ask a question.

REFER TO PEOPLE	who, whoever, whom, whomever
REFER TO THINGS	what, which, whose

Relative pronouns introduce **dependent clauses** that function as adjectives. Relative pronouns refer back to a noun or pronoun that the clause modifies.

REFER TO PEOPLE	who, whoever, whom, whomever, whose
REFER TO THINGS	that, what, whatever, which

A **dependent clause** contains a subject and a verb but does not express a complete thought.

▶ The research *that* caused the literacy test controversy was outdated.

▶ Sylvia Plath was married to Ted Hughes, *who* later became poet laureate of England.

Indefinite pronouns do not refer to specific nouns; rather, they refer to people, places, or things in general (*everyone, anywhere, everything*). Commonly used indefinite pronouns include the following.

Singular

another	either	nobody	somebody
anybody	enough	none	someone
anyone	everybody	no one	something
anything	everyone	nothing	
anywhere	everything	one	
each	neither	other	

Plural

both	many	several
few	others	

▶ Hardly *anyone* had heard of the Sapir-Wharf hypothesis.

▶ Although a number of psychologists have researched brain dominance, *few* have related it to learning style.

Several indefinite pronouns, such as *all, any, more, most, some,* and *none,* can be either singular or plural, depending on their antecedent (see 5e).

The **reciprocal pronouns** *each other* and *one another* indicate an interchange of information or physical objects between two or more parties.

▶ The debate semifinalists congratulated *each other* on their scores.

See Chapter 7 of the Handbook for more on pronoun usage.

EXERCISE 1.2: *Answers*

1. *Our:* personal; *our:* personal; *that:* relative; *we:* personal; *ourselves:* intensive
2. *that:* relative; *us:* personal
3. No pronouns
4. *which:* relative; *these:* demonstrative
5. *Most:* indefinite; *them:* personal

EXERCISE 1.2

Underline the pronouns in the following sentences and identify each one as personal, demonstrative, reflexive, intensive, interrogative, relative, indefinite, or reciprocal. Some sentences may not contain pronouns.

    relative personal   *personal*   *indefinite personal*
▶ The fact <u>that</u> <u>our</u> eyes deceive <u>us</u> is difficult for <u>many</u> of <u>us</u> to accept.

1. Our brains influence our eyes in ways that we ourselves may not realize.
2. Events that surprise us are especially hard to remember accurately.
3. In a famous study, psychologist Elizabeth Loftus staged sudden protests in college classrooms to see how students reacted.
4. The students were later asked to fill out questionnaires in which untrue details of these incidents were suggested.
5. Most of them were wrong about significant details.

1c Verbs

Verbs show action (*type, study*), occurrence (*become, seem*), or a state of being (*be, feel*). There are three types of verbs: action verbs, linking verbs, and helping verbs (also called auxiliary verbs).

Action verbs express physical or mental activities.

▶ My outline *grew* longer and longer.

▶ Amelia *thought* her answer was correct.

Action verbs may be either transitive or intransitive. A **transitive verb** (TV) has a **direct object** (DO) that receives the action and completes the meaning of the sentence. (In the examples, S stands for *Subject.*)

   S TV DO
▶ Juan *wrote* lyrics for songs.

An **intransitive verb** (IV) does not need a direct object to complete the meaning of the sentence.

    S   IV
▶ The lights *flickered.*

Some verbs can be either transitive or intransitive, depending on how they are used in a sentence.

  INTRANSITIVE The student *wrote* quickly.

  TRANSITIVE The student *wrote* a paper on hypnotism.

Linking verbs show existence, explaining what something is, was, or will become. A linking verb connects a word to words that describe it.

▶ Dr. Miller *is* the new college president.

▶ Their answers *were* evasive.

The forms of the verb *be* (*am, is, are, was, were, be, being, been*) are linking verbs. Some action verbs can also function as linking verbs. These include *appear, become, feel, grow, look, prove, remain, seem, smell, sound, stay*, and *taste.*

▶ The weather *grew* bitterly cold.

▶ Something in the kitchen *smells* delicious.

Helping verbs, also called **auxiliary verbs,** are used along with action or linking verbs to indicate tense, mood, or voice or to add further information. A **verb phrase** is a combination of one or more helping verbs and a main verb.

SIMPLE VERB	The newspaper *reports* the incident.
SIMPLE VERB + HELPING VERB	The newspaper *should report* the incident.

Helping verbs include the different forms of *do, be,* and *have* (which can also serve as main verbs in a sentence) along with *can, could, may, might, must, shall, should, will,* and *would.*

EXERCISE 1.3: *Answers*

1. *swept:* action-intransitive
2. *had:* helping; *arrived:* action-intransitive
3. *traveled:* action-intransitive; *faced:* action-transitive
4. *grew:* linking
5. *left:* action-transitive; *were:* linking

EXERCISE 1.3

Underline the verbs in the following sentences and identify each one as action, linking, or helping; for action verbs, identify the verb as transitive or intransitive.

               action-intransitive   *helping action-intransitive*

▶ The California gold rush <u>began</u> when gold <u>was</u> <u>discovered</u> at Sutter's Mill in 1848.

1. Gold fever swept across the United States.
2. A few months later, over four thousand miners had arrived.
3. Some traveled west in wagons and faced hardship and disease.
4. Most "forty-niners" soon grew disillusioned.
5. Those prospectors who left mining for agriculture and storekeeping were better off.

Verb Forms

All verbs except *be* have five forms: the base form, the past tense, the past participle, the present participle, and the *-s* form for the present tense when the subject is singular and in the third person.

     The first three forms are called the verb's principal parts. The base form is the form of the verb as it appears in the dictionary: *review, study, prepare.* For regular verbs, the past tense and past participle are formed by adding *-d* or *-ed* to the base form. For regular verbs ending in *y,* the *y* is changed to *i: rely, relied.* For one-syllable regular verbs ending in a vowel plus a consonant, the consonant is doubled: *plan, planned.* See 25c.

	Regular	*Irregular*
Base form	walk	run
Past tense	walked	ran
Past participle	walked	run
Present participle	walking	running
-s form	walks	runs

Irregular verbs follow no set pattern to form their past tense and past participle.

FORMS OF COMMON IRREGULAR VERBS

Base Form	*Past Tense*	*Past Participle*
be	was/were	been
become	became	become

FORMS OF COMMON IRREGULAR VERBS *(continued)*

Base Form	*Past Tense*	*Past Participle*
begin	began	begun
bite	bit	bitten, bit
blow	blew	blown
build	built	built
burst	burst	burst
catch	caught	caught
choose	chose	chosen
come	came	come
dive	dived, dove	dived
do	did	done
draw	drew	drawn
drive	drove	driven
eat	ate	eaten
fall	fell	fallen
feel	felt	felt
fight	fought	fought
find	found	found
fling	flung	flung
fly	flew	flown
get	got	gotten, got
give	gave	given
go	went	gone
grow	grew	grown
have	had	had
know	knew	known
lay	laid	laid
lead	led	led
leave	left	left
lie	lay	lain
lose	lost	lost
make	made	made
ride	rode	ridden
ring	rang	rung

(Continued on next page)

FORMS OF COMMON IRREGULAR VERBS *(continued)*

Base Form	Past Tense	Past Participle
rise	rose	risen
run	ran	run
say	said	said
set	set	set
sit	sat	sat
speak	spoke	spoken
swear	swore	sworn
swim	swam	swum
take	took	taken
tear	tore	torn
tell	told	told
think	thought	thought
throw	threw	thrown
wear	wore	worn
win	won	won
write	wrote	written

If you are unsure of a verb's principal parts, check your dictionary.

EXERCISE 1.4

Correct any errors in verb form in the following sentences. Some sentences may be correct as written.

>   *won*
> ▶ Muhammad Ali, who ~~wonned~~ the world heavyweight boxing title three separate
>
>   *remains*
> times, ~~remain~~ a popular hero.

1. Muhammad Ali begun his boxing career under the name Cassius Clay.
2. Cassius Clay was boxing as an amateur in 1960, when he earned the Golden Gloves title and an Olympic gold medal.
3. In 1964, he defeated Sonny Liston and become the world heavyweight champion.
4. Ali growed increasingly well known for his quick moves in the ring and his quick wit everywhere else.
5. In 1967, Clay joined the Nation of Islam and taked the Muslim name Muhammad Ali.
6. He refused to be drafted that year for religious reasons and was baned from boxing and stripped of his title.
7. Ali returned to boxing in 1971 but losed his title to Joe Frazier the following year.
8. He get the title back in 1974 by defeating George Foreman.

EXERCISE 1.4: *Answers*

1. Muhammad Ali began . . . Cassius Clay.
2. Correct
3. In 1964, he . . . became the world heavyweight champion.
4. Ali grew increasingly well known . . . everywhere else.
5. In 1967, Clay . . . took the Muslim name Muhammad Ali.
6. He . . . was banned from boxing and stripped of his title.
7. Ali . . . lost his title to Joe Frazier the following year.
8. He got the title . . . by defeating George Foreman.
9. Ali . . . fought him again and won it back later that year.
10. Correct

9. Ali lost the title to Leon Spinks in 1978 but fighted him again and won it back later that year.

10. Although Ali retired in 1979 and has been in declining health, many Americans still admire him greatly.

Verb Tense

The **tenses** of a verb express time. They convey whether an action, a state of being, or an occurrence takes place in the present, past, or future. There are six basic tenses: present, past, future, present perfect, past perfect, and future perfect. There are also three groups of tenses: simple, perfect, and progressive.

Simple tenses indicate whether an action occurs in the present, past, or future.

▶ He *loves* Kabuki theater.

▶ I *purchased* their new CD immediately.

▶ Hitchcock's reputation *will continue to grow.*

Perfect tenses indicate that the action was or will be finished by the time of some other action.

▶ By now, Rosa *has taken* the exam.

▶ James Brown *had* already *performed* when they arrived.

▶ The millennium *will have arrived* before he finishes.

Progressive tenses indicate that the action does, did, or will continue.

▶ She *is going* to kindergarten.

▶ When the ambulance arrived, he *was sweating* profusely.

▶ During spring break, we *will be basking* on a sunny beach.

A SUMMARY OF THE TENSES

Present Tense

Simple present: happening now or occurring regularly

▶ He *performs* his own stunts.

Present progressive: happening now; going on (in progress) now

▶ The governor *is considering* a Senate campaign.

Present perfect: began in the past and was completed in the past or is continuing now

▶ The children's benefactor *has followed* their progress closely.

(Continued on next page)

(Continued)

Present perfect progressive: began in the past and is continuing now

▶ She *has been singing* in nightclubs for thirty years.

Past Tense

Simple past: began and ended in the past

▶ The doctor *treated* him with experimental drugs.

Past progressive: began and continued in the past

▶ They *were* not *expecting* any visitors.

Past perfect: occurred before a certain time in the past or was completed before another action was begun

▶ The birds *had eaten* all the berries before we knew they were ripe.

Past perfect progressive: was taking place until a second action occurred

▶ He *had been seeing* a psychiatrist before his collapse.

Future Tense

Simple future: will take place in the future

▶ The play *will begin* on time.

Future progressive: will both begin and end in the future

▶ After we get on the plane, we *will be sitting* for hours.

Future perfect: will be completed by a certain time in the future or before another action will begin

▶ By next month, the new apprentice *will have become* an expert.

Future perfect progressive: will continue until a certain time in the future

▶ By the time she earns her Ph.D., she *will have been studying* history for twelve years.

Most of the time you will not need to think about verb tense; you will use the correct tense automatically. There are, however, a few situations in which you need to pay special attention to verb tense.

- Use the present tense to make a generalization or to state a principle or fact.

    ▶ Thanksgiving *falls* on the fourth Thursday of November each year.
    ▶ Walking *is* excellent exercise.

- Use the present tense to indicate an action that occurs regularly or habitually.

    ▶ My sister *takes* frequent trips to Dallas.

- Use the present tense when referring to literary works and artworks, even though the work was written or created in the past.

  ▶ *Hamlet is* set in Denmark.

- Also use the present tense to refer to authors no longer living when you are discussing their works.

  ▶ Borges frequently *employs* magical realism in his fiction.

Voice

A verb is in the **active voice** when the subject of the clause or sentence performs the action of the verb.

▶ The diplomats *have arrived.*
▶ He *plays* soccer professionally.

A verb is in the **passive voice** when the subject of a clause or sentence is the receiver of the action that the verb describes. Passive verbs are formed using a form of *be* and the past participle of a verb.

▶ The child *was* badly *bitten* by mosquitoes.
▶ Her car *was stolen.*

Since the passive voice may make it difficult for your readers to understand who is performing the action of a sentence, in most writing situations, use the active voice. If you do not know who performed an action, however, or if you want to emphasize the receiver of the action, consider using the passive voice.

PASSIVE VOICE	The evidence had been carefully removed.
ACTIVE VOICE	The defendant carefully removed the evidence.

Mood

The **mood** of a verb indicates whether it states a fact or asks a question (**indicative**), gives a command or direction (**imperative**), or expresses a condition, wish, or suggestion (**subjunctive**). The subjunctive mood is also used for hypothetical situations or impossible or unlikely events.

INDICATIVE	Redwood trees can pull moisture from the air.
IMPERATIVE	Read the play and write an analysis of it.
SUBJUNCTIVE	It would be nice to win the lottery.

The subjunctive mood, often used in clauses that begin with *if* or *that,* expresses a wish, suggestion, or condition contrary to fact. Use the base form of the verb for the present subjunctive. For the verb *be,* the past tense subjunctive is *were,* not *was.*

▶ I suggested that she *walk* to the station.

▶ The new student in class wished that he *were* more outgoing.

EXERCISE 1.6: *Answers*

1. *was eaten:* indicative, passive
2. *spread:* indicative, active
3. *leads:* indicative, active; *attempted:* indicative, active
4. *was concerned:* indicative, passive; *were outlawed:* subjunctive, passive; *went:* indicative, active; *was defeated:* indicative, passive
5. *outlawed:* indicative, active; *say:* imperative, active

EXERCISE 1.6

Underline the verbs in the following sentences and identify the mood (indicative, imperative, or subjunctive) and voice (active or passive) of each verb.

indicative, active
▶ Opiate use and abuse has a long history.

1. Opium was eaten as a folk medicine in India for centuries.
2. In the seventeenth century, the practice of smoking opium spread from Java to China.
3. Smoking opium leads to severe addiction, and Chinese authorities attempted to ban the drug.
4. Great Britain was concerned about losing its trade with China if opium were outlawed; the countries went to war, and China was defeated.
5. In 1914, the U.S. government outlawed opiates in the original campaign telling citizens to "Just say no."

1d Adjectives

Adjectives modify a noun or pronoun by describing it, limiting it, or giving more information about it. They answer the following questions.

WHICH ONE?	The *cutest* puppy belongs to the neighbors.
WHAT KIND?	Use only *scholarly* sources for the paper.

HOW MANY? *Several hundred* protesters gathered at City Hall.

There are three types of adjectives: descriptive, limiting, and proper. **Descriptive adjectives** name a quality of the person, place, thing, or idea that they describe.

yellow backpack   *unfriendly* face   *disturbing* event

Limiting adjectives narrow the scope of the person, place, or thing they describe.

my laptop   *second* building   *that* notebook

Proper adjectives are derived from proper nouns. They are always capitalized.

Japanese culture   *Elizabethan* England

The articles *a, an,* and *the* appear immediately before nouns and are considered adjectives. *The* refers to a specific item, while *a* and *an* do not. *A* is used before words that begin with consonant sounds. *An* is used before words that begin with vowel sounds.

▶ *The* person behind us laughed.

  The refers to a specific person.

▶ *An* answer will be forthcoming.

  Some answer will be provided.

The can also be used to refer to a group or class of items.

▶ *The* cat is *a* playful animal.

For more on the use of adjectives, see Chapter 9 of the Handbook. For more on articles, see Chapter 26 of the Handbook.

EXERCISE 1.7

Underline the adjectives in the following sentences and identify each one as a descriptive, limiting, or proper adjective or an article.

   art. descrip.   **art.**   **descrip.**   **art.**   **descrip.**   **art.**
▶ A disease cluster is a higher-than-usual incidence of an uncommon illness in a
  community.

1. Computer tracking of cancer cases around the country has revealed many apparent clusters of illness.
2. These clusters have led some people to believe that the cancers have environmental causes.
3. In recent years, discoveries of clusters have usually been followed by intensive testing to find the source.

EXERCISE 1.7: *Answers*

1. *Computer:* descriptive; *cancer:* descriptive; *the:* article; *many:* limiting; *apparent:* descriptive
2. *These:* limiting; *some:* limiting; *the:* article; *environmental:* descriptive
3. *recent:* descriptive; *intensive:* descriptive; *the:* article

(Continued on next page)

4. *Love Canal:* proper; *the:*
    article; *first:* limiting;
    the: article; *American:*
    proper
5. *few:* limiting; *an:* arti-
    cle; *identifiable:*
    descriptive

4. The Love Canal site was one of the first clusters to alert the American public.
5. But few cases of clusters have been traced to an identifiable cause.

1e Adverbs

Adverbs modify verbs, adjectives, other adverbs, entire sentences, or clauses by describing, qualifying, or limiting the meaning of the words they modify. They answer the following questions.

HOW?	Andrea Bocelli performed *brilliantly*.
WHEN?	*Later,* they met to discuss the proposal.
WHERE?	The taxi driver headed *downtown*.
HOW OFTEN?	The bobcat is *rarely* seen in the wild.
TO WHAT EXTENT?	He agreed to cooperate *fully* with the investigation.

Most adverbs end in *-ly:*

particular*ly*	beautiful*ly*	secret*ly*

Common adverbs that do not end in *-ly* include *almost, never, quite, soon, then, there,* and *too.* Some words can function as either adjectives or adverbs depending on their use in the sentence.

ADJECTIVE	The flu victims were finally *well*.
ADVERB	His paper was *well* written.

Adverbs that modify adjectives or other adverbs appear next to the word they modify.

▶ Tired sloths move *especially* slowly.

▶ A pregnant woman may feel *extremely* tired.

Adverbs that modify verbs can appear in several different positions, however.

▶ He *carefully* put the toys together.
▶ He put the toys *carefully* together.
▶ He put the toys together *carefully*.

For more on the use of adverbs, see Chapter 9 of the Handbook.

EXERCISE 1.8

Underline the adverbs in the following sentences. Some sentences may not contain adverbs.

▶ <u>Historically</u>, the Japanese art of flower arranging, or Ikebana, was practiced in private homes.

1. Today, Ikebana appears almost everywhere in Japan.
2. Ikebana practitioners follow ancient rules that govern the placement of the chosen elements.
3. Empty spaces, carefully arranged structures, and a natural appearance are all fundamentally important in Ikebana.
4. Ikebana arrangements are typically triangular.
5. Seasonal flowers and foliage are more highly prized than rare or expensive ones.

1f Conjunctions

Conjunctions connect words, phrases, or clauses. **Coordinating conjunctions** connect words or word groups of equal importance. There are seven coordinating conjunctions: *and, but, or, nor, for, yet,* and *so.*

▶ He attended the inauguration *but* looked unhappy.

Coordinating conjunctions must connect words, phrases, or clauses of the same kind. For example, *and* may connect two nouns, but it cannot connect a noun and a clause.

NOUNS	Novels by *Tom Clancy* and *Robert Parker* appeared on the best-seller list.
PHRASES	We searched *in the closets* and *under the beds.*
CLAUSES	*Custer graduated last in his West Point class,* but *he distinguished himself in the Civil War.*

Conjunctions that are used in pairs are called **correlative conjunctions**: *as . . . as, both . . . and, either . . . or, just as . . . so, neither . . . nor, not . . . but, not only . . . but also,* and *whether . . . or.*

▶ *Neither* the strikers *nor* the management was satisfied with the compromise.

Subordinating conjunctions connect **dependent clauses** to **independent clauses**. They connect ideas of unequal importance. Often used at the beginning of a dependent clause, subordinating conjunctions indicate how a less important idea (expressed in a dependent clause) relates to a more important idea (expressed in an independent clause). Here is a list of common subordinating conjunctions and the relationships they express.

Subordinating Conjunctions

Time	before, after, while, until, when
	▶ *While* the sky was still dark, the army prepared for battle.
Cause or effect	because, since, so that
	▶ *Since* he doesn't like math, he should avoid calculus.

A **dependent clause** contains a subject and a verb but does not express a complete thought.

An **independent clause** contains a subject and a verb and can stand alone as a sentence.

Condition	whether, if, unless, even if
	▶ We don't do volunteer work *unless* it is for a good cause.
Circumstance	as, as far as, as soon as, as if, as though, even though, even if, in order to
	▶ In-line skating is a popular sport, *even though* it is somewhat dangerous.

Conjunctive adverbs link sentence parts that are of equal importance; they also serve as modifiers. Conjunctive adverbs show the following relationships between the elements they connect.

Conjunctive Adverbs

Time	afterward, finally, later, meanwhile, next, subsequently, then, when
	▶ The candidates campaigned for months; *finally,* a primary election was held.
Example	for example, for instance, to illustrate
	▶ Some members of the party—*for example,* the governor—supported another candidate.
Continuation or addition	also, furthermore, in addition, in the first place, moreover
	▶ *In addition* to being poorly organized, his arguments are not logical.
Cause or effect	accordingly, as a result, consequently, hence, therefore, thus, unfortunately
	▶ *As a result,* he may convince few voters.
Differences or contrast	however, nevertheless, on the contrary, on the other hand, otherwise
	▶ *Nevertheless,* he has support from some groups.
Emphasis	in fact, in other words, that is, undoubtedly
	▶ *In fact,* some politicians are tired of constantly needing to raise money for campaigns.
Similarities or comparison	likewise, similarly
	▶ They believe their opponents are *similarly* fed up.

EXERCISE 1.9

Underline the conjunctions in the following sentences and identify each one as a coordinating conjunction, correlative conjunction, subordinating conjunction, or conjunctive adverb.

> *subordinating conjunction*
▶ Sometimes academics behave <u>as though</u> there were a gap between the humanities
coordinating conjunction
<u>and</u> the sciences.

1. Writer and scientist C. P. Snow warned of this gap between the arts and sciences decades ago when he wrote *The Two Cultures.*
2. Since Snow wrote his speech, relations between the two groups have changed.
3. Snow addressed both the scientists who were proud of avoiding literature and the humanities professionals who were blissfully ignorant of basic scientific principles.
4. Today, some academics in the humanities have adopted not only scientific terms, but also scientific theories in their work.
5. The gap between the arts and sciences has changed in the last few decades; unfortunately, it does not seem to be any smaller.

1g Prepositions

A **preposition** is a word or phrase that links and relates a noun or a pronoun (the object of the preposition) to the rest of the sentence. A **prepositional phrase** includes the preposition along with its object and modifiers. Prepositions often show relationships of time, place, direction, or manner.

▶ Steve Prefontaine could run *despite* excruciating pain.

▶ The continental shelf lies *beneath* the ocean.

Common Prepositions

against	beneath	for	over	until
along	beside	from	past	up
among	between	in	since	upon
around	beyond	near	through	with
as	by	off	till	within
at	despite	on	to	without
before	down	onto	toward	
behind	during	out	under	
below	except	outside	underneath	

Compound prepositions consist of more than one word.

▶ *According to* historical records, the town is three hundred years old.

▶ The department gained its reputation *by means of* its diversity.

Common Compound Prepositions

according to	by means of	in spite of	with regard to
aside from	in addition to	instead of	with respect to
as of	in front of	on account of	
as well as	in place of	out of	
because of	in regard to	prior to	

EXERCISE 1.10: *Answers*

1. After Satyajit Ray earned a degree in economics, his mother persuaded him to go to art school.
2. Prior to that time, he had been interested in Western thought, but he became fascinated with Indian art.
3. Ray was an early fan of movies and helped to found the Calcutta Film Society in 1947.
4. Ray's first film, *Pather Panchali,* won a prize at the Cannes Film Festival in 1955.
5. His film career lasted for four decades, and Ray may be remembered as India's greatest filmmaker.

EXERCISE 1.10

Underline the prepositions in the following sentences.

▶ **Generations of filmgoers have admired the work of Indian director Satyajit Ray.**

1. After Satyajit Ray earned a degree in economics, his mother persuaded him to go to art school.
2. Prior to that time, he had been interested in Western thought, but he became fascinated with Indian art.
3. Ray was an early fan of movies and helped to found the Calcutta Film Society in 1947.
4. Ray's first film, *Pather Panchali,* won a prize at the Cannes Film Festival in 1955.
5. His film career lasted for four decades, and Ray may be remembered as India's greatest filmmaker.

1h Interjections

Interjections are words that express surprise or some other strong feeling. An exclamation point or a period often follows an interjection, or a comma may precede or follow it. The choice depends on whether the interjection stands alone or serves as part or all of a sentence.

▶ *Oh,* it wasn't important.

▶ *Ouch!*

▶ There were no fires reported last month, *by the way.*

EXERCISE 1.11: *Answers*

1. The local team did badly last year, but oh well, it's time for a fresh start.
2. Coaching is an area where the team, alas, needs improvement.
3. No interjections
4. Oh, yes, a few good runners wouldn't hurt either.
5. Thank goodness, it's time to get fired up for a brand new season!

EXERCISE 1.11

Underline the interjections in the following sentences. Some sentences may not contain interjections.

▶ **Hooray, baseball season starts soon!**

1. The local team did badly last year, but oh well, it's time for a fresh start.
2. Coaching is an area where the team, alas, needs improvement.
3. The three things that the team lacks most desperately are pitching, batting, and coaching.
4. Oh, yes, a few good runners wouldn't hurt either.
5. Thank goodness, it's time to get fired up for a brand new season!

2 SENTENCE STRUCTURE

2a Sentence parts

A **sentence** is a group of words that expresses a complete thought about something or someone. Every sentence must contain two basic parts: a subject and a predicate.

Subjects

The **subject** of a sentence names a person, place, or thing and tells whom or what the sentence is about. It identifies the performer or receiver of the action expressed in the predicate.

▶ *Carmen Miranda,* the flamboyant performer, made savvy decisions about her career.

▶ The *clock* on the mantel was given to her by her grandmother.

The noun or pronoun that names what the sentence is about is called the **simple subject.**

▶ *Mozart* began composing at the age of four.

▶ The postal *worker* was bitten by a dog.

The simple subject of an imperative sentence is understood as *you,* but *you* is not stated directly.

▶ Be quiet.

　　The sentence is understood as *[You] be quiet.*

The **complete subject** is the simple subject plus its modifiers — words that describe, identify, qualify, or limit the meaning of a noun or pronoun.

　　┌──── complete subject ────┐
▶ A series of very bad *decisions* doomed the project.

　　　┌──────── complete subject────────┐
▶ There are too many *books* to fit on the shelves.

A sentence with a **compound subject** contains two or more simple subjects joined by a coordinating conjunction (*and, but, or, nor, for, yet,* or *so*).

▶ *Joel <u>and</u> Ethan Coen* produce and direct their films.

▶ *A doctor <u>or</u> a physician's assistant* will explain the results.

Predicates

The **predicate** of a sentence indicates what the subject does, what happens to the subject, or what is said about the subject. The predicate, then, can indicate an action or a state of being.

ACTION	Plant respiration *produces* oxygen.
STATE OF BEING	Stonehenge *has existed* for many centuries.

A **helping verb** (also called an **auxiliary verb**) combines with a main verb to indicate tense, mood, or voice or to add further information.

A **complement** is a word or group of words that describes or renames a subject or an object.

The **simple predicate** is the main verb along with its **helping verbs**.

▶ Reporters *should call* the subjects of their stories for comment.

▶ A snow bicycle for Antarctic workers *has been developed*.

The **complete predicate** consists of the simple predicate plus its modifiers and any objects or **complements**. (See p. 23 for more about **complements**.)

```
                            ┌──────────── complete predicate ──────────────
▶ The growth of Los Angeles depended to a large extent on finding a way to get water
  ─────────────────
  to the desert.
```

```
                        ┌──────────── complete predicate ──────────────┐
▶ Watching fishing boats is a relaxing and pleasant way to spend an afternoon.
```

A **compound predicate** contains two or more predicates that have the same subject and that are joined by *and, but, or, nor,* or another conjunction (see 1f).

▶ AIDS drugs *can save many lives <u>but</u> are seldom available in poor countries that need them desperately*.

▶ President Johnson *<u>neither</u> wanted to run for a second term <u>nor</u> planned to serve if elected*.

EXERCISE 2.1: Answers

1. [<u>Wildlife</u> and the Maasai tribe's <u>herds</u> of livestock] (<u>share</u> much of the land at Amboseli Nature Reserve in Kenya). Compound subject
2. (<u>Would</u>) [this <u>kind</u> of human and wildlife cooperation] (<u>work</u> in other areas)?
3. [The Maasai <u>people</u>] (customarily <u>do not kill</u> local wildlife except during severe drought emergencies).
4. [This <u>custom</u>] (both <u>ensures</u> the workability of the Amboseli Reserve's unusual system and <u>indicates</u> the difficulty of trying the same system elsewhere). Compound predicate
5. [The <u>Maasai</u>] (neither <u>need</u> nor <u>wish</u> to destroy the wild animals with whom they share the land). Compound predicate

EXERCISE 2.1

In each of the following sentences, underline the simple subject and the simple predicate, put the complete subject in brackets, and enclose the complete predicate in parentheses. Then identify and label any compound subjects and compound predicates that appear.

```
           compound subject
▶ [Wildlife parks and nature preserves] (should be off-limits to human inhabitants).
```

1. Wildlife and the Maasai tribe's herds of livestock share much of the land at Amboseli Nature Reserve in Kenya.
2. Would this kind of human and wildlife cooperation work in other areas?
3. The Maasai people customarily do not kill local wildlife except during severe drought emergencies.
4. This custom both ensures the workability of the Amboseli Reserve's unusual system and indicates the difficulty of trying the same system elsewhere.
5. The Maasai neither need nor wish to destroy the wild animals with whom they share the land.

Objects

A **direct object** is a noun or pronoun that receives the action of a verb. A direct object answers the question "What?" or "Whom?"

▶ The fiddler played a lively *reel*.

The noun *reel* answers the question, "What did he play?"

▶ The crowd in the stadium jeered the *quarterback*.

The noun *quarterback* answers the question, "Whom did they jeer?"

An **indirect object** is a noun or pronoun that names the person or thing to whom something is done.

▶ Habitat for Humanity gave *him* an award for his work.

▶ A woman on a bench tossed the *pigeons* some crumbs.

Complements

A **complement** is a word or group of words that describes a subject or object and completes the meaning of the sentence. There are two kinds of complements: subject complements and object complements.

A **linking verb** (such as *be, become, seem, feel,* or *taste*) connects the subject of a sentence to a **subject complement**, a noun, a noun phrase, or an adjective that renames or describes the subject.

▶ Bill T. Jones is *a well-known choreographer.*

▶ She was *too disorganized to finish her science project.*

An **object complement** is a noun, a noun phrase, or an adjective that modifies or renames the **direct object**. Object complements appear with transitive verbs (such as *name, find, make, think, elect, appoint, choose,* and *consider*), which express action directed toward something or someone.

A **direct object** receives the action of the verb: *He drove me home.*

▶ The council appointed him *its new vice president.*

▶ The undercooked meat made several children *sick.*

EXERCISE 2.2

Underline the objects and complements in the following sentences and identify each one as a direct object, an indirect object, a subject complement, or an object complement.

              indirect object   *direct object*

▶ A group of pioneers gave their neighbors | most of their belongings and headed west in 1846.

1. They were an inexperienced but hopeful group.
2. The travelers made the head of the wealthy Donner family their official leader.
3. Their untested route was more dangerous than they realized.
4. Unfortunately, heavy snows trapped the few remaining wagons in the Sierra Nevada mountains in October.
5. When some members of the Donner party died, cannibalism gave the others a way to survive.

EXERCISE 2.2: *Answers*

1. *an inexperienced but hopeful group:* subject complement
2. *head of the wealthy Donner family:* direct object; *their official leader:* object complement
3. *more dangerous than they realized:* subject complement
4. *wagons:* direct object
5. *others:* indirect object; *way:* direct object.

2b Phrases

A **phrase** is a group of related words that lacks either a subject, a predicate, or both. A phrase cannot stand alone as a sentence. Phrases can appear at the beginning, middle, or end of a sentence and can help make your writing more detailed and interesting.

WITHOUT PHRASES   The burglars escaped.

Bus travel is an inexpensive choice.

WITH PHRASES   Startled by the alarm, the burglars escaped without getting any money.

For adventurers on a budget, bus travel, while not luxurious, is an inexpensive choice.

There are four common types of phrases: prepositional phrases, verbal phrases, appositive phrases, and absolute phrases.

Prepositional Phrases

A **prepositional phrase** consists of a preposition (*in, above, with, at, behind*), the object of the preposition (a noun or pronoun), and any modifiers of the object. Prepositional phrases usually function as adjectives or adverbs to tell more about people, places, objects, or actions. They can also function as nouns. A prepositional phrase generally adds information about time, place, direction, or manner.

ADJECTIVE PHRASE   The plants *on the edge of the field* are weeds.

On the edge and *of the field* tell *where.*

ADVERB PHRASE   New Orleans is very crowded *during Mardi Gras.*

During Mardi Gras tells *when.*

NOUN PHRASE   *Down the hill* is the shortest way to town.

Down the hill acts as the subject of the sentence.

Each of the following sentences has been edited to include a prepositional phrase or phrases that expand the meaning of the sentence by adding detail.

▶ He fell, *on the icy sidewalk.*

▶ The ship suddenly appeared, *through the mist near the shore.*

Verbal Phrases

A **verbal** is a verb form used as a noun (the *barking* of the dog), an adjective (a *barking* dog), or an adverb (continued *to bark*). It cannot be used alone as the verb of a sentence, however. The three kinds of verbals are participles, gerunds, and infinitives. A **verbal phrase** consists of a verbal and its modifiers.

Participles and Participial Phrases. All verbs have two participles: present and past. The **present participle** is the *-ing* form of a verb (*being, hoping, studying*). The **past participle** of most verbs ends in *-d* or *-ed* (*hoped, consisted*). The past participle of irregular verbs has no set pattern (*been, ridden*). Both the present participle and the past participle can function as adjectives modifying nouns and pronouns.

▶ The planes flew over the foggy airport in a *holding* pattern.

▶ The pot was made of *molded* clay.

A **participial phrase**, which consists of a participle and its modifiers, can also function as an adjective in a sentence.

▶ The suspect, *wanted for questioning* on robbery charges, had vanished.

Gerunds and Gerund Phrases. A **gerund** is the present participle, or *-ing* form, of a verb that functions as a noun in a sentence.

▶ *Driving* can be a frustrating activity.

▶ The government has not done enough to build *housing*.

A **gerund phrase** consists of a gerund and its modifiers. Like a gerund, a gerund phrase is used as a noun and can therefore function in a sentence as a subject, a direct object, an indirect object, an object of a preposition, or a subject complement.

SUBJECT	*Catching the flu* is unpleasant.
DIRECT OBJECT	All the new recruits practiced *marching*.
INDIRECT OBJECT	One director gave his *acting* a chance.
OBJECT OF A PREPOSITION	An ambitious employee may rise by *impressing* her boss.
SUBJECT COMPLEMENT	The biggest thrill was the *skydiving*.

Infinitives and Infinitive Phrases. An **infinitive** is the base form of a verb preceded by *to: to study, to sleep*. An **infinitive phrase** consists of the infinitive plus any modifiers or objects. An infinitive phrase can function as a noun, an adjective, or an adverb.

SUBJECT	*To sleep* was impossible during the music festival.
ADJECTIVE	She had a job *to do*.
ADVERB	I have not yet begun *to fight*.

Sometimes the *to* in an infinitive phrase is understood but not written.

▶ Her demonstration helped me learn the software.

Note: Be sure to distinguish between infinitive phrases and prepositional phrases beginning with the preposition *to*. In an infinitive phrase, *to* is followed by a verb (*to paint*); in a prepositional phrase, *to* is followed by a noun or pronoun (*to a movie*).

Appositive Phrases

An **appositive** is a word that explains, restates, or adds new information about a noun. An **appositive phrase** consists of an appositive and its modifiers.

▶ Phil Spector, *creator of the "wall of sound,"* produced dozens of hit records in the 1960s.

> The appositive phrase adds information about the noun *Phil Spector.*

Absolute Phrases

An **absolute phrase** consists of a noun or pronoun and any modifiers, usually followed by a participle. An absolute phrase modifies an entire sentence, not any particular word or words within the sentence. It can appear anywhere in a sentence and is set off from the rest of the sentence with commas.

▶ *Their shift completed,* the night workers walked out at sunrise.

▶ *An unsuspecting insect clamped in its mandible,* the praying mantis, *its legs folded piously,* appears serenely uninvolved.

EXERCISE 2.3: *Answers*

1. *a modern nation in many ways:* appositive phrase; *in many ways:* prepositional phrase
2. *living in the United States:* participial phrase; *in the United States:* prepositional phrase; *to maintain ties with their homeland:* infinitive phrase; *with their homeland:* prepositional phrase

---

EXERCISE 2.3

Underline the phrases in the following sentences and identify each one as a prepositional phrase, participial phrase, gerund phrase, infinitive phrase, appositive phrase, or absolute phrase. If a phrase occurs within a phrase, double underline the overlapping phrase.

     prepositional   *participial* / *prepositional*
       phrase   *phrase*   *phrase*

▶ In Indian culture, marriages arranged by the couple's parents are still very common.

1. India, a modern nation in many ways, still has ancient customs.
2. Young Indians living in the United States often try to maintain ties with their homeland.

3. A custom practiced for centuries, arranged marriages are one way to find a compatible mate.
4. In some cases, parents may approach their adult children with a proposed match.
5. In other instances, parents arrange the marriage when their children are quite young.

3. *A custom practiced for centuries:* absolute phrase; *to find a compatible mate:* infinitive phrase
4. *In some cases:* prepositional phrase; *with a proposed match:* prepositional phrase
5. *In other instances:* prepositional phrase

2c Clauses

A **clause** is a group of words that contains a subject and a predicate. A clause is either independent (also called *main*) or dependent (also called *subordinate*). An **independent clause** can stand alone as a grammatically complete sentence.

▶ Einstein was a clerk at the Swiss Patent Office.

▶ Ethnic disputes followed the disintegration of Yugoslavia.

A **dependent clause** has a subject and a predicate, but it cannot stand alone as a grammatically complete sentence because it does not express a complete thought. A dependent clause usually begins with either a subordinating conjunction or a relative pronoun that connects it to an independent clause.

Common Subordinating Conjunctions

after	in as much as	that
although	in case that	though
as	in order that	unless
as if	in so far as	until
as far as	in that	when
as soon as	now that	whenever
as though	once	where
because	provided that	wherever
before	rather than	whether
even if	since	while
even though	so that	why
how	supposing that	
if	than	

Relative Pronouns

that	whatever	who (whose, whom)
what	which	whoever (whomever)

┌── dependent clause ──┐
▶ *When the puppies were born,* the breeder examined them carefully.

dependent
┌── clause ──┐
▶ Van Gogh's paintings began to command high prices *after he died.*

```
          ┌────── dependent clause ──────┐
```
▶ Isadora Duncan, *who personified modern dance,* died in a bizarre accident.

When joined to independent clauses, dependent clauses can function as adjectives, adverbs, or nouns and are known as **adjective clauses** (also called **relative clauses**) **adverb clauses,** or **noun clauses.** A noun clause can function as a subject, an object, or a complement.

```
          ┌────── adjective clause ──────┐
```
▶ Comic art, *which was once considered "kid stuff,"* is now taken seriously.

```
          ┌────── adverb clause ──────┐
```
▶ The whistle blew *as the train approached the crossing.*

```
          ┌────── noun clause ──────┐
```
▶ The starving artist ate *whatever he could get.*

Relative pronouns are generally the subject or object in their clauses. *Who* and *whoever* change to *whom* and *whomever* when they function as objects. Sometimes the relative pronoun or subordinating conjunction is implied or understood rather than stated.

▶ African rituals are among the subjects [that] the essay discusses.

That is the understood relative pronoun in the subordinate clause.

A dependent clause may contain an implied predicate. When a dependent clause is missing an element that can be inferred from the context of the sentence, it is called an **elliptical clause.**

```
          ┌────── elliptical clause ──────┐
```
▶ The Watergate coverup disturbed Americans *more than the Iran-Contra hearings.*

The predicate *disturbed them* is implied.

EXERCISE 2.4

Underline the dependent clauses in the following sentences.

▶ An illness <u>that is believed to affect a high percentage of children</u> is attention deficit disorder, or ADD.

1. Children who have ADD are easily distracted and may be hyperactive.
2. If a child has difficulty concentrating on ordinary tasks such as homework, he or she may have ADD.
3. Although treatment of ADD has become more commonplace recently, some people have started to ask questions.
4. Some people wonder whether ADD might be a phenomenon connected to modern life.
5. Other researchers believe that ADD is the result of a chemical deficiency in the brain.

EXERCISE 2.4: *Answers*

1. Children <u>who have ADD</u> are easily distracted and may be hyperactive.
2. <u>If a child has difficulty concentrating on ordinary tasks such as homework,</u> he or she may have ADD.
3. <u>Although treatment of ADD has become more commonplace recently,</u> some people have started to ask questions.
4. Some people wonder <u>whether ADD might be a phenomenon connected to modern life.</u>
5. Other researchers believe <u>that ADD is the result of a chemical deficiency in the brain.</u>

2d Types of sentences

A sentence can be classified as one of four basic types: simple, compound, complex, or compound-complex.

Simple Sentences

A **simple sentence** has one main or **independent clause** and no subordinate or **dependent clauses.** A simple sentence contains at least one subject and one predicate. It may have a compound subject, a compound predicate, and various phrases, but it has only one clause.

> ▶ She sprints.

> ▶ She and her teammates sprint.

> ▶ She and her teammates sprint and run laps.

> ▶ She and her teammates in the track and field events sprint and run laps to achieve their goal of winning medals.

An **independent clause** contains a subject and a verb and can stand alone as a sentence.

A **dependent clause** contains a subject and a verb but does not express a complete thought.

Compound Sentences

A **compound sentence** consists of two or more independent clauses and no dependent clauses. The two independent clauses are usually joined with a comma and a coordinating conjunction (*and, but, nor, or, for, so,* or *yet*).

> ▶ She runs laps, but her teammates practice throwing the javelin.

Sometimes the two clauses are joined with a semicolon and no coordinating conjunction.

> ▶ She runs laps; her teammates practice throwing the javelin.

Or they may be joined with a semicolon and a conjunctive adverb (such as *nonetheless* or *still*), followed by a comma.

> ▶ She runs laps; however, her teammates practice throwing the javelin.

Complex Sentences

A **complex sentence** has one independent clause and one or more dependent clauses. The dependent clauses usually begin with a subordinating conjunction or a relative pronoun (see 2c for a list).

> ▶ They are training *while he recovers from a sprained ankle.*

▶ Runners *who win their event at more than one local track meet* will be eligible for the district trials.

Compound-Complex Sentences

A **compound-complex sentence** contains two or more independent clauses and one or more dependent clauses.

▶ She and her teammates won the meet, and as they were celebrating, a reporter approached for an interview.

▶ A reporter approached while they were celebrating their victory, and after they doused him with champagne, they answered his questions.

EXERCISE 2.5

Identify each of the following sentences as simple, compound, complex, or compound-complex.

▶ Trumpeter Louis Armstrong was a major influence on jazz music. *simple*

1. Armstrong, who was born in New Orleans, played the cornet at first.
2. While he was a member of Fletcher Henderson's band, he began to create innovative jazz forms, and later, in Chicago, he switched to the trumpet.
3. He made important recordings in Chicago in 1925 to 1928.
4. Many jazz historians contend that he is the most influential jazz musician in the twentieth century.
5. Armstrong was also a singer and a film actor, but his contributions as a musician are his most enduring legacy.

3   SENTENCE FRAGMENTS

A **sentence fragment** is a group of words that cannot stand alone as a complete **sentence.** A fragment is often missing a subject, a complete verb, or both.

> FRAGMENT   **Are hatched in sand every year.**

This group of words does not tell *who* or *what* are hatched in sand every year. It lacks a subject.

> FRAGMENT   **Jamal is a basketball player of many talents.** *Especially his rebounding ability.*

The second group of words has a subject, Jamal's rebounding ability, but lacks a verb.

> FRAGMENT   **To notice a friendly smile.**

This group of words lacks both a subject and a verb. *To notice* is not a complete verb. It is an infinitive.

A group of words can have both a subject and a verb but still be a fragment because it does not express a complete thought.

>   **subject**   **verb**
> FRAGMENT   **Because the *number* of voters *has* declined.**

This group of words does not tell what happened as a result of the voter decline. Its meaning is incomplete.

Notice that the preceding fragment begins with the subordinating conjunction *because.* A clause that begins with a subordinating conjunction cannot stand alone as a complete sentence. Here is a list of common subordinating conjunctions.

after	even if	unless
although	even though	until
as soon as	if	whether
because	once	while
before	since	
during	so that	

(For a more complete list of subordinating conjunctions, see 2c.)
    Word groups that begin with a relative pronoun (*that, which, who*) are also not complete sentences.

> A **sentence** is a group of words that must include at least one independent clause (a subject and a verb that express a complete thought).

                                  subject   verb

FRAGMENT   Which *scientists studied* for many years.

The group of words does not tell *what* the scientists studied.

Finally, when a word group begins with a transitional word or phrase (*for example, also*), make sure that it includes both a subject and a verb.

                                         subject

FRAGMENT   For example, the Gulf *Coast* of Florida.

Use the accompanying flowchart to help you decide whether a particular word group is a complete sentence or a sentence fragment. Also try reading your essays

HOW TO IDENTIFY A FRAGMENT

Does the word group have a subject? (Note that the subject may be understood as *you*. Example: [*You*] Close the door.) — **No** → It is a fragment. Revise.

Yes ↓

A **verbal** is a verb form used as a noun (*the barking of the dog*), an adjective (*a barking dog*), or an adverb (*continued to bark*).

Does the word group have a complete verb? (Note that **verbals** are not complete verbs.) — **No** → It is a fragment. Revise.

Yes ↓

Does the word group express a complete idea? If it begins with a subordinating word (*although, since, if*), a relative pronoun (*that, which, who*), or a transitional word or phrase (*for example, likewise, also*), does the word group contain an **independent clause**? — **No** → It is a fragment. Revise.

An **independent clause** contains a subject and a verb and can stand alone as a sentence.

Yes ↓

It is a sentence.

backward from the end to the beginning, sentence by sentence, to check for fragments. This method allows you to evaluate each sentence in isolation, without being distracted by the flow of ideas throughout the essay. You might also try turning each sentence into a *yes* or *no* question by adding a helping verb, such as *do, does,* or *did.* A complete sentence can be turned into a *yes* or *no* question, but a fragment cannot.

SENTENCE	Sociology has wide applications.
YES/NO QUESTION	Does sociology have wide applications?
FRAGMENT	While sociology has wide applications.
YES/NO QUESTION	[Cannot be formed]

A sentence fragment can be revised in two general ways: (1) by attaching it to a nearby sentence or (2) by rewriting the fragment as a complete sentence. The method you choose depends on the element the fragment lacks as well as your intended meaning.

▶ *Eggs are*
  ~~Are~~ hatched in sand each year.

▶ Jamal is a basketball player of many talents~~.~~ *e*~~E~~specially his rebounding ability.

▶ *Sam was too busy to*
  ~~To~~ notice a friendly smile.

▶ *The*
  ~~Because the~~ number of voters has declined.

3a Join a fragment lacking a subject to another sentence, or rewrite it as a complete sentence.

Attach a fragment lacking a subject to a neighboring sentence if the two are about the same person, place, or thing.

▶ Jenny speaks Italian fluently~~.~~ *and*~~And~~ reads French well.

As an alternative, you can add a subject to turn the fragment into a complete sentence.

▶ Jenny speaks Italian fluently. *She also* ~~And~~ reads French well.

3b Add a helping verb to a fragment lacking a complete verb.

Make sure that every sentence you write contains a *complete* verb. For example, verb forms ending in *-ing* need helping verbs to make them complete. **Helping verbs** include forms of *do, be,* and *have* as well as such words as *will, can, could, shall, should, may, might,* and *must.* When you use an *-ing* verb form in a sentence without a helping verb, you create a fragment. To correct the fragment, add the helping verb.

▶   The college *is* installing a fuel cell to heat the library.

3c Join a fragment that lacks both a subject and a verb to another sentence, or add the missing subject and verb.

An **infinitive** is a verb form made up of *to* plus the base form (*to run, to see*).

Often, fragments lacking a subject and verb begin with an **infinitive** such as *to hope, to walk,* and *to play,* which are not complete verbs, or they begin with an *-ed* or *-ing* form of a verb. Revise a fragment that begins with an infinitive or an *-ed* or *-ing* verb form by combining it with a previous sentence.

▶   I plan to transfer next semester, ~~To~~ *to* live closer to home.

▶   Robert E. Lee and Ulysses S. Grant met on April 9, 1865, ~~Bringing~~ *bringing* an end to the Civil War.

You can also revise a fragment beginning with an infinitive or an *-ed* or *-ing* verb form by adding both a subject and a verb to make it a complete sentence.

▶   Linda was reluctant to go out alone at night. *She was unwilling to* ~~To~~ walk across campus from the library.

▶   Kyle was determined to do well on his math exam. *He studied* ~~Studied~~ during every available hour.

Watch out for fragments that begin with a transitional word or phrase. They can usually be corrected by joining them to a previous sentence.

▶   Annie has always wanted to become an orthopedist, *that* ~~That~~ is, a bone specialist.

3d Join a fragment beginning with a subordinating word to another sentence, or drop the subordinating word.

You can correct a fragment beginning with a subordinating word by joining it to the sentence coming before or after.

▶ The students stared spellbound/ ~~While~~ the professor lectured.
while

▶ Until Dr. Jonas Salk invented a vaccine/, ~~Polio~~ was a serious threat to public health.
polio

As an alternative, you can revise this type of fragment by dropping the subordinating word.

▶ ~~Because the~~ 800 area code for toll-free dialing is overused. New codes — 888 and 877 — have been added.
The

3e Join a fragment beginning with a relative pronoun such as *who* or *whom* to another sentence, or rewrite it as a complete sentence.

Another common type of sentence fragment begins with a relative pronoun. **Relative pronouns** include *who, whom, whose, whoever, whomever, what, whatever, which,* and *that.*

▶ My contemporary fiction instructor assigned a novel by Stephen King/, ~~Whose~~ work I admire.
whose

▶ The dodo is an extinct bird. ~~That~~ disappeared in the seventeenth century.
It

Professional writers sometimes use sentence fragments intentionally to achieve special effects, particularly in works of fiction or articles written for popular magazines. An *intentional* fragment may be used to emphasize a point, answer a question, re-create a conversation, or make an exclamation. However, you should avoid using intentional fragments in academic writing. Instructors and other readers may find the fragments distracting or too informal, or they may assume you used a fragment in error.

EXERCISE 3.1

Correct any fragments in the following sentences. Some groups of sentences may be correct as written.

▶ The mail is delivered every afternoon/ ~~While~~ I am at school.
while

1. Your mother may have told you. That a person's mail is private.
2. In these days of computerized mailing lists. Your name and address are certainly not private.
3. The direct-mail business has exploded. Sixty-five billion pieces of unsolicited mail reach American homes and offices each year.

EXERCISE 3.1: *Possible Revisions*

1. Your mother may have told you that a person's mail is private.
2. In these days of computerized mailing lists, your name and address are certainly not private.
3. Both sentences are correct.

4. To put it another way, four trees per person per year contribute to this tide of printed waste.

5. Now you can also get electronic junk mail. Millions of advertisements can be sent . . . a button.

6. Email advertisers can target specific audiences, such as small-business owners or college students.

7. If your online service charges by the hour or the minute, you will pay to read unwanted ads.

8. Companies are choosing . . . lists. For just pennies . . . electronic, and make a profit from a relatively low response.

9. Even though . . . email, the computerized list that spawned it is practically immortal.

10. Your name can be "sold" over and over until it's . . . listed it.

EXERCISE 3.2: *Possible Revision*

Gila trout are endangered in some stretches of water **that** are managed as designated wilderness. A hands-off policy would be their doom **because** exotic trout species now swim in the same streams. Gila trout can survive the competition and the temptation to interbreed only if they swim in isolated tributaries **in** which a waterfall blocks the upstream movement of other fish. Two decades ago, one such tributary was fortified **with**

---

4. To put it another way. Four trees per person per year contribute to this tide of printed waste.

5. Now you can also get electronic junk mail. Millions of advertisements sent over the Internet at the push of a button.

6. Email advertisers can target specific audiences. Such as small-business owners or college students.

7. If your online service charges by the hour or the minute. You will pay to read unwanted ads.

8. Companies choosing from among more than 20,000 mailing lists. For just pennies per name, firms can target recipients with mass mailings, either paper or electronic. And make a profit from a relatively low response.

9. Even though you can toss the printed material or delete the email. The computerized list that spawned it is practically immortal.

10. Your name can be "sold" over and over. Until it's almost impossible to track it to the business that first listed it.

EXERCISE 3.2

Rewrite the following passage as needed to eliminate sentence fragments.

▶ How much and what kind of intervention should be undertaken/~~On~~ behalf of endangered species?   *on*

    Gila trout are endangered in some stretches of water. That are managed as designated wilderness. A hands-off policy would be their doom. Because exotic trout species now swim in the same streams. Gila trout can survive the competition and the temptation to interbreed only if they swim in isolated tributaries. In which a waterfall blocks the upstream movement of other fish. Two decades ago, one such tributary was fortified. With a small concrete dam. In other words, a dam deliberately built in the wilderness. It is often difficult to choose the right way. To manage a wilderness area. A scientific grasp of the way the ecosystem works is essential. Yet not always available.

4   RUN-ON SENTENCES AND COMMA SPLICES

A **run-on sentence** occurs when two or more independent clauses are joined without a punctuation mark or a coordinating conjunction. Run-on sentences are also known as **fused sentences**.

	┌──── independent clause ────┐ ┌── independent clause ──
RUN-ON SENTENCE	A television addict is dependent on television I have suffered this addiction for years.

A **comma splice** occurs when two or more independent clauses are joined with a comma but without a coordinating conjunction (such as *and, or,* or *but*).

COMMA SPLICE

independent clause ———————— independent clause

A typical magic act includes tricks and illusions, both depend on deception.

Notice that only a comma separates the two independent clauses, causing the comma splice.

Another type of comma splice occurs when a word other than a coordinating conjunction is used with a comma to join two or more independent clauses.

COMMA SPLICE

independent clause ————————

A typical magic act includes tricks and illusions, however,

independent clause ————

both depend on deception.

In the preceding sentence, *however* is a conjunctive adverb, not a coordinating conjunction. There are only seven coordinating conjunctions: *and, or, nor, but, for, so,* and *yet.*

RECOGNIZING RUN-ON SENTENCES AND COMMA SPLICES

Many students have difficulty spotting run-on sentences and comma splices in their own writing. Use the accompanying flowchart to help you identify these types of errors in your sentences.

HOW TO IDENTIFY RUN-ON SENTENCES AND COMMA SPLICES

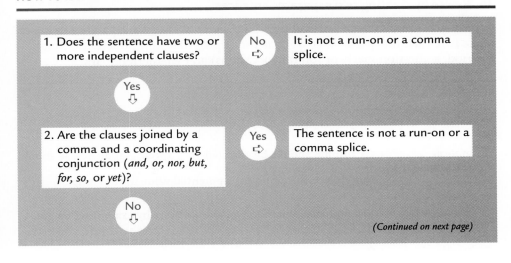

1. Does the sentence have two or more independent clauses? — No ⇨ It is not a run-on or a comma splice.

Yes ⇩

2. Are the clauses joined by a comma and a coordinating conjunction (*and, or, nor, but, for, so,* or *yet*)? — Yes ⇨ The sentence is not a run-on or a comma splice.

No ⇩

(Continued on next page)

---

a small concrete dam. In other words, a dam **was** deliberately built in the wilderness. It is often difficult to choose the right way **to** manage a wilderness area. A scientific grasp of the way the ecosystem works is essential. **Such knowledge is** not always available, **however.**

HOW TO IDENTIFY RUN-ON SENTENCES AND COMMA SPLICES *(continued)*

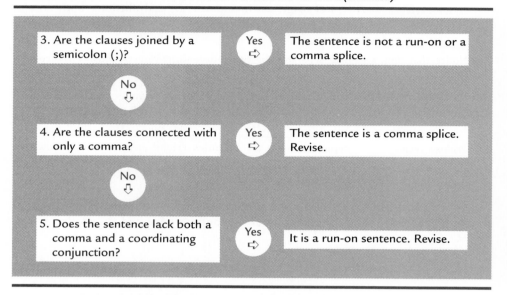

3. Are the clauses joined by a semicolon (;)?

Yes → The sentence is not a run-on or a comma splice.

No ⇩

4. Are the clauses connected with only a comma?

Yes → The sentence is a comma splice. Revise.

No ⇩

5. Does the sentence lack both a comma and a coordinating conjunction?

Yes → It is a run-on sentence. Revise.

CORRECTING RUN-ON SENTENCES AND COMMA SPLICES

There are four basic ways to correct a run-on sentence or comma splice. Choose the method that best fits your sentence or intended meaning.

4a Revise by creating two separate sentences.

Correct a run-on sentence or comma splice by creating two separate sentences. Make sure each independent clause has the appropriate end punctuation mark— a period, a question mark, or (on rare occasions) an exclamation mark.

period   period
↓   ↓

Independent clause . *Independent clause* .

RUN-ON
SENTENCE

A resume should be directed to a specific audience. It ~~it~~ should

emphasize the applicant's potential value to the company.

COMMA SPLICE

To evaluate a charity, you should start by examining its goals ~~,~~ .
T
‸then you should investigate its management practices.

4b Revise by joining the clauses with a semicolon (;).

When the independent clauses are closely connected in meaning, consider joining them with a semicolon. Note that a coordinating conjunction (such as *and, or,* or *but*) is *not* included when you revise with a semicolon (see 4c).

semicolon
↓

| Independent clause | ; | independent clause | . |

RUN-ON SENTENCE	Specialty products are unique items that consumers take time purchasing; these items include cars, parachutes, and skis.
COMMA SPLICE	Studies have shown that male and female managers have different leadership styles; as a result, workers may respond differently to each.

In the second example, the semicolon joins the two clauses connected by the conjunctive adverb *as a result.* When two independent clauses are joined by a conjunctive adverb, a semicolon is needed.

4c Revise by joining the clauses with a comma and a coordinating conjunction.

Two independent clauses can be joined by using *both* a comma and a coordinating conjunction (*and, or, nor, but, for, so,* or *yet*). The coordinating conjunction indicates how the two clauses are related.

comma + coordinating conjunction
↓

| Independent clause | , and | independent clause | . |

RUN-ON SENTENCE	Closed-minded people often refuse to recognize opposing *and* views, they reject ideas without evaluating them.
COMMA SPLICE	Some educators support home schooling, *but* others oppose it vehemently.

4d Revise by making one clause dependent or by turning one clause into a phrase.

A **dependent clause** contains a subject and a verb but does not express a complete thought. It must always be linked to an independent clause. You can correct a run-on sentence or a comma splice by adding a **subordinating conjunction** (such as *because* or *although*) to one of the independent clauses, thereby making it a dependent clause. The subordinating conjunction makes the thought incomplete and dependent on the independent clause.

subordinating conjunction
↓
Because   dependent clause , independent clause .

or   subordinating conjunction
↓
Independent clause   because   dependent clause .

RUN-ON SENTENCE	Facial expressions are very revealing they are an important communication tool.
INDEPENDENT CLAUSE	Facial expressions are very revealing.
DEPENDENT CLAUSE	*Because* facial expressions are very revealing
JOINED TO INDEPENDENT CLAUSE	Because facial expressions are very revealing, they are an important communication tool.

You can also correct a run-on sentence or a comma splice by changing one of the independent clauses to a phrase.

Phrase , independent clause .
or
Independent clause , phrase .
or
Beginning of independent clause , phrase , end of independent clause .

COMMA SPLICE	Medieval peasants in Europe ate a simple, hearty diet, they relied almost totally on agriculture.
INDEPENDENT CLAUSE	Medieval peasants in Europe ate a simple, hearty diet.
CLAUSE REDUCED TO PHRASE	with their simple, hearty diet
EMBEDDED IN INDEPENDENT CLAUSE	Medieval peasants in Europe, with their simple, hearty diet, relied almost totally on agriculture.

Note: A comma or commas may or may not be needed to separate a phrase from the rest of the sentence, depending on how the phrase affects the meaning of the sentence. See 12e. Here are two more examples that show how to revise run-on sentences and comma splices using subordination.

RUN-ON SENTENCE

Distributors open big-budget movies late in the week, ~~they hope~~ *hoping*̂ moviegoers will flock to theaters over the weekend.

COMMA SPLICE

Although the ~~The~~ remote fishing lodge has no heat or electricity, ~~nevertheless~~̂ it is a popular vacation spot.

EXERCISE 4.1

Correct any run-ons or comma splices in the following sentences.

▶ A deadly nerve poison is found on the skin of some Amazon tree frogs̶;̂ native tribes use the poison on the tips of their arrows when they hunt.

1. Disney World is a fantasy nearly every child hopes to experience, it has become part of our popular culture.
2. Shopping at Internet bookstores is convenient, buyers cannot easily evaluate an author's credentials.
3. Openness is one way to build trust in a relationship another is to demonstrate tolerance and patience.
4. In the 1960s many Americans treated Vietnam veterans disrespectfully this situation has changed dramatically since that time.
5. William Faulkner wrote classic novels about life in the U.S. South, Eudora Welty has also written vividly about southern life.
6. With large bodies and tiny wings, bumblebees have long been a puzzle, how do they fly?
7. The Taj Mahal is aptly called the "Pearl Mosque" it glows in the moonlight with unearthly beauty.
8. The Supreme Court often makes controversial decisions, the justices must decide how to interpret the Constitution.
9. Although the clouds were threatening, the storm had not yet struck, however, most boats turned toward shore.
10. Restoring a painting is, indeed, delicate work too much enthusiasm can be dangerous.

EXERCISE 4.2

Correct any run-on sentences and comma splices in the following paragraph. Some sentences may be correct as written.

▶ Some people believe dreams are revealing, *but*̂ others think the brain is simply unloading excess information.

EXERCISE 4.1: *Possible Revisions*

1. Because Disney World is . . . experience, it has . . . culture.
2. Shopping . . . convenient, but buyers . . . credentials.
3. Openness is . . . relationship; another is . . . patience.
4. In the 1960s . . . disrespectfully, a situation that has changed dramatically since that time.
5. William Faulkner wrote . . . the U.S. South, and Eudora Welty . . . southern life.
6. With large bodies and tiny wings, bumblebees have long been a puzzle. How do they fly?
7. Glowing in the moonlight with unearthly beauty, the Taj Mahal is aptly called the "Pearl Mosque."
8. The Supreme Court . . . decisions because the justices must decide how to interpret the Constitution.
9. Although the clouds . . . struck. However, most boats turned toward shore.
10. Restoring a painting is, indeed, delicate work, and too much enthusiasm can be dangerous.

EXERCISE 4.2: *Possible Revision*

Throughout recorded history, people have been fascinated by dreams, **and** they have

(Continued on next page)

wondered what meaning dreams hold. Whether the dreams are ominous or beautiful, people have always wanted to understand them [*correct*]. There are many ancient stories about dream interpretation. **One** of these is the biblical story of Daniel. Daniel is able to interpret a ruler's dream, **a power that** convinces the ruler that Daniel is a prophet. Other early writers considered the topic of dream **interpretation;** to Latin writers, some dreams were meaningful and some were not. Meaningful dreams could reveal the future, these writers argued, but other dreams were simply the result of eating or drinking too much [*correct*]. Sigmund Freud, the founder of psychoanalysis, dramatically changed the field of dream interpretation. **He** believed that dreams come from the subconscious. According to Freud, **because** ideas too frightening for the waking mind often appear in dreams, patients in Freudian therapy **need to** discuss dream images. Today, not everyone agrees with Freud, **but** scientists trying to understand the brain still pay attention to dreams. They are certain that dreams reflect modern life **because** more and more people today dream about computers.

Throughout recorded history, people have been fascinated by dreams, they have wondered what meaning dreams hold. Whether the dreams are ominous or beautiful, people have always wanted to understand them. There are many ancient stories about dream interpretation one of these is the biblical story of Daniel. Daniel is able to interpret a ruler's dream, this power to interpret convinces the ruler that Daniel is a prophet. Other early writers considered the topic of dream interpretation, to Latin writers, some dreams were meaningful and some were not. Meaningful dreams could reveal the future, these writers argued, but other dreams were simply the result of eating or drinking too much. Sigmund Freud, the founder of psychoanalysis, dramatically changed the field of dream interpretation he believed that dreams come from the subconscious. According to Freud, ideas too frightening for the waking mind often appear in dreams, patients in Freudian therapy often discuss dream images. Today, not everyone agrees with Freud, scientists trying to understand the brain still pay attention to dreams. They are certain that dreams reflect modern life more and more people today dream about computers.

5   SUBJECT-VERB AGREEMENT

Subjects and verbs must agree in person and number. **Person** refers to the forms *I* or *we* (first person), *you* (second person), and *he, she, it,* and *they* (third person). **Number** shows whether a word refers to one thing (singular) or more than one thing (plural). In a sentence, subjects and verbs need to be consistent in person and number: *I drive, you drive, she drives.*

Subject-verb agreement errors often occur in complicated sentences, in sentences with compound subjects, or in sentences where the subject and verb are separated by other words or phrases. The following sections will help you look for and revise common errors in subject-verb agreement.

5a   Make sure the verb agrees with the subject, not with words that come between the subject and verb.

▶ The *number* of farm workers *has* remained constant over several decades.

   The subject *number* is singular and requires a singular verb, even though the words *of farm workers* appear between the subject and verb.

5b   Use a plural verb when two or more subjects are joined by *and*.

▶ A dot and a dash represents the letter *A* in Morse code.

▶ Supreme Court Justice Antonin Scalia, media magnate Rupert Murdoch, and news

                                        were
   correspondent Sam Donaldson ~~was~~ born on March 11.

5c **Revise to make the verb agree with the subject closest to it when two or more subjects are joined by *or, either . . . or,* or *neither . . . nor.***

When two or more singular subjects are joined by *or, either . . . or,* or *neither . . . nor,* use a singular verb.

▶ *Math* or *accounting appears* to be a suitable major for you.

▶ Either the *waiter* or the *customer has* misplaced the bill.

▶ Neither the *doctor* nor the *patient is* pessimistic about the prognosis.

When one singular and one plural subject are joined by *or, either . . . or,* or *neither . . . nor,* the verb should agree in number with the subject nearest to it.

▶ Neither the *sailors* nor the *boat was* harmed by the storm.

▶ Neither the *boat* nor the *sailors were* harmed by the storm.

▶ Either my daughters or my wife water^s^ that plant daily.

5d Use a singular verb with most collective nouns, such as *family, couple,* and *class.*

When a **collective noun** refers to a group as one unit acting together, use a singular verb. When the members of the group are acting as individuals, use a plural verb.

▶ The school *committee has* voted to increase teachers' salaries.
   The committee is acting as a unit.

▶ The family ~~are~~ ^is^ living in a cramped apartment.

▶ The *team are* traveling by train, bus, and bike.
   The team members are acting individually.

▶ The jury ~~is~~ ^are^ divided and unable to reach a consensus.

To make their meaning clearer and avoid awkwardness, writers often add *members* or a similar noun.

▶ The members of the jury are divided and unable to reach consensus.

5e Use a singular verb with most indefinite pronouns, such as *anyone, everyone, each, every, no one,* and *something*.

Indefinite pronouns do not refer to a specific person, place, or object. They refer to people, places, or things in general. Singular indefinite pronouns include the following: *each, either, neither, anyone, anybody, anything, everyone, everybody, everything, one, no one, nobody, nothing, someone, somebody, something.*

▶ *Everyone* in this room *is* welcome to express an opinion.

▶ Neither of the candidates ~~have~~ ^{has} run for office before.

Other indefinite pronouns, such as *several, both, many,* and *few,* take a plural verb.

▶ Every year *many succeed* in starting new small businesses.

▶ Several of you jogs̸ at least three miles a day.

Some indefinite pronouns, such as *all, any, more, most, some,* and *none,* take either a singular or a plural verb depending on the noun they refer to. To decide which verb to use, follow this rule: Treat the indefinite pronoun as singular if it refers to something that cannot be counted and as plural if it refers to more than one of something that can be counted.

▶ Most of the water go^{es} into this kettle.
   You cannot count water.

▶ Some of the children in the study chooses̸ immediate rather than delayed rewards.
   You can count children.

5f Revise to make verbs agree with the antecedents of *who, which,* and *that.*

When a **relative pronoun** (*who, which, that*) refers to a singular noun, use a singular verb. When it refers to a plural noun, use a plural verb.

▶ *Toni Morrison, who enjoys* unique success as both a popular and a literary author, won the Nobel Prize in literature in 1993.
   Who refers to Toni Morrison, and because *Toni Morrison* is singular, the verb *enjoys* is singular.

▶ Look for *stores that display* this sign.
   That refers to *stores,* a plural noun.

An **antecedent** is the noun or pronoun to which a pronoun refers.

A **relative pronoun** introduces a dependent clause that functions as an adjective: *the patient <u>who</u> injured her leg.*

Using *one of the* often leads to errors in subject-verb agreement. The phrase *one of the* plus a noun is plural.

▶ A pigeon is *one of the two birds that drink* by suction.

   That refers to *birds,* and since *birds* is plural, the verb *drink* is plural.

However, *only one of the* plus a noun is singular: *The cheetah is the only one of the big cats that <u>has</u> nonretractable claws.*

5g **Revise to make the verb agree with a subject that follows it.**

When a sentence begins with the word *here* or *there* (which cannot function as a subject) or with a **prepositional phrase,** the subject often follows the verb. Look for the subject after the verb and make sure the subject and verb agree.

▶ There *is* a false *panel* somewhere in this room.

▶ Under the stairs *lurks* a solitary *spider.*

5h **Make sure a linking verb agrees with its subject, not a word or phrase that renames the subject.**

Linking verbs, such as forms of *be* and *feel, look,* and *taste,* connect a subject with a word or phrase that renames or describes it. In sentences with linking verbs, the verb should agree with the subject.

▶ The *bluebell is* any of several plants in the lily family.

▶ The worst backyard pest ~~are~~ *is* squirrels, who dig up freshly planted bulbs and plunder bird feeders.

5i **Use a singular verb when the subject is a title.**

▶ *Gulliver's Travels* ~~are~~ *is* a satire by the eighteenth-century British writer Jonathan Swift.

5j **Use singular verbs with singular nouns that end in *s,* such as *physics* and *news.***

▶ *Linguistics deals* with the study of human speech.

A **prepositional phrase** is a group of words that begins with a preposition and includes the object or objects of the preposition and all their modifiers: *above the low wooden table.*

EXERCISE 5.1: *Answers* (p. 812)

1. Many members . . . communicate by speaking English . . .
2. A student . . . expects . . .
3. The United States is different.
4. Working for laws that require . . .
5. In American schools, often . . . has been available . . .
6. Some linguists joke . . . languages is called . . .
7. Some states around the country have begun to change this situation.

(Continued on next page)

8. Correct
9. In a Spanish or French class, children of immigrants . . . learn a new language and perhaps gain . . .
10. Everyone who studies a foreign language is likely to benefit.

EXERCISE 5.2: *Answers*

Everyone in the colder climates **wants** to know if the next winter will be severe. The National Weather Service, however, usually **predicts** the weather only a short time in advance. Another method of making weather predictions **is** popular with many Americans. According to folklore, there **are** a number of signs to alert people to a hard winter ahead. Among these signs **is** the brown stripe on a woolly bear caterpillar. If the brown stripe between the caterpillar's two black stripes **is** wide, some people believe the winter will be a short one. Another of the signs that indicate a hard winter is a large apple harvest [*correct*]. And of course, almost everyone in the United States **has** seen news stories on February 2 about groundhogs predicting the end of winter. Folk beliefs, which are not based on science, **seem** silly to many people. Neither the National Weather Service nor folklore **is** always able to forecast the weather accurately, however.

EXERCISE 5.1

Correct any subject-verb agreement errors in the following sentences. Some sentences may be correct as written.

▶ Most of the people in the world believes that learning a second language is important.

1. Many members of the international business community communicates by speaking English, the international language of business.
2. A student in most non-English-speaking industrialized nations expect to spend six or more years studying English.
3. The United States are different.
4. Working for laws that requires all Americans to speak English is a fairly common U.S. political tactic.
5. In American schools, often neither a teaching staff nor enough money have been available for good foreign language programs.
6. Some linguists joke that a person who speaks two languages are called "bilingual," while a person who speaks one language is called "American."
7. Some states around the country has begun to change this situation.
8. If a class is given lessons in a foreign language, the students feel that they will be better prepared for the new global economy.
9. In a Spanish or French class, children of immigrants for whom English was a second language learns a new language and perhaps gains a new appreciation of their parents' accomplishments.
10. Everyone who study a foreign language are likely to benefit.

EXERCISE 5.2

Correct any sentences with subject-verb agreement errors in the following paragraph. Some sentences may be correct as written.

▶ Watching groundhogs that seeks their shadows is one way to forecast the weather.

Everyone in the colder climates want to know if the next winter will be severe. The National Weather Service, however, usually predict the weather only a short time in advance. Another method of making weather predictions are popular with many Americans. According to folklore, there is a number of signs to alert people to a hard winter ahead. Among these signs are the brown stripe on a woolly bear caterpillar. If the brown stripe between the caterpillar's two black stripes are wide, some people believe the winter will be a short one. Another of the signs that indicate a hard winter is a large apple harvest. And of course, almost everyone in the United States have seen news stories on February 2 about groundhogs predicting the end of winter. Folk beliefs, which are not based on science, seems silly to many people. Neither the National Weather Service nor folklore are always able to forecast the weather accurately, however.

6 VERB FORMS

Except for *be*, all English verbs have five forms.

Base Form	Past Tense	Past Participle	Present Participle	-s Form
move	moved	moved	moving	moves

▶ Many designers *visit* Milan for fashion shows each year.

▶ Reagan and Gorbachev *visited* Iceland for a summit meeting.

▶ Students have *visited* the state capitol every spring for decades.

▶ His cousin from Iowa is *visiting* this week.

▶ Maria *visits* her grandmother in Puerto Rico as often as possible.

6a Use -s or -es endings for present tense verbs that have third-person singular subjects.

The *-s* form is made up of the verb's base form plus *-s* or *-es*.

▶ Mr. King *teaches* English.

A third-person singular subject can consist of a singular noun, a singular pronoun (*he, she,* and *it*), or a singular indefinite pronoun (such as *everyone*).

SINGULAR NOUN	The flower opens.
SINGULAR PRONOUN	He opens the door.
SINGULAR INDEFINITE PRONOUN	Everybody knows the truth.

▶ She ~~want~~ *wants* to be a veterinarian.

▶ None of the townspeople ~~understand~~ *understands* him.

6b Do not omit -ed endings on verbs.

For regular verbs, both the past tense and the past participle are formed by adding *-ed* or *-d* to the base form of the verb. (For more on verb tense, see 1c and 27a.)

▶ She *claimed* to be the czar's daughter, Anastasia.

▶ The defendant *faced* his accusers.

Some speakers do not fully pronounce the *-ed* endings of verbs (*asked, fixed, supposed to, used to*). As a result, they may unintentionally omit these endings in their writing.

> *talked*
> ► He ~~talk~~ to the safety inspectors about plant security.
> ^

> *used*
> ► They ~~use~~ to dance to disco all night long.
> ^

6c Use the correct form of irregular verbs such as *lay* and *lie*.

The verb pairs *lay* and *lie* and *sit* and *set* have similar forms and are often confused. Each verb has its own meaning: *lie* means to recline or rest on a surface, while *lay* means to put or place something; *sit* means to be seated, as in a chair, while *set* means to place something on a surface.

> *lie*
> ► Our dog likes to ~~lay~~ on the couch all afternoon.
> ^

> *sit*
> ► Let me ~~set~~ in this chair for a while.
> ^

For more on irregular verbs, see 1c.

6d Use the active and passive voice appropriately.

When a verb is in the **active voice**, the subject performs the action.

> ACTIVE VOICE The Mississippi River flows into the Gulf of Mexico.

When a verb is in the **passive voice**, the subject receives the action.

> PASSIVE VOICE The computer file was deleted.
>
> Notice that the passive voice sentence does not tell *who* deleted the file.

The active voice expresses ideas more vividly and emphatically than does the passive voice. Whenever possible, use the active voice in your sentences.

> *The colonists threw tea*
> ► ~~Tea was thrown~~ into Boston Harbor. ~~by the colonists.~~
> ^ ^

> *No one is allowed to sell illegal*
> ► ~~Illegal~~ drugs. ~~are not allowed to be sold.~~
> ^ ^

Passive voice sentences may seem indirect, as if the writer is purposely withholding information. In general, use the passive voice sparingly. There are two situations in which it is the best choice, however.

1. When you do not know or do not want to reveal who performed the action of the verb:

   PASSIVE   **Several historic buildings had been torn down.**

2. When you want to emphasize the object of the action rather than the person who causes the action:

   PASSIVE   **The poem "My Last Duchess" by Robert Browning was discussed in class.**

   In this sentence, the title of the poem is more important than the people who discussed it.

6e Use the present tense when writing about literary works, even though they were written in the past.

     depicts
▶ Chaucer's *Canterbury Tales* ~~depicted~~ a tremendously varied group of travelers.
        ^

6f Be sure to distinguish between the immediate past and the less immediate past.

Use the past perfect form of the verb, formed by adding *had* to the past participle, to indicate an action that was completed before another action or a specified time.

   UNCLEAR   **Roberto finished three research papers when the semester ended.**

   Roberto did not finish all three right at the end of the semester.

   REVISED   **Roberto had finished three research papers when the semester ended.**

For more on verb tense, see 1c and 27a.

EXERCISE 6.1

Correct the errors in verb form in the following sentences. Some sentences may be correct as written.

    United States entered the
▶ The Spanish-American War ~~was entered by the United States~~ in 1898.
    ^

1. When the nineteenth century change into the twentieth, many people in the United States became eager to expel Spain from the Americas.
2. Cuba, an island that lays ninety miles off the Florida coast, provided them with an excuse to do so.
3. Cuban rebels were trying to free themselves from Spain, and many Americans wanted to help them.
4. In addition, many people in the United States wanted to take over Spain's territories for a long time.

EXERCISE 6.1: *Answers*

1. When the nineteenth century changed into the twentieth, many people . . .
2. Cuba, an island that lies ninety miles . . .
3. Correct
4. In addition, many people in the United States wanted to . . .

(Continued on next page)

5. The United States
. . . and assumed
control of Cuba . . .
6. Cuba was allowed
. . .
7. Puerto Rico became
a commonwealth in
1952, a position
that placed it . . .
8. Correct
9. They rejected it.
10. Many Puerto Ricans
are worried . . . their
island, and none of
them wants that to
happen.

5. The United States won the war very quickly and assume control of Cuba, the Philippines, Guam, and Puerto Rico.
6. Cuba was allow to take control of its own affairs right away.
7. Puerto Rico became a commonwealth in 1952, a position that place it between statehood and independence.
8. In a 1998 election, the people of Puerto Rico were offered the option of full statehood.
9. It was rejected by them.
10. Many Puerto Ricans are worried that statehood would destroy the native culture of their island, and none of them want that to happen.

EXERCISE 6.2

Correct the errors in verb form in the following paragraph. Some sentences may be correct as written.

▶ Walt Whitman's *Leaves of Grass* ~~contain~~ *contains* long, informally structured poems.

    Walt Whitman was usually considered one of the greatest American poets. He spent almost his whole life in Brooklyn, New York, but he like to write about all of America. He was fired from several jobs for laziness and admitted that he liked to lay in bed until noon. But he had a vision: He wanted to create an entirely new kind of poetry. Rhyme was considered unimportant by him, and he did not think new American poetry needed formal structure. Unfortunately for Whitman, his great masterpiece, *Leaves of Grass,* was not an overnight success. Ralph Waldo Emerson admire it, but Whitman sold very few copies. He revise it continuously until his death. Today, people admires *Leaves of Grass* for its optimism, its strong, beautiful language, its very modern appreciation of the diversity of America, and its astonishing openness about sexuality. Whitman's body of work still move and surprise readers.

7   PRONOUN PROBLEMS

Pronouns are words used in place of nouns. They provide a quick, convenient way to refer to a word that has already been named. Common problems in using pronouns include problems with pronoun reference, agreement, and case.

PRONOUN REFERENCE

    A pronoun should refer clearly to its **antecedent,** the noun or pronoun it substitutes for.

    If an antecedent is missing or unclear, the meaning of the sentence is also unclear. Use the following guidelines to make certain your pronoun references are clear and correct.

7a Make sure each pronoun refers clearly to one antecedent.

▶ The oldies radio station battled the pop rock station for the highest ratings.

                   the pop rock station
Eventually, ~~it~~ won.
        ^

The revised sentence makes it clear which station won: the pop rock station.

7b Be sure to check for vague uses of *they, it,* and *you.*

They, it, and *you* often refer vaguely to antecedents in preceding sentences or to no antecedent at all.

OMITTED   On the Internet, they claimed that an asteroid would collide
ANTECEDENT   with the earth.

On the Internet does not explain what *they* refers to.

CLEAR   On the Internet, a Web page claimed that an asteroid would col-
                 lide with the earth.

Adding the noun *a Web page* clears up the mystery.

                                       they gain
▶ When political scientists study early political cartoons, ~~it provides~~ insight into
                                               ^
historical events.

                    people often talk
▶ In Florida, ~~you often hear~~ about hurricane threats of previous years.
          ^

7c Make sure pronouns do not refer to adjectives or possessives.

Pronouns must refer to nouns or other pronouns. Adjectives and possessives cannot serve as antecedents, although they may seem to suggest a noun the pronoun *could* refer to.

                            he was
▶ He became so depressed that ~~it made him~~ unable to get out of bed.
                          ^

The pronoun *it* seems to refer to the adjective *depressed*, which suggests the noun *depression.* This noun is not in the sentence, however.

                            stocks
▶ The stock market's rapid rise made ~~it~~ appear to be an attractive investment.
                              ^

The pronoun *it* seems to refer to *stock market's,* which is a possessive, not a noun.

7d Make sure the pronouns *who, whom, which,* and *that* refer to clear, specific nouns.

                                    These storms make
▶ Lake-effect storms hit cities along the Great Lakes. ~~That makes~~ winter travel
                                            ^
treacherous.

EXERCISE 7.1: *Possible Revisions* (p. 818)

1. That need for communication is always . . .

2. Because of the importance of the information, it often must be . . .

3. Military strategists . . . because encoded messages baffle the enemy.

4. "Invisible ink," which cannot be seen . . .

5. Lemon juice and vinegar are good choices because they are invisible unless burned.

6. During World War II, U.S. government . . . because Navajo is a difficult and little-studied language.

(Continued on next page)

7. Early code writing involved substituting . . .
8. Because these cryptograms are so simple, they are no longer used to transmit messages.
9. Its complexity was an enormous problem for the Allied forces.
10. Alan Turing, a British civil servant and mathematical genius, finally solved the enigma code.

EXERCISE 7.1

Correct any errors in pronoun reference in the following sentences.

▶ Innovative codes are important because ~~it means that~~ they ~~will be~~ *are* hard to break.

1. A country at war must be able to convey information to military personnel. That is always a challenge.
2. The information's importance often requires it to be transmitted secretly.
3. Military strategists use codes for these transmissions because they baffle the enemy.
4. They say that "invisible ink," which cannot be seen until the paper is heated, was once a popular way to communicate secretly.
5. Lemon juice and vinegar are good choices because you can't see them unless they are burned.
6. During World War II, U.S. government code specialists hired Navajo Indians because it is a difficult and little-studied language.
7. In early code writing, it involved substituting letters throughout the message.
8. These cryptograms are no longer used to transmit messages because they are too simple.
9. The Nazis' enigma code was extremely difficult to crack. This was an enormous problem for the Allied forces.
10. Alan Turing's mathematical genius saved the day. He was a British civil servant who finally solved the enigma code.

PRONOUN-ANTECEDENT AGREEMENT

An **antecedent** is the noun or pronoun to which a pronoun refers.

Person indicates whether the subject is speaking (first person: *I, we*), is being spoken to (second person: *you*), or is being spoken about (third person: *he, she, it, they*). **Number** is a term that classifies pronouns as singular (*I, you, he, she, it*) or plural (*we, you, they*).

Gender is a way of classifying pronouns as masculine (*he, him*), feminine (*she, her*), or neuter (*it, its*).

An **indefinite pronoun** does not refer to a specific person, place, or object. It refers to people, places, or things in general (*anywhere, everyone, everything*).

Pronouns and **antecedents** must agree in **person, number,** and **gender.** The most common agreement error occurs when pronouns and antecedents do not agree in number. If the antecedent is singular, use a singular pronoun. If the antecedent is plural, use a plural pronoun.

In most situations, you will instinctively choose the correct pronoun and antecedent. Here are a few guidelines to follow for those times when you are unsure of which pronoun or antecedent to use.

7e Use singular pronouns to refer to indefinite pronouns that are singular in meaning.

Singular indefinite pronouns include the following.

another	anywhere	everyone	none	other
anybody	each	everything	no one	somebody
anyone	either	neither	nothing	someone
anything	everybody	nobody	one	something

▶ *Each* of the experiments produced *its* desired result.

▶ If *anyone* wants me, give *him or her* my email address.

▶ *Everyone* in America should exercise *his or her* right to vote so *his or her* voice can be heard.

If the pronoun and antecedent do not agree, change either the pronoun or the indefinite pronoun to which it refers. If you need to use a singular pronoun, use *he or she* or *him or her* to avoid sexism.

People
▶ ~~Everyone~~ should check their credit card statement monthly.

his or her
▶ Everyone should check ~~their~~ credit card statement monthly.

An alternative is to eliminate the pronoun or pronouns entirely.

a
▶ No one should lose ~~their~~ job because of family responsibilities.

Note: Overuse of *him or her* and *his or her* can create awkward sentences. To avoid this problem, you can revise your sentences in one of two ways: by using a plural antecedent and a plural pronoun, or by omitting the pronouns altogether.

The indefinite pronouns *all, any, more, most,* and *some* can be either singular or plural, depending on how they are used in sentences. When an indefinite pronoun refers to something that can be counted, use a plural pronoun to refer to it. When an indefinite pronoun refers to something that cannot be counted, use a singular pronoun to refer to it.

▶ **Of the tropical plants studied, *some* have proven *their* usefulness in fighting disease.**

Because the word *plants* is a plural, countable noun, the pronoun *some* is plural in this sentence.

▶ **The water was warm, and *most* of *it* was murky.**

The word *water* is not countable, so *most* is singular.

7f Use a plural pronoun to refer to a compound antecedent joined by *and*.

▶ *The walrus and the carpenter* ate *their* oysters greedily.

Exception: When the singular antecedents joined by *and* refer to the same person, place, or thing, use a singular pronoun.

▶ As *a father and a husband,* **he** is a success.

Exception: When *each* or *every* comes before the antecedent, use a singular pronoun.

▶ *Every* **nut and bolt** was in *its* place for the inspection.

When a compound antecedent is joined by *or* or *nor,* the pronoun should agree with the noun closer to the verb.

▶ Either the panda or the sea otters should have ~~its~~ *their* new habitat soon.

▶ Neither the string quartet nor the soprano needed ~~their~~ *her* sheet music.

7g Use a singular or plural pronoun to refer to a collective noun, depending on the meaning.

A *collective noun* names a group of people or things acting together or individually (*herd, class, team*) and may be referred to by a singular or plural pronoun depending on your intended meaning. When you refer to a group acting together as a unit, use a singular pronoun.

▶ The *wolf pack* surrounds *its* quarry.

   The pack is acting as a unit.

When you refer to the members of the group as acting individually, use a plural pronoun.

▶ After the false alarm, the *bomb squad* returned to *their* homes.

   The members of the squad acted individually.

EXERCISE 7.2: *Answers*

1. Neither the many species of dinosaurs nor the flightless dodo bird could prevent its own extinction.
2. A team of researchers might disagree on their conclusions . . .
3. Correct
4. In one way, animals resemble plants: Some are "weeds" because they have . . .

EXERCISE 7.2

Correct any errors in pronoun-antecedent agreement in the following sentences. Some sentences may be correct as written.

▶ Every scientist has ~~their~~ *his or her* own idea about the state of the environment.

1. Neither the many species of dinosaurs nor the flightless dodo bird could prevent their own extinction.
2. A team of researchers might disagree on its conclusions about the disappearance of the dinosaur.
3. However, most believe that their findings indicate the dodo died out because of competition from other species.

4. In one way, animals resemble plants: Some are "weeds" because it has the ability to thrive under many conditions.
5. Each species that cannot withstand their competitors may be doomed to extinction.
6. When a "weed" and a delicate native species compete for its survival, the native species usually loses.
7. If the snail darter and the spotted owl lose their fight to survive, should humans care?
8. Everyone should be more concerned about the extinction of plants and animals than they seem to be.
9. Every extinction has their effect on other species.
10. The earth has experienced several mass extinctions in its history, but another would take their toll on the quality of human life.

5. Each species that cannot withstand its competitors . . .
6. When a "weed" and a delicate native species compete for their survival . . .
7. Correct
8. People should be more concerned . . .
9. Every extinction has its effect on other species.
10. . . . but another would take its toll . . .

PRONOUN CASE

Most of the time, you will know automatically which form or *case* of a pronoun to use: the **subjective, objective,** or **possessive** case. A pronoun's case indicates its function in a sentence. When a pronoun functions as a subject in a sentence, the subjective case (*I*) is used. When a pronoun functions as a **direct object,** an **indirect object,** or an **object of a preposition,** the objective case (*me*) is used. When a pronoun indicates ownership, the possessive case (*mine*) is used.

A **direct object** receives the action of the verb: *He drove me home.*

Subjective Case	*Objective Case*	*Possessive Case*
I	me	my, mine
we	us	our, ours
you	you	your, yours
he, she, it	him, her, it	his, her, hers, its
they	them	their, theirs
who	whom	whose

An **indirect object** indicates to or for whom an action is performed: *I gave her the keys.*

An **object of a preposition** is a word or phrase that follows a preposition: *with him, above the table.*

Use the following guidelines to correct errors in pronoun case.

7h **Read the sentence aloud without the noun and the word *and* to decide which pronoun to use in a compound construction (*Yolanda and I, Maria and me*).**

INCORRECT   Yolanda and me graduated from high school last year.

If you mentally delete *Yolanda and,* the sentence sounds wrong: *Me graduated from high school last year.*

REVISED   Yolanda and I graduated from high school last year.

If you mentally delete *Yolanda and,* the sentence sounds correct: *I graduated from high school last year.*

INCORRECT   The mayor presented the citizenship award to Mrs. King and I.

If you delete *Mrs. King and,* the sentence sounds wrong: *The mayor presented the citizenship award to I.*

REVISED   The mayor presented the citizenship award to Mrs. King and me.

If you delete *Mrs. King and,* the sentence sounds correct: *The mayor presented the citizenship award to me.*

7i **Read the sentence aloud with the pronoun as the subject when a pronoun follows a form of the verb** *be* (*is, are, was, were*).

INCORRECT   The leader is him.

If you substitute *him* for *the leader,* the sentence sounds wrong: *Him is the leader.*

REVISED   The leader is he.

If you substitute *he* for *the leader,* the sentence sounds correct: *He is the leader.*

▶   The best singer in the group is ~~her~~. *she*

7j **Read the sentence aloud without the noun to determine whether** *we* **or** *us* **should come before a noun.**

▶   If we hikers frighten them, the bears may attack.

If you mentally delete *hikers,* the sentence sounds correct: *If we frighten them, the bears may attack.*

▶   The older children never paid attention to us kindergartners.

If you mentally delete *kindergartners,* the sentence sounds correct: *The older children never paid attention to us.*

7k **Choose the correct pronoun form for a comparison using** *than* **or** *as* **by mentally adding the verb that is implied.**

INCORRECT   Alexandra is a better athlete than me [am].

CORRECT   Alexandra is a better athlete than I [am].

An **object** is the target or recipient of the action described by the verb: *I gave her the keys.*

▶   Juan reads as fast as ~~him~~. *he*

An **object of a preposition** is a word or phrase that follows a preposition: *with him, above the table.*

7l **Use** *who* **or** *whoever* **when the pronoun functions as the subject of a sentence. Use** *whom* **or** *whomever* **when the pronoun functions as the object of a verb or preposition.**

case

To decide whether to use *who* or *whom* in a question, answer the question yourself by using the words *he* or *him* or *she* or *her*. If you use *he* or *she* in the answer, you should use *who* in the question. If you use *him* or *her* in the answer, use *whom* in the question.

QUESTION	(*Who, Whom*) photocopied the article?
ANSWER	*She* photocopied the article.
CORRECT PRONOUN	*Who* photocopied the article?

QUESTION	To (*who, whom*) is that question addressed?
ANSWER	It is addressed to *him*.
CORRECT PRONOUN	To *whom* is that question addressed?

Similarly, to decide whether to use *who* or *whom* in a **dependent clause,** turn the dependent clause into a question. The pronoun you use to answer that question will tell you whether *who* or *whom* should appear in the clause.

> who
> ▶ Aphra Behn's *Oronooko* dramatizes the life of a slave ~~whom~~ came from African
> royalty.

> If you ask the question (*Who, whom*) *came from African royalty?* the answer, *He came from African royalty,* indicates that the correct pronoun is *who*.

> whom
> ▶ The leader ~~who~~ we seek must unite the community.

> If you ask the question (*Who, whom*) *do we seek?* the answer, *We seek him,* indicates that the correct pronoun is *whom*.

A **dependent clause** contains a subject and a verb but does not express a complete thought.

7m Use a possessive pronoun to modify a gerund.

> ▶ *His moralizing* has never been welcome.

The possessive pronoun *his* modifies the gerund *moralizing*.

Gerunds are often confused with **participles** because both end in *-ing*.

PARTICIPLE	Teenagers across the United States watched *them singing* on the *Ed Sullivan Show.*

The teenagers watched them, not the singing.

GERUND	The professor discovered *their cheating* on the final exam.

The cheating was discovered, not the students doing the cheating.

A **gerund** is an *-ing* form of a verb that functions as a noun (*complaining, jogging*).

A **participle** is an *-ing* or *-ed* form of a verb that is used as an adjective (*the terrifying monster*) or with a helping verb to indicate tense (*he was running away*). Pronouns used with participles should be in the objective case; pronouns used with gerunds should be in the possessive case.

EXERCISE 7.3: *Answers*

1. Whoever discovers . . .
2. Correct
3. Correct
4. . . . many Kentucky cavers hoped to make a fortune from their spelunking.
5. Floyd Collins was one Kentucky native who searched . . .
6. In January of 1925, a falling rock trapped Collins, who . . .
7. When his brothers found him, Collins and they worked . . .
8. For several days, the most famous man in Kentucky was he. (*Or:* For several days, he was . . .)
9. Correct
10. Their failing to save Collins was a terrible tragedy . . .

EXERCISE 7.4: *Possible Revision*

Lady Mary Wortley Montagu, **who** was a wealthy aristocrat, was one of the eighteenth century's most interesting characters. Few women then were as well educated as **she. Parents** wanted their **daughters** to be charming, not intellectual, so Lady Mary secretly taught herself Latin. When her husband was appointed ambassador to Turkey, she and he traveled there together [*correct*]. Her letters to friends in London, which were later published, were filled with detail [*correct*]. She described **the atmosphere of a Turkish bath** so vividly that it became a popular setting for paintings and literature. She also learned that

EXERCISE 7.3

Correct any errors in pronoun case in the following sentences. Some sentences may be correct as written.

▶ Cave explorers, ~~whom~~ *who* are called "spelunkers," sometimes find underground rooms no one has seen before.

1. Whomever discovers a large cave is usually able to attract tourists.
2. Much of Kentucky's Mammoth Cave was explored in the 1830s by Stephen Bishop, a slave who worked as a cave guide.
3. Few spelunkers today are better known than he.
4. Following the success of Mammoth Cave, many Kentucky cavers hoped to make a fortune from them spelunking.
5. Floyd Collins was one Kentucky native whom searched his property for caves.
6. In January of 1925, a falling rock trapped Collins, whom was spelunking in a narrow passage in Sand Cave.
7. When his brothers found him, Collins and them worked unsuccessfully to free his trapped leg.
8. For several days, the most famous man in Kentucky was him.
9. The plea to rescue Floyd Collins was answered by whoever could travel to rural Kentucky.
10. Them failing to save Collins was a terrible tragedy for his family and the rescuers.

EXERCISE 7.4

Correct any errors in pronoun reference, agreement, and case in the following paragraph. Some sentences may be correct as written.

▶ ~~Her~~ *She* and her husband married for love, which was unusual at the time.

Lady Mary Wortley Montagu, whom was a wealthy aristocrat, was one of the eighteenth century's most interesting characters. Few women then were as well educated as her. Every parent wanted their daughter to be charming, not intellectual, so Lady Mary secretly taught herself Latin. When her husband was appointed ambassador to Turkey, she and he traveled there together. Her letters to friends in London, which were later published, were filled with detail. She described a Turkish bath's atmosphere so vividly that it became a popular setting for paintings and literature. She also learned that smallpox was rare in Turkey. Of the Turkish people she met, most had gotten his or her immunity to smallpox from a kind of inoculation. This had an effect on Lady Mary herself. Lady Mary's children were among the first British citizens who were inoculated against it.

8   SHIFTS AND MIXED CONSTRUCTIONS

A **shift** is a sudden, unexpected change in point of view, verb tense, voice, mood, or level of diction that may confuse your readers. Shifting from a direct to an indirect question or quotation can also confuse readers. A **mixed construction** is a sentence containing parts that do not sensibly fit together. This chapter will help you identify and correct shifts and mixed constructions in your sentences.

smallpox was rare in Turkey [*correct*]. Of the Turkish people she met, most had gotten **their** immunity to smallpox from a kind of inoculation. **This knowledge** had an effect on Lady Mary herself. Lady Mary's children were among the first British citizens who were inoculated against **the terrible disease.**

SHIFTS

8a Refer to yourself, your audience, and the people you are writing about in a consistent way.

Person shows the writer's point of view. Personal pronouns indicate whether the subject is the speaker (first person: *I, we*), the person spoken to (second person: *you*), or the person or thing spoken about (third person: *he, she, it, they, one*). (For more on person, see 1b and Chapter 4, p. 77.)

INCONSISTENT   *I* discovered that *you* could touch some of the museum exhibits.

Notice that the writer shifts from first-person *I* to the second-person *you.*

CONSISTENT   *I* discovered that *I* could touch some of the museum exhibits.

The writer uses the first-person *I* consistently within the sentence.

> When people study a foreign language, ~~you~~ *they* also learn about another culture.

8b Maintain consistency in verb tense throughout a paragraph or an essay, unless the meaning requires you to change tenses.

INCONSISTENT   The virus *mutated* so quickly that it *develops* a resistance to most vaccines.

The sentence shifts from past to present.

REVISED   The virus *mutates* so quickly that it *develops* a resistance to most vaccines.

Shifts between the present and past tense are among the most common shifts writers make.

> The city's crime rate continues to drop, but experts disagree*d* on the reasons.

8c Change verb tense when you want to indicate an actual time change.

Use the present tense for events that occur in the present; use the past tense for events that occurred in the past. When the time changes, be sure to change the tense. Notice the intentional shifts in the following passage (the verbs are in italics).

Every spring migratory birds *return* to cooler climates to raise their young. This year a pair of bluejays *is occupying* a nest in my yard, and I *spy* on them. The hatchlings *are growing* larger and *developing* feathers. Last spring, robins *built* the nest that the jays now *call* home, and I *watched* them every morning until the young birds *left* home for the last time.

As the events switch from this year (present) to the previous year (past), the writer changes from the present tense (*is occupying*) to the past tense (*built*). (For more on verb tense, see 1c and 27a.)

8d Use a consistent voice.

Needless shifts between the **active voice** and **passive voice** can disorient readers and create wordy sentences.

In the **active voice**, the subject of the sentence performs the action.

In the **passive voice**, the subject receives the action.

> The researchers gave one
> ~~One~~ group of volunteers ~~was given~~ a placebo, and ~~the researchers~~ they treated another group with the new drug.

> Drought and windstorms made farming impossible, and many families ~~were forced~~ the specter of starvation forced to leave Oklahoma. ~~by the specter of starvation.~~

To change a sentence from the passive voice to the active voice, make the performer of the action the subject of the sentence. The original subject of the sentence becomes the direct object. Delete the form of the verb *be*.

PASSIVE	The restraining order was signed by the judge.
ACTIVE	The judge signed the restraining order.

For more on voice, see 1c and 6d.

8e Avoid sudden shifts from indirect to direct questions or quotations.

An indirect question tells what a question is or was.

INDIRECT QUESTION	The defense attorney asked where I was on the evening of May 10.
DIRECT QUESTION	"Where were you on the evening of May 10?"

Avoid shifting from direct to indirect questions.

> he
> Sal asked what could ~~I~~ do to solve the problem.

8f Use a consistent mood throughout a paragraph or an essay.

Mood indicates whether the sentence states a fact or asks a question (**indicative mood**), gives a command or direction (**imperative mood**), or expresses a condition contrary to fact, a wish, or a suggestion (**subjunctive mood**). The subjunctive mood is also used for hypothetical situations or impossible or unlikely events. (For more on mood, see 1c.)

INCONSISTENT

You shouldn't expect to learn ballroom dancing immediately, and remember that even Fred Astaire had to start somewhere. First, find a qualified instructor. Then, you should not be embarrassed even if everyone else seems more graceful than you are. Finally, keep your goal in mind, and you need to practice, practice, practice.

This paragraph contains shifts between the indicative and imperative moods.

CONSISTENT

Don't expect to learn ballroom dancing immediately, and remember that even Fred Astaire had to start somewhere. First, find a qualified instructor. Then, don't be embarrassed if everyone else seems more graceful than you are. Finally, keep your goal in mind, and practice, practice, practice.

This revised paragraph uses the imperative mood consistently.

8g Use a consistent level of diction.

Your level of diction can range from formal to informal. The level you choose should be appropriate for your audience, your subject matter, and your purpose for writing. As you revise your essays, look for inappropriate shifts in diction, such as from a formal to an informal tone or vice versa.

William H. Whyte's studies of human behavior in public space yielded a number of surprises. Perhaps most unexpected was the revelation that people seem to be drawn toward, rather than driven from, crowded spaces. They tend to congregate near the entrances of stores or on street corners. Plazas and shopping districts crowded with pedestrians attract more pedestrians. For some reason, people seem to ~~get a charge out of hanging out where lots of other folks are hanging out, too.~~ *enjoy gathering together in public spaces.*

For academic writing, including class assignments and research papers, use formal language. (For more on levels of diction, see Chapter 8, p. 194).

EXERCISE 8.1

Correct the shifts in person, verb tense, voice, mood, and level of diction in the following sentences.

▶ Experts continue to break new ground in child psychology, and their research. ~~has been studied by many parents.~~ *many parents have studied*

1. A new idea about the development of children's personalities had surprised many American psychologists because it challenges widely accepted theories.
2. We wondered whether our professor knew of the new theory and did she agree with it.
3. Personality is believed by some experts to be the result of parental care, but other specialists feel that biology influences personality more strongly.
4. Most parents think you have a major influence on your child's behavior.
5. The new theory suggests that children's peers are a heck of a lot more influential than parents.
6. Peer acceptance is strongly desired by children, and they want to be different from adults.
7. If adults were to think about their childhood experiences, they realize that this idea has merit.
8. Most adults recall that, in childhood, your friends' opinions were extremely important to you.
9. The way people behave with family members is often different from the way we act with our friends.
10. Jittery moms and dads would be really, really relieved if this hypothesis were proven.

EXERCISE 8.2

Correct the shifts in person, verb tense, voice, mood, and level of diction in the following paragraph.

▶ Some artists long ago used techniques that still ~~surprised~~ *surprise* modern students of their work.

Museum visitors can see paintings by the seventeenth-century Dutch artist Jan Vermeer, but you cannot see how he achieved his remarkable effects. Most of his paintings showed simply furnished household rooms. The people and objects in these rooms seem so real that the paintings resembled photographs. Vermeer's use of perspective and light would also contribute to the paintings' realism. Some art historians believe he used a gizmo called a *camera obscura*. This machine projected an image onto a flat surface so you could draw it. For most experts, Vermeer's possible use of technological aids does not make his totally fabulous results less impressive. It is agreed by art historians that the paintings are masterpieces. Vermeer's paintings are admired even more now than they are in his own lifetime.

MIXED CONSTRUCTIONS

8h Make sure clauses and phrases fit together logically.

A mixed construction contains phrases or clauses that do not work together logically and that cause confusion in meaning.

> MIXED   The fact that the marathon is twenty-six miles, a length that explains why I never have finished it.

The sentence starts with a subject (*The fact*) followed by a dependent clause (*that the marathon is twenty-six miles*). The sentence needs a predicate to complete the independent clause; instead it includes a noun (*a length*) and another dependent clause (*that explains why I never have finished it*). The independent clause that begins with *The fact* is never completed.

> REVISED   The marathon is twenty-six miles long, which is why I never have finished it.

In the revision, the parts of the sentence work together.

To avoid mixed constructions in your writing, it often helps to check the words that connect clauses and phrases, especially prepositions and conjunctions.

8i Make subjects and predicates consistent.

Faulty predication occurs when a subject does not work grammatically with its predicate.

> FAULTY   The most valued trait in an employee is a person who is loyal.

A person is not a trait.

> REVISED   The most valued trait in an employee is loyalty.

>   *the number of people who can afford*
> ▶ Rising health care costs decrease health insurance. ~~for many people.~~

Costs do not decrease health insurance.

8j Avoid the constructions *is when* or *is where* or *reason is . . . because.*

> FAULTY   Indigestion is when you cannot digest food.
> REVISED   Indigestion is the inability to digest food.

>   *the attraction of*   *for*
> ▶ Gravitation is ~~where~~ one body ~~is being attracted by~~ another.

> ▶ ~~The reason~~ I enjoy horseback riding ~~is~~ because it provides outdoor exercise.

EXERCISE 8.2: *Possible Revision*

Museum visitors can see paintings by the seventeenth-century Dutch artist Jan Vermeer, but **they** cannot see how he achieved his remarkable effects. Most of his paintings **show** simply furnished household rooms. The people and objects in these rooms seem so real that the paintings **resemble** photographs. Vermeer's use of perspective and light also **contributes** to the paintings' realism. Some art historians believe he used a **device** called a *camera obscura.* This machine projected an image onto a flat surface so **an artist** could draw it. For most experts, Vermeer's possible use of technological aids does not make his **brilliant** results less impressive. **Art historians agree** that the paintings are masterpieces. **His** paintings are admired even more now than they **were** in Vermeer's own lifetime.

EXERCISE 8.3: *Possible Revisions*

1. Because there are already an estimated 200,000 to 400,000 people building Web sites for a living right now, many young people also want to join this field.
2. Business is booming for independent Web development shops, an industry that grows larger each year.
3. Many companies are going online because they want to communicate with people who use the Web.
4. Once the domain of computer hackers, the online world has become routine for many nontechnical people.
5. Some people think the industry standards require that you know C++ or other programming languages to work with computers.
6. The information technology department is the part of a company where Web projects are often managed.
7. To figure out where in a corporation to look for a Web job, consult its personnel department.
8. Applicants for computer jobs should consider relocating to San Francisco or New York, the primary centers for technology.
9. The most important qualification for applicants is Web experience.
10. By creating a personal Web page, you increase your firsthand knowledge of the Internet.

EXERCISE 8.3

Correct the mixed constructions in the following sentences.

▶ The job that I want is ~~a person who designs~~ designing Web sites.

1. Because there are already an estimated 200,000 to 400,000 people building Web sites for a living right now explains why many young people also want to join this field.
2. The fact that business is booming for independent Web development shops, an industry that grows larger each year.
3. The reason many companies are going online is because they want to communicate with people who use the Web.
4. The online domain of computer hackers has become routine for many nontechnical people.
5. Some people think the industry standards expect that you know C++ or other programming languages to work with computers.
6. The information technology department is where a company hires people to manage Web projects.
7. To figure out where in a corporation to look for a Web job, the personnel department is a resource.
8. Applicants for computer jobs located in San Francisco and New York are the primary centers for technology.
9. The most important qualification is applicants with Web experience.
10. By creating a personal Web page increases firsthand knowledge of the Internet.

9 ADJECTIVES AND ADVERBS

Adjectives and adverbs are powerful. Used appropriately, they can add precision and force to your writing, as the following excerpt demonstrates.

> Seated cross-legged on a brocade pillow, wrapped in burgundy robes, was a short, rotund man with a shiny pate. He looked very old and very tired. Chhongba bowed reverently, spoke briefly to him in the Sherpa tongue, and indicated for us to come forward. —Jon Krakauer, *Into Thin Air*

Adjectives modify nouns or pronouns and indicate which one, what kind, or how many. **Adverbs** modify verbs, adjectives, other adverbs, clauses, or entire sentences and indicate how, when, where, how often, or to what extent. (See also 1d and 1e.)

The two most common errors involving adjectives and adverbs occur when writers use (1) an adjective instead of an adverb (or vice versa) and (2) the wrong form of an adjective or adverb in a comparison. Use the following guidelines to identify and correct these and other common errors in your writing.

9a Use adverbs, not adjectives, to modify verbs, adjectives, or other adverbs.

Although in conversation you may often use adjectives in place of adverbs, you should be careful in your writing to use adverbs to modify verbs, adjectives, or other adverbs.

▶ Those pants are ~~awful~~ *awfully* expensive.

▶ The headlights shone ~~bright~~ *brightly*.

9b Use adjectives, not adverbs, after linking verbs.

Linking verbs, often forms of *be* and other verbs such as *feel, look, make,* and *seem,* express a state of being. A linking verb takes a **subject complement,** a word group that completes or renames the subject of the sentence. Verbs such as *feel* and *look* can also be action verbs. When they function as action verbs in a sentence, they may be modified by an adverb.

If you are not sure whether a word should be an adjective or adverb, determine how it is used in the sentence. If the word modifies a noun, it should be an adjective.

ADJECTIVE   Our *waiter* looked *slow*.

Slow modifies the word *waiter,* a noun. In this sentence, *looked* is a linking verb.

ADVERB   Our waiter *looked slowly* for some menus.

In this sentence, *looked* is expressing an action and is not a linking verb; *slowly* modifies *looked*.

9c Use *good* and *bad* as adjectives; use *well* and *badly* as adverbs.

▶ Einstein was not a *good student*.

The adjective *good* modifies the noun *student*.

▶ Einstein did not *perform well* in school.

The adverb *well* modifies the verb *perform*.

▶ He did ~~bad~~ *badly* in the leading role.

The adverb *badly* modifies the verb *did*.

When you are describing someone's health, *well* can also function as an adjective.

▶ The disease was in remission, but the *patients* were not yet *well*.

9d Be careful not to use adjectives such as *real* and *sure* to modify adverbs or other adjectives.

▶ The produce was crisp and ~~real~~ *really* fresh.

The adverb *really* modifies the adjective *fresh*.

9e   Avoid double negatives.

A sentence with two negative words or phrases contains a **double negative,** which conveys a positive meaning. Do not use two negatives in a sentence unless you want to express a positive meaning (for example, *not uncommon* means "common").

▶ The company is not doing ~~nothing~~ *anything* to promote its incentive plan.

▶ No one under eighteen ~~can't~~ *can* vote in the presidential election.

POSITIVE MEANING INTENDED

Athletic sportswear is not uncommon as casual attire.

9f   Use the comparative form of adjectives and adverbs to compare two things; use the superlative form to compare three or more things.

Adjectives and adverbs can be used to compare two or more persons, objects, actions, or ideas. The **comparative** form of an adjective or adverb compares two items. The **superlative** form compares three or more items. Use the list below to check the comparative and superlative forms of most regular adjectives and adverbs in your sentences.

	Comparatives	*Superlatives*
One-syllable adjectives and adverbs	Add *-er: colder, faster*	Add *-est: coldest, fastest*
Two-syllable adjectives	Add *-er: greasier**	Add *-est: greasiest*
Adjectives with three or more syllables or adverbs ending in *-ly*	Add *more* in front of the word: *more beauti-, ful, more quickly*	Add *most* in front of the word: *most beauti-ful, most quickly*

*To form the comparative and superlative forms of adjectives ending in *-y,* change the *y* to *i* and add *-er* or *-est.*

Irregular adjectives and adverbs form their comparative and superlative forms in unpredictable ways, as the following list illustrates.

	Comparative	*Superlative*
Adjectives		
good	better	best
bad	worse	worst
little	less	least
Adverbs		
well	better	best
badly	worse	worst

	Comparative	Superlative
Words That Function as Adjectives and Adverbs		
many	more	most
some	more	most
much	more	most

Do not use comparative or superlative forms with absolute concepts, such as *unique* and *perfect*. Something cannot be more or less unique, for example; it is either unique or not unique.

>   *a*
> This is ~~the most~~ unique solution to the pollution problem.
>   ^

9g Check your comparisons to be sure they are complete when using comparative and superlative forms.

An incomplete comparison can leave your reader confused about what is being compared.

INCOMPLETE	The Internet works more efficiently.
REVISED	For sending messages, the Internet works more efficiently than the postal service.
INCOMPLETE	The catcher sustained the most crippling knee injury.
REVISED	The catcher sustained the most crippling knee injury of his career.

9h Do not use *more* or *most* with the *-er* or *-est* form of an adjective or adverb.

> The hypothesis must be ~~more~~ clearer.

EXERCISE 9.1

Correct any errors involving adjectives and adverbs in the following sentences.

>   *than any other medium.*
> Events on television seem important because television has more influence/
>   ^

1. Television can have a more immediate impact because it is mainly visual.
2. Televised images from Vietnam made some Americans feel terribly about the war.
3. Military groups are now real careful about allowing reporters to film armed conflicts for television.
4. Politicians who look badly on television tend to perform badly in polls.
5. In 1960, John F. Kennedy was viewed more positively after a televised debate.
6. More Americans get their news from television today.
7. Newspapers may describe important news stories clearer than television.
8. While television is better than newspapers at reporting stories with a strong visual element, it is worst at analyzing them.

EXERCISE 9.1: *Answers*

1. Television can have a more immediate impact than a newspaper . . .
2. Televised images . . . Americans feel terrible . . .
3. Military groups are now really careful . . .
4. Politicians who look bad on television tend to perform badly in polls.
5. In 1960, John F. Kennedy was viewed more positively than his opponent [*or* Richard Nixon] . . .
6. More Americans get their news from television today than from any other source.
7. Newspapers may describe important news stories more clearly than television.
8. While television is better . . . strong visual element, it is worse at analyzing them.
9. News stories that are not visual may be treated very superficially on television.
10. People should never assume . . .

9. News stories that are not visual may be treated very superficial on television.
10. People shouldn't never assume that television provides all the information they need.

EXERCISE 9.2

Correct any errors involving adjectives and adverbs in the following paragraph. Some sentences may be correct as written.

▶ Originating in China, *feng shui* is a traditionally~~-~~art of balancing elements to achieve harmony.

   Feng shui is taken very serious in many Asian societies. Some Hong Kong business executives, for example, will not feel comfortably working in an office until it has been approved by a *feng shui* master. Other people are more interested in *feng shui* for its elegance. A room designed with this idea in mind looks tranquilly. The name *feng shui* means "wind and water," and balancing elements is the more important aspect of the art. Some people believe that this balance brings good luck. Others will admit only that surroundings can have a psychologically effect. It is easier to feel comfortable in a room designed according to *feng shui* principles. The placement of doors, windows, and furnishings contributes to the peaceful effect. Whether *feng shui* is magic or simple great interior design, something about it seems to work.

EXERCISE 9.2: *Answers*

Feng shui is taken very **seriously** in many Asian societies. Some Hong Kong business executives, for example, will not feel **comfortable** working in an office until it has been approved by a *feng shui* master. Other people are more interested in *feng shui* for its elegance [*correct*]. A room designed with this idea in mind looks **tranquil.** The name *feng shui* means "wind and water," and balancing elements is the **most** important aspect of the art. Some people believe that this balance brings good luck [*correct*]. Others will admit only that surroundings can have a **psychological** effect. It is easier to feel comfortable in a room designed according to *feng shui* principles **than in an ordinary room** [*Alternative:* It is easy to feel comfortable in a room designed according to *feng shui* principles.]. The placement of doors, windows, and furnishings contributes to the peaceful effect [*correct*]. Whether *feng shui* is magic or **simply** great interior design, something about it seems to work.

10 MISPLACED AND DANGLING MODIFIERS

A **modifier** is a word or group of words that describes, changes, qualifies, or limits the meaning of another word or group of words in a sentence.

▶ The contestant *smiled delightedly.*

The adverb *delightedly* modifies the verb *smiled.*

▶ *Pretending to be surprised,* he greeted the guests.

The adjective phrase *Pretending to be surprised* modifies the pronoun *he.*

Modifiers that are carefully placed in sentences give your readers a clear picture of the details you want to convey. However, when a sentence contains a **misplaced modifier,** it is hard for the reader to tell which word or group of words the modifier is supposed to be describing.

10a Place modifiers close to the words they describe.

MISPLACED   The mayor *chided* the pedestrians for jaywalking *angrily.*

The adverb *angrily* should be closer to the verb it modifies, *chided.* Here, the adverb appears to be modifying *jaywalking,* so the sentence is confusing.

REVISED The mayor *angrily chided* the pedestrians for jaywalking.

MISPLACED The press *reacted* to the story leaked from the Pentagon *with horror*.

The adverb phrase *with horror* should explain how the press reacted, not how the story was leaked, so the modifier should be closer to the verb *reacted*.

REVISED The press *reacted with horror* to the story leaked from the Pentagon.

10b Make sure each modifier clearly modifies only one word or phrase in a sentence.

When a modifier is placed near or next to the word or phrase it modifies, it may also be near another word it could conceivably modify. When a modifier's placement may cause such ambiguity, rewrite the sentence, placing the modifier so that it clearly refers to the word or phrase it is supposed to modify.

UNCLEAR The film's attempt to portray war accurately depicts a survivor's anguish.

Does the film attempt to portray war accurately, or does it accurately depict a survivor's anguish? The following revisions eliminate the uncertainty.

REVISED *In its* ~~The film's~~ attempt to portray war accurately *, the film* depicts a survivor's anguish.

REVISED The *film* ~~film's attempt to portray war~~ accurately depicts a survivor's anguish, *in its attempt to portray war realistically.*

10c Revise a dangling modifier by rewriting the sentence.

A **dangling modifier** is a word or phrase that does not modify or refer to anything in a sentence. Instead, it seems to modify something that has been left out of the sentence. A dangling modifier can make the meaning of a sentence unclear, inaccurate, or even comical. Most dangling modifiers appear at the beginning or end of sentences.

DANGLING After singing a thrilling aria, the crowd surged toward the stage.

This sentence suggests that the crowd sang the aria.

DANGLING Laying an average of ten eggs a day, the neighboring farmer is proud of his henhouse.

This sentence suggests that the farmer lays eggs.

To revise a sentence with a dangling modifier, follow these steps.

1. Identify the word or words that the modifier is supposed to modify.

2. Revise the sentence to correct the confusion by either changing the modifier into a clause with its own subject and verb or by rewriting the sentence so the word being modified becomes the subject.

▶ After ~~singing~~ a thrilling aria, the crowd surged toward the stage.
   Pavarotti sang

▶ Laying an average of ten eggs a day, the neighboring farmer ~~is~~ proud of his henhouse.
   his prize chickens give ... *reason to be*

EXERCISE 10.1

Correct any misplaced or dangling modifiers in the following sentences.

▶ Hoping to get a message from outer space, a huge telescope. ~~has been built.~~
   scientists have built

1. Solar systems exist throughout the galaxy like our own.
2. So far, no proof on other planets of the existence of life forms has been found.
3. A tremendously powerful telescope searches distant stars for signs of life in the Caribbean.
4. Astronomers monitor signals coming from other parts of the solar system carefully.
5. Wondering whether humans are alone in the universe, the telescope may provide answers.
6. Most of the signals have been caused by cell phone and satellite interference received so far.
7. While trying to intercept signals from other planets, a signal has also been sent from earth.
8. The message is on its way to other parts of our galaxy, containing information about earth.
9. The message will take twenty thousand years to reach its destination or more.
10. A signal sent to earth similarly would take a long time to reach us.

EXERCISE 10.2

Correct any misplaced or dangling modifiers in the following paragraph. Some sentences may be correct as written.

▶ The measurement is now based on atomic vibrations. ~~of one second~~
   of one second

Making sure standard weights and measures are the same all over the world is an important task. To trade internationally, a kilogram in Mexico must weigh the same as a kilogram in Japan. In the past, countries set standards for weighing and measuring individually. One English king declared a yard to be the distance from his nose to his thumb egotistically. Weight was once measured in barleycorns, so unethical merchants soaked barleycorns to make them heavier in water. Today, the metric system is the worldwide standard, and the weight of the U.S. pound is based even on the standard kilogram. In France a cylinder is the world standard kilogram made of platinum.

Securely, this official kilogram is kept in an airtight container. Nevertheless, losing a few billionths of a gram of weight each year, world standards might eventually be affected. Hoping to find a permanent solution, scientists want to base the kilogram measurement on an unchanging natural phenomenon.

weighs the same as a kilogram in Japan. In the past, countries set standards **individually** for weighing and measuring. One English king **egotistically** declared a yard to be the distance from his nose to his thumb. Weight was once measured in barleycorns, so unethical merchants soaked barleycorns **in water** to make them heavier. Today, the metric system is the worldwide standard, and **even** the weight of the U.S. pound is based on the standard kilogram. In France, a cylinder **made of platinum** is the world standard kilogram. **This** official kilogram is kept **securely** in an airtight container. Nevertheless, losing a few billionths of a gram of weight each year, **the platinum kilogram might eventually affect world standards.** Hoping to find a permanent solution, scientists want to base the kilogram measurement on an unchanging natural phenomenon [*correct*].

11 END PUNCTUATION

The end of a sentence can be marked with a period (.), a question mark (?), or an exclamation point (!).

11a Use a period to mark the end of a sentence that makes a statement, gives an instruction, or includes an indirect question; use periods with most abbreviations.

An indirect question is a statement that reports what was asked or is being asked: *He asked where the classroom was.*

Writers seldom omit the period at the end of a sentence that makes a state-ment or gives directions.

STATEMENT	Amnesty International investigates human rights violations.
INSTRUCTION	Use as little water as possible during the drought.

Writers sometimes mistake an indirect question for a direct one, however.

▶ Most visitors want to know where the dinosaur bones were found?.

This sentence states what question was asked; it does not ask the question directly.

Many abbreviations use periods (*M.D., B.C.*). Here are a few exceptions.

NAMES OF ORGANIZATIONS: IBM, CIA, NATO

NAMES OF COUNTRIES: USA, UK

If you are not sure whether an abbreviation should include periods, check a dictionary.

When an abbreviation that uses periods ends a sentence, an additional period is not needed.

▶ The ideal candidate for this job has an M.B.A./

Note: The Modern Language Association (MLA) recommends omitting periods in abbreviations that consist of capital letters (*BC*) but including periods in abbrevi-ations that consist of lowercase letters (*a.m.*).

11b Use a question mark to end a sentence that asks a direct question.

DIRECT QUESTION   Why was the flight delayed?

When a question is also a quotation, the question mark is placed within the quotation marks.

▶ "What did she want?"⸮ Marcia asked.

(See also 15d.)

11c Use an exclamation point to end a sentence that expresses a strong emotion or a forceful command.

▶ Altering experimental results to make them conform to a hypothesis is never ethical!

Use exclamation points sparingly; they lose their impact when used too frequently.

▶ Government officials immediately suspected terrorism!.

EXERCISE 11.1

Correct any errors in the use of end punctuation marks in the following sentences. Some sentences may be correct as written.

▶ Is it possible that hemophilia in the Russian czar's family contributed to the

  Russian Revolution⸮

1. When the daughters of Queen Victoria of England, who carried the gene for hemophilia, married royalty in Germany and Russia, those royal families inherited hemophilia as well?
2. The Russian czar's only son and heir to the throne suffered from hemophilia.
3. You might ask if internal bleeding can occur when a hemophiliac receives a bruise?
4. Czar Nicholas and his wife Alexandra often saw their little boy in terrible pain!
5. A phony monk named Rasputin eased the child's pain, but was he a gifted healer or just a con man.

EXERCISE 11.1: *Answers*

1. When the daughters of Queen Victoria of England . . . those royal families inherited hemophilia as well.
2. Correct
3. You might ask . . . receives a bruise.
4. Czar Nicholas . . . in terrible pain.
5. . . . but was he a gifted healer or just a con man?

12 COMMAS

A comma (,) is used to separate parts of a sentence from one another. Commas, when used correctly, make your sentences clear and help readers understand your meaning.

12a Use a comma before a coordinating word (*and, but, for, nor, or, so, yet*) that joins two independent clauses.

▶ The ball flew past the goalie, but the score did not count.

▶ Her dog was enormous, so many people found it threatening.

An **independent clause** contains a subject and verb and can stand alone as a sentence.

12b Use a comma to separate three or more items in a series.

A **series** is a list of three or more items — words, phrases, or clauses.

▶ Dancing, singing, and acting are just a few of her talents.

▶ Sunflowers grew on the hillsides, along the roads, and in the middle of every pasture.

Some writers omit the comma after the final item in a brief series when using a casual or journalistic style. Occasionally this omission can create confusion, so it is better to include the final comma.

> CONFUSING   She insured her valuable heirlooms, watches and jewelry.

> Do her heirlooms consist entirely of watches and jewelry, or did she insure three kinds of items?

> CLEAR   She insured her valuable heirlooms, watches, and jewelry.

A comma is not used after the last item in a series.

▶ Aphids, slugs, and beetles⸝can severely damage a crop.

(See also 13c on when to use semicolons to separate items in a series.)

12c Use a comma to separate two or more adjectives that modify the same noun when they are not joined by a coordinating word.

▶ Rescue workers found the frightened, hungry child.

To be sure a comma is needed, try reversing the two adjectives. If the phrase still sounds correct when the adjectives are reversed, a comma is needed. If the phrase sounds wrong, a comma is not needed.

▶ The airy, open atrium makes visitors feel at home.

> The phrase *open, airy atrium* sounds right, so a comma is needed.

▶ Local businesses donated the bright red uniforms.

> The phrase *red, bright uniforms* sounds wrong because *bright* modifies *red uniforms* in the original sentence. A comma is not needed.

12d Use a comma to separate introductory words, phrases, and clauses from the rest of a sentence.

> INTRODUCTORY   Above, the sky was a mass of clouds.
> WORD

Without the comma, this sentence would be confusing.

INTRODUCTORY PHRASE	At the start of the project, the researchers were optimistic.
INTRODUCTORY CLAUSE	When alcohol was outlawed, many solid citizens broke the law.

Exception: A comma is not needed after a single word or short phrase or clause when there is no possibility of confusion.

▶ Then a rainbow appeared.

12e Use a comma to set off a nonrestrictive word group from the rest of the sentence.

A **nonrestrictive word group** describes or modifies a word or phrase in a sentence, but it does not change the meaning of the word or phrase. To decide whether a comma is needed, read the sentence without the word group. If the basic meaning is unchanged, a comma is needed.

▶ Most people either love or hate fruitcake, *which is a traditional holiday dessert.*

The meaning of *fruitcake* is not changed by the relative clause *which is a traditional holiday dessert,* so the word group is **nonrestrictive** and a comma is needed.

▶ The child *wearing a tutu* delights in ballet lessons.

The phrase *wearing a tutu* identifies which child delights in ballet lessons, so the word group is **restrictive**, necessary to explain what the word it modifies means, and a comma is not needed.

12f Use a comma to set off parenthetical expressions.

A **parenthetical expression** provides extra information. It can also be a transitional word or phrase (*however, for example, at the beginning*) that is not essential to the meaning of the sentence.

▶ *Furthermore,* his essay had not been proofread.
▶ Islamic countries were, *in fact,* responsible for preserving much classical scientific knowledge.

12g Use commas with dates, addresses, titles, and numbers.

▶ She graduated on June 12, 1994.

When you give only a month and year, a comma is not needed.

▶ She graduated in June 1994.

Place a comma after the date when it appears before the end of the sentence.

▶ Boswell met Johnson on May 16, 1763, in London.

When you give an address within a sentence, do not place a comma between the state and the ZIP code.

▶ Send the package to General Delivery, McPherson, Kansas 67460.

Separate a name from a title with a comma.

▶ The featured speaker was Kate Silverstein, Ph.D.

Use commas in numbers that have more than four digits.

▶ Estimates of the number of protesters ranged from 250,000 to 700,000.

In a number with four digits, the comma is optional: *1500* or *1,500.*

12h Use a comma to separate a direct quotation from the words that explain it.

A direct quotation gives a person's *exact* words, either spoken or written, set off by quotation marks.

▶ She asked, "What's the score?"

Place the comma before the closing quotation mark.

▶ "Wait and see," was his infuriating response.

(See also 15b and 15e.)

12i Use commas to set off the name of someone directly addressed, to set off an echo question, and with a "not" phrase.

DIRECT ADDRESS	"James, answer the question concisely." "Bail has not been granted, your honor."
ECHO QUESTION	More development will require a more expensive infrastructure, won't it?
"NOT" PHRASE	Labor Day, not the autumnal equinox, marks the end of summer for most Americans.

12j Omit unnecessary commas.

As you edit and proofread your papers, watch out for the following common errors in comma usage.

OMIT A COMMA BETWEEN A SUBJECT AND VERB.

      subject   verb

▶ The poet Wilfred Owen, was killed a week before World War I ended.

OMIT A COMMA BETWEEN A VERB AND COMPLEMENT.

             verb   complement

▶ The school referendum is considered, very likely to pass.

> A **complement** is a word or group of words that describes or renames a subject or object.

OMIT A COMMA BETWEEN AN ADJECTIVE AND THE WORD IT MODIFIES.

           adjective noun modified

▶ A growing family needs a large, house.

OMIT A COMMA BETWEEN TWO VERBS IN A COMPOUND PREDICATE.

   compound predicate

▶ We sat, and waited for our punishment.

OMIT A COMMA BETWEEN TWO NOUNS OR PRONOUNS IN A COMPOUND SUBJECT.

        compound subject

▶ Harold Johnson, and Margaret Simpson led the expedition.

OMIT A COMMA BEFORE A COORDINATING WORD JOINING TWO DEPENDENT CLAUSES.

      dependent clause   dependent clause

▶ The band began to play before we arrived, but after the rain stopped.

OMIT A COMMA AFTER THE WORD *THAN* IN A COMPARISON.

▶ The Homestead Act made the cost of land to pioneers less than, the price the government had paid.

OMIT A COMMA AFTER *LIKE* OR *SUCH AS*.

▶ Direct marketing techniques such as, mass mailings and telephone solicitations can be effective.

OMIT COMMAS APPEARING NEXT TO A QUESTION MARK, EXCLAMATION MARK, OR DASH, OR BEFORE AN OPENING PARENTHESIS.

▶ "Where have you been?," she would always ask.

▶ "Stop!," the guard shouted.

EXERCISE 12.1: *Answers* (p. 844)

1. Seneca Village, a crowded shantytown on the Upper West Side, was the home of many poorer black New Yorkers.
2. The city of New York bought the land where the Seneca villagers lived.
3. The land became part of Central Park, and everyone who lived there had to leave in the 1850s.
4. Household items from Seneca Village still turn up in Central Park today, and a museum exhibit . . .
5. In present-day Brooklyn was a middle-class black settlement called Weeksville.
6. James Weeks, an early resident, owned much of the land.
7. Another early landholder, Sylvanus Smith, was a trustee . . .
8. His daughter, Susan Smith McKinney-Steward, was born in Weeksville and was the valedictorian . . .

(Continued on next page)

9. McKinney-Steward became the first female African American physician in New York and the third in the United States.
10. Correct

EXERCISE 12.2: *Answer*

A monument to the Lakota Sioux warrior Crazy Horse is under construction in the Black Hills of South Dakota. Korczak Ziolkowski, a sculptor who also worked on Mount Rush-more, began the project in 1948. Ziolkowski was born on September 6, 1908 — thirty-one years to the day after Crazy Horse died. A Sioux chief asked Ziolkowski if he would create a monu-ment to honor Crazy Horse and other Indian heroes. Ziolkowski designed a sculpture of Crazy Horse on horse-back that, when it is completed, will be the largest statue in the world [*correct*]. The sculpture is being shaped from Thunder-head Mountain, a six-hundred-foot granite rock. Tons of rock have been blasted from the mountain. The sculptor died in 1982, but his widow, children, and grandchildren have car-ried on the work. There has been no government funding, so they have paid for the work entirely with donations and admission fees. By the middle of the twenty-first century, the statue should be fin-ished and will depict the great Sioux hero point-ing at the hills he loved.

▶ Keep spending to a minimum,/— our resources are limited — and throw nothing away.

▶ Fast food,/(which is usually high in fat), is growing in popularity all over the world.

OMIT COMMAS AROUND WORDS THAT RENAME, AND RESTRICT, ANOTHER WORD BEFORE THEM.

If the words are **restrictive** — necessary to explain what the word they modify means — do not enclose them with commas.

▶ The man,/who brought his car in for transmission work,/is a lawyer.

EXERCISE 12.1

Correct any errors in the use of commas in the following sentences. Some sentences may be correct as written.

▶ After slavery was abolished in New York in 1827, several black settlements were
established in what is now New York City.
⌃

1. Seneca Village a crowded shantytown on the Upper West Side was the home of many poorer black New Yorkers.
2. The city of New York, bought the land where the Seneca villagers lived.
3. The land became part of Central Park and everyone, who lived there, had to leave in the 1850s.
4. Household items from Seneca Village still turn up in Central Park today and a museum exhibit was recently devoted to life in the long-gone settlement.
5. In present-day Brooklyn, was a middle-class black settlement called Weeksville.
6. James Weeks, an early resident owned much of the land.
7. Another, early, landholder, Sylvanus Smith, was a trustee of the African Free Schools of Brooklyn.
8. His daughter, Susan Smith McKinney-Steward, was born in Weeksville, and was the vale-dictorian of New York Medical College in 1870.
9. McKinney-Steward became the first, female, African American physician in New York, and the third in the United States.
10. Weeksville was a success story, for some of the houses survived into the twentieth century and have been preserved as historical monuments.

EXERCISE 12.2

Correct any errors in the use of commas in the following paragraph. Some sentences may be correct as written.

▶ In June,/1998, fifty years after Korczak Ziolkowski began sculpting the Crazy Horse monument, the face of Crazy Horse was unveiled.

A monument to the Lakota Sioux warrior, Crazy Horse, is under construction in the Black Hills of South Dakota. Korczak Ziolkowski a sculptor, who also worked on Mount Rushmore, began the project in 1948. Ziolkowski was born on September 6, 1908, — thirty-one years to the day after Crazy Horse died. A Sioux chief asked Ziolkowski, if he would create a monument to honor Crazy Horse, and other Indian heroes. Ziolkowski designed a sculpture of Crazy Horse on horseback that, when it is completed, will be the largest statue in the world. The sculpture is being shaped from Thunderhead Mountain a six-hundred-foot granite rock. Tons of rock have been blasted, from the mountain. The sculptor died in 1982 but his widow, children, and grandchildren have carried on the work. There has been no government funding so, they have paid for the work entirely with donations and admission fees. By the middle of the twenty-first century the statue should be finished, and will depict the great Sioux hero pointing at the hills he loved.

13 SEMICOLONS

A semicolon (;) indicates a stronger pause than a comma but not as strong a pause as a period.

13a Use a semicolon to join two closely related independent clauses.

Use a semicolon to join two closely related independent clauses not connected by a coordinating word (*and, but, for, nor, or, so,* or *yet*).

> ▶ In January and February, sunny days are rare and very short in northern countries; winter depression is common in the north.

An **independent clause** contains a subject and a verb and can stand alone as a sentence.

For advice on other ways to join two independent clauses, see Chapter 4 of the Handbook.

13b Use a semicolon to join two independent clauses linked by a conjunctive adverb or transitional expression.

> ▶ The stunt pilot had to eject from the cockpit; nevertheless, he was not injured.

> ▶ Mass transit is good for the environment; for example, a bus can carry enough people to fill fifteen cars.

A **conjunctive adverb** is a word (such as *also, however,* or *still*) that links two independent clauses.

13c Use semicolons to separate items in a series if commas are used within the items.

Semicolons help prevent confusion in a sentence that contains a series of items with one or more commas within the items.

▶ Fairy tales inspire children by depicting magical events, which appeal to their imaginations; clever boys and girls, who encourage young readers' problem-solving skills; evil creatures, who provide thrills; and good, heroic adults, who make the childhood world seem safer.

Also use a semicolon to separate a series of independent clauses that contain commas.

▶ He is stubborn, selfish, and conservative; she is stubborn, combative, and liberal; and no one is surprised that they do not get along.

(See also 12b on when to use commas to separate items in a series.)

13d Do not use a semicolon to introduce a list, or to separate a phrase or dependent clause from the rest of the sentence.

▶ A growing number of companies employ prison inmates for certain jobs;: selling magazines, conducting surveys, reserving airplane tickets, and taking telephone orders.

(For more on introducing lists, see 14a.)

▶ On the other hand;, taking risks can bring impressive results.

▶ I'll always wonder; if things could have been different.

EXERCISE 13.1

Correct any errors in the use of semicolons in the following sentences. Some sentences may be correct as written.

▶ Many people are in a hurry today;, yet they always seem to feel they are falling further behind.

1. One activity Americans do frequently is driving; to school, to work, to the store, or to leisure activities.
2. When too many people are driving in a hurry; tempers can flare.
3. For years, people have driven while angry, however, now the phenomenon is known as "road rage."
4. Angry drivers can make mistakes, such as forgetting basic safety precautions, they may take unnecessary risks, such as passing recklessly, they often drive too fast, and occasionally they even try to injure other drivers or damage other vehicles.
5. Drivers who are angry at other drivers commit dangerous offenses; following, racing, or even ramming other vehicles.
6. There have been incidents; when one driver has attacked another.
7. As Americans are beginning to realize; road rage endangers all drivers.
8. Drivers under the influence of road rage cause increasing numbers of accidents, and they must be stopped.
9. Public education campaigns are spreading, if people are aware of their reactions, they may control themselves better.

10. Every driver should realize that getting angry is never a solution; and may even make problems worse.

EXERCISE 13.2

Correct any errors in the use of semicolons in the following paragraph. Some sentences may be correct as written.

▶ The word *placebo* is Latin for "I will please,"; placebos have long been used in medical experiments.

In medicine, a placebo is a substance; often a sugar pill, that has no medicinal use. Placebos alone cannot cure any medical problem, nevertheless, many patients improve when taking them. Because patients who receive placebos do not know that the pills are useless, they think they are getting help for their condition; and they get better. This strange but true fact, recognized by doctors; pharmacists; and other professionals; is called the "placebo effect." Chemically, a placebo does nothing, theoretically, the patient should not respond, but somehow, this trick works on many people. The placebo effect is often seen in patients; but it is not widely understood. Since the Middle Ages, people have considered the mind and the body as separate; the placebo effect indicates that this separation may not really exist. The mind can play tricks on the body, for example, the brain produces phantom-limb pain in amputees. Doctors wonder; if the mind can also help to heal the body. If the answer is "yes," then the advances in medical knowledge could be enormous.

14 COLONS

You can use a colon (:) to introduce a list, an explanation, an example, or a further thought within a sentence. The information following the colon should clarify or offer specifics about the information that comes before it.

14a Use a colon to introduce a list or a series.

When you use a colon to introduce a list, make sure the list is preceded by a complete sentence.

▶ The archeologists uncovered several items: pieces of pottery, seeds, animal bones, and household tools.

▶ All students must be immunized against: measles, mumps, and rubella.
common childhood illnesses

14b Use a colon to introduce an explanation, an example, or a summary.

▶ In many ways, Hollywood is very predictable: Action movies arrive in the summer, dramas in the fall.

▶ One tree is particularly famous for its autumn colors: the sugar maple.

▶ Disaster relief efforts began all over the country: Volunteers raised forty million dollars.

Note: If the group of words following a colon is a complete sentence, the first word can begin with either a capital or a lowercase letter. Whichever option you choose, be consistent throughout your paper.

14c Use a colon to introduce a word or phrase that renames another noun.

▶ A hushed group of tourists stared at the most famous statue in Florence: Michelangelo's *David.*

14d Use a colon to introduce a lengthy or heavily punctuated quotation.

A quotation that is more than one or two lines long or that contains two or more commas can be introduced by a colon.

▶ Without pausing for breath, his campaign manager intoned the introduction: "Ladies and gentlemen, today it is my very great privilege to introduce to you the person on whose behalf you have all worked so tirelessly and with such impressive results, the man who is the reason we are all here today—the next president of the United States."

▶ The instructions were confusing: "After adjusting toggles A, B, and C, connect bracket A to post A, bracket B to post B, and bracket C to post C, securing with clamps A, B, and C, as illustrated in figure 1."

14e Use a colon to separate hours and minutes, in salutations for business letters, between titles and subtitles, and in ratios.

HOURS AND MINUTES: 9:15 A.M.

SALUTATIONS: Dear Professor Sung:

TITLES AND SUBTITLES: *American Sphinx: The Character of Thomas Jefferson*

RATIOS: 7:1

14f Use a colon only at the end of an independent clause.

An **independent clause** contains a subject and a verb and can stand alone as a sentence.

A colon should always follow an independent clause, which could stand on its own as a complete sentence. Do not use a colon between a verb and its object, between a preposition and its object, or before a list introduced by such words as *for example, including, is,* and *such as.*

▶ A medieval map is hard to read: The top of the map points to the east, not the north.

A medieval map is hard to read is an independent clause.

▶ Even a small garden can produce/ beans, squash, tomatoes, and corn.

▶ My cat had hidden a ball of twine under/ the sofa.

▶ Bird-watchers are thrilled to spy birds of prey such as/ peregrine falcons, red-tailed hawks, and owls.

EXERCISE 14.1

Correct any errors in the use of colons in the following sentences. Some sentences may be correct as written.

▶ **Young, impeccably dressed couples participated in the latest craze: swing dancing.**

1. The shuttle launch is scheduled for precisely 10.00 A.M.
2. The proposed zoning change was defeated by a margin of 2/1.
3. On early rap records, listeners heard percussion from unusual sources such as: turntables, microphones, and synthesizers.
4. To find out whether a film is historically accurate, consult *Past Imperfect: History According to the Movies*.
5. He believes that the most American of all sports is: roller derby.
6. As the entourage rushed past, the star's press agent snapped her orders: "No questions, no photos, no comment, no kidding!"
7. Travel advisories are in effect for the following areas, the northern Rocky Mountains and the upper Great Plains.
8. The neon lights gleamed: above stores and in diner windows.
9. We were not hungry, we had just eaten lunch an hour earlier.
10. The American songwriting tradition reached its peak in: the 1930s.

15 QUOTATION MARKS

Quotation marks (" ") are used to indicate **direct quotations** or to mark words used as words in your sentences. Quotation marks are always used in pairs. The opening quotation mark (") appears at the beginning of a word or quoted passage and the closing mark (") appears at the end.

15a Place quotation marks around direct statements from other speakers or writers.

Be careful to include the *exact* words of the speaker or writer within the quotation marks.

▶ Lincoln recalled that the United States was "dedicated to the proposition that all men are created equal."

Because *dedicated to the proposition that all men are created equal* repeats Lincoln's exact words, quotation marks are required.

    proposition
▶   Lincoln recalled that the United States was "dedicated to the ~~idea~~ that all men are
      created equal."

      Words in quotation marks must be quoted *exactly* as they appear in the original source.

In dialogue, place quotation marks around each speaker's words. Every time a different person speaks, begin a new paragraph.

> He said, "Sit down."
> "No, thank you," I replied.

With longer passages, indent prose quotations of more than four lines and verse
quotations of more than three lines if you are following MLA style; do not use quotation marks. Indent the quotation ten spaces or one inch from the left margin.
When you quote a poem, follow the line breaks exactly.

```
In "A Letter to Her Husband, Absent upon Public Employment," Ann
Bradstreet poignantly longs for him to return:
            My chilled limbs now numbed lie forlorn;
            Return, return, sweet Sol, from Capricorn;
            In this dead time, alas, what can I more
            Than view those fruits which through thy heat I bore?
            Which sweet contentment yield me for a space,
            True living pictures of their father's face. (11-16)
```

Note: If you are following APA style, indent quotations of forty or more words five
spaces from the left margin. For more on the MLA and APA styles of documentation, see Chapter 20, "Writing a Research Paper," (pp. 682–703).

**15b Place a comma or period that follows a direct quotation *within* the quota-
tion marks.**

▶   "Play it, Sam~~,~~," Rick tells the piano player in *Casablanca*.

▶   Willie Sutton robbed banks because "that's where the money is."

15c Place colons and semicolons *outside* of quotation marks.

▶   The marching band played "Seventy-Six Trombones~~;~~": the drum major's favorite
      song.

▶   A new national anthem should replace "The Star-Spangled Banner~~;~~"; no one can
      sing that song.

15d Place question marks and exclamation points according to the meaning of the sentence.

If the quotation is a question or exclamation, place the question mark or exclamation point *within* the closing quotation mark. If the punctuation mark comes at the end of a sentence, no other end punctuation is needed.

▶ "How does the bridge stand up?", the child wondered.

▶ Poe's insane narrator confesses, "It is the beating of his hideous heart!".

If the entire sentence, of which the quotation is part, is a question or exclamation, the question mark or exclamation point goes *outside* the closing quotation marks at the end of the sentence.

▶ Was Scarlett O'Hara serious when she said, "Tomorrow is another day?"?

15e Use a comma to separate a short quotation from an introductory or identifying phrase such as *he replied* or *she said.*

▶ "Video games improve eye-hand coordination," he replied.

▶ "The homeless population," she reported, "grew steadily throughout the 1980s."

15f Use single quotation marks (' ') to indicate a quotation or a title within a quotation.

▶ The mysterious caller repeatedly insists, "Play 'Misty' for me."

15g Place quotation marks around the titles of short works.

SECTION OF A BOOK: Chapter 1, "Ozzie and Harriet in Spanish Harlem"

POEM: "Ode on a Grecian Urn"

SHORT STORY: "The Yellow Wallpaper"

ESSAY OR ARTICLE: "Their Malcolm, My Problem"

SONG: "I'll Be Around"

EPISODE OF A TELEVISION PROGRAM: "Larry's Last Goodbye"

15h Do not use quotation marks to call unnecessary attention to words or phrases.

▶ The manager who was originally in charge of the project "jumped ship" before the deadline.

Quotation marks can be used to mark words used as words (as an alternative to italics).

▶ The word "receive" is often misspelled.

EXERCISE 15.1

Correct any errors in the use of quotation marks in the following sentences. Some sentences may be correct as written.

▶ The hotel has an excellent restaurant specializing in ⸢fresh⸣ fish.

1. Her essay was entitled, " "Othello's Reputation Is Gone": Shakespeare and Respect."
2. Why did the professor assign "To an Athlete Dying Young?"
3. A movie line many teenagers imitated was "Do you feel lucky, punk"?
4. President Bush admitted he lacked "the vision thing".
5. "I have a dream," Martin Luther King Jr. told the civil rights marchers.
6. Come live with me and be my love, pleads the speaker in Marlowe's poem.
7. The grand jury was not "completely" convinced of the need for a trial.
8. It turned out that the pianist could only play Chopsticks.
9. O'Brien originally published the chapter called "Speaking of Courage" as a short story.
10. Our waitress announced, "The special is prime rib;" unfortunately, we are vegetarians.

16 ELLIPSIS MARKS

An ellipsis mark (. . .) is written as three equally spaced periods. It is used within a direct quotation to indicate where you have left out part of the original quotation. You use an ellipsis mark to shorten a quotation so that it includes just the parts you want or need to quote.

ORIGINAL QUOTATION	"The prison, a high percentage of whose inmates are serving life sentences, looked surprisingly ordinary."
SHORTENED	"The prison . . . looked surprisingly ordinary."

Notice that the two commas were also omitted when the quotation was shortened.

However, when you shorten a quotation, be careful not to change the meaning of the original passage. Do not omit any parts that will alter or misrepresent the writer's intended meaning.

ORIGINAL	"Magicians create illusions, but sometimes audience members want to believe that magic is real."
MEANING ALTERED	"Magicians . . . want to believe that magic is real."

When you omit the last part of a quoted sentence, add a sentence period, for a total of four periods (a period plus the ellipsis mark).

ORIGINAL QUOTATION	"In the sphere of psychology, details are also the thing. God preserve us from commonplaces. Best of all is to avoid depicting the hero's state of mind; you ought to try to make it clear from the hero's actions. It is not necessary to portray many characters. The center of gravity should be in two persons: him and her."

Anton Chekhov, Letter to Alexander P. Chekhov

SHORTENED	"God preserve us from commonplaces. Best of all is to avoid depicting the hero's state of mind. . . . It is not necessary to portray many characters. The center of gravity should be in two persons: him and her."

An ellipsis mark is not needed to indicate that the quoted passage continues after the sentence ends.

▶ He is modest about his contributions to the abolitionist cause: "I could do but little; but what I could, I did with a joyful heart ⌒." (Douglass 54).

Do not use an ellipsis mark at the beginning of a quotation, even though there is material in the original that comes before it.

ORIGINAL QUOTATION	"As was the case after the recent cleaning of the Sistine Chapel, the makeover of the starry ceiling in Grand Central Station has revealed surprisingly brilliant color."
SHORTENED	"[T]he makeover of the starry ceiling in Grand Central Station has revealed surprisingly brilliant color."

Note: The first word of a quoted sentence should be capitalized. If you change from a lowercase to a capital letter, enclose the letter in brackets (see 18d).

If you are following MLA style, enclose ellipsis marks that you add to a quotation in brackets, as in the following shortened version of the Chekhov quotation given above.

SHORTENED	"In the sphere of psychology, details are also the thing. [. . .] Best of all is to avoid depicting the hero's state of mind; you ought to try to make it clear from the hero's actions," (Chekhov 1446).

(For more on MLA style for ellipsis marks, see Chapter 20, p. 676).

EXERCISE 16.1

Shorten each of the following quotations by omitting the underlined portion and adding an ellipsis mark where appropriate.

▶ "Some people who call themselves vegetarians still eat ~~less cuddly creatures such as~~ chicken and fish."

EXERCISE 16.1: *Answers*

1. "The structure of DNA . . . is a double helix."
2. "[M]any critics did not expect *The Silence of the Lambs* to win an Academy Award."
3. Hamlet muses, "To be or not to be. . . ."
4. "[P]eople of all classes receive financial help from the government."
5. "Cole Porter cultivated a suave, sophisticated urban persona. . . ."
6. "Zora Neale Hurston's collections of folklore proved to be very valuable."
7. "[T]wo hundred years ago households . . . had to make their own soap."
8. "Folic acid . . . can help to prevent certain birth defects."
9. "[S]altwater aquariums . . . are difficult and expensive to maintain."
10. "She wrote rather doubtful grammar sometimes [...]" (Thackeray 136–37).

1. "The structure of DNA, <u>as Watson and Crick discovered,</u> is a double helix."
2. "<u>In spite of their admiration for the film,</u> many critics did not expect *The Silence of the Lambs* to win an Academy Award."
3. Hamlet muses, "To be or not to be, <u>that is the question.</u>"
4. "<u>Many Americans do not realize that</u> people of all classes receive financial help from the government."
5. "Cole Porter cultivated a suave, sophisticated urban persona <u>even though he came from a small town in Indiana.</u>"
6. "<u>From an anthropological perspective,</u> Zora Neale Hurston's collections of folklore proved to be very valuable."
7. "<u>We take modern conveniences for granted today, but</u> two hundred years ago households <u>even</u> had to make their own soap."
8. "Folic acid, <u>doctors now believe,</u> can help to prevent certain birth defects."
9. "<u>Although</u> saltwater aquariums <u>are beautiful, they</u> are difficult and expensive to maintain."
10. "She wrote rather doubtful grammar sometimes, <u>and in her verses took all sorts of liberties with the metre</u>" (Thackeray 136–37). (MLA style)

17 APOSTROPHES

An **apostrophe** (') has three functions: to show ownership or possession, to indicate omitted letters in contractions, and to form some plurals.

17a Use an apostrophe to indicate possession or ownership.

Add *-'s* to make a singular noun possessive, including nouns that end with *s* or the sound of *s* and **indefinite pronouns** (*anyone, nobody*).

> The *fox's* prey led it across the field.

> Whether she can win the nomination is *anybody's* guess.

*An **indefinite pronoun** does not refer to a specific person, place, or object. It refers to people, places, or things in general (*anywhere, everyone, everything*).*

Note that the possessive forms of personal pronouns do not take apostrophes: *mine, yours, his, hers, ours, theirs, its.*

> Each bee has it's function in the hive.

The possessive form of *who* is *whose* (not *who's*).

> Marie Curie, *whose* work in chemistry made history, discovered radium.

Add an apostrophe to a plural noun to make it possessive, or add *-'s* if the plural noun does not end in *s.*

> Both *farms'* crops were lost in the flood.

> Our *children's* children will reap the benefits.

To show individual possession by two or more people or groups, add an apostrophe or -'s to each noun.

▶ Sam is equipment manager for both the *boys'* and *girls'* basketball teams.
   Sam works for two different teams.

To show joint possession by two people or groups, add an apostrophe or -'s to the last noun.

▶ The *coaches and players'* dream came true at the end of the season.

Add -'s to the last word of a compound noun to show possession.

▶ My *father-in-law's* boat needs a new engine.
▶ We were ushered into the *chairman of the department's* office.

17b Use an apostrophe to indicate the omitted letter or letters in a contraction.

▶ *I've* [I have] seen the answers.
▶ Jason *didn't* [did not] arrive last night.

17c Use an apostrophe to form the plural of a number, letter, symbol, abbreviation, or word treated as a word.

▶ There are three *5's* on the license plate.
▶ She spells her name with two *C's*.
▶ The *?'s* stand for unknown quantities.
▶ Using two *etc.'s* is unnecessary.
▶ Replace all *can's* in the contract with *cannot's*.

In the sentences above, note that numbers, letters, and words used as themselves are in italics. The -s ending should not be italicized, however. (For more on italics and underlining, see 23d.)

When referring to the years in a decade, an apostrophe is not necessary.

▶ The fashions of the 1970s returned in the 1990s.

Apostrophes are used to signal the omission of the numerals that indicate the century.

the class of '99   music of the '80s

17d **Avoid using apostrophes to form plurals and to form possessives for personal pronouns.**

▶ The trapper's came to town to trade.

▶ She paid for my lunch as well as her's.

EXERCISE 17.1

Correct the errors in the use of apostrophes in the following sentences. Some sentences may be correct as written.

▶ The 1960's was a decade of upheaval.

1. The Vietnam war became the focus of many young peoples' disagreements with their parents.
2. Young Americans felt that their parents' generation was more inhibited than theirs.
3. In the 1960s, "dropping out" was often an activists' choice.
4. Members of the World War II generation were often horrified by their sons and daughters' behavior.
5. When people recall that decade, they tend to remember it's excesses.

---

18 PARENTHESES AND BRACKETS

PARENTHESES

Parentheses—( )—are used to separate nonessential information from the rest of a sentence or paragraph.

18a **Use parentheses to add words, phrases, or sentences that expand on, clarify, or explain the material that precedes or follows.**

▶ The EPA (Environmental Protection Agency) is responsible for developing water pollution standards.

▶ The application fee for the four-day workshop (a total of $100, including the registration fee) is due Friday.

Be sure to use parentheses sparingly; they can clutter your writing.

18b **Use parentheses to insert dates or abbreviations.**

▶ Elizabeth Cady Stanton (1815–1902) helped to organize the first American women's rights convention.

▶ Guidelines for documenting research papers in the humanities are published by the Modern Language Association (MLA).

18c Check the placement of other punctuation used with parentheses.

Parenthetical information that appears at the end of a sentence should be inserted before the period that ends the sentence.

▶ Irish dance has become popular in the United States (probably because of the success of *Riverdance*).

When parenthetical information appears after a word that would be followed by a comma, the comma is always placed after the closing parenthesis.

▶ He called when his plane landed (or so he said), but no one answered.

When a complete sentence appears within parentheses, punctuate the sentence as you would normally unless it is part of another sentence. In that case, the sentence should not begin with a capital letter or be punctuated as a separate sentence.

▶ Timber companies propose various uses for national forests (public land can be leased for commercial purposes).

Exception: If the material within the parentheses is a question, it should end with a question mark.

▶ A few innocent-looking plants (have you heard of the Venus flytrap?) capture and eat insects and animals.

BRACKETS

Brackets ([ ]) are used within quotations and within parentheses.

18d Use brackets to add information or indicate changes you have made to a quotation.

▶ Whitman's preface argued, "Here [the United States] is not merely a nation but a teeming nation of nations."

The explanation tells where *here* is.

▶ "Along came a spider and sat down beside [Miss Muffett]," who apparently suffered from a phobia.

The bracketed name replaces *her* in the original.

Use brackets to enclose the word *sic* when signaling an error in original quoted material.

▶   The incumbent's letter to the editor announced, "My opponant's [sic] claims regarding my record are simply not true."

The Latin word *sic* lets your readers know that the misspelled word or other error in the quoted material is the original author's error, not yours.

Note: If you are using MLA style, enclose ellipsis marks that you add to shorten a quotation in brackets (see Chapter 16 of the Handbook).

18e **Use brackets to enclose parenthetical material in a group of words already enclosed in parentheses.**

▶   The demonstrators (including members of the National Rifle Association [NRA]) crowded around the candidate.

EXERCISE 18.1

Correct the errors in the use of parentheses or brackets in the following sentences. Some sentences may be correct as written.

▶   Typhoid Mary would probably not have infected so many victims if she had stopped working (she was a cook).

1.   Nathan Hale regretted that he had "but one life to give for (his) country."
2.   The Committee for Scientific Investigation of Claims of the Paranormal (CSICOP) tests claims of supernatural abilities.
3.   Malcolm X [1925–1965] was an American political figure assassinated in the 1960s.
4.   The invention of anesthesia made possible many advances in medicine (including lengthy surgery.)
5.   Children believe what they see on television, (at least most of it) and therefore parents should monitor their children's viewing.

19 DASHES

Use a **dash** (—) to separate parts of a sentence. A dash suggests a stronger separation than a comma, colon, or semicolon does. To type a dash, hit the hyphen key twice (--), with no spaces before, between, or after the hyphens. Some word-processing programs automatically convert the two hyphens to a dash (—).

19a **Use a dash or dashes to emphasize a sudden shift or break in thought or mood.**

▶   Computers have given the world instant communication — and electronic junk mail.

19b Use a dash or dashes to introduce an explanation, an example, or the items in a series.

▶ The success of the D-Day invasion was almost miraculous—capturing the beaches of Normandy must have looked impossible in 1944.

When the added thought appears in the middle of the sentence, use two dashes to set it off.

▶ The music-hating monster in *Beowulf*—the poet withholds his name at the beginning—attacks the hall.

19c Use dashes sparingly.

Dashes are emphatic. Do not overuse them or they will lose their effectiveness. Also be careful not to use a dash as a substitute for a **conjunction** or transition.

> but
▶ Einstein's job in Switzerland was dull,~~—~~it offered him plenty of time to think;~~—~~
> *while working there*
> ^he came up with the theory of relativity.

A **conjunction** is a word or words used to connect clauses, phrases, or individual words.

EXERCISE 19.1

Add a dash or pair of dashes where they might be effective, and correct any errors in the use of dashes in the following sentences.

▶ Food, who eats what and why? is now a subject studied by academics.

1. One issue particularly concerns scholars of food; why are certain foods acceptable in some cultures but not in others?
2. Some foods were once popular, but today—hardly anyone has heard of them.
3. In the 1990s, people in Great Britain were alerted to a new danger, mad cow disease.
4. In the 1960s, frozen foods—icy blocks of corn, peas, and string beans—were popular—and convenient—alternatives to fresh produce.
5. Today fresh fruits and vegetables are valued once again, unless a busy cook has no time for peeling and chopping.

20 CAPITALIZATION

A **proper noun** names a particular person, place, thing, or group.

Capitalize the first word of a sentence, **proper nouns,** and the pronoun *I*.

20a Capitalize the first word in a sentence and in a direct quotation.

▶ ~~r~~evision is important. *(R)*

Capitalize the first word in a direct quotation unless it is incorporated into your own sentence or it continues an earlier quotation.

▶ The union representative said, "~~t~~hat meeting did not take place." *(T)*

▶ Sam Verdon complained that "~~N~~o one takes college athletes seriously." *(n)*

▶ "I prefer not to interpret my paintings," replied the famous watercolorist, "~~B~~ecause they should speak for themselves." *(b)*

20b Capitalize proper nouns, including the names of specific people, places, things, and groups.

PEOPLE AND ANIMALS: Franklin Roosevelt, his dog Fala

CITIES, STATES, NATIONS: St. Paul, Minnesota, the United States

WELL-ESTABLISHED GEOGRAPHIC REGIONS: the Gulf Coast, the U.S. Southwest

GOVERNMENT AND OTHER PUBLIC OFFICES, DEPARTMENTS, AND BUILDINGS: the Pentagon, the Supreme Court, the Puck Building

SOCIAL, POLITICAL, BUSINESS, SPORTING, AND CULTURAL ORGANIZATIONS: League of Women Voters, National Basketball Association

MONTHS, DAYS OF THE WEEK, AND HOLIDAYS: February, Thursday, Labor Day

CHAPTER OR SECTION TITLES IN BOOKS: "Why America Has Changed"

NATIONALITIES AND LANGUAGES: Ethiopian, Dutch

RELIGIONS, RELIGIOUS FIGURES, AND SACRED BOOKS: Judaism, the Pope, the Koran

TRADE NAMES: Coca-Cola, Brillo

HISTORIC EVENTS: the Treaty of Versailles, Reconstruction

SPECIFIC COURSE TITLES: Organic Chemistry 101

20c Do not capitalize common nouns.

FAMILY MEMBERS: my uncle, his father

GENERAL AREAS OF THE COUNTRY: southwestern United States

SUBJECTS: I study chemistry.

CENTURIES: seventeenth-century England

GEOGRAPHICAL AREAS: the lake in the park

20d Capitalize the titles of literary and other works, such as books, articles, poems, plays, songs, films, and paintings.

Capitalize the first and last words of the title, the first word following a colon, and all other words except **articles, coordinating conjunctions,** and **prepositions.**

BOOK	*Confusion Is Next: The Sonic Youth Story*
ARTICLE	"Making History at Madison Park"
POEM	"My Last Duchess"
PLAY	*A Raisin in the Sun*
SONG	"Yellow Rose of Texas"
FILM	*Gone with the Wind*
PAINTING	*The Starry Night*

Articles are the words *a, an,* and *the.*

Coordinating conjunctions (*and, but, for, nor, or, so, yet*) connect sentence elements that are of equal importance.

Prepositions (such as *before, on,* and *to*) are used before a noun or pronoun to indicate time, place, space, direction, position, or some other relationship.

20e Capitalize a personal title only when it directly precedes a person's name.

▶ Vice President Maria Washington briefed the stockholders.

▶ Maria Washington was hired from a rival company to be the new vice president.

It is acceptable to capitalize the titles of certain high government officials regardless of whether they precede a name: *the President of the United States.*

EXERCISE 20.1

Correct the capitalization errors in the following paragraph.

▶ The ̶u̶nited ̶n̶ations meets at its headquarters in New York City.
     (U)   (N)

    During world war II, the governments of twenty-six countries pledged their willingness to continue fighting on behalf of the Allies. United States president Franklin Roosevelt came up with a name for the group: the united nations. The "Declaration By United Nations" promised the support of those twenty-six governments for the war effort. The Nations signed this document on New Year's day, 1942. By 1945, the number of countries involved in the united nations had grown to fifty-one. From April through June of that year, fifty Representatives attended the united nations

EXERCISE 20.1: *Answers*

During **World War** II, the governments of twenty-six countries pledged their willingness to continue fighting on behalf of the Allies. United States **President** Franklin Roosevelt came up with a name for the group: the **United Nations.** The "Declaration **by** United Nations"

(Continued on next page)

promised the support of those twenty-six governments for the war effort. The **nations** signed this document on New Year's **Day**, 1942. By 1945, the number of countries involved in the **United Nations** had grown to fifty-one. From April through June of that year, fifty **representatives** attended the **United Nations** Conference on International Organization in San Francisco. There, the **nations** debated the contents of a charter. Although the **war** was nearing an end, the governments foresaw a need to continue international cooperation. The charter was ratified on October 24, 1945, by China, France, **the** Soviet Union, **the** United Kingdom, **the** United States, and a majority of the other **nations**. Every year since then, October 24 has been known as **United Nations Day**.

Conference on International Organization in San Francisco. There, the Nations debated the contents of a charter. Although the War was nearing an end, the governments foresaw a need to continue international cooperation. The charter was ratified on October 24, 1945, by China, France, The Soviet Union, The United Kingdom, The United States, and a majority of the other Nations. Every year since then, October 24 has been known as united nations day.

21 ABBREVIATIONS

Abbreviations are shortened forms of words and phrases. It is acceptable to use abbreviations for some personal titles, names of organizations, time references, and Latin expressions. Most abbreviations use periods, but those composed of all capital letters often do not.

21a Abbreviate titles before and after a person's name.

Ms. Amy Tan	Arthur Rodriguez, M.D.
St. Mary	Bill Cosby, Ph.D.
Dr. C. Everett Koop	Martin Luther King Jr.

21b Abbreviate names of familiar organizations, corporations, and countries.

Use common abbreviations such as *PBS, CIA,* and *MBA* when you are certain that your readers will recognize them.

ABC	AMA	FBI
UNICEF	USA	VCR

21c Abbreviate time references that precede or follow a number.

▶ The meeting will begin at 10:15 A.M. and end at 12 P.M.

▶ The statues were carved in about 300 B.C.E.

The letters B.C.E. stand for "before the common era." An alternative is B.C. ("before Christ").

▶ Alfred became king in A.D. 871.

The letters A.D. stand for the Latin term *anno Domini* and precede the date. The alternative C.E. ("common era") follows the date.

21d Use common abbreviations for Latin terms in parentheses, footnotes, or references.

It is acceptable to use abbreviations for Latin terms in parenthetical comments as well as in source notes or citations. Avoid using these abbreviations outside of parentheses in the text of your essay; spell them out instead.

e.g.	for example
et al.	and others
etc.	and so forth
i.e.	that is
vs. *or* v.	versus

▶ Edison invented the light bulb, the motion picture camera, ~~such items as~~ sound recording devices~~, etc.~~ *and*

21e Do not abbreviate certain words and phrases when they are used in sentences.

Some abbreviations that are acceptable in scientific or technical writing should be spelled out in most other kinds of writing.

UNITS OF MEASUREMENT: ten inches [*not* ten in.]

GEOGRAPHICAL OR PLACE NAMES: I live in New York City [*not* N.Y.C.]. (*Exceptions: Washington, D.C.; U.S.* when it is used as an adjective, as in *U.S. Senate*)

PARTS OF WRITTEN WORKS: chapter 6 [*not* ch. 6]

DAYS, MONTHS, AND HOLIDAYS: Thursday [*not* Thurs.]

NAMES OF SUBJECT AREAS: biology [*not* bio]

PERSONAL TITLES USED WITHOUT A PROPER NAME: doctor [*not* Dr.]

EXERCISE 21.1

Correct the misused abbreviations in the following sentences.

▶ Students of ~~poli sci~~ *political science* know that public opinion often moves in cycles.

1. According to Washington Irving's story, Rip van Winkle fell asleep in the Catskill Mts. for twenty years.
2. The average American woman is five ft. four in. tall.
3. Since it is only ninety pp. long, the text is really a novella, not a novel.
4. The Great Depression began with the stock-market crash on Black Mon.
5. The Coen brothers have a reputation for creating unorthodox films: e.g., *Fargo*.

EXERCISE 21.1: *Answers*

1. Catskill Mountains
2. five feet four inches
3. ninety pages
4. Black Monday
5. . . . unorthodox films such as *Fargo*.

22 NUMBERS

As a general rule, use numbers according to the rules of your field of study. Be sure to represent numbers as numerals or as words consistently.

22a Spell out numbers that begin sentences.

> *Two hundred ten*
> ▶ ~~210~~ students attended the lecture.

22b Spell out numbers that can be written in one or two words.

twenty-six checks   two hundred women

sixty students   one thousand pretzels

Use numerals for numbers that cannot be spelled out in one or two words.

> *375*
> ▶ There are ~~three hundred seventy-five~~ students enrolled this fall.

Use numerals in a sentence with more than one number where one number needs to be written in numerals.

> *28*
> ▶ Of the 420 students in my school, only ~~twenty-eight~~ have a driver's license.

When two numbers appear in succession, spell out one and give numerals for the other.

> *3*
> ▶ Each counselor is in charge of nine ~~three~~-year-olds.

22c Use numerals according to convention.

DATES: August 10, 1993; the 1960s

DECIMALS, PERCENTAGES, FRACTIONS: 56.7, 50% *or* 50 percent, 1¾ cups

EXACT TIMES: 9:27 A.M.

PAGES, CHAPTERS, VOLUMES: page 27, chapter 12, volume 4

ADDRESSES: 122 Peach Street

EXACT AMOUNTS OF MONEY: $5.60, $1.3 million

SCORES AND STATISTICS: 23–6 victory, a factor of 12

EXERCISE 22.1

Correct the errors in the use of numbers in the following sentences. Some sentences may be correct as written.

> *77*
> ▶ The quotation you're looking for is on page ~~seventy-seven~~.

1. 77% of those responding to the poll favored increased taxes on cigarettes.
2. The estimated cost was too low by eighty-seven dollars and fourteen cents.

3. Each window is composed of 100s of small pieces of colored glass.
4. All traffic stopped as a 90-car train went slowly past.
5. February twenty-two is George Washington's birthday, but Presidents' Day is always celebrated on a Monday.

3. hundreds of small pieces
4. a ninety-car train
5. February 22

23 ITALICS AND UNDERLINING

Italic or *slanted type* is used for emphasizing particular words or phrases. It is also used to set off titles of longer works, names of vehicles, non-English words, and words deserving special emphasis.

When writing by hand or using a typewriter, use <u>underlining</u> to indicate italics. Most word-processing programs provide italic type, but your instructor may prefer that you use underlining instead. For example, your instructor may require you to use underlining in a works-cited list. (For more on MLA guidelines, see Chapter 20, p. 682.) In this chapter, most of the examples modeling the use of italics or underlining are shown in italic type.

23a Italicize or underline titles of works published separately.

BOOKS: *Great Expectations*

PLAYS: *Rent*

LONG POEMS: *The Iliad*

MAGAZINES AND JOURNALS: *Entertainment Weekly*; the *New York Review of Books*

NEWSPAPERS: the *Columbus Dispatch*

MOVIES AND VIDEOTAPES: *Titanic*

LONG MUSICAL WORKS, RECORDINGS: *Exile on Main Street*

TELEVISION AND RADIO SERIES: *The Practice*

VISUAL WORKS OF ART (PAINTINGS, SCULPTURES):   *Birth of Venus*

The titles of shorter works, such as the titles of articles, short stories, and songs, should be enclosed in quotation marks (see 15g).

23b Italicize or underline the names of ships, trains, aircraft, and spacecraft.

Titanic	*Spirit of St. Louis*
Orient Express	space shuttle *Challenger*

23c Italicize or underline non-English words not in everyday use.

Words from other languages should be italicized unless they have become a part of the English language, such as "chic" or "taco." If you are unsure, check an English dictionary. If the word is not listed, it should be italicized.

▶ Our instructor lectured on the technique of *Verstehen*.

▶ Tacos are now as much a part of American cuisine as pizza.

23d **Italicize or underline numbers, letters, words, or phrases called out for special emphasis.**

Use italics for numbers, letters, or words used as terms.

▶ Every bottle has *33* on the label.

▶ Hester Prynne is forced to wear a scarlet *A*.

▶ Today, *ain't* is listed in most dictionaries.

Italicize a word or phrase that is being defined or emphasized.

▶ *Alliteration* — the same sounds repeated at the beginning of each word in a group — can be an effective literary device.

Use italics for emphasis only sparingly. When you italicize too many words in a sentence or paragraph, the emphasis is lost.

▶ The U.S. National Park system is *extremely important* (no italics) because it protects some of the most *beautiful* (no italics) and *unusual* (no italics) parts of this country.

EXERCISE 23.1

Correct the errors in the use of italics in the following sentences. Some sentences may be correct as written.

▶ <u>Oedipus</u>, written by Sophocles in the fifth century B.C., is possibly the most famous play of the classical period.

1. The exchange student greeted everyone with a hearty *"Bonjour!"*
2. His professor insisted that TV Guide was not an acceptable research source.
3. Cartoons like The Simpsons have become surprisingly popular with adult audiences.
4. The first European settlers at Plymouth arrived on the Mayflower.
5. His book is discussed in depth in the article *Africa: The Hidden History*.

EXERCISE 23.1: *Answers*

1. Correct
2. *TV Guide*
3. *The Simpsons*
4. *Mayflower.*
5. the article "Africa: The Hidden History."

---

24 HYPHENS

A **hyphen** (-) is used to join compound words, connect parts of words, and to split words at the end of typewritten lines of text.

24a Use a hyphen to join words that function as a unit.

Some compound nouns and verbs are spelled as one word (*download*), some are spelled as two words (*washing machine*), and some are spelled using hyphens (*foul-up*). Check a dictionary when you are unsure; if you do not find the compound listed in your dictionary, spell it as two words.

Use a hyphen to join words that together modify a noun.

▶ An *icy-fingered* hand tapped on her shoulder.

However, when the first word of the compound ends in *-ly* or when the compound adjective follows the noun it modifies, no hyphen is used.

▶ The guard found a *clumsily hidden* duplicate key.
▶ Her voice was *well trained.*

24b Use a hyphen with some prefixes (*all-, ex-, great-, self-*) and suffixes (*-elect*).

▶ Most Americans' parents, grandparents, or *great-grandparents* came from another country.
▶ The *governor-elect* made a stirring victory speech.

Use a hyphen for clarity to prevent confusion with certain combinations of prefixes and base words.

▶ She wants the taxpayers to approve the funding for her ~~recreation~~ *re-creation* of the demolished town hall.

    Recreation has a different meaning from *re-creation.*

24c Use a hyphen when spelling out fractions and the numbers *twenty-one* to *ninety-nine,* in word-number combinations, and to indicate inclusive numbers.

    two-thirds finished   *twenty-two* sources

▶ The *675-yard* path winds through a landscaped garden.
▶ Pages *99-102* cover the military campaigns.

24d Use a hyphen between syllables to split a word at the end of a typewritten line.

Although most word-processing programs automatically break the line before a long word and move the word to the next line, in typewritten or handwritten text you should use a hyphen to divide any words that fall at the end of a line. Divide words between syllables; never break a one-syllable word. Divide a compound word between its parts. Words can also be divided between a prefix and root or between a root and suffix. Check your dictionary if you are uncertain about where to break a word.

```
       Viking invaders failed to conquer Ireland
   because the country was governed by a num-
   ber of petty kings rather than by a central
   authority that could be effectively over-
   thrown; however, by the tenth century this
   situation began to change.
```

EXERCISE 24.1

Correct the errors in the use of hyphens in the following sentences. If you are not sure about a word, check your dictionary. Some sentences may be correct as written.

teenager
▶ Does any ~~teen-ager~~ really need liposuction?

EXERCISE 24.1: *Answers*

1. increasingly popular
   option
2. self-conscious teens
3. sixteen-year-olds
4. nose jobs
5. Correct

1. Adolescents today who are unhappy with their looks can turn to the increasingly-popular option of plastic surgery.
2. For many selfconscious teens and young adults, surgery seems to be the perfect solution.
3. Until recently, very few sixteen year olds considered making permanent surgical changes.
4. But as more adults pay for nose-jobs and tummy tucks, more teens are expressing interest.
5. Are images of people with apparently perfect bodies and faces unduly influencing less-than-perfect young Americans?

25 SPELLING

Misspelled words are among the most common errors for many student writers. Be sure to pay attention to spelling as you edit and proofread your papers, and keep a dictionary close at hand. Misspellings can make your paper appear carelessly written. Use the tips in the accompanying box and the basic spelling rules that follow to help improve your spelling.

25a Remember to put *i* before *e* except after *c* or when pronounced as an *a* as in *neighbor* and *weigh*.

i before *e*: ach*ie*ve, th*ie*f

except after *c*: conc*ei*ve, rec*ei*ve

TIPS FOR IMPROVING YOUR SPELLING

- **Purchase a collegiate dictionary and take the time to look up the correct spellings of words you are unsure of.**
- **Use your word processor's spell-checker function.** Be sure to take advantage of the spell-checker as you edit and proofread your drafts. However, keep in mind that this function will not catch all spelling errors; for example, it cannot detect the incorrect use of *it's* versus *its* or of homonyms such as *there* versus *their* and *weather* versus *whether*. (See 25d for a list of homonyms.)
- **Proofread your drafts for spelling errors.** To avoid being distracted by the flow of ideas in your essays, proofread them backwards, from the last word to the first, looking only for misspellings. For words that sound alike but have different spellings (*to/too/two, their/there*), stop to check their use in the sentence and determine if you have used the correct word.
- **Keep a list of words you commonly misspell.** Whenever you catch spelling errors in a draft or see misspellings marked by your instructor in papers returned to you, add the words to your list. Use your dictionary to locate the correct spelling and pronunciation of each word in the list. Review your list of words periodically and practice pronouncing and writing the words until you master their correct spellings and usage.
- **Develop a spelling awareness.** As you read and write, pay attention to words and how they are spelled. When you encounter a new word, pronounce it slowly and carefully while taking note of its spelling. Try to create a mental image of each word, especially words with silent letters or unusual spellings.

---

or when pronounced as an *a:* fre*i*ght, the*i*r

Memorize the exceptions, such as *either, foreign, height, leisure, neither, seize,* and *weird.*

25b Add *-s* **or** *-es* **to form the plural of most nouns.**

Singular common nouns ending in *-s, -ch, -sh,* or *-x* form the plural by adding *-es.* Nouns ending in *-o* usually form the plural by adding *-s* when the *-o* follows a vowel or *-es* when the *-o* follows a consonant.

Add *-s:*	professor, professors	zoo, zoos
Add *-es:*	sandwich, sandwiches	hero, heroes

To form the plural of common nouns ending in *-y*, change the *y* to *i* and add *-es* when the *y* is preceded by a consonant. Add only *-s* when the *y* is preceded by a vowel.

story	stor*ies*	day	day*s*
baby	bab*ies*	key	key*s*

Compound nouns form the plural by adding *-s* or *-es* to the most important word or, when all the words are equally important, to the last word of the compound.

mother-in-law	mother*s*-in-law
passerby	passerby*s*
stand-in	stand-in*s*

A **proper noun** names a particular person, place, thing, or group.

Proper nouns form the plural by adding *-s* or *-es* without changing the noun's ending.

Thursday	Thursday*s*
Mr. and Mrs. Jones	the Jones*es*

▶ The Gunderson's met us for dinner last night.

25c Drop, keep, change, or double the final letter when adding endings to some words.

Drop the silent *e* when adding an ending that begins with a vowel (*a, e, i, o, u*). Keep the silent *e* when adding an ending that begins with a consonant.

hope	hop*ing*	care	care*ful*
force	for*cing*	encourage	encourage*ment*
advise	advis*able*	love	love*ly*

For words that end in *y*, change the final *y* to *i* before adding an ending when the *y* follows a consonant. Keep the final *y* when the *y* follows a vowel, when the ending is *-ing*, or when *y* ends a proper name.

study	stud*ies*	buy	buy*er*
marry	marr*ied*	marry	marry*ing*
		Fahey	Fahey*s*

Exception: Drop the final *y* whenever you add *-ize*.

memory	memor*ize*
category	categor*ize*

When adding an ending to one-syllable words, double the final consonant if the ending starts with a vowel and the final consonant follows a single vowel. Do *not* double the consonant when two vowels or a vowel and another consonant precede it.

hop	hop*ped*	pair	pair*ed*
trek	trek*ked*	rent	rent*ed*

When adding an ending to words with two or more syllables, double the final consonant if a single vowel precedes it and the stress falls on the last syllable.

transmit	transmit*ted*
refer	refer*ral*

Do *not* double the final consonant when two vowels or a vowel and another consonant precede it.

react	react*ed*
redeem	redeem*ing*

Do *not* double the final consonant if the ending starts with a consonant.

commit	commit*ment*
regret	regret*fully*

25d Watch out for homonyms, groups of words that sound the same but are spelled differently.

The following list includes some commonly confused groups of words.

Homonyms	*Examples of Usage*
accept (take or receive)	Most stores *accept* credit cards.
except (other than)	Everyone has arrived *except* Harry.
affect (to influence)	The new law will *affect* us.
effect (result, outcome)	The *effect* of the storm was frightening.
already (by now)	Miriam is *already* in class.
all ready (fully prepared)	Geoffrey is *all ready*.
allusion (reference to)	The poem contained an *allusion* to Greek mythology.
illusion (not real, a fantasy)	Margaret is under the *illusion* that she is famous.

(Continued on next page)

Homonyms	*Examples of Usage*
cite (to refer to)	Be sure to *cite* your sources.
sight (vision, or tourist attraction)	Her *sight* is failing.
site (place)	We visited the *site* of the accident.
complement (to complete, a counterpart)	The side dishes *complement* the main course.
compliment (praise)	Allison received numerous *compliments*.
elicit (to bring out)	The film *elicits* an emotional response.
illicit (illegal)	The sale of *illicit* drugs is prohibited on campus.
its (possessive of *it*)	The show has found *its* audience.
it's (contraction of *it is*)	*It's* too late to go back.
lead (verb: to guide or direct)	Professor Hong will *lead* the discussion group.
led (past tense of verb *lead*)	Professor Hong *led* the discussion group.
lead (noun: a heavy metal)	*Lead* poisoning is dangerous.
loose (not securely attached)	The button was *loose*.
lose (to fail to keep)	I often *lose* my keys.
principal (most important, or head of a school)	The citizens' *principal* concern is educational costs.
principle (basic rule or truth)	This *principle* should govern all of your actions.
their (possessive of *they*)	The students brought *their* books to class.
there (in that place, opposite of *here*)	*There* is the bus.
they're (contraction of *they are*)	*They're* early.
to (toward)	Please move *to* the front of the class.
too (also, or excessively)	Harry is coming *too*.
two (following *one*)	The *two* speeches were similar.
who's (contraction of *who is*)	*Who's* taking a cab?
whose (possessive of *who*)	*Whose* book is this?
your (possessive of *you*)	*Your* experiment is well designed.
you're (contraction of *you are*)	*You're* passing the course.

25e Watch out for commonly misspelled words.

Commonly Misspelled Words

absence	conscience	fulfill *or* fulfil	noticeable	restaurant
accept	conscious	government	occasionally	rhythm
accessible	convenience	grammar	occurrence	ridiculous
accidentally	criticism	guarantee	omission	roommate
accommodate	criticize	harass	originally	sacrifice
accuracy	curiosity	height	parallel	schedule
achievement	deceive	humorous	particularly	secretary
acquaintance	decision	hypocrisy	permissible	seize
acquire	definitely	imagination	physical	separate
amateur	descendant	immediately	picnicking	sergeant
analysis	disappearance	incredible	pleasant	several
analyze	disappoint	inevitable	possible	similar
apologize	disastrous	intelligence	practically	sincerely
apparent	discipline	interest	precede	sophomore
appearance	efficiency	irresistible	preference	succeed
argument	efficient	judgment	prejudice	successful
ascend	eighth	knowledge	preparation	summary
athlete	eligible	laboratory	prevalent	surprise
attendance	embarrass	leisure	privilege	tendency
beginning	emphasize	length	probably	thorough
believe	environment	library	proceed	through
benefited	especially	license	professor	tragedy
boundary	exaggerate	lightning	pronunciation	truly
Britain	excellence	loneliness	psychology	unanimous
bureaucracy	exercise	maintenance	quantity	usually
business	existence	maneuver	quiet	vacuum
calendar	experience	marriage	receive	vengeance
cemetery	explanation	mathematics	recognize	villain
changeable	familiar	miniature	recommend	weird
characteristic	fascinate	mischievous	reference	writing
column	February	necessary	referred	
committee	foreign	niece	relieve	
conceive	forty	ninety	repetition	

25f Be alert for words that are formed from the same root (they may have different spellings) and for words with silent letters.

heir   heredity

aisle

pneumonia

EXERCISE 25.1

Correct the spelling errors in the following paragraph. If you are not sure about a word, check the list of commonly misspelled words on page 873 or your dictionary. Some sentences may be correct as written.

>   *centuries*
> ▶ After two ~~centurys~~ of isolation, Japan modernized very quickly.

    In 1542, the first European visiters arrived in Japan. Traders and missionarys from the West brought firarms, tobacco, and Christianity to the island nation, which was suffring from internal strife. Japanese rulers welcomed Christianity at first, seing it as a way to reunify the country. However, after large numbers of Japanese converted, some official intolerence toward Christianity appeared. Finally, the rebellion of a Catholic Japanese community ensured that the government would act to prevent Western missionaries and merchants from joining forces with Japanese dissidents. In 1640, a policy of isolation took affect. No foreiners were aloud to enter Japan, and no Japanese were permitted to travel abroad. This policy was finaly relaxed in 1853, and a new era began in 1868, with the arrival of a new imperial government. The new leaders were youthful and visionary, and they wanted to bring their country up to date. Although some Japanese who had enjoied privileges in the old society lost them during modernization, most people where delighted with the country's new direction.

EXERCISE 25.1: *Answers*

In 1542, the first European **visitors** arrived in Japan. Traders and **missionaries** from the West brought **firearms,** tobacco, and Christianity to the island nation, which was **suffering** from internal strife. Japanese rulers welcomed Christianity at first, **seeing** it as a way to reunify the country. However, after large numbers of Japanese converted, some official **intolerance** toward Christianity appeared. Finally, the rebellion of a Catholic Japanese community ensured that the government would act to prevent Western missionaries and merchants from joining forces with Japanese dissidents [*correct*]. In 1640, a policy of isolation took **effect.** No **foreigners** were **allowed** to enter Japan, and no Japanese were **permitted** to travel abroad. This policy was **finally** relaxed in 1853, and a new era began in 1868, with the **arrival** of a new imperial government. The new leaders were youthful and visionary, and they wanted to bring their country up to date [*correct*]. Although some Japanese who had **enjoyed** privileges in the old society lost them during modernization, most people **were** delighted with the country's new direction.

26 NOUNS AND ARTICLES

The two primary types of nouns in English are proper nouns and common nouns. A **proper noun** names a specific, unique person, place, thing, calendar item, or idea and is always capitalized.

Sylvia Plath	Lake Erie	Toyota	Tuesday	Marxism

A **common noun** refers to a person, place, thing, or idea in general and is not capitalized.

writer	lake	car	day	ideology

Common nouns are classified as either count nouns or noncount nouns. A **count noun** names items that can be counted.

artists	books	towns

Count nouns have both singular and plural forms.

Singular Form	*Plural Form*
one artist	three artists
every book	most books
each town	all towns

A **noncount noun** names items that cannot be easily counted.

rain	traffic	mail

Most noncount nouns do not have a plural form.

Incorrect	*Correct*
advices	advice
informations	information
vocabularies	vocabulary

This chapter will help you use these categories — proper noun versus common noun, count versus noncount noun — to avoid errors in your writing, especially in your use of articles (*a, an,* and *the*).

26a **Keep the following guidelines in mind for recognizing and using noncount nouns.**

Nouns in the following categories are likely to be noncount nouns.

> ABSTRACTIONS: advice, courage, grief, information, knowledge, love, satisfaction, wealth
>
> FIELDS OF STUDY OR RESEARCH: chemistry, law, medicine, pollution, sociology, weather
>
> SPORTS AND GAMES: chess, football, soccer, tennis
>
> LIQUIDS: milk, water
>
> THINGS THAT CANNOT BE EASILY COUNTED: rice, sand, snow

▶ He offered some good advices.

Do not use numbers or plural quantity words before noncount nouns.

▶ Many rains hit the windowpane.

Do not use the article *a* or *an* with noncount nouns.

▶ The horses were covered with a mud.

Noncount nouns are used with singular verbs.

▶ The milk were sour.

Some nouns can be noncount or count, depending on whether they refer to something considered as a whole.

> NONCOUNT *Bread* is a staple in almost every cuisine. [*Bread* considered as a kind of food]
>
> COUNT Some *breads* are made without yeast. [Particularly types of bread, such as rye or whole wheat]

26b **Use an article or a demonstrative pronoun (*this, that, these, those*) with a count noun.**

▶ Her client sent her fax.

▶ I found fax on my chair.

26c **Use *a* or *an* before a singular count noun that does not refer to a specific person, place, object, or concept.**

▶ *A* computer is *a* useful tool.

▶ This country needs *an* electric car.

When using the articles *a* and *an,* remember that *a* is used before words beginning with a consonant sound and *an* is used before words beginning with a vowel sound.

a baby	an eagle
a city	an hour
a fish	an island
a hope	an orange
a unicycle	an outrage

26d Use *the* before a noun that refers to something specific.

▶ Mohammad pointed out *the* planets in *the* evening sky.

▶ *The* lamp on my desk is an antique.

Be sure not to omit the article.

▶ He was awake before ^the^ alarm rang.

26e Use *a, an,* or *the* with most singular count nouns considered as general examples; no article is necessary for plural count nouns considered as general examples.

▶ *A* bird feeder is an entertaining addition to any yard.

▶ *The* cat is among the most agile creatures on earth.

▶ *Plants* add a cheery note to any room.

26f Use *the* with plural proper nouns (*the United States, the Joneses, the Koreans*) and certain types of singular proper nouns.

Singular Proper Nouns That Use The

PROPER NOUNS THAT CONSIST OF *THE,* A COMMON NOUN, AND *OF:* *the* Arch of Triumph, *the* state of Vermont, *the* University of Florida

NAMES OF BUILDINGS: *the* Eiffel Tower, *the* White House

COUNTRIES NAMED WITH A PHRASE: *the* Dominican Republic, *the* United Kingdom

NAMES OF HIGHWAYS: *the* Kensington Expressway

NAMES OF HOTELS AND MUSEUMS: *the* Guggenheim Museum, *the* Hilton Hotel

PARTS OF THE GLOBE:　*the* Equator, *the* Northwest, *the* South Pole

HISTORICAL PERIODS AND EVENTS:　*the* Industrial Revolution, *the* Renaissance

NAMES OF SEAS, OCEANS, GULFS, RIVERS, AND DESERTS:　*the* Atlantic Ocean, *the* Gulf of Mexico, *the* Missouri River, *the* Red Sea, *the* Sahara

GROUPS OF ISLANDS:　*the* Hawaiian Islands

MOUNTAIN RANGES:　*the* Alps

26g Do not use an article with most other singular proper nouns.

▶ The houses are beautiful on ~~the~~ Maple Street.

EXERCISE 26.1

For each of the following sentences, choose the correct article. Note that X = no article.

▶ For many Americans, (a/**the**) civil rights movement began when (**X**/the) Rosa Parks refused to give up her seat on a bus to a white man.

1. Rosa Parks, (an/the) African American woman living in Montgomery, Alabama, was riding (a/the) bus with sections reserved for white passengers.
2. (X/The) back of the bus, where African Americans were supposed to sit, was crowded.
3. Parks sat in (X/The) front of the bus, which took tremendous courage.
4. (A/The) bus driver forced her to get off (a/the) bus, but (X/the) incident set off the Montgomery bus boycott.
5. (X/The) people all over United States heard (a/the) story of Rosa Parks, and the civil rights movement had its first hero.

27 VERBS

A **verb** shows an action, an occurrence, or a state of being. ESL writers need to pay special attention to their use of verb tenses, helping or modal verbs (also called auxiliary verbs), and verbs followed by an infinitive or a gerund.

27a Use the appropriate verb tense to express time accurately.

Verb tenses express time. They indicate when an action occurs, occurred, or will occur. The following sections will help you to understand and form the simple, perfect, and progressive tenses.

The Simple Tenses

The simple tenses are used to show clear and simple time relationships. The following chart summarizes how each of the simple tenses is formed and used.

THE SIMPLE TENSES

Tense	How It Is Formed	Examples
Simple present		
Expresses an action or condition occurring at the time of speaking or writing, a statement of fact, or a habitual action	First and second person singular and plural, third person plural: **base form**	I *cook* for five people. They *cook* many unusual dishes.
	Third person singular: base form + *-s* or *-es*	He *cooks* for a family of five.
Simple past		
Indicates that an action occurred in the past and was completed in the past	Regular verbs: base form + *-d* or *-ed*	We *played* field hockey yesterday.
	Irregular verbs: Forms vary; check the list on pp. 774–76 or a dictionary.	He *became* agitated when the doctor approached.
Simple future		
Indicates that an action will take place in the future	*will* or form of *be* + *going to* + base form	His doctor *will try* a new approach.
		Ron *is going to find* a way out.

> The **base form** is the form of a verb as it appears in the dictionary.

The Perfect Tenses

The perfect tenses are also used to show time relationships. A verb in one of the perfect tenses indicates an action that was or will be completed by or before some specified time. The perfect tenses are formed by using a form of *have* along with the verb's **past participle**.

The following chart summarizes how each of the perfect tenses is formed and used.

> The **past participle** of regular verbs is formed by adding *-d, -ed,* or *-en* to the verb's base form. It can be used as an adjective.

THE PERFECT TENSES

Tense	How It Is Formed	Examples
Present perfect		
Indicates that a past action took place at an unspecified time or is continuing to the present	*has* or *have* + past participle	The landlord *has offered* to repair the damage. I *have worked* in this office for two years.

(Continued on next page)

THE PERFECT TENSES *(continued)*

Tense	How It Is Formed	Examples
Past perfect Indicates that an action was completed in the past before some other past action	*had* + past participle	Rafika *had offered* to babysit, but she got sick.
Future perfect Indicates that an action will take place before some specified time in the future	*will* + *have* + past participle	By Monday, the team *will have offered* him a new contract.

The Progressive Tenses

The simple progressive tenses describe actions in progress, indicating that an action did, does, or will continue. They are formed by using a form of *be* along with the **present participle.**

The perfect progressive tenses are used to describe actions that continue to the present or until another action takes place. They are often used to emphasize the length of time involved.

The following chart summarizes how the progressive and perfect progressive tenses are formed and used.

The **present participle** is the *-ing* form of a verb; it shows an action that is in progress or ongoing. It can be used as an adjective.

THE PROGRESSIVE AND PERFECT PROGRESSIVE TENSES

Tense	How It Is Formed	Examples
Present progressive Indicates that an action began in the past, is happening now, and will end sometime in the future	form of *be* + present participle	Consultants *are changing* the workforce.
Past progressive Indicates that an action was in progress at a specified time in the past	*was* or *were* + present participle	He *was changing* a light bulb when the ladder collapsed. They *were driving* to the beach when their car stalled.

(Continued on next page)

THE PROGRESSIVE AND PERFECT PROGRESSIVE TENSES *(continued)*

Tense	How It Is Formed	Examples
Future progressive		
Indicates that an action will begin and continue in the future. The time is often specified.	*will be* + present participle, or present tense of *be* + *going to be* + present participle	New parents *will be changing* diapers for at least two years. Exams *are going to be changing* under the new principal.
Present perfect progressive		
Emphasizes the ongoing nature of an action that began in the past and continues into the present	*has* or *have been* + present participle	Her secretary *has been running* errands all morning. They *have been planning* this party for several weeks.
Past perfect progressive		
Emphasizes the duration of an action that began and continued in the past and was completed before some other past action	*had been* + present participle	He *had been running* two miles a day until he broke his toe.
Future perfect progressive		
Emphasizes the duration of an action that will continue in the future for a specified amount of time before another future action	*will have been* + present participle	When she takes over, her family *will have been running* the company for four generations.

EXERCISE 27.1

Choose the correct verb tense in the following sentences.

▶ Ever since the invention of computers, people (predicted/(have been predicting)) that books would disappear.

1. Most people (enjoy/enjoyed) reading off a computer screen, but not for long periods of time.
2. When computer books become easier to read, some people predict that paper books (will disappear/have disappeared).
3. Until recently, most book lovers (had purchased/purchase) their books in local bookstores.
4. Now, however, publishers (are offering/will be offering) online editions of their books.
5. Books and computers both serve a purpose, and the demand for both probably (increase/will be increasing) for years to come.

EXERCISE 27.1: *Answers*

1. enjoy
2. will disappear
3. had purchased
4. are offering
5. will be increasing

27b Use helping verbs to form tenses and express your meaning precisely.

Helping verbs are used before main verbs to form certain tenses. Some helping verbs—*have, do,* and *be*—change form to indicate tense. (See 27a.) The helping verb *do* indicates tense in questions, inverted phrases, and negative sentences. *Do you know her? Little did I realize what would happen. She does not like him.* It is also used for emphasis: *The sentence does need a comma.* The forms of these helping verbs are as follows.

> have, has, had
> be, am, is, are, was, were, being, been
> do, does, did

Other helping verbs, called **modals,** do not change form. Modal verbs include *can, could, may, might, must, shall, should, will,* and *would.* Modals are used to express ability, necessity, permission, intention, and so forth. The accompanying chart summarizes the common uses of modals.

HOW TO USE MODALS

Meaning	Present or Future Time	Past Time
Ability	*can* Most five-year-olds *can* tie their own shoes.	*could* + *have* + past participle Jim *could have registered* early if he wanted to.
Necessity	*must* or *have to* International travelers *must* carry passports. Students *have to* read critically.	*had to* The governor *had to* work with other officials.
Permission	*may, can* Anyone with a ticket *may* see the film. You *can* come in now.	*might* + *have* + past participle *could* + *have* + past participle You *might have waited* inside, out of the rain. We *could have gone* to the movies.
Intention	*will* He *will* encourage real estate development.	*would* + *have* + past participle I *would have hiked* last weekend, but it rained.

(Continued on next page)

HOW TO USE MODALS *(continued)*

Meaning	Present or Future Time	Past Time
Advisability	*should, had better* Everyone *should* get an education. She *had better* buy a ticket.	*should* + *have* + past participle The trainee *should have read* the manual.
Possibility	*may, might* An accountant *may* work long hours during tax season.	*may* or *might* + *have* + past participle *could* + *have* + past participle The burglar *might have entered* through the window. They *could have lost* their keys.
Speculation	*would* He *would* like her.	*would* + *have* + past participle No one *would have recognized* him without his moustache.

EXERCISE 27.2

In each sentence, fill in the blank with a modal from the list below. In most cases, more than one modal will work in the sentence. Use each modal only once.

can	may	should	would
could have	might	will	would have

▶ Busy professionals who are looking for a husband or wife _*can*_ try videodating.

1. Other people feel that they _____ meet their potential mate in person.
2. The Internet _____ be another way to find romance.
3. In the past, few _____ imagined such uses for technology.
4. Now people fear that technology _____ soon replace many human activities, including matchmaking.
5. Human matchmakers _____ become obsolete if videodating grows more popular.

EXERCISE 27.2: Answers

1. should
2. may *or* might
3. could have *or* would have
4. will, may *or* might
5. will, may, *or* might

27c Use gerunds or infinitives following verbs according to convention.

Often, you will need to use an **infinitive** or a **gerund** as the object of a verb in a sentence, as in the following examples.

An **infinitive** is a verb form made up of *to* plus the base form (*to run, to see*).

A **gerund** is an *-ing* form of a verb that functions as a noun (*complaining, jogging*).

▶ Mustafa needs *to find* his lecture notes.

▶ Lara avoids *studying* in her dormitory.

When you use an infinitive or a gerund as an object, you need to remember that some verbs are followed by infinitives, some verbs are followed by gerunds, and some can be followed by either form without a change in meaning. The following guidelines will help you determine which form to use.

Verbs Followed by Infinitives

Some verbs, including the verbs listed here, are usually followed by an infinitive in English.

agree	claim	manage	promise
ask	decide	need	refuse
beg	expect	offer	venture
bother	fail	plan	want
choose	hope	pretend	wish

In general, use these verbs with an infinitive, not a gerund.

▶ Margaret managed ~~finishing~~ the project.
                 to finish

Some verbs are followed by a noun or a pronoun and then by an infinitive. These verbs include *allow, cause, convince, hire, instruct, order, remind, tell,* and *warn.*

▶ The bank *reminded your office to send* proof of employment.

When using a negative word (such as *no* or *not*) in a sentence containing a verb followed by an infinitive, place the word carefully; its position in the sentence often affects meaning.

▶ Bella did *not* decide to attend.

    She never considered it.

▶ Bella decided *not* to attend.

    She made the decision not to attend.

The causative verbs *have, let,* and *make* are followed by a noun or a pronoun and the base form of the verb (without the word *to*).

▶ The noise made her *lose* her concentration.

▶ The hotel lets visitors *bring* pets.

▶ Have your assistant *type* those letters.

Verbs Followed by Gerunds

The following verbs are often followed by a gerund.

admit	dislike	postpone
appreciate	enjoy	practice
avoid	finish	recall
consider	imagine	resist
delay	keep	risk
deny	mention	suggest
discuss	miss	tolerate

Use these verbs with a gerund, not an infinitive.

> ▶ The zoning committee considered $\overset{approving}{\underset{\wedge}{\text{to approve}}}$ the proposal.

In a sentence containing a gerund, place a negative word (such as *no* or *not*) between the verb and the *-ing* form.

> ▶ Some vacationers consider *not* returning to work.

Verbs Followed by Infinitives or Gerunds

Some verbs (such as *begin, continue, intend, like,* and *prefer*) can be followed by an infinitive or a gerund with little or no change in meaning.

> INFINITIVE   Anita likes to jog.
>
> GERUND   Anita likes jogging.

Other verbs (such as *forget, remember, stop,* and *try*) can be followed by either an infinitive or a gerund, but the meaning of the sentence changes.

> INFINITIVE   Dien remembered to answer the letter.
>
> He remembered that he had an obligation to do something.
>
> GERUND   Dien remembered answering the letter.
>
> He remembered (the action of) doing something.

EXERCISE 27.3

Correct the errors in the use of gerunds and infinitives in the following sentences. Some sentences may be correct as written.

> ▶ Archeologists hope $\overset{to\ discover}{\underset{\wedge}{\text{discovering}}}$ when the first Americans arrived.

EXERCISE 27.3: *Answers*

1. considered changing
2. expect to find
3. suggested changing
4. Correct
5. keep digging

1. Many archeologists have considered to change the date they estimate that humans arrived in the Americas.
2. Until recently, scientists didn't expect finding evidence of human inhabitants older than 11,000 years, the age of stone tools found in Clovis, New Mexico, in the 1930s.
3. Recently, however, after discovering older evidence in Monte Verde, Chile, and other sites, some scientists have suggested to change this date.
4. Archeologists began to reexamine their assumptions after it was established that Monte Verde was older than the Clovis site.
5. One site in Virginia may be over 15,000 years old, and archeologists who keep to dig deeper may find even older evidence.

28 THE PREPOSITIONS *IN, ON,* AND *AT*

These three common prepositions are used before nouns or pronouns to indicate time or location.

Time

Use *in* with
   Months: *in* April
   Years: *in* 1999
   Seasons: *in* the winter
   Certain parts of the day: *in* the morning, *in* the afternoon

Use *on* with
   Days of the week: *on* Tuesday
   Dates: *on* June 20, 1998

Use *at* with
   Specific times: *at* 8 P.M., *at* noon
   Other parts of the day: *at* night, *at* dawn, *at* dusk

Location

Use *in* with
   Geographic places: *in* San Francisco, *in* rural areas
   Enclosed areas: *in* the stadium

Use *on* with
   A surface: *on* a shelf
   Forms of public transportation: *on* the bus
   Street names: *on* Main Street
   Floors of buildings: *on* the fourth floor
   Areas of the country: *on* the Gulf Coast

Use *at* with
   Specific addresses (number and street): *at* 130 Washington Street
   Named locations: *at* Juanita's house
   General locations: *at* the college
   Locations with specific functions: *at* the library

For more on prepositions, see 1g.

EXERCISE 28.1

In the following sentences, fill in the blank with either *in, on,* or *at*.

▶ Every year _*in*_ the spring, filmmakers gather in Hollywood for the Academy Awards ceremony.

1. The Academy Awards ceremony was first televised _____ 1953.
2. The participants gathered in the RKO Pantages Theater _____ Hollywood, California.
3. In recent years, stars have arrived in limousines _____ the Dorothy Chandler Pavilion _____ Los Angeles.
4. The participants have to arrive _____ the middle of the afternoon because the show is timed for the evening _____ the East Coast.
5. The ceremony appears on television around the world, and many members of the audience watch it very late _____ night or early _____ the morning.

29 ADJECTIVES

When using **adjectives,** ESL writers need to pay special attention to how adjectives are arranged when they modify the same noun and how adjectives are combined with prepositions. (For more on adjectives, see 1d and Chapter 9 of the Handbook.)

An **adjective** modifies a noun or pronoun.

29a Follow the conventional order when two or more adjectives modify the same noun.

Possessives come before numbers.

▶ *Anita's three* papers were accepted.

Ordinal numbers (*first, second*) come before cardinal numbers (*one, two*).

▶ James's *first three* requests were denied.

Descriptive adjectives should appear in the following order.

1. Article or possessive noun: *an, Dr. Green's, these*
2. Opinion: *favorite, hideous, lovely*
3. Size: *big, enormous, tiny*
4. Shape: *circular, rectangular, round*
5. Age: *elderly, teenaged, three-year-old*
6. Color: *black, blue, maroon*
7. National origin: *English, Nigerian, Vietnamese*
8. Religion: *Christian, Jewish, Muslim*
9. Matter or substance: *crystal, onyx, tweed*

(Continued on p. 888)

10. Noun used as an adjective: *book* (as in *book jacket*), *picture* (as in *picture frame*), *record* (as in *record producer*)

▶ *beautiful large white* horse

▶ *Juan's old* coat

▶ *a valuable new red British* car

▶ *small oval* table

29b Combine adjectives with specific prepositions to express your meaning precisely.

Prepositions (such as *before, on,* and *to*) are used before a noun or pronoun to indicate time, place, space, direction, position, or some other relationship.

Keep a list of adjective-**preposition** combinations that you hear in conversation or notice in your reading. Consult an ESL dictionary when you are not sure whether a particular combination expresses the meaning you intend. Here are some common adjective-preposition combinations.

afraid of	responsible for (thing or action)
ashamed of	responsible to (person)
full of	satisfied with
grateful for (thing)	sorry for
grateful to (person)	suspicious of
interested in	tired of
proud of	

EXERCISE 29.1: *Answers*

1. Caligula made his favorite horse a Roman senator.
2. He was also responsible for declaring war on the sea god Neptune.
3. Caligula's brief, violent reign made many Roman citizens afraid of their emperor.
4. The emperor's notorious temper led to the deaths of those unfortunate Romans who angered him.
5. Many upstanding citizens were relieved when assassins left Caligula dead.

EXERCISE 29.1

Correct the errors in the order of adjectives and in adjective-preposition combinations in the following sentences.

    insane Roman emperor
▶ The ~~emperor Roman insane~~ Caligula succeeded his uncle, the emperor Tiberius.

1. Caligula made favorite his horse a Roman senator.
2. He was also responsible to declaring war on the sea god Neptune.
3. Brief Caligula's violent reign made many Roman citizens afraid for their emperor.
4. The emperor's notorious temper led to the deaths of unfortunate those Romans who angered him.
5. Upstanding many citizens were relieved when assassins left Caligula dead.

30 COMMON SENTENCE PROBLEMS

As you edit and proofread your writing, watch out for the following problems involving word order, relative pronouns, and negatives.

30a Place sentence elements in the correct order.

Place words and phrases that indicate time or place at the beginning or at the end of a clause. Do not place them between the verb and its direct object (D.O.).

> INCORRECT We did this afternoon our homework.
>
> CORRECT We did our homework this afternoon.

Place the indirect object (I.O.) after the verb and before the direct object (D.O.).

> ▶ Ramon bought his sister a videotape.
>
> ▶ Ramon bought her a videotape.

Exception: When a prepositional phrase takes the place of an indirect object, the phrase should follow the direct object.

> ▶ Ramon bought a videotape for his sister.

Some verbs (such as *describe, explain, illustrate, mention, open,* and *say*) cannot be followed by an indirect object.

> INCORRECT Lu described us the figurine.
>
> CORRECT Lu described the figurine to us.

EXERCISE 30.1

Correct the errors involving the placement of sentence elements in the following sentences. Some sentences may be correct as written.

> *to the visitors*
> ▶ A park ranger explained ~~the visitors~~ the habits of the cave's bats.

1. Every evening at sunset, thousands of bats hunt from the entrance of Carlsbad Caverns in New Mexico mosquitoes.
2. Bat experts tell people that bats are actually helpful to humans.
3. One bat can eat in a single night a huge number of insect pests.
4. At the cave entrance at dusk, the bats provide to curious onlookers a spectacular show.
5. They give the crowds who come to see them when they fly out of the cave a thrilling experience.

EXERCISE 30.1: *Answers*

1. Every evening at sunset, thousands of bats hunt mosquitoes from the entrance of Carlsbad Caverns in New Mexico.
2. Correct
3. One bat can eat a huge number of insect pests in a single night.
4. At the cave entrance at dusk, the bats provide a spectacular show to curious onlookers. [*Or:* At the cave entrance at dusk, the bats provide curious onlookers a spectacular show.]
5. When they fly out of the cave, they give the crowds who come to see them a thrilling experience. [*Or:* When they fly out of the cave, they give a thrilling experience to the crowds who come to see them.]

A **relative pronoun** is a noun substitute that relates groups of words to nouns or other pronouns: *the patient who injured her leg.*

A **dependent clause** contains a subject and a verb but does not express a complete thought.

30b Do not omit a relative pronoun when it is the subject of a relative clause or the object of a verb or preposition within a relative clause.

A **relative clause** is a **dependent clause** that begins with a relative pronoun (such as *that, which, who, whom,* or *whose*) and modifies a noun or pronoun. Sometimes a relative clause begins with a preposition followed by a relative pronoun (the reason *for which* I am writing).

INCORRECT	The firefighter rescued the child was given a hero's welcome.
REVISED	The firefighter *who* rescued the child was given a hero's welcome.
INCORRECT	Juanita found the book for she had been searching all morning.
REVISED	Juanita found the book for *which* she had been searching all morning.

Exception: The relative pronoun and the verb *be* are often omitted in relative clauses when the clause is restrictive (essential to the meaning of the word or phrase it modifies); they should usually be included in a nonrestrictive clause (not essential to the meaning of the word or phrase it modifies). For more on restrictive and nonrestrictive word groups, see 12e.

RESTRICTIVE	Michael grabbed the newspapers [that were] on the table.

That were is optional because the clause is restrictive; it tells which newspapers are meant.

NONRESTRICTIVE	Michael tripped over the stack of day-old newspapers, which were ready to be recycled.

The clause supplies additional but nonessential information about the newspapers. It is nonrestrictive, so *which were* should be included.

Use the relative pronoun *whose* to show possession with a relative clause.

INCORRECT	The committee sat at a table that its surface was scratched.
REVISED	The committee sat at a table whose surface was scratched.

Use relative pronouns, not personal pronouns, to introduce relative clauses.

INCORRECT	Computer terminals, they are scarce at certain times of the day, are an obsession for many students.
REVISED	Computer terminals, *which* are scarce at certain times of the day, are an obsession for many students.

EXERCISE 30.2

Correct the errors in the use of relative pronouns in the following sentences. Some sentences may be correct as written.

that
▶ The United States is a nation ˄ was founded by settlers from other lands.

1. Immigration in the United States is a controversial subject that its implications have been debated for a century.
2. Early laws, they were sometimes discriminatory, restricted immigrants from certain countries.
3. Both legal and undocumented immigrants, who continue to come to the United States in record numbers, often seek employment.
4. Some Americans want to limit immigration fear that new arrivals will compete for scarce jobs.
5. New immigrants, their dreams and wishes resemble those of many previous generations of Americans, continue to arrive.

30c Make a sentence negative by adding *not* or a negative adverb such as *never* or *seldom*.

Place *not* after the first helping verb.

▶ The speech will *not* begin on time.

In questions, the helping verb should be followed by *not* or the contraction for *not* (*-n't*). Place the helping verb and *not* before the subject and the main verb.

▶ *Didn't* I read that story in the newspaper yesterday?

Place negative adverbs before the main verb. In a sentence with a helping verb, place the negative adverb after the first helping verb.

▶ Arthur *seldom forgets* an assignment.
▶ Marguerite *may never play* the violin again.

If a negative adverb is used at the beginning of a clause, the helping verb *do* is needed.

▶ *Rarely* does one see a bald eagle.

EXERCISE 30.3

Correct the errors in the use of negatives in the following sentences. Some sentences may be correct as written.

not
▶ Most reports of UFO sightings and aliens ~~not~~ are believed. ˄

1. Reputable scientists have confirmed never a UFO sighting.
2. A simple explanation for a sighting is difficult seldom to find.
3. People who believe aliens have contacted them offer convincing proof almost never.

EXERCISE 30.2: *Answers*

1. Immigration in the United States is a controversial subject whose implications have been debated for a century.
2. Early laws, which were sometimes discriminatory, restricted immigrants from certain countries.
3. Correct
4. Some Americans who want to limit immigration fear that new arrivals will compete for scarce jobs.
5. New immigrants, whose dreams and wishes resemble those of many previous generations of Americans, continue to arrive.

EXERCISE 30.3: *Answers*

1. Reputable scientists have never confirmed a UFO sighting.
2. A simple explanation for a sighting is seldom difficult to find.
3. People who believe aliens have contacted them almost never offer convincing proof.
4. Correct
5. Aliens may exist, but they probably have not arrived on earth yet.

SUMMARY EXERCISE FOR CHAPTERS 26–30 (p. 892): *Possible Revisions*

Bilingual education, **whose** value is questioned by some educators, is very widespread in **the** United States. In bilingual education theory, students **who do not speak** English learn most subjects in their native language. **At the** same time, they receive **English** instruction from a teacher who also speaks their language so that eventually they will be [*or* **they are**] able to join native speakers in a regular class. **The** reality of bilingual education is often different. **In** California, some parents of students in bilingual education classes protested **that** their children were not learning English. They **went** [*or* **have gone**] to court to abolish bilingual education classes. It is true that some students who **are** taught mainly in their native language **have** difficulty ever learning English well enough to function in an English-language environment. Educators **do** not agree about the reason for this apparent problem with bilingual education. Some **feel that** students should learn most subjects in English immediately, even if they **are not** comfortable at first. They argue that this method **gives** [*or* **would give**] students the advantage of learning English quickly. Other professionals blame **students' previous** education in their native countries. They argue that without bilingual education, **many** students **would drop** out. In addition, they claim that forcing **students** to learn English **makes** [*or* **would make**] them **forget** their native language. People on both sides of the issue have contributed **some useful information to this argument,** but the controversy continues.

4. Isn't it possible that many people simply want to convince themselves that humans are not alone?

5. Aliens may exist, but they probably not have arrived on earth yet.

SUMMARY EXERCISE FOR CHAPTERS 26–30

Review Chapters 26–30, then correct the errors in standard English usage in the following paragraph.

▶ In United States, educational ~~one~~ idea is very controversial.
      the   *one*

Bilingual education, that its value is questioned by some educators, is very widespread in United States. In bilingual education theory, students that are not speaking English learn most subjects in their native language. On the same time, they receive the English instruction from a teacher who also speaks their language so that eventually they will be able to join native speakers in a regular class. Reality of bilingual education is often different. At California, some parents of students in bilingual education classes protested their children were not learning English. They go to court to abolish bilingual education classes. It is true that some students who were taught mainly in their native language has difficulty ever learning English well enough to function in an English-language environment. Educators not agree about the reason for this apparent problem with bilingual education. Some felt students should learn most subjects in English immediately, even if they not are comfortable at first. They argue that this method should give to students the advantage of learning English quickly. Other professionals blame previous students' education in their native countries. They argue that without bilingual education, the many students had dropped out. In addition, they claim that forcing student to learn English has been making them to forget their native language. People on both sides of the issue have contributed to this argument some useful informations, but the controversy continues.

Appendix A

Writing Assessment

The two assessment tests in Appendix A will help you and your instructor determine aspects of your writing that you need to improve. The first test (pp. A-1–A-2) assesses your ability to develop and support ideas about a topic and express them clearly and correctly in an essay. The second test (pp. A-2–A-9) measures your ability to recognize and correct errors in grammar, punctuation, and mechanics.

WRITING ASSESSMENT: WRITING ESSAYS

CONNECTIONS

You might also consider using the Chapter Quick Start for Chapter 22 (p. 753) as an alternative essay assignment.

Choose either Essay Assignment A or Essay Assignment B for this writing assessment test. Although the essay assignments are from courses in interpersonal communications and sociology, you do not need any background in these subject areas to write the essay. For whichever option you choose, then, draw from your personal experience for ideas for the essay. Be sure your essay is about the topic you choose and that it states, develops, and supports one main point about your topic. When you have finished drafting your essay, be sure to revise, edit, and proofread it. Your instructor will evaluate your final essay and identify any writing skills that need improvement. With your instructor's feedback, you will then be able to use the Action Plan Checklist (p. A-9) to find help with those skills needing improvement.

Essay Assignment A

Suppose you are taking a course in interpersonal communications and have been assigned to write a two-page paper on *one* of the following topics. Choose a topic, develop a thesis statement, and support your thesis with evidence.

1. Describe a communication breakdown you have observed or experienced, telling what happened, why it happened, and what could have been done to prevent it.

2. Describe the communication and leadership skills you would bring to the position of assistant manager at a department store in preparation for a job interview.

3. Recall a conflict, disagreement, or argument you have had with someone. What feelings and emotions did you and the other person express? Explain how you communicated those feelings to each other and how the conflict was (or was not) resolved.

4. Explain how you can tell when a person doesn't mean what he or she says, using people you know as examples.

Essay Assignment B

Suppose you are taking a sociology course and your instructor has assigned a two-page essay on one of the following topics. Choose a topic, develop a thesis statement, and support your thesis with evidence.

1. Describe one important function of the family in American life. Explain why it is important and what is expected of family members. Use your own family as an example.

2. Explain one important function of dating in the United States. Support your ideas with your own dating experiences.

3. Examine one major function of the wedding ceremony. Why is this function important? Use weddings that you have attended or been involved in as evidence to support your thesis.

WRITING ASSESSMENT: RECOGNIZING AND CORRECTING SENTENCE ERRORS

Most of the following sentences contain errors; some are correct as written. Look in the underlined part of each sentence for errors in usage, punctuation, grammar, capitalization, or sentence construction. Then choose the one revision that corrects the sentence error(s). If the original sentence contains no errors, select "d. NO CHANGE." Circle the letter of the item you choose as your answer.

1. Lonnie and Robert should put his ideas together and come up with a plan of action for the class project.

    a. Lonnie and Robert should put his idea together
    b. Lonnie and Robert should put her ideas together
    c. Lonnie and Robert should put their ideas together
    d. NO CHANGE

2. The school district newsletter informs all parents of beneficial programs for you and your children.

    a. all parents of beneficial programs for your children.
    b. each parent about beneficial programs for you and your children.
    c. you of all beneficial programs for you and your children.
    d. NO CHANGE

3. Margaret earned an A <u>on her term paper, consequently, she</u> was excused from taking the final exam.

   a. on her term paper; consequently, she
   b. on her term paper, consequently; she
   c. on her term paper consequently, she
   d. NO CHANGE

4. Some students choose courses <u>without studying degree requirements these students often make</u> unwise choices.

   a. without studying degree requirements, these students often make
   b. without studying degree requirements. These students often make
   c. without studying degree requirements; so these students often make
   d. NO CHANGE

5. Twenty-five band members <u>picked up their instruments from their chairs which were tuned and began to play</u>.

   a. picked up their tuned instruments from their chairs and began to play.
   b. picked up their instruments from their chairs tuned and began to play.
   c. picked up and began to play their instruments from their chairs which were tuned.
   d. NO CHANGE

6. I am sure I <u>did good on my midterm exam</u> because it seemed easy to me.

   a. did awful good on my midterm exam
   b. did real good on my midterm exam
   c. did well on my midterm exam
   d. NO CHANGE

7. In many American families, the financial decisions are made jointly by <u>husband and wife, the wife</u> makes most of the routine household decisions.

   a. husband and wife, in contrast the wife
   b. husband and wife the wife
   c. husband and wife. The wife
   d. NO CHANGE

8. Professor Simmons <u>pace while he lectures</u>.

   a. pacing while he lectures.
   b. pace while he lecture.
   c. paces while he lectures.
   d. NO CHANGE

9. When Tara set <u>the cup on the glass-topped table, it broke</u>.

   a. her cup on the glass-topped table, she broke it.
   b. the cup on the table with a glass top; it broke.
   c. it on the glass-topped coffee table, the cup broke.
   d. NO CHANGE

10. Swimming to shore, my arms got tired.

    a. My arms got tired swimming to shore.
    b. When I was swimming to shore, my arms got tired.
    c. My arms, swimming to shore, got tired.
    d. NO CHANGE

11. Thousands of fans waited to get into the stadium. Swarmed around the parking lot like angry bees until security opened the gates.

    a. to get into the stadium. Swarming around the parking lot
    b. to get into the stadium; swarmed around the parking lot
    c. to get into the stadium. They swarmed around the parking lot
    d. NO CHANGE

12. After I left the college library I went to the computer lab.

    a. After I left the college library, I went
    b. After leaving the college library I went
    c. After I left the college library; I went
    d. NO CHANGE

13. To be honest is better than dishonesty.

    a. Being honest is better than dishonesty.
    b. To be honest is better than being dishonest.
    c. It is better to be honest than dishonest.
    d. NO CHANGE

14. The amount of time students spend researching a topic depends on his familiarity with the topic.

    a. students spend researching a topic depends on his or her familiarity
    b. students spend researching a topic depends on their familiarity
    c. a student spends researching a topic depends on their familiarity
    d. NO CHANGE

15. After Carlos completed his term paper, he seems less tense.

    a. his term paper, he seemed
    b. his term paper, he will seem
    c. his term paper, he is seeming
    d. NO CHANGE

16. When Maria tried to sign up for those courses in the fall, but they were full.

    a. When Maria tried to sign up for those courses in the fall; however, they were full.
    b. Although Maria tried to sign up for those courses in the fall, but they were full.
    c. Maria tried to sign up for those courses in the fall, but they were full.
    d. NO CHANGE

17. A course in nutrition <u>may be useful; it may help you make</u> wise food choices.

    a. may be useful, it may help you make
    b. may be useful it may help you make
    c. may be useful; because it may help you make
    d. NO CHANGE

18. According to the reporter, <u>many pets are run over by automobiles roaming around untended.</u>

    a. many pets are run over roaming around untended by automobiles.
    b. many pets roaming around untended are run over by automobiles.
    c. many pets who are run over by automobiles roaming around untended.
    d. NO CHANGE

19. You need to take <u>life more serious if you hope to do well</u> in school.

    a. life more serious if you hope to do good
    b. life more seriously if you hope to do well
    c. life seriouser if you hope to do well
    d. NO CHANGE

20. Leon has already taken <u>three social sciences courses, Introduction to Psychology,</u> Sociology 201, and Anthropology 103.

    a. three social sciences courses; Introduction to Psychology,
    b. three social sciences courses: Introduction to Psychology,
    c. three social sciences courses. Introduction to Psychology,
    d. NO CHANGE

21. <u>There's several people who can</u> advise you about the engineering program.

    a. There are several people who can
    b. There is several people who can
    c. There's two people who can
    d. NO CHANGE

22. <u>In chapter 6 of your book it describes</u> the causes of mental illness.

    a. In chapter 6 of your book, they describe
    b. Chapter 6 of your book describes
    c. In chapter 6 of the book, it describes
    d. NO CHANGE

23. <u>Flood damage was visible crossing the river.</u>

    a. Flood damage was visible, crossing the river.
    b. Crossing the river, the flood damage was visible.
    c. Flood damage was visible as we crossed the river.
    d. NO CHANGE

24. She had to leave the <u>van in the driveway. The heavy, wet snow halfway up</u> the garage door.
    a. van in the driveway. The heavy, wet snow had piled halfway up
    b. van in the driveway. Because of the heavy, wet snow halfway up
    c. van in the driveway; the heavy, wet snow halfway up
    d. NO CHANGE

25. Mail <u>carriers who have been bitten by dogs are</u> wary of them.
    a. carriers, who have been bitten by dogs, are
    b. carriers who have been bitten, by dogs, are
    c. carriers who, having been bitten by dogs, are
    d. NO CHANGE

26. Alfonso <u>need to practice</u> his clarinet every day.
    a. needing to practice
    b. needes to practice
    c. needs to practice
    d. NO CHANGE

27. <u>Everyone should be sure to bring their notebook</u> to class on Wednesday.
    a. Everyone should be sure to bring their notebooks
    b. Everyone should be sure to bring his or her notebook
    c. Everyone should be sure to bring his notebook
    d. NO CHANGE

28. The <u>television program ended Janelle read a book</u> to her son.
    a. When the television program ended, Janelle read a book
    b. The television program ended and Janelle read a book
    c. The television program ended, Janelle read a book
    d. NO CHANGE

29. Georgia <u>replied "The way to a man's heart is through his stomach."</u>
    a. replied "The way to a man's heart is through his stomach".
    b. replied; "The way to a man's heart is through his stomach."
    c. replied, "The way to a man's heart is through his stomach."
    d. NO CHANGE

30. The <u>plan to travel to three cities in two days seem</u> overly ambitious.
    a. plan to travel to three cities in two days are
    b. plan to travel to three cities in two days seems
    c. plan to travel to three cities in two days do seem
    d. NO CHANGE

31. You discover that <u>your concentration improves</u> with practice, so now I can study more in less time.
    a. I discovered that my concentration improves
    b. You discover that concentration improves
    c. You discovered that your concentration improves
    d. NO CHANGE

32. I couldn't watch the <u>rest of the football game. Because there was no chance that we could win</u> now. We were behind by three touchdowns.

    a. rest of the football game and there was no chance that we could win
    b. rest of the football game because there was no chance that we could win
    c. rest of the football game; because there was no chance that we could win
    d. NO CHANGE

33. <u>"Shopping" Barbara explained "is</u> a form of relaxation for me."

    a. "Shopping" Barbara explained, "is
    b. "Shopping," Barbara explained "is
    c. "Shopping," Barbara explained, "is
    d. NO CHANGE

34. A <u>balanced diet, exercising regularly, and to get enough sleep</u> are essential to good health.

    a. Eating a balanced diet, exercising regularly, and to get enough sleep
    b. A balanced diet, regular exercise, and enough sleep
    c. To eat a balanced diet, exercising regularly, and to get enough sleep
    d. NO CHANGE

35. <u>The use of air bags was designed</u> to increase driver and passenger safety.

    a. Airbags were designed
    b. The use of air bags were designed
    c. Increased use of air bags was designed
    d. NO CHANGE

36. The <u>articles and the book contains</u> the information I need.

    a. book and the articles contains
    b. articles and the book contain
    c. articles and the book has contained
    d. NO CHANGE

37. Top firms are always <u>looking for skilled managers. People who can adapt</u> to changing times and rise to new challenges.

    a. looking for skilled managers; people who can adapt
    b. looking for skilled managers. People, who can adapt
    c. looking for skilled managers who can adapt
    d. NO CHANGE

38. <u>Individuals and community groups can assist students in financial need, and</u> help them secure a good education.

    a. Individuals and community groups, can assist students in financial need and
    b. Individuals, and community groups can assist students in financial need, and
    c. Individuals and community groups can assist students in financial need and
    d. NO CHANGE

39. Someone left their briefcase under the table.

    a. Everyone left their briefcase
    b. Someone left their briefcases
    c. Someone left his or her briefcase
    d. NO CHANGE

40. Mustard is a versatile seasoning and it can be used to enhance the flavor of many dishes.

    a. seasoning; and it can be
    b. seasoning, and it can be
    c. seasoning, therefore it can be
    d. NO CHANGE

41. We spent our most happiest days in the little cottage on the lake.

    a. spent our happiest days
    b. spent our more happiest days
    c. spent our more happy days
    d. NO CHANGE

42. Swimming is an excellent form of exercise, it produces a good aerobic workout.

    a. excellent form of exercise it produces
    b. excellent form of exercise and it produces
    c. excellent form of exercise because it produces
    d. NO CHANGE

For a guide to scoring your assessment, turn to p. A-10.

ACTION PLAN CHECKLIST

The Action Plan Checklist (p. A-9) will help you find the appropriate resources for improving the writing skills that you and your instructor have identified as problem areas.

Resources

1. **Part Six, "Handbook: Writing Problems and How to Correct Them."** The Handbook section of this text contains a systematic review of the rules that correspond to most of the topics listed under "Sentence Skills" in the Action Plan Checklist, as well as exercises to help you understand and apply the rules.

2. **Additional Exercises for *Successful College Writing*.** The student exercise book that accompanies this text offers you practice in applying the principles presented in Part Six, "Handbook: Writing Problems and How to Correct Them." The exercise book contains additional exercises for all the topics listed

in the Action Plan Checklist as well as other topics you may wish to review. It is designed so that you can check your answers immediately after completing an exercise. As you work through each exercise, be sure to take the time to discover *why* you answered any items incorrectly and, if you are still uncertain, to check with a classmate or your instructor.

3. *Writing Guide Software for Successful College Writing.* This interactive computer program provides a comprehensive review of many of the topics included in the Action Plan Checklist as well as other key topics. The software includes a tutorial for most of the problem areas identified under "Sentence Skills."

ACTION PLAN CHECKLIST

Directions: **Place a check mark next to each skill that you or your instructor has identified as a problem area.**

Skills Needing Improvement	✔	*Text/Handbook**	*Exercise Book*	*Computer Program*
Paragraph Skills				
Details–Relevant		Ch. 6, p. 135	Exercise P-2	Tutorial 1
Details–Specific		Ch. 6, p. 136	Exercise P-3	Tutorial 2
Topic Sentences		Ch. 6, p. 128	Exercise P-1	Tutorial 4
Transitions		Ch. 6, p. 138	Exercise P-4	Tutorial 5
Sentence Skills				
Adjective and Adverb Usage		H9	Exercise 9.1	Tutorial 6
Capitalization		H20	Exercise 20.1	
Colon Usage		H14	Exercise 14.1	
Comma Splices		H4	Exercise 4.1	Tutorial 7
Comma Usage		H12	Exercise 12.1, 12.2	Tutorial 8
Dangling Modifiers		H10	Exercise 10.1	Tutorial 9
Sentence Fragments		H3	Exercise 3.1	Tutorial 10
Misplaced Modifiers		H10	Exercise 10.1	Tutorial 9
Mixed Constructions		H8	Exercise 8.2	Tutorial 11
Parallelism		Ch. 8, p. 191	Exercise E.4	Tutorial 12
Pronoun-Antecedent Agreement		H7	Exercise 7.2	Tutorial 13
Pronoun Reference		H7	Exercise 7.1	Tutorial 14
Punctuation of Quotations		H15	Exercise 15.1	
Run-on Sentences		H4	Exercise 4.1	Tutorial 15
Semicolon Usage		H13	Exercise 13.1	Tutorial 16
Shifts		H8	Exercise 8.1	Tutorial 17
Subject-Verb Agreement		H5	Exercise 5.1	Tutorial 18
Spelling		H25	Exercise 25.1	Tutorial 19
Verb Forms		H6	Exercise 6.1	Tutorial 20

*Handbook chapters are preceded by the letter *H* in this chart.

Working through Your Action Plan

Once you have filled in the check marks in your Action Plan Checklist, use the following suggestions to achieve maximum success with using it to improve your writing skills.

1. Begin by reading the appropriate section(s) in Chapters 6 and 8 and in Part Six and studying the examples. You may have to read the material several times to grasp it fully.

2. Test your understanding of a particular rule or explanation by looking away from the text and writing the rule or principle in your own words in your journal (see p. 7). If you cannot do so, you do not fully understand the rule. Try discussing it with a classmate and your instructor and recording what you learn from them in your own words. When you can explain the principle or rule in your own words, you are more apt to understand and remember the material.

3. Once you are confident that you understand a rule or explanation for a sentence skill or problem, complete the corresponding exercise in the Handbook, the student exercise book, or both. (The computer tutorials also include links to additional exercises.)

4. Set a deadline by which you will understand the rules and complete the exercises for all of your problem areas. Try to complete everything within the next two to three weeks. The sooner you understand this essential material, the sooner you will be fully prepared to write clear, effective essays.

ADDITIONAL RESOURCES

Exercise Central, which can be accessed at <http://www.bedford stmartins.com /composition /successfulwriting>, provides multiple exercise sets for each sentence-level skill. The exercises are at two levels and include customized feedback.

SCORING AND INTERPRETING YOUR GRAMMAR ASSESSMENT

Score your assessment by using the answer key that follows. Each question assesses your ability to recognize and correct a particular sentence problem. In the answer key, circle the number of each item you answered incorrectly.

Answer Key: Error Correction Self-Assessment

	Answer	Sentence Skill or Problem		Answer	Sentence Skill or Problem
1.	c	Pronoun-Antecedent Agreement	11.	c	Sentence Fragment
2.	c	Shift in Person	12.	a	Comma Usage
3.	a	Comma Splice	13.	c	Parallelism
4.	b	Run-on Sentence	14.	b	Pronoun-Antecedent Agreement
5.	a	Misplaced Modifier	15.	a	Shift in Tense
6.	c	Adverb and Adjective Usage	16.	c	Mixed Construction
7.	c	Comma Splice	17.	d	Semicolon Usage
8.	c	Subject-Verb Agreement	18.	b	Misplaced Modifier
9.	c	Pronoun Reference	19.	b	Adverb and Adjective Usage
10.	b	Dangling Modifier	20.	b	Colon Usage

Answer		Sentence Skill or Problem	Answer		Sentence Skill or Problem
21.	a	Subject-Verb Agreement	32.	b	Sentence Fragment
22.	b	Pronoun Reference	33.	c	Comma Usage
23.	c	Dangling Modifier	34.	b	Parallelism
24.	a	Sentence Fragment	35.	a	Mixed Construction
25.	d	Comma Usage	36.	b	Subject-Verb Agreement
26.	c	Verb Form	37.	c	Sentence Fragment
27.	b	Pronoun-Antecedent Agreement	38.	c	Comma Usage
28.	a	Run-on Sentence	39.	c	Pronoun-Antecedent Agreement
29.	c	Punctuation of Quotation	40.	b	Comma Usage
30.	b	Subject-Verb Agreement	41.	a	Adverb and Adjective Usage
31.	a	Shift in point of view	42.	c	Comma Splice

Five Steps to Academic Success

Organization, planning, knowledge, and communication — these are essential skills for academic success. In your writing course as well as in your other college courses, these skills will make you a better student, enabling you to learn more in less time and to derive the maximum benefit from every course you take. Following are a few steps you can take right away to make your college experience a success.

STEP 1: ORGANIZE A WRITING/STUDY AREA

To get work done efficiently, it is best to work in the same location daily. As you become accustomed to working there each day, you will form a psychological association between the place and the tasks to be done within it — namely, reading and writing. Eventually, you will come to *expect* to work as soon as you enter this area, and your mind will shift easily to academic tasks.

Choose a setting that is conducive to writing and studying. It should be relatively free of distractions, well lit, comfortable, and equipped with all the necessary tools — pens, pencils, scratch pads, a clock, a computer, a calculator, and so forth. Be sure to keep such reference tools as a dictionary and a thesaurus nearby as well. A collegiate dictionary (a hardcover, a paperback, or an online version), is an essential tool. Avoid small pocket dictionaries; they are of only limited use since they contain fewer words, offer only the most common meanings for words, and may not list variant spellings.

If you live on campus, your dormitory room probably includes a desk or work area. If you live off campus, finding the right place may be more difficult but is well worth the extra effort. Your work area need not be a separate room, but it should be a place where you can spread out your materials and find them undisturbed when you return. Otherwise, you may waste a great deal of time setting up your work, figuring out where you left off, and getting started again. If you are a commuting student, you should organize a place to work at home, but you should also find a quiet place on campus where you can study between classes.

Once you choose and organize your writing/studying area, you will find that your ability to concentrate will improve. To further strengthen your concentration skills, use the following tips.

- Vary your activities. Do not complete three reading assignments consecutively; instead, for example, read one assignment, then write, then work on math problems, then read another assignment, and so on.

- Highlight and annotate as you read. These processes will keep you mentally alert. (See Chapter 2.)

- Challenge yourself with deadlines. Before beginning an assignment, estimate how long it should take and work toward completing the task within that time limit.

- Keep a list of distractions. When working on an assignment, stray thoughts about other pressing things are bound to zip through your mind: You remember that you have to get your car inspected tomorrow or that your mother's birthday is next week. When these thoughts occur to you, jot them down in a notepad as reminders. Then get back to work.

STEP 2: PLAN YOUR VALUABLE TIME

Many first-year college students find it difficult to manage their time. Some find a flexible schedule of twelve to eighteen class or lab hours per week too unstructured, and as a result, they never seem to get organized. Others are overwhelmed by the workload and the challenge of integrating college study into an already busy lifestyle. Still others tend to study nonstop, never finding free time for relaxation.

In order to manage your time effectively, you must first decide which things in your life are most important to you and which are less so. Ask yourself, "What do I want out of life, and how will college help me achieve those goals?" Try to establish positive, realistic goals and set a time frame for them. For example, your goal may be to earn a bachelor's degree in elementary education by a certain date. Defining goals and priorities in this way will help you determine the tasks you should spend the most time on.

Planning is another key to time management. If you just let days "happen," you're not likely to get much accomplished. But if you use some sort of organizing plan, you'll find that you get more done; you'll also spend less time worrying about whether and how you'll finish all of your assignments. Depending on your learning style (see p. 10), you may prefer a tightly structured or loosely structured plan—or something in between. Following are three types of plans—term, weekly, and daily—for you to consider. Choose the one that works best for you. Or if you are not sure, experiment by trying out all three.

The* term *plan. Once you have a sense of the workload in each of your courses, block out four to six hours per week for each course. (The rule of thumb is that for every hour spent in class you should plan to work two hours outside of class.) Study for each course during the same time period each week. For instance, you

◄ *Learning Style Options*

might reserve Monday, Wednesday, and Thursday evenings (8–10 P.M.) for your writing course. The tasks you work on each week will vary, but you will always be certain you have enough time to get everything done. This plan establishes a routine for study. If you have trouble getting started on assignments, this plan may be the best one for you.

The* weekly *plan.   Take ten minutes at the beginning of each week to specify the times during which you'll work on each course, taking into account upcoming assignments. For instance, for a Tuesday through Thursday morning writing class, you might reserve the following time slots.

> Mon., 7–9 P.M.: Read and highlight chapter
> Tues., 7–8:30 P.M.: Start draft of paper
> Wed., 7–8 P.M.: Do assigned reading
> Thurs., 3–4 P.M.: Work on draft
> Sat., 12–1 P.M.: Revise paper

The* daily *plan.   Each evening, before you begin studying, assess what needs to be done and determine the order in which you will do these tasks. Although you may be tempted to tackle shorter or easier tasks first, it is usually best to work on the most challenging assignments first, when your concentration and attention span are at their peak.

Regardless of which plan you choose, purchase a calendar notebook or pocket calendar in which you can record assignments, due dates for papers, and upcoming exams.

STEP 3: LEARN ABOUT COLLEGE SERVICES

Every college offers a wide range of academic and nonacademic services to students. Give yourself an advantage by knowing and using what is available at your school. Academic services include writing centers, computer labs, library tours, free workshops, academic skills centers, counseling services, and peer tutoring in specific courses. You can find out when and where these services are offered and how to use them by checking the campus bulletin boards and newspaper. Don't hesitate to use these valuable services—they can give you an important academic advantage. Many or all of these services are free; all you need to do is request them.

In particular, be sure to visit your college's writing center and learn what services it offers. Writing centers offer individualized help with planning, organizing, drafting, and revising papers, usually for any college course, not just your writing class. Computers are often available for your use; if necessary, the writing center's staff or tutors can help you learn how to use them.

STEP 4: COMMUNICATE WITH YOUR INSTRUCTORS

Initially, some of your instructors may seem distant or unapproachable. Most are not; they have a job to do, and they are concentrating on doing it well. In fact, they enjoy teaching and working with students. All you need to do is take the time to get to know them. Most instructors post office hours — times during which they are available and ready to talk with you and answer your questions. However, *you* have to take the initiative. After all, an instructor cannot knock on each student's door and ask if he or she has any questions about today's assignment. On some campuses, you can communicate with your instructor by computer, using email. You will find that your instructors are happy to help you with immediate problems and to serve as valuable sources of information on research, academic decisions, and careers in their respective fields.

STEP 5: BUILD A POSITIVE ACADEMIC IMAGE

Be sure to project a positive academic image of yourself to your instructors and classmates. Communicate — through your words and actions — that you are a hard-working student who takes the college experience seriously. Use the following tips to establish and communicate a positive image.

- Arrive to classes promptly.
- Participate in class discussions.
- Ask or answer questions during class.
- Sit near the front of the room.
- Make eye contact with your instructors.
- Complete reading assignments *before* class.
- Complete all assignments on time.
- Turn in neat, complete, well-organized papers and essays.
- Say "hello" when you meet your instructors on campus.

ANSWERS TO EVEN-NUMBERED EXERCISES

Chapter 1

EXERCISE 1.1 *page 769*

Answers

2. They invaded England from northern Europe. [proper, proper]

4. The Normans, who came from France, later conquered England. [proper, proper, proper]

EXERCISE 1.2 *page 772*

Answers

2. Events that surprise us are especially hard to remember accurately. [relative, personal]

4. The students were later asked to fill out questionnaires in which untrue details of these incidents were suggested. [relative, demonstrative]

EXERCISE 1.3 *page 774*

Answers

2. A few months later, over four thousand miners had arrived. [helping, action-intransitive]

4. Most "forty-niners" soon grew disillusioned. [linking]

EXERCISE 1.4 *page 776*

Answers

2. Correct

4. Ali grew increasingly well known for his quick moves in the ring and his quick wit everywhere else.

6. He refused to be drafted that year for religious reasons and was banned from boxing and stripped of his title.

8. He got the title back in 1974 by defeating George Foreman.

10. Correct

EXERCISE 1.5 *page 779*

Answers

2. While its writers were developing the Constitution, they studied important documents from other societies. [past progressive, simple past]

4. The Constitution is adaptable and has been amended — for example, to ensure that female and nonwhite citizens have the right to vote. [simple present, present perfect, simple present]

EXERCISE 1.6 *page 780*

Answers

2. In the seventeenth century, the practice of smoking opium spread from Java to China. [indicative, active]

4. Great Britain was concerned about losing its trade with China if opium were outlawed; the countries went to war, and China was defeated. [indicative, passive; subjunctive, passive; indicative, active; indicative, passive]

EXERCISE 1.7 *page 781*

Answers

2. These clusters have led some people to believe that the cancers have environmental causes. [limiting, limiting, article, descriptive]

4. The Love Canal site was one of the first clusters to alert the American public. [proper, article, limiting, article, proper]

EXERCISE 1.8 *page 782*

Answers

2. No adverbs

4. Ikebana arrangements are typically triangular.

EXERCISE 1.9 *page 784*

Answers

2. Since Snow wrote his speech, relations between the two groups have changed. [subordinating conjunction]

4. Today, some academics in the humanities have adopted not only scientific terms, but also scientific theories in their work. [correlative conjunction]

EXERCISE 1.10   *page 786*

Answers

2. Prior to that time, he had been interested in Western thought, but he became fascinated with Indian art.

4. Ray's first film, *Pather Panchali,* won a prize at the Cannes Film Festival in 1955.

EXERCISE 1.11   *page 786*

Answers

2. Coaching is an area where the team, alas, needs improvement.

4. Oh, yes, a few good runners wouldn't hurt either.

Chapter 2

EXERCISE 2.1   *page 788*

Answers

2. (Would) [this kind of human and wildlife cooperation] (work in other areas)?

4. [This custom] (both ensures the workability of the Amboseli Reserve's unusual system and indicates the difficulty of trying the same system elsewhere). Compound predicate.

EXERCISE 2.2   *page 789*

Answers

2. The travelers made the head of the wealthy Donner family [direct object] their official leader [object complement].

4. Unfortunately, heavy snows trapped the few remaining wagons [direct object] in the Sierra Nevada mountains in October.

EXERCISE 2.3   *page 792*

Answers

2. *living in the United States:* participial phrase; *in the United States:* prepositional phrase; *to maintain ties with their homeland:* infinitive phrase; *with their homeland:* prepositional phrase

4. *In some cases:* prepositional phrase; *with a proposed match:* prepositional phrase

EXERCISE 2.4   *page 794*

Answers

2. If a child has difficulty concentrating on ordinary tasks such as homework, he or she may have ADD.

4. Some people wonder whether ADD might be a phenomenon connected to modern life.

EXERCISE 2.5   *page 796*

Answers

2. Compound-complex

4. Complex

Chapter 3

EXERCISE 3.1   *page 801*

Possible Revisions

2. In these days of computerized mailing lists, your name and address are certainly not private.

4. To put it another way, four trees per person per year contribute to this tide of printed waste.

6. Email advertisers can target specific audiences, such as small-business owners or college students.

8. Companies are choosing from among more than 20,000 mailing lists. For just pennies per name, firms can target recipients with mass mailings, either paper or electronic, and make a profit from a relatively low response.

10. Your name can be "sold" over and over until it's almost impossible to track it to the business that first listed it.

Chapter 4

EXERCISE 4.1   *page 807*

Possible Revisions

2. Shopping at Internet bookstores is convenient, but buyers cannot easily evaluate an author's credentials.

4. In the 1960s many Americans treated Vietnam veterans disrespectfully, a situation that has changed dramatically since that time.

6. With large bodies and tiny wings, bumblebees have long been a puzzle. How do they fly?

8. The Supreme Court often makes controversial decisions because the justices must decide how to interpret the Constitution.

10. Restoring a painting is, indeed, delicate work, and too much enthusiasm can be dangerous.

Chapter 5

EXERCISE 5.1   *page 812*

Answers

2. A student in most non-English-speaking industrialized nations expects to spend six or more years studying English.

4. Working for laws that require all Americans to speak English is a fairly common U.S. political tactic.

6. Some linguists joke that a person who speaks two languages is called "bilingual," while a person who speaks one language is called "American."

8. Correct

10. Everyone who studies a foreign language is likely to benefit.

Chapter 6

EXERCISE 6.1   *page 815*

Answers

2. Cuba, an island that lies ninety miles off the Florida coast, provided them with an excuse to do so.

4. In addition, many people in the United States had wanted to take over Spain's territories for a long time.

6. Cuba was allowed to take control of its own affairs right away.

8. Correct

10. Many Puerto Ricans are worried that statehood would destroy the native culture of their island, and none of them wants that to happen.

Chapter 7

EXERCISE 7.1   *page 818*

Possible Revisions

2. Because of the importance of the information, it often must be transmitted secretly.

4. "Invisible ink," which cannot be seen until the paper is heated, was once a popular way to communicate secretly.

6. During World War II, U.S. government code specialists hired Navajo Indians because Navajo is a difficult and little-studied language.

8. Because these cryptograms are so simple, they are no longer used to transmit messages.

10. Alan Turing, a British civil servant and mathematical genius, finally solved the enigma code.

EXERCISE 7.2   *page 820*

Answers

2. A team of researchers might disagree on their conclusions about the disappearance of the dinosaur.

4. In one way, animals resemble plants: Some are "weeds" because they have the ability to thrive under many conditions.

6. When a "weed" and a delicate native species compete for their survival, the native species usually loses.

8. People should be more concerned about the extinction of plants and animals than they seem to be.

10. The earth has experienced several mass extinctions in its history, but another would take its toll on the quality of human life.

EXERCISE 7.3   *page 824*

Answers

2. Correct

4. Following the success of Mammoth Cave, many Kentucky cavers hoped to make a fortune from their spelunking.

6. In January of 1925, a falling rock trapped Collins, who was spelunking in a narrow passage in Sand Cave.

8. For several days, the most famous man in Kentucky was he. [*Or:* For several days, he was the most famous man in Kentucky.]

10. Their failing to save Collins was a terrible tragedy for his family and the rescuers.

Chapter 8

EXERCISE 8.1   *page 828*

Possible Revisions

2. We wondered whether our professor knew of the new theory and whether she agreed with it.

4. Most parents think they have a major influence on their children's behavior.

6. Children strongly desire peer acceptance, and they want to be different from adults.

8. Most adults recall that, in childhood, their friends' opinions were extremely important to them.

10. Anxious parents would be greatly relieved if this hypothesis were proven.

EXERCISE 8.3   *page 830*

Possible Revisions

2. Business is booming for independent Web development shops, an industry that grows larger each year.

4. Once the domain of computer hackers, the online world has become routine for many nontechnical people.

6. The information technology department is the part of a company where Web projects are often managed.

8. Applicants for computer jobs should consider relocating to San Francisco or New York, the primary centers for technology.

10. By creating a personal Web page, you increase your firsthand knowledge of the Internet.

Chapter 9

EXERCISE 9.1   *page 833*

Answers

2. Televised images from Vietnam made some Americans feel terrible about the war.

4. Politicians who look bad on television tend to perform badly in polls.

6. More Americans get their news from television today than from any other source.

8. While television is better than newspapers at reporting stories with a strong visual element, it is worse at analyzing them.

10. People should never assume that television provides all the information they need.

Chapter 10

EXERCISE 10.1   *page 836*

Possible Revisions

2. So far, no proof of the existence of life forms on other planets has been found.

4. Astronomers carefully monitor signals coming from other parts of the solar system.

6. Most of the signals received so far have been caused by cell phone and satellite interference.

8. The message, containing information about earth, is on its way to other parts of our galaxy.

10. A signal sent to earth would take a similarly long time to reach us.

Chapter 11

EXERCISE 11.1   *page 839*

Answers

2. Correct

4. Czar Nicholas and his wife Alexandra often saw their little boy in terrible pain.

Chapter 12

EXERCISE 12.1   *page 844*

Answers

2. The city of New York bought the land where the Seneca villagers lived.

4. Household items from Seneca Village still turn up in Central Park today, and a museum exhibit was recently devoted to life in the long-gone settlement.

6. James Weeks, an early resident, owned much of the land.

8. His daughter, Susan Smith McKinney-Steward, was born in Weeksville and was the valedictorian of New York Medical College in 1870.

10. Correct

Chapter 13

EXERCISE 13.1   *page 846*

Answers

2. When too many people are driving in a hurry, tempers can flare.

4. Angry drivers can make mistakes, such as forgetting basic safety precautions; they may take unnecessary risks, such as passing recklessly; they often drive too fast; and occasionally they even try to injure other drivers or damage other vehicles.

6. There have been incidents when one driver has attacked another.

8. Correct

10. Every driver should realize that getting angry is never a solution and may even make problems worse.

Chapter 14

EXERCISE 14.1   *page 849*

Answers

2. The proposed zoning change was defeated by a margin of 2:1.

4. Correct

6. Correct

8. The neon lights gleamed above stores and in diner windows.

10. The American songwriting tradition reached its peak in the 1930s.

Chapter 15

EXERCISE 15.1   *page 852*

Answers

2. Why did the professor assign "To an Athlete Dying Young"?

4. President Bush admitted he lacked "the vision thing."

6. "Come live with me and be my love," pleads the speaker in Marlowe's poem.

8. It turned out that the pianist could only play "Chopsticks."

10. Our waitress announced, "The special is prime rib"; unfortunately, we are vegetarians.

Chapter 16

EXERCISE 16.1   *page 853*

Answers

2. "[M]any critics did not expect *The Silence of the Lambs* to win an Academy Award."

4. "[P]eople of all classes receive financial help from the government."

6. "Zora Neale Hurston's collections of folklore proved to be very valuable."

8. "Folic acid . . . can help to prevent certain birth defects."

10. "She wrote rather doubtful grammar sometimes [. . .]" (Thackeray 136–37).

Chapter 17

EXERCISE 17.1   *page 856*

Answers

2. Correct

4. Members of the World War II generation were often horrified by their sons' and daughters' behavior.

Chapter 18

EXERCISE 18.1   *page 858*

Answers

2. Correct
4. The invention of anesthesia made possible many advances in medicine (including lengthy surgery).

Chapter 19

EXERCISE 19.1   *page 859*

Answers

2. Some foods were once popular, but today hardly anyone has heard of them.
4. In the 1960s, frozen foods—icy blocks of corn, peas, and string beans—were popular and convenient alternatives to fresh produce.

Chapter 21

EXERCISE 21.1   *page 863*

Answers

2. The average American woman is five feet four inches tall.
4. The Great Depression began with the stock-market crash on Black Monday.

Chapter 22

EXERCISE 22.1   *page 864*

Answers

2. The estimated cost was too low by $87.14.
4. All traffic stopped as a ninety-car train went slowly past.

Chapter 23

EXERCISE 23.1   *page 866*

Answers

2. His professor insisted that *TV Guide* was not an acceptable research source.
4. The first European settlers at Plymouth arrived on the *Mayflower.*

Chapter 24

EXERCISE 24.1   *page 868*

Answers

2. For many self-conscious teens and young adults, surgery seems to be the perfect solution.
4. But as more adults pay for nose jobs and tummy tucks, more teens are expressing interest.

Chapter 26

EXERCISE 26.1   *page 878*

Answers

2. The
4. The; the; the

Chapter 27

EXERCISE 27.1   *page 881*

Answers

2. will disappear
4. are offering

EXERCISE 27.2   *page 883*

Answers

2. may *or* might
4. will, may *or* might

EXERCISE 27.3   *page 885*

Answers

2. Until recently, scientists didn't expect to find evidence of human inhabitants older than 11,000 years, the age of stone tools found in Clovis, New Mexico, in the 1930s.
4. Correct

Chapter 28

EXERCISE 28.1   *page 887*

Answers

2. in
4. in; on

Chapter 29

EXERCISE 29.1   *page 888*

Answers

2. He was also responsible for declaring war on the sea god Neptune.

4. The emperor's notorious temper led to the deaths of those unfortunate Romans who angered him.

Chapter 30

EXERCISE 30.1   *page 889*

Answers

2. Correct

4. At the cave entrance at dusk, the bats provide a spectacular show to curious onlookers. [*Or:* At the cave entrance at dusk, the bats provide curious onlookers a spectacular show.]

EXERCISE 30.2   *page 890*

Answers

2. Early laws, which were sometimes discriminatory, restricted immigrants from certain countries.

4. Some Americans who want to limit immigration fear that new arrivals will compete for scarce jobs.

EXERCISE 30.3   *page 891*

Answers

2. A simple explanation for a sighting is seldom difficult to find.

4. Correct

Credits

Index

FIGURES, FLOWCHARTS, AND BOXES

REVISION SYMBOLS

The numbers and letters refer to chapters and sections in the handbook. Page numbers are provided for references to sections outside of the Handbook.

abbr	Faulty abbreviation **21**		**p**	Punctuation **11–19**
ad	Misuse of adjective or adverb **1d, 1e, 9, 29**		$\overset{\wedge}{,}$	Comma **12**
agr	Faulty agreement **5, 7e, 7f, 7g**		**no$\overset{\wedge}{,}$**	No comma **12j**
appr	Inappropriate language *p. 194, 196*		**;**	Semicolon **13**
art	Article **26**		**:**	Colon **14**
awk	Awkward **7, 8, 10**		$\overset{\vee}{,}$	Apostrophe **17**
cap	Capital letter **20**		**" "**	Quotation mark **15**
case	Error in pronoun case **7h–7m**		**. ? !**	End punctuation **11**
cliché	Cliché *p. 198*		**—**	Dash **19**
coh	Coherence *p. 138*		**( )**	Parentheses **18a, 18b, 18c**
cs	Comma splice **4**		**[ ]**	Brackets **18d, 18e**
coord	Coordination *p. 186,* **1f**		**. . .**	Ellipsis mark **16**
dm	Dangling modifier **10c**		**ref**	Reference, pronoun **7a–7d**
ESL	ESL problem **26–30**		**run-on**	Run-on sentence **4**
exact	Inexact word *p. 197*		**sexist**	Sexist language **7e**
frag	Fragment **3**		**shift**	Shift **8a–g**
fs	Fused sentence **4**		**sl**	Slang *p. 194, 196*
hyph	Error in use of hyphen **24**		**sp**	Spelling **25**
irreg	Error in irregular verb **1c**		**sub**	Subordination *p. 187,* **1**
ital	Italics **23**		**t**	Error in verb tense **1c, 6e, 6f, 27a**
lc	Lowercase letter **20**		**trans**	Transition *p. 138*
mix	Mixed construction **8h, 8i, 8j**		**v**	Voice **6d**
mm	Misplaced modifier **10a, 10b**		**var**	Sentence variety *p. 185*
num	Number **22**		**vb**	Verb error **6, 27**
para, ¶	New paragraph *p. 128*		**wrdy**	Wordiness *p. 183*
pass	Ineffective passive *p. 192,* **6d**		**//**	Faulty parallelism *p. 191*
			$\smile$	Close up
			∧	Insert
			X	Obvious error

PROOFREADING CHECKLIST

The following proofreading checklist will help you systematically review your essays for errors.

1. Does each sentence end with the appropriate punctuation (period, question mark, or exclamation point)? For help, see Chapter 11 of the Handbook.
2. Is the punctuation within each sentence correct (commas, colons, semicolons, apostrophes, dashes, and quotation marks)? For help, see Chapters 11–19 of the Handbook.
3. Is each word spelled correctly? For help, see Chapter 25 of the Handbook.
4. Have you used capital letters where needed? For help, see Chapter 20 of the Handbook.
5. Are abbreviations and numbers used correctly? For help, see Chapters 21 and 22 of the Handbook.
6. Are any words omitted?
7. If your paper is typed, have you corrected all typographical errors?
8. If your paper is handwritten, is your handwriting legible throughout?
9. Does your paper meet the format guidelines you are required to follow? (For help, see page 703.)
10. Are your pages in the correct order and numbered?

HANDBOOK CONTENTS